The Complete Handbook of
GARDEN PLANTS

Michael Wright
assisted by Sue Minter
and Brian Carter

Facts On File
New York • Oxford • Sydney

To Ray Elton, who has long set an example and
given warm-hearted encouragement

THE COMPLETE HANDBOOK OF GARDEN PLANTS

Copyright © 1984 by The Rainbird Publishing Group Limited

First published in the United States of America in 1984 by
Facts On File Publications
460 Park Avenue South
New York, New York 10016

Library of Congress Cataloging in Publication Data
Wright, Michael, 1941 –
    The complete handbook of garden plants.
    Includes index.
    1. Plants, Ornamental – Handbooks, manuals, etc.
I Title
SB407.W73 1984 635.9'02'02 83-14133

This book was designed and produced by
The Rainbird Publishing Group Limited
29 Wrights Lane, London W8 5TZ

Jacket illustration by Sarah Fox-Davies. Clockwise from top left:
garden pansy (*Viola × wittrockiana* hybrid),
giant bellflower (*Campanula latifolia*),
mossy saxifrage (*Saxifraga* hybrid),
common European honeysuckle (*Lonicera periclymenum*),
Parrotia persica,
Iris reticulata,
mountain hemlock (*Tsuga mertensiana*),
Japanese cherry (*Prunus* hybrid).

Text set by Bookworm Typesetting, Manchester, England
Colour originated by Bridge Graphics Limited, Hull, England
Printed and bound by Toppan Printing Co. (S) PTE., Singapore

Contents

Introduction	4
Abbreviations	5
Choosing plants for your garden	5
Hardiness zone map	6
Glossary	8
Pests and diseases	11
Trees and shrubs	14
Perennial climbers	228
Border and bedding perennials	252
Bulbs, corms and tubers	362
Rock plants	426
Annuals and biennials	486
Water plants	528
Acknowledgments	534
Consultants	534
Illustration credits	534
Index	535

Introduction

This book attempts what is probably impossible: to provide in a pocketable (or at least easily portable) format a comprehensive guide to all the kinds of decorative outdoor garden plants you are likely to encounter or wish to grow anywhere in the temperate world, and to give all the basic information needed to choose and grow such plants. Tropical and subtropical plants (houseplants in cooler climes) are excluded, as are fruit and vegetables. It does not aim to give detailed instruction on garden design and techniques, for that readers are referred to the vast number of books available that deal with these topics. But what it does do is cover a more comprehensive range of plants – many thousands of species and varieties, with well over 2,500 of them illustrated by watercolour paintings – than any comparable illustrated book yet published.

The book is organized in a way designed to help you choose the plants you want to grow: Firstly, it is divided into major parts dealing with plants of different basic types: trees and shrubs, climbers, perennials, bulbs, rock plants, annuals and biennials and water plants. Then, within each part, there are separate articles for each major botanical family (whose members generally have features or cultural needs in common that gardeners as well as botanists can recognize). At the end of each part, a "miscellaneous" article deals with families having few members of interest. The families are covered in alphabetical order of their botanical name (printed top right of each text page), and within each article the plants are described in alphabetical order of their botanical name.

Key numbers are used to identify illustrations (which always appear on the opposite page unless a page number is specified). If you want to refer to a particular plant whose name you know, rather than a generalized grouping, refer to the index.

Naming names: Botanical rather than "common" names (which are also given) have the advantage of being precise and of being understandable by gardeners and botanists speaking any language. The main botanical names of a plant are printed in italics. The major division of a botanical family is a genus (plural, genera), and its name comes first. Each genus may have anything from one to many hundreds of species, or distinct types; the species name comes second. So long as there is no ambiguity, the genus name is abbreviated after the first occurrence; eg, *Hedera canariensis* & *H. helix* are two species of the genus *Hedera*, the ivies. In most articles, each genus has a separate section, with a bold heading, and each species a separate paragraph.

Subdivisions of species – relatively minor variations (eg, of size or flower colour) – can be named in two ways. Natural geographical varieties and subspecies have Latin-type names in italics after the species name (eg, *Viburnum opulus americanum*, the American cranberry bush, a variety of the guelder rose). Garden-raised varieties (cultivated varieties, or cultivars) have Latin or "fancy" names in Roman (upright) type within quotation marks and with an initial capital letter (eg, *Hedera helix* 'Glacier'). In this book, both categories are simply called varieties.

Hybrids (crosses) between two species or varieties are generally different from either parent and do not usually breed true from seed; they are given names in cultivar style, often without a species name since they belong to no single species (eg, *Rhododendron* 'May Day'). Some true-breeding hybrids are, however, known and these may be given species-style names with the addition of the × sign (eg, *Rosa* × *alba maxima*, the Jacobite rose); the same style may be used for a series or race of similar hybrids. Common names are always printed in Roman type without quotation marks.

A final point on names: Even botanical names do change sometimes, or a plant may be widely grown and sold under an incorrect name; such alternatives, where important, are given in the text.

Other points to note: To save space, a number of abbreviations are widely used in the text; see the key on p5.

General statements in the introduction to an article or to a section of it refer only to the plants listed below – not necessarily to other members of the family or genus not covered.

Always read the information on a species or genus in conjunction with the introduction(s) above it; to save space, general facts are not repeated.

Dimensions: If only one size is given, it is the height; otherwise, height is followed by spread or planting distance. Sizes are the maximum to be expected (not record sizes) in good growing conditions (eg, not on the borderline of hardiness) – unless stated, at about 10–12 years for shrubs, 20–25 years for trees. Leaf sizes are of length followed by width; where only one size is given it is the longest dimension. Brief colour descriptions in listings of varieties refer to flowers unless it is obviously a foliage plant.

Abbreviations

A:	Annual	
B:	Biennial	
H:	Hardy	(in relation to treatment of
HH:	Half-hardy	seed, not frost-hardiness)

fl(s):	flower(s)
fld:	flowered
flg:	flowering
fr(s):	fruit(s)
infl(s):	inflorescence(s)
lf:	leaf
lft(s):	leaflet(s)
lvd:	leaved
lvs:	leaves
sp:	species (singular)
spp:	species (plural. Note: *Hedera* spp means

Hedera species in general)

var(s):	variety/varieties (including natural varieties, subspecies and cultivars – see Introduction)
v:	very
yr(s):	year(s)
*:	flowers notably fragrant ⎫ (set next to
**:	flowers strongly fragrant ⎭ plant name)
lvs*:	leaves aromatic (often only when crushed)
/:	or (Note: semi-/evergreen means semi-evergreen or evergreen)
×:	indicates hybrid (a cross grown originally from seed)
+:	indicates graft hybrid or chimaera (formed originally by grafting one species on another so that their tissues become united).

Choosing plants for your garden

As already noted, this book is arranged in sections to help you choose plants for specific purposes or parts of the garden – shrubberies, rock gardens, etc – but there is still a huge range to choose from. (Remember too that a plant listed in one section may be usable in another – eg, a dwarf shrub in a rock garden.) Apart from cultural needs (see below) & the big differences between one species & another, varieties of one species may differ in size, habit & vigour, in leaf, flower &/or fruit colour & size, in flowering season, etc. Information in the listings should help you choose, but also look for the plants growing live at public gardens, nurseries, etc. Study nursery & seed merchants' catalogues, which often give details of awards given to species or varieties at trials or by horticultural societies. (Specialist nurseries offer a much wider choice than most garden centres.)

Climate: One of the major factors governing what you can grow. As noted in listings, some spp & vars prefer continental climates (with greater extremes of heat & cold) or maritime (more equable) conditions. Some tolerate drought, wet winters, hot summer sun, etc, better than others. For all plants, the amount of cold they can survive – their hardiness – is a limiting factor. This is not an absolute measure. A plant may survive much lower temperatures if it grows in v well-drained soil with little rain, is well-ripened by summer sun & sheltered from cold winds, or is kept constantly cold under snow, dry lvs, straw, etc, rather than alternately frozen & thawed, & so on. However, all plants listed have been graded for *approximate* hardiness (see box). By referring to the maps (pp6–7), you can see the degree of winter cold you can expect, but remember that an open, exposed garden in a low-lying "frost pocket" in the country will be much colder than a sloping city garden with plenty of shelter from overhanging trees. Even within a garden there are cold & warm spots. Unless sure of a plant's hardiness, be prepared to give winter protection or move it into a greenhouse.

Soil: Understand your soil type & if necessary improve it. For greatest choice, the ideal is moist but well-drained, well-cultivated medium loam, not too clayey nor too sandy, containing ample humus (rotted organic matter from dead lvs, peat, etc). A few plants accept waterlogged, boggy soil; some prefer heavy, rather clayey soil to light sandy soil – or vice versa. More or less neutral soil (neither too acid nor too alkaline) suits most plants; some (eg, gypsophila) like alkaline soil (caused by lime or chalk); others (eg, rhododendrons & heathers) need lime-free acid soil (generally peaty, leafy &/or sandy soils). You can check soil acidity/alkalinity with a simple test kit.

Other conditions: Note also in plant listings whether a plant likes full sun, partial shade, light shade or heavy shade; whether it needs shelter from wind or winter wet, & other special requirements.

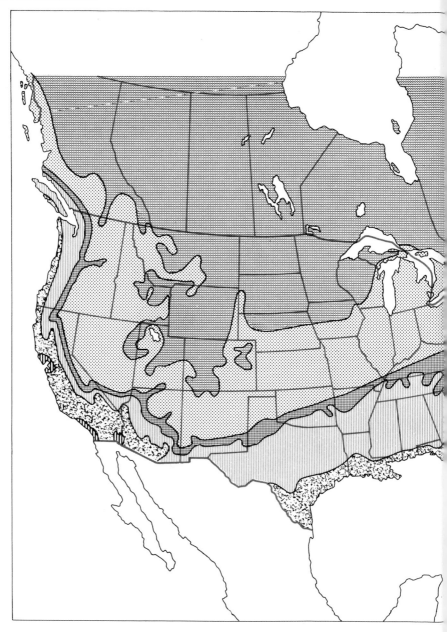

Plant hardiness: In this book, plants are graded approximately for hardiness as follows (assuming normal garden environment & no special winter protection given):

Ultra-hardy: Generally able to survive temperatures below −29°C (−20°F), in some cases to −40°C (−40°F) or lower.

Very hardy: Generally hardy below −18°C (0°F), in some cases to nearly −29°C (−20°F).

Moderately to very hardy: Hardy to about −15 to −18°C (5 to 0°F).

Moderately hardy: Hardy to below −6°C (21°F) & in many cases to −12 to −15°C (10 to 5°F).

Semi-hardy: Able to withstand frosts to −6°C (21°F) at most (& in some cases rather less).

Tender: Not hardy below −1°C (30°F), thus needing to be moved under frost-free cover.

Glossary

Acid: opposite of alkaline; also called sour.

Air layering: Slow method of propagation for azaleas, camellias, holly, lilac, magnolias, etc; done in spring with yr-old wood or in late summer with ripe new wood. Strip lvs from section of shoot 15-30cm (6-12in) from tip; make shallow cut upwards just below bud to form tongue, or remove 1-2.5cm (½-1in) ring of bark in same place; dust cut with hormone rooting powder & pack with moist sphagnum moss; wrap whole in clear plastic sleeve (bag without bottom) tied top & bottom; support with stake or adjacent branch tied above & below; ensure moss remains moist. When roots visible (up to 2 yrs), sever & pot up; grow on in frame or propagator with mist or frequent spraying.

Alkaline (of soil): generally containing lime or chalk; also called sweet.

Alternate (of lvs etc): staggered along stem.

Annual: plant grown from seed to flg in 1yr, then generally dying or discarded.

Hardy annuals: Sow spring or early summer (with many spp where winters not too harsh, sowing in autumn produces earlier fls) thinly in drills or scatter seeds thinly over bed, then cover lightly with soil. When seedlings big enough to handle, pull out surplus to leave correct distance apart; do not overcrowd. **Half-hardy annuals:** Sowing time depends on speed of growth; aim for small vigorous plants to plant out after last frost. Sow seeds v thinly in prepared seed trays (flats) or pots in proprietary seed-raising soil mixture, & raise in temperature of 16–18°C (60–65°F). When big enough to handle replant 5cm (2in) apart in new containers of potting mixture, and grow on in light shade at same temperature. Harden off in cold frame before planting out.

Anther: pollen-bearing part of stamen.

Aril: outer fleshy coat around some seeds.

Awn: bristle-like attachment, as on some seeds, frs & seed-heads of some grasses.

Axil: angle between lf/petiole & stem, or between side shoot & main stem. Hence, axillary.

Back-cross: offspring arising from cross between hybrid & one of its parents.

Bearded: having stiff hairs, as on the lower petals of some irises.

Bicoloured: having 2 colours on same petals.

Biennial: plant grown from seed 1yr, flg the next, then dying or discarded.

Hardy biennials: Treat as for hardy annuals, (see annual), but sow in "reserve" bed, generally in early summer. May be transplanted 15cm (6in) apart at thinning stage. Transplant to flg site late autumn. Where winters v cold, overwinter in pots in cold frame & plant out v early spring.

Bigeneric: derived from 2 different genera.

Bipinnate: describes pinnate lf with lfts further pinnately divided.

Bisexual: having male and female fls on same plant; hence even solitary specimens bear frs.

Bracts: modified lvs surrounding fl; sometimes major decorative feature.

Budding: method of propagation for trees & shrubs used mainly by nurserymen. Small slices of desired var (scion) with bud/s attached joined onto another related sp or var (stock), the tissues growing together to form plant with top-growth of scion on base & roots of stock. Often used where scion difficult to root or where stock healthier or more vigorous/dwarf.

Bulb: swollen underground bud by which some plants rest when dormant.

Bulbil: small, immature bulb, generally at base of parent bulb, but sometimes (aerial bulbil) in lf axil. Can be detached and grown on.

Calcifuge: same as lime-hater.

Calyx: outer ring of fl parts (sepals). Plural calyces.

Chimaera: same as graft hybrid.

Clone: group of identical plants produced by vegetative propagation (eg, cuttings); ancestry can be traced back to single parent.

Composite: member of daisy family, having compound fl heads with outer ray florets ("petals") & inner disc florets.

Compound: describes lvs, fls or frs made up of a number of distinct, similar parts.

Continental: describes climate little influenced by sea, with big difference between summer & winter temperatures, etc.

Corm: underground storage organ similar to bulb but consisting of swollen stem base.

Cormlet: small immature corm. Can be detached and grown on.

Corolla: inner ring of fl parts (petals).

Corymb: more or less flat-topped infl.

Crest: fan-like appendage, as on some fern fronds.

Crisped: curly-edged, as in some fern fronds.

Cross: offspring of 2 distinct parents.

Cross-pollination: pollination of fl by pollen from different plant.

Crown: upper part of roots of herbaceous perennial, from which shoots grow.

Cultivar: cultivated variety; see p4.

Cuttings: see Hardwood cuttings, Internodal cuttings, Leaf-bud cuttings, Root cuttings, Semi-ripe cuttings, Softwood cuttings. See also Propagation.

Cyme: rounded branching infl in which inner or topmost fls open first.

Daisy: see Composite.

Deciduous: describes plant that sheds all lvs at once.

Decumbent: having stems that lie horizontally, rising at tip.

Dioecious: having male and female fls on different plants.

Disbudding: removal of fl buds around a central bud to induce extra-large bloom.

Divided (of lf): having several distinct segments.

Division: easiest method of propagation for most clump/crown-forming perennials (including alpines) & multi-stemmed shrubs. Best done in spring for summer/autumn-flg spp, in autumn for spring-flg. Lift crown; pull apart fibrous-rooted clumps, but use forks for tougher crowns; cut woody crowns with sharp spade or knife & dust cut with fungicide. Discard old, worn-out centre before replanting.

Dormancy: temporary cessation of growth.

Double (of fl): having (much) more than the usual number of petals.

Entire (of lf): having smooth untoothed edges.

Evergreen: plant that retains lvs at all seasons.

F1 hybrid: first-generation cross between 2 pure-bred strains; usually v vigorous.

F2 hybrid: second-generation cross between 2 F1 hybrids.

Falls: pendulous outer petals, as in iris fls.

Farinose: covered in waxy whitish powder.

Fastigiate: having branches that grow almost vertically, forming column shape.

Fertilizer: synthetic or natural organic substances providing essential plant foods including nitrogen (N), especially for stem growth & lvs; phosphorus (phosphate; P), mainly for root growth; potassium (potash; K), especially for fls & frs; & various "trace elements" (proprietary fertilizers generally give analysis of N:P:K content). Some (including bonemeal) contain lime & must not be given to lime-hating plants. A base fertilizer (or dressing) is one mixed with soil before planting; a top dressing is sprinkled on the soil around plant. Liquid fertilizers, diluted with water, are applied to roots or sprayed on foliage.

Floret: individual fl forming part of compound fl, as in composites.

Fimbriated: margins divided to form fringe.

Fruit: the whole seed-bearing organ, whatever its form (eg, pod, capsule, etc).

Glaucous: having bluish sheen.

Graft hybrid: plant formed of mingled tissues of 2 different spp & intermediate in characters.

Grafting: Method of propagation for trees & shrubs used mainly by nurserymen; similar to budding, but using lengths of stem.

Haft: narrow stalk-like base to some petals, as in irises.

Hardwood cuttings: method of propagation used for most hardy trees & many shrubs; generally taken in late autumn. Choose strong, well-ripened shoots & lower lvs of evergreens & trim below bud at bottom. Length varies from 10–15cm (4–6in) for many flg shrubs to 30cm (1ft) for trees. Where winters moderate & soil well drained, plant longer cuttings immediately in slit trench with 2.5cm (1in) of sand at bottom; tread in firmly. Where winters v cold &/or soil heavy, store wrapped in plastic at 0–4°C (37–39°F) & plant in early spring. Smaller cuttings may be best inserted in pots of peat & sand in cold frame. In case of shrubs with v slender shoots, use short side-shoots with short segment ("mallet") of main shoot attached. The following autumn transfer rooted cuttings to nursery beds or pots & grow on until planted out.

Heaving: alternate freezing and thawing of soil causing root damage.

Herbaceous: dying down to ground when dormant.

Hose-in-hose (of fl): having 1 perfect set of petals within another; also called cup-and-saucer.

Humus: substance formed when organic matter rots; important for good soil structure.

Hybrid: plant resulting from crossing 2 distinctly different plants.

Inflorescence: structure made up of several fls.

Internodal cuttings: method of propagation v similar to leaf-bud cuttings but having length of stem attached below; bottom end trimmed between 2 nodes.

Internode: portion of stem between 2 nodes.

Keel: a boat-shaped petal found in pea fls.

Lateral: side shoot, bud, etc.

Layering: propagation technique – inducing shoots to develop roots while attached to parent plant; used mainly for lax-stemmed shrubs, stooled trees & climbers. Peg down branch 15cm (6in) from tip in autumn or late winter & cover pegged part with soil/sand/peat mixture (in ground or pot); stake tip upright. Twisting &/or notching pegged part may assist rooting. Treat border carnations & pinks similarly, pegging down shoots in summer. Layers should be rooted by autumn; sever from parent, carefully lift & overwinter in pots in cold frame; or leave until following spring. See also Air layering.

Leaf-bud cuttings: method of propagation used for camellias. Consist of v small sections of stem with 1 lf & its axillary bud (plump); taken in spring & treated like softwood cuttings. Stem segment may simply be heel.

Leaflet: individual "lf", part of compound lf.

Lime-hater: plant unable to thrive in alkaline soil.

Maritime: describes climate mainly influenced by sea, generally with mild winters & cool summers & often much rain.

Monocarpic: describes plant that dies after flg & frg once (may take several yrs).

Monoecious: having separate male and female fls, but on same plant.

Mulch: soil covering of peat, leaf-mould, etc.

Naturalize: permanently plant; particularly applied to bulbs allowed to grow undisturbed.

Neutral: neither acid nor alkaline.
Node: joint in stem.
Offset: young plant growing from side of parent. Can be detached & grown on.
Opposite (of lvs, etc): in pairs along stem.
Palmate (of lf): having lobes or lfts radiating hand-like from centre.
Panicle: similar to raceme, but with branched clusters of fls along stem.
Peat: in US, called peat moss.
Pedicel, peduncle: fl stalk.
Perennial: plant (especially soft-stemmed) that grows for a number of yrs, generally flg each yr.
Perfoliate: having 2 opposite lvs fused together around stem.
Petaloids: modified stamens, resembling petals.
Petiole: lf stalk.
Phylloclade, phyllode: lf-like short shoot.
Pinna: lft of a fern frond or pinnate lf.
Pinnate (of lf): having lfts in 2 rows.
Pinnatifid: pinnately lobed.
Pinnule: lobe of a lft in bipinnate lf.
Pistil: female part of fl.
Pleaching: training branches of row of trees horizontally to form tall screen.
Pleated (of lf): creased along its length.
Plume: feathery infl.
Pollarding: severe pruning of tree almost to trunk, inducing growth of new young branches.
Pompon: small globular fl or fl head.
Procumbent: creeping.
Propagation: production of new plants in 2 main ways: by growing from seed (bought or collected yourself) & by vegetative methods – dividing up plants or growing new plants from pieces of existing ones. Seed may be sown where plants are to grow (as with hardy annuals) or in trays or pots indoors or out, the seedling plants then being planted out. Temperatures needed vary widely. Generally, germinate hardy perennials, alpines & woody plants in cold frame, tender & semi-hardy plants in warmth. Where seed coat v hard, chip or scrape &/or soak in warmish water before sowing. Seeds of many hardy trees & shrubs need stratifying, others best sown fresh. There are many vegetative methods, the best depending on the sp (or even var) being grown, in 3 main categories: cuttings & layering; division; budding & grafting.
Pruning: Cutting back to control or adjust plant size/shape, encourage profuse fls/frs, or to remove dead/diseased parts. Use sharp tools & cut cleanly; paint large scars with sealant. Make cuts just above (& sloping downwards away from) a side branch or bud pointing in the direction you want new growth to develop. TREES: reduce twinned leading shoots to single; remove lowest branches to leave trunk, especially in broadleaves, when tall enough. SHRUBS: for those flg early on yr-old wood, cut out old, worn-out &

weak stems completely when flg finished, & cut back other fld shoots to vigorous young growth. For those flg from mid-summer on new wood, remove weak shoots in late winter occasionally thinning out a few of oldest stems & cut back yr-old shoots of 2 or 3 buds. For shrubs grown for coloured young shoots, cut back almost to ground in v early spring. Some small-lvd shrubs can be trimmed by shearing, generally after flg. All other shrubs can be thinned out when necessary in spring.
Raceme: unbranched infl having fls on stalks along stem.
Reversion: growth of normal type on sport (eg green lvs on variegated var).
Rhizome: underground stem serving same purpose as bulb or tuber. Use in propagation as for tubers.
Root cuttings: used for fleshy-rooted perennials & woody plants that commonly grow suckers (but not for grafted plants). Lift plant when dormant, or expose roots. Cut 8cm (3in) segments of roots about 1cm (½in) thick; plant vertically (correct way up) in pots of moist peat & sand or of potting mixture. With thin roots, cut 2.5cm (1in) sections; plant flat & shallowly. Keep moist in cold frame.
Scandent: climbing, but not self-supporting.
Scree: v gritty free-draining soil.
Self: having 1 pure colour with no markings.
Self-fertile: able to pollinate its own fls.
Semi-double: having a few more than normal number of petals.
Semi-evergreen: shedding some, but not all, lvs in winter, or only in extreme cold.
Semi-ripe cuttings: method of propagation used for most shrubs & many other woody plants (including many conifers); taken mid summer to early autumn. Choose vigorous, healthy non-flg shoots. Pinch out soft tip growth & trim below a node to give total length of 8cm (3in), less for heathers; or use short lateral shoots pulled off with heel of old wood attached (trim heel tidy). Treat as for softwood cuttings, but no artificial heat needed; or plant under plastic tunnel in open if soil light.
Sepal: any of the lf-like segments of calyx, usually green but often showy and coloured.
Shrub: woody plant without distinct trunk.
Simple: opposite of compound.
Single: having normal number of petals for sp.
Softwood cuttings: method of propagation used for most perennials, sub-shrubs & alpines (all taken in spring or summer) & conifers (late summer). Choose healthy, young, vigorous non-flg shoots (from base of plant in case of dahlias, chrysanthemums, delphiniums, lupins & some others). Cut 2.5–8cm (1–3in) section from tip; trim cleanly just below a node (bud of lf joint). Remove 1 or 2 lowest pairs of lvs, dip cut end in hormone rooting powder & insert in mixture of moist peat &

sand (or proprietary cutting mixture) in propagating unit or pot with plastic cover to retain humidity. Keep in good light at about 18°C (65°F). Once well rooted, transfer to small pots of potting mixture, water & keep in greenhouse for few days. Grow on in cold frame until planting time.

Spadix: thick, fleshy fl spike with small fls; as in members of arum family.

Spathe: showy bract around spadix.

Specimen: plant placed on its own in focal spot.

Spikelet: cluster of fls and bracts in grasses.

Spike: raceme with semi-/stalkless fls.

Spired: having crown with several points.

Sport: sudden change of plant's characteristics (eg, fl colour), due to genetic mutation.

Spur: hollow appendage at base of petal, often long and projecting from rest of fl.

Stamen: male part of fl.

Standard: uppermost, usually erect, petals of some fls; plant grown on single tall stem.

Stigma: pollen-receiving part of pistil.

Stipule: scaly/leafy appendage at base of petiole.

Stolon: runner – shoot that grows along ground, rooting to form new plants.

Stool: clump of shoots growing from near ground.

Stooling: cutting down to ground level to induce tightly packed new growth.

Stopping: pinching out tip to induce branching.

Stratification: exposure of seeds to winter conditions (or refrigeration) for some months in pots of damp sand to induce germination.

Sub-shrub: partly woody, partly herbaceous plant, or plant that is woody where summers hot.

Succulent: having fleshy stems &/or lvs that store water, as in cacti, etc.

Sucker: shoot growing from underground stem/ root. With suckering trees & shrubs growing on own roots (i.e. not grafted), can be used for propagation by digging up with section of roots attached & replanting (best when dormant).

Tendril: twining appendage of some climbers.

Tetraploid: having twice normal number of chromosomes; such plants are mostly vigorous.

Trifoliate: having lvs in 3s.

Trifoliolate (of lf): having 3 lfts.

Tripinnate: describes bipinnate lf with lfts further divided pinnately.

Tuber: swollen underground food storage organ; may derive from stem or root. Can be used for propagation by division much like crowns. Lift when dormant (immediately after flg for rhizomatous irises) & cut up, ensuring at least 1 "eye" (bud) on each piece. Where tuber has no eyes (eg, dahlias, paeonies), each piece must have section of stem with buds. Discard old woody parts, dust with fungicide & replant.

Tufted: having many stems in close cluster at ground level; not spreading.

Umbel: round or flat-topped infl with all fl stalks from one point.

Variegated: patterned with 2 or more distinct colours.

Whorl (of lvs, fls, etc): arranged like spokes of a wheel.

Zoning: ring of contrasting colour on lf.

Pests and diseases

Where only a small part of the plant is affected, it is best first to remove & destroy that part. If this is not enough, in a few cases the whole plant must be destroyed; otherwise, treat it with a suitable pesticide. There are many brands of these, containing various chemicals. Try first to identify your problem, then refer to recommendations below or seek expert advice from a good garden centre or store on the best remedy. (Key to recommended pesticides lists generic or chemical names, which generally appear on labels with any trade names; not all may be available in all countries.)

Most pesticides come as liquids or wettable powders to be mixed with water or sprayed on plants (or sometimes sprinkled on soil); dry powders may be dusted on plants or applied to soil to counter root pests. "Systemic" pesticides attack from within; they are absorbed into the plant's tissues & poison the pest or disease organism that attacks it, remaining effective after normal types would have been washed away by rain. Always follow exactly the manufacturer's instructions on mixing & usage (including warnings on sensitive plants). Spray in calm, preferably dull weather, if possible in early morning or late afternoon. Avoid spillage on skin or inhaling spray/dust; wash hands afterwards; keep out of children's reach – mostly poisonous.

PESTS: Main types are sucking or sap-feeding types (often transmit virus diseases), lf-eaters & those that attack roots or stems.

Ants: A nuisance, but rarely harm plants. Treatment: **E, F, G, J, N, S, X**.

Aphids: (plant lice): Small, plump, often wingless insects that suck sap; multiply v rapidly; excrete honeydew (often infected by sooty moulds). Include greenfly & blackfly (attack lvs, distorting & stunting growth), root aphids (attack roots, often causing wilt) & woolly aphid (attacks branches of ornamental trees). Treatment (start early; systemics often best): **A, B, J, K, L, M, N, P, Q, U, V, S, T**.

Borers: Numerous types; insect larvae that tunnel into stems & trunks of shrubs, trees, etc.

Treatment (apply to trunk/holes): **E, H, J, K, P, S**; if necessary remove wilted portion above attack.

Capsid bugs & relatives: 1cm (½in) green or brown bugs that suck sap of young growth, causing distortion of lvs & fls some time later. Treatment (repeat & also spray in winter): **D, E, H, J, K, L, N, P, S, V.**

Caterpillars: Larvae of butterflies, moths, etc; mostly feed on lvs; some (tortrix) spin webs, rolling lvs. Treatment: **A, B, D, H, J, K, L, M, N, P, S, V, X**; also hand picking.

Chafers & related beetles: Adults may eat lvs & fls, but larvae (to 6cm [2½in] long) attack roots, bulbs, etc, sometimes killing plants. Treatment (apply to soil): **J, K, L, M, N, P, S, X.**

Cutworms: Soil-living brownish caterpillars to 4cm (1½in) long that feed at night, often severing stems of annuals & perennials. Treatment (apply to soil): **C, G, J, N, X**; keep soil well cultivated.

Earwigs: Make ragged holes (at night) in fls & lvs. Treatment (to plants & soil beneath): **D, N, S, X**; keep borders clear of dead lvs, etc.

Eelworms: Microscopic organisms that enter tissues of daffodils, tulips & other plants (stem & bulb eelworm), causing softening, rotting & collapse of plants; also of chrysanthemums, paeonies, etc (chrysanthemum eelworm), causing black patches on lvs. No treatment; destroy infected & neighbouring plants & do not replant with susceptible spp.

Flea beetles: Eat small holes in lvs, etc, of young wallflowers & relatives, mainly in spring. Treatment: **D, H, N, S.**

Froghoppers: (cuckoospit, spittle bugs): Suck sap, distorting growth; live in blob of foam. Treatment (spray forcefully): **N, P.**

Galls: Corky swellings; may be caused by midges (treatment **N**), mites (treatment **J**) & certain wasp larvae (treatment rarely necessary). Can only be controlled when adults on move in spring or early summer.

Leafhoppers: Lf-sucking small insects that jump when disturbed; leave white spots on lvs. Treatment: **H, J, K, L, M, N, P, Q, S, V.**

Leaf miners: Tiny grubs that tunnel in lvs, leaving whitish blotches or trails. Treatment (only needed if serious): **A, J, K, L, M, N, P, S, U, V, X.**

Leatherjackets: Tough-skinned fat grubs (larvae of craneflies [harvestmen, daddy-long-legs]), that feed on roots; mostly lawn pests, but may attack border plants. Treatment (apply to soil): **C, D, F, N**; frequent cultivation to expose to birds.

Millipedes: Generally blackish, to 5cm (2in) long; curl up when disturbed (beneficial centipedes run for cover). Attack roots & shoots of seedlings. Treatment: **J, N.**

Narcissus flies: Larvae bore into daffodil & other bulbs, killing or severely stunting growth. No effective treatment, but keep bulbs well covered with soil in early summer.

Sawflies: Larvae of various types feed on lvs, like caterpillars, sometimes rolling them. Treat as for caterpillars.

Scale insects: Sap-feeders that live under shell-like scales on stems, bark, lvs, etc, laying eggs there; only larvae ("crawlers") move, in summer. Treatment (at crawler stage): **J, K, L, M, P, S**; give shrubs & trees tar-oil winter wash.

Slugs & snails: Feed on lvs, fls, bulbs & other soft tissues, mainly at night. Treatment (best on warm humid nights): **R.**

Tarsonemid mites: Small mites living & feeding on young plant tissues (mainly in buds, under bulb scales, etc), causing distortions, scarring, etc. Treatment **J** may arrest spread.

Thrips: V small, thin sap-feeders causing silvery mottling of lvs & fls; worst in hot summers. Treatment (easy): **A, J, K, L, M, N, P, U, V.**

Whiteflies: Adults resemble tiny moths but are related to aphids; suck sap from lvs & excrete honeydew. Treatment: **A, B, J, P, V.**

Wireworms: Long, thin, leathery, beetle larvae that attack roots & stems; rare in well-cultivated ground. Treatment (apply to soil): **B, C, G, J, N.**

Others: Include various birds & mammals. If scarers &/or physical barriers (netting, etc) not effective, seek local advice on trapping.

DISEASES: More difficult to diagnose. Effects include discoloration, spotting or distortion of lvs, coatings of mould, etc, on shoots, lvs &/or fls, abnormal growth, wilting & death of all or parts of the plant. Apart from chemical treatment, always remove & burn severely affected parts.

Anthracnose: Greyish/whitish spots on lvs &/or stems of various trees & shrubs, especially in wet weather. Treatment (as lvs open): **b, c, f, p.**

Black spot: Large, fuzzy black spots on rose lvs, especially in wet weather, causing lf-fall. Other plants similarly attacked. Treatment (repeat): **b, c, d, g, h, k, l, p, q, r, s.**

Canker: Sunken dead patches on trunk or branches of trees & shrubs; if girdles limb, kills all growth above. Caused by bacteria or fungi. Cut out all dead growth to healthy tissue as soon as noticed & seal wound.

Chlorosis: Yellowing between veins of lvs caused by waterlogged soil or lack of nutrients (eg, iron deficiency in lime-haters growing on alkaline soil – may be helped by feeding sequestered iron).

Club root: Poor growth & swollen, knobbly roots in stocks, wallflowers & other members of cabbage family. Treatment: **b, n, p**; do not replant in same site.

Crown gall: Woody 2.5cm (1in) galls on shoots &/or roots of shrubs, etc, especially of rose family; due to soil bacteria. Cut out infected parts.

Damping-off: Collapse of small seedlings due to fungi attacking stem at soil level. Sterilize soil mixture & treat with **d, e, q, s**.

Downy mildew: Greyish downy patches, generally on underside of lvs with yellow or blackish spots on upper, rotting tissues. Treatment: **b, c, k, l, p, q, s**.

Dutch elm disease: Fungus spread by bark beetles, causing yellowing & wilt of lvs & dieback of branches. Fell tree & burn all bark & twigs on site.

Fireblight: Serious bacterial disease of rose family, especially apples, pears, cotoneasters & hawthorns; notifiable in UK. Starts in fls, spreading backwards, turning stems & lvs brown then black as they die. Cut away & burn to well below affected part, or whole plant if necessary; antibiotic sprays available in some countries.

Grey mould (botrytis): Attacks wide range of plants, especially in wet/humid conditions, causing rotting with grey furry coating. Treatment: **b, d, p, q, s** (after removing affected parts).

Honey fungus (armillaria root rot): Underground fungus attacking all types of plants through roots; seen as honey-coloured toadstools, but living plants infected only via rotting wood, roots, etc, eventually killing. Remove dead plants, including roots; sterilize soil with formalin before replanting.

Powdery mildew: White powdery coating on shoots, lvs & often fls &/or frs, especially in hot, dry weather. Treatment (from spring, repeating): **b, c, f, g, h, j, p, r**; cut out & burn affected parts in winter.

Rots: Apart from grey mould & other diseases listed, rhizoctonia fungi may cause rotting of roots, stems & bulbs, mainly in poor cultural conditions. Remove dead parts, improve cultivation & treat soil with **b, d, e, n, p, q, s**.

Rust: Yellowish spots on upper surface (& cushions of rust-coloured mould on lower) of lvs of roses & many other plants; can be v damaging. Treatment: **a, k, l, m, q, s** & burn diseased lvs.

Tulip fire (tulip blight): Grey or "scorched" patches on tulip lvs, leading to rotting, & deformed fls; worst if spring cold & wet. Destroy diseased plants & bulbs; do not replant tulips in same site; dust/dip bulbs in **b, n**; protect young plants with **b, k, l, p, q, s**.

Virus diseases: May cause distorted or abnormally-shaped growth, mottling of lvs, discolouring or streaking of fls (as in Rembrandt tulips), etc. Spread by sucking insects, handling, soil; passed to offspring by vegetative propagation. No treatment; destroy infected plants & do not replant same spp; control pests.

Wilt: Collapse due to various soil fungi (also root pests, etc), especially in asters, carnations, clematis, paeonies & pansies. Affected plant may regrow if cut back & soil drenched with **b, p, q**; do not replant susceptible spp in same site.

Key to suitable pesticides

Insecticides

A Acephate*
B Bioresmethrin†
C Bromophos
D Carbaryl
E Carbophenothion
F Chlordane‡
G Chlorpyrifos‡
H Derris† (rotenone)
J Diazinon‡
K Dimethoate*†
L Fenitrothion‡
M Formothion*
N Gamma-HCH‡ (benzene hexachloride, BHC, gamma-BHC, hexachlorohexane, HCH, lindane)
P Malathion†
Q Menazon*
R Metaldehyde
S Methoxychlor
T Pirimicarb†§
U Propoxur‡
V Pyrethrum† (pyrethrins)
W Tetradifon†
X Trichlorphon†

Fungicides

a Benodanil
b Benomil*
c Bordeaux mixture
d Captan
e Cheshunt compound
f Dinocap
g Fenarimol
h Folpet
j Lime-sulphur¶
k Mancozeb
l Maneb
m Oxycarboxin*
n Quintozene
p Thiophanate-methyl*
q Thiram
r Triforine*
s Zineb

Key: *systemic; †safe &/or non-persistent; ‡persistent or relatively so in environment; §highly specific against aphids – harmless to most beneficial insects; ¶also attacks mites.

Cypress trees & their close relatives

The most important group of garden conifers, with numerous vars of all sizes. Generally dense, with evergreen foliage persisting almost to base, in sprays or plumes; adult leaves scale-like; juvenile leaves (persistent in some vars) needle-like. Excellent as specimens or for tall screens & background plantings; many good for hedges. **Cultivation**: Very hardy unless stated, but some vars prone to winter scorch. Generally for any well-drained soil in sun or moderate shade (golden vars best in full sun). **Pruning**: Generally unnecessary except to reduce forked leaders to a single, or for hedging (start trimming when young). **Propagation**: Semi-ripe cuttings; some vars by grafting on seedlings of sp; seed (may not breed true). For slow-growing vars and true dwarfs, see pp20–22.

"False" cypresses (*Chamaecyparis* spp; formerly *Cupressus* spp): v popular, generally more or less conical or columnar trees best in moderate climates with adequate moisture; dislike drying winds. Unlike *Cupressus* spp, have foliage in flattened sprays; globular cones less than 12mm (½in) long.

C. lawsoniana **1** (Lawson's cypress; in US, Port Orford cedar): sp to 15×3.5m (50×12ft)/25yrs, eventually to 30m (100ft) or more; rarely grown in gardens but numerous vars v popular. Reddish-brown fissured bark; lvs* in fan-like sprays; male fls crimson, female blue to green. Easy to transplant even when quite mature; resent hard pruning. Vars: 'Allumii' **2** (narrowly conical, to 9×2.5m [30×8ft]; dense; blue-grey); 'Columnaris' **3** ('Columnaris Glauca'; narrowly columnar, to 6×1m [20×3ft]; glaucous); 'Fletcheri' (slow-growing, to 3.5×1.5m [12×5ft]; broadly columnar; semi-juvenile greyish-green lvs, bronze in winter); 'Grayswood Pillar' (dense & v narrow, to 9×0.75m [30×2½ft]; grey); 'Green Pillar' **4** (slow-growing, to 6×1.5m [20×5ft]; dense; bright green); 'Kilmacurragh' (columnar, to 6×1.5m [20×5ft]; dark green; resists snow damage); 'Lanei' ('Lane'; columnar, to 6×2.5m [20×8ft]; bright golden-yellow feathery foliage); 'Lutea' (broadly columnar, to 7.5×2.5m [25×8ft]; drooping crown; pale yellow lvs maturing darker); 'Pembury Blue' (conical, to 6×3m [20×10ft]; delicate silvery-blue); 'Pottenii' (slow-growing, to 5.5×1.5m [18×5ft]; neat & conical; sea-green partially juvenile lvs in soft sprays); 'Stardust' (columnar to narrowly conical, to 6×1.5m [20×5ft]; yellow suffused bronze); 'Stewartii' (elegant & conical, to 7.5×3m [25×10ft]; large flat sprays of golden lvs, greening in winter); 'Triomf van Boskoop' ('Triomphe de Boskoop'; conical, to 9×2m [30×7ft]; steely-blue; open habit, best trimmed regularly); 'Winston Churchill' **5** (to 6×2.5m [20×8ft]; dense & conical, upswept at base; rich golden-yellow); 'Wisselii' **6** (fast-growing, to 9×2.5m [30×8ft]; columnar but open; sparse upright branches; blue-green; profuse male fls).

C. nootkatensis (Nootka cypress; in US, Alaska cedar): conical tree, to 9×3m (30×10ft)/25yrs, eventually to 30m (100ft); branchlets drooping; long flattened sprays of green foliage (pungent when crushed); male fls yellow. Dislikes cold dry winds & v hot summers. Var 'Pendula' **7** has v long drooping branchlets like streamers.

C. obtusa (Honoki cypress): slow-growing broadly conical Japanese tree, to 7.5×3m (25×10ft)/25yrs, eventually to 25m (80ft); rather open; reddish-brown fissured bark; glossy green v short blunt-tipped resinous lvs* in thick flattened sprays, distinctively white-marked beneath. Beautiful specimen for large gardens; popular for Japanese-style gardens; excellent bonsai subject. Var 'Crippsii' **8** (golden Honoki cypress) is slow-growing, to 6×2.5m [20×8ft]; pyramid-shaped & rather open, with spreading branches; frond-like sprays of golden young lvs, greening later; v elegant.

C. pisifera (Sawara cypress; juvenile-lvd forms originally listed as *Retinispora* spp): slow-growing conical Japanese tree, to 6×2.5m (20×8ft)/25yrs, eventually to 20–30m (65–100ft); spreading branches, lower lost when old, showing distinct bole; brownish-red bark; horizontal sprays of dark green foliage, adult lvs sharp-pointed. Numerous vars v popular. Trim in spring if necessary to promote dense growth. Vars: 'Aurea' **9** (young lvs gold, greening in summer); 'Filifera' (broadly pyramid-shaped tree, to 4.5×3m [15×10ft], or large bush; branchlets & foliage whip/thread-like); 'Plumosa' (*R. plumosa*; slow-growing conical tree, to 7.5×3m [25×10ft], or large bush; v dense; awl-shaped semi-juvenile lvs, soft to touch); 'Plumosa Aurea' (bright yellow young lvs becoming yellow-green); 'Squarrosa' **10** (*R. squarrosa*, moss cypress; broadly conical, to 6×3m [20×10ft]; irregular but v dense; sprays of soft juvenile glaucous foliage).

Leyland cypresses (×*Cupressocyparis leylandii* vars): bigeneric hybrids of *Chamaecyparis nootkatensis* & *Cupressus macrocarpa*; v vigorous trees, to 15–18×4.5m (50–60×15ft)/25yrs, eventually to 30m (100ft), but can be kept trimmed as low as 1.2m (4ft) for hedging. Dense & columnar, with conical crown; flattened/irregular slightly drooping sprays of scale-like lvs; cones to 2cm (¾in) across, rare. Combine hardiness of 1st parent listed with wind-tolerance of 2nd; tolerate chalk soils. Vars: 'Castlewellan' **11** (foliage plume-like, tipped gold); 'Haggerston Grey' (greyish-green foliage

14

in irregular dense sprays; commonest var); 'Leighton Green' (dense; green ferny foliage; v common); 'Robinson's Gold' (compact; golden, bronzed in spring).

True cypresses (*Cupressus* spp): generally columnar to pyramid-shaped trees, moderately hardy unless stated, differing from *Chamaecyparis* spp in their irregularly arranged (not flattened) sprays of foliage. Adult lvs* tiny, scale-like; globular, lumpy cones 1.5–4cm (⅝–1½in) long. Difficult to transplant (best pot-grown) but tolerate most except v wet soils.

C. (Chamaecyparis) funebris (mourning or Chinese weeping cypress): elegant pyramid-shaped tree, to 7.5×3m (25×10ft); erect, becoming pendulous when mature; juvenile lvs soft glaucous-green, adult sage-green in flattened sprays. Sometimes grown as pot-plant when young.

C. glabra **1** (*C. arizonica bonita*, smooth Arizona cypress; often sold incorrectly as *C. arizonica*): dense & conical, to 9×3m (30×10ft); mature bark purplish, peeling to show smooth red to yellow inner bark; branchlets cord-like; lvs grey-green to grey-blue, resin-speckled; masses of golden-yellow male fls, spring. Var 'Pyramidalis' **2** is v dense; bright silvery bluish-grey; profuse yellow male fls. True *C. arizonica* (rough Arizona cypress) is v similar but bark rough & lvs yellowish-green; rare in gardens. Both spp drought-resistant.

C. lusitanica (Mexican cypress; mistakenly, Portuguese cypress, cedar of Goa): semi-hardy spreading tree, to 9×3m (30×10ft)/25yrs, eventually to 25m (80ft); drooping branchlets; grey-green lvs. Vars: *benthamii* (narrowly conical; shining green fern-like foliage; rather tender); 'Glauca' (columnar; blue-green); 'Glauca Pendula' (compact & weeping, to 6×5.5m [20×18ft]; glaucous-blue).

C. macrocarpa (Monterey cypress): fast-growing, to 13.5×3.5m (45×12ft)/25yrs, eventually to 30m (100ft); conical to broadly columnar, often becoming flat-topped like cedar of Lebanon (*Cedrus libani*; p30); dense bright to dark green foliage. Good for shelter, hedging; tender when young. Vars: 'Donard Gold' **3** (deep golden-yellow); 'Goldcrest' (rich yellow; juvenile); 'Lutea' (soft yellow to green; good near sea).

C. sempervirens 'Stricta' **4** ('Fastigiata', Italian or Mediterranean cypress): narrowly columnar, to 7.5×0.75m (25×2½ft); long-lived & eventually to 30m (100ft) or more in Mediterranean climates; dark green foliage. Other vars: 'Glauca' (blue-green).

Incense cedar (*Libocedrus decurrens* **5**; correctly, *Calocedrus decurrens*): wild sp irregularly columnar or conical, but usual garden form is var 'Columnaris' ('Fastigiata'): v narrow columnar tree, to 10×1.5m (33×5ft)/25yrs,

eventually to 25m (80ft) or more; crowded erect fan-like sprays of dark green scale-like lvs*; oval 2.5cm (1in) cones. Excellent for formal plantings, backgrounds. Tolerates heat & poor, dry soils if watered infrequently but deeply when young. Var 'Aureovariegata' is speckled yellow.

Thujas (arbor-vitae, *Thuja* spp [pronounced & sometimes spelled *Thuya*]): generally dense conical trees with flattened fronds of scaly foliage, rather like *Chamaecyparis* spp but distinctively fragrant; small narrow cones have oblong overlapping scales hinged at base.

T. occidentalis (American arbor-vitae, northern white cedar): ultra-hardy, slow-growing but not long-lived columnar to pyramid-shaped tree, to 7.5×2.5m (25×8ft)/25yrs, eventually to 15m (50ft); dull yellowish-green lvs*, bronzed in winter. Sp not often grown in gardens, but good for hedging, especially in v cold areas. Tolerates v wet soils. Vars: 'Fastigiata' (narrowly conical, to 7.5×1.2m [25×4ft]); 'Lutea' ('George Peabody'; narrow & dense, to 6×1.2m [20×4ft]; golden all yr); 'Malonyana' (v narrowly columnar & fast-growing, to 7.5×1m [25×3ft]; dark green all yr); 'Spiralis' (to 6×0.75m [20×2½ft]; sprays of dark green foliage in spirals).

T. (Biota) orientalis **6** (Chinese thuja or arbor-vitae; sometimes classified as *Platycladus orientalis*): compact slow-growing conical or columnar tree, to 4.5×1.2m (15×4ft), or tall shrub; branches & branchlets upright; vertical sprays of bright green lvs (not v aromatic). Var 'Elegantissima' is narrowly conical & dwarf when young, eventually growing to 6m (20ft) & broadening; greenish-yellow, bronze in winter.

T. plicata **7** (*T. lobbii*, western red cedar, giant arbor-vitae) handsome & fast-growing narrowly conical tree, to 12×3.5m (40×12ft)/25yrs, eventually to 30m (100ft) or more & broadening, with upswept lower branches; pale to reddish-brown shredding bark; glossy green lvs* in drooping sprays. Excellent as specimen or for hedging or screening, but dislikes strong cold winds. Vars: 'Fastigiata' ('Pyramidalis', 'Stricta'; narrow & dense); 'Semperaurescens' (yellowish-green); 'Zebrina' **8** (foliage barred gold, appearing golden-green from distance; slower-growing than sp but one of tallest golden conifers).

Thujopsis (Hiba arbor-vitae, *Thujopsis* [*Thuja*] *dolabrata* **9**): moderately to v hardy slow-growing conical tree, to 5.5×3.5m (18×12ft)/25yrs, or large shrub; v similar to *Thuja* spp but larger branchlets & lvs in large flattened sprays; lvs shiny dark green. Excellent specimen if sheltered.

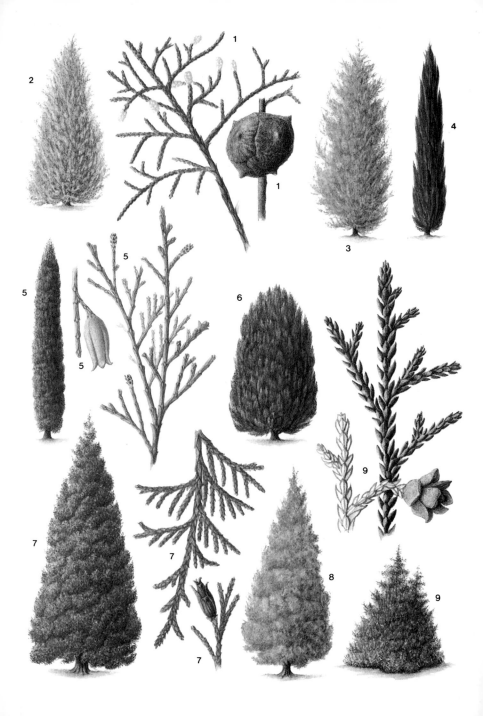

Juniper trees

Juniperus spp & vars. Very useful & varied evergreens, generally tough & hardy, withstanding extremes of heat & cold, drought & poor (even alkaline) soils, & serving many landscaping purposes. Usually rather slow-growing, with thin peeling bark & finely divided branchlets. Juvenile leaves needle- or awl-shaped, 3–25mm (1/8–1in) long; adult leaves usually scale-like & very small. (Some spp & vars have all juvenile leaves, some have both types on same plant.) Sexes generally separate; unique fleshy berry-like fruits, generally black or bluish, with bloom. Spp & vars covered here are trees or upright plants eventually reaching at least 4.5m (15ft); for shrubby & dwarf types, see p22. **Cultivation**; Ultra-hardy unless stated. For any well-drained soil. Lime tolerant. Prone to caterpillars, scale insects, spider mites, rusts causing gall-like growths. Pruning generally unnecessary. **Propagation**: Semi-ripe or hardwood heel cuttings; seed (slow-germinating; may need stratification); grafting. For bushy forms, see p22.

J. chinensis **1** (Chinese juniper): variable, usually columnar tree, to 4.5×1.2m (15×4ft)/25yrs, eventually to 18m (60ft), but sometimes shrubby; generally adult & juvenile lvs on same plant, greyish-green; male fls yellow. Vars: 'Aurea' **2** (Young's golden juniper; less hardy than sp [v hardy]; v slow-growing, to 3×1.2m [10×4ft]/25yrs, but eventually to 6m [20ft] or more; lvs gold, adult brightest; male); 'Columnaris Glauca' (narrowly columnar, to 6×1m [20×3ft]; glaucous-green; greener forms may be sold as 'Columnaris'); 'Keteleeri' **3** (narrowly conical, to 4.5×1m [15×3ft]; bright green adult lvs; profuse frs); 'Spartan' (fast-growing conical or columnar tree, to 6×1.5m [20×5ft]; rich green); 'Stricta' **4** (incorrectly, *J. excelsa stricta*; v often incorrectly sold as 'Pyramidalis' (p22); slow-growing & conical, to 6×1.2m [20×4ft]; blue-grey prickly juvenile lvs). Var 'Kaizuka' ('Torulosa'; p22) is normally a large shrub but forms irregular tree if leader trained.

J. communis (common juniper): slow-growing, v variable shrub or tree; lvs* juvenile, awl-shaped; frs used to flavour gin, etc. Sp rarely grown as too variable. Vars: 'Hibernica' **5** ('Stricta', Irish juniper; narrowly conical to columnar tree, to 3.5×0.75m [12×2½ft]; dark green); *suecica* (Swedish juniper; similar to 'Hibernica' but branchlets nod; bluish-green).

J. deppeana pachyphlaea **6** (alligator juniper): handsome moderately hardy tree, to 4.5×1.5m (15×5ft); bark cracks into small square plates; lvs adult & juvenile, silver-blue; frs 1cm (½in) long. Needs hot dry summers.

J. drupacea **7** (Syrian juniper): moderately to v hardy distinctive pyramid- to column-shaped tree, to 5.5×0.75m (18×2½ft); orange-brown bark; shiny bright green awl-shaped lvs to 22mm (7/8in) long.

J. excelsa (Greek juniper): moderately hardy narrow pyramid-shaped tree, to 6×1m (20×3ft); adult foliage grey-green, in long thread-like sprays. Vars 'Perkinsii' (v glaucous) & 'Stricta' (columnar; not same plant as *J. chinensis* 'Stricta' [above]) retain semi-juvenile lvs.

J. recurva (drooping or Himalayan juniper):

moderately to v hardy graceful tree, to 4.5×2.5m (15×8ft), or large shrub; broadly conical, with branches drooping at ends; dull green awl-shaped lvs; bisexual. Best in wet climates. Vars: 'Castlewellan' (long pendulous branchlets); 'Coxii' **8** (*J. coxii*, coffin juniper; v drooping, like weeping willow; rich sage-green dense foliage).

J. rigida (needle or temple juniper): v hardy graceful tree, to 6×2.5m (20×8ft), or large shrub; spreading branches, drooping at ends; stiff, sharp-pointed bright green lvs, bronzed in winter. Best sheltered from cold winds.

J. scopulorum (Rocky Mountain juniper, Colorado red cedar): rather cypress-like, slow-growing pyramid-shaped tree, to 6×1.8m (20×6ft)/25yrs, eventually to 12m (40ft); reddish-brown bark; adult lvs v small & scale-like, pale green to glaucous. Ultra-hardy but likes hot summers. Vars: 'Blue Heaven' **9** ('Blue Haven'; narrow; bright silvery-blue); 'Gray Gleam' (narrowly columnar; slow-growing; grey-blue); 'Pathfinder' (narrowly conical; blue-grey); 'Skyrocket' **10** (often listed under *J. virginiana*; v narrowly columnar, to 6×0.3m [20×1ft]; blue-grey); 'Springbank' (columnar; grey-green).

J. virginiana ([eastern] red cedar, pencil cedar): broadly conical tree closely related to *J. scopulorum*; to 6×1.8m (20×6ft), becoming round-topped when old; slender branchlets; adult lvs sharp-pointed, dark green; some glaucous juvenile lvs even on mature trees. Best N American sp in W Europe & most of N America; provides fragrant wood. Prone to cedar-apple rust; do not plant near orchards. Vars: 'Burkii' **11** (narrowly pyramid-shaped; steel-blue, purplish in winter); 'Canaertii' (columnar & compact; rich green; free-frtg); 'Cupressifolia' ('Hillspire'; dense & narrow; dark green); 'Elegantissima' (foliage tipped golden, bronze in autumn); 'Glauca' (dense & columnar; silvery-grey, greener in summer); 'Helle' (soft dense foliage; green); 'Manhattan Blue' (compact & conical; bluish-green); 'Pendula' (elegant & drooping, to 6×2.5m [20×8ft]; green). For var 'Skyrocket', see under *J. scopulorum*.

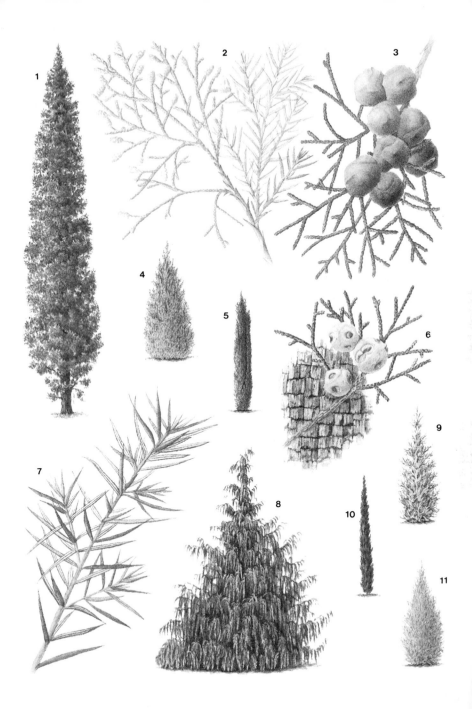

Low-growing cypresses and thujas

Range from rock garden plants to spreading types & substantial bushes, all slow-growing forms of tall spp (p14). Those termed dwarf should remain less than 1.2–1.5m (4–5ft) tall (often much less) even after 15–20 years; good for rock gardens, etc. Others useful for general & specimen planting (sizes given at about 10 years). Unless stated, other features resemble parent. **Cultivation & propagation**: As for tall spp & vars (p14): seeds will not breed true.

"False" cypresses (*Chamaecyparis* spp): v hardy.

C. lawsoniana (Lawson's cypress) vars: MEDIUM-SIZED UPRIGHT & BUSHY VARS: 'Ellwoodii' **1** (slow-growing at first, to 1.8×0.6m [6×2ft]/ 10yrs, eventually to 6m [20ft]; columnar; blue-green semi-juvenile lvs; colour sports include 'Bleu Nantais', 'Blue Gem' & 'Chilworth Silver' [all silvery-blue], 'Ellwood's Gold' [gold in summer] & 'Ellwood's White' [slower-growing; variegated white]); 'Little Spire' (columnar, to 1.2×0.6m [4×2ft]; bluish-green).
SLOW-GROWING SPREADING VARS: 'Dow's Gem' **2** (to 1×1.5m [3×5ft]; drooping branch tips; dense fern-like foliage); 'Duncanii' (domed, to 1×1.8m [3×6ft]; glaucous-green thread-like foliage); 'Nidiformis' (bird's-nest cypress; to 1×1.5m [3×5ft]; arching branches; grey-green); 'Tamariscifolia' (rounded & flat-topped, to 1×2m [3×7ft]; flat triangular sea-green sprays).
DWARF VARS: 'Aurea Densa' **3** (conical, to 60×30cm [2×1ft]; golden-yellow; 'Minima Aurea' is similar but more rounded); 'Forsteckensis' (dense & globular, to 30×40cm [12×16in]; moss-green); 'Gimbornii' **4** (dense, globular & neat, to 60×60cm [2×2ft]; blue-green; 'Minima Glauca' is similar but foliage coarser); 'Nana Albospica' **5** (dense & conical, to 60×30cm [2×1ft]; pale green, young growth white; best in rich soil in shelter); 'Pygmaea Argentea' **6** (rounded, to 40×40cm [16×16in]; bluish-green tipped creamy-white); 'Pygmy' (dense & bun-shaped, to 30×30cm [1×1ft]; grey-green).
C. obtusa (Hinoki cypress) vars: MEDIUM-SIZED UPRIGHT & BUSHY VARS. 'Filicoides' (fernspray cypress; small open tree best kept pruned to 1.5×1.2m [5×4ft]; flat fern-like sprays of moss-green foliage; 'Fernspray Gold' **7** is similar but golden-yellow); 'Nana Gracilis' **8** (conical & slow-growing, to 1×0.75m (3×2½ft)/10yrs, eventually to 2.5×1.5m [8×5ft]; rich glossy green foliage in rounded sprays; 'Tempelhof' is similar but lvs bronzed in winter); 'Tetragona Aurea' (dense but irregular, to 1.5×1m [5×3ft]; angled curving branches; dense golden foliage in full sun; 'Kojolcohiba' is similar but more vigorous).
DWARF VARS: 'Caespitosa' (v slow-growing & dense, to 8×10cm [3×4in]; bun-shaped; rich green; best in pot); 'Juniperoides' (globular, to 15×12cm [6×5in]; dark green; 'Juniperoides

Compacta' is similar but denser); 'Kosteri' (rather sprawling, to 1×1.2m [3×4ft], but best with leader trained up to give layered effect; twisted sprays of lustrous green foliage); 'Nana' **9** (dense & flat-topped, to 25×30cm [10×12in]; v dark green); 'Nana Aurea' (more vigorous than 'Nana', to 50×30cm [20×12in]; new growth golden-yellow); 'Nana Lutea' **10** (neat & compact, to 30×30cm [1×1ft]; bright golden); 'Pygmaea' **11** (low & spreading, to 45×75cm [1½×2½ft]; fan-shaped foliage sprays, bronzed in winter); 'Repens' (semi-prostrate, to 0.3×1.2m [1×4ft]; bright green).
C. pisifera (Sawara cypress) vars: MEDIUM-SIZED UPRIGHT & BUSHY VARS: 'Boulevard' **12** ('Cyanoviridis'; dense & conical, to 2×1m [7×3ft]/10yrs, eventually much larger but can be kept trimmed; silvery blue-grey, best on moist lime-free soil); 'Filifera Aurea' **13** (rather sprawling, to 2×1.5m [7×5ft]/10yrs, but eventually broadly conical, to 4.5×3m [15×10ft]; thread-like golden foliage); 'Plumosa Aurea Nana' (rounded, to 1.2×0.6m [4×2ft]; golden-yellow semi-juvenile foliage; 'Plumosa Rogersii' is similar, but foliage juvenile); 'Squarrosa Sulphurea' (conical, to 2×1m [7×3ft]; soft juvenile foliage, pale sulphur-yellow in spring & early summer, greening).
DWARF VARS: 'Compacta' (bun-shaped, to 20×30cm [8×12in]; blue-green, bronzing in winter); 'Filifera Nana' (rounded & flat-topped, to 0.6×1.2m [2×4ft]; drooping thread-like green foliage; 'Golden Mop' is golden form, to 60×90cm [2×3ft], with finer foliage; 'Sungold' is similar but hardier); 'Nana' (bun-shaped, to 20×50cm [8×18in]; much denser than 'Compacta', with crowded dark green foliage; 'Nana Aureovariegata' **14** is similar but has golden sheen; 'Plumosa Compressa' (v slow-growing & dense bun, to 20×30cm [8×12in]; blue-green parsley-like foliage); 'Squarrosa Intermedia' (globular, to 50×50cm [20×20in]; congested juvenile blue-grey foliage; remove any adult foliage that appears).
C. thyoides 'Andelyensis' (white cypress var): ultra-hardy narrowly conical to columnar bush, v slow-growing to 90×30cm (3×1ft)/10yrs, eventually to 5m (16ft); crowded branchlets with sprays of dark bluish-green foliage; male fls red, tiny; profuse small cones. Hates lime, dry soil. Var 'Ericoides' is compact, to 90×60cm (3×2ft), with sea-green juvenile lvs, purple in winter.

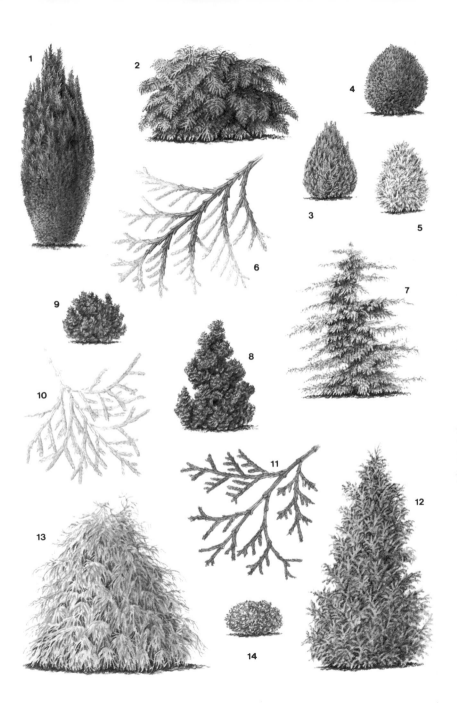

True cypresses (*Cupressus* spp): moderately hardy.

C. glabra 'Compacta' (dwarf Arizona cypress): rounded-conical dwarf bush, to 60×60cm (2×2ft); dense grey-green adult foliage.

C. macrocarpa 'Horizontalis Aurea' ('Gold Spread'; Monterey cypress var): low, spreading shrub, to 1×3m (3×10ft); angled branches; fast-growing; bright golden foliage.

C. sempervirens 'Swane's Golden' **1** (Mediterranean cypress var): compact & narrowly columnar, to 1.8×0.45m (6×1½ft)/10yrs, finally to 4.5m (15ft); golden; best on poor soil in sun.

Thujas (*Thuja* spp):

T. occidentalis (American arbor-vitae) vars: ultra-hardy unless stated.

MEDIUM-SIZED UPRIGHT & BUSHY VARS: 'Ellwangerana Aurea' (sometimes sold incorrectly as 'Rheingold' [below]; rounded, becoming pyramid-shaped, to 3×1.5m [10×5ft]; foliage juvenile at first becoming adult, golden-yellow, bronzing in winter); 'Ericoides' (rounded/spreading, to 1.5×2.5m [5×8ft]; dull green juvenile foliage, rich brown in winter; prone to snow damage; 'Holmstrup' **2** (conical, dense & slow-growing, to 2×1m [6×3ft]/10yrs, eventually to 3.5m [12ft]; rich green); 'Lutea Nana' (dense & pyramid-shaped, to 2×1.5m [7×5ft]; golden-yellow adult foliage, brightest in winter; 'Sunkist' **3** is similar); 'Woodwardii' (compact & globular, to 1.2×1.2m [4×4ft]/10yrs, eventually to 1.5m [5ft]; vertical sprays of rich green foliage).

DWARF VARS: 'Caespitosa' (bun-shaped, to 40×50cm [16×20in]; mid-green); 'Danica' **4** (compact & rounded, to 1×1m [3×3ft]; dark green, bronzing in winter); 'Golden Globe' (globular & rather open, to 1×1m [3×3ft]; golden-yellow); 'Hetz Midget' (v compact & globular, to 30×30cm [1×1ft]; dark green); 'Little Gem' (dense & globular, to 60×60cm [2×2ft]; rich green); 'Rheingold' **5** (dense & rounded, to 1×0.75m [3×2½ft]; remains like a young 'Ellwangerana Aurea', retaining juvenile foliage).

T. orientalis (Chinese arbor-vitae) vars: MEDIUM-SIZED UPRIGHT VARS: 'Conspicua' (columnar, to 2×1m [7×3ft], eventually to 4.5m [15ft]; golden-yellow, colour retained well in winter); 'Elegantissima' (see p16).

DWARF VARS: 'Aurea Nana' **6** (dense & oval, to 60×45cm [2×1½ft]; beautiful golden-yellow in spring & summer, greening later); 'Juniperoides' **7** (dense & rounded, to 60×45cm [2×1½ft]; greyish-green juvenile foliage, purple in winter); 'Rosedalis' (rounded, to 60×45cm [2×1½ft]; soft juvenile foliage, yellow in spring, turning green, then purple-brown by winter).

T. plicata (western red cedar) dwarf vars: 'Cuprea' **8** (to 1×1m [3×3ft]; broadly pyramid-shaped; dark green foliage tipped yellow); 'Rogersii' **9** (v dense, to 75×45cm [2½×1½ft]; dark green tipped golden-bronze); 'Stoneham Gold' **10** (upright bush, to 90×60cm [3×2ft]/10yrs, eventually to 2m [7ft] or more; v dark green tipped bright orange-yellow).

Low-growing and shrubby junipers

Very varied *Juniperus* spp & vars, many derived from tall spp (p18). Those termed dwarf can be expected to remain less than 1.2–1.5m (4–5ft) tall (often much less) even after 15–20 years; can remain permanently in rock gardens, etc. Prostrate vars good for ground cover & as substitutes for heathers on chalky soils. Others include slow-growing tree-shaped & bushy types not generally exceeding 2.5–4.5m (12–15ft); some useful for several years in rock gardens, others often architectural & useful as specimens or for general planting & landscaping. Sizes given at about 10 years; unless stated, other features resemble parent. **Cultivation & propagation**: As for tall spp (p18), but seeds of vars will not breed true; very slow-growing types often grafted. Ultra-hardy unless stated.

J. chinensis (Chinese juniper) vars: v hardy. MEDIUM-SIZED VARS: 'Ames' (dense & pyramid-shaped, to 1.8×1m [6×3ft]; bluish-green); 'Japonica' (bushy & spreading, to 1×1m [3×3ft]/10yrs, with v prickly juvenile lvs, becoming small upright tree with adult lvs when old; rich green); 'Kaizuka' **11** ('Torulosa', Hollywood juniper; irregular upright shrub, to 1.8×1.8m [6×6ft], with slanting branches & clustered mop-like foliage; bright green adult lvs; may eventually become small tree); 'Kaizuka Variegata' ('Torulosa Variegata' is more erect & slow-growing, with creamy patches); 'Maney' (bushy & spreading, to 1.5×1.5m [5×5ft], with upright branches; bluish); 'Obelisk' (narrowly pyramid-shaped, to

3×1.2m [10×4ft]; dense bluish-green prickly foliage); 'Pyramidalis' **12** (often incorrectly sold as 'Stricta' [p16]; compact round-topped column, to 1.5×0.6m [5×2ft]; silver-blue juvenile foliage); 'Variegata' (slow-growing & conical, to 1.5×1m [5×3ft]; blue-green splashed creamy). Var 'San José' is dense & prostrate, to 0.6×1.8m (2×6ft); sage-green mainly juvenile lvs.

J. communis (common juniper): sp slow-growing & v variable, often shrubby, to 3×1.8m (10×6ft), but sometimes tree (p16). Numerous vars. Dwarf vars: 'Compressa' **13** (perfect dwarf column, to 45×15cm [18×6in]/20yrs; v dense, with tiny dark green juvenile lvs); 'Sentinel' ('Pencil Point'; v narrow column, to 1.8×0.3m [6×1ft]); 'Suecica

Nana' (similar to 'Compressa' but looser, rounder-headed & faster-growing, to 1.5×0.3m [5×1ft]/20yrs). PROSTRATE VARS: 'Depressa Aurea' (to 0.3×1.2m [1×4ft]; young lvs golden-yellow, turning bronze then greenish); 'Depressed Star' (to 0.3×1.2m [1×4ft]; bright green feathery foliage browning in winter); 'Hornibrookii' (mat-forming, to 10×90cm [4×36in]; silvery-green); 'Repanda' **1** (dense & mounding, to 0.25×1.8m [10in×6ft]; dark green).

J. conferta (shore juniper): v hardy low-growing shrub, to 0.3×1.8m (1×6ft); crowded awl-shaped lvs, apple-green; 8–12mm (⅓–½in) black frs. Var 'Emerald Sea' is emerald-green, yellow-green in winter.

J. davurica 'Expansa' (*J. chinensis* 'Parsonsii', *J. squamata* 'Parsonsii'): wide-spreading & eventually dome-shaped, to 0.6×2m (2×7ft), with horizontal branches; grey-green juvenile & adult lvs. Do not plant too deeply. Var 'Expansa Variegata' is splashed creamy-white.

J. horizontalis (creeping juniper): variable prostrate sp, generally mat-forming, to 15–30cm×2–3m (6–12in×7–10ft), though often slow-growing at first; lvs mainly juvenile, needle-like, green to blue. Excellent for covering banks, etc; leaders best pinched back when young. Vars: 'Bar Harbor' **2** (v prostrate; grey-green, purplish in winter); 'Blue Chip' **3** (silvery-blue); 'Douglasii' (Waukegan juniper; dense; lvs juvenile & adult, rich grey-green, purplish in winter); 'Emerald Spreader' (bright green feathery juvenile foliage); 'Glomerata' (compact, to 15×90cm [6×36in]; bright green tiny lvs in dense sprays); 'Grey Pearl' (compact, to 15×40cm [6×16in]; grey); Hughes' (vigorous; grey-green); 'Plumosa' (flat-topped spreading bush, to 0.6×1.8m [2×6ft], with angled branches; grey-green lvs in plumes, plum-purple in winter; 'Plumosa Compacta' is denser).

J.×media vars: hybrids of *J. chinensis* & *J. sabina* still often listed under *J. chinensis*; small to medium shrubs with pungent-smelling lvs . PFITZERANA GROUP VARS: (strong spreading branches rising at angle, drooping at tips; lvs mainly semi-juvenile): 'Armstrongii' **4** (compact, to 1×1.2m [3×4ft]; yellowish-green soft lvs); 'Gold Coast' (dense & semi-prostrate, to 1.2×1.8m [4×6ft]; foliage tipped golden-yellow, deepening in winter); 'Hetzii' (vigorous, to 1.8×2m [6×7ft]; glaucous); 'Mint Julep' (semi-prostrate, to 0.75×1.2m [2½×4ft]; rich green); 'Old Gold' **5** (dense & semi-prostrate, to 0.75×1.5m [2½×5ft]; bronze-gold); 'Pfitzerana' **6** (Pfitzer juniper; semi-prostrate, to 1×2m [3×7ft]/10yrs, eventually to 2–3×3–4.5m [7–10×10–15ft]; v popular); 'Sea Spray' (dense & prostrate, to 0.2×2m [8in×7ft]; blue-green); 'Sulphur Spray' (sport of 'Hetzii'; smaller & pale sulphur-yellow). PLUMOSA GROUP VARS: (similar to above but less

spreading & lvs mainly adult, in dense tufts, giving ostrich-plume effect): 'Blaauw' **7** (dense & vase-shaped, to 1.5×1.2m [5×4ft]; bluish grey-green); 'Plumosa' (sometimes sold incorrectly as *J. japonica*; spreading, to 1×1.5m [3×5ft]; deep green; 'Plumosa Aurea' **8** is similar but green-gold deepening to golden-bronze in winter); 'Shimpaku' (v slow-growing, to 40×75cm [16×30in]/10yrs; grey-green.

J. procumbens (often sold incorrectly in US as *J. squamata* 'Prostrata'): sturdy spreading shrub, to 0.6×2m (2×7ft); blue-green juvenile lvs. Best garden var is 'Nana' **9** (slower-growing & denser, to 0.3×1.8m [1×6ft], forming mat).

J. recurva 'Embley Park' **10**; low-growing, spreading var of *J. recurva*, to 40×75cm (1½×2½ft), eventually wider; rich green; best in semi-shade. Var 'Coxii' (p18) is small for yrs.

J. sabina (savin): wild spp generally spreading or prostrate, but v variable & rarely cultivated; sp & vars generally have juvenile & adult lvs on same plant, strong-smelling if crushed. Prone to juniper blight, especially in N American Midwest (resistant vars marked †). Low, spreading vars (all eventually wider than stated): 'Arcadia'† (to 0.45×1.2m [1½×4ft]; rich green); 'Blue Danube' (to 0.6×2m [2×70ft]; grey-blue); 'Broadmoor'† (to 0.3×1.2m [1×4ft]; bright green); 'Buffalo'† (to 0.3×1.2m [1×4ft]; rich green feathery lvs); 'Tamariscifolia' **11** (to 0.45×1.5m [1½×5ft]; dense; blue-green; widely used but v prone to blight). Var 'Hicksii' is bushy, to 1.2×1.5m (4×5ft); semi-erect branches; grey-blue foliage.

J. sargentii (*J. chinensis sargentii*, Sargent juniper); v hardy; prostrate & carpet-forming, to 0.3×2m (1×7ft); lvs mainly adult, greyish pale green. Var 'Glauca' is blue-green.

J. scopulorum (Rocky Mountain juniper) vars: 'Globe' ('Lakewood Globe'; upright & rounded, to 1.5×1.5m [5×5ft]; feathery grey-blue juvenile foliage); 'Silver King' (dense & spreading, to 0.3×2m [1×7ft]; silvery-blue); 'Table Top Blue' (spreading & semi-prostrate, to 1×2m [3×7ft]; flat-topped; grey-blue).

J. squamata vars (intense silver-blue juvenile foliage): 'Blue Carpet' (prostrate, to 0.3×1.5m [1×5ft]); 'Blue Star' **12** (slow-growing, dense & rounded, to 40×50cm [16×20in]); 'Meyeri' (v handsome semi-erect shrub, to 2×2m [7×7ft]/10yrs, eventually to 4.5m [15ft] or even small tree if trained; angled branches; short branchlets, nodding at tips; best pruned regularly.

J. virginiana (eastern red cedar or pencil cedar) vars (lvs mainly adult, on narrow shoots): 'Blue Cloud' (dense & spreading, to 0.45×1.5m [1½×5ft]; protruding twisted branches; silvery-grey); 'Globosa' (dense & neatly rounded, to 1×1m [3×3ft]/10yrs, eventually to 4.5×4.5m [15×15ft]; bright green); 'Gray Owl' **13** (dense & spreading, to 0.6×2.5m [2×8ft]; silver-grey).

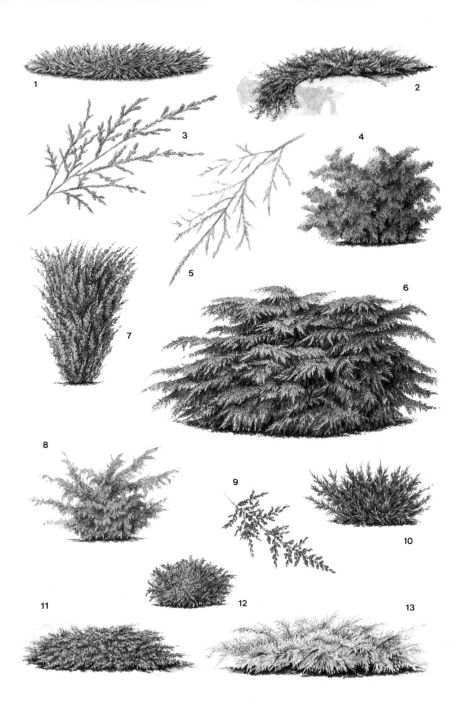

Fir, spruce and hemlock trees

Evergreens with needle-like leaves (sometimes flattened) arranged spirally or in 2 ranks on shoots. Trees conical unless stated, with branches in tiers. Many very tall when old, often losing lower branches, but useful for some years for screening, background planting, etc, or as handsome specimens. **Cultivation**: Very hardy unless stated, most preferring cool moist conditions with some shelter but in full sun. For most fertile soils except shallow chalk; most dislike air pollution. Pruning generally unnecessary and undesirable except to reduce forked leaders to a single. **Propagation**: Best by seed; vars by cuttings, grafting. For low-growing & dwarf types, see pp34–36.

True or silver firs (*Abies* spp): dense & rigidly symmetrical resin-scented trees; winter buds generally resinous; flattened lvs, 1.5–4cm (⅝–1½in) long & glossy green unless stated, white-lined beneath, mainly on top & sides of shoots; male & female fls on separate branches of same tree; attractive upright barrel-shaped cones. 5–10cm (2–4in) long unless stated (distintegrate on tree).

A. amabilis **1** (Pacific or red fir): fast-growing where suited, to 11×3.5m (36×12ft)/25yrs, eventually to 20–30m (65–100ft), or much more in wild; beautifully graceful where thrives, with drooping branches; resinous lvs*; purple 10–15cm (4–6in) cones. For lime-free soil.

A. bracteata **2** (Santa Lucia or bristlecone fir): moderately to v hardy; fast-growing where suited, to 9×4.5m (30×15ft)/25yrs, eventually to 30m (100ft); broadly pyramid-shaped, narrow spiring crown; gracefully curving branches with drooping branchlets; stiff spine-tipped lvs to 5cm (2in) long; purple-brown cones with long bristles. Prone to late frost, especially when young.

A. cephalonica **3** (Greek fir): to 7.5×3.5m (25×12ft)/25yrs, eventually to 30m (100ft) or more; rich green lvs all around shoots; narrow brown cones to 15cm (6in) long. Handsome and lime/pollution tolerant, but prone to late spring frost.

A. concolor (Colorado white fir): v to ultra-hardy; to 10×4.5m (33×15ft)/25yrs, eventually to 30m (100ft) or more; smooth grey bark; glaucous-green lvs* 2.5–8cm (1–3in) long; green to purplish cones. Vars: 'Candicans' **4** (lvs silvery-white); 'Violacea' (lvs glaucous-blue). Var *lowiana* is intermediate form with *A. grandis*.

A. delavayi forrestii **5** (*A. forrestii*): vigorous but rather short-lived in gardens, to 9×3.5m (30×12ft)/25yrs, eventually to 15m (50ft) or more; red resinous buds & reddish-brown young growth; lvs v silvery beneath; purple-black 9cm (3½in) cones with short bristles. Distinctive & beautiful, but sensitive to drought.

A. fargesii **6**: vigorous, to 9×4.5m (30×15ft)/25yrs, eventually to 15–25m (50–80ft) or more; leathery lvs to 5cm (2in) long; cones purple or reddish-brown.

A. homolepis **7** (Nikko fir): to 11×3.5m (36×12ft)/25yrs, eventually to 25m (80ft); handsome & sturdy, becoming domed when old;

finely shredding pinkish bark; rich purple to brown cones.

A. koreana **8** (Korean fir): slow-growing, neat & compact, to 4.5×1.8m (15×6ft)/25yrs, rarely exceeding 10m (33ft) & often only bushy; short blunt lvs; blue-purple to pale brown 7cm (2½in) cones.

A. lasiocarpa arizonica (cork fir): to 10×3.5m (33×12ft)/25yrs, eventually to 12–15m (50–65ft) or more; may develop "candelabra" crown if leader broken; thick creamy-grey corky bark; silvery-blue lvs*; short-lived brown cones. Handsome when young.

A. nordmanniana (Caucasian fir): fast-growing, to 10×4.5m (33×15ft)/25yrs, eventually to 30m (100ft) or more; dense & well tiered; buds not resinous; v dark green lvs*; 10–15cm (4–6in) green to orange-brown cones. May be prone to aphids.

A. pinsapo (Spanish or hedgehog fir): moderately to v hardy; rather slow-growing, to 6×2.5m (20×8ft)/25yrs, eventually to 25m (80ft) or more; sometimes has several trunks; densely packed stiff greyish-green lvs all around shoots; purple-brown cones. Tolerates chalk & dryish conditions. Var 'Glauca' **9** is bluish.

A. procera **10** (*A. nobilis*, noble fir): to 10×3.5m (33×12ft)/25yrs, eventually to 30–40m (100–130ft) or much more; columnar when old; lvs glaucous-green; large purple-brown cones 20–25cm (8–10in) long with conspicuous green bracts, from quite young age. For lime-free soil; prone to aphids. Var 'Glauca' **11** is beautiful blue-grey.

A. veitchii **12**: ultra-hardy; v fast-growing at first, to 10×4.5m (33×15ft)/25yrs, but short-lived, maximum 20–25m (65–80ft)/80yrs; broadly conical; lvs bright white beneath; profuse blue-purple to brown cones.

Spruces (*Picea* spp): sometimes rather open & gaunt when old, but often v graceful; short, hard, usually spiny lvs, generally arranged spirally on shoots but often denser on top than beneath (leave tiny peg-like stumps when shed); cones oval or cylindrical, generally pendulous & rather elegant, 4–8cm (1½–3in) long unless stated, with soft leathery scales, ripening 1st yr.

P. abies (*P. excelsa*, Norway or common spruce): ultra-hardy; fast-growing, to 12×4.5m (40×15ft)/25yrs, eventually to 35m (115ft) or more; glossy

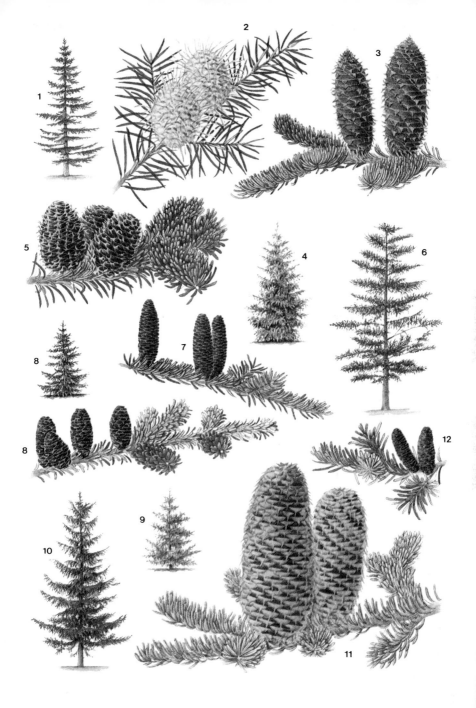

deep green lvs; cones 10–18cm (4–7in) long.
Too big for permanent use, but good as short-
term filler/windbreak. Vars: 'Acrocona' 1 (to
4.5×0.6m [15×2ft] or large shrub; pendulous
branches, many ending in large cones);
'Cupressina' (dense & columnar, to 7.5×2.5m
[25×8ft]); 'Pyramidata' (narrowly conical, to
9×1.2m [30×4ft]).

P. breweriana 2 (Brewer's weeping spruce):
slow-growing, to 6×2.5m (20×8ft)/25yrs,
eventually to 12–30m (40–100ft), tallest in cool
wet mountainous areas; upswept branches with
v long weeping branchlets when mature; dark
green rather sparse lvs; reddish-brown cones.
V beautiful where suited, but needs cool maritime
climate.

P. engelmannii: ultra-hardy; generally slow-
growing at first, to 6×3m (20×10ft)/25yrs,
eventually to 18m (60ft); dense & pyramid-
shaped; lvs* grey-green, or bluish in var
'Glauca'. Best in moist continental climates.

P. glauca 3 (*P. alba*, white or Canadian spruce):
ultra-hardy; similar to *P. abies* but greyer-green
and not so tall, to 9×2.5m (30×8ft)/25yrs,
eventually to 20m (65ft). Var 'Densata' (Black
Hills spruce) grows slowly, to 6m (20ft)/30yrs.

P. jezoensis hondoensis (Hondo or Yeddo
spruce): to 7.5×3.5m (25×12ft)/25yrs,
eventually to 25m (80ft) or more; elegantly
layered; dense deep green foliage, new growths
bright green & prone to late frost damage; young
cones crimson.

P. likiangensis 4: to 9×5.5m (30×18ft)/25yrs,
eventually to 20m (65ft) or more; broadly conical,
with widely spaced upturning branches; lvs
glaucous/green; profuse fls, male crimson,
female scarlet, on mature trees. Prone to late
frost damage when young. Vars *balfouriana* &
purpurea have purple cones; narrow.

P. mariana 5 (*P. nigra*, black spruce): ultra-hardy;
generally slow-growing after first few yrs, to
6×2.5m (20×8ft)/25yrs, eventually to 15m
(50ft); dark bluish-green lvs*; bunched cones
ripening reddish-brown.

P. omorika 6 (Serbian spruce): v to ultra-hardy
fast-growing but slender conical tree, to
10×1.8m (33×6ft)/25yrs, eventually to 25m
(80ft); short curving branches; dark bluish-green
glossy lvs; young cones purple-blue. Tolerates
lime. Var 'Pendula' has long drooping branchlets.

P. orientalis 7 (oriental or Caucasian spruce):
slow-growing at first, to 9×4.5m (30×15)/25yrs,
to 20m (65ft)/50yrs, then slowly to 30m (100ft) or
more; neat, dense & leafy when young; small
dark shining green lvs; cones purple when
young. Var 'Aurea' is slow-growing, to 9m (30ft),
with bright yellow new growth greening in
summer.

P. pungens (Colorado spruce): ultra-hardy;
generally quite slow-growing, to 7.5×2.5m

(25×8ft)/25yrs, eventually to 25–30m (80–100ft)
or more; pyramid-shaped, with tiered horizontal
branches; lvs blue-green, green or greyish;
cylindrical cones to 10cm (4in) long. Best sp for
dryish conditions; in gardens, best replaced after
20–25yrs, before loses lower branches. Main
garden vars are forms of var *glauca* 8 (blue
spruce; all smaller than sp): 'Hoopsii' (dense;
glaucous-blue); 'Koster' ('Kosteriana', Koster's
blue spruce; intense silver-blue); 'Moerheim'
('Moerheimii'; narrowly conical; bluish-white);
'Thomsen' (v pale intense silver-blue). Var
'Argentea' (silver Colorado spruce) is silvery-
white.

P. smithiana 9 (Himalayan weeping spruce):
moderately to v hardy; quite fast-growing when
established, to 10×3m (33×10ft)/25yrs,
eventually to 30m (100ft) or more; horizontal
branches with long drooping branchlets; dark
green lvs to 4cm (1½in) long; 12–18cm (5–7in)
green cones maturing brownish-purple. More
gaunt than *P. breweriana* but grows better in
continental climates; young trees may be
damaged by late frosts.

Douglas fir (*Pseudotsuga menziesii*,
P. douglasii, *P. taxifolia*): ultra-vigorous but
beautiful slender tree, to 25×5.5m (80×18ft)/
25yrs, to 50m (160ft)/70yrs where suited – too
big for most gardens unless sheared as tall
hedge. Flat-topped when old, with furrowed trunk
& plume-like branches with drooping branchlets;
soft pale to dark green flattened 2–2.5cm (¾–1in)
lvs* mainly in 2 ranks, white-banded beneath;
green to brown 5–10cm (2–4in) narrowish
hanging cones with conspicuous 3-pronged
bracts. Prone to aphids in some areas. Var *glauca*
(*P. glauca*, blue Douglas fir) is v to ultra-hardy;
broader & slower-growing than sp, to 7.5×2.5m
(25×8ft)/25yrs; lvs blue-grey/green.

Hemlocks (*Tsuga* spp): extremely beautiful &
elegant in areas with high rainfall & deep soil, with
spreading, upswept branches & drooping
v slender branchlets; close-set & rather yew-like
flattened & blunt lvs, generally less than 2.5cm
(1in) long & in 2 ranks, generally white-banded
beneath; solitary woody cones, generally less
than 2.5cm (1in) long, drooping from ends of
twigs. Good for hedging. Tolerate some shade;
dislikes lime.

T. canadensis (eastern hemlock): v to ultra-
hardy; to 9×6m (30×20ft)/25yrs, eventually to
20–30m (65–100ft); often round-headed, with
several leading shoots; dark green lvs,
undersides twisted uppermost. Tolerates lime.
Var 'Fremdii' is slow-growing, becoming broad,
to 6×5.5m (20×18ft); dense foliage.

T. caroliniana (Carolina hemlock): to 7.5×3.5m
(25×12ft)/25yrs, eventually to 15–25m (50–80ft)
where suited; lvs rather sparse & slender; cones
orange-brown. Best in continental climates.

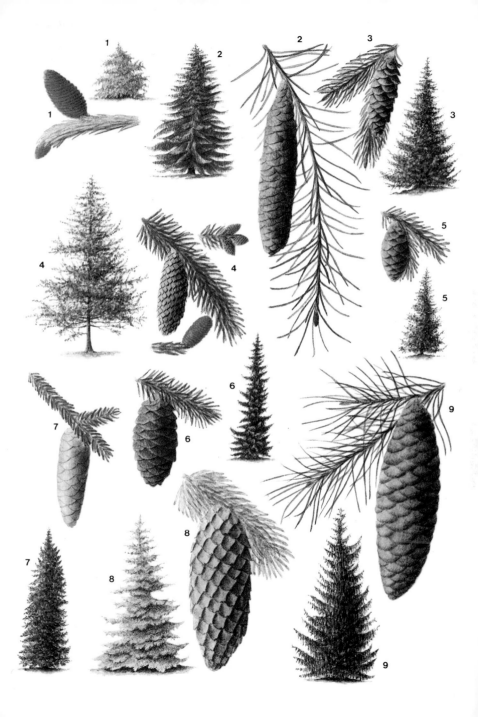

T. diversifolia 1 (northern Japanese hemlock): to 6×4.5m (20×15ft)/25yrs, eventually to 25m (80ft) where suited; usually multi-trunked, rounded & dense; bark & young shoots orange-brown; shining deep green long-lived lvs. Best in continental climates; v slow in UK, but attractive lawn specimen. *T. sieboldii* (southern Japanese hemlock) is similar but more open & pyramidal.
T. heterophylla 2 (western hemlock): moderately to v hardy; v vigorous in damp climates, to 15×6m (50×20ft)/25yrs, eventually to 45m (150ft) or more but slender & graceful, with drooping leader; bark flaking when young, later furrowed; profuse cones. Good specimen. Dislikes continental climates.
T. mertensiana 3 (mountain hemlock): rather slow-growing at first, to 7.5×1.8m (25×6ft)/25yrs, eventually to 20–30m (65–100ft) where suited; elegantly spiring; grey-green to grey-blue lvs all around shoots; violet-purple to brown cones 5–8cm (2–3in) long. Best in cool moist conditions.

Cedar and larch trees

Large shapely trees differing from other members of the pine family in having their needle-like leaves arranged singly & spirally on the long, thin terminal shoots but in crowded tufts on the short spur-like laterals. Excellent as specimens on large lawns. **Cultivation**: Very hardy unless stated. For deep, moist but well-drained loamy soil, preferably in some shelter. Dislike polluted air. Pruning generally unnecessary except to maintain single leader. **Propagation**: Best by seed; vars by grafting.

Cedars (*Cedrus* spp): evergreens, conical when young but becoming flat-topped, with massive trunk & spreading branches, giving majestic effect. Fat barrel-shaped erect cones, purplish when young, with closely overlapping scales, disintegrating on tree after 2yrs.
C. atlantica (Atlas cedar): moderately to v hardy; fast-growing, to 12×12m (40×40ft)/25yrs, eventually to 30m (100ft); silvery to green 1–2.5cm (½–1in) lvs; cones to 8cm (3in) long. Vars: 'Fastigiata' (narrow & upright); 'Glauca' 4 (blue cedar; lvs bright blue-grey; commonest form of sp); 'Glauca Pendula' (probably same as 'Pendula'; to 6–9×6–9m [20–30×20–30ft] or wider if well trained; prostrate if not trained).
C. deodara 5 (deodar, Himalayan cedar): moderately hardy; fast-growing once established, to 9×6m (30×20ft)/25yrs, eventually to 30m (100ft); branch tips droop; 3–5cm (1¼–2in) bluish- to dark green lvs; cones to 10cm (4in) long. Most elegant when young. Vars: 'Aurea' (golden deodar; slow-growing, to 3×1.8m [10×6ft]/25yrs; young lvs golden); 'Pendula' (naturally prostrate, forming small weeping tree if top-grafted).
C. libani (cedar of Lebanon): rather slow-growing, to 7.5×6m (25×20ft)/25yrs, eventually to 25–30m (80–100ft), with huge branches & characteristic tiered habit; lvs 2–3cm (¾–1¼in) long; 8–12cm (3–5in) cones. *C. brevifolia* (Cyprus cedar; sometimes listed as *C. libani brevifolia*) is similar but lvs smaller.
Larches (*Larix* spp): deciduous neatly conical trees with graceful feathery foliage on drooping branchlets & attractive twiggy winter profile; fast-growing unless stated, to 18×7.5m (60×25ft)/25yrs, eventually to 30m (100ft) or more. Soft lvs 2–4cm (¾–1½in) long, fresh green in spring, golden in autumn; male fls yellow, female red, pink or yellow, before lvs; small erect cones generally 2–4cm (¾–1½in) long with thin woody scales, opening 1st yr but not disintegrating (good for decorations). Good for tall screens/hedges. Most spp prone to canker in many areas.
L. decidua 6 (*L. europaea*, European larch): ultra-hardy but may be damaged by late spring frosts; freshest-green foliage.
L.×eurolepis (hybrid or Dunkeld larch): hybrid of *L. decidua* & *L. kaempferi*; v vigorous when young, to 20×9m (65×30ft)/25yrs; resists disease, pests.
L. griffithii (Sikkim larch): semi-hardy; rather slow-growing, to 8×5.5m (30×18ft)/25yrs, eventually to 20m (65ft); v elegant, with long pendulous branchlets; narrow 8cm (3in) cones.
L. kaempferi 7 (*L. leptolepis*, Japanese larch): generally broader than other spp; branchlets do not hang; lvs greyish-green; rounded cones with scales curved back when ripe, looking like woody fls. Resists canker; tolerates poor soils. Vars: 'Blue Haze' (glaucous-blue); 'Der Vaes', 'Pendula' (both weeping & v elegant).
L. laricina (American larch, tamarack): ultra-hardy; rather short-lived, to 7.5×4.5m (25×15ft)/25 yrs, rarely exceeding 25m (80ft); reddish scaly bark; v small cones to 1.5cm (⅝in) long. Tolerates wet, even marshy soil.
Golden larch (*Pseudolarix amabilis* 8, *P. kaempferi*): deciduous pyramid-shaped tree v similar to true larches but cones disintegrate on tree when ripe. Rather slow-growing & broad, to 3.5×3.5m (12×12ft)/25yrs, rarely exceeding 15m (50ft) in cultivation; lvs to 6cm (2½in) long, yellowish-green in spring, rich golden in autumn; cones 5cm (2in) long, with pointed scales. Pest/disease-resistant but prone to late spring frosts when young; hates lime.

Pine trees

Pinus spp. Evergreen trees, mainly conical when young, becoming round/flat-headed, often losing lower branches, when mature. Needle leaves (5–10cm [2–4in] long unless stated) in tight "bundles" of 2, 3 or 5, the bundles often grouped in clusters or bottlebrush-like tufts; new growth in form of "candles" at branch tips. Woody cones, to 5–8cm (2–3in) long & oval unless stated. Many make noble specimens for large lawns, etc; some excellent as windbreaks near sea. **Cultivation**: Very hardy unless stated. Best in open, well-drained soil; except for 5-needled spp, drought-tolerant. Dislike shade, pollution.
Pruning: Only for containment and/or shaping (cut "candles" of new growth by half or more).
Propagation: Spp by seed; vars by grafting on parent sp. For low-growing & dwarf types, see p34.

P. aristata **1** (bristlecone pine): v slow-growing, to 3×1.5m (10×5ft)/30yrs, eventually to 12m (40ft); dense & narrow; "fox-tails" of dark glaucous-green 2–4cm (¾–1½in) lvs in 5s, resin-flecked.
P. ayacahuite (Mexican white pine): usually moderately hardy; to 12×9m (40×30ft)/25yrs, eventually to 25m (80ft); graceful, with conical crown; blue- to grey-green 12–15cm (5–6in) lvs in 5s; narrow cones 20–40cm (8–16in) long.
P. bungeana **2** (lace-bark pine): slow-growing, to 3.5×1.5m (12×5ft)/25yrs, eventually to 20m (65ft) or more; rounded crown but often several trunks; flaking bark showing pale inner bark; dark green lvs in 3s; 4cm (1½in) cones.
P. canariensis (Canary Island pine): semi-hardy; to 9×6m (30×20ft)/25yrs, eventually to 25m (80ft); conical when young, becoming round-crowned; narrow 20–30cm (8–12in) lvs, glaucous to bright green; narrow cones to 20cm (8in) long. Tolerates dry/limy soils.
P. cembra (Arolla pine, Swiss stone pine): ultra-hardy; to 6×1.8m (20×6ft)/25yrs, finally to 20m (65ft); columnar to conical, becoming round-crowned; dense dark green lvs* in 3s.
P. densiflora (Japanese red pine): to 9×4.5m (30×15ft)/25yrs, eventually to 15m (50ft); flat-topped or domed when mature; reddish bark; bright green lvs in 2s; pointed cones in clusters. Hates lime. 'Umbraculifera' is a good var.
P. halepensis (Aleppo pine): semi- to moderately hardy & best in hot climates; to 6×3m (20×10ft); domed crown when mature; sparse bright green lvs in 2s & 3s; pointed cones. Tolerates drought.
P. koraiensis (Korean pine): ultra-hardy; to 7.5×3m (25×10ft)/25yrs, eventually to 20m (65ft); rather open, columnar; deep glossy green lvs in 5s; pointed cones to 15cm (6in) long.
P. leucodermis (*P. heldreichii leucodermis*, Bosnian pine): to 9×4.5m (30×15ft)/25yrs, eventually to 20m (65ft) or more (v slow/final); dense & oval to pyramid-shaped, with upswept branches; grey bark; dense whorls of v dark green lvs in 2s; pointed cones, blue when young.
P. montezumae **3** (Montezuma pine): moderately hardy; to 6×3m (20×10ft)/25yrs; uniquely broad & round-headed; thick furrowed bark; grey-blue 15–25cm (6–10in) lvs mainly in 5s; cones 6–25cm (2½–10in) long (biggest in hot climates).
P. nigra: ultra-hardy; to 7.5×3m (25×10ft)/25yrs,

eventually to 30m (100ft). Var *nigra* (*austriaca*, Austrian pine); is more typical; rounded crown; dark green 10–15cm (4–6in) lvs in 2s.
P. parviflora (Japanese white pine): quite tall in wild, but garden form generally to 5.5×3m (18×10ft)/25yrs, eventually to 18×7.5m (60×25ft); broadly pyramid-shaped; tufts of blue-green lvs in 5s, inner surface silvery; clusters of egg-shaped cones, bluish-green when young.
P. pinea **4** (Italian stone pine, umbrella pine): moderately hardy; to 6×3.5m (20×12ft)/25yrs, eventually to 15m (50ft), sometimes much more; rather short-lived; v distinctive asymmetrical umbrella shape; greyish-green 12–15cm (6–8in) lvs in 2s; egg-shaped 12cm (5in) glossy cones.
P. resinosa (red pine): ultra-hardy; to 7.5×4.5m (25×15ft)/25yrs, eventually to 20m (65ft); dense conical crown; reddish bark; glossy dark green 10–15cm (4–6in) lvs*; small cones. Hates lime.
P. strobus (white pine): ultra-hardy; to 12×5.5m (40×18ft)/25yrs, eventually to 25–30m (80–100ft) or more, but can be sheared; bluish-green 8–12cm (3–5in) lvs in 5s; slender cones 8–20cm (3–8in) long. Hates lime; prone to blister-rust disease. Var 'Pendula' has drooping branches.
P. sylvestris **5** (Scots pine): ultra-hardy; to 12×4.5m (40×15ft)/25yrs, eventually to 20–30m (65–100ft); pyramid-shaped when young becoming attractively irregular, with rather sparse semi-drooping branches; mature bark orangish; bluish grey-green lvs in 2s. Vars: 'Argentea' (silvery lvs); 'Aurea' **6** (slow-growing, to 4.5×2.5m [15×8ft]; young lvs yellowish-green); 'Fastigiata' **7** (v narrowly columnar, to 7.5×1m [25×3ft], with almost vertical branches).
P. thunbergii (*P. thunbergiana*, Japanese black pine): to 7.5×4.5m (25×15ft)/25yrs, eventually to 25–30m (80–100ft), but easily kept smaller by regular pruning; broadly conical, with stiff spreading branches, becoming irregular; bright green stiff lvs in 2s. Best near coast.
P. wallichiana **8** (*P. excelsa*, *P. griffithii*, Himalayan or Bhutan pine): fast-growing, to 15×9m (50×30ft)/25yrs, eventually to 25m (80ft) or more; conical, becoming broadly columnar with round crown; lower branches kept if tree isolated; slender drooping blue-green lvs to 20cm (8in) long, in 5s; banana-shaped resinous cones 15–30cm (6–12in) long.

Low-growing members of the pine family

Generally slow-growing vars of tree spp forming prostrate or bushy plants useful for rock gardens (smallest types), as focal points on lawns & other places, for ground cover (prostrate & spreading types), for contrast in heather gardens, etc. (Those termed dwarf can be expected not to exceed 1.2–1.5m [4–5ft] even after many years; others may remain "dwarf" for some years; sizes given at about 10 years.) Unless stated, other features resemble parent sp (p26–32), though usually smaller. **Cultivation** (including hardiness): As for parent sp unless stated. **Propagation**: *Tsuga* & some *Picea* vars by cuttings; others by grafting.

Silver firs (vars of *Abies* spp):
A. amabilis 'Spreading Star' ('Procumbens'; red fir var): low & spreading, to 1×5m (3×16ft); horizontal branches; rich green lvs. Hates lime.
A. balsamea 'Hudsonia' **1** (dwarf balsam fir): ultra-hardy; dwarf & rounded to prostrate, to 30×45cm (1×1½ft); rich green lvs* mainly in 2 ranks; tolerates some lime. Var 'Nana' is similar but v short lvs* arranged radially on twigs.
A. cephalonica 'Meyer's Dwarf' ('Nana'; Greek fir var): dwarf & prostrate, to 30×60cm (1×2ft); horizontal branches; short lvs.
A. concolor 'Compacta' ('Glauca Compacta'; Colorado white fir var): irregularly rounded, to 1×1m (3×3ft)/10yrs, eventually to 2m (7ft); silvery-blue lvs.
A. lasiocarpa 'Compacta' **2** ('Arizonica Compacta'; cork fir var): dense & conical, to 90×45cm (3×1½ft)/10yrs, eventually to 2–2.5m (7–8ft); lvs intensely silver-blue.
A. nordmanniana 'Golden Spreader' **3** ('Aurea Nana'; Caucasian fir var): dwarf & spreading, to 30×90cm (1×3ft); clear golden-yellow lvs, brightest in winter. Protect from spring frosts when young. Likes partial shade.
A. procera 'Glauca Prostrata' **4** (noble fir var): flat-topped & spreading, to 30×90cm (1×3ft); intense blue-grey lvs. Prone to revert to tall habit, so cut out any upright leaders; hates lime.
Cedars (vars of *Cedrus* spp):
C. brevifolia (Cyprus cedar): see p30.
C. deodara (deodar) vars: 'Golden Horizon' **5** (graceful & semi-prostrate, to 0.75×1.2m [2½×4ft], with pendulous branches; golden lvs); 'Pendula' (prostrate, making spreading bush, to 3×6m [10×20ft] if not top-grafted & any upright leaders removed; see p30); 'Pygmy' **6** ('Pygmaea'; v dwarf & bun-shaped, to 15×20cm [6×8in]; blue-grey lvs).
C. libani (cedar of Lebanon) vars: 'Nana' (slow-growing, dense & conical, to 90×75cm [3×2½ft]/10yrs, eventually flat-topped & spreading, to 4.5m [15ft]; 'Comte de Dijon' is v similar); 'Sargentii' **7** ('Pendula Sargentii'; naturally prostrate, to 0.3×1.8m [1×6ft], but best trained to form dome-shaped weeping bush).
Spruces (vars of *Picea* spp):
P. abies (Norway spruce) vars (may need coarse growth cutting away to maintain character):
'Clanbrassiliana' **8** (dense & generally globular to

flat-topped, to 50×50cm [20×20in]/10yrs, eventually to 2×3m [7×10ft]; lf size variable; prominent brown winter buds); 'Elegans' (Knight's dwarf spruce; similar to 'Clanbrassiliana' [& sometimes incorrectly sold as it or as 'Clanbrassiliana Elegans'] but denser, globular to squat-conical & lvs smaller); 'Gregoryana' **9** (v dense, bun-shaped to globular dwarf, to 20×20cm [8×8in]/10yrs, eventually to 60×60cm [2×2ft]; grey-green lvs); 'Inversa' **10** (naturally prostrate but best trained as upright, weeping bush, to 3.6×0.9m [12×3ft], or can cascade over rock); 'Little Gem' (dwarf, dense & bun-shaped, to 30×40cm [12×16in]); 'Nidiformis' **11** (dense & spreading, to 40×60cm [16×24in]/10yrs, eventually to 1×2m [3×7ft]; dark green); 'Ohlendorffii' (globular to conical, to 60×50cm [24×16in]/10yrs, eventually to 2×1.5m [7×5ft]; lvs yellowish-green in summer); 'Procumbens' **12** (spreading & flat-topped, to 0.45×2m [1½×7ft], with horizontal branches); 'Pumila Nigra' (dense & spreading, to 0.6×1.5m [2×5ft]; v dark green); 'Pygmaea' (v slow-growing, dense, irregular & dwarf, to 20×15cm [8×6in]/10yrs, rarely exceeding 1m [3ft]; globular to broadly conical); 'Reflexa' (naturally prostrate, forming low dome, to 1.5×6m [5×20ft], with upturned branch tips; or can be trained to form small weeping tree to 3m [10ft] tall).
P. glauca (white spruce) & *P. g. albertiana* (Alberta spruce) vars: 'Alberta Globe' (dwarf & rounded, to 25×15cm [10×6in]); 'Albertiana Conica' ('Conica'; dense & neatly conical, to 90×50cm [36×20in]/10yrs, eventually to 2m [7ft]; bright green in early summer; 'Laurin' & 'Lilliput' are dwarf versions, to 30×20cm [12×8in]); 'Echiniformis' (compact & dense dwarf, to 40×40cm [16×16in]; grey-green lvs concealing stems).
P. mariana (black spruce) vars: 'Ericoides' (dwarf & rounded, to 40×60cm [16×24in]; soft grey-green heath-like lvs); 'Nana' (v slow-growing & rounded, to 20×30cm [8×12in]; blue-green).
P. omorika 'Nana' (Serbian spruce var): rounded to conical, to 90×75cm (3×2½ft), with irregular outline; yellow-green lvs showing glaucous undersides.
P. orientalis 'Gracilis' (oriental spruce var): dense & slow-growing, to 75×60cm (2½×2ft)/10yrs,

eventually to 3m (10ft) or more; round-topped, becoming pyramid-shaped; grass-green. Var 'Skylands' ('Compacta Aurea') is rather similar but lvs golden-yellow, tend to scorch in strong sun.

P. pungens glauca (blue spruce) vars: 'Globosa' **1** ('Glauca Globosa'; dwarf, dense & rounded, to 60×60cm [2×2ft]; silvery-blue; 'Montgomery' is similar); 'Prostrata' ('Glauca Procumbens', 'Glauca Prostrata', 'Procumbens'; names given to variable but similar prostrate vars, generally to 0.6×2–3m [2×7–10ft]/10yrs, eventually to 1×4.5m [3×15ft]; blue-grey to silver-blue; 'Koster's Prostrate' is intense silver-blue var of this type).

Pines (*Pinus* spp & vars):
P. aristata: see p32.
P. densiflora 'Umbraculifera' **2** ('Tagyosho'; incorrectly, 'Tanyosho'; Japanese red pine var): slow-growing domed bush, to 1×1m (3×3ft)/10yrs, eventually miniature umbrella-shaped tree, to 3×3m (10×10ft); profuse tiny cones.
P. leucodermis (*P. heldreichii leucodermis*, Bosnian or red-cone pine) vars: 'Compact Gem' **3** ('Compacta'; slow-growing rounded to conical bush, to 2×1.5m [7×5ft]; v dark green); 'Schmidtii' ('Pygmy'; v slow-growing & dense globular to pyramid-shaped dwarf, to 25×25cm [10×10in], rarely exceeding 50cm [20in]; bright green).
P. mugo **4** (mountain pine): ultra-hardy slow-growing but variable sp, generally dense bushy or prostrate shrub, to 1.5×1.5m (5×5ft)/10yrs, sometimes a small tree; v resinous buds; crowded 2–5cm (¾–2in) lvs in 2s; cones to 5cm (2in) long. Lime-tolerant. Best grown as dwarf named vars: 'Corley's Mat' (prostrate & mat-forming, to 0.2×1.2m [8in×4ft]); 'Gnom' **5** (dense globular mound, to 50×75cm [20×30in]); 'Humpy' (v compact & rounded, to 40×50cm [16×20in]; red-brown winter buds); 'Mops' (dense & globular, to 40×50cm [16×20in]).
P. nigra 'Hornibrookiana' **6** (Austrian pine var): slow-growing but spreading, to 45×90cm (1½×3ft)/10yrs, eventually to 1.5×2m (5×7ft); rich dark green.
P. parviflora 'Adcock's Dwarf' (Japanese white pine var): slow-growing, to 1.5×0.75m (5×2½ft)/10yrs; congested foliage. Var 'Brevifolia' is narrow, to 1.5×0.6m (5×2ft)/10yrs, but eventually forms small tree; crowded short blue-green lvs in 5s.
P. pumila **7** (dwarf Siberian pine, Japanese stone pine): ultra-hardy variable shrub, prostrate to bushy but usually dense, mounding & spreading, to 1×1m (3×3ft); crowded 4–8cm (1½–3in) lvs, silvery inner surfaces, in 5s; 5cm (2in) cones. Hates lime. Vars: 'Dwarf Blue' (slow-growing but spreading, to 0.6×1.2m [2×4ft]; lvs brightly white-banded); 'Globe' (globular, to 75×75cm

[2½×2½ft]; blue-grey; male fls red; cones when young).
P. strobus 'Nana': name used loosely for variable small bushy forms of white pine, generally to 0.75×1m (2½×3ft)/10yrs, eventually to 2×3m (7×10ft) but variable; dense bluish-green foliage.
P. sylvestris (Scots pine) vars: 'Beuvronensis' (dense & domed or flat-topped, to 0.75×1m [2½×3ft]/10yrs, eventually to 1.5×2m [5×7ft]); Doone Valley (irregularly conical, to 1.2×1m [4×3ft]; glaucous lvs); 'Hibernia' (dense & rounded, to 1×1m [3×3ft]; blue-grey); 'Waterei' **8** (slow-growing pyramid-shaped bush, to 1.5×1.2m [5×4ft]/10yrs, eventually more rounded, forming a small tree, to 7.5m [25ft]).

Dwarf Douglas fir (*Pseudotsuga menziesii* 'Fletcheri' **9**): slow-growing flat-topped, attractively irregular bush, to 0.75×1m (2½×3ft)/10yrs, eventually to 2×3m (7×10ft); blue-green soft lvs.

Eastern hemlocks (*Tsuga canadensis* vars): 'Bennett' **10** ('Bennett's Minima'; slow-growing & semi-prostrate, to 30×75cm [1×2½ft]/10yrs, eventually to 1×3m [3×10ft]; arching branches, drooping at tips; 'Minima' is same or v similar); 'Cole' ('Cole's Prostrate'; prostrate or trailing, forming carpet to 15×90cm [6×36in], or can be trained higher or top-grafted; lvs in flat sprays; best shaded when young); 'Jeddeloh' **11** (dense & gracefully semi-prostrate, to 0.45×1m [1½×3ft], with depressed centre; pale green); 'Jervis' ('Nearing'; v slow-growing dwarf, to 60×30cm [2×1ft]; congested & twiggy; 'Minuta' (v dwarf & bun-shaped, to 25×25cm [10×10in]; congested, with crowded lvs); 'Nana' (irregular slow-growing bush, to 75×50cm [30×20in]/10yrs, rarely exceeding 1.5m [5ft]; congested terminal growth); 'Nana Gracilis' (mounding, to 45×90cm [1½×3ft], with slender arching stems); 'Pendula' **12** (name sometimes used for various forms, but correctly a prostrate to mounding var best trained when young to form low weeping bush, to 1×1.5m [3×5ft]/10yrs, eventually to 2×3.5cm [7×12ft]; dense & rich green); 'Von Helm's Dwarf' (dense & irregularly conical, to 60×45cm [2×1½ft]; v dark green; contrasting bright green young growth in spring).

The podocarp family

Rather varied evergreen trees & shrubs related to yews (*Taxus* spp; p40), mainly from S Hemisphere. Generally have narrow leaves & fleshy fruits; males & females usually separate. **Cultivation**: Unless stated, moderately hardy & for any moist but well-drained soil in sun or partial shade. **Propagation**: Seed; semi-ripe cuttings.

Dacrydiums (*Dacrydium* spp): Australasian conical weeping trees, becoming more rounded when mature & reaching 30m (100ft) in wild, but slow-growing in cool climates; slender arching & pendulous branches; cypress-like foliage – juvenile lvs awl-shaped, adult scale-like.
D. cupressinum **1** (rimu): to 6×1.8m (20×6ft)/25yrs in moderate climates; pale green foliage, bronzed in winter in exposed situations. Dislikes transplanting. Moderately hardy if well ripened, but less so where summers cool.
D. franklinii **2** (Huon pine): tree, to 3×2.5m (10×8ft)/25yrs, or large graceful shrub in moderate climates; bright green foliage.
Microcachrys (*Microcachrys tetragona* **3**): v hardy dwarf prostrate Tasmanian plant, to 15×90cm (6×36in); whipcord foliage with minute scale-like lvs in 4 ranks; bright red frs. Good for rock garden if allowed to trail or with main stem trained upright to form pendulous bush.
Alpine celery pine (*Phyllocladus alpinus* **4**): curious moderately hardy shrub with insignificant true lvs but flattened lf-like phylloclades (modified shoots), diamond-shaped or lobed, to 2–4×0.5–2cm (¾–1½×¼–¾in); female fls red. Generally narrowly conical to 1.5×1m (5×1ft)/10yrs, eventually to 3m (10ft) or more, though stunted in mountains. Native to New Zealand. Var 'Silver Blades' has silvery-blue phylloclades.
Podocarps (*Podocarpus* spp): rather slow-growing trees & shrubs with flattened, often yew-like narrow lvs (though sometimes larger & brighter green); frs generally bright red. Tree sizes below refer to warm/mild maritime areas; elsewhere form only shrubs. Even ultimately tall spp will not outgrow tubs for some yrs in most areas; low-growing types good for ground cover or large rock gardens.
P. alpinus **5**: moderately to v hardy low, straggling bush, to 1×2m (3×7ft), sometimes to 3m (10ft) in wild; whorls of slender arching branches; yew-like dark green lvs to 1cm (½in) long.
P. andinus **6** (plum-fruited or Chilean yew): v slow-growing tree, to 5.5×3m (18×10ft)/25yrs, eventually to 12m (50ft); somewhat yew-like; lvs 1–2.5cm (½–1in) long; frs like small green to yellowish-white plums.
P. dacrydioides (New Zealand white pine): semi-hardy beautiful weeping tree, to 6×1.8m (20×6ft)/25yrs in warm areas, eventually over 30m (100ft) in wild; juvenile lvs to 8mm (⅓in) long, in 2 rows; adult lvs scale-like.

P. gracilior (fern podocarp; sometimes sold incorrectly as *P. elongatus*): semi-hardy elegant tree, to 6×3m (30×10ft); branches pendulous when mature; juvenile lvs to 10cm (4in) long, glossy dark green; adult lvs shorter, glaucous-green, more crowded.
P. macrophyllus **7** (yew podocarp, yew pine; in US, southern or Japanese yew): narrow upright shrub or tree to 4.5×1m (15×3ft)/25yrs, eventually to 12m (50ft); glossy dark green lvs to 10cm (4in) long, paler beneath, spirally on stems, excellent as specimen or for hedge or tub; trainable. One of hardiest spp but hates lime.
Vars: *angustifolius* (narrow, tapering lvs); *maki* (shrubby or Chinese podocarp; generally slow-growing shrub, to 2×1m [7×3ft]; lvs to 8×0.5cm [3×¼in]; often grown indoors).
P. nivalis **8** (alpine totara): variable in hardiness & habit, but generally moderately to v hardy low, dense bush, to 1×1.8m (×6ft)/20yrs, but sometimes more erect, to 3m (10ft) in wild; olive-green leathery lvs spirally & in rows, to 2cm (¾in) long. Good on chalky soil.
P. nubigenus: moderately to v hardy but needs v wet climate and shelter to thrive; then eventually reaches 15m (50ft), but in gardens usually a slow-growing attractive shrub, to 4.5×3m (15×10ft)/25yrs; rich green, stiff, sharp-pointed lvs 2–4.5cm (¾–1¾in) long, spirally on shoots, glaucous beneath.
P. salignus (*P. chilinus*, willow-leaved podocarp): fairly vigorous tree in mild moist areas, to 5.5×3m (18×10ft)/25yrs, eventually to 12m (50ft), with drooping branches; strap/sickle-shaped shiny deep green lvs to 11cm (4½in) long, pale beneath.
P. totara (totara): irregularly conical tree, to 5.5×2.5m (18×8ft)/25yrs, eventually to 25m (80ft) in wild; furrowed peeling bark; sharp-pointed lance-shaped leathery lvs to 2–2.5cm (¾–1in) long. Var 'Aureus' **9** is smaller; lvs golden. *P. hallii* is similar but smaller, with thinner bark & longer lvs.
Prince Albert yew (*Saxegothaea conspicua* **10**): v slow-growing open weeping tree, to 3.5×1.8m (12×6ft)/25yrs, eventually to 12m (50ft) in wild; rather yew-like dark-green lvs to 3cm (1¼in) long; small cones 1cm (½in) across.

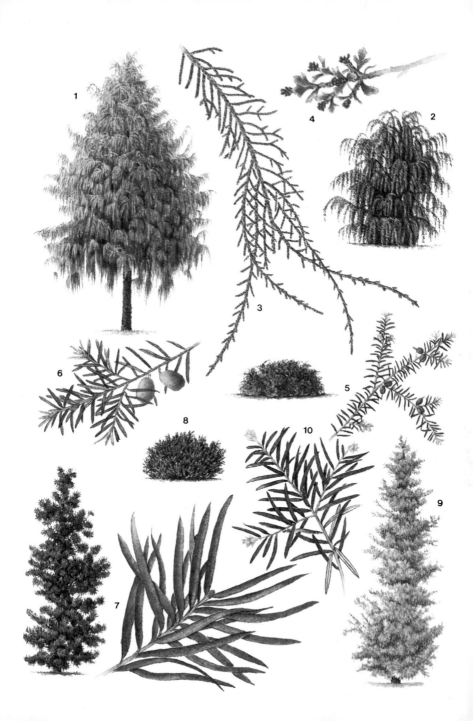

The plum-yew and yew families

Closely related families differing in botanical details. Generally slow-growing bushy evergreen trees or shrubs, mostly with dense foliage, good for backgrounds, screens, hedges, etc (*Taxus* spp used for topiary); dwarf & prostrate forms for rock gardens, ground cover, etc. (Unless stated, sizes given at about 25 years.) Narrow leaves generally in 2 rows. Males & females usually separate; fleshy fruits on females (marked †). **Cultivation**: For any normal, well-drained soil, even chalky, in sun or shade. Most spp best where summers not too hot, but *Taxus* spp tolerate wind & drought once established. Prune lightly only to shape. **Propagation**: Semi-ripe or hardwood cuttings; grafting; spp by seed.

Plum yews (*Cephalotaxus* spp; Cephalotaxaceae): v hardy shrubs or small shrubby trees (generally former in cultivation), v like yews but with larger lvs & frs lacking fleshy cups. Leathery glossy-green narrow lvs, silvery beneath; brownish-green egg-shaped frs 2–3cm (¾–1¼in) long on females.
C. fortunei **1** (Chinese plum yew): bushy & spreading, to 3×3m (10×10ft)/25yrs; soft lvs to 9cm (3½in) long, sharp-pointed.
C. harringtonia drupacea **2** (*C. drupacea*, Japanese plum yew, cow's-tail pine): shrubby, to 3×3m (10×10ft)/25yrs, occasionally to 6m (20ft); mounding, with drooping branchlets; 5cm (2in) long lvs arranged in V shape along shoots. Var 'Fastigiata' is columnar, broadening in warm climates.
Yews (*Taxus* spp; Taxaceae): slow-growing, long-lived dense bushy trees & shrubs with narrow dark green lvs to 3cm (1¼in) long, greyish/yellowish beneath; frs scarlet, to 1.5cm (⅝in) long, on females. V poisonous.
T. baccata **3** (common or English Yew): moderately to v hardy; bushy, to 3.5×1.8m (12×6ft), rarely exceeding 12m (40ft), or large shrub; v thick trunk when old. UPRIGHT & BUSHY VARS: 'Adpressa'† (sometimes sold wrongly in US as *T. brevifolia*; bushy & rounded, to 3×3m [10×10ft]; short lvs; 'Adpressa Variegata'† is slower- & lower-growing, with yellow-edged lvs); 'Amersfoort' (erect open shrub, to 1.8×1.5m [6×5ft]; oval lvs to 10mm [⅜in] long); 'Aurea' (golden yew; compact, to 2.5×1.8m [8×6ft]; golden-yellow lvs, greening); 'Dovastoniana'† **4** (Westfelton yew; wide-spreading tiered tree, to 3.5×4.5m [12×15ft], or vase-shaped shrub with drooping branchlets; v dark green; 'Dovastonii Aurea' has lvs edged yellow); 'Elegantissima'† **5** (dense & upright, to 2.5×1.5m [8×5ft]; lvs golden to straw-coloured, green in shade); 'Fastigiata'† **6** ('Hibernica', 'Stricta', Irish yew; columnar, to 3.5×0.6m [12×2ft], broader in drier areas; v dark green lvs all around shoots; 'Fastigiata Aurea'† is variably golden version; 'Fastigiata Aureomarginata' has yellow-edged lvs; 'Standishii'† **7** is similar, with golden lvs, but v slow-growing, to 3×0.3m [10×1ft]/25yrs); 'Lutea'† **8** ('Fructu-luteo'; orange frs); 'Semperaurea'† (upright but slow, to 1.8×1.8m [6×6ft]; lvs old gold to yellow).

LOW-GROWING & PROSTRATE VARS: 'Repandens'† **9** (v hardy; wide-spreading & flat-topped, to 0.6×1.5m [2×5ft]/10yrs; blue-green lvs; 'Repens Aurea' is similar but less hardy & golden-lvd); 'Summergold' (semi-prostrate, to 0.45×1.5m [1½×5ft]/10yrs; golden-yellow).
T. canadensis (Canadian or American yew; in US, ground hemlock): ultra-hardy spreading shrub, to 1.2×1m (4×3ft)/10yrs, var 'Stricta' more upright.
T. cuspidata (Japanese yew): v hardy spreading shrub or tree, to 4.5×3.5m (15×12ft), to 15m (50ft) in wild; lvs yellowish beneath, often arranged in V shape along shoots; profuse frs. Popular in northern N America; best pruned regularly. Vars: 'Capitata' (name used for conical tree form of sp); 'Densa'† (compact dense bush, to 1.2×1m [4×3ft]/10yrs); 'Expansa' (name used for spreading shrubby form of sp); 'Nana' (slow-growing but eventually large, to 1.8×3m [6×10ft]); 'Thayerae'† (may be *T.×media* var; dense & spreading, to 2.5×4.5m [8×15ft]/25yrs).
T.×media vars: v hardy hybrids of *T. baccata* & *T. cuspidata*, generally intermediate in features; usually vigorous & compact. Popular in N America. Vars: 'Brownii' (slow-growing, dense & columnar at first, then rounded, to 3.5×4.5m [12×15ft]); 'Hatfieldii'† (dense & upright, to 4.5×3.5m [15×12ft]); 'Hicksii'† **10** (columnar, to 6–7.5m×2.5m [20–25×8ft]; v dark green); 'Kelseyi'† (bushy & erect, to 4.5×3.5m [15×12ft]; profuse frs even when young); 'Viridis' (v slow-growing & narrow, to 3×0.6m [10×2ft]; bright green; young growth yellowish).
Nutmeg trees (*Torreya* spp; Taxaceae): rather open pyramid-shaped to rounded trees with stiff, hard, sharp-pointed narrow lvs set rather sparsely in 2 rows, shiny dark green with brighter edges, glaucous bands below; females may have egg-shaped green frs to 4cm (1½in) long with purple markings/shading.
T. californica **11** (Californian nutmeg): moderately to v hardy, but may be deciduous in cold areas; rather slow-growing, to 6×6m (20×20ft), eventually to 15–20m (50–65ft); lvs* to 8cm (3in) long. Like cool summers with adequate moisture.
T. nucifera (kaya, Japanese torreya): v hardy; generally large shrub or slender tree in moderate climates, to 6×6m (20×20ft)/25yrs, eventually to 20m (65ft) in wild; lvs* to 3cm (1¼in) long.

Swamp cypresses and their relatives

A rather diverse family of conifers (some deciduous), many extremely tall when mature, others making striking specimen trees for gardens. **Cultivation**: Generally like moist but well-drained soil. **Propagation**: Seed; semi-ripe or hardwood cuttings.

Tasmanian cedars (*Athrotaxis* spp): uncommon small to medium-sized moderately hardy trees with rather cypress-like lvs. Small green cones, orange-brown in autumn. Need warm maritime climate & shelter.
A. cupressoides: to 6×3m (20×10ft); dense; rounded crown when mature; lvs v small & scaly, pressed to stems; 1cm (½in) cones.
A. laxifolia **1** (summit cedar): to 7.5×4.5m (25×15ft); rather lax & open; intermediate in features between other spp; best sp in gardens.
A. selaginoides (King William pine): most tender sp; to 6×3m (20×10ft); coarser but more conical than other spp; fibrous red-brown bark; sharp-pointed awl-shaped lvs 1cm (½in) long around stems; cones to 2.5cm (1in) wide.
Japanese cedar (*Cryptomeria japonica*): elegant, fast-growing tree for specimen planting. Moderately to v hardy; to 12×5m (40×16ft), fastest in wet climate (can be restricted by pruning); conical, open when old; trunk buttressed when mature; thin reddish-brown bark, peeling in strips; awl-shaped bright green lvs to 2cm (¾in) long; 1.5cm (⅝in) round cones, brown in autumn, at shoot tips (sprays good for cutting). Vars: 'Cristata' (slow-growing, to 3.5×2.5m [12×8ft]; conical; some branchlets form flattened crested sprays); 'Elegans' **2** (*C. elegans*; to 6×4.5m [20×15ft]; bushy, with lax trunk [may bend to ground]; soft feathery lvs, always juvenile, bronze in autumn/winter); 'Lobbii' (slower than sp, to 9×4.5m [30×15ft]; longer branchlets; deep green lvs). Dwarf vars: see p44.
Chinese fir (*Cunninghamia lanceolata* **3**): moderately hardy shapely tree looking rather like some *Araucaria* spp (p44). Quite fast-growing, to 9×4.5m (30×15ft); v long sharp-pointed lvs to 6cm (2½in) long; clustered 4cm (1½in) cones. Best in sheltered maritime areas or woodland.
Chinese swamp cypress (*Glyptostrobus lineatus*): v rare tender to semi-hardy, slow-growing tree; to 6×3m (20×10ft); conical; deciduous, with blue-green pinnate lvs (scaly on cone-bearing twigs), glowing red in autumn; pear-shaped cones to 2.5cm (1in) long.
Dawn redwood (*Metasequoia glyptostroboides*): v fast-growing broadly cone-shaped open tree. V hardy, but may be damaged by early autumn/late spring frosts; to 18×5m (60×16ft)/25yrs; cinnamon-brown shaggy bark; deciduous, with plume-like flattened pinnate lvs 2cm (¾in) long, fresh green turning pinkish-bronze & golden in autumn; drooping 2.5cm (1in) cones.

Umbrella pine (*Sciadopitys verticillata* **4**): v slow-growing v hardy pyramid-shaped tree with whorls of 8–12cm (3–5in) dark green needles like umbrella spokes along branchlets; good as specimen on lawn. To 9×5m (30×16ft)/50yrs; dense, young bark reddish; oval cones 5–10cm (2–4in) long, green when young, maturing 2nd yr. Dislikes lime, air pollution, hot dry situations.
Californian redwood (*Sequoia sempervirens*): tallest known tree, to 12×5m (40×16ft)/25yrs, eventually over 100m (330ft), but dwarf vars suitable for gardens; moderately hardy in maritime climates. Var 'Adpressa' **5** ('Albospica') is slow-growing at first, eventually to 20×6m (65×20ft), less if leading shoot pruned; bushy to untidy column-shaped; lvs to 10mm (⅜in) long in 2 rows; tips of shoots creamy-white in spring & summer. Var 'Cantab' ('Prostrata'; see p44) is usually dwarf but may send a shoot up to 6m (20ft) or more. Var 'Pendula' is eventually tall but narrow, to 9×1.8m (30×6ft); branches weep.
Californian big tree (giant sequoia, giant redwood, wellingtonia; *Sequoiadendron giganteum*; incorrectly, *Sequoia gigantea*): less tall but bulkier than *Sequoia* sp, to 9×3.5m (30×12ft)/25yrs, eventually 75m (250ft); moderately to v hardy, needing slightly less maritime climate; blue-green lvs 1cm (½in) long, close to stems. Var 'Pendulum' is slower-growing & v narrow, to 7.5×1–3m (25×3–10ft)/50yrs; strange shapes when young; branches sometimes v pendulous.
Taiwania (*Taiwania cryptomerioides* **6**): rare semi-hardy conical tree rather like *Cryptomeria* sp. Rather slow-growing, to 5×2m (16×7ft) in cultivation; sparse upswept branches with gracefully drooping branchlets; sickle-shaped juvenile lvs to 2cm (¾in) long, shorter & more scale-like in adult; 1cm (½in) cones at shoot tips.
Swamp or **bald cypresses** (*Taxodium* spp): beautiful deciduous trees, becoming tall but quite slow-growing, with bright green young lvs turning rich brown in autumn. Generally v hardy; grow in ordinary soil as well as wet/swampy land.
T. adscendens **7** (pond cypress): smallest sp, to 7.5×2.5m (25×8ft); column-shaped or conical; 5–10mm (¼–½in) awl-shaped lvs, pressed close to shoots. Var 'Nutans' is narrow, with lax branchlets.
T. distichum **8** (common swamp cypress, bald cypress); to 11×5m (36×16ft); broadly conical, crown becoming domed; trunk buttressed; bark reddish; lvs to 1.5cm (⅝in) long, in 2 rows; 2.5cm (1in) round cones, purple when young.

Low-growing Japanese cedars and redwoods

Vars of tall members of the swamp cypress family (p42), suitable for rock gardens, as dwarf specimens, etc; prostrate forms for ground cover. Sizes given at about 10 years. **Cultivation**: For moist but well-drained soil. **Propagation**: Semi-ripe cuttings; grafting.

Japanese cedars (*Cryptomeria japonica* vars): v hardy; bright green awl-shaped lvs 3–20mm (⅛–¾in) long. Vars: 'Bandai-sugi' (rounded, to 90×75cm [3×2½ft]/10yrs, eventually to 2m [7ft]; lvs irregularly congested on branchlets, bronzed in winter); 'Compressa' (compact & globular, to 1×1m [3×3ft]; dense foliage, red-bronze in winter); 'Elegans Compacta' (slow-growing form of 'Elegans' [p42], to 2×1.5m [7×5ft], with v soft curly juvenile foliage, purple in winter); 'Elegans Nana' (sometimes listed incorrectly as 'Lobbii Nana'; rounded & graceful, to 1×1.5m [3×5ft]; stiff juvenile foliage, bronzed in winter); 'Globosa Nana' **1** (sometimes listed as 'Lobbii Nana'; compact domed bush, to 1×1.5m [3×5ft]; lvs yellowish-green, bluish in winter);

'Jindai-sugi' (compact & conical, to 1.2×1m [4×3ft]; soft green v regular foliage); 'Spiralis' **2** (spreading, to 1×1.5m [3×5ft]; foliage twisted spirally around stems); 'Vilmoriniana' **3** (v similar to 'Compressa' but less neat & less colourful in winter; to 45×60cm [1½×2ft]).

Redwoods (*Sequoia sempervirens* vars): moderately hardy; dense glaucous-green yew-like lvs to 1.5cm (⅝in) long, in 2 rows. Vars: 'Nana Pendula' (prostrate form of 'Pendula' [p42]; can be trained to form weeping bush 1m [3ft] or more tall); 'Prostrata' **4** ('Cantab'; wide-spreading, to 0.75×2m [2½×7ft], or taller if trained; may produce strong leader & grow v tall [prune if necessary]). Var 'Adpressa' (p42) can be kept dwarf by regular pruning.

Other conifers and related trees

Include some of the most distinctive, unusual and primitive trees – all gymnosperms, though only *Agathis* & *Araucaria* spp are conifers in the strict sense. Evergreen unless stated.

Kauri (*Agathis australis* **5**; Araucariaceae): tender New Zealand tree, quite fast-growing in warm climates, to 12×6m (40×20ft)/25yrs, eventually over 30m (100ft) in wild, but much slower in cool areas; columnar to narrowly conical when young; thick scaly bark, weeping resin when damaged (fossilized resin, "kauri gum", valuable); large leathery pale green stalked lvs to 8×2cm (3×¾in), shorter & stalkless on mature trees; rounded cones to 8cm (3in) across. For moist soil.

Araucarias (*Araucaria* spp; Araucariaceae): S American & Australasian trees distantly related to swamp cypress family; striking as specimens. Like moist soil; tender spp can be grown in tubs when young & overwintered under glass. Propagate by seed, semi-ripe cuttings.
A. araucana **6** (*A. imbricaria*, monkey puzzle, Chile pine): moderately to v hardy; quite fast-growing at first, to 9×3m (30×10ft)/25yrs, eventually to 20m (65ft) or more; unique, with rope-like twisted branches in whorls around trunk; open habit, forming wide column at first, later domed; dark green leathery lvs, sharp-pointed & overlapping in spirals along branchlets; cones 12–18cm (5–7in) long. Resists wind.
A. bidwillii **7** (bunya-bunya): tender; to 7.5×2m (25×7ft)/25yrs, eventually to 30m (100ft) or more; narrow conical habit; thick juvenile lvs 4cm (1½in) long in 2 rows; adult lvs wider, overlapping in spirals; cones to 22cm (9in) long,

rather like pineapples.
A. heterophylla **8** (Norfolk Island pine; v often labelled incorrectly *A. excelsa*): tender; to 6×3.5m (20×12ft)/25yrs, eventually to 30m (100ft) or more; pyramid-shaped & open, with tiered branches arranged symmetrically in 4s; needle-like juvenile lvs, adult wider & overlapping.

Sago palm (fern palm, *Cycas revoluta* **9**; Cycadaceae): v primitive, v slow-growing palm-like semi-hardy plant grown for its glossy dark green fern-like fronds; highly ornamental. To 1.8×1.5m (6×5ft)/25yrs, eventually to 3m (10ft); trunk usually short, topped by rosette of pinnate lvs to 1m (3ft) long with narrow lfts to 15cm (6in) long; cones v large (male to 60cm [2ft] tall). Propagate by seed, suckers. Can be grown in tub & overwintered under glass.

Maidenhair tree (*Ginkgo biloba* **10**; Ginkgoaceae): unique descendant of prehistoric family with lvs like maidenhair fern's. V hardy; fairly slow-growing, to 7.5–10×3–6m (25–33×10–20ft)/25yrs, eventually to 25m (80ft); open habit, conical when young; deciduous; fan-shaped pale green lvs 5–8cm (2–3in) long, yellow in autumn; plum-shaped unpleasant-smelling frs on females (kernels edible). Easy to grow & good in cities. Propagate by seed, cuttings, grafting. Vars: 'Fastigiata' **11** (sentry ginkgo; v erect & column-shaped, with almost erect branches); 'Pendula' (branches weep).

The maples

Acer spp. Apart from conifers, the most important foliage trees & shrubs, with most varied & beautiful foliage of all broadleaves. Generally deciduous, usually with palmate leaves, often brilliantly coloured in autumn (varies with climate; NE America ideal). Some spp have attractive bark (striped in snakebark, peeling in paperbark maples). Flowers generally insignificant; fruits (keys or samaras) are paired winged nutlets. Size & habit vary widely; tall spreading spp are good for summer shade in large gardens, parks, streets, etc; medium & small spp (the majority) suitable for smaller gardens; dwarfs for shrub & mixed borders, rock gardens, etc. Many suitable for bonsai training. **Cultivation**: Unless stated, very hardy. For any well-drained but moist soil in sun or partial shade; most smaller spp prefer some shelter. Prone to various insect pests, including leaf miners, scale insects, borers & gall mites; also fungal diseases. **Propagation**: Seed (stratify); vars by budding/grafting onto parent sp.

A. argutum: erect, to 7.5×5m (25×16ft); graceful pale green 5/7-lobed toothed lvs to 10cm (4in) across, yellow in autumn. Likes cool, partial shade; dislikes lime.

A. buergeranum (*A. trifidum*, trident maple): bushy, to 7.5×6m (25×20ft); glossy, deep green ivy-like 3-lobed lvs, glaucous beneath, 4–8cm (1½–3in) across, reddish when young. Pest & disease-resistant. Favourite bonsai subject.

A. campestre (field or hedge maple): round-headed, to 6×4.5m (20×15ft), or as hedging shrub if sheared; can also be pleached; lvs 3/5-lobed, 5–10cm (2–4in) across, clear yellow in autumn.

A. capillipes **1**: erect, to 7.5×6m (25×20ft); mature bark brown striped white; 3-lobed lvs to 12cm (5in) long, open reddish, turn deep green then red/orange in autumn; frs in drooping racemes.

A. cappadocicum (Caucasian maple; sometimes sold as *A. pictum*): fast-growing, to 10×7.5m (33×25ft); spreading; glossy 5/7-lobed lvs, 8–15cm (3–6in) across, rich yellow in autumn. Vars: 'Aureum' (lvs open reddish, then yellow, then green, then yellow in autumn; can be pruned hard when young); 'Rubrum' (lvs open dark red).

A. carpinifolium **2** (hornbeam maple): erect, to 6×3.5m (20×12ft); unlobed hornbeam-like toothed lvs 8–12cm (3–5in) long, brownish-gold or yellow in autumn.

A. circinatum **3** (vine maple): round-headed tree or large bush, to 4.5×4.5m (15×15ft); branches sprawl & twist; 7/9-lobed almost round lvs, orange & red in autumn; fls purplish & white, mid spring; frs red. Good in partial shade.

A. davidii **4**: to 6×5m (20×16ft); variable habit; bark grey-green striped white (best in semi-shade); glossy toothed lvs, generally heart-shaped & unlobed, to 18cm (7in) long, rich yellow in autumn, on red stalks. One of the best snakebark maples. Vars: 'Ernest Wilson' (compact, with branches upright then arching); 'George Forrest' (more open, with spreading branches).

A. diabolicum (horned maple): round-headed, to 6×4.5m (20×15ft); lvs 5-lobed & toothed, to 18cm (7in) across, not colouring in autumn;

yellow fls in drooping infls before lvs. Var *purpurascens* is best form, with salmon to red fls, purple young lvs & frs, & red autumn colour.

*A. ginnala** (Amur maple): ultra-hardy tree or large bush; vigorous & spreading, to 4.5×4.5m (15×15ft); 3-lobed bright green lvs, to 9cm (3½in) long, orange & brilliant crimson in autumn on good forms; red frs, late summer.

A. griseum **5** (paperback maple): beautiful slow-growing tree or large bush, to 5×3m (16×10ft); cinnamon-brown flaking & peeling bark (orange underneath); compound lvs of 3 soft green toothed lfts, silvery beneath, bright red & orange in autumn. Scarce because seed not v fertile.

A. grosseri: spreading tree or large shrub similar to *A. davidii*; to 6×4.5m (20×15ft); shoots grey-green or yellowish, becoming striped white; lvs toothed, 3-lobed or unlobed, to 12cm (5in) long, brilliant red in autumn. Var *hersii* (*A. hersii*) is hardier & has marbled bark & distinctly lobed lvs.

A. japonicum (full-moon maple, Japanese maple): slow-growing, elegant bushy tree or large shrub: to 4.5×4.5m (15×15ft); lvs 8–14cm (3–5½in) long, soft green turning rich crimson in autumn, often quite rounded, with 7–13 lobes & downy stalks; fls purplish-red. Vars: 'Aconitifolium' **6** (lvs deeply cut, almost pinnate, crimson in autumn); 'Aureum' **7** (lvs golden-yellow, prone to sun-scorch; not colouring in autumn); 'Vitifolium' (lvs fan-shaped, with 10–12 lobes, brilliant range of colours in autumn). Need shelter from cold winds.

A. lobelii **8**: moderately hardy; to 10.5×2m (35×8ft); v erect, with upswept branches, good for close planting in avenues; lvs 5-lobed, to 18cm (7in) across, rich green, turning yellow in autumn.

*A. macrophyllum** (Oregon maple): to 10×7.5m (33×25ft); erect to spreading, forming round head; largest lvs of genus, to 30cm (12in) across with 3/5 lobes, glossy green turning bright orange in autumn; yellow fls in long hanging racemes; frs red when young. Dislikes continental climate.

A. monspessulanum (Montpelier maple): neat round-headed tree or large bush rather like

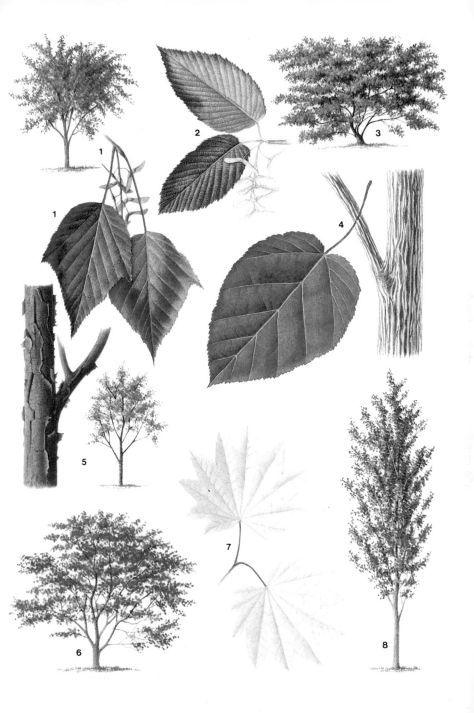

A. campestre; to 6×4.5m (20×15ft); lvs 4–8cm (1½–3in) across, 3-lobed & rather leathery.

A. negundo (box-elder): ultra-hardy, withstanding extreme climates; v fast-growing, to 12×10m (40×33ft); spreading & open; lvs pinnate with 3–5 toothed lfts to 10cm (4in) long; yellowish-green hanging infls before lvs. Vars: 'Aureum' (golden-yellow lvs); *californicum* (lfts hairy beneath); 'Elegans' **1** ('Elegantissimum', 'Aureomarginatum'; lvs yellow at edges; may revert to green if not pruned); 'Variegatum' ('Argenteomarginatum', silver-leaved box-elder; lvs have wide white margin; may revert to green if not pruned); *violaceum* (young shoots purplish & downy; fls pink). All forms can be stooled to form clump of young shoots.

A. nikoense (Nikko maple; may be listed as *A. maximowiczianum* [not *A. maximowiczii*, a different sp]): small bushy tree or spreading shrub, to 6×4.5m (20×15ft); lvs compound, with 3 lfts 8–12cm (3–5in) long, deep red & orange in autumn, on hairy stalks & branchlets; fls before lvs; frs felted.

A. opalus **2** (Italian maple): rounded tree or sometimes large bush, to 9×6m (30×20ft); shallowly 5-lobed dark green glossy lvs to 11cm (4½in) wide; profuse clear yellow drooping infls in spring before lvs.

A. palmatum **3** (Japanese maple): the most popular garden maple, an elegant small tree (often only bush-sized) with delicately lobed palmate lvs in wide range of forms & colours, almost all brilliantly coloured in autumn; tolerate shade, like some shelter; lvs may be damaged by late frost or sun-scorch. Sp grows to 4.5×4.5m (15×15ft) or more; rounded or spreading; lvs 5/7-lobed & toothed, 5–10cm (2–4in) across, bright green turning scarlet, orange or yellow in autumn. Numerous vars in 3 main groups. Vars with 5-lobed lvs: 'Atropurpureum' (lvs bronze-crimson all summer); 'Aureum' **4** (lvs yellow to golden); 'Corallinum' (slow-growing, forming compact dwarf bush; young stems & lvs coral-pink, lvs turning pale green); 'Sanguineum' (lvs blood-red, turning olive-green); 'Versicolor' (lvs variegated green, white & pink; may revert to green). Vars with large (to 12cm [5in]) generally 7-lobed lvs (Heptalobum or Septemlobum group; generally quite vigorous): 'Elegans' (lvs deeply lobed & toothed, pink-tinged when young); 'Elegans Purpureum' ('Purpureum'; red-purple-lvd form of 'Elegans'); *heptalobum* (wild 7-lobed form; lvs green); 'Osakazuki' **5** (lvs yellowish-green, brilliant blood-red in autumn); 'Reticulatum' (lvs yellowish-green, dark green veins); 'Rubrum' (lvs purplish-red fading purplish-green); 'Senkaki' ('Sangokaku', coral-bark maple; young branches coral-red; lvs pale green, yellowish-orange in autumn). Vars with finely dissected lvs with 7–11 lobes, each finely

cut & toothed (Dissectum group, or thread-leaved Japanese maples; low-growing, forming graceful domed bush with drooping branches): 'Dissectum' (lvs green); 'Dissectum Atropurpureum' **6** (lvs purplish); 'Dissectum Flavescens' (lvs yellow-green when young); 'Ornatum' (lvs dark red fading bronzy-green); 'Palmatifidum' (lvs green, v finely cut).

A. pensylvanicum (moosewood; striped or snake-bark maple of N America): ultra-hardy; fast-growing & v erect, to 7.5×4.5m (25×15ft); bark jade-green striped white; lvs 3-lobed, to 18cm (7in) long, yellow in autumn. Dislikes chalk. Var 'Erythrocladum' (may be listed under *A. rufinerve*) has pink young shoots turning red in winter.

A. platanoides (Norway maple): ultra-hardy & withstands city conditions, making good street tree; fast-growing, to 12×9m (40×30ft); dense & round-headed; bright green lvs sharply 5-lobed, 10–18cm (4–7in) wide, usually yellow in autumn; conspicuous bunched yellow fls before lvs. Numerous vars, including: 'Columnare' (narrow column shape); 'Crimson King' **7** (lvs v dark crimson-purple all summer); 'Drummondii' (lvs variegated white at edges); 'Globosum' (slower-growing, to 6×5m [20×16ft], forming dense rounded head); 'Laciniatum' (eagle's-claw maple; erect & tall; lobes of lvs extend to claw-like points); 'Reitenbachii (lvs open reddish, turn green, dark red in autumn); 'Schwedleri' (lvs open crimson, becoming green).

A. pseudoplatanus (sycamore; in Scotland, plane); v tough, withstanding pollution & extreme exposure, providing good wind shelter; fast-growing, to 12×10m (40×33ft); round-headed; dark green lvs, 5-lobed & toothed, 10–18cm (4–7in) wide; fls in long drooping racemes. Bark prone to squirrel damage. Vars: 'Atropurpureum' ('Spaethii'; lvs purple beneath); 'Brilliantissimum' **8** (slow-growing, to 4.5×3.5m [15×12ft]; lvs open pinkish-gold, turning yellow then green); 'Erectum' ('Fastigiatum'; narrow & erect); 'Leopoldii' (lvs open yellowish-pink, later green splashed yellow & pink); 'Prinz Handjery' (rather like 'Brilliantissimum' but lvs tinged purple beneath); 'Worleei' (golden sycamore; lvs rich yellow, greenish in shade).

A. rubrum (red maple): ultra-hardy; fairly fast-growing, to 10×7.5m (33×25ft); dense & round-headed; lvs distinctly 3/5-lobed, 5–12cm (2–5in) across, dark green turning brilliant red & orange early in autumn (best in N America, poor on chalky or dry soils); fls red, before lvs; frs red when young. Vars: 'Columnare' (narrow column-shaped); 'Scanlon' (tall column; good autumn colour); 'Schlesingeri' (richest autumn colour).

A. rufinerve: to 7.5×6m (25×20ft); young shoots bluish-grey, becoming green & white striped; 3-lobed dark green lvs 8–15cm (3–6in) long with

red hairs on veins, bright yellow & red in autumn.
A. saccharinum **1** (*A. dasycarpum*, silver maple);
ultra-hardy, but may be damaged in severe
storms; fast-growing, to 12×9m (40×30ft); v
graceful, with rounded head & long drooping
branches; deeply 5-lobed 10–15cm (4–6in) lvs,
bright green with silvery reverse, clear yellow in
autumn. Vars: 'Laciniatum' ('Wieri'; v pendulous
branches; lvs deeply & narrowly lobed &
toothed); 'Pyramidale' ('Fastigiatum'; narrow).
A. saccharum **2** (sugar maple): ultra-hardy; to
9×7.5m (30×25ft); sturdy but v ornamental, with
round head; 5-lobed palmate lvs 10–15cm (4–

6in) across, brilliant gold, orange & red shades in
autumn (best in N America); maple syrup made
from sap. Vars: 'Globosum' (small & round-
headed); 'Newton Sentry' (extremely narrow, to
15×3.5m [50×12ft]/40yrs, with central leading
shoot); 'Temple's Upright' ('Monumentale'; v
narrow but slow-growing, with no central leader).
A. sterculiaceum (*A. villosum*): moderately hardy;
to 7.5×6m (25×20ft); leathery palmate lvs to
18cm (7in) across; large frs in drooping clusters.
A. tchonoskii: graceful & bushy, to 6×4.5m
(20×15ft); 5/7-lobed toothed lvs 5–10cm (2–4in)
across, bright yellow in autumn. Dislikes lime.

The yucca family

Some spp sometimes classed in Liliaceae. Evergreen shrubby or tree-like plants with rosettes of
sword-like tough leaves – some almost stemless, looking like evergreen perennials, others with stout
trunk topped by tuft of leaves. Striking, "architectural" plants useful for formal gardens or to give
subtropical effect. Tender spp often grown in tubs for summer display, overwintering under glass.
Flowers in large inflorescences. **Cultivation**: See below. **Propagation**: Seed; stem cuttings. *Yucca* spp
also by offsets, root cuttings.

Cordylines (in US, dracaenas; *Cordyline* spp;
sometimes incorrectly sold as *Dracaena* spp);
semi-hardy; tree-like, with long sharp-pointed lvs
at top of strong stem; v large panicles 0.6–1.2m
(2–4ft) long of small whitish fls, early summer.
Need mild moist climate, but hardy to at least
−6°C (21°F).
C. (*D.*) *australis** **3** (cabbage tree; in US, giant
dracaena or grass palm): to 3.5×2.5m (12×8ft);
branching when flg size; lvs 45–90×2.5–6cm
(1½–3ft×1–2½in); infl erect or slightly drooping.
Var 'Atropurpurea' ('Lentiginosa') has lvs partly
purple.
C. (*D.*) *indivisa*: to 3.5×1.8m (12×6ft); normally
unbranched; lvs 1–1.8m×10–15cm (3–6ft×4–
6in); infl pendulous. Var 'Rubra' (red palm lily)
has lvs flushed red.
Yuccas (*Yucca* spp): include some of the
hardiest plants of "tropical" appearance. Tree-
like or stemless, with stiff, tough, sharp-pointed
lvs; drooping cup-shaped fls, generally whitish,
often purple-tinged, in large erect panicles or
racemes (best in hot summer). Prefer well-
drained sandy soil & ample sun. Stemless spp
form offsets at base.
Y. aloifolia (Spanish bayonet): semi- to
moderately hardy (hardiest where summers hot);
tree-like, to 3×1.5m (10×5ft) or more; slender
trunk; lvs to 75×5cm (30×2in), v sharp-pointed
& toothed; infl to 60cm (2ft) long, late summer.
Vars 'Marginata', 'Tricolor' & 'Variegata' are
variegated.
Y. filamentosa (Adam's needle): v hardy; almost
stemless, forming clump; foliage to 0.6×1.2m
(2×4ft); stiff sharp-pointed glaucous lvs to
75×5cm (30×2in) with curly white 8cm (3in) long

fibres at edges; creamy-white 5–8cm (2–3in) fls
in infl 1–1.8m (3–6ft) tall, summer. Var 'Variegata'
4 has lvs striped/edged creamy-white.
Y. flaccida: v hardy; similar to (& often sold as)
Y. filamentosa but lvs less rigid, narrower &
marginal fibres less curly; elegant infl to 1.2m
(4ft) tall. Vars: 'Golden Sword' **5** (lf centres
creamy-yellow); 'Ivory' (large infl of cream fls).
Y. glauca* (*Y. angustifolia*, soapweed): ultra-
hardy; low/prostrate stem, forming clump; foliage
to 0.6×1.2m (2×4ft); v narrow tapering glaucous
lvs to 75×2cm (30×¾in), whitish margins with
fibres; greenish-white 6–8cm (2–3in) fls in infl to
1.1m (3½ft) tall, summer.
Y. gloriosa **6** (Spanish dagger): moderately
hardy; tree-like but slow-growing, to 1.8×1.2m
(6×4ft); usually unbranched; stiff, straight lvs to
60×8cm (24×3in), v sharply pointed; 10cm (4in)
creamy-white or red-flushed fls in infl to 2.5m
(8ft) tall, summer. Vars: 'Medio-striata' (lf centres
striped white); 'Nobilis' ('Ellacombei'; lvs
glaucous, sometimes twisted; fls flushed red
outside); 'Variegata' (lvs striped yellow).
Y. recurvifolia **7**: moderately hardy; similar to
Y. gloriosa, but freer-branching & lvs narrower &
arching; fls creamy-white, late summer. Vars:
'Elegans Marginata' (lvs edged pale yellow);
'Variegata' (lvs striped dull yellow).
Y. smalliana: similar to, and often sold as,
Y. filamentosa, but lvs thinner & narrower.
Y. whipplei* (Our Lord's candle): semi-hardy;
usually stemless, foliage to 1×1.8m (3×6ft); stiff,
tapering glaucous lvs to 90×2.5cm (3ft×1in),
v sharply pointed & toothed; greenish-white 8cm
(3in) fls in dense infl on 2–4m (7–14ft) stem.
Generally monocarpic, dying after flg.

Sumachs and their relatives

A group of striking trees & shrubs including some of the finest autumn-colouring plants for poor, dry soils. Unless stated, deciduous, with alternate, compound leaves. Females may bear attractive fruits, generally persisting to late autumn/winter. **Cultivation**: Best in poorish soil in full sun (but water well to establish). Regular pruning unnecessary. **Pests & diseases**: See below. **Propagation**: Seed; semi-ripe cuttings; *Cotinus* spp & vars also by layering; *Rhus* spp also by root cuttings, suckers.

Smoke trees (smoke bushes, *Cotinus* [*Rhus*] spp): v hardy shrubs of bushy habit; rounded simple lvs, brilliant yellow/red in autumn; feathery panicles with sparse small purple fls, mid summer (then small frs), but mostly sterile, the purplish hairy fl stalks elongating & paling to pink then grey, giving hazy "smoke" appearance in late summer.

C. coggygria **1** (*R. cotinus*, Venetian sumach, European smoke tree/bush): to 3×3m (10×10ft); light green lvs, 4–8cm (1½–3in) long; profuse infls 15–20cm (6–8in) long. Vars: 'Flame' (best autumn lf colour); 'Foliis Purpureis' (lvs purple, turning green then light red); 'Purpureus' ('Atropurpureus'; lvs green; infls pinkish-purple); 'Royal Purple' **2** ('Kromhout'; dark wine-purple lvs, reddening in autumn); 'Velvet Cloak' (purple lvs, reddening in autumn). Purple-lvd forms prone to powdery mildew.

C. obovatus **3** (*C. americanus*, American smoke tree/bush, chittam wood): to 9×4.5m (30×15ft) or small tree; 5–12cm (2–5in) lvs, often reddish when young; infls larger but sparser than above sp, but autumn lf colour better.

Pistachios (*Pistacia* spp): moderately hardy fast-growing trees or large shrubs; pinnate lvs; insignificant greenish fls. Stake and shape when young. Drought- and heat-tolerant; good shade trees even on chalk. Wilt-prone if drainage poor.

P. chinensis (*P. sinensis*, Chinese pistachio): to 6×4.5m (20×15ft); lvs with glossy green lfts to 8×2cm (3×¾in), brilliant scarlet-orange in autumn; red-brown frs to 4cm (1½in) across, turning blue.

P. terebinthus **4** (Cyprus-turpentine): to 9×6m (30×20ft); dark green lvs* with 7–9 lfts to 6cm (2½in) long; reddish fruits to 1cm (¾in), turning purplish-brown.

Sumachs (sumacs, *Rhus* spp): unless stated, ultra-hardy, rather coarse suckering shrubs with lvs & young growth hairy; lvs compound, generally 20–45cm (8–18in) long with lfts 5–10cm (2–4in) long, useful for dramatic effect & all colouring superbly in autumn; fls in conical panicles, generally greenish to dull white; hairy frs in pyramid-shaped clusters unless stated.

R. glabra & *R. typhina* can be coppiced early spring for lush foliage effect. Some spp extremely irritating to skin, especially *R. radicans* (poison ivy), *R. toxicodendron* (poison oak) & *R. vernix* (poison sumach) – never plant in gardens. Wood brittle, prone to storm damage; also prone to wilt (in wet soil), coral spot fungus.

R. aromatica (*R. canadensis*, fragrant sumach): spreading, to 1–1.5×2.5m (3–5×8ft); toothed lfts* in 3s; small yellow fls, spring (before lvs).

R. chinensis (Chinese sumach, nutgall tree): round-headed v hardy tree to 6×5m (20×15ft) or large shrub; winter buds velvety-brown; lvs of 7–13 toothed lfts to 10–15cm (4–6in) long; 20–25cm (8–10in) panicles of creamy-white fls, late summer (best in continental climates); small orange frs.

R. copallina **5** (dwarf, shining or flame-leaf sumach): v hardy; to 2.5×2.5m (8×8ft) or small tree; lvs of 9–21 shining dark green lfts; greeny-yellow fls in 15cm (6in) infls, mid summer.

R. glabra (smooth sumach): to 6×6m (20×20ft); not hairy; lvs of 15–29 toothed lfts; dense infls to 25cm (10in) tall; persistent hairy red frs. Var 'Laciniata' **6** has deeply cut ferny lvs; may revert.

R. succedanea (wax tree): semi- to moderately hardy tree, to 10×8m (30×25ft); lvs of 9–15 long-pointed lfts, glossy above; thick clusters of v small yellowish fls; drooping clusters of berry-like frs (source of candle wax). Irritant.

R. trichocarpa: moderately hardy slow-growing shrub, to 2.5×2.5m (8×8ft), or small tree; lvs of 13–17 v downy lfts, coppery when young; fls insignificant; yellowish prickly frs. Irritant.

R. typhina **7** (stag's-horn sumach): gaunt, flat-topped small tree or large shrub, to 7.5×7.5m (25×25ft); lvs to 60cm (2ft) long of 13–31 toothed lfts; greenish fls in infls to 20cm (8in) tall; frs persistent & v red-hairy. Var 'Laciniata' (correctly, 'Dissecta') has deeply cut ferny lfts; v rich autumn colour.

Pepper trees (*Schinus* spp): evergreen trees of spreading habit grown as street & shade trees in areas with Mediterranean-type climate (though drop messy litter). Lvs pinnate, lfts to 6cm (2½in) long; red pea-like frs on females (attract birds). Tolerate heat & drought. Prone to scale insects.

S. molle (Californian, Peruvian or Australian pepper tree): semi-hardy; fast-growing, to 9×9m (30×30ft); trunk & limbs becoming gnarled, but branchlets droop gracefully; lvs to 25cm (10in) long, with 15–41 bright green lfts; profuse tiny yellowish-white fls, summer; frs in pendent clusters. Invasive roots. Prone to root rot.

S. terebinthifolius (Brazilian pepper tree): tender to semi-hardy; to 7.5×7.5m (25×25ft); non-drooping; lfts fewer, coarser & darker green than *S. molle*; frs v conspicuous. Prone to wilt.

The holly family

Handsome trees & shrubs best known for their spiny leaves & colourful autumn/winter fruits (berries) – though some spp & vars have neither. Evergreen unless stated. Flowers mostly insignificant; berries borne on female plants (female vars marked †) only if male planted within about 30m (100ft) or if male branch grafted onto female; bisexual spp & vars (marked ‡) are self-fertile & bear berries without separate male. Many vars suitable for hedging; generally tolerate pollution & salty winds. **Cultivation**: Unless stated, moderately to v hardy. For moist but well-drained soil in sun or shade (sun best for variegated vars); tolerate lime unless stated. May be prone to leaf miners & some fungal diseases. **Pruning**: Unnecessary except to shape specimens & trim hedges; remove plain-coloured shoots on variegated vars. **Propagation**: Spp by seed (stratify; slow to germinate); evergreens by hardwood cuttings; deciduous spp by semi-ripe cuttings; grafting.

True hollies (*Ilex* spp):

I.×altaclarensis: race of hybrids of *I. aquifolium* & *I. perado*, often listed under *I. aquifolium*; unless stated, vigorous conical/column-shaped trees, to 7.5×3m (25×10ft); handsome leathery lvs 6–10cm (2½–4in) long, moderately spiny, dark green unless stated; large red frs on yr-old wood. Vars: 'Belgica Aurea'† ('Silver Sentinel'; v handsome flat lvs with few spines, deep green mottled pale green & grey, edged cream); 'Camelliifolia'† **1** (lvs almost spineless); 'Golden King'† **2** (golden-edged almost spineless lvs; female); 'Hendersonii'† **3** (similar to 'Golden King' but lvs green); 'Hodginsii' (stems purple; large-spined lvs; v pollution-resistant); 'Lawsoniana'† **4** (lf centres splashed yellow but may revert; long-lasting orange-red frs); 'Mundyi' (large lvs, prominent veins).

I. aquifolium (European holly): densely leafy shrub or small pyramidal tree, to 7.5×4.5m (25×15ft; vars similar unless stated); lvs glossy, 2.5–8cm (1–3in) long, dark green unless stated, usually wavy with sharp spines but almost spineless at top of mature plants; frs generally red, on yr-old wood (v good for cutting). Good for shelter, hedging. Vars: 'Angustifolia'† (slow-growing & neatly conical, to 6×2.5m [20×8ft]; narrow small-spined lvs; also male form); 'Argenteo-marginata'† (also male form; silver-edged lvs); 'Argento-marginata Pendula'† **5** ('Argentea Pendula', 'Perry's Silver Weeping'; to 4.5×4.5m [15×15ft]; dome-shaped, with weeping branches; silver-edged lvs); 'Aureo-marginata'† (variable; gold-edged lvs; also male form); 'Aurea Medio-picta'† ('Golden Milkmaid'; to 4.5×2.5m [15×8ft]; lvs blotched yellow in centre; also male form, 'Aurea Medio-picta Latifolia' or 'Golden Milkboy'); 'Bacciflava'† **6** ('Fructu-luteo'; frs yellow); 'Balkans'† (v hardy); 'Ferox' (hedgehog holly; slow-growing & bushy, to 2.5×1.5m [8×5ft]; lf surfaces spiny); 'Ferox Argentea' **7** (silver hedgehog holly; similar to 'Ferox', but lf edges & spines creamy-white); 'Golden Queen' (gold-edged lvs; male); 'J. C. van Tol'† (dark, glossy, almost spineless lvs; profuse frs; 'Golden van Tol'† is sport with gold-edged lvs); 'Mme Briot'† (shoots purple; lvs

mottled pale green & gold, edged gold); 'Ovata Aurea' (slow, to 4.5×2.5m [15×8ft]; purple twigs; thick, gold-edged lvs, short spines); 'Pendula'† (weeping holly; domed & spreading, to 4.5×4.5m [15×15ft]; long weeping branches); 'Pyramidalis'† **8** (lvs spiny to spineless; profuse frs; 'Pyramidalis Fructo-luteo'† is similar, with yellow frs); 'Watererana' (compact, to 2.5×2m [8×7ft]/30yrs; lvs edged yellow).

I.×aquipernyi 'Brilliant'‡: hybrid of *I. aquifolium* & *I. pernyi*; dense tree, to 6×4.5m (20×15ft); shiny spiny-edged, deeply toothed lvs 5–10cm (2–4in) long; profuse large red frs.

I.×attenuata 'Fosteri' ('Foster's Hybrids'; may be sold as *I. opaca fosteri*): hybrid of *I. cassine* & *I. opaca*; open tree, to 7.5×3m (25×10ft); light green narrowish lvs, sparse teeth; profuse scarlet frs on new wood. Var 'East Palatka' is similar.

I. cornuta (horned or Chinese holly): dense, bushy & slow-growing, to 2.5×2.5m (8×8ft); spined rectangular lvs to 10cm (4in) long, glossy dark green; large red frs. Vars: 'Burfordii'‡ (compact; lvs spined only at tip); 'China Boy' & 'China Girl'† (v hardy); 'Nellie R. Stevens'† (hybrid with *I. aquifolium*; large shrub or small tree, to 7.5×3m [25×10ft]; lvs have few spines; profuse orange-red frs); 'Rotunda' (dwarf; compact rounded habit).

I. crenata (Japanese holly); v hardy; dense shrub to 2.5–3×2–2.5m (8–10×7–8ft) or small tree; leathery glossy green lvs to 2.5cm (1in) long, toothed but spineless; black frs. Can be clipped or bonsai trained. Vars: 'Convexa'† (v hardy; spreading; small convex lvs; good for low hedging); 'Golden Gem' **9** (dwarf & spreading; lvs golden [best in sun]); 'Green Lustre' (low-growing, to 60×40cm [24×16in]; good for low hedging); 'Mariesii'† ('Nummularia'; v dwarf & slow-growing, to 90×30cm [3×1ft]).

I. decidua (possum haw): v hardy shrub, to 3×3.5m (10×12ft) or small tree; deciduous dull green toothed lvs to 3cm (8in) long, crowded on branchlets; frs red or yellow, persistent. Var 'Warren's Red' is v heavy fruiter.

I. glabra (inkberry, gallberry): v to ultra-hardy; dense rounded shrub to 1.2×1.2m (4×4ft); slow-growing but spreads by stolons; dark

shining spineless lvs to 5cm (2in) long; black frs. Hates lime. Var 'Compacta't is dwarf & free-frtg.
I. opaca **1** (American holly): v hardy; large shrub or column-shaped to conical tree, to 7.5×4.5m (25×15ft); spiny dull green lvs, yellowish beneath, to 10cm (4in) long; large red frs on new wood. Needs lime-free soil. Vars: 'Arden't (dark red oval frs); 'Canary't (yellow frs); 'Chief Paduke't (columnar; large lvs & frs); 'Cumberland't (bright red frs); 'Delia Bradley't (v profuse frs); 'Goldie't (profuse yellow frs); 'Jersey Knight' (ultra-hardy); 'Manig't (v large orange-red frs); 'Merry Christmas't (compact; v good for cutting); 'Miss Helen't (dense & conical; profuse large frs).
I. pedunculosa: v hardy; large shrub or small tree, to 4.5×3m (15×10ft); spineless & toothless glossy dark green lvs to 8cm (3in) long; bright red frs on drooping stalks on new wood. Dislikes lime.
I. pernyi **2**: large shrub or pyramid-shaped tree, to 4.5×3m (15×10ft); distinctively spined glossy olive-green lvs to 5cm (2in) long, almost

stalkless; small bright red frs. Var 'Lydia Morris't is a hybrid with *I. cornuta* 'Burfordii'; grows to 1.8m (6ft); large red frs.
I. verticillata **3** (winterberry): ultra-hardy; large spreading shrub, to 3×2.5m (10×8ft); deciduous; toothed purple-tinged lvs to 10cm (4in) long, yellowing in autumn; persistent red frs. Needs lime-free soil. Vars: 'Christmas Cheer't (profuse red frs); 'Chrysocarpa't (yellow frs).
I. vomitoria (yaupon): moderately hardy; shrub or small tree to 6×6m (20×20ft); stiff branches; glossy, leathery lvs to 4cm (1½in) long, toothed but spineless; profuse red frs on yr-old wood.
I. yunnanensis: v hardy; bushy shrub, to 3.5×3.5m (12×12ft); young shoots hairy; young lvs brownish-red becoming glossy green, to 4cm (1½in) long, toothed but spineless; frs red.
Mountain holly (catberry; *Nemopanthus mucronatus*): differs from *Ilex* spp in fl structure. Ultra-hardy but frs best if summers hot; shrub, to 3×3m (10×10ft); spreads by stolons; deciduous, with thin lvs to 6cm (1½in) long, yellowing in autumn; frs dull red (some plants‡).

The ivy family

Trees and shrubs mostly with bold, exotic-looking foliage – compound or deeply lobed – good as specimens & for subtropical effects (though sometimes rather coarse for small gardens). **Cultivation**: Generally for any normal well-drained soil in sun or shade. Often hardier where wood is ripened by hot summers. **Propagation**: Seed; semi-ripe cuttings; root cuttings; where produced, suckers; *Acanthopanax* & × *Fatshedera* spp also by hardwood cuttings.

Acanthopanax (*Acanthopanax sieboldianus, Aralia pentaphylla*; often sold as *Acanthopanax spinosus*): v hardy shrub, to 1.8×2.5m (6×8ft); slender arching stems, few thorns; deciduous; palmately compound lvs with 5/7 lfts to 4cm (1½in) long, white-edged in var 'Variegatus'. Best in shelter.
Japanese angelica tree (*Aralia elata* **4**): v to ultra-hardy tree/suckering shrub, to 4.5×4.5m (15×15ft); stems spiny; deciduous; compound lvs to 1m (3ft) long clustered at branch ends; numerous hairy lfts to 12cm (5in) long; large panicles of small creamy-white fls, early autumn. Vars: 'Aureo-variegata' (lfts edged yellow); 'Variegata' ('Albo-marginata'; lfts edged white). Longer-lived on poor soil.
Fatshedera (×*Fatshedera lizei* **5**): hybrid of *Fatsia japonica* 'Moseri' & *Hedera helix* 'Hibernica'; moderately hardy vigorous but weak-stemmed shrub, to 1.8×1.8m (6×6ft); evergreen; deeply 3/5-lobed glossy, leathery lvs to 20×25cm (8×10in). Good in shade, cities; needs support; often grown indoors. Var 'Variegata' has cream lf blotches; less hardy.
Japanese fatsia (false castor-oil plant, *Fatsia japonica* **6**; often listed as *Aralia sieboldii, A. japonica*): moderately hardy shrub, to 2×2m

(7×7ft); evergreen; leathery, dark green deeply 7/9-lobed lvs 30cm (1ft) across or more; erect panicles of small white fls, autumn; small blackish frs. Best in sheltered semi-shade; good near sea.
Tree ivies (*Hedera helix* vars): non-climbing forms of the popular evergreen climber (p228). Vars include 'Conglomerata' **7** (dwarf, to 90×60cm [3×2ft]; stiff stems; wavy-edged lvs.)
Kalopanax (*Kalopanax pictus* **8**): v hardy, round-headed, rather maple-like tree, to 7.5×6m (25×20ft); young branches & suckers thorny; deciduous; 5/7-lobed lvs to 30cm (1ft) across, less on mature tree, reddish in autumn; clustered umbels of white fls, late summer.
Devil's club (*Oplopanax horridus*): v hardy suckering shrub, to 3×1.8m (10×6ft); stems v spiny (may injure); deciduous; 7/9-lobed & toothed lvs to 25cm (10in) wide, prickly; long infls of greenish fls, late summer; small scarlet frs.
Lancewood (*Pseudopanax crassifolius*): semi-hardy evergreen tree to 4.5×2m (15×7ft); lvs 5cm (2in) diamond-shaped to 75cm (2½ft) sword-shaped, leathery.
Rice-paper tree (*Tetrapanax papyriferus* **9**): tender evergreen shrub, to 3×3m (10×10ft); deeply cut & toothed lvs to 40cm (16in) across, silvery beneath; large panicles of white fls.

The barberry family

Yellow-flowered berrying shrubs popular for hedging or specimen planting. Deciduous spp have fine autumn colours; evergreens include showy winter-flowering plants with dramatic leaf shapes. Most are drought-tolerant and useful close to house foundations. **Cultivation**: Easy; unless stated, v hardy & for any well-drained soil, even shallow chalk; like sun (partial shade for evergreens). For hedging, plant 45–60cm (1½–2ft) apart; trim in autumn (evergreens after flg); otherwise pruning unnecessary. Some *Berberis* spp harbour black stem rust of wheat & cultivation banned in some parts of N America (spp known to be resistant marked †); otherwise healthy. **Propagation**: Semi-ripe or hardwood cuttings; seed; *Mahonia* spp by leaf-bud cuttings or suckers.

Barberries (*Berberis* spp): bushy, dense-lvd shrubs, generally of arching habit; thorny. Evergreen spp grown for attractive lvs & fls; deciduous spp for autumn colour & red, yellow, black or blue berries (often with grape-like bloom & persisting into winter). Lvs usually whorled or clustered in tufts along stems. Unless stated: spines in 3s, to 2–4cm (¾–1½in) long; evergreen toothed or spiny lvs; pendent yellow fls to 0.5–2cm (¼–¾in) across in 2.5–8cm (1–3in) clusters or drooping infls, spring; frs about 1.5cm (½–⅝in) long.
B. calliantha† **1**: to 1×1m (3×3ft); small spines; holly-like lvs to 5cm (2in) long, white beneath; blue-black frs. *B.×bristolensis*† is hybrid with *B. verruculosa*; warty stems; solitary fls; excellent as dwarf hedge.
B. candidula† **2**: to 1×1m (3×3ft); neat & slow-growing, forming dome; small spines; narrow lvs to 3cm (1¼in) long, white beneath; solitary fls, late spring; frs blue-black. Useful for large rock gardens or hedging.
B.×carminea: hybrid group derived partly from *B. aggregata*; deciduous; brilliant autumn colour; fls in panicles. Vars: 'Bountiful' **3** (to 1×1m [3×3ft]; profuse coral-red frs, fine bloom); 'Buccaneer' (to 1.5×1.2m [5×4ft]; berries deep red, persisting to mid winter).
B. concinna†: to 1×1m (3×3ft); deciduous or semi-evergreen holly-like lvs to 2.5cm (1in) long, white beneath; solitary fls; red frs.
B. coxii: to 60×75cm (2×2½ft); yellowish stems with flattened spines; lvs to 5cm (2in) long, grey beneath; blue frs with glaucous bloom.
B. darwinii† **4**: moderately hardy; to 3×3m (10×10ft); holly-like lvs to 2.5cm (1in) long; racemes of 10–30 golden-orange fls tinged red (may repeat in autumn); purple pea-like frs, blue bloom. Good for hedging.
B. dictyophylla: erect, to 2×1.2m (7×4ft); red young branches with white bloom; deciduous oval lvs to 2cm (¾in) long, white beneath, red & gold in autumn; showy, usually solitary fls; red frs with white bloom.
B. empetrifolia†: dwarf or trailing, to 30–45×60cm (1–1½×2ft); small spines; young shoots red; narrow lvs to 2.5cm (1in) long; fls singly or in 2s; black frs. Not common; good rock-garden shrub but not on shallow chalk.

B. gagnepainii† **5**: to 1.8×1.5m (6×5ft); narrow lvs to 10cm (4in) long; profuse fls in large clusters; black frs, blue bloom. Good for hedging.
B. hookeri†: moderately to v hardy; to 1.5×1.2m (5×4ft); angled stems; holly-like lvs to 8cm (3in) long, blue-white beneath; persistent frs, green turning black.
B. insignis†: moderately hardy; to 1.5×1.8m (5×6ft); usually thornless; shiny dark green lvs to 8–12cm (3–5in) long; showy clusters of 15–25 fls; black 8mm (⅓in) frs. Fine foliage shrub.
B. julianae†: vigorous & erect, to 2.5×2m (8×7ft); angled stems, stout spines; lvs to 8cm (3in) long, coppery when young; fls in profuse clusters; black frs about 8mm (⅓in) long, blue bloom. Good for hedging, screening.
B. koreana†: to 1.8×1.5m (6×5ft); flattened spines, often forked; deciduous v spiny lvs to 6cm (2½in) long, often marked red, red in autumn; long infls; glossy red persistent frs to 5mm (¼in) long.
B. linearifolia† **6**: moderately to v hardy; erect, to 2.5×1.2m (8×4ft); small spines; narrow leathery lvs to 4cm (1½in) long; showy orange-crimson fls; black frs, blue bloom.
B.×lologensis† **7**: natural hybrid of *B. darwinii* & *B. linearifolia*; moderately hardy; to 3×3m (10×10ft); variable lvs, usually resembling *B. darwinii*; large orange fls; frs black, blue bloom.
B.×mentorensis†: hybrid of *B. julianae* & *B. thunbergii*; v to ultra-hardy; to 1.5–2×2m (5–7×7ft); dark semi-evergreen lvs to 2.5cm (1in) long, rich red in autumn; dark red frs.
B.×ottawensis: hybrid of *B. thunbergii* & *B. vulgaris*: to 2×1.8m (7×6ft); yellowish stems; deciduous lvs to 2.5cm (1in) long; red frs. Var 'Superba' has bronzed lvs, crimson in autumn.
B. pruinosa **8**: to 2.5×1.8m (8×6ft); lvs to 6cm (2½in) long; small black frs, grey bloom.
B. sargentiana†: to 1.8×1.5m (6×5ft); dense & erect; leathery, v spiny narrow lvs to 10cm (4in) long; fls greenish-yellow; black 8mm (⅓in) frs.
B. sieboldii: compact & rounded, to 1×1m (3×3ft); suckering; small weak spines; bristly deciduous lvs to 6cm (2½in) long, red in autumn if in dry sunny spot; tiny yellow-red shining frs.
B. soulieana†: to 1.8×1.5m (6×5ft); narrow lvs to 10cm (4in) long; purple-black frs to 5mm (¼in)

wide, glaucous bloom.

B.×stenophylla† : hybrid of *B. darwinii* &
B. empetrifolia; dense, graceful & arching, to
3×3m (10×10ft); simple spines; v narrow lvs to
2.5cm (1in) long; profuse small fls; sparse purple
frs, 5mm (¼in) across, white bloom. Showy
specimen; popular for informal hedging. Vars:
'Coccinea' (to 1.2×1m [4×3ft]; crimson buds;
orange fls); 'Corallina' (to 90×60cm [3×2ft];
coral buds; yellow fls); 'Corallina Compacta' (to
30×30cm [1×1ft]); 'Irwinii' (*B.×irwinii*; to 1×1m
[3×3ft]; deep yellow fls); 'Pink Pearl' **1** (to
1.8×1.8m [6×6ft]; lvs green or mottled white &
pink; fls cream, yellow, pink or bicoloured);
'Prostrata' (*B. darwinii* 'Prostrata'; to 60×60cm
[2×2ft]; orange buds; yellow fls);
'Semperflorens' (to 1.8×1.8m [6×6ft]; red buds;
orange fls, long season).

B. temolaica: to 2.5×2m (8×7ft); handsome;
stems glaucous, ageing purple; small spines;
deciduous glaucous lvs to 5cm (2in) long, white
beneath; fls solitary; red frs to 1cm (⅜in) long,
white bloom.

B. thunbergii† (Japanese barberry): v to ultra-
hardy; to 1.5–1.8×1.8m (5–6×6ft); neat habit;
small single spines; oval deciduous lvs to 3cm
(1¼in) long, brilliant red in autumn; fls flushed
red, usually solitary; red frs 8m (⅓in) long. V
popular; excellent hedging shrub, especially on
poor, dryish soils; tolerates shade (except purple
& golden forms). Vars: 'Atropurpurea' (red-
purple lvs, redder in autumn); 'Atropurpurea
Nana' **2** ('Crimson Pygmy'; to 60cm [2ft]; red-
purple lvs; good for ground cover, dwarf
hedging); 'Aurea' (to 60cm [2ft]; yellow lvs,
greening during summer); 'Erecta' (in US, true-
hedge barberry; dense & erect, for hedging);
'Kobold' (to 22×30cm [9×12in]; bright green
lvs); 'Red Chief' (wine-red lvs); 'Red Pillar'
(narrow, to 1.5×0.2m [5ft×8in]; lvs reddish-
purple); 'Rose Glow' **3** (lvs purple-bronze,
mottled pink & silver when young).

B. valdiviana **4**: moderately hardy; to 3×1.5m
(10×5ft); leathery lvs to 8cm (3in) long; racemes
of 20–30 fls; small purple frs.

B. verruculosa† (warty barberry): slow-growing,
to 1.2×1.2m (4×4ft); warty shoots; slender
spines; dark green lvs to 2.5cm (1in) long,
glaucous beneath; fls usually solitary; black frs,
purple bloom. Useful on banks & for hedging.

B. wilsoniae: dense & mounding, to 1×1.5m
(3×5ft); blue-green deciduous lvs to 2cm (¾in)
long, bright red in autumn; fls mid summer; v
profuse coral-red frs.

Mahoberberis (× *Mahoberberis aquisargentii*
5): bigeneric hybrid of *Mahonia aquifolium* &
Berberis sargentiana; moderately to v hardy; to
1.8×1.2m (6×4ft); stems usually spineless;
evergreen spiny lvs (some simple, to 8cm [3in]
long; others trifoliate, terminal lft to 8cm [3in]

long); fls (rare) yellow, in clusters.
× *M. miethkeana* is similar but freer-flg.

Mahonias (*Mahonia* spp; sometimes listed as
Berberis spp): evergreen shrubs with thornless
erect stems and pinnate lvs of paired holly-like
lfts (sometimes bronzing in winter); fragrant
yellow fls in showy clustered racemes, winter
unless stated; frs blue-black, grape-like & edible.

M. (B.) aquifolium* (Oregon grape): to 1×1.5m
(3×5ft) or more; suckering; lvs of 5–9 lfts to 8cm
(3in) long, shiny dark green, reddish-purple in
autumn; infls to 5–8cm (2–3in) long, spring.
Useful for underplanting; tolerates wind &
exposure. Vars: 'Atropurpurea' **6** (lvs dark
purple-red in winter); 'Compacta' (dwarf);
'Moseri' (young lvs pink or red-tinted).

M. (B.) japonica* **7**: moderately hardy; to
3×3.5m (10×12ft); erect, leafy towards top; lvs
of 13–19 leathery lfts to 10cm (4in) long; infls
mainly pendent or spreading, to 25cm (10in)
long, all winter. Good specimen plant. *M. bealei**
(in US, leatherleaf mahonia) is similar but slightly
smaller & hardier, with shorter erect infls.

M. lomariifolia* **8**: semi-hardy; erect & stately, to
3×1.5m (10×5ft); lvs in rosettes towards top of
gaunt stems, to 60cm (2ft) long with 19–37
narrow lfts; erect infls to 15–25cm (6–10in) long.

M.×media: hybrids of *M. japonica* &
M. lomariifolia; to 2.5–3×1.8–2.5m (8–
10×6–8ft); lvs to 60cm (2ft) long of up to 21 rich
green lfts, yellow-green beneath; profuse infls to
35cm (14in) long, late autumn to mid winter.
Among finest winter-flg specimen shrubs. Vars:
'Buckland'* (groups of up to 14 lax branched
infls); 'Charity'* **9** (groups of up to 20 erect &
spreading infls); 'Winter Sun' (erect infls).

M. (B.) nervosa: to 60×90cm (2×3ft) or wider;
suckering; lvs to 45cm (1½ft) long of 11–15
leathery lfts to 8cm (3in) long; erect infls to 20cm
(8in) long, late spring to early summer. Dislikes
lime.

M. pumila: to 30×60cm (1×2ft) or wider;
suckering; lvs of 5–9 small grey-green lfts,
glaucous beneath; infls to 5cm (2in) long, spring;
for ground cover in sun.

Chinese sacred bamboo (heavenly bamboo,
Nandina domestica **10**: sometimes classed in
Nandinaceae): moderately hardy but root hardier;
to 1.8×1m (6×3ft); upright, bamboo-like stems;
evergreen bipinnate or tripinnate lvs to 30–45cm
(1–1½ft) long; narrow green lfts flushed red in
spring, purple in autumn; white fls 1cm (½in)
across in erect panicles to 30cm (1ft) tall, mid
summer; clusters of persistent red frs to 5mm
(¼in) across where summers hot, best when
plants grouped. For rich, moist soil in sunny,
sheltered site. Useful for airy effect; good in tubs.
Var 'Nana Purpurea' grows to 30cm (1ft); young
lvs purplish.

The birch family

Deciduous catkin-bearing trees mostly of cool climates variously valued for their colourful bark, showy male catkins or nuts, some for their airy grace. Some good for hedging. Leaves are single & toothed; all except *Alnus* spp turn gold in autumn. **Cultivation**: Unless stated, very hardy & for any well-drained soil in sun or partial shade. **Propagation**: Seed (stratify); layering where suitable; vars by hardwood cuttings, grafting.

Alders (*Alnus* spp): fast-growing moisture-lovers useful as alternatives to poplars or willows. Unless stated, lvs rounded, to 10cm (4in) long, & male catkins to 5–10cm (2–4in) long, before lvs. Frs are striking blackish woody "cones".

A. cordata (Italian alder): to 12×5.5m (40×18ft); pyramid-shaped; heart-shaped glossy dark green lvs; frs to 3cm (1¼in) long, erect. Tolerates chalk, dryish soils.

A. glutinosa **1** (black or common European alder): ultra-hardy; to 9×4.5m (30×15ft); young growth sticky; pear-shaped glossy lvs; profuse frs. Var 'Imperialis' **2** has deeply cut lvs.

A. incana (grey or white alder): ultra-hardy; to 12×5.5m (40×18ft), or large shrub; young shoots & lvs downy-grey; profuse frs. Var 'Aurea' **3** has young lvs yellowish; catkins orange.

A. rubra (*A. oregona*, red or Oregon alder): to 12×4.5m (40×15ft); pyramid-shaped, with drooping branches; lvs & male catkins to 15cm (6in) long.

Birches (*Betula* spp): graceful airy trees, casting little shade, with attractive bark (often white, usually peeling). Shallow-rooted & not long-lived; prone to stem-borers, leaf-miners.

B. albo-sinensis (in US, Chinese paper birch): to 7.5×3m (25×10ft); peeling orange-red bark, grey-blue bloom; oval lvs to 8cm (3in) long. Var *septentrionalis* has silky lvs.

B. alleghaniensis (*B. lutea*, yellow birch): ultra-hardy; to 7.5×4.5m (25×15ft); yellowish-brown peeling bark; oval lvs to 12cm (5in) long.

B. ermanii: to 9×4.5m (30×15ft); cream or pinkish peeling bark, brown on branches; oval 5–8cm (2–3in) lvs. Ultra-hardy but prone to late frosts.

B. maximowicziana (monarch birch): fast-growing, to 11×6m (36×20ft); orange-grey peeling bark; heart-shaped lvs to 15×10cm (6×4in); male catkins to 12cm (4in) long.

B. nana: ultra-hardy neat shrub, to 60×60cm (2×2ft); 1cm (½in) rounded lvs.

B. nigra (river, black or red birch): to 7.5×4.5m (25×15ft); often forks low; peeling reddish or grey bark, becoming blackish & rugged; diamond-shaped lvs to 8cm (3in) long, white beneath. Tolerates waterlogged soil.

B. papyrifera **4** (paper, canoe or white birch): ultra-hardy; to 9×4.5m (30×15ft); sometimes weeping; thick, peeling white bark; lvs to 8cm (3½in) long; male catkins to 10cm (4in) long.

B. pendula **5** (*B. alba*, *B. verrucosa*, silver birch;

European white birch): ultra-hardy; graceful, to 11×4.5m (36×15ft); branch tips weep; white bark, becoming rough & blackened; diamond-shaped 2.5–6cm (1–2½in) lvs. Tolerates poor soil. Cut-lvd vars: *crispa*; 'Dalecarlica' (pendulous; lvs deeply cut); 'Laciniata'. Weeping vars: 'Tristis'; 'Youngii' (Young's weeping birch).

B. populifolia (grey birch): to 9×4.5m (30×15ft); often forks low; grey-white bark; 5–9cm (2–3½in) lvs. Good on poor soil.

B. utilis (Himalayan birch): to 7.5×4.5m (25×15ft); flaking red/brown bark; 5–9cm (2–3½in) oval lvs. *B. jaquemontii* has white bark.

Hornbeams (*Carpinus* spp): dense-headed trees with oval, pointed, neatly corrugated lvs; male catkins to 5cm (2in) long, with lvs; hop-like frs 2.5–8cm (1–3in) long. Can be used for hedging (plant 45cm [1½ft] apart); clip each summer; dead lvs retained over winter).

C. betulus **6** (common European hornbeam): to 9×4.5m (30×15ft); pyramid-shaped becoming rounded; grey fluted trunk; lvs to 9cm (3½in) long. Vars: 'Columnaris' (slow-growing, dense & columnar, to 3m [10ft]/25yrs); 'Fastigiata' ('Pyramidalis'; conical, becoming rounded & open). *C. caroliniana* (American hornbeam) is similar but ultra-hardy & slower-growing, to 6×4.5m (20×15ft).

C. japonica (Japanese hornbeam): slow-growing, to 5.5×3.5m (18×12ft); branches spread; lvs to 10cm (4in) long, red in autumn.

C. turczaninowii: slender, to 4.5×3.5m (15×12ft); lvs to 5cm (2in) long, rich orange/brown in autumn.

Hazels (filberts, *Corylus* spp): mostly shrubby & suckering, with rounded lvs 10–15cm (4–6in) long; male catkins to 6cm (2½in) long, before lvs; clusters of edible nuts. Good on chalk.

C. avellana (European hazel, cobnut): ultra-hardy; to 4.5×4.5m (15×15ft). Vars: 'Aurea' (lvs yellow); 'Contorta' **7** (corkscrew hazel; to 2.5m [8ft]; branches & twigs twisted); 'Pendula' (weeping; often top-grafted).

C. colurna (Turkish hazel): tree, to 7.5×4.5m (25×15ft); grey bark. Remove suckers.

C. maxima 'Purpurea' **8** (purple-leaved filbert): to 5.5×5.5m (18×18ft); lvs & catkins dark purple.

Hop hornbeam (*Ostrya carpinifolia* **9**): rough-barked hornbeam-like tree, to 7.5×6m (25×20ft); lvs to 10cm (4in) long; frs enclosed in bladder-like husk. *O. virginiana* (American hop hornbeam) is similar but smaller.

Catalpas and their relatives

Some of the showiest flowering trees for temperate & warm regions, often with large leaves (generally deciduous). Flowers of most species funnel-shaped or foxglove-like, in large inflorescences. **Cultivation**: for any good, well-drained soil in sun. **Propagation**: Semi-ripe heel cuttings; seed.

Catalpas (catawbas, *Catalpa* spp): spreading, rounded, densely branched N American & Chinese trees, fast-growing but not long-lived, with large long-stalked lvs, erect panicles of foxglove-like fls, summer, & narrow bean-like pods 30–60cm (1–2ft) long. V hardy but like warm summers; need training up when young. *C. bignonioides* * **1** (southern or common catalpa, Indian bean tree): to 6×7.5m (20×25ft); ovate light green lvs, hairy beneath, opening v late to 10–25×8–20cm (4–10×3–8in); largest on young trees, smell bad if crushed; 25cm (10in) infls of fls to 5cm (2in) across, white spotted yellow & purple. Var 'Aurea' **2** has rich yellow lvs. *C.×erubescens** (*C.×hybrida*; sometimes listed as var 'J. C. Teas'): hybrid of *C. bignonioides* & *C. ovata*; to 6×7.5m (20×25ft); some lvs lobed, opening purple (v dark in var 'Purpurea'), to 30cm

(1ft) long; fls like *C. bignonioides* but smaller. *C. speciosa** (western or northern catalpa, Indian bean tree): similar to *C. bignonioides* but more upright, to 7.5×6m (25×20ft), & lvs leathery, to 30×22cm (12×9in); fls to 6cm (2½in) across.
Foxglove tree (princess tree, *Paulownia tomentosa** **3**, *P. imperialis*): rounded catalpa-like tree, to 9×9m (30×30ft); lvs ovate to lobed, to 30×25cm (12×10in), woolly beneath; erect 30cm (1ft) panicles of foxglove-like pale violet fls to 5cm (2in) long, spring. V hardy when mature but herbaceous when young; can be stooled.
Tecoma (yellow-bells, *Tecoma* [*Bignonia*] *stans* **4**): semi-hardy erect shrub or tree to 5.5×3.5m (18×12ft); evergreen; pinnate lvs with up to 13 lfts to 15cm (6in) long; racemes of bright yellow funnel-shaped fls to 5cm (2in) long, early summer; seed pods to 20cm (8in) long.

The box family

Except for *Pachysandra* spp, generally neat evergreen shrubs grown mainly for their glossy, leathery foliage (good for cutting). **Cultivation**: Easy, in any soil in sun or semi-shade; very hardy unless stated. Prune/shear to shape late summer. Some spp prone to leaf miners. **Propagation**: Semi-ripe cuttings; many spp by division/suckers; seed (may be slow to grow).

Box (*Buxus* spp): rather slow-growing shrubs, sometimes small trees, with glossy, leathery, untoothed lvs in pairs along stems. Good for hedging, topiary, etc.
B. microphylla (in US, little-leaf boxwood): dense & rounded, to 1×1m (3×3ft); lvs thin & narrow. Vars: 'Compacta' (v dense & twiggy, to 1.2×0.3m [4×1ft]; lvs to 2cm [¾in]); 'Green Pillow' (to 40×75cm [16×30in]; lvs to 1.5cm [½in]); *japonica* (Japanese box; open & spreading, to 1.8×1.8m [6×6ft]); *koreana* (Korean box; hardiest var; loose & open, to 0.6×1m [2×3ft]; lvs bronzed in winter).
B. sempervirens **5** (common box of Europe): long-lived; to 3×3m (10×10ft)/25yrs or small tree; spreading but dense; profuse dark green lvs 1.5–3cm (½–1¼in) long (poisonous). Many vars, including: 'Aureovariegata' **6** (to 2×1.8m [7×6ft]; lvs splashed/mottled creamy-yellow); 'Elegantissima' (slow-growing, to 1×0.6m [3×2ft]; lvs small, edged silver); 'Handsworthensis' (robust & erect, to 3×1.2m [10×4ft]; lvs large, dark green); 'Myrtifolia' (low & compact, to 1.5×0.6m [5×2ft]; lvs small, dark green); 'Rosmarinifolia' ('Thymifolia'; compact, to 60×20cm [24×8in]; lvs sage-green, v narrow);

'Suffruticosa' (edging box; dense, to 90×30cm [3×1ft] or can be trimmed to 15cm [6in]; lvs to 2cm [¾in]; bright green).
Pachysandras (*Pachysandra* spp): tufted prostrate sub-shrubs good for ground cover in partial or deep shade; toothed lvs 5–8cm (2–3in) long, dull green; spikes of small greenish-white or purplish petalless fls, spring.
P. procumbens (Allegheny spurge): to 30×90cm (1×3ft); semi-evergreen rounded lvs; fls smell unpleasant, in 5–10cm (2–4in) spikes.
P. terminalis (Japanese spurge): to 25×60cm (10×24in); evergreen diamond-shaped lvs; small infls; white berries. Var 'Variegata' **7** has cream-edged lvs.
Sweet box (*Sarcococca* spp): dwarf often suckering shrub; lvs often narrowish, to 8cm (3in) long, staggered along stems; fls white, v small, late winter–early spring; berries often black.
S. confusa** **8**; dense and bushy, to 1×1.2m (3×4ft); lvs dark glossy green, privet-like.
S. hookeriana**; erect and suckering, to 1.2×0.6m (4×2ft); lvs narrow. Var *digyna*** is hardier and more slender.
S. humilis** **9**; dwarf and spreading, to 60×90cm (1×3ft); lvs dark green.

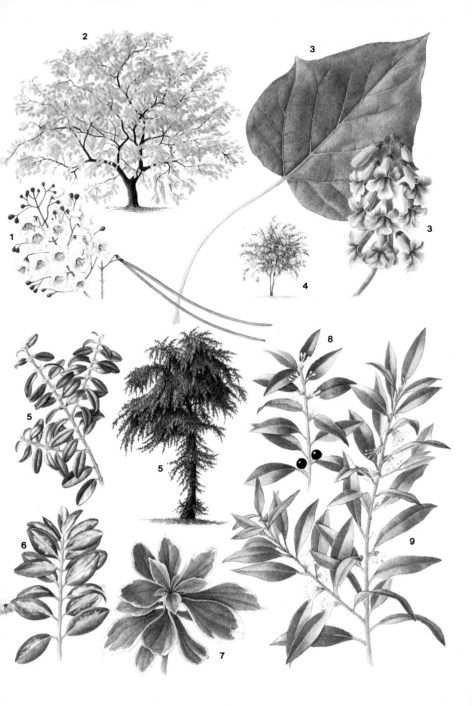

Abelias, weigelas and their relatives

Generally easy, mostly very hardy, free-flowering shrubs, generally of arching habit, good for mixed shrub plantings. Deciduous unless noted. Flowers tubular to funnel-shaped with 5 flaring lobes, mainly in white, pink or red shades. **Cultivation**: Moderately hardy unless stated. For any good well-drained but moist soil in sun or semi-shade. Unless noted, prune after flowering, generally cutting back a few old stems hard. **Propagation**: Semi-ripe or hardwood cuttings; seed; suckers where produced.

Abelias (*Abelia* spp): generally graceful & spreading, with arching branches; lvs in 2s & 3s; free-flg, all summer unless noted. Best in sheltered sunny site; may be cut back by frost but generally regrow.

A. floribunda **1** (Mexican abelia): semi- to moderately hardy; to 1.8×1.5m (6×5ft), more in v mild areas; semi-/evergreen; glossy lvs to 4cm (1½in) long; drooping clusters of brilliant crimson-red fls to 5cm (2in) long, all along branches, late spring & early summer.

A.×grandiflora (in US, glossy abelia): hybrid of *A. chinensis* & *A. uniflora*; moderately to v hardy; to 1.8×1.5m (6×5ft); dense; semi-/evergreen; brilliant glossy green lvs to 6cm (2½in) long; profuse clusters of 2cm (¾in) pink-tinged white fls, summer into autumn. Sometimes used for informal hedge. *A.* 'Edward Goucher' is hybrid with *A. schumannii*; smaller, with deeper lilac-pink fls.

A. schumannii **2**: to 1.5×1.5m (5×5ft); dark green lvs to 3cm (1¼in) long; lilac-pink 2.5cm (1in) fls, summer into autumn.

A. triflora*: moderately to v hardy; tall & graceful, to 3.5×2.5m (12×8ft); young shoots bristly; lance-shaped dark green lvs to 8cm (3in) long; clusters of 2cm (¾in) rosy-white fls, generally in 3s, early summer (not always profuse).

Dipeltas (*Dipelta* spp): rather weigela-like tall shrubs, generally graceful & spreading, with downy young shoots & lvs (to 10–12cm [4–5in] long); showy, somewhat bell-shaped tubular fls, late spring, bracts expanding to become wings of frs.

D. floribunda*: v hardy; to 3×1.8m (10×6ft); peeling bark; abundant clusters of up to 6 pink fls 2.5–3cm (1–1¼in) long, throat flushed yellow.

D. ventricosa: to 3×1.8m (10×6ft); 2.5–3cm (1–1¼in) rose-pink fls, orange throat, inflated.

D. yunnanensis **3**: to 3×1.8m (10×6ft); lvs dark glossy green above; clusters of creamy-white pink-flushed 2–2.5cm (¾–1in) fls, orange throat.

Beauty-bush (*Kolkwitzia amabilis*): v hardy; upright, suckering & gracefully arching, to 3×2.5m (10×8ft); dense & twiggy; peeling bark; dark green lvs to 8cm (3in) long, reddish in autumn; profuse 5–8cm (2–3in) clusters of paired abelia-like fls to 1.5cm (⅝in) long, pale pink with yellow throat, late spring & early summer. Likes lime, sun. Good vars: 'Pink Cloud' **4** & 'Rosea'

Leycesterias (*Leycesteria* spp): to 1.8–2.5×1.2–1.8m (6–8×4–6ft); somewhat bamboo-like habit, with many erect hollow stems (hairy when young), arching towards top; deep green, somewhat glaucous lvs to 15–18cm (6–7in) long; fls in tiered whorls forming drooping racemes; small gooseberry-like frs. Good near sea; prune early spring, removing all previous yr's fld shoots. Self-seed freely where hardy.

L. formosa **5** (Himalayan honeysuckle): 5–10cm (2–4in) infls of 2cm (¾in) white fls, prominent wine-red bracts, mid summer; red-purple frs (attract birds).

Weigelas (*Weigela* [formerly *Diervilla*] spp): v popular free-flg shrubs, generally to 1.8–2×1.8m (6–7×6ft), with lvs to 8–10cm (3–4in) long & clusters of bright 2.5–4cm (1–1½in) fls on short side-shoots from yr-old wood, late spring to early summer (sometimes repeating later). Tolerate pollution; cut back all old fld shoots hard after flg. Spp largely replaced by hybrids.

W. (*D.*) *florida* (*W. rosea*): v hardy; vigorous & spreading, to 1.8×1.8m (6×6ft); suckering; fls deep rose, inside paler fading to almost white. Parent of many hybrids. Vars: 'Foliis Purpureis' **6** (compact; lvs dark metallic-green flushed purple; fls pink); 'Variegata' **7** (compact; lvs edged creamy-white; fls pink); *venusta* (*W. venusta*; graceful; profuse large fls, bright rose-pink; hardiest of genus).

W. hortensis: young shoots hairy; lvs velvety-white beneath; fls of sp carmine-red, but white-fld var 'Nivea' (*albiflora*) is commoner.

W. middendorffiana: to 1.2×1.2m (4×4ft); wrinkled lvs; sulphur-yellow fls blotched orange, mid–late spring. V hardy but fls damaged by spring frosts, so best sheltered.

W. hybrids: derived from *W. florida* & various other spp; showy & free-flg. Vars: 'Abel Carrière' (rosy-carmine fls, throat flared gold, from darker buds: 'Bristol Ruby' **8** (erect & vigorous; bright ruby-red fls from v dark buds; 'Newport Red' ['Vanicek', 'Cardinal Red'] is similar but paler red); 'Bristol Snowflake' (vigorous; white); 'Candida' **9** (incorrectly, 'Avalanche'; white); 'Conquête' (sparse & spreading; large deep rose-pink fls); 'Dame Blanche' (white flushed pink); 'Eva Rathke' (compact; bright crimson-red fls from dark buds; 'Eva Supreme' is similar but more vigorous); 'Féerie' ('Fairy'; profuse large rose-pink fls); 'Floréal' (rosy-pink, deep carmine throat); 'Looymansii Aurea' (young lvs pale golden-yellow; fls pink; best in light shade); 'Styriaca' (carmine-red).

Shrubby honeysuckles and snowberries

Shrubs grown mainly for their flowers (not v showy, but often fragrant in *Lonicera* spp; attract bees) &/or their attractive fleshy berries (attract birds). Deciduous unless stated. Flowers tubular to funnel-shaped, with 4 or 5 lobes. Mostly for mixed borders & shrubberies; *Symphoricarpos* & evergreen *Lonicera* spp good for hedging or ground cover. **Cultivation**: Unless noted, very hardy & for any well-drained soil in sun. **Propagation**: Semi-ripe or hardwood cuttings; seed; suckers where produced.

Honeysuckles (*Lonicera* spp): bushy relatives of well-known climbers (p230) with paired 2-lipped fls generally to 1–2.5cm (½–1in) long, late spring or early summer unless stated; berries red unless noted (best in continental climates where fls not damaged by late frosts). Do not plant in frost pockets; when necessary, prune after flg, thinning out old wood.
L. chrysantha: ultra-hardy; to 3×2.5m (10×8ft); lvs to 12cm (5in) long; pale yellow fls, deepening; coral-red frs. V ornamental.
*L. fragrantissima*** **1**: rather open, to 1.8×1.8m (6×6ft); semi-/evergreen, deciduous in hard winters; leathery lvs to 5cm (2in) long; creamy-white fls, late winter or early spring, before new lvs (or autumn in warm climates; good for cutting). *L.×purpusii** is hybrid with *L. standishii*; similar, but dense & rounded, with bristly lvs.
L. involucrata (twinberry): ultra-hardy; dense, to 2.5×2.5m (8×8ft); dark green lvs to 12cm (5in) long; small yellow or red-tinged fls, red bracts; glossy purple-black frs. Good near sea.
L. korolkowii: graceful & arching, to 2.5×2.5m (8×8ft); glaucous-green downy lvs to 3cm (1¼in) long; pink fls (best where summers hot).
L. morrowii: ultra-hardy; loose & spreading, to 2.5×3m (8×10ft); young shoots downy; lvs to 5cm (2in) long, woolly beneath; fls cream to yellow. Best in wild garden. *L.×bella* vars are hybrids with *L. tatarica* with larger lvs & pink or red fls.
*L. nitida** (box honeysuckle): moderately to v hardy; vigorous & dense, to 1.8×1.8m (6×6ft); evergreen; dark green 1cm (½in) lvs, bronzed in winter; v small creamy-white fls, mid spring; purplish-blue translucent frs. Good for hedging; tolerates wind, salt spray, shade. Vars: 'Baggesen's Gold' **2** (to 1.2×1.8m [4×6ft]; yellow lvs, greening later); 'Elegant' (to 1×1.2m [3×4ft]; arching branches; deep green lvs).
*L. pileata** **3** (privet honeysuckle): low & spreading, to 1×1.8m (3×6ft); stiff horizontal branches; semi-/evergreen; glossy privet-like lvs to 3cm (1¼in) long; inconspicuous creamy fls; translucent violet frs (sparse). Good ground cover; tolerates shade, salt spray.
L. pyrenaica: erect, to 1.2×1.2m (4×4ft); glaucous lvs to 3cm (1¼in) long; fls white flushed red. Attractive dwarf shrub.
*L. setifera**: to 1.8×1.5m (6×5ft); bristly stems, fls & frs; downy, coarsely toothed lance-shaped lvs to 8cm (3in) long; white fls, late winter & early

spring (before lvs).
*L. standishii***: to 1.8×1.8m (6×6ft), more against wall; sometimes semi-evergreen; bristly lvs to 10cm (4in) long; creamy-white fls, early winter to early spring depending on climate. V hardy, but often grown on wall to protect fls.
*L. syringantha*** **4**: spreading & graceful, to 1.8×1.8m (6×6ft); densely branched; glaucous-green lvs to 2.5cm (1in) long; soft lilac fls.
L. tatarica **5** (Tartarian honeysuckle): ultra-hardy; vigorous & bushy, to 3×2.5m (10×8ft); densely twiggy; dark green lvs to 6cm (2½in) long, smaller on flg branches; profuse white to red fls. Showy shrub for background planting, screening, etc; naturalized in some areas. Vars: 'Arnold Red' **6** (v dark red); 'Grandiflora' (large white fls); 'Hack's Red' (purplish-red); 'Morden Orange' (pale pink; orange frs); 'Zabelii' (ruby-red).
L. xylosteum **7** (fly honeysuckle): bushy, to 3×3.5m (10×12ft); downy lvs to 6cm (2½in) long; yellowish fls, sometimes tinged red.
L. 'Clavey's Dwarf' ('Claveyi') is probably hybrid with *L. tatarica*; dense & rounded, to 1×1m (3×3ft); glaucous lvs; white fls; good hedger.
Snowberries (*Symphoricarpos* spp): suckering, thicket-forming plants grown mainly for clusters of glistening berries, to 1cm (½in) across, persisting over winter (good in arrangements); lvs generally grey-green, on v slender stems; fls rather insignificant. Tolerate poor soil & shade.
S. albus laevigatus **8** (*S. rivularis*, common snowberry): ultra-hardy; to 1.8×2m (6×7ft); erect; lvs to 8cm (3in) long; pink fls, early summer; white marble-like frs.
S.×chenaultii: hybrid of *S. microphyllus* & *S. orbiculatus*; erect & much-branched, to 1.5×1.2m (5×4ft); lvs to 2cm (¾in) long; pinkish-white frs tinged red. Var 'Hancock' is prostrate, to 0.6×1.8m (2×6ft); good ground cover.
S.×doorenbosii vars ('Doorenbos Hybrids'): hybrids of *S. albus laevigatus, S.×chenaultii* & *S. orbiculatus*. Vars: 'Magic Berry' **9** (bushy, to 1.2×1.5m [4×5ft]; frs rosy-lilac); 'Mother of Pearl' **10** (vigorous & arching, to 1.8×1.8m [6×6ft]; white frs tinged pink); 'White Hedge' (stiff & erect, to 1.5×1m [5×3ft]; white frs).
S. orbiculatus (coralberry, Indian currant): ultra-hardy; dense & bushy, to 1–2×2–3m (3–7×7–10ft); branches downy; lvs to 3cm (1¼in) long, hairy beneath; whitish fls, late summer; small coral/purplish-red frs (best where summers hot).

Viburnums

Viburnum spp & hybrids. Popular, generally easy shrubs grown for their often fragrant white or pink flowers (some in winter), their colourful fruits (attract birds) &/or their foliage (with fine autumn colours in many deciduous spp). Toothed leaves, to 10cm (4in) long & deciduous unless noted. Flowers generally tubular, with 5 lobes, borne in flat or dome-shaped inflorescences. (Some spp have showy sterile & small fertile flowers like lacecap hydrangeas [p200]; a few vars ["snowballs"] have entirely sterile flowers.) Berry-like red, blue or black fruits, best if cross-pollinated. **Cultivation**: Very hardy unless stated. Best in deep, rich, moist soil in sun or partial shade. May be attacked by aphids. Regular pruning not necessary but cut out overgrown old wood after flowering; evergreens can be trimmed in spring. **Propagation**: Semi-ripe cuttings; seed (stratify); lax spp by layering.

V. betulifolium **1**: to 3×3m (10×10ft); dark green diamond-shaped lvs; white fls in cymes to 10cm (4in) wide, late spring & early summer; profuse bright red translucent frs, persistent.

V.×bodnantense vars: hybrids of *V. farreri* & *V. grandiflorum*; to 2.5–3×2.5m (8–10×8ft); stiff & erect; young lvs bronzed; fls in 2.5–8cm (1–3in) clusters, all winter, on naked twigs. Vars: 'Dawn'** **2** (v frost-resistant pink-flushed white fls from rosy-red buds); 'Deben'** **3** (white fls flushed pink from shell-pink buds; best in mild spells).

*V.×burkwoodii**: hybrids of *V. carlesii* & *V. utile*; to 2.5×3m (8×10ft), semi-/evergreen; dark green lvs, brown felt beneath; 6–9cm (2½–3½in) heads of white fls from pink buds, spring or earlier. Tolerates pollution. 'Park Farm Hybrid'** is similar but more spreading, with larger fls from pinker buds; old lvs colour in autumn. *V.* 'Anne Russell'** **4** is back-cross with *V. carlesii*; compact, to 1.8×1.5m (6×5ft); 8cm (3in) infls.

*V.×carlcephalum** **5** (fragrant snowball): hybrid of *V. carlesii* & *V. macrocephalum keteleeri*; fast-growing, to 2.5×2.5m (8×8ft); stiff habit; glossy bright green lvs, often bright red in autumn; dense round heads to 15cm (6in) across of white fls, pink flush, from pink buds, spring.

*V. carlesii** **6** rounded & bushy, to 1.5×1.5m (5×5ft); downy lvs, greyish beneath, often purple-red in autumn; rounded 5–8cm (2–3in) clusters of white fls from pink buds (formed autumn, open spring); black frs. V popular. Vars: 'Aurora'** **7** (pink fls from red buds); 'Diana'** (purplish-pink fls from red buds). *V.×judii** is hybrid with *V. bitchiuense*; more vigorous, with larger infls of pink-tinted fls.

V. cassinoides (withe-rod): ultra-hardy; rounded, to 1.8×1.8m (6×6ft); thick lvs, bronzed when young, crimson & scarlet in autumn; cream fls in cymes to 10cm (4in) across, early summer; frs red to blue-black, edible. Dislikes shallow chalk.

V. cylindricum: moderately hardy; to 3×1.8m (10×6ft); sometimes a small tree; evergreen wax-coated lvs to 20cm (8in) long; 8–12cm (3–5in) cymes of white fls, lilac stamens mid–late summer; black frs.

V. davidii **8**: moderately to v hardy; mounding, to 1×1.5m (3×5ft); evergreen leathery lvs to 12cm (5in) long, prominently 3-veined; cymes to 8cm (3in) wide of white fls, early summer; fine purple-blue frs if cross-pollinated.

V. cinnamomifolium is v similar but much bigger, to 2.5×1.8m (8×6ft), with loose infls to 15cm (6in) wide.

V. dilatatum: to 2.5×1.5m (8×5ft); rounded hairy lvs to 12cm (5in) long, dark red in autumn; profuse 8–12cm (3–5in) cymes of pure white fls, early summer; profuse bright red frs if cross-pollinated. *V. wrightii* is similar but hairless.

*V. erubescens gracilipes**: moderately to v hardy; to 2.5×1.5–1.8m (8×5–6ft); narrowish lvs; pink-flushed white fls in drooping panicles to 8–10cm (3–4in) long, summer; frs red to black.

*V. farreri** (*V. fragrans*): dense & erect, to 3×3m (10×10ft); lvs bronze when young; white or pink-tinged fls in 5cm (2in) clusters on naked twigs, all winter, or early spring where winters harsh; red frs (rare). Var *candidissimum* (*album*) has pure white fls & green young lvs.

*V. grandiflorum**: stiffly erect, to 3×2m (10×7ft); lvs downy beneath; carmine buds open to rose-pink fls 1cm (½in) long, fading white, in infls to 8cm (3in) across, late winter & early spring (prone to frost damage); frs dark purple.

V.×hillieri 'Winton'*: hybrid of *V. erubescens* & *V. henryi*; moderately to v hardy; rather lax, to 1.8×2.5m (6×8ft); semi-evergreen lvs, coppery when young, bronzed in winter; loose panicles of creamy fls, early summer; frs red to black.

V. hupehense: to 2.5×1.8m (8×6ft); dark green downy lvs to 8cm (3in) long, colouring early autumn; 5cm (2in) corymbs of white fls, early summer; orange-red to red frs.

*V. japonicum**: moderately hardy; to 1.8×1.8m (6×6ft); evergreen leathery lvs to 15cm (6in) long; rounded 8–10cm (3–4in) cymes of white fls, early summer, when mature; red frs.

V. lantana **9** (wayfaring tree): ultra-hardy; vigorous, to 3×2.5m (10×8ft), sometimes tree-like; grey-green hairy lvs, dark crimson in autumn; flat 5–10cm (2–4in) cymes of white fls, late spring & early summer; showy red to black frs. Good on chalk, dry soil.

V. macrocephalum (Chinese snowball): moderately to v hardy; rounded, to 2.5×2.5m (8×8ft); deciduous or semi-evergreen lvs,

downy beneath; 8–15cm (3–6in) globular infls of white sterile fls, late spring.

V. odoratissimum* (sweet viburnum): semi- to moderately hardy; to 3×2.5m (10×8ft); evergreen glossy leathery lvs to 20cm (8in) long, often colouring in winter; 8–15cm (3–6in) panicles of white fls, late summer, when mature; red to black frs. Good on wall.

V. opulus (guelder rose; in US, European cranberry bush): ultra-hardy; to 4.5×4.5m (15×15ft); maple-like lobed lvs, rich red in autumn; 5–8cm (2–3in) lacecap cymes of white fls; profuse glossy red pungent frs (persistent). Tolerates wet soil; prone to aphids. Vars: 'Aureum' **1** (yellow lvs; for semi-shade); 'Compactum' **2** (to 1.8×1.5m [6×5ft]); 'Notcutt's Variety' (large fls & frs); 'Roseum' **3** ('Sterile', snowball bush; globular infls of sterile fls); 'Xanthocarpum' **4** (frs golden). *V. trilobum* (*V. opulus americanum*; in US, American cranberry bush) is v similar.

V. plicatum (*V. tomentosum plicatum*, Japanese snowball): spreading, to 3×3m (10×10ft); horizontal branches; lvs hairy beneath, red in autumn; white sterile fls in 8cm (3in) globular infls all along branches, early summer. Vars of *V. p. tomentosum* (lacecap-fld form): 'Lanarth' (vigorous & tiered; large fls); 'Mariesii' **5** (similar to 'Lanarth'; profuse small infls); 'Pink Beauty' **6** (sterile fls mature pink); 'Rowallane' (compact; profuse fls).

V. prunifolium (black haw): ultra-hardy vigorous shrub, to 4.5×3m (15×10ft), or handsome small tree; lvs red & yellow in autumn; white fls in cymes to 10cm (4in) wide, early summer; blue-black frs (used for preserves).

V. rhytidophyllum **7**: robust & fast-growing, to 4.5×3.5m (15×12ft); evergreen; dark glossy green lvs to 18cm (7in) long, wrinkled, grey felt beneath; whitish fls in 10–20cm (4–8in) infls (form autumn, open late spring); shiny red frs ripening black, profuse if cross-pollinated. Handsome only on good soil in shelter.

V. 'Pragense' is hybrid with *V. utile*; smaller lvs.

V. sieboldii: vigorous & spreading, to 2.5×1.8m (8×6ft); pungent dark glossy green lvs to 12cm (5in) long, bronze in autumn; creamy-white fls in 8–10cm (3–4in) cymes, late spring & early summer; pink frs ripen blue-black, persistent red stalks. Fls & frs best in continental climates.

V. tinus (laurustinus): moderately hardy; bushy & rounded, to 3×3m (10×10ft); dense & leafy; evergreen dark glossy green lvs, toothless but variable size & shape; 5–10cm (2–4in) cymes of white fls from pink buds, winter to early spring; metallic-blue frs ripen black. Thrives in shade or sun; good for hedges & screens. Vars: 'Eve Price' **8** (compact, to 1.8×1.8m [6×6ft]; pinkish fls); 'Lucidum' (vigorous & open but less hardy); 'Variegatum' (semi-hardy; lvs variegated creamy).

V. utile*: moderately to v hardy; to 1.8×1.8m (6×6ft); open & graceful, with slender branches; glossy evergreen lvs to 8cm (3in) long, white down beneath; dense rounded 8cm (3in) infls of white fls, spring; blue-black frs. Tolerates lime.

Elders

Sambucus spp; sometimes classified in Sambucaceae. Vigorous, rather coarse deciduous shrubs generally best in wild garden, but vars with ornamental leaves make fine specimens, screens, etc. Leaves pinnate, with toothed leaflets. Small creamy-white starry flowers, generally in flat heads to 20cm (8in) across, followed by profuse berries (attract birds). Flowers & blue-/black berries popular for wine-making, latter also for pies, cordials, etc; red berries may be poisonous. **Cultivation:** Very hardy unless noted. Best in moist soil in sun or partial shade (golden leaves colour quicker in sun but retain colour longer in shade). For lush foliage, prune hard (or even coppice) in winter or early spring. **Propagation:** Seed; semi-ripe or hardwood cuttings.

S. caerulea (blue elder): vigorous, to 3×3m (10×10ft), sometimes a tree to 9m (30ft) or more; lvs with 5–9 lfts to 15cm (6in) long; fls early summer; black frs, intense glaucous bloom.

S. canadensis (American elder): ultra-hardy; to 3×3m (10×10ft); suckering; lvs with 7-11 lfts to 15cm (6in) long; fls early summer; frs purple-black. Vars: 'Acutiloba' (lfts deeply divided); 'Aurea' (yellow lfts; red frs); 'Maxima' **9** (large lvs; infls to 40cm [16in] wide). Good frtg vars also available in N America.

S. nigra* (European elder): to 4.5×4.5m (15×15ft), or small tree; lvs with 3–7 lfts to 12cm (5in) long, pungent if bruised; fls early summer (heavy odour); frs black. Tolerates chalk, deep shade. Self-seeds via birds. Vars: 'Aurea' (golden elder; deep yellow lfts); 'Aureomarginata' **10** (lfts edged yellow); *laciniata* (fern/parsley-leaved elder; finely divided lfts); 'Pulverulenta' (lfts striped & mottled white).

S. racemosa (European red elder): to 3×3m (10×10ft); lvs with 5–7 lfts to 10cm (4in) long, coarsely toothed; fls in conical infls to 8cm (3in) tall, spring; scarlet frs, early. Vars: 'Plumosa Aurea' **11** (slow-growing, to 2.5×1.8m [8×6ft]; deeply toothed golden lfts; yellow fls); 'Tenuifolia' (mounding, to 0.6×1.2m [2×4ft]; finely cut lfts).

Spindle trees and their relatives

Widely varying shrubs (some becoming small trees), deciduous unless noted, grown mainly for their foliage &/or fruits; flowers generally inconspicuous. Some colour well in autumn; evergreens have fine lush foliage. Used for various structural landscaping purposes; low-growing evergreens for ground cover & hedges, taller types as backgrounds, screens, etc. **Cultivation**: Unless stated, very hardy & for any well-drained fertile soil in sun or partial shade. Little pruning needed except to thin out deciduous spp if necessary late winter; trim hedges spring & late summer. **Propagation**: Semi-ripe cuttings; deciduous spp by seed; prostrate types by layering.

Spindles (*Euonymus* spp): range from creepers to trees; colourful pendulous frs 1–2cm (½–¾in) across, lobed & sometimes winged, bursting to show colourful seed arils (most profuse if cross-pollinated). Like chalk; variegated forms best in some shade; evergreens tolerate full shade; most spp prone to scale insects, aphids & caterpillars.

E. alatus **1** (winged euonymus): ultra-hardy; slow-growing & spreading, to 2.5×3m (8×10ft); open & stiff; branches have conspicuous corky wings; dark green lvs to 8cm (3in) long, rich rosy-scarlet in autumn; purplish frs, scarlet arils. Var 'Compactus' is compact, to 1.5m (5ft).

E. bungeanus (in US, winterberry euonymus): slender & erect, to 3×2.5m (10×8ft), or small tree; pale green lvs to 10cm (4in) long, lemon-yellow tinged pink in autumn; creamy frs tinged pink, orange arils (best where summers hot).

E. europaeus (common [European] spindle tree): ultra-hardy; vigorous & bushy, to 3×3m (10×10ft); or small tree; stems green; narrowish lvs to 9cm (3½in) long, pinkish in autumn; scarlet frs, orange arils. Vars: 'Albus' (frs white); 'Aldenhamensis' (frs bright pink); *intermedius* (large lvs; large bright red frs); 'Red Cascade' **2** (profuse rosy-red frs; best if cross-pollinated).

E. fortunei radicans (*E. radicans*): juvenile form trailing or creeping, to 1.8×3m (6×10ft), or can be trained on wall, climbing to 3–6m (10–20ft), with lvs 1–3cm (½–1¼in) long; adult form bushy & spreading, to 1×1.5m (3×5ft), with lvs 2.5–5cm (1–2in) long; both evergreen, lvs dark glossy green; pinkish frs, orange arils on adults. Juvenile vars: 'Coloratus' (lvs reddish-purple in winter); 'Emerald Charm' (deep green lvs veined white); 'Kewensis' (dwarf; lvs 0.5–1.5cm [¼–⅝in] long); 'Variegatus' ('Gracilis', 'Silver Edge'; grey-green lvs edged white, pink tinge in winter). Adult vars: *carrierei*; 'Emerald and Gold' **3** (lvs edged gold, tinged pink in winter; 'Emerald Gaiety' **4** is more rounded, lvs edged white); 'Silver Queen' **5** (young lvs creamy, becoming green edged creamy-white); *vegetus* **6** (small rounded lvs; free-frtg; can be trained up wall).

E. japonicus (Japanese spindle tree): moderately hardy; bushy & upright, to 3×1.8m (10×6ft), or small tree; evergreen; dark shiny leathery lvs to 8cm (3in) long; pinkish frs, pale orange arils (rare in gardens). Leafy; good for hedging, especially near sea. Prone to mildew. Vars: 'Albomarginatus' ('Pearl Edge'; lvs edged white); 'Aureopictus' **7** ('Aureus'; lvs centred gold; may revert); 'Duc d'Anjou' ('Viridivariegatus'; lvs variegated greyish- & yellowish-green); 'Latifolius Albomarginatus' **8** ('Latifolius Variegatus', 'Macrophyllus Albus'; wide white-edged lvs); 'Microphyllus' (dwarf, to 1m [3ft]; small lvs, suffused gold in 'Microphyllus Pulchellus', edged white in 'Microphyllus Variegatus'); 'Ovatus Aureus' **9** ('Aureovariegatus'; lvs marked pale-yellow).

E. kiautschovicus (*E. patens*): moderately to v hardy; spreading, to 2.5×2.5m (8×8ft); deciduous or semi-evergreen; bright green lvs to 8cm (3in) long; frs pink, orange arils (late). Vars 'Du Pont' & 'Manhattan' have dark green lvs.

E. latifolius: loose & spreading, to 3×2.5m (10×8ft), or small tree; lvs to 12cm (5in) long, brilliant red in autumn; large scarlet winged frs, orange arils. *E. sachalinensis* (correctly, *E. planipes*) is v similar but frs not winged.

E. nanus: dwarf & semi-prostrate, to 8×90cm (3in×3ft); deciduous or semi-evergreen; v narrow rosemary-like lvs to 4cm (1½in) long; pink frs, orange arils, if summers hot. Good ground cover.

E. obovatus: ultra-hardy; trailing, fast-growing & self-rooting, to 0.3×1.8m (1×6ft); lvs to 6cm (2½in) long, bright red in autumn; crimson warty frs, scarlet arils. For ground cover.

E. oxyphyllus: slow-growing, to 1.8–2.5×1.8–2.5m (6–8×6–8ft), or small tree; lvs to 8cm (3in) long, rich purplish-red in autumn; brilliant carmine-red frs, orange arils.

E. yedoensis (correctly, *E. hamiltonianus sieboldianus*): vigorous, to 3×3m (10×10ft), or small tree; lvs to 12cm (5in) long, varied pink & red shades in autumn; pink frs, orange to blood-red arils. 'Coral Charm' **10** is good var.

Pachistimas (*Paxistima* spp; sometimes spelled *Pachistima*): low-growing evergreen shrubs, neat & tufted, with leathery narrowish lvs to 2.5–3cm (1–1¼in) long, fls & frs small. For edging, ground cover, dwarf hedges. Need moist acid soil, preferably in semi-shade; good near sea.

P. canbyi **11**: decumbent, to 30×90cm (1×3ft); lvs bronze in winter. Can be divided.

P. myrsinites: spreading, to 0.6×1.5m (2×5ft); dense growth; glossy lvs.

Rock roses and their relatives

Sun-loving, somewhat tender evergreen shrubs, generally mounding & compact, with beautiful 5-petalled rose-like flowers, ephemeral but very freely produced, late spring to mid summer. Flowers usually have prominent boss of stamens & crinkly paper-like petals. Generally best grouped on hot, dry banks, raised beds, large rock gardens, etc; also for path edgings, taller types for informal screens. **Cultivation**: Moderately hardy unless stated. For light, very well-drained preferably limy soil in full sun; tolerate wind & salt spray. Transplant poorly. Give winter protection where necessary. Little pruning needed except to pinch back young plants & cut out old stems. **Propagation**: Seed (hybridize freely); semi-ripe cuttings; layering. For *Helianthemum* spp (also called rock roses), see 478.

Rock roses (sun roses, *Cistus* spp):
C.×aguilari **1**: hybrid of *C. ladanifer* & *C. populifolius*; vigorous & erect, to 1.5×1.5m (5×5ft); lance-shaped bright green lvs* to 10cm (4in) long; white 8cm (3in) fls, blotched crimson in var 'Maculatus'.
C. albidus **2**: bushy, to 1.8×1.8m (6×6ft); white-woolly lvs to 5cm (2in) long; rosy-lilac 6cm (2½in) fls blotched yellow.
C.×corbariensis (*C.×hybridus*): hybrid of *C. populifolius* & *C. salviifolius*, moderately to v hardy; bushy & spreading, to 1×1.8m (3×6ft); wavy dark green lvs to 5cm (2in) long; 4cm (1½in) white fls, blotched yellow, reddish buds.
C.×cyprius: hybrid of *C. ladanifer* & *C. laurifolius*; vigorous & gracefully spreading, to 1.8×2.5m (6×8ft); lance-shaped dark green lvs* to 10cm (4in) long, greyish in winter; white 8cm (3in) fls, large blood-red blotches.
C. ladanifer **3** (gum cistus): erect, to 1.5×1m (5×3ft); narrow lance-shaped lvs* to 10cm (4in) long; 8–10cm (3–4in) white fls blotched red.
C. laurifolius: moderately to v hardy; stiff & erect, to 1.8×1.8m (6×6ft); peeling bark; dark green lvs* to 8cm (3in) long; white 6–8cm (2½–3in) fls. Hardiest sp. *C.* 'Silver Pink' **4** is beautiful hybrid with *C. creticus* (*C. villosus*); moderately to v hardy on good well-drained soil, less so on poor soil; to 75×75cm (2½×2½ft); lance-shaped lvs to 8cm (3in) long; 8cm (3in) silvery-pink fls.
C.×lusitanicus: hybrid of *C. hirsutus* & *C. ladanifer*; erect, to 60×60cm (2×2ft); lance-shaped dark green lvs* to 6cm (2½in) long; white 6cm (2½in) fls, crimson blotches. Var 'Decumbens' is more spreading, to 0.6×1.2m (2×4ft); fls more prominently blotched.
C. palhinhae: compact & dense, to 60×75cm (2×2½ft); dark green lvs to 5cm (2in) long, dense white down beneath; satiny-white fls 8–10cm (3–4in) wide. Parent of various garden hybrids: 'Anne Palmer' **5** (with *C. crispus*; upright, to 1×1m [3×3ft]; pink fls); 'Elma' (with *C. laurifolius*; bushy & sturdy, to 2×1.8m [7×6ft]; glossy lance-shaped lvs; 9cm [3½in] pure white fls); 'Paladin' & 'Pat' (both with *C. ladanifer*; bushy & spreading, to 1.8×1.8m [6×6ft]; large maroon-blotched fls).
C. populifolius: vigorous, to 1.8×1.5m (6×5ft);

long-stalked lvs to 9×6cm (3½×2½in), prominently net-veined; 5cm (2in) yellow-stained white fls, larger in var *lasiocalyx*.
C.×pulverulentus **6**: compact, to 60×60cm (2×2ft); sage-green wavy lvs to 5cm (2in) long; deep cerise-pink 5cm (2in) fls.
C.×purpureus **7**: hybrid of *C. creticus* (*C. villosus*) & *C. ladanifer*; bushy & rounded, to 1.2×1.2m (4×4ft); greyish-green lvs* to 5cm (2in), downy beneath; reddish-purple 6–8cm (2½–3in) fls blotched dark red.
C. villosus (*C. incanus*; correctly *C. creticus*): variable bushy shrub, to 0.6–1.2×1–1.2m (2–4×3–4ft); young stems often hairy or downy; lvs* to 8cm (3in) long, variable shape, hairy & often wavy; 5–6cm (2–2½in) rose-pink to purple fls, yellow centre.
Halimiocistus (×*Halimiocistus* spp): intergeneric hybrids of *Cistus* & *Halimium* spp.
×*H. ingwersenii* **8**: natural hybrid of *C. hirsutus* & *H. umbellatum*; semi-prostrate, to 45×90cm (1½×3ft); stems hairy; narrow lance-shaped dark green lvs to 4cm (1½in) long; 2.5cm (1in) pure white fls, long season.
×*H. wintonensis* **9**: garden hybrid of *C. salviifolius* & probably *H. ocymoides*; bushy & spreading, to 0.6×1.2m (2×4ft); young shoots & lvs white-woolly, both becoming dull green; lance-shaped lvs to 5cm (2in) long; 5cm (2in) white fls, crimson-maroon zone & yellow eye.
Halimiums (*Halimium* spp): low-growing hairy/downy shrubs closely related to (& sometimes listed as) *Helianthemum* spp.
H. lasianthum formosum **10**: moderately to v hardy; spreading, to 1×1.2m (3×4ft); grey-downy; lvs to 4cm (1½in) long; 4cm (1½in) rich bright yellow fls blotched brownish-purple.
H. libanotis (correctly, *H. commutatum*): erect, to 60×45cm (2×1½ft); v narrow lvs to 4cm (1½in) long, white felt beneath; 2.5cm (1in) golden-yellow fls. *H. umbellatum* is similar, with rosemary-like lvs & white fls blotched yellow, in 10–15cm (4–6in) racemes.
H. ocymoides **11**: usually erect, to 1×1.2m (3×4ft); young shoots densely white-downy; downy lvs to 1.5–3cm (⅝–1¼in) long, green & deciduous on flg shoots; 8–20cm (3–8in) panicles of rich yellow 2.5cm (1in) fls blotched black & purple.

The daisy family

Various tribes of Composites. Range from silver-leaved low shrubs good for ground cover & border contrast (offsetting stronger colours) to large specimen or screening shrubs (some eventually becoming small trees). Evergreen unless stated. Flowers often small or insignificant & button-like (often best removed), or showy & daisy- or aster-like. (All daisy "flowers" are compound; sizes refer to whole flower heads.) Often good in coastal gardens. **Cultivation**: Unless stated, moderately hardy & for any well-drained (even poor) soil in sunny spot. No regular pruning except to trim untidy plants in early spring. **Propagation:** Semi-ripe cuttings; seed.

Artemisias (*Artemisia* spp; Anthemis tribe): bushy aromatic shrubs with more or less grey, generally finely divided foliage; yellow button fls.
A. abrotanum (southernwood, old man, lad's love): v hardy; to 1.2×1.2m (4×4ft); erect; somewhat soft-stemmed; shoots & lvs grey-downy; deciduous or semi-evergreen lvs* to 5cm (2in) long, finely divided; fls yellow, autumn.
A. arborescens **1**: rounded, to 1.2×1.2m (4×4ft); silky white down on shoots & lvs; silvery filigree lvs*; fls bright yellow, summer. Good near sea.
A. tridentata (sage brush): v hardy; open & somewhat lax, to 2×1.5–1.8m (7×5–6ft); old bark shreds; young shoots & lvs densely grey-felted; wedge-shaped 3-toothed lvs* 1–4.5cm (½–1¾in) long; yellowish fls, grey-felted bracts, autumn.

Coyote bush (chaparral broom, *Baccharis pilularis* **2**; Aster tribe): dense & spreading, to 0.6×1.8m (2×6ft); or wider; closely set dark green toothed lvs to 2cm (¾in) long; fls inconspicuous; messy cottony seed-heads on females. Excellent cover for banks, etc, in hot sun.

Brachyglottis (*Brachyglottis repanda*** ; Senecio tribe); semi-hardy exotic-looking New Zealand shrub, to 4.5×4.5m (15×15ft), or small tree; young shoots densely felted; large dark green purple-tinged leathery lvs to 10–30×8–20cm (4–12×3–8in), irregularly lobed/toothed, dense white felt beneath, on long stalks; panicles to 30×40cm (12×16in) of v small greenish-white mignonette-scented fls, early spring. Vars: 'Purpurea' (lvs purple above); *rangiora* (*B. rangiora*; larger glossier lvs).

Cushion bush (*Calocephalus brownii*; Inula tribe): semi-hardy; dense & mounding, to 1×1m (3×3ft); white-woolly; intricate wiry stems with tiny clinging thread-like 3mm (⅛in) lvs; yellow button fls 1cm (½in) across, summer. Best in sandy/gravelly soil exposed to wind.

Eupatorium (*Eupatorium ligustrinum*** **3**; *E. micranthum*; Eupatorium tribe): semi-hardy; dense & dome-shaped, to 2.5×2.5m (8×8ft); bright green lvs to 10×4cm (4×1½in); flattish infls to 20cm (8in) wide of small creamy-white fls, late summer. Can be grown in tub & moved under glass in winter.

Euryops (*Euryops acraeus* **4**; sometimes grown

incorrectly as *E. evansii*; Senecio tribe): moderately hardy; neat & mounding, to 0.6×1.2m (2×4ft); grey stems; clustered silvery-grey narrow lvs to 2.5cm (1in) long; canary-yellow 2.5cm (1in) daisy fls from late spring. Best in gritty soil; dead-head.

Helichrysums (*Helichrysum* spp; many Australasian spp often listed as *Ozothamnus* spp; Inula tribe): bushy, densely leafy shrubs with small fls in summer surrounded by "everlasting" papery bracts.
H. (*O.*) *ledifolium* (kerosene bush): moderately to v hardy; rounded, to 1×1.5m (3×5ft); young shoots downy; v narrow leathery lvs* to 1cm (½in) long, yellowish beneath; white fls with yellow, brownish or red bracts, in corymbs; honey-scented seed heads. Stems & underside of lvs coated with aromatic, inflammable gum.
H. (*O.*) *rosmarinifolium* **5** (sometimes grown incorrectly as *H.* [*O.*] *purpurascens*): erect, to 1.8×1.2m (6×4ft); young stems white-woolly; close-set v narrow dark green lvs to 4cm (1½in) long, rough upper surface, woolly beneath; white fls with light brown bracts richly tinged red, in dense corymbs.
H. splendidum **6** (sometimes grown incorrectly as *H. alveolatum, H. trilineatum*): moderately to v hardy; rounded, to 1×1.8m (3×6ft), but can be kept more compact by regular hard pruning in spring; all parts white-woolly; narrow lvs to 4cm (1½in) long; rounded infls of small yellow fls.
H. (*O.*) *thyrsoideum* **7** (snow in summer; sometimes grown incorrectly as *H.* [*O.*] *rosmarinifolium*): semi- to moderately hardy; to 2.5×1.5–1.8m (8×5–6ft); spreading branches; v narrow close-set lvs* to 5cm (2in) long, resinous above, downy beneath; profuse 1–2cm (½–¾in) corymbs of white fls.

Daisy bushes (tree daisies, tree asters, *Olearia* spp; Aster tribe): showy Australasian shrubs of v varied habit, some eventually small tree; lvs downy/felted beneath; generally corymbs or panicles of daisy- or aster-like fls. Thrive on chalk; wind-tolerant & good for hedges/screens near sea. If straggly, prune hard in spring.
O. avicenniifolia: to 4.5×4.5m (15×15ft); greyish-green lvs to 10cm (4in) long; small white fls, late summer. Good hedger.
O. chathamica: semi-hardy; to 1.8×2.5m

(6×8ft); leathery lance-shaped lvs 5–12cm (2–5in) long; solitary 5cm (2in) aster-like fls, white/purplish & dark purple, spring & early summer.

O.×haastii **8**, p79: hybrid of *O. avicennifolia* & *O. moschata*; moderately to v hardy; bushy & rounded, to 2.5×3m (8×10ft); young shoots downy; crowded dark shiny green lvs to 2.5cm (1in) long; 8mm (⅓in) white & yellow daisy fls, summer. *O.* 'Waikariensis' is similar but more compact, with lance-shaped lvs to 8cm (3in) long.

O. ilicifolia*: spreading, to 3×3m (10×10ft); leathery grey-green lvs to 10cm (4in) long, sharply toothed; 1cm (½in) white & yellow daisy fls, early summer.

O. (Pachystegia) insignis: robust & spreading, to 1×1.8m (3×6ft); young shoots felted; stout leathery lvs to 18cm (7in) long; solitary white & yellow fls to 6cm (2½in) across, late summer.

O. macrodonta* **1** (New Zealand holly): vigorous, to 3×3m (10×10ft); holly-like glossy grey-green lvs* to 12cm (5in) long, spiny teeth; 1cm (½in) white & reddish daisy fls, early summer.

O. nummulariifolia* **2**: dense & bushy, to 1.5×1.8m (5×6ft); crowded leathery lvs to 1cm (½in) long; small solitary creamy fls, summer.

O. phlogopappa (O. gunniana; often grown incorrectly as *O. stellulata*): dense & upright, to 1.8×1.5m (6×5ft); crowded narrow lvs* to 5cm (2in) long; 2.5cm (1in) daisy fls, mid spring, generally white & yellow but sometimes (in 'Splendens' vars **3**) pink, mauve, purple or blue. True *O. stellulata* is less compact.

O.×scilloniensis **4**: hybrid of *O. lyrata* & *O. phlogopappa*; compact, to 2×1.5m (7×5ft); deep green narrowish lvs to 11cm (4½in) long; white & yellow daisy fls; late spring to summer.

O. semidentata: semi-hardy; rounded, to 2.5×2.5m (8×8ft); grey-green lance-shaped lvs to 8cm (3in) long; nodding solitary aster-like lilac fls 5cm (2in) wide, deeper centre, early summer.

Santolinas (*Santolina* spp; Anthemis tribe): dense & mounding, with soft stems & finely divided foliage; 1–2cm (½–¾in) button-like yellow fls on long stems, summer. Good for ground cover, low hedging. Best clipped regularly; may become straggly when old (cut back hard in spring); drought-tolerant.

S. chamaecyparissus **5** (lavender cotton): moderately to v hardy; to 60×90cm (2×3ft), less if clipped; all parts intensely silver-white-felted; thread-like crowded lvs* to 4cm (1½in) long; profuse bright yellow fls. Var 'Nana' (*corsica*) is more compact.

S. neapolitana **6** (often grown incorrectly as *S. rosmarinifolia*; correctly, *S. pinnata neapolitana*): moderately to v hardy; to 60–75×90cm (2–2½×3ft); similar to *S. chamaecyparissus* but looser habit & lvs* longer & more finely divided, green on flg shoots; fls lemon-yellow. Vars: 'Edward Bowles' (lvs greenish-grey; fls creamy); 'Sulphurea' (lvs grey-green; fls primrose-yellow).

S. virens (*S. viridis*; correctly, *S. rosmariniifolia*): spreading, to 0.6×1.2m (2×4ft); bright rich green thread-like lvs* to 5cm (2in) long; bright yellow fls (primrose-yellow in var 'Primrose Gem' **7**).

Senecios (*Senecio* spp; Senecio tribe): wind-tolerant New Zealand shrubs with leathery, often grey lvs &, unless noted, bright yellow daisy fls, summer, in loose infls. Good near sea; like lime.

S. compactus: compact but spreading, to 1.2×2.5m (4×8ft); young shoots white-felted; dark green white-edged lvs to 5cm (2in) long, white felt beneath; 2.5cm (1in) fls. 'Dunedin Hybrids' are series of hybrids with *S. greyi* & *S. laxifolius*; bushy & somewhat lax; lvs greyish becoming green, no white edge; best-known var is 'Sunshine' **8** (long sold incorrectly as *S. greyi* or *S. laxifolius*, both rare in cultivation).

S. monroi **9**: semi- to moderately hardy; dense & domed, to 1.2×1.5m (4×5ft); young shoots felted, narrowish wavy/wrinkled lvs to 5cm (2in) long, whitish felt beneath; 2cm (¾in) fls.

S. reinoldii: dense & rounded, to 3×3m (10×10ft); thick, leathery rounded lvs to 12×10cm (5×4in), dark shining green above, white felt beneath; large infls of small yellowish-white button fls, unpleasant scent.

The dogwood family

Shrubs & trees grown variously for their form, foliage, autumn colour, colourful stems &/or flowers. **Cultivation**: Generally easy. Unless stated, very hardy & for any fertile soil in sun or partial shade. No regular pruning unless noted. **Propagation**: Seed; semi-ripe cuttings; suckers where produced; vars sometimes by budding/grafting.

Aucuba (*Aucuba japonica* **1**, p83 variegated forms called spotted laurel, gold-dust plant): moderately hardy bushy evergreen shrub, to 3×3m (10×10ft) or more (less if pruned); glossy lvs to 8–20×4–8cm (3–8×1½–3in), few teeth; small purplish spring fls on males; clusters of 1–1.5cm (½–⅝in) persistent scarlet berries on females if male nearby. Probably easiest broad-lvd evergreen; tolerates deep shade, pollution; good in tubs, etc. Vars (females marked †): 'Crotonifolia' (lvs boldly speckled yellow); 'Crassifolia' (broad deep green lvs); 'Fructu-albo'† (lvs variegated gold; frs creamy); 'Gold Dust' (lvs boldly spotted gold); *longifolia* (narrow

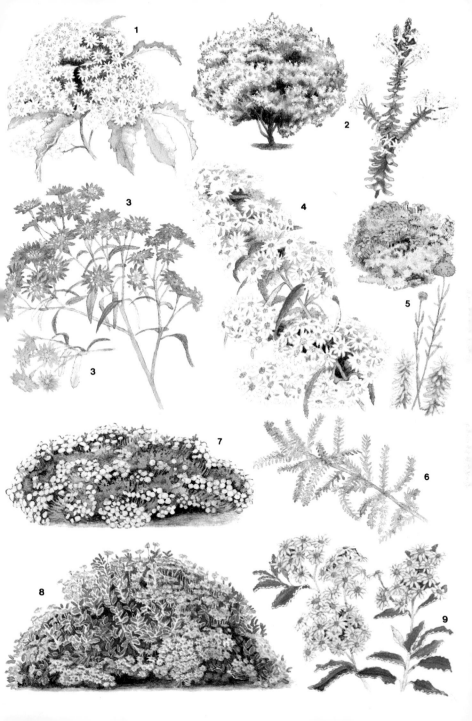

green lvs to 12×3cm [5×1¼in]; male & female forms; 'Salicifolia'† (is similar); 'Nana Rotundifolia'† (compact; small rich green lvs); 'Picturata' (lvs centrally blotched yellow); 'Sulphurea'† (lvs edged pale yellow); 'Variegata'† **2** ('Maculata'; lvs spotted yellow; oldest, best-known var; true 'Maculata' is male).

Dogwoods (cornels, *Cornus* spp; most spp may be correctly *Benthamidia* or *Swida* spp): unless stated, deciduous shrubs with dark green lvs 5–12cm (2–5in) long, small white/yellowish fls on yr-old wood & small berries. Shrubby spp like moist soil.

COLOURED-STEMMED SPP: generally osier-like & thicket-forming, best if pruned hard or to ground every spring; often also have attractive foliage. Can be propagated by hardwood cuttings.

C. (*S.*) *alba* (Tartarian dogwood): ultra-hardy; v vigorous & suckering, to 3×3m (10×10ft); stems rich red in winter; dark green lvs, glaucous beneath, red & orange in autumn; frs white/ bluish. Sp & most vars rampant; best as isolated specimens on lawn, by water, etc; less vigorous vars best in well-cultivated soil. Vars: 'Elegantissima' ('Sibirica Variegata'; lvs edged & mottled white); 'Kesselringii' (less vigorous; winter stems dark purple); 'Sibirica' **3** ('Westonbirt', Siberian dogwood; less vigorous; winter stems glossy crimson); 'Spaethii' (lvs boldly variegated gold).

C. (*S.*) *amomum* (silky dogwood): compact, to 3×3m (10×10ft); young shoots downy, becoming purple; dark green lvs, reddish down beneath; porcelain blue frs.

C. (*S.*) *sanguinea** (common dogwood of Europe; in US, bloodtwig dogwood): erect, to 3×2.5m (10×8ft); young shoots green, becoming flushed red; lvs to 8cm (3in) long, rich red to purple in autumn; frs shiny black.

C. (*S.*) *stolonifera* (*C. sericea*, red osier dogwood): ultra-hardy; rampant & suckering, to 3×3m (10×10ft); spreads by stolons; young shoots dark purplish-red; dark green lvs, often red in autumn; frs white. Vars: 'Flaviramea' (stems greenish-/yellow); 'Nitida' (stems green).

OTHER SPP:

C. (*S.*) *alternifolia* (in US, pagoda dogwood): ultra-hardy; to 4.5×2.5–3m (15×8–10ft), or small multi-trunked tree with tiered spreading branches; bright green lvs, often rich red in autumn; clustered fls, early summer; frs blue-black. Best where summers hot. Var 'Argentea' ('Variegata') grows to 2.5–3m (8–10ft), with small lvs edged creamy-white; v handsome.

C. (*B.*) *capitata*: semi- to moderately hardy evergreen bushy tree, to 6×4.5m (20×15ft), or large shrub; young shoots grey-downy; leathery grey-green densely downy lvs; fls with showy sulphur-yellow bracts, early summer; crimson strawberry-like 2.5–4cm (1–1½in) frs.

C. (*S.*) *controversa* (giant dogwood): elegant tree, to 6×5.5m (20×18ft); horizontal tiered branches; young shoots rich red; glossy lvs, often red & purple in autumn; profuse white fls in 8–18cm (3–7in) cymes, early summer; blue-black frs. Var 'Variegata' **4** has variegated lvs.

C. (*B.*) *florida* (flowering dogwood): bushy tree, 4.5×4.5m (15×15ft), or large shrub; lvs to 15cm (6in) long, often rich orange & red in autumn; flowers with showy white bracts, late spring; brilliant red frs. Best in sunny, dryish or continental climate. Vars: 'Apple Blossom' (bracts flushed pale pink); 'Cherokee Chief' (bracts ruby-red); 'Pendula' (branches pendulous); *rubra* **5** (young lvs reddish; bracts rosy-pink); 'Spring Song' (bracts bright rose-red); 'Welchii' ('Tricolor'; lvs variegated creamy-white, flushed pink, rich rose-red in autumn; may scorch in hot sun); 'White Cloud' (white bracts).

C. (*B.*) *kousa* **6**: to 3.5×3m (12×10ft), or small bushy tree; peeling bark; narrowish lvs to 10cm (4in) long, bronze & crimson in autumn; profuse fls, showy creamy-white lance-shaped bracts, early summer; strawberry-like fleshy frs. Var *chinensis* (Chinese dogwood) is taller & more open, with larger lvs & bracts.

C. mas **7** (Cornelian cherry): spreading & rather open, to 3×3m (10×10ft), or small tree; shiny lvs, red-purple in autumn; profuse tiny yellow fls, late winter & early spring (before lvs; bright red 2cm (¾in) cherry-like frs (edible; used for preserves). Vars: 'Aurea' (lvs flushed yellow); 'Aurea Elegantissima' ('Elegantissima'; lvs edged/variegated gold, often flushed rose); 'Variegata' (lvs edged white).

C. (*B.*) *nuttallii* (Pacific dogwood): moderately hardy tree, to 7.5×4.5m (25×15ft), or large shrub; lvs yellow & scarlet in autumn; fls with showy creamy-white to pinkish bracts, late spring (sometimes repeating late summer); frs orange-red. Beautiful but not easy; may be short-lived. Var 'Gold Spot' has yellow-flecked lvs.

Corokia (wire-netting bush, *Corokia cotoneaster*): moderately hardy rounded shrub, to 1.5×1.8m (5×6ft), smaller in tub; tangled wiry stems, downy when young; sparse evergreen spoon-shaped lvs 2cm (¾in) long, white felt beneath; bright yellow 1cm (½in) starry fls, late spring; red 8cm (⅓in) frs. *C.×virgata* is hybrid with *C. buddleoides*; more leafy, graceful & upright, to 2.5×1.8m (8×6ft); free flg/frtg.

Griselinia (*Griselinia littoralis*): semi- to moderately hardy evergreen shrub, to 4.5×3m (15×10ft), or tree eventually to 12m (50ft); dense & shapely; leathery apple-green rounded lvs to 2.5–10cm (1–4in) long; fls insignificant. Good for hedge near sea. Vars: 'Dixon's Cream' (lvs splashed creamy-white); 'Variegata' (lvs edged white). *G. lucida* is similar but more tender, with deeper green lvs.

The oleaster family

Bushy shrubs (sometimes small trees) grown mainly for their foliage and/or berry-like fruits; flowers insignificant but often strongly fragrant. Wind-resistant, making good hedges or screens (inland or near sea). **Cultivation**: Unless stated, ultra-hardy. For any well-drained soil, preferably light, in sun (evergreens shade-tolerant). Pruning not essential, but tidy late spring or early summer; trim hedges summer. **Propagation**: Semi-ripe cuttings; layering; spp by suckers; deciduous spp by seed (stratify).

Elaeagnus (oleasters, *Elaeagnus* spp): v ornamental, with attractive foliage (evergreens good for cutting); lvs generally pointed, 5—10cm (2—4in) long; frs edible, good for birds.
*E. angustifolia** **1** (oleaster, Russian olive): wide-spreading, to 3.5×3.5m (12×12ft); deciduous willow-like lvs, silvery beneath; fls late spring; frs silvery-yellow, sweet. Can be trained as tree.
*E. commutata*** *(E. argentea*, silverberry): thin & erect, to 3×1.2m (10×4ft); suckering; deciduous; lvs silver both sides; fls late spring; frs silvery.
*E.×ebbingei*** **2**: hybrids of *E. macrophylla* & *E. pungens*; moderately to v hardy; fast-growing, to 3×3m (10×10ft); evergreen leathery lvs, shiny silver beneath, to 12cm (5in) long; fls autumn; frs orange/red. Vars: 'Gilt Edge' **3** (lvs edged gold); 'Limelight' **4** (lvs blotched greenish-yellow).
*E. macrophylla*** *: moderately to v hardy; robust & spreading, to 3×3.5m (10×12ft); young shoots silvery; broad evergreen lvs, silvery when young, becoming lustrous; fls autumn; frs red.
*E. multiflora** * (cherry elaeagnus): v hardy; to 3.5×4.5m (12×15ft); deciduous or semi-evergreen; lvs dark green, silvery beneath; fls

spring; frs blood-red, acid.
*E. pungens*** (thorny elaeagnus): moderately to v hardy; dense & spreading, to 3.5×3.5m (12×12ft); shoots often spiny; evergreen; lvs leathery, glossy dark green; fls autumn; frs red or orange. Vars: 'Aurea', 'Dicksonii' & 'Goldrim' have yellow-edged lvs; 'Frederici' & 'Maculata' **5** ('Aureovariegata') have lvs blotched yellow. *E. glabra** * is similar but semi-climbing; lvs thinner, narrower-pointed & metallic-brown beneath.
*E. umbellata*** *: vigorous, to 4.5×4.5m (15×15ft); often thorny; deciduous pale green lvs, silvery beneath; fls spring; frs silvery to red.
Sea buckthorn (sallow thorn, *Hippophaë rhamnoides*): vigorous thorny shrub, to 4.5×4.5m (15×15ft); deciduous willow-like v narrow lvs to 8cm (3in) long, silvery beneath; fls spring; profuse bright orange-yellow sour frs on females if male planted nearby. Prefers sandy soil.
Buffalo berry (*Shepherdia argentea*): often thorny shrub, to 3×2m (10×7ft); young shoots silvery; deciduous; narrow paired lvs to 5cm (2in) long, silvery beneath; fls early spring; scarlet frs on females (best if summer hot) if male nearby.

Species rhododendrons

Rhododendron spp. After roses, the most spectacular, important & popular genus of flowering shrubs (sometimes trees) – the most important of all for semi-shade on lime-free soil, particularly in maritime climates. Best grouped together or with other lime-hating shrubs. Those covered here are almost all evergreen, with mid—dark green leathery leaves (generally oval to lance-shaped, often smaller than maximum sizes given), often felted or scaly beneath, mainly near end of shoots. Flowers tubular to saucer-shaped with lobed corolla, generally in trusses at end of shoots, mainly spring & early summer, most colours except true blue. **Cultivation**: Unless stated, moderately to very hardy (to −15 to −20°C [5 to −4°F]). For moist but well-drained lime-free acid soil with ample peat or leaf-mould, preferably in semi-shade & sheltered from hot & cold winds; shelter early spp from spring frosts. Plant shallowly; cultivate carefully; mulch. Spray leaves in evening if hot. Give sequestered iron if soil not acid. Dead-head. Prune (rarely necessary) in spring. **Propagation**: Layering; seed; small-leaved spp by semi-ripe cuttings.

Giant species: eventually (after perhaps 40yrs) reaching tree-like dimensions of 6—9m (20—30ft), sometimes more; v large, handsome lvs; large fl trusses; generally need woodland shelter.
R. arboreum **6**: semi- to moderately hardy large shrub or tree, to 9×6m (30×20ft); dark shiny lvs, white to brown felt beneath, to 25×6cm (10×2½in); dense trusses of 15—20 narrow bell fls, 5cm (2in) long, blood-red, pink or white (paler forms hardier), late winter to mid spring. Var

cinnamomeum has lvs felted cinnamon-brown; fls white; moderately hardy.
R. barbatum **7**: moderately hardy spreading shrub or small tree, to 7.5×4.5m (25×15ft); bristly shoots, reddish bark; shiny dark green lvs, paler below, to 20×8cm (8×3in); globular trusses of 10—20 narrow bell fls to 8cm (3in) long, glowing scarlet, early spring.
R. calophytum: v hardy large shrub or tree, to 7.5×4.5m (25×15ft); bright green narrowish

lance-shaped lvs to 30cm (1ft) long; 15–20cm (6–8in) trusses of 15–20 white to pink wide bell fls 5cm (2in) long, blotched maroon, early spring.

*R. falconeri** **1**: moderately hardy stiff-branched large shrub or tree, to 9×6m (30×20ft); shoots woolly; wrinkled dark green lvs, rusty felt below, to 30×15cm (12×6in); dense 15–20cm (6–8in) clusters of 20–25 bell-shaped fls to 6cm (2½in) long, creamy, blotched purple, mid spring.

R. eximium (correctly, *R. falconeri eximium*) is similar, lvs felted rusty-brown on top; fls pink.

R. fictolacteum (correctly, *R. rex fictolacteum*): large shrub or small tree, to 7.5×4.5m (25×15ft) or more; shoots woolly; dark shiny green lvs to 30×10cm (12×4in), brown-woolly beneath; trusses of up to 25 bell-shaped fls to 5cm (2in) long, white or pink-tinged, blotched/spotted crimson, mid spring. *R. arizelum* (correctly, *R. rex arizelum*) is similar, lvs smaller; fls yellow or pink.

R. macabeanum **2**: moderately hardy large, broad shrub or tree, to 9×6m (30×20ft); leathery dark green lvs to 40×20cm (16×8in), whitish felt beneath; dense trusses of 20 or more bell-shaped fls 5–8cm (2–3in) long, creamy- to deep yellow, blotched purple, mid spring.

R. sinogrande **3**: moderately hardy magnificent large shrub or tree, to 7.5×6m (25×20ft) or more; shoots silvery; huge shiny dark green lvs to 75×30cm (2½×1ft), silvery or fawn felt beneath; trusses to 25cm (10in) wide of 20–30 bell-shaped creamy-white to yellow fls 5cm (2in) wide, blotched crimson, mid spring.

Large species: generally reaching 3–6m (10–20ft) in cultivation (dimensions given after 15–20yrs); unless stated, lvs dark green, to 10–15cm (4–6in) long, & fls to 5–8cm (2–3in) long; generally for shady or open sites.

R. augustinii **4**: bushy, to 4.5×2.5m (15×8ft); shoots hairy; narrowish lvs; trusses of 2–6 funnel-shaped fls, violet, lavender-blue, pink or almost white, spotted greenish, mid spring. Several named vars. Needs shelter.

*R. auriculatum**: spreading shrub, to 6×3.5m (20×12ft), or small tree, bigger in mild areas; lvs to 30×12cm (12×5in), brownish hairs beneath; trusses of 7–15 funnel-shaped white or pink fls to 10cm (4in) long, mid–late summer.

R. campanulatum: to 3.5×3.5m (12×12ft) or more; lvs brown-felted beneath; trusses of 8–12 bell-shaped fls, rosy-purple to white, mid spring. Var *aeruginosum* has young lvs silvery green.

*R. crassum**: moderately hardy shrub, to 4.5×2.5m (15×8ft), or small tree; wrinkled leathery lvs, rusty scales beneath; trusses of 3–6 funnel-shaped creamy- to pinkish-white fls to 10cm (4in) long, early summer. Needs shelter.

*R. decorum** **5**: beautiful variable shrub, to 6×3m (20×10ft), or small tree, or sometimes dense & bushy; leathery light green lvs; trusses of 8–14 wide funnel-shaped white fls, often tinged pink or green, late spring.

R. fargesii **6**: v hardy; bushy, to 3.5×2.5m (12×8ft) or more; greyish-green lvs to 9cm (3½in) long, glaucous beneath; trusses of 6–10 bell-shaped rosy-pink to white fls, early spring.

*R. fortunei**: v hardy; spreading, to 3.5×3m (12×10ft); matt green lvs to 20×8cm (8×3in); loose trusses of 6–12 wide funnel-shaped 7-lobed fls, pink fading paler, late spring.

*R. discolor** (correctly, *R. fortunei discolor*) is similar; fls white to pale pink, early summer.

R. fulvum: shrub, to 4.5×2.5m (15×8ft), or small tree; shoots felted brownish-yellow; shiny lvs to 20×8cm (8×3in), thickly felted fawn, cinnamon or red-brown beneath; rounded trusses of up to 20 narrow bell-shaped deep rose- to pale pink fls 4cm (1½in) wide, early spring. Needs shelter.

*R. griffithianum**: semi- to moderately hardy magnificent spreading shrub, to 4.5×4.5m (15×15ft), or small tree; peeling reddish-brown bark; narrow pale green lvs to 30cm (1ft) long; trusses of 3–6 wide bell-shaped fls, white tinged pink, to 15cm (6in) across, mid spring. Shelter.

R. ponticum (common naturalized rhododendron of UK): v hardy spreading shrub, to 4.5×7.5m (15×25ft), or small tree; shiny lvs to 20×6cm (8×2½in), paler beneath; trusses of 10–15 wide funnel-shaped reddish-purple to lilac-pink fls, early summer. Withstands deep shade.

R. rubiginosum **7**: stiff & erect, to 6×3m (20×10ft); lance-shaped lvs* to 9cm (3½in) long, rusty-brown scales beneath; profuse small trusses of funnel-shaped fls, pink or rosy-lilac spotted brown, mid spring. Good for hedge.

R. strigillosum **8**: shrub, to 3.5×3m (12×10ft), or small tree; shoots & lf stalks bristly; drooping bright green lvs, hairy beneath; trusses of 8–12 narrow bell-shaped brilliant crimson fls, late winter to mid spring; needs woodland shelter.

R. sutchuenense **9**: v hardy shrub, to 4.5×3.5m (15×12ft), or small tree; stout shoots; drooping lvs to 30×8cm (12×3in), paler beneath; trusses of 8–12 wide bell-shaped rose-pink or lilac fls, sometimes spotted purple, late winter to mid spring; needs woodland shelter.

R. thomsonii **10**: moderately hardy shrub, to 4.5×2.5m (15×8ft) or wider, or small tree; rounded lvs, glaucous or silvery beneath; loose trusses of 6–12 deep blood-red fleshy bell-shaped fls, large calyx, mid spring; likes shelter.

R. wardii: beautiful variable shrub to 3.5×2.5m (12×8ft), some forms smaller; variable leathery lvs; loose trusses of up to 14 cup/saucer-shaped fls to 6cm (2½in) wide, clear yellow often blotched crimson, late spring. Best in shelter.

R. yunnanense **11**: rather straggling, to 4×2m (14×7ft); semi-deciduous in cold conditions; bright green bristly lvs; profuse small trusses of funnel-shaped lavender, pink or white fls, often spotted crimson, late spring.

Medium-sized species: mature cultivated
height generally 1.5–3m (5–10ft); unless stated,
lvs to 5–10cm (2–4in) & fls to 4–5cm (1½–2in)
long; generally suitable for open or shady sites.
R. aberconwayi **1**: to 2×1.5m (7×5ft); lvs
leathery & brittle; loose trusses of 6–12 saucer-
shaped fls 5–8cm (2–3in) across, white tinged
pink & spotted maroon, late spring. Likes sun.
R. bureavii: v hardy; to 1.8–2.5×1.5–2m (6–
8×5–7ft); young shoots felted rusty-red;
beautiful dark green lvs to 12cm (5in) long, thickly
felted rusty-red beneath; trusses of 10–15
narrow bell-shaped fls, white or pink marked
crimson, mid–late spring. Likes shelter & shade.
R. callimorphum: rounded, to 2×2m (7×7ft);
rounded shiny lvs; small loose trusses of bell-
shaped rose-pink fls, mid spring. Likes shelter.
R. carolinianum **2** (correctly, *R. minus minus*):
ultra-hardy; compact, to 1.8×1.2m (6×4ft); lvs
shiny green; profuse trusses of 4–10 bell-shaped
fls 2.5cm (1in) long, pink to rosy-purple (white in
var *album*), late spring.
R. catawbiense: ultra-hardy; dense & spreading,
to 1.8–3×3m (6–10×10ft); lvs to 15cm (6in)
long; large clusters to 15cm (6in) across of 15–20
funnel-shaped fls, lilac-purple to pink or white,
spotted greenish, late spring to early summer.
R. cinnabarinum: compact & upright, to 3×2.5m
(10×8ft); lvs* greyish-green; small trusses of
tubular fls, bright cinnabar-red, late spring. Vars:
blandfordiiflorum (fls v narrow, red outside,
greenish or yellow inside); *roylei* (*R. roylei*; fls
shorter & more open, rosy-red to dark crimson).
R. concatenans (fls bell-shaped, apricot-yellow)
& *R. xanthocodon* (lvs* dull green; fls creamy to
yellow) are both now correctly forms of *R.
cinnabarinum xanthocodon*.
R. concinnum **3**: to 3×2m (10×7ft) or more; lvs*
scaly; smallish trusses of wide funnel-shaped fls,
purple (wine-red in var *pseudoyanthinum*), mid–
late spring.
R. edgeworthii* **4** (*R. bullatum*): semi-hardy;
straggling, to 2.5×2.5m (8×8ft); shoots felted
tawny; lvs wrinkled, shiny; small trusses of wide
funnel-shaped fls to 10cm (4in) across, white or
pink flushed red outside, mid spring. Needs
shelter.
R. griersonianum: moderately hardy; lax & open,
to 2.5×2.5m (8×8ft); shoots bristly; winter buds
have long scales; lvs 10–20cm (4–8in) long,
olive-green, pale brown wool beneath; trusses of
5–12 trumpet-shaped geranium-scarlet fls to
10cm (4in) wide, v early summer. Best in
sheltered position with some sun.
R. insigne: slow-growing, to 2×1.8m (7×6ft);
attractive shiny lvs to 12cm (5in) long, bronzed
beneath; round trusses of 8–15 or more bell fls,
soft pink, spotted maroon, striped rosy-pink
outside, late spring.
R. lindleyi**: semi-hardy; rather lax, to 2.5×1.8m

(8×6ft); lvs to 15cm (6in) long, olive-green; small
trusses of narrow funnel-shaped fls 8–10cm
(3–4in) long, white, often tinged pink, blotched
yellow, spicy lemon scent, late spring.
R. dalhousiae* is similar, but young shoots
bristly; fls pale yellow fading white.
R. lutescens **5**: straggling, to 3×2m (10×7ft);
shoots reddish; lvs bronzed when young; small
infls of wide funnel-shaped lemon- to primrose-
yellow fls, 2.5cm (1in) wide, spotted light green,
late winter to mid spring. Likes sun & shelter.
R. mucronulatum: a deciduous true
rhododendron; v hardy; rather sparse, to
2.5×1.5m (8×5ft); lvs pointed, thinnish; solitary
wide funnel-shaped fls, pink to rosy-purple,
winter to early spring (before lvs). Best in
woodland shelter. Var 'Cornell Pink' is pure
mid-pink.
R. neriifolium **6**: spreading, to 2.5×2.5m (8×8ft);
shoots hairy; lvs glaucous-white beneath;
trusses of 6–12 narrow bell-shaped fleshy fls,
rich crimson to scarlet, mid spring. Likes shelter.
R. orbiculare: to 2.5×2.5m (8×8ft); dense; lvs
almost round; trusses of 7–10 wide bell-shaped
pink fls to 6cm (2½in) long, mid spring.
R. oreotrephes (*R. exquisitum*): to 3×2.5m
(10×8ft); v variable; semi-deciduous in cold
winters; attractive narrowish to rounded lvs,
green, grey-green or often glaucous; trusses of
3–11 funnel- to bell-shaped fls, rose-pink to
mauve or purple, sometimes spotted, mid spring.
R. pseudochrysanthum **7**: v hardy; slow-growing
& variable, to 2.5×1.8m (8×6ft), often less;
shoots grey-hairy; lvs grey/white-woolly when
young; dense trusses of 10–20 bell-shaped pink
to white fls, mid spring. Best in some shade.
R. souliei **8**: beautiful shrub, to 1.8–3×1.5–2.5m
(6–10×5–8ft); lvs rather rounded, bluish-green
to sea-green; clusters of 5–8 saucer-shaped fls
5–8cm (2–3in) wide, rosy-pink to almost white,
late spring. Best in light shade; fls young.
Small species: mature height 1–1.5m (3–5ft);
unless stated, lvs to 5–10cm (2–4in), fls to
2–4cm (¾–1½in) long; for open or shady sites.
R. caloxanthum **9**: to 1–1.5×1.2–1.8m (3–4×4–
6ft); rounded lvs; profuse trusses of 4–9 bell-
shaped fls, scarlet in bud, opening pale to
orange-yellow, mid–late spring. Likes woodland.
R. ciliatum **10**: rounded, to 1.2–1.5×1.8m (4–
5×6ft); bristly shoots & lvs; profuse small trusses
of bell-shaped fls to 5cm (2in) long, rosy-red in
bud, opening pale pink to white, early–mid
spring. Best in sheltered light shade.
R. ferrugineum (alpenrose, alpine rose): v hardy;
dense & rounded, to 1–1.2×1.2m (3–4×4ft); lvs
rusty beneath; trusses of 6–12 trumpet-shaped
fls, rose-red to white, early summer. Likes cool
conditions. *R. hirsutum* is similar, but shoots & lf
edges bristly; tolerates lime.
R. glaucophyllum: bushy, to 1–1.5×1.5m (3–

5×5ft); shoots have reddish-brown scales; lvs*
glaucous-grey beneath; trusses of 4–10 bell-
shaped fls, rosy-red to lilac, large calyx, mid
spring. Var *luteiflorum* (*R. luteiflorum*) is golden-
yellow.

R. haematodes **1**: slow-growing but spreading, to
1–1.2×1.8m (3–4×6ft), sometimes taller; shoots
brown-woolly; lvs leathery, reddish-brown felt
beneath; trusses of 6–10 narrow bell-shaped fls
to 5cm (2in) long, blood-red, late spring.

R. hanceanum: to 1.2×1.2m (4×4ft); shoots
bronze; trusses of 5–11 funnel-shaped fls,
creamy or pale yellow, mid spring. Var *nanum* is
dwarf, to 45cm (1½ft).

R. hippophaeoides **2**: ultra-hardy; erect, to 1–
1.5×1–1.5m (3–5×3–5ft); suckering; small lvs,
greyish beneath; tight trusses of 4–8 saucer-
shaped fls to 2.5cm (1in) wide, purplish-blue, lilac
or pink, early spring. Tolerates wet soil.

R. moupinense*: to 1–1.5×1–1.2m (3–5×3–4ft);
shoots bristly; lvs small, shiny; small trusses of
funnel-shaped fls, white, sometimes flushed rose
or blotched red/purple, late winter to early spring.
Best in light woodland.

R. racemosum **3**: variable, generally to 1.5×1.2m
(5×4ft); shoots deep red; lvs glaucous beneath;
trusses of wide funnel-shaped fls along stems,
pale/rose-pink to white, all spring. Var 'Forrest's
Dwarf' (F19404) grows to 60cm (2ft); 'Rock
Rose' is erect, to 1.5m (5ft).

R. russatum **4**: v hardy; bushy & dense, to
1.2×1.2m (4×4ft); shoots scaly; lvs to 4.5cm
(1¾in) long, rusty-yellow beneath; tight trusses
of 5–10 wide funnel-shaped fls, indigo-blue,
purple or rose-pink, white throat, early spring.

R. tephropeplum: to 1.2×1m (4×3ft); lvs
glaucous beneath; trusses of 3–9 narrow bell-
shaped fls, pink to crimson-purple, mid spring.
Needs shelter.

R. trichostomum **5**: to 1.2×1m (4×3ft); rather
lax; shoots bristly; narrow olive-green lvs* to
3cm (1¼in) long; dense trusses of 10–20
trumpet-shaped daphne-like fls to 1cm (½in)
wide, white to rose-pink, late spring. Best in
some sun.

R. williamsianum: dense & rounded, to 1.2×1.5m
(4×5ft); young shoots & lvs bronzed; lvs
rounded, glaucous beneath; loose trusses of
dainty bell-shaped fls to 5cm (2in) long, pink to
soft rosy-red, mid spring. Best in some shelter.

R. yakushimanum **6**: ultra-hardy; compact &
rounded, to 1.2×1.2m (4×4ft); shoots white-
felted; lvs narrow to lance-shaped, thick brown
wool beneath; dense trusses of 10–12 beautiful
bell-shaped fls to 5cm (2in) wide, deep rose in
bud opening pale pink to pure white, late spring.
Var 'Koichiro Wada' is among best forms. Parent
of many modern hybrids.

Dwarf species: less than 1m (3ft) tall when
mature; unless stated, lvs to 2.5–5cm (1–2in), fls

2–3cm (¾–1¼in) long; for open or shady sites
unless stated; most spp good for rock gardens.

R. calostrotum: rounded & compact, to 90×90cm
(3×3ft); grey-green lvs, reddish-brown beneath;
usually paired saucer-shaped fls, reddish-purple
to scarlet, spotted crimson, mid–late spring.

R. keleticum (now correctly *R. calostrotum
keleticum*) is similar but smaller, often semi-
prostrate, to 30×45cm (1×1½ft), with small lvs;
R. radicans (now considered a form of *R. c.
keleticum*) is even smaller & mat-forming, to
15×30cm (6×12in); both v hardy.

R. campylogynum **7**: very hardy; dense, to
45×45cm (1½×1½ft); small trusses of nodding
wide bell-shaped fls, white, salmon-pink, red,
purple or almost black, late spring.

R. fastigiatum: v hardy; to 60–90×60cm (2–
3×2ft); v small glaucous-green lvs; small trusses
of funnel-shaped fls, purple or bluish, mid spring.
R. impeditum is similar but smaller; lvs dark
green; fls mauve.

R. forrestii (*R. f. repens*, *R. repens*): creeping &
self-rooting, to 0.3×1.2m (1×4ft); rounded lvs;
solitary or paired narrow bell-shaped fls to 4cm
(1½in) long, scarlet or crimson, mid spring.

R. imperator (correctly, *R. uniflorum imperator*):
prostrate & mat-forming, to 40×45cm (16×18in);
dark green lvs*; solitary or paired funnel-shaped
fls, pinkish-purple, mid spring.

P. keiskei: v variable; dwarf form is v hardy, to
30×30cm (1×1ft); lvs olive-green, reddish &
semi-deciduous in winter; small trusses of
lemon-yellow bell-shaped fls, mid spring.

R. lepidostylum: mounding, to 0.6–0.9×1–1.2m
(2–3×3–4ft); young shoots & lvs intensely blue-
green; lvs semi-evergreen, edges bristly; solitary
or paired wide funnel-shaped yellow fls, late
spring.

R. leucaspis **8**: to 30–60×60–90cm (1–2×2–3ft);
lvs bristly; small clusters of saucer-shaped fls
5cm (2in) wide, white, brown anthers, late winter
to early spring. Needs shelter.

R. pemakoense **9**: mounding, to 30×60cm
(1×2ft), often spreading by suckers; profuse
solitary or paired funnel-shaped fls, orchid-pink,
early spring. Best in some shelter.

R. saluenense: variable habit, to 45–90×60–
90cm (1½–3×2–3ft); shiny lvs*; small trusses of
wide funnel-shaped fls to 4.5cm (1¾in) wide,
pinkish/reddish-purple, spotted darker, mid
spring.

R. scintillans **10** (correctly, *R. polycladum*): to
60×60cm (2×2ft); twiggy; v small lvs, yellow
scales; small trusses of funnel-shaped fls,
lavender/purplish-blue, mid spring.

R. tsangpoense **11** (correctly, *R. charitopes
tsangpoense*): to 30–60×60–90cm (1–2×2–3ft);
lvs v scaly beneath; profuse trusses of wide
bell-shaped fls, pink or pinkish-purple, late
spring.

Hybrid rhododendrons

Evergreen *Rhododendron* hybrids, often of complex parentage, though important modern race of dwarf vars are derived from *R. yakushimanum* (listed separately below). Generally similar to species rhododendrons (p84) but often more profuse flowers over longer season (unless stated, late spring to early summer); flowers generally bell- to funnel-shaped, in large trusses. Some 10,000 registered vars (often variable; one name may cover grex, or group of hybrids of same parentage); selection only listed. **Cultivation** (including hardiness): As for species rhododendrons (p84); generally for open or shady sites. **Propagation**: Layering; grafting on *R. ponticum*, etc; small-leaved vars by semi-ripe cuttings.

Very tall hybrids: to 4.5–6×3.5–5m (15–20×12–16ft), sometimes more; large lvs, generally to 15–20cm (6–8in) long; fls to 10–15cm (4–6in) across. Vars: 'Albatross'* (white to v pale pink; late); 'Angelo', 'Exbury Angelo' (blush-pink to white; best in woodland); 'Beauty of Littleworth' (white speckled red; v large infls); 'Cornish Cross' (crimson-pink; early); 'Fastuosum Flore Pleno' (v hardy; double, mauve); 'Loderi King George'** (among best of Loderi group; v large fls, blush-pink to white); 'Loder's White' (blush- to pure white); 'Mrs A. T. de la Mare' (v hardy; pink to white, speckled green); 'Mount Everest'* (dense; white marked maroon); 'Naomi', 'Exbury Naomi'* **1** (pink to lilac, shaded yellow); 'Pink Pearl' (rose-pink fading paler); 'Polar Bear'* (v vigorous & tree-like; lvs to 30cm [1ft] long; fls white speckled green, v late); 'Sappho' (v hardy; white blotched purple); 'Snow Queen'* (pure white).
Tall hybrids: to 3–4.5×2.5–3.5m (10–15×8–12ft); lvs generally to 12–18cm (5–7in) long; fls to 8–10cm (3–4in) across. Vars: 'A. (Arthur) Bedford' (lavender, dark blotch); 'Azor' (lvs narrow; fls salmon-pink, red throat; late); 'Babylon' (v hardy; satiny-white blotched chocolate); 'Betty Wormald' (pink speckled crimson); 'Cotton Candy' (pastel-pink; tall infls); 'David' (deep blood-red); 'Faggetter's Favourite' (creamy-white flushed pink); 'Furnivall's Daughter' **2** (pale pink blotched crimson); 'Gomer Waterer' **3** (v hardy; blush-white); 'Lady Clementine Mitford' (peach-pink); 'Lavender Girl' (pale lavender); 'Mrs Charles E. Pearson' **4** (pale mauve spotted brown); 'Mrs G. W. Leak' (pink, darker eye; likes shade); 'Queen of Hearts' (deep crimson, black spots); 'Sugar Pink' (candy-pink; v tall infls); 'Susan' (amethyst-violet).
Medium-sized hybrids: to 1.5–3×1.2–2.5m (5–10×4–8ft); lvs generally to 10–15cm (4–6in) long; fls to 4–8cm (1½–3in) across. Vars: 'Alison Johnstone' (amber flushed pink); 'America' (v to ultra-hardy; bright crimson); 'Blue Diamond' **5** (small lvs; violet-blue fls); 'Blue Peter' (v hardy; cobalt-violet, pale centre); 'Boule de Neige' (ultra-hardy; snow-tolerant; white); 'Bow Bells' (young lvs bronze; fls bright pink); 'Christmas Cheer' (v hardy; blush-pink; early); 'Corona' (rose- to coral-pink); 'Cream Glory' (v hardy; rounded lvs; creamy-yellow fls); 'Crest' ('Hawk Crest'; large lvs; v wide primrose-yellow fls, shading deeper); 'Damaris', 'Damaris Logan' (bright yellow); 'Earl of Athlone' (bright blood-red, early; best in shelter); 'Goldsworth Orange' (spreading; yellowish-orange; late); 'Hallelujah' (v hardy; strong rose-red); 'Lady Chamberlain' **6** (orange-pink shades); 'Lady Rosebery' (pink shaded crimson); 'May Day' **7** (lvs brown beneath; fls scarlet); 'Mrs Furnivall' (v hardy; pale rosy-pink blotched dark brown & crimson); 'Nobleanum Venustum' (pink shading to white; ultra-early [from mid winter if mild]; best in woodland); 'Nova Zembla' (v to ultra-hardy; red); 'Purple Splendour' **8** (deep purple, black blotch); 'Romany Chal' (deep glowing red; late; best in woodland); 'Trude Webster' (v hardy; clear pink; large infls); 'Unique' (small lvs; pink buds opening pale yellow); 'Vanessa' (pink, deeper eye); 'Vanessa Pastel' (cream flushed pink).
Small hybrids: to 1–1.5×1–1.2m (3–5×3–4ft); lvs generally to 4–6cm (1½–2½in) long; fls to 4–6cm (1½–2½in) wide, in smallish trusses. Vars: 'April Glow' (v hardy; deep pink; early); 'Arthur Osborn' (large lvs; v dark red fls; late); 'Bluebird' (small lvs; rich violet-blue fls; early); 'Blue Diamond' (large lvs; fls white spotted purple); 'Blue Tit' (small lvs; fls pale lavender-blue); 'Bo-Peep' (pale creamy-yellow; v early); 'Bric-a-Brac' (creamy-white, v early; needs shelter); 'Chink' **9** (pale primrose-yellow, v early); 'Cilpinense' **10** (large pale pink fls, deeper at edges; v early); 'Elizabeth' **11** (large scarlet fls; early; taller in shade); 'Fabia' (orange-red, orange or salmon-pink); 'Humming Bird' (carmine-pink); 'Praecox' (rosy-lilac; v early); 'Seta' (narrow fls, white to pink, shaded crimson; early; best in shelter); 'Songbird' (v small lvs; small flat fls, deep violet-blue; early); 'Temple Belle' (soft pink; early); 'Tessa' (purplish-pink; v early); 'Yellow Hammer' (tubular fls; early).
Dwarf Yakushimanum hybrids: derived from *R. yakushimanum* (p94); v hardy; vigorous & compact, generally to 60–90×60–90cm (2–3×2–3ft); lvs large, to 9–12cm (3½–5in) long; v free-flg, with dense trusses of 12–20 spotted fls to 6cm (2½in) wide. Vars: 'Caroline Allbrook' (lavender frilled fls); 'Diana Pearson' (palest pink flushed magenta); 'Dopey' (rich red); 'Ernest Inman' (mauve, silvery throat); 'Grumpy' (cream tinged pink); 'Hoppy' (white); 'Hydon Ball' (pale

cream), 'Hydon Hunter' (to 1.1m [3½ft]; white tinged pink); 'Pink Cherub' (spreading, to 0.75×1.2m [2½×4ft]; white flushed fuchsia-pink); 'Seven Stars' (palest pink flushed darker); 'Starshine' (compact, to 45×45cm [1½×1½ft]; pink); 'Venetian Chimes' (dark reddish-pink). **Other dwarf hybrids**: unless stated, to 0.6×1.2m (2×4ft); lvs & fls as in small vars

(above). Vars: 'Carmen' **1** (deep blood-red); 'Chikor' **2** (to 30×60cm [1×2ft]; soft yellow); 'Curlew' (light yellow); 'Jenny' ('Creeping Jenny', 'Elizabeth Jenny'; prostrate form of 'Elizabeth'); 'Princess Anne' (sometimes sold in US as 'Golden Fleece'; v hardy; clear yellow); 'Ptarmigan' (to 30×60cm [1×2ft]; white; early); 'Sapphire' **3** (v small lvs; fls purplish-blue, early).

Deciduous azaleas

Deciduous *Rhododendron* (formerly *Azalea*) spp & hybrids, among the most free-flowering and colourful of all deciduous shrubs. Trusses of wide trumpet-shaped flowers with distinct sharp lobes ("petals"), often fragrant, in wide colour range (especially good in yellows, oranges & flame-red – colours not much seen in evergreen azaleas). Leaves often brilliantly coloured in autumn. **Cultivation**: As for rhododendrons (p84), but generally less demanding & best in open (even full sun if watered well). Unless stated, very hardy. Prone to bud blast & petal blight. **Propagation**: Layering; grafting on *R. luteum*, etc; semi-ripe cuttings under mist; spp (also colour strains of hybrids) by seed.

Species: unless stated, fls 4–6cm (1½–2½in) wide.
R. (A.) albrechtii **4**: to 2.5×1.8m (8×6ft); lvs to 10cm (4in) long, clustered at shoot tips, yellow in autumn; small trusses of intense pink to purplish-rose fls, spotted olive-green, mid–late spring (sometimes before lvs). Best in woodland.
*R. (A.) arborescens*** : to 3.5×3m (12×10ft) or more; lvs glossy, to 9cm (3½in) long; small trusses of white fls, often flushed pink, summer.
*R. (A.) atlanticum*** (coast azalea of eastern N America): to 1×1.5m (3×5ft); spreads by stolons; lvs small, bright or bluish-green; trusses of 4-10 white fls, often flushed mauve, late spring.
R. (A.) calendulaceum (flame azalea): to 3×2.5m (10×8ft); downy lvs to 10cm (4in) long, orange & crimson in autumn; profuse trusses of 5–7 fls in brilliant shades of yellow, orange & scarlet, late spring to early summer. *R. bakeri* (Cumberland azalea of eastern N America) is similar but dwarfer & later-flg.
R. canadense (rhodora): ultra-hardy; to 1×1m (3×3ft); lvs small, bluish-green; small trusses of rose-purple fls, mid spring. Thrives in wet soil.
*R. luteum*** **5** (*A. pontica*, common yellow azalea of Europe): to 3×3m (10×10ft) or more; spreads by self-seeding & suckering; lvs to 12cm (5in) long, scarlet & purple in autumn; trusses of 7–12 yellow fls, late spring to early summer.
R. (A.) occidentale * **6** (western azalea of N America): moderately to v hardy; to 2.5–3×2.5m (8–10×8ft); shiny lvs to 10cm (4in) long, hairy beneath; trusses of 6–12 fls 4–8cm (1½–3in) wide, creamy-white or pale pink, blotched yellow & often tinged pink, early summer.
R. prinophyllum (*R. [A.] roseum*; in US, rose-shell azalea): ultra-hardy; to 3×3m (10×10ft); lvs small, grey, woolly beneath; trusses of 5–9 bright pink to violet-red fls, usually blotched brownish-red, late spring.

R. quinquefolium **7**: moderately to v hardy; usually bushy, to 1.2×1m (4×3ft), sometimes small tree; dainty appearance; small lvs, often rounded-diamond shape, in umbrella-like whorls of 5 at shoot tips, pale green often edged purple, colouring in autumn; fls solitary or in 2s or 3s, white spotted green, mid spring (with young lvs). Needs shelter & some shade.
R. reticulatum **8** (*R. rhombicum*): to 3.5×2.5m (12×8ft) or more; young shoots brown-woolly; lvs small, diamond-shaped, net-veined beneath, purple-red in autumn; solitary or paired bright purple fls, mid–late spring (before lvs).
R. schlippenbachii **9** (in US, royal azalea): to 3.5×2.5m (12×8ft); whorls of lvs 5–12cm (2–5in) long at shoot tips, good autumn colour; small trusses of fls to 9cm (3½in) wide, white to beautiful rose-pink, spotted reddish-brown, mid–late spring. V hardy but prone to spring frost damage & sunscorch. Best in warm semi-shade.
R. (A.) vaseyi **10** (in US, pink-shell azalea): to 3.5×3m (12×10ft); narrow tapering lvs 5–10cm (2–4in) long, brilliantly coloured in autumn; trusses of 4–8 fls, generally clear pale pink spotted reddish-brown, mid–late spring (before lvs). Good even on poor sandy soil.
*R. (A.) viscosum*** (swamp azalea, swamp honeysuckle): ultra-hardy; to 3.5×2.5m (12×8ft); young shoots hairy; small lvs, often glaucous or silvery beneath; clusters of 6–12 sticky narrow fls 3cm (1¼in) long, white sometimes suffused pink, early–mid summer.
Hybrids: generally fl late spring to early summer (Mollis first, Knap Hills & some Ghents last).
Ghent hybrids: first bred in early 19th-century Belgium from *R. luteum* & various N American spp; v to ultra-hardy & long-lived; generally to 3–3.5×2.5m (10–12×8ft); lvs often coloured in autumn; brilliant long-tubed fls, 4–6cm (1½–2½in) wide, good for cutting. Vars: 'Bouquet de

Flore' (bright pink striped white); 'Coccinea Speciosa' **1** (brilliant orange-red); 'Corneille'* (pink, double); 'Daviesii'* **2** (creamy to white, blotched yellow); 'Fanny' ('Pucella'; purplish-rose blotched orange); 'Gloria Mundi' (bright orange; best in shade); 'Nancy Waterer' (golden-yellow); 'Narcissiflora'* **3** (soft yellow, double); 'Unique' (v large trusses of up to 50 buff-yellow fls flushed orange).

Knap Hill, Slocock, Exbury & Ilam hybrids: bred mainly this century in UK, US & New Zealand; complex parentage, involving Ghent & Mollis azaleas & various spp (including *R. arborescens, R. calendulaceum, R. molle & R. occidentale*); generally to 1.5–2.5×1.8–2.5m (5–8×6–8ft); young lvs often bronzed, generally colour well in autumn; trusses of up to 18 wide-open fls, often scented, to 8cm (3in) wide, in bright colours, late spring. Sold as unnamed seedlings & as named vars: 'Ballerina' (white, orange mark); 'Balzac'** (orange-red, flame blotch); 'Berryrose'* (salmon-pink, yellow blotch); 'Brazil' (intense orange-red); 'Cecile' (salmon-pink, yellow blotch); 'Chelsea Reach' (creamy-white flushed lilac, double); 'Coronation Lady' (salmon-pink, orange blotch); 'Dorothy Corston' (lvs bronzed; fls deep red); 'Fireglow' (vermilion-orange); 'Gibraltar' (brilliant orange flushed red); 'Golden Oriole'* (deep yellow; early); 'Harvest Moon' (primrose-yellow, darker blotch); 'Homebush' **8** (deep carmine-pink, double); 'Hotspur' (flame-red, orange blotch); 'Klondyke' **9** (bronzed lvs; deep golden-yellow fls); 'Lady Rosebery' (crimson, orange blotch; v large infls); 'Lapwing'* **10** (creamy-yellow tinted pink); 'Marion Merriman' (pale yellow flushed darker, blotched orange-yellow; v large infls); 'Oxydol' (white, pale yellow blotch); 'Persil' (white, deep yellow blotch); 'Pink Ruffles' (carmine-rose, orange blotch); 'Pink William'* (dwarf; silvery-pink, orange blotch); 'Satan' (scarlet; late); 'Silver Slipper'* (white flushed pink, yellow blotch); 'Strawberry Ice' (flesh-pink, flushed & veined rose-pink, yellow throat; v large

infls); 'Tintoretto' (orange suffused pink); 'Whitethroat' **11** (compact; pure white, double); 'Wryneck' (sulphur-yellow tinged pink).

Mollis (Mollis-Sinensis) hybrids: first bred in mid 19th-century Belgium & Holland, mainly from Japanese *R. japonicum* (incorrectly, *A. mollis*), also Chinese *R. molle* (*A. sinensis*); originally for forcing under glass but generally v hardy; to 1.5–2.5×1.5–2.5m (5–8×5–8ft); lvs narrow, hairy, brilliant orange & scarlet in autumn; trusses of 6–12 generally scentless fls to 6cm (2½in) wide, brilliant colours (mainly orange to red), mid–late spring (may be damaged by late frosts in frost pockets). Vars: 'Dr M. Oosthoek' **4** (deep orange-red); 'Floradora' (orange, brownish spots); 'Hamlet' (orange tinged pink; late); 'Koster's Brilliant Red' (orange-red); 'Spek's Orange' (orange; late).

Occidentale hybrids: first bred in late 19th-century England & Holland from *R. occidentale* & mainly Mollis azaleas; to 2–2.5×2.5m (7–8×8ft); fls 5–8cm (2–3in) wide, delicately coloured & blotched, scented. Vars: 'Delicatissima'* (cream tinged pink, yellow blotch); 'Exquisita'* **7** (cream flushed pink, orange blotch); 'Graciosa'* (pale yellow tinged pink, orange blotch); 'Irene Koster'* (white flushed crimson-pink, yellow blotch); 'Superba'* (white flushed pink, large yellow blotch).

Rustica (Rustica Flore Pleno) hybrids: first bred in late 19th-century Belgium from double Ghent & Mollis azaleas; to 2.5–3×2.5m (8–10×8ft); similar to Ghents but v double long-lasting fls in tight trusses; good in open, exposed spots. Vars: 'Aida' (rose tinged lilac); 'Byron' (white tinged carmine-rose); 'Freya' **5** (shell-pink tinged carmine-rose); 'Norma' **6** (buff-pink); 'Phoebe' (sulphur-yellow).

Viscosum hybrids: modern hybrids, mainly from Holland, of *R. viscosum* & Mollis azaleas; v to ultra-hardy; similar to Mollis but v fragrant. Vars: 'Antilope'** (pink flushed salmon); 'Carat'** (orange-red); 'Jolie Madame'* (fls large, rose-pink); 'Rosata'** (carmine-rose).

Evergreen azaleas

Sometimes called Japanese azaleas (first bred there). Semi-evergreen *Rhododendron* (formerly *Azalea*) spp & hybrids (often of complex parentage) with limited colour range but excellent for massed planting. Flowers generally funnel-shaped or flattish, 4–6cm (1½–2½in) wide, with distinct lobes, in profuse small clusters at end of shoots, generally mid–late spring; spp & vars marked † have hose-in-hose flowers. Leaves generally small, 2–4cm (¾–1½in) long unless stated, sometimes colouring in autumn; early ("spring") leaves generally larger & thinner than "summer"; only latter retained over winter. **Cultivation:** As for rhododendrons (p84); best in some shelter & shade **Propagation:** Semi-ripe cuttings; spp by seed.

Species: unless stated, moderately to v hardy.
R. (A.) indicum (incorrectly, Indian azalea [in fact from Japan]): semi- to moderately hardy; to

1–1.8×1–1.2m (3–6×3–4ft); bushy or semi-prostrate; paired or solitary rosy-red to scarlet fls, early summer. Var 'Balsaminiflora' has salmon-

red double fls, rose-like in bud.

R. kaempferi **1** (torch azalea): to 2.5×1.8m (8×6ft); spring lvs to 5cm (2in) long; fls salmon-pink to brick-red, late spring.

R. kiusianum **2** (Kyushu azalea): v hardy; compact, to 1×1.2m (3×4ft); fls small, lilac-purple to magenta-pink, late spring.

R. nakaharae: prostrate & creeping, to 20×60cm (8×24in); lvs v small; fls scarlet, darker blotch, early–mid summer. Good for rock gardens.

R. (A.) obtusum (correctly, *R.* 'Obtusum'; probably natural hybrid of or intermediate between *R. kaempferi* & *R. kiusianum*): to 1×1.2m (3×4ft); fls scarlet to crimson, late spring. Var 'Amoenum'† has brilliant magenta fls.

R. simsii (incorrectly, Indian azalea [in fact from China]; often sold incorrectly as *A. indica*): semi-hardy; to 1.5×1.5m (5×5ft); spring lvs to 5cm (2in) long; fls rose- to dark red, late spring.

*R. yedoense poukhanense** (Korean azalea): v hardy; to 1.8×1.2m (6×4ft); often deciduous; lvs lance-shaped, to 9cm (3½in) long; rosy-purple fls, late spring.

Hybrid azaleas: unless stated, to 1–1.5×1–1.8m (3–5×3–6ft); groups variable (many classed by breeder, not parentage); v free-flg.

Glen Dale hybrids: v hardy but best where summers warm; v varied origin & form. Vars: 'Ambrosia' (begonia-pink fading apricot); 'Aphrodite' (pale pink); 'Buccaneer' (orange-red blotched brick-red); 'Challenger' (orange-red suffused lavender, blotched red); 'Chanticleer' (brilliant reddish-purple); 'Dauntless' (mauve-purple, red eye); 'Dragon' (brilliant red); 'Eros' (pink); 'Everest' (white blotched chartreuse-green); 'Gaiety' (rose-pink, darker blotch); 'Geisha' (white striped red); 'Glacier' (glistening white tinged green); 'Harbinger' (rose, darker blotch); 'Louise Dowdle' (brilliant pink, purplish-pink blotch); 'Martha Hitchcock' (white edged magenta); 'Pixie' (white, red eye); 'Silver Moon' (fls frilled, white blotched pale green); 'Tanager' (red, dark blotch); 'Treasure' (white tinged pink).

Indian (Indica) azaleas: bred largely from *R. indicum* & *R. simsii*; mostly semi-hardy & often grown under glass (fl from early winter); good outdoors in warm areas; fls large. Vars 'Hexe'† ('Firefly'; crimson) & 'Satsuki' (pink, dark blotch) are moderately hardy.

Kaempferi, Malvatica & Vuykiana hybrids: bred from *R. kaempferi*, *R.* 'Malvaticum' & others; v hardy; vigorous. Vars: 'Addy Wery' (bronzy-red); 'Alice' (salmon-red); 'Bengal Fire' (hybrid with *R. oldhamii*; young lvs hairy; fls orange-red); 'Betty' (salmon-pink, darker eye); 'Blue Danube' **3** (violet-blue); 'Double Beauty' (large double pink fls); 'Eddy' **4** (salmon-red); 'Favorite' (crimson-pink); 'Fedora' (phlox-pink); 'Florida' (semi-double; red shaded vermilion); 'John Cairns' (brownish-scarlet); 'Leo' (dwarf &

spreading; orange-pink); 'Naomi' (tall; soft salmon-pink); 'Orange Beauty' (salmon-orange; best in some shade); 'Palestrina' **5** (white, faint green markings); 'Purple Triumph' (deep purple); 'Vuyk's Rosy Red' (large rose-red fls); 'Vuyk's Scarlet' **6** (dwarf; large crimson fls).

Kurume azaleas: originated in Japan, mainly from *R. kaempferi* & *R. kiusianum*; moderately hardy; dwarf, forming dense mounds; small lvs & fls; good in sun if soil moist. Gable hybrids (marked ‡) are similar but hardier. Vars: 'Azuma-Kagami' **7** ('Pink Pearl'; tall; phlox-pink, pale throat); 'Coral Bells'† (coral-pink); 'Hatsugiri' (magenta-purple); 'Hino-crimson' (lvs red in winter; fls bright crimson-red); 'Hinodegiri' ('Red Hussar'; bright crimson); 'Hinomayo' (tallish; phlox-pink); 'Hoo' ('Apple Blossom'; white edged pink); 'Kirin'† **8** ('Daybreak'; silvery-pink); 'Kure-no-yuki'† ('Snowflake'; white); 'Lorna'†‡ (pastel-pink); 'Louise Gable'‡ (salmon-pink, semi-double); 'Mother's Day' **9** (large semi-double fls, crimson; late); 'Rosebud'†‡ (rose-pink, double); 'Sherwood Orchid' (red-violet); 'Shin-seikai'† ('Old Ivory'; creamy-white); 'Snow'† (tall; white blotched chartreuse); 'Stewartstonian'‡ (lvs wine-red in winter; fls brownish-red); 'Vida Brown'† (rose-pink). Vars 'Anna Kehr' (pastel-pink) & 'White Rosebud' (white) are double-fld, similar habit; v hardy.

Macrantha, Satsuki & similar hybrids: derived largely from *R. indicum* & *R. simsii*; moderately hardy; low-growing; largish fls, latish, often variable on one plant. Vars: 'Beni Kirishima' (orange-red); 'Bunkwa' (blush-pink); 'Eikan' (white to salmon-pink); 'Flame Creeper' (creeping; intense orange-red); 'Gumpo' series (white, pink or bicoloured); 'Heiwa' (purple); 'Higasa' (v large fls, rose-pink & white); 'Kagetsu Muji' (white, sometimes tinged/marked rose); 'Kudusama' (purplish-red, paler throat); 'Rukizon' (salmon-orange); 'Shinnyo-no-hikari' (white spotted red-purple); 'Shinnyo-no-tsuki' (white spotted pink).

Nakaharae (North Tisbury) hybrids: derived from *R. nakaharae*; v hardy; v dwarf & mounding; fl early–mid summer. Good for rock gardens, etc. Vars: 'Alexander' (bright red); 'Joseph Hill' (red); 'Michael' (bright pink); 'Red Fountain' (red-orange); 'Wintergreen' (light salmon-pink).

Azaleodendrons: moderately to v hardy hybrids of evergreen rhododendrons & deciduous or evergreen azaleas; generally to 1.5–2.5×1.2–1.8m (5–8×4–6ft); lvs retained over winter (rather untidy); large trusses of fls. Vars: 'Broughtonii Aureum' (soft yellow); 'Dr Masters' (v hardy; rose-red tinged lilac); 'Fragrans' * * (white tinged lilac); 'Glory of Littleworth' * **10** (creamy-white blotched orange); 'Govenianum' * * (lavender-purple); 'Hardijzer Beauty' (clear pink); 'Martine' (dwarf; pink).

Other members of the heath family

Important and varied group of shrubs (& a few trees), almost all for lime-free soil, mostly with small bell-shaped to globular flowers. Evergreen unless stated. **Cultivation**: Unless stated, very hardy and for moist but well-drained lime-free peaty soil, or sandy loam with ample leaf-mould, in sun or partial shade. Regular pruning unnecessary, but old wood can be thinned out in early spring. **Propagation**: Generally by seed, semi-ripe cuttings or layering; division/suckers where appropriate; *Arbutus* vars by grafting.

Strawberry trees (*Arbutus* spp): moderately hardy small trees or large shrubs with leathery dark lvs, panicles of pitcher-shaped generally whitish fls, spring unless stated, followed by decorative orange-red strawberry-like frs (edible but insipid). Among most handsome of small evergreen trees but drop litter. Tolerate lime unless noted; best in warm sunny site sheltered from cold winds, especially when young. Difficult to transplant.
A. andrachne: to 6×4.5m (20×15ft) in warm climates, smaller & shrubby where cool; dense; reddish-brown peeling bark; lvs to 10×5cm (4×2in), generally toothless; erect infls to 10cm (4in) long; 1cm (½in) smoothish frs. Rather tender when young.
A.×andrachnoides **1** (*A.×hybrida*; often sold incorrectly as *A. andrachne*): hybrid of *A. andrachne* & *A. unedo* & intermediate in most characteristics; branches often twisted; cinnamon-red bark; fls late autumn or early spring.
A. menziesii (madrona): generally to 7.5×6m (25×20ft), often more in warm climates; peeling bark, cinnamon-brown beneath; lvs to 15×8cm (6×3in), generally toothless; erect infls to 20×15cm (8×6in); small orange frs. Needs free-draining lime-free soil.
A. unedo **2** ([Killarney] strawberry tree): moderately to v hardy; spreading, to 4.5×3m (15×10ft); suckering; gnarled when old; shredding rough bark, bright red beneath; shiny lvs to 10×4.5cm (4×1¾in), toothed; 5cm (2in) drooping infls, autumn; rough 2cm (¾in) frs ripening autumn (with fls). Var 'Rubra' **3** is compact; pink-flushed fls.
Manzanita (*Arctostaphylos manzanita* **4**): moderately to v hardy distinctive shrub, to 3×1.8m (10×6ft), often tree-like in warm climates; stiff crooked branches; peeling bark, red beneath; stiff grey-green lvs to 5cm (2in) long; small panicles of white or deep pink pitcher-shaped fls, spring; 1cm (½in) frs ripening deep red, only where summers hot. Likes sun.
Leather-leaf (*Chamaedaphne calyculata* **5**): ultra-hardy, rather gaunt shrub, to 1.2×1m (4×3ft); wiry arching branches; narrowish lvs to 5cm (2in) long, brown scales beneath; heath-like white fls along stems, spring.
Enkianthus (*Enkianthus* spp): distinctive deciduous shrubs with branches & lvs in whorls, often giving layered appearance. Grown for

brilliant red, orange or yellow autumn colour & generally bell-shaped fls in drooping umbels or racemes, late spring. Best in light/partial shade.
E. campanulatus **6**: to 2.5×1.5m (8×5ft) or more; erect; lvs to 6cm (2½in) long, dull green; 8mm (⅓in) creamy-yellow fls veined red. Var 'Red Bells' has deep red fls.
E. cernuus: to 1.8×1.2m (6×4ft); lvs to 4cm (1½in) long; 5mm (¼in) white fls (deep red in best-known form, var *rubens* **7**).
E. perulatus **8**: to 1.8×1.2m (6×4ft); narrowish lvs to 5cm (2in) long; 5–8mm (¼–⅓in) white pitcher-shaped fls.
"Tree" heaths (*Erica* spp): generally moderately hardy medium-sized to tall shrubs (rarely true trees) with small needle-like lvs in whorls & racemes of small tubular to globular fls like those of the better-known dwarf spp (p444). For sheltered sunny spot.
*E. arborea** (tree heath): bushy, to 3.5×2.5m (12×8ft), or eventually a tree, to 6m (20ft) or more, where winters v mild; young growth hairy; lvs in 3s; panicles to 45cm (1½ft) long of white fls, early spring. Var *alpina* is v hardy; erect & spreading, to 2.5×2.5m (8×8ft); lvs bright green; infls to 30cm (1ft) long when mature.
E. australis **9** (Spanish or southern heath): rather open, to 1.8×1.2m (6×4ft); spired; young shoots downy; rich dark green lvs in 4s; clusters of bright purplish-red fls, mid spring to early summer (white in var 'Mr Robert').
E. lusitanica **10** (*E. codonodes*, Portugal heath; in US, Spanish heath): dense & erect, to 3×1m (10×3ft); young shoots hairy; feathery light green foliage; v profuse clusters of long-lasting white fls from v early spring (or winter if mild) from pink buds.
*E. mediterranea** (*E. hibernica*, Mediterranean or Irish heath; correctly, *E. erigena*): dense & bushy, to 2.5×1.2m (8×4ft); branches erect; dark green lvs in 4s; dense 2.5–5cm (1–2in) racemes of rosy-red fls all spring. Tolerates lime. Vars (generally to 60–90cm [2–3ft]): 'Alba' (white); 'Brightness' (pink fls from bronzy-red buds); 'Golden Lady' (lvs golden-yellow; sparse white fls); 'Superba' (to 2m [7ft]; clear pink); 'W. T. Rackliff' **11** (larger white fls, brown anthers).
E. terminalis (*E. corsica, E. stricta,* Corsican heath): erect, to 2.5×1.2m (8×4ft); dark glossy green lvs in 4s, 5s or 6s; small umbels of pale rose-pink fls, all summer. Thrives even on

shallow chalk soils.
E. × *veitchii* 'Exeter' * : hybrid of *E. arborea* &
E. lusitanica; to 3 × 1.8m (10 × 6ft); bright green
lvs; racemes to 15cm (6in) long of white fls, early
spring.
Gaulnettya (× *Gaulnettya* [*Gaulthettia*]
wisleyensis 'Wisley Pearl' **1**): intergeneric hybrid
of *Gaultheria shallon* & *Pernettya mucronata*;
bushy & suckering, to 1 × 1m (3 × 3ft); leathery
net-veined lvs to 4cm (1½in) long; 4–6cm
(1½–2½in) racemes of pearly-white fls, late
spring to early summer; dark blood-red 5mm
(¼in) frs, decorative through winter. Var 'Pink
Pixie' is back-cross with *Gaultheria shallon*; more
compact; pink-tinged fls; purplish-red frs.
Gaultherias (*Gaultheria* spp): moderately to
v hardy shrubs similar to *Vaccinium* spp
(especially in lf); generally tufted, often spreading
by underground stems; leathery lvs; small urn-
shaped or globular fls, white unless stated, late
spring or early summer, followed by decorative
berry-like frs 5–10mm (¼–½in) across. For moist
semi-shade.
G. antipoda: generally to 1.2 × 1m (4 × 3ft), or may
be prostrate; young shoots bristly & downy;
rounded apple-green lvs to 1.5cm (⅝in) long,
wavy; white or red frs (edible).
G. hookeri (*G. veitchiana*): generally dense &
mounding, to 1 × 1m (3 × 3ft), but sometimes
rather erect, to 1.8m (6ft); branchlets downy &
bristly; dark glossy green hard lvs to 9cm (3½in)
long, wrinkled; fls in small dense racemes; small
indigo-blue frs.
G. shallon **2** (salal): v hardy; suckering & thicket-
forming, to 1.2 × 1.2m (4 × 4ft); young branches
reddish & bristly; lvs to 10 × 6cm (4 × 2½in),
bristly teeth; 4–12cm (1½–5in) racemes of
pinkish-white fls; dark purple frs-shaped hairy frs
(edible). Good for tall ground cover.
G. wardii: moderately hardy; spreading, to
1.2 × 1m (4 × 3ft); young shoots & lvs hairy; lvs to
9 × 3cm (3½ × 1¼in), conspicuous sunken veins;
fls in small dense racemes; frs purplish, white
bloom.
Huckleberries (*Gaylussacia* spp): small
vaccinium-like shrubs with fls in dense small
racemes, late spring, followed by edible frs where
summers hot.
G. baccata (black huckleberry): dense & erect, to
1 × 0.6m (3 × 2ft); deciduous deep green lvs* to
5cm (2in) long, yellowish beneath, crimson in
autumn; fls dull red; shiny black frs (good
flavour).
G. brachycera (box huckleberry): dwarf &
creeping, to 45 × 60cm (1½ × 2ft); evergreen;
dark glossy green leathery lvs to 2.5cm (1in)
long; white fls marked red; blue frs. Neat &
dainty.
Kalmias (American laurels): handsome shrubs
with leathery lvs & showy clusters of saucer-

shaped 5-lobed fls, late spring or early summer,
on yr-old wood. Foliage poisonous. Like cool
moist roots.
K. angustifolia (sheep laurel, lambkill): ultra-
hardy; generally spreading & open, to 1 × 1.2m
(3 × 4ft), but sometimes dwarf; suckering; bright
green lvs to 5cm (2in) long; rosy-red fls 8mm
(⅓in) across. Var 'Rubra' has deep green lvs &
deeper red fls.
K. latifolia **3** (calico bush, mountain laurel): dense
& thicket-forming, to 3 × 2.5m (10 × 8ft) or wider;
glossy rich green lvs to 12cm (5in) long; 8–10cm
(3–4in) clusters of white, blush- or rose-pink fls
2–2.5cm (¾–1in) across. Vars 'Clementine
Churchill' **4** and 'Ostbo Red' have red fls.
Ledums (*Ledum* spp): low-growing & aromatic,
with neat dark green lvs, generally woolly
beneath, & dense clusters of white, rather starry
fls 1–2cm (½–¾in) across, mid–late spring. Like
moisture.
L. groenlandicum (Labrador tea): ultra-hardy; to
1 × 1m (3 × 3ft); young shoots woolly; lvs* to
5 × 1cm (2 × ½in), rusty wool beneath.
L. palustre (marsh ledum; in US, wild rosemary):
ultra-hardy; open, to 1 × 0.45m (3 × 1½ft); young
shoots brown-woolly; v narrow lvs* to 3cm
(1¼in) long, rusty wool beneath (wider in var
dilatatum **5**).
Leucothoës (*Leucothoë* spp): attractive pieris-
like small shrubs with racemes of small urn-
shaped or cylindrical, generally white fls, early
summer unless stated. Best in semi-shade.
L. fontanesiana **6** (drooping leucothoë; often sold
incorrectly as *L. catesbaei*): to 1.8 × 1.2m
(6 × 4ft); elegant, with arching zigzag branches;
semi-/evergreen leathery lance-shaped lvs to
12cm (5in) long, often tinged red or bronze-
purple in autumn; drooping 2.5–8cm (1–3in) infls.
Vars: 'Rainbow' **7** ('Multicolor'; has young
growths crimson & lvs variegated pink to cream);
'Rollissonii' **8** (to 60 × 45cm [2 × 1½ft]; smaller
leaves).
L. keiskei: to 1.2 × 0.45m (4 × 1½ft); slender
zigzag, often arching stems; young shoots &
lvs bright red; leathery lance-shaped lvs to 9cm
(3½in) long, deep red in autumn; rather sparse
fls to 1.5cm (⅝in) long, mid summer.
Menziesias (*Menziesia* spp): slow-growing
deciduous shrubs with clusters of bell/urn-
shaped waxy fls, late spring. Best sheltered from
late frosts.
M. ciliicalyx **9**: to 90 × 60cm (3 × 2ft); often
somewhat tiered; lvs to 8cm (3in) long; nodding
1.5cm (⅝in) fls, yellowish-green shading to
purplish. Var *purpurea* (often sold incorrectly as
M. purpurea) is showier, with purplish-pink fls.
M. pilosa: erect, to 1.5 × 1m (5 × 3ft); young
shoots & lvs downy; old bark shredding; lvs to
5cm (2in) long; small creamy fls flushed red.
Sorrel tree (sourwood, *Oxydendrum*

[*Andromeda*] *arboreum* **10** p103): beautiful, rather slow-growing tree, to 12×4.5m (40×15ft) where summers hot, smaller or often only a large shrub in cool climates; slender trunk; generally pyramid-shaped crown; deciduous lance-shaped lvs 10–20cm (4–8in) long, brilliant scarlet in autumn provided receives some sun; clusters of slender drooping racemes 15–25cm (6–10in) long of small urn-shaped white fls, mid–late summer.

Pernettya (*Pernettya mucronata*): moderately to v hardy S American gaultheria-like shrub grown for profuse heath-like small fls & (mainly) persistent colourful berries. Suckering & thicket-forming, to 1×1m (3×3ft), or taller in shade; young shoots wiry & often red; densely packed toothed & spiny lvs to 2×0.5cm (¾×¼in); white fls, late spring; females bear berries to 1cm (½in) across, ripening early autumn, white, pink, crimson, purple or almost black (persist to spring). Best in full sun; plant 1 male to every 5–10 females to ensure frtg. Excellent ground cover. Female vars (colours refer to frs): 'Alba' (white tinged pink); 'Atrococcinea' **1** (ruby-red); 'Bell's Seedling' (self-pollinating; dark carmine-red); 'Lilacina' **2** (reddish-lilac); 'Mulberry Wine' (magenta to purple); 'Pink Pearl' (lilac-pink); 'Rosie' (pink flushed rose); 'Sea Shell' **3** (shell-pink); 'White Pearl' (large white frs). 'Thymifolia' is neat male form with small lvs.

Pieris (*Pieris* [*Andromeda*] spp): v ornamental compact shrubs with profuse panicles or racemes of small waxy, generally white fls (buds form autumn, sometimes decorative over winter, open spring) & often bright red/bronze-tinted young lvs. Prone to spring frost damage, so best sheltered & in light shade.

P. (*A.*) *floribunda*: slow-growing, to 1.8×1.8cm (6×6ft); rounded & bushy; dark green leathery lvs to 8cm (3in) long; erect 5–12cm (2–5in) infls (to 20cm [8in] long in var 'Elongata' ['Grandiflora']), early spring.

P. (*A.*) *formosa*: moderately to v hardy; to 3.5×4.5m (12×15ft), even more in v mild climates; dark glossy green leathery lvs to 15cm (6in) long, coppery-red when young; more or less erect infls to 15cm (6in) long, late spring.

P. forrestii **4** (correctly, *P. formosa forrestii*): moderately hardy; similar to *P. formosa* but less tall, with somewhat pendent habit; lvs brilliant red when young; larger fls in long conical infls, mid spring. Vars: 'Charles Michael' (young lvs bronze; fls 1cm [½in] long, in panicles to 20×10cm [8×4in]); 'Jermyns' (young shoots & lvs dark red; showy red buds all winter opening to white fls); 'Wakehurst' (vigorous, with shorter broader lvs, vivid red when young; glistening white fls). *P.* 'Forest Flame' **5** is hybrid with *P. japonica*; compact, to 2×2m (7×7ft); lance-shaped lvs to 12cm (5in) long, brilliant red when young, fading to pink, creamy then green; large drooping infls; v hardy.

P. japonica: to 2×2m (7×7ft); bushy; glossy dark green lvs to 9×2cm (3½×¾in), coppery when young; drooping 8–15cm (3–6in) infls, early spring. Vars: 'Bert Chandler' **6** (young lvs salmon-pink, paling to creamy-white then green); 'Blush' **7** (fl buds rose opening pale pink); 'Christmas Cheer' (v early rose-flushed fls from deep pink buds); 'Flamingo' (deep pink); 'Mountain Fire' (deep red young lvs); 'Purity' (large pure white fls); 'Red Mill' (hardiest var; later-flg); 'Variegata' **8** (slow-growing; narrow lvs edged cream, tinged pink when young).

P. taiwanensis: compact, to 1.8×1.8m (6×6ft); deep green lvs to 12×2.5cm (5×1in), bronze-red when young; clustered semi-erect infls 8–15cm (3–8in) long, early–mid spring.

Blueberries (bilberries, whortleberries, *Vaccinium* spp): moisture-loving shrubs thriving on v acid soils; grown mainly for decorative, generally edible, 5–10mm (¼–½in) frs & (deciduous spp) autumn lf colour; fls small & less showy than others of family, generally white tinged pink or red. Like some shade; can be pruned early spring to maintain bushiness.

V. arctostaphylos (Caucasian whortleberry): slow-growing & spreading, to 3×3m (10×10ft); young shoots reddish; dull green deciduous lvs to 10cm (4in) long, purplish-red in autumn; racemes of white fls tinged purplish, early summer (sometimes repeating); purple-black shiny frs.

V. corymbosum **9** (swamp or high-bush blueberry): ultra-hardy; dense & thicket-forming, to 1.8×2.5cm (6×8ft) or more; deciduous lvs to 9cm (3½in) long, brilliant red shades in autumn; clusters of white or pale pink fls, late spring; v sweet black frs, blue bloom. Numerous frtg vars available, especially in N America.

V. glauco-album (*V. glaucalbum*): moderately hardy; suckering, to 1×1m (3×3ft); hard lvs to 6×3cm (2½×1¼in), vivid blue-white beneath, finely toothed; 5–8cm (2–3in) infls of pinkish-white fls, late spring; blue-black edible frs, blue-white bloom.

V. ovatum (California or evergreen huckleberry): moderately hardy; dense & compact, to 1.2×1m (4×3ft), less in sun; young shoots purple & downy; close-set dark glossy green leathery lvs to 4cm (1½in) long, pinkish when young & purplish in winter; small clusters of white fls, late spring or summer; red frs ripening black, edible.

Zenobia (*Zenobia pulverulenta** **10**): beautiful but rather open & irregular shrub, to 1.5×1.5m (5×5ft); young shoots covered in glaucous-white bloom; deciduous or semi-evergreen lvs to 8cm (3in) long, glaucous-white bloom; clusters of pendent white bell-shaped fls 10mm (⅜in) wide, aniseed-scented, early summer. Needs moisture.

The beech family

Mainly large & handsome specimen trees suitable only for large gardens, parks, etc; some spp & vars smaller & some useful for hedging if regularly trimmed. Grown mainly for foliage, some for nuts; some have good autumn colours. **Cultivation**: Generally for deep, well-drained but moist soil in sunny, open position; lime-tolerant unless stated. **Propagation**: Seed; vars by grafting onto rootstock of parent.

Chestnuts (*Castanea* spp): distinctive, round-headed, long-lived deciduous trees with ribbed bark & lance-shaped coarsely toothed lvs to 22cm (9in) long; catkin fls (smell unpleasant); well-known edible nuts in prickly burrs. V hardy & drought resistant (like hot summers); many spp prone to chestnut blight in N America, & borers.
C. mollissima **1** (Chinese chestnut): to 7.5×6m (25×20ft); young shoots downy; lvs sometimes felted beneath; self-sterile; blight-resistant.
C. sativa (sweet or Spanish chestnut): fast-growing, to 15×12m (50×40ft)/25yrs; best nuts. Vars: 'Albomarginata' (lvs edged creamy-white); 'Marron de Lyon' ('Macrocarpa'; best frtg var).
Beeches (*Fagus* spp): noble round-headed deciduous trees with smooth grey bark & toothed/wavy-edged oval lvs, rich yellow to bronze in autumn; small angular frs ("masts"); shallow-rooted & deep shading.
F. englerana: v hardy; to 7.5×6m (25×20ft); handsome, often with several trunks; slender branches; glaucous lvs 10cm (4in) long, wavy-edged.
F. grandifolia (American beech): ultra-hardy; to 20×15m (65×50ft)/40yrs, less in maritime climates; suckering & good for hedging; lvs to 12cm (5in) long, coarse-toothed.
F. sylvatica (common beech of Europe): v hardy; to 9×9m (30×30ft)/25yrs; good for hedging (retains dead lvs if late clipped); wavy-edged lvs to 10cm (4in) long, fresh green when young; tolerates some pollution. Vars: 'Aspleniifolia' (fern-leaved beech; lvs narrow & deeply cut; var 'Heterophylla' ['Laciniata'] is similar); 'Aurea Pendula' (slender & erect, to 4.5×1.5m [15×5ft]; hanging branches; young lvs yellow [best in shade]); 'Dawyck' **2** ('Fastigiata', v narrow at first; to 9×2m [30×7ft]; 'Dawyck Purple' is purple-lvd form); 'Purpurea Pendula' **3** (round-headed, weeping & v slow-growing, to 3×1.8m [10×6ft]; dark purple lvs); 'Riversii' ('Rivers' Purple'; best form of copper beech, with dark red lvs all summer); 'Zlatia' **4** (slow-growing, to 5.5×5.5m [18×18ft]; young lvs yellow).
Southern beeches (*Nothofagus* spp): fast-growing, densely-lvd S Hemisphere spp with smaller lvs than true beeches. Moderately hardy, but best in moist maritime climate; dislike lime & exposure.
N. antarctica: dense shrub or open tree, to 12×6m (40×20ft); elegant, with slender trunk; deciduous; dark green glossy toothed lvs, yellow in autumn.

N. betuloides **5**: dense evergreen shrub or compact tree, to 9×6m (30×20ft); ascending branches; dark green glossy toothed lvs.
Oaks (*Quercus* spp): unless stated, deciduous trees, some v large & long-lived; most evergreen spp good for hedging; many spp have typically round-lobed lvs; catkin fls; typical acorn frs.
Q. canariensis: moderately hardy; fast-growing, to 9×4.5m (30×15ft); narrow when young; semi-evergreen; boldly toothed lvs to 15cm (6in) long.
Q. cerris 'Variegata' **6** (variegated Turkey oak): moderately to v hardy; slower-growing than sp, to 6×3m (20×10ft); narrow when young; deeply lobed lvs to 12cm (5in) long, creamy-white edge.
Q. coccifera (kermes oak): moderately hardy; v slow-growing dense shrub to 1.5×1.5m (5×5ft); evergreen; glossy variable lvs, usually prickly.
Q. coccinea (scarlet oak): ultra-hardy; rounded & open, to 12×9m (40×30ft); deeply & sharply lobed lvs to 15cm (6in) long, brilliant scarlet in autumn (best in vars 'Splendens' **7** & 'Superba'). Hates lime.
Q. ilex (holm or evergreen oak): moderately hardy but best near sea; round-headed, handsome & spreading, to 6×6m (20×20ft) or good as hedge; leathery lvs to 10cm (4in) long, variable (young lvs often toothed like holly), woolly beneath.
Q. palustris (pin oak): v hardy; dense & pyramid-shaped, to 11×9m (36×30ft); slender drooping branches; deeply & sharply lobed shiny lvs to 12cm (5in) long, brilliant red in autumn. Hates lime.
Q. phillyreoides: moderately to v hardy; rounded shrub, to 3.5×3m (12×10ft), or small tree; evergreen; leathery oval lvs 5cm (2in) long, v small teeth.
Q. robur (*Q. pedunculata*, English oak): v hardy; v long-lived & spreading, to 20×15m (65×50ft)/50yrs, eventually to 30m (100ft); lvs 5–10cm (2–4in) long, round-lobed. Vars: 'Concordia' **8** (golden English oak; rounded & slow-growing, to 4.5×4.5m [15×15ft]; lvs golden-yellow); 'Fastigiata' (cypress oak; column-shaped, to 9×1.5m [30×5ft]).
Q. rubra 'Aurea' **9** (var of red oak): v hardy; rounded, to 9×9m (30×30ft); deeply & sharply lobed lvs to 20cm (8in) long, open yellow, red in autumn. Needs lime-free soil in shelter.
Q. suber **10** (cork oak): moderately hardy; round-headed, to 6×3.5m (20×12ft); thick bark (source of cork); evergreen; leathery oval lvs, toothed, to 6cm (2½in) long.

106

Azaras & idesia

Shrubs & trees grown for their foliage, small but fragrant flowers and berries. **Cultivation**: For any normal soil. **Propagation**: Seed; semi-ripe cuttings; *Idesia* sp also by root cuttings.

Azaras (*Azara* spp): S American evergreen shrubs or small trees with clusters of small fls with conspicuous yellow stamens, early spring, then berries. Generally semi-hardy & best grown against warm wall sheltered except in v mild climates; prune lightly if necessary in summer.
A. dentata* : to 3×2.5m (10×8ft); shiny lvs to 4cm (1½in) long, felted beneath.
A. lanceolata* **1**: usually elegant small tree, to 3.5×3m (12×10ft); lance-shaped bright green lvs to 6cm (2½in) long; berries white to mauve.
A. microphylla** **2**: moderately hardy; to 5×3m (16×10ft); sprays of v small lvs, variegated in var 'Variegata'; berries violet or red.

A. petiolaris* (*A. gilliesii*): to 3×2.5m (10×8ft); holly-like lvs 8cm (3in) long; showiest-fld sp.
A. serrata* : similar to (& confused with) *A. dentata*, but lvs not felted.
Idesia (*Idesia polycarpa** **3**): moderately to v hardy deciduous tree for streets, lawns, etc, rather like a small-lvd catalpa (p64); to 4.5–6× 3–4.5m (15–20×10–15ft); branches horizontal; dark green heart-shaped lvs, to 15×12cm (6×5in) or more, with attractive red stalks; tiny yellowish fls in 15cm (6in) panicles, summer; hanging bunches of red berries on females if male nearby (some trees bisexual). Pruning unnecessary. Var *vestita*; lvs felted beneath.

Shrubby hypericums

St John's worts; *Hypericum* spp; sometimes classified in Hypericaceae. Small shrubs often useful for ground cover, with profuse buttercup-like flowers with boss of stamens, mid summer to autumn. Unless stated, evergreen or semi-evergreen in mild winters. **Cultivation**: Easy, in any well-drained (even poor) soil, in sun or semi-shade; very hardy unless stated. Shorten old growth in early spring. **Propagation**: Seed; semi-ripe cuttings; *H. calycinum* by division. For rock garden shrublets, see p454.

H. balearicum* : semi-hardy; to 60×60cm (2×2ft); v small lvs; 4cm (1½in) yellow fls.
H. beanii (*H. patulum henryi*): vigorous, to 1.2×1.5m (4×5ft); arching; ovate 8cm (3in) lvs; bowl-shaped 5cm (2in) yellow fls. Var 'Gold Cup' has lance-shaped lvs (pale red in autumn) & golden-yellow cup-shaped fls 6cm (2½in) across.
H. bellum: to 60×90cm (2×3ft); dense; almost round 2.5cm (1in) lvs, colouring late summer; golden-yellow cup-shaped 4cm (1½in) fls.
H. calycinum **4** (Aaron's beard; in UK, rose of Sharon): vigorous ground cover, to 0.45×1.5m (1½×5ft) or wider; creeping & self-rooting; bright green lvs to 8cm (3in) long; bright yellow 8–10cm (3–4in) fls. Good under trees; cut back hard in spring every few yrs.
H. forrestii (*H. patulum forrestii*; sometimes sold incorrectly as *H. patulum henryi*): to 1.5×1.8m (5×6ft); lvs to 5cm (2in) long, almost (or sometimes fully) deciduous, orange & red in autumn; saucer-shaped 6cm (2½in) fls, golden-yellow; bronze-red frs.
H. frondosum (*H. aureum*): to 1×1m (3×3ft); rounded, often with tree-like trunk; deciduous; blue-green lvs to 8cm (3in) long; 2.5cm (1in) bright yellow fls.
H. 'Hidcote' **5** (*H. patulum* 'Hidcote'): hybrid possibly of *H. calycinum* & *H. forrestii*; compact, to 1.5×1.8m (5×6ft); dark green lance-shaped lvs; profuse golden-yellow saucer-shaped fls to

8cm (3in) wide. Young growth may be frost-damaged.
H.×inodorum (*H. elatum*): hybrid of *H. androsaemum* & *H. hircinium*; to 1.2×1.5m (4×5ft); arching; lvs* to 8cm (3in) long; yellow 2.5cm (1in) fls; red frs (brilliant salmon-red in var 'Elstead' **6**; prone to rust). Prune hard in spring.
H. kalmianum: ultra-hardy; to 1×1m (3×3ft); dense; narrow glaucous lvs to 5cm (2in) long; bright yellow 2cm (¾in) fls.
H. kouytchense (sometimes sold as *H. penduliflorum, H. patulum grandiflorum, H. patulum* 'Sungold'): to 1×1.2m (3×4ft); lax branches; lvs to 8cm (3in) long; pale golden-yellow 6cm (2½in) fls, bold stamens.
H.×moseranum: hybrid of *H. calycinum* & *H. patulum*; moderately hardy; low & spreading, to 0.75×1.2m (2½×4ft); arching shoots; lvs to 5cm (2in) long; golden yellow 5–6cm (2in) fls; good for ground cover. Var 'Tricolor' **7** is less vigorous & has smaller lvs, edged white & pink, & smaller fls.
H. 'Rowallane' **8**: hybrid of *H. hookerianum* 'Rogersii' & *H. leschenaultii*; moderately hardy; often best against warm wall; vigorous & graceful, to 2×2m (7×7ft); rich green lvs to 6cm (2½in) long; long-lasting bowl-shaped rich golden fls 5–8cm (2–3in) across. Regrows if cut down by frost.

The witch hazel family

Shrubs and trees with very early flowers (often scented) or brilliant autumn colours or both. Deciduous unless noted. **Cultivation**: Unless stated, very hardy. For rich, moist but well-drained soil, lime-free unless stated. Earliest spp best in some shelter. **Propagation**: Seed (stratify); semi-ripe cuttings; lax spp by layering; *Hamamelis* & *Parrotia* spp by grafting onto *Hamamelis virginiana*.

Winter hazels (*Corylopsis* spp): shrubs with small primrose-yellow fls in drooping racemes, generally early spring (before lvs); may be frost-damaged; lvs roundish to heart-shaped, to 10cm (4in) long, rather like hazel lvs (*Corylus* spp; p62). Most spp tolerate lime.

C. glabrescens*: spreading, to 3×2.5m (10×8ft); infls to 5cm (2in) long, mid spring; hardiest sp *C. gotoana* is same or similar.

C. pauciflora* **1**: dense & wide-spreading, to 1.5×1.8m (5×6ft); small lvs, pinkish when young; short infls of 2cm (¾in) fls. Hates lime; prefers shelter.

C. spicata*: spreading, to 1.8×1.8m (6×6ft); large glaucous lvs; infls to 8cm (3in) long.

C. willmottiae: upright, open & graceful, to 2.5×1.8m (8×6ft); lvs often purplish when young (plum-purple in var 'Spring Purple' **2**); dense infls to 8cm (3in) long.

Disanthus (*Disanthus cercidifolius*): shrub grown mainly for brilliant red to orange & purple autumn colours; best in deciduous woodland. To 2.5×1.8m (8×6ft); lvs roundish or heart-shaped, to 10cm (4in) long; v small purplish fls, autumn.

Fothergillas (*Fothergilla* spp): shrubs with early petal-less fls with prominent creamy-white stamens in bottlebrush-like spikes, before lvs; yellow to crimson autumn colours (best in full sun). For light peaty soil.

F. gardenii* (witch alder): to 1×1.2m (3×4ft); lvs to 6cm (2½in) long; infls to 4cm (1½in) long, mid spring.

F. major* **3** (*F. monticola*): to 1.8–3×2m (6–10×7ft); lvs to 10cm (4in) long, glossy; infls to 5cm (2in) long, late spring.

Witch hazels (*Hamamelis* spp): distinctive shrubs (sometimes small trees) with angular branches & spidery v narrow-petalled yellow or reddish fls, generally 2–3cm (¾–1¼in) across or more, mainly mid winter to early spring, before lvs (good for cutting); lvs hazel-like, generally 8–12cm (3–5in) long, yellow or red in autumn. For sun or light shade; tolerate some air pollution.

H.×intermedia vars (sometimes listed under *H. japonica*): hybrids of *H. japonica* & *H. mollis*; vigorous, to 2.5×2.5m (8×8ft); fl from late winter. Vars: 'Arnold Promise' (golden); 'Carmine Red' (large bronze fls, tipped red); 'Diane' (coppery-red); 'Hiltingbury' (copper tinted red); 'Jelena' **4** ('Copper Beauty'; clustered yellow fls tinted red); 'Magic Fire'* ('Feuerzauber'; copper-red); 'Moonlight'* (sulphur-yellow tinged red).

H. japonica (Japanese witch hazel): open & spreading, to 2.5×2.5m (8×8ft), or small tree; lvs yellow, often flushed red, in autumn; fls yellow, red centre, petals curled, mid–late winter. Vars: 'Arborea' (tall-growing); 'Flavopurpurascens' (petals suffused red); 'Zuccariniana' (fls lemon-yellow, late).

H. mollis** **5** (Chinese witch hazel): to 2.5×2.5m (8×8ft), or small tree; lvs yellow in autumn; clustered large golden fls, wide petals, from mid winter. Vars/hybrids: 'Brevipetala'** (small deep yellow fls, reddish centre); 'Goldcrest'** (fls deep yellow, suffused crimson at base; late); 'Pallida'** (fls sulphur-yellow).

H. vernalis** (Ozark witch hazel): erect suckering shrub, to 2×2m (7×7ft); lvs yellow in autumn; profuse small fls, yellow to reddish, from mid winter. Var 'Sandra' has pale yellow fls & young lvs purplish, brilliant orange & red in autumn.

Sweet gums (*Liquidambar* spp): handsome, rather maple-like trees, broadly column/pyramid-shaped, grown for foliage & autumn colour.

L. formosana (Formosan gum): moderately to v hardy; to 10×5m (33×16ft); 12cm (5in) 3/5-lobed lvs, hairy beneath, red-tinted when young & crimson in autumn.

L. styraciflua (common sweet gum): v hardy; to 10×5m (33×16ft); 15cm (6in) 5/7-lobed shiny lvs, brilliant orange, crimson & purple in autumn; fragrant resin. Vars: 'Aurea' **6** (lvs marked yellow); 'Golden Treasure' (lvs edged yellow); 'Variegata' (lvs edged cream, later flushed pink).

Loropetalum (*Loropetalum chinense* **7**): semi-to moderately hardy bushy shrub, to 2×2m (7×7ft); evergreen; oval lvs 5cm (2in) long; white fls v like witch hazel, late winter or early spring.

Parrotia (*Parrotia persica* **8**): spreading, slow-growing tree, to 4.5×7.5m (15×25ft), with short trunk, or large spreading, suckering shrub; flaking mature bark; lvs to 10cm (4in) long, beautiful yellow to scarlet in autumn; petal-less fls, red stamens, early spring (before lvs). Tolerates some lime. Var 'Pendula' has pendulous branches, forming domed mound.

Parrotiopsis (*Parrotiopsis* [*Parrotia*] *jacquemontiana*): moderately hardy small tree, to 3×2.5m (10×8ft), or shrub; rounded, toothed 8cm (3in) lvs, yellow in autumn; petal-less fls, yellow stamens & white bracts, spring & summer.

Sycopsis (*Sycopsis sinensis*): shrub, to 3×2m (10×7ft), or small tree; evergreen; leathery lance-shaped lvs to 10cm (4in) long; petal-less fls, yellow & red stamens, brown bracts, spring.

Horse chestnuts and buckeyes

Aesculus spp. Vigorous round-headed deciduous trees (sometimes large shrubs) mostly too large for small gardens. Compound palmate leaves, usually of 5–7 often lance-shaped leaflets to 15–30cm (6–12in) long. Candle-like upright panicles of flowers, mainly late spring or early summer. Smooth, warty or spiny fruits containing 1 or more large nuts (often poisonous). **Cultivation**: Easy, in any soil; generally very to ultra-hardy. **Propagation**: Seed; vars by grafting.

A. californica * **1** (Californian horse chestnut or buckeye): moderately to v hardy; to 4.5×4.5m (15×15ft); lfts narrow & pointed; 15–20cm (6–8in) infls of white or pink-tinged fls; large rough frs.

A.×carnea (red horse chestnut): hybrid of *A. hippocastanum* & *A. pavia*; to 7.5×7.5m (25×25ft); 15–20cm (6–8in) infls of rose-red fls (deeper in var 'Briottii' **2**); spiny frs; prone to canker.

A. flava (*A. octandra*, sweet or yellow buckeye): to 7.5×6m (25×20ft); 10–15cm (4–6in) infls of yellow fls; smooth frs.

A. glabra (Ohio buckeye): to 6×6m (20×20ft); lvs orange in autumn; 10–15cm (4–6in) infls of greenish-yellow fls; frs spiny.

A. hippocastanum (common horse chestnut of Europe): fast-growing, to 12×10m (40×33ft); infls to 30cm (12in) tall of white fls marked red & yellow; large warty or spiny frs. Var 'Baumanii' ('Flore Pleno') has double fls & no frs.

A. indica (Indian horse chestnut): moderately to v hardy, but young growth tender; to 9×7.5m (30×25ft); pointed glossy lfts; 15–40cm (6–16in) infls of pink-flushed white fls; rough frs. Var 'Sydney Pierce' is v free-flg.

A. neglecta (*A. sylvatica*) 'Erythroblastos' (sunrise horse chestnut): slow-growing, to 6×6m (20×20ft); lfts open shrimp-pink, turn yellow-green, then orange & yellow in autumn; infls to 15cm (6in) long of pale yellow fls; late frosts may damage lfts.

A. parviflora **3** (small-flowered or bottlebrush buckeye): shrub, to 3.5×3.5m (12×12ft), or small tree; lfts downy beneath; 20–30cm (8–12in) infls of white fls, red stamens, mid summer; frs only in long hot summers.

A. pavia (red buckeye): shrub, to 3×2.5m (10×8ft), or small tree; 15–25cm (6–10in) infls of crimson fls (deeper red in var 'Atrosanguinea'); smooth frs. *A. discolor* (*A. pavia* 'Discolor'; red & yellow fls) & *A. d.* 'Mollis' (*A. pavia* 'Mollis'; red fls) are same or similar, but have lfts downy beneath.

Hickories, walnuts and wingnuts

Deciduous trees, often large (especially in continental climates), grown for autumn colour & nuts (most edible). Long pinnate leaves; flowers generally catkins. **Cultivation**: Generally very hardy. For any preferably deep soil. Often difficult to transplant. Prone to various insect pests. **Propagation**: Seed (stratify); grafting.

Hickories (*Carya* spp.): large, stately, rather slender trees with rounded head; lvs generally of 5–9 lfts, each 5–20cm (2–8in) long, yellow to golden-brown in autumn; catkins insignificant. Nuts usually edible.

C. cordiformis **4** (bitternut, swamp hickory): to 7.5×5.5m (25×18ft); yellow winter buds; lvs 25cm (10in) long; bitter grey nuts.

C. glabra (pignut): to 7.5×5.5m (25×18ft); lvs 20–30cm (8–12in) long; bitter nuts.

C. illinoinensis (pecan): to 9×6m (30×20ft); 30–45cm (12–18in) lvs of 11–17 lfts; smooth light brown edible nuts. Best if summers hot.

C. laciniosa (shellbark hickory): to 9×6m (30×20ft); shaggy bark; lvs 30–50cm (12–20in) long; yellow or reddish ridged nuts.

C. ovata **5** (shagbark hickory): to 9×5.5m (30×18ft); flaking, shaggy bark; lvs 20–35cm (8–14in) long; white to dark brown nuts.

C. tomentosa (mockernut, big-bud hickory): to 9×6m (30×20ft); large winter buds; lvs* 20–50cm (8–20in) long; light brown nuts.

Walnuts (*Juglans* spp.): mostly fast-growing trees with large aromatic lvs usually of 11–19 lfts, each to 12–20cm (5–8in) long; long catkins; ridged edible nuts.

J. cinerea (butternut): ultra-hardy; to 7.5×7.5m (25×25ft); hairy lvs* 25–50cm (10–20in) long; v large nuts.

J. nigra (black walnut): v fast-growing in hot climates, to 12×6m (40×30ft); lvs* 30–60cm (1–2ft) long, 15–23 glossy lfts.

J. regia **6** (common, English or Persian walnut): moderately to v hardy; to 7.5×6m (25×20ft); lvs* 20–45cm (8–18in) long, lfts leathery.

Caucasian wingnut (*Pterocarya fraxinifolia* **7**, *P. caucasica*): fast-growing spreading tree, to 10×9m (33×30ft), similar to walnuts but with decorative small winged frs clustered along drooping branchlets; 30–60cm (1–2ft) lvs with 7–27 shiny lfts to 20cm (8in) long; female catkins to 50cm (20in) long. Likes moist soil.

1

2

3

3

3

4

6

5

6

7

Lavender, rosemary, sage and their relatives

Generally quite small shrubs, often aromatic &/or rather soft stemmed, evergreen unless stated. Characteristic 2-lipped flowers, generally small, in spikes or leafy racemes. Most best in mixed borders. **Cultivation**: Unless noted, moderately hardy. Best in light, well-drained (even poor) soil in warm sunny spot. Trim after flowering; if necessary, remove frost-damaged wood in spring. **Propagation**: Semi-ripe cuttings; seed; clump-forming spp by division; *Lavandula* vars best by hardwood cuttings. For sub-shrubby perennial spp, see p294.

Colquhounia (*Colquhounia coccinea* **1**): lax & rather straggly, to 2.5–3×1.8–2.5m (8–10×6–8ft); downy shoots; v variable downy lvs*, 5–20×2.5–12cm (2–8×1–5in), grey felt beneath; slender spikes to 30cm (1ft) long of funnel-shaped orange-red fls 2.5cm (1in) long, late summer & autumn.

Lavenders (*Lavandula* spp): favourite aromatic dwarf shrubs with fragrant lvs & fls; lvs v narrow, grey-green; fls grey-blue to almost purple, generally in spikes on slender stems, summer. Good for ground cover or as low hedge, but not long-lived. Trim after flg; cut back straggly plants hard in spring.
*L. angustifolia*** (*L. officinalis, L. spica,* English or common lavender): v hardy; to 0.6–1×1–1.2m (2–3×3–4ft); lvs* to 4cm (1½in) long; fls in dense spikes. Vars (generally hybrids with *L. latifolia*): 'Alba'** (robust; pinkish-white); 'Grappenhall'** (vigorous; lavender-blue); 'Hidcote'** **2** (compact; violet-purple); 'Munstead'** **3** (compact; green lvs*; bluish-purple fls); 'Nana Alba'** (to 30cm [1ft]; white); 'Vera'** (Dutch lavender; often sold incorrectly as *L. vera;* robust; latish-flg).
*L. lanata*** : to 60×90cm (2×3ft); similar to above but shoots & lvs white-woolly; lvs* to 5cm (2in) long.
*L. stoechas*** **4** (French lavender): to 60–90×60–90cm (2–3×2–3ft); grey-downy; lvs* to 3cm (1¼in) long; deep purple fls in dense spikes topped by leaf-like purple bracts, from late spring.

Lion's ear (lion's tail, *Leonotis leonurus* **5**): semi-to moderately hardy S African shrub; erect, to 1.8×1.5m (6×5ft); square grey-woolly stems; coarsely toothed lance-shaped lvs to 10cm (4in) long; crowded whorls of tubular orange to near-red fls to 6cm (2½in) long, autumn. Pinch out &/or prune after flg to promote bushiness.

Phlomis (*Phlomis* spp): rather coarse low-growing hairy shrubs with wrinkled lvs & fls in whorls up leafy stems in summer.
P. fruticosa **6** (Jerusalem sage): to 1.2×1m (4×3ft); dull green lvs to 12×4.5cm (5×1¾in), grey-hairy; 5cm (2in) whorls of yellow fls.
P. chrysophylla is similar, with yellow-tinged lvs*.

Mint bush (*Prostanthera rotundifolia* **7**): semi-to moderately hardy Australian shrub; dense & bushy, to 1.5×1.5m (5×5ft); young branchlets v slender, with grey down; tiny dark green rounded lvs* to 8mm (⅓in) long; profuse

clusters of small, rather bell-shaped deep lilac to blue-purple fls, spring. Dislikes shallow chalk soils. *P. ovalifolia* is elegant, with drooping branches & olive-green lvs*.

Rosemary (*Rosmarinus officinalis*): moderately to v hardy bushy shrub; generally to 2×2m (7×7ft); may form short rugged trunk when old; young shoots downy; v narrow lvs* to 5cm (2in) long, white-felted beneath, all along shoots; small clusters of generally lilac-blue fls, late spring, on yr-old wood. Good for hedging, dwarf vars for ground cover. Tolerates drought. Vars: 'Benenden Blue' **8** ('Collingwood Ingram'; low-growing, to 0.75×1.2m [2½×4ft]; fls bright blue); 'Miss Jessup's Upright' ('Fastigiatus'; erect & v vigorous; deep bluish-green lvs*; pale mauve fls); 'Prostratus' (often sold, probably incorrectly, as *R. lavandulaceus*; semi-hardy; dense & mat-forming, to 1.8×3m [6×10ft]; fresh green lvs*; lavender-blue fls; good draping dry wall); 'Severn Sea' (semi-hardy; low & spreading, to 1×1.8m [3×6ft], with arching branches; bright blue fls); 'Tuscan Blue' (semi-hardy; erect; light green lvs*; clear blue fls).

Sages (*Salvia* spp): rather sub-shrubby aromatic plants with fls in whorls or clusters up square stems, from early summer.
S. microphylla (*S. grahamii*): to 1.2×1.2m (4×4ft); young shoots slender & soft, reddish; lvs* to 4–8cm (1½–3in) long, downy; red fls 2.5cm (1in) fading magenta-purple. Var *neurepia* **9** (*S. neurepia*) has larger, light green thin lvs* & bright red fls.
S. officinalis (common sage): ultra-hardy in warm dry spot; to 0.6×1.5m (2×5ft), sometimes more; young shoots semi-woody, grey-downy; semi-evergreen wrinkled grey-green lvs* to 8×2.5cm (3×1in), downy; bluish-purple fls 2cm (¾in) long. Ancient culinary & medicinal herb. Vars: 'Icterina' **10** ('Variegata'; lvs* variegated gold); 'Purpurascens' **11** (purple/red-leaved sage; young shoots & lvs* purplish); 'Tricolor' **12** (lvs* variegated yellowish-white & tinted pink/purple when mature).

Shrubby germander (*Teucrium fruticans*): tender; loose & open, to 1.5×1.2m (5×4ft) or more; shoots white-felted; bright green lvs* to 4cm (1½in) long, white felt beneath; unusual lavender to purple prominently lipped fls in upper lf axils, summer. Var 'Azureum' has darker blue fls; semi-hardy.

The laurel family

Often aromatic trees & shrubs, evergreen unless noted, grown mainly for their foliage. Flowers generally greenish or yellowish & insignificant. **Cultivation**: Unless stated, for any well-drained fertile soil in sunny position. **Propagation**: Seed; semi-ripe cuttings; suckers where produced.

Camphor tree (*Cinnamomum camphora* **1**): semi-hardy handsome spreading tree, to 5.5×3.5m (18×12ft) where summers hot, often only shrubby elsewhere; roots invasive; slender-pointed dark green leathery lvs* to 15×8cm (6×3in).

Sweet bay (true or bay laurel, *Laurus nobilis* **2**): moderately hardy dense pyramid-shaped shrub, to 3.5×1.8m (12×6ft), eventually a tree, to 9m (30ft) or more, but can be clipped to almost any shape or size; sometimes suckering; firm dark green lance-shaped variable lvs* to 4–10×½–4cm (1½–4×½–1½in), used as culinary herb; shiny black frs on females. Trained specimens often grown in tubs in formal settings. Vars: *angustifolia* **3** (willow-leaved bay; narrowly lance-shaped lvs); 'Aurea' **4** (lvs golden-yellow). *L. azorica* (*L. canariensis*, Azores or Canary Island bay) is similar but semi-hardy; lvs* to 12×8cm (5×3in).

Linderas (*Lindera* spp): deciduous spp colour well in autumn; fls in dense clusters, spring; attractive frs on females if male nearby. Like moist lime-free soil.

L. benzoin (*Benzoin aestivale*, spice bush): v hardy spicily aromatic rounded shrub, to 3×1.8m (10×6ft); deciduous lvs* to 12×6cm (5×2½in), yellow in autumn; small red frs.

L. obtusiloba **5** (sometimes grown incorrectly as *L. triloba*): v hardy shrub, to 2.5×1.8m (8×6ft), or small tree; deciduous dark shiny green 3-lobed lvs to 12×10cm (5×4in), butter-yellow in autumn; mustard-yellow fls before lvs; small red frs. *L. cercidifolia* is similar but lvs rarely lobed.

Sassafras (*Sassafras albidum* **6**): v hardy broadly conical tree, to 7.5×3.5m (25×12ft)/25yrs, often only shrubby in cool climates; sparsely branched but handsome, with variable, often lobed deciduous lvs* 8–18×5–10cm (3–7×2–4in), glossy dark green, paler beneath, sometimes orange & scarlet in autumn. May grow suckers. Needs well-drained lime-free soil.

California laurel (California bay, *Umbellularia californica* **7**): moderately to v hardy dense round-headed tree, to 7.5×7.5m (25×25ft) or more, but often only a shrub in cool climates; bright glossy green lance-shaped lvs* to 12cm (5in) long; frs ripen purple. Tolerates shade.

Brooms

Generally deciduous sun-loving shrubs, sometimes almost leafless but with green stems, grown for their graceful form &/or profuse, generally yellow pea flowers (with erect "standard" petal, 2 "wing" petals & 2 lower petals united into pouch or "keel"). Unless stated, leaves/leaflets, to 1–2cm (½–¾in) long, flowers 8–15mm (⅓–⅝in) long. Taller spp & vars good as specimens or in groups, against walls or in mixed plantings; smaller for rock gardens, dry walls, banks & general ground cover. Seed pods best removed (may be poisonous). **Cultivation**: Very hardy unless stated. Best in light, not too fertile soil in sun; most spp tolerate some lime; tolerate wind & drought. Transplant poorly from open ground. Unless stated, prune young & mature plants after flowering to maintain bushiness. **Propagation**: Seed; semi-ripe heel cuttings.

Cytisus (brooms, *Cytisus* spp): include best-known garden spp & vars, & all those with red fls; thornless; lvs trifoliolate unless noted.
SPECIES & BOTANICAL HYBRIDS:
C. albus: see *C. multiflorus*.
C. ardoinii **8**: decumbent & mat-forming, to 15×40cm (6×16in); v small hairy lfts; profuse bright yellow fls, spring.
*C. battandieri** **9**: moderately to v hardy; erect but somewhat lax, to 3.5×3.5m (12×12ft); young shoots silky-downy; grey silky-hairy lfts to 8cm (3in) long; golden-yellow pineapple-scented fls in 12cm (5in) racemes, early summer. Good against wall. Cut back v old shoots hard after flg.
C.×beanii: hybrid of *C. ardoinii* & *C. purgans*; semi-prostrate, to 0.45×1m (1½×3ft); solitary

narrow lfts; v profuse golden-yellow fls, late spring, in sprays to 30cm (1ft) long.
*C. (Genista) canariensis** (florists' genista): semi-hardy; dense & much-branched, to 2.5×1.8m (8×6ft) in warm areas; evergreen; dense racemes of bright yellow fls, spring & early summer. Often grown in pots under glass.
C. decumbens: v prostrate, to 15×30cm (6×12in); solitary lfts; rich yellow fls, late spring & early summer.
C.×kewensis **10**: hybrid of *C. ardoinii* & *C. multiflorus*; moderately to v hardy; trailing, to 0.3×1.2m (1×4ft) or wider; narrow lfts; profuse creamy-yellow fls, late spring.
C. multiflorus (white Spanish broom; often listed incorrectly as *C. albus*): upright, to 1.8–3×1.8–

3m (6–10×6–10ft); arching branches; slender, little-branched branchlets; narrow downy lfts; profuse small white fls, late spring. Dislikes lime.

C. nigricans: upright, to 1.5×1m (5×3ft); downy shoots; lfts to 2.5cm (1in) long; erect racemes to 30cm (1ft) long of yellow fls, mid–late summer, on new wood. Prune spring; dead-head.

C.×praecox (Warminster broom; original hybrid correctly *C.×p.* 'Warminster'): hybrid of *C. multiflorus* & *C. purgans*; to 1.8×1.8m (6×6ft) or more; densely branched & arching; stems green; usually solitary downy lfts (soon drop); v profuse creamy-yellow fls, heavy unpleasant scent, late spring. Good for massing, hedge, path edging, etc. Other vars: 'Albus' **1** (white); 'Allgold' **2** (deep yellow); 'Gold Spear' (to 1m [3ft]; golden).

*C. purgans** (Provence broom): bushy & mounding, to 1×1m (3×3ft); green stems; usually solitary lfts (soon drop); chrome-yellow fls, mid–late spring. Needs full sun.

C. purpureus **3** (purple broom): semi-prostrate, to 0.45×1.2m (1½×4ft); dark green lfts to 2.5cm (1in) long; abundant 2cm (¾in) lilac-purple fls, late sprng & early summer. Good ground cover. Vars: 'Albus' (white); 'Atropurpureus' (purple).

C. (*Genista*)×*racemosus* (often sold incorrectly as *C.* [*G.*] *fragrans*; correctly, *C.×spachianus*): hybrid probably of *C. canariensis* & *C. stenopetalus*; semi- to moderately hardy; to 1.8–3×1.5–2m (6–10×5–7ft); v leafy & luxuriant; dark green evergreen lfts, silvery beneath; 5–15cm (2–6in) racemes of rich yellow fls, from mid winter in mild areas or under glass.

C. scoparius (common broom; in US, Scotch broom): erect, to 2.5×2.5m (8×8ft) or more; angled green branchlets; rich golden-yellow 2.5cm (1in) fls, late spring & early summer. May naturalize & become weedy. Vars: 'Andreanus' (wing petals brownish-crimson; standard yellow marked brownish-crimson); 'Cornish Cream' **4** (cream & yellow); 'Firefly' (standard yellow; wings yellow stained bronze); 'Golden Sunlight' (vigorous; rich yellow); *prostratus* (prostrate, to 1.8×1.8cm [6×6ft]; yellow); *sulphureus* (sulphur-yellow; 'Moonlight' is selected form). GARDEN HYBRIDS: derived from various spp & hybrids, including *C. ardoinii*, *C.×beanii*, *C.×dallimorei* (hybrid of *C. scoparius* 'Andreanus' & *C. multiflorus*), *C.×praecox* & *C. scoparius*; unless noted, to 1.5–2.5×1.5–2.5m (5–8×5–8ft). Vars: 'Burkwoodii' (cerise, wings crimson edged yellow); 'Donard Seedling' (pale yellow, standard pinkish-mauve, wings flushed red); 'Dorothy Walpole' (dark cerise & crimson); 'Goldfinch' **5** (crimson & yellow, wings pink & yellow); 'Hollandia' **6** (pale cream & cerise); 'Johnson's Crimson' (graceful; clear crimson); 'Killiney Red' (dwarf, compact, to 1–1.2×1–1.2m [3–4×3–4ft]; bright red); 'Lady

Moore' (creamy-yellow, standard flushed rose, wings flushed flame-red); 'Lord Lambourne' (pale cream, wings red); 'Minstead' (white flushed lilac-purple); 'Porlock'** (hybrid of *C. monsplessulanus* & *C.×racemosus*; moderately hardy; semi-evergreen; golden-yellow); 'San Francisco' (yellow, pinkish-red & orange-red); 'Windlesham Ruby' **7** (mahogany-crimson); 'Zeelandia' (cream & lilac, wings pinkish).

Genistas (brooms, *Genista* spp): similar to *Cytisus* spp but fls always yellow or cream; some spp spiny; lvs simple, generally narrow, sparse.

*G. aetnensis** **8** (Mount Etna broom): tall & elegant, to 4.5×4.5m (15×15ft) or more, becoming tree-like; slender green branches, drooping when young; almost leafless; profuse golden-yellow fls, mid summer, on new wood.

G. hispanica **9** (Spanish gorse, Spanish broom): moderately to v hardy; dense & mounding, to 0.6×1.5m (2×5ft); tangled spiny green branches; v small lvs only on flg twigs; v profuse clusters of rich golden-yellow small fls, late spring & early summer.

G. lydia **10**: lax & arching, to 0.6×1.8m (2×6ft); angled green shoots; small lvs; profuse bright yellow fls, late spring & early summer. V hardy.

G. pilosa: more or less prostrate, to 45×90cm (1½×3ft); tangled twiggy shoots; abundant bright yellow fls in racemes to 15cm (6in) long, early summer.

G. sagittalis **11**: prostrate, with erect side-shoots, to 20×90cm (8×3ft); slender green stems, prominent wings; few lvs; small dense racemes of yellow fls, early summer.

G. sylvestris (*G. dalmatica*, Dalmatian broom): dwarf & tufted, to 15×30cm (6×12in); thin spiny green branches; small lvs; small golden-yellow fls in dense clusters, early summer.

*G. tenera** (*G. virgata*, Madeira broom): moderately to v hardy; bushy, to 3×3m (10×10ft); grey-green lvs, silky-hairy beneath; abundant bright yellow fls, early–mid summer. Var 'Golden Shower'* (often grown incorrectly as *G. cinerea*) is sterile form with drooping branches. True *G. cinerea* is similar but lvs smaller.

G. tinctoria (dyer's greenweed): ultra-hardy; variable, to 0.15–0.6×1.2m (6–24in×4ft); semi-prostrate or erect; narrow lance-shaped lvs to 2.5cm (1in) long; bright yellow fls, all summer. Var 'Plena' is semi-prostrate, double.

Spanish broom (*Spartium junceum** **12**): moderately hardy, often rather gaunt shrub, to 3×2.5m (10×8ft); green rush-like stems; almost leafless; loose 30–45cm (1–1½ft) racemes of rich yellow 2.5cm (1in) fls, all summer, on new wood. All parts poisonous. Good in hot, dry spots or near sea. Best pruned gently late autumn or early spring to keep bushy.

Other trees and shrubs of the pea family

Large family of sun-lovers grown for their attractive, often frond-like foliage & showy flowers. Many are fast-growing but short-lived; some are mainstays of plantings in dry areas because they tolerate drought & poor soil. Leaves finely divided & deciduous unless stated; sometimes in 3s. Nearly all have typical pea flowers (erect "standard" petal, 2 "wing" petals, 2 lower petals united into a pouch or "keel"), usually in racemes. Seed pods often very long, sometimes inflated & often attractive. **Cultivation**: Unless stated, for warm, well-drained, dryish soil in full sun. **Propagation**: Unless stated, seed (scarify and/or soak in hot water); vars by budding. For *Wisteria* spp (trainable as free-standing trees), see p232.

Wattles (*Acacia* spp; sometimes listed incorrectly as *Mimosa* spp): beautiful yellow-fld mainly Australian trees & shrubs for warm climates. Generally semi-hardy; evergreen; adult lvs often reduced to lf-like phyllodes; long-stamened fls clustered into small ball-like heads to 1cm (⅜in) across or small "bottle-brushes", spring unless stated. Generally fast-growing but rather short-lived; good for screening or hedging in warm climates, as wall shrubs in cool regions. For acid soils unless stated; prune as necessary after flg; prone to mimosa webworm in warm climates. Can be propagated by semi-ripe cuttings over heat.

A. armata **1** (kangaroo thorn): dense, twiggy shrub, to 3.5×3.5m (12×12ft) or more; spiny; dark green phyllodes; fl heads solitary or paired; frs silky. Formidable hedging shrub.

A. baileyana (Cootamundra wattle): graceful tree, fast-growing in good soil to 6×4.5m (20×15ft); drooping branches; bipinnate glaucous lvs; profuse fl heads in racemes to 10cm (4in) long, late winter to spring. Handsome but short-lived. Var 'Purpurea' has purple-tinged lvs.

A. dealbata** **2** (*A. decurrens dealbata*, silver wattle, florists' mimosa): best-known sp; semi- to moderately hardy fast-growing tree, to 9×6m (30×20ft); grey bark; bipinnate silvery-green, downy lvs; profuse fl heads in panicles to 10cm (4in) long, late winter to spring.

A. (M.) longifolia **3** (Sydney golden wattle): fast-growing shrub or tree, to 7.5×6m (25×20ft); willow-like leathery phyllodes to 15cm (6in) long; fls in erect racemes to 8cm (3in) long. Lime-tolerant. Var *floribunda* has v narrow phyllodes & profuse fls. *A. mucronata* is similar but somewhat hardier; phyllodes v narrow.

A. melanoxylon (blackwood): semi- to moderately hardy tree, to 12×4.5m (40×15ft); phyllodes curved; fl heads in small clusters.

A. podalyriifolia* (Queensland silver wattle): shrub, to 4.5×3m (15×10ft); young shoots downy; stems & phyllodes silvery-grey; fl heads in long racemes, late winter to early spring.

A. riceana (Rice's wattle): graceful weeping tree, to 7.5×5.5m (25×18ft); narrow dark green phyllodes; slender drooping spikes of yellow fls.

A. (M.) verticillata **4** (prickly Moses): dense shrub, to 6 × 5.5m (20×18ft); phyllodes prickly, in whorls; fls massed in "bottle-brushes" to 2.5cm (1in) long. Good for hedging.

Adenocarpus (*Adenocarpus decorticans* **5**): moderately hardy shrub, to 3×2.5m (10×8ft); small narrow lvs in 3s; gorse-like golden-yellow fls along branches, early summer. Short-lived.

Silk tree (pink siris tree, *Albizia* [*Acacia*; incorrectly, *Albizzia*] *julibrissin*): spreading acacia-like tree or large shrub, to 6×6m (20×20ft); moderately hardy if wood well ripened or if against warm wall; bipinnate feathery lvs (fold at night); long-stamened pink fls (brightest in var 'Rosea' **6**), clustered like bottle-brushes to 5cm (2in) across, mid summer. Blooms young. Prone to mimosa wilt in warm climates.

Anthyllis (*Anthyllis hermanniae* **7**): moderately hardy dwarf shrub, to 60×90cm (2×3ft); branches spine-tipped; narrow hairy lvs; clusters of small yellow & orange fls, early summer. Propagate by semi-ripe cuttings.

Bauhinias (orchid trees, *Bauhinia* spp): tender vigorous trees or shrubs with 2-lobed evergreen lvs; often v showy orchid-like 5-petalled fls to 12cm (5in) across. Propagate by seed, suckers, semi-ripe cuttings over heat.

B. blakeana (Hong Kong orchid tree): to 6×4.5m (20×15ft); fls rosy-purple to crimson, all winter; flat frs (sterile).

B. purpurea (butterfly tree): v fast-growing, to 9×6m (30×20ft); fls white to deep purple, autumn. *B. variegata* is similar but winter-flg; best-known sp; semi-hardy where summers hot.

Brachysema (scimitar shrub, Swan River pea shrub, *Brachysema lanceolatum*): tender spreading shrub, to 1×1m (3×3ft); narrow evergreen lvs, silver beneath; red pea fls, long curved keel petals, all year. For poor, dry soil.

Caesalpinias (*Caesalpinia* [*Poinciana*] spp): fast-growing scrambling shrubs (or small trees), best grown on walls; prickly bipinnate lvs; v showy 5-petalled fls, prominent red stamens to 8cm (3in) long, in erect racemes to 30cm (1ft) long, summer.

C. (P.) gilliesii **8** (bird of paradise shrub): semi- to moderately hardy; to 9m (30ft) on wall; fls yellow.

C. japonica (*C. sepiaria japonica*): moderately hardy; to 3×4.5m (10×15ft), taller on wall; v thorny; fls canary-yellow, upper petal striped red.

Powder-puffs (*Calliandra* spp): tender evergreen shrubs with fls in globular heads of prominent stamens like powder-puffs.

C. haematocephala **1** (*C. inaequilatera*, red powder-puff): to 3×3m (10×10ft); fast-growing; young lvs copper-tinted; red to watermelon-pink fl heads to 8cm (3in) across, winter to spring.
C. tweedii (flame bush): to 2.5×2.5m (8×8ft); ferny lvs; fls yellow, red stamens, late winter to autumn. Root is semi-hardy.

Pea trees & pea shrubs (*Caragana* spp): attractive ultra-hardy central Asian shrubs; usually spiny (especially in dry climates); pinnate lvs; yellow pea fls, spring & early summer. Best in sandy soil.
C. arborescens (Siberian pea tree): vigorous & erect, to 6×2.5m (20×8ft). Best-known sp; good as windbreak, hedge in exposed sites. Vars: 'Lorbergii' **2** (lvs grass-like; fls less showy); 'Nana' (dwarf); 'Pendula' (branches droop stiffly).
C. frutex (Russian pea shrub): to 3×1.8m (10×6ft); twiggy & spineless.
C. maximowicziana: dense & spreading, to 1.8×2.5m (6×8ft) or wider; bright green lvs.
C. microphylla: similar to *C. arborescens* but spreading, to 2.5×3m (8×10ft); lfts v small.
C. pygmaea: to 1.2×1.5m (4×5ft); slender shoots; hanging fls. Best from semi-ripe cuttings.

Carmichaelias (*Carmichaelia* spp): moderately hardy New Zealand shrubs; generally leafless but stems flattened. (Other spp semi-hardy.)
C. enysii: hummock-forming, to 25×30cm (10×12in); violet fls, summer. For rock gardens.
C. petriei*: erect, to 1.8×1.5m (6×5ft); thick stems; violet-purple fls, early summer.

Sennas (*Cassia* spp): good wall shrubs or trees, spp listed semi-hardy; evergreen pinnate lvs; clustered saucer-shaped yellow fls to 2.5cm (1in) across or more, prominent stamens. Spur prune hard after flg; raise from semi-ripe cuttings.
C. corymbosa **3**: to 2.5×3m (8×10ft); pale yellow fls, spring to autumn in warm sunny areas.
C. obtusa **4** (correctly, *C. candolleana*; often incorrectly sold as *C. corymbosa*): to 3×4.5m (10×15ft); lfts rounded at tips; golden-yellow fls, late summer to autumn.

Carob (St John's bread, locust bean, *Ceratonia siliqua* **5**): tender to semi-hardy drought-tolerant evergreen tree, to 6–9×4.5–6m (20–30×15–20ft); dense; lfts rounded, to 10cm (4in) long; small red fls, spring; brown leathery frs to 30cm (1ft) long on females. Does not transplant well.

Cercis (redbuds, *Cercis* spp): beautiful & distinctive early-flg small trees or spreading shrubs. Moderately hardy unless noted; broad, prominently veined lvs 8–12cm (3–5in) long, often pointed, yellow in autumn; showy, usually clustered fls on naked twigs (young or old wood, even on trunk), spring. Like sandy loam; dislike transplanting; prone to coral spot.
C. canadensis **6** ([eastern] redbud): v hardy; to 9×6m (30×20ft); heart-shaped bright green lvs; fls rose-pink, profuse in warm climates, edible.

Vars: 'Alba' ('White Texas'; white); 'Forest Pansy' (purple lvs, especially when young); 'Oklahoma' (deep red); 'Plena' ('Flame'; double).
C. chinensis (Chinese redbud): shrub, to 3.5×2.5m (12×8ft), or small tree; heart-shaped glossy bright green lvs; fls deep rose. Needs hot summers.
C. siliquastrum **7** (Judas tree): moderately to v shrub, to 4.5×3m (15×10ft), or small tree; vivid green heart-shaped & rounded lvs; fls rose to magenta; wide frs. Drought-tolerant; needs warm summers but winter cold to fl well.
C. racemosa: to 9×6m (30×20ft); heart-shaped lvs, downy when young; fls rose-pink, in drooping racemes to 10cm (4in) long, on mature trees.
C. siliquastrum **7** (Judas tree): moderately to v hardy; to 7.5×6m (25×20ft); flat-topped; distinctive, nearly round glaucous lvs; profuse lavender-pink fls (edible); green/purplish frs to 12cm (5in) long. Vars: 'Alba' (white); 'Bodnant' (deep purple).

Chordospartium (*Chordospartium stevensonii*): rare but striking semi- to moderately hardy shrub or tree, to 4.5×3.5m (15×12ft); branches pendent, almost leafless; lilac fls from woolly buds, early summer, in 8cm (3in) long racemes.

Flame pea (*Chorizema cordatum*): tender to semi-hardy evergreen Australian shrub, to 1.5×1.5m (5×5ft); prickly, dark green lvs; fls orange-red flushed purple, in 15cm (6in) racemes, late winter or spring. For ground cover cut back after flg.

Yellowwood (virgilia, *Cladrastis lutea** **8**, *C. tinctoria*): ultra-hardy tree, to 9×9m (30×30ft); slow-growing & spreading; silvery-grey bark; handsome foliage with up to 11 broad lfts (yellow & orange in autumn); wisteria-like drooping panicles to 25cm (10in) long of white pea fls, early summer, on mature trees (sometimes sparse). Can be propagated by root cuttings.

Sturt's desert pea (glory pea, *Clianthus speciosus* **9**, *C. dampieri*; correctly, *C. formosus*): tender evergreen shrub, to 1.2×1.2m (4×4ft); silver-haired; lvs with many 2.5cm (1in) lfts; clusters of spectacular claw-shaped fls to 8cm (3in) long, red blotched purple, early summer. Difficult; short-lived.

Bladder senna (*Colutea arborescens*): v hardy, rather untidy shrub, to 1.8×2.5m (6×8ft); open habit; light green lvs; yellow fls marked red, all summer, on new wood; bladder-like red or coppery frs to 8cm (3in) long, becoming papery by autumn (burst loudly when squeezed). Self-seeds; best pruned quite hard in winter.

Coronillas (*Coronilla* spp): shrubs, to 3×2.5m (10×8ft); yellow fls in umbels, spring–autumn. Easy. Propagate by softwood or semi-ripe cuttings.

C. emerus **1** (scorpion senna): v hardy; pinnate grey-green lvs; fls marked reddish-brown, clawed petals; frs slim, jointed like scorpion's tail.
C. glauca* (*C. valentina glauca*): moderately hardy evergreen; v glaucous lvs; fls profuse. Var 'Variegata' is variegated cream. *C. valentina** is similar but smaller.

Rattlebox (canary-bird bush, *Crotalaria agatiflora* **2**): tender to semi-hardy evergreen shrub, fast-growing to 3×3m (10×10ft); grey-green lvs; showy greenish-yellow fls, marked purple, in erect racemes to 35cm (14in) long, all summer & autumn. Prune hard twice-yearly.

Hedgehog broom (blue broom, *Erinacea anthyllis*, *E. pungens*, *Anthyllis erinacea*): v hardy dwarf shrub, to 30×30cm (1×1ft); dense & v slow-growing; lvs inconspicuous, on green, spine-tipped stems; fls violet or slate-blue, spring. Good for hot, dry banks; likes lime.

Coral trees (*Erythrina* spp): showy tender to semi-hardy shrubs or trees, some coppiced in cooler zones; thorny; lvs in 3s; red pea fls in racemes. For fertile, moist but well-drained soil; winter protection needed; grow as wall shrubs or in pots except in warm climates. Prune after flg. Seeds of some spp poisonous.
E.×bidwillii: hybrid of *E. crista-galli* & *E. herbacea*; to 2.5×1.8m (8×6ft); v thorny; fls in 3s, spring & summer.
E. crista-galli **3** (cockspur coral tree): to 4.5–6×4.5–6m (15–20×15–20ft) in warm climates; to 2.5×1.8m (8×6ft) if coppiced; glaucous spiny lvs; dark red waxy fls to 5cm (2in) long, late summer.
E. humeana (Natal coral tree): to 6×6m (20×20ft); semi-evergreen; orange-red fls held above lvs, late summer to autumn, even when young.

Honey or **sweet locust** (*Gleditsia* [incorrectly *Gleditschia*] *triacanthos*): handsome pollution-tolerant foliage tree good for shade & specimen planting on lawns & (especially non-frtg vars) streets. V hardy once established; to 12×9m (40×30ft)/25yrs, eventually over 30m (100ft); generally v thorny, especially in continental climates; ferny acacia-like light green lvs, often bipinnate, clear yellow in autumn; fls greenish, insignificant; glossy brown persistent frs to 45cm (1½ft) long (best in hot climates). Prone to mimosa webworm & gall midge in some areas. Vars: 'Bujoti' ('Pendula'; shrub or small tree, to 4.5–6×2.5m [15–20×8ft]; drooping branches); 'Elegantissima' (slow-growing shrub, to 3m [10ft]; thornless); *inermis* (thornless); 'Moraine' (good non-frtg form of *inermis*, excellent for streets); 'Rubylace' (young lvs purplish becoming bronze-green); 'Shademaster' (fast-growing; upright); 'Skyline' (v narrow); 'Sunburst' **4** ('Inermis Aurea'; thornless; young lvs bright yellow; not drought-tolerant).

Kentucky coffee tree (*Gymnocladus dioica*, *G. canadensis*): v handsome foliage tree, attractive winter outline. V hardy; slow growing, to 6×3m (20×10ft), eventually to 15m (50ft) or more; twigs pale grey; lvs bipinnate, to 90cm (3ft) long, lfts pinkish when young, becoming dark green, yellow in autumn; fls inconspicuous; brown-red frs to 25cm (10in) long on female plants in warm climates. For rich soil. Grows from root cuttings.

Mongolian sweet vetch (*Hedysarum multijugum apiculatum*): v hardy shrub, to 1.5×2m (5×7ft); floppy zigzag growth; glaucous lvs; rosy-purple fls in erect racemes to 30cm (1ft) long, all summer (cuttable). Propagate by layering.

Indigo (*Indigofera* spp): long-flg shrubs, to 1.8×1.5–1.8m (6×5–6ft), taller against wall; pinnate lvs; pink pea fls in racemes to 15cm (6in) long throughout hot summers into autumn. Good on dry soils. Raise by root or semi-ripe cuttings.
I. amblyantha (pink indigo; sometimes sold incorrectly as *I. potaninii*): v hardy; fls rose or deep pink.
I. gerardiana **5** (Himalayan indigo; correctly, *I. heterantha*): moderately hardy; lvs slightly hairy; fls rosy-purple. Can be coppiced (often done naturally by frost).

Laburnocytisus (+ *Laburnocytisus adamii* **6**): graft hybrid or chimaera of *Cytisus purpureus* on *Laburnum anagyroides*; v hardy small tree, to 6×4.5m (20×15ft); own fls coppery-pink, in racemes to 18cm (7in) long, late spring to early summer, but plant also reverts to both parents, producing yellow laburnun fls from core tissue & tufts of cytisus lvs with purple fls from surface tissue. Grown as botanical curiosity. Propagate by budding onto *L. anagyroides*.

Laburnums (golden rain, golden chain, *Laburnum* spp): v hardy small trees grown for their long drooping racemes of yellow pea fls, late spring to early summer (showy but rather transient); lvs in 3s. Whole plant (especially seeds) poisonous. Easy but not long-lived; for any soil, even shallow chalk; stake when young.
L. alpinum* (Scotch laburnum): to 6×4.5–6m (20×15–20ft); infls to 40cm (16in) long. Var 'Pendulum' is slow-growing & pendulous, to 1.8×1m (6×3ft).
L. anagyroides **7** (*L. vulgare*, common laburnum, golden chain): to 6×3–4.5m (20×10–15ft); infls 10–25cm (4–10in) long. Vars: 'Aureum' (golden-leaved laburnum; lvs yellow in summer, greening by autumn); 'Pendulum' (elegant weeping form, to 3–4.5×3–4.5m [10–15×10–15ft]).
L.×watereri*: hybrid of *L. alpinum* & *L. anagyroides*: to 6×4.5m (20×15ft); dense infls to 25cm (10in) long or more, finest in form 'Vossii' **8** (*L. ×vossii*; infls to 60cm [2ft] long; good lawn tree as frs sparse).

Tree lupin (tree lupine, *Lupinus arboreus** **1**): moderately hardy semi-woody shrub; fast-growing & luxuriant, to 1.5–2.5×1.5–2.5m (5–8×5–8ft)/4yrs, but short-lived; fingered grey-green lvs; fls usually sulphur-yellow, rarely purple or blue, in erect 15–25cm (6–10in) racemes, late spring to mid summer. Drought-resistant but best in rich soil; good near coast; dead-head. Self-seeds. Propagate by semi-ripe cuttings.

Ononis (*Ononis fruticosa*): v hardy compact shrub, to 60×90cm (2×3ft); toothed lfts in 3s; small purplish-pink pea fls in 3s, early–mid summer. Not long-lived.

Jerusalem thorn (*Parkinsonia aculeata** **2**): semi-hardy shrub or tree, to 4.5–6×4.5–6m (15–20×15–20ft); open habit, with spiny, zigzag growth; green bark; sparse compound lvs, tiny lfts; fls deep yellow spotted red, in racemes to 18cm (7in) long, spring & repeating (cuttable).

Evergreen laburnum (*Piptanthus laburnifolius* **3**; correctly, *P. nepalensis*): moderately hardy semi-/evergreen shrub, to 2.5–3×1.8–3m (8–10×6–10ft); dark green lance-shaped lfts, glaucous beneath, in 3s; bright yellow laburnum-like fls in erect racemes, late spring. Good wall shrub but short-lived. Can be layered.

Podalyrias (sweet pea bushes, *Podalyria* spp): semi-hardy evergreen shrubs; silky-hairy lvs to 5cm (2in) long; pea fls, pink & mauve/purple, winter &/or spring; prune lightly after flg.
P. calyptrata*: vigorous, to 3×2.5m (10×8ft).
P. sericea* (satin bush): to 75×60cm (2½×2ft).

Mesquite (*Prosopis glandulosa* **4**; often sold incorrectly as *P. chilensis*): moderately hardy slow-growing tree, to 9×12m (30×40ft); spiny, with crooked branches; profuse tiny lfts; fls orange-yellow (attract bees). Deep-rooted; drought-tolerant; good for shade in desert areas.

Scurfy peas (*Psoralea* spp): shrubs, to 3×3–4.5m (10×10–15ft); blue & white pea fls, summer. Propagate by division, softwood cuttings.
P. glandulosa: moderately hardy; bushy; covered with small black glands; lfts in 3s.
P. pinnata: semi-hardy; dense habit; narrow lfts.

Locusts (*Robinia* spp): N American fast-growing, drought- & pollution-tolerant trees & shrubs with brittle, often spiny branches, pinnate lvs & drooping 8–15cm (3–6in) racemes of rose, pink or white pea fls, early summer. V hardy unless stated; some spp suckering. For ordinary or poor soil; stake when young; not for windy spots. Can be grown from root cuttings, suckers.
R.×ambigua* (*R.×hybrida*): hybrids of *R. pseudacacia* & *R. viscosa*; trees, to 12×4.5–6m (40×15–20ft). Vars: 'Decaisneana' (v handsome; fls rose-pink, best in hot summers); 'Idahoensis' ('Idaho'; showy pink to purplish fls in racemes to 20cm [8in] long).

R. hispida* **5** (moss locust, rose acacia): thornless suckering shrub, to 2.5×1.8m (8×6ft), but often top-grafted on *R. pseudacacia* to make round-headed tree, to 4.5×3m (15×10ft); branches & stalks red-bristled & glandular; lvs smooth; v showy rose-pink fls. Can be invasive; rarely sets seed. Vars: *macrophylla* (no bristles; larger pinker fls); 'Monument' (dense, to 3–3.5×1.8m [10–12×6ft]).

R. kelseyi* (Allegheny moss locust): non-invasive shrub, to 2.5×2m (8×7ft); fls lavender to bright rose; frs have purple hairs.

R. pseudacacia* **6** (black locust, common or false acacia): ultra-hardy suckering tree, to 12×6–9m (40×20–30ft); upright, open & round-headed; blackish, furrowed bark; light green pinnate lvs; white fls in racemes to 20cm (8in) long (attract bees); frs red-brown. Poisonous. Prone to stem borers, leaf miners. Vars: 'Appalachia' (strong straight trunk); 'Frisia' **7** (thorns & young growth red; lvs golden); 'Pyramidalis' ('Fastigiata'; v narrow); 'Semperflorens' (repeat-flg); 'Umbraculifera' (parasol or mop-head acacia; incorrectly, 'Inermis'; thornless dense shrub, to 3×3m [10×10ft], often grown as round-headed standard; rarely fls).

Scarlet wisteria tree (*Sesbania* [*Daubentonia*] *tripetii*): semi-hardy shrub or small tree, to 3×2.5m (10×8ft); fast-growing but short-lived; ferny lvs; brownish-orange fls in racemes to 10cm (4in) long from late spring. Good tub plant or standard. Spur prune in spring.

Sophoras (*Sophora* spp): showy trees & shrubs from China & Pacific area; elegant pinnate lvs; fls in pendent clusters. Some good as wall shrubs.
S. davidii (*S. viciifolia*): v hardy graceful shrub, to 1.8×1.8m (6×6ft); young branches downy, becoming spiny; v small lfts, silky hairs beneath; violet-blue & white pea fls, early summer. Propagate by semi-ripe heel cuttings or seed.
S. japonica (Japanese pagoda tree, Chinese scholar tree): v hardy tree, to 7.5×6m (25×20ft), eventually to 20m (65ft); rich green lvs to 30cm (1ft) long, 2.5–5cm (1–2in) lfts; creamy 1.5cm (½in) fls in loose panicles to 40cm (16in) long, late summer & autumn, on mature trees (best in hot summers). Tolerates pollution. Vars: 'Pendula' **8** (weeping pagoda tree; top-grafted pendent form, to 3–4.5×3–4.5m [10–15×10–15ft]; good for lawns; pretty winter silhouette); 'Regent' (best flg var).
S. tetraptera (kowhai): moderately hardy shrub or small tree, to 4.5–6×4.5–6m (15–20×15–20ft); semi-evergreen; golden-yellow almost tubular fls to 5cm (2in) long, often on naked twigs, spring; hanging winged frs. For moist but well-drained soil; dislikes v hot summers. Var 'Grandiflora' has larger fls. *S. microphylla* **9** (*S. tetraptera microphylla*) is similar but lfts v small; dense when young, becoming tree, to 6×6m (20×20ft).

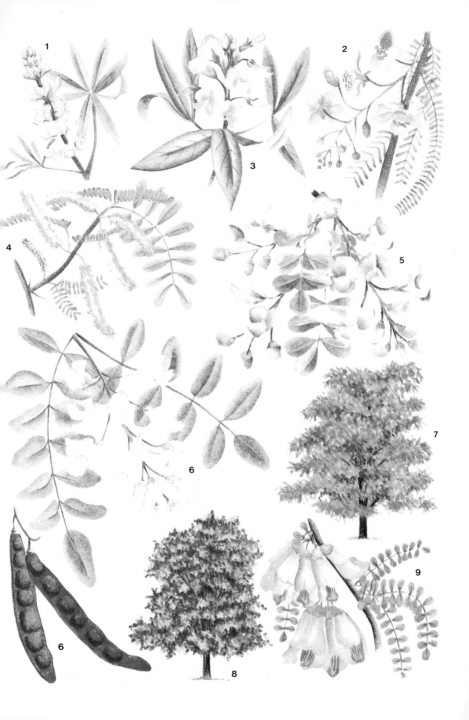

Buddleias and desfontainea

Mainly summer-flowering shrubs, most with profuse tubular flowers, generally clustered & often fragrant. **Cultivation**: Unless stated, for any soil in full sun. **Pruning**: Depends on flowering habit; see below. **Propagation**: Semi-ripe heel cuttings; seed; *B. davidii* & vars by stem tip or hardwood cuttings.

Buddleias (butterfly bushes, *Buddleia* spp): generally deciduous bushy or arching shrubs; lvs mostly lance-shaped, sometimes attractively felted; fls in dense globular or plume-like infls (good for cutting; often attract butterflies). Less hardy spp may regrow if cut down by frost.
*B. alternifolia** **1** (fountain buddleia): v hardy; to 3.5×3.5m (12×12ft); arching; dark green lvs, grey beneath; lilac fls in clusters to 2.5cm (1in) across all along previous yr's growth, early summer. Prune lightly after flg. Var 'Argentea' has lvs densely silver-haired.
B. colvillei **2**: semi-hardy when young, moderately hardy when mature; to 7.5×3.5m (25×12ft); young growths felted; lvs to 20cm (8in) long; large deep red fls, white eye, in pendent clusters to 45cm (1½ft) long, early summer, best in var 'Kewensis'. Do not prune.
*B. crispa**: moderately hardy; to 3×2.5m (10×8ft); bushy; lvs & stems white-felted; toothed lvs to 12cm (5in) long; fls lilac, white eye, in panicles to 10cm (4in) long, all summer. Prune in spring. Good wall shrub.
*B. davidii** (butterfly bush, summer lilac): v hardy; to 4.5×4.5m (15×15ft), more against wall; lvs to 25cm (10in) long, downy beneath; clusters of lilac to purple fls, orange eye, in panicles 15–75cm (6–30in) long, mid summer to autumn, on new wood. Prune hard every spring. Tolerates pollution; good near sea. May self-seed. Vars: 'Black Knight'** (v deep purple); 'Empire Blue'**

3 (violet-blue); 'Fascinating'** ('Fascination'; vivid lilac-pink); 'Fortune'** (lilac); 'Harlequin'** (wine-red; lvs variegated cream); 'Pink Pearl'** (lilac-pink); 'Royal Red'** **4** (reddish-purple); 'White Profusion'**.
*B. fallowiana***: semi-hardy; to 3×3m (10×10ft); open; young shoots woolly; lvs to 25cm (10in) long, silvery; pale lavender fls in panicles to 25cm (10in) long, late summer & autumn, on new wood. Prune in spring. Var 'Alba' **5** has creamy-white fls, orange eye. Vars 'Lochinch'** (violet-blue, orange eye) & 'West Hill'** (pale lavender, orange eye) are hybrids with *B. davidii*.
*B. globosa** **6** (orange ball tree): moderately hardy; to 4.5×2.5m (15×8ft); open; semi-evergreen; deep yellow fls in globular heads along yr-old wood, early summer. Prune after flg.
B.×weyerana: hybrids of *B. davidii magnifica* & *B. globosa*; v hardy; to 4×4m (13×13ft); panicles of globular fl heads on new wood. Prune in spring. Vars: 'Golden Glow' (orange & yellow, shaded pink & mauve); 'Moonlight' (pale cream, orange-yellow throat); 'Sun Gold' **7** (saffron-yellow & orange, shaded buff & rose).
Desfontainea (*Desfontainea spinosa, D. hookerii*; sometimes classed in Potaliaceae): semi-hardy evergreen shrub, to 2.5×1.5m (8×5ft); holly-like lvs to 6cm (2½in) long; tubular waxy fls, scarlet edged yellow, to 4cm (1½in) long, late summer (best in var 'Harold Comber' **8**). For cool, peaty soil in half-shade.

Magnolias and their relatives

Exotic-looking hardy trees and shrubs, highly valued for their large flowers & distinctive, often large leaves (deciduous unless stated). Good as specimens, some against walls. **Cultivation**: Very hardy unless stated; for moist, deep, rich soil, lime-free unless stated. Early-flowering & large-leaved spp need shelter. Pruning generally unnecessary and undesirable. **Propagation**: Layering; grafting; semi-ripe heel cuttings; spp by seed (may need stratification).

Tulip tree (tulip poplar, *Liriodendron tulipifera* **9**): ultra-hardy stately tree; fast-growing, to 7.5×4.5m (25×15ft)/25yrs, eventually over 30m (100ft); grey bark, orange-tinted with age; distinctive light green 4-lobed lvs, golden in autumn; tulip-like greenish-yellow fls, orange inside, prominent stamens, early summer on mature trees. Tolerates lime. Vars: 'Aureomarginatum' **10** (lvs edged yellow); 'Fastigiatum' ('Pyramidale'; columnar).
Magnolias (*Magnolia* spp; incorrectly, tulip trees): trees & shrubs, often large, with beautiful, large globular to chalice- or star-shaped solitary

fls, generally opening flattish, mostly in spring but often only when mature (unless stated, from 5yrs or less); lvs often large & leathery, ovate to lance-shaped or oblong, often hairy beneath; resent transplanting except when young.
*M. acuminata** (cucumber tree): long-lived & fast-growing tree, to 7.5×3.5m (25×12ft), eventually to 25m (90ft); pyramid-shaped, becoming rounded; orange, brown & purplish bark; pale yellow-green lvs to 25cm (10in) long; greenish-yellow fls to 8cm (3in) tall, late spring & early summer, after 12yrs; purplish-red frs to 10cm (4in) long. Tolerates lime.

M. campbellii **1** (pink tulip tree): moderately hardy spreading tree, to 10×5.5m (33×18ft); shiny grey-green lvs to 30cm (1ft) long, glaucous beneath; pink fls, paler inside, opening to 25cm (10in) wide, from late winter (before lvs), usually after 20yrs. Vars: *alba* (white); 'Charles Raffill' (pinkish-purple, edged white); 'Darjeeling' (dark rose); *mollicomata* (mauve-pink, from 10–12yrs); 'Wakehurst' (darkest fls).

M. cordata* (*M. acuminata cordata*): slow-growing shrub or bushy tree, to 4.5×3.5m (15×12ft); lvs to 15cm (6in) long; greenish or yellow fls to 8cm (3in) tall, golden inside, summer, repeating autumn. Tolerates lime.

M. delavayi*: semi- to moderately hardy evergreen bushy tree, to 7.5×6m (25×20ft); lvs to 30cm (1ft) long; short-lived creamy-white cup-shaped fls to 20cm (8in) across, late summer. Best as wall shrub; tolerates lime.

M. denudata* (*M. conspicua*, *M. heptapeta*, yulan, lily tree): slow-growing rounded tree, to 5.5×4.5m (18×15ft); lvs to 15cm (6in) long; profuse pure white fls to 15cm (6in) across, early spring (before lvs), after 7yrs. Tolerates shade.

M. grandiflora** **2** (bull bay, laurel or southern magnolia): moderately to v hardy evergreen tree to 7.5×4.5m (25×15ft)/25yrs, eventually to 15×12m (50×40ft); shiny thick dark green lvs to 20cm (8in) long, red-brown felt beneath; waxy cream fls to 25cm (10in) across, summer & autumn (earlier in hot climates), from 15yrs. Tolerates lime. Vars: 'Exmouth' ('Exoniensis', 'Lanceolata'; narrow lvs; fls v large, borne when young); 'Goliath' (broad lvs; fls v large, borne when young). Grafted vars (often fl within 3yrs): 'Majestic Beauty'; 'Russet'; 'St Mary' (lvs rusty-red beneath); 'Samuel Sommer'.

M. hypoleuca** **3** (*M. obovata*): erect tree, to 7.5×5.5m (25×18ft); bark purple-brown when young; lvs to 25cm (10in) long, bluish-white beneath; creamy-white fls to 20cm (8in) across, red stamens, early summer, after 15yrs; red frs.

M. liliiflora (*M. quinquepeta*, lily magnolia): moderately to v hardy shrub, to 3×3m (10×10ft); lvs to 20cm (8in) long; red-purple tulip-shaped fls opening white, spring to early summer (good for cutting). Var 'Nigra' **4** is compact; large dark purple fls; excellent for small gardens. Vars 'Betty'* & 'Susan'* (both white stained purple outside) are hybrids with *M. stellata*; to 3×1.8m (10×6ft); fl mid spring.

M.×*loebneri**: hybrids of *M. kobus* & *M. stellata*; fast-growing shrubs, to 7.5×7.5m (25×25ft); lance-shaped or obovate lvs; profuse many-petalled starry fls, early spring (before lvs). Tolerate lime. Vars: 'Leonard Messel' **5** (lilac-pink, purple buds); '(Dr) Merrill'** (white).

M. macrophylla*: open tree, to 6×5.5m (20×18ft); v large light green lvs to 90×30cm (3×1ft), downy beneath; ivory fls to 30cm (1ft)

across, with purple blotch, summer, after 12yrs. Needs shelter.

M. salicifolia* (anise or willow-leaf magnolia): fast-growing conical tree, to 7.5×4m (25×13ft); narrow lvs* to 10cm (4in) long; creamy fls to 10cm (4in) across, spring (before lvs), best in var 'Jermyns'. Plant lemon-scented if bruised.

M. sargentiana: moderately hardy tree, to 7.5×4m (25×13ft); leathery lvs to 18cm (7in) long, hairy beneath; rose-pink water-lily-like nodding fls to 20cm (8in) across, paler inside, early spring (before lvs), from 15–20yrs. Var *robusta* **6** has profuse fls from 12yrs.

M. sieboldii** (*M. parviflora*, Oyama magnolia): moderately to v hardy shrub, to 4.5×4.5m (15×15ft); lvs to 15cm (6in) long; inclined cupped white fls to 10cm (4in) across, with crimson stamens, late spring & summer (intermittent); frs crimson.

M.×*soulangiana** (in US, saucer magnolias): hybrids of *M. denudata* & *M. liliiflora*; shrubs, to 5×6m (16×20ft), or small trees; lvs to 15cm (6in) long; tulip-shaped fls to 12cm (5in) across, white suffused purple, mid spring. For any soil except shallow chalk. Numerous vars, including: 'Alba Superba'* (white); 'Alexandrina' (vigorous & erect); 'Brozzonii' (fls to 25cm [10in] across); 'Burgundy' (early); 'Lennei' (*M.*×*lennei*; lvs broad; fls rose-purple, cream flushed purple inside; may repeat); 'Picture' **7** (purple, white inside); 'Rustica Rubra' **8** ('Rubra'; rosy-red); 'San José'* (large early fls).

M. stellata* **9** (*M. halliana*, *M. kobus stellata*, star magnolia): dense rounded shrub, slow-growing to 2.5×2.5m (8×8ft); young bark aromatic; lvs to 10cm (4in) long; prominent hairy buds opening to starry white many-petalled fls to 10cm (4in) across, narrow petals, early–mid spring (before lvs); frs red. Likes peaty soil; shelter from late frosts. Vars: 'Rosea' (pink star magnolia; pink buds; fls fading white); 'Royal Star' (large fls); 'Waterlily' (even more petals; pale pink in bud).

M.×*veitchii* ('Peter Veitch'): hybrid of *M. campbellii* & *M. denudata*; vigorous tree, to 12×7.5m (40×25ft), eventually to 25m (80ft); young growth hairy; dark green lvs to 25cm (10in) long, purplish when young; blush-pink fls to 25cm (10in) wide, mid spring (before lvs), from 10yrs. Var 'Isca' is creamy-white.

M. virginiana** (*M. glauca*, sweet bay): shrub or tree, to 6×3m (20×10ft); semi-evergreen in warm areas; lvs glossy, glaucous beneath, to 12cm (5in) long; waxy globular fls to 8cm (3in) across, creamy-white, all summer, from 10yrs; frs red. For partial shade; tolerates lime.

M. wilsonii* **10**: moderately to v hardy shrub, to 6×7.5m (20×25ft), or small tree; lvs to 15cm (6in) long, brown-haired beneath; saucer-shaped fls to 10cm (4in) across, white with red stamens, early summer from 10yrs. For partial shade.

The mallow family

Showy, free-flowering shrubs, deciduous unless noted, generally with large more or less funnel-shaped 5-petalled flowers, often over long season; stamens usually united to form prominent central column. Often somewhat soft-wooded & tender, & best in warm sunny position sheltered by wall, etc; most also good as tubbed patio plants overwintered under glass. **Cultivation**: For any well-drained soil in sun. Generally need only frost-damaged wood pruning in spring. **Propagation**: Seed; semi-ripe cuttings; layering.

Abutilons (*Abutilon* spp; spp with bell-shaped fls often called Chinese lanterns): generally semi- to moderately hardy fast-growing soft-wooded shrubs good trained on sunny wall; lvs generally lobed & rather maple/vine-like; evergreen in mild winters; free-flg, late spring to autumn. Maintain bushiness by regular pinching back; prone to scale insects, whitefly. May be short-lived.

A. × *hybridum* vars: hybrids mainly of *A. darwinii* & *A. striatum*; arching, to 2.5×2.5m (8×8ft) or more; broad lvs; drooping bell-shaped fls 5cm (2in) long, shades of white, pink, red, orange & yellow. Vars: 'Ashford Red' (puce); 'Boule de Neige' **1** (white); 'Canary Bird' **2** (yellow); 'Golden Fleece' (deep yellow); 'Savitzii' (lvs edged white; fls yellow).

A. megapotamicum: lax & graceful, to 2.5×2.5m (8×8ft); arrow-shaped lvs to 10cm (4in) long (mottled yellow in var 'Variegatum'); drooping red & yellow lantern-like fls to 4cm (1½in) long, prominent stamens.

A. striatum (correctly, *A. pictum*): semi-hardy; slender, to 2.5×1.8m (8×6ft); lvs to 15cm (6in) long (blotched & mottled yellow in var 'Thompsonii' **3**); pendulous bell-shaped orange-/yellow fls to 5cm (2in) long.

A. × *suntense* vars: hybrids of *A. ochsenii* & *A. vitifolium*; moderately hardy; vigorous, to 3×2.5m (10×8ft); felted lvs; 4–5cm (1½–2in) saucer-shaped fls. Vars: 'Jermyns' **4** (dark mauve); 'White Charm'.

A. (*Corynabutilon*) *vitifolium*: moderately hardy; to 4.5×3.5m (15×12ft); dense in warm areas; young shoots & lvs (to 10–15cm [4–6in] long) downy; clustered saucer-shaped pale purplish-blue fls to 5–8cm (2–3in) across. Vars: 'Album' (white); 'Tennant's White'; 'Veronica Tennant' (mauve).

Hibiscus (*Hibiscus* spp): generally v hardy bushy shrubs with widely trumpet-shaped fls to 10cm (4in) across, prominent column, mid/late summer often to autumn (best where summers hot). If pruned hard in spring, fewer larger fls produced; if left unpruned, profuse smaller fls. Prone to aphids.

H. rosa-sinensis (Chinese or tropical hibiscus): tender to semi-hardy, but good tub plant where summers hot if overwintered frost-free; to 2.5×2.5m (8×8ft) where hardy, smaller in tub; glossy evergreen lvs to 15cm (6in) long; fls to 12cm (5in) or more wide, profuse in hot summers, shades of white, pink, red, orange or yellow. Numerous single & double vars available where hardy.

H. sinosyriacus **5**: similar to better-known *H. syriacus* but lvs wider & petals thicker; fls lilac in sp. Vars: 'Autumn Surprise' (white, cerise centre); 'Lilac Queen' (white flushed lilac, garnet-red centre).

H. syriacus (in US, rose of Sharon, shrub althaea): to 1.8–3×1.2–1.8m (6–10×4–6ft); can be trained like tree; generally 3-lobed lvs to 10cm (4in) long; fls in v wide colour range from white to purple. Best on sunny wall where summers cool or autumn early. Single vars: 'Blue Bird' **6** ('Oiseau Bleu'; violet-blue, dark centre); 'Coelestis' (light violet-blue, reddish centre); 'Diana' (pure white); 'Dorothy Crane' (white, crimson centre); 'Hamabo' (not same as *H. hamabo*; white flushed blush-pink, crimson centre); 'Mauve Queen' (mauve, crimson centre); 'Monstrosus' (white, maroon centre); 'Red Heart' (white, red centre); 'Snowdrift' (white; early); 'Totus Albus' (white); 'Woodbridge' **7** (rose-crimson, carmine centre); 'W. R. Smith' (white; crimped petals). Double & semi-double vars: 'Admiral Dewey' (white); 'Ardens' (rosy-purple, maroon centre); 'Duc de Brabant' (deep purplish-pink); 'Elegantissimus' (pale purplish-pink, blotched & streaked pink-red); 'Jeanne d'Arc' (white); 'Lady Stanley' **8** (white shaded pink, crimson centre); 'Violet Clair Double' ('Violaceus Plenus'; blue-purple).

Hoherias (lacebarks, *Hoheria* spp): moderately hardy free-flg New Zealand plants with solitary or clustered white fls in lf axils, mid–late summer. Generally shrubs, to 3–4.5×2.5–3m (10–15×8–10ft), but eventually trees, to 9m (30ft) or more, in warm climates. Young plants grown from seed have v variable juvenile lvs.

H. (*Plagianthus*) *lyallii* * **9**: somewhat heart-shaped downy adult lvs to 10cm (4in) long, coarsely toothed; fls to 4cm (1½in) wide.

H. glabrata * is v similar (once thought same sp) but lvs smooth, softer-wooded & more shrubby; prefers more maritime climate.

H. sexstylosa: v graceful as tree; evergreen; glossy lance-shaped evergreen lvs to 8cm (3in) long; 2cm (¾in) fls. *H.* 'Glory of Amlwch' is hybrid with *H. glabrata*; semi-evergreen; profuse 4cm (1½in) fls.

Lavateras (tree mallows, *Lavatera* spp): rather

soft-wooded semi- to moderately hardy
Mediterranean shrubs good for warm spots near
sea; 3/5-lobed lvs; hollyhock-like fls to 5cm (2in)
wide, early summer to autumn.
L. maritima: to 1.8×1.5m (6×5ft); young growth

grey-downy; evergreen 10cm (4in) lvs; pale
lilac-pink fls blotched crimson.
L. olbia: vigorous, to 2×1.5m (7×5ft); young
growth softly white-hairy; 15cm (6in) lvs; purplish
fls, pink in var 'Rosea' **10**, p133. Likes lime.

Eucalypts

Gum trees, *Eucalyptus* spp. Magnificent, graceful Australian evergreen trees, often very fast-growing &
tall (to 30m [100ft]/25yrs in some cases, depending on soil & climate) but some forming multi-stemmed
coppice-like shrubs (mallees). (Sizes given are ultimate expected in good conditions; can be kept
smaller by hard pruning.) Bark of many spp (gumbarks) shed in flakes or strips; in others, thick, hard &
furrowed (ironbarks) or fibrous (stringybarks). Leaves aromatic; juvenile generally rather broad, opposite
& often rounded & stalkless, to 5–10×5–8cm (2–4×2–3in) unless stated (can be maintained by hard
pruning); adult usually pendulous & alternate, lance-shaped & to 12–20×2.5–4cm (5–8×1–1½in)
unless stated. Flowers generally in small umbels, prominent stamens creamy-white unless noted. Fruits
woody. Widely grown, especially in warm areas, for form, foliage & bark. Over 500 recognized spp,
many in cultivation; selection, mainly of hardier types, listed. **Cultivation**: Unless stated, moderately
hardy (but varies with origin of seed; hardiest if wood well sun-ripened). For most soils in full sun;
generally drought-tolerant but grow better if soil moist. Plant as young seedlings; protect from cold
winds when young. **Propagation**: Seed (treat like HHAs); selected forms rarely by grafting.

E. camaldulensis (river or Murray red gum):
spreading, to 30×7.5–9m (100×25–30ft);
weeping branches; smooth grey bark; mid green
lvs*; rather insignificant fls, summer. Tolerates
lime.
E. camphora (broad-leaved Sally): moderately to
v hardy; to 20×7.5m (65×25ft); dark peeling
bark; fls autumn. Thrives in wet soil.
E. cinerea (Argyle apple, mealy stringybark): to
15×9m (50×30ft); reddish-brown rough bark;
v glaucous juvenile lvs* (persistent; good for
cutting); adult lvs* glaucous & leathery; fls
spring–summer.
E. citriodora **1** (lemon-scented gum): tender to
semi-hardy; to 30×7.5m (100×25ft); v graceful,
with slender trunk; white or bluish flaking bark;
juvenile lvs** lance-shaped, to 12×2.5cm
(5×1in), adult to 15×2cm (6×¾in), both lemon-
scented; fls winter.
E. coccifera **2** (Tasmanian snow gum, Mount
Wellington peppermint): compact & upright, to
7.5×3m (25×10ft); low-altitude form larger but
less hardy; bark peels in long strips, white
beneath; glaucous juvenile lvs* to 5×3cm
(2×1¼in), adult to 6×2cm (2½×¾in), hooked
point, peppermint-scented; fls summer.
E. dairympleana **3** (mountain gum, broad-leaved
kindling bark): vigorous, to 30×7.5m (100×25ft)
or more; patchy smooth bark, grey, white &
pinkish; juvenile lvs* grey-green, adult to
22×2.5cm (9×1in), glossy light green; fls
autumn. Tolerates lime.
E. ficifolia **4** (red-flowering gum): tender to semi-
hardy; to 9×7.5m (30×25ft); dense & round-
headed; grey rough bark; juvenile lvs* bristly,
adult thick & dark glossy green, to 15×5cm
(6×2in); showy red fls, summer. Good near sea.

E. glaucescens **5** (Tingiringi gum): mallee or tree,
to 12×4.5m (40×25ft); peeling dark bark, white
beneath; silvery-glaucous juvenile lvs* to
3×3cm (1¼×1¼in), adult leathery, to 12×2cm
(5×¾in); fls autumn.
E. globulus **6** ([Tasmanian] blue gum): semi- to
moderately hardy; vigorous, to 50×12–15m
(165×40–50ft) or more; dense crown; bluish
bark peeling in long strips; glaucous juvenile lvs*
to 15×8cm (6×3in), adult glossy blue-green, to
30×4cm (12×1½in); fls winter–spring; warty
2.5cm (1in) frs. Var 'Compacta' is more bushy,
eventually to 20×9m (65×30ft); can be sheared.
E. gunnii **7** (cider gum): moderately to v hardy; to
30×12m (100×40ft); greenish to white peeling
bark; juvenile lvs* glaucous & rounded, adult
leathery, to 8×3cm (3×1¼in); fls spring–
summer. Among hardiest spp. Good shade tree.
E. leucoxylon **8** (white ironbark): to 15×7.5m
(50×25ft) or more; branches usually pendulous;
bark mottled bluish & white, flaking; lvs* grey-
green; fls white, pink or red, winter & spring. Var
macrocarpa is bushy, to 6×4.5m (20×15ft);
red-fld form v ornamental.
E. nicholii (narrow-leaved peppermint): graceful
& weeping, to 20×9m (65×30ft); fibrous brown
bark; grey-green juvenile lvs* to 5×0.5cm
(2×¼in), adult dark green, to 12×1cm (5×½in),
purplish bloom when young; fls autumn.
E. niphophila **1**, p137 (snow gum; correctly a var of
E. parviflora): moderately to v hardy; to 9×4.5m
(30×15ft); often leaning; peeling bark mottled
bluish, grey & white; juvenile lvs* pale green, to
4×2.5cm (1½×1in), adult leathery & grey-green,
to 8×2.5cm (3×1in); fls summer. Among
hardiest spp.
E. parvifolia (small-leaved gum): moderately to

v hardy; to 9×6m (30×20ft); dense & elegant; grey bark; lvs* grey-green, juvenile to 3×1.5cm (1¼×⅝in), adult to 6×1cm (2½×½in); fls summer. Tolerates lime.

E. pauciflora (cabbage gum): to 18×9m (60×30ft), often with several crooked trunks; flaking bark, mottled white & dark grey; juvenile lvs* thick & grey-green, adult bright green; fls summer. Var *nana* is shrubby, to 6×3m (20×10ft); narrower lvs.

E. perriniana **2** (spinning gum): to 7.5×4.5m (25×15ft); blotched bark; glaucous lvs*, juvenile perfoliate & persistent even when dead (spin on stems in wind), adult thick; fls summer.

E. polyanthemos **3** (red box, silver-dollar gum): to 20×7.5m (65×25ft); round head; reddish-brown scaly or fibrous bark; grey-green lvs*, juvenile rounded, to 8×10cm (3×4in), adult to 14×4.5cm (5½×1¾in); fls spring–summer.

E. pulverulenta (powdered or silver-leaved mountain gum): semi- to moderately hardy; sprawling, to 12×7.5m (40×25ft) or more; grey & white bark peeling in strips; juvenile & adult lvs similar, to 6×5cm (2½×2in), silvery-grey & stalkless (good for cutting); fls spring.

E.×rhodantha (rose mallee): hybrid of *E. macrocarpa* & *E. pyriformis*; sprawling mallee, to 2.5×2m (8×7ft); greenish-white bark; grey-blue rounded juvenile lvs 5–10cm (2–4in) long, perfoliate; large showy carmine-red fls, v long

season. Can be trained on wall.

E. rudis (desert or flooded gum): to 15×9m (50×30ft); spreading & often weeping; rough grey bark, peeling on branches; lvs grey-green; fls spring–summer, quite showy. Tolerates wind, drought, moisture.

E. sideroxylon (mugga, red ironbark): variable, to 25×9m (80×30ft); hard furrowed black bark, often stained red; dull grey-green lvs, juvenile to 8×1.5cm (3×⅝in), adult to 11×2cm (4½×¾in); fls mainly autumn to late spring, cream, pink or red.

E. torquata **4** (coral gum): tender to semi-hardy; to 7.5×6m (25×20ft) or more; spreading & drooping; rough dark grey bark; juvenile lvs glaucous, to 6×3cm (2½×1¼in), adult grey-green; profuse white to pink & crimson fls, coral-red buds, mainly summer but often almost all yr, from young age.

E. urnigera (urn-fruited gum): vigorous, to 15×6m (50×20ft) or more; drooping branches; peeling bark mottled red-brown & creamy-white; juvenile lvs v glaucous, adult dark glossy green; fls late summer to autumn.

E. viminalis **5** (manna or ribbon gum): vigorous, spreading & weeping; to 45×12m (150×40ft); rough whitish bark peeling in long strips; juvenile lvs dark green, to 10×3cm (4×1¼in), adult pale green; fls most seasons. Good shade tree, best in moist soil.

Bottlebrushes, myrtles and their relatives

Evergreen sun-loving shrubs & trees, mainly Australasian, with generally small but very showy flowers & often handsome foliage. Mostly for very mild to warm climates. **Cultivation**: Semi-hardy unless stated, but may be more tender if summers not hot & sunny. Generally for most soils, but best in hot dry positions. **Propagation**: Seed; semi-ripe cuttings.

Bottlebrushes (*Callistemon* spp): spectacular shrubs with narrow leathery lvs & profuse cylindrical spikes of fls with small petals but long colourful stamens ("bristles" of "bottlebrush"), mainly in summer but almost all year where warm; persistent woody frs. Young shoots (often bronze/red & silky-hairy) grow from end of infls. Attract humming birds in N America. Tolerate drought, lime, salty or moist soils; best pruned hard every few yrs.

C. citrinus (*C. lanceolatus*, crimson or lemon bottlebrush): stiff & rather straggly, to 4.5×2m (15×7ft), but can be kept bushy or trained as tree; lance-shaped lvs* to 8×2cm (3×¾in), lemon-scented; 10–15cm (4–6in) red to crimson infls (large & bright crimson in var 'Splendens' **6**). Best-known sp.

C. linearis: spreading, to 3×2m (10×7ft); v narrow lvs to 10cm (4in) long; 10–12cm (4–5in) bright crimson infls.

C. macropunctatus (*C. rugulosus*): dense &

tangled, to 4.5×4.5cm (15×15ft); narrow lance-shaped lvs to 6cm (2½in) long; 8–10cm (3–4in) scarlet to pink infls, golden anthers.

C. phoeniceus **7** (fiery bottlebrush): moderately hardy; bushy, to 2.5×2m (8×7ft); narrow grey-green lvs to 9cm (3½in) long; brilliant crimson 10cm (4in) infls.

C. rigidus: stiff & erect, to 3×2m (10×7ft); rigid narrow lvs to 10cm (4in) long; 10cm (4in) red infls. Tolerates poor drainage.

C. salignus **8** (white bottlebrush): moderately hardy; tree, to 9×4.5m (30×15ft), or large shrub; papery bark; narrow lance-shaped lvs to 10×1cm (4×½in), red when young; 5–8cm (2–3in) creamy (sometimes pink) infls. Likes moisture. Can be used for hedging.

C. sieberi (alpine bottlebrush): moderately hardy; erect, to 2×1.5m (7×5ft), smaller & more rounded in alpine form, thick narrow dark green lvs to 3cm (1½in) long; narrowish creamy infls to 5cm (2in) long. Probably hardiest sp.

C. speciosus: erect shrub, to 2.5×2m (8×7ft); or small tree; lvs to 12×1cm (5×½in), often glaucous; deep crimson infls to 15×8cm (6×3in), golden anthers. Likes moisture.

C. subulatus **1**: moderately hardy; dense & spreading, to 1.2×1.5m (4×5ft); glossy green needle-like lvs to 4cm (1½in) long; profuse crimson infls 5–8cm (2–3in) long. Likes moisture.

C. viminalis (weeping bottlebrush): weeping tree, ·to 6–9×4.5m (20–30×15ft), or large shrub; scaly bark; light green lance-shaped lvs to 10cm (4in) long, bronze-hairy when young; bright red 5–9cm (2–3½in) infls (v good for cutting). Fine specimen but rather tender.

Geraldton wax plant (*Chamelaucium uncinatum*): spreading shrub, to 3×4.5m (10×15ft); arching branches; narrow bright green lvs to 2.5cm (1in) long, hooked tip; showy infls of 2cm (¾in) 5-petalled waxy white, pink, red or purple fls, spring (good for cutting). Needs perfect drainage; best on sandy soils.

Feijoa (*Feijoa sellowiana* **2**; in US, pineapple guava): semi- to moderately hardy bushy S American shrub, to 4.5×4.5m (15×15ft) or more if not cut back by frost; young shoots & buds white-felted; dark glossy green lvs to 8×4cm (3×1½in), white felt & prominent veins beneath; solitary 4cm (1½in) fls, fleshy white petals shading to red (edible in fruit salads), prominent rich crimson stamens, summer; red-tinged green egg-shaped frs to 5–8cm (2–3in) long, whitish flesh, edible & richly aromatic. Frs rarely where summers not hot; may need cross-pollination except for self-fertile frtg vars. Can be pruned/trained late spring. Var 'Variegata' has white-edged lvs.

Tea trees (*Leptospermum* spp): generally semi- to moderately hardy informal shrubs or small trees with small crowded lvs (used by early Australian settlers to make beverage) & abundant 5-petalled white or pink fls generally 1cm (½in) across, early summer (good for cutting). Useful hedging, screen or specimen plants. Best in well-drained lime-free soils.

L. flavescens: generally to 3×2m (10×7ft); light green 2cm (¾in) lvs; white 1.5cm (⅝in) fls.

L. humifusum (often grown incorrectly as *L. scoparium prostratum*): moderately to v hardy; prostrate, to 0.2×1.8m (8in×6ft); reddish shoots; dark glossy green 10mm (⅜in) lvs; white fls. Good for draping dry wall or rock garden.

L. laevigatum (coastal [in US, Australian] tea tree): vigorous & bushy, to 6×4.5m (20×15ft), or small twisted tree; rough shredding bark; grey-green lvs to 2cm (¾in) long; white 1.5cm (⅝in) fls. Tolerates wind & salt spray; good for coastal hedge/windbreak or as specimen.

L. lanigerum **3** (*L. pubescens*, woolly tea tree): moderately hardy variable erect columnar to spreading shrub, to 3×1–3m (10×3–10ft); young

shoots & lvs generally hairy; lvs to 2cm (¾in) long, usually grey-green; white fls.

L. scoparium (manuka, New Zealand tea tree): generally bushy & twiggy, to 3×2m (10×7ft) or more; lance-shaped narrow lvs* to 1cm (½in) long, sharp-pointed; white fls. Best-known sp, but prone to scale insects in some areas. Vars: 'Album Flore Pleno' (compact; double white rosette fls): 'Chapmanii' (lvs bronze; fls deep rose-red); 'Keatleyi' **4** (rather tender; grey-green lvs; soft pink fls to 2.5cm [1in] wide); 'Nanum' **5** (dense & dwarf, to 30cm [1ft]; rose-pink fls; 'Kiwi' is similar but fls crimson); 'Nichollsii' **6** (bronze-purple lvs; deep crimson fls); 'Red Damask' (free-flg; double, bright red); 'Ruby Glow' (bronze lvs; profuse deep red double fls).

Melaleucas (honey myrtles, *Melaleuca* spp **7**; sometimes called bottlebrushes): v similar to *Callistemon* spp, with bottlebrush fls, but stamens in clusters & slightly less hardy. Numerous spp cultivated in warm areas, mostly medium-sized to large shrubs or small trees; bark often papery; lvs narrow, sometimes needle-like; fls white, cream, lilac, pink, purple or red, generally long season. Best in lime-free soil.

Myrtles (*Myrtus* spp): generally semi- to moderately hardy handsome trees & shrubs with usually solitary 2–2.5cm (¾–1in) white fls, prominent stamens. Good near sea; for any well-drained soil.

M. (Lophomyrtus) bullata: shrub, to 4.5×3.5m (15×12ft), or small tree; puckered leathery rounded lvs to 3cm (1¼in) long, usually bronze/purple-tinged; fls summer; blackish-red 8mm (⅓in) frs. Foliage & fls good for cutting.

M. (L.)×ralphii is hybrid with *M. (L.) obcordata*; lvs smaller, less puckered.

M. communis * **8** (true or common myrtle of S Europe): to 4.5×3m (15×10ft); dense & leafy; dark glossy green lvs* 2.5–5cm (1–2in) long; fls late summer; purple-black 1cm (½in) frs. Can be trained on wall. Vars: *tarentina* **9** (Tarentum myrtle; v dainty, with small lvs; white frs); 'Variegata' (lvs grey-green edged creamy-white).

M. luma **10** (*Luma apiculata*): beautiful shrub, to 6×4.5m (20×15ft), or tree to 12m (40ft); striking flaking cinnamon-brown bark, creamy-white beneath; leathery deep green lvs to 2.5×1.5cm (1×⅝in); fls sometimes clustered, late summer; dark purple 10mm (⅜in) frs (edible).

M. (Eugenia) ugni * (*Ugni molinae*, Chilean guava): moderately hardy; bushy, to 1.8×1.8m (6×6ft); slender stems; dark glossy green lvs to 2.5cm (1in) long; pink-tinged fls, early summer; reddish-brown 1cm (½in) edible frs*. Neat & useful for hedges.

Forsythia, lilac and their relatives

Very popular, generally deciduous early-flowering shrubs with profuse starry 4/5-lobed flowers generally 2–4cm (¾–1½in) wide (very good for cutting). Many good grown against wall. **Cultivation**: Generally easy. Unless stated, very hardy & for fertile, well-drained soils in sun or semi-shade. Annual pruning not usually needed, but thin out old wood occasionally & if necessary trim after flowering. **Propagation**: Semi-ripe or hardwood cuttings; layering; seed; suckers where appropriate. *Syringa* vars often grafted on *S. vulgaris* or *Ligustrum ovalifolium*.

Abeliophyllum (*Abeliophyllum distichum** **1**; incorrectly, white forsythia): forsythia-like but slow-growing, to 1.2×1.2cm (4×4ft), more on wall; lvs 5–8cm (2–3in) long; clusters of white or pink-tinged small fls, late winter (before lvs). Best where summers hot.

Forsythias (*Forsythia* spp): among most colourful of early-spring-flg shrubs, generally fountain-shaped, with clusters of yellow fls all along branches (before lvs; best on yr-old wood). *F.×intermedia* vars: hybrids of *F. suspensa* & *F. viridissima*; vigorous, to 2–2.5×2–2.5m (7–8×7–8ft); branches erect or arching; lance-shaped toothed lvs; free-flg. Vars: 'Beatrix Farrand' (v vigorous; coarse lvs; large soft yellow fls); 'Karl Sax' (bushy; large deep yellow fls); 'Lynwood' **2** (v free-flg; broad-petalled deep yellow fls); 'Spectabilis' **3** (profuse somewhat brassy-yellow fls); 'Spring Glory' (profuse primrose-yellow fls). *F.* 'Arnold Dwarf' is hybrid with *F. japonica*; low & spreading, to 1×2m (3×7ft); self-rooting; bright green lvs; rather sparse yellow-green fls; useful ground cover. *F. ovata* (Korean forsythia): compact, to 1.5×1.5m (5×5ft); lvs to 6cm (2½in) long; v early small bright yellow fls (not v profuse but buds less prone to frost damage in cold areas). *F. suspensa sieboldii* (weeping forsythia): dense, rambling & weeping, to 3×2.5m (10×8ft), taller trained on wall; branch tips self-root; lvs generally simple, to 10cm (4in) long; long-lasting golden-yellow fls. *F. s. fortunei* is more erect; *F. s. atrocaulis* **4** has purplish young shoots & lvs.

Jasmines (*Jasminum* spp): lax, green-stemmed shrubs generally best trained against wall; yellow 5-lobed fls.
J. humile 'Revolutum'* **5** (*J. revolutum*): moderately hardy; to 1.8×1.8m (6×6ft); semi-/evergreen lvs, 5–7 dark green leathery lfts to 5–6cm (2–2½in) long; clusters of yellow fls, early summer.
J. nudiflorum **6** (winter jasmine): semi-prostrate, to 0.6–1×1.5m (2–3×5ft), or to 3.5m (12ft) or more trained on wall; trifoliolate lvs, deep glossy green lfts to 3cm (1¼in) long; bright yellow fls on leafless branches from mid winter on yr-old wood. Prune fld shoots after flg.

Lilacs (*Syringa* spp): generally vigorous, often suckering upright shrubs, sometimes tree-like; lvs generally simple, deep green; fls white to deep purple, in showy panicles to 15–25cm

(6–10in) long unless noted, generally late spring. Like rich, moist soil; remove suckers if grafted. Prone to bacterial blight.
S.×chinensis* (Rouen or Chinese lilac): ultra-hardy hybrid of *S. laciniata* & *S. vulgaris*; dense, rounded & graceful, to 3×2m (10×7ft); lvs to 6cm (2½in) long; arching infls of lilac-purple fls (reddish-lilac in var 'Saugeana').
S.×josiflexa vars: ultra-hardy hybrids of *S. josikaea* & *S. reflexa*; to 3–3.5×3–3.5m (10–12×10–12ft); lvs to 15–20cm (6–8in) long; arching infls. Vars: 'Bellicent'* **7** (clear pink); 'Guinevere'* (lilac-purple to pink).
S. josikaea (Hungarian lilac): ultra-hardy; to 3×2m (10×7ft); glossy lvs to 12cm (7in) long, whitish beneath; slender infls, deep violet-mauve, early summer.
S. laciniata* **8** (cut-leaved lilac): open & graceful, to 1.8–2.5×1.8–2.5m (6–8×6–8ft); dissected feathery lvs to 6cm (2½in) long, 3–9 lobes; 8cm (3in) infls of violet-purple fls.
S. microphylla**: spreading, to 1.5–1.8×1.5–1.8m (5–6×5–6ft); dark green 1–5cm (½–2in) lvs, greyish beneath; 5–10cm (2–4in) infls of pinkish-lilac fls (rose-pink & v profuse in var 'Superba' **9**).
S.×persica* (Persian lilac): hybrid of uncertain parentage; bushy & rounded, to 2×2m (7×7ft); lance-shaped lvs to 6cm (2½in) long; erect broad 8–10cm (3–4in) infls of lilac fls (white in var 'Alba').
S.×prestoniae* vars: ultra-hardy hybrids mainly of *S. reflexa* & *S. villosa*; generally to 3×3m (10×10ft); dense & upright; lvs to 18cm (7in) long; rather loose infls of slender fls. Vars: 'Elinor' (purple-red buds opening pale lilac); 'Ethel M. Webster' (flesh-pink); 'Isabella' **10** (pale lilac-purple infls to 30cm [1ft] long); 'Kim' (broad purplish infls); 'Virgilia' (compact; magenta-purple buds opening pale lilac).
S. reflexa **11**: 3.5×3m (12×10ft); lvs to 20cm (8in) long; dense narrowish, often pendulous infls of purplish-pink fls, pale inside. V free-flg.
S. 'Fountain' is hybrid with drooping pale pink infls.
S. reticulata* (*S. amurensis japonica*, *S. japonica*, Japanese tree lilac): vigorous shrub, to 3.5×2.5m (12×8ft), or tree to 9×4.5m (30×15ft); lvs to 20cm (8in) long; creamy-white infls to 30cm (1ft) long.
S. villosa*: ultra-hardy; to 3.5–4.5×3m (12–

15×10ft); dense; dark green lvs to 15cm (6in) long; profuse erect infls to 30cm (1ft) long or more of lilac-rose fls, early summer.

*S. vulgaris*** (common lilac): ultra-hardy suckering shrub, to 3.5×3m (12×10ft), or small tree; lvs to 15cm (6in) long; pyramid-shaped infls (v large in some vars) of lilac fls. Numerous vars & hybrids with *S. oblata* (latter often listed as *S.×hyacinthiflora*). Single vars: 'Blue Hyacinth'** (mauve to pale blue); 'Clarke's Giant'** **1** (rosy-mauve to lilac-blue); 'Esther Staley'** (red to pink); 'Lamartine'** (lilac-blue); 'Massena'** (deep red-purple); 'Maud Notcutt'** (pure white); 'Sensation'** **2** (purple-red edged white; may revert); 'Vestale'** **3** (pure white). Double vars: 'Charles Joly'** (deep purple-red, fading); 'Katherine Havemeyer'** (purple-lavender fading pinkish); 'Mme Lemoine'** (creamy-yellow to white).

Ashes, privet and their relatives

A large & varied group ranging from large trees best in large gardens & parkland to ornamental shrubs suitable for specimen, border & hedge planting. Flowers 4/5-lobed & generally white; sometimes inconspicuous. **Cultivation**: Unless stated, very hardy & for any well-drained fertile soil in full sun. Pruning not needed unless grown as hedge (trim spring & later if necessary). **Propagation**: Seed; semi-ripe cuttings; *Ligustrum* spp also by hardwood cuttings; some vars also by grafting on parent sp.

Fringe tree (*Chionanthus virginicus* **4**; in US, old man's beard): shrub, to 3.5×3.5m (12×12ft), or tree to 9m (30ft); stout downy shoots; deciduous lv to 20×8cm (8×3in), bright green; densely clustered drooping panicles of narrow-petalled white fls forming mop-like heads, early summer (best where summers hot). Likes moist loamy soil. *C. retusus* (Chinese fringe tree) is smaller, with smaller lvs & shorter, more erect infls.

Ash trees (*Fraxinus* spp): elegant, fast-growing stately trees with fine pinnate lvs (deciduous) & generally inconspicuous fls in spring, then winged frs (samaras). Good shade trees for streets, lawns, etc. Best in rich, moist soil, but not essential; tolerate heat, wind, pollution.

F. americana **5** (white ash): ultra-hardy; to 11–12×6–7.5m (36–40×20–25ft)/25yrs, eventually to 30m (100ft) or more; grey furrowed bark; lvs to 45cm (1½ft) long, 7–9 lfts, often yellow to purple in autumn.

F. excelsior **6** (common ash of Europe): ultra-hardy; to 12×6m (40×20ft)/25yrs, eventually to 30m (100ft) or more; grey bark; black buds; lvs to 30cm (1ft) long, 9–13 lfts, yellow in autumn; conspicuous clusters of frs. Invasive roots; do not plant near buildings. Vars: 'Diversifolia' ('Monophylla', one-leaved ash; large solitary lfts); 'Jaspidea' **7** (golden ash; often grown incorrectly as 'Aurea'; lvs yellow when young & in autumn); 'Pendula' **8** (weeping ash; umbrella-like); 'Westhof's Glorie' (vigorous & upright; dark glossy green lvs).

F. holotricha: to 7.5–9×4.5–5.5m (25–30×15–18ft); velvety shoots; lvs to 25cm (10in) long, 5–13 lfts, downy beneath. Var 'Moraine' is non-frtg.

F. latifolia (*F. oregona*, Oregon ash): moderately to v hardy; to 7.5–9×4.5–6m (25–30×15–20ft); rough, downy reddish-brown shoots; lvs to 30cm (1ft) long, 5–9 dark green lfts, downy beneath.

Tolerates wet soil.

F. ornus **9** (flowering or manna ash): spreading & round-headed, to 6×6m (20×20ft); dense & leafy; dark grey bark oozing sugary sap when cut; lvs to 20cm (8in) long, 5–9 lfts; dense 8–10cm panicles of creamy-white fls, narrow petals, late spring (with young lvs).

F. pennsylvanica (green or red ash): ultra-hardy; compact, to 9–11×4.5–6m (30–36×15–20ft); similar to *F. americana* but young shoots downy. Vars: 'Marshall's Seedless' (non-frtg); *subintegerrima* (*lanceolata*; thicker lfts & smooth shoots).

F. velutina (Arizona or velvet ash): to 7.5–9×4.5–6m (25–30×15–20ft); ridged bark; young shoots usually velvety; thick lvs to 15cm (6in) long, 3–7 lance-shaped lfts, velvety often both sides. Drought-tolerant.

Privets (*Ligustrum* spp): well-known shrubs with neat entire lvs (evergreen unless stated) & panicles of white fls in summer (rather unpleasant heavy scent) followed by poisonous black berries. V often used for hedges & screens but larger & large-lvd spp good as specimens; sizes given unsheared. Tolerate shade.

L. amurense (Amur privet): ultra-hardy; to 3×3m (10×10ft); deciduous or semi-evergreen lvs to 6cm (2½in) long; 5cm (2in) infls.

L. japonicum (Japanese privet): moderately to v hardy; dense & bushy, to 2.5×2m (8×7ft); dark glossy green lvs to 10×5cm (4×2in); infls to 20cm (8in) long. Var 'Rotundifolium' ('Coriaceum') has leathery rounded lvs.

L. lucidum **10** (Chinese or glossy privet): moderately hardy; tree, to 7.5×6m (25×20ft), or large shrub; dark glossy green lvs to 15×6cm (6×2½in); 15–20cm (6–8in) infls, late. Vars: 'Excelsum Superbum' **11** (broad yellow-edged lvs); 'Tricolor' (grey-green white-edged lvs, tinged pink when young).

L. obtusifolium (sometimes sold incorrectly as *L. ibota*): ultra-hardy; to 2.5×3m (8×10ft); deciduous lvs to 6×2.5cm (2½×1in); small nodding infls. Var *regelianum* grows to 1.5m (5ft), with spreading branches.

L. ovalifolium (oval-leaved privet; in US, California privet): dense & erect, to 4.5×3m (15×10ft); glossy oval lvs to 6×3cm (2½×1¼in), generally semi-evergreen; dense 5–10cm (2–4in) infls. Var 'Aureum' **1** (golden privet) has lvs broadly edged yellow. *L.* 'Vicaryi' **2** is hybrid with *L. vulgaris*; lvs all-yellow (best in sun).

L. sinense: moderately hardy; rounded, to 4.5×4.5m (15×15ft); deciduous or semi-evergreen lvs to 8×2.5cm (3×1in), edged white in var 'Variegatum'; profuse 8–10cm (3–4in) infls.

Olive (*Olea europaea* * **3**): semi- to moderately hardy slow-growing evergreen tree, to 4.5×3m (15×10ft)/25yrs, eventually to 7.5m (25ft), commonly grown in Mediterranean climates for frs & as ornamental; rugged grey bark; leathery grey-green lvs to 8×2cm (3×¾in), silvery beneath; small racemes of white fls, spring; green to black 2–4cm (¾–1½in) frs where summers hot.

Osmanthus (*Osmanthus* spp): somewhat holly-like, generally moderately hardy evergreen shrubs with usually white fragrant fls in clusters, spring unless noted; olive-like, usually deep purple-black frs produced only in warm areas. Excellent specimens for sun or semi-shade.

O. delavayi * * **4**: beautiful, slow-growing & spreading, to 2×2m (7×7ft); sharply toothed 2.5cm (1in) lvs; profuse fls.

O. fragrans * * (sweet olive): semi- to moderately hardy; 3×3m (10×10ft); glossy lance-shaped lvs to 10cm (4in) long, often toothed; fls small but

v fragrant, orange in var *aurantiacus*.

O.×fortunei * * is moderately hardy hybrid with *O. heterophyllus*.

O. heterophyllus *: moderately to v hardy; dense & bushy, to 3×3m (10×10ft), more in warm areas; generally holly-like glossy spiny lvs to 6cm (2½in) long, but some adult lvs entire; fls early autumn. Useful as hedge. Vars: 'Gulftide' (deeply spined lvs); 'Variegatus' **5** (lvs edged cream).

O. yunnanensis * (*O. forrestii*): vigorous & magnificent shrub, to 4.5×4.5m (15×15ft), or small tree; lance-shaped lvs to 20×5cm (8×2in), sometimes spiny; creamy-white fls from late winter.

Osmarea (×*Osmarea burkwoodii* * *; correctly, *Osmanthus*×*burkwoodii*): hybrid of *Osmanthus delavayi* & *Phillyrea* (correctly, *Osmanthus*) *decora*; moderately to v hardy rounded evergreen shrub, to 3×3m (10×10ft); dense & bushy; glossy dark green lvs to 5cm (2in) long, slightly toothed; profuse clusters of white fls, spring.

Phillyreas (*Phillyrea* spp): generally moderately hardy evergreen shrubs closely related to *Osmanthus* spp; usually greenish-white fls, late spring to early summer, in clusters; frs blue-black.

P. angustifolia *: to 3×3m (10×10ft); dense; narrow lance-shaped dark green lvs to 6×1cm (2½×½in), even narrower in var *rosmarinifolia*.

P. decora * (correctly, *Osmanthus decorus*): moderately to v hardy; vigorous & bushy, to 3×3m (10×10ft); dark glossy green leathery lvs to 12×4cm (5×1½in), usually entire; dense clusters of pure white fls, spring.

P. latifolia: shrub, to 3×3m (10×10ft), or small tree; drooping branches; glossy dark green lvs, variable shape & size. Rather olive-like.

Fuchsias

Fuchsia spp & vars. Popular though often somewhat tender shrubs grown for their neat foliage & profuse characteristic nodding flowers, all summer to frosts. Leaves generally to 5cm (2in) long, deciduous unless frost-free. Flowers have spreading/reflexing sepals, tubular to bell-shaped corolla & protruding stamens & pistil (sepal colour given 1st in descriptions). Unless noted, upright & bushy, to 1.2–1.8×1.2–1.8m (4–6×4–6ft) or more in warm areas or under glass (many vars can be trained as standards). Often cut to ground by frost, but hardier spp & vars regrow, generally to 60–90cm (2–3ft). Hardier types good for mixed & shrub borders, or for hedging in mild areas; tender popular for window boxes, hanging baskets, tubs & summer bedding. **Cultivation**: Unless noted, roots moderately to very hardy (especially if mulched). For any well-drained moist, fertile soil in sun or light shade; syringe regularly where summers hot & dry. Pinch out young plants for bushiness. Cut back tender vars in autumn; overwinter frost-free. Prune hardier vars spring; remove dead wood & cut back last year's growth to 2–3 buds. **Propagation**: Easy by softwood cuttings in cold frame, summer.

F. fulgens: tender to semi-hardy; shoots red; lvs to 5–12cm (2–5in) long; narrow 5–8cm (2–3in) red fls, sepal tips yellowish.

F.×hybrida vars: hybrids mainly of *F. coccinea*, *F. fulgens* & *F. magellanica*; fls 5–10cm (2–4in)

long. Hardier named vars include: 'Achievement' (cerise & magenta); 'Alice Hoffman' (compact; young lvs purplish; fls pinkish-scarlet & white); 'Cardinal Farges' **6** (small fls, cerise & white); 'Chillerton Beauty' (rose-pink & violet-purple);

'Display **7**, p145 (carmine & rose-pink); 'Dr Foster' (stems reddish; fls scarlet & violet-mauve); 'Genii' (cerise & violet-rose); 'Lena' (low & arching; semi-double, flesh-pink & purple); 'Mme Cornelissen' (semi-double, rich crimson & white); 'Margaret' **8**, p145 (crimson & red-veined purple); 'Mrs Popple **9**, p145 (scarlet & deep purple); 'Mrs W. P. Wood' (flesh-pink & white); 'Phyllis **10**, p145 (pinkish-scarlet, darker corolla); 'Pixie' pinkish-scarlet & red-veined lavender; 'Pumila' (*F. magellanica* 'Pumila'; dwarf, to 20cm [8in]; tiny crimson-scarlet & violet-blue fls); 'Riccartonii' **1** (*F. magellanica* 'Riccartonii'; v vigorous & hardy; scarlet &

purple); 'Rose of Castile Improved' **2** (flesh-pink & purple); 'Tom Thumb' **3** (dwarf, to 40cm [16in]; carmine-pink & violet-purple); 'Trase' (cerise & white).

F. magellanica: to 2.5m (8ft) or more in mild areas; young stems reddish; narrow fls, bright red & purple or blue-violet. Hardiest sp. Vars: 'Gracilis' (v slender & graceful); 'Gracilis Variegata' **4** ('Variegata'; moderately hardy; lvs edged creamy-yellow & flushed pink); *molinae* ('Alba'; white & pale lilac-pink); 'Thompsonii' (similar to 'Gracilis' but more erect); 'Versicolor' (lvs grey-green edged creamy-white, flushed crimson when young).

Tree paeonies

Paeonia spp & vars; formerly classified in Ranunculaceae. Shrubby (never truly tree-like) relatives of the well-known border perennials, with sometimes very large showy flowers, often with crinkly petals (& prominent boss of stamens in single & semi-double vars) in late spring & early summer. Deciduous, with deeply divided leaves. Excellent long-lived specimens. **Cultivation**: Very hardy, but young growth very prone to spring frost damage (especially where winters mild), so best sheltered &/or protected with sacking, etc, when necessary. For any moist but well-drained fertile soil in semi-shade; plant deeply (especially grafted vars); mulch & feed. Dead-head; cut back any damaged wood in spring. Prone to paeony blight (botrytis), especially in damp crowded conditions. **Propagation**: Spp by seed; *P. potaninii* by division; vars usually by grafting on herbaceous *P. lactiflora* but divide if established on own roots.

P. delavayi: suckering, to 1.8×1.8m (6×6ft); doubly divided dark green lvs, lfts to 10cm (4in) long; cup-shaped deep red fls 6–10cm (2½–4in) across, golden stamens. *P.* 'Black Pirate' **5** is hybrid with maroon-crimson fls. *P. potaninii* (*P. delavayi angustiloba*) is similar but smaller, with smaller fls & more finely divided lvs; spreads by stolons; var *alba* is creamy-white.

P.×lemoinei vars: hybrids of *P. lutea* & *P. suffruticosa*, sometimes listed as Lutea hybrids; fls 15–20cm (6–8in) wide, single to fully double, in various yellow shades. Vars: 'Age of Gold' (semi-/double, creamy-gold); 'Alice Harding' (double, lemon-yellow); 'Argosy' (single, primrose-yellow blotched carmine); 'Chromatella' (double, sulphur-yellow); 'L'Esperance' **6** (semi-double, pale yellow marked crimson); 'Souvenir de Maxime Cornu'** **7** (v double, yellow tinged brownish/red). *P. lutea* (*P. delavayi lutea*): to 1–1.2m×1–1.2m (3–4×3–4ft); rather soft-wooded & somewhat herbaceous; lvs like *P. delavayi*; cup-shaped

golden-yellow fls 6cm (2½in) across. Var *ludlowii* **8** is more robust 1.8–2.5×1.8–2.5m (6–8×6–8ft), with larger, flatter, earlier fls. *P.* 'Anne Rosse' is hybrid with *P. delavayi*; fls lemon-yellow, reverse streaked red.

P. suffruticosa (*P. arborea, P. moutan,* moutan or common tree paeony): to 1.8×1.8m (6×6ft); stiff habit; doubly pinnate/divided lvs with deeply divided lfts; fls of sp to 15cm (6in) wide, but to 30cm (1ft) or more in garden vars; silky petals. Natural vars: 'Banksii' (double, purplish red shading to almost white); 'Rock's Variety'* **9** (single or semi-double, white, maroon blotch); 'Rosea Plena'* (double, pink). Japanese garden vars have finely divided lvs & beautiful single to double erect fls with silky, crinkled petals in shades of white, pink, red, lilac & purple. Chinese & European garden vars have v large & heavy fully double fls, often drooping, mainly in pink shades; vars include: 'Bijou de Chusan' (blush white, rose centre); 'Comtesse de Tuder' (blush pink); 'Elizabeth' ('Reine Elisabeth'; crimson).

Palms

Uniquely spectacular "architectural" evergreens long favoured for creating exotic effect, mainly in warm areas but some remarkably hardy. (Where winters cold most can be grown in tubs & moved under glass in winter.) Range from low-growing types usable for ground cover to tall graceful trees with unbranched trunk crowned by cluster of often huge leaves (fronds) generally divided pinnately (in "feather" palms) or palmately ("fan" palms). Inflorescences grow from among or beneath leaves (spp marked † have males & females separate; latter produce fruits [often decorative] only if male nearby). **Cultivation**:

Unless stated, semi-hardy (to about −6°C [21°F] if well-ripened) & for any well-drained soil in sun or (especially when young) light shade. Transplant easily in spring. Remove dead leaves early spring; hose down to remove dust, pests, salt, etc. **Propagation**: Seed; clump-forming spp by division.

Queen palm (*Arecastrum romanozoffianum, Cocos plumosa*): fast-growing, to 7.5×4.5m (25×15ft); v straight grey trunk; arching feathery lvs to 3–4.5m (10–15ft) long, bright glossy green.

Blue hesper palm (*Brahea* [*Erythea*] *armata* **1**): slow-growing, to 4.5–6×2.5m (15–20×8ft); stout, rough trunk; fan-like silvery-blue lvs 1–1.5m (3–5ft) across; arching plumes to 4.5m (15ft) long of grey-white fls; frs brown.

Pindo or jelly palm (*Butia capitata*†): semi- to moderately hardy; slow-growing, to 3–4.5×3–4.5m (10–15×10–15ft); stout trunk with dead lf bases; arching feathery lvs to 3.5–4.5m (12–15ft) long; infls to 1.5m (5ft) long of small yellow to red fls; large edible pineapple-flavoured frs.

European fan palm (*Chamaerops humilis*† **2**): moderately hardy; generally multi-stemmed, to 1.5×2.5m (5×8ft), but single-stemmed form taller; stiff fan-like lvs 60–90cm (2–3ft) wide; 12cm (5in) infls of small yellow fls; small frs.

Chilean wine palm (*Jubaea chilensis, J. spectabilis*): slow-growing & robust, to 3–4.5×3m (10–15×10ft); thick trunk with scars of lf bases; feathery lvs to 2–3.5m (7–12ft) long; dense dropping infls; yellow 4cm (1½in) frs.

Date palms (*Phoenix* spp): feather palms with folded lfts, lowest reduced to spines.
P. canariensis† **3** (Canary Island date palm): robust, to 3–4.5×3.5–5.5m (10–15×12–18ft); stout trunk with dead lf bases; dense crown of lvs to 6m (20ft) long, drooping when mature; fls on 2m (7ft) stalks; heavy clusters of orange frs.
P. dactylifera† (date palm): to 4.5–6×7.5–11m

(15–20×25–36ft); often suckering when young; slender trunk; rather sparse crown; glaucous lvs to 6m (20ft) long; white fls on 1.2m (4ft) stalks; deep orange frs. Propagated by suckers.

Needle palm (*Rhapidophyllum hystrix*): moderately hardy; bushy & slow-growing, to 1.5×2.5m (5×8ft); suckering; fan-shaped dark green lvs to 1m (3ft) across, silvery beneath (bases have needle-like spines); wine-red fls.

Lady palm (*Rhapis excelsa*†): bamboo-like & clump-forming, to 2.5–3×1.8–2.5m (8–10×6–8ft); slender green cane-like stems; dark glossy green fan-like lvs to 60cm (2ft) wide, lfts finely toothed, slender stalk. Likes shade. *R. humilis* is similar but taller & more slender. Good in tubs.

Palmetto (cabbage palm, *Sabal palmetto*): slow-growing, to 3–4.5×3.5–4.5m (10–15×12–15ft) or more; dense globular head; fan-shaped lvs to 2.5cm (8ft).

Windmill palm (Chusan palm, *Trachycarpus fortunei* **4**, *T.* [*Chamaerops*] *excelsa*): moderately hardy; to 2.5–3×1.8–2.5m (8–10×6–8ft) where winters mild; trunk covered with lf bases & dark fibres; stiff fan-like lvs to 1m (3ft) across, toothed stalk.

Washington palm (California fan palm, *Washingtonia filifera* **5**): to 4.5–5.5×3–3.5m (15–18×10–12ft); distinctive, with dense hanging thatch ("petticoat") of dead lvs below crown; grey-green fan-shaped lvs to 2m (7ft) across with numerous long threads; numerous white fls; frs black & shiny. *W. robusta* (Mexican fan palm) is similar but taller & more slender.

Pittosporums

Pittosporum spp. Somewhat tender, mostly Australasian evergreen shrubs or small trees grown for their attractive foliage (good for cutting) & small but fragrant flowers (generally in clusters). Leaves generally to 10×2.5–4cm (4×1–1½in). Handsome specimen/hedging plants, for mild areas, often grown against wall where colder; good in tubs. **Cultivation**: Semi- to moderately hardy unless stated. Best in light loamy soil in sun or semi-shade. Trim to restrict size. **Propagation**: Seed; semi-ripe cuttings; grafting.

P. crassifolium* **6** (karo): to 3.5–4.5×3m (12–15×10ft); thick dark green lvs, dense down beneath; reddish-purple fls, spring. Var 'Variegatum' has grey-green lvs edged white.
P. tenuifolium**: moderately hardy; fast-growing bushy tree, to 7.5×2.5m (25×8ft) or more; columnar when young; pale glossy green wavy lvs to 6×2cm (2½×¾in); dark red fls, spring. Makes good tall hedge. Vars: 'Irene Paterson' **7** (young lvs creamy, becoming green marbled white, tinged pink in winter); 'Purpureum' (mature lvs reddish-purple); 'Silver Queen' (lvs edged whitish); 'Tom Thumb' (dwarf version of

'Purpureum'). *P.* 'Garnettii' **8** is probably hybrid with *P. ralphii*; lvs grey-green edged white, often tinged pink.
P. tobira** **9** (tobira): bushy, to 4.5×3.5m (15×12ft); dark leathery lvs; creamy-white 2.5cm (1in) fls from late spring. Var 'Variegatum' has grey-green lvs edged creamy-white.
P. undulatum** **10** (Victorian box): semi-hardy; generally a tree, to 9×6m (30×20ft) or more; dark glossy green wavy lvs to 15×5cm (6×2in); creamy-white fls, late spring or early summer; showy orange frs. Var 'Variegatum' has lvs edged creamy-white.

The protea family

Generally rather tender evergreen trees & shrubs from S Hemisphere with striking & distinctive flowers, often having prominent styles, some forming large cone-shaped heads (generally good for cutting, many also for drying). Generally like Mediterranean-type climate, with hot dry summers & warm moist winters; good near sea but most need conservatory treatment in cool temperate regions. Many smaller spp good for hedging where hardy. **Cultivation:** Unless stated, tender to semi-hardy & for very well-drained lime-free soil in sun. Pruning not needed. **Propagation:** Semi-ripe cuttings; seed (spring-sown unless stated); *Embothrium* sp by suckers; *Protea* spp also sometimes by softwood cuttings, grafting.

Australian honeysuckles (*Banksia* spp): mainly Australian shrubs with handsome, variable lvs & broad bottlebrush infls often at branch tips, late winter or spring unless stated, followed by woody cone-like frs. V drought-tolerant.
B. coccinea: to 3.5×1.8m (12×6ft); usually bushy; dark green toothed, oval lvs; bright red infls to 8×5cm (3×2in). V showy.
B. collina: to 1.8–3×1.8m (6–10×6ft); narrow, toothed deep green lvs, silver reverse; honey-buff infls to 15cm (6in) long, long stamens (purple-brown, red or yellow-green).
B. ericifolia 1: to 4.5×4m (15×13ft); dense & bushy; heath-like bright green lvs; slender golden-yellow infls to 25cm (10in) long, silky styles, autumn & winter. Good for hedging.
B. grandis (bull banksia): variable shrub or tree, to 1.5–9×3–6m (5–30×10–20ft); lvs to 30cm (1ft) long, dark green & toothed down to midrib; yellow infls to 30×8cm (12×3in).
B. integrifolia: tree, to 6–12×3–6m (20–40×10–20ft); dense; leathery lance-shaped lvs, white beneath; yellow-brown 15cm (6in) infls.
B. littoralis 2: tree, to 7.5–12×3–6m (25–40×10–20ft); narrow, toothed lvs, white beneath; orange-yellow infls to 25cm (10in) long, prominent purple or yellowish styles.
B. menziesii (honey flower): to 3.5–12×2–6m (12–40×7–20ft); narrow toothed lvs, brown hairs beneath; pink/red & gold infls to 12cm (5in) long.
B. occidentalis: to 1.5×1.8m (5×6ft); narrow lvs, white beneath; red infls to 15cm (6in) long.
B. serrata 3: shrub/tree, to 9×3.5m (30×12ft); rough bark; wavy, toothed lvs; grey-green infls to 15×8cm (6×3in), autumn. Tolerates salt spray.
Chilean fire bush (*Embothrium coccineum*): semi- or moderately hardy slender & erect shrub or tree best in light woodland (needs moist fertile soil) in cool moist climate. To 6–12×4m (20–40×13ft); suckering; dark green glossy lvs 5–8cm (3–4in) long; profuse brilliant scarlet fls in cylindrical racemes to 10cm (4in) long, late spring & early summer. Var *lanceolatum* 'Norquinco Valley' 4 is hardier, semi-evergreen & v free-flg.
Chilean nut (Chilean hazel, *Gevuina avellana*; sometimes incorrectly spelled *Guevina*): fine leafy tree, to 12×4.5m (40×15ft); brown, downy shoots; handsome glossy green pinnate lvs to 40×25cm (15×10in); racemes to 10cm (4in) long of white fls, prominent stamens, mid

summer; red edible nuts ripening black only in warm moist areas. For sheltered woodland.
Grevilleas (spider flowers, *Grevillea* spp): distinctive Australian trees & (mainly) shrubs having tubular fls with long curved styles, clustered loosely or in erect or toothbrush-like spidery heads, all year unless stated. Lvs v variable; frs pod-like. Drought-tolerant. Hybridize freely.
G. alpina 5: semi- to moderately hardy; compact & bushy, to 30–60×90cm (1–2×3ft); variable; lvs usually grey-green & needle-like, to 2.5cm (1in) long; fls red & yellow, in terminal clusters. For rock gardens or pots.
G. asplenifolia: fast-growing, to 3×4m (10×13ft); fine, narrow, fern-like lvs to 25cm (10in) long; deep red toothbrush-like infls to 5cm (2in) long.
G. banksii 6 (often sold as *G. banksii forsteri*): shrub, to 3×2m (10×7ft), or small tree; dark green pinnate lvs to 15cm (6in) long; bright red fls (rarely cream) in erect spikes 18cm (7in) tall. Popular specimen plant; wind-tolerant.
G. bipinnatifida: sprawling, to 1×1.5m (3×5ft); attractive v divided prickly lvs to 10cm (4in) long; infls to 15cm (6in) long of red toothbrush-like fls, winter–spring.
G. buxifolia: to 1.5×1.5m (5×5ft); hairy lvs to 2cm (¾in) long; woolly grey fls in clusters.
G. lanigera: to 1×1.5m (3×5ft); narrow, hairy lvs to 2cm (¾in) long; red & cream fls, late winter or spring. Useful on banks.
G. robusta (silky oak): semi-hardy (more so when mature); tree, to 18×9m (60×30ft), or can be clipped as hedge; fine, ferny, compound lvs (many drop in spring); orange toothbrush-like infls to 10cm (4in) long, spring. Useful timber & street tree in warm climates; seedlings popular foliage pot/bedding plants in temperate zones. Branches brittle; stake when young. Tolerates poor soil.
G. rosmarinifolia 7: semi- to moderately hardy; to 1.8×1.8m (6×6ft); narrow rosemary-like lvs to 4cm (1½in) long, hairy beneath; red fls. Can be clipped as formal hedge.
G. sulphurea 8 (*G. juniperina sulphurea*): moderately hardy; to 2×2m (7×7ft); needle-like lvs to 2cm (¾in) long; fls variable, usually canary-yellow, spring to early summer.
G. wilsonii (firewheel): to 1×1.5m (3×5ft); prickly, divided lvs; red fls in spring.

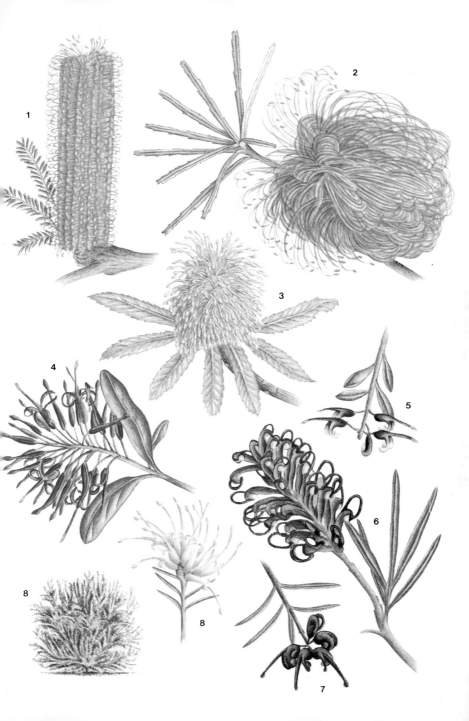

G. hybrids: 'Canberra Gem' (to 2×2m [7×7ft]; waxy pink & red fls); 'Sandra Gordon' (to 4×2.5m [13×8ft]; bright yellow fls); 'Shirley Howie' (to 1.2×1.2m [4×4ft]; deep pink fls).

Hakeas (pincushion trees, *Hakea* spp): large group of Australian trees & (mainly) shrubs with fls like *Grevillea* spp but borne in leaf axils & followed by attractive woody frs. Lvs needle-like unless stated, these spp conifer-like. Tolerate poor, dry soil & lime; good near coast.

H. laurina **1** (sea-urchin tree): tree, to 6–9×3–6m (20–30×10–20ft), or large shrub; lance-shaped lvs to 15cm (6in) long; crimson fls, yellow styles, in dense clusters, autumn & winter. Best-known sp, popular in Mediterranean area.

H. lissosperma: moderately hardy; to 3×2m (10×7ft); lvs to 15cm (6in) long; white fls, summer; frs to 2.5cm (1in) long. Makes good screen. *H. sericea* (*H. acicularis*) is similar.

H. microcarpa*: moderately hardy; to 3×3m (10×10ft); lvs to 8cm (3in) long; white fls, late spring; pale brown frs to 1cm (½in) long.

H. suaveolens* (sweet hakea): to 3×3m (10×10ft); lvs to 10cm (4in) long; white fls, autumn & winter. Good for screening.

Silver tree (*Leucodendron argenteum** **2**): slow-growing S African tree, to 9×6m (30×20ft), or large shrub grown mainly for foliage (good in arrangements); fine lance-shaped lvs to 15cm (6in) long, densely silver-haired & shimmering; male fls* orange, to 6cm (2½in) across, females (unscented; on separate trees) in silvered cone-like heads, mid summer. Fine specimen tree but not long-lived. Prone to root rot. Sow seed autumn.

Nodding pincushion (*Leucospermum nutans* **3**, *L. cordifolium*): S African shrub, to 1–1.5×1.5m (3–5×5ft); oval lvs to 6cm (2½in) long; profuse pink to purple or orange-red fls to 10cm (4in) across with prominent tubular styles, late winter & early spring (v good for cutting). Not long-lived; roots resent disturbance, prone to rot; tolerates lime. Sow seed autumn.

Lomatias (*Lomatia* spp): semi- to moderately hardy shrubs with attractive lvs & grevillea-like fls, mid summer (valued for arrangements). For any soil (except shallow chalk) in partial shade.

L. ferruginea: to 9×4.5m (30×15ft), or small tree; shoots covered with brown-red down; deep green divided lvs to 40cm (15in) long; buff & scarlet fls in racemes to 5cm (2in) long.

L. myricoides** (*L. longifolia*): to 2.5×3m (8×10ft); dark green lance-shaped lvs to 15cm (6in) long; white fls.

L. tinctoria* **4**: to 1×1.8m (3×6ft); dark green divided lvs to 8cm (3in) long; pale yellow fls. Hardiest sp.

Proteas (*Protea* spp): rather difficult S African shrubs with tiny fls massed in dense, showy artichoke-like heads with colourful, sometimes hairy bracts & usually opening to a goblet shape, winter to late spring unless stated (S African national fl; important commercial cut fl; good for drying). For group planting, or larger spp as specimens; fl best when young. Most need cool humidity of coastal sites; must have perfect drainage but regular watering; prone to root rot, borers, leaf miners. Dead-head unless seed wanted (slow maturing; sow autumn).

P. aristata (Christmas or Ladysmith protea): to 1.5×1.2m (5×4ft); needle-like lvs; dusty-pink fl heads to 12cm (5in) long, spring & summer.

P. barbigera (*P. magnifica*, bearded or giant woolly protea): to 1.5×1.5m (5×5ft); grey-green pink-edged lvs to 20cm (8in) long; fl heads to 15cm (6in) wide, silver tipped black, white-bearded pink, yellow-green or white bracts.

P. compacta: to 3×1.5–2m (10×5–7ft); erect & compact; neatly overlapping oval leathery lvs to 11cm (4½in) long, light green; profuse softly hairy rose-pink fl heads to 10cm (4in) long, autumn to mid summer.

P. cynaroides **5** (giant or king protea): to 1×1m (3×3ft); variable lvs to 12cm (5in) long, long stalks; profuse bowl-shaped fl heads to 25cm (10in) across, silver or pink inside, dark red to rose or silver-pink velvety bracts. Magnificent; the finest cut fl.

P. longiflora **6**: to 3×2.5m (10×8ft); oval lvs to 10cm (4in) long; slender pointed buds to 10cm (4in) long opening greenish-white, cream or pink, silky styles, spring & summer (short-lived).

P. neriifolia **7**: to 3×2.5m (10×8ft); slender lvs to 15cm (6in) long; fl heads to 12cm (5in) long, not opening wide, bracts iridescent pink or red, fringed & bearded with brown hairs, winter.

P. mellifera (*P. repens*, sugarbush, honey flower): to 2×1.8m (7×6ft); erect; slender lvs to 10cm (4in) long; fls to 12×8cm (5×3in) like inverted cone, bracts pale green, white or rose (attract bees).

P. susannae: to 2×2m (7×7ft); pungent grey-green lvs to 12cm (5in) long; fls to 10×6cm (4×2½in), rose or white within, bracts pink, brown base. For limy soils.

Firewheel tree (*Stenocarpus sinuatus* **8**): tree, to 9×4.5m (30×15ft); dark green glossy lvs, sometimes lobed, to 30cm (1ft) long; red fls, yellow stamens, in radiating umbels to 8cm (3in) wide, mainly autumn; pod-like frs to 10cm (4in) long. Tolerates lime.

Waratahs (*Telopea* spp): Australasian shrubs with striking brilliant red fls in bracted infls. For moist soils; prune after flg.

T. speciosissima **9** (New South Wales waratah): to 3×1.5m (10×5ft); toothed lvs to 15cm (6in) long; infls 15cm (6in) across, spring.

T. truncata (Tasmanian waratah): moderately hardy; to 3×3m (10×10ft); lvs & early summer fls smaller than above.

Californian lilacs and their relatives

A varied group including perhaps the finest (though somewhat tender) blue-flowered shrubs.
Cultivation: For light, well-drained soil in sun. Pruning unnecessary unless stated. **Propagation**: Seed, sown autumn; *Ceanothus*, *Paliurus* & *Rhamnus* spp & vars also by semi-ripe heel cuttings.

Californian lilacs (*Ceanothus* spp & hybrids, many of doubtful parentage): fast-growing Californian shrubs with tiny blue (or rarely pink) fls in profuse showy panicles. Unless stated, moderately hardy, semi-/evergreen & fl on yr-old wood late spring to early summer (prune after flg only for containment). Late-flg spp fl on new wood (prune early spring, deciduous spp hardest). Best against sunny wall in borderline areas; sizes given are for free-standing specimens. Not long-lived; in N America, flourish only on W Coast.
C. arboreus 'Trewithen Blue'*: semi-hardy; often tree-like, to 6×6m (20×20ft); dark green lvs to 10cm (4in) long, grey beneath; infls to 10×5cm (4×2in), blue, long season.
C. 'Burkwoodii': hybrid of *C. floribundus* & *C.* 'Indigo'; moderately to v hardy; to 2×2m (7×7ft); shiny oval lvs to 3cm (1¼in) long, greyish beneath; 5cm (2in) infls of dark blue fls, mid summer to autumn. *C.* 'Autumnal Blue' is similar but lvs glossier; infls larger, paler blue.
C. caeruleus (*C. azureus*): to 2.5×2.5m (8×8ft); 5cm (2in) lvs, brown-haired beneath; 15cm (6in) fluffy infls of sky-blue fls, summer to autumn.
C.×delilianus vars: hybrids of *C. americanus* & *C. caeruleus*; moderately to v hardy; deciduous; fl mid summer to autumn. Best-known var is 'Gloire de Versailles' **1**: to 1.8×1.8m (6×6ft), or can be clipped in formal plantings; oval lvs; showy infls to 20cm (8in) long of powder-blue fls. Other vars (to 1.5×1.8m [5×6ft]): 'Mairie Simon' **2** (probably *C. ovatus* hybrid; rose-pink); 'Perle Rose' (rose-pink); 'Topaz' (indigo-blue).
C. dentatus: to 3×3m (10×10ft); shiny dark green lvs to 1cm (½in) long, grey beneath; 4cm (1½in) clusters of bright blue fls.
C. foliosus 'Italian Skies': may be hybrid; to 1.5×2.5m (5×8ft); dark green lvs to 2cm (¾in) long; branching infls of bright blue fls.
C. gloriosus (in US, Point Reyes ceanothus): prostrate & carpeting, to 0.1×3m (4in×10ft); leathery 4cm (1½in) lvs; lavender-blue fls.
C. griseus horizontalis (in US, Carmel creeper): prostrate, to 0.15×3m (6in×10ft); bright green 5cm (2in) lvs; light blue fls. *C.* 'Edinburgh' **3** ('Edinensis') is hybrid of upright form of *C. griseus*; bushy, to 2.5×3m (8×10ft); olive-green lvs; clusters of rich blue fls.
C. impressus **4** (Santa Barbara ceanothus): to 1.5×1.8m (5×6ft); crowded dark green lvs to 1cm (½in) long; profuse deep blue fls.
C.×lobbianus: hybrid probably of *C. dentatus* & *C. griseus*; to 1.8×2.5m (6×8ft); oblong lvs, pale beneath; dark blue fls. Vars 'Russellianus' & 'Southmead' have bright blue.
C. rigidus: semi-hardy; to 1.2×1.8m (4×6ft); dense; dark glossy green wedge-shaped lvs to 1cm (½in) long; 2.5cm (1in) infls of purplish-blue fls. *C.* 'Delight' (hybrid with *C. papillosus*) is moderately hardy; to 2.5×3m (8×10ft); deep green lvs; 5–8cm (2–3in) infls of rich blue fls.
C. thyrsiflorus **5** (blue-blossom): moderately to v hardy; to 3.5×5m (12×15ft), or small tree; glossy lvs to 4cm (1½in) long; 2.5–8cm (1–3in) clusters of pale blue fls. Vars: 'Cascade' (arching habit); *repens* (prostrate, to 0.1×3m [4in×10ft], or mounding to 1m [3ft]).
C.×veitchianus: hybrid of doubtful parentage; to 2.5×2.5m (8×8ft); wedge-shaped glossy lvs; profuse 2.5–5cm (1–2in) infls of deep blue fls.
Colletias (*Colletia* spp): curious moderately hardy shrubs, almost leafless when adult; profuse 1–4cm (½–1½in) spines; tubular petalless fls 3mm (⅛in) long, autumn.
C. armata*: to 2.5×1.8m (8×6ft); young growth solely spines; fls white (pink in var 'Rosea' **6**).
C. cruciata*: slow-growing, to 2.5×2m (8×7ft); spines triangular/bodkin-shaped; fls yellowish.
Japanese raisin tree (*Hovenia dulcis*): deciduous tree, v hardy if ripened; to 6×4.5m (20×15ft); glossy, toothed, heart-shaped lvs to 18×15cm (7×6in); fls greenish; fleshy fr stalks.
Christ's thorn (*Paliurus spina-christi* **7**): moderately to v hardy thorny shrub, to 3.5×3.5m (12×12ft), or small tree; deciduous oval lvs to 4cm (1½in) long, yellow in autumn; profuse greenish-yellow fls, summer; flat yellow frs. Good for hedging.
Buckthorns (*Rhamnus* spp): foliage shrubs (those listed thornless) with dark green oval lvs to 5cm (2in) long; inconspicuous whitish-green fls; frs to 5mm (¼in) across, red ripening black.
R. alaternus (Italian buckthorn): moderately hardy evergreen, fast-growing to 3×2.5m (10×8ft). Tolerates pollution, salt, shearing. Var 'Argenteovariegata' **8** has narrow lvs edged cream.
R. frangula **9** (alder buckthorn): ultra-hardy; to 4.5×3.5m (15×12ft); deciduous. May self-seed. Vars: 'Asplenifolia' (thread-like lvs); 'Columnaris' ('Tallhedge'; to 3.5×1.2m [12×4ft]; for hedging).
Jujube (Chinese date, *Ziziphus jujuba* **10**): v hardy spiny tree for any dry soil where summers hot; to 6×3.5m (20×12ft); deciduous glossy lvs to 5cm (2in) long; plum-like edible frs, ripen black.

Rose species and their close varieties

New classification: Wild roses. *Rosa* spp & vars, including natural and similar man-made hybrids, usually with 5-petalled single flowers, also some semi-doubles and doubles; generally once-flowering, in late spring or early summer. Deciduous, with pinnate leaves and oval leaflets. Many have decorative fruits (hips) in autumn. Mostly medium to large open shrubs, best for shrub plantings or as specimens. **Cultivation**: Unless stated, moderately to very hardy. For well-drained, well-prepared fertile soil in full sun. Generally more pest- and disease-resistant than bush roses. **Pruning**: Little needed except removal of dead growth. Do not dead-head if hips wanted. **Propagation**: Hardwood cuttings; seed (hand-pollinate). For certain species, see also other rose articles.

R. californica plena* **1**: to 1.8×1.5m (6×5ft); wiry, arching stems; lvs fern-like; semi-double pink fls 4cm (1½in) across, in clusters; hips edible after frost.

R. 'Canary Bird'* **2** (*R. xanthina* 'Canary Bird'): to 2×2m (7×7ft); bushy, with arching stems; bright green ferny lvs; 5cm (2in) canary-yellow fls, early; may die back on heavy soils.

R.×dupontii** ('Dupontii', *R. moschata nivea*): to 2×2m (7×7ft); lax; few thorns; grey-green lvs; fls to 8cm (3in) across, creamy-pink fading white; hips orange.

R. ecae: moderately hardy; to 1.5×1.2m (5×4ft); fine fern-like lvs; rich yellow 2.5cm (1in) fls.

R. farreri persetosa **3** (*R. elegantula* 'Persetosa', threepenny-bit rose): to 1.5×1.8m (5×6ft); dense & thorny; v small ferny lvs; profuse pink fls 2cm (¾in) across; profuse coral-red hips.

R. fedtschenkoana*: v hardy; to 2.5×1.8m (8×6ft); vigorous & suckering; glaucous lvs; white fls throughout summer.

R. foetida bicolor **4** (*R. lutea punicea*, *R. lutea bicolor*, Austrian copper brier): moderately hardy; to 1.5×1.2m (5×4ft); arching; bright green lvs; brilliant copper-red fls 5–8cm (2–2½in) across, yellow reverse; strange scent.

R. forrestiana*: to 2×1.8m (7×6ft); lax & arching; clusters of white-eyed pink fls 4cm (1½in) across; hips bright red.

R. 'Golden Chersonese'*: hybrid of *R. ecae* & 'Canary Bird'; to 1.8×1.5m (6×5ft); wiry stems; dainty lvs; bright golden-yellow fls 4cm (1½in) across.

R.×harisonii** **5** ('Harison's Yellow'): probably a hybrid of *R. spinosissima* & *R. foetida* 'Persiana'; v hardy; to 1.8×1.2m (6×4ft); semi-double bright yellow fls 5cm (2in) across.

R. 'Highdownensis' (*R.×highdownensis*): *R. moyesii* seedling; vigorous, to 3×3m (10×10ft); clustered cerise-crimson fls 6cm (2½in) across; v large orange-red bottle-shaped hips.

R. moyesii 'Geranium' **6**: to 3×2.5m (10×8ft); fls blood-red, 5cm (2in) across; v large orange-red bottle-shaped hips.

R. moyesii rosea (*R. holodonta*): similar to above, but fls pink, clustered; largest hips, to 8cm (3in) long.

R.×paulii** ('Paulii', *R. rugosa repens alba*):

hybrid of *R. rugosa* & *R. arvensis*; ultra-hardy; spreading, to 1.2×3.5m (4×12ft), making dense ground cover; v thorny; profuse clustered starry white fls 5cm (2in) across. Var *rosea*** **7** ('Paulii Rosea') is similar but less vigorous; pink.

R. pomifera (*R. villosa*, apple rose): to 2×2m (7×7ft); stiff habit; lvs rosy-pink, 5cm (2in) across; hairy, gooseberry-like crimson hips to 2.5cm (1in) across, edible. Var *duplex* (Wolley-Dod's rose) is semi-double; hips fewer & smaller.

R. primula* (incense rose): to 1.8×1.8m (6×6ft); stiff red thorns; glaucous lvs, aromatic after rain; profuse pale yellow fls 4cm (1½in) across, early.

R. roxburghii* **8** (*R. microphylla*): chestnut, burr or chinquapin rose): sturdy, to 2×1.8m (7×6ft); greyish shredding bark; many lfts; fls pink, 6cm (2½in) across, double; yellowish-green tomato-shaped hips 4cm (1½in) across, prickly.

R. rubiginosa (*R. eglanteria*) hybrids (Penzance sweet-briers): v hardy; to 1.8×1.8m (6×6ft) or more; thorny & tangled; fls fleeting, 5cm (2in) across. Vars: 'Amy Robsart'* (pink); 'Lord Penzance'* (buff-yellow); 'Meg Merrilees' (crimson).

R. rubrifolia **9** (*R. glauca*): ultra-hardy; to 1.8×1.5m (6×5ft); arching; young stems plum-coloured, few thorns; lvs purplish/reddish-grey; pink fls 4cm (1½in) across; red-brown hips.

R. sericea pteracantha **10** (*R. omeiensis pteracantha*): to 2.5×1.8m (8×6ft); flat wing-like thorns to 4cm (1½in) wide, red when young; 4-petalled white fls 5cm (2in) across, early.

R. spinosissima altaica* (*R. pimpinellifolia altaica*, *R. altaica*): v hardy; to 1.8×1.2m (6×4ft); stems bristly; creamy-white 6cm (2½in) fls; hips almost black.

R. virginiana* (*R. lucida*): ultra-hardy; to 1.8×1.8m (6×6ft); dense & suckering; few thorns; glossy lvs, colouring well in autumn; fls cerise-pink, 5cm (2in) across; hips scarlet.

'Williams' Double Yellow'* (*R. spinosissima* [*R. pimpinellifolia*] *lutea plena*): v hardy; to 1×1m (3×3ft); prickly; double mimosa-yellow fls, green carpels in centre, early.

Old garden roses

Rosa hybrids derived from various species. New classification generally same as traditional groupings; groups originated before development of Hybrid Teas in late 19th century. Unless stated, mainly for general shrub plantings. **Cultivation**: Generally as for species (p156), but some rather disease-prone. **Propagation**: Hardwood cuttings; budding. For climbing vars, see pp242–4.

Albas: ancient, probably cross of *R. corymbifera* & a Damask; v hardy; vigorous; sparse thorns; grey-green lvs; summer-flg. Prune after flg; ⅔ of laterals & if necessary ⅓ of main stems.
R.×*alba maxima*** 1** (Jacobite rose): to 1.8×1.5m (6×5ft); double white fls 8cm (3in) across; oval hips.
R. 'Félicité Parmentier'*: to 1.2×1m (4×3ft); clusters of flesh-pink 5cm (2in) fls.
R. 'Königin von Dänemarck'** ('Queen of Denmark'): 1.5×1.2m (5×4ft); lax; lvs bluish; v double carmine-centred pink 6cm (2½in) fls.
R. 'Maiden's Blush'*: to 1.5×2m (5×7ft); blush-pink loosely double 7cm (2¼in) fls.
Bourbons: from cross of China & Damask roses; moderately hardy; some vars lax; smooth lvs; large globular double fls, most repeating. Prune as for Albas, but in spring.
R. 'Ferdinand Pichard'** 2**: to 1.5×1.2m (5×4ft); cupped fls 5cm (2in) across, pink striped crimson. Often classed as Hybrid Perpetual.
R. 'Mme Isaac Pereire'** 3**: to 2×1.5m (7×5ft); cerise-pink 10cm (4in) fls.
R. 'Mme Pierre Oger'**: to 1.8×1m (6×3ft); 8cm (3in) fls, blush-pink, deeper at edges.
R. 'Zéphirine Drouhin': see p244.
Centifolias (Provence or cabbage roses): possibly derived from Albas & Damasks; v hardy; lax, most needing support; lvs limp; fls nodding, double, summer. Prune ⅓ of main canes after flg.
R.×*centifolia**** (cabbage, Holland or Provence rose): to 1.5×1.2m (5×4ft); globular pink fls 8cm (3in) across.
R. 'Chapeau de Napoleon'** 4** (*R.*×*centifolia cristata*, 'Crested Moss'): not a true Moss rose, though mossy calyx; to 1.5×1.2m (5×4ft); rose-pink 8cm (3in) across.
R. 'Fantin-Latour'**: to 1.8×1.5m (6×5ft); erect; pale blush-pink fls 7cm (2¾in) across.
China roses: derived from *R. chinensis*; moderately hardy; light & airy habit; few thorns; dainty semi-evergreen lvs; perpetual-flg, spring to late autumn. Prune old or weak stems only.
R. 'Mutabilis'* **5** (*R. chinensis mutabilis*, 'Tipo Ideale'): to 1×1m (3×3ft), much more on a wall; bronze-tinted lvs; 6cm (2½in) single fls, flame to yellow to pink to coppery-red.
R. 'Old Blush'* ('Parsons' Pink China'): to 1.2×1.2m (4×4ft) or more against a wall; twiggy; soft pink semi-double fls; long season.
Damasks: ancient; derived from *R.*×*damascena*; most v hardy; lax & open; except 'Autumn Damask' (*R.*×*damascena*

semperflorens), summer-flg only; strongly fragrant; used for rose-water & attar of roses. Prune as for Albas.
R. 'Ispahan'**: to 1.5×1.2m (5×4ft); pink semi-double fls 6cm (2½in) across, long season.
R. 'Mme Hardy'** 6**: to 1.8×1.5m (6×5ft); 6cm (2½in) double white fls, green centre.
Gallicas: ancient; derived from *R. gallica*; v hardy; usually erect, bristly & suckering; rough lvs prone to mildew; can be used for hedges or (short vars) bedding. Prune as for Albas.
R. 'Charles de Mills'* **7** ('Bizarre Triomphant'): to 1.5×1.2m (5×4ft); flat v double fls 9cm (3¾in) across, crimson to purple.
R. 'Complicata': to 1.8×2.5m (6×8ft) or will scramble; pointed lvs; pink & white 7cm (2¾in) single fls.
R. 'Rosa Mundi'* **8**: to 1.2×1.2m (4×4ft); semi-double 6cm (2½in) fls, pink striped crimson.
Hybrid Perpetuals: derived from Bourbons, Portlands & China roses; v hardy; variable habit (low vars for bedding; peg down canes); double, rather globular fls, most repeating. Prune tall types as Albas, others as Hybrid Teas (p162).
R. 'Général Jacqueminot'** ('General Jack'): to 1.2×1m (4×3ft); bright crimson 8cm (3in) fls.
R. 'Paul Neyron' **9**: to 1.5×1m (5×3ft); deep rose-pink paeony-like fls 12cm (5in) across.
Moss roses: mainly derived from *R.*×*centifolia* 'Muscosa', and like Centifolias except for moss-like growth on sepals & flower stalk; some are Damask Mosses. V hardy.
R. 'Henri Martin' **10**: to 1.8×1.5m (6×5ft); globular crimson fls 8cm (3in) across.
R. 'Muscosa'* (*R.*×*centifolia* 'Muscosa', common or old pink moss rose): to 1.2×1.2m (4×4ft); pink globular 6cm (2½in) fls.
Portland roses: sometimes called Perpetual Damasks; similar origins to Bourbons; compact habit; repeat-flg; prune like Bourbons. V hardy.
R. 'Comte de Chambord'** 11**: to 1.2×1m (4×3ft); double pink 7 cm (2¾in) fls, tinted lilac.
Tea roses: derived from Chinese vars probably of *R. gigantea* (*R. odorata gigantea*); most tender or semi-hardy, best where summers are hot, otherwise under glass; few thorns; large lvs; often high-centred elegant fls, supposedly scented like fresh-picked tea; recurrent. Prune in spring, removing any frost-damaged wood. Hardiest vars include 'Général Schablikine'* (coppery-red) & 'Lady Hillingdon'* (apricot-yellow; usually grown as climbing sport) – both moderately hardy.

Modern shrub roses

New classification: Shrub roses, recurrent & non-recurrent. Diverse group of *Rosa* hybrids originating mainly in 20th century. Usually medium to large shrubs for general or specimen planting. Deciduous; pinnate leaves. Unless stated, flowers 5–8cm (2–3in) across, in clusters, generally in two main seasons: early summer & early autumn. **Cultivation**: As for species roses (p156). **Pruning**: Unless stated, remove dead wood, shorten laterals & if necessary main canes, late winter. **Propagation**: Hardwood cuttings; budding.

Hybrid Musks: only distantly related to musk rose (*R. moschata*) but most v fragrant & free-flg. Many good for hedging. Moderately to v hardy.
R. 'Ballerina' **1**: to 1×1m (3×3ft); single pink & white fls 2.5cm (1in) across.
R. 'Belinda' * : to 1.5×1.2m (5×4ft); small soft pink semi-double fls.
R. 'Buff Beauty' * **2**: to 1.5×1.5m (5×5ft); lax; double buff-apricot fls; prone to mildew.
R. 'Felicia' ** : to 1.5×1.5m (5×5ft); silvery-pink loosely double fls, shaded salmon.
R. 'Penelope' ** : to 1.8×1.2m (6×4ft); sturdy; creamy-apricot semi-double fls.
R. 'Prosperity' ** : to 1.8×2.5m (6×8ft); rosette fls, pink fading ivory.
R. 'Vanity' ** **3**: to 1.8×1.8m (6×6ft); open; single or semi-double pink fls.
Rugosas: derived from *R. rugosa*. Ultra- to v hardy; thorny, dense & vigorous; good for hedges; generally little pruning needed. Lvs typically wrinkled (rugose); generally v healthy; often yellowing in autumn. Almost continuous-flg early summer to autumn; large hips on single & semi-double vars.
R. 'Blanc Double de Coubert' ** : to 1.8×1.5m (6×5ft); semi-double white fls.
R. 'Conrad Ferdinand Meyer' * : to 2.5×1.5m (8×5ft); silvery-pink double 9cm (3½in) fls.
R. 'Fru Dagmar Hastrup (Hartopp)' ** : to 1.5×1.5m (5×5ft); clear pink single fls; red hips.
R. 'Hansa' ** : to 1.5×1.5m (5×5ft); double crimson-purple fls.
R. 'Max Graf': see p240.
R. 'Pink Grootendorst' **4**: to 1.5×1.2m (5×4ft); pink 3cm (1¼in) double fls, frilled edge.
R. 'Roseraie de l'Hay' ** **5**: to 1.8×1.5m (6×5ft); loose wine-red 10cm (4in) double fls.
R. 'Sarah van Fleet' ** : to 2.5×1.5m (8×5ft); cupped pink 10cm (4in) double fls.
R. 'Thérèse Bugnet' * : to 1.8×1.5m (6×5ft); double red fls, fading pink.
Other modern shrub roses: generally moderately to v hardy. Include some Floribunda-shrubs (p164).
R. 'Angelina' * : to 1.5×1.2m (5×4ft); rounded; semi-double carmine-pink fls.
R. 'Bonn' * : sometimes classed as Hybrid Musk; to 1.2×1.5m (4×5ft); upright; loose semi-double orange-scarlet fls; red hips.
R. 'Cerise Bouquet' ** : v hardy; to 1.8×2.5m (6×8ft); arching; grey-green lvs; semi-double

cerise-crimson fls in one long season.
R. 'Chinatown' ** ('Ville de Chine'): Floribunda-type; to 1.5×1.2m (5×4ft); golden double fls.
R. 'Constance Spry' * **6**: to 1.8×1.5m (6×5ft); lax; globular rose-pink fls; once-flg.
R. 'Dorothy Wheatcroft': Floribunda-type; to 1.8×1.2m (6×4ft); upright; semi-double orange-scarlet fls.
R. 'Frank Naylor' * **7**: to 1.2×1.2m (4×4ft); bushy; dark lvs; single deep maroon-crimson fls, golden eye.
R. 'Fred Loads' * : Floribunda-type; to 2×1.5m (7×5ft); semi-double fls, vermilion-orange.
R. 'Fritz Nobis' ** : v hardy; to 1.8×1.8m (6×6ft); large thorns; high-centred double pink fls; once-flg.
R. 'Frühlingsgold' * ('Spring Gold'): v hardy; to 2×2m (7×7ft); arching; 8–10cm (3–4in) single or semi-double yellow fls; once-flg, early.
R. 'Frühlingsmorgen' * **8**: v hardy to 1.8×1.5m (6×5ft); single 10cm (4in) fls, pink with golden centre; some repeat; maroon hips.
R. 'Golden Wings' * : to 1.8×1.5m (6×5ft); single 11cm (4½in) pale yellow fls, darker centre.
R. 'Kathleen Ferrier' ** : to 1.5×1.5m (5×5ft); semi-double salmon-pink fls.
R. 'Lavender Lassie' * **9**: sometimes classed as Hybrid Musk; to 1.5m (5ft) or more; rather globular double rosette fls, lilac-pink.
R. 'Marguerite Hilling' ('Pink Nevada'): similar to 'Nevada' but fls pink.
R. 'Marjorie Fair': to 1.2×1.2m (4×4ft); single deep carmine fls, pale eye.
R. 'Nevada' **10**: to 2×2.5m (7×8ft); arching & magnificent; single or semi-double 8–10cm (3–4in) fls, creamy-white to pinkish, all along canes; some repeat; may be prone to black spot.
R. 'Nymphenberg' * : to 1.8×1.8m (6×6ft) or will climb; semi-double 10cm (4in) fls, salmon-pink shaded orange.
R. 'Queen Elizabeth': Floribunda-type; to 2.5×1.2m (8×4ft) or more; few thorns; cupped double pink fls.
R. 'Raubritter' * : *R.×macrantha* hybrid; spreading, to 1×1.8m (3×6ft); semi-double globular pink 5cm (2in) fls; once-flg; good for ground cover; prone to mildew.
R. 'Sally Holmes' **11**: to 1.2×1m (4×3ft); single or semi-double blush-white fls.
R. 'Sea Foam': to 1×1.8m (3×6ft); semi-prostrate; double white fls, shaded cream to pink.

Hybrid Tea roses

New classification: Bush roses, large-flowered. *Rosa* hybrids of complex parentage originating in crosses of Teas & Hybrid Perpetuals. Combine Teas' large, elegant high-centred double blooms, one/few to a stem, with Hybrid Perpetuals' greater robustness. Almost continuous-flowering early summer to autumn, but two main flushes. The best roses for cut flowers; often strongly scented. Generally small shrubs 0.6–1m (2–3ft) tall; best for bedding. Also standards ("tree" roses). Leaves pinnate; deciduous. Flowers average 8cm (3in) long in bud, opening 10cm (4in) wide. **Cultivation**: As for species roses (p156), but prepare ground & feed well – rose fertilizer spring & summer, potash-rich fertilizer late summer. Moderately hardy; need protection (especially budding union) below about −10°C (14°F). Plant with union just below soil, lower in cold areas, higher if frost-free. Planting distance: 45–60cm (1½–2ft), more in warm climates. many vars prone to diseases (especially black spot, mildew & rust) & insect pests. **Pruning**: Late autumn or late winter. Remove dead or weak canes & those crossing centre of bush; shorten others to 20–25cm (8–10in), longer with very vigorous vars or in warm areas; prune thin canes harder than thick. **Propagation**: Budding on *R. canina*, *R. corymbifera* 'Laxa', *R. multiflora*, etc. For climbing sports, see p244.

R. 'Adolf Horstmann': deep yellow, edged pink.
R. 'Alec's Red'** **1**: cherry-red full fls.
R. 'Alexander': tall; orange-vermilion.
R. 'Alpine Sunset'**: peach-pink, flushed yellow.
R. 'Blessings'* **2**: full coral-pink fls, opening cupped.
R. 'Blue Moon'** ('Mainzer Fastnacht', 'Sissi'): lilac-mauve (best "blue" rose so far); semi-hardy but healthy.
R. 'Bonsoir'**: glossy lvs; full peach-pink fls, poor in rain; healthy.
R. 'Century Two'*: tall; medium pink, deeper reverse.
R. 'Champion'* **3**: v large fls, yellow & pink blends.
R. 'Chrysler Imperial'**: compact, deep crimson.
R. 'Color Magic'*: creamy-pink to cherry-red; healthy.
R. 'Doris Tysterman'*: gold, shaded bronze; prone to mildew.
R. 'Double Delight'** **4**: fls globular, red & white.
R. 'Duet'*: pale pink, darker reverse.
R. 'Elizabeth Harkness'*: creamy-buff, tinged pink; paler in autumn.
R. 'Ernest H. Morse'**: free-flg; turkey-red, fading duller.
R. 'Fragrant Cloud'** **5** ('Duftwolke'): large dusky geranium-red fls.
R. 'Garden Party'*: tall; loose, full fls, creamy-white tinged pink.
R. 'Granada'* ('Donatella'): cupped fls, blended pink, red & yellow.
R. 'Grandpa Dickson'* ('Irish Gold'): large pale yellow fls sometimes flushed pink at edges.
R. 'Harriny'**: pale pink, shaded salmon.
R. 'John Waterer'*: tall; large crimson fls.
R. 'Josephine Bruce'*: sprawling; fls dusky-crimson; prone to mildew.
R. 'Just Joey'* **6**: coppery-orange fls, red veins.
R. 'King's Ransom'*: rich pure yellow; healthy; somewhat tender.
R. 'Korp': see p164.
R. 'Lady X'*: pale mauve.

R. 'Maria Callas'** **7** ('Miss All-American Beauty'): tall; large, cupped dark carmine-pink fls, shaded lighter.
R. 'Mischief'*: salmon- to shrimp-pink; may be prone to rust.
R. 'Mister Lincoln'**: tall; large dark dusky-red fls opening cupped.
R. 'Mullard Jubilee'** ('Electron'): full cerise fls.
R. 'National Trust': free-flg; crimson-red.
R. 'Papa Meilland'**: deep velvety-crimson; v prone to mildew.
R. 'Pascali'*: tall & free-flg; smallish creamy-white fls; healthy & rain-resistant.
R. 'Peace' **8** ('Gioia', 'Gloria Dei', 'Mme A. Meilland'): v popular; tall; v large fls, pale yellow flushed pink; prune lightly; v healthy.
R. 'Piccadilly': best scarlet & gold; healthy.
R. 'Pink Favorite': large rose-pink fls; v healthy.
R. 'Precious Platinum'**: full bright crimson-red fls; rain-resistant; prone to mildew.
R. 'Pristine'* **9**: vigorous, to 1.1m (3½ft); blush-white fls.
R. 'Red Devil'** ('Coeur d'Amour'): tall; large light red fls, paler reverse; healthy, but fls poor in rain.
R. 'Rose Gaujard': tall; cherry-red fls, reverse pale pink & silvery-white; healthy.
R. 'Royal Highness'* ('Königliche Hoheit'): soft pale pink; dislikes prolonged rain.
R. 'Silver Jubilee' **10**: coppery-pink shaded peach; healthy.
R. 'Silver Lining'**: silvery-pink.
R. 'Sunblest': tall; golden-yellow, unfading.
R. 'Super Star'* ('Tropicana'): brilliant pale vermilion; prone to mildew.
R. 'Sutter's Gold'**: tall; free-flg; large fls, golden-yellow fading creamy-yellow; dislikes heat.
R. 'Swarthmore'*: rose-red.
R. 'Tiffany'** **11**: large rosy-salmon fls.
R. 'Troika'** ('Royal Dane'): free-flg; apricot to orange, edged scarlet.
R. 'Wendy Cussons'**: free-flg; bright cerise.

Floribunda, Grandiflora and Polyantha roses

New classification: Bush roses, Polyanthas & cluster-flowering. *Rosa* hybrids, generally of complex parentage but all with cluster-flowering habit inherited from *R. multiflora* (*R. polyantha*). Generally small, bushy bedding shrubs 0.6–1m (2–3ft) tall; Grandifloras taller. Some also grown as standards ("tree" roses). Leaves pinnate; small leaflets. Flowers generally small (but up to Hybrid Tea size in Grandifloras); double or semi-double unless stated; borne continuously from early summer to autumn. **Cultivation**: As for Hybrid Teas (p162). Moderately hardy (more so than Hybrid Teas), needing winter protection below about −12°C (10°F). **Pruning**: As for Hybrid Teas but less hard. With tall-growing Floribundas & Grandifloras shorten main canes by one-third. **Propagation**: Hardwood cuttings; budding. For tall-growing Floribunda-shrubs, see p160; for climbing sports of Floribundas, see p244.

Floribundas & Grandifloras: derived from crosses of Polyanthas with Hybrid Perpetuals & (mainly) Hybrid Teas. Fls generally 6cm (2½in) across; vars marked † have large fls like Hybrid Teas' (taller vars of this type sometimes classed as Grandifloras). Generally healthier than Polyanthas or Hybrid Teas.

R. 'Allgold': buttercup-yellow; v healthy.
R. 'Anabell'**† ('Korbel'): salmon-orange.
R. 'Anne Cocker': bright vermilion; thorny.
R. 'Anne Harkness': vigorous, to 1.1m (3½ft); fls coppery-yellow, late; v healthy.
R. 'Arthur Bell'**†: yellow, fading paler.
R. 'Betty Prior'* **1**: to 1.2m (4ft); profuse single carmine-pink fls.
R. 'Chinatown': see p162.
R. 'City of Belfast': velvety vermilion-scarlet fls, frilled petal edges.
R. 'City of Leeds'†: rich salmon.
R. 'Dame of Sark': upright, to 1.1m (3½ft); fls golden-yellow, flushed scarlet.
R. 'Dearest'*: large salmon-pink fls opening flat; poor in rain; prone to rust & black spot.
R. 'Dream Waltz': upright, to 1.1m (3½ft); large velvety-red fls.
R. 'Elizabeth of Glamis'** **2** ('Irish Beauty'): large coral-salmon fls; poor in cold areas or on heavy soil.
R. 'Escapade'*: large rosy-magenta fls, pale centre.
R. 'Europeana'*: large trusses of deep crimson fls; prone to mildew.
R. 'Evelyn Fison'* ('Irish Wonder'): bright unfading scarlet-red.
R. 'Eye Paint': Floribunda-shrub, to 1.2m (4ft), suitable for bedding if pruned hard; small single scarlet fls, white eye. Prone to black spot.
R. 'First Edition' **3**: large trusses of coral-orange fls, fading.
R. 'Fred Loads': see p162.
R. 'Friesia'**('Korresia', 'Sunsprite'): bright yellow.
R. 'Iceberg'* ('Schneewittchen'): vigorous, to 1.2m (4ft), or less if pruned hard; white fls; prone to mildew & black spot.
R. 'Ivory Fashion'*†: ivory-white.
R. 'Korp'† **4** ('Prominent'): bright red.
R. 'Lilli Marlene': bright crimson.

R. 'Liverpool Echo'†: pale salmon-pink.
R. 'Living Fire': orange shading to scarlet & golden-yellow; healthy.
R. 'Margaret Merril'** **5**: pearly-white.
R. 'Masquerade': tall; fls yellow, turning salmon-pink, then bronze-red.
R. 'Matangi'* **6**: orange-vermilion, silver eye & reverse; v healthy.
R. 'Molly McGredy': cherry-red, silver reverse.
R. 'News'*†: dark red to purple.
R. 'Orangeade': vermilion to reddish-orange; may be prone to black spot.
R. 'Orange Sensation'**: orange-vermilion.
R. 'Pink Parfait'* † **7**: tall, to 1.1m (3½ft); fls pink shaded cream.
R. 'Queen Elizabeth': see p160.
R. 'Redgold' ('Rouge et Or'): fls golden-yellow, edged cherry-red.
R. 'Rob Roy'†: vigorous, to 1.1m (3½ft); scarlet-crimson fls.
R. 'Rose Parade'*: fls coral-peach, cupped.
R. 'Sarabande': scarlet-red; healthy.
R. 'Sea Pearl'* † ('Flower Girl'): vigorous; to 1.1m (3½ft); orange-pink fls, yellow reverse.
R. 'Sonia'* † ('Sweet Promise'): tall; rose-pink.
R. 'Southampton'† **8**: vigorous, to 1.1m (3½ft); fls apricot-orange, flushed scarlet; v healthy.
R. 'Sue Lawley': carmine, white eye.
R. 'Sunsilk'†: pure lemon-yellow.
R. 'Tip Top'*: dwarf; profuse salmon-pink fls; prone to black spot.
R. 'Tony Jacklin'† **9**: orange-salmon.
R. 'Topsi': dwarf; brilliant scarlet fls; prone to black spot.

Polyanthas: derived from *R. multiflora* crossed with China & Tea roses; few now cultivated. Good for edging or small beds. Fls generally 2–4cm (¾–1½in) across. Many prone to mildew.
R. 'Cécile Brunner'* (sweetheart rose): soft pink.
R. 'Little White Pet' ('White Pet'): not true Polyantha but same habit; red buds; white fls.
R. 'Margo Koster'* ('Sunbeam'): to 45cm (1½ft); largish salmon-pink fls.
R. 'Perle d'Or': to 1.2m (4ft); fls apricot-yellow, opening paler.
R. 'The Fairy' **10**: not true Polyantha but same habit; v profuse soft pink globular fls.
R. 'Yesterday': Floribunda-Polyantha; lilac-pink.

Miniature roses

New classification: same. *Rosa* hybrids, mostly of complex parentage; many originating with *R*. 'Rouletii', found about 1920 but much older. Unless stated, 20–30cm (8–12in) tall, with dwarf pinnate leaves (deciduous) and flowers to 2.5cm (1in) across; double unless stated. Also Miniature standards ("tree" roses) on 30cm (1ft) stem. Cross-breeding with Floribundas has resulted in some larger-flowered, often taller vars (marked †). All recurrent, with long flowering season. For miniature bedding schemes, edging beds & paths, wall pockets, rock gardens, pots & tubs, etc. **Cultivation**: As for Hybrid Teas (p166) but on smaller scale; planting distance about 20cm (8in). Generally moderately to very hardy. Grow indoors only in cool greenhouse or for temporary display in well-lit room; rest outdoors after flowering. **Pruning**: Minimal. **Propagation**: Hardwood cuttings. For climbing Miniatures, see pp242–4.

R. 'Angela Rippon' **1** ('Ocarina', 'Ocaru'): salmon-pink.

R. 'Anna Ford'†: orange-red to pink.

R. 'Baby Betsy McCall'*: pale pink.

R. 'Baby Darling': orange to orange-pink; somewhat tender.

R. 'Baby Faurax'* **2**: Polyantha (p164), but only 30cm (1ft) tall; lavender-purple.

R. 'Baby Masquerade'*† ('Baby Carnival'): to 40cm (16in); fls yellow, darkening to red, like 'Masquerade' (p164) but more subdued; v hardy & healthy.

R. 'Beauty Secret'**: crimson-red high-centred fls; v hardy.

R. 'Bo-Peep': pale pink.

R. 'Chipper': to 40–45cm (16–18in); salmon-pink; somewhat tender.

R. 'Cinderella'* **3**: thornless; v double blush-pink small fls; healthy.

R. 'Colibri': bright orange-yellow double fls; may be prone to black spot.

R. 'Darling Flame': to 35cm (14in); vermilion.

R. 'Dreamglo': red & white bicolour.

R. 'Dresden Doll' **4**: miniature Moss rose (p158); to 60cm (2ft); v double soft pink mossed fls, largish.

R. 'Easter Morning'†: largish ivory-white fls.

R. 'Eleanor': deep coral pink. Good as a standard.

R. 'Fairlane'*: glossy lvs; creamy pink/yellow fls.

R. 'Gloriglow'†: brilliant orange, creamy-white reverse.

R. 'Gold Pin'*: largish semi-double golden-yellow fls.

R. 'Green Diamond' **5**: pink buds; soft green fls.

R. 'Heidi'**: medium pink 4cm (1½in) fls.

R. 'Honest Abe': crimson-red 4cm (1½in) fls.

R. 'Judy Fischer': small rose-pink fls.

R. 'Kathy'*: orange-scarlet.

R. 'Lavender Jewel': mauve.

R. 'Little Buckeroo'†: to 35-40cm (14-16in); small fls, bright red centred white.

R. 'Magic Carrousel' **6**: white edged bright red.

R. 'Mary Adair' **7**: apricot blends.

R. 'Mary Marshall'*: coral-orange high-centred fls, yellow base.

R. 'My Valentine': rich red.

R. 'Nozomi': see p242.

R. 'Opal Jewel'*: pink, darker centre.

R. 'Over the Rainbow': red & pink, reverse & base gold.

R. 'Party Girl'*: soft yellow flushed salmon-pink.

R. 'Peaches 'n' Cream': pink blends.

R. 'Peachy': free-flg; pale peach-pink.

R. 'Pink Cameo' ('Climbing Cameo'): see p244.

R. 'Pink Mandy': lilac-pink.

R. 'Poker Chip': scarlet-orange.

R. 'Pompon de Paris': bright pink; for 'Climbing Pompon de Paris', see p244.

R. 'Pour Toi' ('For You', 'Para Ti', 'Wendy'): to 15-20cm (6-8in); semi-double white fls tinted yellow at base.

R. 'Rise 'n' Shine' **8**: to 35cm (14in); clear yellow.

R. 'Robin': v double rich red fls.

R. 'Rosmarin'*: globular, soft pale pink, fls, light red reverse.

R. 'Rouletii' **9** (*R. rouletii*, *R. chinensis minima*, 'Fairy Rose'): semi-evergreen; v small semi-double fls, rose-red; v hardy.

R. 'Royal Salute': free-flg; carmine-pink.

R. 'Scarlet Gem'* ('Scarlet Pimpernel'): to 30–40cm (12–16in); free-flg; v double orange-scarlet fls.

R. 'September Days': deep yellow.

R. 'Sheri Anne': to 40cm (16in); orange-red.

R. 'Simplex'†: to 40cm (16in); apricot buds opening white; single.

R. 'Snow Carpet' **10**: spreading, for ground cover; v double white fls 4cm (1½in) across.

R. 'Snow Magic': white 3cm (1¼in) fls.

R. 'Stacey Sue': to 18cm (7in); spreading; v double soft pink fls.

R. 'Starina': large, vivid orange-scarlet fls, good for cutting; somewhat tender.

R. 'Stars 'n' Stripes' **11**: to 60 cm (2ft); single fls, red & white striped.

R. 'Swedish Doll'†: to 40cm (16in); coral-pink 4cm (1½in) fls.

R. 'Top Secret'*: medium red 4cm (1½in) fls.

R. 'Toy Clown' **12**: to 40–45cm (16–18in); few thorns; semi-double fls, white edged red.

R. 'Willie Winkie': to 15–25cm (6–10in); rose-pink.

R. 'Yellow Doll'*: pale yellow to cream.

Shrubby potentillas, brambles and their relatives

Mainly deciduous, often stool-forming shrubs grown for their showy flowers &/or decorative stems. Good as specimens or for shrub borders; some for ground cover. **Cultivation**: Generally easy in any well-drained soil in full sun or partial shade. Very hardy unless stated. **Pruning**: Occasionally thin out old flowered shoots after flowering (each year with some *Rubus* spp). **Propagation**: Softwood cuttings; layering; division where appropriate.

Kerria (*Kerria japonica*): bushy & arching, to 1.5×1.8m (5×6ft), more against wall; fresh green stems; toothed, rather triangular lvs 5–10cm (2–4in) long; golden-yellow rather buttercup-like fls to 4.5cm (1¾in) wide, mid–late spring, on yr-old wood. Vars: 'Pleniflora' **1** (to 3m [10ft]; 5cm [2in] v double fls); 'Variegata' (to 1.5m [5ft]; lvs edged white).

Potentillas (cinquefoils, *Potentilla* spp; all often listed under *P. fruticosa*): ultra-hardy small dense shrubs with peeling bark & showy fls 2–3cm (¾–1¼in) wide, long season generally late spring to late summer or autumn; lvs generally pinnate, with 3–7 lfts 1–2.5cm (⅜–1in) long. Excellent in sunny border or rock garden; taller vars good for hedging; low, spreading vars for ground cover.
P. arbuscula (*P. f. arbuscula*): to 1×1m (3×3ft); green, silky-haired lvs; deep yellow fls.
P. davurica (*P. f. davurica, P. glabra*): 1×1m (3×3ft); dark glossy green lvs; white fls. Vars: 'Abbotswood' (spreading; free-flg); 'Farrer's White' (upright; profuse fls, summer); 'Manchu' (incorrectly, *mandshurica*; semi-prostrate & mounding, to 30×60cm [1×2ft]; greyish hairy lvs); *veitchii* (gracefully arching; lvs hairy; small fls).
P. fruticosa: bushy, to 1.2×1.2m (4×4ft); lvs mid/glaucous-green; fls bright yellow. Sp rarely grown but parent of many hybrids (see below).
P. parvifolia (*P. f. parvifolia*): to 1×1m (3×3ft); v small narrow lfts, grey-green; small deep yellow fls. Vars: 'Gold Drop' (dwarf & bushy; bright green lvs; golden-yellow fls); 'Klondike' **2** (like 'Gold Drop' but taller, with larger fls).
P. hybrids: unless stated, to 0.75–1.2×1–1.2m (2½–4×3–4ft); large fls. Vars: 'Daydawn' **3** (peach-pink flushed cream); 'Elizabeth' **4** (incorrectly, *P. arbuscula*; rich yellow fls, long season; prone to mildew, red spider mites); 'Goldfinger' (compact; deep yellow); 'Gold Star' (v large yellow fls); 'Katherine Dykes' (vigorous; canary-yellow); 'Moonlight' **5** ('Maanelys'; vigorous; soft creamy-yellow); 'Primrose Beauty' (dense & arching; hairy lvs; primrose-yellow fls, darker eye); 'Red Ace' **6** (low & spreading, to 60×90cm [2×3ft]; bright red fls, yellow reverse [fade in extreme heat]); 'Royal Flush' (to 40×75cm [16×30in]; rose-pink [fade in hot weather]); 'Tangerine' (mounding, to 1×1.5m [3×5ft]; coppery-yellow to orange, best in semi-shade); 'Vilmoriniana' **7** (to 1.5m [5ft]; silvery lvs;

creamy-white fls, yellow centre); 'William Purdom' (incorrectly, 'Purdomii'; to 1.5×2m [5×7ft]; bright green lvs; pale yellow fls).
Rhodotypos (jetbead, white kerria, *Rhodotypos scandens* **8** *R. kerrioides*); kerria-like shrub, to 1.5×2m (5×7ft); toothed dark green lvs to 10×5cm (4×2in); 4-petalled white fls to 5cm (2in) wide, rather like small dog rose, late spring & summer; shiny black pea-sized frs (poisonous).
Rubus (brambles, *Rubus* spp): varied, generally vigorous shrubs with prickly stems, lobed or compound lvs, fls in early summer, & edible blackberry/raspberry-like frs. Spp marked † fl on yr-old wood or grown for decorative young stems; cut out old stems after flg/frtg. Stems of many spp can be trained over pergolas, etc.
R. calycinoides (often grown incorrectly as *R. fockeanus*; correctly a var of *R. pentalobus*): prostrate & self-rooting, to 2.5cm×1m (1in×3ft); 3/5-lobed evergreen lvs to 4cm (1½in) long, wrinkled; small white fls; scarlet frs.
R. cockburnianus† (*R. giraldianus*): to 2.5×2m (8×7ft); white-bloomed shoots; pinnate lvs, 7–9 lfts, white beneath; rose-purple fls.
R. deliciosus†: to 3×3m (10×10ft); thornless; brown peeling bark; 3/5-lobed lvs to 8cm (3in) long; pure white 5cm (2in) fls. *R.* 'Benenden'† **9** (*R.×tridel* 'Benenden') is hybrid with *R. trilobus*; v vigorous; white fls to 7cm (2¾in) wide.
R. laciniatus (cut-leaved bramble): to 3×4.5m (10×15ft); arching; stout spines; semi-evergreen pinnate lvs, lobed & toothed lfts; pale pink fls; large sweet black frs.
R. odoratus*† **10** (flowering raspberry): ultra-hardy; to 2.5×3m (8×10ft); suckering; thornless; vine-like velvety lvs to 30cm (1ft) wide; large clusters of 5cm (2in) rose-purple fls, summer; red frs where summers long. Best in semi-shade.
R. phoenicolasius† **11** (wineberry): to 3×3m (10×10ft); young shoots densely red-bristled; trifoliate lvs, white-hairy beneath; small pink fls, hairy calyx; bright red raspberry-like frs.
R. spectabilis*† (salmonberry): to 1.5×1.5m (5×5ft); suckering; trifoliate lvs; magenta-rose 2.5cm (1in) nodding fls, spring; orange frs.
R. ulmifolius 'Bellidiflorus' **12**: v vigorous, to 2×3m (7×10ft); arching; semi-evergreen pinnate lvs, white beneath; large panicles of double pink fls, mid summer. Best in wild garden.

Spiraeas and their relatives

Free-flowering deciduous shrubs with large, sometimes plume-like inflorescences of generally small white or pink flowers. Handsome plants for sunny borders, the larger spp as specimens. **Cultivation**: Unless stated, very hardy & for any soil, preferably in full sun. Regular pruning unnecessary unless noted. **Propagation**: Seed; semi-ripe cuttings; suckering spp by division.

Exochordas (pearl bushes, *Exochorda* spp): large, with narrowish lvs to 8–10×2.5–4cm (3–4×1–1½in) & racemes of showy white fls to 2.5–4cm (1–1½in) across, late spring. Can be restricted by pruning after flg.
E. giraldii: vigorous & spreading, to 3×4.5m (10×15ft); young shoots pinkish. Var *wilsonii* has fls to 5cm (2in) wide.
E.×macrantha 'The Bride' **1**: hybrid of *E. korolkowii* & *E. racemosa*; mounding, to 1×2m (3×7ft); arching branches; free-flg.
E. racemosa (*E. grandiflora*): bushy & spreading, to 3×3m (10×10ft); v large infls, best if old fld shoots thinned out. Not good on shallow chalk.
Holodiscus (cream-bush, ocean spray, *Holodiscus* [*Spiraea*] *discolor*): spreading shrub, to 3.5×3.5m (12×12ft); arching branches; deeply lobed & toothed lvs to 9cm (3½in) long, grey felt beneath; drooping plume-like 30cm (1ft) infls of tiny creamy fls, summer.
Ninebark (*Physocarpus opulifolius*): ultra-hardy; vigorous, to 3×3m (10×10ft) or more; bark peels in many layers; toothed & 3-lobed lvs to 8cm (3in) long; rounded clusters of small white fls tinged pink, early summer. Best in semi-wild garden. Var 'Luteus' **2** has yellow young lvs.
Sorbarias (false spiraeas, *Sorbaria* spp): v vigorous, suckering, spiraea-like shrubs with elegant bright green pinnate lvs, 13–23 lfts to 5–10cm (2–4in) long; small white fls in pyramid-shaped panicles to 30–45cm (1–1½ft) long, mid summer. Like moist soil; cut back late winter or early spring & thin out old fld shoots.
S. (*Spiraea*) *aitchisonii* **3**: spreading, to 2.5×2.5m (8×8ft); young shoots red; large branching infls.
S. (*Spiraea*) *sorbifolia*: ultra-hardy; to 2×3m (7×10ft); stiffly erect infls.
Spiraeas (*Spiraea* spp): v popular, with profuse small fls in dense corymbs or panicles & often attractive foliage (lvs simple & toothed unless stated). Spp & vars marked † fl late on young wood; cut back hard late winter or early spring. Others fl on yr-old wood; thin out weak & old fld shoots after flg.
S. albiflora: see *S. japonica* 'Albiflora'.
S.×arguta **4** (*S.* 'Arguta'; in UK, bridal wreath, foam of May): hybrid of *S.×multiflora* & *S. thunbergii*; bushy & rounded, to 2×2m (7×7ft); slender shoots; narrowish lvs to 4cm (1½in) long; small clusters of white fls, spring.
S.×billiardii 'Triumphans'† **5**: hybrid of *S. douglasii* & *S. salicifolia*; suckering, to 2×2.5m

(7×8ft); narrowish 8cm (3in) lvs; bright rose-purple fls in pyramid-shaped infls to 20×10cm (8×4in), summer. Var 'Macrothyrsa' has wider lvs & bright pink fls.
S.×bumalda: see under *S. japonica*.
S. cantonensis (*S. reevsiana*): moderately to v hardy; spreading, to 1.8×3m (6×10ft); arching shoots; lvs to 6cm (2½in) long; 5cm (2in) clusters of white fls, early summer.
S. japonica†: erect, to 1.5×1m (5×3ft); lvs to 8cm (3in) long; pink fls in wide flat infls, mid–late summer. Vars/hybrids: 'Albiflora' (*S. albiflora*; to 60cm [2ft]; white); 'Anthony Waterer' **6** (*S.×bumalda* 'Anthony Waterer'; to 1.2m [4ft]; lvs often variegated white/pink; fls bright crimson); 'Bullata' (compact, to 45cm [1½ft]; small puckered lvs; rose-crimson fls); 'Bumalda' (*S.×bumalda*; to 1m [3ft]; lvs often variegated; fls deep pink); 'Goldflame' (*S.×bumalda* 'Goldflame' **7**; to 60cm [2ft]; young lvs orange-red becoming yellow [may revert]; fls rose-pink); 'Nana' **8** ('Alpina'; dense & mounding, to 0.6×1.5m [2×5ft]; small lvs; lilac-pink fls); 'Shirobana' (to 75cm [2½ft]; white and pink fls).
S. nipponica 'Snowmound' **9** (incorrectly, *S. n. tosaensis*): dense & bushy, to 2×2.5m (7×8ft); lvs to 4×1cm (1½×½in), almost toothless; dense rounded clusters of white fls, early summer.
S. prunifolia (*S. p.* 'Plena' **10**; in US, bridal wreath): dense, to 1.8×2.5m (6×8ft); arching shoots; 5cm (2in) lvs, orange or red in autumn; double white fls in profuse clusters, late spring.
S. thunbergii: dense & twiggy, to 1.5×2m (5×7ft); v narrow 4cm (1½in) lvs; profuse clusters of white fls, early–mid spring.
S. trichocarpa: vigorous, to 1.8×1.8m (6×6ft); fresh green lvs to 6×2.5cm (2½×1in); rounded 5cm (2in) corymbs of white fls, early summer.
S.×vanhouttei: hybrid of *S. cantoniensis* & *S. trilobata*; vigorous & arching, to 2×3m (7×10ft); clusters of white fls, early summer.
Stephanandra (*Stephanandra incisa*): dense, suckering, spiraea-like shrub grown mainly for foliage; to 1.5×2.5m (5×8ft); rich brown shoots (attractive in winter); deeply lobed & toothed lvs to 8×5cm (3×2in), rich yellow in autumn; greenish or creamy-white fls, early summer. Prefers moist soil; cut back old shoots hard early spring. Var 'Crispa' grows to 60cm (2ft); smaller, more deeply toothed crinkly lvs; good for ground cover. *S. tanakae* **11** is similar but generally larger, with larger shallowly lobed lvs.

Cotoneasters

Cotoneaster spp. Among best of berrying shrubs (sometimes small trees), ranging from prostrate to tall bushy & arching types. Neat entire leaves, deciduous or evergreen (former unless stated, these often colouring well in autumn). White or pinkish 8–12mm (⅓–½in) fls, late spring or early summer, followed by conspicuous 5–10mm (¼–⅜in) fruits, bright red unless stated. Large spp good specimens & for hedging, others for ground cover or wall shrubs. **Cultivation**: Moderately to very hardy unless stated. Easy in any well-drained soil, preferably in full sun; thrive in poor soil. Prone to fireblight. No regular pruning needed except as hedge. **Propagation**: Seed (stratify; may not come true); semi-ripe heel cuttings; prostrate spp by layering.

C. adpressus: v hardy; slow-growing & prostrate, to 1×1.8m (1×6ft); 1.5cm (⅝in) wavy-edged lvs, red in autumn. Good for rock garden. Var *praecox* (*C. praecox*) is more vigorous.

C. affinis bacillaris: arching shrub, to 3×3m (10×10ft), or small tree; variable lvs to 8cm (3in) long; profuse clusters of fls; frs purple-black.

C. bullatus floribundus: v hardy; open & arching, to 2.5×2.5m (8×8ft); lvs to 8cm (3in) long, conspicuous veins, bright red in autumn; large clusters of pinkish fls.

C. congestus: dense & mounding, to 7.5×30cm (3in×1ft); dull blue-green 8mm (⅓in) evergreen lvs; pinkish fls. V good for rock garden.

C. conspicuus: usually dense & arching, to 1.8×2.5m (6×8ft); small v dark green evergreen lvs. Var 'Decorus' **1** is lower growing.

C. dammeri: v hardy; prostrate & vigorous, to 1×1.8m (3×6ft); bright green evergreen lvs to 3cm (1¼in) long. Excellent carpeter. Var 'Skogholm' ('Skogsholmen') is slightly taller, to 0.45×3m (1½×10ft).

C. divaricatus: v hardy; to 1.8×1.8m (6×6ft); shining dark green 1–2cm (½–¾in) lvs, colouring well in autumn; bright rose-pink fls; profuse frs. Good for hedging.

C. franchetii: graceful & arching, to 2.5×2.5m (8×8ft); grey-green 2–3cm (¾–1¼in) semi-/evergreen lvs, thickly felted beneath; small infls of pinkish fls; oblong orange-red frs. Var *sternianus* (often sold as *C. wardii*) has rounded frs; older lvs often colour in autumn; v hardy.

C. frigidus **2**: rounded shrub or tree, to 6×4.5m (20×15ft); deep green deciduous or semi-evergreen lvs to 12×5cm (5×2in), woolly beneath when young; dense flat infls; heavy clusters of frs, creamy-yellow in var 'Fructu-luteo'. Hybrids with *C. salicifolius* & related spp: 'Cornubia' **3** (vigorous & spreading, to 4.5×4.5m [15×15ft], sometimes tree-like; lance-shaped 12cm [5in] semi-evergreen lvs; v free-frtg); 'Hybridus Pendulus' **4** (semi-prostrate shrub, to 0.3×3m [1×10ft], or can be trained as small weeping tree, to 1.8m [6ft] tall; evergreen lvs to 8cm [3in] long; profuse frs); 'John Waterer' (*C.×watereri*; hybrid with *C. henryanus*; vigorous, to 4.5×4.5m [15×15ft]; semi-/evergreen narrowish lvs to 8cm [3in] long; large fl & fr clusters); 'Rothschildianus' **5** (to 4.5×4.5m

[15×15ft]; semi-/evergreen lance-shaped lvs; creamy-yellow frs); 'Saint Monica' (to 5.5×4.5m [18×15ft]; semi-evergreen lvs to 15cm [6in] long; frs in drooping clusters).

C. glaucophyllus serotinus: vigorous, to 2.5×2.5m (8×8ft); dark green evergreen lvs to 8cm (3in) long; infls to 8cm (3in) wide, mid–late summer; frs v persistent.

C. horizontalis: v hardy; low & spreading, to 0.6×2.5m (2×8ft); higher against wall; characteristic "herringbone" branching; small rounded dark green lvs, bright orange-red in late autumn. Vars: 'Variegatus' **6** (lvs edged creamy-white, pink in autumn); 'Saxatilis' (v prostrate). *C. apiculatus* is similar but more bushy.

C. lacteus: v hardy; to 2.5×2.5m (8×8ft); dark green evergreen 5cm (2in) lvs, dense white down beneath; infls 5–8cm (2–3in) wide, early–mid summer. Good for hedging.

C. microphyllus (in US, small-leaved cotoneaster): semi-prostrate, to 0.3×1.8m (1×6ft); dark glossy evergreen lvs 1cm (½in) long. Excellent on bank. Vars: *cochleatus* (more prostrate & compact); *thymifolius* (v small, narrow lvs; excellent for rock garden).

C. moupinensis **7**: to 2.5×2.5m (8×8ft); similar to *C. bullatus*, but frs black; lvs downy beneath.

C. multiflorus: v hardy; to 3×3m (10×10ft); slender arching branches; thin lvs to 6cm (2½in) long; profuse branching infls (showiest sp in fl).

C. racemiflorus soongoricus: ultra-hardy; to 2.5×2.5m (8×8ft); slender downy shoots; greyish-green 3cm (1¼in) lvs, downy beneath; profuse persistent frs, often rose-pink.

C. salicifolius: vigorous & spreading, to 3×3m (10×10ft); lance-shaped semi-/evergreen wrinkled lvs to 8×2cm (3×¾in), downy beneath; profuse fls & small frs. Vars: 'Autumn Fire' ('Herbstfeuer'; low & spreading, to 0.45×2.5m [1½×8ft]; v profuse frs); *floccosus* **8** (v hardy; graceful; can be trained as tree, to 3×3m [10×10ft]; glossy lvs, grey-white beneath, on fan-like stems; v profuse fls & frs); 'Gnom' (dense, prostrate & mounding, to 0.6×1.8m [2×6ft]; excellent ground cover). Hybrids: see under *C. frigidus*.

C. simonsii **9**: v hardy; erect, to 2.5×1.8m (8×6ft); dark green rounded deciduous or semi-evergreen lvs 2.5cm (1in) long; persistent frs.

Pyracanthas and their allies

Rather varied shrubs & small trees (former unless stated) grown for their flowers & decorative fruits (often eaten by birds) &/or their spring &/or autumn foliage colour. Evergreen unless noted, generally with toothed leaves. Mostly best as specimens or for hedging; some good against walls. **Cultivation**: Unless stated, very hardy & for any well-drained soil, preferably in full sun. **Propagation**: Seed; semi-ripe cuttings; layering; suckering spp by division.

Serviceberries (Juneberries, shadbushes, *Amelanchier* spp): deciduous, with lvs to 5–8cm (2–3in) long; profuse racemes of small white fls, spring (as lvs open); small black or purplish edible frs. Prefer lime-free soil.
A. asiatica* : graceful tree, to 6×4.5m (20×15ft); erect infls.
A. laevis* **1** (Allegheny serviceberry): spreading tree, to 7.5×5.5m (25×18ft), or large shrub; young lvs yellowish-bronze, brilliant orange & red in autumn; drooping infls. *A. lamarckii* **2** (sometimes listed incorrectly as *A. canadensis*) is similar; *A.* 'Rubescens' (*A.×grandiflora* 'Rubescens') is pink-fld hybrid.
A. stolonifera: ultra-hardy; spreading & suckering, to 1.5×2m (5×7ft); lvs brilliant orange-red in autumn; short erect infls.

Chokeberries (*Aronia* spp): bushy & suckering; deciduous, with lvs to 8cm (3in) long, red or purplish in autumn; white or pink-tinged small fls in corymbs, late spring, followed by small frs.
A. arbutifolia (red chokeberry): vigorous, to 2×2m (7×7ft); lvs downy beneath; persistent bright red frs, v profuse in var 'Brilliantissima' (brilliant autumn colour). Var 'Erecta' is narrow & upright.
A. melanocarpa (black chokeberry): to 1×1.5m (3×5ft); frs black. Var 'Brilliant' **3** has fine autumn colour. Tolerates dryish soil.
A. prunifolia (*A. floribunda*): similar to *A. arbutifolia* but frs purple.

Loquat (Japanese medlar, *Eriobotrya japonica** **4**): bushy tree, to 5.5×4.5m (18×15ft), or large shrub; stout, densely hairy young shoots; dark glossy green leathery lvs to 20–30×10–12cm (8–12×4–5in), brown-woolly beneath, prominent veins; 8–15cm (3–6in) erect panicles of white hawthorn-like fls 2cm (¾in) wide, autumn; rounded to pear-shaped orange or yellow frs* to 5cm (2in) long, ripening winter–spring (edible; used for pies, preserves, etc). Moderately hardy but fls only after hot summers & frs damaged below −6°C (21°F); in cooler areas makes handsome wall shrub. Prone to fireblight.

Photinias (*Photinia* spp): shrubs & small trees with lvs generally to 8–12×4.5cm (3–5×1¾in), corymbs or short panicles of small white fls usually in spring, & small red frs (best where summers hot). Generally moderately hardy; deciduous spp hate lime. May need pruning to maintain compact habit.
P. arbutifolia (toyon; in US, Christmas berry;

correctly, *Heteromeles arbutifolia*): vigorous & spreading, to 3.5×3m (12×10ft); or small tree; leathery toothed lvs; fls summer; frs winter.
P.×fraseri vars: hybrids of *P. glabra* & *P. serrulata*; vigorous, to 4.5×4.5m (15×15ft); young lvs bright bronze-red, becoming dark glossy green. Vars: 'Birmingham' (original hybrid); 'Red Robin' **5** (young growth brilliant red); 'Robusta' (vigorous).
P. glabra: to 3×2.5m (10×8ft); young lvs bronze, becoming dark glossy green; infls to 15cm (6in) wide. Var 'Rubens' has young lvs bright red.
P. serrulata: to 4.5×4.5m (15×15ft), or small tree; leathery lvs to 20×8cm (8×3in), bronzy-red when young; infls to 15cm (6in) wide.
P. villosa **6**: v hardy deciduous shrub, to 3×3m (10×10ft), or small tree; lvs scarlet & gold in autumn. Var *maximowicziana* (*P. koreana*) has leathery lvs, prominent veins, golden in autumn.

Firethorns (*Pyracantha* spp): spiny, with narrow toothed lvs to 5–8cm (2–3in) long, profuse small corymbs of white fls, early summer, & v profuse persistent red to yellow small frs. Generally moderately to v hardy (hybrids less so), fireblight.
P. angustifolia: moderately hardy; to 1.8×1.8m (6×6ft); downy shoots; lvs grey-felted beneath; frs bright orange-yellow, v persistent.
P. atalantioides **7** (*P. gibbsii*): v vigorous, to 3×3m (10×10ft); often nearly spineless; lvs dark glossy green; late scarlet frs in dense clusters (yellow in var 'Aurea' **8**). *P.* 'Watereri' is hybrid with *P. rogersiana*; to 3m (10ft); small lvs.
P. coccinea (common pyracantha): vigorous & dense, to 2.5×2.5m (8×8ft); dark glossy green lvs; profuse dense bunches of dark red frs. Vars & hybrids: 'Golden Charmer' (orange-yellow frs); 'Kasan' (v hardy; orange-red frs); 'Lalandei' (v hardy; upright; orange-red frs); 'Mohave' (v hardy; spreading; large orange-red frs); 'Orange Charmer' (upright; profuse deep orange frs); 'Orange Glow' **9** (dense; bright orange-red persistent frs).
P. rogersiana (*P. crenulata rogersiana*): dense & erect, to 2.5×2.5m (8×8ft); bright green 4cm (1½in) lvs; showy infls; v profuse golden-yellow to reddish-orange frs. *P. koidzumi* is similar but less hardy; var 'Santa Cruz' is semi-prostrate, to 1×2.5m (3×8ft), & good for covering banks, etc.

Rhaphiolepis (*Rhaphiolepis* spp; sometimes spelled *Raphiolepis*): sun-lovers with shiny leathery lvs to 8cm (3in) long & racemes or

panicles of 1–2cm (½–¾in) fls, summer in cool climates, winter to late spring in v warm areas; dark blue small frs. Best in hot sun, against wall.

R. indica **1** (Indian hawthorn): semi- to moderately hardy; to 1.5×1.8m (5×6ft); lance-shaped pointed lvs, reddish when young; fls white to deep pink (variable). Numerous vars available in warm areas (eg, California).

R. umbellata: moderately hardy; vigorous, to 1.2×1.5m (4×5ft); thick rounded lvs; white fls.

R.×delacourii is hybrid with *R. indica*; pink fls

(rose-crimson in var 'Coate's Crimson' **2**).

Stranvaesia (*Stranvaesia* [*Photinia*] *davidiana* **3**): moderately to v hardy vigorous shrub, to 3×3m (10×10ft), or small tree; dark green lance-shaped lvs to 12×2.5cm (5×1in; turn bright red before falling); 8cm (3in) corymbs of white fls, early summer; profuse bright red persistent frs (yellow in var 'Fructu Luteo'). ×*Stranvinia* 'Redstart' **4** is hybrid with *Photinia×fraseri* 'Robusta'; young lvs coppery-red; red frs tipped yellow.

Hawthorns, medlar and their hybrids

Dense deciduous trees (& some shrubs), generally spiny & with attractive foliage (often colouring well in autumn), flowers (white unless stated) & fruits. Attractive specimens or lawn trees, many good for small gardens &/or streets. **Cultivation**: Very hardy unless stated. For any well-drained fertile soil in sun. Prone to fireblight. **Propagation**: Best by seed (stratify); vars by grafting/budding on parent sp.

Hawthorns (thorns, *Crataegus* spp): unless stated, round-headed or rather spreading trees, to 4.5–6×4.5–6m (15–20×15–20ft); lvs toothed &/or lobed, to 5–8cm (2–3in) long unless stated; corymbs of 8–20mm (⅓–¾in) fls, generally late spring & v early summer; rounded frs ("haws"), red & 1.5–2.5cm (⅝–1in) across unless stated, often persistent, used for preserves. Tolerate pollution, salty winds.

C. azarolus (azarole): moderately to v hardy; shoots & undersides of lvs downy; dense infls; frs usually yellowish, good flavour.

C. crus-galli **5** (cockspur thorn): thorns 8cm (3in) or more long; leathery lvs to 10×4cm (4×1½in), orange & scarlet in autumn; frs persistent.

C. durobrivensis: shrub, to 4.5×3.6m (15×12ft); 5cm (2in) thorns; deeply lobed lvs; fls to 2.5cm (1in) across; frs large, persistent. V ornamental.

C. laciniata **6** (*C. orientalis*): branches almost thornless, tips often pendulous; lvs narrowly lobed, grey beneath; frs large, yellowish-red.

C. laevigata* (*C. oxyacantha*, English hawthorn, may): 2.5cm (1in) thorns; dark green 3/5-lobed lvs; profuse fls & frs. Vars & hybrids with *C. monogyna*: 'Aurea' (frs yellow); 'Gireoudii' (young lvs mottled pink & white); 'Paul's Scarlet' **7** ('Coccinea Plena', 'Paulii'; double, scarlet); 'Plena' (double, white ageing pink); 'Punicea' (crimson); 'Toba' (*C.×mordensis*; double, white ageing pink).

C.×lavallei (*C.×carrierei*): hybrid of *C. crus-galli* & *C. stipulacea*; dense & leafy, with stout 4cm (1½in) thorns; dark glossy green lvs to 10×6cm (4×2½in), downy beneath, coppery-red in autumn, often persisting into winter; fls to 2.5cm (1in) across; bright orange-red persistent frs. V handsome.

C. mollis: to 3×3.5m (10×12ft); stout 5cm (2in) thorns; lvs to 10cm (4in) long, downy; fls to 2.5cm (1in) across; frs large but drop early.

C. monogyna* (common English hawthorn, may, quick): to 7.5×6m (25×20ft); v similar to *C. laevigata* but more thorny & larger, more deeply 3–7-lobed lvs. Often used for hedging. Vars: 'Biflora' ('Praecox', Glastonbury thorn; fls mid winter if mild, repeating spring); 'Stricta' ('Fastigiata'; v narrow, to 5.5×2.5m [18×8ft]).

C. pedicellata (*C. coccinea*): 5cm (2in) thorns; lvs to 10cm (4in) long, often colouring well in autumn; bright scarlet frs in large bunches.

C. phaenopyrum **8** (Washington thorn): slender 8cm (3in) thorns; glossy green rather maple-like lvs, brilliant orange & red in autumn; dense infls, early summer; profuse dense clusters of 5mm (¼in) deep crimson frs, v persistent.

C.×prunifolia **9**: probably hybrid of *C. crus-galli* & *C. macracantha*; rigid 8cm (3in) thorns; bright glossy green lvs, rich crimson in autumn.

C. tanacetifolia* **10**: erect; few thorns; lvs narrowly lobed, grey-downy; small infls of 2.5cm (1in) fls, early summer; yellow or red-flushed frs like tiny apples, good flavour.

Hybrid medlar-thorn (×*Crataemespilus* [*Crataegomespilus*] *grandiflora*): bigeneric hybrid of *Mespilus germanica* & *Crataegus laevigata* or *C. monogyna*; vigorous rounded leafy tree, to 4.5×5.5m (15×18ft); finely toothed & often lobed lvs to 8×5cm (3×2in), orange & yellow in autumn; 2.5cm (1in) fls in 2s & 3s, late spring; yellowish-brown 2cm (¾in) frs. Fine foliage tree.

Medlar (*Mespilus germanica* **1**, p179): picturesque tree, to 4.5×5.5m (15×18ft); with crooked branches; small thorns; finely toothed downy lvs to 12cm (5in) long, reddish-brown in autumn; solitary white or pink-tinged fls 2.5–4cm (1–1½in) across, late spring or v early summer; brown 2.5cm (1in) frs, conspicuous calyx, edible when over-ripe. Selected frtg vars (eg, 'Dutch', 'Nottingham') generally thornless.

Mountain ashes, whitebeams and their relatives

Sorbus spp. Popular deciduous trees (& a few shrubs) grown mainly for their handsome foliage (often pinnate, with leaflets generally 2.5–5cm [1–2in] long, &/or colouring brilliantly in autumn) & usually profuse clusters of showy & colourful berry-like fruits from late summer – among the most spectacular fruiting display of all temperate trees. Flowers generally small & white, in corymbs, late spring unless stated. Excellent garden & street trees; fruits attract birds. **Cultivation**: Unless stated, very hardy & for any fertile soil in sun or partial shade. Pinnate-leaved spp dislike drought. Prone to fireblight, borers. **Propagation**: Seed; vars by budding/grafting on parent or related sp.

S. alnifolia: to 5.5×3.5m (18×12ft); dense; doubly toothed, sometimes shallowly lobed lvs to 10×4cm (4×1½in), orange & scarlet in autumn; 1cm (½in) white fls; bright red frs.
S. aria **2** (whitebeam): to 5.5×4.5m (18×15ft); doubly toothed glossy green lvs to 10×6cm (4×2½in), dense white felt beneath, orange & yellow in autumn; 1cm (½in) scarlet frs. Good on shallow chalk; tolerates pollution, salty winds. Vars: 'Aurea' (lvs yellowish-green); 'Chrysophylla' (lvs yellow); 'Lutescens' (young lvs silver-hairy); 'Majestica' **3** ('Decaisneana'; large lvs & frs).
S. aucuparia (rowan, European mountain ash): ultra-hardy; to 5.5×4.5m (18×15ft); pinnate lvs, 13–15 sharply toothed lfts; infls to 15cm (6in) across; large clusters of bright orange-red frs (used for preserves). Vars: 'Asplenifolia' (deeply cut ferny lvs); 'Beissneri' **4** (compact & erect; young shoots red; bark coppery-orange; young lvs yellow); 'Edulis' (large lvs & frs; frs sweet; best var for preserves); 'Fastigiata' (narrow & upright, to 4.5×1.5m [15×5ft]); 'Pendula' (broad & weeping, to 3×4.5m [10×15ft]).
S. cashmiriana: to 4.5×3m (15×10ft); open & graceful; pinnate lvs, 13–19 sharply toothed lfts, rich green; large infls of 1cm (½in) pink-flushed fls; persistent white frs to 1.5cm (⅝in) wide.
S. domestica **5** (service tree): spreading, to 7.5×5.5m (25×18ft); rough bark; pinnate lvs, 13–21 sharply toothed lfts; pear/apple-shaped frs to 3cm (1¼in) long, green tinged red.
S. hupehensis **6**: to 5.5×4.5m (18×15ft); pinnate lvs, 9–17 bluish-green lfts, often orange & red in autumn; white or pinkish persistent frs on red stalks.
S. hybrida: may be of hybrid origin but breeds true; to 5.5×4.5m (18×15ft); lobed dark green lvs to 9×6cm (3½×2½in), grey felt beneath, usually with basal lfts; wide infls; deep scarlet frs to 1.5cm (⅝in) wide.
S. intermedia (Swedish whitebeam): to 5.5×5.5m (18×18ft); dense; lobed & toothed dark green lvs to 10×8cm (4×3in), grey felt beneath; infls to 12cm (5in) wide; bright red 1cm (½in) frs.
S. 'Joseph Rock' **7**: vigorous & erect, to 6×3.5m (20×12ft); pinnate lvs, 15–21 sharply toothed narrow lfts, red, orange & purple in autumn; large clusters of persistent yellow frs.

S.×*kewensis*: hybrid of *S. aucuparia* & *S. pohuashanensis* (sometimes listed as latter): to 5.5×5.5m (18×18ft); pinnate lvs, 11–15 sharply toothed lfts, grey beneath; v large heavy clusters of bright orange-red frs.
S. pygmaea (*S. poteriifolia*): dwarf suckering shrub, to 8×30cm (3×12in); pinnate lvs, 9–15 sharply toothed lfts to 1cm (½in) long; fls pink; frs white or pink-tinged. Best in moist, peaty soil.
S. reducta: spreading, suckering shrub, to 0.6×1.8m (2×6ft); pinnate lvs, 9–15 deeply toothed 2–3cm (¾–1¼in) dark glossy green lfts, bronze & purple in autumn; pink frs. Best in moist fertile soil.
S. sargentiana: moderately to v hardy; to 6×4.5m (20×15ft); open; stout branches; large sticky crimson winter buds; lvs to 30cm (1ft) long, 9–13 lfts to 12cm (5in) long, open mahogany-brown, brilliant orange-red in autumn; infls to 25cm (10in) wide; v large clusters of orange-red frs.
S. scalaris: to 4.5×6m (15×20ft); spreading & flat-headed, with long arching branches; ferny pinnate lvs, up to 33 narrow, crowded dark green lfts, cobwebby beneath, often orange, red & purple in late autumn; infls to 18cm (7in) wide; dense clusters of bright red small frs.
S. thibetica 'John Mitchell' (*S.* 'Mitchellii'): vigorous, narrow, to 9×4m (30×13ft); large dark green rounded lvs to 12×10cm (5×4in), silvery-felted beneath; brown 1.5cm (⅝in) frs.
S.×*thuringiaca*: hybrid of *S. aria* & *S. aucuparia*, sometimes confused with *S. hybrida* but does not breed true; to 5.5×3m (18×10ft); densely branched; dark green lvs to 15×10cm (6×4in), grey beneath, toothed at end, deeply lobed at base, sometimes with basal lfts; bright red frs. Var 'Fastigiata' is narrow, to 5.5×5.5m (18×18ft).
S. tianshanica: slow-growing tree, to 3.5×3m (12×10ft), or large shrub; pinnate lvs, 11–15 glossy green lfts, colouring in autumn; fls to 2cm (¾in) wide & red frs in continental climates.
S. torminalis (wild service tree): rounded to 6×5.5m (20×18ft); maple-like lobed & toothed lvs to 12×10cm (5×4in), dark glossy green above, yellow or crimson in autumn; fls early summer; brown frs to 1.5cm (⅝in) long.
S. vilmorinii: elegant & spreading, to 3×3.5m (10×12ft); ferny pinnate lvs, up to 29 lfts to 2cm (¾in) long, orange & red in autumn; persistent deep pink frs paling to almost white.

178

Quinces

All formerly *Cydonia* spp. Deciduous shrubs (& a few trees), often spiny, grown mainly for their showy spring flowers followed by ornamental, often fragrant apple/pear-shaped fruits (edible but sour; used for preserves). Often grown as wall shrubs, but not essential. **Cultivation**: Very hardy unless stated, but *Cydonia* spp need v warm summers to ripen fruits & wood. For any fertile soil in sunny spot. **Pruning**: Little needed unless trained on wall; then prune after flowering, cutting back side shoots to 2 or 3 buds. **Propagation**: Semi-ripe cuttings; layering; spp by seed.

Flowering quinces (cydonia, *Chaenomeles* [*Cydonia*] spp): stout-branched spiny shrubs; toothed lvs; saucer-shaped fls to 4cm (1½in) across, often in clusters, all spring (often also in mild winter spells); yellowish frs. Good for borders, hedging, walls.
C. cathayensis **1**: moderately to v hardy; to 3×3m (10×10ft); lance-shaped 8–12cm (3–5in) lvs, downy beneath; white fls flushed pink; frs to 15–20cm (6–8in) long. Hybrids with *C.×superba* (listed as *C.×californica*): 'Enchantress' (shell-pink); 'Pink Beauty' (purplish-pink).
C. japonica (Maule's quince, lesser flowering quince): low & spreading, to 1.2×2.5m (4×8ft); rounded lvs to 5cm (2in) long; profuse orange- to blood-red fls; 4cm (1½in) frs*, stained red.
C. speciosa **2** (*C. lagenaria*, japonica, Japanese quince; long incorrectly listed as *Cydonia japonica*): spreading, to 1.8×2.5m (6×8ft) or more; saw-toothed glossy lvs to 8cm (3in) long; fls red; 5–6cm (2–2½in) green-yellow frs*. Vars include: 'Cardinalis' (crimson-scarlet);

'Moerloosei' **3** (dense clusters of pink & white fls); 'Nivalis' **4** (pure white); 'Rosea Plena' (double, rose-pink); 'Rubra Grandiflora' (v large crimson fls); 'Simonii' (low-growing; semi-double blood-red fls); 'Snow' (pure white); 'Versicolor Lutescens' (cream flushed pink).
C.×superba vars: hybrids of *C. japonica* & *C. speciosa*; generally low & spreading, to 1–1.5×1.8–2.5m (3–5×6–8ft). Vars include: 'Coral Sea' (unusual salmon-coral shade); 'Crimson & Gold' **5** (deep red, golden anthers); 'Hever Castle' (shrimp-pink); 'Incendie' (distinctive orange-red); 'Jet Trail' (dwarf; white); 'Knap Hill Scarlet' (profuse large brilliant red fls); 'Pink Lady' **6** (rose-pink); 'Rowallane' (brilliant crimson).
Common quince (*Cydonia oblonga* **7**): spineless tree, to 4.5×3.5m (15×12ft), or large shrub; young shoots downy; dark green lvs to 10×5.5cm (4×2¼in), grey-woolly beneath; white or pale pink 5cm (2in) fls, late spring; yellow frs* to 10cm (4in) long.

Ornamental crab apples and pears

Among the most important deciduous trees for small gardens, with attractive blossom mid–late spring unless stated, often followed by colourful fruits. Foliage often attractive, sometimes colouring in autumn. Excellent specimens, but often fruit best if several vars grown nearby. **Cultivation**: Unless stated, very hardy & for any well-drained fertile soil in full sun. As with edible spp, prone to various pests & diseases, including fireblight, scab, canker, rust, mildew. **Propagation**: Seed (may well not breed true); grafting on various stocks, including dwarfing types.

Crab apples (*Malus* spp): lvs generally 5–10cm (2–4in) long; clusters of 5-petalled fls generally 2.5–4cm (1–1½in) across; frs round or oval, good for preserves.
SPECIES & BOTANICAL HYBRIDS:
M.×arnoldiana: hybrid of *M. baccata* & *M. floribunda*; graceful round-headed tree, to 4.5×4.5m (15×15ft), or large shrub; pink fls from red buds, inside fading white; 2cm (¾in) oval frs, yellow flushed red.
*M. baccata** **8** (Siberian crab): ultra-hardy; round-headed & spreading, to 5.5×6m (18×20ft); white fls; small bright red or yellow frs. Healthy. Var *mandshurica** (Manchurian crab) fls early.
*M. coronaria*** (American crab): spreading & open, to 4.5×5.5m (15×18ft); rose-tinged white fls to 5cm (2in) across, late spring & v early summer; v acid yellowish-green 2.5–4cm (1–

1½in) frs. Vars 'Charlottae'* **9** & 'Nieuwlandiana'* are semi-double; resist scab.
M. florentina **10**: may be intergeneric hybrid of *M. sylvestris* & *Sorbus torminalis* (wild service tree); to 4.5×4.5m (15×15ft); round-headed; hawthorn-like lobed & toothed lvs, orange & scarlet in autumn; 2cm (¾in) white fls, early summer; rather oval 1cm (½in) frs, yellow to red.
*M. floribunda** **11** (Japanese crab): probably hybrid; dense & spreading, to 4.5×6m (15×20ft); long arching branches; some lvs may be lobed; profuse blush-pink fls from red buds; yellow 2cm (¾in) frs. Popular.
M. halliana: to 4.5×4.5m (15×15ft); dark glossy green lvs; deep rose-pink semi-double pendulous fls; v small purple-red frs. Var 'Parkmanii' is more double. *M.×atrosanguinea* is hybrid with *M. sieboldii*; to 4.5×6m (15×20ft);

rose-pink fls from crimson buds; scab-resistant.

M. hupehensis*: vigorous & spreading, to 6×6m (20×20ft); stiffly ascending branches; white fls from pink buds, often profuse only in alternate yrs; red-tinged yellow 1cm (½in) frs. Breeds true from seed; scab-resistant. Var *rosea* is rosy-pink.

M.×purpurea **1**: hybrid of *M.×atrosanguinea* & *M. niedzwetzkyana*; spreading when mature, to 4.5×5.5m (15×18ft); young growth & lvs purplish; profuse rosy-crimson fls; 2.5cm (1in) wine-red frs. Closely related hybrids/vars (often only large bushes; lvs purplish becoming bronzed; fls wine-red; frs purplish-red): 'Aldenhamensis' (fls late spring; flattened 2.5cm [1in] frs); 'Eleyi' **2** (*M.×eleyi*; conical 2.5cm [1in] frs); 'Lemoinei' (erect habit; fls single or semi-double, best on mature trees, 1.5cm [⅝in] frs).

M.×robusta (cherry crab; incorrectly, Siberian crab): hybrid of *M. baccata* & *prunifolia*; vigorous & spreading, to 5.5×6m (18×20ft); fls white or pink-flushed; persistent cherry-like red or yellow 2.5cm (1in) frs. Vars: 'Red Siberian' **3**; 'Yellow Siberian'.

M. sargentii* **4**: bushy shrub, to 1.8×3.5m (6×12ft); lvs often lobed; profuse pure white fls; bright red flattened frs 8mm (⅓in) across.

M. sieboldii (Toringo crab): arching, spreading shrub, to 2.5×3.5m (8×12ft); smallish sharply toothed lvs; small pale to deep pink fls on v thin stalks; v small red or yellowish frs.

M. spectabilis: round-headed tree, to 4.5×4.5m (15×15ft), or tall shrub; glossy green lvs; blush-pink fls to 5cm (2in) across from deep rosy-red buds; v acid yellow 2.5cm (1in) frs. Var 'Riversii' has large lvs & large double fls, deeper pink.

M. trilobata: conical, to 5.5×1.5m (18×5ft), with erect branches; maple-like lobed glossy lvs, colouring in autumn; large white fls, late spring; red or yellow 2cm (¾in) frs.

M. tschonoskii **5**: ultra-hardy; vigorous & narrowly conical, to 6×1.8m (20×6ft); coarsely toothed lvs to 12cm (5in) long, brilliant orange, scarlet & purple in autumn; white fls flushed rose at first; rather insignificant brownish-yellow frs.

M.×zumi: hybrid of *M. baccata mandshurica* & *M. sieboldii*; to 3.5×3m (12×10ft); pyramid-shaped; white fls from pink buds; red 1cm (½in) frs. Var 'Calocarpa' is more spreading; lvs lobed on young shoots; frs persistent.

GARDEN HYBRIDS: round-headed & to 4.5–6×3–5.5m (15–20×10–18ft) unless stated.

M. 'Bob White'*: profuse white fls from red buds; persistent 1.5cm (⅝in) yellow frs.

M. 'Brandywine'*: purple-tinted lvs, russet in autumn; semi-double deep rose-pink fls; red frs.

M. 'Dartmouth': profuse white fls; reddish-purple frs to 5cm (2in) across.

M. 'Dolgo'*: ultra-hardy; vigorous & white 4.5cm (1¾in) fls, profuse in alternate yrs; bright red 3cm (1¼in) frs. Resists scab.

M. 'Dorothea': profuse silvery-pink semi-double fls 4–5cm (1½–2in) across from crimson buds; bright yellow 1cm (½in) frs.

M. 'Echtermeyer': weeping; young lvs bronzed; pale carmine-red fls; purplish-red 2.5cm (1in) frs.

M. 'Flame': ultra-hardy; white fls from pink buds; 2cm (¾in) bright red frs. Resists scab.

M. 'Golden Hornet' **6**: spreading; white fls; profuse 2–2.5cm (¾–1in) golden-yellow frs.

M. 'John Downie' **7**: erect, spreading later; white fls from pink buds; showy bright orange & red conical frs 3cm (1¼in) long (good flavour).

M. 'Katherine': dense; semi-double 5cm (2in) fls, pink fading white; 5mm (¼in) bright red frs flushed yellow.

M. 'Prince George': 5cm (2in) double rose-pink fls, late. Resists scab.

M. 'Profusion': spreading; young lvs purplish becoming bronzed; profuse deep red-purple fls, pink centre; blood-red 1cm (½in) frs.

M. 'Radiant': weeping; young lvs tinted reddish; white fls; profuse 1cm (½in) cherry-like red frs.

M. 'Red Jade' **8**: weeping; white fls; profuse bright red persistent frs 1cm (½in) across.

M. 'Red Sentinel': white fls; deep red glossy 2.5cm (1in) frs, v persistent.

M. 'Red Silver': vigorous; young lvs flushed reddish; rose-pink fls; deep red 2cm (¾in) frs.

M. 'Snowdrift': ultra-hardy; v profuse white fls from pink buds; orange-red 1cm (½in) frs.

M. 'Van Eseltine' **9**: v narrow & erect, to 5.5×1.2m (18×4ft); semi-double shell-pink fls 5cm (2in) across from scarlet buds; yellow frs.

Pears (*Pyrus* spp): grown mainly for lvs (to 8–10cm [3–4in] long) & white 5-petalled fls, generally 2.5–4cm (1–1½in) across; 2.5–4cm (1½–2in) frs, rounded or pear-shaped, generally not showy. Tolerate dry or wet soils, salty winds.

P. calleryana: strong-growing, to 6×3.5m (20×12ft); often thorny; glossy green lvs, often colouring well in autumn; small fls; frs brownish. Resists fireblight. 'Bradford' (neat, to 5.5×3.5m [18×12ft]) & 'Chanticleer' **10** (conical, to 5.5×3m [18×10ft]) are free-flg thornless vars.

P. communis 'Beech Hill' (a common wild pear var): v narrow, to 6×1.8m (20×6ft); glossy lvs, orange & yellow in autumn; brown frs.

P. nivalis (snow pear): sturdy, to 6×5.5m (20×18ft); young shoots & lvs silvery-grey; profuse fls; rounded yellowish-green frs.

P. salicifolia (willow-leaved pear): more or less weeping (especially in var 'Pendula' **11**), to 5.5×4.5m (18×15ft); young shoots downy; narrow lance-shaped lvs, silvery when young, becoming grey-green; creamy-white fls; yellowish-brown frs. Excellent lawn specimen.

P. ussuriensis (Chinese pear): vigorous & elegant, to 7.5×5.5m (25×18ft); bristly-toothed lvs, bronze-crimson in autumn; profuse early fls; rounded yellow frs. Resists fireblight.

Cherry laurels

Prunus spp (subgenus *Laurocerasus*). Evergreens often used for hedging but seen best as isolated specimens; some vars useful as ground cover. Small whitish flowers in racemes. **Cultivation**: Generally for any well-drained soil in sun or shade. For hedge, plant 1m (3ft) apart; trim spring or autumn. **Propagation**: Seed; hardwood cuttings; layering. For true laurel (bay, *Laurus nobilis*), see p116.

P. caroliniana (Carolina cherry laurel): semi- to moderately hardy bushy tree, to 7.5×6m (25×20ft); entire dark glossy green lance-shaped lvs to 10cm (4in) long; infls to 2.5cm (1in) long, early spring; plum-like 1cm (½in) black frs.

P. laurocerasus **1** ([English] laurel, common cherry laurel): moderately to v hardy vigorous spreading shrub, to 4.5×6m (15×20ft), or small tree; dark shining green leathery lvs to 15cm (6in) long; infls to 12cm (5in) long, mid–late spring; purple-black 1cm (½in) frs. Shoots, lvs & seeds poisonous. Dislikes shallow chalk soils; prone to leaf spot, mildew. Vars: 'Greenmantle' (spreading, to 1.5×3m [5×10ft]); 'Magnoliifolia' (vigorous, to 6×6m [20×20ft]; lvs to 30×10cm

[12×4in]); 'Otto Luyken' **2** (dense & bushy, to 0.6×1.5m [2×5ft]) narrow lvs; free-flg); 'Schipkaensis' (v hardy; compact & spreading, to 2.5×1.8m [8×6ft]); 'Zabeliana' (low & spreading, to 1.2×3m (4×10ft); narrow lvs; free flg; good ground cover).

P. lusitanica **3** (Portugal laurel): moderately to v hardy (more so than *P. laurocerasus*); bushy shrub, to 4.5×3m (15×10ft), or small tree; dark glossy green lvs to 12×5cm (5×2in), paler beneath, reddish stalks; narrow infls to 25cm (10in) long, early summer; 8mm (⅓in) red to purple-black frs. Prone to silver leaf disease. Var 'Variegata' **4** is moderately hardy; lvs edged white, often pinkish in winter.

Ornamental cherries

Prunus spp (subgenera *Cerasus* & *Padus*). Probably the best-loved & most important spring-flowering trees (& some shrubs); some also having good autumn colour or attractive bark. Deciduous, with narrow-pointed toothed lvs, to 5–10cm (2–4in) long unless stated. Flowers on stalks, to 2.5–4cm (1–1½in) across unless stated, in dense clusters, racemes or corymbs. Trees excellent as specimens or for avenues & streets, smaller-flowered types in groups; shrubs for borders, etc. **Cultivation**: Very hardy unless noted. For any well-drained soil in full sun, preferably sheltered from cold winds. Regular pruning generally unnecessary except for shrubs flowering on year-old wood (cut back flowered shoots hard after flowering). Trim hedges after flowering. **Pests & diseases**: Blackfly; canker; silver leaf; witches' brooms; birds (attack winter buds). **Propagation**: Seed; semi-ripe cuttings; large-flowered hybrids by budding/grafting on *P. avium,* etc.

Tree species (including close vars): generally round-headed.

P. avium (wild or mazzard cherry, gean): ultra-hardy; vigorous, to 11×9m (36×30ft); lvs to 12cm (5in) long, crimson in autumn; white fls, mid spring; blackish-red 2cm (¾in) frs, sweet/bitter. Var 'Plena' **5** has v profuse large double fls.

P. campanulata (Formosan or bell-flowered cherry): semi- to moderately hardy; to 6×6m (20×20ft); bell-shaped deep rose fls 2cm (¾in) across, early spring before lvs.

P. cerasus 'Semperflorens' (All-Saints cherry; sour cherry var): ultra-hardy; to 5.5×3.5m (18×12ft); branches rather pendulous; white fls, mid spring, repeating throughout summer on new growth; acid edible frs.

P. conradinae* **6**: elegant & rather open, to 6×6m (20×20ft); white or pale pink fls, late winter or early spring (before lvs), semi-double & longer lasting in var 'Semi-plena'*; small red frs.

P. maackii **7** (Manchurian or Amur cherry): ultra-hardy; pyramid-shaped, to 6×4.5m (20×15ft); grown for peeling honey-brown

glossy bark; small white fls, late spring, not showy.

P. padus* (bird cherry): ultra-hardy; vigorous, to 11×6m (36×20ft); lvs to 12cm (5in) long; drooping or spreading infls of 1cm (½in) white fls, late spring; small black bitter frs. Vars: 'Colorata' (stems purple; young lvs bronze-purple becoming purplish-green; fls deep pink, fading); commutata (early-flg); 'Plena' (double); 'Watereri' **8** ('Grandiflora'; large infls).

P. sargentii **9** (Sargent cherry): spreading, to 7.5×9m (25×30ft); lvs coppery-red when young, brilliant orange & red in early autumn; bright pink 4–5cm (1½–2in) fls, mid spring. One of best spp but hates pollution. Var 'Rancho' is narrower, with larger, deeper pink fls.

P. serotina* **10** (black or rum cherry): ultra-hardy; vigorous & elegant, to 11×9m (36×30ft), less in moderate climates; dark green glossy lvs to 15cm (6in) long, yellow in autumn; white 1cm (½in) fls in 12cm (5in) infls, late spring to early summer; sour red to black frs. 'Pendula' is gracefully weeping var; usually top-grafted.

P. serrula* : to 4.5×4.5m (15×15ft); grown for glossy reddish mahogany-brown peeling bark (best if loose flakes removed occasionally); narrowish lvs; small white fls, not showy.

P. serrulata spontanea (Japanese/Chinese hill cherry): to 6×6m (20×20ft); young lvs usually reddish-brown, often colouring well in autumn; pink or white fls, mid spring; frs dark purple-red. Parent (with *P. serrulata* & others) of large-fld hybrid Japanese cherries (see below) but beautiful in own right.

P. subhirtella (Higan or spring cherry): to 6×6m (20×20ft); twiggy; profuse pale pink 2cm (¾in) fls, early spring (before lvs); black frs. Dislikes pollution. Vars (generally smaller): 'Autumnalis' (autumn cherry); semi-double pale pink or white fls, mild spells in late autumn & winter, sometimes repeating spring; 'Autumnalis Rosea' is deeper pink); 'Fukubana' (semi-double, deep pink); *pendula* (branches weep to ground, vars: 'Pendula Plena Rosea' [semi-double, deep pink]; 'Pendula Rosea' [flesh-pink]; 'Pendula Rubra' **1** [deep pink]); 'Stellata' ('Pink Star'; large starry fls).

P. virginiana (choke cherry, Virginia bird cherry): ultra-hardy; to 6×3m (20×10ft); lvs to 12cm (5in) long; dense 15cm (6in) infls of 8mm (⅓in) white fls, late spring. Var 'Schubert' has green lvs turning purple early summer.

P.×yedoensis (Yoshino cherry): may be hybrid of *P. speciosa* & *P. subhirtella*; to 5.5×7.5m (18×25ft); rather drooping branches; lvs bronze to orange in autumn; profuse white or pink fls, early–mid spring (usually before lvs). Var 'Ivensii' is arching & weeping; fls white.

Tree hybrids: includes Japanese cherries often listed under *P. serrulata* but generally of complex parentage. Unless stated, to 4.5–6×4.5–6m (15–20×15–20ft) & fl mid–late spring; lvs generally bronzed when young, often colouring in autumn. Vars: 'Accolade' **2** (open habit; semi-double, pale pink); 'Amanogawa'* **3** (v narrow & upright, to 6×1.5m [20×5ft]; semi-double, shell-pink); 'Asano' (Yoshido cherry; broad; mauve-pink double 6cm [2½in] fls); 'Cheal's Weeping' **4** (often sold incorrectly as 'Kiku Shidare Zakura'; branches weep to ground; double, rose-pink); 'Daikoku' **5** (incorrectly, 'Beni-fugan'; spreading; double bright purplish-pink 5cm [2in] fls); 'Fudan Zakura' (pink buds, white fls, winter & early spring); 'Fugenzo' ('James H. Veitch'; dense & flat-topped; 5cm [2in] double rose-pink fls, late); 'Hally Jolivette' (slender shoots; hairy lvs; pink buds, semi-double white fls before lvs); 'Hillieri' (broad; lvs bright red in autumn; blush-pink fls; 'Spire' [*P.×hillieri* 'Spire'] is similar but narrow, to 5.5×2.5m [18×8ft]); 'Hokusai' (spreading; lvs orange & red in autumn; 5cm [2in] semi-double pale pink fls, long season); 'Horinji' (erect; 5cm [2in] semi-double deep pink fls, paler centre);

'Jo-nioi' (vigorous; white); 'Kansan' ('Kwanzan', 'Sekiyama'; incorrectly 'Hisakura'; vigorous & vase-shaped; double, purplish-pink; 'Pink Perfection' **6** is similar but clear pink); 'Kursar' (bushy; lvs orange in autumn; vivid deep pink small fls, early); 'Mikurama-gaeshi' (open; 5cm [2in] single/semi-double pale pink fls); 'Ojochin' ('Senriko'; vigorous; good autumn colour; pale pink to white fls); 'Okama' (small lvs, colouring in autumn; carmine-pink fls); 'Pandora' (compact & vase-shaped; dark brown shiny bark; white or pale pink fls, early); 'Shimidsu' **7** ('Shogetsu'; flat crown; lvs orange & red in autumn; 5cm [2in] double white frilly fls, late); 'Shirofugen' (in US, 'White Goddess'; vigorous; drooping branches; lvs orange in autumn; double white 5–6cm [2–2½in] fls fading mauve-pink, late); 'Shirotae'* ('Kojima', 'Mount Fuji'; spreading; drooping branches; long lvs; 5cm [2in] single/semi-double white fls); 'Tai Haku' (great white cherry; v vigorous, to 7.5×7.5m [25×25ft]; 20cm [8in] lvs; white 6cm [2½in] fls); 'Tao-yoma' (lvs red & orange in autumn; semi-double shell-pink fls, deeper edge & reverse, fading); 'Ukon' (lvs red, copper & purple in autumn; 5cm [2in] semi-double greenish-yellow fls); 'Umineko' (narrow & erect, to 6×2.5m [20×8ft]; good autumn colour; white fls); 'Yedo Zakura' (semi-double rich shell-pink 5cm [2in] fls).

Shrubs: generally bushy.

P. besseyi (Rocky Mountains or western sand cherry): ultra-hardy; to 1.2×1.5m (4×5ft); grey-green lvs, bronze-purple in autumn; profuse clusters of 1.5cm (⅝in) white fls, spring; black edible frs, best where summers hot.

P.×cistena **8** (*P.* 'Crimson Dwarf'; purple-leaved sand cherry): hybrid of *P. cerasifera* 'Pissardii' (p188) & *P. pumila*; ultra-hardy; to 1.8×1.8m (6×6ft); reddish-purple lvs; white fls, spring; blackish-purple frs. Excellent for hedging.

P. glandulosa **9** (Chinese bush cherry; in US, dwarf flowering almond [misnomer]): neat, to 1.2×1.5m (4×5ft); profuse solitary or paired pink or white 1cm (½in) fls, mid spring, on yr-old wood; showy red frs. Vars 'Alba Plena' ('Alboplena'; white) & 'Sinensis' ('Rosea Plena'; pink) are much showier, with 3cm (1¼in) double fls, late spring, & larger lvs.

P. incisa **10** (Fuji cherry): to 3×1.5m (10×5ft), or small tree; deeply toothed lvs, red when young; profuse nodding white or pale pink 2cm (¾in) fls, early spring; small black frs. Popular for bonsai. Var 'Praecox' fls from winter.

P. tomentosa (downy cherry, Manchu or Nanking cherry): ultra-hardy; to 1.8×1.5m (6×5ft); young shoots downy; dark green lvs, woolly beneath; profuse but often fleeting solitary or paired 2cm (¾in) fls, pale pink or white, early spring on yr-old wood; bright red frs where summers hot.

Ornamental almonds, apricots, peaches and plums

Prunus spp. Deciduous small trees & shrubs (former unless stated), relatives of popular stone fruits grown mainly for their showy 5-petalled early flowers (solitary or in small clusters along branches) & often attractive foliage. Excellent specimens for moderate-sized gardens (best against dark background); shrubs for borders, hedging or against walls. **Cultivation**: Very hardy unless stated. For any well-drained soil (even shallow chalk) in full sun. Regular pruning generally not needed; trim hedges after flowering. **Pests & diseases**: Red spider mites; aphids; borers; peach leaf curl; mildew; scale; silver leaf. **Propagation**: Seed; vars by budding/grafting (often on plum stocks); many by semi-ripe cuttings.

Almonds & peaches (subgenus *Amygdalus*): fls almost stalkless, before lvs.

P.×amygdalo-persica 'Pollardii' **1**: hybrid of *P. dulcis* & *P. persica*, similar to former but lvs sharper-toothed & fls brighter pink, 5cm (2in) across, early spring; to 4.5×3m (15×10ft).

P. davidiana (Père David's peach): ultra-hardy; upright, to 5.5×3m (18×10ft); fine-toothed lance-shaped lvs to 12×4cm (5×1½in); white or pale pink 2.5cm (1in) fls, winter to early spring; 3cm (1¼in) rounded yellowish frs. Best sheltered. Vars 'Alba' (white); 'Rubra' (rose).

P. dulcis **2** (*P. amygdalus*, almond): moderately to v hardy; to 4.5×4.5m (15×15ft); fine-toothed lance-shaped lvs to 12×4cm (5×1½in); 2.5–5cm (1–2in) generally soft pink fls, early spring; frs green at first, giving good-quality nuts only where summers hot. Vars: 'Alba' (white); 'Praecox' (early); 'Roseoplena' (double).

P. persica (peach & nectarine): bushy, to 3.5×2.5m (12×8ft); long-pointed lance-shaped lvs to 15×4cm (6×1½in); fls pale pink to red, 2.5–4cm (1–1½in) or more wide, early–mid spring; juicy 5–8cm (2–3in) frs (larger in frtg vars) where summers hot. Vars: 'Cardinal' (double red rosette fls): 'Foliis Rubris' (in US, 'Royal Redleaf'; lvs reddish-purple becoming bronzed green; fls pink); 'Helen Borchers' (large semi-double rose-pink fls); 'Iceberg' **3** (profuse large white semi-double fls); 'Klara Mayer' **4** (double, peach-pink); 'Peppermint Stick' (double, white striped red; 'Versicolor' is similar); 'Prince Charming' (upright; double, rose-red); 'Russell's Red' (double, crimson); 'Windle Weeping' (pendulous; semi-double, purplish-pink).

P. tenella (dwarf Russian almond): ultra-hardy suckering shrub, to 1.2×1.5m (4×5ft); bright green narrow lvs to 8cm (3in) long; profuse rosy-pink 2cm (¾in) fls, mid spring; small almond-like frs if summers hot. Var 'Fire Hill' **5** has brilliant rose-red fls.

P. triloba **6** (*P. t.* 'Multiplex'; in US, flowering almond): dense shrub, to 2.5×2.5m (8×8ft), or small tree; doubly toothed lvs to 8cm (3in) long; peach-pink double rosette fls to 4cm (1½in) across, early spring, along yr-old shoots (often forced under glass). Cut back fld shoots hard after flg (especially if trained on wall). Var *simplex* is wild single form.

Apricots & plums (subgenus *Prunus*): fls on short stalks, before or with lvs.

P.×blireana **7**: hybrid of *P. cerasifera* 'Pissardii' & *P. mume* 'Alphandii'; to 3.5×4.5m (12×15ft); arching branches; young lvs bronzy-red, to 5cm (2in) long, becoming almost green; double 3cm (1¼in) rose-pink fls, early spring, with or just before lvs; purplish-red frs.

P. cerasifera (cherry or myrobalan plum): ultra-hardy; bushy, to 5.5×5.5m (18×18ft); thin lvs to 6cm (2½in) long; profuse clusters of white 2–2.5cm (¾–1in) fls, early spring; sweet red frs (cherry plums) to 3cm (1¼in) across (good for tarts, etc). Sp & purple-lvd vars good for hedging. Vars: *divaricata* (*P. divaricata*; small yellow frs); 'Hollywood' (young lvs green, becoming purple); 'Nigra' **8** (lvs v dark purple; fls pink; 'Vesuvius' is similar); 'Pissardii' **9** ('Atropurpurea', purple-leaved plum; lvs reddish-purple; fls white, from pink buds); 'Thundercloud' (lvs coppery-purple).

P. 'Trailblazer' is hybrid of *P. c.* 'Nigra' & probably *P. salicina*; bronze-green lvs; profuse white fls.

P.×cistena: see p186.

P. maritima (beach or sand plum): ultra-hardy compact shrub, to 1.5×1.5m (5×5ft); narrow saw-toothed lvs to 8cm (3in) long; small clusters of 1cm (½in) white fls, late spring, before lvs; red, purple or yellow frs to 2.5cm (1in) across (used for preserves). Useful for exposed coastal sites, sandy soil. Var 'Flava' has yellow frs.

P. (*Armeniaca*) *mume* * (Japanese apricot): moderately to v hardy; to 4.5×4.5m (15×15ft); round-headed & open, with slender branches; sharp-pointed lvs to 10cm (4in) long; profuse pale pink 3cm (1¼in) fls, late winter or early spring, sour bitter yellowish frs to 3cm (1¼in) wide after hot summers. Vars: 'Albo-plena' ** (semi-double, white); 'Alphandii' ** **10** (semi-double, pink); 'Beni-shidon' *** (double, deep pink, mid spring); 'Pendula' ** (weeping; pale pink); 'Rosemary Clarke' * (semi-double white fls, red calyx).

P. spinosa **11** (blackthorn, sloe): dense suckering shrub, to 3.5×3m (12×10ft), or small tree; spiny shoots; lvs to 4cm (1½in) long; white 2cm (¾in) fls, early spring, usually before lvs; blue-black 1cm (½in) bitter frs Useful for hedging; good on poor soils. Vars: 'Plena' (double); 'Purpurea' (lvs red becoming purple; fls pink).

Gardenias and their relatives

Generally rather tender shrubs grown for their showy, usually highly fragrant tubular to cup-shaped flowers or for their berries. Evergreen unless stated. Used as specimens or for hedging in warm zones, some for temporary summer display outdoors where winters cold. **Cultivation**: Generally for rich, peaty, rather acid soils in partial shade; feed & water well unless stated. Can be pruned after flowering. **Propagation**: Unless stated, semi-ripe or hardwood cuttings; spp also by seed.

Sweet bouvardia (*Bouvardia longiflora*** 1**): semi-hardy lax shrub, to 1×1m (3×3ft); paired lvs; 8cm (3in) tubular white fls in loose infls, any season in warm climates, autumn elsewhere, good for cutting. Good in tub to move under glass in winter. Propagate by softwood cuttings.

Coprosmas (*Coprosma* spp): New Zealand shrubs grown for berries (female plants only), some for glossy lvs; fls insignificant. Good near sea; taller spp for windbreaks. Moderately hardy unless stated; drought-tolerant once established.

C. acerosa: to 0.25×1.5m (10in×5ft); prostrate & twiggy; lvs small, v narrow; pale blue frs. Best in rock garden.

C. lucida **2**: tender to semi-hardy; to 3.5×3m (12×10ft); leathery glossy lvs to 12cm (5in) long; bright orange-red frs.

C. propinqua: to 3×2.5m (10×8ft); slender, spreading habit; small, v narrow lvs; pale blue to almost black frs. Prefers moist soils.

C. repens **3** (*C. baueri*, mirror plant): semi-hardy; fast-growing, to 3×2.5m (10×8ft); v glossy oval lvs to 8cm (3in) long; yellow to orange-red clustered frs. Good for hedge (can be clipped). Vars: 'Marginata' **4** (lvs edged yellow); 'Variegata' **5** (to 1×0.6m [3×2ft]; lvs marked yellow-green).

Gardenias (*Gardenia* spp): showy shrubs grown for waxy white fragrant fls (generally good for cutting) & glossy narrowish lvs. For hedging & containers in warm zones; best under glass where summers cool (withstand some frost but need humid hot summers; syringe daily to prevent bud drop).

*G. jasminoides*** 6** (common gardenia, Cape jasmine): semi- to moderately hardy; to 1.8×1.8m (6×6ft); leathery lvs to 10cm (4in) long; fls usually double, v good for bouquets.

Vars: 'August Beauty' (large fls, late spring to late autumn); 'Florida' (*G. florida*; fls early–mid summer); *fortuniana* (8cm [3in] fls, early–mid summer); 'Mystery' (to 2.5m [8ft] unless pruned; 10–12cm [4–5in] fls, late spring & early summer); 'Radicans' (to 30×90cm [1×3ft]; small fls; for ground cover); 'Veitchii Improved' **7** (prolific 5cm [2in] fls, late spring to late autumn).

*G. thunbergia*** *: semi-hardy; slow-growing, to 2.5×3m (8×10ft); lvs v dark green; funnel-shaped fls to 8cm (3in) long, mid winter to early spring, best on older plants, not good for cutting. Tolerates poorer soil than other sp.

Luculias (*Luculia* spp): semi-hardy shrubs or small trees with large semi-evergreen lvs & showy clusters to 20cm (8in) across of fragrant fls. In cool areas grow under glass except in summer.

*L. grandifolia*** *: to 2×1.5m (7×5ft); lvs v veined, to 40cm (16in) long, colouring in autumn; white fls to 6cm (2½in) long, early summer.

*L. gratissima*** 8**: to 2×1.5m (7×5ft); lvs to 20cm (8in) long; pink or mauvish fls to 2.5cm (1in) long, autumn & winter (good under glass).

*L. pinceana*** *: to 2.5×2m (8×7ft); lvs to 15cm (6in) long; white fls, tinted pink, to 5cm (2in) long, later spring to early autumn.

Rondeletias (*Rondeletia* spp): semi- to moderately hardy shrubs, to 2–3×1.5–2.5m (7–10×5–8ft); oval glossy lvs; dense clusters of rather transient tubular salmon-pink fls from late winter. Good near coast; protect from hard frost.

R. amoena (*R. versicolor*): lvs yellowish to dark reddish-green, bronze when young, hairy beneath.

R. cordata **9**: lvs bright green.

The citrus family

Trees & shrubs with pungent foliage, some thorny, some berrying or fruiting, & generally with star-like flowers (often fragrant). Evergreen unless stated. Oranges, lemons, etc, are commercial crops also prized in gardens in warm areas for their heavily fragrant flowers & showy edible fruits; can be grown in tubs in cool temperate regions and overwintered under glass. **Cultivation**: Generally for fertile, moist but free-draining soil in sun. **Propagation**: Semi-ripe cuttings; spp by seed; some *Citrus* spp & vars by grafting.

Boronias (*Boronia* spp): very tender to semi-hardy Australian shrubs with pinnate lvs, needle-like lfts & spring fls. For lime-free soil in part-shade; prune freely after flg. Rather short-lived.

B. elatior: to 1.8×1.2m (6×4ft); hairy; fls carmine or purplish, 5mm (¼in) long.

*B. heterophylla**: to 1.5×1m (5×3ft); lvs & fls in whorls; profuse drooping rosy-crimson fls 1cm

(½in) across.

*B. megastigma*** **10**, p191 (sweet or scented boronia): to 60×30cm (2×1ft); nodding brown fls, yellow inside (cuttable; used for perfumes). Replace every 2-3yrs.

*B. serrulata*** (in Australia, Sydney rose boronia): to 1.2×1m (4×3ft); simple, toothed lvs; fls lilac-mauve, clustered.

Mexican orange (*Choisya ternata** **1**): moderately hardy, but may be damaged by late frosts; rounded shrub, fairly fast-growing, to 2×2.5m (7×8ft), or more in warm climates; glossy dark green lvs; white starry fls, rather like orange blossom, in profuse clusters, spring & sometimes later. Can be pruned hard after flg; tolerates shade, coastal conditions; useful hedging shrub.

Citrange (×*Citroncirus webberi**): intergeneric hybrid of *Citrus sinensis* & *Poncirus trifoliata*; moderately hardy if grafted on *P. trifoliata* but best against sunny wall; shrub or small tree, to 3.5×3m (12×10ft); spiny; evergreen or semi-deciduous; fls like parents'; 5–8cm (2–3in) sour bitter frs, from late summer.

Oranges, lemons, etc (*Citrus* spp): spp listed generally semi-hardy if well ripened (hardiest if grafted on *Poncirus trifoliata*); generally spiny small trees or large shrubs (to 1.2–3m [4–10ft] on dwarfing rootstock); lvs oval, generally dark green & glossy; white fls, spring to early summer, some used for perfumes; frs slow-maturing (to 1yr; generally ripen winter–spring). Good for hedging, streets, lawns & landscaping in warm areas, tub or conservatory plants elsewhere (need moist air under glass). Water & feed freely outdoors; prune weak growth. Prone to various pests & diseases.

*C. aurantium*** **2** (sour or Seville orange): hardiest large-fr sp (to −6°C [21°F]); to 7.5×6m (25×20ft); lvs* to 10cm (4in) long; orange-red frs to 8cm (3in) diameter, acid & bitter. V ornamental; good for hedging (prune hard).

*C. limon*** **3** (lemon): most tender of spp listed (to −3°C [27°F]) but needs least summer heat; to 6×4.5m (20×15ft); spnes to 2cm (¾in) long; fls tinged purple; sour frs, green turning yellow, to 10cm (4in) long, v slow-ripening. Vars: 'Eureka' (frs ripen all year); 'Improved Meyer' (hardiest var; thin-skinned yellow-orange frs, all year); 'Lisbon' (vigorous; heat-tolerant); 'Ponderosa' (wonder lemon; huge, thick-skinned frs, mainly winter; good ornamental).

*C. mitis*** **4** (calamondin; correctly, ×*Citrofortunella mitis*, intergeneric hybrid of *C. reticulata* & *Fortunella* sp); hardiest sp (to −7°C[19°F] or lower); to 3×1.8m (10×6ft); spineless; sour orange 3cm (1¼in) persistent frs, even on v young plants. Popular for pots & tubs. *C. reticulata* (*C. nobilis*, mandarin, tangerine, satsuma): to 4.5×2.5m (15×8ft); 5–8cm (2–3in)

sweet yellow to orange-red frs, globular or flattened, loose peel. Vars: 'Clementine' (early-ripening); 'Dancy' (tangerine; frs seedy; good in tub); 'Kara' (large frs); 'Kinnow'; 'Owari' (satsuma var; hardy to −5°C [23°F]; ripens autumn).

*C. sinensis*** (sweet orange): to 7.5×6m (25×20ft); small spines; fls spring to early summer; frs sweet, to 10cm (4in) diameter. Navel vars (frs thick-skinned): 'Robertson' (v prolific on dwarfing stock); 'Skaggs Bonanza' (prolific on young trees); 'Washington'. Valencia vars (frs thin-skinned): 'Arizona Sweets' (hardiest); 'Seedless Valencia' (ripens from late spring); 'Shamouti' (popular on dwarfing stock). Blood vars (frs red flesh): 'Maltese'; 'Sanguinelli' (red-skinned); 'Tarocco'.

Breath of heaven (Cape may, *Coleonema* spp): often sold as *Diosma* spp): heath-like branching shrubs, to 1.8×1.2m (6×4ft); tender to semi-hardy; like hot summers; glossy v narrow lvs*; profuse fls to 5mm (¼in) across, winter & spring. Clip lightly after flg. Good on free-draining bank.

C. album (*D. alba, D. reevesii*): white fls.

C. (correctly, *D.*) *ericoides**: white fls.

C. pulchrum **5** (*D. pulchra*): pink fls.

Australian fuchsias (*Correa* spp): tender to semi-hardy shrubs with small rounded lvs, grey-felted beneath, & fuchsia-like bell fls in clusters. Best in poor dryish soil; useful ground cover on banks in warm regions or for containers.

C. alba: arching, to 1.2×1m (4×3ft); white fls to 1cm (½in) long, summer.

C. backhousiana **6** (may be sold as *C.×magnifica*): upright, to 1.5×1.5m (5×5ft); greenish-yellow fls to 2.5cm (1in) long, winter.

C. pulchella **7**: spreading, to 0.6×1.5m (2×5ft); pink fls to 2.5cm (1in) long, winter.

Euodia (*Euodia* [*Evodia*] *danielii* **8**): v hardy late-flg tree; fast-growing, to 6×5m (20×16ft); deciduous; compounds lvs, leathery lfts to 10cm (4in) long; corymbs to 15cm (6in) wide of small white fls, late summer; showy red frs. Good on any soil; pollution-tolerant. *E. hupehensis* is similar but taller.

Kumquats (*Fortunella* spp): shrubs, to 2–3×1.5–2.5m (7–10×5–8ft), less on dwarfing rootstock, or small trees, closely related to *Citrus* spp. Semi- to moderately hardy (to −10°C [14°F] if well ripened); dark green glossy lvs to 8–10cm (3–4in) long; white fls, spring; 2.5–3cm (1–1¼in) deep orange edible frs (sour & aromatic) after warm summers. Attractive in lf or fr; good in tub when on dwarfing rootstock.

*F. japonica*** (Marumi kumquat): spiny; globular frs.

*F. margarita*** (Nagami kumquat): spineless; oblong frs.

Amur cork tree (*Phellodendron amurense* **9**): ultra-hardy wide-spreading graceful tree, to

7.5×9m (25×30ft); bark corky on mature trees; deciduous; bright green pinnate lvs to 35cm (14in) long, lfts* grey-green beneath, yellow in autumn; fls inconspicuous; black frs on females (messy litter). Good for light shade, especially on chalky soils. Best in continental climates (spring frosts damage shoots); elsewhere, vars *japonicum* (*P. japonicum*; bark not corky), *lavallei* (*P. lavallei*) & *sachalinense* (*P. sachalinense*; bark not corky) are better (all smaller than sp).

Hardy or trifoliate orange (*Poncirus* [*Citrus*] *trifoliata*** **1**): v hardy deciduous shrub; slow-growing, to 3×3m (10×10ft); v thorny green stems; lvs usually in 3s; white fls to 5cm (2in) wide, late spring (before lvs); aromatic yellow-orange globular frs to 5cm (2in) diameter, bitter & acid. Makes formidable hedge (can be sheared).

Skimmias (*Skimmia* spp): compact, low-growing shrubs grown for their glossy leathery lvs to 10cm (4in) long, usually fragrant fls in spring (best on males) & small bright red frs (generally only on females [marked †] if male nearby; best if hand-pollinated); good for massing. Moderately hardy in extreme climates, more so elsewhere; easy; for any soil unless stated; tolerate shade.

S. japonica*: to 1×1.5m (3×5ft); white fls in panicles to 8cm (3in) long; frs 1cm (⅓in) across. Vars: 'Foremanii'*† **2** (probably hybrid with *S. reevesiana*, correctly *S.*×*foremanii*; vigorous; fls & frs in large clusters); 'Fragrans'** (dome-shaped; free-flg); 'Fructu-Albo'† (dwarf; frs white); 'Nymans'† (profuse fls & large frs); 'Rubella'* **3** (*S. rubella*; pink buds; large infls).

S. laureola*: to 1×1.5m (3×5ft); lvs clustered at shoot tips; greenish-yellow fls in panicles to 10cm (4in) long. Females not grown.

S. reevesiana (*S. fortunei*): to 60×90m (2×3ft); dull green lvs; bisexual white fls in panicles to 5–8cm (2–3in) long; oval crimson frs on all plants, persistent. Dislikes lime.

The poplars

Populus spp. Fast-growing, deciduous catkin-bearing trees (sexes mostly separate) useful for rapid screens & windbreaks, but roots very invasive (damage drains; dry out foundations) so plant at least 30m (100ft) from buildings. **Cultivation**: Easy; tolerate poor conditions. Ultra-hardy unless stated. Prone to leaf diseases, canker. **Propagation**: Hardwood cuttings; suckers; seed (hybridize freely).

White poplar (abele, *P. alba* **4**; Leuce group): to 12×9m (40×30ft); suckering; lvs lobed, white felt beneath. Tolerates lime, salt spray, drought; good for windbreaks. Vars: 'Pyramidalis' ('Bolleana'; conical); 'Richardii' (lvs yellow).

Aspens (Leuce group): similar to above but lvs smooth beneath, on long thin quivering stalks.

P. tremula **5** ([European] aspen): to 12×9m (40×30ft); open; lvs grey-green, coarse teeth. Var 'Pendula' (weeping aspen) droops; to 4.5×7.5m (15×25ft); profuse fls.

P. tremuloides (quaking or American aspen): to 6–9×4.5m (20–30×15ft); lvs small, fine teeth. Hardy below −45°C (−50°F). Var 'Pendula' weeps; to 3×3.5m (10×12ft).

Chinese poplar (*P. lasiocarpa* **6**; Leucoides group): v hardy; to 7.5×5m (25×16ft); heart-shaped leathery lvs to 25×20cm (10×8in), downy beneath, red veins & stalks.

Balsam poplars (Tacamahacca group): resinous winter buds; balsam scent as lvs open; lvs whitish beneath.

P. balsamifera (*P. tacamahacca*, balsam poplar; sometimes listed as *P. candicans*): to 12×6m (40×20ft); suckering; lvs** to 10cm (4in) long. Best in continental climates.

P. candicans (*P.*×*gileadensis*; balm of Gilead): may be hybrid of *P. balsamifera* & *P. deltoides*; similar to *P. balsamifera* but broader; suckering; lvs** to 15cm (6in) long. Prone to canker. Var 'Aurora' **7** has lvs variegated cream & pink; best pollarded or coppiced.

P. szechuanica: v hardy; to 12×6m (40×20ft); dark green lvs* to 30×20cm (12×8in).

P. trichocarpa (black cottonwood, western balsam poplar): v hardy; v vigorous, to 18×6m (60×20ft); lvs** to 25cm (10in) long. Best in rather maritime climates; prone to canker.

Black poplars (Aegiros group): corrugated bark; lvs all-green, on thin stalks (move constantly).

P.×*berolinensis* (Berlin poplar): hybrid of *P. laurifolia* & *P. nigra* 'Italica': to 18×4.5m (60×15ft); narrowly columnar; drought-tolerant.

P.×*canadensis* (*P.*×*euramericana*) vars (hybrid black poplars): hybrids of *P. deltoides* & *P. nigra*. Vars: 'Eugenei' (Eugene or Carolina poplar; columnar, to 18×6m [60×20ft]; canker-resistant); 'Robusta' **8** (vigorous, to 18×7.5m [60×25ft]; young lvs bronze); 'Serotina' (incorrectly, Canadian or black Italian poplar; v vigorous, to 18×12m [60×40ft]; open habit; young lvs bronze becoming grey-green; good pollarded). Var 'Serotina Aurea' **9** young lvs yellow.

P. deltoides ([northern] cottonwood): to 15×12m (50×40ft); broad crown; glossy lvs*; fluffy seeds; tolerates drought, extreme climates.

P. nigra (black poplar) vars: *betulifolia* (Manchester or downy black poplar; to 15×9m [50×30ft]; young shoots downy; v pollution-tolerant); 'Italica' (Lombardy poplar; v narrow, to 15×2.5m [50×8ft]; prone to canker [crown dies]); 'Plantierensis' **10** (similar to 'Italica').

Willows

Salix spp. Mostly vigorous deciduous trees & shrubs generally with lance-shaped leaves, to 10cm (4in) long unless stated. Catkins generally appear spring, sexes on separate plants; males often very fluffy ("pussies"; best on shrubby spp [sallows]); females greenish, now showy. Tree spp grown mainly for shelter & as specimens (especially weeping forms, often planted near water though not essential); shrubs often for colourful young shoots (best if stooled or pollarded every 1–2 years) & catkins, also as ground cover or for soil stabilization. **Cultivation**: Very hardy unless stated; for any deep, preferably moist soil in sun. Prone to aphids, scale insects, fungal canker & some other diseases. Some spp prone to storm damage. Unless stooling, prune only to remove dead wood. **Propagation**: Hardwood cuttings; seed; weeping forms sometimes by top-grafting. For dwarf spp, see p468.

Tree types (including those good stooled):
S. alba **1** (white willow): ultra-hardy; fast-growing, to 12×7.5m (40×25ft); branches erect, tips weep; downy lvs to 8cm (3in) long. Good windbreak. Var *argentea* (*regalis, sericea*) has v silvery lvs; less vigorous. Vars with colourful young shoots: 'Britzensis' **2** (scarlet willow; incorrectly, 'Chermesina'; shoots bright red); 'Chrysostela' (shoots gold, tips orange-red); *vitellina* (golden/yellow willow; yellow shoots).
S. babylonica (weeping willow): spreading & v weeping, to 11×12m (36×40ft). Resists canker. Var 'Crispa' ('Annularis') has twisted lvs.
S.×blanda (in US, Wisconsin weeping willow): hybrid probably of *S. babylonica* & *S. fragilis*; ultra-hardy; to 9×5.5m (30×18ft); somewhat weeping but branchlets shortish; dark green leathery lvs to 15cm (6in) long.
S.×chrysocoma **3** (golden weeping willow; sometimes sold as *S. alba* 'Tristis' or *S.a.* 'Vitellina Pendula'): beautiful weeping tree, to 12×9m (40×30ft); yellow young growth.
S. daphnoides **4** (violet willow): upright & fast-growing, to 11×5.5m (36×18ft); young shoots purple, white bloom (best if stooled); dark green leathery lvs, bluish beneath; showy silky male catkins to 5cm (2in) long, early spring.
S.×elegantissima (in US, Thurlow weeping willow): probably hybrid of *S. babylonica* & *S. fragilis*; ultra-hardy; fast-growing & v weeping, to 11×5.5m (36×18ft); dark green lvs to 12×2.5cm (5×1in).
S. matsudana (Peking willow): conical or rather rounded tree, to 9×4.5m (30×15ft); young shoots yellowish; narrow bright green lvs. Tolerates drought. Vars: 'Pendula' (weeping; young growth green); 'Tortuosa' **5** (corkscrew or dragon's-claw willow; branches & lvs twisted.
S. pentandra (bay willow): erect tree, to 5.5×2.5m (18×8ft), or large shrub; glossy laurel-like brilliant green lvs. Handsome.
Shrubby types (sometimes making small trees):
S. aegyptiaca (*S. medemii*, musk willow): to 4.5×2.5m (15×8ft); young shoots downy; oval lvs, downy beneath; yellow male catkins to 4cm (1½in) long, late winter (before lvs).
S. bockii: neat, to 1.2×1.2m (4×4ft); young shoots grey-downy; small bright green lvs to

1.5×0.5cm (⅝×¼in), white-haired beneath; greyish male catkins late summer & autumn.
S. caprea **6** (goat willow, great sallow; male form, pussy willow): bushy, to 4.5×3.5m (15×12ft); variable grey-green lvs, woolly beneath; male catkins silky-grey, females greenish, early spring (before lvs; males v good for arrangements). Can be stooled. Vars 'Kilmarnock' ('Pendula'; male) & 'Weeping Sally' (female) are pendulous.
S. discolor is similar N American sp; ultra-hardy.
S. elaeagnos **7** (*S. incana*, hoary willow): ultra-hardy; dense & leafy, to 1.8×1.8m (6×6ft); young shoots woolly; v narrow lvs to 12cm (5in) long, white-felted beneath; 2.5cm (1in) yellow male catkins with lvs.
S. fargesii **8**: spreading, to 1.5×1.8m (5×6ft); young bark shining brown; red winter buds; glossy prominently veined lvs to 15×8cm (6×3in); catkins erect, before lvs. Showy.
S. gracilistyla: spreading, to 3×4.5m (10×15ft); silky grey-green lvs, conspicuous veins; reddish-grey to yellow male catkins to 4cm (1½in) long, before lvs. *S.* 'Melanostachys' **9** (*S. melanostachys*, black pussy willow) has almost black male catkins, brick-red anthers becoming yellow.
S. hastata 'Wehrhahnii' **10**: spreading, to 1.2×1.5m (4×5ft); young shoots purplish; oval lvs, fresh green when young; profuse woolly white male catkins to 4cm (1½in) long, with lvs.
S. purpurea (purple osier): open & graceful, to 3.5×3.5m (12×12ft), young shoots often purplish; dark green glossy lvs to 8cm (3in) long. Vars: 'Nana' (incorrectly, 'Gracilis'; bushy, to 1.2×1.2m [4×4ft]; can be kept dense by clipping); 'Pendula' (branches droop; sometimes top-grafted to form small weeping tree).
S. repens (creeping willow): creeping, to 1.8×2.5m (6×8ft), lower in wild; young shoots silky; grey-green silky lvs to 4×2cm (1½×¾in), often smaller; silvery-grey male catkins 2cm (¾in) long, before lvs. Good for moist or dry rocky positions (smaller in latter), or by sea.
S. sachalinensis 'Sekka' ('Setsuka'): to 3×3m (10×10ft) if stooled; some stems curiously flattened & twisted; lance-shaped glossy green lvs to 15cm (6in) long; male 4cm (1½in) catkins before lvs. Best stooled every spring.

Mock oranges and their close relatives

Sometimes classed in Philadelphaceae. Apart from *Carpenteria* sp, deciduous shrubs of arching habit popular for their profuse, often fragrant white or pink flowers generally with golden stamens, unless stated early summer on year-old wood. Much hybridized. Best in mixed shrub plantings. **Cultivation**: Unless noted, very hardy & for any well-drained soil in sun or partial shade; tolerate lime & drought. **Pruning**: When needed, remove only old flowered wood of deciduous spp after flowering. Old plants can be pruned hard. **Propagation**: Semi-ripe or hardwood cuttings; layering.

Carpenteria (*Carpenteria californica** **1**; in US, tree anemone): moderately hardy bushy evergreen, to 1.8×1.8m (6×6ft); lance-shaped dark green glossy lvs to 10cm (4in) long, felted beneath; clusters of 3–7 anemone-like white fls 5–8cm (2–3in) wide, early–mid summer. Best against warm sunny wall. Pruning unnecessary.

Deutzias (*Deutzia* spp): unless stated, to 1.2–1.8×1.2–1.8m (4–6×4–6ft), with lance-shaped to oval grey-green lvs & profuse panicles or racemes of rather starry 5-petalled fls 1–2cm (½–¾in) across, golden stamens. Young growth may be injured by late frosts.

D. chunii: white fls, pink reverse, mid summer.

D. ningpoensis is similar.

*D. compacta** **2**: neat habit; dense infls of small white fls from pink buds, mid summer.

*D. corymbosa**: moderately to v hardy; vigorous, to 2.5×2.5 (8×8ft); large infls of white fls.

D.×elegantissima vars: hybrids of *D. purpurascens* & *D. sieboldiana*; compact. Vars: 'Elegantissima'* (white flushed rose, reverse pink); 'Fasciculata' (bright rose-pink); 'Rosealind' **3** (carmine-pink).

D. gracilis **4**: profuse early white fls in erect infls (may be damaged by late frosts, but can be cut for forcing indoors). *D.×candelabra* is hybrid with *D. sieboldiana*; larger, denser infls.

D.×hybrida vars: hybrids of *D. longifolia* & probably *D. discolor*; v free-flg. Vars: 'Contraste' (fuchsia-pink, reverse striped darker); 'Joconde' (white 3cm (1¼in) fls, reverse purplish); 'Magicien' **5** (purplish-pink edged white, reverse purplish); 'Mont Rose' (purplish-pink shaded darker); 'Perle Rose' (small pale pink fls).

D.×lemoinei vars: hybrids of *D. gracilis* & *D. parviflora*; white fls. Vars: 'Avalanche'* (sometimes listed under *D.×maliflora*; small clusters of fls along stems); 'Boule de Neige' (compact; dense rounded infls); 'Lemoinei' (erect infls, early [prone to late frost damage]).

D. longifolia: moderately to v hardy; 2.5cm (1in) pale purplish-pink fls. Var 'Veitchii' has larger, deeper pink fls.

D. pulchra: semi- to moderately hardy; panicles of drooping white bell-shaped fls, late spring.

D.×rosea vars: hybrids of *D. gracilis* & *D. purpurascens*; generally compact, to 1×1m (3×3ft); fls rather bell-shaped. Vars: 'Campanulata' (white, purple calyx); 'Carminea' (pale rosy-pink, darker reverse); 'Eximea' (white,

reverse pinkish); 'Pink Pompon' (double, pink); 'Rosea' (pale pink, darker reverse).

D. scabra (*D. crenata*; often confused with *D. sieboldiana*): vigorous, to 3×2m (10×7ft); profuse white fls, sometimes flushed pink on reverse. Vars: 'Candidissima' (double, pure white); 'Flore Pleno' **6** (double, white flushed purplish on rerverse); 'Pride of Rochester' (double, white flushed rose-pink). *D.×magnifica* ('Magnifica') is hybrid with *D. vilmoriniae*; showy dense infls of double white fls.

D. setchuenensis corymbiflora: moderately hardy; v profuse white fls, early–mid summer. Needs full sun to ripen wood.

Mock oranges (*Philadelphus* spp; often incorrectly called syringas): free-flg shrubs grown for the orange-blossom scent of the clusters of white 4-petalled cup-shaped to flattish fls (cuttable); lvs oval.

*P. coronarius** **7**: to 2.5×2m (8×7ft); lvs to 8cm (3in) long; creamy 2.5cm (1in) fls, prominent stamens. Var 'Aureus' **8** has bright yellow young lvs; fls insignificant.

*P. delavayi***: vigorous, to 3×2.5m (10×8ft); dark green lvs 10–18cm (4–7in) long; dense infls of 4cm (1½in) fls. Best in light shade.

*P. microphyllus***: dense & bushy, to 1.2×1m (4×3ft); bright green lvs to 2.5cm (1in) long; usually solitary 2.5cm (1in) fls. Best in warm sunny areas.

P. hybrids of various spp (to 1.2–1.8×1.2–1.8m [4–6×4–6ft] unless stated): 'Avalanche'* (v profuse 2.5cm [1in] fls); 'Beauclerk'** (6cm [2½in] fls, centre flushed pink); 'Belle Etoile'** **9** (5cm [2in] fls, reddish blotch); 'Bouquet Blanc'* (large clusters of 2.5cm [1in] double fls); 'Conquête'** (5cm [2in] single/semi-double fls); 'Enchantment'* (profuse crowded infls of 2.5cm [1in] double fls); 'Etoile Rose'* (4cm [1½in] fls marked rose); 'Frosty Morn'** (ultra-hardy; double fls); 'Manteau d'Hermine'** **10** (compact, to 1×1m [3×3ft]; 4cm [1½in] double creamy fls); 'Minnesota Snowflake'* (ultra-hardy; 4cm [1½in] double fls); 'Norma'* (5cm [2in] fls along arching branches); 'Silver Showers'** (bushy, to 1×1m [3×3ft]; 4.5cm [1¾in] solitary fls); 'Sybille'* (graceful; to 1×1.8m [3×6ft]; 5cm [2in] fls stained purplish-rose); 'Virginal'* (vigorous, to 3m [10ft]; rather gaunt; double/semi-double 5cm [2in] fls; v popular); 'Voie Lactée'* (5cm [2in] fls, sometimes with 5 or 6 petals).

Hydrangeas

Hydrangea spp; sometimes classed in Hydrangeaceae. Popular deciduous shrubs flowering summer into autumn unless noted, with showy panicles or flat or domed corymbs, often of "lacecap" type with showy sterile ("ray") flowers surrounding small fertile flowers. Colour, except of white fls & some *H. serrata* vars, depends on soil acidity – blue if acid, pink or red if neutral or alkaline. Leaves to 15cm (6in) or more long, generally toothed. Excellent for wall/foundation plantings or (where fully hardy) isolated beds or as specimens. **Cultivation**: Unless stated, moderately hardy & for rich moist soil in semi- or light shade. Best in sheltered position or near sea (young growth often damaged by spring frosts); protect in cold winters. Mulch in spring; dead-head. To ensure true blue flowers on neutral soil water with blueing compound, aluminium sulphate or alum. **Pruning**: In late autumn or early spring, cut back *H. arborescens* & *H. paniculata* by half or more; thin out 2/3-year-old shoots of *H. macrophylla* vars. Little needed for other spp except to remove dead or damaged shoots early spring. **Propagation**: Semi-ripe cuttings; layering; suckers or division where appropriate.

H. arborescens 'Grandiflora' (in US, hills of snow hydrangea): v hardy; to 1.8×1.8m (6×6ft) or more; loose habit; rich green lvs; profuse heavy globular infls 10–18cm (4–7in) across, white or creamy, all sterile fls. V showy. Var 'Annabelle' **1** is similar, with some fertile fls; snow-white.

H. aspera **2** (*H. villosa*): to 2.5×2.5m (8×8ft); young stems hairy; lvs velvety beneath; flattish lacecap infls to 25cm (10in) wide, fertile fls bluish, sterile white, pink or purple. Tolerates dry soil.

H. heteromalla 'Bretschneideri' (*H. bretschneideri*): v hardy; bushy, to 2.5×2.5m (8×8ft); peeling dark brown bark; flattish white lacecap infls to 30cm (1ft) wide. Var 'Snowcap' is sturdy, with large lvs; tolerates wind & drought.

H. involucrata: to 1.2×1.2m (4×4ft) where hardy, less if cut down by frost; 8–12cm (3–5in) lacecap infls, white & blue, prominent bracts. Var 'Hortensis' has more sterile fls, double, buff-pink to whitish.

H. macrophylla (*H. hortensia*, *H. opuloides*, common or French hydrangea) vars: many probably hybrids; some vars (marked †) v hardy; generally to 1–1.8×1–1.8m (3–6×3–6ft), more in mild climates. HORTENSIA (mop-headed) VARS (rounded 12–20cm [5–8in] infls, almost all sterile fls): 'Altona'† (rose-pink to mid blue); 'Ami Pasquier' (dwarf; deep red to purplish); 'Deutschland' (lvs colour in autumn; fls deep pink to mid blue); 'Domotoi' (double, pale pink to pale blue); 'Europa' (large fls, pink to clear blue); 'Forever Pink'† (dwarf; rosy-pink to pale blue); 'Générale Vicomtesse de Vibraye'† **3** ('Vibraye'; free-flg; pink to clear blue); 'Goliath' (large fls, deep pink to lilac-blue; good near coast); 'Hamburg' (large fls, deep rose to purplish, dry metallic-purple); 'Mme E. Mouillère' **4** (white; best out of sun); 'Maréchal Foch' **5** (free-flg & early, deep pink to gentian-blue); 'Niedersachsen' (late, pale pink to pale blue); 'Nigra'† ('Mandshurica'; stems almost black; fls pink to blue); 'Nikko Blue' (rose or blue); 'Parsifal' (toothed sepals, crimson-pink to deep blue, or mixed); 'Sister Therese' (white); 'Westfalen' **6** (dwarf; free-flg, vivid crimson to

deep purple-blue). LACECAP VARS (flattened lacecap infls 10–15cm [4–6in] wide, mainly mid summer): 'Blue Wave' **7** (fertile fls blue, sterile pink or lilac to rich blue); 'Lanarth White' (compact; fertile fls pink to bright blue, sterile white); 'Mariesii' (large sterile fls, rose-pink to rich blue, mixed among sterile); 'Tricolor' **8** ('Variegata', 'Variegated Mariesii'; lvs variegated green, greyish & pale yellow; fls pale pink to blue); 'Veitchii' (fertile fls blue, sterile white; needs light shade); 'White Wave' ('Mariesii Alba', 'Mariesii Grandiflora'; fertile fls pinkish or bluish, sterile white).

H. paniculata: v hardy; to 3.5×3.5m (12×12ft), less if hard pruned but sometimes tree-like; pyramid-shaped panicles generally 15–20cm (6–8in) long, fertile fls yellowish-white, sterile white fading purple-pink. Vars: 'Grandiflora' **9** (in US, pee-gee hydrangea; v vigorous; almost all sterile fls in dense infls, to 45×30cm [1½×1ft] if shoots pruned hard & thinned & plant fed well, but also v showy with normal treatment); 'Praecox' (fls mainly sterile, early).

H. quercifolia **10** (oak-leaved hydrangea): v hardy when mature &/or well-ripened; to 1–1.8×1.2–1.8m (3–6×4–6ft); suckering; large 5/7-lobed lvs, downy beneath, rich orange, crimson or purple in autumn; 10–25cm (4–10in) panicles of white fertile & sterile fls fading purplish. Can be pruned to keep compact. Takes sun.

H. sargentiana **11** (correctly, *H. aspera sargentiana*): upright, to 3×3m (10×10ft); suckering; young shoots hairy & bristly; velvety dull green lvs to 25cm (10in) long; flattish lacecap infls to 20cm (8in) wide, fertile fls pinkish-white, sterile lilac-pink. Shade from midday sun.

H. serrata (*H. Macrophylla serrata*): v hardy; dainty, to 1×1m (3×3ft), with slender shoots & lvs; flat lacecap infls to 8cm (3in) across, pink or bluish. Vars: 'Bluebird' (*H. acuminata* 'Bluebird'; to 1.5m [5ft]; reddish-purple to deep blue); 'Grayswood' (to 1.5cm [5ft]; white ageing to pink or bright red); 'Preziosa' **12** (young growths reddish-purple; hortensia-type infls, rose-pink ageing crimson, blotched darker).

Escallonias and iteas

Sometimes classed in Escalloniaceae. Attractive, mainly evergreen flowering shrubs with glossy leaves & abundant small flowers generally in racemes or panicles. **Cultivation**: See below; moderately hardy unless stated. Tolerate some drought & lime. **Propagation**: Semi-ripe cuttings.

Escallonias (*Escallonia* spp): generally fast-growing, with smallish often clustered lvs (sometimes resinous) & somewhat tubular white to red fls with 5 spreading petals & small central disc, late summer into autumn unless stated. Best grown against warm wall (easily trained) except where winters mild; elsewhere make good hedges, screens & windbreaks near sea. For well-drained, not too rich soil in sun or partial shade (latter best in hot climates). Prune smaller spp & vars gently after flg to maintain compact habit; thin out old wood of tall spp in spring.
E. bifida (*E. montevidensis*): to 3×2.5m (10×8ft), or small tree; bright green lvs* to 8cm (3in) long; rounded infls to 15cm (6in) or more long of pure white fls.
E.×exoniensis: hybrid of *E. rosea* & *E. rubra*; to 3×3m (10×10ft), or small tree; lvs 1–4cm (½–1½in) long; white or rose-tinted fls from early summer. Var 'Balfourii' is fine form with drooping branchlets. *E.* 'Iveyi' **1** is hybrid with *E. bifida* with v dark green lvs & white fls in infls to 15×10cm (6×4in); among best of escallonias.
E. laevis (*E. organensis*): semi-hardy; robust, to 1.8×1.8m (6×6ft); stiff lvs to 8cm (3in) long; dense infls of small clear rosy-red fls, late summer to autumn.
E.×langleyensis vars: hybrids derived from *E. rubra*, *E. macrantha* (*E. rubra macrantha*) & *E. virgata*; generally to 1.8–2.5×2.5m (6–8×8ft); long arching shoots; semi-/evergreen; fls in smallish infls from early/mid summer. Vars: 'Apple Blossom' **2** (compact & slow-growing, to 1.5m [5ft]; pink & white chalice-shaped fls); 'Donard Beauty' **3** (profuse rose-red fls); 'Donard Brilliance' (large rich rose-red fls); 'Donard Gem'* (lvs* coarsely toothed; light pink fls); 'Donard Radiance' **4** (compact; lvs coarsely toothed; rich rose-pink chalice-shaped fls);

'Donard Seedling'* (vigorous; fls white flushed pink, from pink buds); 'Donard Star' (compact; large deep rosy-pink fls); 'Glory of Donard' **5** (large deep carmine-pink fls); 'Langleyensis' (original hybrid; small bright rosy-carmine fls); 'Peach Blossom' (similar to 'Apple Blossom' but peach-pink); 'Slieve Donard' **6** (pale pink marked carmine).
E. macrantha (correctly, *E. rubra macrantha*): dense & luxuriant, to 1.8–3×2.5m (6–10×8ft); deeply toothed lvs* to 8cm (3in) long; 5–10cm (2–4in) infls of bright rosy-red fls. Excellent maritime hedging shrub. Var 'C. F. Ball' **7** has profuse crimson fls.
E. rubra: dense & upright, to 3×2.5m (10×8ft); variable lvs* to 5cm (2in) long, prominent veins; pink to deep crimson fls. Var 'Woodside' ('Pygmaea') is dense & compact, to 0.6×1.5m (2×5ft), but may revert; rosy-crimson fls; remove vigorous shoots.
E. virgata: 1.8×1.8m (6×6ft); robust & leafy, with gracefully arching branches; deciduous; white fls, early–mid summer. Hates chalk.
Iteas (*Itea* spp; in US, sweetspires): summer-flg shrubs for moist, rich soil in sun or semi-shade.
*I. ilicifolia** * **8**: arching shrub, to 3×3m (10×10ft) or more; holly-like spiny lvs 5–10cm (2–4in) long, dark glossy green; elegantly drooping racemes to 30cm (1ft) long of small greenish-white fls, late summer. Good near water or as informal screen where hardy; elsewhere against warm wall.
*I. virginica** **9**: v hardy; to 1.5×1.5m (5×5ft); erect stems branch near top; deciduous bright green lvs to 8cm (3in) long, finely toothed, brilliant red in autumn; dense erect 8–15cm (3–6in) racemes of creamy-white fls, mid summer, on yr-old wood. Prune autumn or spring, cutting out enough old shoots for new growth. Can be propagated by division.

Ornamental currants and gooseberries

Ribes spp; gooseberries sometimes listed as *Grossularia* spp; both sometimes classed in Grossulariaceae. Mostly deciduous bushy shrubs with 3/5-lobed leaves. Currants generally spineless, with flowers & small fruits in racemes; gooseberries spiny, with flowers in small clusters & hairy fruits. Flowers long-tubed to cup/bell-shaped, with 4 or 5 flaring sepals, sometimes with prominent stamens rather like fuchsias, spring unless stated. **Cultivation**: Generally easy in well-drained fertile soil in sun or partial shade. Very hardy unless stated. Occasionally thin out old wood in spring. Prone to aphids & (in US) white pine blister rust (cultivation forbidden in certain areas). **Propagation**: Seed; hardwood or (especially currants) semi-ripe cuttings; layering.

R. alpinum **10** (mountain currant): ultra-hardy; dense & twiggy, to 1.8×1.2m (6×4ft); lvs to 4cm (1½in)

long, early; greenish-yellow fls; red frs. Neat & good for hedging in sun or shade. Var 'Aureum'

has yellow young lvs.

R. bracteosum (Californian black currant): moderately to v hardy; to 1.8×1.5m (6×5ft); large maple-like lvs* to 18cm (7in) or more wide; erect infls of greenish-yellow fls; black frs, whitish bloom, unpleasant taste.

*R. fasciculatum**: to 1.2×1.5m (4×5ft); lvs downy, to 5×8cm (2×3in); yellow fls; persistent scarlet frs.

*R. gayanum**: moderately to v hardy; to 1.2×1.8m (4×6ft); suckering; evergreen; velvety grey-green lvs to 5cm (2in) long; short dense infls of bell-shaped yellow fls, early summer; purple-black frs.

R. henryi: semi-prostrate, to 1×1m (3×3ft); young shoots bristly; evergreen unlobed pale green lvs 5–10cm (2–4in) long; greenish-yellow fls, late winter or early spring, on mossy stalks; dark red frs to 1cm (½in) long. *R. laurifolium* 1 is similar but shoots smooth & lvs leathery.

R. lacustre 2 (bristly black currant, swamp gooseberry): ultra-hardy; to 1.2×1.2m (4×4ft); slender stems with spines & brown bristles/prickles; gooseberry-like deeply cut lvs to 5cm (2in) long; currant-like infls of crimson fls, creamy/pinkish reverse, late spring to early summer; bristly black frs. For cool, damp sites.

*R. odoratum*** (buffalo currant): to 2×1.5m (7×5ft); erect, with arching branches near top; pale green 5cm (2in) lvs turning red in autumn; bright golden-yellow spicily fragrant fls; purple-black frs. *R. aureum* is similar & often confused, but fls smaller; frs yellow, red or black, edible.

R. sanguineum ([red] flowering currant): to 2×2.5m (7×8ft); heart-shaped lobed lvs to 10cm (4in) wide, downy beneath; pink to deep rosy-red 1cm (½in) fls in racemes to 10cm (4in) long; frs black, blue bloom. Most decorative sp, but pungent smell. Vars: 'Albescens' 3 (whitish, tinged pink); 'Brocklebankii' 4 (to 1.2m [4ft]; golden-yellow lvs (best if pruned hard late winter); pink fls); 'King Edward VII' 5 (to 1.8m [6ft]; intense crimson); 'Pulborough Scarlet' 6 (vigorous, to 3m [10ft]; profuse deep red fls).

R. (G.) speciosum 7 (fuchsia-flowered gooseberry): moderately hardy; to 1.8×1.5m (6×5ft); spiny; semi-evergreen glossy lvs to 3cm (1¼in) long; profuse rich red pendulous fls, rather fuchsia-like, with prominent stamens; bristly red frs to 1cm (½in) long.

Hebes and their relatives

Evergreen shrubs grown in warm or mild areas for both foliage & flowers. Leaves generally in rows along stems, stalkless or almost so. Flowers more or less tubular, often lipped or with unequal-sized lobes, generally in showy inflorescences. **Cultivation**: Moderately hardy unless stated. For well-drained soil in sunny site. **Pruning**: Little needed, but dead-head. If necessary cut back after flowering to maintain bushiness; leggy plants can be cut back hard early spring. **Propagation**: Semi-ripe or hardwood cuttings; seed. For dwarf shrubs grown mainly in rock gardens, see p474.

Hebes (shrubby veronicas, *Hebe* spp; formerly *Veronica* spp): bushy, mainly New Zealand shrubs with leathery lvs generally in 4 rows along stems (v small & scale-like in "whipcord" spp); small 4-lobed fls in panicles, racemes or spikes, early summer unless stated. Grown for form, foliage & fls; useful landscaping plants, smaller types for edging & ground cover, taller for shrub borders, hedging, etc. Hardiest on poorish, light soil or with wall protection; dislike extreme climates & best near coasts; tolerate pollution & salty winds. Less hardy types can be grown in containers & overwintered under glass.
SPECIES (including botanical hybrids):

H. (V.) albicans 8: dense & rounded to 0.6×1.5m (2×5ft); glaucous 2.5cm (1in) lvs; 5cm (2in) infls of white fls.

H. (V.) ×andersonii: hybrid of *H. salicifolia* & *H. speciosa*; semi-hardy; to 1.8×1.8m (6×6ft), less if grown in pots for summer bedding; fleshy deep green 10cm (4in) lvs; 10–15cm (4–6in) infls of soft lavender-blue fls fading white, late summer. Var 'Variegata' 9 (*H.* 'Andersonii Variegata') has lvs edged & mottled creamy-white; more common.

H. (V.) anomala 10: compact & bushy, to 1×1.2m (3×4ft); bright green 1–2cm (½–¾in) lvs; small clustered spikes of white fls.

H. (V.) armstrongii: see *H. ochracea*.

H. (V.) brachysiphon 11 (sometimes grown incorrectly as *H.* [V.] *traversii*): rounded & spreading, to 1.8×2.5m (6×8ft); close-set dark green 1–2.5cm (½–1in) lvs; profuse 8cm (3in) racemes of white fls. Popular; good lawn specimen.

H. (V.) buxifolia: neat & upright, to 1.5×1m (5×3ft); stiff 1cm (½in) lvs, dark glossy green; clustered infls of white fls. Good for hedging. Among hardiest & most heat/drought-tolerant spp.

H. (V.) canterburiensis: dainty & hummock-forming, to 1×1m (3×3ft); densely packed dark glossy green 0.5–1cm (¼–½in) lvs; profuse 2.5cm (1in) racemes of white fls.

H. (V.) cupressoides: dense, rounded & slow-growing, to 1.8×1.8m (8×8ft), less in cool climates; bright green cypress-like whipcord foliage; 2.5cm (1in) clusters of pale blue fls (not

reliable). Var 'Nana' is dwarf. *H.* (*V.*) *propinqua* is similar but lvs closer-set & fls white; grows to 1×1m (3×3ft).

H. (*V.*)×*franciscana* vars: hybrids of *H. elliptica* & *H. speciosa*; dense, to 1.2×1.2m (4×4ft) or wider; light green regularly arranged lvs; 5–8cm (2–3in) racemes of fls to 1cm (½in) wide, violet-blue, purple or white. Rather tender when young. Vars: 'Blue Gem' **1** (compact & dome-shaped; bright violet-blue); 'Variegata' (lvs edged creamy-white; fls mauve-blue).

H. (*V.*) *hulkeana* (New Zealand lilac): often considered rather tender but moderately hardy in poor soil or against sunny wall; to 1×1.2m (3×4ft), more against wall; rather straggly; pale green glossy lvs 2.5–5cm (1–2in) long; profuse panicles to 30cm (1ft) or more long of lavender-blue fls, late spring & early summer. Dead-head regularly. Fls in 1yr from cuttings, so can be treated like bedding perennial, overwintering cuttings under glass. *H.* (*V.*) *lavaudiana* is similar but dwarfer, to 30×30cm (1×1ft), with smaller lvs & infls (sometimes white).

H. (*V.*) *lycopodioides**: to 60×30cm (2×1ft); rigid, erect branches; dense whipcord foliage; small clusters of white fls, mid summer (not reliable in cool climates).

H. ochracea **2** (often grown incorrectly as *H.* [*V.*] *armstrongii*): dense, to 60×60cm (2×2ft); characteristic ochre or coppery-brown whipcord foliage; short spikes of white fls, mid summer. True *H.* (*V.*) *armstrongii* **3** is yellowish-green.

H. (*V.*) *rakaiensis* **4** (often grown incorrectly as *H.* [*V.*] *subalpina*): to 1×1.2m (3×4ft); dense; glossy green narrow lvs to 2cm (¾in) long; 5cm (2in) racemes of white fls. True *H.* (*V.*) *subalpina* is taller, with lvs 2.5cm (1in) long.

H. recurva **5** (*H.* 'Aoira'): rounded & spreading, to 1×1.5m (3×5ft); narrow glaucous-grey lvs to 4–5cm (1½–2in) long; abundant white fls in 5cm (2in) racemes, mid summer. Attractive.

H. (*V.*) *salicifolia* **6**: 3×3m (10×10ft); erect; lance-shaped bright green lvs 5–15cm (2–5in) long; white or lilac-tinged fls in narrow racemes to 15–25cm (6–10in) long. Parent of many hybrids.

H. (*V.*) *speciosa*: semi-hardy; dense & robust, to 1.5×1.5m (5×5ft); stout; spreading branches; leathery dark glossy green lvs 5–10cm (2–4in) long; dense 4–8cm (1½–3in) racemes of dark reddish-purple fls, all summer. Parent of many hybrids. Best near sea.

GARDEN HYBRIDS: generally long-flg.

H. 'Alicia Amherst' **7** ('Royal Purple' incorrectly, 'Veitchii'): hybrid of *H. speciosa* but hardier; to 1.2×1.5m (4×5ft); dark green leathery 8cm (3in) lvs; 8–10cm (3–4in) racemes of deep violet fls, late summer.

H. 'Autumn Glory' **8**; may be *H. pimeleoides* hybrid; loosely mounding, to 1×1m (3×3ft); dark glossy green 2.5–4cm (1–1½in) lvs, red-edged

when young; dense 5cm (2in) racemes/panicles of deep violet fls, late summer & autumn.

H. 'Bowles' Hybrid' ('Eversley Seedling'): to 60×60cm (2×2ft); narrow pale green lvs; graceful 5–10cm (2–4in) panicles of mauve fls, all summer & autumn.

H. 'Ettrick Shepherd': to 1×1.2m (3×4ft); lance-shaped dull green lvs; dense 8–10cm (3–4in) racemes of reddish-purple fls fading fast to white, so infl looks bicoloured.

H. 'La Seduisante' **9** ('Diamant'): *H. speciosa* hybrid; semi-hardy; to 1.5×1.5m (5×5ft); mid-green leathery lvs 5-8cm (2–3in) long; dense 10cm (4in) spikes of magenta-purple fls, summer into autumn.

H. 'Margery Fish': dense & compact, to 1×1m (3×3ft); wavy narrowish lvs to 3cm (1¼in) long, edges tinged red, young lvs bronzed in winter; dense 8–10cm (3–4in) racemes of violet-blue & white fls, summer & autumn.

H. 'Marjorie': v hardy; bushy & spreading, to 1×1.2m (3×4ft); rather fleshy lvs to 8cm (3in) long; 5–8cm (2–3in) racemes of clear light blue fls, mid summer to early autumn.

H. 'Midsummer Beauty' **10**: hybrid of *H. salicifolia* & *H. speciosa*; to 1.2×1.5m (4×5ft); 10cm (4in) lvs, red beneath when young; profuse 12cm (5in) racemes of lavender-purple fls, mid summer to early winter.

H. 'Mrs Winder': dense, to 1.2×1.5m (4×5ft); stems reddish-brown; narrow lvs to 3cm (1¼in) long, edged & tinged red; profuse 5cm (2in) racemes of violet fls, white tube.

H. 'Patty's Purple': *H. buxifolia* hybrid; to 1×1m (3×3ft); dark red stems; dark green 1cm (½in) lvs; narrow spikes of purple fls, summer.

H. 'Waikiki': bushy & spreading, to 0.6×1m (2×3ft); lvs to 2.5cm (1in) long, bronzed when young; small racemes of violet-blue fls, early summer.

Leucophyllum (ceniza; in US, Texas ranger, *Leucophyllum frutescens*): v drought/heat-tolerant hedging & specimen shrub good in desert conditions; slow-growing, to 1.5–2.5×1.2–1.8m (5–8×4–6ft), felted silvery-grey lvs to 2.5cm (1in) long; sporadically profuse rosy-lavender bell-shaped lipped fls 2.5cm (1in) wide, hot summer weather often after rain showers. Moderately hardy if well ripened; needs v good drainage (killed by over-watering).

Shrubby penstemon (*Penstemon cordifolius*): semi- to moderately hardy straggly shrub, to 2×2m (7×7ft); semi-/evergreen; dark glossy green heart-shaped coarsely toothed lvs to 5cm (2in) long; pyramid-shaped panicles to 30×20cm (12×8in) of 4cm (1½in) tubular, lipped scarlet fls, summer (earlier in hot climates). Best grown or trained against sunny wall (branches lax).

The potato family

Very decorative, generally evergreen flowering shrubs mainly for Mediterranean & similar warm climates, though some will survive in cooler areas on sunny protected wall & all can be grown in tubs & overwintered under glass. (Sizes given for plants grown in open where hardy; tubbed plants smaller; on wall often taller.) **Cultivation**: Unless stated, semi-hardy (to about −4°C [25°F]) & for well-drained fertile soil in sun or partial shade. **Propagation**: Softwood or semi-ripe cuttings.

Brunfelsia (yesterday, today and tomorrow plant, *Brunfelsia pauciflora** **1**): tender; to 1×1m (3×3ft); lance-shaped leathery lvs to 10cm (4in) long; profuse clusters of 5cm (2in) rich purple fls fading to near-white, spring & summer. Best in lime-free soil; prune late winter to keep bushy.
Cestrums (*Cestrum* spp): tender; generally to 2–3×2m (7–10×7ft), often semi-climbing; lvs to 10–15cm (4–6in) long, narrowish or lance-shaped; clusters of showy tubular fls 2.5cm (1in) long, summer unless noted. May freeze to ground but regrow from base. Feed well; thin out 2/3yr-old shoots & pinch back early spring.
C. aurantiacum: bright orange fls; white berries.
C. elegans **2** (*C. purpureum*): arching branches; purplish-red fls from late spring; red berries.
C. fasciculatum: similar to *C. elegans* but fls purer red & earlier. *C.* 'Newellii' may be hybrid with *C. elegans*; fls brilliant crimson.
C. nocturnum** (night jessamine): lvs to 20cm (8in) long; creamy-white fls, white berries.
C. parqui** **3**: semi- to moderately hardy; deciduous willow-like lvs to 12cm (5in) long; yellowish-green fls, fragrant at night; violet-brown berries. Probably poisonous. Grows to 1.5m (5ft) if cut down by frosts.
Angel's trumpets (*Datura* [*Brugmansia*] spp **4, 5**): large shrubs, generally to 3×3m (10×10ft) & often tree-like, grown for large dangling trumpet-shaped summer fls (generally fragrant in evening); lvs large, often coarsely toothed. Rather coarse though spectacular. Fls & seeds poisonous. Shelter from winds; cut back early spring. Various spp have white, yellow, pink or red & yellow fls, 5–30cm (6–12in) or more long.
Fabiana (*Fabiana imbricata*): semi- to moderately hardy rather heath-like shrub, to 2×2m (7×7ft), plume-like branches with tiny needle-like lvs; profuse tubular white fls to 2cm (¾in) long along branches, late spring or early summer. Prefers moist lime-free soil. Var *violacea* **6** is bluish-mauve.
Potato bush (*Solanum rantonnetii*): spreading & arching, to 2×2m (7×7ft), or can be trained as tree or on wall; semi-evergreen; bright green 10cm (4in) lvs; clusters of violet-blue 2.5cm (1in) fls, yellow eye, summer into autumn; red heart-shaped dangling frs. Prune to keep neat.

Snowbell and snowdrop trees and their relatives

Deciduous small trees (generally rather spreading & loose-branched) & shrubs grown for their attractive, generally white flowers (often bell-shaped & pendulous). Fine specimens. **Cultivation**: Very hardy unless stated. For moist but well-drained lime-free soil in sunny spot, preferably sheltered from strong winds. Regular pruning not necessary. **Propagation**: Seed (stratify); semi-ripe cuttings; layering.

Snowdrop tree (silver-bells, *Halesia carolina*; correctly, *H. tetraptera*): tree, to 7.5×7.5m (25×25ft) where summers hot, often shrubby in cool areas; lvs to 12cm (5in) long, downy beneath; abundant clusters of drooping snowdrop-like 1–2cm (½–¾in) fls along naked branches, late spring; conspicuous 4-winged frs 4cm (1½in) long. *H. monticola* **7** (mountain snowdrop/silverbell tree) is similar but more vigorous, with slightly larger lvs & fls (pale pink in var 'Rosea'); to 12×9m (40×30ft).
Pterostyrax (epaulette tree, *Pterostyrax hispida**): moderately to v hardy shrub, to 6×5.5m (20×18ft), or small tree; vigorous & spreading; lvs to 20×10cm (8×4in); drooping panicles to 25cm (10in) long of creamy-white fls, early summer; hairy 1cm (½in) frs.
Rehderodendron (*Rehderodendron macrocarpum*): moderately to v hardy tree, to 6×3m (20×10ft); finely toothed narrowish red-stalked lvs to 10cm (4in) long; lax clusters of creamy-white fls, conspicuous yellow anthers, late spring (before lvs); ribbed red frs to 8cm (3in) long. Rare.
Snowbells (storaxes, *Styrax* spp): beautiful, with pure white pendulous fls, conspicuous yellow anthers, early summer. Need care & possibly winter protection when young.
S. japonica **8** (Japanese snowbell): to 6×6m (20×20ft); graceful, with spreading branches often drooping at tips; dark glossy green lvs to 8cm (3in) long; 2cm (¾in) fls hang in clusters beneath branches. Shade from morning sun.
S. obassia* **9** (fragrant snowbell): round-headed or rather narrow, to 6×4.5m (20×15ft); almost round deep green lvs to 20cm (8in) long, downy beneath; 15–20cm (6–8in) racemes of 2.5cm (1in) fls. Handsome in lf & fl.

Camellias

Camellia spp. Among best of evergreen flowering shrubs (sometimes becoming trees), with glossy small-toothed leaves & profuse beautiful white, pink or red flowers, mainly late winter to mid spring. Good as specimens, in mixed borders, against walls, or in tubs (can move under glass in winter). Thousands of vars, many very similar; flowers classified as single, semi-double, anemone-formed, paeony-formed, rose-formed or formal double. **Cultivation**: Generally moderately to very hardy. Plant shallowly in neutral or acid humus-rich soil in light or partial shade (not facing E; morning sun scorches frozen blooms). Mulch with peat. Thin excess buds; dead-head. Prune if necessary after flowering. **Propagation**: Semi-ripe stem or leaf-bud cuttings; *C. reticulata* vars by grafting on *C. japonica*.

C. japonica (common camellia): bushy, generally to 2–3×1.5–2m (7–10×5–7ft), eventually larger; lvs glossy deep green, 8–10cm (3–4in) long; fls 5–12cm (2–5in) across (8–10cm [3–4in] unless stated). Vars (sizes refer to fls): 'Adolphe Audusson' (large semi-double, blood-red); 'Alba Plena' **1** ('Alba Grandiflora'; large formal double, white; v early); 'Alba Simplex' (large single, white); 'Anemonaeflora' (anemone-formed, dark crimson); 'Apollo' (semi-double, rose-red, sometimes blotched white); 'Arejishi' (lvs coarsely toothed; fls paeony-formed, dark rose-red); 'Chandleri' (large semi-double to anemone-formed, bright red, sometimes blotched white); 'C. M. Wilson' (large anemone-formed, light pink); 'Contessa Lavinia Maggi' **2** (large formal double, white or pale pink, striped red); 'Coquetti' (large formal double, deep red); 'Donckelarii' (large semi-double, red marbled white); 'Elegans' **3** ('Chandleri Elegans'; large anemone-formed, deep pink); 'Fred Sander' **4** ('Fimbriata Superba'; semi-double, fimbriated, crimson); 'Furoan' (single, soft pink); 'Gloire de Nantes' (large semi-double, rose-pink); 'Jupiter' ('Juno'; single to semi-double, scarlet, sometimes marked white); 'Lady Clare' (semi-prostrate; large semi-double, clear pink); 'Lady Vansittart' (semi-double, wavy-edged petals, white striped pink); 'Magnoliaeflora' (semi-double, blush-pink); 'Mathotiana' **5** ('Julia Drayton', 'Mathotiana Rubra'; large rose-formed, crimson); 'Mathotiana Alba' (large formal double, white); 'Mathotiana Rosea' (large formal double, pink); 'Mathotiana Supreme' (large semi-double, crimson); 'Nagasaki' ('Lady Audrey Buller'; lvs often mottled yellow; large semi-double fls, carmine marbled white); 'Nobilissima' **6** (anemone-formed, white shaded yellow); 'Preston Rose' **7** ('Duchesse de Rohan'; paeony-formed, salmon-pink); 'Prof Charles S. Sargent' (anemone-formed, dark red); 'Rubescens Major' (large formal double, rose-red veined darker); 'White Swan' (single, white, golden stamens). Var *rusticana* (*C. rusticana*, snow camellia) & its named forms from Japan have v small fls.
C. reticulata: generally semi/moderately hardy; open & erect, to 3–4×2.5–3.5m (10–13×8–12ft) or more; lvs narrowish, leathery, prominently veined; fls 12–15cm (5–6in) across. Vars:

'Buddha' (semi-double, wavy petals, rose-red); 'Captain Rawes' **8** (semi-double, glistening pink); 'Crimson Robe' ('Tataochung'; semi-double, crinkled petals, crimson); 'Mary Williams' (moderately hardy; single, crimson-pink, yellow stamens); 'Noble Pearl' ('Paochucha'; semi-double, Turkey-red); 'Pagoda' ('Sungtzelin'; rose-formed to formal double, deep scarlet); 'Shot Silk' ('Tayinhung'; semi-double, wavy petals, brilliant pink); 'Trewithen Pink' (moderately hardy; semi-double, deep rose-pink). Hybrids (moderately to v hardy): 'Inspiration' (semi-double, deep pink); 'Leonard Messel' (semi-double, rich clear pink); 'Salutation' **9** (semi-double, soft silvery-pink).
C. saluenensis: moderately hardy; rather similar to *C. reticulata*, but denser, & lvs & fls smaller; fls single, soft pink, profuse. Var 'Cornish Snow' has single fls, white flushed pink on reverse.
C. sasanqua: variable habit, to 3–4×2.5–3.5m (10–13×8–12ft) or more; lvs rather thin & narrow, to 8cm (3in) long; fls 4–5cm (1½–2in) across, v early (from autumn in warm climates, winter elsewhere); best in warm sunny spot. Vars (those marked † sometimes listed under *C. hiemalis*; later, with thicker petals): 'Cleopatra' (semi-double, rose-pink); 'Crimson King' (single, bright red); 'Duff Allan' (single, white); 'Hugh Evans' (single, pink); 'Narumigata'* (large single, white tinged pink at edges); 'Shishigashira'† (compact; semi-double to double, rose-red; long season); 'Showanosakae'† (arching; semi-double to paeony-formed, soft pink); 'Sparkling Burgundy' (paeony-formed, rose-red); 'White Doves' **10** ('Minenoyuki'; spreading; paeony-formed, white); 'Yuletide' (single, bright red).
C.×williamsii vars: race of hybrids of *C. japonica* & *C. saluenensis*; form & lvs like former, fls like latter; free-flg even in cold areas, from winter; dead fls generally drop. Vars: 'Caerhays' (anemone-formed, lilac-pink); 'Citation' (semi-double, silvery blush-pink); 'Donation' **11** (large semi-double, orchid-pink); 'Francis Hanger' (single, white); 'Golden Spangles' **12** (lvs blotched yellowish; small single fls, phlox-pink); 'Hiraethlyn' (single, v pale pink); 'J. C. Williams' (single, phlox-pink); 'Mary Christian' (small single, clear pink); 'November Pink' (single, phlox-pink); 'St Ewe' (single, rose-pink).

Other members of the tea family

Somewhat neglected shrubs (& some trees), generally with camellia-like creamy-/white flowers. Deciduous unless noted, these spp having fine autumn colour & attractive bark. **Cultivation**: Very hardy unless stated. For lime-free moist peaty soil in sheltered sites in sun or partial shade. **Propagation**: Seed; semi-ripe cuttings; layering.

Cleyera (*Cleyera japonica*): moderately hardy; to 2.5×3m (8×10ft); evergreen; dark green glossy lvs to 10cm (4in) long; 1cm (½in) fls, early summer; pea-sized red to black frs. *C. fortunei* (*C. japonica* 'Tricolor') is dwarf, to 1×1.5m (3×5ft); yellow-edged lvs often flushed rose.

Franklinia (*Franklinia* [*Gordonia*] *alatamaha* **1**): shrub or tree, rather slow-growing to 4.5×3m (15×10ft); reddish bark; lvs to 15cm (6in) long, scarlet in autumn; fls to 8cm (3in) across, late summer & autumn. Needs long hot summers.

Gordonia (*Gordonia axillaris* **2**, *G. anomala*): semi-hardy; to 6×3.5m (20×12ft); evergreen; dark green glossy lvs to 18cm (7in) long; fls 8–15cm (3–6in) wide, intermittently early winter to late spring if sheltered. *G. lasianthus* (loblolly bay) is magnolia-like tree, to 12m (50ft) or more; moderately hardy where summers long & hot.

Stewartias (*Stuartia* [*Stewartia*] spp): rather slow-growing, with peeling bark & lvs 5–10cm (2–4in) long; profuse short-lived fls, mid summer.

S. malacodendron: moderately hardy; to 3.5×3.5m (12×12ft); fls to 9cm (3½in) wide, purple stamens; lvs reddish-purple in autumn. Needs warm summers.

S. ovata **3**: to 4.5×4.5m (15×15ft); bushy; lvs orange or yellow in autumn; fls to 10cm (4in) wide, frilled petals. Var *grandiflora* has fls to 11cm (4½in) wide, purple stamens.

S. pseudocamellia **4**: to 6×4.5m (20×15ft), or tree eventually to 12m (50ft); pyramid-shaped; red flaking bark; lvs yellow, red & sometimes purple in autumn; cup-shaped fls to 6cm (2½in) across. Var *koreana* (*S. koreana*) is smaller, with broader lvs & flat fls; good for small gardens.

S. sinensis **5**: moderately to v hardy tree, to 6×3.5m (20×12ft); beautiful brown & purplish peeling bark; lvs crimson in autumn; fls to 5cm (2in) across.

The daphne family

Generally highly scented, rather slow-growing shrubs with clusters of 4-lobed tubular flowers to 1.5cm (⅝in) long, winter & spring. Evergreen unless noted. **Cultivation**: Very hardy unless stated. For moist but well-drained loamy soil in sun or partial shade. Little or no pruning needed. **Propagation**: Semi-ripe heel cuttings; seed; grafting; lax spp by layering. For dwarf spp usually grown in rock garden, see p484.

Daphnes (*Daphne* spp): flowers usually showy, with thick glistening petals, spring unless stated; berry-like frs. All parts (especially frs) poisonous. Rather short-lived & prone to viruses; resent root disturbance.

D. bholua **: erect & open, to 1.8×1.5m (6×5ft); usually evergreen; lance-shaped lvs to 10cm (4in) long; purplish fls, paler inside, mid–late winter; black frs. Var 'Gurkha' is deciduous with white flushed purple fls.

D.×burkwoodii **: hybrid of *D. caucasica* & *D. cneorum*; dense & rounded, to 1–1.2×1.2–1.5m (3–4×4–5ft); semi-evergreen narrow pale green lvs to 3cm (1¼in) long; pink fls in 5cm (2in) clusters along branches; frs red. Popular & easy. Vars: 'Arthur Burkwood'; 'Somerset' **6**.

D. genkwa *: slender, to 1×1m (3×3ft); deciduous lance-shaped lvs to 5cm (2in) long; lilac fls (before lvs); frs white. Short-lived & difficult; needs warm summers.

D. laureola * **7** (spurge laurel): moderately to v hardy; to 1.2×1.2m (4×4ft); glossy laurel-like lvs to 11cm (4½in) long; yellowish-green fls (not showy), from late winter; frs blue-black.

D. mezereum ** **8** (mezereon): erect, to 1.2×1.2m (4×4ft); deciduous narrow lvs to 9cm (3½in) long, greyish beneath; rosy-purple fls along leafless branches from late winter; frs red. Short-lived & v prone to viruses; likes cool moist conditions. Var 'Bowles' White' is white; frs yellow.

D. odora **: moderately hardy; to 1.8×1.8m (6×6ft); lance-shaped dark glossy green lvs to 8cm (3in) long; red-purple fls, mid winter to spring (cuttable; can be forced). Var 'Aureo-marginata' is hardier; lvs rimmed yellow.

D. pontica *: moderately to v hardy; to 1–1.2×1.8m (3–4×6ft); vase-shaped; glossy lvs to 8cm (3in) long; yellowish-green fls.

D. tangutica * **9**: rounded & sturdy, to 90×60cm (3×2ft); leathery bright green lvs to 8cm (3in) long; rosy-purple fls, white inside; frs red.

Edgeworthia (paperbush, *Edgeworthia chrysantha* * **10**, *E. papyrifera*): moderately hardy; to 1.8×1.5m (6×5ft); tough supple branches; deciduous lance-shaped lvs to 12cm (5in) long, clustered; dense clusters of deep yellow fls, late winter (before lvs).

Limes or lindens

Tilia spp & hybrids. Mostly large, fast-growing deciduous trees mainly for landscaping, streets, shade. Take hard pruning, pollarding; can be pleached to make tall screen. Leaves thin & limp, toothed & often heart-shaped, to 10–12cm (4–5in) long unless noted. Small creamy-white flowers in long cymes with wing-like bract; attract bees. **Cultivation**: Very hardy unless stated. Best on rich moist soil. Many spp prone to aphids (drip honeydew, infected by sooty moulds). **Propagation**: Seed; layering; grafting.

T. americana* (American lime, basswood): ultra-hardy; to 11–12×5.5–7.5m (36–40×18–25ft)/ 25yrs, eventually to 30m (100ft). Vars: 'Fastigiata' (narrowly columnar); 'Redmond' (dense conical).

T. cordata* (*T. parvifolia*, small-leaved lime): ultra-hardy; to 9×4.5m (30×15ft)/25yrs, eventually to 25m (80ft); finely toothed rounded lvs to 8cm (3in) long. Vars 'Greenspire' & 'Swedish Upright' are narrow.

T.×euchlora* **1** (Caucasian lime): hybrid of uncertain origin; to 6–7.5×3–5.5m (20–25×10–18ft)/25yrs, eventually to 20m (65ft); somewhat pendulous; glossy lvs. Aphid-resistant.

T.×europaea* **2** (*T.×vulgaris*, common European lime): hybrid of *T. cordata* &

T. platyphyllos; ultra-hardy; to 7.5–11×4.5–6m (25–36×15–20ft)/25yrs, eventually to 40m (130ft); may grow profuse water-shoots; lvs drop early. V prone to aphid attack. Vars: 'Pallida' (conical; lvs yellowish beneath); 'Wratislaviensis' **3** (young lvs yellow).

T. mongolica* **4** (Mongolian lime): dense &

compact, to 6–7.5×3–4.5m (20–25×10–15ft)/ 25yrs, eventually to 18m (60ft); graceful; reddish shoots; glossy, often deeply lobed lvs to 8cm (3in) long, reddish when young, yellow later.

T. oliveri* **5**: to 6–7.5×3–4.5m (20–25×10–15ft)/25yrs, eventually to 15m (50ft); smooth grey bark; branches somewhat pendulous; finely toothed pale green lvs, silvery-white felt beneath.

T. petiolaris** (weeping silver lime; probably correctly, *T. tomentosa* var/hybrid): weeping, to 6–9×3–5.5m (20–30×10–18ft)/25yrs, eventually to 30m (100ft); fluttering dark green lvs, white felt beneath. Intoxicates bees.

T. tomentosa** **6** (silver lime) is similar but erect; lvs short-stalked.

T. platyphyllos (broad-leaved lime): ultra-hardy; to 9–12×4.5–6m (30–40×15–20ft)/25yrs, eventually over 30m (100ft); rounded lvs, downy beneath. Vars (generally less vigorous): 'Aurea' (winter shoots yellow); 'Laciniata' ('Asplenifolia'; lvs deeply lobed & coarsely toothed); 'Rubra' (red-twigged lime; winter shoots red).

The elm family

Elegant, often stately deciduous trees generally with toothed leaves, often asymmetrical at base. Flowers inconspicuous. Good street & landscape trees, but virulent strain of Dutch elm disease attacks most *Ulmus* spp, so no longer planted in most areas. **Cultivation**: Unless stated, very hardy & for any well-drained fertile soil in open site. **Propagation**: Seed; layering; grafting; suckers where produced.

Nettle trees (hackberries, *Celtis* spp): round-headed trees, generally to 6×4.5m (20×15ft)/ 25yrs, eventually to 12–18m (40–60ft); lvs often yellow in autumn; rounded fleshy frs.

C. australis (European hackberry): moderately to v hardy; smooth grey bark; lance-shaped lvs to 12×4cm (5×1½in), downy beneath; frs brown. Best where summers hot. *C. caucasica* **7** is similar but lvs smaller; likes cool summers.

C. laevigata (*C. mississippiensis*, sugarberry, Mississippi hackberry): sometimes eventually to 25m (80ft); warty bark; often toothless tapering lvs to 8×3cm (3×1¼in); frs orange to purple.

C. occidentalis (common hackberry): ultra-hardy; eventually to 30m (100ft) in some areas; grey corky bark; lvs to 12cm (5in) long, glossy & sharply toothed; frs orange to purple.

Elms (*Ulmus* spp): lvs doubly toothed; frs winged. Spp listed generally resist Dutch elm disease.

U.×elegantissima 'Jacqueline Hillier' **8**: hybrid of

U. glabra & *U. plotii*; dense suckering shrub, to 1.5×2m (5×7ft); rough lvs to 4cm (1½in) long.

U. parvifolia **9** (Chinese elm): round-headed, to 7.5×7.5m (25×25ft)/25yrs, eventually to 20m (65ft); sometimes semi-evergreen glossy leathery lvs to 6×3cm (2½×1¼in), persistent.

U. pumila (Siberian elm): variable tree, to 3–9×3–6m (10–30×10–20ft), or shrub; lvs almost symmetrical, to 6×2.5cm (2½×1in).

Zelkovas (*Zelkova* spp): smooth-barked, with toothed symmetrical lvs & wrinkled nut-like frs.

Z. carpinifolia **10**: vigorous, to 7.5–9×3–4.5m (25–30×10–15ft)/25yrs, eventually to 25–30m (80–100ft); trunk usually divides into many erect branches/trunks, making ovoid head; lvs to 8×4.5cm (3×1¾in), orange-brown in autumn.

Z. serrata (Japanese zelkova): round-headed & spreading, to 4.5–6×4.5–7.5m (15–20×15–25ft)/25yrs, eventually to 30m (100ft); sharply toothed tapering lvs to 11×5cm (4½×2in), red, orange & yellow in autumn.

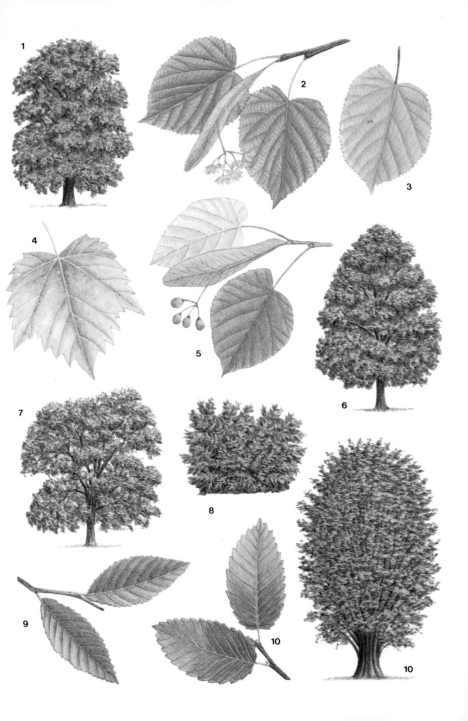

Lantanas, clerodendrums and their relatives

Generally deciduous shrubs (some sometimes becoming small trees) often with aromatic leaves. Flowers usually small but showy, produced on the young growths, sometimes followed by attractive fruits. Most are suitable for shrub borders or as specimens, the more tender spp against a wall in colder areas. **Cultivation**: For any well-drained soil in full sun. See below for hardiness; generally hardier if wood well ripened by hot sun. **Propagation**: Seed; semi-ripe or hardwood cuttings.

Callicarpas (beauty-berries, *Callicarpa* spp): attractive erect shrubs, v hardy unless noted, grown mainly for their densely clustered small, brightly coloured (usually lilac) frs (best if cross-pollinated) and often good autumn lf colour; small pink or purplish fls in dense clusters, summer.
C. americana (American beauty-berry, French mulberry): moderately hardy; to 1.8×1.2m (6×4ft); shoots downy; lvs to 15cm (6in) long, white/rusty felt beneath; bluish fls; profuse purple frs.
C. bodinieri giraldii **1** (*C. giraldiana*): to 2.5×1.5m (8×5ft); lance-shaped slender-pointed lvs to 12×5cm (5×2in), rose-purple in autumn; profuse deep lilac frs. Var 'Profusion' is v free-frtg.
C. japonica: to 2×1.5m (7×5ft); stems not fully woody; rather lance-shaped, often long-tapered lvs to 12×5cm (5×2in); frs violet. Vars: 'Leucocarpa' (white frs); *luxurians* (larger lvs & infls). *C. dichotoma* **2** is similar but more compact, to 1.5×1m (5×3ft).

Caryopteris (*Caryopteris* spp; in US, bluebeards): small moderately hardy shrubs with often toothed or lobed grey-green lvs* & densely clustered blue fls, prominent stamens, mid/late summer often into autumn. Rather soft-stemmed & often cut down by frost; in any case best pruned hard in spring.
C.×clandonensis vars: hybrids of *C. incana* & *C. mongolica*; to 60×75cm (2×2½ft); lvs* to 5–8cm (2–3in) long. Vars: 'Arthur Simmonds' (lvs dull green, few teeth; fls bright blue); 'Ferndown' (darker green lvs; deeper blue fls); 'Heavenly Blue' **3** (more erect & compact; deep blue fls); 'Kew Blue' (darker blue).
C. incana: spreading, to 1×1.2m (3×4ft); deeply lobed dull green lvs*; pretty bright violet-blue fls, autumn.

Clerodendrums (glory-bowers, *Clerodendrum* spp): soft-stemmed shrubs grown for their attractive fls in broad infls, late summer & autumn; lvs smell unpleasant if crushed. Can be treated as perennials where cut down by frost.
C. bungei* **4**: semi- to moderately hardy suckering shrub, to 2×2m (7×7ft); vigorous erect shoots with large heart-shaped lvs to 20×18cm (8×7in); deep purplish-red fls in 10–12cm (4–5in) corymbs. Propagate by division.
C. trichotomum*: moderately to v hardy shrub, to 3.5×4.5m (12×15ft), or small tree; soft lvs to 22×12cm (9×5in), downy beneath; starry white

fls to 4cm (1½in) across in 15–22cm (6–9in) cymes; bright blue to black small frs, crimson calyx. Var *fargesii* **5** has brighter green, less downy lvs. Propagate by suckers, root cuttings.

Duranta (golden dewdrop, pigeon berry, skyflower, *Duranta repens, D. plumieri*): tender to semi-hardy evergreen shrub, to 4.5×5m (15×18ft); stems often spiny; lvs to 10cm (4in) long, dark glossy green; beautiful lilac-blue tubular fls in slender, drooping racemes, most of yr in warm climates; 1cm (½in) translucent yellow frs (poisonous). Good hedger in Mediterranean & other warm climates; can be trimmed after flg to restrict size. Vars: 'Alba' (white); 'Variegata' **6** (lvs edged creamy-white).

Lantanas (*Lantana* spp): tender to semi-hardy fast-growing semi-/evergreen shrubs used for hedging, ground cover, etc, where hardy; elsewhere often treated as herbaceous or bedding plants (or grown under glass). Lvs pungent when crushed; fl almost all yr. Prune hard early spring.
L. camara **7** (common lantana, yellow sage): to 2×2m (7×7ft); square prickly stems; scalloped lvs to 4–6cm (1½–2½in) long; dense 5cm (2in) clusters of small changeable orange-yellow, orange, red &/or white fls; blue-black poisonous frs. Numerous vars & hybrids with *L. montevidensis* sold in warm-climate zones.
L. montevidensis **8** (*L. sellowiana*, trailing lantana): semi-prostrate, to 1.8×1.8m (6×6ft); toothed lvs to 2.5cm (1in) long; 2.5cm (1in) clusters of rosy-lilac fls. Good ground cover.

Lemon verbena (*Lippia citriodora* **9**; correctly, *Aloysia triphylla*): moderately hardy shrub, to 3×3m (10×10ft), or small tree; lance-shaped bristly pale green lvs** to 10×2cm (4×¾in), strongly lemon-scented; tiny lilac fls in slender 12cm (5in) panicles, late summer.

Vitex (*Vitex* spp): moderately hardy shrubs, to 3×3.5m (10×12ft), sometimes becoming small trees, with palmately divided lvs, 5–7 lfts; small violet fls in racemes or panicles to 15–20cm (6–8in) long, late summer to early autumn. Need hot sun to ripen wood.
V. agnus-castus **10** (chaste tree): narrow lance-shaped lfts* to 15cm (6in) long, toothless. Var *alba* has white fls.
V. negundo: narrow lfts to 10cm (4in) long, sometimes toothed (to 5cm [2in] long & deeply lobed in var *heterophylla*).

Miscellaneous trees and shrubs

Listed alphabetically by family name. Deciduous unless stated. **Cultivation & propagation**: See below; unless stated, very hardy & for any well-drained fertile soil in sun or semi-shade. For shrubby climbers, see pp228–250, for sub-shrubs, see pp252–360; for dwarf shrubs usually grown in rock gardens, see pp426–484.

American pawpaw (*Asimina triloba* **1**; Annonaceae): shrub, to 3.5×2m (12×7ft), or small tree where summers hot; drooping lvs to 20–30cm (8–12in) long, yellow in autumn; 5cm (2in) purple fls, spring (before lvs); bottle-shaped frs to 12cm (5in) long, green ripening brown, fleshy & edible (rare unless summers hot). Likes moist soil in hot sun; transplants poorly. Propagate by seed, layering.

Natal plum & oleander (*Carissa* & *Nerium* spp; Apocynaceae): showy leathery-lvd evergreen sun-loving shrubs for warm areas (good for hedges & screens) or elsewhere in tubs, moving under glass for winter. Prune as needed in spring to control. Propagate by semi-ripe cuttings.
*Carissa grandiflora*** (Natal plum): tender to semi-hardy; to 2×2m (7×7ft); spiny; glossy lvs to 8cm (3in) long; waxy-white starry fls to 5cm (2in) across, all yr; plum-like 5cm (2in) red frs, edible. Good near sea. Various erect, dwarf & prostrate vars available in warm areas.
Nerium oleander **2** (oleander; fragrant vars often listed as *N. indicum*; *N. odorum*): moderately hardy where summers hot, less so elsewhere; bushy & suckering; to 3×3m (10×10ft) or more; lance-shaped lvs 10–25cm (4–10in) long, often in 3s; clusters of single or double 2.5-5cm (1–2in) fls, shades of red, pink, salmon, white or yellowish, spring & summer. All parts poisonous. Tolerates salt, pollution; prone to scale insects. Can be pruned hard. Var 'Variegata' has yellow-variegated lvs; double pink fls.

Fremontia (flannel bush, *Fremontodendron* [*Fremontia*] *californicum* **3**; Bombacaceae; sometimes classed in Sterculiaceae): semi- to moderately hardy semi-/evergreen shrub, to 4.5×3.5m (15×12ft), more on wall & sometimes a small tree in warm areas; dark green, usually 3-lobed lvs to 10cm (4in) long, pale brown felt beneath; profuse solitary yellow cup-shaped fls opening flat to 6cm (2½in) wide, late spring & all summer. *F.* 'California Glory' is hybrid with *F. mexicana*; vigorous & v free-flg; fls lemon-yellow flushed red outside. Both best on sunny wall in well-drained soil; drought-tolerant. Propagate by seed, semi-ripe cuttings.

The wintersweet family (*Calycanthus* & *Chimonanthus* spp; Calycanthaceae): shrubs grown for their distinctive fragrant fls with numerous petals & sepals. Propagate by seed, layering, division.
Calycanthus floridus **4** (Carolina allspice, sweetshrub): rather straggly, to 2.5×2.5m

(8×8ft); bark, wood, roots & lvs aromatic; dark green rough lvs* to 12cm (5in) long, downy beneath; reddish-purple fls to 5cm (2in) wide, summer. *C. fertilis** is similar but less fragrant.
Chimonanthus praecox** **5** (*C. fragrans*, wintersweet): moderately to v hardy; bushy, to 2.5×2.5m (8×8ft), more against wall; glossy green lance-shaped lvs to 12cm (5in) long, rough above; purple-centred yellowish fls to 2.5cm (1in) wide, winter to early spring, depending on weather. Prune early spring if grown on wall. Vars: 'Grandiflorus'* (large lvs; large deep yellow fls stained red); 'Luteus'** **6** (pure yellow).

Katsura tree (*Cercidiphyllum japonicum* **7**; Cercidiphyllaceae): elegant tree, to 9×7.5m (30×25ft)/25yrs, eventually to 20m (65ft) or more, with twisted, furrowed trunk(s) & somewhat pendulous branches; rather heart-shaped lvs to 10cm (4in) long, rich yellow, orange, pink or red (variable) in autumn; fls inconspicuous. Propagate by seed, softwood cuttings. Var *magnificum* (*C. magnificum*) has larger lvs.

Tree purslane (sea orach, *Atriplex halimus* **8**; Chenopodiaceae): moderately hardy semi-evergreen shrub, to 1.8×2m (6×7ft); loose & bushy; stems & lvs bright silvery-grey; lvs diamond-shaped, to 6×3cm (2½×1¼in). One of best silver shrubs, excellent near sea in full sun. Propagate by semi-ripe cuttings.

Clethras (summer-sweets, *Clethra* spp; Clethraceae): shrubs (most eventually small trees) grown for slender racemes/panicles of small fragrant fls, generally creamy-/white, mid–late summer; lvs to 12–15cm (5–6in) long unless noted. Unless noted, v hardy where well summer-ripened but moderately hardy in cool climates; for lime-free moist (even wet) peaty soil; tolerate salty winds. Propagate by seed, semi-ripe cuttings.
C. alnifolia** **9** (sweet pepper bush): v hardy; erect, to 2×2m (7×7ft); lvs to 10cm (4in) long, yellow to orange in autumn; dense erect 5–15cm (2–6in) infls, branching in var 'Paniculata'**. Var 'Rosea'* has pink-tinted fls & glossy lvs.
C. barbinervis*: bushy, to 3×1.8m (10×6ft); clustered lvs, red & yellow in autumn; horizontal 10–15cm (4–6in) infls.
C. delavayi * **1**, p221: to 4.5×2.5m (15×8ft); lance-shaped lvs, downy beneath, yellow in autumn; dense one-sided 10–15cm (4–6in) infls of cupped fls, red calyx.
C. fargesii*: to 3.5×2.5m (12×8ft); lance-

shaped deep bright green lvs, rich yellow in autumn; branching 20–25cm (8–10in) infls of pure white fls.

Bush morning glory (*Convolvulus cneorum* **2**; Convolvulaceae): moderately hardy leafy evergreen shrub, to 1×1m (3×3ft); stems & lvs silvery-grey, with silky hairs; narrow lvs to 6cm (2½in) long; funnel-shaped pink-tinged white fls 4cm (1½in) wide, opening in succession all summer. Excellent front-row shrub for sunny well-drained site, or against sunny wall in colder areas. Propagate by semi-ripe cuttings.

Leatherwood (*Cyrilla racemiflora*; Cyrillaceae): moderately hardy shrub, to 1.8×1.2m (6×4ft), tender forms in warm areas tree-like & evergreen; glossy green lance-shaped lvs to 10cm (4in) long, crimson in autumn; small white fls in profuse slender racemes to 15cm (6in) long, late summer & autumn (attract bees). For lime-free preferably peaty soil. Propagate by seed, semi-ripe cuttings.

Persimmons (*Diospyros* spp; Ebenaceae): trees grown for their attractive foliage & (especially where summers hot) edible frs; small cream fls, summer, males clustered, females (on separate trees) solitary; frs fleshy & sweet, with persistent calyx. Propagate by seed, semi-ripe cuttings, grafting.

D. kaki **3** (Chinese or Japanese persimmon): moderately hardy; to 9×6m (30×20ft); glossy green lvs to 20×9cm (8×3½in), downy beneath, orange to red & purple in autumn; usually yellow tomato-like frs to 8cm (3in) across. Numerous frtg vars available in warm areas.

D. virginiana **4** (American or common persimmon): to 9×4.5m (30×15ft); dark grey rugged bark; dark glossy green lvs to 15cm (6in) long; 2.5–5cm (1–2in) yellow to orange frs.

Crinodendrons (*Crinodendron* [*Tricuspidaria*] spp; Elaeocarpaceae): semi- to moderately hardy erect evergreen shrubs, to 4.5×2.5m (15×8ft), or small trees; dark green hanging bell/urn-shaped fls, early summer. For moist, lime-free soil in semi-shade. Propagate by semi-ripe cuttings.

C. hookeranum **5** (*C.* [*T.*] *lanceolata*, lantern tree): rigid lance-shaped lvs to 12cm (5in) long; crimson urn-shaped fls to 3cm (1¼in) long.

C. patagua (*C.* [*T.*] *dependens*; lily-of-the-valley tree): more vigorous; lvs to 8cm (3in) long; white bell-shaped fls 2cm (¾in) long.

Richea (*Richea scoparia*; Epacridaceae): moderately hardy evergreen shrub, to 1.5×1m (5×3ft) or more; erect stems clothed with narrow rigid tapering lvs to 6cm (2½in) long; erect spikes 5–10cm (2–4in) long of small white, pink or red fls, late spring. For moist acid soil. Propagate by seed, semi-ripe cuttings.

Eucryphias (*Eucryphia* spp; Eucryphiaceae): generally evergreens, moderately hardy unless stated, grown for attractive foliage & beautiful white fls with conspicuous stamens. Best in moist acid/neutral soil (though lime-tolerant unless noted) in shelter, with roots shaded. Propagate by seed, semi-ripe cuttings, layering.

E. cordifolia **6**: semi- to moderately hardy shrub, to 3.5×2m (12×7ft), or tree eventually to 15m (50ft) or more; narrowish dull green lvs to 8cm (3in) long, wavy edges; 5cm (2in) fls, late summer to autumn.

E. glutinosa **7**: large shrub or small tree, to 4.5×3m (15×10ft); deciduous or semi-evergreen pinnate lvs, 3–5 shiny dark green lfts to 6cm (2½in) long, orange-red in autumn; 6cm (2½in) fls, mid summer. Hardiest sp; not lime-tolerant.

E.×intermedia 'Rostrevor' * **8**; hybrid of *E. glutinosa* & *E. lucida*; tree, to 6×1.8–2m (20×6–7ft); lvs simple or trifoliolate, dark green; 3cm (1¼in) fls, late summer to early autumn.

E. lucida * (*E. billardieri*, leatherwood): columnar tree, to 6×3m (20×10ft); more in wild; rich glossy green lvs* to 8×1.5cm (3×⅝in); 2.5–5cm (1–2in) pendulous fls, summer.

E.×nymansensis vars: hybrids of *E. cordifolia* & *E. glutinosa*; dense trees with simple or pinnate lvs, 1–5 glossy green lfts; profuse 6cm (2½in) fls, mid–late summer. Vars 'Mount Usher' (to 4.5×2.5m [15×8ft]; fls often double); 'Nymansay' (vigorous, to 6×2.5m [20×8ft] or more).

Chinese tallow tree (*Sapium sebiferum* **9**; Euphorbiaceae): round-headed or conical tree, to 6×6m (20×20ft), sometimes shrubby or suckering; long-stalked fluttering poplar-like lvs to 8cm (3in) long, brilliant red, purple, orange &/or yellow in autumn; tiny yellowish fls in 10cm (4in) spikes, summer. Seed coating yields candle wax. Moderately hardy where well sun-ripened, making good street tree; semi-hardy in cool climates. Propagate by seed, semi-ripe cuttings, grafting.

Silk tassel bush (*Garrya elliptica* **10**; Garryaceae): moderately hardy fast-growing dioecious evergreen shrub, to 3.5×3m (12×10ft) or more; dense & bushy; dark glossy green roundish lvs to 8cm (3in) long, wavy edges, grey-woolly beneath; tiny fls in drooping catkins, on male plants growing in winter to 15cm (6in) long, or to 30cm (1ft) in mild areas, with prominent yellow anthers; female catkins 4–10cm (1½–4in) long. Good on sunny/shady wall. Propagate by semi-ripe cuttings.

Decaisnea (*Decaisnea fargesii* **1**, p223; Lardizabalaceae): erect shrub, to 4.5×2.5m (15×8ft), grown for handsome foliage & unusual fls & frs; pinnate lvs to 1m (3ft) long, 13–25 lfts to 15cm (6in) long; yellowish-green fls to 3cm (1¼in) long in drooping 30–45cm (1–1½ft) panicles; pod-like metallic-blue frs to 10cm (4in)

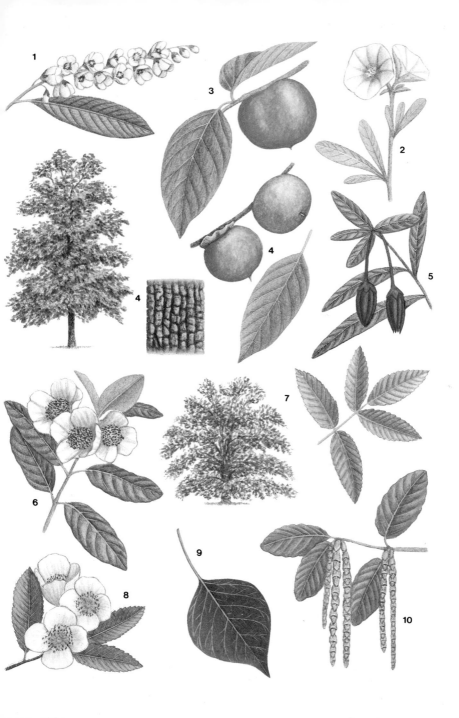

long. Likes rich soil; propagate by seed.

The lily family (*Danaë, Philesia* & *Ruscus* spp; Liliaceae): moderately hardy suckering, slender-stemmed evergreen shrubs, *Danaë* & *Ruscus* spp having lf-like phylloclades in axils of tiny scale-like true lvs. Like moist semi-shade.

Danaë (*Ruscus*) *racemosa* (Alexandrian laurel): elegant, erect & rather bamboo-like, to 1.2×1m (4×3ft); stems green; bright glossy green tapering phylloclades to 10×4cm (4×1½in); clusters of greenish-yellow fls; red berries. Good cut for arrangements. Propagate by seed, division.

Philesia magellanica **2** (sometimes classed in Philesiaceae): thicket-forming, to 1.2×1.2m (4×4ft) or more, sometimes climbing up trees, rocks; dark green narrow rigid lvs to 4cm (1½in) long; rosy-crimson nodding tubular fls to 6cm (2½in) long, mid–late summer. Propagate by suckers, hardwood cuttings.

Ruscus aculeatus **3** (butcher's broom): rhizomatous, to 1×1m (3×3ft); branching stems; rigid spine-tipped phylloclades to 4×2cm (1½×¾in); bright red berries on females if male nearby. Stems good for cutting. Tolerates hot sun or dense shade; propagate by division, seed.
R. hypoglossum: dense & dwarf, to 25×60cm (10in×2ft); arching unbranched stems; phylloclades to 10×4cm (4×1½in), not spiny.

Crape myrtle (*Lagerstroemia indica* **4** ; Lythraceae): moderately hardy tree, to 6×3m (20×10ft), shrubby in selected forms or if pruned hard; privet-like glossy lvs to 6cm (2½in) long, sometimes colouring well in autumn; beautiful 2.5–4cm (1–1½in) fls with 6 crinkled petals in panicles to 20×12cm (8×5in) on new wood, mid–late summer. Fls freely only where summers long & hot; prone to mildew in some areas. Can be pruned hard in spring. Propagate by seed, semi-ripe cuttings. Sold by colour & as named vars in shades of red, rose, pink, lilac, purple & white. Seedlings sometimes treated as bedding plants.

The mahogany family (*Cedrela* & *Melia* spp; Meliaceae): good street & shade trees, best in full sun, with pinnate lvs & small fls in panicles.
Cedrela (*Toona*) *sinensis** (toon, Chinese cedar): to 9×4.5m (30×15ft)/25yrs, eventually to 15m (50ft) or more; lvs to 60cm (2ft) long, up to 23 lfts to 10cm (4in) long, onion-scented when crushed; white fls in drooping infls to 30cm (1ft) long, summer. Propagate by seed, root cuttings.
*Melia azedarach** **5** (bead tree, China-berry): moderately hardy if well ripened, less so in cool climates; spreading, to 9×9m (30×30ft); bipinnate lvs to 1m (3ft) long, lfts to 5×2cm (2×¾in); erect 10–20cm (4–8in) infls of lilac fls 2cm (¾in) across, violet central column, late spring; persistent creamy-yellow egg-shaped frs 1cm (½in) long (poisonous in quantity).

Propagate by seed, semi-ripe cuttings. Var 'Umbraculiformis' (in US, Texas umbrella tree) is dome-shaped.

The mulberry family (*Broussonetia, Ficus, Morus* & *Maclura* spp; Moraceae): trees grown for ornament & shade, some for frs.
Broussonetia papyrifera **6** (paper mulberry): round-headed, to 9×7.5m (30×25ft), with twisted trunk, & vigorous shrub; olive-green v variable lvs to 20cm (8in) long, entire to deeply lobed, rough above, woolly beneath; male fls in 8cm (3in) catkins; females (on separate trees) in rounded clusters; orange-red 2cm (¾in) frs on females if male nearby. Useful street tree in hot, dry areas. Propagate by seed, suckers, semi-ripe heel cuttings.
Ficus carica **7** (common fig): moderately hardy shrubby tree, to 4.5×3.5m (15×12ft) or more, or large shrub where cut back by hard frosts (root moderately to v hardy); lvs to 20×20cm (8×8in), deeply 3/5-lobed; well-known edible frs ripen best in long hot summers. Often grown as picturesque wall shrub in cool areas; can be grown in tub & moved under glass in winter. Prune in winter. Propagate by hardwood cuttings, grafting, layering. Numerous frtg vars available in warm areas. Many other ornamental *Ficus* spp grown in frost-free zones.
Maclura pomifera **8** (Osage orange): spiny tree, fast-growing where summers hot, to 7.5×3m (25×10ft), but can be pruned hard for hedge or screen; dark green lvs to 10cm (4in) long, yellow in autumn; fls inconspicuous, yellowish-green; 10cm (4in) inedible frs like yellow-green oranges on female plants if male nearby. Good on poor soils. Propagate by seed, layering, root cuttings.
Morus nigra **9** (black or common mulberry): picturesque & rugged, to 4.5×4.5m (15×15ft), with dense head; coarsely toothed rough lvs to 20cm (8in) long, sometimes lobed; inconspicuous green fls in catkins; dark reddish-purple blackberry-like sweet frs to 2.5cm (1in) long (stain paths). Propagate by seed, hardwood cuttings, layering, budding. *M. alba* (white mulberry) has rather insipid white/pinkish frs; more commonly grown for ornament in N America & S Europe; food for silkworms.

Wax myrtles (bayberries, *Myrica* spp; Myricaceae): aromatic shrubs with lance-shaped lvs, small catkins in early summer & small generally greyish/yellowish-white wax-coated frs on females if male nearby. Propagate by seed, layering.
M. californica (California bayberry): moderately hardy; to 3.5×2.5m (12×8ft) or more; evergreen dark glossy green lvs* to 10cm (4in) long; purplish frs. Tolerates drought, v poor soil.
M. gale (bog myrtle, sweet gale): ultra-hardy; to 1.5×1m (5×3ft); lvs* to 6cm (2½in) long, dark glossy green; good on wet soil.

M. pensylvanica **1** (bayberry): v to ultra-hardy; to 2.5×1.5m (8×5ft); deciduous or semi-evergreen lvs* to 10cm (4in) long. Good on poor, dry soils. *M. cerifera* (wax myrtle) is similar but less hardy & taller.

The tupelo family (*Davidia* & *Nyssa* spp; Nyssaceae): v ornamental trees grown for their conspicuous fl bracts or autumn colour. Propagate by seed, semi-ripe cuttings, layering. *Davidia involucrata* (dove or handkerchief tree; sometimes classed in Davidiaceae): spectacular tree, to 7.5–9×4.5m (25–30×15ft)/25yrs, eventually to 15m (50ft) or more; bright green rather heart-shaped lvs to 15×11cm (6×4½in), thick grey down beneath except in var *vilmoriniana* **2** (commoner); dense rounded fl heads, late spring, with paired creamy-white unequal lf-like bracts, to 20×10cm (8×4in) long. Best on moist soil in shelter. *Nyssa sylvatica* **3** (tupelo, black gum): pyramid-shaped, to 7.5–9×3–5.5m (25–30×10–18ft)/25yrs, eventually to 25m (80ft) or more; dark glossy green lvs to 15×8cm (6×3in), brilliant red & yellow in autumn. Best in moist soil where summers hot; transplants poorly. *N. sinensis* has narrow lvs to 15×5cm (6×2in), purple when young, crimson & orange in autumn.

Tree poppy (*Dendromecon rigida** **4**; Papaveraceae): semi- to moderately hardy evergreen shrub, to 3×3.5m (10×12ft); shoots glaucous, soft-wooded; leathery glaucous lvs to 8×2.5cm (3×1in); poppy-like bright yellow fls 5–8cm (2–3in) across, most of yr in warm climates but mainly summer. Needs well-drained soil in full sun. Propagate by seed, semi-ripe cuttings. *D. harfordii* (*D. rigida harfordii*) is similar but taller, with deep green lvs. For the sub-shrubby *Romneya coulteri* (California tree poppy), see p314.

Planes (*Platanus* spp; in US, sycamores; Platanaceae): vigorous large trees with flaking creamy-grey bark & palmately lobed rather maple-like large lvs; fls inconspicuous; ball-shaped pendulous woody frs. Grown for ornament & shade, often in streets. Like sun; can be pruned hard or pollarded; prone to anthracnose (wilt), especially in cool damp weather. Propagate by seed, hardwood cuttings, layering (from stooled plants), grafting. *P.×acerifolia* **5** (*P.×hybrida, P. occidentalis acerifolia,* London plane): probably hybrid of *P. occidentalis* & *P. orientalis*; to 12×9m (40×30ft)/25yrs, eventually to 30m (100ft) or more; deeply 3/5-lobed variable lvs, to 18×25cm (7×10in), blotched white in var 'Suttneri'. *P. occidentalis* (American plane, buttonwood; in US, sycamore): v to ultra-hardy; to 12×9m (40×30ft)/25yrs, eventually to 40m (130ft) or more; lvs shallowly 3/5-lobed, to 20×20cm (8×8in). Best in continental climate.

P. orientalis **6** (oriental plane): to 12×9m (40×30ft)/25yrs, eventually to 25m (80ft) or more; lvs deeply 5/7-lobed, to 20×25cm (8×10in), narrower & more deeply cut in var 'Digitata'. Generally healthy.

Ceratostigmas (*Ceratostigma* spp; Plumbaginaceae): small free-flg shrubs with bristly lvs (generally red in autumn) & attractive blue fls in clusters. Need sunny well-drained spot, against wall in cold areas; old shoots can be cut out early spring. Propagate by semi-ripe cuttings. For *Plumbago capensis*, shrubby if not supported, see p250.
C. griffithii: semi- to moderately hardy; to 1×1m (3×3ft); evergreen lvs to 4×1.5cm (1½×⅝in), purplish edges; fls late summer.
C. willmottianum **7** (Chinese plumbago): moderately hardy; to 1.2×1.5m (4×5ft); deciduous lvs to 5×2cm (2×¾in); fls mid summer & autumn. Soft-wooded; herbaceous in cold areas.

Cantua (magic flower of the Incas, *Cantua buxifolia* **8**; Polemoniaceae): beautiful tender to semi-hardy evergreen shrub, to 2×2.5m (7×8ft); rather open & straggly; variable lvs to 5cm (2in) long, to 2cm (¾in) on flg shoots; drooping corymbs of 4–8 tubular rosy-red fls 8–10cm (3–4in) long, streaked yellow, mainly late spring but on & off all yr in warm areas. Often grown under cool glass. Propagate by seed, semi-ripe cuttings.

Pomegranate (*Punica granatum* **9**; Punicaceae): semi- to moderately hardy shrub (moderately hardy if well sun-ripened), to 3×2m (10×7ft) or more, sometimes a small tree, grown for showy fls & edible frs (only in warm areas); shoots often spiny; glossy green lvs to 8×2.5cm (3×1in), brilliant yellow in autumn; scarlet funnel-shaped fls to 4cm (1½in) across, crinkly petals, summer to early autumn; frs yellowish/red, to 8cm (3in) across. Best in good soil in full sun; in colder areas can be trained on wall or grown in tub & overwintered under glass. Propagate by seed, layering, semi-ripe or hardwood cuttings. Vars: 'Alba Plena' (double, creamy-white); 'Chico' **10** (compact; large double fls, long season; no frs); 'Nana' (dwarf, to 1×1m [3×3ft]; small lvs, fls & frs; good low hedge or tub plant); 'Wonderful' (best frtg var).

Yellowroot (*Xanthorhiza simplicissima* **1**, p227; Ranunculaceae): suckering shrub, to 0.6×1m (2×3ft), grown for attractive foliage & early fls; lvs pinnate, 3–5 deeply toothed 2.5–8cm (1–3in) lfts, bronze-purple in autumn; small purple fls in drooping 10cm (4in) panicles, early spring. Good ground cover in damp shade. Propagate by division, seed.

The soapberry family (*Koelreuteria* & *Xanthoceras* spp: Sapindaceae): trees & shrubs grown for their attractive pinnate foliage, fls (in

panicles) &/or frs. Propagate by seed.

Koelreuteria paniculata **2** (golden rain tree, pride of India, varnish tree): tree, to 6×4.5m (20×15ft)/25yrs, eventually to 12m (40ft) or more; often gaunt at first, becoming denser; pinnate (sometimes bipinnate) lvs to 45cm (1½ft) long, 12–18 coarsely toothed/lobed lfts; pyramid-shaped 20–30cm (8–12in) panicles of yellow fls, summer, then inflated bladder-like yellowish-brown frs. Good in hot, dry, exposed positions; prone to coral-spot fungus. Var 'Fastigiata' is narrowly columnar. *K. bipinnata* (moderately hardy where well ripened) & *K. elegans* (*K. formosana*; semi-hardy) have bipinnate lvs & pink frs.

Xanthoceras sorbifolium: beautiful shrub, to 3×1.5m (10×5ft), or small tree; lvs to 30cm (1ft) long, 9–17 sharply toothed dark green lfts; erect panicles to 20cm (8in) long of 3cm (1¼in) white fls blotched yellow or pink, late spring; green top-shaped 5cm (2in) frs. Best with ample summer sun; may be damaged by late spring frosts; prone to coral-spot fungus.

Tree of heaven (*Ailanthus altissima* **3**; Simaroubaceae): vigorous round-headed tree, to 9–12×4.5–9m (30–45×15–30ft)/25yrs, eventually to 20m (65ft) or more, or can be stooled; rather ash-like pinnate lvs to 1m (3ft) long, sometimes over 30 lfts 8–15cm (3–6in) long; small greenish fls in panicles, unpleasantly scented on male trees; reddish-brown winged frs in large bunches. Excellent street tree, handsome in lf & fr. Propagate by suckers, grafting, seed.

Stachyurus (*Stachyurus praecox* **4**; Stachyuraceae): moderately to v hardy early-flg shrub, to 2×2m (7×7ft) or more; reddish-brown glossy branches; lance-shaped lvs to 15cm (6in) long; pale yellow fls in slender drooping 8cm (3in) racemes, formed autumn but opening before lvs v early spring (sometimes earlier). Likes humus-rich acid soil; fls may be damaged by hard frost after opening. Propagate by semi-ripe heel cuttings. *S. chinensis* is similar but more vigorous, with broader lvs; fls slightly later.

Chinese parasol tree (*Firmiana simplex* **5**; Sterculiaceae): semi- to moderately hardy handsome tree, to 9×6m (30×20ft)/25yrs in warm areas, eventually to 18m (60ft); smooth grey-green bark; shallowly 3/5-lobed lvs to 20–30cm (8–12in) long, on long stalks; small yellowish fls in panicles to 45×20cm (18×8in), summer. Good shade, street or lawn tree. Propagate by seed.

Symplocos (Asiatic sweetleaf, *Symplocos paniculata* * **6**; Symplocaceae): shrub, to 2.5×2m (8×7ft), or small elegant tree; variable finely toothed lvs to 10×5cm (4×2in), slightly hairy; small white fls in 4–6cm (1½–2½in) panicles, late spring; small frs ripening bright blue, most

profuse if cross-pollinated. Best in acid soil in full sun. Propagate by seed.

Tamarisks (*Tamarix* spp; Tamaricaceae): elegant shrubs or small trees with slender arching branches & tiny lvs. Grown for their graceful habit, attractive somewhat juniper-like foliage & plumes of pink fls. Best in full sun; v good near sea (used for hedging). Propagate by hardwood or semi-ripe cuttings. Nomenclature often confused.

T. hispida: to 1.2×1.2m (4×4ft); downy shoots; glaucous downy lvs; bright pink fls in erect 8cm (3in) racemes, late summer. Prune in spring. Needs hot summers.

T. parviflora **7** (sometimes sold incorrectly as *T. africana, T. tetrandra*): to 4.5×4.5m (15×15ft); brown-purple branches; lvs bright green; rosy-pink fls in 2.5–5cm (1–2in) racemes along yr-old stems. Prune after flg.

T. pentandra (correctly, *T. ramosissima*): ultra-hardy; to 4.5×4.5m (15×15ft); fls late summer, in profuse 2.5–12cm (1–5in) racemes along shoots, forming panicles to 1m (3ft) long. Prune in spring. Vars: 'Pink Cascade' (vigorous; rich pink); 'Rosea' (rosy-pink); 'Rubra' **8** (dark pink).

Bupleurum (*Bupleurum fruticosum*; Umbelliferae): moderately hardy semi-/evergreen lax shrub, to 2×2m (7×7ft); slender shoots, purplish when young; blue-green leathery lance-shaped lvs to 8×2.5cm (3×1in); small yellow fls in 8–10cm (3–4in) umbels, mid–late summer. Good on poor, dry soils exposed to sea winds. Propagate by semi-ripe cuttings.

The winter's-bark family (*Drimys* & *Pseudowintera* spp; Winteraceae): evergreens with leathery lvs*. Prefer moist soil. Propagate by semi-ripe cuttings, layering.

Drimys lanceolata (mountain pepper tree): moderately hardy dense shrub, to 1.8–2.5×1.8–2.5m (6–8×6–8ft), or small tree; young shoots rich red; glossy lance-shaped lvs* to 1.5–8cm (⅝–3in) long; clusters of small white fls, spring, followed by small frs on females.

D. winteri * **9** (winter's bark): semi- to moderately hardy tree, to 7.5×4.5m (25×15ft), or large conical shrub; aromatic bark; soft green lvs* to 18×6cm (7×2in), glaucous beneath; clusters of 4cm (1½in) creamy-white fls, spring.

Pseudowintera colorata **10**: semi-hardy compact shrub, to 1.5×1.5m (5×5ft); lvs* to 6×2.5cm (2½×1in), pale yellow-green flushed pink, deep reddish-purple edge, glaucous beneath; yellowish-green fls in small clusters. Best in woodland.

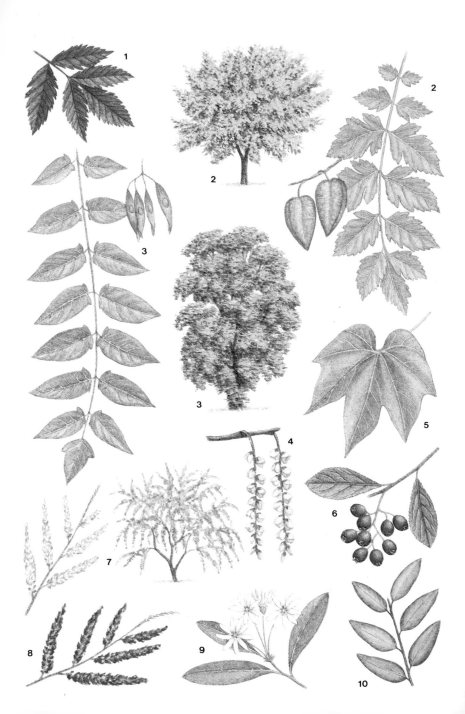

Chilean jasmine and its relatives

Pretty, sun-loving, rather tender, twining woody climbers with fragrant white flowers in summer. **Cultivation**: Prefer light, acid soil in sheltered spot. Provide support. Aphids may infest young shoots. **Propagation**: Softwood cuttings.

Chilean jasmine (*Mandevilla laxa*** 1**, *M. suaveolens*): semi-hardy; to 4.5–6m (15–20ft); deciduous; white to pinkish 5cm (2in) funnel-shaped fls in corymbs.
Trachelospermums (star jasmines, *Trachelospermum* spp): evergreen; glossy, dark green lvs; small, jasmine-like fls in cymes.
T. (*Rhyncospermum*) *asiaticum** (*T. divaricatum*,

yellow star jasmine): moderately hardy; to over 6m (20ft); yellow-white fls.
T. (*R.*) *jasminoides*** (star jasmine, Confederate jasmine): semi-hardy; self-clinging; to 7.5m (25ft); white to cream fls; survives salt spray. Vars: 'Japonicum' (*T. japonicum*; lvs white-veined, bronze in autumn); 'Variegatum' **2** (lvs variegated cream-white).

The ivies

Hedera spp. Vigorous, self-clinging evergreen woody climbers excellent for covering walls, fences, stumps, etc. Also for ground cover (especially vars marked †). Flowers insignificant; leaves and berries poisonous. Climbing, lobed-leaved forms are juvenile; adult is bushy, with rounded or ovate leaves. **Cultivation**: Easy; for any soil or aspect; tolerate shade and pollution. Stop leading shoots to encourage branching; can be pruned hard in late winter. **Propagation**: Semi-ripe or hardwood cuttings of typical shoots. For Boston ivy (*Parthenocissus tricuspidata*), see p246.

H. canariensis (*H. algeriensis*, *H. helix canariensis*, Canary Island or Algerian ivy): moderately hardy; to 4.5–6m (15–20ft); stems dark red; lvs to 20cm (8in) long, bronzing in autumn. Vars: 'Azorica' (bright green); 'Canary Cream' (lvs blotched cream); 'Gold Leaf' (lf centres yellow); 'Variegata' **3** ('Gloire de Marengo'; lvs edged silver-grey & creamy).
H. colchica (Persian ivy): v hardy; to 6–9m (20–30ft); heart-shaped dark green lvs to 15×25cm (6×10in). Vars: 'Dentata' (elephant's ear ivy; lvs dark green, toothed); 'Sulphur Heart' (incorrectly, 'Paddy's Pride'; lvs splashed yellow); 'Variegata' **4** ('Dentata Variegata'; as 'Dentata' but lvs margined cream).
H. helix (common or English ivy): generally v hardy, but some vars less so; some vars to 15m (50ft) or more. Numerous vars, including: 'Adam'† (small variegated lvs); 'Atropurpurea' (lvs purple in winter); 'Aureovariegata' ('Chrysophylla'; variegated yellow; may revert to green); 'Baltica' (ultra-hardy); 'Bulgaria'

(drought-resistant); 'Buttercup' **5** ('Golden Cloud', 'Russell's Gold'; yellow to yellowish-green); 'Chicago' (dark green well-lobed lvs); 'Conglomerata'† (bushy form; see p56); 'Deltoidea'† ('Sweetheart'; heart-shaped lvs); 'Digitata' ('Palmata'; lvs have five finger-like lobes); 'Discolor' ('Marmorata'; lvs small, mottled white); 'Glacier'† **6** (lvs greyish, edged cream); 'Goldheart' **7** ('Golden Jubilee'; lvs yellow edged green); 'Green Ripple' (frilled lf edges); 'Hibernica'† (*H. helix hibernica*, *H. hibernica*, Irish ivy; large dark green lvs); 'Ivalace'† ('Green Gem', 'Little Gem', lace ivy; dark green crimped lvs); 'Little Diamond'† (small diamond-shaped/lobed lvs, variegated white); 'Manda's Crested'† (green curled lvs); 'Parsley Crested'† (pale green parsley-like lvs); 'Pin Oak'† (lvs like bird's foot); 'Pittsburgh' (like 'Chicago' but lvs smaller); 'Sagittifolia' **8** ('Sagittaefolia'; lvs arrow-shaped); 'Shamrock'† (bright green); 'Tricolor'† ('Elegantissima', 'Marginata-rubra'; variegated cream, lf edges red in autumn).

Wax plant and its relatives

Twining or clinging woody climbers for mildest areas with small, fragrant, generally waxy whitish flowers in summer. **Cultivation**: For warm, sheltered spots in well-drained soil. Provide support. **Propagation**: Cuttings; layering; seed under glass.

Araujia (*Araujia sericofera*, cruel plant): tender; vigorous, to 7.5m (25ft); evergreen; creamy-white fls; yellow-green seed pods.
Wax plant (*Hoya carnosa** **9**): tender; self-clinging, to 6m (20ft); also for ground cover;

evergreen; leathery lvs (variegated in some vars); white to pink starry fls in umbels.
Wattakaka (*Wattakaka* [*Dregea*] *sinensis** **10**): to 3m (10ft); deciduous; creamy-white fls in umbels.

Trumpet creepers and their relatives

Attractive twining or clinging woody climbers with profuse, colourful trumpet-shaped or tubular flowers, mainly from late summer. Some are rather tender. **Cultivation**: Prefer moist but well-drained soil in sun. Provide support; tie in *Campsis* spp as aerial roots may not give enough support. Prune early spring to encourage flowering and remove frost-damaged stems. **Propagation**: Semi-ripe cuttings; seed (especially *Eccremocarpus scaber*); *Campsis* spp by root cuttings.

Cross vine (*Bignonia* [*Doxantha*] *capreolata* **1**): moderately to v hardy, but may be cut down by hard frost; rampant, to 15m (50ft); evergreen or semi-evergreen; 3–5cm (1½–2in) long orange-red to yellow tubular fls, late spring.

Trumpet creepers (*Campsis* spp): deciduous; pinnate lvs; orange & red trumpet fls 5–10cm (2–4in) long.

C. grandiflora (*C. chinensis*, Chinese trumpet creeper): moderately hardy; to 9m (30ft).

C. radicans **2** (American trumpet creeper, trumpet vine): v hardy; vigorous, to 12m (40ft).

C.×tagliabuana: v hardy; to 10m (33ft); hybrid of two spp above & v similar. Best var: 'Mme Galen' (salmon-red).

Chilean glory flower (*Eccremocarpus scaber* **3**): moderately hardy; may be treated as HHA; vigorous, to 3–4.5m (10–15ft); evergreen but cut down by frost (protected roots may survive); 2.5cm (1in) long scarlet to yellow tubular fls in racemes, summer & autumn.

Cape honeysuckle (*Tecomaria capensis* **4**): semi-hardy; vigorous, to 4.5m (15ft); racemes of brilliant orange 5cm (2in) trumpet fls.

Climbing honeysuckles

Lonicera spp. Vigorous, twining woody climbers at their best rambling over bushes, tree stumps, pergolas, etc. Whorls of trumpet-shaped, often sweetly fragrant flowers, mainly in summer. Some spp evergreen, but few of these are fragrant. Fleshy berries eaten by birds but toxic to humans. **Cultivation**: For any soil, but prefer cool, moist roots. Many like semi-shade. Provide support. If control needed, prune after flowering or cut out old stems in winter. Aphids are worst pest. **Propagation**: Semi-ripe or hardwood cuttings; layering; seed.

L.×americana**: hybrid of *L. caprifolium* & *L. etrusca*; moderately to v hardy; vigorous, to 9m (30ft); deciduous; prolific white to yellow, purple-tinged fls 4–5cm (1½–2in) long.

L.×brownii (scarlet trumpet honeysuckle): hybrid of *L. hirsuta* & *L. sempervirens*; v hardy; to 3–4.5m (10–15ft); deciduous or semi-evergreen; fls orange-scarlet, 2.5–4cm (1–1½in) long, late spring, repeating late summer. Var 'Dropmore Scarlet' is scarlet-red & long-flg.

L. caprifolium** (goat-leaf honeysuckle, sweet honeysuckle, Italian woodbine): v hardy; to 6m (20ft); deciduous; yellowish-white fls 4–5cm (1½–2in) long.

L. henryi: v hardy; to 9m (30ft); semi-/evergreen; yellow and purplish-red 2.5m (1in) fls.

L. hildebrandiana** **5** (giant honeysuckle): semi-hardy; v vigorous, to 25m (80ft) in good conditions; evergreen oval lvs 8–15cm (3–6in) long; creamy to orange fls 10–15cm (6–8in) long & 5–8cm (2–3in) wide; berries 2.5cm (1in) long.

L. japonica** (Japanese honeysuckle): v hardy; rampant, to 9m (30ft); semi-/evergreen; lvs 8cm (3in) long; fls 2.5–4cm (1–1½in) long, white to yellow. Vars: 'Aureo-reticulata' **6** (less vigorous than sp; bright green lvs netted golden-yellow; often cut back by hard frost); 'Halliana'** (v vigorous).

L. periclymenum** (common European honeysuckle, woodbine): v hardy; vigorous, to 6m (20ft); invasive; deciduous; fls creamy-white and purplish, 4–5cm (1½–2in) long. Vars: 'Belgica'** **7** (early Dutch honeysuckle; more compact; late spring-flg, repeating); 'Serotina'** (late Dutch honeysuckle; similar to 'Belgica' but later-flg, & more vigorous).

L. sempervirens **8** (trumpet honeysuckle): considered hardiest sp in N America (ultra-hardy), but semi- to moderately hardy in British Isles; to 6m (20ft) or more; evergreen or semi-evergreen; 4–5cm (1½–2in) fls, orange-scarlet; larger and brighter in var 'Superba' ('Magnifica').

L.×tellmanniana **9**: hybrid of *L. sempervirens* 'Superba' & *L. tragophylla*; v hardy; to 4.5m (15ft); deciduous; slender 5cm (2in) orange-yellow fls.

L. tragophylla (Chinese woodbine): v hardy; vigorous, to 6m (20ft); deciduous; showy, with bright golden fls 5–9cm (2–3½in) long in large clusters.

The pea family

Generally sun-loving climbers – some very vigorous – grown mainly for their clusters (often racemes) of colourful flowers. These are generally of typical pea shape, with standard & keel petals at top & bottom, wing petals at sides. Many species have attractive pinnate leaves with many leaflets. They vary considerably in vigour and habit, some being rather sprawling but others reaching as much as 30m (100ft). Most are woody, but *Lathyrus* spp are herbaceous. **Cultivation**: Grow in any well-drained soil, in sheltered spots for tender types in marginal areas. Provide support for stems or tendrils. **Pruning**: Cut back *Lathyrus* spp to ground in late autumn. Prune side-shoots of *Wisteria* spp in late winter & shorten leafy growths in summer. Prune others as needed in late winter or after flowering. Dead-heading prolongs flowering. **Propagation**: Seed, nicking coats of hard seeds. Tender species by softwood or semi-ripe cuttings. *Wisteria* spp by semi-ripe cuttings, layering, grafting (very slow to flower from seed). For *Cassia obtusa* (often grown as wall shrub), see p122; for *Dolichos lablab* (grown as annual in warm zones), see p508.

Glory pea (parrot's bill, lobster claw, *Clianthus puniceus* **1**): semi-hardy; sprawling, to 1.8–3.5m (6–12ft); evergreen or semi-evergreen fern-like pinnate lvs; red claw-shaped pea flowers with dark blotches, 10cm (4in) long, in clusters, early summer (white in var 'Albus'). See also *C. formosus* (p122).

Coral peas and their relatives (*Hardenbergia* spp; *Kennedia* spp): tender or semi-hardy Australasian spp; evergreen; make quick cover on trellis or ground.
H. (K.) comptoniana **2**: twining, to 2.5m (8ft); pinnate lvs; 1cm (½in) blue to violet fls, blotched green & white, in 15–20cm (6–8in) spikes, spring.
H. violacea **3**: shrubby climber similar to above, but lvs not divided; fls violet to rose or white, blotched yellow.
K. (H.) ovata: similar to above; lvs pinnate; fls red.

Perennial peas (*Lathyrus* spp): vigorous climbers with leaf tendrils, herbaceous perennial relatives of sweet peas (p508); prefer cool atmosphere, so start early in first year in areas with hot summers, to flower before summer heat; fls freely produced in clusters throughout summer (good for cutting).
L. cirrhosus: v hardy; to 1.5–1.8m (5–6ft); lvs pinnate; fls rose-purple, 2cm (¾in) across.
L. grandiflorus: v hardy; to 1.2–1.8m (4–6ft); fls rose-red, 4cm (1½in) across.
L. latifolius **4** (everlasting pea, perennial pea): ultra-hardy; to 1.8–3m (6–10ft); fls 4cm (1½in) across, rose to purple (white in var 'White Pearl' [*albus*]).
L. rotundifolius (Persian everlasting pea): v hardy; to 1.8m (6ft); creeping rootstock; fresh green round lfts; fls rose-pink, to 2.5cm (1in) across.
L. tuberosus: v hardy; to 1.2–1.5m (4–5ft), or will sprawl over bank; creeping tuberous root (edible); clear pink fls on long stalk.
Kudzu vine (*Pueraria lobata* * **5**, *P. hirsuta*, *P. thunbergiana*): v hardy, but often grown as HHA; sub-shrubby twining climber; v fast-growing &

vigorous, to 20m (65ft) or more in warm areas; to 3–4.5m (10–15ft) as HHA; spreads by underground runners; drought-resistant; large hairy lvs 15cm (6in) long, providing good shade in hot areas; small purple to red fls in 30cm (12in) racemes on established plants, late summer. Good for quick camouflage but may be invasive.

Wisterias (*Wisteria* spp; sometimes wrongly spelled *Wistaria*): beautiful, tall-growing twining climbers with gracefully drooping racemes of pea fls, generally bluish, in late spring; good for walls, pergolas, etc, but need space; can also be trained as free-standing trees; deciduous; lvs pinnate, with up to 19 lfts; seeds poisonous.
*W. floribunda** (*W. multijuga*, Japanese wisteria): v to ultra-hardy; to 9m (30ft); fls violet-blue, in 20–50cm (8–20in) racemes, opening from base with early lvs. Vars: 'Alba' * (white); 'Kuchi Beni' ** (pinkish-white); 'Longissima' * (violet); 'Macrobotrys' ** **6** ('Multijuga'; violet to purple fls in v long racemes, to 1m [3ft] or more); 'Rosea' ** (pink); 'Violacea Plena' * (violet-blue; double).
*W. × formosa***: cross of above with
W. sinensis; v hardy; to 9m (30ft); fls violet-blue to violet-pink in 30cm (12in) racemes, opening all together.
W. sinensis (*W. chinensis*, Chinese wisteria): v hardy; v vigorous, to 20–30m (65–100ft); fls mauve or lilac, freely produced in 20–30cm (8–12in) racemes, opening simultaneously before lvs. Vars: 'Alba' (white); 'Black Dragon' **7** (dark purple; double); 'Jako' ** (white); 'Plena' (mauve; double); 'Prolific' ('Oosthoek's Variety'; v free-flg).
W. venusta **8**: v hardy; to 9m (30ft); large white fls, each 2.5cm (1in) long, in 10–15cm (4–6in) racemes. Var 'Violacea' is violet.

Bougainvilleas

Bougainvillea spp. Among the showiest climbers for areas with a Mediterranean climate, with brilliantly coloured 2.5cm (1in) papery bracts over a long period around inconspicuous flowers; usually red to purple, also white, yellow, orange or rust. Woody; climb vigorously with hooked thorns to 9m (30ft) or more; good for covering walls, pillars, trees, trellis, etc; can be trained as standard or hedge. Deciduous. **Cultivation**: Tender to semi-hardy; prefer dry summers. Any soil in full sun. Provide support and tie in. Prune main shoots and laterals late winter. **Propagation**: Half-ripe cuttings.

B.×buttiana: hybrid of *B. glabra* & *B. peruviana*; bracts crimson or orange, fading purple. Vars: 'Brilliant' **1** (orange, fading cerise); 'Golden Glow' (yellow, fading apricot); 'Kiltie Campbell' (orange); 'Mrs Butt' ('Crimson Lake'; crimson, fading magenta); 'Mrs Helen McClean' (orange). *B. glabra* **2**: long-flg; bracts purple fading magenta. Var 'Sanderana' is bright purple. *B. spectabilis*: v vigorous; bracts 5cm (2in) long, pink, red or purple.

Climbing jasmines

Jasminum spp, also called jessamine. Include some of the most sweetly scented climbers. The small trumpet-shaped flowers are mainly white or yellow. Good for training on walls, pergolas, etc. Woody. Hardy types are pollution-resistant. **Cultivation**: Almost any soil in sun or light shade. Provide support and tie in as necessary. Unless stated, no regular pruning needed, but thin out old growths. Prone to scale insects. **Propagation**: Seed; semi-ripe or hardwood cuttings; layering. For shrubby jasmines and related forsythias, some often grown as semi-climbing wall shrubs, see p140; for the unrelated Chilean jasmine and star jasmine, see p228.

J. beesianum*: moderately to v hardy; vigorous, to 3.5m (12ft); deciduous; rose-pink to red fls 2cm (¾in) long, late spring or early summer. *J. mesnyi* **3** (*J. primulinum*, Japanese jasmine, primrose jasmine): moderately hardy; to 4.5m (15ft); semi-evergreen; semi-double yellow fls 4cm (1½in) long throughout spring. Cut back flg growths hard after flg. *J. officinale*** **4** (common white jasmine, summer jasmine, poet's jessamine): moderately to v hardy; vigorous, to 9m (30ft), but stems weak; deciduous or semi-evergreen; lvs pinnate; white fls 4cm (1½in) long, summer. Vars: 'Affine'** ('Grandiflorum'; fls larger, tinged pink in bud);

'Aureovariegatum'** (lvs variegated creamy-yellow). *J. polyanthum*** **5** (Chinese jasmine): moderately hardy; vigorous, twining to 7.5m (25ft); deciduous or semi-evergreen; lvs pinnate; panicles of white fls, flushed pink, to 2.5cm (1in) long, spring to late summer; can be pruned hard after flg. *J.×stephanense***: hybrid of *J. beesianum* & *J. officinale* 'Affine'; moderately hardy; vigorous, twining to 7.5m (25ft); deciduous or semi-evergreen; lvs often variegated; clusters of pale pink fls 1.5cm (½in) long, early summer.

Passionflowers

Passiflora spp. South American tendrilled woody climbers with unusual short-lived summer flowers 5–10cm (2–4in) across (said to symbolize crucifixion). Colour descriptions below refer first to outer tepals (petals and sepals), then inner fringe-like corona. Most species are rather tender and may be cut down by frost; otherwise evergreen, reaching 4.5–9m (15–30ft). Leaves generally lobed. Some species produce edible fruits (passionfruits or granadillas) in warm areas. **Cultivation**: Any well-drained soil in warm position. Provide support. Water well in summer. Prune frost-damaged and excessive old growths in late winter. Main pest: eelworms. **Propagation**: Semi-ripe cuttings; seed.

P.×allardii: hybrid of *P. caerulea* 'Constance Elliott' & *P. quadrangularis*; semi-hardy; fls white and pink/blue. *P. caerulea* **6** (common blue passionflower): moderately hardy; fls white/blue & purple; frs orange/yellow. Var 'Constance Elliott' is white. *P. edulis* **7** (purple granadilla): semi-hardy; fls white/purple & white; frs yellow to purple. Var

'Crackerjack' is good fruiter. *P.* (*Tacsonia*) *mollissima* **8** (curuba, banana passionfruit): moderately to semi-hardy; fls white & pink, corona small; frs yellowish. *P. quadrangularis** **9** (granadilla): tender to semi-hardy; lvs not lobed; fls white to violet/purple, blue and white; frs yellow.

Clematis species and their varieties

Clematis spp, sometimes called the virgin's bower. Among the most popular genera of climbers, but wild species and their close varieties are less well known (but easier to establish and usually more vigorous) than large-flowered hybrids (p238). Flowers less showy, mostly single, cup- or bell-shaped; cuttable. All are woody climbers with twining petioles, good for trellis, pergolas, stumps, etc. Deciduous unless stated. **Cultivation**: Unless stated, very hardy. Like alkaline soil with cool roots (protect with paving, ground cover or mulch) but top growth in sun (less vigorous types may need some shade). Provide support. Mulch annually. Not so prone to wilt as hybrids. **Pruning**: Unnecessary for early and mid-season types, but may be cut back after flowering; late types flower on new wood, so may be cut back hard in late winter. **Propagation**: Half-ripe cuttings (internodal preferred in UK, nodal in US); layering; spp by seed.

Very early sp: late winter- to spring-flg.
C. cirrhosa: to 6m (20ft); fern-like evergreen lvs; white bell-shaped fls to 5cm (2in) wide; silken seed-heads. Var *balearica* **1** (*C. calycina*) is moderately hardy & less vigorous; fls greenish-yellow, spotted purple.

Early spp: spring-flg.
C. (*Atragene*) *alpina*: to 2.5m (8ft); 2.5–4cm (1–1½in) bell-like violet-blue fls with whitish stamens; silky seed-heads. Vars: 'Columbine' (lavender-blue; pointed sepals); 'Frances Rivis' **2** ('Blue Giant'; v large fls); 'Pamela Jackman', (dark blue); 'Ruby' (rosy-red); 'Sibirica' ('Alba'; whitish); 'White Moth', (white; double).
C. armandii **3**: moderately hardy; to 6–9m (20–30ft); lvs evergreen, glossy; white fls 5cm (2in) across. Vars: 'Apple Blossom' * (pink & white); 'Snow Drift' * (white).

Mid-season spp: late spring- to summer-flg.
C. chrysocoma: moderately hardy; to 3m (10ft); downy lvs & shoots; pale pink 5cm (2in) fls. Var *sericea* (*C. spooneri*) is hardier; to 6m (20ft); fls white, to 8cm (3in) across.
C. macropetala: to 2.5–3.5m (8–12ft); violet-blue 5–8cm (2–3in) semi-double fls; silky seed-heads. Vars: 'Lagoon' (deep lavender); 'Maidwell Hall' (deep blue); 'Markham's Pink' **4** ('Markhamii'; rose-pink).
C. montana *: v easy; to 12m (40ft); profuse white 5–6cm (2–2½in) fls. Vars: 'Elizabeth' * (pink); 'Rubens' * **5** (rosy-pink); 'Tetra-rose' * (v vigorous; lilac-pink fls to 8cm [3in] wide); 'Wilsonii' (white; late-flg).

Late spp: summer- to autumn-flg.
C. fargesii souliei (correctly, *C. potaninii fargesii*): to 6m (20ft); 5cm (2in) pure white fls; feathery seed-heads.
C. flammula *: moderately to v hardy; to 3m (10ft); panicles of pure white fls to 2.5cm (1in) across; silky seed-heads. Var 'Rubro-marginata' * (sometimes listed as *C.×violacea* 'Rubro-marginata') has white fls fringed violet-red.
C. florida: moderately to v hardy; to 1.8–2.5m (6–8ft); sometimes semi-evergreen; creamy-white 6–8cm (2½–3in) fls with greenish stripes on reverse. Var 'Sieboldii' **6** ('Bicolor') has

semi-double 8cm (3in) white fls centred purple.
C.×jouiniana: hybrid of *C. heracleifolia davidiana* & *C. vitalba*; vigorous, to 3.5m (12ft) or more; non-twining, so tie in; panicles of 2.5cm (1in) lilac-tinted white fls. Good for ground cover.
C. maximowicziana * (*C. dioscoreifolia robusta*, sweet autumn clematis; for long known incorrectly as *C. paniculata*): v vigorous, to 6–9m (20–30ft); semi-evergreen; white fls to 3cm (1¼in) across, v profuse where summers hot; silvery seed-heads. (True *C. paniculata* is better known as *C. indivisa*, a semi-hardy New Zealand sp; evergreen [lvs lobed in var 'Lobata']; panicles of 8cm [3in] white fls; feathery seed-heads.)
C. orientalis **7**: to 6m (20ft); hanging bell-shaped fls, 2.5–5cm (1–2in) across, with thick orange-yellow sepals like orange peel; silky seed-heads.
C. rehderana * **8** (*C. nutans*): moderately to v hardy; to 7.5m (25ft); lvs pinnate, silky beneath; erect panicles of nodding 2cm (¾in) bell-shaped primrose-yellow fls.
C. tangutica **9**: to 3m (10ft); lvs singly or doubly pinnate; bright yellow lantern-shaped fls 5cm (2in) long, deep yellow in var 'Gravetye'; fluffy seed-heads.
C. texensis: to 1.8–3.5m (6–12ft); lvs glaucous, pinnate; brilliant scarlet urn-shaped fls, 2.5cm (1in) long, with leathery sepals. May die to ground in winter. Vars: 'Duchess of Albany' (pink); 'Etoile Rose' **10** (cerise-pink with silver margins); 'Gravetye Beauty' (crimson-red); 'Sir Trevor Lawrence' (carmine).
C. viticella: to 3.5m (12ft); lvs singly or doubly pinnate; profuse 4cm (1½in) violet, reddish-purple or blue fls. Vars: 'Abundance' (light wine-red, deep red veins); 'Alba Luxurians' (creamy-white, tinted mauve and tipped green); 'Kermesina' (crimson or wine-red); 'Minuet', **11** (large creamy-white fls, edged purple); 'Purpurea Plena Elegans' **12** ('Elegans Plena'; violet-purple; double); 'Royal Velours' (velvety-purple); 'Rubra' (wine-red; vigorous).

Large-flowered hybrid clematis

Derived from various *Clematis* spp. Generally longer-flowering and showier than species clematis (p236) but less vigorous – 2.5–4.5m (8–15ft) unless stated. Flowers mainly single, opening flat, 10–15cm (4–6in) to 20–25cm (8–10in) across; descriptions below refer to flowers. Flowering season and habit (hence pruning) vary. Deciduous; leaves entire or pinnate. **Cultivation**: As for species, but often more difficult to establish; prone to clematis wilt (sudden collapse; cut back and drench with fungicide). Unless stated, very hardy. **Propagation**: Half-ripe cuttings (internodal preferred in UK, nodal in US); layering; grafting on to rootstock of *C. flammula*, *C. vitalba* or *C. viticella*.

Early vars: fl from late spring or early summer, may repeat late summer or autumn. Pruning not essential but best pruned lightly to strong buds in late winter.

C. 'Alice Fisk': low-growing; wisteria-blue.

C. 'Barbara Dibley' **1**: petunia-red, barred.

C. 'Barbara Jackman': mauve, barred crimson.

C. 'Bee's Jubilee': mauve-pink, barred carmine.

C. 'Belle of Woking': silvery-mauve; double.

C. 'Charissima': pink, centred & barred maroon.

C. 'Countess of Lovelace' **2**: lilac-blue; first flush double.

C. 'Daniel Deronda': violet-blue; first flush semi-double.

C. 'Duchess of Edinburgh': white; double; small.

C. 'Edo Muraski' ('Bluebird'): deep violet.

C. 'Herbert Johnson': reddish-mauve.

C. 'H. F. Young': Wedgwood-blue.

C. 'Kathleen Dunford': rosy-purple; first flush semi-double.

C. 'Kathleen Wheeler': rosy-mauve; large.

C. 'Lasurstern': deep blue; wavy sepals.

C. 'Lincoln Star': bright pink, paler edges.

C. 'Lord Nevill': purplish-blue; wavy edges.

C. 'Marcel Moser': rosy-mauve, barred carmine.

C. 'Miss Bateman': creamy-white; small.

C. 'Mrs N. Thompson' **3**: low-growing; violet, barred scarlet; small.

C. 'Mrs Spencer Castle': bluish-pink; first flush semi-double.

C. 'Nelly Moser': pale pink, barred carmine.

C. 'Proteus': rosy-lilac; first flush double.

C. 'P. T. James': deep blue; semi-double.

C. 'Richard Pennell': rosy-mauve; wavy sepals.

C. 'Susan Allsop': rosy-purple, magenta bars.

C. 'The President': deep purple-blue, pale bars.

C. 'Violet Elizabeth': mauve-pink; first flush double.

C. 'Vyvyan Pennell' **4**: violet-blue, tinged red; first flush double.

C. 'Walter Pennell': deep pink, tinged mauve; first flush double.

Late vars: fl from mid summer, on new wood; fls generally smaller than early vars; vars marked † may have some larger early fls if pruned lightly; otherwise prune hard to 1m (3ft) late winter.

C. 'Ascotiensis': bright lavender-blue.

C. 'Comtesse de Bouchaud': pinkish-mauve.

C. 'Ernest Markham'†: petunia-red; v late.

C. 'Etoile Violette': vigorous; deep purple; small.

C. 'Gipsy Queen'†: vigorous; violet-purple; v late.

C. 'Hagley Hybrid': low-growing; shell-pink.

C. 'Huldine': vigorous; white, mauve reverse; small.

C. 'Jackmanii Alba'†: vigorous; white; first flush sometimes double, bluish-white.

C. 'Jackmanii Rubra'†: vigorous; crimson; first flush sometimes double.

C. 'Jackmanii Superba' **5**: vigorous; purple.

C. 'Lady Betty Balfour': vigorous; violet-blue; v late.

C. 'Mme Edouard André': low-growing; wine-red.

C. 'Mme Julia Correvon': wine-red; small.

C. 'Margaret Hunt' **6**: vigorous; mauve-pink.

C. 'Margot Koster': mauve-pink; small.

C. 'Niobe': low-growing; dark ruby-red.

C. 'Perle d'Azur' **7**: sky-blue; nodding.

C. 'Pink Fantasy': shell-pink, darker bars.

C. 'Rouge Cardinal': crimson.

C. 'Star of India': vigorous; reddish-purple, barred red.

C. 'Tillicum': pale blue; v large.

C. 'Twilight': petunia-mauve.

C. 'Venosa Violacea': bipinnate lvs; violet-blue, white veins.

C. 'Victoria': rosy-purple, barred.

C. 'Ville de Lyon' **8**: carmine, edged crimson; v late.

Dual-purpose vars: equally good early- or late-flg, depending on pruning; if pruned lightly, large early fls on old wood, then smaller fls on new wood later; if pruned hard, big display from mid summer on new wood only.

C. 'Elsa Späth' ('Xerxes'): lavender-blue.

C. 'General Sikorski': vigorous; mid-blue.

C. 'Henryi': creamy-white.

C. 'Lady Caroline Nevill': lavender, barred darker; first flush may be semi-double.

C. 'Lady Northcliffe': low-growing; deep Wedgwood-blue.

C. 'Marie Boisselot' **9** ('Mme le Coultre'): white.

C. 'Mrs Cholmondeley': lavender-blue.

C. 'Ramona' ('Hybrida Sieboldii'): lavender-blue.

C. 'Sealand Gem': rosy-mauve, barred carmine.

C. 'Silver Moon': silvery-grey.

C. 'W. E. Gladstone': lavender-blue; large.

C. 'William Kennett': vigorous; lavender-blue, reddish bars; wavy edges.

Rambler roses

New classification: Climbing roses, non-recurrent (though some have a second minor flush). *Rosa* spp & vars, many derived from *R. wichuraiana*. Woody, with thin, pliable canes that scramble with hooked thorns. Used also for making weeping standards when budded on tall stems. Leaves usually small & glossy, pinnate, deciduous. Generally flower mid summer only (a few vars earlier), best on year-old shoots from base. Blooms mainly small, to 4cm (1½in) across, in clusters or trusses; single unless stated. **Cultivation**: Except where stated, moderately to very hardy. Prepare soil well; feed regularly. Rather prone to rose diseases (especially mildew), so best grown where air can circulate freely (not against wall or solid fence). Provide support & tie in canes (easy to train). Vigorous types good for climbing into large, strong trees. Some good for ground cover; peg down canes to promote rooting. **Pruning**: Generally, cut out all or most old canes to near ground immediately after flowering. Thin out old wood of early-flowering vars to where new laterals have sprouted & shorten weaker laterals to 5–8cm (2–3in). Little pruning needed for vigorous tree-climbers except occasional removal of old wood. **Propagation**: Hardwood cuttings; layering.

R. 'Aimée Vibert'* ('Bouquet de la Mariée', 'nivea'): to 4.5m (15ft); medium-large white double fls in small clusters; recurrent.

R. 'Albéric Barbier'**: vigorous, to 7.5m (25ft); large pale yellow double fls fading cream.

R. 'Albertine'** **1**: vigorous, to 6m (20ft) or more; large coppery-pink double fls; v prone to mildew; good on arch or pergola.

R. 'Alister Stella Gray'** ('Golden Rambler'): to 4.5m (15ft); pale yellow, fading white; recurrent.

R. 'American Pillar': to 6m (20ft); large fls, carmine-pink with white eye, in large trusses.

R. 'Bobbie James'**: vigorous, to 7.5m (25ft); semi-double creamy-white fls in large trusses.

R. brunonii 'La Mortola' ** (a Himalayan musk rose var): moderately hardy; v vigorous, to 9m (30ft) or more; creamy-white fls in large trusses; red hips.

R. 'Crimson Shower' **2**: to 3m (10ft); crimson pompon fls in large trusses, late.

R. 'Dr W. van Fleet'*: to 4.5m (15ft); early-flg; large pale pink double fls fading lighter, mainly on old wood; prune lightly.

R. 'Dorothy Perkins': to 4.5m (15ft); double rose-pink fls in large clusters; prone to mildew.

R. 'Easlea's Golden Rambler'*: to 3.5m (12ft); large, deep creamy-yellow semi-double fls, singly & in clusters.

R. 'Emily Gray' **3**: moderately hardy; to 4.5m (15ft); lvs bronze-tinted, almost evergreen; fls double, buff-yellow.

R. 'Excelsa' ('Red Dorothy Perkins'): to 5.5m (18ft); rose-red to crimson double fls in large clusters.

R. 'Félicité et Perpétue'* **4**: to 4.5m (15ft); almost evergreen; white pompon fls; prune lightly.

R. filipes 'Kiftsgate'**: v vigorous, to 9m (30ft) or more; huge corymbs of creamy-white small fls; small red hips.

R. 'François Juranville'*: vigorous, to 7.5m (25ft); large double salmon-pink fls (may recur).

R. 'Goldfinch'**: to 4.5m (15ft); button-like semi-double pale yellow fls, fading white.

R. 'Hiawatha': to 6m (20ft); crimson, white centre. Good for ground cover.

R. 'Jersey Beauty'*: to 5.5m (18ft); buff-yellow fading cream; may repeat.

*R. longicuspis*** **5**: moderately hardy; vigorous, to 6m (20ft); white fls in large corymbs; small red hips.

R. 'Max Graf'* **6**: trailing Rugosa, best for ground cover; bright pink, paler centre.

R. 'May Queen'**: to 4.5m (15ft); large double pink fls, flushed lilac (may repeat); v healthy.

R. 'Paul's Himalayan Musk Rambler'**: moderately hardy; v vigorous, to 9–12m (30–40ft); lilac-white.

R. 'Purity': vigorous, to 9m (30ft); semi-double, white.

R. 'Rambling Rector'*: vigorous, to 6m (20ft); semi-double, white.

R. 'Ramona'* **7** ('Red Cherokee'): semi-hardy; to 4.5m (15ft); early crimson clematis-like fls.

R. 'Rose-Marie Viaud': to 4.5m (15ft); few thorns; semi-double, amethyst to violet; prone to mildew.

R. 'Sander's White Rambler'*: to 4.5m (15ft); white rosette fls in large clusters; v healthy.

R. 'Seven Sisters' (*R. multiflora* 'Platyphylla' ['Grevillei']): moderately hardy; rampant, to 9m (30ft); largish fls, supposedly in seven shades from crimson to lilac-white; mildew likely.

R. 'Silver Moon'** **8**: vigorous, to 6m (20ft) or more; large single/semi-double creamy-white fls.

R. 'Temple Bells': whitish, sometimes tinged pink; best for ground cover.

R. 'The Garland'** ('Wood's Garland'): to 3m (10ft); semi-double pink fls, fading white, in large clusters.

R. 'Veilchenblau'** **9** ('Violet Blue'): to 4.5m (15ft); semi-double, violet-blue, white centre.

R. 'Violette': to 4.5m (15ft); few thorns; semi-double crimson-purple fls in large clusters.

R. 'Wedding Day'** **10**: v vigorous, to 6m (20ft) or more; creamy to white star-like fls, flushed & spotted pink, in large clusters.

R. 'White Dorothy' ('White Dorothy Perkins'): to 4.5m (15ft); double white fls in large clusters; prone to mildew.

Climbing roses

New classification: Climbing roses, recurrent & non-recurrent (former unless stated). *Rosa* spp & vars, mostly hybrids of complex parentage. Scrambling shrubs with hooked thorns. Differ from Rambler roses (p240) in having a permanent framework of (generally stiff) stems with lateral flowering shoots; little or no new growth from base. Generally less vigorous than many Ramblers, some making shrubs if pruned hard. (Low-growing types often termed pillar roses.) Leaves larger, pinnate; generally deciduous. Flowers generally large, solitary or in small clusters, from late spring or early summer often until autumn; unless stated, double & 8–10cm (3–4in) across. Good for walls, fences, pergolas, etc, in sun.
Cultivation: Generally moderately to very hardy. Prepare soil well; feed regularly. Provide supporting wires or trellis & tie in. Train main stems horizontally (spirally around pillars) to encourage flowering laterals. **Pruning**: None first year. Dead-head regularly. Prune laterals to two or three buds from stem in autumn or winter. Remove very old, weak or damaged wood but otherwise leave main stems.
Propagation: Hardwood cuttings; budding.

True climbers: not climbing sports of bush roses.
R. 'Allen Chandler' **1**: v vigorous, to 6m (20ft); large semi-double velvety-crimson fls, early.
R. 'Aloha'** **2**: to 3m (10ft), less as shrub; pink fls on long stems.
R. 'Altissimo': sturdy, to 3.5m (12ft), less as shrub; large single fls, deep red shaded crimson.
R. 'America'**: to 3m (10ft); large peachy-apricot fls; almost perpetual-flg.
R. 'Aurora': vigorous, to 4.5m (15ft); large orange-yellow fls.
*R. banksiae lutea** (yellow Banksian rose): semi- to moderately hardy; vigorous, to 7.5m (25ft); semi-evergreen; v small yellow fls in large sprays; non-recurrent; prune minimally.
R. 'Bantry Bay' **3**: to 3m (10ft); fls semi-double, pink.
R. 'Céline Forestier'**: semi-hardy; to 4.5m (15ft); small pale orange-yellow fls in clusters.
R. 'Compassion'** **4**: to 2.5m (8ft); pale orange-salmon fls, paler on outside; v healthy.
R. 'Copenhagen'**: to 3m (10ft); lvs coppery-tinged; fls scarlet, large and v double.
R. 'Coral Dawn'*: to 3m (10ft); large deep coral-pink fls, pale pink at edges; perpetual-flg.
R. 'Danse du Feu'* **5** ('Spectacular'): v hardy; to 3m (10ft); scarlet semi-double fls; early.
R. 'Don Juan'***: to 3m (10ft); large, dark velvety-red fls.
R. 'Dortmund'* **6**: v hardy; to 3m (10ft); large single fls, crimson-red with white eye, in large. clusters; v healthy.
R. 'Elegance'*: vigorous, to 4.5m (15ft); large pale yellow fls, fading cream at edges; prone to mildew.
R. 'Galway Bay': to 2.5m (8ft); profuse large salmon-pink fls; good for pillars.
*R. gigantea**: semi- to moderately hardy; v vigorous, to 9m (30ft) or more; red-tinted lvs; v large lemon-white single fls; non-recurrent.
R. 'Gloire de Dijon'** **7**: good strains vigorous, to 4.5m (15ft); buff-yellow fls all summer.
R. 'Golden Showers'*: to 3m (10ft), less as shrub in cold areas; almost thornless; large golden-yellow early fls, opening loosely; v healthy.
R. 'Grand Hotel': to 2.5m (8ft); fls bright scarlet, opening cupped.
R. 'Guinée'**: to 6m (20ft); large dark maroon-crimson early fls; not v recurrent; prone to mildew.
R. 'Hamburger Phoenix': v hardy; to 3m (10ft); semi-double dark crimson fls; v healthy.
R. 'Handel' **8**: to 4.5m (15ft); coppery-tinged lvs; cupped fls, cream flushed pink at edges.
R. 'Highfield'**: to 3m (10ft); primrose-yellow fls; v healthy.
R. 'Joseph's Coat' **9**: to 3m (10ft), less as shrub; trusses of semi-double fls, yellow & orange flushed red at edges. Good on pillar.
R. 'Karlsruhe': v hardy; to 4.5m (15ft); fls deep rose-pink.
R. 'Lawrence Johnston'* ('Hidcote Yellow'): vigorous, to 6m (20ft), or 3m (10ft) as shrub; semi-double bright yellow fls; not v recurrent; needs shelter.
R. 'Leverkusen': v hardy; to 2.5m (8ft); pale yellow fls in large clusters.
R. 'Mme Alfred Carrière'** **10**: v vigorous, to 7.5m (25ft); large cupped fls, white tinted pink; needs full sun.
R. 'Mme Grégoire Staechelin'* ('Spanish Beauty'): vigorous, to 6m (20ft); v early large pink fls, darker on reverse; non-recurrent; occasionally prune old stems hard.
R. 'Maigold'**: v hardy; to 3m (10ft); v thorny; semi-double bronze-yellow fls; non-recurrent.
R. 'Maréchal Niel'**: semi-hardy; to 4.5m (15ft); large golden drooping fls.
R. 'Mermaid' **11**: moderately hardy; v vigorous once established, to 9m (30ft); semi-evergreen; large thorns; v large single sulphur-yellow nearly sterile fls, little or no pruning.
R. 'New Dawn'* ('The New Dawn', 'Everblooming Dr W. van Fleet'): to 6m (20ft), less if pruned as shrub; blush-pink fls; perpetual-flg.
R. 'Nozomi' **1**, p245: climbing Miniature, to 1.2m (4ft), or for ground cover; small pointed lvs; small

single fls, pink fading white, in trusses.

R. 'Parade'*: to 3.5m (12ft); reddish-tinted lvs; deep carmine fls.

R. 'Parkdirektor Riggers': v hardy; semi-double glowing crimson fls in large trusses; perpetual-flg; may be prone to mildew and black spot.

R. 'Paul's Scarlet Climber': to 3–4.5m (10–15ft); semi-double bright crimson fls; non-recurrent; sometimes classed as Rambler.

R. 'Pink Cameo' ('Climbing Cameo'): climbing Miniature; to 1.5m (5ft); small glossy lvs; v small rich rose-pink fls.

R. 'Pink Perpétue'* 2: to 3.5m (12ft); pink fls, carmine reverse; v recurrent.

R. 'Royal Flush'*: vigorous, to 4.5m (15ft); semi-double cream fls edged pink.

R. 'Royal Gold'* 3: to 2.5m (8ft); deep yellow fls.

R. 'Schoolgirl' 4: to 4.5m (15ft); large apricot-orange fls.

R. 'Swan Lake' 5 ('Schwanensee'): to 3m (10ft); large white fls tinged pink.

R. 'Sympathie'*: to 3.5m (12ft); velvety-red fls.

R. 'White Cockade'*: to 2.5m (8ft); white fls.

R. 'Zéphirine Drouhin'** 6: climbing Bourbon; v hardy; vigorous, to 4.5m (15ft), less as shrub; almost thornless; young lvs coppery; loose cerise-pink fls, repeating autumn; prone to mildew & black spot.

Climbing sports of bush roses: have prefix 'Climbing' (abbreviated 'Cl'); generally similar to parent (see pp156–166) except for habit & often poor fl repeat; generally moderately hardy.

R. 'Cl Blessings'*: Hybrid Tea; to 6m (20ft); soft coral-pink fls.

R. 'Cl Cécile Brunner'* ('Cl Sweetheart Rose'): Tea-Polyantha; vigorous, to 6m (20ft); small pink fls in sprays.

R. 'Cl Etoile de Hollande'**: Hybrid Tea; to 1.8m (6ft); large dusky-red fls; prone to mildew.

R. 'Cl Iceberg'*: Floribunda; to 2.5–3m (8–10ft); trusses of white fls.

R. 'Cl Lady Hillingdon'**: Tea; semi- to moderately hardy; vigorous, to 6m (20ft); coppery lvs; orange-yellow fls.

R. 'Cl Mme Caroline Testout'**: Hybrid Tea; to 2.5m (8ft); large globular fls, silvery-pink shaded carmine.

R. 'Cl Masquerade': Floribunda; to 2.5m (8ft); semi-double red, pink & yellow fls in trusses; not v recurrent.

R. 'Cl Pompon de Paris' (sometimes sold as 'Cl Rouletii'): Miniature; to 2.5m (8ft); v small bright pink fls; not v recurrent.

R. 'Cl Shot Silk'**: Hybrid Tea; to 3.5m (12ft); cherry-pink fls shading to orange-yellow.

Climbing hydrangeas and their relatives

Sometimes classified as Hydrangeaceae. Decorative self-clinging woody climbers with aerial roots and inflorescences of small white or creamy-white flowers, mainly in early summer. Most withstand pollution and grow well in sun or semi-shade. Good for walls or old trees or tree-trunks; will make ground cover if no support. **Cultivation**: For any fertile soil but preferably moist loam. No pruning needed except to cut out weak or dead growths in late winter; dead-head. **Propagation**: Semi-ripe cuttings; seed.

Decumarias (*Decumaria* spp): moderately to v hardy.

D. barbara*: to 9m (30ft); deciduous or semi-evergreen; glossy lvs; fls in corymbs 10cm (4in) across.

D. sinensis** 7: to 5m (16ft); evergreen; matt lvs; fls in corymbs, profuse.

Climbing hydrangeas (*Hydrangea* spp): v pollution-tolerant.

H. anomala (*H. altissima*): moderately to v hardy; vigorous, to 12m (40ft) or more; deciduous; lvs coarsely toothed, 12cm (5in) long; fls in flattish corymbs, 15–20cm (6–8in) across.

H. anomala petiolaris 8 (*H. petiolaris*, *H. scandens*, common or Japanese climbing hydrangea): v hardy; strong-growing when established, to 20–25m (65–80ft); also grown as shrub; deciduous; lvs finely toothed, 5–10cm (2–4in) long; fls in flat corymbs 18–25cm (7–10in) across.

H. integerrima (correctly, *H. serratifolia*): moderately to v hardy; to 6m (20ft); evergreen;

lvs dark green, leathery; fls in domed panicles 5–8cm (2–3in) across.

Pileostegia (*Pileostegia viburnoides* 9): moderately hardy; rather slow-growing, to 7.5m (25ft); evergreen; lvs leathery, 8–15cm (3–6in) long; fls in panicles 10–15cm (4–6in) wide in late summer. Likes full sun.

Schizophragmas (*Schizophragma* spp): all slow-growing at first; deciduous; similar to hydrangeas, but fls in large flat cymes, each with several creamy bracts; may be propagated by layering.

S. hydrangeoides (in US, Japanese hydrangea vine): v hardy; to 12m (40ft); lvs coarsely toothed; infls 20–25cm (8–10in) across; bracts 2.5–4cm (1–1½in) long. Var 'Roseum' has pink-flushed bracts. Sometimes confused with *Hydrangea anomala petiolaris*.

S. integrifolium 10: moderately to v hardy; to 6m (20ft); lvs with no or small teeth; infls to 30cm (12in) across; bracts 6–10cm (2½–4in) long.

The potato family

Rather tender woody climbers for warm walls in mild climates, grown for their trumpet- or star-shaped flowers followed by berry-like fruits. Evergreen or semi-evergreen, but may be cut to ground by frost.
Cultivation: Any well-drained soil. Provide support and tie in as necessary. Prune in late winter.
Propagation: Half-ripe cuttings; layering.

Chalice vines (*Solandra* spp): tender; lvs leathery, 15cm (6in) long; apricot-scented trumpet- or chalice-shaped fls, spring.
S. grandiflora*: to 9m (30ft); fls cream, fading brownish, 10–15cm (4–6in) long.
S. maxima* **1** (*S. nitida, S. hartwegii*, cup of gold): to 3.5–4.5m (12–15ft); bushy; fls yellow, purple markings, 20–25cm (8–10in) long.
Potato vines (*Solanum* spp): fls star-shaped, from mid or late summer.
S. crispum **2** (Chilean potato tree): moderately hardy; to 4.5–6m (15–20ft); herbaceous in cold areas; lvs glossy, 10cm (4in) long; corymbs of

purple-blue fls 2.5cm (1in) across, yellow stamens. Var 'Glasnevin' ('Autumnale') is slightly hardier & freer-flg.
S. jasminoides **3** (jasmine nightshade, potato vine): semi-hardy; twining, to 3–4.5m (10–15ft) or more if warm; lvs glossy, 5cm (2in) long; fls pale blue with yellow stamens, 2–2.5cm (¾–1in) across, in cymes. Vars: 'Album' (white); 'Grandiflorum' (larger infls).
S. wendlandii **4** (giant potato vine): tender; to 15m (50ft); prickly stems; glossy lvs 10–25cm (4–10in) long; lilac-blue fls 5–6cm (2–2½in) across in hanging clusters; large frs.

Grape vines and their relatives

Some confusion and name changes between genera *Ampelopsis, Cissus, Parthenocissus* and *Vitis*. Mainly sun-loving tendrilled (some self-clinging) woody climbers grown for their foliage and/or attractive (sometimes edible) fruits. Some have intense autumn leaf colours. Flowers insignificant. Strong-growing; good for covering walls, fences, old trees, stumps, etc. **Cultivation**: For any well-drained soil, preferably not acid. Provide support. Many species prone to mildew, other fungal diseases and various insect pests. **Pruning**: As necessary in autumn or early spring; special method for grape production. **Propagation**: Seed; semi-ripe or hardwood cuttings; layering. *Vitis* spp by eye cuttings of ripe dormant wood; *V. coignetiae* by layering.

Ampelopsis (*Ampelopsis* spp): v hardy, but attractive pea-size frs produced only if hot summer and mild autumn; deciduous.
A. aconitifolia (may be sold as *V. vinifera* 'Ciotat'): to 10m (33ft); lvs delicate, palmate or pinnate, 10–12cm (4–5in) across; frs orange or yellow.
A. brevipedunculata **5** (*A. heterophylla*): vigorous, to 20m (65ft); 3/5-lobed lvs 5–15cm (2–6in) across; porcelain-blue frs. Var 'Elegans' is less vigorous; lvs variegated.
Grape ivies (*Cissus* spp): evergreen or semi-evergreen; glossy lvs.
C. antarctica (kangaroo vine): tender; vigorous, to 4.5–6m (15–20ft); lvs 8–10cm (4–5in) long.
C. striata (*A. sempervirens*, miniature grape ivy): semi-hardy; to 3.5m (12ft); lvs of 4/5 lfts, each 2.5cm (1in) long; purplish frs in hot climates.
Boston ivy and Virginia creepers
(*Parthenocissus* spp): most spp self-clinging; deciduous, with rich autumn colours; small frs if summers hot.
P. henryana **6** (Chinese Virginia creeper): moderately to v hardy; to 7.5–9m (25–30ft); lvs of 3/5 lfts, each 6cm (2½in) long, white veins.
P. himalayana (*V. semicordata*, Himalayan Virginia creeper): moderately hardy; to 7.5–9m (25–30ft); lvs of 3 lfts, each 5–15cm (2–6in) long.

P. inserta (*P. vitacea*): ultra-hardy; not self-clinging; vigorous, to 12m (40ft); lvs of 5 glossy lfts, each 15cm (6in) long.
P. quinquefolia **7** (*V. hederacea*, true Virginia creeper): ultra-hardy; v vigorous, to 20m (70ft); lvs of 5 lfts, each 5–12cm (2–5in) long.
P. tricuspidata **8** (*V. inconstans*, Boston ivy, Japanese ivy; incorrectly, Virginia creeper): v hardy; v vigorous, to 15m (50ft); lvs variable, to 20cm (8in) long. Var 'Veitchii' (*A. veitchii, V. inconstans* 'Purpurea') has smaller lvs.
Grape vines (*Vitis* spp): deciduous, often colouring in autumn; frs best if summers hot.
V. amurensis (Amur grape): v hardy; vigorous, to 15m (50ft); lvs lobed, 10–25cm (4–10in) across, colouring; small black frs.
V. coignetiae **9** (crimson glory vine): v hardy; spectacular, to 25m (80ft); rounded/lobed lvs to 30cm (12in) across, colour well; black sour frs.
V. labrusca (fox grape, skunk grape): v hardy; vigorous, to 6m (25ft) or more; lvs variable, 8–20cm (3–8in) across, colouring; sweet, musky amber to black frs.
V. riparia* (*V. odoratissima*, riverbank grape; incorrectly, *V. vulpina*): ultra-hardy; to 3.5m (12ft); lvs lobed, 8–20cm (3–8in) across, colouring; yellow-green fls; purple-black acid frs.

V. vinifera (wine grape): v hardy; vigorous, to 15m (50ft) unless pruned hard; lvs lobed, 10–22cm (4–9in) across; frs variable, green to black. Decorative vars: 'Apiifolia' ('Laciniosa', parsley vine; deeply cut lvs); 'Brant' **10**, p247 ('Brandt';

hybrid with *V. riparia*; lvs deeply lobed, colouring well; sweet black frs); 'Incana' (dusty miller grape; lvs downy-white; frs reddish-purple); 'Purpurea' (teinturier grape; lvs red, turning purple; frs black).

Miscellaneous climbers

Listed alphabetically by family name. Unless stated, all woody, need support & for almost any soil. For annual climbers, including perennials normally treated thus, see p486–526. **Propagation**: See below.

Clock vine (*Thunbergia grandiflora* **1**; Acanthaceae): semi-hardy; vigorous, to 6m (20ft) or more; twining; evergreen lvs to 20cm (8in) long; purplish-blue trumpet fls 6–8cm (2½–3in) across, spring and summer. For sun; prune lightly after flg. Propagate by seed (can be grown as HHA), softwood cuttings.
Actinidias (*Actinidia* spp; Actinidiaceae): twining; grown for lvs (deciduous), early summer fls & edible frs (if male & female planted). Propagate by seed, semi-ripe cuttings.
A. arguta: v hardy; vigorous, to 15m (50ft); toothed 8–12cm (3–5in) lvs; white fls 2cm (¾in) across; frs 2.5cm (1in) long, insipid. Var *cordifolia* has heart-shaped lvs.
*A. chinensis** **2** (Chinese gooseberry, Kiwi fruit): moderately hardy; vigorous, to 9m (30ft); heart-shaped lvs to 20cm (8in) long; creamy-white fls 4cm (1½in) across; hairy frs 5cm (2in) long.
A. kolomikta **3** (Kolomikta vine): v hardy; to 6m (20ft); heart-shaped 12cm (5in) lvs, variegated white & pink at tips (best in full sun); small white fls; 2.5cm (1in) sweet frs.
Aristolochias (*Aristolochia* spp; Aristolochiaceae): twining; grown as screen; curious funnel-shaped curved fls in early summer; pollution-tolerant. Propagate by semi-ripe cuttings, layering, seed.
A. altissima (*A. sempervirens*): semi-hardy; root moderately hardy; to 5.5m (18ft); evergreen unless cut down by frost; lvs 5–10cm (2–4in) long; fls 4cm (1½in) long, yellowish-brown, dark stripes.
A. durior **4** (*A. macrophylla*, *A. sipho*, Dutchman's pipe): v hardy; v vigorous, to 9m (30ft); deciduous; lvs heart-shaped, to 30cm (1ft) long; fls 2.5cm (1in) long, yellow, brown & green.
Codonopsis (*Codonopsis convolvulacea* **5**; Campanulaceae): v hardy herbaceous twiner; to 1.8m (6ft); pale green lvs to 8cm (3in) long; bell-shaped to starry lavender-blue fls to 5cm (2in) wide, summer. Best in cool partial shade. Propagate by seed, basal cuttings. *C. vinciflora* is similar or same sp; fls narrower.
Hop (*Humulus lupulus*; Cannabaceae): v to ultra-hardy herbaceous twiner; fast-growing, to 3–6m (10–20ft), making good summer screen; lvs 8–15cm (3–6in) long, lobed (yellow in var

'Aureus' **6**); fls have greenish bracts. Propagate by seed, root cuttings.
Climbing bittersweets (*Celastrus* spp; Celastraceae): vigorous; twining; deciduous; fls insignificant, but showy red seeds on females. Main pest: scale insects. Propagate by semi-ripe or hardwood cuttings, layering, root cuttings, seed.
C. hypoleucus (*C. hypoglaucus*): moderately hardy; to 6m (20ft); lvs to 15cm (6in) long, glaucous beneath.
C. orbiculatus **7** (*C. articulatus*, oriental bittersweet): v hardy; to 9–12m (30–40ft); lvs to 10cm (4in) long, yellow in autumn.
C. scandens (American or false bittersweet, staff vine): ultra-hardy; to 6m (20ft); may choke young tree; lvs to 10cm (4in) long, may be poisonous.
Climbing gazanias (*Mutisia* spp; Compositae): semi- to moderately hardy, but thrive only in hot summers; tendrilled; evergreen; gazania-like daisy fls. For well-drained soil. Propagate by seed, softwood cuttings.
M. decurrens: to 3m (10ft); fls yellow & orange, 10–12cm (4–5in) across.
M. oligodon **8**: best sp for cool climate; to 1.5m (5ft); 6cm (2½in) yellow & pink fls.
Perennial morning glory (blue dawn flower, *Ipomoea acuminata* **9**, *I. learii*; Convolvulaceae): semi-hardy to tender perennial, but tuberous root can overwinter indoors in frosty areas; twining, to 3m (10ft); deciduous; showy short-lived fls to 12cm (5in) across, blue fading pink, all summer. For sun. Propagate by seed, softwood cuttings.
Coral plant (*Berberidopsis corallina* **10**; Flacourtiaceae): semi-hardy; to 1.5–3m (5–10ft); twining & scrambling, but tie in; evergreen; 8cm (3in) leathery, dark green lvs; drooping racemes of small red fls, late summer. Hates lime. Propagate by seed, softwood cuttings, layering.
The akebia family (*Akebia* & *Lardizabala* spp; Lardizabalaceae): vigorous twining evergreens or semi-evergreens grown for lvs & fls; fleshy edible sausage-shaped frs, 5–15cm (2–6in) long, after hot summers. For sun. Prune hard (especially *Akebia* spp) in late winter when necessary. Propagate by half-ripe cuttings, seed, layering.
*Akebia quinata** **1**, p251 (five-leaf akebia): v hardy;

rampant, to 9–12m (30–40ft); palmate lvs with 5 lfts; small reddish-purple fls in racemes, spring; frs purple, insipid.

A. trifoliata (*A. lobata*, three-leaf akebia): v hardy; to 9m (30ft); trifoliate lvs; fls dark purple, in racemes, spring; frs pale violet.

Lardizabala biternata: semi-hardy; to 12m (40ft) in warm areas; pinnate lvs; leathery lfts 10cm (4in) long; fls chocolate-purple & white, males in racemes, females larger & solitary, winter; frs purple.

The lily family (*Asparagus, Gloriosa* & *Lapageria* spp; Liliaceae): Propagate by seed, division.

Asparagus plumosus (asparagus fern; correctly, *A. setaceus*): semi-hardy perennial often grown indoors as juvenile (non-climbing); adult to 3m (10ft); evergreen; bright green feathery phylloclades (not true lvs); fls v small; frs purple-black berries.

A. sprengeri (correctly, *A. densiflorus* 'Sprengeri'): semi-hardy perennial often grown indoors; arching & semi-prostrate, to 1.8m (6ft) if trained; evergreen; mid-green foliage coarser than in *A. plumosus*; fls v small; red frs.

Gloriosa rothschildiana **2** (glory lily): tender tuberous perennial; to 1.8–2.5m (6–8ft); deciduous; lvs 12–18cm (5–7in) long, tendril-like tips; lily-like fls 8cm (3in) long, red shading to yellow, all summer. Grows best in long, hot summers; lift tubers before first frost & store indoors; start growth in greenhouse & plant out early summer; tie in. Propagate also by offsets.

G. superba: similar to *G. rothschildiana* but fls yellow, turning red.

Lapageria rosea **3** (Chilean bellflower): tender or semi-hardy; to 3–4.5m (10–15ft); evergreen; lvs leathery, 5–8cm (2–3in) long; rose-crimson bell fls to 8cm (3in) long, summer. Var 'Albiflora' is white. For semi-shade in moist, lime-free soil. Propagate by layering, half-ripe cuttings, seed.

Carolina jessamine (yellow jessamine, *Gelsemium sempervirens** **4**; Loganiaceae): moderately hardy twiner; to 6m (20ft); semi-evergreen; glossy lance-shaped lvs to 10cm (4in) long; trumpet-shaped bright yellow fls to 4cm (1½in) long, spring. All parts poisonous. For full sun; cut back hard if top-heavy. Propagate by seed, semi-ripe cuttings.

Cape leadwort (Cape plumbago, *Plumbago capensis* **5**; correctly, *P. auriculata*; Plumbaginaceae): semi-hardy S African lax climber often grown under glass; to 3.5m (12ft) or more if supported, otherwise bushy; semi-evergreen; narrow lvs to 8cm (3in) long; panicles of pale blue primrose-shaped fls 2.5cm (1in) wide, all summer (all year where warm & frost-free). For well-drained soil in sun; tie in. Propagate by semi-ripe heel cuttings.

The knotweed family (*Muehlenbeckia* & *Polygonum* spp; Polygonaceae): twining

deciduous or semi-evergreen climbers.

Muehlenbeckia complexa (wire-vine, maidenhair vine): moderately hardy; to 1.8m (6ft) or prostrate, making dense cover; wiry-stemmed; lvs variable, round to fiddle-shaped, to 2cm (¾in) long; fls v small; frs white. Tolerates salty coastal soil. Propagate by semi-ripe cuttings, seed.

Polygonum (*Bilderdykia*) *aubertii* (China fleece flower, silver lace vine; often sold as *P. baldschuanicum*): v hardy; extremely vigorous, to 12m (40ft) or more, growing up to 6m (20ft) a yr; bright green lvs; large panicles of small greenish-white fls, summer to autumn. Good for covering old trees, stumps, etc, in full sun; thin each winter to control. Propagate by semi-ripe heel cuttings, hardwood cuttings.

P. (*B.*) *baldschuanicum* **6** (Russian vine, Bokhara fleece flower): v similar to *P. aubertii* and often confused; fls pink-tinged, in drooping racemes.

P. multiflorum: moderately hardy tuberous perennial; to 4.5m (15ft); evergreen in mild climates; lvs dark green, glossy, 5–12cm (2–5in) long; slender panicles of small greenish-white fls, summer. For full sun; protect crown in cold winters; cut back hard early spring. Propagate by division.

Schisandras (magnolia vines, *Schisandra* spp; Schisandraceae, formerly Magnoliaceae): deciduous twining climbers with cup-shaped fls usually late spring, then, if both sexes planted, long spikes of red berries. Prefer acid or neutral soil. Propagate by seed, softwood cuttings, root cuttings, layering.

S. chinensis*: v hardy; to 6–9m (20–30ft); lvs 5–10cm (2–4in) long; fls 1–2cm (½–¾in) across, white to pale pink.

S. glaucescens: moderately hardy; to 4.5m (15ft); lvs glaucous beneath; fls orange-red, 2.5cm (1in) across. *S. henryi* is similar; fls white.

S. rubriflora **7** (*S. grandiflora rubriflora*): moderately hardy; to 4.5m (15ft); lvs leathery, 8–10cm (3–4in) long; 2.5cm (1in) crimson fls.

Perennial nasturtiums (*Tropaeolum* spp; Tropaeolaceae): tuberous herbaceous perennials grown for their brilliant red, orange or yellow spurred trumpet fls, summer. For any light soil in sun; cut down top growth in winter; if necessary, overwinter tubers indoors. Main pest: aphids. Propagate by seed, cuttings, division.

T. polyphyllum **8**: moderately hardy; to 1.8m (6ft) if trained, otherwise prostrate; lvs glaucous; fls yellow to orange, 2.5cm (1in) across.

T. speciosum **9** (flame creeper): moderately hardy; to 3–4.5m (10–15ft); fls scarlet, 4cm (1½in) across. Prefers cool, moist climate; dislikes pollution. Spreads by creeping rhizome.

T. tuberosum **10**: semi-hardy; vigorous, to 1.8–3m (6–10ft); lvs palmate; fls yellow & red, late; tuber edible. 'Early Flowering Variety' fls from early summer.

Agaves and phormiums

Formerly classed in Amaryllidaceae & Liliaceae respectively. Evergreen perennials grown mainly for their bold form and tough, decorative leaves. Excellent though rather tender focal & contrast plants. **Cultivation**: See below. **Propagation**: Seed; *Agave* spp by offsets; *Phormium* spp by division.

Agaves (century plants, *Agave* spp): tender to semi-hardy, generally stemless rosette-forming succulents with fleshy, fibrous, strap-shaped lvs (sharp-pointed & often spiny-edged): slow-growing; after 10-25yrs or more may grow tall branching infl with generally greenish or white bell-shaped fls, then die, generally leaving offsets. For v well-drained sandy soil in full sun; withstand slight frost if dry. Good in containers or for summer bedding in cold-winter areas.
A. americana (common century plant): to 1×2m (3×7ft) or more; v sharp-pointed curved grey-green lvs to 15–25cm (6–10in) wide, hooked spines; infl to 4.5–6m (15–20ft) or more tall. Vars: 'Marginata' **1** (lvs edged yellowish-white); 'Medio-picta' (yellow central lf stripe).
A. filifera **2**: to 45×90cm (1½×3ft); stiff tapering lvs, edges thread-bearing; infl to 1.8m (6ft) tall.
A. stricta: to 40×75cm (16×30in); eventually forms thick stem; lvs v narrow, green, v sharp-pointed; infl to 1.8–2.5m (6–8ft) tall.
A. univittata: to 0.6×1.2m (2×4ft); stiff sword-shaped lvs, dark green, pale stripe, long hooked teeth; infl to 3m (10ft) tall or more.
A. victoriae-reginae **3**: tender; to 15×30cm (6×12in); dark green stiff lvs, white lines; infl to 1.2m (4ft) tall; no offsets.
A. vilmoriniana: to 0.6×1.2m (2×4ft); pale green arching & twisting lvs to 10cm (4in) wide in loose rosette; infl to 5m (16ft) tall.
Phormiums (New Zealand flax, *Phormium* spp): moderately hardy stemless fleshy-rooted perennials forming clumps of sword-like

evergreen lvs; tubular fls, summer, then seed pods, on tall branching stems. For any fertile soil, preferably moist, in sun; protect with deep mulch if winters cold; tolerate pollution, salty winds.
P. cookianum (mountain flax correctly, *P. colensoi*): compact, to 0.6–1.5×0.3m (2–5×1ft); lvs green, to 6cm (2½in) wide, rather lax; fls brown, pale green inside; seed pods nodding. Vars (generally to 0.75–1m [2½–3ft]; descriptions refer to lvs): 'Cream Delight' **4** (green, cream stripe); 'Dark Delight' (maroon-purple); 'Emerald Green' (30cm [1ft]; bright green); 'Tricolor' (green, edges striped creamy-white & red).
P. tenax (New Zealand flax): sp to 1.8–3×1.2–1.5m (6–10×4–5ft); lvs stiff & tough, to 12cm (5in) wide, olive-green; fls rusty-red, on purple stem; seed pods to 10cm (4in) long. Vars & hybrids with *P. cookianum* (generallly to 1–2m [3–7ft]; descriptions refer to lvs): 'Aurora' (bronze striped red, orange & apricot); 'Bronze Baby' (dwarf; bronze); 'Dazzler' **5** (to 50cm [20in]; arching; red-brown striped carmine); 'Goliath' (to 3m [10ft]; olive-green); 'Purpureum' (brownish-purple); 'Radiance' (creamy-yellow & green, edged dark green); 'Sundowner' **6** (bronze-green edged pink); 'Thumbelina' (to 30cm [1ft]; purple-bronze); 'Variegatum' (dark green, edged creamy-white); 'Veitchii' (creamy-yellow & green, edged dark green); 'Yellow Queen' (yellow, narrow green edge); 'Yellow Wave' **7** (to 75cm [2½ft]; yellow to lime-green, edged emerald-green).

The mesembryanthemum family

Succulent sub-shrubby relatives of well-known annual (p520), all once classed as *Mesembryanthemum* spp. Often called ice plants (lvs of many spp glisten with tiny crystals). Drought-resistant. Narrow fleshy lvs; profuse satiny daisy-like fls, singly or clustered, open daytime all summer (earlier where warm). Good for summer bedding or containers if winters frosty, elsewhere for borders, ground cover etc; good on coasts; *Carpobrotus* spp bind soil. **Cultivation**: Tender to semi-hardy. For very well-drained soil (even sand) in full sun. Dead-head. Overwinter frost-free, dryish. **Propagation**: Cuttings; seed.

Hottentot fig (*Carpobrotus edulis* **8**): trailing & mat-forming, to 8×90cm (3×36in); lvs 3—sided, to 12cm (5in) long; fls to 10cm (4in) across, yellow, pink or purple; frs edible.
C. chilensis (sea fig) is similar but fls smaller, magenta.
Drosanthemum (*Drosanthemum hispidum*): hummock-forming, to 30–60×90cm (1—2×3ft); cylindrical glistening lvs 2.5cm (1in) long; deep purple fls 2.5cm (1in) across.

D. floribundum is trailing, with pale pink fls.
Lampranthus (ice plants, *Lampranthus* spp): lvs generally 2–5cm (¾–2in) long, cylindrical to 3-sided; fls profuse, from early spring if warm.
L. amoenus **9**: to 25×30cm (10×12in); lvs bright green; fls brilliant purple, 5cm (2in) across.
L. aurantiacus **10**: to 40×30cm (16×12in); lvs glaucous-green; fls bright orange, to 4cm (1½in).
L. coccineus: to 40×30cm (16×12in); lvs grey-green; fls 4 cm (1½in) across, carmine-red.

L. conspicuus: to 45×30cm (1½×1ft); shrubby; lvs to 8cm (3in) long, bright green, reddish tip; fls to 5cm (2in) across, reddish-purple.
L. emarginatus: to 45×45cm (1½×1½ft); lvs glaucous-green, translucent spots; fls to 3cm (1¼in) across, violet-pink.
L. roseus (*L. multiradiatus*): to 45×30cm

(1½×1ft); bushy; lvs glaucous; fls to 4 cm (1½in) across, rose-pink to purplish.
L. spectabilis **11**, p253; prostrate, to 30×60cm (1×2ft); lvs to 8cm (3in) long, grey-green; fls 5–6cm (2–2½in) across, pink, red or purple.
Oscularia (*Oscularia deltoides**): to 20×20cm (8×8in); lvs small & 3-sided, bluish-grey, reddish teeth; fls 1cm (½in) across, pink.

Alstroemerias

Peruvian lilies, *Alstroemeria* spp; sometimes classed in Amaryllidaceae. Somewhat tender S American clump-forming herbaceous perennials with fleshy spreading roots (sometimes listed with bulbs). Loose clusters of showy 4–5cm (1½–2in) wide azalea/lily-like flowers (very good for cutting) on thin, upright leafy stems, late spring & early summer. Leaves narrow, limp. Die down mid–late summer but seed heads decorative. **Cultivation**: Unless stated, moderately hardy. For rich, well-drained soil in sun in cool climates, semi-shade where hot. Plant young plants spring or (where hardy) dormant roots autumn, 15cm (6in) deep. Where winters cold, treat like tender bulbs; in marginal areas mulch thickly in winter. **Propagation**: Seed (hybridize freely); division.

A. aurantiaca **1**: rather invasive, to 90×40cm (36×16in); fls rich yellow to orange-scarlet, upper petals veined red. Vars: 'Dover Orange' (rich orange); 'Lutea' (yellow); 'Moerheim Orange' (vigorous; rich orange). Hardiest sp.
A. caryophyllaea*: to 45×30cm (1½×1ft); fls red & white, upper petals streaked & spotted.
A. chilensis: semi-hardy; to 60–90×30cm (2–3×1ft); fls red or pink, marked yellow.
A. haemantha **2** to 90×45cm (3×1½ft); fls deep orange-red, upper petals streaked yellow.
A. ligtu: to 90×30cm (3×1ft); fls pale pink to deep red, upper petals streaked white. 'Ligtu

Hybrids' **3** (with *A. haemantha*) are best known; to 1–1.2m (3–4ft); fls in shades of pink, salmon, coral, orange, yellow, red & white, streaked & spotted (sold as mixtures).
A. pelegrina: semi-hardy; to 45×30cm (1½×1ft); fls generally lilac-pink, flushed yellow & spotted purple. Var 'Alba' **4** (Inca lily) is white.
A. pulchella **5** (parrot lily; may be correctly *A. psittacina*): to 90×30cm (3×1ft); fls dark red, tipped green & spotted brown.
A. violacea: semi-hardy; to 45–60×30cm (1½–2×1ft); fls violet-mauve, upper petals almost white, spotted purple.

Epimediums

Barrenworts, bishop's hats, *Epimedium* spp. Low-growing, slowly spreading evergreen or semi-evergreen perennials grown mainly for their attractive compound leaves. Leaflets leathery, 5–8cm (2–3in) long, heart-shaped & often sharply toothed, on wiry stems; generally fresh green tinted pink or red when young, becoming deep glossy green & veined in summer & yellow/bronze/red-tinted in autumn. Flowers waxy, generally saucer-shaped & 1–2cm (⅜–¾in) across, often spurred & multicoloured, in airy sprays, spring. Unless stated, foliage 20–30×25–40cm (8–12×10–16in), flowers slightly taller. Excellent for ground cover under trees, shrubs, etc, & edges of borders. Flowers & leaves good for cutting. **Cultivation**: Very to ultra-hardy unless stated. For rich moist soil, preferably in semi-shade but tolerate deep shade or sun (if moist). Remove dead leaves. **Propagation**: Division.

E. alpinum: lfts often flecked brown & red; fls red & yellow, short-spurred.
E. grandiflorum (*E. macranthum*): fls to 5cm (2in) across, white, pink red or violet, long-spurred. Var 'Rose Queen' is crimson-pink; to 15cm (6in).
E. perralderianum: to 40cm (16in); evergreen glossy lfts; fls bright yellow, short-spurred.
E. pinnatum: v hardy; lfts brightly tinted autumn; fls bright yellow, short red spurs. Var *colchicum* **6** (*elegans*) has profuse large fls.
E.×rubrum **7** (*E. alpinum rubrum*, *E×coccineum*): hybrid of *E. alpinum* &

E. grandiflorum; fls to 2.5cm (1in) across, crimson & yellow, starry.
E.×versicolor 'Sulphureum' **8** (*E. sulphureum*): hybrid of *E. grandiflorum* & *E. pinnatum colchicum*; vigorous; fls pale yellow, drooping, spurs tinged red.
E.×warleyense **9**: hybrid of *E. alpinum* & *E. pinnatum colchicum*; fls flame, short-spurred.
E.×youngianum hybrids of *E. diphyllum* & *E. grandiflorum*. Vars: 'Niveum' **10** (sometimes listed as *E. grandiflorum* 'Niveum'; pure white); 'Roseum' (lilac-pink).

The forget-me-not family

Border or ground-cover plants, many of woodland origin, some providing the richest blues of early summer. Flowers tubular, saucer-shaped or starry, in dense cymes, held above coarse (generally hairy) leaves. **Cultivation:** Generally ultra-hardy in free-draining soils. For rich, moist soil (well drained to prevent root rot) in semi-shade unless noted. **Propagation:** Root cuttings; division; spp by seed.

Alkanets (bugloss, *Anchusa* spp): lance-shaped lvs; fls deep rich blue, saucer-shaped, to 1.5cm (½in) across. Self-seed freely. For full sun.
A. angustissima: to 30×25cm (12×10in); fls early summer (cut back for autumn repeat).
A. azurea (*A. italica*, Italian bugloss): to 1.5×0.45m (5×1½ft); fls in panicles, early–mid summer. Stake. Vars: 'Little John' (to 45cm [1½ft]); 'Loddon Royalist' **1** (to 1m [3ft]); 'Morning Glory' (to 1.5m [5ft]); 'Opal' (to 1.2m [4ft]); sky-blue).

Prophet flower (*Arnebia echioides* **2**; correctly, *Echioides longiflorum*): v hardy; to 30×25cm (12×10in); basal lvs; fls tubular, bright yellow blotched maroon when young, early summer (& sometimes autumn). For full sun.

Siberian bugloss (*Brunnera macrophylla*, *Anchusa myosotidiflora*): to 45×45cm (1½×1½ft); heart-shaped lvs; blue forget-me-not-like fls in dainty sprays, early summer (cuttable). Useful ground cover. Vars: 'Langtrees' **3** (lvs spotted silver); 'Variegata' (lvs splashed white; must have shade; remove green stems).

Hound's-tongues (*Cynoglossum* spp): easy but lax perennials with mainly basal lvs; intense blue forget-me-not-like fls, early-mid summer. For sun; stake.
C. grande: to 90×30cm (3×1ft); fls white-centred.
C. nervosum **4**: to 45×30cm (1½×1ft).

Mertensias (*Mertensia* spp; in US, bluebells): easy plants with tubular blue fls (usually pink in bud), early summer unless stated.
M. ciliata: to 75×45cm (2½×1½ft); oval glaucous lvs; fls sky-blue. Tolerates some sun.
M. echioides: to 20×45cm (8×18in); fls deep blue (may repeat autumn); lax, for ground cover.
M. paniculata: to 90×60cm (3×2ft); sprawling; lvs grey-green; pale blue fls in drooping sprays.
M. virginica **5** (Virginia cowslip, Virginia bluebells): to 60×30cm (2×1ft); bluish-grey lvs (die down summer); drooping pure blue fls, late spring (cuttable). Var 'Rubra' is pink.

Moltkia (*Moltkia* [*Lithospermum*] × *intermedia*): hybrid of *M. petraea* & *M. suffruticosa*; to 40×30cm (16×12in); bushy & sub-shrubby; bright blue fls, early summer. Raise from softwood cuttings.

Giant or **Chatham Island forget-me-not** (*Myosotidium hortensia*, *M. nobile*): semi-hardy evergreen perennial; to 45×45cm (1½×1½ft); oval, glossy, veined lvs to 30cm (1ft) long; profuse blue fls, edged white, spring. For cool

sheltered spots; good near sea. Mulch; give winter protection.

Forget-me-nots (*Myosotis* spp): see pp426 & 486.

Lungworts (*Pulmonaria* spp): mostly evergreen early-flg perennials useful for ground cover. To 30×30cm (1×1ft) unless stated; green/silver-spotted lance-shaped lvs; fls tubular, pink or blue (colour sometimes unstable; may indicate acidity changes within plant), spring. For partial shade.
P. angustifolia (blue cowslip): lvs unspotted; fls sky-blue, best in var 'Azurea' **6**. 'Mawson's Variety' & 'Munstead Blue' are deep blue vars.
P. longifolia: narrow lvs spotted white; fls bright blue or white, late spring to summer.
P. mollis (correctly, *P. montana*): to 45×60cm (1½×2ft); velvety lvs; fls deep blue, fading purple or coral.
P. officinalis (Jerusalem cowslip, Jerusalem sage, soldiers and sailors, spotted dog): lvs spotted white; fls pink turning lilac-blue.
P. saccharata (Bethlehem sage): handsome lvs densely silver-marbled; fls pink turning blue. Vars: *alba* (white); 'Bowles Red' **7**; 'Highdown' (rich blue); 'Margery Fish'; 'Pink Dawn'.

Comfrey (*Symphytum* spp): easy spreading plants for ground cover, all with coarse, hairy lvs; tubular fls in drooping cymes. Dislike heat.
S. caucasicum (blue comfrey): to 60×45cm (2×1½ft); fls pink turning blue, spring to early summer.
S. grandiflorum **8**: to 20×40cm (8×16in); creamy-yellow transient fls, spring. Invasive. Vars: 'Hidcote Blue'; 'Hidcote Pink'.
S. officinale (common comfrey, boneset): to 1.2×0.6m (4×2ft); fls yellowish-white, pink or purple, early summer. Weedy; for wild gardens.
S. orientale **9**: to 60×45cm (2×1½ft); white fls, early summer. Short-lived; self-seeds.
S. rubrum: may be hybrid; to 40×45cm (16×18in); crimson fls all summer.
S.×uplandicum (*S. peregrinum*, Russian comfrey): hybrid of *S. asperum* & *S. officinale*; to 1.2×1.2m (4×4ft); fls rose turning blue-purple, on winged stems, early-mid summer. Var 'Variegatum' **10** has grey-green lvs edged white; fls purplish-pink.

Eastern borage (*Trachystemon orientale*, *Nordmannia cordifolia*): invasive ground-cover plant useful beneath trees. To 45×60cm (1½×2ft); hairy heart-shaped lvs to 30cm (1ft) across; starry blue-purple fls in short spikes, spring (before lvs). For any soil in sun or shade.

Desert cacti

Succulent plants with stout stems or bodies, adapted to withstand heat & drought. Grown for their architectural form, decorative spines, hair or wool, and/or large colourful (though rather transient) flowers (generally more or less funnel-shaped, with many petals, early–mid summer unless stated). Mostly grown in pots under glass in cool regions but many spp remarkably hardy if summers hot & winters dry. (Winter resting in cool dry conditions encourages better flowering.) Larger spp used for landscaping, patios, etc, where hardy; smaller for rock gardens, raised beds, pots (even tender spp can spend summers outdoors). **Cultivation:** For extremely free-draining soil & at least 4–6 hours direct sun daily. In summer water freely & feed (high potash promotes flowering); in winter keep dry with cloche if necessary. If pot-grown do not over-pot. Hardiness noted below refers to ideal wild conditions of low humidity, but many very hardy spp will survive lesser frosts in wetter areas if drainage perfect. Prone to mealy bugs, root bugs, scale insects, mushroom flies, eelworms (nematodes) & rot fungi. **Propagation:** Seed, spring-sown; offsets; cuttings (let wound dry).

Cephalocerei (*Cephalocereus* spp): tender to semi-hardy; slow-growing & eventually v tall; erect & column-shaped; stem ribbed, spiny & often hairy; fls nocturnal, only on mature plants. Numerous spp, including fast-growing *C. polylophus* and slow-growing *C. senilis* **1** (old man cactus; young growth v hairy); both reach 12m (40ft) in wild.

Peruvian apple cactus (*Cereus peruvianus*): semi-hardy; eventually to 9m (30ft); upright & branching, becoming shrub/tree-like; angled glaucous stems, clustered short brownish spines; white nocturnal fls to 12cm (5in) across. Var 'Monstrosus' **2** (giant club) is slower-growing, with v branching knobbly stems.

Beehive cacti (*Coryphantha* spp; sometimes listed as *Neobesseya* spp; correctly *Escobaria* spp): small globular to cylindrical, knobbly, spiny plants similar to *Mammillaria*; often clump-forming; include some of hardiest dwarf cacti. *C. (E., N.) missouriensis** (Missouri pincushion cactus): moderately hardy; to 6×8cm (2½× 3in); yellow-green fls to 5cm (2in) across. *C. (E.) vivipara* **6**: moderately hardy; to 15×8cm (6×3in) but usually shorter; pink to purple fls to 5cm (2in) across.

Barrel cacti (*Echinocactus* spp): slow-growing but eventually quite large globular to cylindrical cacti with prominent ribs & large spines; fl only when mature; semi-hardy but v good for tubs, summer bedding. *E. grusonii* **3** (golden barrel [ball] cactus): eventually to 1.2×1m (4×3ft); golden spines to 5cm (2in) long; fls yellow. *E. ingens* (giant barrel cactus): eventually to 1.2×1.2m (4×4ft); brown spines to 3cm (1¼in) long; fls yellow.

Hedgehog cacti (*Echinocereus* spp): to 40×10cm (16×4in); generally cylindrical, often forming clumps; ribbed & spiny; fls (usually close at night). Hate humidity; short-lived if over-watered. Numerous spp & vars; among hardiest (all moderately hardy) are *E. reichenbachii* (lace cactus; pink to purple), *E. triglochidiatus* (scarlet to crimson) &

E. viridiflorus* (yellowish-green). *E. pectinatus rigidissimus* **4** (rainbow cactus) is moderately hardy; spines pink, white & yellow in bands up stem; fls magenta.

Sea-urchin cacti (*Echinopsis* spp **5**): generally semi-hardy; fast-growing, to 25×10cm (10×4in); globular to cylindrical, often forming clumps; ribbed & spiny; profuse showy, large fls on long tubes (open at night). Numerous spp, mainly with white, pink or red fls.

Fish-hook or barrel cacti (*Ferocactus* spp): semi- to moderately hardy slow-growing ribbed cacti closely related to *Echinocactus* spp; globular, becoming cylindrical; large colourful spines, often flattened, hooked or twisted; yellow to red fls when 30cm (1ft) tall. *F. (E.) acanthodes* **7**: to 1.8×0.3m (6×1ft); spines pink to bright red, hooked. *F. hamatacanthus*: to 60×12cm (24×5in); spines brown to grey, some hooked. *F. (E.) wislizeni*: v slow-growing, to 1.8×0.45cm (6×1½ft); some spines brown or red & hooked.

Lobivias (cob cacti, *Lobivia* spp **8**): semi- to moderately hardy; to 8–15×5cm (3–6×2in); globular to cylindrical, often forming clumps; ribbed & spiny; profuse short-lived fls to 10cm (4in) across when young. Easy. Numerous spp; mainly red or yellow fls.

Mammillarias (pincushion cacti, *Mammillaria* spp **9**): diverse genus of mainly globular small cacti; generally semi- to moderately hardy; to 12–20×10–15cm (5–8×4–6in); often form clumps; ribless but have conical spiny tubercles; some spp hairy; fls to 2.5cm (1in) long, in rings around top of stem; frs red or black. Easy though some prone to root rot. V numerous spp; fls generally cream, magenta or red.

Prickly pears (chollas, *Opuntia* spp): include hardiest large cacti, v hardy unless stated; branching stems jointed, in flattened segments ("pads") unless stated; ribless; tufts of spines & hooked glochids; red or yellow fls to 8cm (3in) wide when mature. Needs a little water in winter. *O. basilaris* **10** (beaver-tail cactus): to 1m (3ft); clump-forming; pads purplish, few spines.

O. erinacea ursina (grizzly bear cactus): to 45cm (1½ft); profuse bristly spines.

O. fragilis: to 10cm (4in); prostrate and spreading; short flattened joints (v fragile).

O. humifusa (*O. compressa*): prostrate & spreading; oval pads 9–17cm (3½–6½in) long; few spines; showy yellow fls 10cm (4in) across.

O. imbricata (*O. arborescens*, chain-link cactus): tree-like, to 3m (10ft); woody trunk to 8cm (3in) thick; narrow, warty cylindrical joints, spiny.

O. microdasys **1** (bunny ears): semi- to moderately hardy; spreading, to 0.6×1.2m (2×4ft); spineless but many clusters of glochids, yellow, white or red-brown in vars.

O. polyacantha **2**: low, spreading; spines 2–5cm (¾–2in) long.

Crown cacti (*Rebutia* spp **3**): semi-hardy; low-growing, forming clusters of globular stems to 8cm (3in) across, spirally tubercled & spiny; profuse long-tubed fls, usually red or orange, spring to autumn (close at night). Numerous spp.

Organ-pipe cactus (*Stenocereus* [*Lemaireocereus*] *thurberi* **4**): tender to semi-hardy; slow-growing, to 4.5m (15ft); tree-like, with cylindrical branching stems to 20cm (8in) thick, ribbed & spiny; white to purplish nocturnal fls to 8cm (3in) long when mature; edible red frs.

Forest cacti

Often wrongly called leaf cacti (except for *Aporocactus* spp) because of flattened, drooping, virtually spineless branching stems. Epiphytes, growing wild on tree branches or rocks. Flowers very showy. Grown mainly in pots under glass in cool regions, but good outdoors in summer in hanging baskets under trees, porches, etc. **Cultivation**: Tender. Easy; unless stated, for humus-rich, lime-free, well-drained potting mixture, moist all year, in semi-shade. Spray if humidity low. **Propagation**: Seed (may not breed true); cuttings; grafting on *Pereskia* spp.

Rat-tail cactus (*Aporocactus flagelliformis* **5**): cylindrical green stems to 1m (3ft) long, 2.5cm (1in) thick, ribbed & with short yellow or brown spines; pink to magenta fls to 8cm (3in) long, spring (close at night). Tolerates lime, dry air & gritty soil; likes sun; water v sparingly in winter.

Epicacti (orchid cacti, *Epiphyllum* hybrids **6** of complex parentage): smooth, notched stems to 1m (3ft) long, 2.5–8cm (1–3in) wide; v large fls opening 6–25cm (2½–9in) wide, mainly spring & summer, sometimes repeating later, wide colour range (not blue). Numerous named vars, some scented.

Easter cactus (*Rhipsalis* [*Rhipsalidopsis*] *gaertneri* **7**): rather upright, to 30×30cm (1×1ft); stem segments to 5×2.5cm (2×1in); profuse bright red or pink fls to 8cm (3in) long, spring (may repeat late summer).

Christmas cactus (*Schlumbergera* × *buckleyi* **8**): often sold incorrectly as *Zygocactus truncatus*: arching & drooping; jointed stems to 45cm (1½ft) long, 2.5cm (1in) wide; narrow satiny-cerise fls 6–8cm (2½–3in) long, winter. Vars in shades of white, pink, salmon & orange. True *Z. truncatus* (crab cactus, correctly *S. truncata*) is similar to *S.* × *buckleyi* but stem joints toothed & fls earlier.

Campanulas and their relatives

Easy and popular plants, herbaceous unless stated, mostly with lovely nodding flowers in shades of blue, white or soft pink. Many produce erect flower spikes from rosettes of basal leaves & are good cut flowers. **Cultivation**: Ultra-hardy unless stated; for any well-drained soil in sun or partial shade unless noted. Dead-head unless seed wanted; if necessary protect more tender spp in winter. **Propagation**: Seed, sown late spring; division (spring). For dwarf spp more often grown as rock plants, see p426; for perennials treated as biennials, see p522.

Ladybells (*Adenophora* spp): fleshy-rooted plants otherwise similar to campanulas. Bell-shaped nodding fls to 1.5cm (⅝in) long, mid summer. For full sun; resent disturbance.

A. liliifolia* : to 60–90×45cm (2–3×1½ft); pale blue fls in erect branching spikes arising from heart-shaped basal lvs.

A. tashiroi: to 25–60×30cm (10–24×12in); procumbent stems; fls violet-blue, solitary or in racemes.

Bellflowers (*Campanula* spp): easy, with broadly

cup- or bell-shaped fls, unless stated in erect spikes, early summer; lvs generally more or less rounded and toothed. All have milky sap. Tall vars need shelter (or stake); self-seed.

C. alliariifolia (spurred bellflower): graceful & clump-forming, to 45–60×45cm (1½–2×1½ft); grey-green lvs to 12cm (5in) long, long stalks; creamy-white fls to 5cm (2in) long, early–mid summer. Can be propagated from basal shoot cuttings. Var 'Ivory Bells' **1**, p263, has larger fls.

C. barbata (bearded bellflower): v hardy; to

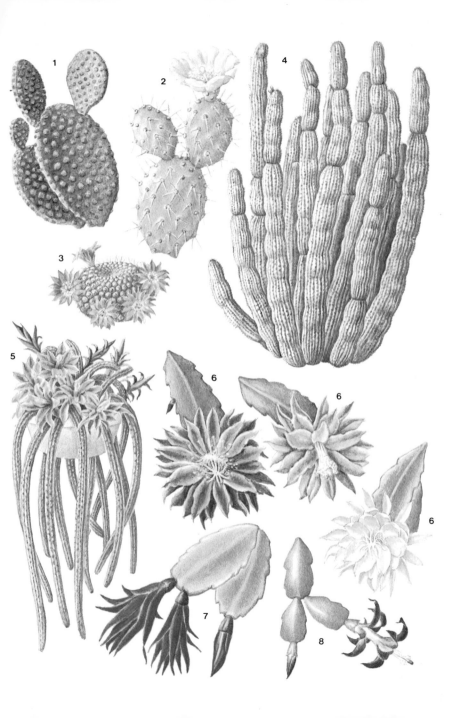

45×15–30cm (18×6–12in); rosette-forming; lance-shaped hairy lvs; bluish-purple or white fls to 4cm (1½in) long, woolly hairs drooping from bells. Short-lived.

C. bononiensis: to 75×30cm (2½×1ft); lance-shaped grey-green lvs; starry lilac fls to 2cm (¾in) long.

C. collina: clump-forming, to 30×30cm (1×1ft); oval basal lvs to 8cm (3in) long; fls deep purple-blue, to 4cm (1½in) long.

C. glomerata (clustered bellflower): variable, to 30–90×30–60cm (1–3×1–2ft); globular heads of purple-blue fls to 2.5cm (1in) long, white pistils (good for cutting). Vars: 'Acaulis' (to 12cm [5in]; nearly stemless fls); 'Alba' (to 45cm [1½ft]; white); *dahurica* (to 60cm [2ft]; rich violet; invasive); 'Joan Elliott' (violet, from late spring); 'Purple Pixie' (to 30cm [1ft]; violet, late); 'Superba' **2** (to 75cm [2½ft]; violet; invasive but long-flg).

C. isophylla (Italian bellflower, star of Bethlehem): semi- to moderately hardy; trailing, to 15×30–45cm (6×12–18in); lvs to 4cm (1½in) long; v profuse star-shaped mid blue fls to 2.5cm (1in) wide, mid–late summer. Deservedly popular for hanging baskets, pots; protect from winter wet. Vars: 'Alba' (white); 'Caerulea' (pale blue); 'Mayii' (greyish hairy lvs; large China-blue fls).

C. lactiflora (milky bellflower): v hardy; to 1–1.5×0.6m (3–5×2ft); oval lvs to 12cm (5in) long along arching stems; bell-shaped lavender-blue or milk-white fls to 4cm (1½in) across in dense panicles, all summer. Long-lived; can be naturalized. Vars: 'Loddon Anna' **3** (to 1.2m [4ft]; soft pink); 'Pouffe' (to 25×45cm [10×18in]; profuse fls); 'Prichard's Variety' (to 90cm [3ft]; violet-blue; self-seeds).

C. latifolia (giant bellflower): clump-forming, to 1.2–1.5×0.6m (4–5×2ft); oval lvs to 15cm (6in) long; purple-blue fls to 6cm (2½in) long, mid summer. Self-seeds freely. Vars (to 1–1.1m [3–3½ft]): 'Brantwood' (violet-purple); 'Gloaming' **4** (smoky-blue); 'White Ladies' (white).

C. persicifolia (*C. grandis, C. latiloba*, peach-leaved or willow bellflower): to 90×30–45cm (3×1–1½ft); rosette-forming; evergreen basal lvs to 20cm (8in) long; blue fls to 5cm (2in) wide (good for cutting). Vars: 'Alba' (white); 'Blue Bells' (rich blue); 'Percy Piper' **5** (deep blue); 'Pride of Exmouth' (to 60cm [2ft]; semi-double, pale blue); 'Snowdrift' (white); 'Telham Beauty' (v large light blue fls); 'White Pearl' (double).

C. punctata: to 30×45cm (1×1½ft); oval lvs; fls to 5cm (2in) long, cream flushed pink, red-dotted within, in leaf axils. Invasive; unusual. Prefers sandy soil, full sun. Var 'Burghaltii' **6** (*C.×burghaltii*) is probably a hybrid with *P. latifolia*; to 45–60cm (1½–2ft); purple buds open to pale greyish-lilac fls to 8cm (3in) long on

wiry stems, all summer; needs support. Var 'Van Houttei' is similar but purple-lilac.

C. pyramidalis: see p522.

C. rapunculoides: to 90×60cm (3×2ft); stem lvs nettle-like; violet starry fls to 2.5cm (1in) long on graceful stems, late spring to early summer. V invasive & self-seeding; a beautiful weed only for the wild garden.

C. rhomboidalis: to 60×30cm (2×1ft); lvs to 5cm (2in) long; blue-purple fls to 2.5cm (1in) long.

C. sarmatica: v hardy; clump-forming, to 30–60×30cm (1–2×1ft); hairy; grey-green lvs to 8cm (3in) long; fls to 2.5cm (1in) long, grey-blue & downy. Unusual & showy; for full sun.

C. trachelium (*C. urticifolia*, nettle-leaved bellflower, Coventry bells): spreading, to 60×30cm (2×1ft); lvs nettle-like; blue-purple fls to 4cm (1½in) long, late summer. Vars: 'Alba' (white); 'Albo Plena' (double, white); 'Bernice' **7** (double, powder-blue).

Bonnet bellflowers (*Codonopsis* spp): v hardy sprawling perennials; oval, pungent lvs to 2.5cm (1in) long; nodding bell-shaped fls to 4cm (1½in) long, usually solitary, early–mid summer. Prefer acid soils. Good for banks or rock gardens. Can be propagated from basal shoot cuttings.

C. clematidea **8**: to 60×30cm (2×1ft); broad bell fls, bluish-white marked gold & black inside.

C. ovata: to 25–45×30cm (10–18×12in); narrow bell fls, pale blue marked orange & purple inside.

Horned rampions (*Phyteuma* spp): border plants for v sharply drained soil or large rock gardens; toothed lvs mainly in basal rosettes; small bright blue fls in dense globular heads, early summer.

P. orbiculare: v hardy; to 30×30–45cm (1×1–1½ft); oval lvs; infls to 4cm (1½in) across. Protect from slugs.

P. scheuchzeri **9**: moderately hardy; to 30×30cm (1×1ft); lvs nearly lance-shaped; infls to 2.5cm (1in) across.

Balloon flower (*Platycodon grandiflorum*): to 60–90×45cm (2–3×1½ft); clump-forming; toothed oval lvs to 8cm (3in) long, glaucous; clustered balloon-like buds open to light blue saucer-shaped fls to 5–8cm (2–3in) across, all summer. Long-lived. Do not disturb roots; divide only old plants. Vars: 'Album' (white); 'Apoyama' (to 10–12cm [4–5in]; deep mauve); 'Mariesii' **10** (to 30–45cm [1–1½ft]; pale to deep blue fls, early; commonest form); 'Mother of Pearl' (pale pink, semi-double); 'Plenum' (light blue, semi-double); 'Shell Pink'; 'Snowflakes' (white, semi-double).

Common throatwort (*Trachelium caeruleum*): moderately hardy; to 90×45cm (3×1½ft); toothed oval lvs to 8cm (3in) long; dense heads of v narrow lavender-blue fls, prominent styles, mid summer. Can be propagated by basal shoot cuttings; often treated as HHA in cold areas.

Carnations and pinks

Dianthus spp & vars (many of complex parentage). Charming cottage garden plants loved for their fragrance & useful for edging, raised beds, etc; taller vars for borders. Leaves evergreen, grass-like & generally grey-green, blue-green or blue-grey. Flowers flattish & rounded, single or double, often frilled, in shades of pink, red, purple, white or yellow; associate well with grey-leaved plants; good for cutting & exhibition. Flowers classed as selfs, bicolours (with contrasting eye), fancies (with contrasting flecks or stripes), picotees with contrasting outer zone, & laced vars (each petal edged with contrasting "lacing"). Bloom best when young; replace every few years. **Cultivation**: For well-drained neutral or alkaline (not too fertile) soil in full sun (or partial shade in hot climates). Tolerate pollution & coastal sites but dislike v hot dry summers & cold wet winters. Plant firmly but shallowly; do not mulch. Dead-head or shear after flowering. Protect from excessive winter wet; in severe winters cover with conifer branches. Prone to wilt & root rot in poorly-drained soils. **Propagation**: Easy, by cuttings of non-flowering shoots or layering, summer; seed sown spring or summer (will not breed true). For dwarf spp & vars, see p488.

Carnations (in US, clove pinks): tall, with branching stems; lvs bluish-green; fls double. Need staking.
D. caryophyllus** (wild carnation, gilliflower, clove pink): moderately to v hardy; to 30–60×45cm (1–2×1½ft); clusters of 2–5 purplish fls to 4cm (1½in) across, mid summer. Main parent of vars below.
Perpetual-flowering (florists') carnations* **1**, **2**: tender to semi-hardy; to 1.2×0.3m (4×1ft); fls crinkly edged, to 8cm (3in) across if disbudded, less as sprays, in various shades; if warm enough; mainly under glass.
Border carnations: moderately to v hardy; to 60–90×30–45cm (2–3×1–1½ft); clusters of smooth-edged fls to 5cm (2in) across (more if disbudded), often scented (especially "clove" vars), mid summer. Replace every 2–3yrs. Sold as unnamed seedlings & named vars: 'Beauty of Cambridge' (pale yellow); 'Bookham Grand' (crimson); 'Bookham Lad' (white striped scarlet); 'Candy Clove'** (white marked rosy-red); 'Catherine Glover' (yellow market scarlet); 'Cherry Clove'** (cherry-rose); 'Clarinda' (salmon); 'Consul' (apricot); 'Dainty Lady' (white lined red); 'Dwarf Grenadin' (dwarf seed strain; mixed); 'English Giants'** (seed strain; mixed); 'Eudoxia' (white); 'Eva Humphries' (white edged wine-red); 'Fiery Cross' (scarlet); 'Fingo Clove'** (deep crimson); 'Harmony' (grey-purple flecked cerise); 'Horsa' (apricot marked salmon); 'Imperial Clove'** (violet-carmine); 'Juliet' (dwarf; scarlet); 'Lavender Clove'** (lavender); 'Leslie Rennison'* (purple flushed rose); 'Lustre' **3** (golden-apricot); 'Merlin Clove Improved'** **4** (white marked crimson); 'Oppenheimer's Red'; 'Orange Maid' (apricot marked bronze); 'Perfect Clove'** (deep crimson); 'Pixie Delight' (dwarf seed strain; mixed); 'Portsdown Perfume'** (white striped lavender & pink); 'Robin Thain'** (white marked crimson); 'Salmon Clove'** (salmon-coral); 'Santa Claus' **5** (yellow edged purple); 'Scarlet Fragrance'** (scarlet-red); 'Thomas Lee' (pale

yellow, edged & flecked scarlet); 'Violet Clove'** (deep violet); 'Warrior'* **6** (white marked blood-red); 'Zebra' **7** (yellow marked crimson).
Pinks: generally smaller than carnations; fls double unless stated; generally cuttable.
D. × *allwoodii* vars (modern garden pinks): hybrids of old-fashioned pinks (*D. plumarius* vars) & perpetual-flg carnations (*D. caryophyllus* vars); generally ultra-hardy; fast-growing but short-lived, to 25–40×25cm (10–16×10in); grey-green lvs; profuse fls to 5cm (2in) across, early summer repeating autumn (into winter in mild areas; vars marked † v good for cutting). Replace every 2–3yrs; stop young plants to bush out. Self vars: 'Aqua'* (white); 'Charles' (bright crimson); 'Danielle'* (orange-red); 'David' (bright scarlet); 'Diane'† (deep red); 'Doris Majestic'*† (bright salmon-pink); 'Haytor White'*† (white; larg fls); 'Helen'*† (salmon-pink); 'Ian'**† (dark crimson); 'Jacqueline' (rose-vermilion); 'Oliver'* (rose-cerise); 'Sandra'** (sugar-pink). Bicoloured vars: 'Angela' (cream, coral-red eye); 'Daphne' (single; pale pink, crimson eye); 'Doris'*† **8** (pale salmon-pink, red eye); 'Ruby Doris'*† (bright rose, ruby eye). Laced vars: 'Constance' (pale pink, carmine lacing); 'Laced Joy' (pink, crimson eye & lacing); 'Laced Monarch' (pink, chestnut lacing); 'Laced Prudence' (white, crimson lacing); 'Laced Romeo' (creamy-white, chestnut-red lacing); 'Susan'† (pale lilac, darker eye & lacing). Fancy vars: 'Doris Supreme'*† (pale salmon-pink, carmine flakes & stripes); 'Freckles' **9** (silver-pink flecked red); 'Paul' (shell-pink veined crimson). Var 'Rainbow Loveliness' is a seed-raised mixture; fringed fls. Show pinks are hybrids with border carnations; to 60×30cm (2×1ft); long-stemmed fls, mid–late summer (v good for cutting); vars: 'Show Aristocrat' (pink, buff eye); 'Show Beauty'* **10** (deep rosy-pink, maroon eye); 'Show Charming' **11** (semi-double; pink, coral-red centre); 'Show Emblem'* (soft pink); 'Show Enchantress' (salmon-pink); 'Show Ideal' (cream, salmon-red centre); 'Show Magnificence' (apple-blossom-pink); 'Show

Pearl' (white).

D.× latifolius (button pink): hybrid, v hardy; to 25–40×25cm (10–16×10in); grass-like lvs; v profuse rose-pink to dark red fls to 2.5cm (1in) across, all summer.

*D. plumarius*** (cottage or common pink; in US, grass pink): ultra-hardy; to 40×30cm (16×12in); mat-forming; glaucous lvs; small clusters of single, often fringed, pink, purple or white fls to 4cm (1½in) across, late spring & early summer. Sp rarely grown, but main parent of numerous vars (generally sold as old-fashioned pinks; to 25–40cm [10–16in]; self-branching, so stopping not needed; longer-lived than modern vars, needing replacement every 5yrs). Self vars: 'Earl

of Essex'** (rose-pink, fringed); 'Fortuna' (cerise); 'Freda' (mauve); 'Inchmery'** (pale pink); 'Mrs Sinkins'** **1** (white); 'Pink Princess' (coral-pink); 'Priory Pink'* (mauve-pink); 'White Ladies'** (pure white; vigorous). Bicoloured vars: 'Charles Musgrave' **2** ('Musgrave's Pink'; single; white, greenish eye); 'Pink Mrs Sinkins'** ('Excelsior'; carmine, dark eye); 'Red Emperor' (mahogany, dark red eye); 'Sam Barlow'** (white, almost black eye). Laced vars: 'Dad's Favourite' **3** (white, purple-maroon lacing); 'London Glow' (crimson, white lacing); 'London Lovely' (white, dark eye, mauve lacing); 'London Poppet' (pale pink, ruby eye & lacing). Var 'Spring Beauty'* is a mixed seed strain.

Other plants of the pink family

Easy border plants providing good cut flowers. Campion flowers mainly shades of red, some associated with grey leaves. Gypsophila useful for its airy habit and masses of tiny flowers for cutting or contrasting with heavy-leaved perennials; also good for filling spaces left by spring-flowering bulbs. **Cultivation**: Ultra-hardy unless stated. For any well-drained soil (alkaline for *Gypsophila* sp) in sun. **Propagation**: See below. For rock garden spp (some suitable for border edging) see p488.

Baby's breath (chalk plant, *Gypsophila paniculata*): mounding, to 60–90×60cm (2–3×2ft); non-invasive fang-like roots; lance-shaped glaucous lvs to 8cm (3in) long; profuse tiny single white fls to 5mm (¼in) across in wiry panicles to 25cm (10in) long, early-midsummer (repeating autumn if cut back after first flg), cuttable, dryable. Not for cold/damp soil; do not disturb; plant grafted vars with graft below soil for gradual stem rooting. Propagate by seed; vars by semi-ripe cuttings or grafting on sp. Vars & hybrids: 'Bristol Fairy' (double, white; rather short-lived); 'Compacta Plena' **4** ('Bodgeri'; to 45cm [1½ft]; double, white); 'Dantziger' (white; good in poor light); 'Flamingo' (double, pale pink); 'Perfecta' (double, white); 'Pink Star' **5** (to 45cm [1½ft]; double, pale pink); 'Rosy Veil' (to 30cm [1ft]; double, v pale pink).

Campions (catchflies, *Lychnis* spp; some often listed as *Agrostemma*, *Silene* or *Viscaria* spp): border perennials with scarlet or magenta fls usually with distinctive calyx; lvs often in basal rosettes. Generally not long-lived; must have good drainage. Propagate by seed, division.

L.× arkwrightii **6**: hybrid of *L. chalcedonica* & *L.× haageana*: to 30×25cm (12×10in); lvs flushed purple; scarlet toothed fls to 4–5cm (1½–2in) across, inflated calyx, early–mid summer. Protect from slugs. Var 'Vesuvius' is dark red.

L. chalcedonica **7** (Maltese cross, Jerusalem cross): to 60–90×30–40cm (2–3ft×12–16in); lvs lance-shaped; brilliant scarlet cross-shaped fls to 2.5cm (1in) across in heads 8–12cm (3–5in) wide, mid summer. Var 'Plena' is double, rare.

L. (A.) coronaria (rose campion, mullein pink): to 60×30cm (2×1ft); lvs silvery-grey, woolly, to 10cm (4in) long, basal & along stems; clusters of magenta fls to 4cm (1½in) across, mid–late summer. Good on dry, poor soils. Vars: 'Abbotswood Rose' **8** (cerise); 'Alba' (white); 'Oculata' **9** (white centred cerise).

L. (correctly, S.) dioica (*Melandrium diurnum*, red campion): v hardy; to 50×40cm (20×16in); basal & stem lvs hairy; fls reddish-purple or rose, inflated calyx, spring–mid summer. Vars: 'Rosea Plena' (pink); 'Rubra' (*M. rubrum*; red).

L. (A.) flos-jovis (flower of Jove): v hardy; to 60×30cm (2×1ft); dense tufts of white-haired lvs & stems; loose, rounded infls of 1cm (½in) purple or red fls, inflated calyx, early–mid summer. Vars: 'Alba' (to 45cm [1½ft]; white); 'Hort's Variety' (to 30cm [1ft]; rosy-pink).

L.× haageana: hybrid of *L. coronata* & *L. fulgens*; to 20–30×20cm (8–12×8in); lvs mid-green; orange or scarlet fls to 5cm (2in) across, toothed.

L. viscaria (*L. [V.] vulgaris*, German catchfly): to 30×40cm (12×12–16in); tufted, grass-like lvs to 8cm (3in) long; dense infls of carmine fls to 2cm (¾in) wide, tubular calyx, late spring–early summer. Vars: 'Alba' (white); 'Splendens Plena' **10** (dark lvs; double fls).

Bouncing Bet (soapwort; *Saponaria officinalis* **11**): to 60–90×60cm (2–3×2ft); lance-shaped lvs to 10cm (4in) long; pink or white carnation-like fls to 4cm (1½in) across, mid–late summer if dead-headed. Can be invasive; good for wild garden. Provide twiggy support. Propagate by division. Best-known vars double: 'Alba Plena' (white); 'Rosea Plena' (pink).

Florists' chrysanthemums

Hybrids of complex parentage, classed as *Chrysanthemum* ×*morifolium*, probably derived from *C. indicum, C. makinoi* & other Chinese & Japanese spp; members of Anthemis tribe of daisy family. Somewhat tender perennials valued for late summer & autumn display & long-lasting cut flowers. In most areas, only early vars (flowering late summer to early autumn) grown outdoors; late vars (flowering late autumn & winter) grown under glass except in warm frost-free areas; mid-season (October-flowering) types can be used either way in mild areas. Plants more or less branching, depending on type & treatment (see below). Leaves lobed, pungent. Flowers in wide colour range, very varied in size & form. (As with all daisies, flowers are compound; sizes refer to whole flower heads.) **Cultivation**: Semi-to moderately hardy unless noted. For moist but well-drained fertile soil in open position. Plant shallowly late spring; stake tall vars. Stop when 15–20cm (6–8in) tall to induce branching. No further treatment needed for bushy plants of Spray, Mum, Korean & Pompon vars (produce many small flowers for display/cutting). With other vars grown for large blooms (mainly for cutting), disbud to leave 1 terminal bud per stem. Except where winters mild, cut down after flowering, lift crowns (stools) before hard frosts & overwinter frost-free. **Pests & diseases** include: eelworms; leaf miners; caterpillars; aphids; whitefly; virus & fungal diseases. **Propagation** (for vigour, raise afresh each year): Basal cuttings from stools brought into growth under glass, spring; Koreans, Charm & Cascade types also by seed. **Classification** (varies internationally): By season, flower type & flower size. Selection of early vars listed; mid-season & late vars classified in same way.

Large/medium-flowered (disbudded) types 1: to 1.2–1.5×0.6m (4–5×2ft); must be disbudded; fls 10–12cm (4–5in) across.

INCURVED **2**: fls double; petals forming tightly globular blooms. Vars: 'Cheerleader' (bronze); 'Coppersmith' (bronze); 'Peter Rowe' (yellow); 'Quarterback' (pink); 'Stadium Queen' (red).

REFLEXED **3**: fls double; petals fall outwards, overlapping to give umbrella effect. Vars: 'French Vanilla' (white); 'Parador' (purple); 'Ruth Lehman' (white); 'Snowflake' (white).

INTERMEDIATE **4**: fls double; loosely incurving, or incurving towards top & reflexed below. Vars: 'Acacia' (yellow); 'Fall Charm' (pink); 'Ginger Nut' (light bronze); 'Irish Linen' (white); 'Peace' (yellow).

DECORATIVES: fls double; outer petals generally reflexing and often laciniated at tips, inner petals sometimes slightly incurving, forming rather flattened blooms. Vars: 'Bunkerhill' (orange); 'Flying Saucer' (white); 'Mojave Gold' (bronze); 'Ruby Breithaupt' (yellow).

ANEMONE-FLOWERED **5**: semi-double fls 10–12cm (4–5in) wide rather like annual scabious (p522), with short outer petals & "pincushion" centre. Vars: 'Catina' (bronze); 'Premiere' (yellow).

SINGLE & SEMI-DOUBLE **6**: daisy-like fls 8–12cm (3–5in) across with small golden central disc & long outer petals. Vars: 'Daisy Bronze'; 'Daisy Gold'; 'Daisy Red'.

OTHERS: Spoon, Quill, Spider, Brush & Thistle vars have rather loose fls, to 10–12cm (4–5in) across, with long tubular quill-like petals, tip flattened in Spoon **7**, straight in Quill **8**, hooked in Spider, arranged nearly parallel to the stem in Brush, or flattened and twisted in Thistle vars. No early disbudded vars available.

Spray types 9: to 1–1.2×0.6m (3–4×2ft); dwarf, to 0.6–1×0.6m (2–3×2ft) in Mum vars; freely branching, with sprays of fls in similar forms to disbudded vars but 5–10cm (2–4in) across.

DECORATIVE vars **10**: 'Best Regards' (bronze); 'Betsy Ross' (white); 'Confetti' (pink); 'Golden Regards' (yellow); 'Jewel Box' (lavender); 'Redheart' (red); 'Ruby Mound' (red).

ANEMONE-FLOWERED vars: 'Ann Ladygo' (pink); 'Autumn Bride' (white); 'Muted Sunshine' (yellow).

SINGLE vars: 'Daisy Bronze'; 'Daisy Pink'; 'Daisy Red'; 'Daisy Royal' (purple); 'Daisy Yellow'.

SPOON vars: 'Early Starlet' (bronze); 'Happy Face' (yellow); 'Yellow Starlet'.

QUILLED vars: 'Apogee' (purple); 'First Lady' (pink); 'Pioneer Lady' (pink); 'Sea urchin' (yellow).

Koreans: moderately to v hardy vars similar in form to Sprays, with single or double fls to 5cm (2in) across. Can be grown as semi-permanent border plants in many areas. Often better raised from seed. Named vars in range of colours, though not commonly available.

Pompon types 11: low & bushy or cushion-like, to 30×60cm (1×2ft), with compact semi-/globular double fls 2.5–7.5cm (1–3in) across. Good for bedding or front of border. Vars: 'Baby Tears' (white); 'Brown Eyes' (bronze); 'Gypsy Wine' (rose); 'Sunloving' (yellow).

Charm types 12: bushy, to 1×1–1.2m (3×3–4ft), with v profuse fls to 2.5cm (1in) across (up to 3,000 per plant). Named vars late-flg, for growing in pots in cool greenhouse, but early-flg strains can be grown from seed as HHAs.

Cascade types 13: trailing, with flexible stems to 1–1.5m (3–5ft) long covered with profuse 2.5cm (1in) fls. For hanging pots, pedestals, etc; can be trained into specimen shapes. As with Charms, named vars late-flg, but seed of early vars available.

Chrysanthemum species and their relatives

Anthemis tribe of the daisy family. Easy border perennials (some evergreen), yielding long-lasting cut flowers (compound), some dryable. Leaves generally feathery, often silver, many aromatic when crushed. **Cultivation**: Unless stated, very hardy & for any well-drained soil in full sun. Pest- & disease-free. **Propagation**: Division unless noted. For rock garden spp, see 434.

Yarrows (*Achillea* spp): erect, with flattish or loose corymbs of rayless fls (good for cutting & drying); unless stated, lvs feathery, often aromatic. Excellent for mid borders. For hot dry places unless stated; divide regularly.

A. clypeolata: probably a hybrid; to 45×40cm (18×16in); evergreen pinnate lvs*, v silver-haired; tiny yellow fls in dense corymbs to 12cm (5in) across, early summer. Divide every spring. Var 'Moonshine' **1** is a hybrid with *A. taygetea*; to 60×45cm (2×1½ft); grey-green lvs*; canary-yellow fls; v popular.

A. filipendulina (*A. eupatorium*, fern-leaved yarrow): ultra-hardy; to 1.2×1.2m (4×4ft); grey-green toothed lvs* to 25cm (10in) long; tiny deep yellow fls in corymbs 10–15cm (4–6in) across, late summer. Vars: 'Coronation Gold' (hybrid with *A. clypeolata*; to 1m [3ft]; evergreen); 'Gold Plate' **2** (to 2m [6ft]; wide infls).

A. millefolium (common yarrow, milfoil): ultra-hardy weedy sp with some cultivated vars; to 75×60cm (2½×2ft); mat-forming; lvs dark green; fls in flat heads, early–mid summer. Invasive. Vars: 'Cerise Queen' **3**; 'Fire King' (bright red); 'Flower of Sulphur' ('Schwefelblüte'; pale yellow); 'Red Beauty' (rosy-red).

A. ptarmica (sneezewort, sneezeweed): ultra-hardy; to 75×60cm (2½×2ft); dark green narrow lvs; white fls (double in garden vars) in loose corymbs to 10cm (4in) wide, summer. For cool, moist soil; needs twiggy support; can be invasive. Vars: 'Snowball' ('Boule de Neige', to 40cm [16in]; 'Perry's White' (v white fls, early-mid summer); 'The Pearl' (mid-late summer).

A. serrata (*A. decolorans*) 'W. B. Child' **4**: to 75×45cm (2½×1½ft); dark green lvs; flat heads of single white fls, late spring (cuttable).

A. taygetea: probably hybrid of *A. clypeolata* & *A. millefolium*: to 45×15cm (18×6in); evergreen lvs*, slightly silvered; fls pale yellow in flat heads to 10cm (4in) across.

Anthemis (*Anthemis* spp): ultra-hardy; finely divided pungent lvs; daisy-like 5–6cm (2–2½in) fls, early–mid summer (cuttable). Cut back after flg. Propagate also by cuttings.

A. cupaniana **5**: to 30×40cm (12×16in); mat-forming; evergreen silver-grey lvs*; yellow-eyed white fls. Good for edging but can be invasive.

A. nobilis (common, garden, Roman or Russian chamomile; correctly, *Chamaemelum nobile*): 25×40cm (10×16in); can be sheared to 5–8cm (2–3in); finely cut evergreen lvs*; small white fls. Non-flg 'Treneague' best for fragrant lawns.

A. sancti-johannis **6** (St John's chamomile): to 45×40cm (18×16in); bushy; grey-green semi-evergreen lvs*; bright orange fls.

A. tinctoria (ox-eye chamomile, golden marguerite): to 75×45cm (2½×1½ft); lvs* woolly beneath; fls yellow. Short-lived. Vars & hybrids with *A. sancti-johannis*: 'E. C. Buxton' **7** (primrose); 'Grallagh Gold' (golden-yellow); 'Moonlight' (soft yellow); 'Wargrave Variety' (light yellow).

Artemisias (*Artemisia* spp): ultra-hardy; dissected silver foliage, often aromatic. For poor soils unless noted. For shrubby spp, see p78.

A. absinthium (wormwood, absinthe): to 90×60cm (3×2ft); sub-shrubby; silky-grey lvs*; small fls. Trim after flg. Best vars: 'Lambrook Giant'; 'Lambrook Silver' **8** (to 75cm [2½ft]).

A. lactiflora (white mugwort): to 1.5×0.45m (5×1½ft); erect; green lvs; grown for plumes of creamy, rather granular fls to 20cm (8in) long, mid summer (cuttable). For moist soils.

A. ludoviciana (*A. gnaphalodes*, *A. purshiana*, western mugwort, white sage, cudweed): to 1.2×0.45m (4×1½ft); narrow silvery-grey lvs*; sprays of v small grey-white fls, mid summer. Prune hard in autumn. Var *albula* **9** ('Silver Queen', 'Silver King', *A. albula*) grows to 90×60cm (3×2ft); profuse finely cut foliage*.

A. maritima (*A. nutans*): to 45×30cm (1½×1ft); finely-divided silver-woolly lvs*; fls yellowish. Var 'Powys Castle' is non-flg.

A. splendens **10** (often listed as *A. canescens*, *A. armeniaca*): to 45×30cm (1×1½ft); sub-shrubby; dainty filigree lvs*. Cut back in spring.

A. stellerana **11** (dusty miller, old woman, beach wormwood): to 45–60×45cm (1½–2×1½ft); lax; shrubby evergreen in mild areas; grey-white lvs; tiny yellow fls, late summer. Good near sea. Propagate also by semi-ripe heel cuttings.

A. valesiaca: to 45×45cm (1½×1½ft); filigree lvs* & white fls, both in arching sprays.

Chrysanthemums (*Chrysanthemum* spp): grown for showy daisy-like fls, white with yellow eye unless stated, cuttable. For fertile soil; healthiest with regular division. Propagate also by cuttings. For florists' chrysanthemums, see p268; for *C. parthenium* (usually grown as HHA), see p492.

C. coccineum (pyrethrum, painted daisy; often sold as *Pyrethrum roseum* or *P. hybridum*): ultra-hardy; to 75–90×45cm (2½–3×1½ft); bright green feathery lvs; daisy-like fls, early summer. For fertile alkaline soil; give twiggy

support; divide only after 3–4yrs. Single vars: 'Avalanche' (white); 'Brenda' (cerise-pink); 'Bressingham Red' (crimson-scarlet); 'Buckeye' (semi-double; scarlet); 'Corrillion' (salmon); 'Eileen May Robinson' (clear pink); 'Evenglow' (salmon); 'Kelway's Glorious' **1** (crimson); 'Robinson's Dark Crimson'; 'Silver Challenger' (white); 'Taurus' (blood-red). Double vars: 'Aphrodite' (white); 'Carl Vogt' (white); 'Helen' (light pink); 'J. N. Twerdy' (deep red); 'Lord Rosebery' (red); 'Mont Blanc' (white); 'Poinsettia' (large, red); 'Princess Mary' (deep pink); 'Progression' (pink); 'Prospero' (salmon); 'Red Dwarf' ('Roteszwerg'; to 30cm [12in]; carmine-red); 'Senator' (red flecked silver); 'Snowball' (white); 'Vanessa' **2** (pink flushed gold).

C. (*Pyrethrum, Tanacetum*) *corymbosum*: to 90×45cm (3×1½ft); daisy fls, mid summer.

C. *frutescens* (white or French marguerite, Paris daisy; sometimes listed as *Anthemis frutescens*): semi-hardy; sub-shrubby; to 45×45cm (1½×1½ft); dark green lvs; yellow-centred white fls all summer if dead-headed. For bedding, containers (raise annually from cuttings or treat as HHA). Can be trained as standard, to 1.2×0.6m (4×2ft). Var 'Jamaica Primrose' is light yellow.

C. *leucanthemum* (*Leucanthemum vulgare*, ox-eye daisy, moon daisy): ultra-hardy; to 60×45cm (2×1½ft); profuse 2.5–5cm (1–2in) daisy fls, early summer. Vars: 'Little Silver Princess' (dwarf); 'Maistern' (large fls).

C. *maximum* (Shasta daisy; probably correctly C.×*superbum*, a hybrid with C. *lacustre*): v hardy but not for hot, dry climates; to 90×45cm (3×1½ft); daisy fls, mid summer. Vars: 'Aglaia' (semi-double); 'Alaska' (single, ultra-hardy); 'Diener's Giant Double Strain' (double, semi-double & frilled fls); 'Esther Read' (double); 'Horace Read' (double, creamy); 'Little Miss Muffet' (to 40cm [16in]); 'Mrs Cornell' (semi-double); 'Polaris' (v large single); 'Röggli's Super Giant' (v large single); 'H. Seibert' **3** (frilled); 'Snowcap' (to 50cm [20in]); 'Thomas Killin' (semi-double); 'Wirral Supreme' **4** (double).

C. *rubellum* (C. *erubescens*; correctly, C. *zawadskii latilobium*): to 75×45cm (2½×1½ft); lobed lvs; fls pink, yellow eye, late summer/autumn. Vars: 'Clara Curtis' (clear pink); 'Duchess of Edinburgh' (bright crimson); 'Mary Stoker' **5** (yellow); 'Royal Command' (semi-double, purple-red).

C. *serotinum* **6** (C. *uliginosum*, Hungarian or giant daisy): ultra-hardy; to 1.8×0.45m (6×1½ft); single fls centred greenish-yellow, late autumn.

Asters, Michaelmas daisies and their relatives

Aster and Vernonia tribes of the daisy family. Easy (sometimes invasive) border perennials (herbaceous unless stated) all with daisy-like flowers (compound), singly or in sprays (all cuttable). **Cultivation:** Any fertile soil, moist but well drained, in sun. Most spp must be divided regularly. **Propagation:** Division; most spp by seed; *Celmisia* spp also by cuttings.

Asters & Michaelmas daisies (*Aster* spp): ultra-hardy and late summer/autumn flg unless noted; lvs narrow; fls golden-centred & daisy-like (except A. *linosyris*); colours noted refer to outer ray "petals". Some vars (especially A. *novi-belgii*) prone to powdery mildew & aster wilt.

A. *acris* (A. *sedifolius*): to 75×40cm (30×16in); bushy & non-invasive; fls lavender-blue, starry, to 2.5m (1in) across, in dense corymbs. May need staking. Vars: 'Nanus' (commonest form; to 45cm [18in]); 'Roseus' (lilac-pink).

A. *amellus**** (Italian aster): to 60×40cm (24×16in); stems woody; lvs rough, grey-green, to 12cm (5in) long; fls to 6cm (2½in) across. Fairly disease-resistant; slow-growing, non-invasive but long-lived. Divide every 3yrs. Vars: 'Brilliant' (bright pink); 'King George' **7** (violet-blue); 'Nocturne' (lavender); 'Pink Zenith' **8** (clear pink); 'Sonia' (rose-pink); 'Violet Queen' (to 45cm [1½ft]; violet).

A. *cordifolius*: to 1.2×0.45m (4×1½ft); silvery-blue fls to 2cm (¾in) across in wide heads. Vars: 'Ideal' (pale blue); 'Silver Spray' (silvery-blue).

A. *ericoides*: to 90×60cm (3×2ft); twiggy stems; profuse v late fls to 1.5cm (½in) across in panicles. Disease-resistant. Vars: 'Blue Star' (pale blue); 'Brimstone' (creamy-yellow); 'Delight' (white); 'Esther' (pale pink); 'Ringdove' (rosy-mauve).

A. *farreri*: v hardy; to 45×30cm (1½×1ft); solitary violet fls to 5cm (2in) across, early summer.

A.×*frikartii**** : hybrid of A. *amellus* & A. *thomsonii*; v hardy; to 75×40cm (30×16in); lavender-blue 5cm (2in) fls, v long season from mid summer. Excellent for borders (especially var 'Mönch' **9**). Other vars: 'Flora's Delight' (to 40cm [16in]; lilac-pink; cut back after flg); 'Wonder of Stafa' ('Wunder von Stafa'; pale lavender; may need staking). Divide every 3yrs.

A. *linosyris* (*Lynosyris vulgaris*, goldilocks): to 60×30cm (2×1ft); button-like rayless yellow fls to 1.5cm (½in) across in dense corymbs. Best var: 'Gold Dust' **10**.

A. *novae-angliae* (Michaelmas daisy, New England aster): to 1.2×0.45m (4×1½ft); pink to

mauve 2.5–5cm (1–2in) fls in loose terminal corymbs on woody stems; non-invasive. Useful autumn-flg plant for moist sites, but limited colour range; disease-free; divide every 2yrs. Vars: 'Alma Potschke' **11**, p273 (bright rose tinged salmon); 'Harrington's Pink' (clear pink): 'Lye End Beauty' (lavender); 'September Ruby' (rosy-crimson); 'Treasure' (lilac).

A. novi-belgii (true Michaelmas daisy, New York aster): to 0.3–1.2×0.3–0.45m (1–4×1–1½ft); fls in wide colour range, 4–5cm (1½–2in) across, in branched infls. Useful autumn-flg group for borders (dwarf types for edging), though some can be invasive; may self-seed. Susceptible to aster wilt and mildew; divide every 2yrs. Tall vars (to 1–1.2m [3–4ft] unless stated): 'Amanda' (rich violet); 'Blondie (semi-double, pure white); 'Carnival' **1** (to 60cm [2ft]; semi-double, red): 'Crimson Brocade' (vivid red); 'Eventide' (semi-double, violet); 'Freda Ballard' (semi-double, red); 'Marie Ballard' **2** (double, light blue); 'Mount Everest' (pure white); 'Royal Velvet' (to 60cm [2ft]; double, rich violet-blue); 'Sonata' (sky-blue); 'Winston S. Churchill' **3** (to 75cm [2½ft]; ruby-red). Dwarf vars (to 30cm [1ft]): 'Chatterbox' (red); 'Dandy' **4** (purplish-red); 'Jenny' (double, violet-purple); 'Lady in Blue' **5** (semi-double, blue); 'Little Pink Beauty' (to 40cm [16in]; semi-double, pink); 'Professor Kippenberg' (blue-purple); 'Purple Feather' (violet-purple); 'Royal Amethyst' (pale pink); 'Royal Opal' (icy-blue); 'Snowsprite' **6** (white); 'Victor' (lavender).

A. spectabilis: mat-forming, to 20×20cm (8×8in); deep green leathery lvs; blue fls to 4cm (1½in) across, early autumn. Disease-resistant.

A. thomsonii 'Nanus': to 40×40cm (16×16in); grey-green lvs; lavender-blue 4–6cm (1½–2½in) fls over long period. Trouble-free; do not divide.

A. tongolensis (*A. subcaeruleus*; often listed incorrectly as *A. yunnanensis*): v hardy; to 45×30cm (1½×1ft); mat-forming; hairy lvs; fls blue centred orange, to 6cm (2½in) across, early summer. Divide every 2–3yrs. Vars: 'Berggarten' (violet-blue); 'Napsbury' (deep blue); 'Shining Mountain' (lavender-blue).

Boltonias (*Boltonia* spp): easy ultra-hardy perennials, large & branching (stake); lvs insignificant; fls to 2cm (¾in) across, starry, in profuse panicles. Summer. Divide every 2yrs.

B. asteroides **7** (white boltonia): to 1.5×0.6m (5×2ft); fls white to violet.

B. latisquama (violet boltonia): to 2.5×0.6m (8×2ft); fls pinkish-purple.

Celmisias (*Celmisia* spp): moderately hardy evergreen perennials (v hardy if protected from winter wet) forming handsome rosettes of silver-haired lvs; mat-forming (spread by runners): fls white centred yellow, mid-summer.

C. coriacea **8**: to 30×60cm (1×2ft); woolly

stems; glaucous lvs, woolly below, to 60cm (2ft) long; fls to 8cm (3in) across.

C. spectabilis: to 40×30cm (16×12in); pointed woolly lvs; profuse fls to 5cm (2in) across.

Fleabanes (*Erigeron* spp): v to ultra-hardy plants for front of borders; mid-green lance-shaped lvs; fls 5–6cm (2–2½in) across, early–mid summer.

E. aurantiacus (double orange daisy): to 25×25cm (10×10in); mat-forming; velvety lvs; fls orange-yellow. Short-lived.

E.×hybridus: hybrids of various N American spp, including *E. speciosus macranthus*; generally to 60×40cm (24×16in); leafy stems; profuse fls. Best erigerons for borders & cuttings. Vars (often listed under *E. speciosus*): 'Adria' (amethyst-violet); 'Amity' (single, lilac-rose); 'Dimity' (to 25cm [10in]; pink); 'Double Beauty' (double, violet-blue); 'Foerster's Liebling' (to 45cm [1½ft]; semi-double, deep pink); 'Gaiety' **9** (bright pink); 'Prosperity' **10** (to 45cm [1½ft]; semi-double, light blue); 'Quakeress' (light mauve-pink); 'Rotes Meer' **11** (semi-double, red); 'Schwartzes Meer' (lavender-violet); 'Vanity' (clear pink).

Golden rods (*Solidago* spp): vigorous v to ultra-hardy border plants; spp tall but many vars shorter & less invasive; serrated narrow lvs; fls yellow, tiny but in dense sprays 10–30cm (4–12in) long, late summer/autumn. Divide and replant regularly. Self-seed.

S. canadensis: vigorous, to 1.8×0.75m (6×2½ft); suitable for wild gardens. Best-known var is 'Golden Wings'.

S.×hybrida (*S.×arendsii*): non-invasive hybrids mainly of *S. virgaurea* &×*Solidaster luteus*; best golden rods for gardens; golden-green lvs. Vars: 'Cloth of Gold' (to 45cm [1½ft]); 'Crown of Rays' **12** (to 45cm [1½ft]); 'Golden Dwarf' (to 30cm [1ft]); 'Golden Gates' (to 1m [3ft]); 'Goldenmosa' (to 1m [3ft]; fluffy sprays); 'Golden Shower' (to 75cm [2½ft]); 'Golden Thumb' ('Queenie'; to 30cm [1ft]); 'Lemore' **13** (to 60cm [2ft]; primrose); 'Mimosa' (to 1.5m [5ft]); 'Peter Pan' ('Goldstrahl'; to 1m [3ft]).

Solidaster (×*Solidaster luteus*,×*S. hybridus*, *Asterago lutea*, *Aster hybridus luteus*): v hardy; to 75×30cm (2½×1ft); lance-shaped lvs to 15cm (6in) long; small starry canary-yellow fls in 15cm (6in) panicles from mid summer.

Stokes's aster (cornflower aster, *Stokesia laevis*, *S. cyanea*): v hardy border plant to 45×45cm (1½×1½ft); glossy lvs; solitary cornflower-like fls to 8cm (3in) across with notched florets, white, pink & blue shades, late summer & autumn. Divide every 3yrs. Vars: 'Alba' (to 30cm [1ft]; white); 'Blue Danube' (light blue); 'Blue Star' **14** (to 30cm [1ft]; light blue); 'Wyoming' (to 40cm [16in]; deep blue).

Heleniums, sunflowers and their relatives

Helenium & Helianthus tribes of the daisy family. Long-flowering N American herbaceous border perennials with mainly yellow to bronze daisy flowers (compound); good for cutting; single unless stated. Best for massed planting. **Cultivation**: Easy; unless stated, for any well-drained fertile soil in full sun. Dead-head. Divide every few years in spring. **Propagation**: Division; spp by seed; cuttings; *Echinacea* & *Gaillardia* spp by root cuttings.

Chrysogonum (*Chrysogonum virginianum* 1): moderately to v hardy; to 30–60×25cm (12–24×10in); stems elongate late in season; hairy; bright green toothed lvs; starry golden fls to 2.5–4cm (1–1½in) wide, spring to autumn. For lime-free soil.

Coreopsis (tickseeds, *Coreopsis* spp): unless stated, to 45–60×45cm (1½–2×1½ft); golden-yellow fls, yellow or orange disc, all summer. *C. auriculata*: v hardy; 5cm (2in) fls, blotched maroon in var 'Superba'. Var 'Nana' grows to 15cm (6in); for front of border.

C. grandiflora (tickseed): v hardy; bushy but needs support; leafy stems; 6cm (2½ft) fls; rather short-lived & may be grown as HB; may self-seed. *C. lanceolata* is similar but ultra-hardy; basal lvs. Vars (may be listed under either sp): 'Goldfink' 2 ('Goldfinch'; to 30cm [1ft]; reliably perennial); 'Mayfield Giant' (to 1.1m [3½ft]; large fls); 'New Gold' (to 75cm [2½ft]; double); 'Sunburst' (to 75cm [2½ft]; semi-double); 'Sunray' (double; free-flg; can be grown as HA).

C. verticillata 3: moderately to v hardy; to 60cm (2ft); finely divided lvs; 2.5cm (1in) fls, long season. Vars: 'Grandiflora' ('Golden Shower'; fls to 4cm [1½in] wide); 'Zagreb' 4 (to 35cm [14in]).

Purple coneflower (*Echinacea* [*Rudbeckia*] *purpurea* 5): ultra-hardy; to 1–1.2×0.45m (3–4×1½ft); sturdy; crimson-purple 10–15cm (4–6in) fls, conical orange-brown disc, mid–late summer. Vars (generally to 75–90cm [2½–3ft]): 'Bressingham Hybrids' (free-flg); 'Bright Star' (rosy-red); 'Crimson Star' (to 60cm [2ft]); 'Robert Bloom' (intense cerise-purple); 'The King' (to 1.2m [4ft]; coral-maroon); 'White Lustre' (white).

Blanket flower (*Gaillardia aristata*): ultra-hardy where drainage perfect; to 60–90×45cm (2–3×1½ft); grey-green lvs; yellow & brownish-red 8–10cm (3–4in) fls, summer to autumn. Sp rarely grown; vars (correctly, *G.×grandiflora*; hybrids with annual *G. pulchella*; free-flg but may be short-lived): 'Burgundy' (deep wine-red); 'Croftway Yellow'; 'Dazzler' (yellow, maroon centre); 'Goblin' 6 (to 25cm [10in]; yellow & red); 'Mandarin' (orange-flame & red); 'Wirral Flame' 7 (browny-red & gold); 'Yellow Queen'.

Helenium (sneezeweed, *Helenium autumnale*): ultra-hardy; to 1.5×0.45m (5×1½ft); profuse 2.5–4cm (1–1½in) yellow fls, conical disc, from mid/late summer; may need staking. Most garden vars are hybrids with *H. biglovii*. Tall vars (to 1–1.2m [3–4ft]): 'Bressingham Gold' (gold

suffused crimson); 'Bruno' (crimson-mahogany); 'Butterpat' (yellow); 'Coppelia' 8 (coppery-orange); 'Latest Red' ('Spätrot'; bronze-red); 'Moerheim Beauty' (bronze-red); 'Riverton Beauty' (yellow, maroon eye). Short vars (to 60–75cm [2–2½ft]): 'Crimson Beauty' (mahogany); 'Golden Youth' (yellow; early); 'Mme Canivet' (yellow); 'Mahogany' (gold & brownish-red); 'Pumilum Magnificum' (butter-yellow); 'Wyndley' (orange, brown flecks).

Perennial sunflowers (*Helianthus* spp): bushier than well-known annuals (p496) but most rather coarse; generally to 1.2–1.8×0.6m (4–6×2ft); fls deep yellow.

H. decapetalus & hybrids (*H.×multiflorus*): v hardy; rough 20cm (8in) lvs; 5–8cm (2–3in) fls. Vars: 'Capenoch Star' (lemon); 'Flore-Pleno' (double, clear yellow); 'Loddon Gold' 9 (double).

H. salicifolius (*H. orgyalis*) to 2.5m (8ft); narrow willow-like lvs to 20cm (8in) long; sprays of 4–5cm (1½–2in) fls, early autumn.

Heliopsis (*Heliopsis scabra*; correctly, *H. helianthoides scabra*): ultra-hardy; to 1–1.2×0.6m (3–4×2ft); rough stems & lvs; 8cm (3in) yellow fls, all summer. Vars: 'Desert King' (single); 'Gigantea' (semi-double); 'Golden Plume' 10 (double); 'Gold Greenheart' (double, pale yellow, centre tinged green); 'Incomparabilis' (double, orange-yellow); 'Patula' (double, gold-yellow); 'Summer Sun' (short; semi-double).

Rudbeckias (coneflowers, *Rudbeckia* spp): fls generally golden-yellow, conical black or brown disc, from mid/late summer.

R. fulgida: v to ultra-hardy; to 60–90×45cm (2–3×1½ft); 6cm (2½in) orange-yellow fls. Vars: 'Deamii' (*R. deamii*, *R. speciosa deamii*; 8–10cm [3–4in] fls); 'Goldsturm' 11 ('Goldstorm'; 8cm [3in] narrow-petalled fls); 'Speciosa' (*R. newmanii*, *R. speciosa newmanii*; 8cm [3in] fls).

R. laciniata: ultra-hardy; to 2×0.6m (7×2ft); lvs deeply divided; yellow fls, greenish cone, 8–10cm (3–4in) across. Vars: 'Golden Glow' ('Hortensia'; double); 'Goldquelle' (often listed under *R. nitida*; to 1m [3ft]; fls double); 'Herbstsonne' 12 ('Autumn Sun'; often listed under *R. nitida*; 10cm [4in] fls, green cone).

R. maxima: moderately hardy; to 1–1.5×0.6m (3–5×2ft) or more; grey-green lvs; fls 12–15cm (5–6in) across.

R. subtomentosa: v hardy; to 90×45cm (3×1½ft); 8cm (3in) fls, button-like disc.

Knapweeds and their relatives

Carduus tribe of the daisy family. Trouble-free plants, many silver-leaved; compound flowers, generally purple, in globular thistle- or cornflower-like heads within papery bracts. **Cultivation**: For well-drained soil in sun. Lift & divide every 3–4 years. **Propagation**: Division; spp by seed.

Knapweeds (*Centaurea* spp): unless stated, v to ultra-hardy plants with dissected grey-green to silver lvs; fls cuttable. For dryish, alkaline soils.
C. cineraria (*C. candidissima*, dusty miller): to 45×45cm (1½×1½ft); white-lvd plant for edging. Moderately hardy if protected from winter wet, but best propagated by cuttings taken early autumn, overwintered under glass & planted out spring.
C. dealbata (perennial cornflower): to 60×60cm (2×2ft); lvs silver beneath; rose-pink cornflower-like fls, early summer (may repeat autumn). Stake; dead-head. Vars: 'John Coutts' (fls centred pale yellow); 'Steenbergii' **1** (to 75cm [2½ft]; fls deep pink, white centre; invasive roots).
C. gymnocarpa (dusty miller): moderately hardy; to 60×60cm (2×2ft); sub-shrubby; silvery lvs; v small purple fls, mid summer. Useful as foliage "dot" plant. Best treated like *C. cineraria.* Var 'Colchester White' is v silver.
C. hypoleuca: to 45×45cm (1½×1½ft); grey lvs; cornflower-like pink fls, late spring to early autumn; frs silvery.
C. macrocephala **2** (globe centaurea): erect & vigorous, to 1.8×0.6m (6×2ft); lvs lance-shaped, light green; fls like yellow thistles, early summer (good for drying).
C. montana **3** (mountain bluet): to 60×30cm (2×1ft); lax; lance-shaped greyish lvs; fls blue, early summer. For poorish soil. Vars: 'Alba' (white); 'Carnea' (pink); 'Violetta' (deep blue).
C. pulcherrima (*Aetheopappus pulcherrimus*): moderately hardy; to 30×30cm (1×1ft); pink fls, early summer. Needs warm position.
C. pulchra 'Major' **4**: moderately hardy; to 60×30cm (2×1ft); profuse pink fls, mid summer (dryable).
C. ragusina (dusty miller): moderately hardy; white-felted lvs; bright yellow fls, mid summer.
C. rhaponticum (giant knapweed): to 90×90cm (3×3ft); grey-white oblong lvs; lilac fls to 12cm (5in) across, mid-summer.
C. ruthenica: to 1×0.45m (3×1½ft); dark green lvs; lemon-yellow thistle-like fls, mid summer.
C. simplicicaulis: to 25×25cm (10×10in); profuse small silvery lvs; silvery-pink cornflower-like fls, late spring to mid summer. For edging or rock garden in sun.
Cirsium (*Cirsium rivulare*): ornamental thistle, to 1.2×0.6m (4×2ft); spiny-edged pinnate lvs, hairy beneath; purple fls in clusters, mid summer. Var *atropurpureum* **5** (*Cnicus atropurpureus, C. ruthenicus*) grows to 90cm (3ft); fls red-purple.

Globe artichoke (*Cynara scolymus* **6**): moderately hardy vegetable often grown as stately specimen or border plant; to 1.5×1.5m (5×5ft); much divided glaucous foliage, white-haired beneath; fls thistle-like, within large prickly bracts, mid summer (cuttable; dryable; bract-bases edible). Propagate by suckers.
Globe thistles (*Echinops* spp): ultra-hardy erect plants with globular, prickly metallic-blue fl heads, mid summer (dryable); lvs divided. Tolerate poor soil and drought; propagate by root cuttings or division.
E. banaticus: to 1.2×0.6m (4×2ft).
E. humilis: to 1.5×0.6m (5×2ft); lvs cobwebbed above, hairy beneath. Best var: 'Taplow Blue' **7**.
E. ritro **8**: to 1.2×0.6m (4×2ft); stems woolly; lvs glossy, downy beneath. Vars: *tenuifolius* (*E. ruthenicus*); 'Veitch's Blue'.
Serratula (*Serratula shawii* **9**): to 25×25cm (10×10in); finely divided lvs; bright purple cornflower-like fls, late summer & autumn.

Other members of the daisy family

Various tribes of Composites, some invasive but many showy border plants. Flowers are compound, mostly cuttable (some "everlasting") and usually either yellow or blue/purple. **Cultivation**: Unless stated, for light, well-drained soil in sun. **Propagation**: Division; spp by seed. For tender & semi-hardy perennial spp normally treated as annuals, see pp490–499.

Pearly everlastings (*Anaphalis* spp; Inula tribe): silver-lvd plants with yellow-eyed white fls in bunched heads, mid–late summer (good for cutting & drying; sometimes dyed). For moister soil and more shade than most silver-lvd plants, but ultra-hardy only if dryish in winter; otherwise v hardy. Divide every 3–4yrs.
A. margaritacea **1**: to 45×45cm (1½×1½ft); narrow lvs; profuse fls in loose heads.
A. nubigena (correctly, *A. triplinervis monocephala*): to 20×30cm (8×12in); compact var for dry places, rock gardens.
A. triplinervis: to 30×40cm (12×16in); lvs densely haired beneath, to 20cm (8in) long. Not drought-tolerant. Var 'Summer Snow' is good form.
A. yedoensis **2** (*A. cinnamomea*): erect, to 60×40cm (24×16in); fls in flattish heads, long season.
Mountain tobacco (*Arnica montana* **3**; Senecio tribe): v hardy alpine meadow plant, showy but invasive in borders; to 30×30cm (1×1ft); hairy lvs in basal rosette; dandelion-like orange/yellow fls to 8cm (3in) across, early summer.
Yellow or **willow-leaf ox-eye** (*Buphthalmum salicifolium* **4**; sometimes listed as *Inula* 'Golden Beauty'; Inula tribe): ultra-hardy showy border plant, to 60×60cm (2×2ft); lance-shaped lvs, dark green to greyish; large deep yellow daisy fls, early–mid summer.
Cupid's dart (blue cupidone, blue succory, *Catananche caerulea* **5**; Cichorium tribe): v hardy short-lived sparse perennial, to 75×45cm (2½×1½ft); wiry stems; narrow lvs; cornflower-like blue fls in papery calyx (cuttable, dryable), mid–late summer. Vars: 'Bicolor' (white, blue centre); 'Blue Giant' (pale blue); 'Major' (deep blue); 'Perry's White'.
Chicory (wild succory, Belgian or French endive, *Cichorium intybus* **6**; Cichorium tribe): ultra-hardy vegetable sometimes used as decorative border plant; erect & vigorous, to 1.5×0.6m (5×2ft); sky-blue daisy fls on sparse, branched stems, late summer & autumn. Prefers limy soils. Grow from seed. Pink & white forms exist.
Leopard's banes (*Doronicum* spp; Senecio tribe): v hardy spring-flg plants with yellow daisy fls (v good for cutting); toothed, heart-shaped lvs (die down in hot summers). Easy in moist soils in sun or partial shade; not for hot climates; divide every 2-3yrs.
D. austriacum: to 60×30cm (2×1ft).
D. cordatum (*D. caucasicum* , *D. columnae*): to

45×30cm (1½×1ft). Vars: 'Magnificum' (fls to 8cm [3½in] across); 'Spring Beauty' **7** ('Frühlingspracht'; v double fls). Var 'Miss Mason' ('Madame Mason') is probably hybrid of this sp; clump-forming; lvs persistent.
D. pardalianches (great leopard's bane): to 90×45cm (3×1½ft); branched flg stems; rather invasive. Var 'Gold Bunch' grows to 75cm (2½ft).
D. plantagineum: to 75×45cm (2½×1½ft); hairy; best in form 'Excelsum' **8** ('Harpur Crewe'; fls to 8cm (3in) across, 3 or 4 per stem).
Eupatoriums (bonesets, *Eupatorium* spp; Eupatorium tribe): easy erect perennials best in moist soils; all have toothed lvs & fluffy, usually blue-purple fls in corymbs, late summer & autumn (cuttable). Some are weedy, for naturalizing.
E. cannabinum (hemp agrimony): v hardy; to 1.2×0.6m (4×2ft); palmate lvs; reddish-purple fls in heads to 12cm (5in) across, commonest in double form 'Plenum'. Weedy, for wild gardens.
E. coelestinum (mistflower, blue boneset, hardy ageratum): v hardy; to 60×30cm (2×1ft); triangular lvs; fls blue, violet or white. Rhizomatous; invasive. Var 'Wayside' is compact, to 30cm (1ft); fls pale lavender.
E. purpureum ([sweet or green-stemmed] Joe Pye weed): ultra-hardy; to 1.8×1m (6×3ft); lvs* vanilla-scented; fls rose-purple, mid-late summer. Striking at rear of borders. Var 'Atropurpureum' **9** has purple lvs.
E. rugosum (*E. ageratoides*, white snakeroot, white sanicle): ultra-hardy; to 1.2×0.6m (4×2ft); white fls; poisonous to cattle.
Gerbera (Transvaal daisy, Barberton daisy, *Gerbera jamesonii* **10**; Mutisia tribe): semi-hardy S African plants with brilliant single or semi-double daisy fls to 12cm (5in) across, early–mid summer (v good for cutting). To 45×30cm (1½×1ft); lobed lvs, woolly beneath. Showy, for pots or bedding, or permanent planting in warm areas or if protected in winter; also grown under glass. Likes moist, well-drained soil; divide every 3–4yrs. Sold in mixtures (probably hybrids with *G. viridifolia*; white, pink, salmon, yellow, red, violet) – eg, 'Duplex Hybrids', 'Fantasia', 'Happipot'.
Helichrysums (perennial everlastings, *Helichrysum* spp): sub-shrubby perennials grown mainly for their grey-green or silvery foliage (evergreen in warm areas); clusters of small "everlasting" fls with papery bracts, summer. Generally moderately hardy, but need

protection from winter wet.

H. angustifolium (curry plant, white-leaved everlasting): to 40×60cm (16×24in); semi-shrubby; needle-like silvery-grey lvs*, curry-scented; fls mustard-yellow.

H. orientale: to 40×30cm (16×12in); narrow grey-felted lvs to 8cm (3in) long; lemon-yellow fls, late summer, best in var 'Sulphur Light' **1** ('Schwefel Licht'; sulphur-yellow fls).

H. petiolatum (liquorice plant): semi- to moderately hardy; lax, to 60×60cm (2×2ft) or more; stems semi-trailing; grey-felted rounded lvs to 4cm (1½in) long; fls creamy. Good in hanging baskets.

H. plicatum: upright, to 60×60cm (2×2ft); silvery-grey v narrow lvs to 10cm (4in) long; fls golden-yellow.

Hawkweeds (*Hieracium* spp; Cichorium tribe): ultra-hardy plants useful for poor dry soil; to 30–60×30cm (1–2×1ft); silvery hairy lvs forming basal rosettes; dandelion-like yellow fls, early-mid summer, on stiff stems. Self-seed; most spread by stolons.

H. bombycinum: lvs grey-green.

H. lanatum: densely silvered lvs; best when fls removed.

H. maculatum (spotted hawkweed): stems reddish; lvs spotted dark purple.

H. villosum **2** (shaggy hawkweed): clump-forming; lvs greyish, woolly.

Inulas (*Inula* spp; Inula tribe): ultra-hardy unless stated; grown for yellow daisy fls, usually with narrow "petals". For moist soil.

I. acaulis: v hardy; mat-forming, to 10×30cm (4×12in); stemless fls, early summer; for front of border or rock garden.

I. ensifolia: to 60×30cm (2×1ft); clump-forming; narrow, pointed lvs; fls mid summer (often 1st yr from seed). Var 'Compacta' to 25cm (10in).

I. hookeri **3**: to 60×60cm (2×2ft); hairy lvs; fls greenish-yellow, all summer. Spreads quickly.

I. magnifica **4**: to 1.8×1m (6×3ft); large lvs, hairy beneath; fls to 15cm (6in) across, late summer. For large borders & waterside gardens.

I. orientalis: to 60×45cm (2×1½ft); fls orange-yellow, early summer.

I. royleana (*I. macrocephala*, Himalayan elecampane): to 60×60cm (2×2ft); orange-yellow fls to 11cm (4½in) across, late summer. Dislikes heat, winter wet.

Gayfeathers (blazing stars, *Liatris* spp; Eupatorium tribe): striking upright border plants with v narrow grass-like lvs & tall dense spikes like bottle-brushes of generally pink to purple thistle-like fls. Unless stated, ultra-hardy; fl spikes to 30cm (1ft) long, opening from top (good for cutting). Tuberous-rooted; divide every 3–4yrs.

L. elegans: moderately hardy; to 1.2×0.45m (4×1½ft); fls all summer.

L. graminifolia: moderately v hardy; to 1×0.45m (3×1½ft); v narrow lvs.

L. pycnostachya (Kansas or cat-tail gayfeather): to 1.2×0.3m (4×1ft); fls mid–late summer. Var 'Alba' is white.

L. scariosa **5** (tall gayfeather): to 1.8×0.45m (6×1½ft); fls late summer. Vars: 'September Glory' (deep purple); 'Snow White' (to 1.2m [4ft]); 'White Spire'.

L. spicata (spike gayfeather; often sold incorrectly as *L. callilepis*): to 1×0.45m (3×1½ft); fls mid–late summer. Tolerates wetter conditions than other spp. Vars: *alba* (white); 'August Glory' (deep blue-purple); 'Kobold' **6** ('Gnome'; to 60cm [2ft]; mauve-pink); 'Silver Tips' (lavender).

Ligularias (golden rays, *Ligularia* spp; some previously included in *Senecio*; Senecio tribe): v hardy robust perennials for moist or boggy soil, useful for vertical accent; handsome mounds of large, long-stalked, leathery rounded lvs to 30cm (1ft) long or more, some dark-tinted; orange or yellow daisy fls on erect, branching stems. Prone to slugs & snails.

L. dentata (*S. clivorum*): to 1.5×1m (5×3ft); toothed heart-shaped lvs, flushed purple beneath; orange fls, mid-summer. Vars: 'Desdemona' **7** (lvs & stems purplish; fls orange-red); 'Orange Queen' (green lvs); 'Othello' (lvs red-purple). Var 'Gregynog Gold' (sometimes listed under *L. ×hessei*) is hybrid with *L. veitchiana*; to 1.8×1m (6×3ft); heart-shaped lvs; orange fls in huge spikes, mid summer.

L. (S.) przewalskii: to 1.8×0.75m (6×2½ft); purple-black stems; triangular, toothed lvs; ragged yellow fls in erect racemes, mid–late summer, best in var 'The Rocket' **8**.

Senecios (*Senecio* spp; Senecio tribe): v hardy moisture-loving perennials.

S. doronicum: to 45×30cm (1½×1ft); mat-forming; dark green lvs; yellow daisy fls to 5cm (2in) across, early summer. Var 'Sunburst' **9** is orange-yellow.

S. (Ligularia) tanguticus: to 2×1m (7×3ft); much divided foliage; tiny yellow fls in erect plumes to 30cm (1ft) tall, late summer; frs pale, fluffy. Invasive.

Venidio-arctotis (× *Venidio-arctotis*; Arctotis tribe): intergeneric hybrid of *Arctotis grandis* & *Venidium fastuosum*; tender bedding perennial; to 45×45cm (1½×1½ft); greyish lobed lvs, woolly beneath; pastel-coloured daisy fls to 8cm (3in) across, all summer (cuttable). Sterile, so no dead-heading needed; overwinter frost-free. Propagate by semi-ripe cuttings. Vars: 'Aurora' (pale bronze); 'Bacchus' (purple); 'Champagne' (cream & purple); 'China Rose' **10** (rose-pink); 'Flame' **11** (orange-red); 'Mahogany' (brownish-crimson); 'Sunshine' (brownish-yellow & crimson); 'Torch' (bronze & crimson).

Echeverias and sedums

Succulent-leaved sun-lovers providing contrast to other plants. **Cultivation & propagation**: See below.

Echeverias (*Echeveria* spp **1**, **2**): tender to semi-hardy rosette-forming evergreens often massed in formal summer bedding schemes; lvs v fleshy, blue-grey or -green, sometimes tinted reddish in strong sun; tubular or bell-shaped yellow to red fls in cymes or spikes on slender upright or arching stems, summer. For rich but gritty soil in full sun. Propagate by offsets, leaf cuttings, seed. Numerous spp & vars, generally less than 25cm (10in) tall, but *E. gibbiflora* grows to 1m (3ft), with rosettes to 60cm (2ft) wide.

Sedums (*Sedum* spp; sometimes called stonecrops, but name mainly used for mat-forming spp [see p438]): generally ultra-hardy, with rounded stalkless lvs on flg stems forming compact hummocks; small starry fls in flat or domed cymes, mainly shades of pink or red, summer unless stated. For any well-drained (even poor) soil in full sun. Propagate by stem cuttings, division. (Some smaller spp generally grown in rock gardens [p438].)
S. 'Autumn Joy' **3** ('Herbstfreude'): hybrid probably of *S. spectabile* & *S. telephium*; to 60×60cm (2×2ft); lvs pale grey-green; infls to 20cm (8in) wide of pink fls fading salmon to copper-red, late summer & autumn.
S. maximum (*S. telephium maximum*): to 60–

90×60cm (2–3×2ft); dark green 12cm (5in) lvs; yellowish-green fls, autumn. Vars: 'Atropurpureum' **4** (lvs & stems purple-red; fls pink); 'Variegatum' (*S. telephium* 'Variegatum'; lvs variegated yellow/cream; fls bronze-red).
S. morganianum **5** (donkey's tail): tender; prostrate, trailing stems to 1m (3ft) long, "braided" with overlapping grey-green lvs 2–2.5cm (¾–1in) long; sometimes clusters of rose-red fls. Good hanging basket plant; overwinter frost-free.
S. (*Rhodiola*) *rosea* **6** (*S. rhodiola*, rose-root): to 30×30cm (1×1ft); close-packed blue-grey lvs to 4cm (1½in) long; 8cm (3in) infls of pale yellow fls from coppery buds, late spring.
S. 'Ruby Glow' **7**: to 25×30cm (10×12in); blue-green lvs; 10cm (4in) infls of ruby-red fls.
S. spectabile **8**: to 45×45cm (1½×1½ft); grey-green lvs to 8cm (3in) long; fluffy 12–15cm (5–6in) infls of pink fls, late summer & autumn, on sturdy stems. Vars: 'Brilliant' (deep rose-pink); 'Carmen' (carmine-pink); 'Meteor' (carmine-red).
S. telephium (orpine): to 45–60×45cm (1½–2×1½ft); deep green narrowish lvs to 8cm (3in) long; flat 10cm (4in) infls of dusky red-purple fls on floppy stems, late summer. Var 'Munstead Red' is v dark.

The cress family

Often somewhat coarse perennials (herbaceous unless stated) with basal clumps or mats of leaves below profuse small cross-shaped 4-petalled flowers. Some good for ground cover, others best in wild garden. **Cultivation**: Unless noted, very hardy & for any reasonably well-drained soil in sun or semi-shade. **Propagation**: Seed; division; *Crambe* sp by root cuttings.

Cardamines (*Cardamine* spp): moisture-lovers forming mats of pinnate lvs, rounded watercress-like lfts; clusters of white, pink or purplish fls.
C. latifolia **9**: evergreen; to 45×60cm (1½×2ft); bright green lvs, darkening; lilac fls, late spring.
C. pratensis (lady's smock, cuckoo flower, meadow cress): to 50×25cm (20×10in); stem lvs narrow; small single/double white or rose-lilac fls, yellow anthers, spring.
Crambe (*Crambe cordifolia** **10**): to 1.8×1.2m (6×4ft); huge limp heart-shaped lvs to 75cm (2½ft) wide, lobed & toothed; open panicles to 75cm (2½ft) across of tiny white fls, summer.
Toothwort (*Dentaria pinnata*): to 45×30cm (1½×1ft); tufted light green divided lvs; racemes of white or mauve fls, spring. Likes shade.
Sweet rocket (dame's rocket, dame's or damask violet, *Hesperis matronalis***): ultra-hardy; evergreen; branching, to 1×0.6m (3×2ft); dark green lance-shaped lvs to 10cm (4in) long; loose

panicles to 45cm (1½ft) long of 1–2.5cm (½–1in) white, lilac or pale purple fls, early summer. Short-lived; self-seeds.
Perennial honesty (*Lunaria rediviva** **11**): similar to *L. annua* (p502) but taller & bushier, to 1.1×0.6m (3½×2ft); lvs sharply toothed; fls v pale lilac, almost white, spring. May be short-lived.

Spurges

Euphorbia spp. Curious spring- & summer-flowering plants (herbaceous unless noted) grown for showy heads of long-lasting bracts (often sulphur/greenish-yellow) surrounding insignificant flowers. Leaves narrow or lance-shaped, usually crowded on unbranched fleshy stems (exude irritant & often poisonous sap when cut). Useful for border contrast. **Cultivation**: Moderately hardy unless stated. For any reasonably well-drained soil in sun or partial shade. **Propagation**: Seed; basal cuttings; division.

E. charias **1**: to 1.2×1m (4×3ft); sub-shrubby & often evergreen; dark blue-grey lvs to 10cm (4in) long; column-shaped heads of sulphur-yellow to greenish bracts, centred brown, early spring. *E. wulfenii* **2** (*E. c. wulfenii*) is similar, with broader heads of yellowish-green bracts.
E. cyparissias (cypress spurge): ultra-hardy; creeping, to 30×60cm (1×2ft); grey-green 4cm (1½in) lvs; 5cm (2in) heads of green-yellow bracts, spring–summer. Likes lime.
E. epithymoides (*E. polychroma*): clump-forming & rounded, to 45×45cm (1½×1½ft); bright green lvs, reddish in autumn; 8cm (3in) heads of bright yellow bracts, spring.
E. griffithii: to 75×60cm (2½×2ft); pink-veined bright green lvs; 10cm (4in) heads of brick-red bracts (brightest in var 'Fireglow' **3**), yellow true

fls, late spring to early summer.
E. myrsinites **4**: trailing, to 15×40cm (6×16in); evergreen fleshy blue-grey sharp-tipped lvs in spirals; 5–10cm (2–4in) heads of greenish-yellow bracts, spring.
E. palustris: to 1×1m (3×3ft); bright green lvs, yellow-orange in autumn; 15cm (6in) heads of canary-yellow bracts, early summer. Likes moisture.
E. robbiae: spreading, to 60×60cm (2×2ft); rather leathery evergreen dark lvs; 8cm (3in) heads of greenish-yellow bracts, early summer. Good ground cover; tolerates poor soils, shade.
E. sikkimensis **5**: to 1.2×0.6m (4×2ft); young shoots & lf veins red; lvs to 10cm (4in) long; 8cm (3in) flat heads of deep yellow bracts, early summer. Best in moist soil.

Cranesbills

Geranium spp. Tough clump-forming border perennials (herbaceous unless noted) with deeply cut/lobed leaves & 5-petalled saucer-shaped flowers, to 2.5–5cm (1–2in) wide & early–mid summer unless stated. Good also for ground cover. **Cultivation**: Unless stated, very hardy & for any well-drained soil in sun or partial shade. Cut back taller spp after flg. **Propagation**: Seed; division. For smaller spp usually (but not essentially) grown in rock gardens, see p450.

G. endressii: to 45×60cm (1½×2ft); evergreen; 2.5cm (1in) pale rose fls veined darker, from late spring. Vars: 'A. T. Johnson' (silvery-pink); 'Claridge Druce' (hybrid; vigorous; lilac-pink 5cm [2in] fls); 'Rose Clair' (rose-salmon veined purple); 'Wargrave Pink' **6** (clear salmon).
G. 'Russell Prichard' is prostrate hybrid with *G. traversii*; moderately hardy; grey-green lvs; carmine fls, long season.
G. grandiflorum **7** (correctly, *G. himalayense*): spreading, to 30×60cm (1×2ft); lvs colour in autumn; violet-blue fls veined red. Vars: 'Alpinum' (dwarf; fls centred reddish); 'Plenum' ('Birch Double'; double). *G.* 'Johnson's Blue' is hybrid with dark-veined bright lavender-blue fls.
G. macrorrhizum: ultra-hardy; to 30×60cm (1×2ft); semi-evergreen lvs*, colouring in autumn; 2.5cm (1in) deep magenta fls, early. Vars: 'Album' (white); 'Walter Ingwersen' ('Ingwersen's Variety'; rose-pink).
G.×magnificum **8**: hybrid of *G. ibericum* & *G. platypetalum*, often sold as former; ultra-hardy; to 60×60cm (2×2ft); 2.5cm (1in) violet-blue fls.
G. phaeum **9** (mourning widow): to 60×45cm

(2×1½ft); small deep maroon-purple to blackish nodding fls, reflexed petals. Good in shade. Vars: 'Album' (white); *lividum* (dark lilac-grey).
G. pratense (meadow cranesbill): to 60×60cm (2×2ft); lvs colour in autumn; small red-veined blue-purple fls, mid–late summer. Vars: 'Album' (white); 'Album Plenum' (double, white); 'Coeruleum Plenum' (double, pale blue); 'Mrs Kendall Clarke' (pearly-grey tinted pink); 'Purpureum Plenum' (double, deep blue).
G. psilostemon **10** (*G. armenum*): bushy, to 90×75cm (3×2½ft); lvs colour in autumn; profuse intense magenta fls, black centre (softer lilac-pink in var 'Bressingham Flair').
G. sylvaticum: to 75×60cm (2½×2ft); grey-green lvs; white-centred violet fls, late spring, on hairy stems. Vars: 'Album' (white); 'Mayflower' (pale violet-blue); 'Wanneri' (pink).
G. wallichianum: semi-prostrate, to 30×90cm (1×3ft); white-centred light blue fls (clearest in 'Buxton's Blue' **11**), dark stamens, on hairy stems, early summer to autumn.
G. wlazzovianum: to 60×60cm (2×2ft); lvs & stems soft-hairy; dark violet to lavender-blue fls veined purple, all summer.

Pelargoniums

Pelargonium spp & vars, many of complex parentage; commonly called geraniums, but not true *Geranium* spp (p286). Tender evergreen sub-shrubs from S Africa. Stems semi-succulent, woodier in hot climates. Generally very free-flowering, late spring into autumn (all year under glass above 13°C [55°F]), in shades of white, pink, red, orange & purple; flowers single or semi-double unless stated. Some grown mainly for variegated &/or scented leaves. Numerous vars; selection listed below. **Cultivation:** For any free-draining soil in full sun or partial shade. Do not over-feed, -water or -pot; prune for bushiness; dead-head. Lift & take under glass before frosts to give propagating material. Prone to various diseases (seed-raised/young plants less so). **Propagation:** Cuttings, any season; seed sown over heat mid–late winter after chipping/soaking 48 hours (F1 hybrids grown as HHAs – main large-scale method).

Regal pelargoniums (*P.* × *domesticum* vars; in US Martha/Lady Washington geraniums, show geraniums): hybrids of various spp; to 45–60×40cm (18–24×16in); lobed, toothed, fluted lvs to 10cm (4in) across; 5–15cm (2–6in) umbels of v showy fls to 5cm (2in) across, often frilly. Best in pots. Vars: 'Applause' (pink, frilled); 'Aztec' **1** (pink, veined dark maroon, white base); 'Black Magic' (nearly black); 'Georgia Peach' (apricot-pink); 'Grand Slam' (red); 'Lavender Grand Slam' **2** (mauve marked maroon).

Zonal geraniums (common or garden geraniums, *P.* × *hortorum* vars): hybrids mainly of *P. inquinans* & *P. zonale*; to 30–60×30cm (1–2×1ft), but to 1.5×1m (5×3ft) where hardy; rounded/kidney-shaped lvs 8–12cm (3–5in) across, generally scallop-edged & often with ring-shaped bronze zoning (v colourful in fancy-lvd vars); umbels to 15cm (6in) across of single, semi-double or double fls to 2.5cm (1in) across. Best type for bedding; some can be trained as standards. Vars from cuttings: 'A. M. Mayne' (purple); 'Appleblossom Rosebud' (double, white edged green & pink); 'Burgenland Girl' (reddish-pink); 'Deacon' series (bushy, size depends on container size; double, various colours including 'Deacon Lilac Mist' **3**); 'Highfield's Festival' (rose-lavender, white eye); 'Irene' series 'Modesty' [double, white]; 'Penny' [neon-pink, white eye]; 'Treasure Chest' **4** [orange-scarlet]); 'Kathleen Gamble' (salmon); 'King of Denmark' (salmon); 'Morval' (pink); 'Orangesonne' (double orange); 'Regina' (pink); 'Stellar' series **5** (lobed lvs; starry fls).
Seed vars (F1 hybrids unless stated; generally fl in 4 months under glass at 21°C[70°F]): 'Carefree' (mixed & separate colours); 'Fleuriste Mixed' (F2 hybrid); 'Mustang' (brilliant scarlet); 'Orange Punch'; 'Picasso' (cerise, orange eye); 'Ringo' (scarlet); 'Sprinter' series, including 'Bright Eyes' (red, white eye), 'Cherie (blush-pink flushed salmon), 'Cherry Glow' (cerise), 'Debutante' (salmon), 'Showgirl' (rose-pink), 'Snow White', 'Sooner Red' (early; scarlet); 'Sprinter' (scarlet).
Fancy-leaved vars: 'A Happy Thought' **6** (lvs marked yellow; red fls); 'Caroline Schmidt' (lvs

green & white; double red fls); 'Chelsea Gem' (lvs green & white; double pale pink fls); 'Freak of Nature' (lvs cream or white, splashed green; red fls); 'Mrs Henry Cox' **7** (lvs green, yellow, red & copper; fls salmon); 'Prince Regent' (lvs pale green & chestnut; large salmon-pink fls).
Miniature vars (to 15×10cm [6×4in], more where hardy; good for edging, etc): 'Bridesmaid' (large double fls, cream marked orange & pink); 'Chieko' (double, crimson-purple); 'Fantasie' (double, white); 'Fleurette' (deep salmon); 'Jane Eyre' (deep lavender); 'Mr Pickwick' (salmon-pink); 'Red Black Vesuvius' **8** (red; near-black lvs); 'Sunstar' (orange); 'Sweet Sue' (deep red, white eye); 'Variegated Kleine Liebling' (red; lvs edged white); 'Virgo' (white).

Ivy-leaved geraniums (*P. peltatum* vars): trailing; stems to 1m (3ft) long; 5–8cm (2–3in) ivy-like fleshy lvs; smallish umbels of 2.5cm (1in) fls. V good for hanging baskets, window boxes, ground cover. Vars: 'Carlos Uhden' (double, deep red, white eye); 'Crocodile' (pink; lvs meshed white); 'L'Elegante' **9** (white & mauve; lvs marbled white & pink); 'Mexican Beauty' (dark red); 'Patricia' (double, pale lilac); 'Rouletta' **10** (red & white); 'Santa Paula' (double, mauve); 'Sybil Holmes' (double, rose-pink); 'Yale' (red).

Scented-leaved pelargoniums: to 60–90×45–60cm (2–3×1½–2ft) unless stated; lvs v fragrant when brushed or crushed; fls generally small. Good for pots. Spp & vars: 'Attar of Roses' (lvs** rose-scented); *P. crispum* (lemon or Prince Rupert geranium; crinkled lemon-scented lvs**, edged cream in var 'Variegatum' **11**; lavender fls); *P.* × *fragrans* (nutmeg geranium; 3-lobed nutmeg-scented lvs**; white fls; spotted & veined red); 'Lady Plymouth' (rose-scented lvs**, lobed & toothed, edged cream); 'Mabel Grey' (rough serrated lvs**, v lemon-scented); 'Prince of Orange' (similar to *P. crispum* but lvs** orange-scented); *P. quercifolium* **12** & vars such as 'Royal Oak' (oak-leaved geraniums; glossy oak-like pungent sticky lvs; mauve fls spotted & veined purple); *P. tomentosum* (peppermint geranium; shallowly lobed velvety pale green lvs** to 10cm [4in] across, peppermint-scented; tiny white fls).

Ornamental perennial grasses

Spp & vars of wild grasses with attractive leaves and/or graceful feathery flower- & seed-heads, early or mid summer unless stated (those marked † especially good for drying). Herbaceous unless stated. Grown for contrast in mixed borders, for ground cover & edging, as specimens & in pebble gardens; erect forms for screening & to provide vertical accent or arching grace. (Lawn grasses not covered here.) **Cultivation**: Easy; unless stated, very hardy & for any well-drained soil in sun. Tolerate pollution. Confine rhizomatous spp in sunken containers. **Propagation**: Division, spring; spp by seed, sown spring.

Golden foxtail (*Alopecurus pratensis* 'Aureus' **1**): to 50×50cm (20×20in); rhizomatous; lvs striped gold & green, brightest if clipped in spring to prevent flg. For ground cover.

Variegated oat grass (*Arrhenatherum elatius* [*A. bulbosum*] 'Variegatum' **2**): to 60×30cm (2×1ft); lvs striped & heavily edged white; forms aerial bulbils. For edging. Divide regularly.

Blue grama (mosquito grass, *Bouteloua gracilis*†): to 50×30cm (20×12in); tufted; v narrow mid green lvs; dainty infls held horizontally. Needs v good drainage; drought-tolerant (may die down).

Quaking grass (*Briza media*† **3**): to 60×30cm (2×1ft); tuft of green lvs; dainty open panicles of drooping heart-shaped green to purplish spikelets to 8mm (⅓in) long (tremble in breeze).

Pampas grass (*Cortaderia selloana*†, *C. argentea*): moderately to v hardy; to 3×1.8m (10×6ft); clump-forming; evergreen (herbaceous if v cold); arching, glaucous saw-toothed lvs; erect feathery panicles to 75cm (2½ft) long, silvery-white (best on females), late summer into autumn, best against dark background. Fine specimen. Drought-tolerant; mulch in winter in cold areas. Vars: 'Gold Band' **4** (to 1.5m [5ft]; lvs striped gold); 'Pumila' **5** (to 1.2m [4ft]; free-flg; good for small gardens); 'Rendatleri' (purplish infls; shelter from wind); 'Roi des Roses' (large pink infls); 'Sunningdale Silver' (to 3.5m [12ft]; strong stems).

Tufted hair grass (*Deschampsia caespitosa*†): to 90×90cm (3×3ft); tufted; evergreen; profuse graceful panicles to 50×20cm (20×8in), silvery, gold or purplish. For moist soil in semi-shade. Self-seeds.

Fescues (*Festuca* spp): evergreens with quill-like lvs, good for edging, banks. For sandy soil. *F. alpina*: to 15×15cm (6×6in); bright green lvs; pale green slender infls.
F. amethystina: to 45×30cm (1½×1ft); glaucous lvs; panicles to 15cm (6in) long of green or purplish spikelets.
F. glacialis: to 15×15cm (6×6in); silvery-blue lvs; greyish or violet-tinged infls.
F. glauca **6** (blue fescue; correctly, *F. ovina glauca*): to 25×25cm (10×10in); blue-grey lvs; purplish infls. 'Sea Urchin' is good tufted var.

Blue oat grass (*Helictotrichon* [*Avena*] *sempervirens* **7**; often sold as *A. candida*): to 1.2×1m (4×3ft); evergreen narrow glaucous lvs; slender upright infls. Graceful specimen in sun.

Variegated creeping soft grass (*Holcus mollis* 'Albovariegatus' **8** ['Variegatus']): to 25×25cm (10×10in); rhizomatous; lvs edged white; few infls. Good for edging, ground cover.

Koeleria (*Koeleria glauca* **9**): to 60×30cm (2×1ft); tufted; evergreen glaucous-blue lvs; narrow infls.

Bowles' golden grass (*Milium effusum* 'Aureum' **10**): to 45–60×30cm (1½–2×1ft); slender; arching bright yellow lvs (good for arrangements); loose yellowish infls. Makes fine highlight; self-seeds (breeds true). For rich moist soil in part shade.

Silver grasses (*Miscanthus* spp): vigorous & erect often variegated grasses useful as windbreaks or for specimen planting (good by water); flat lvs to 2.5cm (1in) wide, usually late developing; silky-white infls flushed red or purple, mid summer into autumn (best where summers hot); lvs & fls attractive through winter, so cut down in spring. For moist soils; for screens/windbreaks plant 60cm (2ft) apart.
M. sacchariflorus† (Amur silver grass): to 2–3×1m (7–10×3ft); rhizomatous but not invasive; gracefully curving toothed lvs, pale midrib. Var 'Variegatus' has lvs striped white.
M. sinensis† (*Eulalia japonica*, eulalia): v to ultra-hardy; to 1.8–3×1m (6–10×3ft); clump-forming; toothed blue-green lvs, white midrib, hairy beneath. Vars: 'Giganteus' (tallest var for screening); 'Gracillimus' (to 1–1.2m [3–4ft]; v narrow lvs); 'Silver Feather'† ('Silberfeder'; arching sprays of silky infls, to 2m [7ft]); 'Variegatus' (to 1.2m [4ft]; lvs striped yellowish & silver-white); 'Zebrinus'† **11** (zebra grass; to 1.2m [4ft]; yellow bands across lvs; striking).

Moor grass (Indian grass, *Molinia caerulea*): to 60×60cm (2×2ft); tapering green lvs; purplish branching infls, late summer & autumn. Likes moist soil. Var 'Variegata' is neat & tufted, with cream-striped lvs, beautiful in autumn & winter.

Switch grass (*Panicum virgatum*†): vigorous & erect, to 1.5×1m (5×3ft); flat lvs to 15mm (⅝in) wide, yellow in autumn; profuse feathery infls, late summer & autumn. Vars (to 1–1.2m [3–4ft]): 'Rubrum' (lvs & infls tinged red); 'Strictum' (lvs narrow).

Pennisetums (*Pennisetum* spp†): moderately

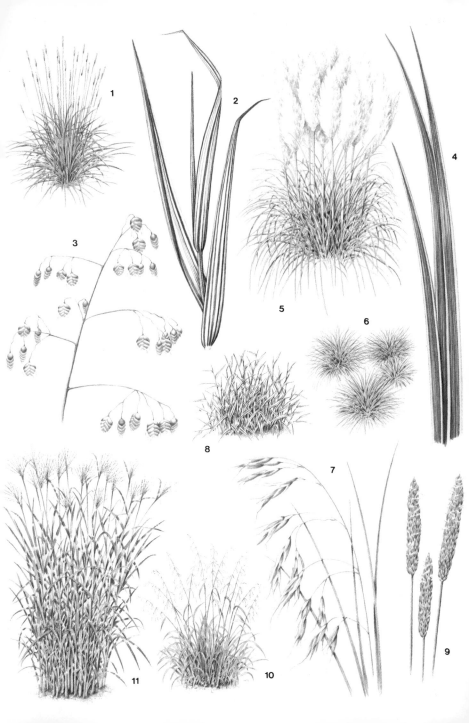

hardy; graceful arching lvs; feathery bottlebrush infls on tall curving stems, summer–autumn. Good as specimens. Mulch in winter in frosty areas.

P. alopecuroides (Chinese pennisetum, rose fountain grass): to 90×60cm (3×2ft); purplish or reddish infls. Var 'Woodside' is free-flg.

P. orientale **1**: to 45×30cm (1½×1ft); hairy lvs; fine silvery-pink infls, long season. Often grown as HHA.

P. setaceum (*P. ruppelii*, fountain grass): semi-hardy; to 90×60cm (3×2ft); pinkish or purplish silky infls to 30cm (1ft) long.

P. villosum **2** (feathertop; incorrectly, *P. longistylum*): to 60×45cm (2×1½ft); white to brownish infls. Often grown as HHA.

Gardener's garters (ribbon grass, *Phalaris arundinacea picta*† **3**, *P. a. variegata*): to 1–

1.5×0.6m (3–5×2ft); invasive; narrow lvs striped green & cream/white, brightest in spring; infls profuse but small, attractive in winter.

Variegated cord grass (*Spartina pectinata* 'Aureo-marginata'): to 1.8×1m (6×3ft); invasive; arching pale green lvs edged yellow; narrow green & purplish infls. Good near water (salt or fresh).

Feather or needle grasses (*Stipa* spp†): tufted, with narrow lvs & arching feathery infls to 30cm (1ft) long. Good as specimens. Moderately hardy.

S. (correctly, *Achnatherum*) *calamagrostis*: to 1–1.2×0.6m (3–4×2ft); greyish-green lvs; infls silvery to golden-brown. May need support.

S. gigantea **4**: to 1.2–2×1m (4–7×3ft); near-evergreen; profuse purplish infls turning yellow.

S. pennata (common feather grass of Europe): to 90×45cm (3×1½ft); silvery infls, v long awns.

Bamboos

Graceful & elegant giant grasses often thought of (& used) as shrubs but actually woody-stemmed evergreen or semi-evergreen perennials, mainly from Far East. Many spp too vigorous or invasive for small gardens, but others make fine specimens; some good in tubs or as screens; some spp dwarfs good for ground cover. Arching jointed stems (usually hollow) of upright spp bend in breeze, rustling leaves. Leaves lance-shaped, variegated in some vars. Most flower rarely at long intervals but may then die. Nomenclature confused. **Cultivation**: Moderately to very hardy unless stated, but protect from cold winds. Best in moist, fertile soil in sun or partial shade. Check spread of invasive types by confining roots in tub, or by severing underground rhizomes. **Propagation**: Division, late spring or early autumn; root cuttings; seed (see above). For Chinese sacred bamboo (*Nandina domestica*), see p60.

Arundinarias (*Arundinaria* spp): unless stated, good specimen/tub plants.

A. anceps: invasive, to 3–4.5m (10–15ft) or more; graceful & arching, forming dense thicket; bright green lvs 4–10cm (1½–4in) long. Good for screening.

A. (*Pleioblastus*) *humilis*: invasive, spreading, to 0.6×1.2m (2–4ft); stems v slender; bright green lvs to 18cm (7in) long. For ground cover. *A.* (*P.*) *pumila* is similar.

A. (*Pseudosasa*) *japonica* (*Bambusa metake*, arrow bamboo, metake): invasive, vigorous, to 2–4.5m (7–15ft); erect canes to 2cm (¾in) thick; lvs to 30×5cm (12×2in). Good for screening.

A. (*Sinarundinaria*) *murielae* **5** (correctly, *Thamnocalamus spathaceus*): non-invasive, clump-forming, to 2–3m (7–10ft); arching green to yellowish canes; dark green lvs to 10cm (4in) long. Excellent specimen.

A. (*Sinarundinaria*) *nitida*: non-invasive, to 2.5–4m (8–13ft); similar to *A. murielae* but canes dark purple. Needs semi-shade.

A. vagans (*Pleioblastus viridistriatus vagans*): v invasive, to 0.3m (1ft) or wider, forming dense carpet; v narrow stems; narrow lvs to 10cm (4in) long. For ground cover in wild garden.

A. (*Pleioblastus*) *variegata* **6** (*A. fortunei*): moderately invasive, spreading & thicket-forming, to 1m (3ft); white & dark green striped lvs to 15cm (6in) long. Attractive.

A. (*Pleioblastus*) *viridistriata* **7**: non-invasive, clump-forming, to 1.2m (4ft); lvs to 20cm (8in) long, brightly striped green & gold.

Phyllostachys (*Phyllostachys* spp): densely clump-forming spp with zigzag canes to 4cm (1½in) thick or more.

P. aurea **8** (golden bamboo): invasive, to 4.5m (15ft); yellowish-green canes used for umbrella handles; profuse dark green narrow lvs to 10cm (4in) long.

P. nigra: invasive, to 3–6m (10–20ft); old canes black; profuse dark green lvs to 12cm (5in) long.

P. viridiglaucescens **9**: invasive, to 4.5–6m (15–20ft); canes bright green flushed purple, arching at edge of clump; bright green lvs to 12cm (5in) long. *P. flexuosa* is similar but much more compact.

Sasa (*S. palmata*: v invasive, to 2.5m (8ft); glaucous canes; v large bright green lvs to 30×8cm (12×3in). *S. veitchii* **10** is dwarf but equally invasive; lvs edged white.

Shibataea (*Shibataea kumasasa*): non-invasive, moderately hardy; compact & clump-forming, to 75cm (2½ft); zigzag flattened canes; lvs to 10×2.5cm (4×1in), with stalks. Good for ground cover; distinctive.

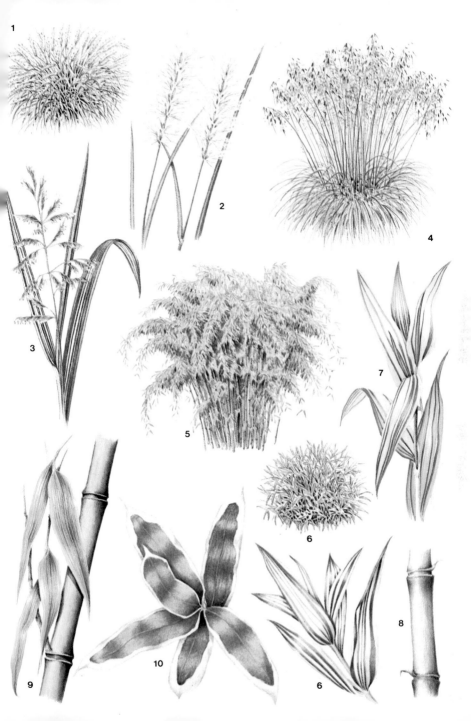

The mint family

Generally herbaceous perennials, often hairy, with square stems & usually toothed leaves (often aromatic; some used as culinary herbs or source of aromatic oils). Hooded flowers, usually in whorls along erect stems. Some spp invasive but useful for ground cover. **Cultivation**: Easy; for well-drained soil in sun unless stated. **Propagation**: Division; cuttings; spp by seed. For bugles (*Ajuga* spp), see p454.

Mexican giant hyssop (*Agastache mexicana* **1**): moderately hardy; erect, to 30–60×30cm (1–2×1ft); lvs* to 6cm (2½in) long; 10cm (4in) spikes of profuse pink or crimson fls, early–mid summer. Short-lived; striking in warm, dry spot.

Calamints (*Calamintha* spp): v hardy dwarf mint-like plants with profuse small fls.
C. (*Satureja*) *grandiflora*: to 45×45cm (1½×1½ft); lvs* to 6cm (2½in) long; pink sage-like fls to 2.5cm (1in) long, early summer.
C. nepetoides **2** (correctly, *C. nepeta nepeta*): to 30×30cm (1×1ft); mint-scented lvs* 2.5cm (1in) long; thyme-like lilac fls to 1.5cm (⅝in) long, late summer & autumn. Attracts bees.

Horehound (*Ballota pseudodictamnus*): moderately hardy plant grown for greyish woolly rounded lvs; sprawling, to 30–60×60cm (1–2×2ft); sub-shrubby; insignificant pale mauve fls, summer. Dislikes winter wet; cut back late winter.

Elsholtzia (mint shrub, *Elsholtzia stauntonii*): v hardy sub-shrub, to 1.2×0.6m (4×2ft); lance-shaped mint-scented lvs* to 15cm (6in) long; panicles to 20cm (8in) long of purplish-pink fls, late summer & autumn. Cut back late winter.

Hyssop (*Hyssopus officinalis* **3**): ultra-hardy; to 45×30cm (1½×1ft); sub-shrubby; lance-shaped lvs* to 4cm (1½in) long; purple-blue fls to 1cm (½in) long in spikes to 12cm (5in) tall, mid–late summer. Can be grown as low hedge (trim spring). Best on dry, chalky soils. Vars: 'Albus' (white); 'Roseus' (pink).

Dead nettles (*Lamium* spp): rather invasive plants for ground cover; evergreen nettle-like lvs; fl late spring & early summer. Shade-tolerant; good under trees. Shear after flg.
L. (correctly, *Lamiastrum*) *galeobdolon* (*Galeobdolon luteum*, yellow archangel, golden dead nettle): v hardy; sprawling, to 30–60×60cm (1–2×2ft); lvs to 8cm (3in) long; yellow fls. Rampant; for wild garden. Vars: 'Silver Carpet' ('Silberteppiche'; non-invasive; lvs speckled silver); 'Variegatum' **4** (lvs marbled silver).
L. garganicum: v hardy; to 15×40cm (6×16in); neat habit; pink to red fls. For moist shade.
L. maculatum (spotted dead nettle): ultra-hardy; to 30×60cm (1×2ft); crinkled lvs 4cm (1½in) long, central silver markings; purplish-pink fls in 5cm (2in) spikes. Vars: 'Album' (white); 'Aureum' (to 20×20cm [8×8in]; yellow semi-evergreen lvs, white stripe; best in moist shade); 'Beacon Silver' **5** (lvs completely silvered; fine carpeting plant); 'Chequers' (to 20×45cm [8×18in]; small

lvs); 'Roseum' (pale pink).
L. orvala **6** (giant dead nettle): v hardy; to 60×30cm (2×1ft); clump-forming & non-invasive; herbaceous; heart-shaped 6cm (2½in) lvs; white, buff-pink or purplish fls.

Lemon balm (common balm, *Melissa officinalis*): v hardy; dense & erect, to 60×45cm (2×1½ft); hairy lemon-scented oval lvs* to 8cm (3in) long, deeply veined; insignificant white fls. Self-seeds; shade-tolerant. Vars: 'All Gold' (lvs golden); 'Aurea' **7** (lvs splashed gold).

Bastard balm (*Melittis melissophyllum* **8**): v hardy; to 45×45cm (1½×1½ft); wrinkled lvs* to 8cm (3in) long; white & pink-striped fls to 4cm (1½in) long, late spring to mid summer. Takes shade.

Mints (*Mentha* spp): v hardy culinary & medicinal herbs, mostly invasive & few ornamental; lvs* generally pointed, to 6cm (2½in) long; rather insignificant pink to purplish fls, mid–late summer. Like moist soil; roots best confined in sunken containers; prone to rust.
M.×*gentilis* (red or Scotch mint): hybrid of *M. arvensis* & *M. spicata*: to 45×60–90cm (1½×2–3ft); reddish stems. Var 'Variegata' has lvs splashed yellow; best ornamental form.
M. longifolia (horsemint): variable, to 0.3–1.2×0.6m (1–4×2ft); whole plant grey-green; lvs* to 9cm (3½in) long; spikes to 10cm (4in) long of pink, lilac or white fls.
M.×*rotundifolia* (apple mint): hybrid of *M. longifolia* & *M. suaveolens*, but plants sold are probably *M. suaveolens*; to 60–90×60cm (2–3×2ft) or wider; hairy; pale green rounded lvs* (v good flavour). Var 'Variegata' **9** (pineapple mint) has lvs* edged & splashed white.

Sweet bergamot (Oswego tea, bee balm, *Monarda didyma*): v hardy; to 60–90×45cm (2–3×1½ft); hairy mint-like lvs* to 10cm (4in) long; sage-like scarlet fls, hooded & in heads to 8cm (3in) across, all summer if dead-headed. For moist soil; can be invasive; divide every few yrs. Vars & hybrids with *M. fistulosa*: 'Adam' (cerise-scarlet); 'Cambridge Scarlet' **10**; 'Croftway Pink' **11** (rosy); 'Mahogany' (deep red-brown); 'Prairie Glow' (salmon-red); 'Prairie Night' (rich purple-violet); 'Snow Maiden' (white).

Catmint & ground ivy (*Nepeta* spp): ultra-hardy spreading plants for ground cover; semi-evergreen; fl all summer if dead-headed.
N.×*faassenii* (often sold incorrectly as *N. mussinii*): hybrid of *N. mussinii* & *N. nepetella*;

sprawling, to 30–45×45cm (1–1½×1½ft); greyish lvs* to 3cm (1¼in) long; racemes to 15cm (6in) tall of sterile lavender fls. Var 'Six Hills Giant' (often sold as *N. gigantea*) to 60cm (2ft). Need v good drainage; dislike cold wet winters.
N. (*Dracocephalum*) *govaniana*: compact & erect, to 90×60cm (3×2ft); pointed lvs; profuse spikes of yellow tubular fls.
N. (correctly, *Glechoma*) *hederacea* 'Variegata' (*N. glechoma* 'Variegata', variegated ground ivy): mat-forming & trailing, to 0.1×1.2m (4in×4ft); evergreen kidney-shaped lvs* to 1cm (½in) long, pale green splashed white; lavender fls in lf axils, spring to early summer.
N. nervosa **1**: bushy, to 30–60×30cm (1–2×1ft); narrow lvs to 10cm (4in) long; blue fls in dense spikes to 15cm (6in) tall. Showy.
N. sibirica (*N. macrantha*): spreading, to 90×45cm (3×1½ft); lvs* to 9cm (3½in) long; violet-blue fls on erect stems. Var 'Blue Beauty' ('Souvenir d'André Chaudron') grows to 45cm (1½ft); lavender-blue fls; invasive.
Common or wild marjoram (oregano, *Origanum vulgare*): ultra-hardy; to 30–45×30cm (1–1½×1ft); rounded lvs* to 4cm (1½in) long up wiry stems; rosy-purple fls in clusters to 10cm (4in) tall, mid summer. Culinary herb. Var 'Aureum' **2** has yellow young lvs fading green.
Russian sage (*Perovskia atriplicifolia*): v hardy; to 1–1.5×0.45m (3–5×1½ft); sub-shrubby; whole plant downy; grey-green lvs* to 5cm (2in) long; panicles to 30cm (1ft) long of small violet-blue fls, late summer. Vars: 'Blue Mist' (pale blue; early); 'Blue Spire' (lvs finely lobed).
Phlomis (*Phlomis* spp): generally moderately hardy bushy plants with hairy heart-shaped lvs & spikes of fls on erect stems in early summer.
P. russeliana **3** (sometimes sold incorrectly as *P. viscosa*): to 1.2×0.45m (4×1½ft); yellow fls.
P. samia: to 90×60cm (3×2ft); yellowish fls.
P. tuberosa: ultra-hardy; to 1.5×1m (5×3ft); tuberous; lvs to 25cm (10in) long; pinkish fls.
Obedient plant (lion's heart, false dragonhead, *Physostegia virginiana*): ultra-hardy; slender & upright, to 0.75–1.2×0.6m (2½–4×2ft); lance-shaped lvs to 12cm (5in) long; snapdragon-like mauve-pink fls in erect spikes, mid–late summer. For moist soil. Vars: 'Rose Bouquet' (pink); 'Summer Snow' **4** (white); 'Summer Spire' **5** (lilac-purple); 'Vivid' (to 50cm [20in]; rose; late).
Brazilian coleus (Swedish ivy, *Plectranthus oertendahlii* **6**): tender S African prostrate foliage plant, for semi-shade; to 15×45cm (6×18in); hairy; rounded evergreen lvs to 5cm (2in) across, bronze-green with silvered veins; clustered white & purple fls, summer & autumn.
Salvias (sage & clary, *Salvia* spp): sun-loving easy border plants, some short-lived; hairy & aromatic; fls in erect spikes, many useful for late flg, good for cutting. Divide every 3–4yrs.

S. azurea (blue sage): moderately hardy; to 1–1.8×0.6m (3–6×2ft); narrow grey-green lvs to 8cm (3in) long; clear blue fls, autumn. Var *grandiflora* (*S. pitcheri*) has larger fls.
S. blepharophylla: semi-hardy; to 45×45cm (1½×1½ft); sub-shrubby; dark green glossy lvs; bright red fls, summer. Rather invasive roots.
S. fulgens (cardinal sage): tender to semi-hardy; to 90×60cm (3×2ft); sub-shrubby; lvs to 8cm (3in) long; spikes of vivid red fls 5cm (2in) long, purplish-red calyx, summer & autumn.
S. guaranitica (*S. ambigens*): semi- or moderately hardy; to 1.5×0.6m (5×2ft); dark green lvs to 12cm (5in) long; deep blue fls in branched spikes, mid summer to autumn.
S. pratensis (meadow clary): ultra-hardy; to 0.3–1.2×0.6m (1–4×2ft); basal clump of lvs* to 15cm (6in) long; pink, lavender, blue or violet-purple fls in branched spikes, early summer. Short-lived. Vars: 'Rosea' **7** (rosy-purple).
S.×superba (often sold incorrectly as *S. nemorosa* or *S. virgata nemorosa*): hybrid of *S.×sylvestris* & *S. villicaulis*; v hardy; to 90×45–60cm (3×1½–2ft); bushy; grey-green lvs* to 8cm (3in) long; spikes of violet-blue fls, crimson-purple bracts, mid summer to autumn. Vars & related hybrids: 'East Friesland' (to 75cm [2½ft]); 'Lubeca' **8** (to 45cm [1½ft]); 'Indigo' **9** (to 1.1m [3½ft]; deep blue, branching spikes); 'May Night' ('Mainacht'; to 40cm [16in]; dark violet; v early).
S. uliginosa (bog sage): moderately hardy; to 1.5×0.45m (5×1½ft); broad toothed lvs to 10cm (4in) long; sky-blue fls in branching spikes, autumn. For moist soils; needs support.
Betonies (*Stachys* spp): easy border & edging plants mostly with purple, cuttable lvs.
S. (*Betonica*) *grandiflora* (*B.* [*S.*] *macrantha*, woundwort): ultra-hardy; to 60–90×30cm (2–3×1ft); rosettes of dark green corrugated lvs to 6cm (2½in) long; fls rosy-violet, early–mid summer. Divide every few yrs. Variable; good vars: 'Robusta' **10** (vigorous; lilac-mauve); 'Rosea Superba' (rich rose-purple).
S. lanata **11** (*S. olympica*, lamb's tongue, lamb's ear, woolly betony; correctly, *S. byzantina*): v hardy evergreen mat-forming perennial, to 30–45×30cm (1–1½×1ft); grown for tongue-shaped densely silver-haired lvs to 15cm (6in) long; purple fls on woolly spikes from mid summer. Tolerates drought. Vars: 'Olympica' (silvery-white lvs; pinkish fls); 'Sheila McQueen' (larger lvs & fls); 'Silver Carpet' **12** (non-flg).
S. (*Betonica*) *officinalis* (*S. betonica*, bishop's-wort, wood betony): v hardy; to 60×30cm (2×1ft); lvs to 12cm (5in) long; fls red-purple, mid–late summer. Tolerates hot, dry soil.
S. spicata: compact, to 45×45cm (1½×1½ft); puckered lvs; pink fls in spikes to 8cm (3in) tall, early–mid summer. Vars: 'Densiflora' (dense infls); 'Rosea' (to 30cm [1ft]; bright pink).

The pea family

Easy border perennials with typical pea flowers (erect "standard" petal, 2 "wing" petals, 2 lower petals united into a pouch or "keel") often in showy spikes, some highly developed by hybridization. Generally herbaceous, the sub-shrubby spp deciduous unless stated; leaves compound. Seed pods sometimes inflated. **Cultivation**: Unless stated, very hardy & for any well-drained soil in sun. **Propagation**: Division; seed, sown spring after chipping/soaking; sub-shrubs & *Lupinus* vars by cuttings.

False indigoes (*Baptisia* spp): bushy & upright, to 1.2×0.6m (4×2ft); blue-green lvs in 3s; lupin-like fls, early summer, good for cutting; frs inflated, dryable. Prefer deep, moist, lime-free soil; resent disturbance.
B. australis **1**: ultra-hardy; fls indigo-blue.
B. tinctoria (horsefly, wild indigo): moderately to v hardy; bright yellow fls in branched spikes. Useful in wild garden. Drought-tolerant.
Wild senna (*Cassia marilandica*): ultra-hardy sub-shrub, to 1–1.2×1m (3–4×3ft); pinnate lvs; 8cm (3in) racemes of yellow fls, summer; frs to 10cm (4in) long.
Desmodium (*Desmodium tiliifolium*): moderately to v hardy sub-shrub, to 1.2×1.2m (4×4ft); lvs in 3s; 30cm (1ft) panicles of pale lilac to dark pink fls, late summer into autumn, best in hot summers.
Canary clover (*Dorycnium* [*Lotus*] *hirsutum*): moderately to v hardy broom-like sub-shrub, to 60×60cm (2×2ft); silver-haired; clover-like lvs; small heads of white, pink & purple fls, all summer. Best in hot, poor soil.
Goat's rue (*Galega officinalis*): ultra-hardy vetch-like perennial, to 1–1.5×0.75m (3–5×2½ft); light green pinnate lvs; 30cm (1ft) branched spikes of white to rosy-mauve fls, summer. For borders (need support) or wild garden. Vars (most correctly *G.×hartlandii*; hybrids with *G. patula*): 'Alba' **2** (white); 'Carnea' (pinkish-mauve); 'Her Majesty' **3** (lilac-pink); 'Lady Wilson' (mauve & cream). *G. orientalis* is similar but smaller, with clear violet-blue fls; invasive root.
Vetchlings (wild peas, *Lathyrus* [*Orobus*] spp): non-climbing relatives of perennial peas (p232); dense & bushy, with pinnate lvs & spring fls.
L. (*O.*) *aureus* (often listed as *O. aurantiacus*; correctly, *L.* [*O.*] *luteus aureus*): to 60×60cm (2×2ft); fresh green lvs; amber fls.
L. (*O.*) *vernus* **4**: to 30–45×30cm (1–1½×1ft); rather ferny pale green foliage; small infls of purple & blue fls. Charming with spring bulbs. Var 'Spring Charm' is creamy-pink.
Bush clover (*Lespedeza thunbergii* **5**, *L. sieboldii*, *Desmodium penduliflorum*): moderately to v hardy arching sub-shrub, to 1.2–2.5×3m (4–8×10ft); lvs in 3s, appearing late; rosy-purple fls in drooping panicles to 60cm (2ft) long, late summer to early autumn. Splendid late display. Cut to ground early spring.
Parrot's beak (winged pea, *Lotus berthelotii* **6**):

semi-hardy evergreen trailing or scrambling sub-shrub, to 30–60×90cm (1–2×3ft); lvs hairy, silver-grey; scarlet fls, hooked standards, early summer. For ground cover in v well-drained soil where hardy; elsewhere for pots, hanging baskets. Trim for bushiness; dies back in cold.
Garden or Russell lupins (lupines, *Lupinus* hybrids* **7** derived mainly from blue-fld *L. polyphyllus*): to 1–1.2×0.6m (3–4×2ft); clump of rich green palmately divided lvs on long stalks with 12–18 lfts to 12cm (5in) long; dense spikes to 60cm (2ft) long of self or bicoloured fls in shades of white, yellow, orange, red-purple & blue, early summer. Among best of tall early fls; dead-head to encourage repeat. Not long-lived; best on light lime-free soil; protect from slugs. Named vars of original 'Russell Hybrids' raised by cuttings now generally weakened by virus disease; seed-raised plants best (good forms can be continued by cuttings). More or less true-breeding seed strains include: 'Chandelier' (yellow shades): 'Dwarf Lulu' (to 60cm [2ft]; mixed colours); 'My Castle' (brick-red); 'Noble Maiden' (white & cream); 'The Chatelaine' (pink & white); 'The Governor' (blue & white); 'The Pages' (carmine).
Ononis (*Ononis rotundifolia* **8**): rather short-lived bushy sub-shrub, to 45×45cm (1½×1½ft); zig-zag stems; almost round hairy lfts in 3s; small clusters of 2cm (¾in) clear rose fls, standard streaked red, all summer. Trim after flg.
False lupins (*Thermopsis* spp): ultra-hardy lupin-like plants with palmate trifoliate lvs & racemes of yellow fls, early–mid summer. For deep soil.
T. angustifolia: to 1.5×0.6m (5×2ft); arching; canary-yellow fls.
T. caroliniana **9**: to 1.5×0.6m (5×2ft); upright; dense infls to 25cm (10in) long.
T. lupinoides (*T. lanceolata*): to 90×60cm (3×2ft); clear yellow fls in compact infls.
T. mollis: to 90×45cm (3×1½ft); compact; tapering infls.
T. montana: to 90×60cm (3×2ft); 20cm (8in) infls of straw-yellow fls. Invasive.

The lily family

Vary widely, from shade/moisture lovers to plants for open sunny sites, often with attractive leaves (mainly basal, but important group with leafy stems) &/or flowers often in racemes or spikes. Many are fine border perennials, others good for ground cover, bedding or cutting. Herbaceous unless noted; many have fleshy or rhizomatous roots. Some spp recently reclassified in family Trilliaceae, but retained here for convenience. **Cultivation**: Unless stated, very hardy & for any well-drained soil in sun or partial shade. Protect shade/moisture lovers from slugs. **Propagation**: Division, spring unless stated; seed.

St Bernard's lilies (*Anthericum* spp): moderately to v hardy easy clump-forming plants with 30cm (1ft) grassy lvs & profuse starry white fls in slender erect racemes (cuttable). Keep moist in summer; fleshy root can be lifted for winter in v cold areas. See also *Chlorophytum* & *Paradisea* spp.
A. liliago **1**: to 60×30cm (2×1ft); 4cm (1½in) fls, late spring & early summer. Self-seeds.
A. ramosum **2** (*A. graminifolium*): to 90×30cm (3×1ft); airy branching spikes of 2cm (¾in) fls, early summer.
Jacob's rod (yellow asphodel, *Asphodeline* [*Asphodelus*] *lutea** **3**): moderately to v hardy rhizomatous plant, to 1.2×0.3m (4×1ft); grassy glaucous lvs to 30cm (1ft) long; stiff dense spikes of yellow fls, late spring; decorative seed spikes.
Asphodel (*Asphodelus albus*): moderately to v hardy tuberous-rooted plant, to 90×30cm (3×1ft); similar to above but fls white, tinted brownish.
Aspidistra (cast-iron plant, *Aspidistra elatior* **4**; sometimes sold incorrectly as *A. lurida*): usually grown indoors, but moderately hardy if dryish in winter; forms dense clumps, to 60×45cm (2×1½ft); evergreen, with tough dark green glossy lvs to 60×10cm (24×4in) on stalks direct from ground; rarely, stemless brown-purple fls. Tolerates shade, poor soil. Var 'Variegata' **5** has lvs striped white.
Astelia (*Astelia nervosa**): moderately to v hardy clump-forming plant, to 0.6×1.5m (2×5ft); arching evergreen grassy lvs to 1.8m (6ft) long, silvery-grey, woolly beneath; short spikes of inconspicuous fls. *A. cockaynei* is similar but smaller, with silky lvs.
Spider plants (St Bernard's lilies, *Chlorophytum* spp; sometimes listed as *Anthericum* spp): easy semi-hardy rhizomatous evergreens usually grown indoors but useful for summer bedding or hanging baskets. Lvs arching & strap-like, in tufts; fls white, insignificant.
C. capense **6** (*C. elatum*): to 25×40cm (10×16in); mid green lvs; few plantlets.
C. (A.) comosum: sp rarely grown; vars (generally to 30×60cm [1×2ft]): 'Mandaianum' (*C. [A.] mandaianum*; dwarf, to 10×15cm [4×6in]; lvs striped yellow); 'Picturatum' (lvs striped yellow); 'Variegatum' (lvs edged white); 'Vittatum' **7** (*C. vittatum*; lvs striped white).
Bluebeard lilies (*Clintonia* spp): rosette-forming

rhizomatous plants with broad rich green lvs; clusters of bell-like 2cm (¾in) fls on leafless stems, late spring & early summer; glossy blue berries. Cool, humus-rich, shady, moist soil.
C. andrewsiana **8**: to 60×30cm (2×1ft); fls carmine-pink or purplish.
C. borealis **9** (corn lily): ultra-hardy; to 30×30cm (1×1ft); glossy lvs; yellowish-green fls.
C. umbellulata*: to 30×30cm (1×1ft); fls white spotted green & purple; berries black.
Lily of the valley (*Convallaria majalis*** **10**): ultra-hardy woodland plant; to 20×30cm (8×12in); spreads by rhizomes & often treated like bulb; paired rich green lvs to 15×8cm (6×3in), arching & partly enfolding fl stems; gracefully drooping racemes of nodding bell-shaped fls, waxy-white or sometimes pink, late spring, sometimes followed by red berries. V good for ground cover in partial shade (may also thrive in sun); fls best pulled, not cut. Likes moist, humus-rich soil; divide/plant rhizomes ("pips") shallowly but firmly, late autumn. Can be forced in pots at 20°C (68°F) after cold dormant period for winter display indoors (pre-chilled "prepared" pips sometimes available). Vars: 'Fortin's Giant' (large fls); 'Prolificans' ('Plena'; double); 'Rosea' **11** (pink); 'Variegata' ('Striata'; lvs striped gold).
Fairy bells (*Disporum hookeri, D. oreganum*): rhizomatous woodland plant rather like Solomon's seal; to 30×30cm (1×1ft); leafy stems with stalkless heart-shaped light green lvs to 10cm (4in) long & nodding creamy-white or greenish bell-shaped fls 1cm (½in) long, spring; orange-red berries. *D. smithii* (fairy lantern) is similar but fls longer. Plant rhizomes 8cm (3in) deep in autumn in humus-rich soil in cool shade.
Foxtail lilies (desert candles, *Eremurus* spp): generally moderately to v hardy tall, showy plants with strap-shaped basal lvs (die down in summer) & striking feathery spikes of starry fls like miniature lilies with prominent stamens, early summer; fl & seed heads excellent for cutting. Best seen against dark green evergreens. Divide/plant late summer in sand pocket in fertile soil in sheltered sunny site; brittle fleshy roots, leave undisturbed till crowded; mulch for winter protection; stake tall spp.
E. elwesii (*E. elwesianus*): may be hybrid; to 1.8–3×1m (6–10×3ft); fls salmon, sometimes white, centred green. Var 'Albus' is pure white.
E. himalaicus: ultra-hardy; to 1–1.2×0.75m (3–

4×2½ft); dense infls to 60×10cm (24×4in) of white fls, v early.

E. olgae: to 1.2–2×1m (4–7×3ft); white or pink fls, early–mid summer.

E. robustus: ultra-hardy; vigorous, to 2.5×1–1.2m (8×3–4ft); lvs to 1.2m (4ft) long, die down before flg; dense infls to 1.2m (4ft) long of pink fls marked brown & green. V showy.

E. stenophyllus **1** (*E. bungei*): to 1–1.5×0.6m (3–5×2ft); slender; 45cm (1½ft) infls of yellow fls fading orange. Var *aurantiacus* (*E. aurantiacus*) is orange.

E. hybrids: derived from various spp but largely *E. olgae* & *E. stenophyllus*; generally to 1.5–2×0.6–1m (5–7×2–3ft); fls white or shades of pink, amber, orange & yellow, in long spikes. Vars & strains: 'Highdown Hybrids'; 'Himrob' (hybrid of *E. himalaicus* & *E. robustus*; to 2.5m [8ft]; pink); 'Ruiter Hybrids' **2**; 'Shelford Hybrids'.

Swamp pink (*Helonias bullata**): moderately to v hardy bog plant, to 60–90×60cm (2–3×2ft); rhizomatous; narrow basal lvs to 30cm (1ft) long; pink or purplish fls in 8cm (3in) clusters, spring. For wet soil in sun.

Daylilies (*Hemerocallis* spp & hybrids): v popular, generally ultra-hardy clump-forming plants. Arching strap-shaped glossy lvs; lily-like trumpet-shaped fls (transient but borne in succession, generally early–mid summer) in open branched clusters on strong stems. Good for herbaceous & mixed borders in sun or partial shade in dry or moist soil; tough, easy & pest-free; divide only after 5–6yrs. Dead-head.

H. aurantiaca: moderately to v hardy; to 90×75cm (3×2½ft); rhizomatous; semi-evergreen; burnt-orange fls to 10cm (4in) wide.

H. citrina*: to 1.1×0.75m (3½×2½ft); lemon-yellow nocturnal fls to 12cm (5in) wide.

H. fulva **3**: to 90×75cm (3×2½ft); rhizomatous; rusty orange-red fls 9cm (3½in) wide.

H. minor*: to 45×30cm (1½×1ft); yellow 10cm (4in) fls.

H. multiflora*: v hardy; to 90×60cm (3×2ft); profuse golden-yellow fls to 8cm (3in) wide, late summer & autumn.

H. hybrids **4** (generally of complex parentage): generally to 60–90×45cm (2–3×1½ft) but dwarf vars to 20–45×30cm (8–18×12in); fls generally 10–15cm (4–6in) wide, v bold & heavy-textured in tetraploid vars, but only 5–8cm (2–3in) wide & v profuse in miniature-fld vars (usually on standard-size plants). V many named vars in shades of cream, yellow, gold, bronze, orange, peach, pink, rose, red, maroon, purple, lilac & lavender, often shading to different colour in throat; some with frilled petals, many glistening & waxy, some semi-/double, some flg into autumn, some scented. Also sold as mixed seedlings.

Plantain lilies (*Hosta* spp): generally ultra-hardy moisture-lovers grown mainly for clumps of large

lance-shaped to almost round lvs, prominently veined & often glaucous or variegated (good for arrangements). Racemes of bell- to trumpet-shaped white to purple fls 4–6cm (1½–2½in) long, above foliage, summer. Popular ground cover; spread slowly. For sun or shade; fl best in sun but lvs generally best in shade (especially variegated forms).

H. crispula **5**: to 75×45cm (2½×1½ft); dark green waxy lvs to 20cm (8in) long, edged white; lilac fls, early summer.

H. decorata (sometimes sold as *H. d. marginata*): to 60×45cm (2×1½ft); dark green rounded lvs to 15cm (6in) long, edged white; deep lilac fls, mid summer.

H. elata (*H. fortunei gigantea, H. montana*): to 90×75cm (3×2½ft); rich dark green wavy-edged lvs to 25cm (10in) long; fls pale lilac to deep lavender-blue. Var 'Aureomarginata' has lvs with wide yellow-cream edges.

H. fortunei: to 75×60cm (2½×2ft); grey- to sage-green heart-shaped pointed lvs to 12cm (5in) long, on long stalks, yellow in autumn; lilac fls. Vars: 'Albopicta' **6** (creamy-yellow lvs edged & striped pale green, fading to green); 'Aureomarginata' **7** (green lvs edged yellow); 'Marginato-alba' ('Albomarginata'; green lvs edged white, glaucous-grey beneath); 'Obscura Marginata' (green lvs edged creamy-yellow).

H. lancifolia **8**: compact, to 60×45cm (2×1½ft); narrowish dark green glossy lvs to 12cm (5in) long; deep lilac fls, late summer.

H. plantaginea*: to 60×60cm (2×2ft); heart-shaped pale green glossy lvs to 25cm (10in) long; pure white trumpet-shaped fls to 12cm (5in) long, late summer & autumn. Var 'Grandiflora'* has longer & narrower lvs & fls.

H. rectifolia: to 90×45cm (3×1½ft); erect lance-shaped dark green lvs to 30cm (1ft) long; profuse blue-violet fls, late summer. Var 'Tall Boy' has heart-shaped lvs & infls to 1.2m (4ft).

H. sieboldiana (*H. glauca*): to 75–90×60cm (2–3×2ft); magnificent grey-green to bluish lvs to 30–40cm (12–16in) long, heavy veining, making dense clump, yellow in autumn; low infls of white to lilac fls, early summer. Vars: 'Elegans' **9** (finest form, with blue-green lvs to 30cm [1ft] wide); 'Frances Williams' ('Gold Edge'; lvs edged yellow; 'Gold Circle' is same or v similar); 'Helen Doriot' (to 90cm [3ft]; selection of 'Elegans' with distinctly puckered lvs).

H. sieboldii (*H. albomarginata*): to 50×40cm (20×16in) or more; narrowish green lvs to 15cm (6in) long, narrow white edge; lilac fls marked violet. Spreads by rhizomes. Var 'Alba' has green lvs & white fls.

H.×tardiana vars: hybrids of *H. sieboldiana* 'Elegans' & *H. tardiflora*; to 40×25cm (16×10in); bluish lvs. Var 'Halcyon' (original hybrid) has white fls; other vars sometimes available.

H. tardiflora (*H. lancifolia tardiflora*): similar to
H. lancifolia but smaller, to 25×25cm (10×10in);
mauve trumpet-shaped fls, autumn.
H. undulata (*H. lancifolia undulata*): to 60×60cm
(2×2ft); creamy-centred mid green lvs to 15cm
(6in) long, wavy & twisted; lavender fls. Vars:
'Erromena' (*H. erromena*; to 1.2m [4ft]; lvs
all-green; fine lilac fls on tall stems);
'Mediovariegata' **1** (to 30cm [1ft]; lvs striped
yellow); 'Univittata' (vigorous; lvs less wavy,
narrowly striped).
H. ventricosa (*H. caerulea*): to 90×60cm (3×2ft);
glaucous, heart-shaped lvs to 20cm (8in) long,
shiny beneath; rich violet fls, dark veins. Vars:
'Aureomaculata' **2** (to 75cm [2½ft]; lvs splashed
yellow, fading); 'Variegata' (lvs strikingly edged
cream-yellow).
H. hybrids of various spp (to 60–90×60cm
[2–3×2ft] unless stated): 'Gold Leaf' (golden lvs,
almost unfading); 'Gold Standard' (upright,
puckered blue-green lvs, broad golden-green
centre); 'Honeybells'* (light green wavy lvs to
30cm [1ft] long; lilac fls striped violet); 'Krossa
Regal' (vase-shaped, with 25cm [10in] glaucous-
blue lvs on arching stalks; lavender fls on 1.5m
[5ft] stems, late summer); 'Royal Standard'* **3**
(heart-shaped green lvs, wavy & puckered; white
fls, late summer); 'Thomas Hogg' **4** (glossy dark
green lvs to 20cm [8in] long, edged cream; pale
lilac fls, early summer).

Red-hot pokers (torch lilies, *Kniphofia* [*Tritoma*]
spp & hybrids): generally moderately to v hardy
sun-lovers, to 75–90×60cm (2½–3×2ft) unless
stated; tufts of grassy lvs (rather coarse in some
spp); erect spikes of close-packed pendent
tubular fls on stout stems, mainly in summer.
Good as specimens, for herbaceous & mixed
borders, or for cutting. Dead-head; in cold areas
mulch or bunch old lvs to protect crown in winter,
or lift & store in cool place. Nomenclature
confused; many plants grown as spp may be
hybrids; many named vars eventually weakened
by viruses & superseded; unnamed seedlings
often stronger.
Early spp & vars (fl early summer): 'Atlanta' **5** (to
1.2m [4ft]; broad evergreen glaucous lvs; yellow
& red fls); 'Earliest of All' (flame-red); 'Goldelse'
(soft yellow); *K. primulina* (red & yellow; v early);
'Tubergeniana' (often sold as *K. tubergenii*;
creamy-yellow).
Mid season spp & vars (fl mid-late summer):
'Ada' (to 1.1m [3½ft]; deep orange-yellow);
'Alcazar' (orange); 'Bressingham Comet' (yellow
& red); 'Bressingham Flame' **6** (deep orange);
'Brimstone' **7** (canary-yellow); 'Fiery Fred' (fiery
red); 'Goldmine' (to 1.1m [3½ft]; orange-yellow);
'Maid of Orleans' (cream); 'Royal Standard' (to
1.2m [4ft]; red & yellow); 'Samuel's Sensation'
(to 1.5m [5ft]; scarlet).
Late spp & vars (fl late summer to autumn):

K. caulescens (to 1.2m [4ft]; evergreen glaucous
lvs from prostrate woody stems; fls coral-red
fading yellow); 'C. M. Prichard' (to 1.8m [6ft];
bronze-orange); *K. galpinii* **8** (probably a form of
K. triangularis; orange; *K. macowanii* &
K. nelsonii are probably similar, both orange/
flame-red); *K. praecox* (*K. uvaria* 'Nobilis'; to
1.8m [6ft]; scarlet); *K. uvaria* **9** (original red-hot
poker; to 1.5m [5ft]; coarse evergreen lvs; fls
orange to yellow).

Liriopes (lily-turfs, *Liriope* spp): drought- &
salt-tolerant evergreen plants forming tufts of
dark green broad grassy lvs; small bead-like lilac
fls closely clustered in erect spikes above lvs,
mid summer into autumn, then black berries.
Easy in sun or shade; good for ground cover &
borders.
L. muscari **10**: moderately to v hardy; to
45×40cm (18×16in); 12cm (5in) infls of dark
violet fls. Vars: 'Majestic' (large infls); 'Silvery
Sunproof' (lvs variegated gold [fades white]);
'Variegata' (sometimes sold incorrectly as
Ophiopogon jaburan 'Variegatus'; lvs striped
yellow, becoming all-green).
L. spicata (creeping lily-turf): to 25×45cm
(10×18in); rhizomatous & spreading; 8cm (3in)
infls of white or pale lilac fls. Shear back each
spring.

Ophiopogon (lily-turf, mondo grass,
Ophiopogon spp): moderately hardy evergreens
closely related & similar to *Liriope* spp; grassy
dark green lvs almost conceal short spikes of
bell-shaped fls, mid summer; blue berries. For
sun or shade (latter especially in hot climates).
O. jaburan: to 60×60cm (2×2ft); lvs striped
yellow in variegated forms **11**; white fls. Best in
shade.
O. japonicus (mondo grass): to 30×45cm
(1×1½ft); spreads by stolons; fls white to violet.
Good carpeter.
O. planiscapus: to 45×45cm (1½×1½ft);
spreads slowly; fls white or purplish-pink. Var
'Nigrescens' **12** (to 20×30cm [8×12in]) has lvs
soon turning purple-black; unusual, contrasting
well with silver lvs; tolerates shade.

St Bruno lily (*Paradisea* [*Anthericum*]
*liliastrum**): ultra-hardy plant with fleshy
rhizomatous roots; to 60×45cm (2×1½ft); clump
of grassy lvs to 60cm (2ft) long; loose 1-sided
racemes of up to 10 lily-like funnel-shaped fls
5cm (2in) long, white tipped green, early
summer. Plant roots autumn or spring 8cm (3in)
deep in damp humus-rich soil in partial shade.

Paris (*Paris* spp; now correctly classified in
Trilliaceae): rhizomatous plants similar to *Trillium*
spp but with lvs & petals in whorls of 4
(sometimes more) at top of stems; v long-lasting
starry solitary fls with prominent stamens;
attractive berries. Fine woodland plants for damp
shady sites; tolerate lime. All parts poisonous.

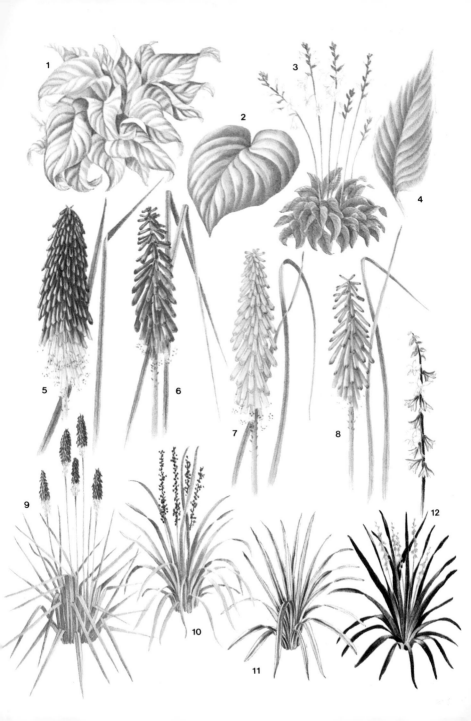

P. polyphylla: to 90×45cm (3×1½ft); lvs to 15cm (6in) long; 10cm (4in) yellow & green fls, violet stigmas, summer; red frs.

P. quadrifolia (herb paris): to 15–30×25cm (6–12×10in); lvs to 6–12cm (2½–5in) long; yellowish-green fls, late spring & early summer; black frs.

Solomon's seals (*Polygonatum* spp): ultra-hardy rhizomatous plants with graceful arching stems carrying ranks of generally pale green rounded lvs held horizontally above dangling white narrow bell fls edged green, late spring; blue or black berries. Easy in deep, rich, moist soil in light shade; mulch in spring. Nomenclature somewhat confused.

P. biflorum (*P. canaliculatum*): to 90×45cm (3×1½ft); pointed lvs to 10cm (4in) long, glaucous beneath; 1cm (½in) fls, usually paired.

P. commutatum (*P. giganteum*, giant Solomon's seal; often sold incorrectly as *P. canaliculatum*): vigorous, to 1.2–1.8×0.75m (4–6×2½ft; biggest in rich, moist soil); lvs to 18cm (7in) long; clusters of 2–10 fls to 2cm (¾in) long.

P.×hybridum (common Solomon's seal of gardens; often listed as *P. multiflorum*, sometimes as *P. odoratum*, but correctly a hybrid of these spp): to 75–90×30–45cm (2½–3×1–1½ft); lvs to 8cm (3in) long; clusters of 2–5 fls 1.5–2.5cm (⅝–1in) long, late spring to early summer. Vars: 'Flore Pleno' (double); 'Variegatum' **1** (lvs striped cream).

P. japonicum **2** (correctly, *P. odoratum thunbergii*): to 90×30cm (3×1ft); lvs to 15cm (6in) long; fls to 2.5cm (1in) long, in 2s & 3s.

P. verticillatum: erect, to 1.1×0.45m (3½×1½ft); narrow 10cm (4in) lvs in whorls at intervals up stem; clusters of 8mm (⅓in) fls.

False Solomon's seals (*Smilacina* spp): ultra-hardy rhizomatous woodland plants with leafy, often arching stems bearing racemes or panicles of fluffy greenish-white, creamy or pinkish fls, late spring & early summer. For deep, rich, moist lime-free soil in partial shade.

S. racemosa* **3** (false spikenard): to 75–90×45cm (2½–3×1½ft); lance-shaped bright green lvs to 15cm (6in) long; arching 10–15cm (4–6in) infls of whitish/creamy fls; red berries.

S. stellata (star-flowered lily of the valley): to 60×45cm (2×1½ft); invasive in light soil; narrowly lance-shaped lvs to 15cm (6in) long; sprays of whitish starry fls; dark red berries.

Streptopus (twisted-stalks, *Streptopus* spp): ultra-hardy plants similar to Solomon's seals in needs & appearance, but stems twisted & sometimes branched; fls to 1cm (½in) long, with distinct petals, early summer; red berries.

S. amplexifolius: to 60×30cm (2×1ft); whitish.

S. roseus: to 45×30cm (1½×1ft); rose-pink.

Toad lilies (*Tricyrtis* spp): erect rhizomatous plants with oval pointed lvs 12–15cm (5–6in) long

& branched infls of strikingly spotted fls, funnel-shaped but opening widely to 4–5cm (1½–2in) across, prominent stamens & style, early autumn (good for cutting). For cool, rich, moist soil in semi-shade; sometimes grown in pots.

T. formosana **4**: moderately hardy; to 60×45cm (2×1½ft); dark green lvs; white fls spotted purple. Var *stolonifera* (*T. stolonifera*) spreads.

T. hirta: to 90×60cm (3×2ft); hairy lvs; white fls spotted lilac.

T. macropoda: to 75×45cm (2½×1½ft); fls greenish-yellow to creamy, spotted purple.

Trilliums (wood lilies, wake robins, *Trillium* spp; now correctly classified in Trilliaceae): distinctive rhizomatous plants with whorls of 3 lvs under solitary 3-petalled fls at top of each stem. Unless stated, to 30×30cm (1×1ft); lvs to 10–15cm (4–6in) long; fls to 4cm (1½in) across, spring. Plant rhizomes 5–10cm (2–4in) deep in humus-rich moist soil in partial/light shade; increase slowly.

T. cernuum (nodding trillium): ultra-hardy; to 45×30cm (1½×1ft); nodding white/pinkish fls, maroon centre.

T. chloropetalum: moderately to v hardy; to 75×30cm (2½×1ft); lvs mottled; large pink, maroon, pale yellow or cream fls.

T. erectum **5**: to 60×30cm (2×1ft); nodding fls, usually red-purple, unpleasant scent.

T. grandiflorum **6** (wake robin): fls white fading pale pink, to 8cm (3in) wide. Var 'Plenum' is double.

T. ovatum: to 20×25cm (8×10in); white fls becoming pink.

T. sessile **7** (toadshade): moderately to v hardy; lvs marbled; erect maroon fls to 8cm (3in) long.

T. undulatum **8** (painted lady): ultra-hardy; fluted fls, white veined purple.

Merrybells (bellwort, *Uvularia grandiflora* **9**): ultra-hardy plant related & needing similar conditions to Solomon's seals; to 60×30cm (2×1ft); arching stems with 12cm (5in) lance-shaped lvs, glaucous beneath; nodding lemon-yellow fls to 5cm (2in) long, narrow (sometimes twisting) petals, late spring. Dainty & easy.

False hellebores or helleborines (*Veratrum* spp): stately ultra-hardy rhizomatous plants with fine pleated lvs to 30×15–20cm (12×6–8in), opening like fans, & erect branched & downy plumes of small starry fls, mid summer. For shady borders or woodland gardens in v moist, rich soil. Poisonous.

V. album (white helleborine): to 1.2×0.45cm (4×1½ft); 30–60cm (1–2ft) infls of greenish-white fls.

V. nigrum **10**: to 1.2×0.45m (4×1½ft); infls to 90cm (3ft) long of dark maroon fls; attractive seed heads. V striking.

V. viride (Indian poke): to 2×0.6m (7×2ft); 30–60cm (1–2ft) infls of yellow-green fls.

The mallow family

Sun-loving, long-flowering, mainly quite tall herbaceous perennials with 5-petalled satiny flowers.
Cultivation: For any normal to poor soil; *Callirhoe* spp need dry soil, but *Hibiscus moscheutos* must not dry out. **Propagation**: Seed; clump-forming spp by division; *Callirhoe* & *Malva* spp by stem cuttings. For spp best grown as annuals/biennials, see p510.

Poppy mallows (wine cups, *Callirhoe* spp): ultra-hardy sprawling plants with deep tap roots; good for dry banks, rock walls etc. Lvs deeply divided; 5cm (2in) fls, deep pink to reddish-purple, from early summer.
C. digitata: to 45×60cm (1½×2ft).
C. involucrata 1: to 30×60cm (1×2ft); lvs hairy.
Rose mallow (*Hibiscus moscheutos, H. palustris*): considered v hardy in US but semi- to moderately hardy in UK (often grown in greenhouse). To 1.5–2.5×1–1.5m (5–8×3–5ft), largest in v moist soil; sub-shrubby; lvs to 20cm (8in) long, sometimes lobed; huge white, pink or crimson satiny fls 15–30cm (6–12in) across, mid summer to frosts. Good near coast. Sold as named vars, including F1 hybrids (fl 1st yr from seed; often grown as HHAs; see p510).
True mallows (*Malva* spp): easily grown v to ultra-hardy bushy border plants; may need staking if soil rich. May be prone to rust.
M. alcea (hollyhock mallow): to 1.2×0.6m

(4×2ft); deeply lobed lvs; bowl-shaped rose-pink 5cm (2in) fls, mid summer to late autumn. Var *fastigiata* 2 is shorter fls crowded near top of stem.
M. moschata 3 (musk mallow): to 60–90×45cm (2–3×1½ft); doubly divided lvs; 5cm (2in) fls, pink to lavender, from early summer; musky smell. Short-lived; self-seeds. Var 'Alba' is white.
Sidalcea (chequer mallow, *Sidalcea malviflora* & hybrids): graceful & upright moderately hardy border plants, to 0.75–1.2×0.45m (2½–4×1½ft); basal clump of lvs; tall branching spikes of 4–5cm (1½–2in) cup-shaped silky fls, shell-pink to crimson, all summer. Cut down to 30cm (1ft) soon after flg; tall vars may need support. Vars (to 0.75–1.1m [2½–3½ft] unless stated): 'Croftway Red' 4 (deepest pink; early); 'Loveliness' 5 (shell-pink); 'Nimmerdor' (deep pink; early); 'Oberon' (clear rose-pink); 'Pink Pinnacle' (clear pink; late); 'Puck' (to 60cm [2ft]; clear pink); 'Rose Queen' 6 (to 1.2m [4ft]; rose-pink); 'William Smith' (salmon-pink).

The evening primrose family

Summer-flowering, sun-loving herbaceous perennials generally with long season. Larger spp suitable for wild gardens or herbaceous borders, smaller for front of borders, dry slopes or large rock gardens.
Cultivation: Unless stated, very hardy. Generally for well-drained soil. **Propagation**: Division; spp by seed. For *Zauschneria californica* (Californian fuchsia) & other rock garden spp also suitable for borders, see p482; for *Oenothera* spp raised each year from seed, see p510.

Epilobiums (*Epilobium* spp): less invasive relatives of showy but weedy rosebay willow herb. Ultra-hardy; may self-seed.
E. fleischeri: often confused with *E. rosmarinifolium* but smaller, to 75×45cm (2½×1½ft); lax & clump-forming; narrow greyish lvs; corymbs of rose-red 2.5cm (1in) fls.
E. rosmarinifolium (correctly, *E. dodonaei*): to 1.2×0.6m (4×2ft); similar to above but more upright; fls in lax infls.
E. latifolium: to 45×45cm (1½×1½ft); glaucous lvs; large rose-pink fls; likes moist soil.
Gaura (*Gaura lindheimeri* 7): bushy & graceful, to 1.2×1m (4×3ft); open panicles of pinkish-white fls, 4cm (1½in) across, summer & autumn (1st yr from seed). Good in dry, sandy soil; v hardy. Dislikes wet winters on heavy soil.
Oenotheras (evening primroses [night-flg spp] & sundrops [day-flg]; *Oenothera* spp): long-flg N American natives with cup-shaped yellow fls; need v well-drained soil & ample watering.
O. fruticosa 8 (*O. linearis*, common sundrops of

eastern N America; often confused with *O. tetragona*): ultra-hardy; to 30–60×30cm (1–2×1ft); narrow lvs; yellow fls 2.5–4cm (1–1½in) across, daytime.
O. missouriensis 9 (*O. macrocarpa*, Ozark sundrops): prostrate, to 25×40cm (10×24in); forms mats of narrow dark green lvs; beautiful pale yellow fls 8–10cm (3–4in) across on short stems, opening evening, summer to early autumn. Prefers poor soil.
O. tetragona (*O. fruticosa youngii, O. youngii*; often sold incorrectly as *O. fruticosa*): ultra-hardy; to 90×30cm (3×1ft); dark lvs; clear yellow silky fls 2.5–4cm (1–1½in) across, daytime. Natural vars: *cinaeus* (*O. cinaeus*; lvs bronzed in spring; large deep yellow fls); *fraseri* (*O. fraseri*; lvs glaucous; 5cm [2in] fls); *riparia* (*O. riparia*; lax, to 20×40cm [12×15in]; good for rock garden). Garden vars (neat & mounding, to 45–60cm [1½–2ft]; fls to 6cm [2½in] wide): 'Fireworks' 10 ('Fyrverkeri'; golden-yellow); 'Highlight' ('Höheslicht'; bright yellow); 'Yellow River' (rich yellow).

Paeonies

Paeonia spp; formerly classified in Ranunculaceae. Among the best, most ancient & most important herbaceous perennials for temperate regions. V long-lived, with attractive foliage (often reddish in spring &/or colouring in autumn) remaining neat after flowers die. Latter are large & beautiful, bowl-shaped, single unless stated, late spring & early summer; good for cutting (in bud), but take few stems per plant. Associate well with many bulbs. If left, colourful seeds in opening pods. **Cultivation**: Very to ultra-hardy unless stated. For any rich, well-drained soil in sun (or partial shade where summers hot). Plant crown 4cm (1½in) deep. Water well in hot dry weather; top-dress & mulch in autumn. Divide in autumn if flowering poor. Stake tall vars. **Propagation**: Division, autumn; seed. For shrubby "tree" paeonies, see p146.

P. anomala to 60×60cm (2×2ft); finely divided dark green lvs; intense crimson-red 8–10cm (3–4in) fls, yellow stamens, early.

P. arietina * **1** (correctly, *P. mascula arietina*): to 75×60cm (2½×3ft); spreading; greyish-green lvs, hairy beneath; rose- to magenta-pink 8–12cm (3–5in) fls, creamy-yellow stamens, early. Vars: 'Mother of Pearl' (light pink); 'Northern Glory' (silky magenta-pink); 'Rose Gem' (red).

P. cambessedesii: moderately hardy; to 45×45cm (1½×1½ft); leathery lvs, purple beneath; deep rose-pink 6–10cm (2½–4in) fls, red stamens & purple pistils, early.

*P. emodi** : moderately to v hardy; to 90×90cm (3×3ft); dark green lvs, paler beneath; pure white 8–12cm (3–5in) fls, yellow stamens.

*P. lactiflora** (*P. albiflora*, Chinese paeony): to 60–90×60cm (2–3×2ft); mid–dark green lvs, often tinged bronze-red when young; fls of sp silky-white, 8–10cm (3–4in) wide, yellow stamens. Main parent of hundreds of vars/hybrids (generally 0.75–1m [30–40in]; fls to 10–15cm [4–6in] wide); selection listed. Single vars (generally with yellow/orange stamens): 'Beersheba'* (rose-pink); 'Krinkled White' (v large crepe-like white petals); 'Lord Kitchener' (crimson); 'Scarlett O'Hara' (warm red); 'White Wings'**2**; 'Whitleyi Major'* ('The Bride'; white). Semi-double vars (including "Japanese" vars, with large petals & enlarged petaloid stamens, & anemone-fld vars, with even larger petaloids half-filling cup of fl): 'Aureole' (cherry-pink, cream & white centre); 'Bowl of Beauty'* **3** (pale pink, creamy-white centre); 'Bridal Veil' **4** (light pink, centre creamy-white & pink); 'Chocolate Soldier'* (purple-red, centre mottled yellow); 'Globe of Light'* (rose-pink, gold centre); 'Honey Gold' (white, centre gold & white); 'Pink Lemonade'** (pink, centre pink, yellow & cream); 'Primevere'* (creamy-white, centre sulphur-yellow; almost fully double); 'Sword Dance' **5** (strong unfading red); 'Whopper'* (v large soft pink fls, almost fully double). Fully double vars: 'Baroness Schroeder'* (flesh-pink to white); 'Bonanza' (dark red); 'Bowl of Cream'* (v large creamy-white fls); 'Claire Dubois'** (satiny-pink); 'Dinner Plate'* (v large shell-pink fls); 'Edulis Superba'* (rosy-lilac); 'Edulis

Supreme'* (vivid pink); 'Félix Crousse'* (carmine-red); 'Félix Supreme' (ruby-red); 'Festiva Maxima'* (white flecked crimson); 'First Lady'* (rich pink; early); 'Inspector Lavergne' (crimson); 'Jay Cee'* (strong red; rich green lvs); 'Karl Rosenfeld'* (crimson); 'Laura Dessert'* (pink to creamy-white, pale yellow centre); 'Lillian Wild' (white flushed flesh-pink); 'Martin Cahuzac' (dark crimson-maroon); 'Mrs F. D. Roosevelt'** (deep pink); 'Monsieur Jules Elie'* **6** (silvery rose-pink); 'Moonstone' (blush-pink); 'President Poincare'* (ruby-red); 'Red Charm' (vivid red; early); 'Sarah Bernhardt'* **7** (apple-blossom pink); 'Shirley Temple'* (pale pink to whitish); 'Solange'* (creamy buff-pink, paler centre); (late).

P. lobata (correctly, *P. peregrina*): v hardy; to 60×60cm (2×2ft); spreading; deeply cut glossy lvs; cup-shaped deep red fls 8–10cm (3–4in) wide, red stamens, early. Vars: 'Fire King' (brilliant crimson-scarlet); 'Sunshine' (salmon-scarlet).

P. mlokosewitschii **8**: v hardy; to 75×75cm (2½×2½ft); soft grey-green lvs, downy beneath; 8–10cm (3–4in) lemon-yellow fls, golden stamens, v early.

P. obovata alba: to 60×60cm (2×2ft); dark green lvs; pure white 8cm (3in) fls, golden stamens, early. Var 'Grandiflora' has larger creamy-white fls.

P. officinalis (wild paeony of Europe): to 60×60cm (2×2ft); spreading; deeply cut mid–dark green lvs; crimson fls to 12cm (5in) wide, red stamens, early. Vars (to 75×90cm [2½×3ft]): 'Alba Plena' (semi-double, white); 'Anemonaeflora Rosea' (rosy-red, semi-double, central petaloids crimson edged gold); 'Rosea Plena' (double, bright pink); 'Rubra Plena' **9** (deep crimson, double).

*P.×smouthii** **10** (sometimes sold incorrectly as *P. anomala*): hybrid of *P. lactiflora* & *P. tenuifolia*; to 60×60cm (2×2ft); finely dissected dark green lvs; crimson 8cm (2in) fls, early.

P. tenuifolia (fern-leaved paeony): to 45×45cm (1½×1½ft); spreading; v finely cut fern-like dense foliage; shiny deep crimson fls to 8cm (3in) wide, golden stamens, resting on foliage. Vars: 'Plena' (double); 'Rosea' **11** (pink).

The poppy family

Beautiful & bold herbaceous border perennials, most (except *Macleaya* spp) having large, often silky or crepe-like flowers of typical poppy shape. Leaves often deeply cut & hairy. Cut stems weep white or yellow sap (may be poisonous). Most have fleshy roots & some spread quickly, but may resent root disturbance; some short-lived. **Cultivation:** Two distinct groups: some for hot, dry conditions; others for cool, moist shade. **Propagation:** Root cuttings; division (not *Romneya* spp); seed (especially *Meconopsis* spp); *Macleaya* & *Romneya* spp by suckers. For the short-lived alpine & Icelandic poppies (*Papaver alpinum* & *P. nudicaule*), best treated as HAs or HBs, see p512.

Hylomecon (*Hylomecon japonicum* **1** [often listed as *H. vernalis*]): moderately to v hardy woodland perennial for rich, moist soil; to 30×25cm (12×10in); lvs fern-like, fresh green; 5cm (2in) yellow poppy fls, spring.

Plume poppies (*Macleaya* [*Bocconia*] spp): tall, spreading ultra-hardy perennials for large borders or specimen planting mainly in sun; to 1.5–2×1m (5–7×3ft); deeply cut lvs to 20cm (8in) across, white beneath (extend to ground, so best not fronted by other plants); small petal-less fls in 90cm (3ft) plume-like panicles.

M. (*B.*) *cordata* **2**: fls silvery, from mid summer.

M. (*B.*) *microcarpa*: v similar to above; tiny pink fls (richest in var 'Coral Plume'), earlier.

Himalayan blue poppies & relatives

(*Meconopsis* spp): beautiful but often short-lived moderately to v hardy perennials for humus-rich, moist soil in cool shade. Some are monocarpic (die after flg) & best raised from seed every 1–2yrs.

M. betonicifolia **3** (*M. baileyi*, Himalayan blue poppy): to 1–1.5×0.45m (3–5×1½ft); lvs hairy; beautiful sky-blue 6–8cm (2½–3in) poppy fls with yellow stamens, early summer; colour poorer in dry conditions. May be monocarpic if allowed to fl 1st yr. Var 'Alba' is white.

M. cambrica **4** (Welsh poppy): only European sp; to 45×30cm (1½×1ft); ferny lvs at base; 5cm (2in) lemon-yellow to orange poppy fls, all summer. Easily grown in any soil & position; self-seeds freely (except double forms).

M. chelidonifolia: to 90×40cm (36×16in); deeply lobed hairy lvs; pale yellow 2.5cm (1in) bell fls, early summer. For cool woodland.

M. grandis: to 60–90cm×45cm (2–3×1½ft); toothed hairy lvs at base; nodding 8–10cm (3–4in) poppy fls, deep blue to purplish (white in var 'Miss Dickson'), late spring. Divide regularly.

M. integrifolia (yellow Chinese poppy): to 60×40cm (24×16in); rosette of hairy lvs; 12cm (5in) cup-shaped yellow fls, early summer; usually monocarpic.

M. napaulensis (*M. wallichii*): to 1.2–1.8×0.6m (4–6×2ft); lvs deeply lobed; 8cm (3in) blue, purple, red or white nodding fls, early summer; usually monocarpic.

M. quintuplinerva **5** (harebell poppy): to 45×30cm (1½×1ft); mat of hairy lvs; dangling lavender-blue 5cm (2in) bell fls on arching hairy stalks. For well-drained soil.

M. regia **6**: to 1–1.5×0.6m (3–5×2ft); rosette of deeply cut lvs to 50cm (20in) long with bronze hairs; 8cm (3in) cup-shaped golden fls, early summer; usually monocarpic.

M.×*sheldonii* 'Branklyn' **7** (often listed as *M. grandis* 'Branklyn'): hybrid of *M. betonicifolia* & *M. grandis*; to 1.2–1.5×0.45m (4–5×1½ft); rich blue fls 10cm (4in) or more across. Divide regularly.

M. superba: to 1×0.6m (3×2ft); white poppy fls to 13cm (5½in) across, mid summer. Rather rare.

M. villosa: to 60×30cm (2×1ft); rosette of hairy lvs; clear yellow, nodding, globular poppy fls, 5cm (2in) across.

True poppies (*Papaver* spp): well known for their brilliant though short-lived fls with prominent stamens on long stems; cuttable if picked in bud & stems sealed in hot water; stems & lvs generally hairy. Like hot sun & dry, poor soil.

P. lateritium: moderately hardy; to 75×45cm (2½×1½ft); lobed lvs in rosette; orange to brick-red fls 8cm (3in) across, early summer.

P. orientale **8** (oriental poppy): rather sprawling & robust, but one of best & most popular border perennials. Ultra-hardy; to 60–90×60cm (2–3×2ft); deeply cut lvs; 8–12cm (3–5in) fls, v early summer, scarlet in sp but vars also pink, white & deep red, often blotched black, some fringed or double. Foliage dies down mid summer; cut back hard after flg to produce new growth. Short-lived where winters warm. Vars: 'Black and White' **9** (white, black central zone); 'Curlilocks' (vermilion, black throat, ruffled); 'Fireball' (*nanum plenum*; dwarf; orange-scarlet double fls; early); 'Goliath' **10** (blood-red); 'Indian Chief' (maroon); 'Marcus Perry' (deep scarlet); 'Mrs Perry' **11** (salmon-pink); 'Perry's White'; 'Persepolis' (v big bright orange fls); 'Picotee' (salmon & white frilled fls); 'Salmon Glow' (deep salmon-pink, double); 'Salome' (shining pink); 'Stormtorch' ('Sturmfackel'; fiery-red); 'Sultana' (glistening pink); 'Turkish Delight' (flesh-pink).

P. pilosum: moderately hardy; to 90×60cm (3×2ft); bushy; toothed lvs; 5cm (2in) brick-red fls, early summer.

P. rupifragum (Spanish poppy): moderately hardy; to 45×45cm (1½×1½ft); deeply cut lvs; silky 8cm (3in) brick-red fls, mid summer.

P. spicatum (*P. heldreichii*): moderately hardy; to

75×45cm (2½×1½ft); v hairy lvs; spikes of orange-red fls to 8cm (3in) across, early summer.
California "tree" poppy (Matilija poppy, *Romneya coulteri** **1**): semi- to moderately hardy invasive sub-shrubby perennial for light, well-drained soil in warm, sunny spot. To 1.2–1.8×1.2m (4–6×4ft); glaucous pinnate lvs; short-lived 8–15cm (3–6in) poppy-like brilliant white fls with boss of golden stamens, from mid summer (cuttable if stem ends seared in flame).

Resents transplanting; cut down top growth in winter; protect crown in cold winters. Var *trichocalyx* is similar but shorter. 'White Cloud' is good US var. For true tree poppy (*Dendromecon rigida*), see p224.
Celandine poppy (wood poppy, *Stylophorum diphyllum* **2**): v hardy perennial for rich soil in partial shade; to 40×30cm (16×12in); downy; lvs lobed; clusters of yellow poppy-like fls, 5cm (2in) across, from late spring; silvery seed-pods.

Border phlox and polemoniums

Easily grown herbaceous border perennials with colourful, often spectacular, flowers. Phlox particularly are among the most useful late summer perennials for colour association. **Cultivation**: For light, fertile soil that does not dry out, in full sun or partial shade. Thin out or replant phlox every 3–4 years, polemoniums every 1–2 years. Phlox (especially *Phlox paniculata*) prone to stem eelworm.
Propagation: Spp by seed; *Phlox* spp & vars by stem cuttings, root cuttings (best – avoids eelworm infestation); *Polemonium* spp & vars by division.

Phlox (*Phlox* spp): ultra- to v hardy N American border perennials (best in groups) with showy panicles of fls, cuttable but short-lived in water; lvs generally narrow. Thin out weak shoots in spring; dead-head.
P. carolina (*P. suffruticosa*): to 75–90×30cm (2½–3×1ft); fls purple to pink or white, 2cm (¾in) across, early to mid summer. 'Rosalinde', is good pink var.
P. divaricata **3** (*P. canadensis*, blue phlox): spreading, to 30×30–45cm (1×1–1½ft); fls violet-blue to lavender & pink, 2.5cm (1in) across, in loose clusters, early summer. For edging & ground cover. Var 'Laphamii' is a good blue. Hybrids with *P. paniculata* (often listed as *P.×arendsii*; free-flg): 'Anja' (purple); 'Hilda' (lavender, pink eye); 'Lisbeth' (lavender-blue); 'Susanne' (white, red eye).
P. maculata* : to 75–90×45cm (2½–3×1½ft); fls mauve-pink, 2cm (¾in) wide, in narrow cylindrical spikes. Vars: 'Alpha' **4** (pink); 'Miss Lingard' (white); 'Omega' **5** (white, tinged violet).
P. paniculata* (*P. decussata*, garden phlox): to 0.6–1.2×0.45–0.6m (2–4×1½–2ft); dense panicles of 2.5cm (1in) fls, purple in sp but white & pink to red & purple in vars, mid & late summer. Vars (generally to 0.75–1.1m [2½–3½ft]): 'Balmoral' (rosy-lavender); 'Border Gem' (violet-blue); 'Brigadier' (orange-scarlet); 'Bright Eyes' (pink, red eye); 'Caroline Vandenberg' (lavender-blue); 'Chintz' (pink, red eye); 'Endurance' (salmon-orange); 'Fairy's Petticoat' (mauve, darker eye); 'Hampton Court' (amethyst-blue); 'Harlequin' **6** (purple-violet; variegated lvs); 'Marlborough' (violet-purple); 'Mary Fox' (salmon-pink, red eye); 'Fujiyama' (white); 'Mother of Pearl' **7** (white suffused pink); 'Orange Perfection'; 'Pastorale' (pink, purple eye); 'Prime Minister' (white, red eye); 'Prince of

Orange' (orange-salmon); 'Progress' (light blue); 'Rembrandt' (white); 'Russian Violet' (violet-purple); 'Sandra' (scarlet); 'Sandringham' (pink, darker eye); 'Sir John Falstaff' (salmon-pink); 'Starfire' **8** (deep red); 'Tenor' (red); 'Vintage Wine' (purplish-red); 'White Admiral' **9** (white).
Polemoniums (Jacob's ladders, *Polemonium* spp): mainly ultra- to v hardy border perennials, once popular in cottage gardens, with clustered cup- or saucer-shaped mainly blue fls with golden stamens above mound of finely divided ladder-like pinnate lvs.
P. caeruleum **10** (Jacob's ladder, Greek valerian): to 60×30cm (2×1ft); 2cm (¾in) open lavender-blue fls from late spring; self-seeds. Vars & hybrids: 'Album' (white); *P.×richardsonii* (*P.×jacobaea*; to 45cm [1½ft]; violet-blue).
P. carneum: moderately hardy; to 45×45cm (1½×1½ft); pinkish cup-shaped fls, 2cm (¾in) across, from late spring. Var 'Pink Beauty' is purplish-pink.
P. foliosissimum **11**: to 75×45cm (2½×1½ft); cup-shaped lavender-blue or white fls, 1.5cm (⅝in) across, all summer. Best garden sp.
P. humile (correctly, *P. boreale*) 'Sapphire': to 45×45cm (1½×1½ft); pale blue 1cm (½in) saucer-shaped fls from late spring.
P. reptans (creeping Jacob's ladder): spreading, to 30×40cm (12×16in); saucer-shaped blue fls, 1cm (½in) across, late spring. 'Blue Pearl' is good var.

Knotweeds and ornamental rhubarbs

Bold herbaceous border plants with attractive, sometimes large leaves and very small flowers generally in profuse spikes. Many make good ground cover or form large clumps. **Cultivation**: For any soil, preferably rich and moist for clump-forming types. Unless stated, very hardy. **Propagation**: Division; seed.

Knotweeds (fleece flowers, *Polygonum* spp): have characteristic swollen stem joints ("knots"); generally form strong basal clumps of foliage with small fls in profuse dense poker-like spikes. For sun or shade; genus includes invasive weeds.
P. affine: ultra-hardy; spreading, to 25×45–60cm (10×18–24in); low mat of lance-shaped lvs, rusty-brown in autumn & winter; 15–20cm (6–8in) spikes of pink to dark red fls, all summer. Good for front of border, large rock garden, ground cover. Vars: 'Darjeeling Red' (v deep pink); 'Dimity' (dwarf; light pink); 'Donald Lowndes' ('Lowndes' Variety'; compact & free-flg; rose-red).
P. amplexicaule **1** (mountain fleece): variable, to 1–1.2×0.75 (3–4×2½ft); large dark green lvs; 15cm (6in) spikes of crimson to white fls, early summer to autumn. Vars: 'Album' (white); 'Arun Gem' ('Pendula'; to 60cm [2ft]; hanging tassels of bright pink fls); 'Atrosanguineum' (crimson); 'Firetail' (scarlet); 'Inverleith' (to 45cm [1½ft]; short red infls).
P. bistorta 'Superbum' **2** (garden var of bistort, snakeweed): ultra-hardy; to 90×60cm (3×2ft); light green broad lvs; 15cm (6in) spikes of clear pink fls, early summer (may repeat).
P. campanulatum **3**: to 90×75cm (3×2½ft); spreading; soft green pointed lvs; 5–8cm (2–3in) panicles of pink bell fls, early summer to autumn.
P. cuspidatum compactum (sometimes sold incorrectly as *P. reynoutria*): ultra-hardy; spreading, to 1×1m (3×3ft) or wider; rounded leathery lvs to 15cm (6in) long; profuse racemes

of tiny white fls turning pink, late summer; reddish seed heads. Slightly less invasive than *P. cuspidatum*, but only for wild gardens on poor soil.
P. macrophyllum: to 45×45cm (1½×1½ft); erect; strap-like wavy lvs to 20cm (8in) long; blunt spikes 8cm (3in) long of pink fls, all summer to autumn. Needs moisture.
P. milettii **4**: to 30–45×30cm (1–1½×1ft); deep green narrow lvs; 5–8cm (2–3in) spikes of rich crimson fls, all summer. Needs moisture.
P. paniculatum: to 1.5×1m (5×3ft); bushy; tall feathery sprays of v small creamy-white fls, sometimes flushed pink, late summer. Only for wild gardens.
P. sphaerostachyum **5**: to 60×30cm (2×1ft); light green narrow lvs; profuse 6–8cm (2½–3in) spikes of bright rose-pink fls all summer, to autumn if dead-headed.
Ornamental rhubarbs (*Rheum* spp): relatives of culinary rhubarb, with large or v large ornamental lvs & tall infls of small fls (to 2m [7ft]) in rich moist soil; good as specimens. Best in full sun.
R. alexandrae **6**: to 90×60cm (3×2ft); glossy green 30×20cm (12×8in) lvs; 30–45cm (1–1½ft) spikes of fls, late spring, hidden by large pale yellow papery bracts, ageing reddish.
R. palmatum: to 1.5–2.5×1.5m (5–8×5ft); deeply cut glossy lvs to 90×75cm (3×2½ft), purplish-red when young; erect 60–90cm (2–3ft) fluffy panicles of small pink or red fls, early summer. Var 'Atrosanguineum' ('Rubrum') has lvs opening vivid red & cerise-crimson fls.

Loosestrifes

Lysimachia spp. Except for *L. nummularia*, clump-forming (sometimes rather invasive) summer-flowering herbaceous plants with upright leafy stems. **Cultivation**: For any moist soil in sun or part-shade; very hardy unless stated. **Propagation**: Division.

L. ciliata: to 0.6–1.2×0.6m (2–4×2ft); lvs to 15cm (6in) long; clear yellow 2.5cm (1in) nodding fls in lf axils up stems. V invasive.
L. clethroides **7**: ultra-hardy; to 90×60cm (3×2ft); lance-shaped lvs to 15cm (6in) long, often red in autumn; 10–15cm (4–6in) arching racemes of starry greyish-white 1cm (½in) fls, later than other spp. Rather invasive.
L. ephemerum **8**: to 1.2×0.3cm (4×1ft); forms neat clump; narrow grey-green lvs; 30cm (1ft) spikes of starry white fls.
L. nummularia **9** (moneywort, creeping Jenny):

ultra-hardy; trailing & self-rooting, to 5×60cm (2×24in); evergreen; 2.5cm (1in) rounded lvs; yellow 1–2cm (½–¾in) cup-shaped fls along stems. Var 'Aurea' has golden lvs (best in partial shade). Vigorous, making good ground cover even on rather dry soil.
L. punctata **10** (garden or yellow loosestrife): to 60–90×60cm (2–3×2ft); lance-shaped lvs; cup-shaped brassy-yellow fls to 2cm (¾in) across in whorls up stems. Rather invasive.

316

Primulas and polyanthus

Primula spp; sometimes called primroses. Showy rosette/clump-forming plants with umbels of 5-petalled flowers in spring &/or early summer. Leaves &/or stems & flowers of some spp coated with powdery farina. Best massed in shady borders, woodland, etc; excellent near streams or pools.
Cultivation: Unless stated, very hardy. For any soil (preferably rich) that never dries out, preferably in partial shade. (Except for polyanthus, often termed bog primulas, but boggy conditions not essential.)
Propagation: Division; seed (germinates best below 18°C [64°F]). **Classification**: Botanically into some 30 sections; also more generally by geographical origin (except polyanthus, all spp listed here Asiatic). For smaller spp, many good in woodland conditions, see p460.

Candelabra section: vigorous; lvs often semi-erect, lance-shaped to oval, generally toothed; fls 1–2cm (½–¾in) wide, in series of up to 8 umbels or whorls up tall stems, late spring to early summer.

P. aurantiaca **1**: to 45×20cm (18×8in); lvs ragged, to 20cm (8in) long; fls yellow to tawny-red, on brownish-red stems. Var 'Bonfire' (probably a hybrid) is taller & fiery-red.

P. beesiana **2**: to 60×45cm (2×1½ft); lvs light green, slightly farinose, to 25cm (10in) long; fls reddish/lilac-purple, yellow eye; deep-rooted.

P.×bullesiana ('Asthore Hybrids'): strain of hybrids of *P. beesiana* & *P. bulleyana*; to 60–90×45cm (2–3×1½ft); fls in shades of cream, yellow, apricot, orange, pink, crimson & purple.

P. bulleyana **3**: to 60–75×45cm (2–2½×1½ft); dark green lvs to 30cm (1ft) long, reddish midrib; fls golden-yellow to orange-red. V popular.

P. burmanica: to 60×45cm (2×1½ft); lvs to 30cm (1ft) long; dense whorls of reddish-purple fls, yellow eye. Easy.

P. chungensis: to 60×45cm (2×1½ft); tufts of shallowly lobed lvs; yellow/orange fls, red eye.

P. cockburniana **4**: to 30–40×30cm (12–16×12in); rather sparse clumps of lvs to 15cm (6in) long; fls orange-scarlet; rather short-lived.

*P. helodoxa**: moderately hardy; to 90×45cm (3×1½ft); semi-evergreen; glossy light green lvs to 30cm (1ft) long; fls bright golden-yellow; likes lime & needs shade.

P. japonica (Japanese primrose): to 60–75×45cm (2–2½×1½ft); lush pale green lvs to 25cm (10in) long; fls reddish-purple, yellow eye, to 2.5cm (1in) across. Vars (generally breed true from seed): 'Miller's Crimson' (velvety-crimson, black eye); 'Postford White' **5** (white, yellow eye); 'Rosea' (deep pink). Easy & tough, but sometimes rather short-lived.

P. poissonii: to 45×25cm (18×10in); rosettes of shiny glaucous lvs to 15cm (6in) long; fls purplish/plum-red. Tolerates sun & dryish soil.

P. pulverulenta: to 45–60×45cm (1½–2×1½ft); lvs pale green, to 30cm (1ft) long, wrinkled; fls wine-red to crimson, darker eye, on farinose stems. Vars & hybrids: 'Bartley Strain' (shell-pink); 'Inverewe' (vivid orange-scarlet; sterile); 'Rowallane' **6** (salmon-pink; sterile). V robust.

P. smithiana: to 45–60×30cm (1½–2×1ft); lvs thin, to 20cm (8in) long; fls bright yellow.

Drumstick primula (*P. denticulata* **7**; Denticulate section): to 30×25cm (12×10in); robust; compact rosettes of farinose leathery lvs to 15–20cm (6–8in) long; dense globular heads to 8cm (3in) across of 1cm (½in) fls, usually pale lilac to deep purple, yellow eye, all spring. Sold as mixed seed strains & vars: 'Alba' (white); 'Bressingham Beauty' (powder-blue); 'Prichard's Ruby' (ruby-red). Easy; often grown as HHA or HB for bedding; overwinters as dormant bud.

Sikkimensis section: similar to Candelabra spp but nodding bell-shaped fls 1–2cm (½–¾in) across in elegant umbels (sometimes 2 to a stem), late spring & early summer; lvs have distinct stalks.

*P. alpicola** (*P. microdonta alpicola*, moonlight primula): to 30–60×30cm (1–2×1ft); lvs to 15cm (6in) long, wrinkled; fls farinose, v variable: ivory-white, soft yellow, purple or violet.

*P. florindae** **8** (giant cowslip): to 0.6–1.2×0.6m (2–4×2ft): clump of heart-shaped lvs to 25cm (10in) long on long stalks; v large heads of pale yellow (sometimes orange to blood-red) farinose fls, long season. Makes good ground cover; will grow in shallow water; likes lime.

P. secundiflora: to 60×30cm (2×1ft); lvs to 10cm (4in) long, farinose beneath when young, fls deep wine-red, v dark within, farinose.

*P. sikkimensis** **9** (Himalayan cowslip): to 45–60×30cm (1½–2×1ft); lvs pale green, to 12cm (5in) long, wrinkled; fls pale yellow, to 2.5cm (1in) across.

Polyanthus (polyantha primroses; sometimes listed as *P.×polyantha* **10**, *P. veris elatior* or *P. vulgaris elatior*; Vernalis section): garden hybrids of *P. vulgaris*, probably with *P. veris* & *P. elatior* (p464), with bold umbels of colourful fls to 4cm (1½in) across on strong stems, late winter to spring; mainly for spring bedding & pots under glass. To 20–30×20–25cm (8–12×8–10in); semi-evergreen; v wide colour range, including strong & pastel shades, generally with yellow eye, including bicolours & tricolours; some doubles. Sold mainly as seed strains in mixtures, colour series & single colours; many strains (including well-known 'Pacific Giants' **11**) only moderately hardy & best under glass; others v to ultra-hardy; dark colours withstand hot sun best.

Ferns

Primitive, flowerless, generally moisture-loving perennials (herbaceous unless stated) loved for their grace & delicacy. Among the most useful plants, good foils for flowering plants & used as underplanting in woodland or by cold sunless walls, some by waterside; spreading types good for ground cover; small forms for rock gardens, rock walls, peat beds & banks. All are charming in spring, when croziers ("fiddleheads") unfurl; some colour in autumn. Fronds pinnate or bipinnate unless noted. Nomenclature often confusing, with many name changes; family Polypodiaceae unless stated. **Cultivation**: Unless stated, very hardy & for moist but well-drained peaty soil in cool shade sheltered from drying winds; mulch in spring. **Propagation**: Division, spring or early autumn; spores (borne under pinnae, in some spp only on special fertile fronds), sown spring (not easy). Commercially sometimes by tissue culture.

Maidenhair ferns (*Adiantum* spp): rhizomatous; dainty & lacy, with light green filigree fronds with black, wiry, arching stalks. Do not mulch.

A. capillus-veneris (true [in US, southern] maidenhair): semi–moderately hardy; to 40×40cm (16×16in); evergreen; uniquely wedge-shaped pinnules. Often grown under glass; likes lime.

A. pedatum (American/northern maidenhair): ultra-hardy; to 45×30cm (1½×1ft); branching fronds, oblong pinnules. Vars: *aleuticum* **1** (now correctly *subpumilum*; dwarf, to 15×30cm [6×8in]; tolerates some sun); *japonicum* (fronds coppery-pink when young).

A. venustum **2**: v hardy; to 25×25cm (10×10in); similar to *A. capillus-veneris*; triangular pinnules, pink when young. Forms carpet.

Spleenworts (*Asplenium* spp): evergreen lime-lovers generally best planted vertically in rock crevices, walls, etc.

A. adiantum-nigrum (black spleenwort): to 25×25cm (10×10in); rather erect leathery fronds with dark stalks & variable pinnules.

A. ceterach **3** (*Ceterach officinarum*, rusty-back fern): to 15×15cm (6×6in); tufted; distinctive sage-green pinnatifid fronds, alternate pinnae, silvered & becoming brown beneath. Takes sun.

A. platyneuron (ebony spleenwort): ultra-hardy; to 40×35cm (16×14in); semi-evergreen; almost black stalks. Good in woodland.

A. (Phyllitis) scolopendrium (*Scolopendrium vulgare*, hart's-tongue fern): ultra-hardy; to 30–60×30cm (1–2×1ft); v variable, but fronds generally strap-shaped, not divided. Easy in woodland conditions or shady border. Numerous vars include: 'Crispum' (crisped); 'Cristatum' **4** (crested); *laceratum* 'Kaye's Variety' (wide crested fronds with deeply cut edges); 'Undulatum' **5** (dwarf; wavy fronds).

A. trichomanes **6** (maidenhair spleenwort): ultra-hardy; to 25×25cm (10×10in); tufted; curving black stalks with oval pinnae. Pretty & easy.

Athyriums (in US, glade ferns; *Athyrium* spp): ultra-hardy tufted moisture-lovers tolerating some sun; related to *Asplenium* spp.

A. filix-femina **7** (lady fern): to 60–90×60cm (2–3×2ft); v variable; dainty bright green fronds; pretty by water. Hundreds of vars include:

corymbiferum (fronds have bunched tassel-like crests); *cristatum* (fronds have flat crests); 'Fieldii' (tall; pinnae paired in cross-like formation); 'Frizelliae' (tatting fern; to 45cm [1½ft]; pinnae like lacy balls along stalks); 'Minutum' ('Minimum', 'Minutissimum'; dwarf, to 15×15cm [6×6in]); *plumosum* (fronds feathery); 'Vernoniae' (triangular crisped pinnae); 'Victoriae' (tall; criss-crossed crested pinnae, forming lattice-like effect).

A. nipponicum (*A. goeringianum*, *A. iseanum*): to 30–60×45cm (1–2×1½ft); coarsely divided fronds, purplish stalks. Var 'Pictum' **8** ('Metallicum', Japanese painted fern) has dark red stems, greyish or glaucous pinnae, shaded darker; best sheltered.

A. thelypteroides (silvery spleenwort, silvery glade fern; correctly *Diplazium acrostichoides*): to 75×75cm (2½×2½ft); spreading; pale green fronds, yellow hairs beneath.

Hard ferns (*Blechnum* spp): lime-hating evergreens with tough, leathery fronds (fertile & sterile distinct); tolerate dryish air.

B. penna-marina (dwarf hard fern): to 15×30cm (6×12in); creeping; deep green fronds, narrow pinnae. Good for rock garden.

B. spicant **9** (common hard fern, deer fern): to 30–60×45cm (1–2×1½ft); narrow pinnatifid fronds, becoming pinnate on mature plants; sterile fronds spreading; fertile fronds (deciduous) longer & upright, with narrower pinnae. Easy.

Parsley fern (*Cryptogramma crispa* **10**): ultra-hardy; to 20×20cm (8×8in); tufted; triangular parsley-like fronds (fertile & sterile separate but similar). Not easy; for wet, lime-free soil in sun. Var *acrostichoides* (*C. acrostichoides*) is similar N American form.

Japanese holly fern (*Cyrtomium* [*Polystichum*] *falcatum*): moderately hardy tufted evergreen, to 60–90×60–90cm (2–3×2–3ft); dark green fronds with glossy leathery holly-like pinnae. Tough & easy if protected below −4°C (25°F); good in pots. Var 'Rochfordianum' is compact, with deeply notched pinnae. *C. fortunei* is similar but pinnae not glossy.

Bladder ferns (*Cystopteris* spp): dainty ultra-hardy plants with bright green feathery fronds.

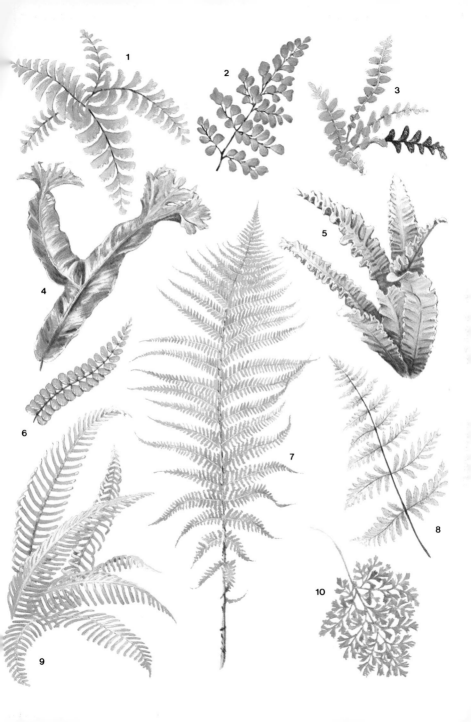

For moist rock garden.

C. bulbifera (berry or bulbil bladder fern): to 30–90×20–40cm (12–36×8–16in), depending on moisture; gracefully arching fronds, brown stalks, bearing bulbils. Likes lime.

C. fragilis (brittle or fragile fern): to 25×20cm (10×8in); slowly spreading; brittle green stems.

Squirrel's-foot fern (hare's-foot fern, *Davallia mariesii* **1**): moderately hardy though usually grown under glass; to 20×20cm (8×8in); creeping hairy rhizome; semi-evergreen much-divided fronds, bronzed in spring.

Hay-scented fern (boulder fern, *Dennstaedtia* [*Dicksonia*] *punctilobula*): ultra-hardy; vigorous, to 60×45cm (2×1½ft); spreading; fresh green finely divided fronds, hay-scented when bruised (fertile & sterile v similar). Sun or shade any soil.

Tasmanian tree fern (*Dicksonia antarctica* **2**; family Dicksoniaceae): semi-hardy evergreen, slow-growing to 4.5×3m (15×10ft), more in wild; brown fibrous trunk topped by rosette of arching dark green fronds to 1.8m (6ft) long. Needs rich soil in damp atmosphere; spray trunk with water daily if necessary.

Buckler ferns (wood or shield ferns, *Dryopteris* spp): large genus of easy tufted woodland ferns; compact & vigorous. Generally ultra-hardy & for any fertile soil.

D. aemula (hay-scented buckler fern): erect, to 30–60×30cm (1–2×1ft); bright green finely divided evergreen fronds, scented of new-mown hay. For lime-free soil in shade.

D. affinis (*D. borreri*): see *D. pseudomas*.

D. cristata (crested buckler/wood fern [misnomer]): to 75×60cm (2½×2ft); non-crested leathery fronds. For moist soil.

D. dilatata **3** (*D. aristata*, broad buckler fern; correctly, *D. austriaca*): to 0.6–1.2×0.6m (2–4×2ft); elegant, with broad, triangular arching fronds. Good by water. Var 'Grandiceps' has v large crests on fronds. See also *D. spinulosa*.

D. erythrosora (Japanese buckler/shield fern): to 90×60cm (3×2ft); evergreen, with broad triangular fronds, coppery when young, scarlet spore capsules beneath. Striking.

D. filix-mas **4** (male fern): to 1–1.2×1m (3–4×3ft); tufted & robust; semi-evergreen; light green fronds, brownish stems. Common European native, making easy ground cover, good in wild gardens. Tolerates dryness, sun & poor soil; self-sows. Numerous vars include: 'Crispa' (to 45cm [1½ft]; crisped); 'Crispa Cristata' (to 40cm [16in]; crisped & crested); *cristata* **5** (variably crested, best in 'Martindale'); 'Grandiceps' (to 60cm [2ft]; v large crests); 'Linearis' (erect, with finely cut fronds); 'Polydactyla' (pinnae have long crests).

D. goldiana (giant wood fern, Goldie's fern): to 1–1.2×0.6m (3–4×2ft); large coarse fronds, yellowish in spring, scaly. Best in cool, shady wild garden.

D. marginalis (marginal shield/buckler fern, leather wood fern): to 45×45cm (1½×1½ft); evergreen; bluish-green shiny leathery fronds from distinct woody crown. Fine specimen.

D. noveboracensis: see *Thelypteris noveboracensis*.

D. pseudomas **6** (*D. borreri*, golden scaled male fern; correctly, *D. affinis*): to 1.2×1m (4×3ft); robust, beautiful semi-evergreen; croziers & young fronds golden-green, becoming rich green, large & arching, scaly golden stems. Fine landscape plant. Tolerates dry soil. Vars: *cristata* 'The King' (superbly crested); 'Cristata Angustata' **7** (to 45cm [1½ft]; narrow, neatly crested fronds).

D. spinulosa (*D. carthusiana*, toothed wood fern; correctly, *D. austriaca spinulosa*): to 75×60cm (2½×2ft); deep green delicate fronds.

D. thelypteris: see *Thelypteris palustris*.

Oak ferns (*Gymnocarpium* spp): ultra-hardy creeping rhizomatous ferns with triangular fronds. Good for rock gardens, peat beds, shady borders.

G. dryopteris (oak fern): to 30×45cm (1×1½ft); bright green fronds, v feathery in var 'Plumosum'.

G. robertianum (northern or limestone oak fern): to 30×45cm (1×1½ft); thicker, darker green fronds than above. Likes lime.

Thousand-leaved fern (*Hypolepis millefolia*): moderately hardy creeping rhizomatous evergreen; to 30×60cm (1×2ft); dark green bracken-like fronds. Dainty but somewhat invasive. Tolerates sun. *H. rugulosa* is similar but larger, with wider-spaced brownish-green pinnae.

Ostrich fern (shuttlecock fern, *Matteuccia struthiopteris*, **8**, *Struthiopteris germanica*): large ultra-hardy moisture-loving fern with fronds rather like ostrich feathers arranged in vase or shuttlecock shape, to 1–1.5×0.6–1m (3–5×2–3ft); fertile fronds (later) form smaller inner "shuttlecock"; both from erect stout stock. Striking & beautiful in late spring, browning late summer; spreads by underground runners. Needs v moist, even boggy soil. Var *pennsylvanica* (*S. pennsylvanica*) of N America is more erect, to 1.8m (6ft), rarely to 3m (10ft).

Sensitive fern (bead fern, *Onoclea sensibilis* **9**): ultra-hardy rhizomatous moisture-lovers; to 60×90cm (2×3ft); pale green triangular sterile fronds with large, toothed pinnae, browning in autumn; persistent narrow fertile fronds with bead-like pinnae (good for winter arrangements). Good ground cover by water, but can be invasive (less so in sun).

Flowering ferns (*Osmunda* spp; family Osmundaceae): ultra-hardy vigorous moisture-lovers with separate sterile & fertile fronds, the fertile pinnae maturing to look like dried fls.

Tufted habit, generally to 1.2×1m (4×3ft); roots form matted peaty clumps (used as orchid growing medium, osmunda fibre). Striking bog plants; hate lime.

O. cinnamomea **1** (cinnamon fern): young fronds white-woolly when young; fertile fronds dark green turning cinnamon-brown. Young croziers edible (treat like asparagus).

O. claytoniana (interrupted fern): fertile fronds bear brown fertile pinnae clustered in centre of frond. Young croziers edible.

O. regalis **2** (royal fern): to 1.8×1.8m (6×6ft), more where suited; fronds coppery when young, becoming fresh green, then yellow-brown in autumn; tufts of fertile pinnae. Magnificent & handsome waterside plant. Vars: 'Purpurascens' **3** (fronds glaucous); 'Undulata' (fronds crisped).

Beech fern (*Phegopteris connectilis*): see *Thelypteris phegopteris*.

Hart's-tongue fern (*Phyllitis scolopendrium*): see *Asplenium scolopendrium*.

Common polypody (*Polypodium vulgare*; v similar N American sp now correctly *P. virginianum*): ultra-hardy small evergreen creeping fern, to 25–40×40cm (10–16×16in); leathery pinnatifid fronds with alternate plane, fresh green new fronds developing late. Often grows as epiphyte; good for ground cover. Easy in dryish, stony soil; tolerates lime. Vars: *australe* (correctly *P. australe*; broader, softer fronds); 'Bifidum' (pinnae forked); 'Cornubiense' **4** ('Elegantissimum'; fronds generally tripinnate or quadripinnate, giving lacy effect; remove reverted fronds); *interjectum* (correctly *P. interjectum*; fronds broader; tolerates wetter soil); 'Longicaudatum' (long pointed fronds); 'Pulcherrimum' (fronds deeply & finely cut; vigorous).

Shield ferns (holly ferns; *Polystichum* spp): tufted, non-invasive woodland ferns. Lime-tolerant; for rich soil in shade.

P. acrostichoides (Christmas fern): ultra-hardy; to 60–90×60cm (2–3×2ft); evergreen; dark glossy green leathery fronds with dagger-like almost opposite pinnae. Likes moisture, lime.

P. aculeatum **5** (prickly or hard shield fern): to 60–90×60cm (2–3×2ft); evergreen; finely divided fronds, with glossy dark green alternate pinnae, leathery & rigid, yellowish in spring. Good in woodland, by water. Vars: 'Pulcherrimum' (fronds v finely divided); 'Pulcherrimum Gracillimum' (v long, thin, tasselled pinnae).

P. braunii (Braun's holly fern): ultra-hardy; to 60–90×60cm (2–3×2ft); lustrous green leathery fronds from crown; deciduous, but dead fronds persistent. Likes moisture.

P. falcatum: see *Cyrtomium falcatum*.

P. lonchitis ([mountain] holly fern): ultra-hardy; to 30–60×60cm (1–2×2ft); evergreen; narrowish

leathery fronds with close-set bristly pinnae. For cool moist rock garden; difficult in lowlands.

P. munitum (giant holly fern, sword fern, Christmas fern): to 90×90cm (3×3ft) or more; evergreen; makes large clump of glossy dark green arching fronds. Likes moisture.

P. setiferum **6** (soft shield fern, hedge fern; sometimes sold incorrectly as *P. aculeatum*): to 0.6–1.2×1–1.5m (2–4×3–5ft); semi-/evergreen; gracefully arching mid green fronds with delicately cut pinnae & scaly stems. Easy in moist or dryish soil. V numerous vars (to 60×60cm [2×2ft] unless stated) include: *acutilobum* ('Proliferum'; narrow, finely divided fronds with bulbils); *congestum* (dense & dwarf, to 20cm [8in]); *divisilobum* (finely divided tripinnate or quadripinnate fronds; 'Iveryanum' is crested form); 'Plumosum' (semi-prostrate; dense feathery fronds).

Thelypteris (*Thelypteris* spp): smallish clump-forming rhizomatous ferns for moist acid soil unless stated.

T. (*Phegopteris*) *hexagonoptera* ([broad] beech fern): ultra-hardy; to 45×45cm (1½×1½ft); broad triangular mid green fronds with deeply cut pinnae. Tolerates some sun & dryness.

T. (*Dryopteris*) *noveboracensis* (New York fern): ultra-hardy; to 60×60cm (2×2ft); yellow-green narrowish fronds with alternate pinnae. Takes sun if moist.

T. palustris (*Dryopteris thelypteris*, marsh fern): to 60×60cm (2×2ft); similar to *T. noveboracensis* but likes boggy neutral soil near pools. Spreads by creeping rhizomes.

T. phegopteris **7** ([long/narrow] beech fern, northern beech fern; correctly, *Phegopteris connectilis*): ultra-hardy; to 45×45cm (1½×1½ft); light green triangular fronds, flimsy & graceful, smaller than *T. hexagonoptera*. Good ground cover but can be invasive.

Woodsias (*Woodsia* spp): small ultra-hardy tufted ferns for rock gardens.

W. ilvensis **8** (rusty woodsia): to 10–20×20cm (4–8×8in); dull green fronds with reddish stalks & deeply cut pinnae. For moist crevice.

W. obtusa (common or blunt-lobed woodsia): to 40×40cm (16×16in); semi-/evergreen; greyish-green fronds, fertile fronds more erect. Easy in dryish, gritty soil in some sun; tolerates lime.

Chain ferns (*Woodwardia* spp): large tufted ferns, easy in v moist or boggy acid soils.

W. radicans **9** (European chain fern): semi-hardy; vigorous, to 1–1.8×1m (3–6×3ft); arching light green fronds from crown. Creates exotic effect.

W. fimbriata (*W. chamissoi*, giant chain fern; may be sold as *W. radicans*) of western N America is similar but moderately to v hardy & taller.

W. virginica (Virginia chain fern): to 1–1.2×1m (3–4×3ft); creeping; erect glossy green fronds, reddish in spring, purple stalks.

Monkshoods and delphiniums

Mainly tall, predominantly blue-flowered herbaceous perennials for full sun or light shade. Include some of the most graceful & arresting of summer border plants, with tall racemes or spikes of flowers over deeply divided foliage, useful for accent. Shorter spp good for front of borders or large rock gardens; *Aconitum* spp also for woodland plantings. Good for cutting. **Cultivation**: Unless stated, ultra-hardy but dislike extreme summer heat. For deep, rich, moist but well-drained soil. Stake tall spp & vars; dead-head & may repeat in autumn. **Propagation**: Seed; division.

Monkshoods (aconites, *Aconitum* spp): have characteristic helmet-like or hooded fls, to 4cm (1½in) high, & dark green, glossy lobed lvs. All parts, particularly roots, v poisonous. Mulch in spring; divide when clumps large.

A. carmichaelii (often sold as *A. fischeri*): to 90×50cm (3ft×16in); erect; short racemes of Wedgwood-blue fls, late summer. Var *wilsonii* (*A. wilsonii*) is taller, to 1.8m (6ft). Other vars: 'Arendsii' **1** (to 1.2m [4ft]; amethyst-blue); 'Barker's Variety' (to 1.8m [6ft]; deep blue); 'Kelmscott' **2** (to 1.8m [6ft]; rich violet-blue).

A. henryi (*A. autumnale*) 'Spark's Variety' (*sparkianum, sparksii*; may be listed under *A. cammarum* or *A. napellus*): v hardy; to 1.2–1.5×0.45m (4–5×1½ft); dark violet-blue fls from mid summer.

A. napellus (common monkshood of Europe, helmet flower; some forms may be listed under *A. cammarum*): erect, to 1.1×0.45m (3½×1½ft); dense racemes of deep blue fls from mid summer. Vars & hybrids: 'Album' (off-white); 'Bicolor' **3** (branching; violet-blue & white); 'Blue Sceptre' (to 75cm [2½ft]; narrow spikes of violet-blue & white fls); 'Bressingham Spire' (narrow spikes of violet-blue fls); 'Carneum' (flesh-pink); 'Newry Blue' (to 1.5m [5ft]; navy-blue; early).

A. vulparia & *A. lycoctonum* (*A. septentrionale*, wolfsbane): v similar spp; to 1–1.2×0.45m (3–4×1½ft); branching spikes of yellowish fls in summer. Var 'Ivorine' is ivory-white.

Delphiniums (larkspurs, *Delphinium* spp): generally have dense spikes of spurred fls, often with contrasting eye ("bee") of small inner petals; some spp (garland larkspurs) more bushy; lvs deeply dissected, mid green. Prefer alkaline soil; prone to crown rot, root rot, slugs. Short-lived as perennials; treat as HHAs in areas with long hot summers.

D.×belladonna (Belladonna hybrids; often listed under *D. elatum*, sometimes *D. formosanum*): hybrids of *D. elatum* & *D. grandiflorum* &/or *D. cheilanthum* (*D. formosanum*); branching & graceful, to 1.1–1.4×0.6m (3½–4½×2ft); thin stems; fls to 5cm (2in) wide in loose racemes, mainly white to dark blue, from early summer. Vars: 'Blue Bees' (bright light blue); 'Bonita' (gentian-blue); 'Lamartine' **4** (deep blue); 'Loddon Blue' (royal-blue); 'Moerheimii' (white); 'Peace' (strong mid blue); 'Pink Sensation'

(hybrid with *D. nudicaule*; to 90cm [3ft]; clear pink); 'Wendy' (gentian-blue, dark flecks).

D. brunonianum: to 45×30cm (1½×1ft); fls 3cm (1¼in) wide, pale lilac-blue with black & yellow "bee", summer.

D. cardinale: moderately hardy; to 60–90×45cm (2–3×1½ft); open racemes of 2cm (¾in) cup-shaped scarlet fls, yellow centre, mid summer.

D. elatum: to 1–1.5×0.6m (3–5×2ft); 30cm (1ft) or longer dense spikes of 2.5cm (1in) blue fls from early summer. Sp rarely grown, but a major parent of large-fld Elatum hybrids (to 1.2–2.5×0.6–0.9m [4–8×2–3ft]; fls to 6cm [2½in] across in v long spikes). Seed strains (generally mixed): 'Blackmore & Langdon Strain'; 'Blue Fountains' (dwarf, to 75cm [2½ft]); 'Connecticut Yankees' (dwarf, to 75cm [2½ft]); 'Pacific Hybrids' ('Pacific Giants'); 'Round Table' series; 'Wrexham' ('Hollyhock') strain. Named tall vars (over 1.4m [4½ft]): 'Astolat' (pink); 'Black Knight' (dark blue, black eye); 'Blue Jay' (mid blue, white eye); 'Blue Nile' **5** (strong mid blue, white eye); 'Butterball' **6** (cream, yellow eye); 'Cherry Pie' (dusky-pink); 'Fanfare' (pale mauve; early); 'Faust' (ultramarine, indigo eye); 'Galahad' **7** (white); 'Gordon Forsyth' (amethyst); 'Icecap' (white); 'Ruby' (mulberry-pink, brown eye); 'Silver Jubilee' (white, dark eye); 'Strawberry Fair' **8** (dusky-pink); 'Summer Skies' (sky-blue, white eye). Dwarf vars (to 1–1.4m [3–4½ft]): 'Baby Doll' (pale mauve, yellowish eye); 'Blue Heaven' (mid blue, double); 'Blue Jade' **9** (sky-blue, brown eye); 'Blue Tit' (indigo, dark eye); 'Mighty Atom' (deep lavender); 'Royal Flush' (dusky-pink, white eye). See also *D.×belladonna*.

D. grandiflorum (*D. chinense*): to 30–60×30cm (1–2×1ft); branching; 25–30cm (10–12in) racemes of violet-blue fls, long spurs, mid summer. Vars & seed strains: 'Album' (white); 'Azure Fairy'; 'Blue Butterfly'.

D. nudicaule **10**: moderately hardy & short-lived; to 60×25cm (24×10in); open racemes of orange-red long-spurred fls from early summer.

D. tatsienense: bushy, to 25–40×15cm (10–16×6in); loose branching infls of deep violet-blue long-spurred fls, orange beard, early summer. Short-lived.

D. zalil (may be sold as *D. sulphureum*; correctly, *D. semibracteatum*): to 30–60×30cm (1–2×1ft); yellow cup-shaped fls in loose racemes, early summer. Needs sun & v good drainage.

Bugbanes and meadow rues

Apart from monkshoods & delphiniums (p326), the tallest border perennials of the buttercup family. Stately yet dainty, both have large inflorescences of tiny flowers (good for cutting) & mostly lacy & elegant fern-like leaves. Some bugbanes flower into autumn. **Cultivation**: For rich, moist soil in sun or (preferably) light shade; bugbanes also adaptable for deep shade. **Propagation**: Division; seed.

Bugbanes (*Cimicifuga* spp): ultra-hardy; lvs generally much divided, sometimes strange scent; mainly white v small fls in v long narrow spikes. Staking not needed.
C. americanum (American bugbane): to 1.8×0.6m (6×2ft); loose infls of creamy-white fls, late summer.
C. dahurica: to 1.5×0.6m (5×2ft); showy branching spikes of creamy-white fls, late summer.
C. foetida: to 1.8×0.6m (6×2ft); arching spikes of greenish-yellow fls, early autumn; handsome green seed pods. Var *intermedia*: see *C. simplex*.
C. japonica: to 1–1.2×0.75m (3–4×2½ft); shiny lobed lvs; long spikes of white fls, late summer.
C. racemosa **1** (black snake-root): to 1.5×0.6m (5×2ft); fresh green divided lvs; showy wand-like racemes to 90cm (3ft) long of pure white fls, mid summer. Var *cordifolia* (*C. cordifolia*) has shiny dark lvs, some heart-shaped, & creamy-green fls.
C. simplex (sometimes listed as *C. foetida intermedia*): to 1.2×0.6m (4×2ft); arching spikes of white fls, mid autumn. Vars: 'Elstead Variety' (buds lilac); *ramosa* (*C. ramosa*; to 2m [7ft]; v late); 'White Pearl' **2** ('Armleuchter').
Meadow rues (*Thalictrum* spp): generally v hardy; lvs often like maidenhair fern's; tiny fls in branching panicles, early summer. Need staking.

T. aquilegifolium **3**: to 90×30cm (3×1ft); columbine-like pale green lvs; fluffy rosy-lilac to purple fls. Vars: 'Album' (white); 'Dwarf Purple' (purple-mauve); 'Purpureum' (to 1.2m [4ft]; pale purple); 'Thundercloud' (deep purple).
T. delavayi **4** (often sold as *T. dipterocarpum*, a different but similar sp): to 1.8×0.6m (6×2ft); dainty lvs; v large panicles of lilac-mauve fls, yellow stamens. Vars: 'Album' (to 1.1m [3½ft]; white); 'Hewitt's Double' **5** (to 90cm [3ft]; mauve double fls; likes shade).
T. flavum (yellow meadow rue): to 1.5×0.45m (5×1½ft); compact infls of fluffy yellow fls.
T. minus (often sold as *T. adiantifolium*): ultra-hardy; to 60–90×30cm (2–3×1ft); grey-green "maidenhair" lvs; insignificant fls with yellowish stamens.
T. rochebrunianum **6** (often spelled *rocquebrunianum*): erect, to 1.2×0.6m (4×2ft); dainty lvs; showy loose panicles of rosy-lavender fls, yellow stamens.
T. simplex (often listed as *T. angustifolium* or *T. lucidum*): erect, to 1.5×0.6m (5×2ft); lvs dark green, shiny; greenish-yellow fluffy fls.
T. speciosissimum (often listed as *T. glaucum* or *T. flavum glaucum*): 1.5×0.6m (5×2ft); lvs blue-grey, deeply divided & good for cutting; fluffy yellow fls.

Other members of the buttercup family

Small to medium-sized border perennials – mostly under 1m (3ft); herbaceous unless stated. Many have nodding flowers, often with spurred petals; others are rounder & more buttercup-like; most except *Anemone* spp good for cutting. Leaves usually compound, attractive. Many spp poisonous. **Cultivation**: Mainly for rich, moist but well-drained soil with ample humus in light/partial shade. **Propagation**: Division; seed; *Anemone* spp also by root cuttings; *Clematis* spp also by stem cuttings. For tuberous anemones & ranunculus, see pp422–4; for dwarf spp best grown in rock gardens, see p466.

Baneberries (*Actaea* spp): generally ultra-hardy, best in cool spot; deeply cut fern-like lvs; racemes of small white/bluish fls, late spring or early summer; decorative but v poisonous 1cm (½in) berries from late summer; other parts also poisonous. Naming of spp confused.
A. pachypoda **7** (often listed as *A. alba* or *A. spicata alba*; white baneberry of N America): to 90×45cm (3×1½ft); berries white/pinkish, scarlet stalks.
A. rubra **8** (*A. spicata rubra*; red baneberry of N America): to 30–60×30cm (1–2×1ft); berries mostly red, held well above lvs.

A. spicata **9** (incorrectly, *A. alba*, *A. spicata alba*; black baneberry of Europe, herb Christopher): v hardy; to 45×45cm (1½×1½ft); shining black berries (most poisonous sp).
Adonis (*Adonis* spp): ultra-hardy early-flg dwarf perennials with large buttercup-like yellow fls & finely cut ferny lvs.
A. amurensis: to 15–30×25cm (6–12×10in); bright yellow 5cm (2in) bowl-shaped fls from late winter; dies down early summer. Vars: 'Fukujukai' (v early); 'Plena' (double green centred fls).
A. vernalis: to 40×25cm (16×10in); yellow 5cm (2in) fls, opening flat, spring. *A. volgensis* is

similar but fls slightly earlier.

Anemones (windflowers, *Anemone* spp):
v hardy & long-lived; good in sun if soil moist;
invasive if soil light. Lvs often vine-like; rounded,
cup-shaped to flat fls with central boss, on wiry
stems, late summer to autumn.

A. hupehensis (Japanese anemone): to
45×45cm (1½×1½ft); rose-pink 5–8cm (2–3in)
fls. Var *japonica* (*A. japonica*) is taller, with
narrower petals; a parent of garden hybrids.

A.×hybrida **1** (Japanese anemone of gardens;
often sold as *A. hupehensis japonica*, *A. japonica*
or *A. elegans*): hybrid of *A. hupehensis japonica*
& *A. vitifolia*; to 1–1.5×0.6m (3–5×2ft); clumps
of dark green lobed lvs; soft rose-pink 8cm (3in)
fls to mid autumn. Vars (generally to 60–90cm
[2–3ft]): 'Bressingham Glow' (to 45cm [1½ft];
rosy-red semi-double fls); 'Honorine Jobert' (to
1.2m [4ft]; white); 'Krimhilde' (blush-pink, semi-
double); 'Lady Gilmour' (nodding almost double
pink fls); 'Lorelei' (delicate pink); 'Louise Uhink'
(white); 'Margarete' **2** (deep pink, almost
double); 'Max Vogel' (pink); 'Mont Rose' (rich
pink); 'Prinz Heinrich' (sometimes sold as
'Profusion'; deep pink; v similar to *A. hupehensis
japonica*); 'Queen Charlotte' (pale pink, semi-
double); 'September Charm' (soft pink; v similar
to *A. hupehensis*); 'Whirlwind' **3** (white, semi-
double); 'White Giant' ('White Queen'; to 1.2m
[4ft]; large fls).

A.×lesseri **4**: hybrid of *A. multifida* & *A.
sylvestris*: to 45×30cm (1½×1ft); ferny lvs;
carmine-rose 5cm (2in) fls, early summer.

A. vitifolia 'Robustissima' (may be correctly *A.
tomentosa*): ultra-hardy; generally to 75×30cm
(2½×1ft), but can be invasive; vine-like lvs; pale
pink 8cm (3in) fls, late summer.

Columbines (*Aquilegia* spp): dainty but ultra-
hardy, with maidenhair-like lfts & profuse graceful
fls, often nodding, from late spring or early
summer; sepals & petals often contrasting
colours; petals extend back to form spurs. For
sun or light shade; short-lived but self-seed.
Prone to leaf-miners.

A. caerulea: to 60×30cm (2×1ft); fls 5–8cm
(2–3in) across, sepals generally blue, petals
creamy-white, spurs to 5cm (2in) long.

A. canadensis (wild columbine of eastern
N America): to 60×30cm (2×1ft); narrow
nodding fls with red sepals & yellow petals; spurs
red, to 2.5cm (1in) long; prominent stamens.

A. chrysantha **5** (often sold as *A. longissima*): to
90×60cm (3×2ft); bright golden-yellow fls 8cm
(3in) wide with narrow spurs to 8cm (3in) long;
prominent stamens.

A. glandulosa: to 30×30cm (1×1ft); fls 8cm (3in)
wide, sepals lilac-blue, petals violet-blue, short
hooked spurs.

A.×hybrida (columbine hybrids): often listed
under *A. vulgaris*, but main parents of long-

spurred vars probably *A. caerulea*, *A. chrysantha*
& others; mostly to 60–90×45cm (2–3×1½ft);
fls 5–8cm (2–3in) wide, usually in wide range of
colours from white & yellow to pink, deep red &
purple. Vars: 'Biedermeier' (to 45cm [1½ft]);
'Crimson Star' (to 45cm [1½ft]; crimson &
white); 'McKana Hybrids' **6**: 'Mrs Scott Elliott'
strain; 'Spring Song' (large vivid fls).

A. longissima: v similar to *A. chrysantha* but fls
paler yellow & spurs 9–15cm (3½–6in) long.
'Longissima Hybrids' have wide range of colours.

A. vulgaris (wild columbine of Europe, granny's
bonnet): to 75×45cm (2½×1½ft); nodding fls
2.5–4cm (1–1½in) wide, with short hooked
spurs; mainly violet, also crimson, pink, plum
&/or white. Poisonous. Var 'Nora Barlow' **7** has
double spurless fls, suffused red, pink & green;
breeds almost true from seed.

Herbaceous clematis (*Clematis* spp): mainly
ultra-hardy; most have fluffy seed-heads after fls;
for cool neutral or alkaline soil in full/part sun;
may need support with twiggy sticks.

C.×durandii: hybrid of *C. integrifolia* &
C. 'Jackmanii' (climber); v hardy; semi-climber,
to 1.8×1m (6×3ft); nodding dark violet 8–10cm
(3–4in) fls, cream stamens, late summer.

C. heracleifolia**: to 1×0.45–1.2m (3×1½–4ft);
sprawling & sub-shrubby; dark green lvs; small
semi-tubular to bell-like purple-blue fls, late
summer. Vars: 'Crépuscule'* (azure-blue;
bushy); *davidiana** **8** (large violet-blue fls);
'Wyevale'* (flax-blue).

C. integrifolia **9**: to 0.6×0.3–1.5m (2×1–5ft);
sprawling if not supported; veined lvs; small
nodding indigo-violet bell fls, summer. Vars:
'Hendersonii' (larger deep blue fls); 'Rosea'
(pink).

C. recta*: to 1.2×0.6m (4×2ft); dark green
pinnate lvs; profuse small white starry fls, early
summer. Poisonous. Vars: 'Edward Prichard'*
(hybrid with *C. heracleifolia*; white suffused blue;
needs support); 'Purpurea' **10** (young lvs
coppery-purple).

Glaucidium (*Glaucidium palmatum* **11**;
sometimes classified in Podophyllaceae): v hardy
clump-forming Japanese woodland plant for
humus-rich soil in sheltered shade; to 30–
60×60cm (1–2×2ft); lobed vine-like lvs to 30cm
(1ft) across; cup-shaped wide-petalled poppy-
like pale lilac fls (white in var 'Leucanthum'
['Album']) to 8cm (3in) wide, with boss of yellow
stamens, late spring.

Hellebores (*Helleborus* spp): generally v to
ultra-hardy; most spp evergreen; large, generally
lance-shaped toothed lfts, often leathery, making
good ground cover; v long-lasting & cold-
resistant fls in winter or early spring (relative
times given below), cup- to bowl-shaped, with
prominent boss of stamens & thick petals;
unusual sombre colours. For semi-shade or

moderate sun. All parts of most spp v poisonous.
H. abchasicus: to 30–45×45cm (1–1½×1ft); 6–
8cm (2½–3in) deep purplish-red drooping fls,
darker spots, early.
H. antiquorum: to 30×30cm (1×1ft); 6cm (2½in)
red-purple fls, green at base, late.
H. atrorubens **1** (*H. orientalis atrorubens*): to
30×45cm (1×1½ft); evergreen only in mild
climates; 5cm (2in) bluish-maroon fls, ageing
violet, v early.
H. foetidus (stinking hellebore): to 45×45cm
(1½×1½ft); drooping pale green bell fls to 3cm
(1¼in) across, edged maroon, late; foetid smell.
H. lividus: semi- to moderately hardy; to
45×30cm (1½×1ft); lvs veined greyish; 6cm
(2½in) greenish to dull purple fls, late. Var
corsicus **2** (often listed as *H. corsicus* or
H. argutifolius) is moderately hardy; to 60×60cm
(2×2ft); greyish lvs; 5cm (2in) yellowish-green
drooping fls, late.
H. niger **3** (Christmas rose): to 30–45×45cm
(1–1½×1ft); 5–8cm (2–3in) white or pink-tinged
nodding fls, v early. Vars: 'Lewis Cobbett' (fls
rose-pink outside, blush-pink flushed green
inside); *macranthus* (*altifolius*; fls to 12cm [5in]
across, white tinted rose-purple outside);
'Potter's Wheel' (white 12cm [5in] fls).
H. orientalis **4** (Lenten rose): to 45–60×45cm
(1½–2×1½ft); lvs prostrate; 5–8cm (2–3in)
cream to plum fls, often flecked crimson, fading
brown, mid season. Hybrids with *H. abschasicus*:
'Heartsease' (maroon); 'Winter Cheer' (pinkish).
H. purpurascens: to 30×30cm (1×1ft);
deciduous palmate lvs; 5cm (2in) nodding
maroon fls, greenish inside, late.
H. viridis (green hellebore): to 30×45cm
(1×1½ft); deciduous lvs; 5cm (2in) bright
yellowish-green fls, mid season.
Buttercups (*Ranunculus* spp): generally
v hardy; non-invasive relatives of the common
weed (mainly double forms grown in borders);
deeply divided or lobed lvs. For moist soil in sun
or light shade. Most spp poisonous.
R. aconitifolius **5**: to 60–90×60cm (2–3×2ft);
profuse white buttercup fls to 2cm (¾in) wide,
late spring. Usual garden var is 'Flore Pleno'
('Plenus', fair maids of France [of Kent]); double
pompon fls, early summer.
R. acris 'Flore Pleno' **6** ('Plenus'; double form of
common meadow buttercup): ultra-hardy; to
75×45cm (2½×1½ft); bright yellow waxy 1–2cm
(½–¾in) double rosette fls, early summer.
R. bulbosus 'Speciosus Plenus' (sometimes sold
as *R. gouanii* 'Plenus'): to 30×30cm (1×1ft);
double yellow fls 2.5–4cm (1–1½in) wide, late
spring to early summer.
Globe flowers (*Trollius* spp): ultra-hardy
moisture-lovers with globe-shaped yellow to
orange fls, late spring & early summer, like large
incurved buttercups; deeply lobed lvs. For sun or
light shade. Poisonous.
T. asiaticus: to 45×30cm (1½×1ft); 4–5cm
(1½–2in) orange-yellow fls.
T. chinensis **7** (usually sold as *T. ledebourii*): to
90×45cm (3×1½ft); similar to *T.×hybridus*
(below) but fls filled with narrow petal-like
stamens, early summer. Vars: 'Golden Queen' &
'Imperial Orange' are deep orange-yellow.
T. europaeus (common globe flower): to
60×45cm (2×1½ft); 5cm (2in) lemon-yellow fls.
Best var is 'Superbus'.
T.×hybridus vars (*T.×cultorum*, garden globe
flowers; often listed under *T. europaeus*, but
probably hybrids with *T. asiaticus* & *T. chinensis*):
to 60–75×45cm (2–2½×1½ft); fls to 6cm
(2½in) across. Vars: 'Alabaster' (ivory-yellow);
'Canary Bird' **8** (lemon-yellow); 'Commander in
Chief' (deep orange); 'Earliest of All' (light
yellow); 'Fireglobe' **9** (deep orange-yellow);
'Goldquelle' **10** (v large mid yellow fls); 'Lemon
Queen' (pale yellow); 'Orange Princess' (tall;
orange-yellow); 'Prichard's Giant' (tall; mid
yellow); 'Salamander' (strong dark orange).
T. yunnanensis: to 60×30cm (2×1ft); upright;
wiry stems; bright yellow single fls 4–5cm (1½–
2in) wide, early summer. *T. stenopetalus* is
similar but later.

Shorter perennials of the rose family

Free-flowering herbaceous plants for middle or front of borders & ground cover, most with typical 5-petalled flowers. **Cultivation**: Prefer moist but well-drained soil in sun or partial shade. Mulch in spring. **Propagation**: Division; seed (especially *Alchemilla, Geum* & *Potentilla* spp).

Lady's mantles (*Alchemilla* spp): v to ultra-hardy ground-cover plants with attractive, generally rounded, lobed & fluted lvs forming saucer shape; sprays of tiny greenish/yellow fls, early summer; good for cutting.
A. alpina (alpine lady's mantle): to 15×25cm (6×10in); pale green silvery lvs with narrow lfts; green fls. Self-seeds.
A. erythropoda: to 15×25cm (6×10in); bluish lvs; sulphur-yellow fls.
A. mollis **1** (common lady's mantle of gardens; sometimes listed incorrectly as *A. vulgaris*): to 30–45×45cm (1–1½×1½ft); rich bluish-green hairy lvs 10cm (4in) across; greenish-yellow fls.
Ornamental strawberries (*Fragaria* spp): generally v hardy ground-cover plants with typical trifoliate semi-evergreen serrated lvs; 5-petalled 2–2.5cm (¾–1in) fls, early summer; red edible frs. For any fertile soil. Spread (& propagated by) runners.
P. californica: moderately hardy; to 10×60cm (4×24in); glossy lvs; white fls; 1cm (½in) frs.
F. chiloensis **2** (beach strawberry): to 15×50cm (6×20in); shiny lvs; white fls; 2cm (¾in) frs. A parent of cultivated strawberries.
F. indica (Indian strawberry; correctly, *Duchesnia indica*): invasive, to 8cm×2.5m (3in×8ft); deep green toothed lvs; yellow fls; small insipid frs.
Avens (geums, *Geum* spp): generally ultra-hardy clump-forming border plants with strongly coloured single/double rosette fls over long season from late spring or early summer; lvs compound (lfts usually rounded & lobed), fresh green & hairy. For any fertile soil; divide clumps every few yrs.
G.×borisii **3**: hybrid of *G. bulgaricum* & *G. reptans*; to 30×30cm (1×1ft); bright orange-scarlet single fls 3cm (1¼in) across.
'Georgenberg' is a similar hybrid with apricot fls suffused red.
G. bulgaricum: to 30–45×30cm (1–1½×1ft); bright yellow/orange nodding bell-like fls.
G. chiloense (Chilean avens; sometimes listed as *G. coccineum*; probably correctly, *G. quellyon*): v hardy, but protect in v cold winters; to 45–60×30–45cm (1½–2×1–1½ft); fls bowl-shaped, scarlet & 2.5cm (1in) across in sp, larger in vars & hybrids; good for cutting. Seed strains (rather short-lived): 'Lady Stratheden' **4** (double, yellow); 'Mrs Bradshaw' **5** (semi-double, scarlet). Hybrids with true *G. coccineum* (longer-lived & hardier than above): 'Dolly North' (double, orange-yellow); 'Fire Opal' **6** (semi-double, flame-red); 'Princess Juliana' (semi-double,

bronze); 'Red Wings' (semi-double, red); 'Rubin' (semi-double, red).
G. rivale **7** (water or purple avens, Indian chocolate): to 30–45×30–45cm (1–1½×1–1½ft); 3cm (1¼in) nodding bell-shaped fls, yellowish-pink with purple sepals. Vars: 'Leonard's Variety' (coppery-pink flushed orange); 'Lionel Cox' (rich yellow). Thrives in wet soil; chocolate-flavoured drink can be made from root.
G. rossii: to 30×30cm (1×1ft); dissected lvs; yellow bowl-shaped fls. Likes cool, moist soil.
Herbaceous potentillas (cinquefoils; *Potentilla* spp): v hardy colourful free-flg border plants for any soil in full sun; most have strawberry-like compound lvs with toothed lfts; loose sprays of saucer-shaped fls. Divide every few yrs; propagate short-lived spp & vars frequently.
P. alba: foliage to 10×30cm (4×12in); vigorous; tufted & mat forming, for ground cover; lfts hairy beneath; golden-eyed white fls 2.5cm (1in) wide, on 25cm (10in) stems, from late spring.
P. argyrophylla: to 60×60cm (2×2ft); low clump of silvery strawberry lvs; yellow 2.5–3cm (1–1¼in) fls, summer.
P. atrosanguinea (*P. argyrophylla* 'Atrosanguinea'): similar to *P. argyrophylla* but fls dark red. Primary parent of many garden hybrids (unless stated, to 45–60×45–60cm [1½–2×1½–2ft]; profuse 4–5cm [1½–2in] fls, summer): 'Blazeaway' (to 40cm [16in]; single, suffused orange-red); 'Flamenco' (single, intense scarlet); 'Gibson's Scarlet' **8** (to 30cm [1ft]; single, brilliant scarlet); 'Glory of Nancy' ('Gloire de Nancy'; semi-double, orange-brown & coral-red); 'M Rouillard' **9** (mahogany); 'Wm. Rollison' (semi-double, orange-red, yellow reverse); 'Yellow Queen' **10** (to 40cm [16in]; semi-double, bright yellow; early).
P. nepalensis: to 60×40cm (24×16in); rather upright; deep green lvs; v profuse branching sprays of single 2.5–4cm (1–1½in) fls, summer, rose-red in sp. Hybrids: 'Firedance' **11** (salmon shading to scarlet at centre); 'Miss Wilmott' **12** (cherry-pink, shading darker); 'Roxana' (rosy-orange). Rather short-lived; best cut back after flg.
P. recta 'Warrenii' (often listed as *P. warrennii*): to 60×45cm (2×1½ft); hairy lfts; clusters of bright yellow 2.5cm (1in) fls.

Taller perennials of the rose family

Moisture-lovers ideal for wild gardens, rear of borders or specimen planting, especially near streams, etc. Most have profuse small flowers in large inflorescences. **Cultivation**: Generally for moist soil in sun or (preferably) partial shade. **Propagation**: Division; seed.

Goat's beard (*Aruncus dioicus, A. sylvester, A. vulgaris*): ultra-hardy; handsome specimen plant, to 2×1–1.2m (7×3–4ft); large compound lvs forming 1.2m (4ft) clump; tall plumes of tiny creamy-white fls, early summer; ornamental seed-heads (poisonous) on females. Var 'Kneiffii' **1** is dwarf (to 75×45cm [2½×1½ft]), with finely divided ferny lvs. *A. plumosus* 'Glasnevin' grows to 1.2m (4ft).

Meadowsweets (*Filipendula* spp; formerly *Spiraea* spp): generally ultra-hardy moisture-loving medium to tall clump-forming plants with large compound lvs (terminal lfts usually lobed, to 20cm [8in] wide) & large feathery flat-topped plumes 15-25cm (6–10in) wide of tiny fls, summer. Nomenclature somewhat confused. *F. (S.) kamtschatica** (sometimes spelled *camtschatica*; sometimes listed as *S. gigantea* or *S. palmata*): to 1.2–2.5×0.6m (4–8×2ft); fls white (reddish-pink in var 'Rosea' **2**). *F. purpurea* (*S. palmata*; incorrectly, *F. palmata*): v hardy; to 60–90×45cm (2–3×1½ft); dark green lvs with 5/7-lobed terminal lfts; fls deep rose-pink, fading paler. Vars: 'Alba' (white); 'Elegans' (light pink); 'Nana' (*F. [S.] digitata* 'Nana'; to 25cm [10in]; cerise-pink). True *F. (S.) palmata* has 7/9-lobed terminal lfts, white-woolly beneath, & pale pink fls. *F. rubra* (*S. lobata*, queen of the prairie): to 1–2×0.6m (3–7×2ft); peach-pink fls in infls to 30cm (1ft) across. 'Venusta' ('Magnifica', *F. venusta*) is best-known var; deep pink. *F. ulmaria** (common meadowsweet of Europe,

queen of the meadow): to 0.6–1.2×0.45m (2–4×1½ft); dark green lvs, hairy beneath; fls creamy-white. Vars: 'Aurea' **3** (to 45cm [1½ft]; young lvs golden-green turning creamy; likes partial shade); 'Plena' ('Flore Pleno'; double; prone to mildew). *F. vulgaris* (*F. hexapetala*, dropwort): to 60–90×45cm (2–3×1½ft); deeply cut, fern-like lvs; fls creamy-white, often tinged red. Vars: 'Flore Pleno' **4** ('Plena'; to 60cm [2ft]; double white fls); 'Grandiflora' (large heads of creamy fls). For any well-drained soil in full sun; likes lime.

Bowman's root (*Gillenia trifoliata* **5**): v hardy graceful woodland plant good in wild garden; also suitable for open sites where soil moist. To 1×0.6m (3×2ft); rather sparse compound lvs; sprays of 2.5cm (1in) starry white fls with reddish sepals, on slender reddish stems, early summer.

Burnets (*Sanguisorba* spp; formerly *Poterium* spp): v to ultra-hardy vigorous moisture-lovers for sun or light shade; elegant pinnate lvs with up to 21 lfts; spikes of small fls in bottlebrush infls (good for cutting). Provide twiggy supports. *S. (P.) canadensis* (Canadian or American burnet): to 1.8×0.6m (6×2ft); pale green lvs; 15cm (6in) infls of white fls, late summer. *S. (P.) obtusa* **6** (Japanese burnet): to 1–1.2×0.75m (3–4×2½ft); greyish lvs; 8cm (3in) infls of rose-pink fls (white in var 'Albiflora') early summer. *S. (P.) tenuifolia*: to 1.2×0.6m (4×2ft); lvs green, fls white to purple-red, in 5cm (2in) infls, early summer.

The saxifrage family

Border, woodland and ground-cover plants generally having low basal clumps of largish, often lobed leaves and tall, often fluffy inflorescences of small flowers. **Cultivation**: Most like moist (some wet) soil in sun or light shade. **Propagation**: Division; seed; where produced, runners.

Astilbes (*Astilbe* spp; often confused with *Aruncus, Filipendula* & *Spiraea* spp & wrongly called goat's beard, meadowsweet or spiraea [see above]): beautiful v hardy border plants with rich green deeply cut compound lvs (bronzed when young) & tapering fluffy heads of minute fls, summer (can be dried), then decorative seed-heads (can be left for winter); for deep, rich, always moist (even boggy) soil in sun or partial shade (mulch in spring if dryish); divide every few yrs.

A.×arendsii vars: race of garden hybrids derived from *A. chinensis davidii, A. astilboides,*

A. japonica & *A. thunbergii*; to 60–90×60cm (2–3×2ft), some to 1.2m (4ft); lvs darkest in red vars; infls upright, pyramid-shaped, to 45cm (1½ft) long. Vars: 'Amethyst' (lilac-pink; early); 'Bressingham Beauty' **7** (rich pink); 'Bridal Veil' ('Brautschleier'; white fading creamy); 'Cattleya' (rose-pink); 'Deutschland' **8** (white; early); 'Fanal' **9** (short; deep crimson-red; early); 'Federsee' (carmine-rose; tolerates drier conditions than other vars); 'Finale' (may be listed under *A. chinensis*; to 45cm [1½ft]; pale pink); 'Fire' **10** ('Feuer'; coral-red; late); 'Hyacinth' **11** (rose-pink); 'Irrlicht' (pure white);

'Salland' (tall; purplish-pink; late); 'Red Sentinel' (intense brick-red; early); 'Rhineland' ('Rheinland'; clear pink; early); 'Venus' (pale pink); 'White Gloria' (early).

A. chinensis (incorrectly, *A. sinensis*): to 90×60cm (3×2ft); lvs coarsely toothed; fls rose-pink to purplish. Vars: *davidii* (*A. davidii*; to 1.5m [5ft]; rose-purple fls, late; a primary parent of *A.×arendsii* hybrids); 'Pumila' **1** (dwarf, to 45×45cm [1½×1½ft]; mauve-pink fls; late; good for ground cover); *taquetii* 'Superba' (see *A. taquetii* 'Superba' [below]).

A.×crispa vars: race of dwarf garden hybrids probably of *A.×arendsii* & *A. simplicifolia*; to 25×20cm (10×8in); crinkled, deeply cut lvs; 15cm (6in) infls. Vars: 'Gnome' (rose-pink); 'Perkeo' (pink); 'Peter Pan' (deep pink).

A. rivularis: to 1.5×1m (5×3ft); spreading & clump-forming; arching plumes of creamy-white fls.

A.×rosea vars: race of hybrids of *A. chinensis* & *A. japonica*; to 45×45cm (1½×1½ft); deeply cut feathery lvs; fluffy infls. Vars: 'Peach Blossom' (pale salmon-pink); 'Queen Alexandra' (deep pink).

A. simplicifolia: to 30×20cm (12×8in); lvs deeply cut but simple; narrow arching infls of white or pale pink fls. Vars & hybrids: 'Atrorosea' (to 45cm [1½ft]; bright pink); 'Bronze Elegance' (to 30cm [1ft]; rose-pink/salmon; dark lvs; needs shade); 'Nana' (to 15cm [6in]; pink); 'Sprite' **2** (to 40cm [16in]; shell-pink).

A. taquetii (*A. chinensis taquetii*) 'Superba': to 1.2×1m (4×3ft); dark lvs; v long spikes of bright rosy-purple fls, late. Tolerates some dryness if shaded, or full sun if soil moist.

A. thunbergii: to 60×60cm (2×2ft); spreading infls with arching side-branches. Hybrids (often listed under *A.×arendsii*; to 90cm [3ft]): 'Professor van der Wielen' (white); 'Ostrich Plume' ('Straussenfeder'; coral-pink).

Bergenias (*Bergenia* spp; formerly *Megasea* or *Saxifraga* spp): generally ultra-hardy semi-evergreen spreading plants with large, leathery, generally rounded lvs, making good ground cover; showy infls of white to red & purple bell-shaped fls 2–2.5cm (¾–1in) long from early spring (good for cutting); for any soil, dry or moist, in sun or shade.

B. cordifolia: to 30×40cm (12×16in); deep green lvs to 25cm (10in) long; mauve-pink fls. Vars: 'Perfecta' (to 50cm [20in]; rosy-red); 'Purpurea' **3** (lvs magenta in winter; fls pinkish-purple).

B. crassifolia: to 30×40cm (12×16in); spoon-shaped lvs to 20cm (8in) long, red-tinted in winter; fls lavender-pink.

B. purpurascens (*B. delavayi*): to 40×60cm (16×24in); 25cm (10in) lvs, dark reddish in winter; fls pink to purplish-red.

B. stracheyi: to 30×25cm (12×10in); lvs to 20cm

(8in) long; fls white to pink (white in var *alba*).

B. hybrids (generally to 30–45×30cm [1–1½×1ft]): 'Abendglut' ('Evening Glow'; to 25cm [10in]; lvs maroon in winter; fls magenta-crimson); 'Baby Doll' (compact; fls clear pink); 'Ballawley' **4** ('Delbees'; to 60cm [2ft]; lvs flabby; fls crimson); 'Morgenröte' ('Morning Blush'; fls carmine-pink, repeating early summer); ×*schmidtii* **5** ('Ernst Schmidt'; toothed rich green lvs; clear rose-pink fls); 'Silberlicht' **6** ('Silver Light'; fls white); 'Sunningdale' (lvs red-brown in winter; fls lilac-carmine).

Heucheras (*Heuchera* spp): ultra-hardy semi-evergreen plants good for ground cover in well-drained soil in sun or partial shade; lvs rounded, lobed & hairy, in dense mat; graceful panicles of tiny bell fls, late spring & summer (good for cutting). Divide every few yrs.

H. cylindrica: to 60–90×30cm (2–3×1ft); dark green lvs; spikes of creamy-white to greenish-yellow fls. Vars & hybrids: 'Chartreuse' (chartreuse-green); 'Greenfinch' (creamy-green); 'Hyperion' (deep pink).

H. sanguinea (coral flower): to 30–60×30cm (1–2×1ft); dark green lvs, often marbled; fls bright coral-red in sp. Vars & hybrids (latter correctly classed as *H.×brizoides*): 'Bressingham Blaze' (coral-flame); 'Bressingham Hybrids' (mixed seed strain); 'Firebird' (deep red); 'Pearl Drops' (white); 'Pretty Polly' (short; clear pink); 'Red Spangles' **7** (crimson-scarlet); 'Scintillation' (pink & red); 'Sparkler' (crimson); 'Splendour' (salmon-scarlet); 'Sunset' (coral-red & pink).

Heucherellas (×*Heucherella* spp): ultra-hardy bigeneric hybrids of *Heuchera* & *Tiarella* spp, rather similar to *Heuchera* spp but earlier-flg; good for cutting. For light peaty soil in sun or light shade.

×*H.* 'Bridget Bloom' **8**: hybrid of *Heuchera×brizoides* & *Tiarella wherryi*; to 45×30cm (1½×1ft); compact foliage; sprays of pink fls, spring & summer.

×*H. tiarelloides*: hybrid of *Heuchera×brizoides* & *Tiarella cordifolia*; to 40×40cm (16×16in); spreading golden-green lvs, spikes of salmon-pink fls, late spring.

Kirengeshomas (*Kirengeshoma* spp): beautiful v hardy late summer- or autumn-flg plants with sharply lobed lvs to 20cm (8in) across & sprays of 3cm (1¼in) waxy yellow fls. For deep, moist soil in partial shade.

K. koreana: to 1.1×0.6m (3½×2ft); dull green lvs; erect infls.

K. palmata **9**: to 90×60cm (3×2ft); clear green lvs; gracefully drooping infls.

Umbrella plant (*Peltiphyllum* [*Saxifraga*] *peltatum* **10**): v hardy bog plant, to 1–1.5×0.6m (3–5×2ft); huge circular lobed & toothed lvs to 60cm (2ft) across, on 90cm (3ft) stalks; white to

pink 1cm (½in) fls, in rounded infls on stems to 1.5m (5ft) tall, spring (before lvs). Var 'Nanum' is dwarf, foliage to 30cm (1ft). For wet soil in sun or shade.

Rodgersias (*Rodgersia* spp): v hardy moisture-lovers with large handsome lvs & showy upright panicles of small whitish or pink fls, early–mid summer. Best in sheltered position in sun or partial shade; good for ground cover.

R. aesculifolia: to 1.8×0.75m (6×2½ft); glossy bronzed lvs like horse chestnut, with 7 toothed lfts to 25cm (10in) long; fls creamy to pink, in infls to 45cm (1½ft) long; reddish seed heads.

R. pinnata **1**: to 1.2×0.6m (4×2ft); pinnate lvs with paired lfts to 20cm (8in) long; fls white to pink, in 25–30cm (10–12in) infls. Vars: 'Elegans'* (creamy-white); 'Irish Bronze' **2** (bronze lvs; creamy-pink fls); 'Superba' **3** (lvs bronzed/ purplish; fls bright pink, in infls to 50cm [20in] long).

R. podophylla: to 1.2×0.75m (4×2½ft); 5-lobed lvs like horse chestnut's with lobes to 25cm (10in) long, bronzed when young, then green, then coppery; fls creamy, in 30–45cm (1–1½ft) infls.

R. sambucifolia: to 90×60cm (3×2ft); compact & neat; pinnate lvs with 3–11 narrow lfts; elegant flat-topped infls of creamy-white fls.

R. (Astilboides) tabularis **4**: to 90×75cm (3×2½ft); almost round scalloped light green lvs to 90cm (3ft) across, on long stalks; creamy-white fls, in infls to 25cm (10in) long.

Border saxifrages (*Saxifraga* spp): generally moderately hardy larger relatives of the well-known rock plants (p470), with rosettes of largish rounded & lobed lvs, & sprays of fls on thin stems; good for edging, etc. Generally like cool, damp semi-shade.

S. fortunei (correctly, *S. cortusifolia fortunei*): to 30–45×30cm (1–1½×1ft); deep green fleshy lvs, red beneath; 2.5cm (1in) white starry fls with long lower petals, late autumn. Dislikes lime. Vars: 'Rubrifolia' **5** (to 25cm [10in]; coppery lvs); 'Wada's Variety' (reddish-purple lvs).

S.×geum: hybrid of *S. hirsuta* & *S. umbrosa*; to 30×45cm (1×1½ft); dark green leathery lvs; tiny white or pinkish fls, late spring.

S. stolonifera (*S. sarmentosa*, mother of thousands, strawberry geranium): often grown indoors, but moderately hardy; to 45×45cm (1½×1½ft); spreads by runners with plantlets at tips; veined & marbled lvs, reddish beneath; 2.5cm (1in) starry white fls with long lower petals, summer. Var 'Tricolor' **6** has lvs variegated yellow & pink; less vigorous than sp.

S. umbrosa (London pride; probably correctly *S.×urbium*, a hybrid with *S. spathularis*): to 45×45cm (1½×1½ft); spreading; fleshy dark green lvs; profuse starry pink fls, late spring. 'Elliott's Variety' ('Clarence Elliott'), 'Primuloides'

& 'Walter Ingwersen' are dwarf vars (to 15cm [6in]). Other vars: 'Rubra' (larger lvs; darker fls); 'Variegata' **7** ('Aurea Punctata'; variegated).

Fringecup (*Tellima grandiflora* **8**): v hardy semi-evergreen plant good for ground cover in cool shade, even in poor soil. To 60×60cm (2×2ft); hairy lobed lvs 10cm (4in) wide; sprays of small greenish-white bell fls ageing reddish, spring & early summer. Lvs of var 'Purpurea' turn purplish in winter.

Tiarellas (foam flowers, *Tiarella* spp): generally v to ultra-hardy low-growing semi-evergreen plants good for ground cover in cool, rich soil in light shade; fluffy racemes of v small starry fls.

T. cordifolia **9** (foam flower): to 30×60cm (1×2ft); spreads by runners; lobed & toothed lvs, bronzed in winter; creamy-white fls from late spring.

T. polyphylla: to 45×30cm (1½×1ft); clump-forming; lobed & toothed lvs; fls white or pinkish, early summer.

T. trifoliata: to 45×30cm (1½×1ft); trifoliate lvs; white fls, early summer.

T. wherryi: to 40×30cm (16×12in); similar to *T. cordifolia* but lacking runners; creamy-white fls all summer.

Piggy-back plant (*Tolmeia menziesii* **10**): often grown indoors, but moderately hardy evergreen ground-cover plant for rich soil in partial shade or sun; produces young plants at lf bases; rather weedy. Foliage to 20×40cm (8×16in); spreading & self-rooting; 10cm (4in) hairy maple-like lvs; rather insignificant brownish fls in racemes to 60cm (2ft) tall, early summer.

Penstemons, speedwells and their relatives

Rather diverse group of perennials with flowers often having larger lower petals (sometimes lipped or pouched) & often in spikes or racemes. **Cultivation**: See below; mostly sun-lovers. **Propagation**: Seed; cuttings; clump-forming types by division; *Verbascum* spp by root cuttings; tender bedding types by stem cuttings in summer or basal cuttings in spring. For snapdragons (*Antirrhinum* spp) & other spp generally treated as annuals or biennials that may be perennial in favourable conditions, see p514.

Bush calceolaria (*Calceolaria integrifolia* **1**, *C. rugosa*): semi-hardy sub-shrub used mainly for summer bedding; bushy, to 45–60×30cm (1½–2×1ft), to 1.2m (4ft) in warm climates (may need support); evergreen where hardy; lvs matt, wrinkled; profuse yellow to red-brown pouched fls to 2.5cm (1in) long, summer. Vars 'Golden Bunch' & 'Sunshine' (F1 hybrid) can be grown as HHAs. Like acid soil.

Turtle-heads (*Chelone* spp): stiff & upright, with spikes of 2.5cm (1in) snapdragon-like fls (said to resemble turtles' heads), good for cutting. Like good but acid soil.

C. barbata: see *Penstemon barbata* (below).

C. lyonii: ultra-hardy; to 45×45cm (1½×1½ft); rose-pink fls, yellow beard, summer.

C. obliqua **2**: v hardy; to 75×45cm (2½×1½ft); deep lilac-pink fls, pale yellow beard, late summer & early autumn.

Perennial foxgloves (*Digitalis* spp): rather short-lived v to ultra-hardy relatives of common biennial foxglove (p516); can also be grown as HBs. Evergreen lance-shaped lvs; spikes of typical tubular fls, summer. Prefer light shade; remove central spike after flg. V poisonous.

D. grandiflora **3** (*D. ambigua*): to 60–90×30cm (2–3×1ft); pale creamy-yellow 5cm (2in) fls marked brown.

D. lutea: to 60×30cm (2×1ft); pale creamy-yellow fls to 2.5cm (1in) long, early.

D.×mertonensis **4**: to 60–90×30cm (2–3×1ft); pink fls 5cm (2in) long. Propagate frequently.

Toadflax (*Linaria* spp): generally moderately to v hardy short-lived upright perennials with narrow lvs & spikes of snapdragon-like fls all summer (good for cutting). For well-drained soil in sun; may need support. Self-seed.

L. dalmatica (correctly, *L. genistifolia dalmatica*): to 1–1.2×0.45m (3–4×1½ft); lvs glaucous; fls bright yellow, 4cm (1½in) long. Var 'Canary Bird' is deep yellow.

L. purpurea: to 1–1.2×0.4m (3–4ft×16in); greyish lvs; purple-blue 1cm (½in) fls, light pink in var 'Canon Went' **5**.

L. triornithophora **6**: semi- to moderately hardy; to 1×0.45m (3×1½ft); glaucous lvs; pink to deep rosy-purple fls, yellow markings. Can be treated as HHA.

Monkey flowers (*Mimulus* spp): moisture-loving short-lived perennials for borders, pool margins, etc; more tender types for summer bedding. Open-mouthed snapdragon-like lipped fls often

spotted/blotched (said to look like monkeys' faces), summer. Divide regularly.

M. cardinalis **7** (scarlet monkey flower): moderately hardy; to 30–90×45cm (1–3×1½ft); sticky downy lvs; narrow fls to 5cm (2in) long, scarlet to cerise, prominent stamens; withstands dryish soil.

M. (*Diplacus*) *glutinosus* **8** (bush monkey flower; correctly, *M. aurantiacus*): semi-hardy evergreen sub-shrub often grown under glass; to 1.2×0.6m (4×2ft), less in cool climates; sticky lvs; trumpet fls 5cm (2in) across, buff-yellow to orange & crimson, petals notched; withstands dryish soil.

M. guttatus (common monkey flower of N America, naturalized widely in Europe): v hardy; to 30–60×45cm (1–2×1½ft); erect or sprawling; racemes of yellow fls to 5cm (2in) across, throat red-spotted.

M.×hybridus (sometimes called *M. tigrinus*): hybrids mainly of *M. guttatus* & *M. luteus*; moderately to v hardy perennials often treated as HHAs; to 30–60×30cm (1–2×1ft); fls 5cm (2in) across, shades of white, yellow & orange, blotched & spotted red, brown & crimson. Vars (to 30–40cm [12–16in]): 'A. T. Johnson' (deep yellow heavily blotched brown-red); 'Firedragon' (orange-red speckled darker); 'Harlequin' (multicoloured, shades of red & yellow); 'Ochrid' (yellow & maroon); 'Shep' (yellow blotched brown).

M. lewisii **9**: v hardy; to 30–60×40cm (12–24×16in); floppy; greyish hairy sticky lvs; fls mainly deep pink, 4cm (1½in) long.

M. luteus: closely related to (& often confused with) *M. guttatus*; similar, with smaller yellow fls with larger red to purple blotches. Moderately hardy; for shallow water or moist soil.

M. ringens (Allegheny monkey flower): ultra-hardy; to 30–90×30cm (1–3×1ft); narrow blue to purple, pink & white fls 2.5cm (1in) long. For water to 15cm (6in) deep or moist soil.

Penstemons (*Penstemon* spp): long-flg colourful border plants for moist but well-drained soil in sun; more tender types often used for summer bedding; tall racemes of lipped tubular fls, drooping & often rather foxglove-like, all summer & often to autumn if dead-headed.

P. barbatus (*Chelone barbata*): ultra-hardy; to 90×45cm (3×1½ft) or more; rosy-red fls 2.5cm (1in) long, lip bearded; vars pink to scarlet & purple.

P. fruticosus: v hardy; to 40–60×40cm (16–

24×16in); dense sub-shrub; profuse lavender-purple fls 4cm (1½in) long. Var 'Catherine de la Mare' is lilac-blue.

P.×gloxinioides (*P.×hybridus*) vars: hybrids of *P. hartwegii*, *P. cobaea* & other spp; generally moderately hardy but best treated as tender bedding perennials or HHAs, especially if soil heavy or winters wet; to 60–90×45cm (2–3×1½ft); 5cm (2in) fls. Vars: 'Cherry Ripe' (warm red); 'Firebird' ('Schönholzeri'; scarlet); 'Garnet' (v hardy; deep red); 'Giant Hybrids' (mixed seed strain); 'King George' (crimson-scarlet marked white); 'Monarch Strain' (mixed seed strain); 'Pennington Gem' (cerise-crimson, white markings); 'Pink Endurance' **1** (v hardy; pink); 'Sour Grapes' (purple); 'Southgate Gem' (blood-red); 'White Bedder' (white).

P. hartwegii (sometimes sold as *P. gentianoides*): semi-hardy; to 60×40cm (24×16in); bushy; rich green lvs; bright scarlet fls 5cm (2in) long. Rarely grown, but main parent of hybrids above.

P. ovatus: ultra-hardy; to 90×45cm (3×1½ft); 2cm (¾in) fls, purple to lavender-blue (white in var 'Albus').

Phygelius (*Phygelius* spp): moderately to v hardy sub-shrubs for sunny border (fully shrubby & taller if frost-free or against sheltered warm wall); also grown under glass. Panicles of drooping narrow tubular fls to 5cm (2in) long with prominent stamens, all summer. Drought-resistant; cut down top growth if frost-killed.

P. aequalis: to 60–90×45cm (2–3×1½ft); rosy buff-red fls.

P. capensis **2** (Cape figwort, Cape fuchsia): to 0.75–1.2×0.6m (2½–4×2ft); coral-red fls.

Water figwort (*Scrophularia aquatica* [correctly, *S. auriculata*] 'Variegata' **3**): moderately hardy variegated form of common European weed; to 60–90×30cm (2–3×1ft); upright; oblong-oval lvs 10cm (4in) long, striped & splashed cream (basal lvs evergreen); stalks & stems winged; fls insignificant (best removed). For moist soil in sun or partial shade.

Mulleins (*Verbascum* spp): tall perennials (sometimes short-lived) with strong branching spikes, 30–60cm (1–2ft) long or more, of mainly saucer-shaped fls, early–mid summer; large, generally hairy lvs, basal & on stems. For any well-drained ordinary or poor soil in sun; may need support; dead-head. Propagate short-lived spp regularly.

V.chaixii (sometimes listed as *V. vernale*): v hardy; to 1–1.5×0.45m (3–5×1½ft); grey-green lvs; slender infls of yellow fls, mauve eye (white & mauve in var 'Alba').

V×hybridum vars: race of hybrids of *V. phoeniceum* & other spp; generally moderately to v hardy; unless stated, to 1–1.2×0.45m (3–4×1½ft). Vars: 'C. L. Adams' (to 1.8m [6ft]; deep yellow, magenta eye); 'Cotswold

Beauty' (biscuit-yellow & lilac); 'Cotswold Gem' (terracotta & yellow); 'Cotswold Queen' (amber & purple); 'Gainsborough' **4** (primrose-yellow); grey lvs); 'Golden Bush' (to 60cm [2ft]; bushy; small clear yellow fls, pink eye; long-flg); 'Mont Blanc' (white; grey lvs); 'Pink Domino' **5** (deep rose; dark lvs).

V. olympicum: v hardy; to 1.8–2.5×0.75m (6–8×2½ft); rosette of grey lvs; bright yellow 2.5cm (1in) fls.

V. phoeniceum **6** (purple mullein): v hardy; to 1–1.4×0.45m (3–4½×1½ft); rosette of dark green lvs; fls white to pink & purple; short-lived; self-seeds freely.

V. thapsiforme (*V. densiflorum*): ultra-hardy; to 1.2–1.5×0.6m (4–5×2ft); rosette of rich green crinkly lvs; erect spikes of 5cm (2in) yellow fls. Short-lived.

Speedwells (*Veronica* spp): easy, generally ultra-hardy border plants usually with slender 15–20cm (6–8in) racemes/spikes of small saucer-shaped fls in summer (good for cutting) & rather narrow lvs (generally basal & on stems). For any well-drained soil in sun; taller spp may need support.

V. exaltata: to 1.2–1.5×0.45m (4–5×1½ft); soft, pale blue fls, late summer.

V. gentianoides **7**: v hardy; to 45×45cm (1½×1½ft); mat of dark green lvs; v pale blue fls, early summer. Vars: 'Alba' (white); 'Variegata' (lvs variegated).

V. incana **8** (woolly speedwell; sometimes listed as *V. candida*): to 30–40×30cm (12–16×12in); semi-evergreen silvery lvs; mid blue fls. Vars & hybrids: 'Rosea' (fls flushed pink); 'Wendy' (to 60cm [2ft]; lvs less grey; fls pale blue).

V. longifolia: v hardy; to 1.2×0.45m (4×1½ft); purplish-blue fls. Vars & hybrids: 'Foerster's Blue' (to 75cm [2½ft]; deep blue); 'Icicle' (to 60cm [2ft]; white); *subsessilis* (*V. subsessilis*, *V. Hendersonii*; to 60cm [2ft]; royal-blue).

V. spicata: to 30–60×45cm (1–2×1½ft); forms neat clump; dense short infls of bright blue fls. Vars & hybrids: 'Alba' (white); 'Barcarolle' (rose-pink); 'Blue Fox' ('Blaufuchs'; bright lavender-blue); 'Icicle' (see above); 'Minuet' **9** (greyish lvs; pink fls); 'Red Fox' ('Rotefuchs'; reddish-pink); 'Saraband' (deep lavender-blue).

V. teucrium (correctly *V. latifolia*): to 60×45cm (2×1½ft); short infls of blue to reddish fls. Vars: 'Blue Fountain' (rich blue); 'Crater Lake Blue' (to 30cm [1ft]; deep blue); 'Kapitan' (to 25cm [10in]; bright blue; early); 'Shirley Blue' **10** (to 20cm [8in]; brilliant blue); 'Trehane' (to 20cm [8in]; lvs golden-green; fls deep blue).

V. virginica (Culver's root; correctly, *Veronicastrum virginicum*): to 1.2–1.5×0.6m (4–5×2ft); erect; long branched infls of pale blue fls, late summer. Vars: 'Alba' (white); 'Rosea' (pink).

Sea hollies and their relatives

Sturdy herbaceous plants with much-branched, generally showy compound umbels of very small flowers, summer unless stated (generally good for cutting & often striking in arrangements). Large basal tufts or hummocks of generally coarsely divided & cut leaves, often spiny. For borders, the larger types as specimens or for wild gardens. **Cultivation**: Unless stated, very hardy & for any well-drained but moist soil in sun or partial shade. **Propagation**: Seed; division; *Eryngium* spp by root cuttings.

Masterworts (*Astrantia* spp): densely clump-forming, with tight umbels backed by spiny bracts.
A. carniolica: to 60×40cm (24×16in); finely divided lvs; 2.5cm (1in) infls of pink-tinged white fls, white bracts. Var 'Rubra' is smaller, to 45×30cm (1½×1ft); infls purplish-red marked green.
A. major **1**: to 60–90×40cm (24–36×16in); 2.5cm (1in) infls of pink, rose or white fls, lance-shaped pink/purple-tinged bracts. Good beside water. Vars: *involucrata* (*A. involucrata*; profuse greenish-white infls, long bracts; 'Shaggy' ['Margery Fish'], has long-lasting shaggy infls); 'Variegata' (lvs variegated).
A. maxima (*A. helleborifolia*); to 90×30cm (3×1ft); 4cm (1½in) infls of pinkish fls, broad rose-pink glossy bracts. Best in rich soil.
Hare's ear (*Bupleurum falcatum* **2**): ultra-hardy; to 90×60cm (3×2ft); narrow lvs to 20cm (8in) long; cow-parsley-like infls of tiny yellow fls, summer & autumn. Short-lived; self-seeds.
Eryngiums (*Eryngium* spp; often called sea hollies, but correct only for *E. maritimum*): somewhat thistle-like, with spiny lvs & dense teasel-like heads of white to blue-purple fls, bracts generally sharply toothed & spiny. Best as small specimens or clumps; v good for cutting/drying. More compact on poorish soil; tolerate lime, drought. Nomenclature rather confused.
E. agavifolium **3** (may be sold incorrectly as *E. bromeliifolium*): to 1.2×0.6m (4×2ft); sword-shaped evergreen lvs to 45cm (1½ft) long; greenish 2.5–5cm (1–2in) infls, rather small bracts. *E. serra* is similar.
E. alpinum **4**: to 75×45cm (2½×1½ft); heart-shaped blue-green basal lvs; 3cm (1¼in) metallic-blue infls, finely divided violet-blue bracts, on stout blue stems.
E. amethystinum (often confused with

E. planum): ultra-hardy; to 60×60cm (2×2ft); narrow 1cm (½in) blue-purple infls on steel-blue stems.
E. bourgattii **5**: to 60×40cm (24×16in); crisped grey-green lvs, white veins; 2cm (¾in) bluish infls, narrow steely-blue bracts. *E.×zabelii* is hybrid with *E. alpinum*; fls late summer.
E. giganteum **6**: to 1.2×0.6m (4×2ft) or more; bluish heart-shaped basal lvs; 5cm (2in) or longer silvery-blue or greenish infls, long bracts, after few yrs. Monocarpic but self-seeds.
E. maritimum (sea holly): to 30×30cm (1×1ft); v glaucous stiff lvs; 2.5cm (1in) steel-blue infls, large silvery bracts. Likes hot, dry spot.
E.×oliverianum: hybrid of unknown parentage; to 1–1.2×0.6m (3–5×2ft); heart-shaped blue-green basal lvs; bluish infls to 4cm (1½in) long, deep mauve-blue narrow bracts.
E. planum: to 90×45cm (3×1½ft); dark green basal lvs; light blue 1cm (½in) infls, blue-green narrow bracts. Better for cutting than border.
E. tripartitum **7**: probably hybrid; to 75×60cm (2½×2ft); dark green basal lvs, few spines; 1cm (½in) globular steel-blue infls on spreading branches. Good border plant.
E. variifolium **8**: to 60×30cm (2×1ft); rounded evergreen basal lvs, glossy dark green marked white; 2cm (¾in) pale bluish infls, silvery bracts.
Giant fennel (*Ferula communis* **9**): handsome & striking moderately hardy plant forming dense mound to 1×1–1.2m (3×3–4ft) of v finely dissected lvs (glaucous or bronzed in some forms); when mature, cow-parsley-like infls 30cm (1ft) or more wide of small yellow fls on stout glaucous stem to 2.5–3.5m (8–12ft) tall.
F. tingitana is similar but smaller, to 2m (7ft).
Himalayan parsley (*Selinum tenuifolium*, *Oreocome candollei*): stately cow-parsley-like plant, to 1–1.5×0.2m (3–5×2ft); finely cut filigree lvs; large flat infls of white fls, black anthers.

The valerian family

Sun-loving herbaceous plants, often unpleasantly scented when bruised, bearing branched heads of small flowers in summer. **Cultivation**: Unless stated, very hardy & for any well-drained soil in full sun or light shade. Cut down in autumn. **Propagation**: Seed; division.

Red valerian (*Centranthus* [*Kentranthus*] *ruber* **10**): bushy, to 60–90×30cm (2–3×1ft); woody rootstock (difficult to divide); rather fleshy grey-green lvs to 10cm (4in) long; 8–10cm (3–4in)

infls of deep pink or red fls, long season. Thrives in hot, dry soil; often naturalized in wall crevices, etc; can be weedy. Vars: 'Albus' (white); 'Atrococcineus' (deep crimson).

Patrinia (*Patrinia triloba**): clump-forming, to 20×15cm (8×6in); tufts of 3/5-lobed lvs to 8cm (3in) long; loose clusters to 10cm (4in) across of golden fls, early summer. Tolerates shade.
Valerians (*Valeriana* spp): easy rhizomatous plants. Tall spp best staked.
V. arizonica: mat-forming & creeping, to 15×15cm (6×6in); dark green fleshy lvs; corymbs to 15cm (6in) across of pale pink or whitish fls, early.

V. officinalis* **11**, p347 (common or cat's valerian): ultra-hardy; to 1–1.2×1m (3–4×3ft); basal clump of deeply cut or compound lvs, lance-shaped lfts; loose flattish infls of white, pink or mauve fls.
V. phu: to 90×45cm (3×1½ft); broad lvs, stem lvs deeply cut; dense panicles to 15cm (6in) long of white fls. Var 'Aurea' has yellow young lvs.
V. sambucifolia: erect & vigorous, to 1.5×0.6m (5×2ft); dark green divided lvs; branched flattish heads of pale pink fls, early summer.

Violas, violettas & violets

Viola spp, true perennial relatives of pansies (p526). Dwarf tufted plants popular for border & path edgings; also for rock gardens or for underplanting trees & shrubs. Leaves ovate or heart-shaped, toothed. Flowers 5-petalled, profuse in spring & early summer (winter & spring in warm climates), often repeating later; often sterile (inconspicuous late summer flowers self-fertile. **Cultivation**: Very to ultra-hardy unless stated. For any moist but well-drained fertile soil in cool semi-shade, or full sun where not too hot. Dead-head violas and violettas where possible & cut back in autumn. May be attacked by slugs, red spider mites, certain caterpillars. **Propagation**: Cuttings, division; seed.

Violas & violettas: like small pansies, with flattish fls generally 2.5–3cm (1–1¼in) across, rounded petals, on branching leafy stems.
SPECIES:
V. aetolica (*V. saxatilis aetolica*): to 12×25cm (5×10in); clear yellow fls.
V. bertolonii: to 25×40cm (10×16in); rather squarish fls, violet or yellow, sometimes white.
V. cornuta: (horned violet; in US, tufted pansy): moderately to v hardy; to 15–25×30cm (6–10×12in); rich green lvs; long-stemmed deep violet-purple fls, long slender spurs. Vars: 'Alba' **1** (white); 'Belmont Blue' ('Boughton Blue', pale sky blue); 'Lilacina' (soft lilac); 'Minor' (to 5cm [2in]; small pale violet fls).
V. gracilis: to 15×30cm (6×12in); deep violet-purple fls, long spurs. Vars: 'Minor' (small pale blue fls on short stems); 'Major' (long-stemmed).
V. lutea **2** (mountain pansy): to 20×40cm (8×16in); yellow fls, brown or purple veins.
HYBRIDS:
Violas*: to 15×35cm (6×14in); fls generally 3–5cm (1¼–2in) across. Vars: 'Admiration' (purple-blue, yellow eye); 'Ardross Gem' (bronze-gold & pale blue); 'Aspasia' (cream & yellow); 'Barbara' (pink-mauve & yellow); 'Bullion' (deep yellow); 'Dobbie's Bronze'; 'Gladys Findlay' (white centred violet); 'Irish Molly' **3** (khaki-yellow, bronzed centre); 'Jackanapes' (yellow & brown-red); 'Jersey Gem' (purple-blue); 'Maggie Mott' (silvery-mauve, cream centre); 'Miss Brookes' (reddish-purple, yellow eye); 'Primrose Dame' (pale yellow).
Violettas*: to 10–15×30cm (4–6×12in); fls generally to 2.5cm (1in) across. Vars: 'Boy Blue'; 'Buttercup' (deep yellow); 'Dawn' (primrose-yellow); 'Calantha' (yellow); 'Little David' (creamy-white); 'Pippa' **4** (mauve, yellow eye);

'Princess Mab' (mauve, freckled); 'Purity'** (white); 'Rebecca'** **5** (cream flecked violet).
Violets: fls rather nodding, about 2.5cm (1in) across, with narrowish petals, generally with pronounced spurs; heart-shaped, stalked lvs.
V. cucullata* (marsh violet): mat-forming, to 8–15×15cm (3–6×6in); violet fls, white base. Tolerates wet soil. See also *V. sororia*.
V. elatior: to 30×15cm (12×6in); lance-shaped lvs to 8cm (3in) long; short-spurred pale blue fls, purple veins. Likes wet soil.
V. hederacea **6** (Australian or trailing violet): moderately hardy; spreads by stolons, to 8×25cm (3×10in); violet-blue almost spurless fls, tipped/shaded white.
V. labradorica 'Purpurea': to 12×30cm (5×12in); dark green lvs suffused purple; mauve fls, spring.
V. odorata** **7** (sweet violet): spreads by stolons, to 15×40cm (6×16in); short-spurred deep violet fls, sometimes rose-pink or white, spring. Hybrids (florists' violets): 'Coeur d'Alsace'* (pink); 'Czar* (violet-purple); 'Governor Herrick' (purple); 'John Raddenbury'* (blue); 'Lianne' (red-purple); 'Mrs R. Barton'* (white); 'Princess of Wales'** (blue-violet); 'White Czar'* (white feathered violet & yellow). Double-fld vars (Parma violets): 'Duchess de Parme'** **8** (mauve); 'Marie Louise'** (violet & white).
V. pedata **9** (bird's-food violet): to 12×25cm (5×10in); palmate lobed lvs; violet-purple flattish fls to 4cm (1½in) across.
V. septentrionalis **10**: mat-forming, to 12×10cm (5×4in); white fls streaked violet-purple.
V. sororia (*V. papilionacea*; to 20×30cm (8×12in); fls variable, generally dark blue or purple. Vars: 'Freckles' **11** (pale blue freckled purple); 'Priceana' (*V. priceana*, Confederate violet; grey-blue).

Miscellaneous perennials

Listed alphabetically by family name. Herbaceous unless stated. Generally for borders, etc; tender & semi-hardy spp for summer bedding in cool areas. **Cultivation & propagation**: See below; unless stated, very hardy & for any well-drained fertile soil in sun or partial shade. For perennial climbers, see pp228–250; for plants growing from bulbs, corms & tubers (including some rhizomatous plants often treated as ordinary perennials), see pp362–424; for short-lived or tender perennials usually grown as annuals or biennials, see pp486–526.

Bear's breeches (*Acanthus* spp; Acanthaceae): stately, with large decorative lobed/divided basal lvs & sturdy spikes of tubular lipped fls with leafy spine-tipped bracts, summer (can be dried). Good specimen/border plants. Propagate by seed, division, root cuttings.

A. longifolius (correctly, *A. balcanicus*): to 1×0.6m (3×2ft); deeply lobed wavy-edged lvs to 60×20cm (2ft×8in); 30cm (1ft) spikes of mauve fls.

A. mollis: moderately to v hardy; to 1.2×1m (4×3ft); deep glossy green lobed lvs to 60×30cm (2×1ft); 45–60cm (1½–2ft) spikes of white fls, pinkish-purple bracts. Var 'Latifolius' is hardier & sturdier.

A. spinosus **1**: moderately to v hardy; to 1.2×1m (4×3ft); dark green leathery lvs to 40×15cm (16×6in), deeply cut & spiny; 45cm (1½ft) spikes of white or mauve-tinted fls, rose-purple bracts.

The amaranth family (*Alternanthera* & *Iresine* spp; Amaranthaceae): bushy bedding plants with richly coloured, often variegated lvs; fls small & rarely formed. For warm, sunny spot; best clipped/pinched to keep compact. Propagate each yr by cuttings, autumn or spring, & overwinter under glass.

Alternanthera ficoidea (parrot-leaf, Joseph's coat, etc): moderately hardy; to 25×20cm (10×8in), less if clipped; lvs to 8cm (3in) long, vividly veined & marked green, yellow, orange & red (some sold as named vars).

Iresine herbstii (blood-leaf, beefsteak plant): tender; to 45×30cm (1½×1ft), less if pinched, taller in frost-free areas if overwintered; evergreen where hardy; 5–12cm (2–5in) rich maroon or green lvs, veined yellowish, notched tip. Var 'Aureo-reticulata' **2** has green & gold lvs veined red; stems bright red. *I. lindenii* **3** (also called blood-leaf) is smaller, with pointed blood-red lvs veined paler red; stems bright red.

The periwinkle family (*Amsonia, Catharanthus, Rhazya* & *Vinca* spp; Apocynaceae): varied, with 5-petalled funnel-shaped fls. Propagate by cuttings, division or seed.

Amsonia tabernaemontana (*A. salicifolia*): ultra-hardy; to 60–90×45cm (2–3×1½ft); arching stems with narrow willow-like lvs to 20cm (8in) long; loose clusters of 2cm (¾in) starry grey-blue fls, summer. Likes sun. *Rhazya* (*A.*) *orientalis* is similar but smaller, with broader grey-green lvs.

Catharanthus roseus (rose or Madagascar periwinkle; better known as *Vinca rosea*): tender erect sub-shrub, to 30–60×30cm (1–2×1ft); evergreen narrow glossy lvs to 5cm (2in) long; rounded 4cm (1½in) rose-pink fls centred deep rose, spring to autumn (or all yr in v warm areas). For rich soil in sheltered sunny site; often treated as HHA. Vars (dwarf): 'Little Bright Eyes' **4** (white centred deep rose-pink); 'Little Pinkie' **5** (deep rose-pink).

Vinca major **6** (greater periwinkle, blue-buttons): moderately to v hardy semi-prostrate self-rooting sub-shrub, to 30×90cm (1×3ft), good for ground cover in semi-/shade; evergreen lvs to 5cm (2in) long, dark glossy green; bright blue-mauve 4cm (1½in) fls, mainly late spring to mid summer, often repeating. Tolerates limy, acid & poor soils. Var 'Variegata' ('Elegantissima') has lvs variegated cream.

V. minor (lesser periwinkle; in US, trailing myrtle): similar to *V. major* but v hardy & grows to 10×90cm (4in×3ft), with narrower lvs & smaller fls. Vars: 'Alba' **7** (white); 'Albo-plena' (double, white); 'Atropurpurea' (deep purple); 'Aureovariegata' (lvs variegated creamy-yellow; 'Aureovariegata Alba' has white fls); 'Azurea Flore Pleno' **8** (double, sky-blue); 'Bowles' Variety' **9** ('La Grave'; profuse large deep blue fls); 'Burgundy' (wine-red); 'Jekyll's White' (profuse white fls); 'Multiplex' ('Flore Pleno'; double, purplish).

Wild gingers (*Asarum* spp; Aristolochiaceae): rhizomatous, stemless & carpet-forming, to 12–20×30cm (5–8×12in); heart-shaped generally evergreen lvs on long stalks; curious bell-shaped brownish/greenish-purple fls, spring, under lvs. Good ground cover in rich, moist soil in shade. Propagate by division, seed.

A. canadense: ultra-hardy; herbaceous; lvs to 18cm (7in) wide, downy (may irritate skin).

A. caudatum: evergreen; lvs to 15cm (6in) wide.

A. europaeum **10**: evergreen; lvs to 8cm (3in) wide.

Milkweeds (*Asclepias* spp; Asclepiadaceae): erect vigorous & spreading, with milky sap, narrow lance-shaped lvs to 12–15cm (5–6in) long & umbel-like 5cm (2in) clusters of unusual showy fls, summer, each with 5 reflexed petals & "crown" with 5 horns; seed pods large & often hairy; seeds have "parachute" of hairs. Ultra-hardy unless noted; best in moist soil; support if

exposed. Propagate by seed, division.

A. curassavica **11**, p351 (blood-flower): semi- to moderately hardy; to 90×45cm (3×1½ft); woody base; glossy lvs; crimson & orange fls. Needs shelter.

A. incarnata* **1** (swamp milkweed): to 1.2×0.6m (4×2ft); deep flesh-pink fls.

A. speciosa: to 75×60cm (2½×2ft); densely white-felted; fls purplish-pink. Invasive.

A. tuberosa **2** (butterfly-weed, pleurisy root): to 60×30cm (2×1ft); woody base; crowded lvs; bright orange-yellow fls (attract butterflies). Difficult to establish; best in deep sandy loam.

Jeffersonias & podophyllums (*Jeffersonia* & *Podophyllum* spp; Berberidaceae; sometimes classed in Podophyllaceae): low-growing & creeping, with lobed lvs & small cup-shaped fls. Most parts poisonous. For peaty, humus-rich soil in partial shade, making good ground cover in woodland. Propagate by seed, division.

Jeffersonia diphylla (twinleaf): to 30×30cm (1×1ft); lvs to 15cm (6in) long, 2 kidney-shaped lfts; white 2.5cm (1in) fls on leafless stalks, spring; frs pear-shaped, lidded.

J. dubia **3**: to 25×25cm (10×10in); lvs to 10cm (4in) across, deeply 2-lobed, coppery-purple when young; lavender-blue fls to 3cm (1¼in) wide, late spring to early summer.

Podophyllum emodi (correctly, *P. hexandrum*): to 30–45×45cm (1–1½×1½ft); rhizomatous; paired deeply 3/5-lobed toothed lvs to 25cm (10in) across, spotted brown when young; nodding waxy white or pale pink fls 5cm (2in) wide, early spring; shiny red 5cm (2in) frs, edible. Vars: *chinensis* (lvs boldly marked; fls pale rose); 'Majus' (vigorous).

P. peltatum (May apple): ultra-hardy; to 45×45cm (1½×1½ft); rhizomatous; bright green palmate lvs to 30cm (1ft) across, 5–9 lobes; waxy creamy-white fls 5cm (2in) wide, spring to early summer; golden-yellow lemon-shaped frs to 5cm (2in) long.

Incarvillea (*Incarvillea delavayi* **4**; Bignoniaceae): to 60×30cm (2×1ft); fleshy root; basal tuft of deep green pinnate lvs to 25cm (10in) long, up to 23 narrow 5cm (2in) lfts; showy rose-pink, rather gloxinia-like fls to 8cm (3in) long, yellow throat, clustered on stout stalks, late spring & early summer. *I. mairei grandiflora* (*I. grandiflora*) is similar but shorter, with sparser cerise-pink fls, orange throat; lfts broader. Both need rich but well-drained soil in sun; plant root 8cm (3in) deep; can be lifted for winter if extremely cold. Propagate by seed, division.

Puya (*Puya berteroniana*; usually sold incorrectly as *P. alpestris*; Bromeliaceae): semi-hardy; to 90×60cm (3×2ft); evergreen rosette of narrow grey-green lvs 60cm (2ft) long, sword-shaped & spiny; when mature, sturdy spikes of metallic blue-green bracted fls, orange anthers, early

summer. Hardiest member of pineapple family. For v well-drained soil in full sun. Propagate by division, seed.

Twinflower (*Linnaea borealis** **5**; Caprifoliaceae): ultra-hardy prostrate sub-shrub, to 8×60cm (3×24in); evergreen lvs to 2.5cm (1in) long; paired nodding bell-shaped soft pink fls 10mm (⅜in) long on slender upright stems, early summer. Good ground cover in cool moist shade. Propagate by division. Var *americana* has narrower fls; more common.

The spiderwort family (*Setcreasea*, *Tradescantia* & *Zebrina* spp; Commelinaceae): generally semi-hardy, with fleshy stems & lvs (evergreen where frost-free), these spp often grown indoors but also for summer bedding, hanging baskets, etc, in warm areas. Propagate by seed, cuttings.

Setcreasea pallida 'Purple Heart' **6** (*S. purpurea*): rather sprawling, to 40×50cm (16×20in); narrow purple-flushed lvs to 15cm (6in) long; inconspicuous clusters of rose-purple fls, large purple bracts, from late spring. For summer bedding. Re-grows if cut down by mild frost.

Tradescantia×andersoniana vars **7** (spiderworts, trinity flowers; v often sold incorrectly as *T.virginiana*): complex v to ultra-hardy herbaceous hybrids of *T. virginiana* & other spp; erect, to 45–90×60cm (1½–3×2ft); rush-like pointed lvs; clusters of short-lived triangular fls to 4cm (1½in) wide opening in succession all summer. For sunny borders. Like moist soil; best supported if exposed. Numerous named vars in shades of blue, purple, carmine, red & white.

T. fluminensis (wandering Jew): prostrate & trailing, to 5×60cm (2×24in); lvs to 4cm (1½in) long, purplish beneath in good light, variegated in some vars. Good in hanging baskets. Similar spp include: *S. striata* (correctly, *Callisia elegans*; dark green hairy 8cm [3in] lvs veined silver); *T. albiflora* (also called wandering Jew; lvs larger); *T. blossfeldiana* (glossy 10cm [4in] lvs, purple & hairy beneath); *Zebrina pendula* **8** (*T. zebrina*, inch plant; silver-banded 8cm [3in] lvs) & its vars.

Convolvulus (bindweeds, *Convolvulus* spp; Convolvulaceae): somewhat invasive ground-cover plants with grey-green hairy lvs & funnel-shaped 2.5–5cm (1–2in) fls like morning glories, all summer (close at night). Best in wild gardens. Propagate by cuttings, division, seed.

C. althaeoides: moderately to v hardy; to 30×90cm (1×3ft); may climb; upper lvs deeply divided; pink to purple fls. *C. elegantissimus* is similar but fls pink striped red.

C. mauritanicus **9**: semi-hardy; to 30×90cm (1×3ft); woody base; small rounded lvs; violet-blue fls, whitish throat.

Bunchberry (dwarf cornel, *Cornus* [*Chamaepericlymenum*] *canadensis* **10**;

Cornaceae): ultra-hardy; rhizomatous &
spreading, to 20×60cm (8×24in) or wider;
crowded 8cm (3in) lvs, red in autumn; clustered
tiny fls surrounded by showy white petal-like
bracts, late spring & early summer, followed by
bright red berries. Good ground cover in cool
lime-free woodland. Propagate by division, seed.

Sedges (*Carex* spp; Cyperaceae): grass-like
tufted plants with gracefully arching lvs; rather
insignificant fls in spikes with leafy bracts, on
triangular stems. Smaller spp useful for bright
evergreen ground cover, edging, etc; tall spp
good specimen plant in cool shade. Propagate by
division, seed.

C. morrowii (Japanese sedge) vars: to 30×30cm
(1×1ft). Vars: 'Evergold' **1** ('Aurea Variegata'; lvs
striped golden-yellow); 'Variegata' (*expallida*; lvs
striped white).

C. pendula (great drooping sedge): to 1.2×1m
(4×3ft); rather broad yellow-green lvs.

C. stricta 'Bowles' Golden': to 60×45cm
(2×1½ft); lvs golden-yellow, greening late
summer. Short-lived.

Galax (*Galax urceolata* **2**, *G. aphylla*;
Diapensiaceae): ultra-hardy rhizomatous
evergreen, to 30–45×30cm (1–1½×1ft);
rosettes of glossy dark green rounded to heart-
shaped lvs 8–12cm (3–5in) across, bronzed in
winter, forming low clump; slender leafless
spikes of small white fls, early summer. Good
ground cover for moist, lime-free peaty soil in
partial shade. Propagate by division.

The scabious family (*Cephalaria, Knautia,
Morina* & *Scabiosa* spp; Dipsacaceae): summer-
flg, most with somewhat daisy-like typical
scabious ("pincushion") fls, with tight bristly disc
surrounded by overlapping ring of outer petals
and bract-like sepals, followed by showy seed
heads (both good for cutting). Like sun; may
need support. Propagate by division, seed.

Cephalaria gigantea (giant scabious; often sold
incorrectly as *C. tatarica*): ultra-hardy; to
1.8×1.2m (6×4ft); clump of large pinnately
divided dark green lvs; long-lasting 5cm (2in)
primrose/creamy-yellow fls on ribbed branching
stems. Can be propagated by root cuttings.

Knautia (*Scabiosa*) *macedonica* **3** (*S. rumelica*):
to 60×60cm (2×2ft); basal clump of often
pinnately lobed lvs; rich deep crimson 5cm (2in)
scabious fls on branched arching stems.

Morina longifolia **4**: to 90×45cm (3×1½ft); basal
rosette of narrow thistle-like rich green lvs* to
30cm (1ft) long, wavy & spiny edges; tubular fls
4cm (1½in) long with 5 flaring lobes, in whorls up
leafy stems with collars of prickly bracts; fls white
becoming pink-flushed, ageing deep crimson.

Scabiosa caucasica (florists' scabious,
pincushion flower): ultra-hardy; to 45–75×45–
60cm (1½–2½×1½×2ft); narrow glaucous lvs,
stem lvs divided; flat fls to 8cm (3in) wide, long

season, pale mauve-blue centred yellowish-
green in sp. Vars: 'Blue Perfection' (lavender-
blue); 'Bressingham White'; 'Clive Greaves' **5**
(rich lavender-blue); 'Floral Queen' (blue); 'Miss
Willmott' **6** (white); 'Moerheim Blue' (deep
mauve-blue); 'White Bonnet'.

S. columbaria: ultra-hardy; to 75×75cm
(2½×2½ft); grey-green lvs, basal usually entire,
stem lvs pinnate; lilac-blue 8cm (3in) fls, dark
purplish central bristles, on hairy stems.

S. graminifolia: to 45×45cm (1½×1½ft); woody
base; mat of grassy silvery-grey lvs; pinkish-
mauve 5cm (2in) fls, pink in var 'Pinkushion' **7**.

S. ochroleuca: to 75×75cm (2½×2½ft); silver-
haired mainly pinnate-lobed lvs; pale yellow 4cm
(1½in) fls. Self-seeds.

Dicentras (bleeding hearts, *Dicentra* spp;
Fumariaceae; formerly in Papaveraceae):
graceful & dainty, with finely divided ferny lvs &
arching racemes of nodding, somewhat heart-
shaped fls, mainly late spring & early summer.
Ultra-hardy & best in cool semi-shade (short-
lived where winters v mild); for moist, peaty,
well-drained soil. Propagate by division, seed.

D. eximia **8** (fringed bleeding heart): clump-
forming to 30–45×30cm (1–1½×1ft); grey-
green lvs; deep mauve-pink 2cm (¾in) fls (may
repeat if cut back after flg). Vars: 'Alba' (white);
'Spring Morning' (to 50cm [20in]; glaucous lvs;
soft pink fls).

D. formosa (western bleeding heart);
rhizomatous, to 30–45×45cm (1–1½×1½ft);
lvs often glaucous, on long stalks; small
dense racemes of 1.5cm (⅝in) deep rosy-
mauve fls. Vars: 'Adrian Bloom' (glaucous
lvs; rich carmine-red fls); 'Bountiful' (blue-green
lvs; crimson fls); 'Luxuriant' (vigorous, to 50cm
[20in]; dark blue-green lvs; cherry-red fls); 'Pearl
Drops' **9** (glaucous lvs; white fls flushed pink);
'Sweetheart' (white).

D. spectabilis **10** (common bleeding heart): to
45–75×45cm (1½–2½×1½ft); glaucous lvs,
less ferny & more paeony-like than other spp;
long racemes of distinctly heart-shaped 2.5cm
(1in) rosy-red fls, protruding white inner petals.
Var 'Alba' ('Pantaloons') has pure white fls.

Gentians (*Gentiana* spp; Gentianaceae): tall
border relatives of well-known alpines (p450),
with leafy stems & fls in upper lf axils, mid
summer. For moist soil in semi-shade. Propagate
by seed, division, basal cuttings.

G. asclepiadea **11** (willow gentian): slender, to
45–60×45cm (1½–2×1½ft); arching or erect
stems with paired broadly lance-shaped lvs to
8cm (3in) long; narrow bell-shaped deep blue fls
to 4cm (1½in) long in 1s, 2s or 3s. Var 'Alba' has
white fls, greenish throat.

G. lutea (yellow gentian): to 1.5×0.6m (5×2ft);
stout stems with lvs to 30cm (1ft) long; whorls of
starry bright yellow 2.5cm (1in) fls; attractive

seed-heads.

Gunneras (*Gunnera* spp; Gunneraceae;
formerly in Haloragaceae): rhizomatous
moisture-lovers, dwarf or giant, grown mainly for
rounded to kidney-shaped foliage; fls small, but
generally in large cone-like brownish or greenish
infls, summer (followed by clusters of red frs). For
rich, moist soil. Propagate by division, seed.
G. chilensis (*G. scabra, G. tinctoria*): to
1.8×1.5m (6×5ft); huge rhubarb-like palmately
lobed & coarsely toothed lvs 1.2–1.5m (4–5ft)
across, stalk & undersides spiny; infls to 1m (3ft)
tall, spiny bracts (largely obscured by lvs).
G. manicata **1** is similar but even larger, to
3×3.5m (10×12ft), with lvs to 2m (7ft) or more
across; spines reddish; infls taller but slimmer.
Crown moderately to v hardy if thickly mulched in
winter, otherwise semi- to moderately hardy.
G. magellanica: moderately hardy; mat-forming,
to 10×45cm (4×18in); spreads by stolons;
kidney-shaped toothed & crinkled lvs to 5cm
(2in) across; infls to 8cm (3in) tall. For cool
semi-shade.

Sisyrinchium (*Sisyrinchium striatum*;
Iridaceae): moderately to v hardy; evergreen;
clump-forming & rather grass-like, to 60×30cm
(2×1ft); sword-shaped grey-green lvs to
30×2.5cm (12×1in); creamy-yellow, rather
primula-like fls 2cm (¾in) across, reverse striped
brownish, clustered along erect spikes, early
summer. Shoots die after flg; plant may be
short-lived unless divided regularly in late
summer, but often self-seeds. For well-drained
soil in sun. Propagate by division, seed.

Flax (*Linum* spp; Linaceae): easy but rather
short-lived dainty sun-lovers with small, narrow,
crowded stem lvs & brightly coloured saucer-
shaped 5-petalled fls, short-lived but appearing
over long season early–mid summer, in branched
clusters. For dwarf spp, also suitable for front of
border, see p480. Propagate by seed, cuttings.
L. austriacum: ultra-hardy; to 60×30cm (2×1ft);
rather lax thin stems with v narrow lvs to 1.5cm
(⅝in) long; clear blue 2cm (¾in) fls. Short-lived.
L. campanulatum: moderately to v hardy; to
35×30cm (14×12in); woody base; lance-shaped
greyish-green lvs, transparent edges; pale yellow
orange-veined fls 3cm (1¼in) wide.
L. flavum (golden flax): to 30–60×30cm (1–
2×1ft); sub-shrubby; lance-shaped to spoon-
shaped lvs; profuse 2.5cm (1in) golden fls.
L. narbonense **2**: to 45–60×30cm (1½–2×1ft);
wiry stems; narrow lance-shaped grey-green lvs
to 2cm (¾in) long (evergreen in mild areas);
deep azure-blue silky fls to 4cm (1½in) wide, all
summer. 'Six Hills' is best var.
L. perenne **3**: to 45–60×30cm (1½–2×1ft);
narrow grey-green lvs 2.5cm (1in) long; profuse
deep blue 2.5cm (1in) fls on gracefully arching
stems. Short-lived.

Lobelias (*Lobelia* spp; Lobeliaceae; sometimes
included in Campanulaceae): erect border plants,
quite different from well-known bedding plants
(p524), with bracted racemes of often brilliantly
coloured tubular 2-lipped fls. For rich, moist soil
in sheltered, partially shaded site; may need
staking. Propagate by division, seed.
L. cardinalis (cardinal flower): to 90×30cm
(3×1ft); stems often purplish; lance-shaped lvs
to 10cm (4in) long; vivid scarlet fls 4cm (1½in)
long, mid–late summer. Ultra-hardy but short-
lived; likes boggy conditions. *L. splendens* **4**
(*L. fulgens*) is similar but moderatey hardy &
hairy, with longer purplish lvs & deep red fls.
L.×hybrida var (lobelia hybrids; correctly,
L.×gerardii & *L.×speciosa*): hybrids of
L. cardinalis, L. syphilitica & *L. splendens*, often
listed under parents; to 1–1.2×0.3m (3–4×1ft);
lvs generally reddish to coppery-tinted. Vars
(v hardy unless noted): 'Bee's Scarlet'
(moderately hardy; large vivid scarlet fls); 'Cherry
Ripe' **5** (cerise-scarlet); 'Dark Crusader' (velvety
dark red); 'Queen Victoria' (moderately hardy;
deep plum-red lvs; vivid scarlet fls);
L.×vedrariensis (dark green lvs; long infls of dark
lavender-purple fls, late summer into autumn);
'Will Scarlet' (bright scarlet).
L. syphilitica **6**: to 1×0.3m (3×1ft); pale green lvs
to 12cm (5in) long; tall infls to 75cm (2½ft) long
of clear blue 2.5cm (1in) fls, mid–late summer.
Short-lived; produces offsets. Var 'Alba' is white.

The loosestrife family (*Cuphea* & *Lythrum* spp;
Lythraceae):
Cuphea ignea **7** (cigar flower, firecracker plant):
tender to semi-hardy bushy evergreen sub-shrub
good for summer bedding, edging, etc,
overwintering under glass. Compact, to
30×30cm (1×1ft); more if not pinched back;
narrow lvs 2.5–8cm (1–3in) long; bright red
tubular "cigar" fls 2cm (¾in) long, violet & white
tip, summer & autumn. Likes full sun. Propagate
by seed, cuttings. *C. miniata* (*C. llavea miniata*;
probably correctly, *C.×purpurea*, a hybrid with
C. procumbens) is similar but lvs broader & fls
vermilion to cerise-scarlet, tipped violet.
Lythrum salicaria (purple loosestrife): ultra-hardy;
vigorous to 1–1.5×0.45m (3–5×1½ft);
erect & bushy, with tough woody rootstock;
lance-shaped lvs to 10cm (4in) long;
long-lasting red-purple starry fls 2cm (¾in) wide
in whorls up leafy stems, all summer. V adaptable
but prefers moist (even boggy) soil. Sp rarely
grown; vars: 'Firecandle' **8** ('Feuerkerze'; vivid
rose-red); 'Lady Sackville' **9** (rose-pink); 'Robert'
(rose-red); 'The Beacon' (intense rose-crimson).
Propagate by division, cuttings.
L. virgatum: ultra-hardy; to 1×0.45m (3×1½ft);
similar to *L. salicaria* but lvs narrower & fls
violet-pink. Vars: 'Morden Pink' (deep phlox-
pink); 'Rose Queen' (rose-pink); 'The Rocket'

(deep rose-pink).

Honey flower (*Melianthus major*; Melianthaceae): semi-hardy pungently aromatic sub-shrub grown mainly for striking foliage. Sprawling, to 2.5×3m (8×10ft); stems hollow; pinnate lvs to 45cm (1½ft) long, 9–11 coarsely toothed glaucous lfts to 15cm (6in) long; brownish-red 2.5cm (1in) fls in racemes to 30cm (1ft) long, summer. Propagate by cuttings, seed.

Bananas (*Ensete* & *Musa* spp; Musaceae): tender to semi-hardy rather palm-like plants with huge arching rich green lvs (sheathing bases form trunk-like pseudostem); 5cm (2in) yellowish fls surrounded by leathery petal-like bracts borne on long drooping stalk, developing into familiar "hand" of frs where v warm (plant dies to root after flg & frtg). Grown in warm areas for subtropical effect. Need rich, moist soil; best sheltered from wind (damages lvs). Even where hardy, may be cut to ground by frost; where winters cold, best in tub moved under glass in winter. Propagate by seed, root cuttings, offsets. Spp include: *Ensete ventricosum* (*Musa ensete*, Abyssinian banana; to 2–6m [7–20ft], with lvs to 3–6×0.6–1.2m [10–20×2–4ft]); *M. acuminata* 'Dwarf Cavendish' **1** (*M. cavendishii*; to 1.8–2.5m [6–8ft]; lvs to 1.5×0.6m [5×2ft]); *M. basjoo* (Japanese banana; hardiest sp, hardy to −6°C [21°F] or lower; to 2.5m [8ft]; lvs to 1.5×0.6m [5×2ft]); *M.×paradisiaca* (edible banana; to 6m [20ft]; lvs to 2.5×1m [8×3ft]).

Orchids (*Orchis* spp; some now correctly *Dactylorhiza* spp; Orchidaceae): beautiful moderately hardy upright slender plants for humus-rich moist soil in sun or semi-shade. Lance-shaped alternate lvs sheath stems; spikes or racemes of typical orchid fls, with prominent 3-lobed broad lip, early–mid summer. Propagate by division of tuber-like pseudo bulbs.
O. (*D.*) *elata* **2**: to 75×30cm (2½×1ft); dull green lvs; dense 25cm (10in) infls of deep lilac-purple, slightly speckled fls. *O.* (*D.*) *foliosa* (*O. maderensis*, Madeira orchid) is similar but shorter, to 45×30cm (1½×1ft), with shiny green lvs & red-purple fls.
O. (*D.*) *fuchsii* **3** (*O. maculata*): to 50×30cm (20×12in); lvs faintly mottled reddish-brown; dense cylindrical to conical 15cm (6in) spikes of lilac-pink to mauve-violet heavily spotted fls. 'Bressingham Bonus' **4** is good violet-mauve form.
O. (*D.*) *latifolia* (marsh orchid): to 60×30cm (2×1ft); narrow maroon-spotted lvs; spikes of rosy-/lilac fls, pale throat. Needs moisture.
O. militaris (military orchid): to 45×30cm (1½×1ft); dense infls of spidery magenta-purple fls, manikin-shaped.
O. purpurea* **5** (*O. fusca*, lady orchid): to 45×30cm (1½×1ft); broad shiny lvs; dense broad infls of manikin-shaped purple & pink fls.

Pokeweed (pokeberry, *Phytolacca americana* **6**, *P. decandra*; Phytolaccaceae): ultra-hardy bold but rather weedy & unpleasant-smelling plant for mixed border or wild garden; vigorous & erect, to 1.2–3×1m (4–10×3ft); tufts of succulent stems; lvs to 20cm (8in) long, rich red to purplish in autumn; erect 8–15cm (3–6in) dense spikes of tiny greenish-white starry fls, summer, ageing reddish & followed by purple-black berries. Root & berries poisonous. Self seeds. May need staking if exposed. Propagate by division, seed.
P. clavigera **7** is similar but smaller, to 1.2×0.6m (4×2ft), & less coarse; stems bright red & lvs bright yellow in autumn; fls pink.

The plumbago family (*Armeria, Ceratostigma* & *Limonium* spp; Plumbaginaceae): low-growing, for front of border or ground cover in full sun. Propagate by division, seed.
Armeria pseudarmeria (border thrift; often grown incorrectly as *A. plantaginea*): moderately to v hardy broad-lvd relative of common thrift (p456); to 60×30cm (2×1ft); tufts of evergreen lance-shaped lvs to 25×2cm (10×¾in); globular 4.5cm (1¾in) heads of deep pink to white fls, early–mid summer. Var 'Bee's Ruby' is deep cerise-pink to ruby-red.
Ceratostigma plumbaginoides **8** (*Plumbago larpentiae*): bushy & clump-forming, to 30×45cm (1×1½ft); woody base, with wiry stems; deep green leathery lance-shaped lvs to 8cm (3in) long, crimson & mahogany in autumn; bristly clusters of 5-lobed tubular fls 2cm (¾in) across, sky-blue to vivid peacock-blue, late summer & autumn. Can be propagated by suckers.
Limonium (*Statice*) *latifolium* (border or broad-leaved sea lavender): ultra-hardy; to 45–60×60–90cm (1½–2×2–3ft); woody base; rosettes of evergreen leathery downy lvs to 25cm (10in) long; airy panicles of profuse tiny blue-mauve fls, white sepals, on wiry stems, mid–late summer. Good by sea. Can be propagated by root cuttings. Vars: 'Blue Cloud' (pale lavender-blue); 'Robert Butler' **9** (compact, to 40×45cm [16×18in]; violet-blue); 'Violetta' (rich violet).
L. (*Goniolimon*) *tataricum* is somewhat similar but more compact & mounding, with 15cm (6in) lvs & sprays of tiny rose-pink to white fls.

Wintergreen (*Pyrola rotundifolia**; Pyrolaceae; sometimes included in Ericaceae): stoloniferous mat-forming evergreen, to 25×30cm (10×12in); rosettes of dark green shiny round lvs to 5cm (2in) across; spikes of 1cm (½in) cup-shaped nodding fls, curious elongated tongue-like style, early–mid summer. For rich, moist, lime-free soil in shade. Var *americana* is slightly larger.
P. asarifolia (crimson to pink), *P. elliptica** (greenish-white) & *P. uliginosa* (correctly, *P. asarifolia purpurea*; pink to reddish-purple) are all similar.

Woodruffs (*Asperula* & *Galium* spp; Rubiaceae):

rather lax, forming cushions or mats, with whorls of rather narrow lvs up square stems & branched cymes of 5mm (¼in) starry fls. Good ground cover for moist lightish soil in semi-shade. Propagate by division, seed.

Asperula hexaphylla: to 45×45cm (1½×1½ft); slender stems; lvs in 6s; pearly-pink fls, early summer.

*Galium odoratum** (*A. odorata*, sweet woodruff, bedstraw): to 25×90cm (10×36in), spreading vigorously by stolons; deep green bristle-tipped lvs* to 4cm (1½in) long in whorls of 6–8; white fls, late spring & early summer (cuttable).

The rue family (*Dictamnus* & *Ruta* spp; Rutaceae): aromatic plants for full sun.

*Dictamnus albus** **1** (*D. fraxinella*, dittany, gas plant): ultra-hardy & v long-lived in cool climates; erect, to 1×0.6m (3×2ft); strongly sharp-scented pinnate lvs*, 9–11 dark glossy green toothed lfts to 8cm (3in) long; erect 20–30cm (8–12in) racemes of irregular 2.5cm (1in) white or pink fls with spreading petals & long curving stamens, early summer, followed by lobed seed capsules (explode when ripe). All parts (especially fls & seed pods) give off inflammable vapour (can be ignited in hot weather, hence other common name, burning bush). All parts (especially seed pods) poisonous. Propagate by seed. Vars: 'Purpureus' (mauve); 'Ruber' (rose-purple).

Ruta graveolens (rue): neat sub-shrub, to 60–90×60cm (2–3×2ft); evergreen deeply divided blue-green filigree lvs* (bitter-tasting; sometimes used as culinary herb; may cause dermatitis); rather insignificant greenish-yellow fls in corymbs, early–mid summer. Good foliage plant for border or low hedge. Best cut back hard in spring. Vars: 'Jackman's Blue' **2** (dense & compact; lvs v glaucous); 'Variegata' (lvs variegated creamy).

Chinese lantern (bladder cherry, *Physalis alkekengi* **3**; Solanaceae): ultra-hardy, rather invasive lax plant, to 45×60cm (1½×2ft), grown for bright orange 5cm (2in) lantern-like inflated calyces around cherry-like orange-red edible frs, late summer; lvs more or less triangular, to 8cm (3in) long; small starry creamy-white fls, mid summer. For full sun. Propagate by division, seed (can be treated as HHA). *P. franchetii* (correctly, *P. alkekengi franchetii*) is taller, to 60×60cm (2×2ft), with larger lvs & frs; better border plant. Var 'Gigantea' is tallest form, to 1m (3ft).

Bird-of-paradise flower (*Strelitzia reginae* **4**; Strelitziaceae, correctly Musaceae): spectacular tender evergreen for frost-free areas, also used as summer bedding or patio tub plant where summers warm; to 1.2×1.2m (4×4ft); stemless & clump-forming; leathery blue-green lvs to 45×15cm (18×6in) on stalks to 1m (3ft) long; long-lasting curious orange, blue & white bird-like infls to 15–20cm (6–8in) long, on & off all yr

in warm areas. For rich soil. Propagate by division, suckers, seed.

Mind-your-own-business (baby's tears, *Helxine* [correctly, *Soleirolia*] *soleirolii*; Urticaceae): moderately hardy, often rather invasive self-rooting carpeter, to 2.5–8×60cm (1–3×24in) or wider, grown solely for 5mm (¼in) bright green rounded lvs, evergreen unless cut back by sharp frost; fls inconspicuous. For cool moist shade (eg, under trees, shrubs); can be weedy (self-seeds & grows from stem or root fragments). Propagate by cuttings (v easy). Vars: 'Argentea' (lvs variegated silver); 'Aurea' **5** (lvs yellow-green).

The ginger family (*Cautleya*, *Hedychium* & *Roscoea* spp; Zingiberaceae): fleshy/ rhizomatous-rooted plants related to *Canna* spp (p424), with broadly lance-shaped lvs sheathing stems, & showy fls. For rich, moist soil in warm sunny spot; where tender, lift & overwinter root in cool but frost-free place, or grow in container & move under cover. Propagate by division, seed. *Cautleya lutea* (correctly, *C. gracilis*): moderately hardy, to 45×25cm (18×10in); glossy lvs to 20cm (8in) long, purplish beneath; small spikes of yellow orchid-like fls, summer.

C. spicata: to 60×45cm (2×1½ft); glossy lvs to 30cm (1ft) long; dense spikes of dark yellow fls, red 2.5cm (1in) bracts, late summer. Var 'Robusta' **6** is good sturdy form.

Hedychium spp (ginger lilies, garland flowers, butterfly lilies): tender to semi-hardy; to 1–1.5×1m (3–5×3ft); lvs to 30–50cm (12–20in) long; bold spikes of 5–8cm (2–3in) butterfly-like fls, long stamens, late summer & early autumn. Spp: *H. coccineum** (coral-red or pink shades); *H. coronarium*** (white); *H. densiflorum** **7** (moderately hardy; orange-red); *H. flavum** (yellow); *H. gardnerianum** **8** (yellow, red stamens).

Roscoea spp: moderately hardy; dormant autumn to early summer; lvs to 10–20cm (4–8in) long; short spikes of showy orchid/iris-like lipped fls, summer. Spp: *R. alpina* (to 15×10cm [6×4in]; pink to purplish); *R. beesiana* (to 40×30cm [16×12in]; yellow fls tipped buff & lilac-purple); *R. cautleoides* **9** (to 45×30cm [18×12in]; soft yellow hooded fls); *R. humeana* **10** (to 45×30cm [18×12in]; large violet-purple fls, yellow throat); *R. purpurea* (to 45×30cm [18×12in]; rich purple fls, white-lipped in var *procera*).

Ornamental onions

Allium spp; often classed in Liliaceae, sometimes in Alliaceae. Decorative relatives of well-known culinary plants, with small flowers in umbels (often large & globular; good for cutting fresh or dried) on leafless stems. Leaves generally narrow to strap-shaped; smell of onions if crushed. Larger types for beds & borders (excellent between shrubs), containers, etc; smaller for edging, rock gardens. May self-seed. **Cultivation**: Generally easy in any well-drained (even poor) soil in sun or partial shade; plant 10–15cm (4–6in) deep, autumn. Support tall spp. Divide large clumps after flowering. Very hardy unless stated. **Propagation**: Offsets; aerial bulbils; seed (may need stratifying).

A. aflatunense: to 0.75–1.2×0.3m (2½–4×1ft); 8–10cm (3–4in) globular infls of star-shaped pinkish-purple fls, late spring.

A. albopilosum **1** (Persian onion; correctly, *A. christophii*): to 45–90×15cm (18–36×6in); lvs hairy beneath; 15–25cm (6–10in) open globular infls of star-shaped silvery-lilac fls, early summer; seed-heads v good for drying.

A. beesianum: to 30–45×15cm (12–18×6in); grassy lvs; 5cm (2in) loose, rounded, nodding infls of bright blue or purple bell fls, mid summer.

A. caeruleum **2** (*A. azureum*): to 45–60×15cm (18–24×6in); 5–8cm (2–3in) rounded infls of deep sky-blue fls, early–mid summer.

A. cernuum (nodding onion, wild onion of N America): ultra-hardy; to 30–45×20cm (12–18×8in); drooping loose infls of rosy-purple to white bell fls, mid summer; bulbs edible.

A. cyaneum: to 15–25×15cm (6–10×6in); grassy lvs; 5cm (2in) sparse infls of intense cobalt-blue nodding fls, mid summer.

A. flavum: ultra-hardy but likes hot sun; to 20–30×15cm (8–12×6in) or taller; grass-like lvs; 4–5cm (1½–2in) loose rounded infls of golden-yellow urn-shaped fls, mid summer.

A. giganteum **3**: to 1–1.5×0.3m (3–5×1ft); 10–15cm (4–6in) dense globular infls of star-shaped bright rosy-lilac fls, early–mid summer.

A. karataviense **4**: to 20–40×20cm (8–16×8in); attractive broad glaucous lvs; globular infls 10cm (4in) or more wide of dull pink to greyish-white starry fls, late spring.

A. moly **5** (golden garlic): ultra-hardy if summers hot; to 30–45×20cm (12–18×8in); 5–8cm (2–3in) clusters of golden-yellow starry fls, late spring/early summer. Invasive.

A. narcissiflorum (*N. pedemontanum*): moderately to v hardy; to 15–25×25cm (6–10×10in); sparse infls of bell-shaped pink to wine-red erect fls, early summer; needs warm position & protection from winter wet.

A. neapolitanum* **6** (sometimes called daffodil garlic): moderately hardy; to 30–45×10cm (12–18×4in); loose infls of white fls, late spring. Usual var sold is 'Grandiflorum'.

A. ostrowskianum **7** (*A. oreophilum ostrowskianum*): ultra-hardy if summers hot; to 20–30×10cm (8–12×4in); 5cm (2in) rounded infls of pink to carmine starry fls, early summer. Var 'Zwanenburg' has richest colour.

A. pulchellum **8**: to 30–60×20cm (12–24×8in); lvs v narrow; graceful loose infls of small reddish-violet fls, mid summer. 'Album' is beautiful white var.

A. rosenbachianum: to 60–90×25cm (24–36×10in); 10–15cm (4–6in) dense globular infls of deep violet-purple star-shaped fls, late spring or early summer.

A. roseum **9**: to 30–45×15cm (12–18×6in); 8–10cm (3–4in) loose globular infls of bright pink star-shaped fls, early summer. Needs warm, sunny position.

A. schubertii: moderately hardy; to 30–60×20cm (12–24×8in); 10–15cm (4–6in) spherical spiky infls of pale rose-pink starry fls, early summer; distinctive seed-heads. For warm, sheltered spot.

A. senescens: ultra-hardy; to 15–30×15cm (6–12×6in) or more; lvs generally wavy or twisted, greyish to glaucous-green; 5cm (2in) spherical infls of pale rose-pink to purplish fls, late summer.

A. siculum (correctly, *Nectaroscordum siculum*): moderately hardy; to 0.6–1.2×0.3m (2–4×1ft); narrow lance-shaped lvs (v strong-smelling if bruised); 8–10cm (3–4in) loose infls of drooping bell-shaped fls, greenish marked purple, late spring or early summer. Spreading.

A. sphaerocephalum: to 60×20cm (24×8in); narrow grass-like lvs; dense egg-shaped infls 2.5cm (1in) wide of wine-purple fls, mid summer.

A. triquetrum* **10**: moderately hardy; to 30–45×15cm (12–18×6in); narrow v strong-smelling lvs; 5cm (2in) wide loose infls of drooping bell-shaped white or greenish fls, late spring. Invasive; best in woodland.

A. tuberosum* (Chinese chives): to 50×25cm (20×10in); flattish infls of white fls, dark eye, late summer. *A. ramosum* is similar.

A. unifolium: moderately hardy; to 60×25cm (24×10in); loose spherical infls of rose-pink fls, early summer. For well-drained sunny site.

A. ursinum (ramsons): to 45×20cm (18×8in); lvs to 5cm (2in) wide, strong-smelling from distance; profuse but sparse flattish infls of snowy-white fls, spring. For woodland; can be weedy.

A. zebdanense (incorrectly, *A. zebadense*): moderately hardy; to 30–50×15cm (12–20×6in); 5cm (2in) infls of largish white bell-shaped fls, late spring.

Wild daffodils and narcissi

Species, natural varieties & wild hybrids of *Narcissus* (Div 10 of official classification [see pp368–370] but nomenclature somewhat confused). Mainly dwarf, small-flowered spring-flowering (some very early) forebears of garden vars, in similar range of flower shapes plus others; unless stated, 1 flower per stem; good for cutting. Leaves narrow to cylindrical. Ideal for rock garden pockets, pots & containers, or naturalizing in short grass (most increase prolifically in good soil); like sun or dappled shade.
Cultivation: As for large-flowered garden vars (p368), but plant 8–10cm (3–4in) deep & about same distance apart; need very good drainage. Lift & divide when clumps very big. Except where stated, very hardy. **Propagation**: Offsets; seed.

N. asturiensis **1** (often sold as *N. minimus*): smallest trumpet daffodil; to 8–15cm (3–5in); fls golden-yellow, 2.5cm (1in) long, late winter.
N. bulbocodium (hoop-petticoat daffodil): fl stems to 15cm (6in); lvs longer, rush-like; fls yellow, with conical 2.5cm (1in) trumpet & v narrow petals, from late winter. Vars: *citrinus* (*vulgaris citrinus*; lemon-yellow large fls, late); *conspicuus* **2** (*vulgaris conspicuus*; deep yellow large fls, late); *nivalis* (small; pale yellow); *obesus* (deep yellow fls 1cm [½in] across); *romieuxii* ; sulphur-yellow to primrose; v early); *tenuifolius* (*N. tenuifolius*; v early & dwarf; golden).
N. canaliculatus ** **3**: probably a dwarf form of *N. tazetta*; to 15cm (6in); erect blue-green lvs; white reflexing fls, globular golden cup, mid spring (3–4 or more per stem). For sunny position.
N. cantabricus: often listed as *N. bulbocodium monophyllus* & v similar; to 8–10cm (3–4in); fls white, v early. Best under cold glass.
N. cyclamineus **4** (cyclamen-flowered narcissus): to 15–20cm (6–8in); golden drooping fls to 5cm (2in) long, v early spring, with v narrow trumpet & back-swept petals. Best in moist light shade. Vars: see p370 (Div 6).
N.×gracilis **: hybrid of *N. jonquilla* & *N. poeticus* or *N. tazetta*: to 30–40cm (12–16in); pale yellow fls 4–5cm (1½–2in) across with short cup, late spring.
N. jonquilla ** **5** (jonquil): to 30cm (1ft); clusters of 2–6 deep yellow fls 3–4cm (1¼–1½in) wide, small cup, mid spring. Var *flore-pleno* (Queen Anne's double jonquil; may be a form of *N. minor*) is double. Other vars: see p370 (Div 7).
N. juncifolius ** (rush-leaved jonquil): to 15cm (6in); rush-like lvs; clusters of 2–5 bright yellow fls 2cm (¾in) across, small cup, mid spring.
N. lobularis **6** (form of *N. obvallaris* [*N. pseudonarcissus obvallaris*] but listed separately in catalogues): to 10–15cm (4–6in); small pale yellow fls, darker narrow trumpet, late winter.
N. minor: to 15–20cm (6–8in); yellow fls to 3.5cm (1⅜in) long, petals paler & twisted, early spring. Var *minimus* (true *N. minimus*) is dwarfer.
N. nanus: to 10–15cm (4–6in); similar to *N. minor* but stiffer & more erect; fls paler & broader.
N. obvallaris **7** (Tenby daffodil; correctly, *N. pseudonarcissus obvallaris*): to 30cm (12in); bright golden trumpet fls, 4–5cm (1½–2in) long,

late winter or early spring.
N.×odorus ** (*N. campernellii*, campernelle jonquil): hybrid of *N. jonquilla* & *N. pseudonarcissus*: to 30–40cm (12–16in); clusters of 2–4 bright yellow fls to 6cm (2½in) across, bell-shaped cup, mid spring. Var *campernellii plenus* (Queen Anne's Irish campernelle) is double.
N. poeticus ** **8** (poet's or pheasant's-eye narcissus): to 40–45cm (16–18in); white fls 5–8cm (2–3in) across, v short yellow cup edged red, late spring. Var *recurvus* ('Old Pheasant's Eye') has swept-back petals. Other vars: see p370 (Div 9).
N. pseudonarcissus (wild daffodil, Lent lily): variable sp incorporating several forms grown in gardens under other names; to 15–30cm (6–12in); yellow trumpet fls 5–6cm (2–2½in) long, petals generally paler than trumpet, early spring. Var *moschatus* is 15cm (6in) tall & has nodding white fls. Other vars: see *N. lobularis* & *N. obvallaris* (above); also p368 (Div 1).
N. rupicola ** (*N. juncifolius rupicola*): to 8–12cm (3–5in); similar to *N. juncifolius* but smaller; rush-lvd; fls late spring.
N. scaberulus: to 8–12cm (3–5in); rush-lvd; deep orange-yellow fls less than 2.5cm (1in) across with narrow trumpet 2.5cm (1in) long, early spring. Needs v good drainage but moisture when flg.
N. tazetta ** (bunch-flowered or polyanthus narcissus): semi- to moderately hardy; to 30–45cm (12–18in); clusters of 4–8 white fls 2.5–5cm (1–2in) across, almost flat with v shallow pale yellow cup, winter. Var *papyraceus* ('Paper White') is best known; all white; earliest-flg narcissus, best in bowls indoors. Other vars: see p370 (Div 8); see also *N. canaliculatus* (above).
N. triandrus (angel's-tears narcissus): to 20cm (8in); lvs longer; clusters of up to 6 pendulous white to yellow fls with 2cm (¾in) globular cup & swept-back petals, early spring. Typical var is *albus* **9** (*triandrus*; to 8–10cm [3–4in]; creamy-white). Other vars: *concolor* * (to 15cm [6in]; pale yellow); see also p370 (Div 5).
N. watieri **10**: to 12cm (5in); rush-lvd; white fls (sometimes flushed pink), 2.5cm (1in) wide with cup 1cm (½in) long, greenish-yellow. Needs moist but well-drained soil.

Other dwarf plants of the amaryllis family

Generally less than 30cm (1ft) tall, with small flowers. For rock gardens, front of borders, underplanting trees & shrubs, etc. **Cultivation**: See below. **Propagation**: Offsets; seed. For dwarf ornamental onions (*Allium* spp), see p362; for dwarf daffodils (*Narcissus* spp), see p364, for blood lilies (*Haemanthus* spp), many of which are rather small, see p372.

Chlidanthus perfumed fairy lily, delicate lily, *Chlidanthus fragrans** **1**): moderately hardy S American large-fld dwarf bulb for sunny rock gardens, etc; to 25–30×15–20cm (10–12×6–8in); strap-shaped lvs; lily-like bright yellow fls 8cm (3in) long in clusters, early summer. Plant 10cm (4in) deep in well-drained soil, spring; protect or lift in winter.

Snowdrops (fair maids of February, *Galanthus* spp): v to ultra-hardy mainly winter- or early spring-flg plants ideal in grass or under deciduous trees; all rather similar, with strap-shaped, generally glaucous lvs & 2–3cm (¾–1¼in) solitary nodding white bell fls, short inner petals all or part green; good for cutting. Like partial shade & moist, rich soil; best planted (10cm [4in] deep, 5–15cm [2–6in] apart) in spring when growing; do not let bulbs dry out.
G. byzantinus: to 25cm (10in); fls mid winter to early spring.
G. caucasicus **2**: ultra-hardy; to 15cm (6in); rounded fls from mid winter.
G. elwesii (giant snowdrop): to 25cm (10in); large fls from late winter.
G. ikariae latifolius: to 15cm (6in); bright green lvs; large fls, mid spring.
G. nivalis (common snowdrop): ultra-hardy; to 20cm (8in); fls from mid-winter. Vars: 'Atkinsii' **3** (large fls, v early); 'Flore Pleno' (double); *reginae-olgae* (fls autumn, before lvs, likes open position); 'Sam Arnott'* (to 25cm [10in]); 'Straffan' (fls mid spring); 'Viridi-apice' ('Viridapicis'; petal tips marked green).
G. plicatus (Crimean snowdrop): to 25cm (10in); similar to *G. byzantinus*, but single green mark at tip of inner petals.

Ipheion (spring star-flower, *Ipheion uniflorum** **4**;often listed as *Brodiaea* or *Triteleia* [sometimes *Leucocoryne, Milla*] *uniflora*; sometimes classed in Liliaceae): easy v hardy spring-flg bulb for well-drained soil in sun or partial shade; to 20×5cm (8×2in); grass-like onion-smelling lvs; profuse 4cm (1½in) wide starry fls, white to violet-blue. Vars: 'Caeruleum' (pale blue); 'Wisley Blue' (violet-blue). Plant 10cm (4in) deep, autumn.

Snowflakes (*Leucojum* spp): v hardy plants with nodding white & green fls like snowdrops (*Galanthus* spp) but more rounded, with petals all same length; good for cutting. Generally plant 8–10cm (3–4in) deep in moist soil in sun or partial shade, autumn.
L. aestivum **5** (summer or giant snowflake,

Loddon lily): to 45–60×15cm (18–24×6in); strap-shaped lvs; umbels of 2–2.5cm (¾–1in) fls, late spring. Var 'Gravetye Giant' is robust, with large fls.
L. autumnale **6** (autumn snowflake): to 25×8cm (10×3in); grass-like lvs; 1cm (½in) pink-flushed fls, late summer to autumn. Plant 5cm (2in) deep in well-drained soil, early spring.
L. vernum (spring snowflake): to 20×10cm (10×4in); strap-shaped lvs; 2cm (¾in) fls, late winter or early spring, yellow-marked in var *carpathicum* **7**.

Sternbergias (*Sternbergia* spp): moderately to v hardy bulbs with strap-shaped lvs & crocus-like fls; for v well-drained soil in full sun; plant 10–15cm (4–6in) deep, mid–late summer.
S. clusiana **8** (*S. macrantha*): to 15×15cm (6×6in); golden-yellow fls to 8cm (3in) long, late summer to autumn (after lvs die down).
S. fischerana: to 15×10cm (6×4in); canary-yellow 4cm (1½in) fls, spring (with lvs).
S. (*Amaryllis*) *lutea* **9** (*S. aurantiaca*, autumn or winter daffodil; may be biblical lily of the field): to 15×10cm (6×4in); rich golden-yellow 4–5cm (1½–2in) fls, early autumn (with or before lvs).

Zephyr lilies (flowers of the west wind, rain lilies, *Zephyranthes* spp): mainly summer/autumn-flg bulbs for warm sunny positions; grass-like lvs; rather crocus-like trumpet-shaped fls usually opening starry. Plant 10cm (4in) deep & apart in moist but well-drained soil, spring. Mulch in winter where hardy; otherwise lift & overwinter frost-free in damp peat. Semi-hardy spp best under glass except where summers v warm.
Z. (*Amaryllis*) *atamasco*: moderately hardy; to 20–30cm (8–12in); fls to 10cm (4in) wide, white or pink-tinged, spring.
Z. (*Amaryllis*) *candida* **10**: best-known sp in UK; moderately hardy; to 10–20cm (4–8in); white, sometimes pink-tinged fls 4cm (1½in) across, early autumn.
Z. drummondii* (*Cooperaria pedunculata*): semi-to moderately hardy; to 20cm (8in); lvs glaucous; fls to 4cm (1½in) wide, white tinged red outside, opening at night, summer. *Z. brazosensis** (*C. drummondii*) is similar; to 25cm (10in).
Z. grandiflora (*Z. carinata*): semi-hardy; to 30cm (12in); fls bright pink, 5cm (2in) wide, summer.
Z. rosea **11** is similar, but fls smaller.
Z. robusta (*Habranthus robustus*): semi-hardy; to 20cm (8in); fls rose-red, to 8cm (3in) wide, summer (before lvs).

Garden daffodils and narcissi

Narcissus hybrids, mostly of complex parentage, generally taller & with showier flowers than wild relatives (p364); among favourite spring flowers. Leaves generally strap-shaped & greyish-green, from ground. Flowers have inner trumpet/cup-shaped corona (crown) surrounded by perianth ("petals"); mainly yellow, white &/or orange, some partly red or pink; one flower per stem unless stated; all good for cutting. (Unless stated, colour descriptions below refer to petals.) Season normally spans spring (earlier in very mild areas, shorter in continental climates). Used for spring bedding, naturalizing in grass or borders, containers, etc; most vars good for gentle forcing in bowls & pots. Bulbs poisonous.
Cultivation: Unless stated, very to ultra-hardy. For any (preferably rich) well-drained soil in sun or partial shade. Plant 10–15cm (4–6in) deep (to 20cm [8in] in permanent borders), 10–25cm (4–10in) apart according to usage, late summer/early autumn. Dead-head; foliar-feed. Do not cut/tie leaves until dead.
Pests & diseases: Eelworms; narcissus fly grubs; basal rot. **Propagation**: Offsets; divide crowded clumps mid summer. **Classification**: By flower form & origin in 12 divisions including wild spp (Div 10; p364) & miscellaneous (Div 12); sometimes (not now officially) subdivided by colour or cup size. Some 15,000–20,000 registered vars; selection listed below.

Trumpet daffodils (Div 1): generally to 35–45cm (14–18in); fls have large trumpet at least as long as petals; early/mid season.
All-yellow vars (formerly Div 1a; petals & trumpet all golden-yellow): 'Arctic Gold'; 'Dutch Master' **1** (v large fls); 'Golden Harvest'; 'Unsurpassable' (v large fls); 'Youth' (to 30cm [1ft]).
Bicoloured vars (Div 1b; cream to white, trumpet darker): 'Foresight' (trumpet lemon-yellow); 'Goblet' (to 30cm [1ft]; trumpet yellow); 'Magnet' **2** (trumpet bright yellow); 'Queen of Bicolours' (trumpet canary-yellow).
All-white vars (Div 1c): 'Beersheba' (large fls, narrow trumpet); 'Cantatrice' (narrow trumpet); 'Mrs E. H. Krelage' (opens creamy-white); 'Mount Hood' **3** (trumpet opens creamy-yellow); 'W. P. Milner' (to 20cm [8in]; yellowish).
Reversed bicoloured vars (Div 1d; trumpet paler than petals): 'Rushlight' (lemon-yellow shading to white); 'Spellbinder' **4** (greenish-yellow, trumpet becoming white).
Large-cupped narcissi (Div 2): generally to 40–50cm (16–20in); corona over ⅓ but less than ½ petal length; unless stated wide & cup-shaped (often ruffled); early/mid season.
All-yellow vars (Div 2a): 'Carlton' (soft yellow); 'Galway' **5**; 'Hyperion' (sulphur-yellow, cup yellow shaded pale orange); 'St Keverne' (narrow trumpet); 'Spectacular' (creamy-yellow, cup orange-yellow); 'Yellow Sun'.
Yellow vars, orange to red cup (Div 2a): 'Confuoco' (cup scarlet); 'Fortune' **6** (cup coppery orange-red); 'Home Fires' (cup orange); 'Red Rascal' (cup orange-red); 'Scarlet O'Hara' (cup scarlet).
White vars, yellow cup (Div 2b): 'Amor' (cup canary-yellow edged orange-yellow, greenish eye); 'Brunswick' (cup primrose-yellow); 'Duke of Windsor' (cup orange-yellow); 'Green Island' **7** (cup greenish-yellow & greenish-white); 'Pontresina' (cup primrose-yellow); 'Rococo' (cup apricot to yellow, centre ivory); 'Tudor Minstrel' (large fls; cup ochre).

White vars, orange to red cup (Div 2b): 'Flower Record' **8** (cup yellowish-orange, darker edge); 'Orange Monarch' (cup diffused orange & yellow); 'Professor Einstein' (orange flat cup); 'Royal Orange' (large fls; brilliant orange flat cup); 'Sempre Avanti' (creamy, cup orange).
White vars, pink cup/trumpet (Div 2b; best in sun): 'Blaris' (cup coral-pink); 'Louise de Coligny'** (trumpet apricot-pink); 'Mrs R. O. Backhouse' (narrow apricot & shell-pink trumpet); 'Roseworthy' (cup rose-pink); 'Salmon Trout' **9** (large salmon-pink trumpet).
All-white vars (Div 2c): 'Easter Moon' (green eye); 'Ice Follies' (cup opens lemon-yellow); 'Pigeon' (latish); 'Snowshill'** (trumpet opens lemon-yellow).
Reversed bicoloured var (Div 2d; petals darker than corona): 'Binkie' (sulphur-yellow shading to white).
Small-cupped narcissi (Div 3): generally to 35–45cm (14–18in); cup less than ⅓ length of petals; mid season.
Yellow-petalled vars (Div 3a): 'Birma' (sulphur-yellow, cup orange-scarlet); 'Edward Buxton' (pale yellow, cup orange edged darker).
White-petalled vars with coloured cup (Div 3b): 'Barrett Browning' **10** (cup orange); 'Clockface' (cup yellow edged orange); 'La Riante' (cup deep orange-red); 'Verger' (cup orange-red).
All-white vars (Div 3c): 'Polar Ice'; 'Verona'.
Double narcissi (Div 4): generally to 35–45cm (14–18in); double fls; generally mid season. Vars (those marked † sometimes listed in Div 8 – moderately hardy & best indoors): *albus plenus odoratus*** (double white Poeticus narcissus; pure white; late); 'Bridal Crown'** (multi-fld; white tinged lemon-yellow); 'Cheerfulness'**† **11** (multi-fld; creamy-white); 'Erlicheer'** (to 20cm [8in]; multi-fld; ivory & primrose-yellow); 'Flower Drift' (semi-double sport of 'Flower Record' [Div 2]; creamy-white, orange centre); 'Yellow Cheerfulness'**† (golden-yellow form of 'Cheerfulness'); 'Golden Ducat' (sport of 'King

Alfred' [Div 1]; large golden-yellow fls); 'Irene
Copeland' (creamy-white & apricot-yellow);
'Mary Copeland' (white & orange); 'Sir Winston
Churchill'**† (sport of 'Geranium' [Div 8]; multi-
fld; yellow & orange-yellow); 'Texas' (tall; large
yellow & orange fls); 'Van Sion' **1** ('Telamonius
Plenus'; yellow; v early); 'White Lion' (white &
soft yellow).
Triandrus narcissi (Div 5): derived from
N. triandrus (p364); generally to 25–30cm (10–
12in); drooping fls with silky back-swept twisted
petals; usually multi-fld; mid/late season.
Long-cupped vars (Div 5a, cup at least ⅔ petal
length): 'Liberty Bells' (soft yellow); 'Thalia' (tall;
white); 'Tresamble' **2** (white, base tinged cream).
Short-cupped vars (Div 5b; cup less than ⅔ petal
length); 'April Tears' (dwarf; deep yellow);
'Hawera' (dwarf; lemon-yellow).
Cyclamineus narcissi (cyclamen-flowered
narcissi; Div 6); derived from *N. cyclamineus*
(p364); generally to 20–25cm (8–10in); lvs
narrow, bright green; drooping fls with back-
swept petals and usually long narrow trumpet;
early. Vars: 'February Gold' **3** (golden-yellow);
'February Silver' (white); 'Jack Snipe' (creamy-
white, trumpet golden-yellow); 'March Sunshine'
(canary-yellow, trumpet golden); 'Peeping Tom'
(to 35cm [14in]; golden-yellow, trumpet slightly
darker); 'Tete-a-Tete' (multi-fld; buttercup-gold).
Var 'Beryl'* is hybrid with a Poeticus var & has
short, globular orange cup; petals primrose.
Jonquils (Jonquilla narcissi; Div 7): derived from
N. jonquilla (p364); to 30–45cm (12–18in); dark
green rush-like lvs; scented fls with broad petals
& shallow cup; usually multi-fld; mid season.

Vars: 'Golden Sceptre'** (golden-yellow; v deep
cup); 'Suzy'** (bright yellow, rich orange cup);
'Sweetness'** (creamy-yellow, darker cup);
'Trevithian'** **4** (lemon-yellow).
Tazetta & Poetaz narcissi (polyanthus narcissi;
Div 8): derived from *N. tazetta* (with *N. poeticus*
in Poetaz vars); vigorous & erect, to 45cm (18in);
small scented fls with petals often crinkled &
v short cup; multi-fld; early/mid season.
Tazetta vars (semi- to moderately hardy): 'Paper
White'** (semi-hardy & v early; best indoors;
white); 'Grand Soleil d'Or'** (early; yellow,
orange cup).
Poetaz vars (moderately hardy): 'Cragford'**
(v early; white, orange cup); 'Geranium'** **5**
(white, orange-red cup); 'Scarlet Gem'
(primrose-yellow, orange-red cup); 'Silver
Chimes' (white, creamy-lemon cup). See double
vars in Div 4.
Poeticus narcissi (poet's narcissi; Div 9):
derived from *N. poeticus* solely; to 35–45cm
(14–18in); flat, lax lvs; scented fls, usually
solitary, with white petals & small flat red-edged
cup; mid/late season. Vars: 'Actaea'** (yellow
cup); 'Cantabile'** (green cup); 'Old Pheasant's
Eye'** (*N. poeticus recurvus*; see p364). See
also Div 4.
Split-corona narcissi (Butterfly, Collar, Papillon
or Split-cup vars; Div 11): to 35–45cm (14–18in);
fls have corona split at least ⅓ of length into
separate petals, usually flat. Vars: 'Baccarat'
(lemon-yellow); 'Canasta' (white, yellow corona);
'Gold Collar' (yellow); 'Papillon Blanc' (white);
'Parisienne' **6** (white, orange corona).

Other taller plants of the amaryllis family

Mostly rather tender and at least 30cm (1ft) tall, with umbels of generally large, rather lily-like flowers on
leafless stems; good for cutting. Leaves generally strap-shaped, growing from ground or neck of bulb.
For sheltered beds & borders, containers, etc. **Cultivation**: Generally for rich, fertile but well-drained
deep soil in a warm, sunny site; protect in winter with glass or thick mulch, or lift smaller dormant bulbs;
keep dryish when dormant. Or grow in tubs or pots & keep under cover in winter. Unless stated, plant in
spring. **Propagation**: Offsets; seed; *Agapanthus* & *Clivia* spp by division.

Agapanthus (African blue lilies, *Agapanthus*
spp; mistakenly, lilies of the Nile; often classed in
Liliaceae, sometimes in Alliaceae): S African
tuberous plants with lvs to 60cm (2ft) long &
rounded infls 15–30cm (6–12in) across of 10–30
or more deep blue to white funnel-shaped fls, late
summer & early autumn, on long stems. Plant
10cm (4in) deep, more if winters cold.
A. africanus (*A. umbellatus*): semi-hardy; to
60–90×45cm (2–3×1½ft); evergreen in mild
climates; fls violet-blue.
A. campanulatus (sometimes incorrectly listed as
A. umbellatus mooreanus): moderately hardy; to
0.6–1.2×0.45m (2–4×1½ft); deciduous; soft

blue fls in rather flat infls. Vars: 'Isis' **7** (deep
blue); *patens* (*A. patens*; fls wide open).
A. inapertus (sometimes listed as *A. weilligii*):
moderately hardy; to 1–1.2×0.6m (2–4×2ft);
deciduous; pendulous blue fls on stiff stems.
A. orientalis (*A. praecox*, *A. praecox orientalis*;
often sold as *A. umbellatus*): commonest sp;
semi-hardy; to 1.2×0.6m (4×2ft); evergreen;
large spherical heads of white to deep blue fls.
Vars (some often listed incorrectly under
A. africanus or *A. campanulatus*; generally
moderately hardy): 'Albus' (white); *flore pleno*
(double); 'Mooreanus' (dwarf, to 45cm [1½ft]);
'Snowball' **8**, (white).

A. hybrids (of various spp above): generally moderately hardy. Vars: 'Blue Giant' (to 1.1m [3½ft]; rich blue); 'Bressingham Blue' (to 90cm [3ft]; deep amethyst-blue); 'Headbourne Hybrids' **9**, p371 (moderately to v hardy seed strain; to 60–90cm [2–3ft]; shades of blue).

Belladonna lily (*Amaryllis belladonna*** **10**, p371); semi- to moderately hardy S African bulb; to 60×30cm (2×1ft); lvs die down mid summer; infls of 6–12 trumpet-shaped pink fls to 12cm (5in) wide, from late summer. Bulb poisonous. Vars: 'Hathor' (white, ivory throat); 'Parkeri' (correctly, × *Amarygia parkeri*; vigorous & free-flg; deep pink, yellow throat). Plant shallowly in frost-free areas, 15–20cm (6–8in) deep elsewhere.

Coral drops (*Bessera elegans*; often classed in Liliaceae or Alliaceae): semi- to moderately hardy Mexican corm; to 60–90×20cm (24–36×8in); sparse narrow lvs; loose infls of 10–20 white-marked orange-red bell fls 2.5cm (1in) across with white centre & prominent purple stamens, all summer. Plant 10cm (4in) deep.

Brodiaeas (*Brodiaea* spp; some spp now correctly *Dichelostemma* or *Triteleia*; often classed in Liliaceae or Alliaceae): generally moderately to v hardy N American corms rather like onions (*Allium* spp p362) with grass-like lvs & umbels of starry to tubular fls, generally 3–4cm (1¼–1½in) long/wide, on slender stems, spring & summer. Plant 10–15cm (4–6in) deep, 5–15cm (2–6in) apart, in full sun. Unless stated, plant autumn except where winters v cold.

B. bridgesii (correctly, *T. bridgesii*): to 45cm (1½ft); tufted; 10cm (4in) infls of 12–20 funnel-shaped lilac or blue fls, opening starry, early summer. Plant spring or autumn.

B. californica: to 60cm (2ft); loose infls of 12–20 tubular lilac to violet fls, early summer. Plant spring or autumn.

B. coronaria (*B. grandiflora*, *Hookera coronaria*): to 30–45cm (1–1½ft); infls of 3–12 violet-blue starry fls from late spring.

B. elegans (incorrectly, *B. coronaria*, *B. grandiflora*): to 40cm (16in); reflexing violet to purple fls from late spring.

B. hyacinthina **1** (*B. lactea*; in US, wild hyacinth; correctly, *T. hyacinthina*): to 45cm (1½ft); infls of 20–30 white or purplish fls, early summer.

B. ida-maia **2** (*B. coccinea*, firecracker flower; correctly, *D. ida-maia*): to 45–60cm (1½–2ft); tufted; infls of up to 20 drooping crimson tubular fls tipped with greenish petals, early summer. Needs v warm position; plant spring or autumn.

B. ixioides (pretty-face, golden brodiaea; correctly, *T. ixioides*): to 30–60cm (1–2ft); infls of 10–20 starry golden-yellow fls, early spring.

B. laxa **3** (grass nut; correctly *T. laxa*): to 60cm (2ft); large infls of 30–50 violet-mauve funnel-shaped fls from spring. Var 'Queen Fabiola' is

deep violet.

B. pulchella (*B. capitata*; in US, blue-dicks, wild hyacinth; correctly *D. pulchellum*): to 45cm (1½ft); large infls of small violet fls, spring. Plant spring or autumn.

B. × *tubergenii* **4** (correctly, *T.* 'Tubergenii'): hybrid of *B.* (*T.*) *laxa* & *B.* (*T.*) *peduncularis*; to 45cm (1½ft); vigorous; open 10cm (4in) infls of blue-violet fls, late spring.

Kaffir lilies (*Clivia* spp): tender S African spring- or early summer-flg evergreen plants with fleshy bulb-like roots, & usually grown in pots or tubs, under glass except in frost-free areas. Lvs to 60cm (2ft) long, in 2 rows; fls in large infls on stout stem. For semi-shade; plant shallowly.

C. miniata **5**: to 45cm (1½ft); fls erect, trumpet-shaped, 8cm (3in) long or more, scarlet, yellow throat. Plant autumn.

C. nobilis: to 30cm (1ft); drooping narrow fls, red & yellow tipped green. Plant autumn.

Crinodonna (× *Crinodonna corsii** **6**, × *Amarcrinum howardii*; correctly, × *A. memoria-corsii*): moderately hardy intergeneric hybrid of *Amaryllis belladonna* & *Crinum moorei*; to 1–1.2m (3–4ft); habit similar to crinum but amaryllis-like clear pink trumpet fls, late summer or early autumn. Grow like amaryllis.

Crinums (*Crinum* spp): generally semi- to moderately hardy bulbs with untidy evergreen lvs to 90cm (3ft) long & v large infls of trumpet-shaped fls, 8–10cm (3–4in) long, summer & early autumn. Plant shallowly.

C. americanum** (in US, southern swamp crinum): semi-hardy; to 45–60×30–45cm (1½–2×1–1½ft); lvs narrow; fls white, early.

C. asiaticum**: to 1.5×1m (5×3ft); fls greenish-white, drooping. Bulb poisonous.

C. bulbispermum** (*C. longifolium*; incorrectly, *C. capense*): moderately hardy; to 0.6–1.2×0.6m (2–4×2ft); fls white, flushed pink outside.

C. moorei**: to 1.2×1m (4×3ft); lvs broad; fls rose-pink (white in var 'Album' **7** ['Schmidtii']).

C. × *powellii*** **8**: hybrid of *C. bulbispermum* & *C. moorei*; moderately hardy; to 1.2×1m (4×3ft); frfee-flg; fls reddish-pink to white.

Blood lilies (*Haemanthus* spp): tender to semi-hardy low-growing S African bulbs with dense umbels of v small fls with prominent stamens, summer; lvs oblong to lance-shaped, generally deciduous & 20–30cm (8–12in) long. Best in pots except in v warm climates; plant shallowly.

H. albiflos: to 30cm (1ft); evergreen; 5cm (2in) brush-like infls of white fls, white bracts.

H. coccineus **9**: to 25cm (10in); lvs to 60cm (2ft) long; 8cm (3in) brush-like infls of red fls, bright red bracts.

H. katharinae (blood flower): to 30cm (1ft); 15cm (6in) round infls of salmon-red fls.

H. multiflorus **10**: to 45cm (1½ft); 15cm (6in) round infls of blood-red fls.

Spider lilies (*Hymenocallis* spp; sometimes confused with *Pancratium* spp): semi- to moderately hardy bulbs whose fls have central trumpet & long narrow reflexing outer petals, summer; lvs arching, to 60cm (2ft) long. Plant 15cm (6in) deep, 25cm (10in) apart.

H.×festalis**: hybrid of *H. longipetala* & *H. narcissiflora*; to 45cm (1½ft); white fls to 12cm (5in) wide.

H. narcissiflora** **1** (*H. calathina*, *Ismene calathina*, basket flower, Peruvian daffodil): to 60cm (2ft); fls white, marked green (markings faint in var 'Advance'), to 15cm (6in) across.

Lycoris (*Lycoris* spp; sometimes called spider lilies; sometimes listed as *Amaryllis* spp); semi- to moderately hardy bulbs with funnel-shaped fls with wavy petals, late summer (after lvs die down). Plant shallowly 30cm (1ft) apart, mid summer.

L. (A.) aurea (golden spider lily): to 45cm (1½ft); fls golden-yellow, 8cm (3in) across.

L. (A.) radiata **2** (red spider lily): to 40cm (16in); orange-red 4cm (1½in) fls.

L. sanguinea: to 45cm (1½ft); 5cm (2in) red fls.

L. squamigera* **3** (*A. hallii*, resurrection lily, autumn amaryllis): v hardy if summers hot but considered moderately hardy in UK; to 60cm (2ft); large infls of 8cm (3in) rosy-lilac fls.

Nerines (*Nerine* spp): generally semi-hardy S African bulbs with trumpet-shaped bright red, pink or white fls with narrow petals (often waved/frilled) & prominent stamens, late summer to autumn; lvs in 2 ranks, after fls, die down in summer. Plant 10–15cm (4–6in) deep, early summer.

N. bowdenii **4**: moderately hardy; to 60×20cm (24×8in); large elegant infls of 8–12 pale pink fls 8cm (3in) across. Vars: 'Fenwick's Variety' (vigorous, with large deep pink fls); 'Pink Beauty' (deep pink); 'Pink Triumph' (silvery-pink).

N. flexuosa: to 60×20cm (24×8in); large infls of 12 or more 5cm (2in) pale pink fls (white in var 'Alba').

N. sarniensis **5** (Guernsey lily): to 45–60×20cm (18–24×8in); large infls of 12–18 vermilion to crimson 8cm (3in) fls.

N. undulata: to 45×15cm (18×6in); infls of 8–10 nodding 2cm (¾in) pink fls.

Sea lilies (*Pancratium* spp; sometimes confused with *Hymenocallis* spp): semi- to moderately hardy bulbs of Mediterranean coast with infls of starry white fls 8cm (3in) across with inner cup-shaped corona & narrow petals, late spring or early summer. Plant 15cm (6in) deep.

P. illyricum* **6**: to 30–45×25cm (12–18×10in); glaucous deciduous lvs; infls of 8–12 fls, green corona. Best outdoor sp; plant autumn.

P. maritimum** **7** (sea lily, sea daffodil): to 30–40×25cm (12–16×10in); semi-evergreen; infls of 4–8 pure white fls.

Jacobean lily (Aztec lily, *Sprekelia* [*Amaryllis*] *formosissima* **8**): semi-hardy Mexican bulb; to 30–45×20cm (12–18×8in); 30cm (1ft) lvs, after fls; striking solitary bright red trumpet-shaped fls 10cm (4in) across, upper petals more spreading, early summer. Plant 10–15cm (4–6in) deep, spring (autumn in warm areas).

Tulbaghias (*Tulbaghia* spp; sometimes called wild garlic; sometimes classed in Liliaceae): semi-hardy S African corms with narrow onion-scented evergreen lvs & globular infls of small lilac to violet fls, long season. For light sandy soil in sunny position; plant shallowly. Or for pots.

T. fragrans* (sweet garlic): to 30–45×20cm (12–18×8in); infls of up to 40 bright lilac funnel-shaped fls, autumn to spring.

T. violacea **9**: to 75×25cm (30×10in); infls of 10–20 pale purplish-lilac bell-shaped fls, spring to autumn.

Scarborough lily (*Vallota speciosa* **10**, *V.* [*Amaryllis*] *purpurea*): tender S African bulb best grown in pots, or for moist fertile soil in full sun in frost-free areas; needs moisture all year. To 60×30cm (2×1ft); bright, glossy evergreen lvs; infls of up to 10 funnel-shaped vermilion-red fls 8cm (3in) wide, summer & early autumn.

The aroid or arum family

Curious tuberous/rhizomatous plants, generally stemless, with large, lush, often spear-shaped leaves. Flower-like spathes surround fleshy spike (spadix) of insignificant true flowers (sometimes unpleasant-smelling), often followed by red or orange berries. **Cultivation**: Unless stated, moderately to very hardy and for moist but well-drained humus-rich soil in shady site. Plant tubers 10–15cm (4–6in) deep, rhizomes 5–8cm (2–3in) deep, autumn where hardy, otherwise spring. If grown in open ground lift tubers where not hardy & store cool & dryish over winter. **Propagation**: Division or offsets; seed.

Arisaemas (*Arisaema* spp): arum-like plants with divided or lobed lvs. Take sun if soil moist.

A. candidissimum **1** p377: to 30×45cm (1×1½ft); glossy trifoliate lvs; 8cm (3in) hooded white spathes veined green outside, throat striped pink, early summer (before lvs); orange frs.

A. consanguineum: moderately hardy; to 90×30cm (3×1ft); umbrella-like cut lvs; green spathes striped brown/purple inside, brown dangling spadix, late summer; red frs.

A. dracontium (green dragon): to 90×45cm (3×1½ft); lvs cut into many segments to 25cm

(10in) long; 8cm (3in) green spathes, projecting yellow spadix, late spring; orange-red frs.

A. sikokianum **2**: to 45×45cm (1½×1½ft); lvs deeply 3/5-lobed; 15cm (6in) white hooded spathes shaded & striped green & red-purple, white clubbed spadix, late spring (as lvs open).

A. speciosum (cobra lily): to 60–90×45cm (2–3×1½ft); 3-lobed rich green lvs edged brownish, on sturdy mottled stalks; deep maroon-purple 8–25cm (3–10in) hooded spathes striped green outside, late spring, creamy spadix with purple dangling tail to 60cm (2ft) long.

A. triphyllum **3** (*A. atrorubens*, N American Jack-in-the-pulpit); v hardy; to 30–60×30cm (1–2×1ft); 3-lobed 20cm (8in) lvs; broad 10–18cm (4–7in) hooded spathes, purplish-brown veined white inside, green tinted purplish outside, greenish-brown spadix, early summer; red frs.

Mouse plant (*Arisarum proboscideum*): rhizomatous, to 20×25cm (8×10in); spear-shaped 8–12cm (3–5in) lvs; small, partly hidden olive-green spathes, tail-like spadix to 15cm (6in) long, spring. Curiosity for shady rock garden.

Arums (*Arum* spp): generally sun-loving plants with spear-shaped lvs developing autumn or early winter; fl spring.

A. creticum **4**: to 45×30cm (1½×1ft); glossy 10–12cm (4–5in) lvs; clear yellow 18cm (7in) hooded spathes, darker yellow spadix.

A. italicum: to 45×30cm (1½×1ft); long-stalked veined lvs to 30cm (1ft) long, marbled grey in vars 'Marmoratum' **5** & 'Pictum' (narrower lvs, more heavily marbled); pale yellowish-green spathes to 30cm (1ft) long, often heavily marked purple, creamy spadix; conspicuous red frs.

A. pictum (*A. corsicum*): to 30×30cm (1×1ft); lvs to 25×8cm (10×3in); 18cm (7in) purple-black spathes & spadix.

Caladiums (angel's wings, *Caladium* ×*hortulanum* vars **6**; hybrids derived from & often listed under *C. bicolor*): tender bedding/pot plants grown for their delicate, beautifully marked & brightly coloured lvs. To 60×30cm (2×1ft); broadly spear-shaped long-stalked lvs to 30cm (1ft) long, sometimes wavy or crinkled, variegated (veined, mottled, spotted, blotched or marbled) in contrasting shades of dark green, yellow-green, crimson, scarlet, rose-pink &/or white (sometimes almost all white or red). For summer bedding in moist light shade; like at least 21°C (70°F) in daytime; best started under warm glass in spring, planted out early summer; lift before 1st hard frost. Sold as mixtures and numerous named vars.

Elephant's ear (Egyptian taro, *Colocasia esculenta antiquorum*): tender foliage plant, to 1.8×1.8m (6×6ft); bright green rounded spear-shaped lvs to 60×30cm (2×1ft), evergreen in warmest areas. For lush tropical effect; good in tub. Treat like *Caladium* sp but takes some sun.

Dragon plant (*Dracunculus vulgaris* **7**, *Arum dracunculus*): to 90×45cm (3×1½ft); fleshy mottled stems; deeply divided fan-shaped lvs to 20cm (8in) long; greenish spathes to 50cm (20in) long, purple-maroon inside, large purple-black spadix, strong putrid smell, early summer; scarlet frs. Likes sun.

Skunk cabbage (bog arum, *Lysichiton* [incorrectly, *Lysichitum*] *americanus*): sturdy rhizomatous moisture-lover, to 1.2×0.6m (4×2ft); paddle-shaped lvs to 1.2×0.3m (4×1ft), winged stalks; yellow 25cm (10in) spathes, greenish protruding spadix, unpleasant scent, spring (with emerging lvs). *L. camtschatcensis** is similar but all parts smaller; spathes white. For moist/wet soil or pool margin in sun or light shade.

Pinellia (*Pinellia ternata*): ultra-hardy; rhizomatous; to 15×15cm (6×6in); small lvs in segments; greenish-purple spathes, late summer.

Voodoo lily (monarch of the East, *Sauromatum guttatum* **8**, *S. venosum*, *Arum cornutum*): to 75×60cm (2½×2ft); deeply lobed handsome umbrella-like lvs to 45cm (1½ft) long on stout mottled stalks, after fls; narrow brownish spathe to 60cm (2ft) long, yellow blotched purple inside, long tail-like purple spadix, spring, unpleasant scent. For sheltered spot in full sun; lift tuber autumn & start in warmth early spring to ensure repeat-flg. Tuber will fl in warm spot without soil/water.

Zantedeschias (*Zantedeschia* spp; in UK, arum lilies; in US, calla lilies): rhizomatous S African plants with arrow-shaped rather leathery lvs & large funnel-shaped recurved spathes generally 12–15cm (5–6in) long, shortish spadix, late spring & early summer. Generally tender to semi-hardy; best grown in large pots (in sun or partial shade) & taken indoors in winter.

Z. aethiopica (common arum/calla lily): semi–moderately hardy; to 90×60cm (3×2ft); white spathes to 25cm (10in) long, spadix yellow. Thrives standing in water. Var 'Crowborough' is moderately hardy.

Z. albomaculata: to 60×45cm (2×1½ft); white-spotted lvs; spathes creamy-white, purple throat.

Z. elliottiana **9**: to 75×45cm (2½×1½ft); white-spotted lvs; spathes bright yellow.

Z. rehmanii: to 60×45cm (2×1½ft); spathes rosy-purple to white tinged pink.

Border dahlias

Dahlia hybrids, classed as *D.×cultorum*; sometimes listed under *D. variabilis* but in fact of complex parentage & derived mainly from *D. coccinea* & *D. pinnata* (*D. rosea, D. variabilis*). Tender tuberous perennials belonging to Helianthus tribe of the daisy family, with profuse single, semi-double or double flowers 5–30cm (2–12in) or more across of very varied form & colour, mid summer to 1st frosts; very good for cutting; largest flower sizes generally tallest. (As with all composites, "flowers" are actually compound flower-heads, "petals" are correctly ray florets. All colours except blue, including shades of white, yellow, bronze, red, pink, mauve & purple, including blends (combinations of 2 or more colours), bicolours (2 distinct colours) & multicolours. Leaves pinnate, with oval leaflets 10–15cm (4–6in) long, generally rich mid green (sometimes bronzed). Smaller vars good for bedding, mixed borders, containers, etc; taller types often grown separately, mainly for cutting, also good for summer screens or fillers between shrubs. **Cultivation**: For rich, well-drained but moist soil in sunny spot. Plant tubers 10–15cm (4–6in) deep, 60–90cm (2–3ft) apart according to height, mid–late spring after last hard frost. (Can be sprouted first under glass.) Stake all except smallest types. Pinch out leading shoot at 3–4 weeks. Keep well watered; mulch in dry weather. Disbud if for exhibition, not for general display & cutting; dead-head regularly. Cut down after 1st autumn frost blackens foliage, lift tubers, dry & store in damp peat, cool but frost-free, over winter. Divide before replanting. **Pests & diseases**: Aphids; borers; cutworms; viruses; fungal diseases. **Propagation**: Division, ensuring each tuber or clump of tubers has at least one strong eye; basal cuttings (taken from tubers brought into growth at 16°C [61°F] in late winter) rooted over warmth. **Classification**: By flower form (see below), subdivided in some groups by flower diameter into Miniature (up to 10cm [4in]), Small (10–15cm [4–6in]), Medium (15–20cm [6–8in]), Large (20–25cm [8–10in]) & Giant (over 25cm [10in]); size of named vars may vary with climate. Some 20,000 registered named vars. For bedding dahlias, botanically identical to border types but comprising seed strains of low-growing types grown as HHAs, see p494.

Single 1: to 45–75×45–60cm (1½–2½×1½–2ft); fls to 10cm (4in) wide (often much less), with single ring of petals around open central disc, generally profuse, with v long season if dead-headed. Need no support; v good for bedding, mixed borders. Includes most strains of seed-raised bedding dahlias. Wide colour range.

Anemone-flowered 2: generally to 0.6–1.1m (2–3½ft); fls to 10cm (4in) wide, with 1 or more rings of flat outer petals around pincushion-like disc of tubular petals (sometimes enlarged to give semi-double appearance). Good for bedding, mixed borders. Rather rare; includes pastel shades.

Collerette 3: to 0.75–1.2m (2½–4ft); fls to 10cm (4in) wide, with outer ring of broad flat petals around inner ring of shorter petals (collar) & central disc, the 2 rows of petals often in contrasting colours. V good for cutting (strong stems). Wide colour range.

Paeony-flowered 4: to 1m (3ft); fls to 10cm (4in) wide, with 2 or more rings of flattish petals, the central petals often small & curled, partly covering the disc. Not v popular in many countries, but sometimes used for bedding. Forerunners of Decorative vars.

Decorative 5: to 1–1.5m (3–5ft); fls range from Miniature to Giant, all fully double, with broad flat or flattish petals, generally blunt-tipped. Sub-divided in some countries into Formal Decorative (with petals arranged regularly) and Informal Decorative (with petals long, twisted or pointed & arranged irregularly). Also includes Water-lily 6 (Nymphaea) types (sometimes classed in Miscellaneous group) with v straight, flat spreading petals. V popular for cutting & exhibition. V wide colour range.

Ball 7: to 1–1.2m (3–4ft); fls Small or Miniature, ball-shaped & fully double, with blunt/round-tipped petals curved inwards for over half length, arranged in spirals. Good for garden display, cutting & exhibition. V wide colour range.

Pompon 8: to 1–1.2m (3–4ft); similar to Ball vars but maximum fl size 5cm (2in); petals curve inwards whole length. V long-lasting when cut.

Cactus 9: to 1–1.5m (3–5ft); fls Miniature to Giant, all fully double though less solid than other vars, with long narrow petals tightly rolled ("quilled"). Sub-divided in some countries into Incurved Cactus (with petals curving inwards towards centre of fl) & Straight Cactus (with petals more or less straight). V showy when cut; easy to grow well.

Semi-cactus 10: to 1–1.5m (3–5ft); fls Miniature to Giant, like Cactus but petals broader & flattish for at least half length; fls fuller & v popular for exhibition & cutting; some vars may grow to 35cm (14in) across in ideal conditions. Wide colour range.

Miscellaneous: all types not classified above, including: Carnation-flowered 11 (petal-ends fimbriated, or split); Chrysanthemum-flowered (fls resemble incurved chrysanthemum; see p268); Lilliput 12 (low-growing, with profuse 2.5cm [1in] single fls; good for pots, tubs, edging); Orchid (with strap-like petals, resemble orchid fl); Rose-flowered (fls resemble opening rosebud).

Crocuses

Crocus spp & vars. Among the most popular & colourful dwarf bulbs (correctly corms), most flowering late winter & early spring but an important group in autumn and early spring. (In warm climates groups merge, season extends over all winter.) Flowers upright & goblet-shaped, with 6 petals, often opening starry or cup-shaped, with or before leaves, in shades of blue, pink, lilac, purple, yellow or white, often narrowly striped/feathered; prominent yellow or orange styles. Leaves grassy & usually erect, mid–dark green often with silvery midrib. Unless stated, height when in flower 8–10cm (3–4in); leaves may later grow taller. Excellent for rock gardens, border edges, around base of specimen trees, window boxes, tubs & other containers, & underplanting low ground cover; spring spp also good for naturalizing in short grass (do not mow before leaves turn yellow) & for forcing in containers indoors. **Cultivation**: Very hardy unless stated. For any well-drained soil in sun or light shade. Some spp (marked †) need dry conditions when dormant; best protected in frame or alpine house in damp climates. A few (marked ‡) prefer moisture, dislike long droughts. Plant 8–10cm (3–4in) deep & apart, spring-flowering spp in autumn, autumn-flowering spp in early summer. Lift & divide every 3–4 yrs. **Pests**: Rodents & leather-jackets eat corms; birds damage flowers (especially yellows). **Propagation**: Seed; cormlets.

Late winter & spring flowers: unless stated, fls appear early spring, with lvs.

C. ancyrensis: to 6cm (2½in); v narrow lvs; long-lasting tangerine or rich yellow fls from late winter (v free-flg in var 'Golden Bunch' **1**).

C. balansae*†: wide-opening orange or yellow fls marked brown or purplish outside. Var 'Zwanenburg' is deep orange, deep bronze outside. *C. olivieri*† & *C. suterianus*† are similar.

C. biflorus† (Scotch crocus [misnomer; Mediterranean]): fls white to pale blue-purple, generally striped purple outside, from late winter. Vars: *adamii* (*annulatus adamicus*; lilac, faint veining); *albus* (*weldenii*; white, flecked purple outside; stronger violet flecking in var 'Fairy' **2**); *argenteus* (silvery-white suffused purple inside, boldly striped purple outside; early).

C. candidus†: broad, sparse, prostrate lvs; fls white, cream, pale yellow or orange, white throat, feathered brown or purplish outside. Var 'Subflavus' is pale yellow striped bronze-purple.

C. chrysanthus: short narrow lvs; profuse variable fls (typically golden-yellow), late winter. Good in alpine house. Vars & hybrids include: 'Advance' (pale yellow marked bronze & mauve outside, creamy-yellow inside); 'Blue Bird' (pale purplish-blue edged creamy-white outside, creamy-white inside); 'Blue Pearl' **3** (soft pale blue, bronze base, silvery inside); 'Cream Beauty' **4** (creamy-yellow); 'E. A. Bowles' (buttercup-yellow, purplish-bronze base); 'Goldilocks' (deep yellow, bronze-purple base); 'Ladykiller' (pointed white fls, outside deep purple-blue edged white); 'Princess Beatrix' (clear blue, golden-yellow base); 'Snow Bunting' (white, golden base, outside feathered purple); 'Ruby Giant' (purplish wine-red); 'Warley' (cream, outer petals suffused blue-purple, yellow base); 'Zwanenburg Bronze' **5** (rich golden-yellow, outside bronze).

C. dalmaticus: to 6cm (2½in); pointed lilac fls, yellow throat, feathered darker outside.

C. etruscus: lilac fls, yellow throat, light purple veining outside, from late winter. Var 'Zwanenburg' **6** is blue-violet.

C. flavus (*C. aureus*): longish lvs; rich orange-yellow cup-shaped fls, late winter. Good for naturalizing but garden forms often sterile.

C. fleischeri: small white starry fls, striped purple outside, scarlet style, late winter.

C. imperati*: moderately hardy; v large wide-opening fls, inner petals violet, outer buff, often veined purple outside, late winter to spring.

C. korolkowii: many lvs; glossy greenish-yellow starry fls veined &/or striped bronze, late winter.

C. minimus† **7**: to 5cm (2in); similar to *C. corsicus*; v narrow lvs; small lilac fls, outer petals buff feathered purple outside.

C. sieberi: starry white to deep purple fls, yellow throat, from late winter (often before lvs). Vars: 'Firefly' (lilac-pink, bright orange style); 'Hubert Edelsten' **8** (pale lilac marked purple); 'Violet Queen' (dark violet-blue; free-flg).

C. susianus (cloth-of-gold crocus; correctly, *C. angustifolius*): starry bright yellow fls marked brown outside, late winter.

C. tomasinianus: slender lavender fls opening starry, mid–late winter. Naturalizes easily. Vars: 'Barr's Purple' (dark lilac-purple); 'Ruby Giant' **9** (red-purple); 'Whitewell Purple' (red-purple).

C. vernus‡: sp has variable white, lilac or purple fls, often feathered or striped darker purple outside, throat white. Sp & vars excellent for naturalizing. Garden vars & hybrids (generally listed as Dutch crocuses; to 12cm [5in]; large fls): 'Early Perfection' **10** (intense violet-blue); 'Flower Record' (rich violet-blue); 'Golden Yellow'; 'Jeanne d'Arc' **11** ('Joan of Arc'; white); 'Kathleen Parlow' (white); 'Large Yellow' **12**; 'Little Dorrit' (silvery lilac-blue); 'Paulus Potter' (deep magenta-purple); 'Peter Pan' (brilliant white); 'Pickwick' **13** (deep lilac striping on silvery-grey); 'Queen of the Blues' (lavender-blue); 'Remembrance' (violet-purple); 'Striped Beauty' (white feathered purple); 'Vanguard' (silvery-lilac; early); 'Yellow Giant'.

C. versicolor: pale mauve-blue fls veined purple, from late winter. Var 'Picturatus' (cloth-of-silver crocus) is white with purplish feathering.
Autumn & early winter flowers: unless stated, fls appear mid autumn, before lvs.
C. byzantinus‡ (*C. banaticus, C. iridiflorus*): fls pale lilac to purple, outer petals darker & twice length of inner. Likes shade.
C. cancellatus: to 12cm (5in); fls white to lilac-blue, feathered purple, yellow throat, early autumn (sometimes with lvs).
C. kotschyanus **1** (*C. zonatus*): fls rose-lilac, white or yellow throat spotted deep yellow.
C. laevigatus*: white to pale lilac fls, feathered purple outside, yellow-orange throat, to early winter. Best protected by cloche. Var 'Fontenayi' is bright rosy-lilac, buff outside; to mid winter.
C. longiflorus**: long-petalled deep lilac fls, orange throat, scarlet style, to late autumn. Var *melitensis* is heavily feathered purple outside.
C. medius **2**: lavender to deep lilac fls open wide, starry basal markings, scarlet style, late autumn.

C. niveus†: white fls, yellow throat, orange-scarlet style, v late autumn. Multiplies rapidly.
C. nudiflorus‡ **3**: large purple fls, orange-scarlet style, early autumn. Spreads by stolons.
C. ochroleucus†: pure/creamy-white fls, deep yellow throat.
C. pulchellus: lilac-blue fls veined darker, hairy yellow throat, early autumn.
C. salzmanii: weather-resistant pale lilac fls, yellowish throat, orange style, with lvs.
C. sativus*† (saffron crocus): rosy-purple fls veined darker, early autumn, usually with lvs, styles & stigmas intense orange-red (source of saffron dye). Var *cartwrightianus* is smaller; easier where summers cool & damp.
C. speciosus **4**: to 12cm (5in); lilac-blue fls veined & speckled darker, white or pale lilac throat. Easy. Vars: *aitchisonii* (pale lavender); 'Albus' (white); 'Artabir' (delicate pale blue marked darker); 'Cassiope' (lavender-blue); 'Oxonian' (dark blue).
C. zonatus: see *C. kotschyanus*.

Gladioli

Sword lilies; *Gladiolus* spp & (mainly) hybrids, usually of complex parentage. Very popular & showy summer-flowering corms with tall one-sided spikes of irregular outward-facing trumpet-shaped flowers in wide range of colours & bicolours. Dark green sword-shaped ribbed leaves, very erect. Good for spot planting in groups in mixed & herbaceous borders, & for cutting. **Cultivation**: Unless stated, semi-hardy; lift before 1st hard frost, overwinter corms cool but frost-free, replant after last hard frost. Plant 10–15cm (4–6in) deep & apart in any well-drained fertile soil in sunny spot, mid–late spring (3-4 batches in succession every 2 weeks for longest display). Can be forced in pots. **Pests & diseases**: Various insect pests & fungal diseases may attack stored corms. **Propagation**: Offsets (cormlets); seed. For *Acidanthera bicolor* (now correctly *Gladiolus callianthus*), see p392.

G. byzantinus: v hardy; to 60cm (2ft); loose 40cm (16in) spikes of reddish-purple, rose-pink or white 6cm (2½in) fls, early summer. Multiply freely. *G. communis* is v similar; fls pinkish.
G. carneus (*G. blandus*): moderately hardy; to 45cm (1½ft); 30cm (1ft) spikes of pale pink or creamy-white 6cm (2½in) fls, pink/purplish blotch, spring to early summer.
G. × colvillei (sometimes sold incorrectly as *G. nanus*) vars: hybrids derived from *G. cardinalis* & *G. tristis*; moderately hardy; to 45–60cm (1½–2ft); loose spikes to 25cm (10in) long of upward-facing 8cm (3in) fls, early summer, scarlet blotched yellow in original hybrids. Other vars (sometimes listed with Miniature Hybrids [below]): 'Amanda Mahy' (rich salmon); 'Peach Blossom' **5** (rose blotched cream); 'Spitfire' (scarlet blotched lilac); 'The Bride' (pure white).
G. × hortulanus (garden gladiolus) vars: hybrids probably of *G. natalensis* & various other spp; sold as mixtures & hundreds of named vars in several major groups: Large-Flowered Hybrids **6**

grow to 1–1.2m (3.4ft); vigorous, with strong 40–50cm (16–20in) dense spikes of somewhat triangular fls 10–18cm (4–7in) wide, mid to v late summer (catalogues list early, mid-season & late vars); colour range v wide, often with contrasting throat, edging or blotching. Primulinus Hybrids **7** (derived in part from *G. primulinus*) grow to 60–90cm (2–3ft); slender spikes to 40cm (16in) long of hooded fls 5–8cm (2–3in) wide, mid summer; wide colour range but generally softer than above. Butterfly Hybrids **8** grow to 60–90cm (2–3ft); dense spikes to 45cm (1½ft) long of 5–10cm (2–4in) often ruffled fls with striking throat markings & blotches. Miniature Hybrids (often listed as *G. nanus* vars) grow to 75cm (2½ft); dense spikes to 40cm (16in) long of usually ruffled fls 4–6cm (1½–2½in) wide, mid summer; see also *G. × colvillei*.
G. tristis*: moderately hardy; to 60cm (2ft) or more; v narrow lvs; loose spikes to 25cm (10in) long of narrowish starry fls, creamy or pale yellow, often marked green or brownish, fragrant in evenings, spring (var *aestivalis* in summer).

Bearded irises

Iris spp & (mainly) hybrids having ruffled flowers with beard of fleshy hairs on lower "fall" petals. Hybrids often called flag or German irises & listed under *I. germanica*, but generally of complex parentage. Striking, though short season (spring & early summer), with many flowers per stem in very wide colour range, often bicoloured. Sword-like grey-green, semi-/evergreen leaves in fans. For border display; dwarfs for rock gardens. Spread slowly by rhizomes. **Cultivation:** Very hardy; for free-draining more or less neutral soil in full sun. Plant firmly, leaving top of rhizome exposed; divide every 3–4 years, after flowering, discarding woody centre. **Pests & diseases:** Slugs & snails; bud flies, borers; rot fungi; scorch. **Propagation:** Division. **Classification:** Into cushion (Arillate) & true bearded (Eupogon) groups, latter sub-divided by height & flower size.

Miniature dwarf bearded: to 20cm (8in); fls 5–8cm (2–3in) across, mid spring.

I. chamaeiris: to 20×20cm (8×8in); yellow, white or purple fls, singly or in pairs.

I. pumila: to 10×15cm (4×6in); stemless purple, white or yellow fls, v early.

Hybrids (to 20×15–20cm [8×6–8in]): 'Bee Wings' **1** (yellow, brown patch); 'Blue Doll' (lavender-blue); 'Boo' (white, violet falls); 'Bright White ' (early); 'Campbellii' (violet blue); 'Chieftain' (blue-black); 'Cyanea' (rosy-purple, blue beard); 'Laced Lemonade' (golden-yellow, wavy petals); 'Little Buccaneer' (red, orange beard); 'Moonlight' (light yellow); 'Path of Gold' (gold); 'Pixie' (creamy-yellow, falls marked bronze); 'Ritz' (yellow, falls blotched maroon); 'Twink' (purple, purple-veined white falls).

Standard dwarf bearded: to 20–40×25–30cm (8–16×10–12in); fls 8–10cm (3–4in) across, mid spring. Hybrids: 'Blue Denim' **2** (pale blue); 'Bronze Babe' (yellow, bronze falls); 'Cherry Garden' (rich velvety-red); 'Church Stoke' (bright purple, lighter beard); 'Forest Light' * (cream, falls marked green & yellow); 'Gingerbread Man' (brown, purplish beard); 'Gleaming Gold' (brassy-yellow); 'Golden Fair' (golden-yellow); 'Green Spot' **3** (cream, falls patched green); 'Hammered Copper' (apricot-copper); 'Irish Sea' (light green, blue beard); 'Katy Petts' (mid blue, falls patched violet, pale blue beard); 'Melon Honey' (soft apricot, falls marked white); 'Red Heart' (lavender-blue, dark red falls); 'Regards' (pink, maroon-red falls); 'Royal Contrast' (rich purple, white beard); 'Ruby Crown' (reddish-purple); 'Sweetie' (pure pink); 'White Gem'.

Intermediate & border bearded: to 40–70×25–30cm (16–28×10–12in); fls 10–12cm (4–5in) across, late spring or (vars marked †) early summer. Vars: 'Apache Warrior' (golden-tan, falls flushed red); 'Brown Lasso'† (tan, falls lavender edged brown); 'Chiltern Gold' (yellow); 'Chocoletto'† (light chocolate); 'Drummer Boy' (light blue, darker falls); 'Frenchi'† **4** (orchid-pink & rose-violet); 'Jungle Shadows'† (brown, grey & purple blend); 'Langport' series (various colours); 'Little Reb'† (purple & white); 'Scintilla' (cream); 'Solent Breeze' (yellow & brown); 'Red Orchid' (dark red, gold beard); 'Solo' (creamy-

yellow patched gold); 'Tulare' (golden-yellow, orange beard).

Tall bearded: to 70–120×30–40cm (28–48×12–16in); fls 10–18cm (4–7in) across, early summer.

*I. florentina** (orris; correctly, *I. germanica florentina*): to 75×30 (2½×1ft); fls bluish-white; ground dried root used in perfumery.

*I. germanica** (flag iris, fleur-de-lys): probably hybrid; to 60–90×30cm (2–3×1ft); evergreen; purple fls 8–10cm (3–4in) across, white beard.

*I. pallida**: to 90×30cm (3×1ft); fls lavender. Vars 'Argentea Variegata' **5** (white-striped lvs) & 'Aurea Variegata' (gold-striped lvs) are grown mainly for foliage.

Hybrids: 'Allegiance' (navy-blue); 'Amigo's Guitar' (buff, violet falls); 'Ancient Egypt' (deep apricot, tangerine beard); 'Annabel Jane' (pale lilac); 'Blue Eyed Brunette' **6** (brown, falls flashed blue); 'Caliente' (red-brown); 'Caramba' (yellow speckled purple); 'Christmas Time' (white, red beard); 'Credo' **7** (maroon, bronze-tipped beard); 'Cup Race' (white); 'Dream Lover' (blue-white, purple falls, lemon beard); 'Dusky Dancer; (black-violet); 'Dutch Chocolate' (mid & dark brown); 'Eleanor's Pride' (pale blue); 'Esther Fay' (pale pink); 'Foggy Dew' (white stippled blue); 'Gaylord' (pure white, falls purple); 'Golden Alps' (ivory, falls yellow); 'Gypsy Jewels' **8** (garnet-red); 'Henry Shaw' (white); 'Joyce Terry' (yellow, white falls); 'Latin Lover' **9** (white veined purple, deep purple falls); 'Loop the Loop' (pure white edged violet); 'Lord Baltimore' (light blue, violet-blue falls); 'Milestone' (buff, falls purple); 'Olympic Torch' (copper-bronze); 'One Desire' **10** (clear pink); 'Patrician' (white, gold hafts); 'Pink Sleigh' (lavender-pink, red beard): 'Post Time' (coppery-red); 'Princess Amarantha' (reddish-purple, red beard); 'Radiant Apogee' (deep yellow, falls white edged brown); 'Radiant Light' (orange); 'Rainbow Gold' (buttercup-yellow, orange beard); 'Raspberry Ripples' (raspberry-pink, red beard); 'Rippling Waters' (pale violet-blue, red beard); 'Rondo' (white edged red-violet); 'Royal Touch' **11** (satiny royal-blue; 'Sea Captain' (sky-blue); 'Shepherd's Delight' (apricot-pink); 'Smart Girl' (apricot, red beard); 'Snow Cloud' (bluish-white, falls pale

blue); 'Spreckles' (yellow speckled red);
'Stepping Out' (white edged violet); 'Study in
Black' (deep red & black); 'Symphony' (sea-blue,
dark veins); 'Tangerine Sky' (orange); 'The
Citadel' (snow-white); 'The Monarch' (plum-
purple, gold beard); 'Topolino' (orchid-pink, gold
beard); 'Touché' (pink, blue falls); 'Touch Up'
(white edged orchid-pink); 'Tuxedo' **1** (blue-
black); 'War Lord' (red); 'Warm Laughter' (rosy
orchid-pink); 'West Coast' **2** (orange-gold);
'White Lightning' (white, yellow beard); 'Wild
Apache' (cinnamon flushed violet, falls white,
edged mulberry).

Cushion & related types (Oncocyclus &
Regelia groups): fl late spring; beard broad &
cushion-like, on both falls & upper "standard"
petals in Regelia spp; lvs die down mid summer.
Spread by stolons. Difficult (especially
Oncocyclus spp); need v good drainage; plant
5cm (2in) deep; cloche after flg to ripen & protect
rhizomes.

I. gatesii (Oncocyclus group): to 60×30cm

(2×1ft); solitary off-white purple-veined fls to
12cm (5in) wide. Best in frame.
*I. hoogiana** **3** (Regelia group): to 50×30cm
(20×12in); lvs bright green; lavender-blue fls to
10cm (4in) across, 2 or 3 per stem.
I. stolonifera (Regelia group): to 60×30cm
(2×1ft); fls 8cm (3in) across, brown marked blue,
blue beard. Var 'Zwanenburg Beauty' **4** is blue,
edged bronze, falls bronze flushed maroon.
I. susiana (mourning iris; Oncocyclus group): to
40×30cm (16×12in); solitary grey fls 10–12cm
(4–5in) across, veined & blotched dark purple.
×Oncogelia (×Regeliocyclus) vars: hybrids
between Oncocyclus & Regelia spp; to
45×30cm (1½×1ft); attractively veined fls 8–
12cm (3–6in) across. Vars: 'Chione' (bluish-
white, standards veined blue, falls blotched
brown); 'Clara' (white veined black); 'Clotho'
(violet, black falls); 'Mercury' (violet, bronze
falls); 'Thor' **5** (grey veined purple); 'Vera' (brown
suffused purple). Also sold as unnamed
seedlings.

Beardless irises

Iris spp & hybrids having elegant flowers with smooth ("beardless") lower petals ("falls"). Flowers often
bicoloured, delicately marked & veined, several per stem; many good for cutting. Evergreen unless
stated, with rather narrow long leaves. Good for moist borders & (smaller types) rock gardens. Spread
by narrow rhizomes below soil surface. **Cultivation**: For moist neutral or lime-free soil unless stated,
generally in full sun. Plant 2.5–5cm (1–2in) deep. **Pests & diseases**: See p384. **Propagation**: Division
(early autumn or early spring; Hexagona types & *I. ruthenica* after flowering); Californica types by seed.
Classification: Botanically into 6 main groups.

Pacific Coast irises (Californica group):
moderately to v hardy free-flg N American spp &
hybrids; lvs dark green; dainty fls 6–10cm (2½–
4in) across, late spring & early summer (good for
cutting). Divide early autumn, only if essential
(keep roots moist).
I. douglasiana **6**: to 50×45cm (20×18in); fls
lilac-purple, lavender, buff or whitish, falls veined,
usually 5 per stem. Tolerates lime.
I. innominata **7**: to 20×25cm (8×10in); fls gold,
buff or cream, veined brown, in 1s or 2s.
I. tenax (Oregon iris): to 40×30cm (16×12in);
herbaceous; fls lavender-blue, cream or pink
shades, in 1s or 2s.
Pacific Coast Hybrids **8** (mainly of *I. douglasiana,
I. innominata* & *I. fernaldii*): to 25–40×30cm
(10–16×12in); fls (2–3yrs from seed) on
branching stems, selfs & bicolours in shades of
blue-purple, yellow (veined brown or purple),
white (veined yellow) & red. Hybridize freely &
self-seed; sold mainly in mixtures or by colour.
Louisiana swamp irises (Hexagona group):
moderately hardy; light green lvs; fls 8–10cm
(3–4in) wide, usually grouped on zigzag stems,
early–mid summer. Spreading; for humus-rich,
moist soil. Mulch in winter.

I. brevicaulis (Lamance iris): to 60×60cm
(2×2ft); fls blue-purple or deep blue.
I. fulva **9** (copper iris): to 60×60cm (2×2ft); fls
copper or pinkish.
*I. giganticaerulea**: to 90×60cm (3×2ft); fls
violet or blue.
I.×nelsonii: natural hybrid of *I. brevicaulis, I. fulva*
& *I. giganticaerulea*; to 90×60cm (3×2ft); fls
bright reddish-purple.
Louisiana hybrids: to 60–90×60cm (2–3×2ft);
showy fls 12–20cm (5–8in) across. Vars: 'Dixie
Deb' **10** (light yellow); 'Fulvala' (*I.×fulvala*;
reddish/bluish-purple); 'Marjorie Brummitt' (pink
& red bicolour): 'Pristine Beauty' (turquoise-
blue); 'Wheelhorse' (red).
Siberian irises (Sibirica group): v hardy unless
stated; grass-like herbaceous lvs; profuse fls
6–10cm (2½–4in) across in groups on slender
stems above lvs, early summer (good for
cutting); fls dryable. Elegant easy plant for moist
borders, the pool-side. For cool rich soil; tolerate
semi-shade; divide only when centre of clump
dies.
I. bulleyana: to 60×45cm (2×1½ft); fls lilac, falls
yellow veined purple.
I. chrysographes **11**: to 60×45cm (2×1½ft); fls

violet-blue or reddish-purple, falls veined gold. Vars: 'Black Knight' (blackish-purple); 'Margot Holmes' (wine-red marked orange).

I. delavayii: to 1.2×0.6m (4×2ft); fls violet-purple marked white.

I. forrestii **1**: to 40×45cm (16×18in), taller in wet soil; fls pale yellow, falls veined brown.

I. sibirica (Siberian iris): ultra-hardy; to 90×60cm (3×2ft); fls blue or white, on branching stems. Sibirica hybrids: to 90×60cm (3×2ft); fls 8–15cm (3–6in) across. Vars (large-fld tetraploids marked †): 'Anniversary' (white, falls marked yellow); 'Cambridge' (light blue); 'Cleve Dodge' (velvety black-purple); 'Ewen'† **2** (velvety wine-red, marked gold); 'Ego' (ruffled, blue); 'Fourfold White'† (waxy-white, flared); 'Gatineau' (light blue, falls marked gold); 'Helen Astor' (pink); 'Lavender Light' (lavender-pink, falls marked white); 'Limeheart' (white, falls marked green); 'Navy Brass'† (navy-blue marked gold); 'Orville Fay'† (mid blue); 'Polly Dodge'† (claret-red); 'Sea Shadows' **3** (pale blue, falls deep blue, turquoise styles); 'Silver Edge'† (mid blue edged white); 'Sparkling Rose' (mauve, falls marked white & pale bronze); 'White Swirl' (flared falls).

Spuria irises (Spuria group): v hardy unless stated; clump-forming; lvs generally reed-like, glaucous; robust waxy fls to 6–15cm (2½–6in) across, early summer (cuttable). Trouble-free; for any soil in full sun; leave undisturbed.

I. graminea**: to 20×25cm (8×10in); grass-like lvs; solitary purple fls, falls veined blue on white.

I. kernerana: to 45×25cm (18×10in); light green lvs; yellow recurved fls.

I. orientalis (*I. ochroleuca*): ultra-hardy; to 1.2×0.6m (4×2ft); fls cream, falls marked gold.

I. spuria (butterfly iris): ultra-hardy; to 90×60cm (3×2ft); fls bluish-purple.

Spuria hybrids (butterfly irises): to 1–1.2×0.6m (3–4×2ft); mainly for warm climates, but vars marked † are moderately hardy; trouble-free. Vars: 'Arbitrator' **4** (purple, falls yellow edged purple); 'Archie Owen' (yellow); 'Chumasch Chief' (velvety chocolate-brown); 'Conquista' (maroon); 'Contradiction' **5** (brown, falls yellow veined brown); 'Driftwood'† (golden-brown);

'Elixir'† (orange); 'Everglow' (golden-yellow flushed brown); 'Farolito' (lavender, falls orange edged lavender); 'Monspur'† (blue); 'Navigator' (pale blue, falls flushed yellow); 'Oroville' (buttercup-yellow); 'Purple Knight' (midnight-blue, falls flushed gold); 'Red Oak' (maroon-red); 'Shelford Giant'† (to 2m [7ft]; cream, falls marked gold); 'Sierra Nevada'† **6** (pure white, falls marked yellow); 'Wadi Zem Zem' (yellow); 'Wake Robin'† (white, yellow patch).

Other beardless irises (various groups):

I. foetidissima **7** (gladdon, stinking gladwyn): moderately to v hardy; to 45×45cm (1½×1½ft); dark green lvs, pungent if bruised; fls pale purple, not showy; pods split open to show scarlet seeds, dryable. Tolerates dry shade & lime. Vars: *lutea* (yellow fls, brown veins); 'Variegata' (lvs striped cream).

I. kaempferi (Japanese iris; correctly *I. ensata*): v hardy; to 90×45cm (3×1½ft); deciduous; clustered single or double fls to 10–20cm (4–8in) across with v broad falls marked yellow, mid summer. Sold in seed mixtures and vars: 'Driven Snow' (v large white fls); 'Hercules' **8** (dark blue); 'Kagari Bi' (rose-pink, silver veins); 'Moonlight Waves' (white shaded blue); 'Nichiko Yama' (violet); 'Repsime' (sky-blue); 'Snowdrift' (white); 'Suehiro' (deep lavender); 'Variegata' (violet; variegated lvs); 'Wake Musha' (double, purple).

I. ruthenica: ultra-hardy; to 15×15cm (6×6in); deciduous grass-like lvs; purple fls, falls white veined blue, spring (not reliable). For rock garden. Tolerates lime.

I. setosa: ultra-hardy; to 75×45cm (2½×1½ft); deciduous grass-like lvs; fls greyish-purple with broad falls, early summer, on branching stems.

I. unguicularis* **9** (*I. stylosa*, Algerian iris): moderately to v hardy; foliage to 60×40cm (24×16in); arching lvs; short-stemmed solitary lilac fls, falls marked white & yellow, all winter (best after hot summers; cuttable in bud). Prefers poor dryish alkaline soil in sheltered sunny spot (good at foot of wall); trim lvs late summer to ripen rhizomes. Vars: 'Mary Barnard' (violet; wide lvs); 'Starker's Pink' (mauvy-pink; narrow lvs).

Crested irises

Iris spp (Evansiana section) with flattish pale/pastel-coloured flowers with showy fringed crest on "fall" petals. Leaves evergreen & sword-shaped unless noted. Larger spp for borders, smaller for rock garden. **Cultivation**: For humus-rich soil, lime-free unless stated, in semi-shade. Plant rhizome just below surface. **Pests & diseases**: See p384. **Propagation**: Division (after flg; *I. gracilipes* mid summer).

I. confusa: moderately to v hardy; to 90×60cm (3×2ft); fls 4–5cm (1½–2in) wide, white flushed mauve, spotted yellow & orange, in groups.

I. cristata **10** ([dwarf] crested iris): ultra-hardy; to

10–20×15cm (4–8×6in); deciduous; lilac fls to 6cm (2½in) wide, falls whitish, white & orange crests, mid spring. Plant with rhizome partly exposed. Vars: 'Alba' (white); 'Caerulea' (blue);

lacustris (to 8cm [3in]).

I. gracilipes: moderately to v hardy; to 20×15cm (8×6in); lvs grass-like; lilac-pink fls to 2.5cm (1in) across, orange crests, late spring.

I. japonica **1**: moderately hardy; to 60×45cm (2×1½ft); fls 5–8cm (2–3in) wide, lilac spotted yellow & deep lilac, yellow crests, on branched stems. Protect in winter; good in pots. 'Ledger's Variety' is hardier.

I. tectorum (wall or roof iris): v hardy; to 30×30cm (1×1ft); fls to 10cm (4in) wide, lavender spotted darker, white crests, late spring. Tolerates lime; divide every 2yrs. Can be raised from seed. Var 'Alba' is white.

Bulbous irises

Herbaceous *Iris* spp & hybrids growing from a bulb rather than rhizome, generally with rather elegant slender-petalled flowers. Juno & Reticulata types good for rock gardens, Xiphium for beds, borders & cutting. Most good in pots under cool glass. **Cultivation:** Unless stated, for light, well-drained soil (alkaline for Juno & Reticulata groups) in full sun & shelter. Plant early autumn; dead-head; feed after flowering. Prone to grey bulb rot & ink disease; mice; mosaic virus. **Propagation:** Offsets.

Juno irises (Juno group): moderately to v hardy unless stated; distinctive but uncommon, with erect stems sheathed by shiny lvs, grey-green beneath, dying down in summer; 4 or more fls to 8cm (3in) wide per stem (in lf axils), spring, "standard" petals often insignificant. Fleshy storage roots, prone to damage; best in dry conditions in summer. Plant 5cm (2in) deep.

*I. aucheri** **2** (*I. sindjarensis*): to 30×20cm (12×8in); fls lavender-blue streaked pale green.

*I. bucharica** **3**: to 45×15cm (18×6in); fls cream marked gold. Easiest sp of group.

I. graeberana: to 40×25cm (16×10in); lvs blue-green; fls blue-mauve, falls silver-blue veined darker.

I. magnifica: to 60×25cm (24×10in); fls pale lilac veined darker.

I. orchioides: moderately hardy; to 30×20cm (12×8in); fls golden-yellow. For pots/shelter.

Netted irises (Reticulata group): v hardy; bulbs netted with fibres; lvs tubular, pointed; fls to 8cm (3in) across, late winter (earliest of all irises). Plant 8cm (3in) deep.

*I. danfordiae** **4**: to 12×8cm (5×3in); fls bright yellow spotted brown, before lvs (2nd flg may be delayed a yr unless planted 12cm [5in] deep).

I. histrioides 'Major' **5**: to 12×8cm (5×3in); fls gentian-blue spotted white, before lvs. Best sp for pots.

I. reticulata: to 15×8cm (6×3in); fls purple, falls marked orange, with lvs. V popular. Vars & hybrids with *I. histrioides* 'Major': 'Cantab' **6** (pale blue, falls marked orange); 'Clairette' (sky-blue, falls deep blue marked white); 'Harmony' (sky-blue, falls marked yellow, before lvs); 'Jeannine'* (purple, falls marked orange); 'Joyce' (sky-blue, falls marked reddish); 'J. S. Dijt'* **7** (red-purple marked orange); 'Pauline' (red-violet marked white); 'Springtime' (pale blue, falls dark blue marked white); 'Violet Beauty' (deep violet marked orange).

I. winogradowii: to 10×8cm (4×3in); fls lemon-yellow, before lvs.

English, Dutch & Spanish irises (Xiphium group): moderately hardy Mediterranean spp & hybrids; generally to 60×15–20cm (24×6–8in); lvs reed-like, rather sparse; fls 10–12cm (4–5in) across, one or two per stem (good for cutting). Plant 10cm (4in) deep; protect if necessary in winter; forced bulbs best discarded.

I. tingitana: fls blue, falls marked yellow, spring. Lvs & buds prone to damage by spring frosts; needs hot summers to fl again. Good for forcing in late winter.

I. xiphioides (English iris; correctly *I. latifolia*; sometimes sold as *I. anglica*): large royal-blue fls, falls marked gold, mid summer. Hybrids (English irises **8**) are white, blue, purple or pink; best bought as unnamed seedlings (named vars often virus-infected, with flecked petals). For rich, moist soils; leave to naturalize.

I. xiphium (Spanish iris; sometimes sold as *I. hispanica*): fls purple, falls streaked yellow, early summer. Hybrids (Spanish irises **9**) grow to 30–45×15cm (12–18×6in); fls yellow, bronze & purple shades, some dusky; best bought as unnamed seedlings. For warm, dryish soil; bulbs best lifted after flg to ripen; replant early autumn. DUTCH HYBRIDS (Dutch irises); hybrids of *I. xiphium*, *I. tingitana* & other spp; to 40–60×15cm (16–24×6in); white, yellow, blue or purple fls (selfs & bicolours), early summer (before Spanish irises); often forced under glass for winter cutting. Sold as unnamed seedlings & named vars: 'Blue Champion'; 'Bronze Queen' (golden brown & bronze flushed blue); 'Frans Hals' (violet, falls violet-bronze); 'Golden Emperor' (golden-yellow); 'Imperator' (midnight-blue, falls marked orange); 'Lemon Queen' **10** (lemon-yellow); 'Marquette' (white, falls canary-yellow); 'Professor Blaauw' (mid blue, falls marked yellow); 'Royal Yellow' (yellow, falls richer yellow); 'Sunshine' (yellow); 'Wedgwood' **11** (pale blue); 'White Van Vliet' (ivory blotched gold); 'White Excelsior' (white, falls streaked greenish-yellow).

Other members of the iris family

Generally rather tender plants growing from corms, bulbs, rhizomes or tubers. Herbaceous unless stated. Flowers mostly in showy spikes, generally good for cutting. For sunny borders; smaller spp good in rock gardens; unless stated can be grown in pots under cool glass. **Cultivation**: Generally for well-drained soil in full sun; plant 8cm (3in) deep in spring unless noted. Treat like gladioli (p382): where hardy, leave in ground over winter, protecting with mulch or cloche if necessary; otherwise lift in autumn or when foliage dies down, dry, store frost-free & replant in spring. **Propagation**: Seed, sown spring; cormous & bulbous spp by offsets; tuberous & rhizomatous spp by division.

Peacock orchid (*Acidanthera bicolor**, *Gladiolus callianthus*): tender E African corm closely related to *Tritonia* & *Gladiolus* spp; to 45–90×15–25cm (18–36×6–10in); sword-shaped gladiolus-like lvs; starry white fls to 8cm (3in) across, up to 10 per spike, late summer or early autumn (graceful & good for cutting). Var *murielae* **1** (*A. murielae*) has reddish-purple fls.

Baboon flower (*Babiana stricta** **2**): S African corm, moderately to v hardy if well mulched in winter; to 25×8cm (10×3in); pleated freesia-like hairy lvs; erect funnel-shaped pale blue, white, violet or reddish-mauve fls to 2.5cm (1in) long in dense spikes, spring. Plant in autumn 15cm (6in) deep; in pots treat as *Freesia* vars.

Blackberry lily (leopard flower, *Belamcanda* [*Pardanthus*] *chinensis* **3**): moderately hardy rhizomatous plant, v hardy in warm sunny spot if well mulched in winter; to 90×20cm (36×8in); iris-like lvs; small red-spotted salmon-orange tigridia-like fls to 5cm (2in) wide in clusters of 4–12, summer; pods split to show clusters of shiny black seeds. A parent of intergeneric hybrids listed as × *Pardancanda norrisii* (v hardy; to 75cm [2½ft]; variable flaring iris-like often spotted fls in shades of blue, purple, yellow, orange & red, all summer to frosts).

Montbretias (*Crocosmia* spp; sometimes listed as *Montbretia* or *Tritonia* spp): moderately to v hardy S African corms with sword-shaped semi-evergreen lvs & arching spikes of funnel-shaped fls 2.5–5cm (1–2in) long from mid summer (v good for cutting). Easy. Trim in spring. Propagate by division.

C. (*T.*) *aurea*: moderately hardy; to 90×30cm (3×1ft); bright yellow fls.

C. (*M.*) × *crocosmiiflora* vars: hybrids of *C. aurea* & *C. pottsii*; to 60–75×25cm (24–30×10in); large yellow to scarlet fls, late summer. Popular. Vars: 'Bressingham Blaze' (flame-red); 'Citronella' **4** (lemon-yellow); 'Earlham Hybrids' (mixed); 'Emily McKenzie' (deep orange, crimson throat); 'Firebird' (flame); 'His Majesty' (scarlet, orange centre); 'Jackanapes' **5** (yellow & orange bicolour); 'Lucifer' (to 1.1m [3½ft]; deep flame-red, early); 'Solfatare' (apricot; bronzed lvs); 'Spitfire' (orange); 'Vulcan' **6** (orange-red).

C. masonorum **7**: to 75×25cm (30×10in); fine lvs; broad orange-red fls held erect.

C. (*M.*) *pottsii*: to 1.2×0.3m (4×1ft); broad lvs; fls bright yellow flushed red, in erect infls.

Curtonus (Aunt Eliza, pleated leaves, *Curtonus* [*Antholyza*] *paniculatus*): moderately hardy montbretia-like S African corm; to 75–90×25cm (30–36×10in); pleated lvs to 8cm (3in) wide; orange-red trumpet fls to 5cm (2in) long on erect zigzag stems, late summer. Plant 15cm (6in) deep in autumn.

Wand flower (angel's fishing rod, *Dierama pulcherrimum* **8**): moderately hardy semi-evergreen corm; to 1.5–1.8×0.45m (5–6×1½ft); grassy, v narrow lvs; wiry arching stems with dangling deep purplish-red trumpet-shaped fls to 2.5cm (1in) long, mid summer into autumn.

D. pendulum is similar but smaller, with white to mauve-pink fls.

Diplarrhena (*Diplarrhena moraea**): semi-hardy rhizomatous Australian plant; clump-forming, to 60×25cm (24×10in); long grassy lvs; clusters of iris-like white fls, inner petals yellow & purple, early summer.

Freesias (*Freesia* × *hybrida*** vars): hybrids of various *Freesia* spp, including *F. refracta*; tender to semi-hardy S African corms widely grown for cut flowers; to 45×10cm (18×4in); sparse sword-shaped lvs; one-sided arching spikes of waxy funnel-shaped fls to 2.5–5cm (1–2in) long on wiry stems, singles & doubles in wide colour range from white & yellow to pink, red, orange & purple. In frost-free zones, corms planted late summer fl late winter & spring; elsewhere prepared corms planted spring outdoors fl from late summer (discard after flg). Corms planted in pots late summer fl from early winter under cool glass. Feed well under glass; provide twiggy support. Easy to raise from seed; sold as unnamed seedlings & named vars (not all fragrant): 'Albion'* (white); 'Aurora'** (creamy-gold); 'Ballerina'** (white); 'Cervin' (creamy-white); 'Cote d'Azur' **9** (lilac, white throat); 'Demeter'** (creamy-yellow); 'Diana'** (double, creamy-white); 'Elegance'* (white); 'Fantasy'** **10** (double, creamy-yellow); 'Midas' (deep yellow); 'Pandora'** (pale magenta, white throat); 'President'** (orange); 'Prince of Orange'** (orange); 'Red Star'* **11** (red, yellow throat); 'Romany'* (double, mauve); 'Rose Marie'** (lilac-pink, white throat); 'Royal Blue'** (blue, white throat); 'Venus'** (rose, ivory-white

throat); 'Vesuvius'* (vibrant red, yellow throat); 'Viking'** (purplish-pink, white throat).

Snake's-head iris (*Hermodactylus* [*Iris*] *tuberosus* **1**): moderately hardy iris-like tuberous perennial; to 30×15cm (12×6in); v narrow lvs; unusual iris-like olive-green fls to 5cm (2in) long, purple-brown falls, mid–late spring. Plant in summer in warm alkaline soil.

African corn lilies (*Ixia* hybrids **2**; often listed as *I. viridiflora*, but derived from various *I.* spp): moderately hardy S African corms; to 45×15cm (18×6in); narrow, sparse, sword-shaped lvs; star-shaped fls to 4cm (1½in) across in spikes on erect wiry stems, in wide colour range mostly with contrasting eye, late spring to early summer if planted in autumn, later if planted in spring, earlier under glass; good for cutting (pick when just open). Sold as unnamed seedlings & vars: 'Afterglow' (buff-orange, centre rimmed red-black); 'Hogarth' (creamy-yellow, purple centre); 'Nelson' (white, purple-red centre); 'Rose Emperor' (soft pink, carmine-pink centre).

Lapeirousia (*Lapeirousia* [*Lapeyrousia*] *laxa* **3**, *Anomatheca cruenta*): moderately hardy freesia-like S African corm; to 30×15cm (12×6in); lvs in flattened fan; starry trumpet-shaped red fls to 2.5cm (1in) wide in one-sided spikes, from mid summer outdoors, winter under glass if treated as freesias. *L. grandiflora* is similar but larger.

Libertia (*Libertia formosa* **4**): moderately hardy; rhizomatous; to 90×15cm (36×6in); grassy lvs; branching spikes of clustered white & greenish fls to 2cm (¾in) across, late spring into summer (earlier under glass). *L. ixiodes* is similar but smaller. For acid soil; plant early autumn.

Butterfly irises (Natal lilies, *Moraea* spp): semi-to moderately hardy iris-like corms; sparse narrow lvs; succession of showy but short-lived iris-like fls on branching stems from late spring (earlier under glass). Plant autumn in warm spot. *M. irioides* * (African iris; correctly, *Dietes vegeta*): to 90×15cm (36×6in); fls white & yellow, styles marked blue.
M. ramosissima ** (*M. ramosa*): moderately hardy; to 60×25cm (24×10in); fls yellow shaded blue.
M. spathulata * (*M. spathacea*): moderately hardy; to 60×25cm (24×10in); solitary lf; fls brilliant yellow.
M. tricuspidata * **5** (peacock iris): to 60×20cm (24×8in); pure white fls, peacock-blue blotch.

Romuleas (*Romulea* spp): moderately hardy crocus-like corms with grassy lvs & clustered fls in early spring, opening only in sun. Plant in groups to naturalize.
R. bulbocodium **6**: to 15×8cm (6×3in); fls usually bright purple, yellow throat, opening to 3cm (1¼in) wide.
R. requienii: to 10×8cm (4×3in); deep violet fls to 2cm (¾in) wide.

Kaffir lily (crimson flag, *Schizostylis coccinea*): moderately hardy S African rhizomatous plant; to 75×25cm (30×10in); long sword-like lvs; starry cup-shaped crimson fls to 4cm (1½in) across in erect spikes, late autumn (good for cutting). Needs shelter & moist soil; plant 10cm (4in) deep in spring; mulch in winter in cold areas; divide ever 4yrs. Vars: 'Major' (large fls); 'Mrs Hegarty' (rose-pink); 'November Cheer' (pink); 'Salmon Charm' (flesh-pink); 'Viscountess Byng' **7** (pale pink).

Harlequin flower (wand flower, *Sparaxis tricolor* & its hybrids **8**): semi-hardy S African corm similar to *Ixia* hybrids; to 30–45×10cm (12–18×4in); narrow, sword-shaped lvs; erect spikes of fls opening flat to 4cm (1½in) across, late spring to early summer (good for cutting); colour variable – white, yellow, orange or red, often marked purple-black & centred yellow. Sold mainly as mixtures.

Tiger flower (shell flower, *Tigridia pavonia* **9**): moderately hardy bulbs from Central America with distinctive & showy spotted fls; to 45–60×15cm (18–24×6in); erect, pleated lvs; fls with 3 broad outer petals opening flat to 10–15cm (4–6in) across & heavily marked central cup, transient but opening in succession, mid–late summer. Sold mainly as unnamed seedlings in white, yellow, orange, lilac or red shades, spotted brown or red. Where winters mild plant in autumn for earlier flg; liquid feed during flg.

Tritonias (*Tritonia* spp; sometimes called montbretias & listed as *Crocosmia* or *Montbretia* spp): moderately hardy S American corms; to 30–45×10cm (12–18×4in); narrow sword-shaped lvs; broadly funnel-shaped fls to 4cm (1½in) wide in arching spikes, late spring to early summer (good for cutting). Best grown under glass where summers not v warm.
T. crocata: best-known sp. Vars: 'Incomparabile' (deep orange); 'Isabella' (flesh-pink tinged yellow); 'Roseline' (pink); 'Salmon Queen' **10** (salmon-orange); 'Tea Rose' (cream, yellow centre); 'White Glory' (white tinged amber).
T. hyalina: tawny-yellow fls, spoon-shaped petals.
T. rubrolucens (*T. rosea*): to 60cm (2ft); rose fls.

Bugle lilies (*Watsonia* spp): moderately hardy S African corms with sword-shaped lvs & tall spikes of narrow-tubed trumpet-shaped fls. Need moisture-retentive soil; plant 10cm (4in) deep; stake. Best under glass in cool climates.
W. ardernei: to 90×15cm (36×6in); white fls to 4cm (1½in) wide, early summer.
W. beatricis: to 90×20cm (36×8in); evergreen; terracotta to apricot fls to 10cm (4in) wide, late summer. Not for pot culture.
W. pyramidata (*W. rosea*): to 1–1.5×0.15m (3–5ft×6in); rose-pink to mauve fls to 8cm (3in) wide on branched stems, early–mid summer.

Erythroniums and fritillaries

Attractive and graceful mostly quite small spring-flowering bulbs with nodding lily-like, cyclamen-like or bell-shaped small flowers & narrow or lance-shaped leaves (die down mid summer). Good for rock gardens, underplanting trees & shrubs, or containers; smaller *Fritillaria* spp may naturalize in grass. **Cultivation**: Unless stated, very hardy; *Erythronium* spp dislike very hot, dry summers. Generally prefer partial shade & humus-rich, moist but well-drained soil. Plant in groups in early autumn, generally 10–15cm (4–6in) deep, same distance apart; do not damage or allow fleshy bulbs to dry. Plant large bulbs on side or aid drainage with sand. **Propagation**: Offsets; seed (may self-sow).

Erythroniums (dog's-tooth violets, adder's-tongues, fawn or trout lilies, *Erythronium* spp): woodland natives with graceful fls, petals generally reflexing like Turk's-head lilies; 2 to 4 basal lvs, often marbled. Do not disturb till clumps v big; mulch in summer.

E. albidum (white fawn lily): to 30cm (1ft); bluish- to pinkish-white 2.5–5cm (1–2in) starry fls, late spring.

E. americanum (yellow adder's-tongue, common fawn lily, trout lily): ultra-hardy; to 30cm (1ft); lvs mottled brown; 5cm (2in) pale yellow starry fls, blotched brown at base, late spring.

E. californicum (Californian fawn lily): to 30–45cm (1–1½ft); lvs mottled purple; clustered creamy-white fls to 8cm (3in) across, early spring.

E. citrinum: to 20–30cm (8–12in); lvs mottled brown; 4cm (1½in) creamy to lemon-yellow fls, early spring.

E. dens-canis (dog's-tooth violet): ultra-hardy; to 15–20cm (6–8in); lvs mottled brown & greyish; fls 5–8cm (2–3in) across, pink to purple, late spring. Vars: 'Frans Hals' (violet); 'Lilac Wonder' **1**; 'Pink Beauty'; 'Pink Perfection'; 'Purple King' (fls cyclamen-purple marked brown); 'Rose Queen'; 'Snowflake' (white); 'White Splendour'.

E. grandiflorum (avalanche lily); to 60cm (2ft); 15cm (6in) racemes of 2–6 bright yellow fls 5–8cm (2–3in) across, early spring.

E. hendersonii: to 30cm (1ft); lvs mottled; 4cm (1½in) mauve-lilac fls, purple base, early spring.

E. oregonum: to 60cm (2ft); lvs mottled; 5–8cm (2–3in) creamy-yellow starry fls, early spring.

E. revolutum: to 30cm (1ft); lvs mottled; 8cm (3in) fls, white to pink & purple, mottled, late spring. Vars: 'Rose Beauty' (pink); 'White Beauty' **2** (white zoned yellow).

E. tuolumnense **3**: to 30cm (1ft); lvs yellowish-green; 4cm (1½in) golden-yellow starry fls, good for cutting. Hybrids with *E. revolutum*: 'Kondo' (sulphur-yellow marked brown); 'Pagoda' (to 45cm [1½ft]; lvs marbled brownish; large yellow fls).

Fritillaries (*Fritillaria* spp): drooping bell-shaped to tulip-like fls, generally 2.5cm (1in) across, often in unusual shades of greenish-yellow and purplish-brown with chequered pattern, singly or clustered near top of stems; often some lvs on stem. Divide & replant every few yrs.

F. acmopetala **4**: to 40–45cm (16–18in); fls yellowish-green, streaked brown-purple.

F. imperialis (crown imperial fritillary): good for mixed borders; to 60–90×25–30cm (24–36×10–12in); clustered yellow to red musty-scented fls on strong stem below terminal "crown" of lvs. Vars: 'Aurora' (orange-red): 'Lutea Maxima' **5** (deep lemon-yellow); 'Premier' (soft orange); 'Rubra Maxima' (burnt orange). Plant 20cm (8in) deep.

F. gracilis: to 40–45cm (16–18in); fls reddish-brown, olive-green inside.

F. lanceolata: (rice-root fritillary): to 60cm (2ft); fls dark purple-brown mottled greenish-yellow, late spring.

F. latifolia: to 30cm (1ft); fls purple to yellow, chequered. Vars: 'Aurea' **6** (correctly, *F. aurea*; yellowish, chequered brown); 'Erasmus' (olive-green chequered vivid brown inside); 'Nobilis' (maroon, yellowish-green inside).

*F. liliacea**: (white fritillary): to 25–30cm (10–12in); 2cm (¾in) white fls streaked green.

F. meleagris (snake's-head fritillary; guinea-hen flower): ultra-hardy; to 30–40cm (12–16in); fls chequered white & reddish-purple. Vars: 'Alba' (white veined green); 'Aphrodite' (almost pure white); 'Artemis' **7** (greyish-purple, chequered green); 'Charon' (purple chequered black, dull sheen); 'Poseidon' (white chequered purple); 'Purple King' (dark wine-purple); 'Saturnus' (red-violet).

F. pallidiflora **8**: ultra-hardy; to 30–40cm (12–16in); glaucous lvs; fls greenish-cream to yellow, flecked brown.

*F. persica**: to 90cm (3ft); glaucous lvs; racemes of 10–30 violet-blue 2cm (¾in) fls. Var 'Adiyaman' **9** is dark purple, to 1.2m (4ft) tall.

F. pluriflora (pink fritillary, adobe lily): to 30–40cm (12–16in); pinkish-purple fls.

F. pontica **10**: to 45cm (1½ft); fls greenish-yellow marked purplish-brown.

F. pudica (yellow fritillary): ultra-hardy but needs v good drainage; to 15cm (6in); 2.5cm (1in) golden-yellow fls sometimes tinged purple.

F. pyrenaica: to 45cm (1½ft); musty-scented dark purple fls, often yellowish inside, chequered.

F. royelii: to 60cm (2ft); yellowish-green fls chequered purple, late spring.

F. verticillata (*F. thunbergii*): to 60cm (2ft); fls creamy-yellow striped green & mottled purple.

Squills and their relatives

Generally spring-flowering small bulbs with bell-shaped or starry flowers in shades of blue; some vars are pink or white. Most have narrow or strap-shaped leaves. Good for planting in groups in borders & wild gardens, on banks, in rock garden pockets (smaller spp), or under light trees & shrubs; most grow in outdoor containers. **Cultivation**: Generally very hardy. For humus-rich, moist but well-drained soil in sun or shade; *Puschkinia* spp like gritty soil. Plant 8–10cm (3–4in) deep, 8–15cm (3–6in) apart in autumn. **Propagation**: Offsets; seed (most spp self-sow).

Chionodoxas (glory of the snow, *Chionodoxa* spp): v early spring-flg alpines, not so tolerant of damp shade as other spp. Clustered wide-open starry fls, upward-facing; good for cutting.
C. gigantea (correctly, *C. luciliae* 'Gigantea'): taller-growing var of *C. luciliae*, to 20cm (8in); pale or gentian-blue 4cm (1½in) fls, white eye. Var 'Pink Giant' (*C. luciliae* 'Pink Giant') is orchid-pink.
C. luciliae **1**: best-known sp; to 8–15cm (3–6in); bright blue 2.5cm (1in) fls, white eye. Vars: 'Alba' (white); 'Rosea' **2** (lilac-pink); 'Tmolii' (*C. tmolii*; dwarf; pale blue, white centre; late). See also *C. gigantea* (above).
C. sardensis: to 10–15cm (4–6in); gentian-blue 2cm (¾in) fls, v small white eye.
English & Spanish bluebells (wild hyacinths, *Endymion* spp; often listed as *Scilla* spp): late spring-flg natives of woodland & hedgerows in Europe, with erect racemes of mainly blue to purple bell fls. When cutting, snap or cut (do not pull) stems. Like acid soil; not suitable for containers.
E. hispanicus **3** (*S. campanulata*, *S. hispanica*, Spanish bluebell, Spanish squill): to 30–45cm (1–1½ft); strong upright racemes of 10–30 violet-blue 2cm (¾in) fls. Vars: 'Excelsior' (v large blue-violet fls in tall spikes); 'La Grandesse' (pure white); 'Myosotis' (clear blue; early); 'Queen of the Pinks' (deep pink); 'White Triumphator' **4** (white).
E. non-scriptus (*S. non-scripta*, *S. nutans*, English bluebell; in Scotland, wild hyacinth): to 30cm (1ft); curving racemes of 4–16 violet-blue 1cm (½in) fls. Vars: 'Alba' (white); 'Rosea' (pink).
Striped squill (*Puschkinia libanotica* **5**; correctly, *P. scilloides libanotica*): v to ultra-hardy; to 10–20cm (4–8in); slender racemes of 6–12 pale blue 1cm (½in) bell fls, darker stripes, spring. Var 'Alba' is white.
True squills (scillas, *Scilla* spp): short, with bell-shaped to starry fls, mainly blue, in racemes or umbels on slender stems from late winter; spread freely.
S. bifolia **6** (twinleaf squill): v to ultra-hardy; to 15–20cm (6–8in); usually 2 or 3 narrow lvs; loose racemes of 3–8 usually nodding gentian-blue star-shaped fls, 1cm (½in) across, from late winter or early spring. Vars: 'Alba' (white); 'Rosea' (shell-pink).
S. monophylla: to 15–25cm (6–10in); usually

single lf 15cm (6in) long; loose racemes of 6–20 lilac-blue 5mm (¼in) bell fls, late spring to early summer.
S. peruviana **7** (Cuban lily [misnomers – from Mediterranean area]): semi- to moderately hardy; to 30cm (1ft); dense umbels of 50–100 deep blue star-shaped 1cm (½in) fls, late spring & early summer. V short dormant season; plant in summer.
*S. pratensis** (meadow squill; correctly *S. litardieri*): to 25cm (10in); dense racemes of 12–35 violet-blue starry bell-like fls, 5mm (¼in) across, spring to early summer. Vigorous form sometimes sold as *S. amethystina*.
S. siberica (Siberian squill): ultra-hardy; to 20cm (8in); loose racemes of 2–5 brilliant violet-blue 1cm (½in) nodding starry bell fls, v early spring. Vars: 'Alba' (white); 'Atrocoerulea' **8** ('Spring Beauty'; v early; fls larger, deeper blue); 'Taurica' **9** ('Multiflora'; v early; pale blue, dark veins).
S. tubergeniana **10**: ultra-hardy; to 8–10cm (3–4in); loose racemes of up to 4 pale blue open bell fls 4cm (1½in) across, darker stripe (more pronounced in var 'Zwanenburg'), from late winter (before lvs).

Hyacinths and their close relatives

Easy, mainly spring-flowering bulbs with narrow basal leaves & erect racemes of globular to bell-shaped & reflexing flowers on strong leafless stalks. Good grouped in borders, & for bedding & containers (*Hyacinthus* vars often forced indoors); smaller spp also for rock gardens. **Cultivation**: For any well-drained soil, preferably in full sun. Generally plant early autumn, 5–8cm (2–3in) deep & apart unless stated. **Propagation**: Seed; division or offsets (latter induced commercially in *Hyacinthus* vars by cutting into basal plate of bulb). Nomenclature somewhat confused.

Summer hyacinth (spire lily, *Galtonia* [*Hyacinthus*] *candicans** **1**): moderately to v hardy (v hardy if mulched thickly in winter); to 1.2×0.3m (4×1ft); strap-shaped lvs to 75×5cm (30×2in); sturdy open infls of nodding 4cm (1½in) bell fls, white tinged green, late summer. Good for back of border, cutting. Plant 15cm (6in) deep, spring; best lifted for winter in cold areas.

Hyacinths (*Hyacinthus* spp): generally v hardy; fleshy strap-shaped lvs to 20–30cm (8–12in) long; fls in cylindrical racemes.

H. (*Scilla*) *amethystinus* (Spanish hyacinth; correctly, *Brimeura amethystina*): to 20–25cm (8–10in); loose infls of up to 15 nodding bell-shaped light blue fls 10mm (⅜in) long, late spring. Var 'Alba' is white.

H. azureus: see *Muscari azureum*.

H. orientalis** (common hyacinth): sp rarely grown, but parent of numerous hybrids (Dutch hyacinths): to 25–30×15–20cm (10–12×6–8in); lvs follow fl buds; v dense infls to 15cm (6in) long of funnel-shaped reflexing fls to 2.5cm (1in) long, waxy petals, mid–late spring (from early winter if forced indoors). Best massed or grouped in beds, containers, etc; "second" ("bedding") size bulbs (or bulbs that have fld once indoors) generally adequate outdoors; plant 15cm (6in) deep. Vars: 'Amethyst'* (amethyst-blue); 'Amsterdam'* (salmon-red); 'Bismark'* (clear blue); 'Blue Jacket'* (deep blue; dark stem); 'Blushing Dolly'** (cherry-blossom pink); 'Carnegie'* (white); 'Chestnut Flower'** (pale pink, double); 'City of Haarlem'** **2** (primrose-yellow); 'Colosseum'* (white); 'Delft Blue'* **3**; 'Eros'* (deep rose-pink); 'General Kohler'** (lavender-blue, double); 'Gipsy Queen'* (yellow flushed apricot-orange); 'Jan Bos'* **4** (carmine); 'King of the Blues'** (indigo-blue); 'Lady Derby'* (shell-pink); 'La Victoire'* (red); 'L'Innocence'** (white); 'Lord Balfour'* (deep heliotrope-blue); 'Madame Kruger'** (white, double); 'Marconi'* (pink); 'Myosotis'* (forget-me-not blue); 'Orange Boven'* ('Salmonetta'; salmon-orange); 'Ostara'** **5** (bright blue, darker bands); 'Perle Brilliante'* (pale blue); 'Pink Pearl'* (deep rose); 'Prince Henry'* (cream-yellow); 'Princess Irene'* (pink); 'Queen of the Blues'* (azure-blue); 'Queen of the Pinks'* (pink, deeper bands); 'Tubergen's Scarlet'** (red); 'Yellow Hammer'* (cream-yellow).

H. orientalis albulus** (Roman or French-Roman hyacinth): moderately to v hardy; to 15–20cm (6–8in); loose, infls of white, pink or blue reflexing bell fls (2 or 3 stems per bulb), early spring.

H. romanus (Roman or Dutch-Roman hyacinth; correctly, *Bellevalia romana*): moderately to v hardy; to 15–30cm (6–12in); loose infls of small bell fls, white/blue-tinged, mid–late spring.

Grape hyacinths (*Muscari* spp): v to ultra-hardy dwarf bulbs with grassy lvs & generally crowded shortish infls of 5–8mm (¼–⅓in) urn-shaped or globular fls, generally mid spring, cuttable. Excellent for naturalizing; multiply freely.

M. armeniacum*: to 25cm (10in); lvs appear autumn, overwinter; tapering spikes of white-edged cobalt-blue fls, mid spring. Vars: 'Blue Spike' **6** (double sterile fls in large dense infls); 'Cantab' (pale blue); 'Early Giant'* (large infls); 'Heavenly Blue' (shy-blue).

M. (*Hyacinthella, Hyacinthus*) *azureum*: to 20cm (8in); bright blue tubular fls, from late winter.

M. botryoides (common grape hyacinth of Europe): to 20cm (8in); white-rimmed deep blue globular fls. Var 'Album' **7** is white.

M. comosum (tassel hyacinth): to 30–45cm (1–1½ft); loose infls of many olive-green fertile fls topped by tuft of upright purple sterile fls, late spring. Bulbs edible. Vars 'Monstrosum' (violet-blue) & 'Plumosum' (reddish-purple; both called feather hyacinths) have only sterile fls, petals cut into fine shreds.

M. latifolium: to 25cm (10in); 1 or 2 lvs per bulb; violet-blue fls, paler & sterile at top.

M. macrocarpum* **8** (*M. moschatum flavum*): to 20cm (8in); arching lvs to 40cm (16in) long; rather loose infls of tubular bright yellow fls 10mm (⅜in) long, edged brown.

M. neglectum*: to 20cm (8in); v dark blue white-edged fls.

M. paradoxum: to 30cm (1ft); lvs to 45×2cm (18×¾in); broad infls of v dark blue fls, inside & edge greenish, late spring, stout stalk.

M. racemosum* **9** (*M. moschatum*, musk hyacinth; often confused with *M. atlanticum*): to 20–25cm (8–10in); lvs to 30×2cm (12×¾in); dark blue-purple white-rimmed fls fading yellowish, early–mid spring. Var 'Majus' ('Major') is larger.

M. tubergenianum **10** (in UK, Oxford & Cambridge grape hyacinth): to 20–25cm (8–10in); tapering infls with fls dark ("Oxford") blue at base, pale ("Cambridge") blue at top, early spring.

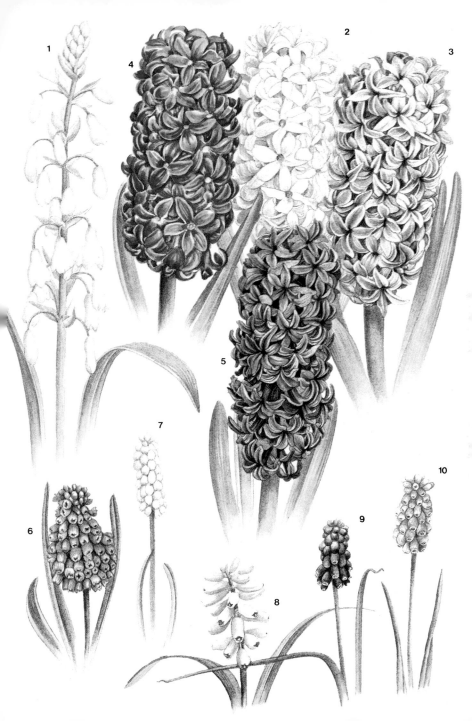

Species tulips

Sometimes called botanical tulips. Wild *Tulipa* spp & closely related vars & hybrids, generally shorter & smaller-flowered than the better-known garden tulip cultivars (p404). Flowers generally goblet-shaped, sometimes opening flat (sizes refer to flower length before fully open); solitary unless stated; taller spp good for cutting. Leaves lance-shaped unless stated. Good for rock gardens, small beds & borders, containers, etc, in sun. **Cultivation**: As for garden hybrids, but can be naturalized in light soil (light soil essential for some spp). Plant 7.5–10cm (3–4in) deep, 8–15cm (3–6in) apart, according to size. Unless stated, very hardy. **Propagation**: Offsets; seed (several years to flower).

T. acuminata **1** (*T. cornuta*, horned or Turkish tulip): to 50cm (20in); narrow lvs; 8cm (3in) fls, yellow streaked red, with narrow twisted petals, mid–late spring. Probably a hybrid.

T. aucherana* **2**: to 10cm (4in); narrow lvs; 3cm (1¼in) fls opening star-shaped, rose-pink with yellow centre, early spring.

T. batalinii **3**: to 15cm (6in); narrow glaucous lvs; 4cm (1½in) pure primrose-yellow fls with pointed petals, mid–late spring. Needs v well-drained soil & summer warmth; best in alpine house or rock garden. Var 'Bronze Charm' (hybrid with *T. linifolia*) is shorter & bronze to apricot.

T. biflora **4**: to 10–15cm (4–6in); narrow greyish lvs; 2cm (¾in) yellow-centred white fls, shaded green & red outside, opening star-shaped, early spring; 1–5 (often 2) fls per stem. Long-lived in well-drained soil.

T. clusiana* **5** (lady tulip): to 25–30cm (10–12in); v narrow erect grey-green lvs; 4cm (1½in) white fls, violet basal blotch, outer petals banded red on outside, opening star-like, mid spring. Likes well-drained soil & hot summers; spreads by underground stolons. Vars: *chrysantha* **6** (often sold incorrectly as *T. chrysantha*; moderately to v hardy; 15–20cm [6–8in] fls yellow banded red outside, no blotch); 'Cynthia' (fls creamy blotched purple, banded red outside); *stellata* (*T. stellata*; fls white blotched yellow, tinged red outside).

T. eichleri: to 30cm (1ft); sturdy; glaucous lvs; 10cm (4in) brilliant scarlet glossy fls with yellow-edged black basal blotch, mid–late spring. Var 'Excelsa' is deeper colour.

T. fosteriana : to 30cm (1ft); grey-green lvs; 10cm (4in) fls, opening flat, brilliant scarlet with yellow-edged black centre, mid spring. Vars: see p406 (Div 13); also involved in breeding Darwin Hybrids (Div 5).

T. greigii: to 25–30cm (10–12in); grey-green lvs striped/mottled purple-brown or bronze; 8cm (3in) fls, orange-scarlet with yellow-edged black basal blotch, early spring. Vars: see p410 (Div 14); also involved in breeding Fosteriana (Div 13) & Kaufmanniana (Div 12) hybrids.

T. hageri: to 20–30cm (8–12in); red-edged narrow lvs; 5cm (2in) coppery-red & greenish fls (sometimes 2 per stem), mid–late spring.

T. kaufmanniana **7** (water-lily tulip): to 15–25cm (6–10in); glaucous-green lvs; 8cm (3in) fls

opening flat & star-like, white to creamy-yellow with yellow centre, flushed red & yellow outside, early spring. Vars: see p406 (Div 12). 'Peacock Hybrids' are hybrids of *T. kaufmanniana* & *T. greigii*, with former's multi-coloured fls & latter's marked lvs; sold as mixtures.

T. kolpakowskiana: ultra-hardy; to 15–20cm (6–8in); 5cm (2in) fls opening flat & starry, then reflexing, yellow shaded cherry-red outside, mid spring.

T. linifolia **8**: to 15–20cm (6–8in); rosette of v narrow red-edged lvs; 5cm (2in) glossy scarlet fls with black basal blotch, late spring.

T. marjolettii **9**: to 60cm (2ft); 4–5cm (1½–2in) primrose-yellow fls shaded red outside, v late spring. Probably a hybrid.

T. maximowiczii: to 15cm (6in); similar to *T. linifolia* but smaller bluish-black blotch & slightly earlier.

T. persica* (*T. celsiana*; may be form of *T. patens*): to 25cm (10in); narrow red-edged dark green lvs; 4cm (1½in) clear yellow bronze-tinged fls opening star-like, v late spring (often 2 or 3 per stem).

T. praecox: to 45–50cm (18–20in); sturdy; glaucous lvs; 9–10cm (3½–4in) red fls with yellow-edged dark basal blotch, opening v wide, early spring; spreads by underground stolons. May be a hybrid.

T. praestans: to 25–30cm (10–12in); grey-green ribbed lvs; 5cm (2in) brick-red fls, early spring (3–5 per stem). Vars: 'Fusilier' **10** (flame-scarlet); 'Zwanenburg' (carmine-red).

T. pulchella: to 10–15cm (4–6in); narrow lvs; 3cm (1¼in) fls opening flat, crimson to purple with white-edged bluish centre, v early spring (up to 3 per stem). Vars: 'Humilis' (violet-pink, yellow centre); 'Violacea' **11** (purple-violet, yellow centre). For well-drained rock garden.

T. sylvestris*: to 30–40cm (12–16in); narrow grey-green lvs; 5cm (2in) yellow fls, nodding in bud, mid–late spring; spreads by underground stolons. Good in partial shade.

T. tarda **1**, p405 (often sold incorrectly as *T. dasystemon*): to 10–15cm (4–6in); rosette of narrow lvs; 5cm (2in) fls opening star-shaped, white with large yellow centre, early–mid spring (often several per stem); spreads by underground stolons. Needs v good drainage.

T. tubergeniana: to 30cm (1ft); glaucous lvs;

9–10cm (3½–4in) glossy vermilion fls with yellow-edged greenish-black basal blotch, mid spring. Var 'Keukenhof' is multi-fld.

T. turkestanica 2 (*T. biflora turkestanica*): to 20–25cm (8–10in); glaucous lvs; 3cm (1¼in) creamy-white fls with orange-yellow centre, opening flat & star-like, early spring (several per stem).

T. urumiensis 3: to 10cm (4in); rosette of prostrate lvs; 4cm (1½in) golden-yellow fls, nodding & bronzed in bud, opening wide & star-like, mid spring (3–5 per stem).

T. wilsoniana: to 20–25cm (8–10in); red-edged glaucous lvs; 5cm (2in) deep blood-red fls with black basal blotch, mid–late spring. *T. montana* is similar; blotch bluish-black.

Garden tulips

Hybrids of various *Tulipa* spp, often of complex parentage; many derived originally from *T. gesneriana* &/or *T. suaveolens*. Long valued for bold colours & flower shapes (unless stated, solitary & single, with 6 petals, cup/goblet-shaped; dimensions given are average fl length & diameter in good conditions, but vary with var & conditions). Used mainly for spring bedding & containers; all except short vars good for cutting; some vars (especially "prepared" bulbs) can be forced in bowls under glass. Leaves generally quite broad & lance-shaped, often with greyish or bluish tinge. **Cultivation**: Very hardy. Prefer rich, well-drained soil in sun. Plant mid autumn to early winter 12–15cm (5–6in) deep; in warm climates first store 8 weeks at 4–7°C (39–45°F). Dead-head. Best lifted when foliage dies, dried & stored till autumn, then replanted in fresh site. Prone to fire disease (protect bulbs with fungicide). **Propagation**: Offsets. **Classification**: By flower form, season & origin into 14 divisions (recently revised) plus wild species (p402). Some 4,000 registered vars; selection listed below.

Single Early (Div 1; includes some vars formerly classed as Darwins): to 25–60×10–15cm (10–24×4–6in); fls cup-shaped, to 8–10×8cm (3–4×3in), sometimes opening flat in sun, early–mid spring. Good for bedding (even in exposed spots), containers, bowls, etc; prepared bulbs can be forced to fl from mid winter. Vars: 'Apricot Beauty' (apricot-pink tinged red, fading soft apricot); 'Bellona'* 4 (golden-yellow); 'Brilliant Star' (orange-scarlet, dark basal blotch); 'Couleur Cardinal' (deep velvety-red tinged purple); 'Diana' (pure white); 'General de Wet'* 5 ('De Wet'; golden-orange stippled scarlet); 'Keizerskroon' ('Grand Duc'; brilliant red, wide yellow edge); 'Pink Beauty' (carmine-pink striped white); 'Pink Trophy' (pink flushed rose); 'Prince Carnival'* (yellow flamed red); 'Ruby Red' (glowing scarlet); 'Van der Neer' (violet-purple).

Double Early (Div 2): to 25–40×15cm (10–16×6in); long-lasting double paeony-like fls opening wide, to 6–8×10cm (2½–3×4in), early–mid spring (generally just after Div 1). V good for massed bedding & tubs, preferably with some shelter; easy to force. Vars: 'Carlton' (deep Turkey-red); 'Electra' (deep cherry-red); 'Hytuna' (buttercup-yellow); 'Orange Nassau' (orange-red shaded mahogany); 'Peach Blossom'* 6 (deep rosy-pink); 'Schoonoord' (shining white); 'Willemsoord' (carmine-red edged white).

Triumph (Div 3; formerly Div 4; includes some vars formerly classed as Mendels): to 40–50×15–20cm (16–20×6–8in); fls conical, opening more rounded, to 8–10×5–8cm (3–4×2–3in), on sturdy stems, mid–late spring (generally weather-resistant). For bedding (even in exposed places) or forcing. Vars: 'Athleet' 7 (white); 'Attila' 8 (violet); 'Bestseller' (coppery-orange); 'Garden Party' 9 (white edged carmine-pink); 'Golden Melody' (butter-yellow); 'Invasion' (orange-red edged cream); 'Kansas' (white); 'Kees Nelis' ('Ringo'; blood-red edged yellow); 'Peerless Pink' (satiny-pink); 'Tambour Maitre' (cardinal-red).

Darwin Hybrids (Div 4; formerly Div 5): hybrids of Darwins & *T. fosteriana* vars; to 55–70×15–20cm (22–28×6–8in); v large cupped fls, to 12×15–20cm (5×6–8in) in some vars, in brilliant colours on strong stems, mid–late spring. Excellent for focal planting. Vars: 'Apeldoorn' 10 (orange-scarlet); 'Elizabeth Arden' (deep salmon tinted violet); 'Golden Apeldoorn' (golden-yellow); 'Gudoshnik' (dark yellow spotted red & speckled rose); 'Holland's Glorie' (v large soft orange-scarlet fls); 'Jewel of Spring' (sulphur-yellow, narrow red edge); 'President Kennedy' (deep yellow faintly flushed red); 'Queen Wilhelmina' (orange-scarlet edged orange); 'Red Matador' (carmine-scarlet flushed scarlet).

Single Late (May-flowering; Div 5; incorporates former Darwin and many Cottage vars): generally to 45–75×15–20cm (18–30×6–8in); fls variable but often large-cupped, squarish or oval, to 10–12×8–10cm (4–5×3–4in), often with pointed petals, late spring to v early summer; some ("Bouquet" vars) multi-fld. Useful for bedding. Normal vars: 'Balalaika' (rich-red); 'Bleu Aimable' (lavender-mauve); 'Clara Butt' (salmon-rose); 'Golden Harvest' 1, p407 (daffodil-yellow); 'Landsaedel's Supreme' ('Wayside'; glowing red); 'Maureen' (white flushed cream); 'Most Miles' (currant-red); 'Niphetos' (creamy-

yellow); 'Princess Margaret Rose' (yellow edged orange-red); 'Queen of Bartigons' (salmon-pink); 'Queen of Night' **2** (velvety-maroon); 'Smiling Queen' (pink, deeper flush); 'Snowpeak' (white); 'Sorbet' (creamy-white feathered red); 'Sunkist' (deep yellow); 'Sweet Harmony' (lemon-yellow edged ivory). Bouquet vars: 'Georgette' (rich yellow edged cerise); 'Orange Bouquet' **3** (vivid red-orange, yellow base).

Lily-Flowered (Div 6; formerly Div 7): to 45–60×15cm (18–24×6in); elegant & graceful, with narrow-waisted fls to 9–12×8cm (3½–5×3in), petals pointed, on wiry but strong stems, late spring. Best for sheltered positions. Vars: 'Aladdin' (crimson edged gold); 'China Pink' **4** (rose-pink); 'Mariette' (deep satin-pink); 'Maytime' (mauve-lilac edged white); 'Queen of Sheba' (bronze-red edged orange); 'Red Shine' (ruby-red); 'West Point' (primrose-yellow); 'White Triumphator'.

Fringed (orchid-flowered; Div 7; formerly incorporated in Cottage div): to 50–75×15–20cm (20–30×6–8in); generally similar to Single Late vars, but petals edged with crystal-shaped fringes. Popular for arrangements. Sold as mixtures & named vars: 'Arma' (cardinal-red); 'Burgundy Lace' (wine-red).

Viridiflora (green tulips; Div 8; formerly incorporated in Cottage div): generally to 25–30×15cm (10–12×6in); generally similar to Single Late vars, but petals partly greenish. Popular for arrangements. Vars: 'Artist' (green shading to rose & apricot; twisted petals); 'Golden Artist' (golden-yellow flushed apricot, green splashes; frilled petals); 'Greenland' **5** (to 60cm [2ft]; green shading to yellow & rich pink); 'Pimpernel' (Turkey-red blazed green & purple).

Rembrandt (Div 9; includes former Bizarre & Bybloemen vars): to 45–70×15–20cm (18–28×6–8in); generally similar to Single Late vars, but colours "broken" into striped/feathered patterns due to virus. Sold as mixtures & named vars: 'Absalon' **6** (mahogany on yellow); 'Black Boy' (chocolate on bronze); 'Dainty Maid' (magenta-purple on white); 'Insulinde' (violet on yellow); 'Victor Hugo' (cherry-pink on white).

Parrot (Div 10): to 50–65×15–20cm (20–26×6–8in); similar to Single Late vars, but fls up to 12cm (5in) wide & petal edges frilled, cut or fringed & often twisted; long-flg. For sheltered positions. Sold as mixtures & named vars: 'Black Parrot' (purplish-black); 'Blue Parrot' (violet); 'Estella Rijnveld' (red & white); 'Fantasy' (rose-pink often streaked green); 'Flaming Parrot' (yellow flamed red); 'Orange Favourite'* (deep orange blotched green); 'Texas Gold' **7** (deep yellow edged red); 'White Parrot'.

Double Late (Paeony-Flowered; Div 11): to 40–60×15cm (16–24×6in); showy, squat, paeony-like double fls, to 8–10×10–12cm

(3–4×4–5in), on sturdy stems, mid–late spring. Best in sheltered position. Vars: 'Angelique' (blush-pink shaded deeper); 'Gold Medal' (golden-yellow); 'Lilac Perfection' (pearly-lilac); 'May Wonder' (clear rose); 'Mount Tacoma' **8** (white); 'Orange Triumph' (dark orange edged gold); 'Symphonia' (carmine-red).

Kaufmanniana Hybrids (water-lily tulips; Div 12): to 10–25×10–15cm (4–10×4–6in); derived from *T. kaufmanniana* (p406) & other spp & vars, with former's starry water-lily-like fls opening flat to 6cm (2½in) across, generally bicoloured, early spring; some (marked †) have striped/mottled lvs. Good for rock gardens, edging, containers, etc; can be naturalized. Vars: 'Daylight'† (scarlet & yellow); 'Heart's Delight'† (pale pink shaded carmine-red outside, red & yellow base); 'Shakespeare' **9** (carmine-red edged salmon outside, salmon flushed scarlet with golden-yellow base inside); 'Stresa'† (bright red edged yellow outside, golden-yellow blotched red inside); 'The First' (v early; ivory-white shaded carmine-red outside).

Fosterana Hybrids (Div 13): derived largely from *T. fosterana* (p402); generally to 30–45×15–20cm (12–18×6–8in); fresh-green lvs; v large vividly-coloured fls, to 15cm (6in) long opening to 18–20cm (7–8in) wide, early–mid spring. Best for focal plantings or contrast with quieter colours. Vars: 'Cantata' (to 25cm [10in]; shiny lvs; scarlet-red fls); 'Easter Parade' (yellow shaded red); 'Galata' (orange-red); 'Princeps' (to 25cm [10in]; orange-scarlet); 'Purissima' ('White Emperor'; white, yellow centre); 'Red Emperor' **10** ('Mme Lefeber'; brilliant vermilion-scarlet); 'Yellow Empress' (yellow-primrose).

Greigii Hybrids (Div 14): derived largely from *T. greigii* (p402); generally to 20–40×15cm (8–16×6in); lvs often wavy, generally striped/mottled purplish or brown; large colourful fls, to 10–12×13cm (4–5×4½in), mid–late spring. For rock gardens, beds, containers, etc. Vars: 'Cape Cod' (apricot edged yellow outside, bronze-yellow inside); 'Dreamboat' (salmon flushed amber); 'Oriental Beauty' (carmine-red outside, vermilion with brownish base inside); 'Oriental Splendour' (to 50cm [20in]; yellow, shaded carmine-red outside); 'Plaisir' **11** (to 15cm [6in]; creamy-white striped vermilion-red); 'Red Riding Hood' (to 20cm [8in]; brilliant red, black base); 'Yellow Dawn' (yellow, shaded rose-red outside); 'Zampa' (primrose-yellow flushed red, bronze base).

Lilies

Lilium spp & hybrids (latter often of complex parentage). Among the most important & stately of all bulbs, with elegant, often very fragrant flowers, unless stated in early summer. Leafy stems are crowned with 6-lobed flowers (narrowly trumpet-shaped to flat or reflexing ["Turk's-cap"]), singly or in loose inflorescences, in most colours except blue, generally spotted inside. Leaves generally narrow to lance-shaped, alternate or in whorls. Bulbs generally large & scaly; many spp & vars grow roots also from stem above bulb (must be planted deeply). Can be grown in groups in mixed borders, among shrubs or in woodland gardens. Very good for cutting; can be forced in large pots under glass. **Cultivation**: Very hardy unless stated, but even these best protected with thick mulch below about −18°C (0°F). Generally for any well-drained (but not dry) soil with ample humus in sun or partial shade; if soil heavy, plant in pocket of sand. Plant autumn or early spring (preferably with some intact growing roots), unless stated 10–15cm (4–6in) deep, 15–25cm (6–10in) apart. **Pests & diseases**: Rodents & squirrels (eat bulbs); slugs & various insect pests; viruses (transmitted mainly by aphids); fungal diseases. **Propagation** (use virus-free stock): Offsets; bulb scales; bulbils from leaf axils or stem bases where produced; seed, sown autumn (named vars will not breed true). **Classification**: By origin & flower form into 9 divisions including spp (Div 9; covered first below). Some 3,500 registered vars & seed strains (latter variable); selection listed. For giant lilies (*Cardiocrinum* spp), see p416.

Species (Div 9; includes close vars): sometimes sub-divided (mainly for exhibition) by shape.

L. amabile **1**: ultra-hardy; to 1m (3ft); lvs to 9cm (3½in) long; racemes of up to 6 pendent rich red Turk's-cap fls 8cm (3in) wide, spotted black, brown anthers; unpleasant scent. Forms underground bulbils. Best in light shade. Var 'Luteum' is clear orange-yellow.

L. auratum* **2** (gold-rayed [-banded] lily): moderately hardy; to 1.5–2.5m (5–8ft); dark green leathery lvs to 22cm (9in) long; racemes of up to 35 crimson-spotted white fls to 30cm (1ft) across, petals banded gold, late summer. Plant deeply; hates lime, susceptible to viruses. Vars 'Pictum' (bands crimson at end); *platyphyllum* (*macranthum*; v large fls); 'Rubrum' (fls banded crimson); 'Tom Thumb' (dwarf, to 40cm [16in]).

L. bulbiferum **3** (*L. aurantiacum*) *croceum* (orange lily): ultra-hardy; to 1.2–1.5m (4–5ft); 15cm (6in) lvs; umbels of up to 20 erect orange-red fls 8cm (3in) long. Produces aerial bulbils.

L. canadense **4** (Canada lily; in N America, wild yellow lily): ultra-hardy; to 1.2–1.8m (4–6ft); whorls of 15cm (6in) lvs; up to 4 umbels, each of up to 20 bell-shaped nodding 8cm (3in) fls, orange-yellow to red, spotted purple-brown, mid summer. Hates lime; best in light shade.

L. candidum** **5** (madonna lily): to 1.2–1.5m (4–5ft); basal lvs to 22cm (9in) long, appear autumn & persist; racemes of 5–20 waxy pure white horizontal trumpet-shaped fls to 8cm (3in) long, golden anthers. Dies down soon after flg. Plant 2.5–5cm (1–2in) deep, early autumn; likes some lime; susceptible to botrytis.

L. cernuum* **6**: ultra-hardy; to 45cm (1½ft); v narrow 15cm (6in) lvs; racemes of up to 6 nodding Turk's-cap fls 5cm (2in) wide, purplish-pink spotted red-purple, lilac anthers.

L. chalcedonicum (scarlet Turk's-cap lily): moderately to v hardy; to 1.2m (4ft); stem crowded with silvery-edged erect 10cm (4in) lvs; racemes of up to 10 pendent waxy vermilion-scarlet Turk's-cap fls to 8cm (3in) wide, mid summer. Plant 2.5–5cm (1–2in) deep; susceptible to botrytis, viruses.

L. columbianum **7** (Columbia lily): moderately to v hardy; to 1.2–1.8m (4–6ft); whorls of 10cm (4in) lvs; racemes of up to 40 nodding Turk's-cap fls to 5cm (2in) across, yellow to reddish-orange, spotted maroon, mid summer.

L. concolor (star lily): v hardy; to 60cm (2ft); v narrow 10cm (4in) lvs; umbels of up to 7 erect starry vermilion fls 5cm (2in) long. Var 'Coridion' is lemon-yellow spotted purple-brown.

L. davidii: to 1.2–1.8m (4–6ft); v narrow finely toothed lvs to 10cm (4in) long; racemes of up to 20 nodding bright orange-scarlet Turk's-cap fls 8–10cm (3–4in) wide, raised black spots, mid summer. Forms bulbils just below soil. Best staked. Vars: *macranthum* (cinnabar-red); *willmottiae* (large pyramid-shaped infls on strong stems).

L. formosanum* **8**: moderately hardy; to 1.2–1.8m (4–6ft); crowded v narrow dark green lvs to 20cm (8in) long; umbels of up to 10 (often less) funnel-shaped white fls 12–20cm (5–8in) long, suffused purple outside, late summer to autumn. Hates lime; susceptible to viruses. Easy & quick from seed.

L. giganteum: see *Cardiocrinum giganteum* (p416); *L. longiflorum takeshima*.

L. hansonii* **9**: to 1.2m (4ft); whorls of dark green waxy lvs to 12cm (5in) long; large racemes of nodding, strongly reflexed thick-textured orange-yellow fls to 6cm (2½in) wide, spotted brown. For lime-free soil in light shade; healthy.

L. henryi** **10**: to 2.5m (8ft); arching stems (best staked); crowded glossy lvs to 15cm (6in) long; loose racemes of 4–20 horizontal orange-yellow to apricot reflexed fls to 9cm (3½in) long, spotted brown, dark orange anthers, mid–late summer.

Plant deeply; best in light shade.

L. japonicum* (Japanese lily): v hardy; to 60–90cm (2–3ft); dark green 15cm (6in) lvs; small racemes of white, pale pink to purple trumpet-shaped fls to 15cm (6in) long, orange-brown anthers, mid summer. For sandy, lime-free soil in semi-shade; susceptible to viruses.

L. lancifolium: see *L. tigrinum*.

L. leichtlinii: v hardy; to 1.2m (4ft); crowded narrow 15cm (6in) lvs; infls of up to 5 nodding lemon-yellow Turk's-cap fls 8cm (3in) long, spotted brown, anthers red, mid summer. Spreads by stolons. For lime-free soil. Var *maximowiczii* (*tigrinum*; more common) is taller; fls cinnabar red spotted purple-brown.

L. longiflorum** **1** (white trumpet lily, Easter lily): moderately hardy; to 1m (3ft); shiny 10cm (4in) lvs; small infls of horizontal trumpet-shaped pure white fls 12–18cm (5–7in) long, golden anthers, mid summer. Often grown in pots & forced for spring flg (hence common name). Susceptible to viruses. Vars: 'Holland's Glory' (hardier); 'Mount Everest' (taller; v large waxy fls); *takeshima* (sometimes sold incorrectly as *L. giganteum*; clusters of up to 10 large fls).

L. martagon **2** (Turk's-cap lily): ultra-hardy; to 1–1.5m (3–5ft); spaced whorls of dark green 15cm (6in) lvs; large racemes of unpleasant-scented nodding Turk's-cap fls to 4cm (1½in) long, usually purple-pink spotted black, but white in var *album*, dark wine-red in *cattaniae* (*dalmatica*). Long-lived; best in partial shade.

L. monadelphum*: ultra-hardy; 1.2m (4ft); crowded 12cm (5in) lvs; large racemes of nodding bell-shaped reflexing bright yellow fls to 12cm (5in) across, often tinged/spotted purple. Best in partial shade. Var *szovitsianum* **3** (correctly, *L. szovitsianum*) is similar but infls generally smaller.

L. nepalense: moderately to v hardy; to 1–1.2m (3–4ft); stem runs underground 30–60cm (1–2ft) before emerging; sparse 12cm (5in) lvs; small infls of trumpet-shaped pendent fls 12cm (5in) long on arching stalks, green-yellow, stained/blotched purple inside, mid summer. Forms bulbils at ground level. Needs long, warm growing season, high humidity. Var 'Robusta' is hardier; fls larger.

L. pardalinum* **4** (leopard or panther lily): ultra-hardy; to 1.5–2m (5–7ft); strong stems; narrow lvs to 18cm (7in) long; solitary or sparse nodding Turk's-cap fls to 10cm (4in) across, bright orange-red shaded crimson, prominently spotted crimson or brown, early–mid summer. Spreads strongly by rhizomes. Best in damp lime-free soil. Var 'Giganteum' (sunset lily; probably hybrid with *L. humboldtii*) has large yellow-centred bright red fls spotted purple-brown.

L. philadelphicum (wood lily of N America): to 1m (3ft); whorls of narrow 10cm (4in) lvs; small infls

of wide-open bell-shaped fls to 10cm (4in) across, orange to scarlet, spotted purple. Best in lime-free soil in light shade; protect from winter wet.

L. pumilum* (*L. tenuifolium*, coral lily): ultra-hardy; to 45–60cm (1½–2ft); wiry stems; crowded grassy lvs 10cm (4in) long; racemes of up to 20 nodding bright scarlet Turk's-cap fls to 5cm (2in) across. For full sun. Var 'Golden Gleam' is golden-orange.

L. pyrenaicum **5**: to 1m (3ft); crowded narrow lvs to 12cm (5in) long; loose racemes of up to 12 unpleasant-scented pendent Turk's-cap fls 4cm (1½in) across, greenish-yellow spotted purple-black, orange-brown anthers, late spring or early summer. Var 'Aureum'** is deeper canary-yellow, greenish throat; scent pleasant.

L. regale** **6** (regal or royal lily): ultra-hardy; to 1.2–1.8m (4–6ft); crowded lvs to 12cm (5in) long; loose umbels of up to 30 horizontal trumpet-shaped fls to 15cm (6in) long, white shaded sulphur-yellow in throat, outside shaded rose or purplish, mid summer. Easy from seed; spreads freely; best in full sun. V popular. Var 'Album'** is pure white, yellowish throat.

L. sargentiae* is similar but forms aerial bulbils; fls shaded purple to greenish outside, mid–late summer.

L. rubellum* **7**: ultra-hardy; to 75cm (2½ft); rather broad, stalked lvs; umbels of up to 9 horizontal bell/funnel-shaped clear rose-pink fls to 8cm (3in) long, late spring & early summer.

L. speciosum** (Japanese or showy lily; sometimes listed incorrectly as *L. lancifolium*): moderately to v hardy; to 1.2–1.5m (4–5ft); rather sparse broad 18cm (7in) leathery lvs; v large leafy panicles of nodding bowl-shaped reflexing fls to 15cm (6in) wide, waxy-white heavily shaded crimson or rose, raised crimson spots, v late summer. Best in lime-free soil. V good in pots under glass. Vars: 'Album'* (white, yellow throat); 'Ellabee'* **8** (pure white); 'Grand Commander'* **9** (crimson, whitish edge, heavily spotted deep crimson); 'Lucie Wilson'* (v large rose-pink fls edged white, red spots); 'Melpomene'* (deep carmine edged white, heavily spotted ruby-red); 'Numazu Beauty'* (large-fld, deeper-coloured form of 'Rubrum'); 'Rosemede'* (even darker form of 'Rubrum'; v large fls); 'Roseum'* (rose, pink spots); 'Rubrum'* **10** (carmine-red); 'Rubrum Magnificum'* (rich ruby-carmine, wide white edge); 'Uchida'* (profuse large deep crimson fls, heavily spotted).

L. superbum ([American] Turk's-cap lily; sometimes sold as *L. canadense superbum*): v hardy; to 1.5–2.5m (5–8ft); whorls of lvs to 15cm (6in) long; sometimes v large infls of nodding Turk's-cap fls to 10cm (4in) wide, orange-scarlet spotted purplish-brown, mid

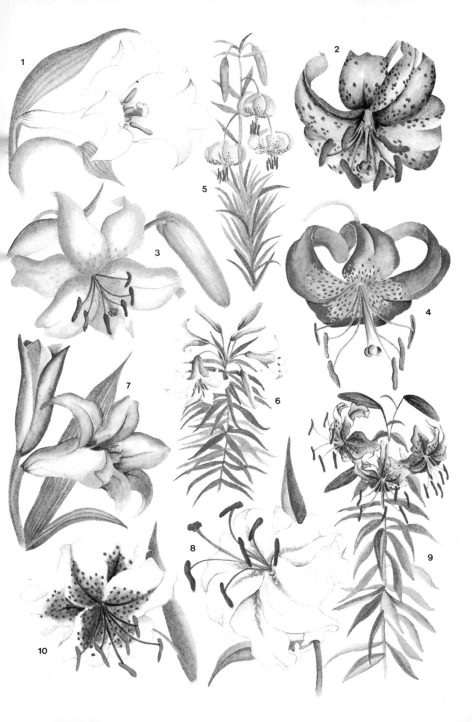

summer. Needs lime-free soil & ample summer moisture.

L. tigrinum (tiger lily; correctly, *L. lancifolium*): ultra-hardy; to 1.2–1.8m (4–6ft); stems cobwebby, with aerial bulbils; crowded 18cm (7in) lvs; racemes of up to 25 nodding Turk's-cap brilliant orange-red fls to 12cm (5in) across, purple-black spots, prominent orange-brown anthers, late summer. Bulbs edible. For lime-free soil in sun; susceptible to viruses. Vars: *flaviflorum* **1** (yellow tiger lily; yellow, purple spots); 'Flore Pleno' (double); *fortunei* (stems woolly; fls salmon-orange, late); 'Splendens' **2** (larger, abundant fls, rich red, bold spots).

L. tsingtauense **3**: v hardy; to 60–90cm (2–3ft); whorls of 10cm (4in) lvs; rather small, open clusters of erect funnel-shaped wide-opening orange fls 5cm (2in) across, mid summer. Hates lime.

L. wallichianum**: moderately hardy; to 1.8m (6ft); stems often run underground before emerging; crowded lvs to 25cm (10in) long; usually solitary horizontal trumpet-shaped creamy-white fls to 20–25cm (8–10in) long, greenish outside, yellow anthers, v late summer.

L. wardii*: to 1–1.5m (3–5ft); stems run underground before emerging; crowded short lvs; racemes of up to 40 nodding Turk's-cap fls to 6cm (2½in) wide, rose-pink spotted reddish-purple, orange anthers, mid summer.

Asiatic hybrids (Div 1): derived from Asiatic spp but excluding those in Div 6; sub-divided by fl shape & carriage. Generally compact, to 0.6–1.2m (2–4ft).

UPWARD-FACING (Div 1a): erect fls singly or in umbels.

L.× hollandicum (*L.× umbellatum*) vars (candlestick lilies): hybrids of *L. bulbiferum croceum* & *L.× maculatum* vars; to 1m (3ft); umbels of red, orange or yellow cup-shaped fls to 9cm (3½in) across. Vars: 'Apricot'; 'Golden Chalice Hybrids' (yellow, apricot & orange shades; 'Golden Wonder' is golden-yellow); 'Orange Triumph' **4** (vivid orange); 'Vermilion Brilliant'.

L.× maculatum (*L. elegans, L. thunbergianum*; incorrectly, *L. aurantiacum*) vars: hybrids of *L. dauricum* & *L. concolor*; to 60cm (2ft); small umbels of lemon-yellow to deep red cup-shaped fls to 10cm (4in) across, usually spotted, early–mid summer. Dislike lime. Vars include 'Wallacei' (rose-apricot, brown spots).

Other hybrids (including Mid-Century Hybrids, derived mainly from *L.× hollandicum* & *L. tigrinum*): reflexed fls 10–12cm (4–5in) across in wide colour range spotted maroon or brown, in wide umbels. Good in pots; can be forced. Vars: 'Bellona' (golden-yellow); 'Brigitta' (yellow); 'Chinook' (salmon); 'Cinnabar' (to 60cm [2ft]; maroon); 'Connecticut King' **5** (clear golden-

yellow, no spots); 'Dayspring' (lemon-yellow, gold blush); 'Destiny' (lemon-yellow); 'Enchantment' **6** (vigorous; nasturtium-red); 'Firecracker' (vivid scarlet); 'Pirate' (vermilion-red); 'Prince Charming' (purple-red, paler throat); 'Red Lion' (orange-red); 'Scarlet Emperor' (to 60cm [2ft]; scarlet); 'Sunkissed' (to 60cm [2ft]; soft orange); 'Tabasco' (chestnut-red).

OUTWARD-FACING (Div 1b): generally similar to above, but reflexed spotted fls more or less outward-facing, in umbels or racemes; include some Mid-Century Hybrids, also Preston Hybrids (derived partly from *L. dauricum* & *L. davidii willmottiae*; prefer lime-free soil in semi-shade). Vars & strains: 'Apricot Beauty' (apricot-orange fls, mid summer); 'Atilla' (creamy-yellow); 'Brandywine'* (apricot-yellow); 'Connecticut Lemonglow' (pale yellow, no spots); 'Corsage' **7** (thick petals, rosy-pink shading to ivory, maroon spots); 'Exception' **8** (narrow petals, deep rose shading paler); 'Fire King' (flame-red); 'Golden Souvenir' (lemon-yellow fls, mid summer); 'Ming Yellow' (bright yellow); 'Paprika' (to 75cm [2½ft]; deep crimson); 'Pastel Hybrids' (to 60cm [2ft]; soft colours); 'Pink Tiger' (rose-pink); 'Prince Constantine' (orange shading darker); 'Prosperity' (lemon-yellow).

PENDENT (Div 1c): generally similar to above, but pendent Turk's-cap spotted fls 8–10cm (3–4in) across on long stalks, in panicles. Major groups include Fiesta Hybrids (up to 30 fls 8cm [3in] wide per stem, yellow to vivid dark red, spotted maroon-black; strains include 'Burgundy' [cherry- to wine-red] & 'Citronella' **9** [lemon- to golden-yellow]) & Harlequin Hybrids (derived from *L. cernuum*; to 1.5m [5ft]; up to 20 fls to 10cm [4in] wide per stem, shades of white, pink, lilac, red, purple, cream, salmon, terracotta, etc); also includes some Mid-Century Hybrids. Named vars: 'Amber Gold' (butter-yellow, reverse reddish-bronze); 'Connecticut Yankee' (waxy, orange-red); 'Discovery' (soft lilac-pink tipped vermilion); 'Fuga' (bright orange, reverse reddish); 'Hornback's Gold' (soft yellow); 'La Bohème' (intense golden-yellow); 'Maxwill' (to 1.5m [5ft]; orange-red; large infls).

Martagon hybrids (Div 2): hybrids of *L. hansonii* & *L. martagon*; to 1.5–1.8m (5–6ft); racemes of 20–30 pendent Turk's-cap fls to 4cm (1½in) long, early. Best in partial shade.

L.× backhousiae vars (Backhouse Hybrids): white, yellow, pink or maroon, marbled/spotted pinkish or purplish. Vars: 'J. S. Dijt' (cream spotted purple); 'Marhan' **10** (bright yellow spotted brown, or orange spotted red-brown); 'Mrs R. O. Backhouse' (orange-yellow spotted purple, reverse flushed pink).

L.× dalhansonii: hybrid of *L. hansonii* & *L. martagon cattaniae* (*dalmatica*); profuse maroon fls, orange spots, unpleasant scent.

Candidum hybrids (Div 3): hybrids of
L. candidum & other European spp other than
L. martagon. Plant early autumn 2.5–5cm (1–2in)
deep.

L.×testaceum** (*L. excelsum*, Nankeen lily):
hybrid of *L. candidum* & *L. chalcedonicum*; to
1.2–1.8m (4–6ft); crowded narrow lvs to 10cm
(4in) long; racemes of up to 12 nodding reflexed
fls to 8cm (3in) wide, waxy apricot-yellow often
flushed pink, sometimes spotted red, orange-red
anthers, mid summer. An old favourite.

American hybrids (Div 4): derived from
L. pardalinum, L. parryi & other N American spp.
Spread by rhizomes.

Bellingham Hybrids*: complex parentage; to
1.5–1.8m (5–6ft); racemes of 20 or more
pendent, strongly reflexed fls to 8cm (3in) wide
on short stalks, shades of yellow, orange & red
(including bicolours), all prominently spotted
brown. Best in lime-free leafy soil in light shade.
Vars: 'Afterglow' **1** (reddish-orange); 'Shuksan'
(yellow-orange flushed red).

Longiflorum hybrids (Div 5): derived from
L. longiflorum & *L. formosanum*; moderately
hardy; horizontal trumpet-shaped fls. Prone to
viruses; few vars grown. Var 'White Queen'**
(may be listed as *L. longiflorum* 'White Queen')
grows to 1m (3ft); elegant pure white fls 12–
20cm (5–8in) long, mid summer; best in pots.

Trumpet & Aurelian hybrids (Div 6): derived
from Asiatic spp (other than those in Div 1),
including *L. henryi, L. regale* & *L. sargentiae*;
many developed from *L.×aurelianense*, a
variable hybrid of *L. henryi* & *L. sargentiae*.
Sub-divided by fl shape.

TRUMPET-SHAPED (Div 6a): generally to 1.5–1.8m
(5–6ft), with candelabra-like umbels of 12–20
trumpet/funnel-shaped fls to 20cm (8in) long,
mid summer. Best in rich, preferably lime-free
soil in semi-shade. Vars & strains (those marked
† belong to the sturdy & lime-tolerant Olympic
Hybrids): 'African Queen' strain **2** (apricot to
tawny-orange); 'Black Dragon'*† **3** (white,
outside rich purple-brown edged white);
'Damson' (silvery fuchsia-pink); 'Golden Clarion'
strain* (pale to deep yellow, reverse often striped
brown/red); 'Golden Splendor' strain **4** (large-fld
deep golden selection of 'Golden Clarion',
reverse striped maroon); 'Green Dragon'*†
(rather bowl-shaped white fls, reverse flushed
chartreuse-green); 'Green Magic' strain**† (v
large white fls, throat tinged green); 'Honeydew'
(yellow, yellowish-green reverse); 'Limelight'*
(lime-yellow); 'Mabel Violet' (purple-violet);
'Moonlight' strain** (greenish-yellow, outside
sometimes veined whitish); 'Pink Pearl' strain*†
(selection from 'Pink Perfection' strain; pink
shades); 'Pink Perfection' strain† **5** (rose- to
fuchsia-pink); 'Royal Gold' strain (*L. regale*
hybrid; glistening golden-yellow); 'Sentinel'

strain*† (white, pale yellow throat).

BOWL-SHAPED (Div 6b): to 1.2–2m (4–7ft); umbels
of shallow bowl-shaped outward-facing fls, mid–
late summer. Like partial shade. Vars & strains:
'Heart's Desire' strain** **6** (cream or yellow,
throat often orange); 'Thunderbolt'* (rich
orange).

PENDENT (Div 6c): to 1.2–1.8m (4–6ft); strong
stems; umbels of nodding trumpet/bowl-shaped
fls, late summer. Vars: 'Nutmegger' (yellow,
vermilion spots); 'Panamint' (white flushed
green, almost black spots).

STAR-SHAPED (Sunburst; Div 6d): to 1.2–1.8m
(4–6ft); rather flat starry fls to 18cm (7in) wide in
clusters at top of stems, mid summer. Best in
partial shade. Vars & strains: 'Bright Star' **7**
(silvery-white, starry orange central markings);
'Golden Sunburst' strain (golden-yellow, reverse
veined green); 'Pink Sunburst' strain (soft pink,
throat often paler, white or greenish).

Oriental hybrids (Div 7): derived from
L. auratum, L. speciosum & other Japanese spp,
including crosses with the Chinese *L. henryi*;
perhaps the most beautiful of all hybrid lilies, with
huge spotted & generally bicoloured fls in v large
racemes or clusters, mid–late summer. Need rich
but v well-drained soil in full sun but best
sheltered (often not so hardy as other vars);
v good in pots/tubs under glass or in open.
Sub-divided by fl shape.

TRUMPET-SHAPED (Div 7a): few if any available.

BOWL-SHAPED (Div 7b): to 1–1.5m (3–5ft);
beautiful bowl-shaped fls to 25cm (10in) across
in tall racemes. Vars & strains: 'Bonfire'
(moderately hardy; crimson edged white, spotted
darker crimson, reverse silvery flushed pink);
'Crimson Beauty' **8** (white banded crimson,
vermilion spots [raised in throat], green star in
throat); 'Empress of India' (moderately hardy;
deep crimson-red veined darker); 'Magic Pink'
(pink); 'Pink Glory' strain (pink or salmon shades,
generally edged white); 'Red Band Hybrids'**
(bright crimson-red to rich vermilion, edged
white).

STAR-SHAPED (Div 7c): to 1.5–2m (5–7ft); racemes
of starry flattish fls to 25cm (10in) wide, recurving
tips. Strains: 'Imperial Crimson' (deep crimson-
red shades, edged white, reverse silvery);
'Imperial Gold' (similar to *L. auratum*; white
banded rich yellow, maroon spots); 'Imperial
Silver' **9** (white, vermilion spots).

RECURVED (Div 7d): to 1.2–1.8m (4–6ft); large
loose clusters of deeply recurved fls to 18cm
(7in) wide. Vars & strains: 'Black Beauty' **10**
(v dark red); 'Jamboree' strain (crinkled petals,
maroon edged silver, crimson spots); 'Journey's
End' (deep rose-pink edged white).

Miscellaneous hybrids (Div 8): includes all
those not classified elsewhere. Few if any
available.

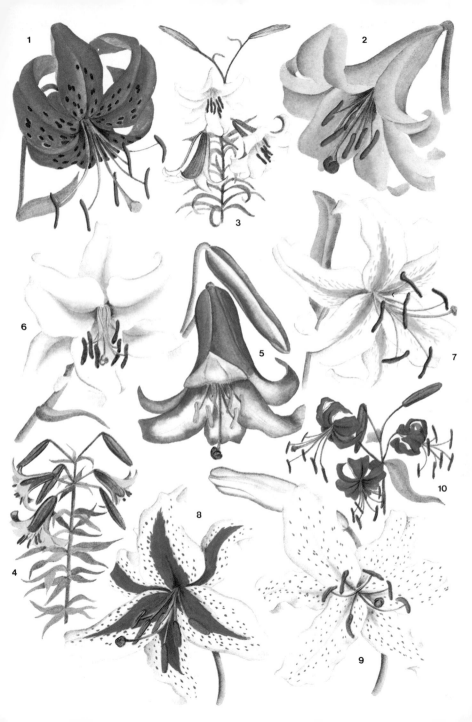

Other taller members of the lily family

Over 30cm (1ft) tall when in flower, often much more. Range from giant lilies with huge flowers to dainty types with tall graceful sprays of small flowers. Mostly summer-flowering. **Cultivation**: See below; very hardy unless stated. **Propagation**: Seed; offsets. For rhizomatous spp generally treated like herbaceous perennials, see pp300–306.

Calochortus (Mariposa lilies, *Calochortus* spp): beautiful, somewhat tulip- or fritillary-like late spring- or early summer-flg N American corms with v long basal lvs & often also narrow or lance-shaped stem lvs; fls in clusters, either globular & nodding (in fairy lanterns or globe tulips), erect & cup-shaped, often with rolled-back petal tips (in star tulips; see p418) or large & cup-shaped, on branching stems (in true mariposa lilies or butterfly tulips). Quite difficult, needing v well-drained poor soil (preferably in rock garden or raised bed) in full sun & dry period when dormant after flg; where summers not dry, best lifted after lvs die & stored till autumn, then replanted 5cm (2in) deep, 25cm (10in) apart; or grow in pots plunged to rim in soil in autumn & lifted after flg. Generally v to ultra-hardy but best mulched thickly in winter to prevent alternate freezing & thawing.

C. albus **1** (white fairy lantern or globe tulip): to 30–60cm (1–2ft); pinkish/white fls to 4cm (1½in) long, early.

C. amabilis* **2** (golden fairy lantern or globe tulip): to 40–50cm (16–20in); 2.5cm (1in) deep yellow fls, early. *C. pulchellus* is similar but fls larger.

C. amoenus (purple globe tulip): to 30–50cm (12–20in); 3cm (1¼in) rosy-purple bell-shaped fls.

C. barbatus: to 60cm (2ft); nodding bell-shaped 2.5cm (1in) mustard-yellow fls, hairy & fringed, late summer. Easy in sunny border.

C. luteus **3** (yellow Mariposa lily): to 30–50cm (12–20in); erect bright yellow fls 5cm (2in) across, usually, marked reddish-brown.

C. venustus **4** (white Mariposa lily): to 25–60cm (10–24in) or more; erect fls to 8cm (3in) across in wide range of colours from white, cream, yellow & orange to red, lilac & purple, always blotched red.

Camasses (*Camassia* spp): moisture-loving N American bulbs with strap-shaped lvs & racemes of starry white to violet-blue fls, late spring or early summer. Good for borders or for naturalizing in grass, wild gardens. Plant early autumn, 8–10cm (3–4in) deep, 15–25cm (6–10in) apart, in moist loamy soil in semi-shade; dead-head if self-seeding unwanted.

C. cusickii **5**: to 1m (3ft); v large bulb; rather fleshy broad lvs to 50cm (20in) long; tall racemes of up to 300 pale lavender to violet-blue fls 4cm (1½in) across. Spreads freely.

C. leichtlinii **6**: to 1–1.2m (3–4ft); lvs to 60cm (2ft) long; large racemes of creamy-white to deep blue fls to 4cm (1½in) across. Vars: 'Atrocaerulea' (deep violet-blue); 'Semiplena' (double, creamy-white).

C. quamash **7** (*C. esculenta*, quamash, common camass): to 45–75cm (1½–2½ft); lvs to 50cm (20in) long, often glaucous; dense racemes of violet-blue, pale blue or sometimes white fls (cuttable).

C. scilloides (*C. fraseri*, eastern camass; in US, wild hyacinth): to 45–60cm (1½–2ft); narrow grassy lvs to 60cm (2ft) long; racemes of 6–10 pale blue, or sometimes white or blue-violet, fls to 2.5cm (1in) wide.

Giant lilies (*Cardiocrinum* spp; formerly *Lilium* spp): majestic plants v similar to lilies but with large heart-shaped dark green lvs; sturdy racemes of long trumpet-shaped white/creamy fls, mid–late summer. Bulb dies after flg, leaving offsets (reach flg size in 3–5yrs), so best to plant several different-sized bulbs for fls each yr. Plant in autumn 1m (3ft) apart, shallowly in humus-rich, moist but well-drained soil in cool shade; best in light woodland among low-growing everygreen shrubs to protect early growth from spring frosts; mulch in winter.

C. (L.) cordatum: to 1.8m (6ft); long-stalked lvs to 30cm (1ft) long, bronzed when young; infls of 4–24 creamy-white drooping fls to 15cm (6in) long, spotted reddish-brown, throat blotched yellow.

C. (L.) giganteum* **8**: to 1.8–2.5m (6–8ft) or more; rosette of oval lvs to 45cm (1½ft) long; racemes of 10–20 drooping white/creamy fls 15cm (6in) or more long, throat streaked reddish-brown or purple.

Pineapple lilies (*Eucomis* spp): semi-hardy stately S African bulbs with dense racemes of starry fls, generally white or greenish, on sturdy stems, mid–late summer; prominent pineapple-like tuft ("coma") of leafy bracts on top of infls; true lvs bright green & strap-like, lax or arching, in basal rosette. Plant 10–12cm (4–5in) deep, 30cm (1ft) apart, in any well-drained sandy soil in sunny or part-shaded sheltered site; plant autumn where winters mild; elsewhere plant spring, lift after lvs die down & store frost-free over winter. Good in pots under glass.

E. autumnalis (*E. undulata*): to 50cm (20in); lvs wavy; greenish-white 2cm (¾in) fls.

E. bicolor **9**: to 60cm (2ft); broad wavy-edged lvs; pale green 2.5cm (1in) fls edged purple. Var 'Alba' is pure creamy-white.

E. comosa* **1** (*E. punctata*): to 60cm (2ft); lvs
spotted crimson; loose infls of 1cm (½in)
greenish-cream fls, lilac throat.

E. pole-evansii: to 1–1.5m (3–5ft); broad crinkly-
edged lvs; dense infls of greenish-white to green
fls; coma to 15cm (6in) wide.

Nomocharis (*Nomocharis* spp): graceful
fritillary/lily-like Himalayan bulbs growing well
only in cool, moist climates. Lvs generally lance-
shaped & glossy, to 10cm (4in) long; fls bell- or
saucer-shaped, often nodding, from upper lf
axils, mid summer. Stem-rooting; plant in spring
15cm (6in) deep, 30–40cm (12–16in) apart, in
moist, peaty soil in semi-shade; do not disturb;
mulch. Apart from spp below, seeds of hybrids
(often listed as *N.* × *hybrida*) sometimes available.

N. aperta **2**: to 60–90cm (2–3ft); slightly nodding
rose-pink fls to 10cm (4in) wide, deep reddish-
purple eye & crimson spots & blotches.

N. farreri: to 1m (3ft) or more; white nodding fls to
8cm (3in) wide with maroon eye & purplish spots.

N. mairei: to 75cm (2½ft); flat nodding fls to
10cm (4in) wide, white with deep red-purple eye
& spotting, inner petals narrower & fringed.

N. pardanthina **3**: to 60–90cm (2–3ft); lvs to 5cm
(2in) long; up to 10 nodding saucer-shaped pale
pink fls to 8cm (3in) wide, inner petals rounded &
fringed, heavy purple spotting. Best-known sp.

N. saluenensis **4**: to 1m (3ft); lvs usually paired;
rather starry saucer-shaped pale rose fls to 9cm
(3½in) wide with dark red-purple eye & freckles,
petals flushed deeper pink at tips; sometimes
white or pale yellow.

Notholirions (*Notholirion* spp): fritillary/lily-like
bulbs that die after flg, leaving offsets (like
Cardiocrinum spp; see p416); to 1.2m (4ft);
narrow, lax basal lvs appear in autumn & remain

over winter; racemes of horizontal flaring funnel-
shaped fls on leafy stems. Plant in autumn, 40cm
(16in) apart, 10cm (4in) deep in v well-drained
peaty soil in cool sheltered spot, preferably
where low evergreen shrubs protect lvs in winter.

N. bulbiferum (*N. hyacinthinum*): lvs to 45cm
(1½ft) long; loose infls of 10–30 flaring pale lilac
fls 2.5cm (1in) long, shading to green at petal
tips, mid summer.

N. thompsonianum*: lvs to 30cm (1ft) long;
dense infls of 10–25 pale rosy-lilac fls 6cm
(2½in) long, late spring or early summer.

Ornithogalums (*Ornithogalum* spp; often called
stars of Bethlehem, especially *O. umbellatum*
[p420] & *O. arabicum*): generally sun-loving
bulbs with narrow basal lvs & racemes of starry
white fls. Plant 5–8cm (2–3in) deep, 8–10cm
(3–4in) apart, in any well-drained soil, in autumn
where hardy, elsewhere in spring (lifting in
autumn). Often grown in pots under glass.

O. arabicum* **5** (*O. corymbosum*, star of
Bethlehem): moderately hardy; to 45–60cm
(1½–2ft); lvs to 60cm (2ft) long; flattish infls of up
to 12 white fls to 6cm (2½in) across, prominent
black pistil, late spring. Will fl again only if bulb
well sun-ripened in summer.

O. nutans **6**: to 30–45cm (1–1½ft); lvs to 60cm
(2ft) long; one-side infls of nodding starry bell-
shaped white fls to 5cm (2in) across, reverse
striped green, spring (cuttable). Thrives in semi-
shade; will naturalize.

O. thyrsoides **7** (chincherinchee): semi-hardy; to
60cm (2ft); lvs to 40cm (16in) long; dense infls of
starry cup-shaped creamy-white fls 2.5cm (1in)
across, greenish eye, v long-lasting when cut. Fls
early spring where hardy; elsewhere spring-
planted bulbs fl in summer.

Other dwarf members of the lily family

Generally less than 30cm (1ft) tall, with goblet-shaped or starry flowers, though in some the leaves grow
taller after flowering. Most good grouped in rock gardens, front of borders, etc; *Colchicum* spp best in
rougher spots. **Cultivation**: See below; very hardy unless stated, & for any well-drained soil in sun or
light shade. **Propagation**: Seed; offsets. For other dwarf bulbs of the family, see pp396–404; for lily of
the valley (*Convallaria majalis*), a rhizomatous perennial often treated like a bulb, see p300.

Spring meadow saffron (*Bulbocodium vernum* **8**,
Colchicum bulbocodium, C. vernum)· crocus-like
corm, to 10–15 × 10cm (4–6 × 4in); lvs narrow,
strap-like; clusters of up to 3 rose-violet funnel-
shaped fls, clawed petals, on v short stalks,
v early spring (before lvs). Plant early autumn,
8cm (3in) deep, in full sun; lift & divide every
3–4yrs.

Dwarf calochortus (star tulips, *Calochortus*
spp): moderately hardy compact spp of mariposa
lilies (p416), with erect, somewhat tulip-like
bell-shaped fls. Cultivation as for taller spp.

C. coeruleus (beavertail grass, cat's ear): to

15 × 10cm (6 × 4in); basal lvs to 15cm (6in) long;
wide-opening 2.5cm (1in) pale mauve-blue fls,
hairs on inner segments, early summer.

C. uniflorus **9** (lilac star tulip): to 25 × 10cm
(10 × 4in); basal lvs to 40cm (16in) long; small
umbels of 5cm (2in) lilac fls, purple spot on each
petal, late spring or early summer. Can be
propagated by aerial bulbils.

Colchicums (*Colchicum* spp; often called
autumn crocuses or meadow saffrons, but these
apply to *C. autumnale* only; not related to
crocuses): showy corms flg autumn unless
stated, with profuse generally white to purplish

crocus-like fls direct from ground without lvs (heights given when in fl); stemless lvs appear spring & die down early summer, rather large, glossy & generally strap-shaped. Lvs of most spp untidy, so best in shrubberies, rough grass, etc; will naturalize. Plant corms (large) 8cm (3in) deep, mid–late summer (when dormant); bare corms will fl indoors without soil or water. Corms & seeds poisonous.

C. agrippinum 1 (sometimes sold incorrectly as C. variegatum): to 8–10×15cm (3–4×6in); lvs to 15cm (6in) long, almost prostrate; starry rose-purple & white chequered fls, long white tube.

C. autumnale (autumn crocus, meadow saffron): to 15×20cm (6×8in); lvs to 30cm (1ft) long; generally lilac fls to 10cm (4in) wide. Vars: 'Album' 2 (white); 'Album Plenum' (double white); 'Major' (robust; lilac-mauve); 'Minor' (small rose-lilac); 'Roseum Plenum' (double rose-pink).

C. byzantinum 3 (often listed as C. autumnale major): to 15–20×25cm (6–8×10in); lvs to 40×10cm (16×4in); profuse pale lilac-pink starry fls to 10cm (4in) wide, early.

C. luteum (yellow spring colchicum): to 10×15cm (4×6in); narrow lvs with fls, later to 30cm (1ft) long; yellow fls to 4cm (1½in) wide, early spring.

C. sibthorpii: moderately hardy; to 15×15cm (6×6in); prostrate lvs to 20cm (8in) long; soft lilac-purple chequered & shaded fls, yellow anthers.

C. speciosum: to 15×25cm (6×10in) or taller; broad lvs to 40cm (16in) long; goblet-shaped rose-pink to purplish fls to 10cm (4in) across, long tube, from late summer. Vars: 'Album' (white); 'Atrorubens' 4 (reddish-purple); bornmuelleri (C. bornmuelleri; large rosy-mauve fls, white throat, early); illyricum (correctly, C. giganteum; large rose-purple fls, white throat, stout tube). Hybrids (derived mainly from vars bornmuelleri & illyricum; generally better than either, with robust fls): 'Autumn Queen' (violet-purple); 'Disraeli' (dark mauve, faint chequering); 'Lilac Wonder' (deep lilac-pink striped white); 'The Giant' (v large violet-mauve fls, white throat); 'Violet Queen' 5 (rosy-violet, paler throat, faint chequering); 'Waterlily' 6 (hybrid with C. autumnale; large wide-opening lilac-mauve double fls).

Star of Bethlehem (Ornithogalum umbellatum): dwarf relative of chincherinchee (O. thyrsoides; p418); to 20–30×15–20cm (8–12×6–8in); v narrow grassy lvs to 30cm (1ft) long; flattish infls of up to 20 starry white fls 2.5cm (1in) across, reverse striped green, late spring (good for cutting but close at night). Plant in autumn 5–8cm (2–3in) deep; will naturalize (may become weedy). O. balansae 7 is generally similar but smaller, to 10–15×10cm (4–6×4in), with 10cm (4in) lvs; fls early–mid spring; likes full sun.

Wood sorrels

Oxalis spp. Low-growing, dainty plants forming mats or tufts of characteristic clover-like leaves with 3 or more leaflets & funnel-shaped 5-petalled flowers often opening wide only in sun. Leaves may close at night with flowers. Good for rock gardens, alpine house; shade-lovers for woodland. **Cultivation**: Moderately hardy unless stated. Plant early-flowering spp autumn, others spring, 8cm (3in) deep & apart in well-drained but moist peaty & gritty soil in warm sunny spot unless stated. Where tender, lift or protect in winter or grow under glass. **Propagation**: Division or offsets; seed.

O. adenophylla 8: to 10cm (4in); grey-green lvs, many lfts; 3cm (1¼in) lilac-pink fls, maroon eye, from late spring.

O. bowiei: to 25cm (10in); downy lvs; umbels of cup-shaped rosy-purple fls to 4cm (1½in) across, summer.

O. braziliensis: to 10cm (4in); carpet of purplish lvs; purplish-red 2.5cm (1in) fls, late spring.

O. deppei (sometimes called good-luck plant): to 15–25cm (6–10in); lvs usually of 4 lfts, blotched reddish-brown; profuse carmine-pink to purplish-red fls in umbels, early summer. Vars: 'Alba' (white); 'Iron Cross' 9 (carmine).

O. enneaphylla*: v hardy; to 8cm (3in); tuberous; fan-like lvs with folding grey-green lfts; white fls to 5cm (2in) across, early summer. Var 'Rosea' 10 is pale pink.

O. inops (correctly, O. depressa): to 10cm (4in); grey-green lvs; 3cm (1¼in) pink fls, yellow centre, early summer. Rather invasive.

O. laciniata* 11: v hardy; to 5–10cm (2–4in); rhizomatous; grey-green lvs, many lfts; pale lavender-purple 2.5cm (1in) fls, veined darker, early summer.

O. lasiandra: to 15cm (6in); red-stalked lvs; umbels of crimson fls, early summer.

O. lobata: to 10cm (4in); tuberous; bright green lvs (die down in summer); golden-yellow fls, autumn.

O. purpurea (O. variabilis): semi-hardy; to 15cm (6in); trifoliate lvs; purple, pink or white fls to 5cm (2in) across; yellow tube, late autumn.

O. rubra (sometimes sold incorrectly as O. rosea or O. floribunda): to 20cm (8in); tuberous; trifoliate lvs; large infls of deep pink 1.5cm (⅝in) fls, from late spring. Good for window box.

Cyclamen

Cyclamen spp. Dwarf tuberous shade-lovers, generally to 10–15×15cm (4–6×6in), forming carpets of rounded heart-shaped leaves generally 5–8cm (2–3in) long, often marbled or blotched silver. Characteristic nodding flowers with 5 backswept petals generally 2–2.5cm (¾–1in) long, in shades of violet, crimson, pink & white. Stalks curl after fertilization. Excellent for underplanting shrubs & trees (even conifers), walls, shady rock gardens etc. **Cultivation**: For moist but well-drained peaty/leafy soil in full or partial shade. Plant tubers 5cm (2in) deep unless stated, smooth domed side downwards (or on side if in doubt), late summer or early autumn. Less hardy spp can be protected by thick winter mulch. **Propagation**: Seed (self-sow).

C. cilicium *: moderately hardy; lvs zoned silver, red beneath; profuse rose-pink fls blotched crimson, autumn.

C. coum **1** (*C. orbiculatum, C. vernum*): v hardy; variable; lvs all-green or marbled silver (latter often listed as var *atkinsii* or, incorrectly, as *C.×atkinsii*); broad-petalled fls, winter to early spring, pink, crimson or white, all blotched purple.

C. europaeum ** **2** (correctly, *C. purpurascens*): v hardy; lvs marked silver, red-purple beneath; deep carmine fls blotched darker, summer.

C. hederifolium * (*C. neapolitanum*): v hardy; lvs to 14cm (5½in) long, often lobed like ivy, v variably marbled silver, after fls; profuse rose-pink fls, blotched deeper, autumn. Tubers grow

v large; plant shallowly 30cm (1ft) apart. Var 'Album' **3** is white.

C. libanoticum *: semi- to moderately hardy; wavy-edged toothed lvs zoned yellowish, red beneath; pale pink 4cm (1½in) fls maturing salmon, late winter to early spring.

C. persicum * **4**: semi- to moderately hardy; to 20×20cm (8×8in); variable, usually marbled lvs; white to pale pink 4cm (1½in) fls, blotched darker, spring. Parent of numerous large hybrids (florists' cyclamen); generally unscented.

C. repandum *: moderately hardy; ivy-shaped faintly marbled lvs to 12cm (6in) long, maroon beneath; pale pink to deep rose or almost carmine fls 3cm (1¼in) long, darker zone, mid–late spring.

Anemones and their relatives

Mainly spring-flowering small tuberous or rhizomatous plants with generally solitary bowl-shaped, sometimes starry flowers often with ring of leaves below. Basal leaves deeply cut. Excellent for rock gardens, border edging & light woodland; taller types good for cutting. **Cultivation**: Unless stated, very hardy & for any moist but well-drained humus-rich soil in sun or partial/light shade. Plant 5cm (2in) deep, late summer or early autumn unless noted. **Propagation**: Division; seed.

Anemones (windflowers, *Anemone* spp): like lime.

A. apennina: to 20×10cm (8×4in); clear deep blue fls 4cm (1½in) across, spring; naturalizes well. Vars 'Alba' (white, bluish reverse); 'Plena' (double).

A. blanda **5**: to 15×10cm (6×4in); lvs rather fleshy; profuse deep blue daisy-like starry fls 4cm (1½in) wide, early spring. For warm, sheltered spot. Vars: 'Atrocaerulea' (dark blue); 'Blue Star' (large fls); 'Charmer' (rose-red); 'Pink Star' (pink, yellow centre); 'Radar' (rose-pink to red, white centre); *scythinica* (white, blue reverse); 'White Splendour'.

A. coronaria: moderately hardy, but can be planted in spring where winters cold; to 15–30×15cm (6–12×6in); rather poppy-like fls to 5cm (2in) wide in shades of blue, red & white, spring. Parent of single-fld (De Caen **6**) & semi-double (St Brigid **7**) florists' anemones, with fls to 8cm (3in) across with central black boss; plants short-lived but v good for cutting; fl almost all year if planted in succession (protect with

cloches in winter, fl 3–6 months from planting). De Caen vars: 'Hollandia' (His Excellency'; scarlet); 'Mr Fokker (purple-blue); 'Sylphide' (rose-magenta); 'The Bride' (white). St Brigid vars: 'Lord Lieutenant' (deep blue); 'Mount Everest' (white); 'The Admiral' (magenta to violet); 'The Governor' (scarlet).

A.×fulgens: hybrids of *A. hortensis* & *A. pavonina* (similar to & often confused with latter); to 30×15cm (12×6in); 6cm (2½in) vivid red starry fls, narrow whitish ring, mid–late spring. 'St Bravo' strain is sturdy; mixed colours.

A. narcissiflora **8**: to 45×30cm (1½×1ft); umbels of 2.5cm (1in) white fls, often flushed pink, spring.

A. nemorosa **9** (European wood anemone): ultra-hardy; to 20×15cm (8×6in); glossy white 2.5cm (1in) starry fls, sometimes flushed pink, spring. Good for naturalizing in light shade. Vars: 'Alba Plena' (double, white); 'Allenii' (large lilac-blue fls); 'Lychette' (large white fls); 'Robinsoniana' (powder-blue); 'Royal Blue'; 'Vestal' (white, central white boss).

Winter aconites (*Eranthis* spp): yellow

buttercup-like fls, v early; die down summer.
E. cilicica: to 8×8cm (3×3in); 2.5cm (1in) deep
yellow fls, early spring.
E. hyemalis **10**, p423: to 10×8cm (4×3in); 2cm
(¾in) pale yellow fls, from late winter.
E.×tubergenii: hybrid of above spp; to 20×10cm
(8×4in); lemon-yellow fls to 4cm (1½in) across,
early spring.
Ranunculus (Persian or turban buttercup,
Ranunculus asiaticus **1**): moderately hardy; to

25–40×15cm (10–16×6in); fresh green ferny lvs
(die down summer); profuse semi-double to
v double fls 5–12cm (2–5in) wide, often several
per stem, in shades of yellow, orange, pink, red &
white, long season. For cutting & borders. Where
winters mild, plant autumn to fl from late winter;
elsewhere plant early spring to fl late spring &
summer, lift late summer & store cool & dry over
winter. Plant tubers "claws" down; need v good
drainage & full sun.

Miscellaneous bulbs, corms and tubers

Listed alphabetically by family name. **Cultivation**: See below. **Propagation**: Offsets or division; seed.
For tuberous/rhizomatous plants normally treated like border perennials, see pp252–360.

Tuberose (*Polianthes tuberosa***; Agavaceae):
tender rhizomatous plant best grown in container
under glass & moved outdoors for summer; to
1.1m (3½ft); grassy lvs to 45cm (1½ft) long;
racemes of waxy white funnel-shaped fls to 6cm
(2½in) long, late summer to autumn (can be
forced indoors almost any season). For light soil
in warm sunny site; plant 5cm (2in) deep, spring.
Var 'The Pearl' **2** is double & more common.
Tuberous begonias (*Begonia* spp;
Begoniaceae): popular summer bedding &
container plants with large fleshy asymmetrical
lvs, hairy beneath, on fleshy hairy stalks, &
separate male & female fls on same plant (latter
small, with winged ovaries; former large, showy
& generally double). For moist but well-drained
peaty soil in sheltered sunny or part-shaded site;
plant 5–8cm (2–3in) deep, late spring. (Start
B.×tuberhybrida vars into growth indoors at 18°C
[64°F] two months before planting out; lift before
hard frosts & store frost-free.) Can be propagated
by stem cuttings.
B. evansiana (correctly, *B. grandis*): moderately
hardy (more so if protected in winter): to 60–
90×45cm (2–3×1½ft); rounded heart-shaped
glossy lvs, red veins, red beneath; drooping
branched infls of flesh-pink fls, male to 4cm
(1½in) wide, all summer.
B.×tuberhybrida vars: tender hybrids of complex
parentage; to 30–60×40cm (12–24×16in);
variable habit & lvs; fls in wide range of colours
except blue & mauve (including bicolours), male
generally 5–10cm (2–4in) across, summer to
early autumn. Sold as mixtures, by colour and (by
specialist growers) as named vars in various
groups classified by form of male fls &/or habit.
Main groups (all double unless stated): Camellia-
Flowered **3** (Cammelliiflora; camellia-like rosette
fls to 15cm [6in] across); Fimbriata Plena
(Carnation-Flowered; carnation-like fls to 12cm
[5in] across, petals fringed); Marginata **4** (sold as
B. crispa marginata vars; single or double fls with
outer band of contrasting colour); Marmorata **5**

(*B.×marmorata* vars; similar to Camellia-
Flowered, but rose-pink fls spotted/blotched
white); Multiflora **6** (*B. ×multiflora maxima* vars;
compact & bushy, with profuse single or double
5–8cm [2–3in] fls; v good for bedding); Pendula
7 (*B.×lloydii*; stems trailing or pendent; smallish
lvs; single or double fls in prolific clusters; good
for hanging baskets, windowboxes); Picotee
(similar to Camellia-Flowered, but fls edged with
different shade of main colour); Rosebud
(Rosiflora; fls to 12cm [5in] across, raised centre
like part-open rosebud); Ruffled Camellia **8** (like
Camellia-Flowered, but petals ruffled).
Canna (Indian shot, *Canna×generalis*,
C.×hybrida; Cannaceae): hybrids of mixed
parentage, mostly tall semi- to moderately hardy
rhizomatous plants, generally to 1.5×0.45m
(5×1½ft), good as dot plants adding tropical
elegance to summer bedding schemes; dwarf
vars (to 60×30cm [2×1ft]) for general bedding,
containers, etc. Lvs to 60×30cm (2×1ft), green
or bronze-purple, on fl stems; crowded racemes
of flaring tubular fls to 10cm (4in) across, bright
shades of red, pink, orange, yellow & white,
summer to autumn. Treat like tender tuberous
Begonia vars (see above), planting 8–12cm
(4–5in) deep in humus-rich, moist but well-
drained soil in full sun; dead-head. Vars (to
1–1.5m [3–5ft] & green-lvd unless stated):
'Bonfire' (orange-scarlet); 'City of Portland'
(rose-pink edged yellow); 'Eureka' (creamy-
white); 'Evening Star' (carmine-pink); 'Lucifer'
(bright crimson edged yellow); 'Miss Oklahoma'
(watermelon-pink); 'Nirvana' (to 45cm [1½ft]; lvs
striped yellow; yellow fls from red buds); 'Orchid'
(vivid pink); 'Pfitzer' series (to 75cm [2½ft];
various colours); 'Red King Humbert' **9** (to 1.8m
[6ft]; bronze lvs; deep red fls); 'Richard Wallace'
10 (canary-yellow); 'Rosamond Cole' (scarlet
edged yellow, reverse golden-yellow flushed
red); 'The President' (bright scarlet); 'Tyrol'
(bronze lvs; pink fls); 'Yellow King Humbert'
(yellow marked red).

The forget-me-not family

Plants mainly of Mediterranean origin, evergreen unless stated, generally with bright blue flowers borne over hoary leaves. Flowers 8–12mm (⅓–½in) across, generally saucer- to star-shaped. **Cultivation**: Unless stated, moderately to very hardy & for well-drained soil in full sun. **Propagation**: Softwood cuttings or seed unless stated.

Tufted alkanet (*Anchusa caespitosa* **1**): v hardy; to 5×20cm (2×8in); dense tufts of narrow deep green lvs; vivid blue fls, white eye, spring. Not easy; for raised bed, scree or alpine house. Propagate by root cuttings.

Lithospermums (*Lithospermum* spp; correctly *Lithodora* spp): carpeting sub-shrubs with profuse, rather starry gentian-blue fls all summer. *L. diffusum*: to 10×60cm (4×24in); dark green lvs. Needs lime-free soil. Vars: 'Grace Ward' (intense blue); 'Heavenly Blue' **2** (deep blue). *L. oleifolium* **3**: to 15×30cm (6×12in); grey-green lvs; pale blue fls from pink buds. Tolerates lime.

Moltkias (*Moltkia* spp; formerly *Lithospermum* spp): bushy sub-shrubs with narrow greyish lvs & clusters of funnel-shaped blue fls to 2.5cm (1in) long, early summer. *M. (L.) doerfleri*: to 40×30cm (16×12in); fls purplish. *M. (L.) petraea*: to 30×30cm (1×1ft); soft blue fls from pinkish buds. *M. (L.)×froebellii* & *M. (L.)×intermedia* are hybrids with *M. (L.) suffruticosa*, with dark green lvs.

Alpine forget-me-not (*Myosotis alpestris*): ultra-hardy true perennial (though short-lived) relative of garden forget-me-not (*M. sylvatica*, often listed as *M. alpestris*, p486); to 20×15cm (8×6in); tufted; azure-blue fls, late spring & early summer. *M. rupicola* **4** (dwarf, to 8cm [3in]) is similar.

Navelworts (*Omphalodes* spp): long-lived carpeting plants with long-stalked heart-shaped lvs & fls like large forget-me-nots. Generally for cool, moist shade. Propagate by division. *O. cappadocica* **5**: to 20×45cm (8×18in); bright blue fls early–mid summer. Var 'Anthea Bloom' has grey-green lvs & profuse sky-blue fls. *O. luciliae* **6**: to 15×45cm (6×18in); oval grey-green lvs; soft blue fls, summer. For free-draining alkaline soil, rock crevice. *O. verna* (blue-eyed Mary): to 15×60cm (6×24in); stoloniferous; herbaceous; white-throated fls, early spring. Var 'Alba' is white.

Golden drop (*Onosma tauricum**; often sold as the similar but rarely grown *O. echioides*): sub-shrub, to 20×25cm (8×10in); grey-green lvs; pendent deep yellow tubular fls to 2–2.5cm long, spring to mid summer. For hot banks, walls.

The campanula family

Free-flowering, generally herbaceous plants with charming more or less bell-shaped blue or white flowers in summer (useful to follow spring alpines). For rock gardens, walls, paving; smaller spp for crevices or pans. **Cultivation**: Very hardy unless stated. Often very easy in any well-drained soil in sun or semi-shade. Protect from slugs & snails. **Propagation**: Division; seed (generally sown spring); softwood or root cuttings. For taller spp, some suitable for large rock gardens, see p260.

Campanulas (bellflowers, *Campanula* spp): unless noted, heart- to kidney-shaped, toothed lvs on long stalks; 5-petalled fls, generally bell-shaped (some starry, some narrow), unless stated blue & appearing early–mid summer. *C. allionii* **7** (*C. alpestris*): to 8×15cm (3×6in); rhizomatous; lance-shaped lvs; blue-purple tubular fls to 4cm (1½in) long, early summer. For lime-free scree or alpine house. *C. arvatica*: mat-forming, to 5×30cm (2×12in), with trailing stems; starry violet-blue fls to 2.5cm (1in) wide, mid summer. Var 'Alba' is white. *C. aucheri*: to 5×10cm (2×4in); tufted; thick roots; downy lvs; solitary deep purple fls to 2.5cm (1in) long, early summer. *C. carpatica* (tussock or Carpathian bellflower): ultra-hardy; to 15–30×30–40cm (6–12×12–16in); forms strong, showy clump covered with shallowy cup-shaped fls to 2.5–5cm (1–2in)

across. Superb & easy. Many vars include: 'Blue Clips' (mid blue); 'Blue Moonlight' **8** (grey-blue); 'Bressingham White'; 'Chewton Joy' (china-blue; late); 'Isobel' **9** (violet); 'Snow Imp' (white; late); 'White Star' **10**. *C. cochleariifolia* **11** (*C. pusilla*, fairy's thimble): to 10–15×30cm (4–6×12in); rhizomatous, making tufted growth as it spreads; thimble-shaped nodding sky-blue fls to 1cm (½in) long on wiry stems, all summer. Dainty & easy. Numerous vars & hybrids include: 'Alba' (white); 'Blue Tit' (white); 'Cambridge Blue' (pale blue); 'Elizabeth Oliver' (double, powder-blue); 'Hallii' (small white fls); 'Oakington' (large deep blue fls). *C. excisa*: to 10×15–30cm (4×6–12in); rhizomatous; narrow lvs; lilac-blue, pleated, rather pendent fls to 2.5cm (1in) long, early summer. Not easy; divide & replant regularly. For lime-free soil.

C. fragilis: moderately hardy; semi-prostrate, to 10×30cm (4×12in); tufts of shiny lvs; showy fls to 4cm (1½in) across.

C. garganica (Adriatic bellflower; correctly, *C. elatines garganica*): to 15×15–30cm (6×6–12in); profuse star-shaped fls in lax panicles to 15cm (6in) long, all summer. Good for wall. Vars: 'Hirsuta' (*C. istriaca*; grey-haired lvs); 'W. H. Paine' **1** (deep blue fls, white centre).

C.×haylodgensis **2**: hybrid of *C. carpatica* & *C. cochleariifolia*; lax, to 8×15cm (3×6in); yellow-green lvs; double fls to 1cm (½in) long.

C. morettiana: moderately hardy; to 8×15cm (3×6in); forms tufted mat of tiny grey-haired lvs; solitary violet fls to 2.5cm (1in) long, early summer. Likes lime; best in alpine house.

C. persicifolia nitida (Planiflora', *C. nitida*, C. planiflora): dwarf var of *C. persicifolia* (p262), to 15×10cm (6×4in); rosettes of crinkly lvs; clustered bell fls (white in var 'Alba'). Seedlings revert to full size.

C. portenschlagiana **3** (*C. muralis*): spreading & mat-forming, to 15×45–60cm (6×18–24in); semi-evergreen; mid blue rather starry bells to 2cm (¾in) long, all summer. Long-lived, v easy & popular; shade-tolerant.

C. poscharskyana (Serbian bellflower): ultra-hardy; rampant, to 30×60–90cm (1×2–3ft); lax stems form dense mats; lavender-blue starry fls to 2.5cm (1in) across in long sprays, all summer. Rather coarse, but useful on v dry banks or to cover rough walls. Vars & hybrids: 'Birch Hybrid' (hybrid with *C. portenschlagiana* & intermediate in form; beautiful & free-flg); 'Constellation' ('Stella' seedling; clump-forming; wide open lavender-blue fls); 'E. H. Frost' (white, tinged blue); 'Stella' (bright blue).

C. pulla **4**: to 10×30cm (4×12in); rhizomatous & tufted; solitary purple, nodding fls to 2cm (¾in) long. Divide & replant regularly; likes lime & some shade.

C.×pulloides: hybrid of *C. carpatica* & *C. pulla*; to 20×20cm (8×8in); rhizomatous; hairy lvs; blue-purple fls to 2.5cm (1in) long, slightly nodding. *C.* 'G. F. Wilson' has same parentage but is smaller, with violet-blue fls.

C. raddeana: to 30×25cm (12×10in); rhizomatous & tufted; narrowish glossy dark green lvs; sprays of deep violet-blue nodding fls 2cm (¾in) long on upright stems. Divide regularly. Likes lime.

C. raineri **5**: to 10×15cm (4×6in); tufted; grey-green lvs; broad bowl-shaped china-blue fls to 4cm (1½in) across, usually solitary, early summer. Likes lime.

C. rotundifolia **6** (harebell; in Scotland, bluebell): ultra-hardy; to 15–30×25–45cm (6–12×10–18in); basal lvs rounded; wiry stems with narrow lvs bear nodding fls 2–2.5cm (¾–1in) long. Widely naturalized. Vars: 'Alba' (white);

'Olympica' (large fls). *C. linifolia* is similar, with grey hairy lvs & purple-blue, blue or white fls.

C.×stansfieldii **7**: hybrid of dubious parentage; to 12×30cm (5×12in); slightly nodding violet fls to 2.5cm (1in) long, in sprays.

C. thyrsoides*: unique yellow-fld sp; to 30×15cm (12×6in); bristly narrow lvs; thick spikes of creamy-yellow fls. Dies after flg but easily raised from seed.

C. zoysii **8**: to 8×15cm (3×6in); tufted growth from thin rhizomes; light blue, urn-shaped fls to 1cm (½in) long, narrowed & ruffled at mouth, mid–late summer. For gritty limy soil in crevice or alpine house.

C. hybrids not listed above: 'Molly Pinsent' (bushy, to 20×30cm [8×12in]; lavender-blue fls); 'Peter Nix' (to 15×30cm [6×12in]; profuse light blue nodding fls).

Cyananthus (trailing bellflowers, *Cyananthus* spp): prostrate, mat-forming plants with solitary blue funnel-shaped fls, bearded throat & brown-haired calyx, late summer & autumn. For lime-free, peaty soil in sun. Fleshy roots; do not divide.

C. lobatus: to 10×40cm (4×15in); pale green lobed lvs. Vars: 'Albus' (ivory-white); 'Kingdon Ward' **9** (deep blue).

C. microphyllus (sometimes listed incorrectly as *C. integer*): to 8×30cm (3×12in); heath-like lvs, white-haired beneath; blue-purple fls with white hairs, to 2.5cm (1in) across.

C. sherriffii: to 5×45cm (2×18in); young growth silver-haired; bright blue fls to 2.5cm (1in) across. High alpine; best under glass.

Edraianthus (grassy-bells, *Edraianthus* [*Wahlenbergia*] spp; sometimes spelled *Hedraeanthus*): tufted mat-forming plants, to 2.5–8×20cm (1–3×8in), with grey-green grassy lvs and upturned stemless blue to purple bell fls to 2–2.5cm (¾–1in) long, late spring to early summer. Short-lived. For full sun in limestone scree, trough or alpine house.

E. graminifolius: needle-like lvs; pale purple fls in clusters.

E. (W.) pumilio: profuse solitary violet-blue fls. Give winter protection.

E. (W.) serpyllifolius: deep green lance-shaped lvs; violet-blue solitary fls. Var 'Major' **10** has deep purple fls to 5cm (2in) across.

Horned rampions (*Phyteuma* spp): tufted plants with tubular fls clustered in dense globular heads to 4cm (1½in) across. For scree. Sow seed autumn.

P. comosum **11** (correctly, *Physoplexis comosa*): to 5–10×15cm (2–4×6in); claw-like purplish fls in stemless clusters each with protruding style, mid summer. Unusual plant for limestone scree or alpine house.

P. hemisphaericum: to 10–15×25cm (4–6×10in); grass-like lvs; blue or near-white fls on short stems, early summer.

Rock pinks

Dianthus spp, vars & hybrids. Showy, easy, free-flowering plants making tufted hummocks or spreading mats. Leaves grassy & grey-green unless noted, evergreen & attractive all year. Profuse flowers (red, pink, white, rarely yellow), single unless noted, on upright stems above foliage. Excellent for rock gardens & dry walls, smaller kinds also for troughs. **Cultivation**: Unless stated, ultra-hardy & for well-drained neutral/alkaline soil in full sun. Short-lived spp best propagated every 2 or 3 years. **Propagation**: Seed, sown spring (variable: select best forms); semi-ripe cuttings.

Species & their varieties (including reasonably true-breeding hybrids):

D. alpinus **1** (alpine pink): mat-forming, to 10×15cm (4×6in); deep green lvs; profuse but variable fls to 4cm (1½in) wide, pale pink to red-purple with white eye, late spring to mid summer. Short-lived. Prone to carnation fly. Vars: 'Albus' ('Waithman's White'; white, centre spotted purple, greenish reverse); 'Red Velvet' (beautiful deep crimson, black centre); 'Rose Velvet' (rose-red).

D. arenarius **** 2** (sand pink): mat-forming, to 20–30×30cm (8–12×12in); v narrow lvs to 5cm (2in) long; fls to 2.5cm (1in) across, white with green eye, v fringed petals often edged purple, early–mid summer, may repeat in autumn.

D.×*arvernensis* (Auvergne pink): may be hybrid of *D. monspessulanus* & *D. sequieri*, or possibly a form of *D. gratianopolitanus*; to 15×15cm (6×6in); hummock of lvs to 1cm (½in) long; rosy-pink toothed fls on branched stems, late spring to mid summer. Var 'Albus' is white.

D.×*calalpinus** : hybrid of *D. alpinus* & *D. callizonus*; to 8×15cm (3×6in); mat-forming; deep green lvs; fls to 4cm (1½in) wide, pink, centre dotted white, early–mid summer.

D. deltoides (maiden pink): mat-forming, to 15–25×40cm (6–10×16in); deep green narrow lvs, often flushed purple-red, especially beneath; profuse variable fls 1–2cm (½–¾in) across, red, pink or white with crimson eye, on narrow, grass-like stems, early–late summer. Self-seeds freely. Useful for rock walls, paving. Vars & hybrids (breed reasonably true from seed): 'Albus' (light green lvs; white fls, crimson centre); 'Brilliancy' (deep crimson); 'Brilliant' (rose-pink); 'Flashing Light' (crimson); 'Hansen's Red' (bright crimson); 'Samos' **3** (brilliant carmine-red; dark purple-green lvs); 'Wisley Variety' **4** (carmine-red).

D. gratianopolitanus **** 5** (*D. caesius*, Cheddar pink): to 10–30×30cm (4–12×12in); mat-forming, rooting as it spreads; profuse fringed pink fls 2.5cm (1in) across, late spring to early summer. Fairly long-lived. Vars (to 10–15cm [4–6in]): 'La Bourboulle'** ('La Bourbille'; tufted habit); 'Flore-Pleno'** (semi-double).

D. haematocalyx: to 15–30×10cm (6–12×4in); rosy-purple fls to 2cm (¾in) across, yellow reverse, opening from red calyx, mid summer.

D. knappii: to 25–40×10cm (10–15×4in); untidy habit; clusters of clear sulphur-yellow fls to 1cm (½in) across, early summer. Free-flg; short-lived.

D. myrtinervis: v compact, to 8×20cm (3×8in), in poor scree conditions but loose & lax if soil too rich; rather like dwarf *D. deltoides*, with light cushions of bright green lvs; profuse almost stemless bright pink fls 10mm (⅜in) across, early summer.

D. neglectus **6** (glacier pink; correctly, *D. pavonius*): v hardy; to 10–20×15cm (4–8×6in); dense grassy cushion; variable fls to 3cm (1¼in) across, pink to crimson with buff reverse, mid summer. Prefers lime-free soil.

D. noeanus** (correctly, *D. petraeus noeanus*; sometimes listed as *Acanthophyllum spinosum*): v hardy; to 20–30×15–20cm (8–12×6–8in); sharp-pointed mid green lvs in tufts; clusters of white fls to 1cm (½in) wide, fringed petals.

D. subacaulis: to 5×20cm (2×8in); woody base; neatly tufted lvs; v short-stemmed 1.5cm (⅝in) carmine-pink fls, summer.

D. superbus** **7** (fringed pink, lilac pink): to 20–45×15cm (8–18×6in); sprawling stems; mid green lvs; lilac or white fls to 4cm (1½in) across with v fringed petals, centre spotted green, from mid summer. Short-lived; fairly shade-tolerant; tall forms need staking. Vars: 'Loveliness'** (hybrid with *D.*×*allwoodii*; less sprawling; good colour range).

D. sylvestris (*D. inodorus*, wood pink [misnomer; alpine]): to 20–30×20cm (8–12×8in); narrow wiry lvs; rosy-pink fls to 2cm (¾in) across, notched petals, early–mid summer.

Hybrids (sometimes listed as *D.*×*allwoodii alpinus* vars): generally of complex parentage; compact, to 8–15×15–20cm (3–6×6–8in); tufted. Numerous vars include: 'Annabel'* (deep pink); 'Bombardier' (semi-double, dark crimson; v free-flg); 'Dainty Maid' (red, crimson eye, white edge, fringed); 'Diana' (magenta-crimson, dark eye, fringed); 'Essex Witch' (rose-pink); 'Fanal' **8** (intense red); 'Fusilier' (crimson, dark centre, fringed); 'Garland' (rose-pink); 'Gravetye Gem' (large rose-pink fls); 'Grenadier' (maroon-scarlet; blue lvs); 'Little Jock'* **9** (semi-double, pink, dark eye); 'Mars' **10** ('Brigadier'; double, crimson-magenta); 'Oakington Hybrid'* (double, deep rose); 'Pike's Pink' **11** (double, pale pink); 'Waithman's Beauty' (crimson flecked white); 'Wisp'* **12** (white, purple eye).

Other members of the pink family

Sun-lovers, generally cushion/mat-forming or prostrate (some mere mossy films), with profuse 5-petalled flowers. Evergreen unless stated. Most excellent for screes, dry walls, etc; smaller spp for troughs. **Cultivation**: Unless stated, very hardy & for very well-drained gritty or sandy soil in full sun. **Propagation**: Seed; division; cuttings. For border spp, some suitable for large rock gardens, see p264.

Sandworts (*Arenaria* spp): bright green mossy mats to 30–45cm (1–1½ft) wide; generally white starry fls on wiry stems, late spring & early summer.

A. balearica: moderately to v hardy; to 2.5cm (1in); profuse tiny fls. Best in shade growing over moist rock.

A. grandiflora: to 5–8cm (2–3in); fls to 2.5cm (1in) wide.

A. montana **1**: to 8–15cm (3–6in); dark green; saucer-shaped 1–2cm (½–¾in) fls.

A. purpurascens (pink sandwort); to 5–8cm (2–3in); 1–2cm (½–¾in) purplish fls, clear pink in 'Elliott's Variety'.

Mouse-ear chickweeds (*Cerastium* spp): ultra-hardy mat-forming plants, often rather invasive; grey-green woolly lvs; 2–2.5cm (¾–1in) white fls on branching stems, early summer.

C. alpinum **2**: to 5–10×30cm (2–4×12in); starry fls. Var 'Lanatum' is compact & v silvery; fls insignificant; protect from winter wet.

C. tomentosum **3** (snow-in-summer): rampant, to 10–15×60cm (4–6×24in) or wider; profuse starry fls. *C. biebersteinii* (also called snow-in-summer); is similar but woollier, with cup-shaped fls. Both too rampant for small rock gardens; best on rough banks.

Gypsophila (*Gypsophila* spp): generally ultra-hardy, with narrow or lance-shaped grey-green lvs.

G. aretioides: tight hard cushion of tiny lvs, to 5×20cm (2×8in); tiny stemless white fls. Var 'Caucasica' is v compact. Both best in alpine house or limestone scree.

G. cerastioides: moderately hardy; tufted & mat-forming, to 8×30cm (3×12in); loose sprays of 10mm (⅜in) purple-veined white fls all summer.

G. repens: trailing & mat-forming, to 15×60cm (6×24in); tangled wiry stems; profuse sprays of 10mm (⅜in) white or pink fls, early summer. Vars: 'Dubia' (*G. dubia*; dark green lvs; pink fls); 'Fratensis' **4** (compact; rich pink); 'Monstrosa' (vigorous; white); 'Rosea' (pink).

Alpine campion (*Lychnis* [*Viscaria*] *alpina* **5**): tufted, to 10×10cm (4×4in); rosettes of dark green narrow lvs; dense heads of purplish, pink or white 1.5cm (⅝in) fls, early summer, on sturdy stems. Var 'Rosea' is rich rose-pink.

Pearlwort (*Sagina glabra*; sometimes sold incorrectly as *Arenaria caespitosa* [*A. verna*, *Minuartia verna*]): ultra-hardy; to 2.5×30cm (1×12in); moss-like mats of v narrow bright

green lvs (yellow-green in var 'Aurea'); white fls, spring & early summer. Takes partial shade.

S. subulata (Corsican pearlwort) is similarly mat-forming, but fl stalks grow to 10cm (4in.).

Soapworts (*Saponaria* spp): generally prostrate & trailing plants forming mats of leafy stems with profuse pink fls in summer. Good for banks or hanging over rocks.

S. 'Bressingham Hybrid' **6**: hybrid of *S. ocymoides* & *S.×olivana*; forms neat, almost prostrate cushion, to 5×15cm (2×6in); hairy lvs, clustered clear deep pink fls, summer.

S. ocymoides **7**: ultra-hardy; vigorous, to 15×60cm (6×24in); v profuse bright to deep rose-pink 1cm (½in) fls, late spring to mid summer. Self-seeds. Vars: 'Alba' (white); 'Compacta' (slower-growing & more compact than sp); 'Rubra Compacta' (compact; rich carmine-pink fls); 'Splendens' (dark pink).

S.×olivana: hybrid of *S. caespitosa* & *S. pumilio*; compact & cushion-forming, to 5×20cm (2×8in); many bright pink 2.5cm (1in) fls, summer. Easier to grow than parents.

Campions (*Silene* spp): tufted plants with narrow lvs & colourful fls, late spring & early summer; generally easy, for any well-drained soil unless stated.

S. acaulis **8** (moss campion, cushion pink): densely mat-forming, to 5×30–45cm (2×12–18in); bright green lvs; almost stemless vivid pink 1cm (½in) fls, profuse in wild but sometimes sparse in gardens unless soil poor & gritty. Var *pedunculata* (*elongata*) has fl stems to 10cm (4in) tall; free-flg.

S. alpestris (*S. quadrifida*): neatly tufted, to 20×15cm (8×6in); pale green glossy lvs; profuse sprays of white starry fls, double in var 'Plena'.

S. maritima (sea campion; *S. vulgaris maritima*): prostrate, to 15×30cm (6×12in); mat of glaucous lvs; small white fls in sp (rarely grown). Vars: 'Plena' **9** (2.5–4cm [1–1½in] double white fls); 'Rosea' (small pink fls).

S. schafta: to 15×30cm (6×12in); spreading tufts of mid green lvs; sprays of starry 2cm (¾in) magenta-pink fls, early summer to autumn.

Tunic flower (*Tunica* [correctly, *Petrorhagia*] *saxifraga* **10**): easy prostrate plant similar to gypsophila; to 15×40cm (6×16in); wiry stems; tiny narrow lvs; numerous tiny rose-pink fls all summer. Vars: 'Alba Plena' (double, white); 'Rosette' (double, pink).

The daisy family

Various tribes of Composites. Sun-lovers grown for flowers and/or foliage (all evergreen; many silver-leaved). Include many alpine & dwarf relatives of well-known border perennials. (All daisy "flowers" are compound; sizes refer to whole flower head.) **Cultivation**: Need full sun & well- or very well-drained soil; silver spp generally dislike winter wet. Dead-head. **Propagation**: Division; seed; stem cuttings.

Dwarf yarrows (Achillea spp; Anthemis tribe): generally ultra-hardy tufted plants, best in poor soil; usually deeply cut, often silvery lvs; small fls, often in flattish corymbs, spring & summer. Like lime.

A. ageratifolia (Anthemis aizoon): to 20×20cm (8×8in); silvery toothed (often deeply) lvs; white fls 2.5cm (1in) across.

A. argentea (may be var of A. clavennae): to 12×12cm (5×5in); mats of fine silvery lvs; small pure white daisy fls.

A. chrysocoma: to 15×25cm (6×10in); carpet of woolly silvery-grey lvs*; 5–8cm (2–3in) infls of mustard-yellow fls.

A. clavennae: to 10–25×25cm (4–10×10in); silver deeply cut lvs; loose infls of 2cm (¾in) white fls.

A.×kellereri **1**: hybrid of A. clavennae; to 15×25cm (6×10in); finely cut silver-grey lvs; white fls in tight infls.

A. 'King Edward' (A.×lewisii): hybrid of A. argentea & A. tomentosa; v hardy; to 15×20cm (6×8in); carpets of grey-green lvs; 4–6cm (1½–2in) infls of lemon-yellow fls.

A.×kobliana: hybrid of A. clavennae & A. umbellata; v hardy; to 20×20cm (8×8in); grey deeply cut lvs; 10cm (4in) infls of white fls.

A. tomentosa **2** (woolly yarrow): best-known alpine yarrow; to 15–25×30cm (6–10×12in); mats of finely cut woolly grey-green lvs*; dense 8cm (3in) infls of bright yellow fls.

Mount Atlas daisy (Anacyclus depressus **3**; Anthemis tribe): v hardy Moroccan alpine for v well-drained soil; dislikes winter wet. Semi-prostrate, to 8×30cm (3×12in); finely cut carrot-like grey-green lvs in rosettes; 5cm (2in) white daisy fls, crimson reverse, from late spring. A. atlanticus & A. maroccanus are similar.

Antennarias (Antennaria spp; Inula tribe): ultra-hardy carpeters for paving, overplanting bulbs, alpine lawns, etc; for any well-drained soil.

A. dioica: foliage to 5×45cm (2×18in) in greyish mats (self-rooting); 5mm (¼in) pink-tipped fluffy white fls in clusters on 15cm (6in) stems, late spring. Vars: 'Minima' (dwarf form); 'Nyewood' (fls crimson); 'Rosea' (correctly, A. rosea; fls pink); tomentosa (A. tomentosa; silvery lvs).

A. parvifolia **4** (often listed as A. aprica or A. dioica aprica): similar to A. dioica, with silvery lvs & white fls.

Dwarf artemisias (wormwoods, Artemisia spp; Anthemis tribe): v to ultra-hardy silvery-lvd

shrubs or sub-shrubs with insignificant fls. For v well-drained soil; dislike winter wet.

A. brachyloba: foliage to 2×15cm (½×6in); dense, finely cut silver lvs*; small yellow fls on 10cm (4in) stems.

A. lanata (A. nitida): to 15×25cm (6×10in); silver deeply cut lvs* with silky hairs; clustered small yellow fls, summer.

A. schmidtiana 'Nana' **5** ('Silver Mound'): to 10×30cm (4×12in); dome of finely cut silver lvs*; small yellowish fls, hairy bracts, autumn.

Alpine asters (Aster spp; Aster tribe): easy, generally ultra-hardy plants for any well-drained soil; form small spreading clumps; narrow lvs; golden-eyed daisy fls with narrow, usually bluish to pink petals, summer.

A. alpinus: to 15–20×30–45cm (6–8×12–18in); 2.5–4cm (1–1½in) fls, white, pink & bluish shades. Vars: 'Albus' (white); 'Beechwood' **6** (free-flg; lavender-blue); 'Wargrave Variety' (pale pink tinged purple).

A. natalensis (correctly, Felicia rosulata): v hardy; to 15×30cm (6×12in); mats of grey-green hairy lvs; clear blue 2.5cm (1in) fls; needs warm position.

A. tibeticus: similar to A. alpinus but more slender; 2.5–5cm (1–2in) bright blue fls.

Stemless thistle (Carlina acaulis **7**; Carduus tribe): v hardy; for dry, v well-drained soil. To 10–20×30cm (4–8×12in); rosettes of spiny greyish lvs to 15cm (6in) long; thistle-like whitish fls with silvery bracts, 5–12cm (2–5in) across, summer; fls stemless in sp, on 10cm (4in) stems in var caulescens.

Alpine chrysanthemums (Chrysanthemum spp; Anthemis tribe): v hardy; for rather poor, well-drained gritty soil.

C. (Pyrethrum) alpinum: to 15×30cm (6×12in); tufted; finely divided deep green lvs; 2.5–3cm (1–1¼in) white to pink fls, yellow disc, summer. Often short-lived.

C. (Tanacetum) haradjanii **8** (often listed as Tanacetum densum 'Amani'): to 25×30–40cm (10×12–16in); sub-shrubby; dense mound of silvery fern-like lvs; clustered small yellow fls, summer (may be removed if grown for foliage). Dislikes winter wet.

C. (Leucanthemum) hosmariense **9**: to 25×30–40cm (10×12–16in); sub-shrubby; finely cut v silver hairy lvs; golden-eyed white daisy fls 4cm (1½in) across, spring to autumn.

C. weyrichii: to 20×25cm (8×10in); fleshy pale

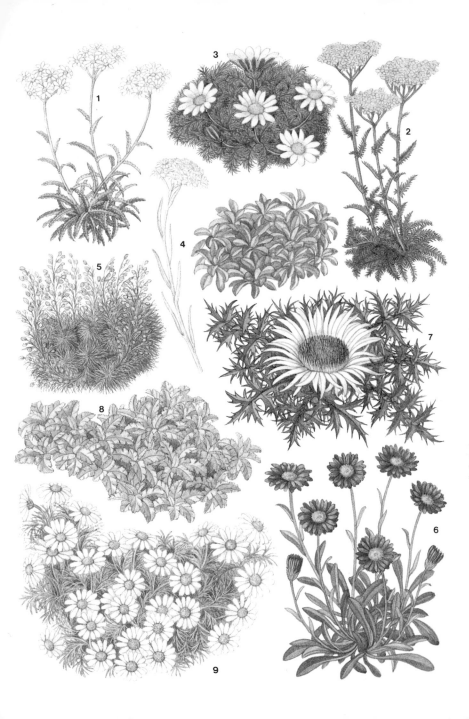

green lvs; 4.5cm (1¾in) pink daisy fls, yellow disc, autumn.

Cotulas (*Cotula* spp; Anthemis tribe): moderately hardy New Zealand carpeters with fern-like lvs; best between paving (rather invasive); for gritty well-drained soil.

C. atrata 'Luteola' **1**: to 5×30cm (2×12in); mat of finely cut fleshy lvs; 2cm (¼in) pinchushion-like dark red & black fls.

C. potentillina: to 2.5×45–50cm (1×18–20in); creeping mat of green lvs.

C. squallida: to 2.5×45cm (1×18in); creeping mat of bronzed green lvs.

Crepis (hawkweeds, *Crepis* spp; Cichorium tribe): v hardy, sometimes weedy, rosette plants with tap roots & dandelion-like lvs & fls; for poor soil.

C. aurea: to 20×25cm (8×10in); fls coppery-orange, summer.

C. incana **2**: to 20×30cm (8×12in); greyish hairy lvs; fluffy pink fls all summer.

Dwarf Cape marigold (*Dimorphotheca* [correctly, *Osteospermum*] *barberae* 'Compacta'): moderately hardy dwarf var of *D. barberae* (p494): to 15×40cm (6×16in); lvs* leathery; rosy-purple 5cm (2in) daisy fls, all summer. For sandy soil.

Dwarf erigerons (fleabanes, *Erigeron* spp; Aster tribe): easy plants for gritty soil with 2cm (¾in) semi-double daisy fls from late spring; generally v hardy.

E. aureus **3**: to 10×20cm (4×8in); golden fls.

E. 'Birch Hybrid': hybrid of *E. aureus* & *E. flettii*; to 10×20cm (4×8in); creamy-yellow fls.

E. compositus (*E. multifidus*): to 10×20cm (4×8in); deeply cut grey-green woolly lvs; white fls.

E. karvinskianus (*E. mucronatus*, *Vitadenia triloba*): moderately hardy; spreading, to 15–25×30cm (6–10×12in); white to pale pink fls; self-seeds.

Haplopappus (*Haplopappus coronipifolius* **4**; correctly, *H. glutinosus*; Aster tribe): v hardy sub-shrubby evergreen for v well-drained soil; to 30×20cm (12×8in); dark green lobed leathery lvs; golden daisy fls, summer. *H. lyallii* is similar.

Helichrysums (strawflowers, *Helichrysum* spp; Inula tribe): generally moderately to v hardy silver/greyish-lvd plants for v well-drained gritty soil (protect from winter wet); fls usually small and button-like, with papery bracts, summer (often removed if grown for foliage).

H. bellidioides: spreading, to 5×45cm (2×18in); small dark green & silver woolly lvs; white fls.

N. coralloides: to 25×20cm (10×8in); shrubby dark green scale-like lvs with white wool along stems; v small yellow fls.

H. milfordiae **5** (sometimes sold incorrectly as *H. marginatum*): to 5×25cm (2×10in); densely clustered rosettes of silvery-green lvs; yellow fls

with red-backed white bracts, 2.5cm (1in) across, late spring.

H. orientale: to 30×30cm (12×12in); sub-shrubby; forms mound of grey-green hairy lvs; 8cm (3in) clusters of yellow fls. V susceptible to winter wet.

H. plumeum: to 30×40cm (12×15in); similar to *H. coralloides* but softer & hairier.

H. virgineum: to 25×15cm (10×6in); shrubby; v woolly silvery lvs; yellow fls with creamy-white bracts, 4cm (1½in) across; best under glass.

Edelweiss (*Leontopodium* spp; Inula tribe): v hardy; grey-green woolly lvs; small white fls with irregular narrow greyish woolly bracts, forming starry fl head 5cm (2in) across, late spring to early summer. For well-drained soil; easy to grow from seed.

L. alpinum **6** (common edelweiss of Swiss Alps): to 15×25cm (6×10in). Var *crassense* has v white lvs & fls & is longer-lived.

L. haplophylloides (often sold as *L. aloysiodorum*): to 25×25cm (10×10in); lvs* lemon-scented.

Raoulias (*Raoulia* spp; Inula tribe): generally moderately to v hardy New Zealand mat-forming plants for ground cover in v well-drained gritty soil; tiny lvs in clustered rosettes, often silver; small almost stemless fls, spring. Protect from winter wet.

R. australis: to 0.5–1×30cm (¼–½×12in); forms silvery mat; fls pale yellow.

R. glabra: to 0.5–1×30–45cm (¼–½×12–18in); bright green mat; fls whitish.

R. hookeri **7**: to 1×30cm (½×12in); similar to *R. australis*; v silver.

R. lutescens **8** (often sold as *R. subsericea*): to 1×30–45cm (½×12–18in); grey-green mat; fls yellow.

R. tenuicaulis: to 0.5×30cm (¼×12in); grey-green mat; fls yellow.

Dwarf golden rods (*Solidago* spp & vars; Aster tribe): v hardy; dwarf forms of popular border plants (p274) narrow lvs; plume-like heads of golden-yellow fls from mid summer. For any soil. Spp & vars suitable for rock gardens: *S. cutleri* **9** (*S. virgaurea alpina*; to 30cm [12in]); *S.* 'Golden Thumb' (to 30cm [12in]; late-flg); *S. virgaurea brachystachys* (*S. brachystachys*; to 20cm [8in]); *S. virgaurea nana* (to 15cm [6in]; early-flg).

Tanacetum: See under *Chrysanthemum* (above).

Townsendias (*Townsendia* spp; Aster tribe): v to ultra-hardy N American alpines for well-drained soil; tufts of narrow lvs; 5cm (2in) yellow-centred aster-like fls, summer.

T. exscapa **10**: to 5×10cm (2×4in); lvs greyish; fls almost stemless, white or pinkish.

T. formosa: to 10×10cm (4×4in); violet-blue.

T. parryi: to 15×10cm (6×4in); lavender-blue; short-lived.

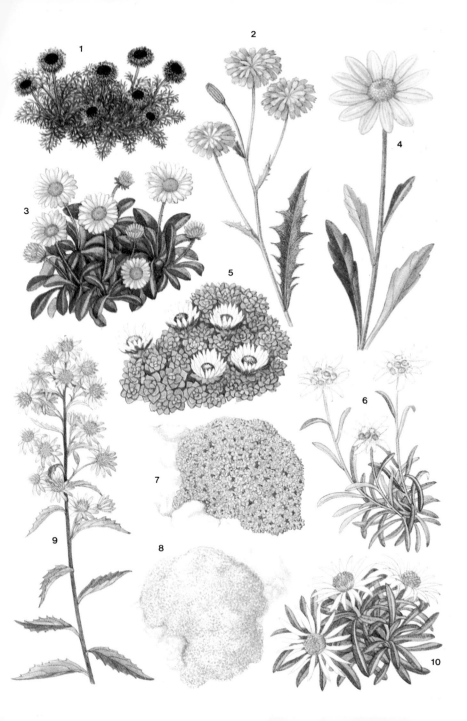

Stonecrops

Sedum spp. Colourful, generally easy, mat-forming or sprawling plants with thick semi-prostrate stems & small fleshy leaves (cylindrical to rounded & triangular). Evergreen unless stated. Abundant 5-petalled starry flowers, generally 0.5–1cm (¼–½in) across, solitary or (usually) in flat cymes, mid summer unless stated. Often rather invasive, but many succeed on v poor soil where little else grows. **Cultivation**: Very to ultra-hardy unless stated. For well-drained, gritty soil in full sun. **Propagation**: Easy, by seed, layering, leaf/stem cuttings, offsets.

S. acre **1** (biting stonecrop, wall-pepper, golden moss): sp invasive, to 5×25cm (2×10in); mat-forming; yellow-green lvs; 2.5–4cm (1–1½in) infls of yellow fls, early summer. Vars (non-invasive): 'Aureum' ('Variegatum'; shoot tips golden); 'Elegans' (shoot tips silver); 'Majus' (large lvs & fls); 'Minus' (dwarf).

S. aizoon: to 30×30cm (1×1ft); herbaceous; 8cm (3in) toothed lvs; 5–8cm (2–3in) infls of golden-yellow fls (orange-yellow in var 'Aurantiacum'). Often grown in borders.

S. album: sp invasive, to 10×25cm (4×10in), used for ground cover; pink stems; grey-green lvs; 8cm (3in) infls of white fls. Vars (non-invasive; mat-forming): 'Coral Carpet' **2** (coral-red lvs; pink fls); *micranthum* (v small lvs & white fls); *murale* (bronze-purple lvs; pink fls).

S. anacampseros: to 15×30cm (6×12in); snake-like prostrate brown stems; sparse blue-grey lvs in terminal rosettes; purplish-pink fls.

S. brevifolium: moderately hardy; creeping, to 4×15cm (1½×6in); powdery crowded lvs, suffused pink; clusters of small white fls, early summer.

S. cauticolum **3**: rather spreading, to 15×30cm (6×12in) or more; herbaceous; arching stems; blue-grey lvs; 10cm (4in) infls of crimson fls, late summer & early autumn.

S. dasyphyllum: to 5×20cm (2×8in); dense mat of tiny grey-green downy lvs; clusters of tiny pale pink or white fls, early summer. Var *glanduliferum* is v woolly.

S. ewersii: to 15×40cm (6×16in); trailing stems; blue-grey rounded lvs; dense infls of pink to violet fls, mid–late summer. Var *homophyllum* ('Haysii') is dwarf form.

S. floriferum 'Weihenstephener Gold' **4**: may be hybrid; to 10×45cm (4×18in); sprawling; profuse starry golden-yellow fls (attract bees).

S. kamtschaticum: to 10×50cm (4×20in); dark green spatula-shaped lvs; infls of bright yellow fls. Vars: *middendorffianum* (*S. middendorffianum*; lvs narrow); 'Variegatum' (lvs variegated; fls ageing orange-red).

S. lydium: mat-forming, to 8×15cm (3×6in); bright green lvs tinged red in summer; dense infls of small white fls, early summer.

S. oreganum **5** (sometimes sold incorrectly as *S. obtusatum*): to 8×25cm (3×10in); loose rosettes of glossy lvs, suffused red in summer; small infls of bright yellow fls.

S. pachyphyllum **6** (jelly-bean plant): tender to semi-hardy succulent sub-shrub, to 30×30cm (1×1ft); blue-green club-shaped lvs, pink tips; 5–8cm (2–3in) infls of yellow fls, spring. Useful in warm areas, elsewhere under glass.

S. pilosum: to 8×10cm (3×4in); forms softly hairy rosettes like sempervivums (p440); monocarpic, producing dense 2.5–8cm (1–3in) infls of rose-red fls, early summer, 2nd or later yr, then dying. Propagate regularly from seed (easy).

S. populifolium*: to 30×25cm (12×10in); sub-shrubby; coarsely toothed lvs (deciduous); infls of white or pink-tinged fls, hawthorn-scented.

S. pulchellum: moderately to v hardy; to 8×15cm (3×6in); red stems; narrow rich green lvs; starry infls of rose-pink fls. Likes moist soil in semi-shade.

S. reflexum (stone orpine): to 20×40cm (8×16in); forms mat of grey-green narrow lvs & reddish stems; 5–8cm (2–3in) infls of yellow fls, drooping in bud.

S. sieboldii: moderately hardy, though often grown indoors; trailing, to 8×40cm (3×16in); herbaceous in cold; striking blue-grey round lvs in 3s along stems; 5–8cm (2–3in) infls of purple-pink fls, autumn. Good in hanging baskets. Var 'Medio-variegatum' **7** has lvs centred yellowish.

S. spathulifolium: v hardy; to 10×30cm (4×12in); forms dense mat of purple-green spoon-shaped lvs in small rosettes, often powdery; 5cm (2in) infls of bright yellow fls, late spring & early summer. Vars: 'Aureum' (lvs splashed yellow & tinted pink); 'Cape Blanco' **8** ('Capa Blanca'; lvs almost white with powder); 'Purpureum' (lvs larger, purple).

S. spurium: creeping & mat-forming, to 10×40cm (4×16in); broad lvs on red stems; 5–8cm (2–3in) dense infls of pink fls. Vars: 'Album' (white); 'Erdblut' (carmine-red); 'Fuldaglut' ('Glow'; red lvs; crimson fls); 'Green Mantle' (fresh green lvs); 'Purple Carpet' (deep purple-red lvs; pink fls); 'Schorbusser Blut' **9** ('Dragon's Blood'; bronzed lvs; crimson fls).

S. 'Vera Jameson' **10**: hybrid of *S. maximum* 'Altropurpureum' & *S.* 'Ruby Glow' (p284); to 25×30cm (10×12in); herbaceous; arching stems with deep purple lvs; infls of dusty-pink fls. Also good at front of border.

Other members of the crassula family

Succulent, rosette-forming plants making spreading mats or congested mounds, grown mainly for form, texture & colour of evergreen leaves. Cluster in crevices, on walls, in troughs or pans. **Cultivation**: For very free-draining gritty soil, in full sun unless stated; surround with chippings. Protect from excessive winter wet and birds. **Propagation**: Leaf cuttings; division or offsets; seed.

Lamb's tail (*Chiastophyllum* [*Cotyledon*] *oppositifolium* **1**; often sold as *Cotyledon simplicifolia*): v hardy rhizomatous creeping & self-rooting plant, to 15×60cm (6×24in); lvs oval, toothed; arching racemes of yellow fls, late spring to summer. Best in cool partial shade.

Crassulas (*Crassula* spp): S African plants often best in alpine house; small starry fls, summer.
C. milfordiae (*C. sedifolia*): moderately hardy; to 5×40cm (2×16in); tiny rosettes of grey-green lvs, tinted bronze in winter; white fls from crimson buds in hot summers. *C. sediformis* is similar; hummock-forming.
C. sarcocaulis: semi-hardy tree-like sub-shrub, to 25×15cm (10×6in); lvs flushed red; pink fls.

Houseleeks (*Sempervivum* spp; some correctly *Jovibarba* spp): v hardy; mat/hummock-forming, clustered rosettes generally to 2.5–8×20–30cm (1–3×8–12in), rosettes elongating to 15–30cm (6–12in) tall when flg; fls starry, mid summer; rosette dies after flg, leaving offsets. Traditionally grown on house roofs. Much hybridized; nomenclature confused.
S. arachnoideum (cobweb or spider houseleek): 1–2cm (½–¾in) rosettes; green lvs edged red, tips joined by attractive cobwebby hairs; showy rose-red fls. Var 'Laggeri' **2** ('Tomentosum') is more densely webbed.
S. (J.) arenarium: 0.5–2cm (¼–¾in) pale green & red rosettes; pale yellow fls.
S.×calcaratum: probably *S. tectorum* hybrid; 2cm (¾in) green & purple rosettes; pink fls.
S. dolomiticum: hairy 1–5cm (½–2in) rosettes, green edged red; fls rose-red striped purple.
S.×funckii: probably hybrid of *S. arachnoideum*,

S. montanum & *S. tectorum*; 2.5–4cm (1–1½in) hairy green rosettes tipped purple; fls rose-purple.
S. grandiflorum **3**: 5–10cm (2–4in) dull green rosettes, sticky-hairy & smelling of goats; large yellow fls, purple spot.
S. (J.) heuffelii **4**: 5–8cm (2–3in) green to grey-green rosettes, sometimes tipped brown/purple or flushed red. No offsets; rosettes divide.
S. (J.) hirtum: 2.5–5cm (1–2in) yellow-green rosettes, often reddish-brown outside; bold infls of yellow fls.
S. marmoreum: 5–10cm (2–4in) rosettes, usually green & red, hairy when young; fls crimson edged white. Var 'Bruneifolium' is brown-lvd.
S. montanum **5**: usually green 2.5–4cm (1–1½in) rosettes; fls red-purple.
S. octopodes: moderately hardy; 2.5cm (1in) hairy rosettes of pale–mid green lvs; fls yellow & red.
S. (J.) soboliferum **6** (hen-and-chicken houseleek): 1–3cm (½–1¼in) bright green rosettes; fls rare.
S. tectorum (common or roof houseleek): flattish 5–15cm (2–6in) green rosettes, usually tipped purple or maroon; fls (rare) purple. V variable; vars & hybrids include: *alpinum* (dwarf); 'Beta' (bronze-red); *calcareum* **7** (compact; grey-green & maroon); 'Commander Hay' **8** (purple-red tipped green); 'Jubilee' (green & crimson); 'Mahogany' **9** (mahogany-red); 'Othello' (v large crimson & green rosettes); 'Rubin' (large reddish-bronze rosettes); 'Triste' (reddish-green; pink fls).

Alyssums, aubrieta and their relatives

Mostly sun-loving plants providing some of the most spectacular sheets of colour in the spring rock garden or dry wall. Evergreen unless stated, generally with narrow or lance-shaped leaves. Small cross-shaped flowers, generally in 2.5–5cm (1–2in) rounded inflorescences (often hiding foliage), spring or early summer unless stated. **Cultivation**: Unless noted, very hardy & for any well-drained soil in full sun. Dead head; cut back more sprawling spp after flowering to promote compact habit. **Propagation**: Cuttings; division; spp by seed.

Stone-cresses (*Aethionema* spp): bushy mounding sub-shrubs with grey-green lvs & profuse, generally pink fls. Like lime.
A. grandiflorum (Persian stone-cress): to 30×30–45cm (1×1–1½ft), fls pale pink.
A. pulchellum is same or similar sp; more compact with richer pink fls.

A. iberideum: to 15×30cm (6×12in); white fls.
A. 'Warley Rose' **10** ('Warley Hybrid'): hybrid probably of *A. coridifolium*; compact, to 15×30cm (6×12in); rich rose-pink fls. *A.* 'Warley Ruber' **11** is similar but rose-red.
Alyssums (*Alyssum* spp): prostrate or trailing sub-shrubs with grey-green lvs & profuse yellow

fls. Generally ultra-hardy.

A. montanum* : mat-forming, to 8–15×30cm (3–6×12in); hairy grey lvs; bright yellow fls.

A. murale (yellow-tuft; often sold incorrectly as *A. argenteum*): to 30×25cm (12×10in); lemon-yellow fls, summer. Short-lived but self-seeds.

A. saxatile (gold dust, common yellow alyssum; correctly, *Aurinia saxatilis*): vigorous & mat-forming, to 20–30×45cm (10–12×18in); v profuse golden-yellow fls. V popular associated with aubrieta, becomes lanky if not trimmed regularly. Vars: 'Citrinum' (lemon-yellow); 'Compactum' **1** (dense & compact); 'Dudley Neville' **2** (compact; silvery lvs; buff-yellow fls); 'Plenum' ('Flore Pleno'; compact; double fls).

A. serpyllifolium: v hardy; prostrate, to 5×20cm (2×8in); tiny grey-green lvs; clear yellow fls.

A. spinosum: see *Ptilotrichum spinosum*.

Rock-cresses (*Arabis* spp): include rampant & dwarf spp, most with grey-green lvs & white fls.

A. blepharophylla **3**: moderately hardy; to 10×20cm (4×8in); tufts of stiff green lvs; white, pink or purplish fls, spring. Best in alpine house.

A. caucasica (*A. albida*, common white arabis; may be listed incorrectly as *A. alpina*): ultra-hardy; to 25×60cm (10×24in); profuse white fls, early spring to early summer. Sp too invasive for most rock gardens, but good on dry banks & walls (with aubrieta, etc). Compact vars (generally to 20×45cm [8×18in]); 'Coccinea' (crimson); 'Flore Pleno' ('Alba Plena', 'Plena'; double snow-white fls); 'Rosabella' **4** (pink); 'Variegata' (lvs variegated gold & white; fls pink).

A. ferdinandi-coburgii 'Variegata' **5**: moderately hardy; to 10×20cm (4×8in); mats of green & white lvs, white fls, late spring.

Aubrieta (*Aubrieta deltoidea*; often mis-spelled *Aubretia*): v popular trailing & mat-forming plant, to 15×45–60cm (6×18–24in); small wedge-shaped toothed lvs; v profuse pink to near-red, purple & violet 2cm (¾in) fls. Excellent for banks, walls & rock-garden crevices; also for border edging. Likes lime; cut back hard after flg. Variable from seed; propagate best forms. Numerous vars include: 'Aurea' **6** ('Aurea Variegata,' lvs edged gold); 'Bob Saunders' (double, reddish-purple); 'Bressingham Pink' **7** (double, pink); 'Bressingham Red' (large rose-red fls); 'Dr Mules' (deep violet-blue); 'Greencourt Purple' (large double fls, purple); 'Gurgedyke' **8** (dark purple); 'Maurice Pritchard' (light pink); 'Mrs Rodewald' (bright rose-red); 'Red Carpet' **9** (deep red); 'Riverslea' (mauve-pink; late); 'Variegata ('Argentea Variegata'; lvs edged silver); 'Wanda' (double, light red).

Drabas (whitlow grasses, *Draba* spp): v neat cushion/mat-forming plants with v small rigid lvs in crowded rosettes & generally yellow fls on wiry stems, spring. Need gritty, well-drained soil; best in alpine house, or protect from winter wet.

D. aizoides **10**: to 10×20cm (4×8in); bristle-tipped lvs; lemon-yellow fls. Easy outdoors.

D. bruniifolia: to 5×20cm (2×8in); hairy lvs; sprays of tiny yellow fls.

D. bryoides (correctly, *D. rigida bryoides*): compact cushion, to 5×8cm (2×3in), sparse golden-yellow fls. Var 'Imbricata' **11** is v compact, to 5×5cm (2×2in); for trough or pan.

D. mollissima: to 5×20cm (2×8in); hairy grey-green lvs; profuse bright yellow fls, late spring; best in alpine house.

D. polytricha: to 5×20cm (2×8in); forms grey-green hummock; profuse golden fls; best in alpine house.

D. rigida: similar to *D. bryoides* but less compact, to 8×15cm (3×6in), & freer-flg.

Dwarf wallflowers (treacle mustards, *Erysimum* [*Cheiranthus*] spp): resemble miniature biennial wallflowers (*Cheiranthus* spp; p506); bushy, with mid–dark green generally lance-shaped lvs & showy fls. Short-lived but often self-seed; thrive on poor soil. Nomenclature sometimes confused.

E. (*C.*) *alpinum** : to 15×15–25cm (6×6–10in); sulphur-yellow fls. Vars/hybrids: 'Moonlight' (primose-yellow); 'Orange Flame' **12** (tangerine).

E. (*C.*) *capitatum** **13**: moderately hardy; to 25×15cm (10×6in); sub-shrubby; cream fls.

E. helveticum* (*E. pumilum*): to 5–15×10–15cm (2–6×4–6in); neatly tufted; clear yellow fls. Var 'Golden Gem' is rich golden-yellow.

E. pulchellum (*E. rupestre*): moderately to v hardy; to 30×25cm (12×10in); mustard-yellow to orange fls.

Hutchinsia (chamois cress, *Hutchinsia alpina*): to 10×25cm (4×10in); similar to *Draba* spp, making neat mound of dark green ferny lvs; tiny white fls, summer.

Iberis (perennial candytufts, *Iberis* spp): easy bushy sub-shrubs; dark green lvs; dense infls of generally white fls. Do well in poor soil.

I. gibraltarica: moderately hardy; to 30×30–45cm (1×1–1½ft); leathery lvs; white fls flushed mauve. Self-seeds.

I. saxatilis (*I. petraea*): ultra-hardy; to 10×25cm (4×10in); v narrow, almost needle-like lvs; white fls, sometimes tinged mauve.

I. sempervirens: ultra-hardy; sp vigorous, to 25×60cm (10×24in); semi-/evergreen; pure white fls. Sp & var 'Snowflake' **14** (to 20×60cm [8×24in]; profuse large infls; best vigorous form) are rather large for many rock gardens. Dwarf vars: 'Little Gem' (to 15×30cm [6×12in]); 'Pygmaea' (*I. pygmaea*; to 5×15cm [2×6in]).

Spiny alyssum (*Ptilotrichum* [*Alyssum*] *spinosum*): moderately to v hardy spiny domed sub-shrub, to 20×25cm (8×10in); wiry tangled stems; dense grey lvs; profuse infls of creamy-white fls, early summer. For scree or trough. Var 'Roseum' is pale to deep pink.

Heaths, heathers and their allies

Low-growing but often sprawling shrubs with very small scale/needle-like evergreen leaves densely clothing shoots. Long-lasting small bell/urn-shaped flowers, usually in spikes or racemes; good for cutting fresh or dried (especially vars marked †). Generally good for ground cover; for moist, peaty rock gardens, peat beds, etc. Some spp too vigorous for small rock gardens unless cut back often, and may swamp smaller plants – ideal in special heath garden/bed (mixed spp colourful all year). **Cultivation**: Unless stated, very hardy. Generally for lime-free peaty soil, in full sun unless stated. May be prone to fungal disease causing dieback. **Pruning**: Dead flower heads of most spp attractive, so trim lightly early spring (after flowering for very early spp). **Propagation**: Semi-ripe heel cuttings; sprawling spp & vars also by layering; seed. For tall-growing "tree" heaths, see p100.

Spike heath (*Bruckenthalia spiculifolia*): dwarf heather-like shrub, to 20×30cm (8×12in); v small & narrow bristle-tipped lvs; 2.5cm (1in) infls of v small rosy-pink bell fls, late spring or early summer.

Heather (ling, *Calluna vulgaris*): well-known heath/moorland plant of N Europe, v variable in cultivation; to 10–60×10–75cm (4–24×4–30in); short scale-like lvs, colourful in some vars; white to deep purple 5mm (¼in) fls in 8–25cm (3–10in) infls, mid summer to autumn. Vars (unless stated spread to 30–45cm [1–1½ft] & fl late summer or early autumn): 'Alba Plena'† (to 30cm [1ft]; double white fls; late); 'Alba Rigida' (to 15×25cm [6×10in]; stiff branches; white); 'Alportii' (to 60cm [2ft]; crimson); 'Barnett Anley' (to 45cm [1½ft]; dense infls of purple fls); 'Beoley Gold' (to 50×60cm [20×24in]; lvs flushed gold & cream; fls white); 'Blazeaway' **1** (to 45cm [1½ft]; lvs golden-green, red in winter; fls purple); 'County Wicklow' ('Camla'; to 20×25cm [8×10in]; pale pink double fls); 'Elsie Purnell'† **2** (to 50cm [20in]; greyish lvs; double silvery-pink fls; latish); 'Foxii Nana' (to 10×15cm [4×6in]; dense cushion of lvs; rarely, purple fls); 'Golden Carpet' (to 10×60cm [4×24in]; gold lvs flecked red & orange; reddish-purple fls); 'Golden Feather' **3** (to 45×60cm [1½×2ft]; golden feathery lvs, orange in winter; mauve fls); 'Gold Haze' **4** (to 45–60cm [1½–2ft]; yellow lvs; white fls); 'Hammondii'† (to 60–75cm [2–2½ft]; long infls of white fls); 'H. E. Beale'† (to 60×75cm [2×2½ft]; greyish-green lvs; long infls of silvery-pink double fls; late); 'Hirsuta Typica' ('Silver Queen'; to 40×25cm [16×10in]; greyish/silvery lvs; purple fls); 'Humpty Dumpty' (to 15×25cm [6×10in]; moss-green lvs tipped golden-yellow; white fls); 'J. H. Hamilton' (to 15cm [6in], large double rose-pink fls); 'Joan Sparkes' (to 20cm [8in]; dark green feathery lvs; profuse mauve-pink double fls); 'Mair's Variety'† (to 60×50cm [24×20in]; white fls; early); 'Mrs Ronald Gray' (to 8cm [3in]; purple; good ground cover); 'Multicolor' **5** ('Prairie Fire'; to 10cm [4in]; lvs golden-green tinged vivid red & orange; fls mauve); 'My Dream'† (to 60×75cm [2×2½ft]; white sport of 'H. E. Beale'); 'Peter Sparkes'† **6** (to 45cm [1½ft]; long spikes of deep pink fls;

latish); 'Robert Chapman' **7** (to 30cm [1ft]; lvs orange-gold, mahogany & brilliant red in winter; fls soft purple); 'Serlei'† (to 60×60cm [2×2ft]; bright green lvs; long infls of white fls; latish); 'Sister Anne' **8** ('Hirsuta compacta'; to 10×25cm [4×10in]; grey lvs; pink fls).

Cassiopes (*Cassiope* spp; some sometimes listed as *Andromeda* spp): v to ultra-hardy neat heath-like shrublets with dense, scale-like overlapping dark green lvs & solitary 5mm (¼in) bell fls on wiry stems, spring. For cool semi-shade; good in pots.
C. lycopodioides: prostrate, to 8×45cm (3×18in); white fls, red calyx, along branches. Var 'Muirhead' **9** (hybrid with *C. wardii*) is more erect, to 20×40cm (8×16in).
C. mertensiana (in US sometimes known as white heather): to 30×40cm (12×16in); creamy-white fls at branch tips.
C. tetragona: tufted & upright, to 10–30×30cm (4–12×12in); ivory-white narrow-mouthed fls. Var 'Edinburgh' **10** (hybrid with *C. fastigiata*) is v free-flg & easy.
C. wardii: upright & branching, to 20×20cm (8×8in); lvs fringed with white hairs; large white fls on short stalks.

St Dabeoc's heaths (*Daboecia* spp): heath-like shrubs with rather oval lvs, silvery beneath, & 8–15cm (3–6in) racemes of relatively large bell fls (dead heads not retained). Like some shelter.
D. azorica: generally considered semi- to moderately hardy, but hardier in mountains of Azores; dense & compact, to 15×15cm (6×6in); lvs to 8mm (⅓in) long; red-purple 8mm (⅓in) fls from v early summer.
D. cantabrica (*D. polifolia*, Irish or Connemara heath): moderately to v hardy; rather sprawling, to 60×60cm (2×2ft); lvs to 10mm (⅜in) long; purplish-pink fls to 12mm (½in) long, mid summer to autumn. Vars: 'Alba' (white); 'Atropurpurea' (rich reddish-purple); 'Bicolor' **11** (white, purple & bicoloured); 'David Moss'† (white); 'Praegerae' (deep pink).
D.×scotica: hybrids of above spp, & intermediate in size & habit, but v hardy; fl v early summer, repeating to autumn. Vars: 'Jack Drake' (garnet-red); 'William Buchanan' **12** (crimson-purple).
Heaths (*Erica* spp): generally slow-growing

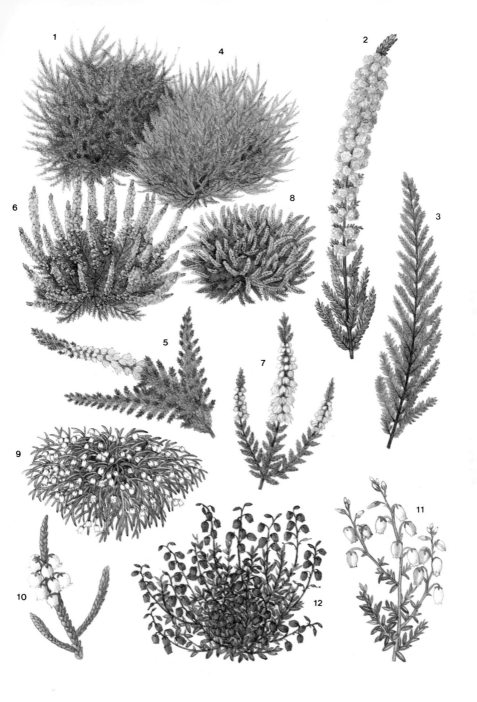

dwarf shrubs with v small needle-like whorled lvs
& profuse 5mm (¼in) fls. Like sandy soil.
E. carnea (winter or spring heath; correctly,
E. herbacea): dense & hummock-forming; lvs
generally pale green; fls in 8–15cm (3–6in)
racemes, rosy-red in sp, generally mid winter to
early spring (later in cold winters). Tolerates lime.
Vars (unless stated, to 15–30×40–60cm [6–
12×16–24in]): 'Alan Coates'† (to 15×35cm
[6×14in]; pink-purple); 'Ann Sparkes' (to
10×40cm [4×16in]; lvs gold, bronze & green; fls
deep carmine); 'Aurea' (lvs golden in spring; fls
pink to white); 'Cecilia M. Beale' (white);
'December Red' (cyclamen-purple; early);
'Eileen Porter' (carmine-red bicoloured fls;
v early); 'Foxhollow' (to 30×75cm [1×2½ft];
golden-yellow lvs; pink fls); 'Heathwood' (to
10×30cm [4×12in]; dark lvs; rosy-purple fls;
late); 'King George' (sometimes sold as 'Winter
Beauty'; deep rose-pink); 'Loughrigg' (to
10×30cm [4×12in]; lvs bluish-green to bronze;
fls rosy-purple; latish); 'Myretoun Ruby' **1**
('Winter Jewel'; dark green lvs; bright red fls);
'Pink Spangles' **2** (purplish-pink; early); 'Pirbright
Rose' (glaucous lvs; red-purple fls; early);
'Praecox Rubra' (deep rose-red; early); 'Ruby
Glow' (lvs dark green; fls carmine-red; late);
'Snow Queen' (fresh green lvs; large white fls);
'Springwood Pink' **3** (to 10×30cm [4×12in];
rose-pink); 'Springwood White' (dark green lvs;
profuse white fls); 'Vivellii' **4** (to 10×30cm
[4×12in]; lvs bronzed winter; fls carmine-red).
E. ciliaris (Dorset or fringed heath): moderately to
v hardy; rather straggly, to 30×45cm (1×1½ft) or
more unless trimmed; pale green lvs; fls in
5–12cm (2–5in) racemes, rosy-red in sp, mid
summer to autumn. Vars: 'Aurea' (golden lvs;
pink fls); 'Corfe Castle' (salmon- to cherry-pink);
'David McClintock' (greyish lvs; white fls tipped
pink); 'Maweane' (sturdy & upright, to 45cm
[1½ft]; purple-pink); 'Mrs C. H. Gill' (dark green
lvs; rich red fls); 'Stoborough' (vigorous, to 60cm
[2ft]; white); 'Wych'† (flesh-pink).
E. cinerea (bell heather, twisted heath): stiff-
branched & bushy; neat glossy lvs; fls in 8cm
(3in) racemes or umbels, purple in sp, early
summer to autumn. Vars (unless stated, to
15–30×30–50cm [6–12×12–20in]): 'Alba Minor'
(compact; white): 'Apricot Charm'† (compact; lvs
yellow to apricot; fls mauve); 'Atrorubens' (ruby-
red); 'Atrosanguinea Smith's Variety' **5** (dark lvs;
profuse scarlet fls); 'C. D. Eason' (dark lvs;
rose-red fls); 'Cevennes' (lavender-pink); 'C. G.
Best' (long infls of salmon-pink fls); 'Coccinea'
(dwarf; carmine-red); 'Eden Valley' (dark lvs; fls
white flushed lilac); 'Foxhollow Mahogany' (dark
lvs; mahogany-red fls); 'Golden Drop' **6** (lvs
coppery-gold, rust-red in winter; sparse pink fls);
'Hookstone White' (to 45cm [1½ft]; long infls of
white fls); 'Knap Hill Pink' (deep green lvs; bright

pink fls); 'Pink Ice' (dark lvs, bronzed in winter;
pink fls): 'P. S. Patrick' (to 40cm [16in]; dark lvs;
reddish-purple fls in long infls); 'Stephen Davis'
(dark lvs; brilliant red fls); 'Velvet Night' **7** (dark
lvs; v dark purple fls); 'Vivienne Patricia' (v dark
lvs, tips tinged red; dark lavender fls).
E.×darleyensis vars: hybrids of *E. carnea* &
E. mediterranea (*E. erigena*: p100); vigorous &
spreading, to 60×90cm (2×3ft) or wider; mid-
green lvs; fls in 8–15cm (3–6in) leafy racemes,
early/mid winter to spring. Tolerate lime. Vars:
'Arthur Johnson' (rose-pink fls in v long spikes);
'Darley Dale' (original hybrid; profuse pinkish-
mauve fls); 'George Rendall' (compact; pinkish-
purple); 'Jack H. Brummage' (lvs greenish-
yellow to gold, tinged red in winter; fls deep
pink); 'Silberschmelze' * **8** ('Molten Silver',
'Silver Beads', 'Silver Bells', 'Silver Mist'; lvs
dark green in winter; fls silvery-white).
E. mackaiana (*E. mackaii*): to 25×25cm
(10×10in); dark green lvs; 5cm (2in) racemes of
rosy-red fls, summer, double in var 'Plena'
('Crawfordii').
E. tetralix (cross-leaved heath): ultra-hardy; to
30×30cm (1×1ft) or more; grey-green lvs in 4s;
dense clusters of fls, summer to early autumn,
soft rose-pink in sp. Needs ample moisture. Vars:
'Alba Mollis' (white); 'Con Underwood' **9**
(crimson); 'L. E. Underwood' (buds terracotta; fls
pink); 'Pink Star' (star-like upright pink fls).
E. vagans (Cornish heath): v vigorous &
spreading, to 0.3–0.6×0.6–1.2m (1–2×2–4ft);
dark green lvs; 15cm (6in) leafy racemes of v
small fls, late summer to autumn. Vars: 'Cream'†
(white); 'Diana Hornibrook' (dwarf; crimson);
'Lyonesse' (white); 'Mrs D. F. Maxwell' **10** (deep
cerise); 'St Keverne' ('Kevernensis'; rose-pink);
'Valerie Proudley' (white; lvs golden to lime-
green; slow-growing).
E.×watsonii vars: hybrids of *E. ciliaris* &
E. tetralix: to 30×60cm (1×2ft); lvs mainly in 4s;
short racemes of rosy-pink fls, mid summer to
autumn. Vars: 'Dawn' (spreading); 'H. Maxwell'
(upright).
E.×williamsii vars: hybrids of *E. tetralix* &
E. vagans; to 30–60×60cm (1–2×2ft); dense &
compact; lvs in 4s, often yellowish; short clusters
of v small pink fls, early summer to autumn. Vars:
'Gwavas' (compact); 'P. D. Williams' (original
hybrid; rather sprawling).
Phyllodoces (mountain heaths, *Phyllodoce*
spp): dainty & compact heath-like dwarf shrubs
for cool, moist semi-shade; thicker stems than
true heaths & dark green narrow lvs to 1.5cm
(⅝in) long; clusters or short racemes of 5mm
(¼in) urn/bell-shaped fls, spring to summer.
P. aleutica **1**, p449: mat-forming, to 8–20×30cm
(3–8×12in); white to greenish fls.
P. breweri: tufted, to 25×30cm (10×12in);
purplish-pink fls.

P. caerulea: ultra-hardy; to 8–30×45cm (3–12×18in); cushion-forming; fls bluish-purple.
P. empetriformis: to 8–25×30–45cm (3–10×12–18in); mat-forming; fls purple.
P. glanduliflora **2**: ultra-hardy; to 20–30×30cm (8–12×12in); stiff, erect branches; fls sulphur-yellow.
P.×intermedia (often sold as *P. empetriformis*): hybrid of *P. empetriformis* & *P. glanduliflora*; to 15–25×30–45cm (6–10×12–18in) or wider; tufted & mat-forming; fls mauve to purple or yellowish-pink. Vars: 'Drummondii' (crimson-purple); 'Fred Stoker' (best-known form; easy).
P. nipponica: to 10–25×25cm (4–10×10in); compact & tufted; white or pink-tinged fls.
Phyllothamnus (×*Phyllothamnus erectus*): bigeneric hybrid probably of *Phyllodoce empetriformis* & *Rhodothamnus chamaecistus*; heath-like dense shrublet, to 30–40×30cm (12–15×12in); glossy green narrow lvs; clusters of funnel-shaped rose-pink fls 1cm (½in) across, spring; for cool, moist position.

Other members of the heath family

Lime-hating evergreen dwarf shrubs related to heaths & heathers (p444) but with broader, leathery leaves. Smaller spp for rock gardens, larger for peat beds, etc. **Cultivation & propagation**: As for heaths, but generally like cool, moist shade; little pruning needed. Dwarf rhododendrons, see pp90, 92.

Bog rosemary (*Andromeda polifolia*): ultra-hardy shrublet, to 30×45cm (1×1½ft); lvs to 4cm (1½in) long; compact clusters of pink to white urn-shaped 5mm (¼in) fls from late spring.
Bearberry (*Arctostaphylos uva-ursi* **3**): ultra-hardy trailing & self-rooting shrub, to 15×90cm (6×36in); lvs to 3cm (1¼in) long; pink-flushed white urn-shaped v small fls in drooping clusters from mid spring; brilliant red berries.
A. nevadensis (pine-mat manzanita) is v similar but only moderately to v hardy.
Epigaeas (*Epigaea* spp): prostrate self-rooting shrubs with lvs to 8cm (3in) long & spring fls often hidden by lvs. Best in semi-shade.
E. asiatica* : v hardy; to 8×30cm (3×12in); short racemes of bright pink 1cm (½in) bell/urn-shaped fls.
E. repens** (trailing arbutus, mayflower): ultra-hardy; to 10×30cm (4×12in); dense clusters of 1.5cm (⅝in) funnel-shaped white to pink fls.
Gaultherias (wintergreens, *Gaultheria* spp): neat & compact dwarf or prostrate shrubs similar to *Vaccinium* spp; small urn/globe-shaped fls, white or pinkish, early summer; showy berries. For semi-shade; generally moderately to v hardy.
G. miqueliana **4**: v hardy; to 20–30×45cm (8–12×18in); bright green 2.5cm (1in) lvs; fls in drooping racemes; white to pinkish frs.
G. nummarioides: moderately hardy; spreading, to 15×45cm (6×18in); dense & tufted; 1cm (½in) glossy lvs; fls solitary; rarely, blue-black frs.
G. procumbens **5** (creeping wintergreen, partridge-berry, checkerberry): ultra-hardy; creeping & mat-forming, to 15×60cm (6×24in) or wider; 2.5–5cm (1–2in) glossy lvs at branch tips, reddish in winter; fls mid summer; red frs.
G. pyroloides: compact & mat-forming, to 15–25×30cm (6–10×12in); 4cm (1½in) bright green lvs at branch tips; fls in short racemes; frs blue-black.

G. trichophylla: dense & prostrate, to 8–15×45cm (3–6×18in); stalkless 1cm (½in) glossy lvs; solitary pink fls; bright blue frs.
Dwarf kalmia (bog kalmia, *Kalmia polifolia*): ultra-hardy dwarf bushy shrub, to 30–45×30cm (1–1½×1ft); dark green rather narrow lvs to 4cm (1½in) long; bright pink-purple saucer-shaped fls 1cm (½in) across from late spring. Alpine form, var *microphylla* **6** (*K. microphylla*) is dwarf, to 15×30cm (6×12in), with smaller lvs & fls.
Kalmiopsis (*Kalmiopsis leachiana* **7**): moderately to v hardy tufted shrub, to 30×30cm (1×1ft); 2cm (¾in) lvs; open bell-shaped rosy-purple fls to 1.5cm (⅝in) wide, in loose clusters, spring; for open position.
Sand myrtle (*Leiophyllum buxifolium*): v hardy variable but usually hummock-forming shrub to 30×45cm (1×1½ft); small rounded box-like lvs; clustered white to pink fls 5mm (¼in) across, late spring. Likes peaty, sandy soil.
Dwarf blueberries (*Vaccinium* spp): dwarf decorative relatives of well-known frtg shrubs; clusters of small narrow to bell-shaped fls, generally late spring; edible frs; for sun or part-shade.
V. myrsinites (evergreen blueberry): moderately hardy; to 30–60×45cm (1–2×1½ft); 2cm (¾in) glossy lvs; white/pinkish fls; blue-black frs.
V. nummularia **8**: moderately hardy; to 30×30cm (1×1ft); stems arching; shiny 2.5cm (1in) lvs; rose-red to pink fls; glossy black frs.
V. oxycoccos (*Oxycoccus palustris*, European or small cranberry): ultra-hardy; prostrate, to 8×45cm (3×18in); wiry stems; v small lvs, silvery beneath; pink fls, reflexed petals; red frs.
V. vitis-idaea **9** (cowberry): ultra-hardy; creeping, to 10–25×45cm (4–10×18in); glossy rounded 3cm (1¼in) lvs; white or pale pink fls; red frs. Var *minus* (mountain cranberry) is v dwarf.

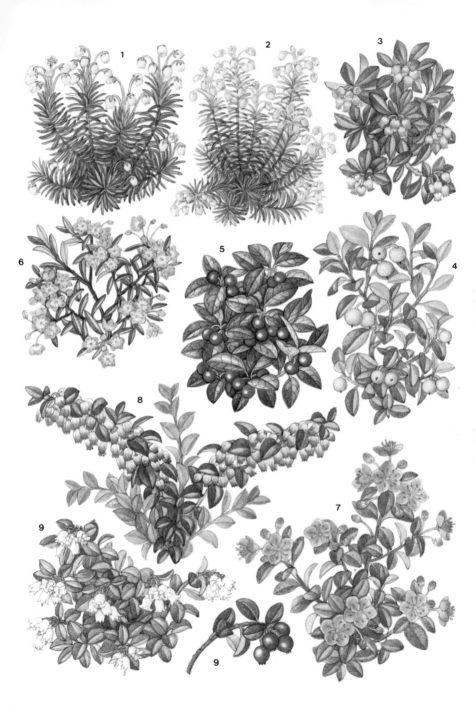

Gentians

Gentiana spp. Among the most well-known groups of alpine & rock garden plants. Leaves generally narrow to lance-shaped, toothless & often stalkless, evergreen unless stated. Flowers generally upright, either bell/trumpet-shaped or long-tubed, all generally 5-lobed, often with fringed or petal-like teeth between lobes. **Cultivation**: Needs vary, but unless stated very hardy & for rich, leafy, moist but very well-drained soil. Spring- & summer-flowering spp (mainly European) generally like open, sunny site; latter easier to grow. Autumn-flowering spp (mainly Asiatic) like cool semi-shade; they & some others must have lime-free soil. **Propagation**: Seed (sown fresh); root division; cuttings.

G. acaulis **1** (trumpet or stemless gentian): ultra-hardy variable sp: to 10×30–45cm (4×12–18in); mat of glossy deep green lvs; brilliant deep blue trumpet fls 5–8cm (2–3in) long, throat often speckled green, late spring. Easy to grow if planted firmly in heavy soil but often erratic flg (unpredictable; may vary with site, season, individual plant). Vars or subsidiary spp: *alpina* (*G. alpina*; dwarf; deep- to sky-blue green-spotted fls; free-flg; dislikes lime); *angustifolia* (*G. angustifolia*; narrow lvs & sky-blue fls; likes lime); *clusii* (*G. clusii*; closest to garden form, with large, often purplish-blue fls, few speckles; likes lime); *dinarica* (*G. dinarica*; broader lvs; unspotted fls; free-flg; likes lime); *kochiana* (*G. kochiana*; deep pure blue; hates lime).

G. farreri **2**: to 10×30cm (4×12in); prostrate stems; v narrow lvs; intense electric-blue fls to 6cm (2½in) long, throat shaded white & spotted greenish, late summer to autumn (colour may vary; best bought in fl). Tolerates lime. Var 'Hexa-Farreri' (hybrid with *G. hexaphylla*), light blue fls.

G. gracillipes **3** (often sold incorrectly as *G. purdomii*): to 15×40cm (6×16in); rosette of narrow lvs; semi-prostrate stems tipped by solitary bell-shaped purple-blue fls, mid–late summer. Hates lime. Var 'Alba' is white.

G. lagodechiana **4**: to 15–20×30cm (6–8×12in); similar to *G. septemfida* but fls solitary, rarely paired, summer.

G.×macaulayi: hybrid of *G. farreri* & *G. sino-ornata*; to 15×30–45cm (6×12–18in); deep blue trumpet-shaped fls to 6cm (2½in) long, early autumn. Hates lime. *G.* 'Kidbrooke Seedling' (vigorous), 'Kingfisher' **5** (large brilliant blue fls, mid–late autumn) & 'Macaulayi Wells' (pale blue).

G. pneumonanthe (marsh gentian): variable, to 15–40×30cm (6–16×12in); herbaceous; basal rosettes of lvs; leafy stems with terminal & axillary 4cm (1½in) bell-shaped blue, spotted fls, mid–late summer. For cool, moist soil.

G. saxosa **6**: semi-hardy; to 10×15cm (4×6in); tufts of glossy green spatula-shaped lvs; small cup-shaped white fls veined grey, late summer.

G. septemfida **7**: ultra-hardy; to 20–30×30cm (8–12×12in); dense tufts of mid green lvs forming dome; clustered bell-shaped deep blue or purplish fls, summer. Easy & free-flg.

G. sino-ornata **8**: to 15×30–40cm (6×12–16in); rosettes of lvs & prostrate leafy stems forming carpet; trumpet-shaped deep pure blue fls 5cm (2in) long, autumn. Easy & free-flg in lime-free acid soil; favourite autumn sp. Divide every 2–3yrs in spring. Vars: 'Alba' **9** (white); 'Angel's Wings' (bright blue, striped & feathered white); 'Brin's Form' (semi-climbing; profuse deep blue fls); 'Mary Lyle' (creamy-white); 'Praecox' (early).

G. veitchiorum: to 15×15cm (6×6in); basal rosettes of dark green blunt lvs & prostrate branching stems; funnel-shaped deep royal-blue fls to 5cm (2in) long, from late summer. For lime-free soil. Hybrids with *G. farreri*: 'Inverleith' (v large clear deep blue fls, early autumn); 'Midnight' (an 'Inverleith' seedling; deep royal-blue fls, autumn). Hybrids with *G. sino-ornata*: 'Bernardii' (vigorous; tubular deep blue fls, banded yellow outside, late summer); 'Stevanagensis' **10** (vigorous; trumpet-shaped 5cm [2in] fls, rich deep purple-blue, green-spotted throat, autumn).

G. verna angulosa **11** (a var of spring gentian): to 8×15cm (3×6in); tufts of glossy mid green lvs; intense azure-blue starry fls 2cm (¾in) across, late spring. For gritty, humus-rich moist soil; likes lime. Short-lived; propagate regularly by seed.

Storksbills and cranesbills

Choice, colourful relatives of the tough border geraniums (p286), all with 5-petalled saucer-shaped flowers & distinctive seed pods produced freely over attractive deeply cut leaves (semi-/evergreen). Useful on walls or for ground cover. **Cultivation**: For well-drained soil (preferably limy for *Erodium* spp) in sun. **Propagation**: Seed; division (spring); *Erodium* spp also by heel cuttings.

Storksbills (heron's-bills, *Erodium* spp): charming compact plants, often with rather woody rootstock; moderately hardy unless stated; lvs generally pinnately lobed or cut; fls

pink, white (often veined) or yellow, to 2–2.5cm (¾–1in) wide unless stated.

E. chamaedryoides (*E. reichardii*): moderately to v hardy; mat-forming, to 2.5–5×25cm (1–2×10in); crinkled, scalloped lvs to 10mm (⅜in) long; white 10mm (⅜in) fls veined pink, early–mid summer. Dainty. Propagate by root cuttings. Vars: 'Bishop's Form' (deep reddish-pink); 'Roseum' **1** (pink veined crimson).

E. chrysanthum: to 15–30×30–40cm (6–12×12–16in); dense tufts of ferny silver lvs; pale yellow fls all summer (best on female plants).

E. corsicum **2**: to 15×25cm (6×10in); tufts of downy grey lvs; pink fls veined red, all summer. Takes salt spray but protect from winter wet; for warm spot. Var 'Rubrum' is red.

E. guttatum: moderately to v hardy; to 15×25cm (6×10in); sub-shrubby; lobed 1cm (½in) lvs; white fls spotted purple, all summer. For scree.

E. macradenum **3**: to 20×30cm (8×12in); ferny mid green lvs*; lilac fls marked purple, early–mid summer. Var 'Roseum' is rose-pink.

Cranesbills (*Geranium* spp): easy, generally v hardy free-flg plants with deeply palmately lobed lvs & red, pink or white fls (to 2.5cm [1in] across unless noted) all summer.

G. argenteum: moderately hardy; to 12×30cm (5×12in); silvery silky-hairy lvs in tufts; pink fls, veined darker. For scree.

G. cinereum: to 10–15×25cm (4–6×10in); cushion of grey-green lvs; profuse deep pink fls, dark centre & stripes, late spring to autumn. Vars & hybrids: 'Appleblossom' (pale pink); 'Ballerina' **4** (lilac-pink, dark centre, red veins); 'Laurence Flatman' (large pink fls, heavily marked crimson); *subcaulescens* (see *G. subcaulescens*).

G. dalmaticum **5**: to 15×60cm (6×24in); cushion-forming; glossy lvs, red & orange in autumn; light pink fls, early–mid summer. Var 'Album' is white tinged pink.

G. farreri: slow-growing, to 15×30cm (6×12in), forming dense mat; grey-green lvs to 2.5cm (1in) across; lilac-rose fls, black anthers, late spring to early summer. Needs v good drainage. Var 'Album' is white.

G. pylzowianum **6**: to 10×25cm (4×10in) or wider; spreads by rhizomes; feathery lvs; clear pink fls, early summer. Pretty.

G. renardii **7**: clump-forming, to 20×30cm (8×12in); soft grey-green lvs; palest lavender fls, veined violet, late spring to mid summer. Best in poorish soil.

G. sanguineum (bloody cranesbill): ultra-hardy; sp vigorous, to 25×45cm (10×18in); magenta fls to 4cm (1½in) across all summer. Too large for most rock gardens; dwarf vars: 'Album' (white); 'Lancastriense' (to 5×15cm [2×6in]; dark green lvs; salmon-pink fls veined crimson; easy & popular).

G. subcaulescens **8** (correctly, *G. cinereum subcaulescens*): to 10–15×30cm (4–6×12in); rounded grey-green lvs; magenta fls, black centre. Vars: 'Giuseppii' (strong crimson-purple); 'Splendens' (salmon-pink).

Ramondas and their relatives

Evergreen, rosette-forming plants with thick, rather succulent hairy leaves and sprays of pretty lilac or blue flowers on erect stems in spring. From mountains of S Europe; extremely useful alpines for shady sites. **Cultivation**: Very hardy. For cool, peaty soil in shade. Dislike water settling on rosettes; best in vertical crevice in shady wall or rock garden (north-facing in N Hemisphere) kept fairly dry in winter; or for alpine house. Protect from slugs. **Propagation**: Leaf cuttings (early–mid summer); seed, sown autumn.

Haberleas (*Haberlea* spp): rosettes of dark green toothed lvs to 8cm (3in) long; tubular, lobed fls, rather frilled, to 2.5cm (1in) across, late spring to early summer.

H. ferdinandi-coburgii **9** (may be form of *H. rhodopensis*): to 10–15×15–25cm (4–6×6–9in); pale lilac fls, white throat spotted gold.

H. rhodopensis: to 8×15–25cm (3×6–9in); silky-hairy lvs; smaller lavender fls, sparsely spotted. Var 'Virginalis' is white, yellow-green throat.

Jankaea (*Jankaea* [*Ramonda*] *heldreichii* **10**): to 8×12cm (3×5in); softly hairy silver-grey lvs to 3cm (1¼in) long, reddish-brown beneath; bell-shaped blue fls, early spring. Rare & difficult; hates winter wet; best in alpine house.

Ramondas (*Ramonda* spp): to 10×25cm (4×10in); rosettes of toothed, roughly hairy lvs; plentiful lavender-blue flattish fls to 2.5–4cm (1–1½in) wide, conspicuous stamens.

R. myconi **11** (*R. pyrenaica*): deep green crinkled lvs to 6cm (2½in) long; fls with golden stamens. Vars 'Alba' (white); 'Rosea' (deep rose-pink).

R. nathaliae: neat habit; mid green glossy lvs to 5cm (2in) long, fringed with hairs; fls with golden stamens.

R. serbica: glossy, lobed lvs; cup-shaped lilac-blue fls, purple stamens.

St John's worts

Hypericum spp & vars. Prostrate or tufted plants with profuse golden-yellow flowers centred by prominent stamens. Easy on rock walls, sunny banks. Deciduous & summer-flowering unless stated. **Cultivation**: Moderately hardy; for well-drained soil in sunny sites. **Propagation**: Softwood cuttings.

H. coris **1**: to 15×30cm (6×12in); evergreen; narrow grey-green heather-like lvs in whorls; fls to 1–2cm (½–¾in) across on sparse wiry stems. Likes lime.

H. empetrifolium 'Prostratum'; dense prostrate shrublet, to 8×30cm (3×12in); evergreen heather-like lvs; fls to 2cm (¾in) across.

H. olympicum **2** (often sold as *H. polyphyllum*): to 15–20×30cm (6–8×12in); erect & bushy; grey-green oval lvs; fls to 5cm (2in) across. Easy & popular. Var 'Citrinum' is pale yellow.

H. repens (correctly, *H. linarioides*): to 15×30cm (6×12in); narrow lvs; fls sometimes red-veined, to 2.5cm (1in) across, early.

H. reptans: to 8×30–45cm (3×12–18in); mat-forming; pale green rounded lvs, red-brown in autumn; solitary fls to 3cm (1½in) wide from scarlet buds.

H. rhodopeum **3** (correctly, *H. cerastoides*): to 15×45cm (6×18in); mat-forming; hairy, evergreen oval lvs; fls to 4cm (1½in) across, late spring to early summer.

Sisyrinchiums

Sisyrinchium spp. Tufted iris-like plants with narrow grassy leaves & star-shaped satiny flowers. For crevices, between paving. May self-seed. **Cultivation**: Moderately hardy unless stated. For moist but well-drained soil in sun. **Propagation**: Division; seed. For *S. striatum*, see p356.

S. angustifolium **4** (blue-eyed grass): ultra-hardy; to 25×20cm (10×8in); transient violet fls to 1cm (½in) across, yellow eye, all summer.

S. bermudiana: to 30×15–25cm (12×6–10in); fls similar to above, late spring to early summer.

S. brachypus **5**: to 15×15cm (6×6in); yellow fls to 2cm (¾in) across, summer & autumn.

S. californicum (golden-eyed grass): to 15–

30×15cm (6–12×6in); yellow fls to 2.5cm (1in) across, late spring to mid summer.

S. douglasii (grass-widow): v hardy; to 25×15cm (10×6in); herbaceous; bell-shaped nodding fls to 2.5cm (1in) long, purple veined darker, spring.

S. macounii: to 15×15cm (6×6in); cupped purple fls, spring & summer. Var 'Album' **6** is white.

Thymes and their relatives

Mat-forming or sub-shrubby plants (deciduous unless stated) with square stems & profuse hooded flowers clustered in whorls along erect spikes. Showy; many useful for ground cover. **Cultivation**: Unless stated, for any well-drained soil in full sun. **Propagation**: Division; woody-stemmed spp by semi-ripe cuttings.

Bugles (bugleweeds, *Ajuga* spp): ultra-hardy; for ground cover in moist soil & partial shade unless stated. Fls mainly blue, early summer. Easy but some invasive; good under trees or shrubs.

A. genevensis: to 15–30×15cm (6–12×6in); toothed lvs to 11cm (4½in) long; blue (rarely pink or white) fls in spikes to 5cm (2in) tall. Prefers sun & good drainage. Var 'Brockbankii' is deep blue.

A. pyramidalis **7**: to 25×15cm (10×6in); toothed lvs to 10cm (4in) long; heads to 10–15cm (4–6in) tall of blue fls, purple bracts, spring.

A. reptans (carpet or common bugle): mat-forming, stoloniferous & invasive, to 10–30×30–45cm (4–12×12–18in); oblong lvs to 4cm (1½in) long; blue fls. Many fine-lvd vars (best in some sun), eg: 'Atropurpurea' **8** ('Purpurea'; purple lvs); 'Burgundy Glow' **9** (purple, bronze & cream lvs); 'Multicolor' **10** ('Rainbow'; bronze, pink &

yellow lvs); 'Variegata' (grey-green & cream lvs).

Corsican mint (menthella, *Mentha requienii*): moderately hardy carpeter, to 2.5×30cm (1×12in); round lvs* to 1cm (⅜in) long, peppermint-scented; tiny pale purple stemless fls, early–mid summer. For cool, moist soil.

Origanums (*Origanum* spp; sometimes listed as *Amaracus* spp): moderately hardy mat-forming or sub-shrubby Mediterranean perennials, aromatic & related to marjoram. Resent winter wet.

O. amanum **11**: slowly mat-forming, to 5–10×15cm (2–4×6in); light green lvs; rose-pink fls to 4cm (1½in) long, mid summer into autumn.

O. (A.) dictamnus **12** (Cretan dittany): to 30×30cm (1×1ft); twiggy; grey-green woolly rounded lvs to 2.5cm (1in) across; pink fls in purple-bracted hop-like heads to 5cm (2in) long, mid summer.

O. laevigatum: to 25×60cm (10×24in), forming twiggy mat; lvs dark green; pink fls, red-purple bracts, late summer.

Self-heals (*Prunella* spp): v hardy spreading plants for ground cover in moist soil in sun or partial shade; fl all summer. Self-seed.
P. grandiflora **1**: to 15×45cm (6×18in); oval lvs; violet-purple fls in 5–8cm (2–3in) spikes.
P.×webbiana: hybrids of complex parentage; to 25–30×40cm (10–12×16in); rosy-purple fls in compact spikes. Vars: 'Alba' (white); 'Loveliness' (pale violet); 'Loveliness Pink' **2** (clear pink); 'Rosea' (rose-pink).

Skullcaps (*Scutellaria* spp): neat rhizomatous v hardy plants with toothed lvs to 2.5cm (1in) long & erect tubular fls; summer. Tolerate semi-shade.
S. alpina: to 15–25×45cm (6–10×18in); mat-forming; purple fls to 2.5cm (1in) long, often marked yellow. Var 'Alba' is white.
S. indica japonica **3**: to 15×30cm (6×12in); lax & tufted; grey-green lvs; purple-blue fls in racemes to 10cm (4in) tall.

Germanders (*Teucrium* spp): v hardy evergreen sub-shrubs; more or less silver-grey lvs, attractive with blue or pink fls. Tolerate poor soil.
T. aroanium: to 10×30cm (4×12in); much-branched & procumbent; oval lvs; profuse grey-blue fls in crowded racemes, mid summer.
T. chamaedrys **4** (wall germander): to 20×45cm (8×18in); deep green oval lvs, grey beneath; pink 2cm (¾in) fls spotted red & white, in spikes, mid–late summer. Can be sheared.
T. pyrenaicum: to 8×40cm (3×16in); trailing, forming woody mats; rounded lvs; mauve & cream fls in heads to 2.5cm (1in) across, early summer.
T. rosmarinifolium (*T. creticum*): to 8×30cm (3×12in); narrow lvs; rosy-purple fls in groups to 5cm (2in) across, woolly calyx, all summer.

Thymes (*Thymus* spp): easy aromatic evergreen plants, v hardy unless stated, with lvs to 5–10mm (¼–½in) long & profuse fls, early summer (attract bees). Good in paving. Shear bushy spp after flg.
T. cilicicus: moderately hardy; to 10–15×25cm (4–6×10in); narrow hairy lvs*; profuse pink fls in clusters to 1cm (½in) across.
T.×citriodorus (lemon-scented thyme): hybrid of *T. pulegioides* & *T. vulgaris*; to 25–30×30–40cm (10–12×12–16in); neat & bushy; oval lvs* to 1cm (½in) long; pale lilac fls. Variegated vars best known: 'Aureus' **5** (gold & green lvs); 'Silver Queen' **6** (silver & green lvs).
T. doerfleri (*T. hirsutus doerfleri*; possibly a form of *T. praecox*): mat-forming, to 8×45cm (3×18in); grey-green woolly lvs; lilac-pink fls in clusters to 10mm (⅜in) wide. Var 'Bressingham Seedling' **7** is clear pink.
T. 'Doone Valley' **8**: hybrid of uncertain parentage; to 12×30cm (5×12in); mat-forming; green & gold variegated lvs*; lavender fls.
T. herba-barona (caraway thyme): to 12×40cm (5×16in); mat-forming; dark green lvs*; lilac fls in clusters to 8cm (3in) tall.
T. nitidus (Sicily thyme; correctly, *T. richardii nitidus*; often confused with *T. carnosus*): to 20×30cm (8×12in); grey-green lvs*, hairy beneath; whitish/pink fls in 4cm (1½in) clusters.
T. serpyllum (*T. drucei*, wild thyme of Europe): ultra-hardy; mat-forming, to 8×60cm (3×24in); grey-green lvs; red, pink or white fls in heads to 1cm (½in) across, forming sheets of colour all summer. Vars: 'Albus' (white; pale lvs); 'Annie Hall' (shell-pink; pale lvs); 'Coccineus' **9** (crimson; dark green lvs); *lanuginosus* (usually lilac; v hairy lvs); 'Pink Chintz' (large rose fls); 'Snowdrift' (white; dark green lvs).
T. vulgaris (garden thyme): to 20×30cm (8×12in); bushy; mauve fls. Vars 'Aureus' & 'Gold Edge' have gold & green lvs.

Prickly heaths and thrifts

Evergreens with tufted, grass-like lvs forming dense cushions. Long-flowering if dead-headed.
Cultivation: For very well-drained soil in full sun. **Propagation**: See below.

Prickly heaths (prickly thrifts, *Acantholimon* spp): moderately hardy; slow-growing, to 15×30cm (6×12in); rigid, spiky lvs; fls 1cm (½in) across in loose erect racemes, all summer. Large genus, some not easy; dislike root disturbance. Propagate by layering.
A. glumaceum: lvs to 6cm (2½in) long; mauve fls.
A. venustum **10** (*A. olivieri*): lvs silver-grey, to 2cm (¾in) long; rose fls. Resents winter wet; best on dry wall or under glass.

Thrifts (*Armeria* spp): easy ultra-hardy plants with long-lasting pink fls in globular heads over

grassy mats, late spring into summer. Good near sea. Propagate by division.
A. caespitosa (correctly, *A. juniperifolia*): to 5–8×15–25cm (2–3×6–10in); sharp-tipped lvs to 2cm (¾in) long; infls to 2cm (¾in) across. 'Bevan's Variety' **11** has deeper pink fls.
A. maritima (common thrift, sea pink): to 15–30×30cm (6–12×12in); lvs to 10cm (4in) long; infls to 2.5cm (1in) across. Vars: 'Alba' (pure white); 'Dusseldorf Pride' (near red); 'Vindictive' **12** (to 10cm [4in]; deep rose-pink).

Rock phlox

Phlox spp. Prostrate or hummock-forming N American plants with woody stems & dense mats of narrow glossy leaves (usually evergreen), covered wth 5-petalled flowers 10–25mm (⅜–1in) across in late spring & early summer. Ideal for carpeting & dry walls. **Cultivation**: Unless stated, very to ultra-hardy. Most spp thrive in any well-drained soil in full sun; some need moist but well-drained peaty or leafy soil and some shade. **Propagation**: Semi-ripe heel cuttings; soft tip cuttings. For *P. divaricata*, see p314.

P. adsurgens **1**: moderately hardy; to 20×30cm (8×12in); tufts of shiny lvs; dense heads of usually salmon-pink fls, late. For cool shade. Var 'Waggon Wheel' has larger fls with petal segments deeply cut like spokes.

P. bifida (sand phlox): to 20×25cm (8×10in); mounding; fls lilac or lavender, petals deeply notched, early.

P. 'Chattahoochee': to 25×35cm (10×14in); heads of large violet fls, purple eye; for cool semi-shade.

P. douglasii **2**: to 10×15–45cm (4×6–18in); tufted hummocks of mid green lvs; profuse white to lavender, pink or red small fls. Vars: 'Boothman's Variety' (spreading; mauve, purple eye); 'Crackerjack' (v compact; crimson-red); 'Eva' (pink, crimson eye); 'Lilac Queen' (vigorous; pale lilac); 'May Snow' ('Snow Queen'; white); 'Red Admiral' (compact; crimson); 'Rosea' (silvery-pink); 'Rose cushion' (v compact; rose-pink).

P.×procumbens **3** (often sold incorrectly as *P. amoena*): hybrid of *P. stolonifera* & *P.*

subulata; to 25×30cm (10×12in); heads of bright purple to deep pink fls. Vars: 'Rosea' (often sold simply as *P. amoena*; lilac-pink); 'Variegata' (lvs variegated silver).

P. stolonifera (*P. reptans*, creeping phlox): to 15–20×30cm (6–8×12in); self-rooting lax stems; loose clusters of large violet to purple fls early. For cool shade. Vars: 'Ariane' (white, yellow eye); 'Blue Ridge' (clear blue); 'Pink Ridge'. Var 'Millstream' is hybrid with *P. amoena*; large pink fls, white eye & central red star.

P. subulata (*P. setacea*, moss phlox, moss pink): vigorous, to 10–15×45cm (4–6×18in); mats of mid green lvs; profuse white to red or purple fls. Vars: 'Alexander's Surprise' (salmon-pink); 'Amazing Grace' (white, red eye); 'Benita' (lavender-blue); 'Betty' (salmon-pink); 'Blue Hills'; 'Brilliant' (deep rose); 'Emerald Cushion Blue' (bright green lvs; clear blue fls); 'G. F. Wilson' (mauve-blue); 'Red Wing' (carmine, dark eye); 'Scarlet Flame'; 'Sky Blue'; 'Temiscaming' **4** (magenta-red); 'White Delight'.

Lewisias

Lewisia spp. N American alpines with starchy tuberous roots & basal rosettes of narrow to spatula-shaped fleshy leaves (evergreen unless stated). Profuse showy flowers – white to rose, red & orange, generally 4–5cm (1½–2in) wide – singly or in panicles on stems above foliage, generally spring to early summer. **Cultivation**: Very hardy, but crown may rot if wet in winter; best grown in rock crevice or on sloping scree with chippings around neck. Need very well-drained but rich soil, preferably lime-free with ample organic matter & grit; like moisture when flowering, then dry conditions. Evergreens like some shade, herbaceous spp full sun. **Propagation**: Seed (stratify; hybridize freely, so may not breed true); offsets, cuttings in spring.

L. brachycalyx: to 5–8×15–25cm (2–3×6–10in); herbaceous; satiny white fls often tinged pink.

L. columbiana: to 15–30×15–25cm (6–12×6–10in); panicles of small pink or white fls with red veins. Var 'Rosea' (may be hybrid) is purple-red.

L. cotyledon: to 25×15–25cm (10×6–10in); dense mat of lvs; panicles of white to pink fls tinged/striped red. Vars: *heckneri* **5** (*L. heckneri*; lvs toothed; fls pink to deep rose, striped darker); *howellii* (*L. howellii*; to 15cm [6in]; lvs crinkled; fls rose-pink striped carmine).

L. nevadensis (*L. pygmaea nevadensis*): to 8×8cm (3×3in); herbaceous; small, almost stemless white fls, late.

L. pygmaea: ultra-hardy; to 8×8cm (3×3in); herbaceous; small white or pink fls, late.

L. rediviva (bitter root): to 8×15cm (3×6in); herbaceous; beautiful, with satiny white or rose-pink many-petalled large fls.

L. tweedyi **6**: to 15×25cm (6×10in); lvs more erect than other spp; beautiful, with large v pale pink to creamy-apricot or salmon-rose fls. Var 'Rosea' is rose-pink.

L. hybrids & seed strains (most derived partly from *L. cotyledon*; colours often include rich yellows & oranges): 'Ashmore Hybrids' (pink to red & copper); 'Ashmore Chastity' (white); 'Birch Hybrids' (pink to crimson); 'George Henley' (brick-red); 'Phyllellia' (dwarf; white to deep rose); 'Rose Splendour' **7** (rose-pink); 'Sunset Strain' (pink, apricot, orange, deep red, etc); 'Trevosia' **8** (long sprays of salmon-red fls).

Primulas

Primula spp; often called primroses. Very large genus of beautiful small rosette/clump-forming plants with 5-petalled flowers, generally singly or in umbels, mainly spring & early summer. Leaves &/or stems of many spp farinose (coated with powdery farina). Mainly for cool, moist, shady parts of rock gardens, woodland, etc (best grouped). Spread 15–25cm (6–10in) unless stated. **Cultivation**: Varied (see below), but generally need constant moisture & some shade; difficult in hot, dry conditions. Unless stated, very hardy, but roots may be damaged by soil heaving. **Propagation**: Seed; short cuttings of side-shoots in early summer; clump-forming types by division after flowering. **Classification**: By botanical characteristics into some 30 sections; also more generally by geographical origin. For taller spp, some suitable for larger rock gardens, etc, see p318.

Auricula section: lvs fleshy, often farinose. European; for rich, moist but v well-drained soil in full but not scorching sun.

P. allionii: to 5cm (2in); sticky 4.5cm (1¾in) lvs; umbels of up to 7 purple, rose-red to white 2.5cm (1in) fls, early spring. Likes lime; dislikes winter wet.

*P. auricula** (auricula, dusty miller): ultra-hardy; to 15cm (6in); pale to grey-green lvs, often farinose; 2cm (¾in) bright yellow fls in large umbels, all spring; often grown under glass for show. Vars: 'Blairside Yellow'* **1** (rich yellow; may be hybrid); 'Blue Fire'* (blue); 'Gold of Ophir'* (yellow); 'Old Yellow Dusty Miller'* (farinose lvs; yellow fls); 'Red Dusty Miller'* (farinose lvs; red fls); 'Willowbrook'* (yellow).

P.×bileckii **2** (correctly, *P.×steinii*): hybrid of *P. minima* & *P. rubra*; to 5cm (2in); tuft of dark green 2.5cm (1in) toothed lvs; umbels of 2–5 deep rose-pink 2.5cm (1in) fls, white eye, late spring.

*P. marginata**: to 10cm (4in); woody base; silver-edged, toothed farinose lvs to 10cm (4in) long; umbels of up to 20 pale lavender to purple & violet fls 2–2.5cm (¾–1in) across, spring. Vars: 'Hycinthia' (deep mauve-blue); 'Linda Pope' **3** (large lavender-blue fls); 'Prichard's Variety' (soft purple); 'Shipton' (pale plue). Best in rock crevice or wall; like lime.

P. minima: to 5cm (2in); rosettes of 2.5cm (1in) glossy toothed lvs; 2.5cm (1in) rose-pink fls, petals deeply notched, 1 or 2 to a stem, spring. Best in crevice or trough.

P.×pubescens vars: series of natural & garden hybrids of *P. auricula*, *P. latifolia* (*P. viscosa*) & *P. rubra*; generally to 10–15cm (4–6in); lvs often farinose; fls in large umbels, spring. Vars: 'Alba' (pure white); 'Argus' (purple, white eye); 'Carmen' (carmine); 'Christine' (rose-pink); 'Faldonside' **4** (bright crimson); 'Marlene' (violet-purple); 'Mrs J. H. Wilson' **5** (violet, white eye); 'Rufus' (to 20cm [8in]; brick-red).

P. rubra (*P. hirsuta*): to 5–10cm (2–4in); rosettes of hairy, sticky lvs to 10cm (4in) long; profuse large umbels of pink to lilac & red 2–2.5cm (¾–1in) fls. 'Boothman's Variety' ('Stuart Boothman') is rich crimson-pink. Good in crevice or trough.

P. spectabilis **6**: to 12cm (5in); rosettes of leathery lvs to 10cm (4in) long; small umbels of flattish rose-pink to -red to 2.5cm (1in) fls, white eye, late spring. For cool, moist, shaded crevice.

Cortusoid section: lvs generally lobed, crinkly & hairy; fls in prominent umbels. Asiatic; for light, humus-rich, moist but well-drained soil in light shade.

P. cortusoides: ultra-hardy; to 20cm (8in); attractive lvs to 8cm (3in) long; large umbels of pink to crimson-purple fls, late spring.

P. polyneura (*P. lichiangensis*, *P. veitchii*): to 15–30cm (6–12in); lvs often silvery beneath; 2.5cm (1in) fls, pale rose to reddish-purple, late spring/early summer, 1–3 umbels per stem.

P. sieboldii: to 15–25cm (6–10in); prominently lobed & toothed lvs; loose umbels of 6–10 white to red or purple 2.5–4cm (1–1½in) fls, white eye, late spring. Vars: 'Geisha Girl' (deep pink); 'Mikado' **7** (rosy-magenta); 'Snowflakes' (white). Good in woodland or boggy soil.

Farinose section: lvs often (not always) farinose. Asiatic & European; generally for cool, moist soil in sun or light shade.

P. clarkei: to 5cm (2in); tufts of small pale green lvs; rose-pink 2cm (¾in) fls, solitary or in small umbels, spring. Divide regularly.

P. farinosa (bird's-eye primrose): to 10–15cm (4–6in); farinose silvery lvs; large umbels of 1cm (⅜in) pink, rosy-lilac or purple fls, yellow eye, early spring. Not long-lived. *P. laurentiana* & *P. intercedens* are v similar N American spp; *P. mistassinica* is also similar but dwarfer.

P. frondosa **8**: similar to *A. farinosa* but sturdier, to 20cm (8in); rosettes of farinose lvs, silvery beneath; umbels of 10–30 rose-lilac or reddish-purple 1cm (½in) fls, yellow eye, spring. Easy. *P. specuicola* of N America is similar; fls violet.

P. rosea: to 30cm (1ft); v showy; lvs not farinose; profuse umbels of 4–12 intense rose-pink 2cm (¾in) fls, yellow eye, early spring (starting before lvs), on gradually lengthening stems. Vars: 'Delight' **9** ('Visser de Geer'; deep carmine-pink large fls); 'Grandiflora' (v large deep pink fls). Easy in v moist, even boggy soil.

P. warshenewskiana: to 8cm (3in); mat of finely toothed lvs; umbels of bright rose-pink 2cm (¾in) fls, yellow eye, spring; spreads by stolons.

P. yargongensis* (*P. wardii*): to 20–30cm (8–12in); rosettes of fresh green lvs; umbels of 3–8 pink, mauve or purple fls, white eye, late spring. **Nivalis section**: lvs leathery, strap-shaped; fls generally fragrant, often on tallish stems. Asiatic; for v well-drained moist soil in cool semi-shade; difficult in dry climates.

P. chionantha* **1**: to 30cm (1ft) or more; lvs farinose at first, to 25cm (10in) long; 1–4 umbels per stem of 2.5cm (1in) white fls, yellow eye, spring. Easiest of section.

P. macrophylla: to 20–25cm (8–10in); narrow lvs, farinose beneath; large umbels of 2.5cm (1in) lilac to violet fls, maroon eye, spring.

P. sinoplantaginea* : to 20cm (8in) or more; lvs v narrow; umbels of 5–12 purple 2cm (¾in) fls, grey eye, early summer. *P. sinopurpurea** is similar but lvs wider & fls to 3cm (1¼in) across.

Petiolaris section: lvs in dense rosettes (some spp evergreen, others dormant winter buds); infls on short stems, early. Asiatic; for v humus-rich well-drained soil in cool humid shade; v hardy but need protection from winter wet; difficult in dry climates.

P. aureata: to 8cm (3in); evergreen; lvs farinose in winter, not in summer; umbel of several large creamy-yellow fls, centre flushed orange, spring.

P. edgeworthii (*P. winteri*): to 8–10cm (3–4in); fat winter bud; early lvs farinose, becoming green; clusters of soft bluish-mauve 2cm (¾in) fls, white/yellow eye, from mid winter.

P. gracilipes **2**: to 8cm (3in); tight winter bud; serrated non-farinose lvs in tight rosettes; profuse solitary lavender-pink fls, white eye, early spring. Among easiest of section.

P. whitei **3** (*P. bhutanica*): to 10cm (4in); v large winter bud; lvs toothed, farinose at first; profuse umbels of pale or deep blue 2.5cm (1in) fls, white eye, spring.

Soldanelloid section: lvs soft-hairy but not farinose; generally pendent bell-shaped fls, often fragrant. Asiatic; often rather difficult, for peaty, gritty, moist soil in cool semi-shade or under glass.

P. nutans* **4**: to 30cm (1ft); rosettes of rather erect grey-green hairy, velvety lvs to 20cm (8in) long; spikes of nodding lavender to violet bell fls to 2.5cm (1in) wide, early summer; easiest of secton, but sometimes short-lived.

P. reidii* : to 10cm (4in); sparse rosettes of pale green softly furry lvs; umbels of 3–10 semi-pendent ivory-white bell fls 2cm (¾in) wide, late spring. Var *williamsii** **5** is more robust, with larger soft blue to white fls.

Vernalis section: the common English primrose & its relatives; fls generally solitary though profuse. European; vigorous in cool humus-rich soil in light shade; divide regularly. For polyanthus (*P. vulgaris* hybrids, sometimes listed as *P.×polyantha*), see p318.

P. juliae: to 5–8×30cm (2–3×12in); mats of creeping stems & dark green rounded toothed lvs to 10cm (4in) long; bright purple 2cm (¾in) fls, yellow eye, spring.

P.×juliae (correctly, *P.×pruhoniciana*): hybrids of *P. juliae* & other Vernalis spp; generally to 8–15cm (3–6in); mid green crinkled lvs; solitary fls, late winter to spring. Numerous vars, including: 'Ariel' (fls blood-red flecked white, green ruff); 'Blue Riband' (blue); 'Garryarde Guinevere' **6** (sometimes listed as *P.×garryarde* 'Guinevere'; lvs bronze; fls soft pink); 'Kinlough Beauty' (salmon-pink striped cream); 'Victory' (purple); 'Wanda' (wine-purple).

P. veris* (*P. officinalis*, cowslip): to 15–25×15cm (6–10×6in); lvs irregularly toothed, to 20cm (8in) long, hairy beneath; umbels (often one-sided) of nodding bright yellow bell fls 1.5cm (½in) across, orange eye, late spring. Good in wild garden, grass, etc. *P. elatior* (oxlip) is similar, but fls larger (to 2.5cm [1in] wide), paler yellow & not fragrant.

P. vulgaris (*P. acaulis*, English primrose): to 15cm (6in); rosettes of bright green wrinkled lvs to 25cm (10in) long; profuse solitary pale yellow fls, darker centre, 2.5cm (1in) across, early spring. Vars: 'Alba Plena' (double, white); *heterochroma* (lvs silvery beneath; fls white, yellow or purple); *sibthorpii* (*P. altaica*; pink or red). See also p318.

Other sections

P. amoena **7** (Bullate section; sometimes confused with *P. vulgaris sibthorpii*) to 20×10cm (8×4in); small crinkled lvs; umbels of 6–10 pink, lavender or violet (sometimes yellow or white) 2.5cm (1in) fls, yellow eye, spring. European; for humus-rich soil in half-shade.

P. capitata* (Capitate section): to 15–30×8cm (6–12×3in); compact rosettes of crinkled, usually farinose toothed lvs; usually flattened globular heads of small tubular to open purplish-blue fls, mid summer to early autumn. Var *mooreana* has lvs white beneath & richly coloured fls. Asiatic; quite easy in light, well-drained humus-rich soil in cool light shade.

P. forrestii* **8** (Bullate section): to 20cm (8in); woody rhizomes; leathery, crinkled dark green 20cm (8in) lvs, farinose beneath; umbels of 10–25 orange-eyed golden-yellow 2cm (¾in) fls, late spring. Asiatic, but likes well-drained dryish position in rock crevice; likes limes.

P. vialii **9** (*P. littoniana*; Muscarioid section): moderately hardy; to 30–50cm (12–20in); tufted; pale green lvs to 20cm (8in) long, slightly farinose; 8–12cm (3–5in) dense spikes (like miniature red-hot poker [*Kniphofia* spp]) of lavender-blue fls, crimson in bud, early summer. Asiatic; for light, rich soil in cool light shade.

Other members of the primose family

Vary from primula-like plants for woodland conditions to tiny hummock-forming high alpines v difficult except in alpine house. **Cultivation**: Generally v hardy. *Androsace, Dionysia* & *Douglasia* spp: well-drained gritty but humus-rich soil in sun. *Cortusa, Dodecatheon* & *Soldanella* spp: rich, moist soil in cool open or semi-shade (very well-drained & gritty for *Soldanella* spp). **Propagation**: Seed; division.

Rock jasmines (*Androsace* spp): beautiful dwarf cushion/mat-forming alpines (former type hate winter wet, v difficult in open); small primrose-like fls, solitary or in small umbels.

A. carnea **1**: to 8×20cm (3×8in); variable; tufts of narrow dark green 2cm (¾in) lvs (wider in var *laggeri*); infls of 5mm (¼in) pale pink or white fls, yellow eye, early summer.

A. chamaejasme: to 2.5–5×15cm (1–2×6in); mat-forming; rosettes of 1cm (½in) softly hairy grey-green pointed lvs; small infls of white 5mm (¼in) fls, turning pink, yellow eye, early summer.

A. imbricata **2** (*A. argentea*; correctly *A. vandellii*): to 2.5×10cm (1×4in); densely tufted cushion of v small felted lvs in rosettes; solitary, almost stemless tiny white fls, late spring. Hates lime; protect from winter wet.

A. lanuginosa **3**: trailing, to 8×30–45cm (3×12–18in); mat of silvery-green 2cm (¾in) lvs with silky hairs; infls of rose- to lavender-pink 10mm (¾in) fls, darker eye, summer to autumn. Var *leichtlinii* is white, pink eye.

A. primuloides **4** (*A. sarmentosa primuloides*; incorrectly, *A. sarmentosa*): ultra-hardy; spreading by stolons, to 10×60cm (4×24in); dense mat of lvs to 5cm (2in) long in rosettes, silvery hairs; infls of pink fls to 1cm (½in) across, spring. Easy, but dislikes winter wet. Var 'Chumbyi' (*A. chumbyi, A. sarmentosa chumbyi*) is more compact & silky. *A. sarmentosa* (*A. sarmentosa yunnanensis*) is similar but lvs hairy only when young & fls smaller, rose-red.

A. sempervivoides: to 5×30cm (2×12in); mat-forming by stolons; 5cm (1in) rosettes of small fleshy bright green lvs; small umbels of 5mm (¼in) pink fls, late spring or early summer.

A. villosa*: to 5–8×25cm (2–3×10in); mat-forming; compact rosettes of v small silvery-green woolly lvs; profuse small umbels of white or pink 10mm (⅜in) fls, yellowish eye, late spring or early summer. Vars: *arachnoidea* (compact; silvery; fls white, pink eye); *jaquemontii* (*A. jaquemontii*; compact; reddish hairs; fls rose-pink).

Cortusa (*Cortusa matthioli* **5**): rather primula-like; to 15–25×30cm (6–10×12in); crinkly, softly hairy rounded & lobed lvs in tufts; one-sided umbels of nodding purplish-pink bell fls, late spring (white in var 'Alba').

Dionysia (*Dionysia aretioides* **6**): to 2.5×10cm (1×4in); cushion of tiny softly hairy primrose-like lvs in rosettes; almost stemless primrose-like golden-yellow fls to 10mm (⅜in) across, spring.

Best under glass to avoid winter wet; likes lime.

Shooting-stars (*Dodecatheon* spp): rather primula-like N American plants, but nodding fls (2–2.5cm [¾–1in] long, in umbels) have cyclamen-like back-swept petals; sizes v variable; lvs narrow to spatula-shaped, smooth, often fleshy, in rosettes; fls have dark eye & ring of yellow.

D. alpinum: to 10–30×15cm (4–12×6in); lvs to 8cm (3in) long; fls lavender to magenta, early summer.

D. dentatum: to 15–40×15cm (6–16×6in); lvs to 10cm (4in) long; fls white, spring/early summer.

D. jeffreyi **7** (Sierra shooting-star): to 15–60×30cm (6–24×12in); lvs to 30cm (1ft) long; fls red-purple, late spring.

D. meadia (common shooting-star of eastern N America): Ultra-hardy; to 20–45×30cm (8–18×12in); lvs to 20cm (8in) long; fls pink, lilac or white, late spring.

D. pulchellum **8** (sometimes sold incorrectly as *D. integrifolium* or *D. pauciflorum*): to 10–45×20cm (4–18×8in); lvs 5–30cm (2–12in) long; fls lavender to magenta, late spring to summer.

Douglasias (*Douglasia* spp, sometimes listed as *Androsace, Gregoria,* etc, spp): similar to androsaces but fls have longer neck.

D. (G.) laevigata **9**: to 5–8×30cm (2–3×12in); tufted & creeping; narrowish smooth lvs to 15mm (⅝in) long; small clusters of 10mm (⅜in) rose-pink fls, late spring.

D. (A., G.) vitaliana*: to 5×30cm (2×12in); mat-forming; rosettes of narrow grey-green lvs to 10mm (⅜in) long; small stemless yellow fls, late spring or early summer. Var 'Praetutiana' is silvery & free-flg.

Soldanellas (snowbells, *Soldanella* spp): neat plants with rounded leathery basal lvs & fringed, bell-shaped, nodding fls 1–2cm (½–¾in) long, singly or in small umbels, early spring. Protect from slugs & winter wet.

S. alpina: to 8–15×20cm (3–6×8in); lvs to 4cm (1½in) across; fls lavender-purple.

S. minima: to 8×15cm (3×6in); lvs 10mm (⅜in) across; fls lilac marked violet inside.

S. montana **10**: to 15–20×30cm (6–8×12in); lvs to 6cm (2½in) across; fls bluish-lilac. *S. villosa* (*S. montana villosa*) is similar, but stems hairy.

S. pindicola: to 10×20cm (4×8in); lvs to 4cm (1½in) across; fls pinkish-lilac.

S. pusilla **11**: to 10×15cm (4×6in); lvs to 1cm (½in) across; fls pale violet.

The buttercup family

Varied dwarf perennials ranging from alpine buttercups to showy columbines & pulsatillas. **Cultivation**: Unless stated, very hardy & for any well-drained soil with peat or leaf mould in sun or part-shade. **Propagation**: Seed (sow fresh); clump-forming spp by division. For dwarf true anemones (tuberous), see p422, for other relatives, some suitable for larger rock gardens, see pp326–332.

Columbines (*Aquilegia* spp): similar except for size to border spp (p330), with lfts like maidenhair fern & spurred fls late spring or early summer; generally tufted; stems often hairy. Not long-lived but self-seed.

A. alpina: ultra-hardy; to 30×30cm (1×1ft); grey-green lvs; bright/deep blue 5cm (2in) fls.

A. bertolonii **1** (*A. reuteri*): to 15×15cm (6×6in); rich violet-blue 5cm (2in) fls.

A. discolor: to 10–15×15cm (4–6×6in); lvs form low cushion; blue & cream 4cm (1½in) fls.

A. (*Semiaquilegia*) *ecalcarata*: to 20–30×20cm (8–12×8in); reddish- or purplish-brown 2.5cm (1in) spurless fls.

A. flabellata (*A. akitensis, A. japonica*): ultra-hardy; to 45×20cm (18×8in); glaucous lvs; bluish-purple to lilac 4cm (1½in) fls, hooked spurs. Vars (better known than sp): 'Nana Alba' (to 20×15cm [8×6in]; creamy-white); *pumila* **2** ('Nana'; sometimes sold as *A. akitensis* or *A. akitensis kurilensis*; to 15cm [6in]).

A. glandulosa: ultra-hardy; to 30×20cm (12×8in); clusters of wide blue & white fls 4cm (1½in) long, hooked spurs.

A. scopulorum: variable, to 25×15cm (10×6in); glaucous lvs; fls variable, usually lavender to violet & cream, long spurs.

Hepaticas (*Hepatica* spp; formerly & sometimes listed as *Anemone* spp): woodland natives good in moist part of rock garden, preferably in part-shade; semi-evergreen; 3-lobed crisp lvs on wiry stalks; anemone-like fls with rounded petal-like sepals from v early spring.

H.×media 'Ballard's Variety' **3** ('Ballardii'): hybrid of *H. nobilis* & *H. transsilvanica*; to 15×25cm (6×10in); mauve 2.5cm (1in) fls.

H. nobilis **4** (*H. triloba, A. hepatica*): to 8–10×25cm (3–4×10in); shallow lf lobes; 2–2.5cm (¾–1in) fls, blue in sp but white, pink, purple or red in vars. *H. americana* is similar.

H. transsilvanica (*H. angulosa*): more slender than above, to 10×25cm (4×10in); lf lobes deep; 2.5–3cm (1–1¼in) pale mauve-blue fls (sky-blue in var 'Loddon Blue').

Pulsatillas (*Pulsatilla* spp; formerly & often listed [especially in US] as *Anemone* spp): beautiful tufted plants with ferny lvs & goblet-shaped nodding fls with prominent yellow stamens, opening starry, mid/late spring; lvs, stems & buds softly hairy. Dislike root disturbance.

P. (*A.*) *alpina*: to 30×15cm (12×6in); 5–6cm (2–2½in) white fls; fluffy seed-heads. Var *sulphurea* **5** (*P.* [*A.*] *sulphurea*) is deep sulphur-

yellow & later. *P.* (*A.*) *occidentalis* is similar; fls white or pinkish.

P. (*A.*) *vernalis*: to 15×15cm (6×6in); silky golden hairs; buds tinged bluish; 5cm (2in) pearly-white (sometimes pink-tinged) fls. Protect from excess winter wet.

P. vulgaris **6** (*A. pulsatilla*, pasque flower): to 20–30×25cm (8–12×10in); 5–8cm (2–3in) purple fls (white, pink, red or blue in vars); silky seed-heads. *P.* (*A.*) *halleri* is similar.

Alpine buttercups (*Ranunculus* spp): tufted or clump-forming; sprays of bowl/saucer-shaped fls, generally 2–2.5cm (¾–1in) wide.

R. alpestris: to 10×15cm (4×6in); glossy, lobed, toothed lvs; white fls, yellow eye, spring to mid summer.

R. amplexicaulis: to 15–20×15cm (6–8×6in); glaucous lance-shaped lvs; white fls, yellow eye, late spring (largest in var 'Grandiflora'); dies down late summer.

R. calandrinioides **7**: to 15×15cm (6×6in); grey-green wavy-edged lance-shaped lvs from autumn; 5cm (2in) white fls, often flushed pink, crepe-like petals, from mid winter; dies down late summer. Best under glass to protect fls.

R. crenatus: to 10×10cm (4×4in); heart-shaped toothed lvs; white fls, yellow eye, early summer.

R. ficaria (lesser celandine): to 30cm (12in); marbled heart-shaped glossy lvs; solitary shining golden-yellow 2.5–5cm (1–2in) fls, spring. Wild form invasive; compact vars include: 'Albus' (white); 'Aurantiacus' **8** ('Cupreus'; coppery-orange); 'Flore Pleno' (double); 'Major' (large golden fls); 'Primrose' (creamy-yellow).

R. gramineus **9**: to 20–30×30cm (8–12×12in); grassy lvs; shiny yellow fls, late spring. Tends to become lanky.

R. montanus: to 15×20cm (6×8in); variable; lobed lvs; solitary bright yellow fls, late spring & summer. Var 'Molten Gold' is dwarf & free-flg.

Dwarf meadow rues (*Thalictrum* spp): tufted plants with deeply divided/lobed lvs on wiry stems & fluffy infls of v small fls, summer. Like part-shade.

T. coreanum: to 15×15cm (6×6in); bronze-tinted lvs; lilac fls.

T. kiusianum **10**: to 15×20cm (6×8in); maidenhair-like lvs; lilac to purple fls.

Dwarf globeflower (*Trollius pumilus*): to 30×25cm (12×10in); glossy deeply lobed basal lvs; shining golden-yellow fls, opening flat to 2.5–4cm (1–1½in), early summer. 'Wargrave Variety' is best var. Like moisture.

The rose family

Generally prostrate sun-loving plants, many useful for ground cover, often sub-shrubby. Evergreen unless stated. Flowers often 5-petalled & rose-like, but sometimes very small. **Cultivation**: Unless stated, very hardy and for any well-drained soil in sun. **Propagation**: Seed; division; cuttings; running spp by layering.

New Zealand burrs (*Acaena* spp): moderately to v hardy, vigorous, sometimes rather invasive carpeting plants, generally to 5–10×60cm (2–4×24in), good between paving or to overplant dwarf bulbs; small pinnate lvs; insignificant fls, summer, followed by bristly seed-heads ("burrs"). Thrive on poor soil. Nomenclature of many garden types uncertain. Spp & hybrids include: *A. adscendens* (to 15cm [6in]; grey-green lvs; reddish burrs); *A.* 'Blue Haze' (grey lvs; brownish burrs); *A. buchananii* (pea-green lvs; orange-brown burrs); *A.* 'Copper Carpet' ('Kuperferteppich'; bronzed lvs; greenish-red burrs); *A. microphylla* **1** (rusty lvs; scarlet burrs); *A. pulchella* (reddish-purple lvs; red burrs).

Mountain avens (*Dryas octopetala* **2**): ultra-hardy sub-shrubby mat-forming plant, to 10×60cm (4×24in); prostrate stems; deep green leathery oak-like lvs, grey-green beneath; saucer-shaped 8-petalled white fls 2.5cm (1in) wide, early summer; silky seed-heads. Var 'Minor' is v dwarf, to 5×25cm (2×10in).
D. drummondii is similar, but lvs more wedge-shaped & fls yellow, nodding, bell-shaped.
D.×suendermannii is hybrid of the above; fls yellow in bud, opening creamy-white.

Avens (*Geum* spp): tufted, with upright pinnate lvs & toothed lfts (terminal lft much larger); large yellow, rather rose-like 5-petalled fls, late spring & early summer.
G. montanum **3**: to 15×30cm (6×12in); no runners; 2.5cm (1in) golden-yellow fls. Var 'Maximum' has larger fls.
G. reptans: to 15×45cm (6×18in); spreads by red runners; 4cm (1½in) bright yellow fls. Difficult & lime-hating; for moist scree.

Rock spiraea (*Petrophytum* [*Spiraea*] *caespitosum* **4**): mat-forming, to 8×60cm (3×24in) or wider; woody prostrate stems; dense tufts of 0.5–1cm (¼–½in) silky-hairy lvs; short spikes of tiny white fls, summer. *P. hendersonii* is more compact & hummock-forming, to 10×30cm (4×12in); lvs dark green or bronzed; fls creamy.

Cinquefoils (*Potentilla* spp): colourful, mainly summer-flg plants with deeply divided or compound lvs & generally yellow, rather rose-like fls, long season.
P. aurea: carpet-forming, to 5–15×30cm (2–6×12in); creeping stems; bright green lvs; clusters of 1–2cm (½–¾in) bright yellow fls. Vars: *chrysocraspedia* (orange); 'Plena' (double).
P. crantzii (*P. alpestris*): tufted, to 8–15×15cm (3–6×6in); deep green lvs; 2.5cm (1in) yellow fls blotched orange.
P. eriocarpa: creeping, to 5×20cm (2×8in); grey-green lvs; rounded yellow fls to 4cm (1½in) wide.
P. nitida: mat-forming, to 5×30cm (2×12in); silvery-hairy lvs; almost stemless 2.5cm (1in) rose-pink to white fls, early summer. Likes lime. Likes scree. Var 'Rubra' **5** is deep pink; free-flg.
P. tabernaemontani **6** (*P. verna*, spring cinquefoil): mat-forming, to 8×60cm (8×24in); dark green lvs; 1cm (½in) bright yellow fls, mid–late spring, some repeat. Var 'Nana' is compact, to 5×15cm (2×6in); good in trough.
P.×tonguei: hybrid of *P. nepalensis*; mat-forming, to 10×45cm (4×18in) or wider; dark green, often bronzed lvs; soft apricot 1cm (½in) fls flushed crimson.

Waldsteinia (*Waldsteinia ternata* **7**): creeping & carpet-forming sub-shrub, to 10×45cm (4×18in) or wider; dark green cinquefoil-like toothed & somewhat hairy lvs; sprays of 1cm (½in) rose-like 5-petalled yellow fls, mid–late spring. Sun or light shade. *W. fragarioides* is similar but larger.

Dwarf willows

Salix spp. Valuable rock garden shrubs; prostrate types hug ground & rocks; upright are bushy or make dwarf trees. Deciduous with glossy leaves 1–2.5cm (½–1in) long. Conspicuous silky erect catkins in spring on male plants (often before leaves), silvery to yellow unless noted. (Female catkins inconspicuous). **Cultivation**: Ultra-hardy unless stated. For almost any soil in sun or partial shade. Prone to various insect pests. **Propagation**: Hardwood cuttings; seed.

S. apoda: v hardy; to 25×60cm (10×24in); spreading or mat-forming; catkins orange-pink.
S.×boydii **8**: hybrid of uncertain parentage; dwarf tree, to 45×40cm (18×16in); crinkly grey-green lvs becoming dark green; female.

S. herbacea: creeping, to 10×25cm (4×10in); bright green lvs; likes moisture.
S. lanata **9** (woolly willow): slow-growing bush, to 60×60cm (2×2ft); sometimes to 1.2–1.5m (4–5ft); branchlets woolly; densely silver-haired lvs

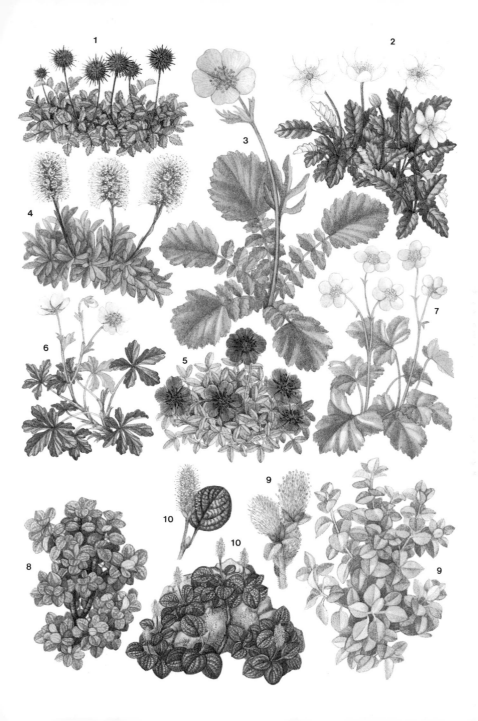

to 6cm (2½in) long; catkins bright golden. Var
'Stuartii' (probably hybrid with *S. lapponum*) is
smaller, with orange winter buds & less hairy lvs;
female.
S. lapponum: twiggy bush, to 1×1m (3×3ft);
narrow lvs to 6cm (2½in) long, white-haired
above; v silky catkins.

S. reticulata **10**, p469: prostrate & v slow-
growing, to 15×60cm (6×24in); dark green
crinkly lvs, glaucous beneath; golden catkins.
S. nivalis is similar.
S. retusa: prostrate & mat-forming, to 5×25cm
(2×10in); shiny lvs; greyish catkins. *S. uva-ursi*
is similar but lvs narrower & catkins red.

Saxifrages

Saxifraga spp. One of largest & most important genera of rock plants, including many hybrids both
natural and garden. Clump/hummock/mat-forming plants with leaves in low rosettes (evergreen unless
stated); 5-petalled flowers singly or in clusters above foliage. **Cultivation**: See below, but generally
need alkaline or neutral soil. Unless stated, very hardy. Spp & vars marked † best in alpine house/frame
over winter. **Propagation**: Seed (hybridize freely); division; rosettes treated as cuttings.
Classification: Botanically into some 15 sections, only a few important horticulturally. For border spp,
most also suitable for larger rock gardens, see p336.

Mossy saxifrages (Dactyloides section): low
mounds or carpets of green, usually deeply
divided lvs; sprays of star/bell-shaped open fls
1cm (½in) across on wiry stems, spring unless
stated. For ordinary moist soil in semi-shade;
divide & replant every few yrs.
S. aquatica: to 45×25cm (18×10in); large
shiny lvs; tall spikes of white fls, summer.
S. moschata: to 5×40cm (2×16in); finely cut lvs;
sprays of creamy-white to yellow fls. Vars:
'Atropurpurea' (fls purple); 'Cloth of Gold' **1** (lvs
bright gold; fls white); 'Compacta' (dense &
neat); 'Variegata' (lvs variegated).
S. rosacea (*S. decipiens*): v variable size & habit,
to 10×40cm (4×16in); 5-lobed lvs; fls open flat,
white, pink or red.
Hybrids of *S. caespitosa*, *S. rosacea*, *S.
moschata*, etc (generally to 8–15×30–45cm [3–
6×12–18in]): 'Bob Hawkins' **2** (lvs variegated
silver, tinted crimson when mature; fls white);
'Carnival' (carmine-rose); 'Elf' (dwarf; carmine;
late); 'Flowers of Sulphur' (lemon-yellow); 'Four
Winds' (to 25cm [10in]; deep crimson); 'Pearly
King' (dwarf; white); 'Peter Pan' **3** (dwarf;
crimson); 'Pixie' (dwarf; rose-red); 'Red Admiral'
(bright red); 'Sanguinea Superba' (deep
crimson); 'Triumph' (large blood-red fls); 'White
Pixie' (dwarf; white); 'Winston Churchill' (pink).
Encrusted or silver saxifrages (Euaizoonia or
Aizoon section): mat-forming, with rosettes of
usually strap-shaped leathery lvs, silvery
encrustations of lime at edges; sprays of star-
shaped fls 1cm (½in) across, late spring. Easy in
well-drained, preferably limy soil in full sun; best
in crevice or wall, or for raised bed, scree, etc.
S. aizoon: see *S. paniculata* (below).
S.×burnatii: hybrid of *S. cochlearis* &
S. paniculata; to 15×30cm (6×12in); bluish lvs;
white fls.
S. callosa **4** (*S. lingulata*): to 40×30cm,
(16×18in); silver-grey lvs, usually narrow;

arching panicles of white fls (pink or red in some
vars). Var 'Kathleen Pinsent' (hybrid) has soft
pink fls.
S. cochlearis **5**: to 25×20cm (10×8in); compact
domes of silvery lvs; plumes of white fls on
red stems. Var *minor* is v compact, to 10 cm (4in).
S. cotyledon: variable, to 45–60×30cm (1½–
2×1ft); large flat rosettes of dark green lvs;
pyramid-shaped infls of profuse white fls. Vars:
'Norvegica' (lvs pointed); 'Pyramidalis' (large
infls); 'Southside Seedling' **6** (hybrid; to 30cm
[1ft]; fls heavily spotted red).
S. hostii: to 30×25cm (12×10in); loose rosettes
of greyish lvs; panicles of creamy-white fls,
sometimes spotted red. Var *altissima* is sturdier,
with red-tinged lvs.
S. longifolia: to 45×30cm (1½×1ft); large
symmetrical rosettes of silver-grey lvs; arching
sprays of white fls. Vars & hybrids: 'Dr Ramsay'
(hybrid with *S. cochlearis*; to 25cm [10in]; large
white fls); 'Tumbling Waters' **7** (hybrid with
S. callosa; to 60cm [2ft]; v large rosettes & infls);
'Walpole's Variety' (to 25cm [10in]; mounds of
small bluish rosettes).
S. paniculata (*S. aizoon*): ultra-hardy; v variable,
to 10–30×40cm (4–12×16in); mats/hummocks
of narrow grey-green lvs; sprays of white, yellow
or pink fls. Vars: *baldensis* (*minutifolia*;
v compact, to 5×10cm [2×4in]; silvery lvs; white
fls); 'Lutea' (clear yellow); 'Rosea' **8** (soft pink).
Cushion saxifrages (Kabschia, including
Engleria, section): slow-growing rosettes of
silvery or greyish lime-encrusted lvs, like
Euaizoonia spp but in small dense hummocks or
mats; profuse large saucer-shaped fls 1–2.5cm
(½–1in) wide, singly or in small clusters, on short
stems, early spring. For v well-drained gritty soil,
preferably limy; good in rock crevices & walls;
protect from summer sun & excess winter wet.
S.×apiculata **9**: hybrid of *S. juniperifolia sancta* &
S. marginata rocheliana; to 10×30cm (4×12in);

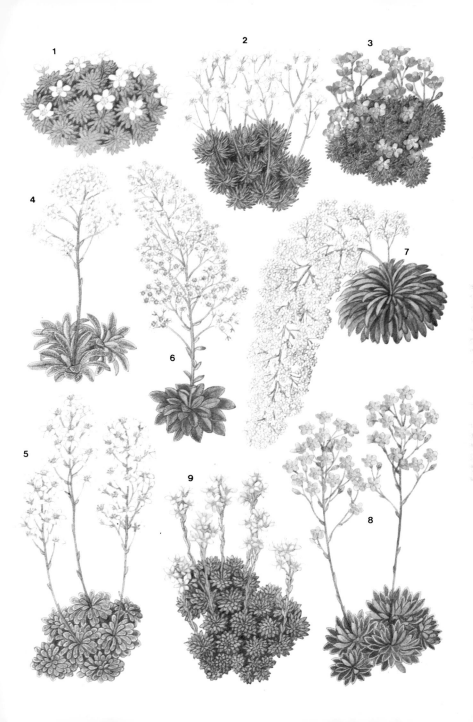

cushions of v small deep green lvs; primose-yellow fls (ivory-white in var 'Alba').

S. × *borisii*: hybrid of *S. ferdinandi-coburgii* & *S. marginata*; to 8×30cm (3×12in); cushions of narrow glaucous lvs; pale yellow fls on reddish stems.

S. burserana: to 8×30cm (3×12in); variable; hard cushions of bluish-grey stiff lvs; large pure white fls on reddish stems. Vars: 'Brookside' **1** (v large fls); 'Crenata' (petals scalloped); 'Gloria' (v large fls, green stems); 'His Majesty' **2** (probably hybrid; fls fade pinkish); 'Major Lutea' (probably hybrid; large pale yellow fls); 'Sulphurea' (probably hybrid; pale yellow fls).

S. diapensioides†: to 8×30cm (3×12in); v hard cushions of grey-green blunt lvs; white fls. Var 'Lutea' (probably hybrid) is yellow.

S. × *elizabethae* **3** (sometimes sold as *S.* × *godseffiana*): hybrid of *S. burserana* & *S. juniperifolia sancta*; to 8×30cm (3×12in); mats of dark green lvs; heads of small yellow fls.

S. grisebachii†: to 20×25cm (8×10in); flat rosettes of heavily encrusted silvery-green lvs; arching sprays of small pink fls part-hidden by hairy red bracts, long season. 'Wisley Variety' **4** is vigorous & colourful form.

S. × *haagii*: hybrid of *S. ferdinandi-coburgii* & *S. juniperifolia sancta*: to 8×25cm (3×10in); loose mats of dark green lvs; profuse small golden starry fls.

S. juniperifolia sancta (*S. sancta*): to 5×15cm (2×6in); mats of dark green pointed lvs; heads of golden-yellow fls (best on poor soil).

S. × *kellereri*: probably hybrid of *S. burserana* & *S. stribrnyi* or *S. sempervivum*; to 15×25cm (6×10in); small rosettes of grey-green encrusted lvs; sprays of tubular pink fls, v early.

S. × *kewensis*: hybrid of *S. burserana macrantha* & *S. porophylla*; to 10×30cm (4×12in); neat cushions of narrow grey-green lvs; sprays of pink fls, red/pink bracts & sepals.

S. lilacina†: to 2.5×30cm (1×12in); flat cushions of v small green lvs; almost stemless lilac fls. Hates lime.

S. marginata **5**: to 8×15cm (3×6in); variable; compact mats of v small silver-grey lvs (larger & in v flat rosettes in var *rocheliana*); white funnel-shaped fls (yellow in var *rocheliana* 'Lutea' [probably hybrid]).

Other Kabschia hybrids (parents given in brackets): 'Boston Spa' (unknown; to 8×25cm [3×10in]; mats of dark green lvs; profuse yellow fls); 'Bridget' (*S. stribrnyi* × *S. marginata* var; to 10×15cm [4×6in]; dense silvery-blue hummocks; drooping heads of rosy-red fls); 'Cranbourne' **6** (unknown; to 5×20cm [2×8in]; hard cushions of grey-green lvs; profuse almost stemless pink fls); 'Faldonside' (*S. aretioides* × *S. marginata* var; to 5×20cm [2×8in]; hard hummocks of narrow grey-green lvs; large rich

yellow fls); 'Harlow Car' (unknown; to 5×15cm [2×6in]; hard hummocks of blue-green lvs; crimson fls, dark eye); 'Iris Pritchard' **7**. (*S. godroniana* × *S. lilacina*; to 8×25cm [3×10in]; compact humps of encrusted grey-green lvs; buff-apricot fls); 'Irvingii' (*S. burserana* × *S. lilacina*; to 5×15cm [2×8in]; compact mounds of spiny glaucous-grey lvs; profuse almost stemless pink fls; early); 'Jenkinsae' (*S. burserana* × *S. lilacina*; similar to 'Irvingii' but looser habit; fls on short stems); 'Megasaeflora' (probably *S. burserana* × other sp; similar to *S. burserana* but large rose-pink fls, darker centre); 'Riverslea' (*S. ferdinandi-coburgii* × *S. lilacina*; to 5×25cm [2×10in]; dense mounds of silvery lvs; sprays of pinkish-purple fls); 'Valerie Finnis' **8** (probably *S. burserana* × other sp; similar to *S. burserana* but profuse primrose-yellow fls); 'Winifred' (*S. lilacina* × other sp; similar to 'Cranbourne' but fls rich crimson).

Other rock saxifrages (various sections):
S. aizoides: to 8×30cm (3×12in); mats of glossy green fleshy lvs; short cymes of red-spotted yellow fls (orange in var *aurantia*; blood-red in var *atrorubens*), summer. For rich, moist soil in semi-shade.

S. brunoniana†: moderately hardy; to 15×30cm (6×12in); rosettes of narrow bristle-edged lvs; loose panicles of 2cm (¾in) yellow fls, summer; spreads by profuse thin runners. For moist but gritty soil in cool position.

S. cuneifolia: to 15×30cm (6×16in); mats of dark green rounded lvs; panicles of v small creamy-white fls, late spring. For any soil in shade.

S. granulata (meadow saxifrage, fair maids of France): to 25×20cm (10×8in); fleshy, kidney-shaped lobed lvs (die down after flg); elegant sprays of 2.5cm (1in) white fls (double in var 'Flore Pleno' **9**), early summer; spreads by bulbils. For moist but well-drained soil in sun.

S. oppositifolia: ultra-hardy; to 5×45cm (2×18in) or wider; variable; dense mats of tiny dark green lvs; stemless cup-shaped fls to 1cm (½in) across, white to crimson & reddish-purple, early spring. For moist but v well-drained soil in sun (protect from scorching). Vars: 'Alba' (white); *latina* (compact; silvery lvs; rose-pink fls); 'Ruth Draper' **10** (large rich red fls); 'Splendens' ('Vaccariana'; deep rose-red fls); 'W. A. Clarke' (rich pink).

S. × *primulaize*: hybrid of *S. aizoides aurantia* & *S. umbrosa* 'Primuloides'; to 8×15cm (3×6in); like dwarf London pride (*S. umbrosa*; p340); sprays of small bright carmine-red to salmon fls, summer. For moist light shade.

S. retusa: to 5×25cm (2×10in); like compact *S. oppositifolia*, but erect clusters of small rich red fls, spring. For gritty humus-rich soil, preferably lime-free, in open shade.

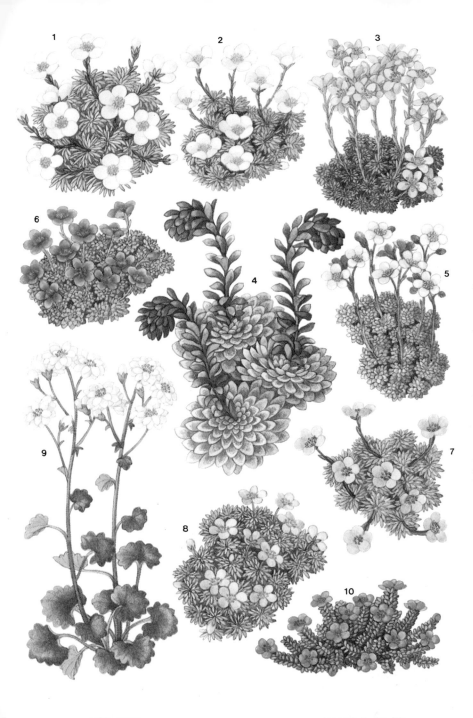

Hebes, penstemons, speedwells and their relatives

Dwarf relatives of the border popular perennials (p342), equally varied but often with snapdragon-like or pouched/lipped flowers, mainly in summer. Evergreen unless stated. **Cultivation**: Unless noted, very hardy & for any well-drained soil in sunny position. **Propagation**: Seed; cuttings (semi-ripe for shrubby spp); division.

Asarina (*Asarina procumbens 1*, *Antirrhinum asarina*): moderately hardy; trailing, to 8×45cm (3×18in); sticky heart-shaped grey-green lvs to 5cm (2in) long; white snapdragon fls tinted yellow/pink, all summer. Likes cool position.

Calceolarias (*Calceolaria* spp): moderately hardy plants with creeping rhizomes; lvs generally to 6cm (2½in) long; characteristic pouched fls 2.5–4cm (1–1½in) long, summer. For cool, humus-rich soil in partial shade; protect in harsh winters or grow in alpine house.

C. biflora: to 25×30cm (10×12in); oval lvs in basal rosettes; paired yellow fls.

C. darwinii 2: to 10×15cm (4×6in); mat of oblong lvs; yellow fls speckled chestnut-brown, with prominent horizontal white bar. *C. fothergillii* is similar but lvs hairy & fls yellow & red. Both difficult & often short-lived.

C. polyrrhiza: to 10×20cm (4×8in); tufted; lance-shaped basal lvs; fls yellow spotted purple. *C. acutifolia* is same or v similar sp. *C.* 'John Innes' 3 is hybrid with *C. biflora*; bright yellow fls on 15cm (6in) stems, early.

C. tenella 4: to 10×25cm (4×10in); prostrate & self-rooting; 1cm (½in) oval lvs; clear yellow fls speckled crimson.

Dwarf Kenilworth ivies (ivy-leaved toadflax, *Cymbalaria muralis* [*Linaria cymbalaria*] vars): dwarf forms of prostrate but invasive ultra-hardy plant best in wild garden or with roots confined in container; kidney-shaped lvs with 5–9 lobes; snapdragon-like fls, generally pink or bluish, all summer. Rock garden vars (tufted, to 5×15–30cm [2×6–12in]): 'Globosa' 5 (pale purple); 'Globosa Rosea' (pink); 'Nana Alba' (white, yellow throat).

Erinus (fairy foxglove, *Erinus alpinus 6*): to 8×15cm (3×6in); tufted; small toothed lvs; 6cm (2½in) racemes of tiny lavender or purple-pink starry fls, spring to mid summer. Rather short-lived but self-seeds. Vars: 'Albus' (white); 'Dr Hanelle' (carmine-red); 'Mrs Charles Boyle' (clear pink).

Dwarf hebes (shrubby veronicas, *Hebe* spp; formerly *Veronica* spp): generally moderately to v hardy dwarf hummock-forming shrubs with leafy stems (sometimes "whipcord", with overlapping scaly lvs) & spikes/racemes of small fls in summer. For sun or partial shade; good near sea, in cities. See also p204.

H. (*V.*) *buchananii* 'Minor': to 8×15cm (3×6in); glossy green lvs; sparse white fls, early summer. Parent sp grows to 30cm (1ft).

H. (*V.*) *pimeleoides*: semi-/prostrate, to 30×60cm (1×2ft); glaucous lvs; dark purple fls. Hybrids: 'Carl Teschner' (to 30×60cm [1×2ft]; dark green lvs; violet-blue fls); 'Edinensis' (to 45×45cm [1½×1½ft]; bright green dense lvs; white fls [rare]).

H. (*V.*) *pinguifolia* 'Pagei' 7 (often listed as *H.* [*V.*] *pageana*): to 30×60cm (1×2ft); glaucous-grey lvs; white fls, late spring (often repeat).

H. tetrasticha: to 15×30cm (6×12in); olive-green whipcord foliage; white fls. Good in trough or scree.

Alpine toadflax (*Linaria alpina 8*): trailing, to 15×25cm (6×10in); mats of fleshy blue-grey narrow lvs in whorls; profuse snapdragon-like purple fls striped orange, all summer. Short-lived but self-seeds. *L. tristis* 'Lurida' is similar but fls yellow-grey, veined maroon & blotched purple; for sunny scree or alpine house.

Mazus (*Mazus* spp): creeping & mat-forming, with toothed lvs & short snapdragon-like fls, summer. Good for paving, overplanting bulbs, etc. Like moist soil; replace when straggly.

M. pumilio: moderately to v hardy; to 5×40cm (2×16in); creeping underground stems; tufts of lvs to 8cm (3in) long; white to lilac fls, marked yellow.

M. (*Mimulus*) *radicans*: moderately to v hardy; to 5×30cm (2×12in); stems self-rooting; bronzed lvs to 5cm (2in) long; fls white blotched violet.

M. reptans 9 (may be sold incorrectly as *M. rugosus*): vigorous, to 5×45cm (2×18in); stems self-rooting; fresh green lvs to 2.5cm (1in) long; purple-blue fls marked white & yellow.

Mimulus (monkey flowers, musks, *Mimulus* spp): moisture-loving, generally mat-forming plants with lush green oval lvs & brilliant, often strikingly blotched trumpet-shaped lipped flowers, late spring & summer. Often rather short-lived; divide regularly.

M.×burnetii 10: hybrid of *M. cupreus* & *M. luteus*; to 20×25cm (8×10in); 3cm (1½in) copper-yellow fls, yellow throat & spotting.

M. cupreus: to 25×25cm (10×10in); tufted; 4–5cm (1½–2in) yellow fls ageing coppery, spotted brown. Often grown as HHA. Vars & hybrids (generally to 15–20cm [6–8in]): 'Bee's Dazzler' (scarlet); 'Red Emperor' (crimson-scarlet); 'Scarlet Bee' (bright flame-red); 'Whitecroft Scarlet' 11 (neat & compact; intense vermilion-scarlet); 'Wisley Red' (rich scarlet).

M. × hybridus vars: see p342.
*M. moschatus** (musk flower): to 20×25cm (8×10in); sticky-hairy; profuse 2cm (¾in) yellow fls marked brown. Most garden forms not scented.
M. primuloides: moderately hardy; to 10×15cm (4×6in); rosettes of tiny hairy lvs; 2.5cm (1in) yellow fls spotted red-brown.

Ourisias (*Ourisia* spp): mat-forming plants for cool, moist semi-shade, preferably in lime-free soil; fls tubular to trumpet-shaped, lipped.
O. elegans **1** (often sold incorrectly as *O. coccinea*): moderately hardy; to 20×25cm (8×10in); light green lvs; racemes of nodding scarlet fls, summer.
O. macrophylla **2**: moderately to v hardy; to 30×40cm (12×16in); leathery dark green lvs; whorls of yellow-centred white fls, early summer.
O. macrocarpa is similar but more robust.

Parahebes (*Parahebe* spp; formerly *Veronica, Hebe* spp): generally moderately to v hardy sub-shrubby relatives to *Hebe* spp; more or less prostrate, with small lvs & summer fls in racemes.
P. (H., V.) cataractae **3**: to 25×75cm (10×25in); toothed lvs; white fls veined pinkish-purple.
P. (H., V.) lyallii is similar but smaller & more prostrate.
P. decora (*V. bidwillii*; probably often sold incorrectly as *P. × bidwillii*): to 20×15cm (8×6in); prostrate stems with tiny rounded lvs; fls white or pale lilac, veined pink. True *P. × bidwillii* is hybrid with *P. lyallii*; lvs larger & often lobed; may not be in cultivation.

Penstemons (*Penstemon* spp): showy N American plants with racemes of tubular lipped fls generally 2.5–4cm (1–1½in) long. For well-drained sheltered positions in sun; protect over winter in v cold areas. Nomenclature often confused.
P. alpinus **4**: clump-forming, to 25×20cm (10×8in); broad lvs; blue or purplish fls, white throat, early summer.
P. confertus (sometimes listed incorrectly as *P. procerus*): variable; dwarf form semi-prostrate, to 15×25cm (6×10in); lance-shaped lvs; 2cm (¾in) cream to sulphur-yellow fls, summer.
P. cristatus (correctly, *P. eriantherus*): bushy, to 25×25cm (10×10in); lvs lance-shaped to oval; reddish-purple fls, summer.
P. davidsonii: mat-forming sub-shrub, to 15×25cm (6×10in); small grey-green lvs; rich pink or ruby-red fls, early summer. *P. 'Six Hills'* is hybrid with *P. cristatus* & intermediate in habit; lvs glaucous; fls lilac.
P. heterophyllus: moderately hardy; to 30–45×30cm (1–1½×1ft); narrowish lvs; pink-tinged blue fls all summer. Var 'Blue Gem' **5** ('True Blue') is pure sky-blue.
P. menziesii (may be correctly *P. davidsonii menziesii*): variable sub-shrub, to 25×40cm

(10×16in) or more; oblong toothed lvs; violet-blue to purple fls, early summer. *P. newberryi* **6** is similar, but fls rose-pink to rose-purple.
P. pinifolius: to 20×30cm (8×12in); v narrow lvs; 2cm (¾in) scarlet fls all summer.
P. roezlii (probably correctly a form of *P. newberryi*): rounded sub-shrub, to 20×30cm (8×12in); lance-shaped lvs; profuse cherry-red fls, early summer. True *P. roezlii* (correctly, *P. laetus roezlii*) has lavender to violet fls.
P. rupicola **7**: prostrate & mat-forming, to 15×25cm (6×10in); sub-shrubby; small leathery lvs; deep carmine-pink fls, late spring & early summer.
P. scouleri (correctly, *P. fruticosus scouleri*): bushy sub-shrub, to 30×45cm (1×1½ft); narrowly lance-shaped leathery lvs; lavender to purple fls to 5cm (2in) long, early–mid summer.

Dwarf mulleins (*Verbascum* spp): moderately hardy dwarf bushy sub-shrubs with grey hairy lvs & short spikes of 2.5cm (1in) yellow fls, early–mid summer. Need v well-drained sunny site & protection from winter wet; best in scree, dry wall or alpine house.
V. dumulosum **8**: to 30×30cm (1×1ft); lvs oval; fls sulphur-yellow, purple eye.
V. spinosum: to 30×30cm (1×1ft); branches spiny; lvs toothed, less hairy than above, fls clear yellow. *V. 'Letitia'* **9** is a hybrid of above spp; to 25×25cm (10×10in); lvs lobed & felted; profuse yellow fls, brown blotch, long season.

Speedwells (*Veronica* spp): generally prostrate & mat-forming, with small lvs & spikes of small saucer-shaped fls, late spring & early summer, mainly in shades of blue & purple. See also *Hebe* & *Parahebe* spp (above); for border spp, some having dwarf vars, see p344.
V. allionii: to 10×25cm (4×10in); creeping & self-rooting; blue-grey lvs; violet fls.
V. armena: to 10×20cm (4×5in); deeply cut lvs; bright blue fls on erect stems.
V. bombycina: to 5×15cm (2×6in); densely white-woolly tiny lvs; china-blue fls. Best in alpine house.
V. cinerea **10**: to 10×40cm (4×16in); mounding; grey-green narrow lvs to 10cm (4in) long; pale blue fls.
V. fruticans (*V. saxatilis*): to 15×20cm (6×8in); sub-shrubby; clear deep blue fls, red eye.
V. fruticulosa is similar but ultra-hardy; fls pink, or blue with reddish markings.
V. pectinata **11**: ultra-hardy; to 8×40cm (3×16in); v hairy grey lvs; deep blue fls, white eye. Var 'Rosea' is pink.
V. prostrata (often listed incorrectly as *V. rupestris*; may be form of *V. teucrium*. to 8–20×40cm (3–8×16in); lvs to 3cm (1¼in) long; profuse deep blue fls. Easy & showy. Vars: 'Blue Sheen' (china-blue); 'Loddon Blue' (compact; rich deep blue); 'Mrs Holt' **12** (soft

pink); 'Nana' (v dwarf); 'Rosea' (pink); 'Royal Blue' (rich gentian-blue); 'Silver Queen' (silvery-blue); 'Spode Blue' (pale china-blue).
V. saturejoides: ultra-hardy; to 8×40cm (3×16in); glossy dark green lvs; dark blue fls marked red.
V. telephifolia: to 5×10cm (2×4in); creeping; silvery-grey waxy lvs; china-blue fls. For gritty soil; best in alpine house.

Wulfenias (*Wulfenia* spp): tufted rhizomatous plants for rich moist soil but protected from winter wet; best in alpine house.
W. carinthiaca **1** to 25×30cm (10×12in); rosettes of scalloped leathery lvs to 20cm (8in) long; dense erect racemes of lipped violet-blue, pink or white fls, early–mid summer.
W. orientalis: to 15×30cm (6×12in); rosettes of fleshy lvs; violet fls, spring or early summer.

Miscellaneous rock plants

Listed alphabetically by family name. Evergreen unless noted. **Cultivation & propagation**: See below; unless stated, very hardy & propagated by division, softwood/semi-ripe cuttings or seed. For dwarf conifers, see pp14–44; for dwarf bulbs, see pp362–424; for dwarf annuals to fill gaps, see pp486–526. Some moderate-sized shrubs (pp46–226) & perennials (pp252–360) are also suitable for larger rock gardens.

Sun roses (rock roses, *Helianthemum* spp; Cistaceae): vigorous semi-prostrate sub-shrubs with small, narrow, softly hairy lvs & profuse but short-lived saucer-shaped 5-petalled fls like small wild roses, early–mid summer. Easy in full sun & dryish soil; thrive on lime. Cut back after flg (encourages repeat flg). For *Cistus* spp (also called sun or rock roses), see p76.
H. alpestre (correctly, *H. oelandicum alpestre*): to 10×30cm (4×12in); 1cm (½in) lvs; profuse 2cm (¾in) golden-yellow fls. Var 'Serpyllifolium' **2** is v prostrate, with v small grey-green lvs.
H. lunulatum: cushion-forming, to 20×30cm (8×12in); grey-green 1.5cm (⅝in) lvs; 1cm (½in) bright golden-yellow fls, orange centre.
H. nummularium (*H. chamaecistus, H. vulgare*): to 15–30×60–90cm (6–12×24–36in); deep green lvs to 2.5cm (1in) long; clusters of up to 12 fls 2.5cm (1in) wide, yellow in sp. Parent of numerous vars & hybrids, including: 'Amy Baring' (buttercup-yellow); 'Ben Afflick' (orange, bronze centre); 'Ben Fhada' (golden-yellow, orange centre); 'Ben Heckla' **3** (bronze-gold); 'Ben Nevis' (deep yellow, bronze-red centre); 'Firedragon' (orange-scarlet; grey-green lvs); 'Henfield Brilliant' **4** (brick-red; greyish lvs); 'Jubilee' **5** (primrose-yellow, double); 'Praecox' (yellow, greyish lvs); 'The Bride' **6** (white, yellow centre; grey lvs); 'Watergate Rose' (rosy-crimson, centre tinged orange; grey-green lvs); 'Wisley Pink' **7** (soft pink, orange centre; grey-green lvs; 'Wisley Primrose' (primrose-yellow; grey-green lvs).
Morisia (*Morisia monanthos* **8**, *M. hypogaea*; Cruciferae): to 2.5×15cm (1×6in); compact tufted rosettes of narrow, coarsely serrated dark green lvs; almost stemless golden-yellow 1cm (½in) cross-shaped fls, all spring. For v well-drained sandy soil in sun; best in scree or trough. Propagate by root cuttings, seed.
Shortias (*Shortia* spp; some formerly

Schizocodon spp; Diapensiaceae): pretty stemless plants spreading by runners & creeping roots; glossy rounded lvs on wiry stalks; nodding 5-lobed bell/funnel-shaped lvs, fringed or toothed petals, on slender stalks, mid–late spring. For cool, lime-free humus-rich soil in partial/full shade.
S. galacifolia: to 15×30cm (6×12in); sharply toothed 8cm (3in) lvs, bronzed in autumn & winter; 2.5cm (1in) white fls fading pinkish.
S. uniflora **9** is similar but lvs more heart-shaped & fls to 4cm (1½in) wide (pale pink in var 'Grandiflora').
S. soldanelloides **10** (fringe-bell): to 12×30cm (5×12in); dark green coarsely toothed 3cm (1¼in) lvs, often dark red in autumn & winter; fringed rose-pink 2.5cm (1in) fls, fading to white or bluish at edges. Vars: *alpina* (dwarf); *ilicifolia* (lvs rather holly-like).
Pterocephalus (*Pterocephalus parnassi* **11**, *Scabiosa pterocephala*; Dipsacaceae): tufted & cushion-forming, to 10×30cm (4×12in); often deeply toothed grey-green hairy lvs to 4cm (1½in) long; scabious-like 2.5cm (1in) fl heads, soft/purplish-pink, late spring & summer. Easy in dryish limy soil in full sun; ideal for dry wall.
Sea heaths (*Frankenia* spp; Frankeniaceae): heather-like carpeting plants, to 8×30cm (3×12in), good near sea; wiry prostrate stems; tiny lvs; tiny 5-petalled fls, summer. For light sandy soil in full sun.
F. laevis: v narrow green lvs; flesh-pink fls.
F. thymifolia **12**: hairy grey-green lvs; rose-pink fls.
The fumitory family (*Corydalis* & *Dicentra* spp; Fumariaceae; formerly in Papaveraceae): tuberous/rhizomatous herbaceous plants with delicately divided ferny lvs & racemes of curious spurred fls to 2.5cm (1in) long, tubular unless noted, generally late spring & early summer. Unless stated, for any soil in sun or partial shade.

Corydalis ambigua: to 10–15×10–15cm (4–6×4–6in); paired lvs, rounded lfts; blue, purple or white fls, upturned spurs.

C. cashmeriana **1**: to 15×25cm (6×10in); blue-green lvs; brilliant blue fls, curved spurs. Hates lime; best in cool humid conditions.

C. cheilanthifolia: to 25×25cm (10×10in); dense racemes of bright yellow 1cm (½in) fls.

C. lutea **2** (common yellow corydalis of Europe): to 20×30cm (8×12in); somewhat glaucous lvs; golden-yellow fls, long season. Tolerates full shade; self-seeds freely, often in old walls.

C. wilsonii **3**: to 25×30cm (10×12in); v glaucous lvs; bright canary-yellow fls.

Dicentra cucullaria **4** (Dutchman's breeches): ultra-hardy; to 8–15×15cm (3–6×6in); pale bluish-green lvs; nodding racemes of yellow-tipped white fls, locket-shaped with 2 long spurs, from mid spring. Likes cool, moist, peaty soil. Dies down soon after flg.

Globularias (globe daisies, *Globularia* spp; Globulariaceae): cushion-forming, with globular fl heads like powder-puffs on erect stalks just above foliage, late spring & early summer. Like sun.

G. cordifolia **5**: to 8×15–22cm (3×6–9in); glossy green notched lvs in rosettes; blue fls in short-stalked 1cm (½in) heads.

G. meridionalis (*G. bellidifolia*): to 22×22cm (9×9in); woody stems with small lance-shaped dark green lvs to 8cm (3in) long; powder-blue to rich blue fls in 2cm (¾in) heads.

Rhodohypoxis (*Rhodohypoxis baurii* **6**; Hypoxidaceae): moderately to v hardy; tufted, to 6×10cm (2½×4in); corm-like root; hairy narrow lvs; starry 2.5cm (1in) fls, white to dark rose-red, late spring & summer. For moist, peaty, lime-free soil in sun. Vars: 'Appleblossom' (pink); 'Garnet' (crimson); 'Harlequin' (white flushed pink); 'Margaret Rose' (flesh-pink).

The pea family (*Lotus, Parochetus* & *Trifolium* spp; Leguminosae): prostrate & mat-forming, with characteristic compound lvs, small rounded lfts, & solitary or clustered pea fls. For full sun.

Lotus corniculatus 'Flore Pleno' (double var of bird's-foot trefoil): to 5×45cm (2×18in); fresh green trifoliolate lvs; clusters of 3–6 bright yellow fls, sometimes tinged reddish, summer. For any soil.

Parochetus communis **7** (shamrock pea, blue oxalis): semi- to moderately hardy; to 10×60cm (4×24in); herbaceous; clover-like lvs; cobalt-blue fls, summer & autumn. For moist soil; protect in winter or overwinter rooted cuttings under glass.

Trifolium repens 'Purpurascens Quadriphyllum'* **8** (purple-lvd var of four-leaf clover): ultra-hardy; often invasive, to 5–10×60cm (2–4×24in) or wider; green-edged purplish lvs, 3–6 (often 4) lfts; typical white clover fls in globular 2cm (¾in)

heads, summer. For any soil.

Butterwort (*Pinguicula grandiflora* **9**; Lentibulariaceae): moderately to v hardy insectivorous bog plant for wet mossy pocket next to rock garden pool; to 10×15cm (4×6in); herbaceous, overwintering as dormant bud; flattened basal rosette of pale yellowish-green lvs to 8cm (3in) long, v sticky; solitary long-spurred & lipped purple-violet fls 2.5cm (1in) wide, early summer, on erect stalks.

Dwarf Solomon's seals (*Polygonatum* spp; Liliaceae): rhizomatous herbaceous plants for rich, moist soil in light shade.

P. falcatum: to 30×30cm (1×1ft); miniature version of common Solomon's seal (p306) with curving stems bearing paired narrow stalkless lvs & dangling creamy-white tubular/bell-shaped fls in lf axils, late spring.

P. hookeri: mat-forming, to 8×30cm (3×12in); crowded rosettes of mid green lvs; almost stemless erect starry rosy-lilac fls to 2cm (¾in) long, late spring.

Dwarf flax (*Linum* spp; Linaceae): mostly hummock-forming shrubby plants with profuse brightly coloured funnel-shaped fls, summer. For full sun.

L. arboreum **10**: moderately hardy; compact, to 30×30cm (1×1ft); blue-green lvs to 4cm (1½in) long; clustered golden-yellow fls 4cm (1½in) wide.

L. perenne alpinum: dwarf var of *L. perenne* (p356), to 15×20cm (6×8in); clear blue 2cm (¾in) fls.

L. salsaloides (correctly, *L. suffruticosum salsaloides*): moderately hardy; semi-prostrate, to 5×22cm (2×9in); v narrow lvs; pearly-white 4cm (1½in) fls. Best-known var is 'Nanum' (prostrate, to 8×45cm [3×18in]).

Pratia (*Pratia angulata* **11**; sometimes grown incorrectly as *P. treadwellii*; Lobeliaceae; sometimes included in Campanulaceae): moderately hardy; mat-forming & self-rooting, to 5×30cm (2×12in); fleshy round-toothed lvs to 1cm (½in) long; solitary purple-veined white early summer fls to 2cm (¾in) long, rather like bedding lobelias (p524); showy 1cm (½in) purplish-crimson berries. For moist shade.

Dwarf jasmine (*Jasminum parkeri*; Oleaceae): moderately hardy twiggy domed shrub, to 30×60cm (1×2ft), or will trail over rock; pinnate lvs, 3–5 dark green 5mm (¼in) lfts; yellow tubular fls to 2cm (¾in) long, 6 flaring lobes, in upper lf axils, early summer. For any well-drained soil in sun.

The evening primrose family (*Epilobium* [willow herb], *Fuchsia, Oenothera* [evening primrose] & *Zauschneria* [Californian fuchsia] spp; Onagraceae; some sometimes classed in Oenotheraceae): generally for any well-drained soil in sun.

Epilobium glabellum **1**: to 30×45cm (1×1½ft);
woody base; many stems, with glossy, often
bronzed, 2cm (¾in) lvs; creamy-white funnel-
shaped fls 2.5cm (1in) wide in loose heads, all
summer.
E. kai-koense: to 15×30cm (6×12in); slender
stems; purplish-green 2.5cm (1in) lvs; 2cm (¾in)
rose-pink to almost white fls, summer.
E. 'Broadwell Hybrid' is hybrid of above spp;
intermediate in character.
Fuchsia procumbens **2** (trailing fuchsia):
moderately hardy; prostrate & trailing, to
5×60cm (2×24in); heart-shaped, rather fleshy
lvs to 2cm (¾in) long; erect orange-yellow
tubular fls to 2cm (¾in) long with purple & green
reflexed sepals, all summer; bright red frs to
2.5cm (1in) long. For sheltered sunny site.
F. 'Pumila' & *F.* 'Tom Thumb' (p146) are also
suitable for rock gardens.
Oenothera acaulis (*O. taraxacifolia*): moderately
to v hardy; to 20×30cm (8×12in); tufted rosettes
of hairy, rather dandelion-like coarsely toothed
lvs to 20cm (8in) long; stemless saucer-shaped
fls to 8cm (3in) wide, white fading pink, opening
in evening, late spring & all summer. Short-lived.
Var 'Aurea' is yellow.
O. caespitosa* **3**: to 15×22cm (6×9in); spreads
by underground runners; tufts of narrow coarsely
toothed lvs to 10cm (4in) long; white fls to 8cm
(3in) wide on short stems, opening in evening,
summer. Needs dry, light, sandy soil; protect
from winter wet.
O. perennis (*O. pumila*, dwarf sundrops):
moderately hardy; to 15×25cm (6×10in); neat &
tufted, with lance/spatula-shaped lvs to 5cm (2in)
long; yellow cup-shaped fls to 2.5cm (1in)
across, opening daytime from nodding buds, in
loose leafy spikes, summer.
Zauschneria californica **4** (Californian fuchsia):
bushy, clump-forming sub-shrub, to 45×45cm
(1½×1½ft); slender, often arching stems;
deciduous or herbaceous where winters cold,
evergreen in v mild areas; narrow grey-green
hairy lvs to 4cm (1½in) long; spikes of vivid
scarlet tubular fls to 4cm (1½in) long, flaring
lobes, late summer into autumn. Moderately to
v hardy, but likes v warm sunny site & light,
v well-drained soil. Where winters cold & damp,
protect rootstock &/or overwinter rooted cuttings
under glass. Vars: 'Dublin' (green lvs; reliable in
cool climates); *latifolia* (broad lvs; v hardy);
mexicana (lance-shaped lvs). *Z. cana*
(*Z. californica microphylla*) is similar but with
v narrow grey lvs.
Terrestrial orchids (*Bletilla, Cypripedium* &
Pleione spp; Orchidaceae): showy herbaceous
plants growing from swollen tuber-like
pseudobulbs; lvs generally broad & thin, often
pleated & in 2 ranks; fls with 3 sepals, often
elongated & tapering, & 3 petals, lowest enlarged

to form lip or pouch. Generally for well-drained
but moist peaty, gritty soil in partial shade;
mulch/protect in winter (best in alpine house).
Bletilla striata **5** (*B. hyacinthina*): moderately
hardy; to 30×15cm (12×6in); pleated lance-
shaped lvs; racemes of rosy-purple to mauve-
pink fls 5cm (2in) wide, darker crisped lip, early
summer. Var 'Alba' **6** is white.
Cypripedium acaule **7** (pink lady's slipper,
moccasin flower): to 25×20cm (10×8in); paired
pleated lvs to 20×4cm (8×1½in); reddish-purple
solitary fls to 8cm (3in) long, pouch purplish-pink
veined crimson, late spring & early summer.
Ultra-hardy but difficult; needs acid soil.
C. pubescens **8** (yellow lady's slipper; correctly,
C. calceolus pubescens): ultra-hardy; to
30×30cm (1×1ft); stems & lvs hairy (may
irritate); pleated lvs to 20×8cm (8×3in); 8cm
(3in) greenish-yellow fls, pouch yellow, summer.
C. reginae **9**: ultra-hardy; to 60×30cm (2×1ft);
densely hairy (may irritate); pleated lvs to
20×11cm (8×4½in); generally paired 8–10cm
(3–4in) pure white fls on leafy stems, pouch
mottled/striped rose-pink or purplish, summer.
Pleione bulbocodioides **10** (*P. formosana*):
moderately hardy; to 8–10×15cm (3–4×6in) in fl,
lvs taller; lvs narrowish to lance-shaped, ribbed;
v showy fls 8–10cm (3–4in) wide, spring (before
lvs; earlier under glass), with lance-shaped
sepals & petals & tubular or trumpet-shaped
fringed & mottled lip, in shades of pink, mauve &
white, often shaded & marked cream or yellow.
Needs winter protection. Vars: 'Alba' (white, lip
marked yellow); 'Blush of Dawn' (pale pink, lip
mottled white); *limprichtii* (*P. limprichtii*; rich
reddish-purple, pale lip blotched reddish; among
easiest); 'Oriental Jewel' (deep pink); 'Oriental
Splendour' (rose-red); *pricei* (*P. pricei*; generally
purple, lip marked brown); 'Polar Sun' (pure
white, lip marked lemon-yellow). *P. humilis* is
similar, with pink-flushed white fls, broad lip
blotched brownish-purple.
Bloodroot (*Sanguinaria canadensis* **11**;
Papaveraceae): ultra-hardy rhizomatous
herbaceous plant, to 20×30cm (8×12in); deeply
lobed & scalloped grey-green lvs to 15cm (6in)
across (die down late summer); pure waxy-white
anemone-like fls 4cm (1½in) wide, boss of
golden stamens, spring. All parts, especially
roots, have bright red sap. For well-drained peaty
soil in cool shaded site. Var 'Flore Pleno' **12**
('Multiplex') has larger double fls.
Milkworts (*Polygala* spp; Polygalaceae):
prostrate & mat-forming, with small rather pea-
like winged fls in 5cm (2in) racemes.
P. calcarea: to 8×30cm (3×12in); small dark
green lvs; bright blue fls, summer. For limy soil or
scree bed in full sun.
P. chamaebuxus (ground box): to 15×30cm
(6×12in); woody stems; leathery box-like lvs to

2.5cm (1in) long; fls yellow & cream, tipped
purple, spring to early summer. For peaty soil in
light shade. Var *grandiflora* **1** ('Atropurpurea',
'Purpurea', *rhodoptera*) has deep red & yellow
fls.

The knotweed family (*Muehlenbeckia* &
Polygonum spp; Polygonaceae): prostrate &
mat-forming. For any soil, generally in full sun.
Muehlenbeckia axillaris **2** (*M. nana*): to 5×30cm
(2×12in); creeping woody stems with tiny
rounded dark green lvs to 1cm (½in) long; fls
insignificant, sometimes followed by small white
berries. For sun or shade.

Polygonum affine: ultra-hardy; to 20×45cm
(8×18in); lance-shaped lvs to 10cm (4in) long,
bronze-red in winter; erect spikes of pink or red
fls, summer into autumn. Vars: 'Darjeeling Red'
(dark green lvs; 15cm [6in] spikes of deep pink
fls); 'Donald Lowndes' **3** (compact; bright green
lvs; 15–20cm [6–8in] spikes of rose-red fls,
darkening).

P. tenuicaule: to 10×30cm (4×12in); small broad
lvs; 5cm (2in) spikes of white fls, spring.

P. vacciniifolium **4**: v hardy; to 15×60cm
(6×24in); woody trailing stems with dark green
leathery lvs to 1cm (½in) long; 8cm (3in) spikes
of rose-pink fls, mid summer/autumn.

The madder family (*Asperula, Houstonia* &
Mitchella spp; Rubiaceae): cushion/mat-forming
plants. *Asperula* spp for gritty, v well-drained soil
in full sun; others for peaty soil in cool semi-
shade.

Asperula lilaciflora caespitosa: to 5×20cm
(2×8in); v narrow bright green 2cm (¾in) lvs in
4s; profuse deep pink tubular fls 1cm (½in) long,
spreading lobes, in clusters, early–mid summer.

A. suberosa **5** (*A. athoa*; correctly, *A. gussonei*):
to 8×20cm (3×8in); mat of narrow hairy grey lvs;
profuse clusters of 1cm (½in) pink fls, early–mid
summer. Dislikes winter wet.

Houstonia (correctly, *Hedyotis*) *caerulea* **6**
(bluets): ultra-hardy; to 15×20cm (6×8in);
tufted; lance-shaped lvs to 1cm (½in) long;
profuse tiny yellow-eyed porcelain-blue to white
fls, late spring. Likes moisture. *H. serpyllifolia*
(creeping bluets; correctly, *Hedyotis michauxii*)
often sold incorrectly as *H. caerulea*; prostrate &
mat-forming, to 8×30–45cm (3×12–18in), with
broader lvs & deeper blue fls. 'Millard's Variety' is
sturdier form.

Mitchella repens (partridge berry): ultra-hardy; to
8×45–60cm (3×18–24in); trailing woody stems
with rounded glossy lvs to 2cm (¾in) long,
whitish veins; paired small pinkish-white funnel-
shaped fls, summer, followed by edible scarlet
berries.

White-cup (*Nierembergia repens* **7** , *N. rivularis*;
Solanaceae): moderately to v hardy prostrate
plant, to 5×45cm (2×18in), spreading by
underground stems; spatula-shaped bright green

lvs to 3cm (1¼in) long; profuse cup-shaped
creamy-white fls to 4cm (1½in) wide, golden-
yellow throat, summer. For sunny site in gritty but
moist soil. *N. caerulea* (p518), usually grown as
annual, can be grown in rock garden where
winters mild.

Daphnes (*Daphne* spp; Thymelaeaceae): dwarf
relatives of well-known shrubs (p212), many of
which are also small enough for many rock
gardens; clustered glistening starry fls to 1.5cm
(⅝in) long, late spring & early summer unless
noted. All parts poisonous. Generally for most but
well-drained neutral or slight alkaline soil.

*D. arbuscula*** **8**: to 15×30cm (6×12in); reddish
stems; dark green lvs to 2.5cm (1in) long; 2.5cm
(1in) infls of rose-pink fls.

*D. blagayana***: mat-forming, to 22×90cm
(9×36in); sparse oval lvs to 4cm (1½in) long;
5cm (2in) heads of creamy fls, spring. Rejuvenate
regularly by covering stems with soil/stones to
promote rooting. For cool conditions.

*D. cneorum*** (garland flower): mat-forming, to
15×60–90cm (6×24–36in); dark green 2.5cm
(1in) lvs; profuse rosy-pink fls in dense heads
(may repeat autumn). For cool, moist soil; layer
like *D. blagayana*. Vars: 'Alba' (white); 'Eximea'
(sturdy; deep pink); *pygmaea* (dwarf).

*D. petraea***: slow-growing, to 8–15×30cm (3–
6×12in); gnarled; narrow dark green leathery lvs
to 1cm (½in) long; rich pink fls (best when
grafted on *D. mezereum* or other sp). Beautiful
plant for gritty, limy, humus-rich soil. Var
'Grandiflora' **9** has larger fls.

*D. retusa** **10**: moderately to v hardy; slow-
growing, to 60×60cm (2×2ft); dense & compact;
dark glossy green lvs to 8cm (3in) long; 8cm (3in)
heads of rose-purple fls, white inside, spring; red
berries.

Tropaeolum (*Tropaeolum polyphyllum*;
Tropaeolaceae): moderately hardy tuberous-
rooted prostrate plant, to 15×90cm (6×36in) or
wider; trailing stems; intensely silver deeply
lobed lvs; clear yellow nasturtium-like
long-spurred funnel-shaped fls to 1.5cm (⅝in)
across, sometimes shaded orange, early–mid
summer. For any well-drained soil; plant tuber
deeply.

Hacquetia (*Hacquetia* [*Dondia*] *epipactis* **11**;
Umbelliferae): to 8×22cm (3×9in); tufted;
deeply palmately lobed dark green lvs preceded
by tight umbels of minute golden-yellow fls, collar
of leafy bracts, early spring. Best in damp heavy
soil in cool shade.

Dwarf valerian (*Valeriana saxatilis*;
Valerianaceae): mat-forming, to 22×22cm
(9×9in); tufted; basal lvs entire, stem lvs pinnate;
small rounded clusters of white or pink fls on
stout stalks, early summer. For any well-drained
soil in full sun. *V. montana* is similar.

The amaranth family

Half-hardy annuals for summer bedding. Most have showy fluffy or papery inflorescences, some colourful leaves. **Cultivation**: For any ordinary soil in sun.

Amaranths (*Amaranthus* spp): grown for fls &/or lvs (edible); lf colour best in poor soil.
A. caudatus **1** (love-lies-bleeding, tassel flower): to 1–1.2×0.45m (3–4×1½ft); lvs pale green; erect or drooping rope-like infls, crimson in sp, green in var 'Viridis'.
A. hybridus (green amaranth): to 1–1.2×0.3–0.45m (3–4×1–1½ft); lvs green flushed copper; erect blood-red infls. Var *erythrostachys* **2** (prince's feather; often listed as
A. hypochondriacus) has deep red brush-like 15cm (6in) infls & reddish or purple lvs.
A. tricolor vars (Joseph's coat): to 60–90×30–45cm (2–3×1–1½ft); bushy; lvs to 30×10cm (12×4in), shades of red, bronze, yellow & green; fls small (best removed). Vars: 'Illumination' **3**; 'Molten Fire' (poinsettia-like); *salicifolius* 'Flaming Fountain' (drooping willow-like narrow lvs, orange, carmine & bronze).

Celosias (*Celosia* spp): to 30–60×30cm (1–2×1ft); feathery or crested infls, shades of red, orange & yellow. For warm spots; drought-tolerant, good in pots.
C. argentea cristata **4** (*C. cristata childsii*, cockscomb): infls crested, 8–12cm (3–5in) across. Vars: 'Fireglow' (deep red); 'Jewel Box' (dwarf; mixed); 'Toreador' (bright red).
C. argentea plumosa (*C. a. pyramidalis*, *C. cristata plumosa*, Prince of Wales' feathers); infls plume-like, to 18cm (7in) long. Vars: 'Fairy Fountains' **5** (dwarf; mixed); 'Fiery Feather' (red); 'Geisha' (dwarf; mixed); 'Golden Feather'; 'Golden Triumph'.
Globe amaranth (*Gomphrena globosa* **6**): to 30×20cm (12×8in); round papery fls 2.5cm (1in) wide, like large clover fl, purple, red, pink, white or yellow (can be dried). Drought-tolerant. Var 'Buddy' is dwarf.

The forget-me-not family

Includes many of the best blue-flowered annuals and biennials (or short-lived perennials treated thus). Mostly summer-flowering, for mixed borders, etc, but forget-me-not is one of the most important biennials for associating with spring bulbs. **Cultivation**: For any fertile soil, generally in sun.

Anchusa (summer forget-me-not, *Anchusa capensis*): HB (give winter protection), HHA or HA for mixed borders & pots; to 45×25cm (18×10in); blue 5mm (¼in) fls, often with white eye. Vars: 'Blue Angel' (dwarf; intense blue); 'Blue Bird' **7** (sky-blue).
Chinese forget-me-not (hound's tongue, *Cynoglossum amabile**): HB, HHA or HA; to 45–60×30cm (1½–2×1ft); turquoise to purple funnel-shaped fls 5–10mm (¼–½in) long, summer; self-seeds. Tolerates light shade.
Echiums (viper's bugloss, *Echium* spp): rather coarse border plants with showy summer fls.
E. lycopsis (*E. plantagineum*): HA (spring/autumn-sown), HHA or HB; to 90×45cm (3×1½ft); 25cm (10in) spikes of white, pink, red, purple or blue tubular fls. Vars: 'Blue Bedder' (violet-blue); 'Dwarf Hybrids' **8** (mixed).
E. rubrum (correctly, *E. russicum*): HB or short-lived v hardy perennial; to 90×30cm (3×1ft); tubular red fls 1cm (½in) long. Var 'Burgundy' is dark red.
E. vulgare (blueweed): HB usually grown as HA (spring/autumn-sown); to 60×25cm (24×10in); profuse purple to violet 1cm (½in) long tubular fls (attract bees); self-seeds.
Heliotrope (cherry pie, *Heliotropium arborescens***; often listed as *H. corymbosum*,

H. hybridum or *H. peruvianum*): tender shrubby perennial generally grown as HHA for pots or summer bedding (also as perennial under glass); to 30–60×40cm (12–24×16in), or to 1.2m (4ft) as perennial; lance-shaped wrinkled lvs to 8cm (3in) long; dense heads 10–30cm (4–12in) across of small blue, purple, lavender or white fls (good for cutting; used for perfume). Likes rich soil; can be propagated from cuttings under glass; can be trained as standard as "dot" plant, for tubs, etc. Vars: 'Lemoine' (tallish; purple); 'Marine' (short; violet-purple); 'Regale' (v large infls, blue shades).
Forget-me-not (*Myosotis sylvatica**, *M. oblongata*; often incorrectly listed as *M. alpestris* [p426]): spring-flg HB (protect in cold winters) or short-lived moderately to v hardy perennial for partial shade; to 15–40×15cm (6–16×6in); dense spikes or sprays of 10mm (⅜in) fls, mainly blue with white eye, also white or pink. Good for edging & underplanting spring bulbs; dwarf vars (marked †) for rock garden. Vars: 'Alba'† (white); 'Blue Ball'† (indigo-blue; compact); 'Blue Bird' (dark blue; cuttable); 'Carmine King'† **9** (carmine-pink); 'Marine'† (bright blue); 'Rose Pink'†; 'Royal Blue' **10** (bright blue; early); 'Ultramarine'† (deepest blue); 'Victoria Blue'† (gentian blue).

The dianthus family

Sun-loving summer-flowering annuals & biennials (& perennials treated thus), singles having typical 5-petalled flowers. For mixed borders & bedding; several good for cutting. Most dislike acid soil.

Corn cockle (*Agrostemma githago* 'Milas' **1**): garden var of field weed; HA (spring/autumn-sown); to 60–90×30cm (2–3×1ft); rosy-lilac fls to 8cm (3in) across, summer. Seeds poisonous.

Dianthus (*Dianthus* spp): mainly tender to moderately hardy short-lived perennials grown as HHAs, HAs or HBs; all have narrow, often greyish, lvs; fls red, pink or white; for mixed borders, bedding, etc, in neutral/alkaline soil.

D. barbatus ** **2** (sweet William): best as HB (protect from extreme cold) or (dwarf vars) HHA; to 15–60×15–25cm (6–24×6–10in); flattened/domed 8–12cm (3–5in) cymes of single or double 1cm (½in) fls, often bicoloured, v early summer; tall vars good for cutting. Vars: various single colours & mixtures including: 'Beauty' series; 'Indian Carpet' (dwarf); 'Messenger'; 'Newport Pink'; 'Sweet Wivelsfield' (loose fl heads); 'Wee Willie' (dwarf; HHA).

D. caryophyllus ** (carnation): see p264. Some vars fl 1st yr from seed as HHAs, with double 4–5cm (1½–2in) fls – eg, 'Dwarf Fragrance' (to 25cm [10in]); 'Enfant de Nice' (to 35cm [14in]); 'Knight' series (F1 hybrids; to 30cm [1ft]); 'Queen' series (to 45cm [1½ft]).

D. chinensis (Indian, Chinese or rainbow pink; some strains listed as *D.×heddewigii* [Japanese pink]): grown as HHA or HA; to 15–30×15–20cm (6–12×6–8in); fls mainly single, 2.5–5cm (1–2in) across, selfs & bicolours. Dead-head. Vars (F1 hybrids marked †; unless stated, mixed & to 15–20cm [6–8in]): 'Baby Doll'; 'Charm' series & 'Magic Charms'† **3**; 'Lace' series & 'Orchid Lace'† (to 30cm [1ft]); 'Persian Carpet' (to

10–15cm [4–6in]); 'Queen of Hearts'† **4** (scarlet; to 30cm [1ft]); 'Queens Court'† (to 25cm [10in]); 'Snowfire'† **5** (white & red); 'Snowflake'† (white).

D. superbus 'Loveliness' ** ('Rainbow Loveliness'): treat as HB or HHA; to 30–40×20cm (12–16×8in); 4cm (1½in) fringed white to plum-red fls.

Gypsophila (baby's breath, *Gypsophila elegans*): graceful lime-loving HA for mixed borders & cutting; to 45–60×30cm (1½–2×1ft); profuse 5–12mm (¼–½in) white or pink fls. Var 'Covent Garden' **6** has v large fls.

Saponaria (*Saponaria vaccaria*; correctly, *Vaccaria pyramidata*): HA for borders & cutting; to 75×25cm (30×10in); deep pink or white 1cm (½in) fls. 'Pink Beauty' is best pink var.

Catchflies & relatives (*Silene* & *Lychnis* spp): treat most as HAs (spring/autumn-sown); for beds & mixed borders. Grey-green lvs.

S. armeria (sweet William catchfly): to 30–60×15cm (12–24×6in); dense clusters of starry 2cm (¾in) fls, purple, pink or white.

S. coeli-rosa (rose of heaven; correctly *L. coeli-rosa*; often listed as *Viscaria elegans*): to 45×15cm (18×6in); 2.5cm (1in) fls, white to crimson, blue & purple; white or (in Oculata vars **7**) dark eye. Sold as mixtures, also vars: 'Blue Angel' (azure), 'Blue Pearl' (lavender); 'Cardinalis' (crimson).

S. compacta (*S. orientalis*): HB or HHA: to 45×15cm (18×6in); loose clusters of 2.5cm (1in) pink fls, late.

S. pendula **8** (nodding catchfly): to 15–25×15cm (6–10×6in); pink or white 1cm (½in) fls.

Everlasting daisies

Also called immortelles. Have daisy flowers (single unless stated) in summer with papery or straw-like petals or bracts; very long-lasting if cut before fully open & hung upside-down to dry. Also for borders. **Cultivation**: best in light (even poor) soil in full sun.

Ammobium (sand flower, winged everlasting, *Ammobium alatum*): perennial grown as HHA or HA; to 60–90×30cm (2–3×1ft); winged stems, silvery lvs; 2.5–5cm (1–2in) white fls, large golden disc. Var 'Grandiflora' has largest fls.

Strawflower (*Helichrysum bracteatum* **9**): perennial grown as HHA; to 30–90×20–30cm (1–3ft×8–12in); double fls with straw-like red, pink, orange, yellow or white bracts, to 5cm (2in) across, more in *monstrosum* vars. Vars: 'Bikini' series, including 'Bright Bikinis' (to 30–40cm [12–16in]; mixed); 'Dwarf Spangle Mixed' (to 30cm [1ft]); 'Monstrosum Double Mixed' (to

75cm [2½ft]).

Helipterums (sunrays, *Helipterum* spp): HAs (do not transplant well).

H. (*Rhodanthe*) *manglesii* **10** (Swan River everlasting): to 40–60×20cm (16–24×8in); 4cm (1½in) red to white fls, yellow disc.

H. (*Acroclinium*) *roseum* **11**: to 40–60×30cm (16–24×12in); grey-green lvs; rose-pink to white fls, to 5cm (2in) across, yellow disc.

Xeranthemum (in US, immortelle; *Xeranthemum annuum* **12**): treat as HA; to 60–90×30cm (2–3×1ft); silver lvs; 4cm (1½in) single or double fls, purple to white.

Other members of the daisy family

The largest & most important family of garden annuals (including some tender perennials treated thus), divided botanically into some 12 tribes. Easy sun-lovers grown mainly for colourful flowers (some for foliage), for borders & beds (dwarfs for edging), containers, etc; many good for cutting. (All daisy "flowers" are compound; sizes refer to whole flower heads.) **Cultivation**: Generally for any well-drained soil in full or partial sun. Pinch out growing tips to promote bushy habit. Dead-head regularly. Support tall types with twiggy sticks. Tender perennial types can be propagated by cuttings in summer, overwintered under glass, then planted out after last frost. For "everlasting" daisies, see p488.

Floss flowers (*Ageratum* spp; Eupatorium tribe): tender summer bedding plants with bunched fluffy double fls. Treat as HHAs, sowing spring, or autumn for early fls.
A. conyzoides: to 60×45cm (2×1½ft); small blue or white fls in clusters 5cm (2in) across, all summer; good for cutting.
A. houstonianum (*A. mexicanum*): to 10–45×15–30cm (4–18×6–12in); most vars compact & bushy; lvs hairy; fls in trusses 8–10cm (3–4in) across, blue, pink & white shades, all summer. Tetraploid and F1 hybrid vars best for vigour & fl size. Vars (generally 15cm [6in] tall): 'Blue Angel' (F1 hybrid; mid blue); 'Blue Cap' (deep blue); 'Blue Chip' (F1 hybrid; clear blue); 'Blue Mink' **1** (tetraploid; pale blue); 'Fairy Pink' (rose-pink); 'North Sea' (reddish-mauve).
Lazy daisy (*Aphanostephus skirrhobasis*; Aster tribe): HHA or HA good for light soils & windy spots; to 50×20–30cm (20×8–12in); narrow grey-green hairy lvs; white & yellow 2.5cm (1in) daisy fls on 45cm (1½ft) stems, late spring & summer; long-lasting when cut.
African daisies (*Arctotis* spp; Arctotis tribe): tender or semi-hardy S African perennials grown as HHAs or (sometimes) HAs. Brightly coloured, sun-loving bedding & pot plants. Fls large, single, daisy-like, with contrasting central disc colour; open only in full sun; cuttable but short-lived in water & close at night; spring-flg in wild. Lvs large, often cut or lobed; woolly & silvery-green. Stem bases may rot in wet conditions.
A. acaulis **2** (*A. scapigera*): to 15–25×30cm (6–10×12in); fls 9cm (3½in) across, orange to deep red, summer.
A. breviscapa **3**: to 15×20cm (6×8in); fls bright orange, black disc, summer & autumn. Var *aurantiaca* is orange-yellow with purplish disc.
A.×hybrida **4** (Arctotis hybrids; sometimes sold under names of other spp): to 30–60×30cm (1–2×1ft); fls to 10cm (4in) across, on long stems, summer & autumn; generally sold as mixtures of ivory, cream, yellow, apricot, orange, red, etc, shades, often with zoning & contrasting disc.
A. stoechadifolia (*A. venusta*, blue-eyed African daisy): to 60–75×30cm (2–2½×1ft); quick-growing, with thick stems; fls 8cm (3in) across, glistening white with blue disc zoned gold, on long stems, summer & autumn. Var *grandis* **5**

(*A. grandis*) sprawls; fls white or pale yellow, 10cm (4in) across.
Tahoka daisy (*Aster* [*Machaeranthera*] *tenacetifolius*; Aster tribe): N American biennial often treated as HHA or (with protection) autumn-sown HA for summer bedding; to 30–60×25cm (12–24×10in); lvs bristly; long-lasting lavender-blue 5cm (2in) daisy fls, golden disc, summer & autumn; sun-loving, heat-tolerant & trouble-free.
Common European or **English daisy** (*Bellis perennis*; Aster tribe): perennial lawn weed with decorative forms grown as HBs for spring & early summer bedding, edging, ground cover between bulbs, etc. Vars to 10–15×15cm (4–6×6in); fls of sp typical 2cm (¾in) daisies, white or pinkish-white & yellow; Monstrosa vars (eg 'Giant Double' **6**) have 5cm (2in) double fls, crimson to pink & white; dwarf double vars (eg 'Dresden China', 'Lilliput', 'Pomponette' **7**, 'Red Buttons', 'Rob Roy') have profuse double 2cm (¾in) button fls, similar colours; all fl spring to mid summer. Dead-head to prevent self-seeding, though some vars (eg 'Dresden China', 'Rob Roy') are sterile (propagate by division). Seedlings may need some winter protection.
Swan River daisy (*Brachycome iberidifolia*; Aster tribe): Australian HHA good for borders, containers, etc, in sun; to 30–45×30–40cm (12–18×12–16in); lvs deeply cut; 2.5cm (1in) daisy fls, pale blue, pink or white, summer & autumn; cuttable. Var 'Purple Splendour' **8** is blue-purple.
Tassel flower (paint brush, *Cacalia* [*Emilia*] *coccinea* **9**, *E. flammea*; correctly, *E. javanica*; Senecio tribe): colourful HHA or HA (late-spring-sown) for summer bedding, good in hot dry spots & coastal gardens; to 30–60×25cm (12–24×10in); low grey-green lvs; tassel-like red or yellow fls, 1cm (½in) across, in loose corymbs on wiry stems, all summer; long-lasting when cut.
Pot marigold (*Calendula officinalis*; Calendula tribe): v easy free-flg HA (spring/autumn-sown) or HHA for sun, even in poor soils; good for bedding or pots. To 30–60×30–40cm (12–24×12–16in); lvs pale green, pungent smell; fls single or double, to 10cm (4in) across, cream to orange, late spring to autumn (all year under glass or in warm climate); cuttable but close at night. Vars: 'Art Shades' (pastel shades);

'Crested Mixed' (quilled centre petals); 'Family Circle' (dwarf; pastel bicoloured fls); 'Fiesta Gitana' **1** (dwarf; pastel shades); 'Geisha Girl' (reddish-orange; incurved); 'Pacific Beauty' **2** (tall; various colours; v large fls); 'Radio' (orange; quilled petals).

China aster (annual aster, *Callistephus chinensis*; Aster tribe): diverse vars of HHAs or late-spring-sown HAs for bedding, containers & cut fls. To 20–75×30–60cm (8–30×12–24in); fls single or double, in wide colour range (mainly white, pink, red, purple & blue), mid summer to autumn in seasons of 1–2 months. Prone to wilt (some vars resistant), so plant in fresh soil each year; also aphids & other insect pests. Sold in numerous vars (in single colours & mixtures; double fls unless stated), including:
Dwarf vars (to 30cm [1ft]): 'Chrysanthemum-Flowered' (early); 'Milady' (early; chrysanthemum-like incurved fls); 'Pepite' (mid-season; semi-double); 'Pinocchio' (late; v double); 'Thousand Wonders' (mid-season; v dwarf; fls large).
Medium vars (to 30–50cm [12–20in]): 'Lilliput' (mid-season; profuse small quill-petalled fls); 'Ostrich Plume' **3** (early; fls large; reflexing feathery petals); 'Pompon' **4** (mid-season; pompon fls).
Tall vars (to 60cm [2ft] or more): 'Bouquet Powderpuffs' (mid-season; round fls like powderpuffs); 'Duchess' **5** (late; large incurved chrysanthemum-like fls); 'Giant Ray' ('Unicum'; mid-season; fls to 15cm [6in] across, thread-like petals); 'Giants of California' (late; fls like 'Ostrich Plume'); 'Princess' **6** (mid-season; fls have quilled cushion-like centre); 'Sinensis' (mid-season; single); 'Super Sinensis' (mid-season; semi-double); 'Totem Pole' (mid-season; 15–18cm [6–7in] shaggy plumed fls).
Cornflowers & relatives (*Centaurea* spp; Carduus tribe): easy & colourful summer-flg border annuals; narrow petals emerge from globular fl base. Treat as spring/autumn-sown HAs or HHAs; some prone to fungus diseases.
C. americana (basket flower): to 1.2m (4ft); fls 10–12cm (4–5in) across, lavender, pink or white.
C. cyanus (cornflower): to 30–90×20–40cm (12–36×8–16in); sprays of 2.5–5cm (1–2in) fls, usually bright blue, also purple, red, pink or white; tall vars good for cutting. Vars: 'Blue Boy' (tall); 'Blue Diadem' (tall; large deep blue fls); 'Jubilee Gem' (dwarf; deep blue); 'Polka Dot' **7** (medium; various colours).
C. moschata* **8** (sweet sultan; sometimes sold as *C. imperialis*): to 45–60×25cm (18–24×10in); grey-green lvs; fringed 8cm (3in) fls, white, pink, mauve, purple or yellow; good for cutting.
Annual chrysanthemums (*Chrysanthemum* spp; Anthemis tribe): free-flg, bushy & colourful

HAs or HHAs for borders (short vars for edging), containers, cutting, etc; fl throughout summer. All have deeply cut lvs; many have single daisy fls with contrasting colour zones.
C. carinatum **9** (*C. tricolor*): to 45–60×20–25cm (18–24×10–12in); fls, usually single, with purple disc & banded petals in bright colours. Vars: 'Court Jesters' (dwarf); 'Double Mixed' (double; bronze, crimson, etc, shades); 'Merry Mixed'; 'Northern Star' (white & yellow).
C. coronarium **10**: to 30–90×30–45cm (1–3×1–1½ft); 5cm (2in) golden-yellow to white fls. Vars: 'Flore Plenum' (tall; semi-double or double); 'Golden Gem' (dwarf; semi-double).
C. multicaule: to 15–30×20cm (6–12×8in); lvs glaucous; 4–5cm (1½–2in) single daisy fls, golden-yellow. Var 'Gold Plate' is v dwarf.
C. paludosum: to 25×20cm (10×8in); grey-green lvs; single 2.5cm (1in) white & yellow daisy fls.
C. parthenium (feverfew; often sold as *Matricaria eximia*): short-lived v hardy perennial grown as HHA for summer bedding or pots; to 20–45×20–40cm (8–18×8–16in); aromatic lvs; profuse yellow &/or white 2cm (¾in) fls, generally double like anemone-flowered florists' chrysanthemums (p268). Vars: 'Golden Ball' **11** (dwarf; golden-yellow); 'Selma' (tall; large white fls; cuttable); 'Snow Dwarf' (dwarf; ivory, yellow centre); 'White Stars' (dwarf; white).
C. segetum (corn marigold): to 45×30cm (1½×1ft); greyish lvs; 6cm (2½in) single daisy fls, generally yellow; cuttable. Vars: 'Eastern Star' (primrose); 'Evening Star' (golden); 'Morning Star' (pale).
C.×spectabile: hybrid of *C. carinatum* & *C. coronarium*; to 1–1.2×0.45m (3–4×1½ft); 8–10cm (3–4in) single daisy fls, good for cutting. Vars: 'Cecilia' (white banded yellow); 'Sunray' (bright yellow).
Cinerarias: see under *Senecio* (p282).
Cladanthus (Palm Springs daisy, *Cladanthus* [*Anthemis*] *arabicus* **12**; Anthemis tribe): HA for borders; to 75×30cm (2½×1ft); mounding habit; feathery aromatic lvs; profuse 5cm (2in) cheerful golden-yellow single fls all summer & autumn.
Blessed thistle (*Cnicus* [*Carduus*] *benedictus*; Carduus tribe): attractive thistle-like HA for borders, etc; to 60×45cm (2×1½ft); lvs to 15×5cm (6×2in), spiny; thistle-like yellow fls 2.5cm (1in) across, spring & summer; dead-head to prevent self-seeding.
Coreopsis (annual tickseed, *Coreopsis* [*Calliopsis*] spp; Helianthus tribe): free-flg bushy plants for massed planting & cut fls. Deeply cut or pinnate lvs; 2.5–5cm (1–2in) daisy fls in summer, yellow with central reddish-brown blotch; withstand pollution; treat as HAs (spring/autumn-sown) or HHAs. For perennial spp, some of which fl freely 1st yr from seed, see p276.

C. drummondii (correctly, *C. basalis*): to 60×30cm (2×1ft); fls have purple disc. 'Golden Crown' is good var.

C. tinctoria **1** (*C. bicolor*): to 60–90×20cm (2–3ft×8in); 20–30cm (8–12in) tall in dwarf *nana* vars; fls profuse. Sold as mixtures (including doubles); also vars 'Dazzler' (dwarf) & 'Tiger Star' (fls yellow & bronze striped & mottled).

Cosmos (cosmea, *Cosmos* spp, Helianthus tribe): mostly tall HHAs with elegant dahlia-like mainly single fls for back of borders & cutting; long season if dead-headed. Prefer hot summers & light, poor soil; attract aphids.

C. bipinnatus: to 1–1.2×0.6m (3–4×2ft) or more; finely-cut lvs; fls to 10cm (3in) across, yellow disc & white, red &/or pink petals. Vars: 'Candystripe' (white & red striped bicolour); 'Radiance' (crimson & deep pink bicolour); 'Sensation' **2** (mixed & single colours).

C. sulphureus: to 60–90×45cm (2–3×1½ft) or more; lvs coarser; fls to 8cm (3in) across, mostly yellow or red. Vars: 'Bright Lights' **3** (short; yellow, orange, scarlet); 'Diablo' (bright red); 'Klondyke' (double, orange); 'Psyche' (semi-double, white to red); 'Sunset' (semi-double, orange-scarlet).

Pincushion plant (*Cotula* [*Cenia*] *barbata*; Anthemis tribe): compact & pretty S African HHA for edging; to 8–15×10cm (3–6×4in); forms tufted clumps with yellow 8mm (⅓in) button fls on 8–15cm (3–6in) stems above foliage.

Crepis (*Crepis rubra*; Cichorium tribe): spring/autumn-sown HA for front of border; to 30×15cm (12×6in); toothed lvs; dandelion-like white or pink fls 2.5–4cm (1–1½in) across, summer.

Bedding dahlias (*Dahlia* hybrids; Helianthus tribe): tender tuberous perennials like border dahlias (p378) but dwarf vars flg 1st yr from seed, grown as HHAs; lift tubers after 1st frost for re-use. To 30–50×30–45cm (12–20×12–18in); fls to 9cm (3½in) across, single, semi-double or double, mid summer to frost if dead-headed; all colours except blue. Sold as mixtures & named forms, including: 'Coltness Hybrids' **4** (single); 'Dandy' **5** (collarette); 'Disco' (semi-double & double; quilled petals); 'Early Bird' (v early & dwarf; semi-double & double); 'Redskin' (dark bronze lvs; double & semi-double); 'Rigoletto' **6** (v compact & double); 'Unwin's Dwarf Hybrids' (semi-double).

Cape marigolds (African daisies, *Dimorphotheca* spp; Calendula tribe): S African annuals & tender perennials treated as HHAs or HAs; glistening daisy fls 5–8cm (2–3in) across, all summer (close at night & in dull weather). For light soil & full sun; dead-head.

D. annua (correctly, *D. pluvialis*): true annual; to 20–30×15cm (8–12×6in); fls creamy with purple reverse & brown disc. Var 'Ringens' has purple zoning.

D. aurantiaca (correctly, *D. sinuata*; star of the veldt): perennial; to 30–45×30cm (1–1½×1ft); fls white to orange-yellow, including pastels; disc yellow-brown. Vars: 'Aurantiaca Hybrids' **7** (mixed); 'Glistening White'; 'Goliath' ('Giant Orange'); 'Las Vegas' (mixed); 'Salmon Beauty'. In frost-free areas fl winter & spring if sown late summer.

D. (correctly, *Osteospermum*) *barberae*: to 45×30cm (1½×1ft); fls white, pink or purple dark eye. Var 'Compactum' is dwarf; pink fls.

D. (correctly, *Osteospermum*) *ecklonis*: perennial (sub-shrubby); to 60×30cm (2×1ft); fls white with blue reverse & pale blue disc.

Blue & kingfisher daisies (*Felicia* spp; Aster tribe): S African annuals or tender perennials treated as HHAs; bright blue marguerite-type daisy fls with yellow disc from mid summer; for bedding, edging, containers, etc, in full sun.

F. amelloides (*Agathaea coelestis*, blue daisy, blue marguerite): to 45×25cm (18×10in); 3cm (1¼in) sky-blue fls held above foliage; perennial in frost-free areas.

F. amoena (*F.* [*Aster*] *pappei*): to 20×40cm (8×16in); lvs semi-succulent; 2.5cm (1in) China-blue fls.

F. bergerana **8** (kingfisher daisy): to 20×15cm (8×6in); mat of grey lvs; steely-blue 2cm (¾in) fls; true annual.

Annual gaillardia (blanket flower, *Gaillardia pulchella*; Helenium tribe): sun-loving HHA or HA for border & cutting; to 45–60×30cm (1½–2×1ft); lvs grey-green; 5cm (2in) fls, single in sp but most vars double, red to bronze & yellow. Vars: 'Lollipop' **9** (dwarf); 'Picta Lorenziana'. For perennial gaillardias see p276.

Gazanias (treasure flowers, *Gazania* spp; Arctotis tribe): S African tender rhizomatous perennials usually grown as HHAs; low-growing, with 5–10cm (2–4in) daisy fls, summer to frosts, most bicoloured in shades of yellow, orange, brown, red & pink (close at night); narrow lvs, often grey-green. Like sun; for bedding, edging, pots, cutting; good near coasts. Prone to grey mould in wet.

G.×hybrida: to 20–30×30cm (8–12×12in). Vars: 'Chansonette' (v bright colours); 'Golden Margarita' **10** (F1 hybrid; early; golden, dark markings); 'Harlequin Hybrids' (almost prostrate); 'Ministar' (upright); 'Monarch Mixed'; 'Rainbow Mixed'; 'Sunshine' **11** (multicoloured).

G. rigens (*G. splendens*): to 25×30cm (9×12in); prostrate; probably main parent of hybrids.

G. uniflora (*G. leucolaena*, trailing gazania; correctly, *G. rigens leucolaena*): creeping, to 10–20×30cm (4–8×12in).

Sunflowers (*Helianthus* spp; Helianthus tribe): tall N American spring-sown HAs (or treat as HHAs) known for huge solitary daisy fls 10–30cm (4–12in) or more wide, with large disc, on stout

stems; some vars shorter & bushier; some doubles; fls mainly yellow or reddish-bronze, from mid or late summer; cuttable. Good for screens, temporary hedges or back of large borders in full sun. Seeds edible (attract birds).
H. annuus **1**: to 1.8–3×0.3–0.45m (6–10×1–1½ft); unbranching; toothed 30cm (1ft) heart-shaped lvs; fls to 35cm (14in) across.
H. debilis cucumerifolius: to 1×0.45m (3×1½ft); bushy; glossy 8cm (3in) oval lvs; fls 12cm (4in) or more across, disc reddish-purple.
Garden vars derived from one or more spp: 'Autumn Beauty' ('Color Fashion'; to 1.2–1.8m [4–6ft]; branching; yellow, red & bronze 15cm [6in] fls); 'Dwarf Sungold' (to 60cm [2ft]; bushy; double 10cm [4in] yellow fls); 'Italian White' **2** (to 1.2–1.5m [4–5ft]; branching; 10cm [4in] white & primrose fls, dark disk); 'Piccolo' (to 1.2m [4ft]; branching; 10cm [4in] golden fls, small dark disc); 'Russian Giant' (to 2.5–3m [8–10ft]; unbranched; yellow 30cm [1ft] fls); 'Sunburst' (to 1.2m [4ft]; branching; 10–15cm [4–6in] fls, shades of yellow, bronze & maroon); 'Sungold' (to 1.8m [6ft]; golden-yellow 15cm [6in] double fls); 'Teddy Bear' (to 60cm [2ft]; bushy; 12cm [5in] v double yellow fls).

Tidy tips (*Layia elegans* **3**; correctly, *L. platyglossa*; Helianthus tribe): bushy HA (spring-sown) with 5cm (2in) yellow daisy fls, petals tipped white. To 45×25cm (18×10in); lvs* grey-green; fls summer & autumn, good for cutting.

Matricaria: see under *Chrysanthemum* (p270).

Giant thistles (*Onopordum* spp; Carduus tribe): tall, branching HB thistles with v spiny silvery-grey lvs; purple 5cm (2in) thistle fls, mid summer (dead-head to prevent self-seeding); for dramatic effect at back of border, in wild garden, etc.
O. acanthium **4** (Scotch or cotton thistle): to 2.5×0.75m (8×2½ft).
O. arabicum (*O. nervosum*, heraldic thistle): to 2.5×0.75m (8×2½ft); thick stems; lvs prominently veined beneath.

Annual rudbeckias & gloriosa daisies
(coneflowers, *Rudbeckia* spp; Helianthus tribe): easy, showy border plants with cone/button-centred daisy fls, mainly yellow & reddish-bronze; good for cutting.
R. bicolor (*R. hirta pulcherrima*): HHA; 60×30cm (2×1ft); small lvs; 8–10cm (3–4in) yellow fls with black cone, mid summer. Var 'Superba' has bolder fls.
R. hirta (black-eyed Susan): short-lived perennial grown as HHA; to 30–90×30–45cm (1–3×1–1½ft); larger lvs; 8cm (3in) golden-yellow fls with maroon or often nearly black centre, late summer & autumn. Normal vars: 'Golden Flame' (to 45cm [1½ft]; profuse large fls); 'Marmalade' (to 60cm [2ft]; fls to 12cm [5in] across); 'Rustic Dwarfs' (to 60cm [2ft]; bushy; fls gold, bronze & mahogany, to 12cm [5in] across). Tetraploid vars (gloriosa

daisies; to 0.75–1.1×0.6m [2½–3½×2ft]; v large fls): 'Double Gloriosa' ('Double Gold'; semi-double golden fls to 11cm [4½in] across); 'Gloriosa' ('Single Gloriosa'; 18cm [7in] single fls, yellow to mahogany shades & bicolours); 'Golden Daisy' (14cm [5½in] golden fls, brown cone); 'Irish Eyes' (12cm [5in] single golden fls, green centre); 'Pinwheel' (single 12cm [5in] fls, mahogany & gold bicolour).

Creeping zinnia (*Sanvitalia procumbens* **6**; Helianthus tribe): HA (autumn-sown in mild areas) for edging, walls, rock gardens, etc, in sun; to 15×15cm (6×6in); trailing; yellow 2cm (¾in) daisy fls, purplish-black disc. Var 'Flore Pleno' is double.

Cinerarias & relatives (*Senecio* spp, some often listed as *Cineraria* spp; Senecio tribe):
S. cineraria (*S.* [*Cineraria*] *bicolor, C. maritima*, silver-leaved cineraria, dusty miller): semi-hardy sub-shrubby perennial usually treated as HHA; to 20–30×30cm (8–12×12in), more as perennial; grown for deeply lobed or dissected silver lvs (make good border contrast); fls yellow, 1cm (½in) across (best removed). Vars: 'Candicans'; 'White Diamond' (white deeply cut lvs); 'Ramparts' **7** (bolder lvs); 'Silver Dust' (v silver fern-like lvs); 'Silver Queen'. For well-drained soil; prone to rot in cold & wet.
S. cruentus (*C. cruenta*, cineraria): tender perennial grown as annual mainly for pots indoors, also outdoors in frost-free areas & for spring window-boxes in sheltered places; to 45×30cm (1½×1ft); colourful daisy fls 2–8cm (¾–3in) across, winter to spring, in shades of pink, carmine, purple & blue, with white zoning.
S. (*Jacobaea*) *elegans* **8**: HHA or HA; to 45×15cm (18×6in); for grouping in borders; showy 2.5cm (1in) purple, crimson or rose daisy fls, yellow disc, summer.

Blessed thistle (Our Lady's milk thistle, St Mary's thistle, *Silybum marianum*; Carduus tribe): HA or HB with bold, attractive foliage for back of border or wild garden; to 1.2×0.6m (4×2ft); rosette of glossy, dark green lvs marbled with white veins; deep violet 5cm (2in) fls, summer.

Marigolds (*Tagetes* spp; Helenium tribe): v easy & most popular of HHAs with long-lasting vivid mahogany-red to pale yellow & near-white fls all summer & autumn. For formal & informal bedding, containers, etc, in full sun; dwarf vars for edging; larger vars good for cutting (remove lvs); all have deeply divided dark green lvs, generally strongly scented; dead-head for longest display.
T. erecta vars (African, American or Aztec marigolds): generally to 60–90×30–45cm (2–3×1–1½ft) but dwarf vars to 25–50×25cm (10–20×10in); vigorous & erect, but more branching if stopped; fls of sp single, but garden vars

double, 8–20cm (3–8in) across, orange to v pale yellow or whitish, mid summer to frosts.
V numerous vars listed in seed catalogues, most with carnation- or chrysanthemum-like fls, largest & most consistent in F1 hybrids **1**.

T. lucida* (sweet-scented marigold): tender perennial grown as HHA; to 45×30cm (1½×1ft); bushy; clusters of 1cm (½in) golden or orange-yellow daisy fls, late summer.

T. patula vars **2** (French marigolds): generally to 20–30×30cm (8–12×12in); compact & bushy; single, semi-double or double fls 4–5cm (1½–2in) or more across, mahogany-red to pale yellow, including bicolours, early summer to frosts. Numerous vars listed in seed catalogues.

T. tenuifolia (*T. signata*, tagetes, signet marigold): to 60cm (2ft), but most garden vars are Pumila type, to 15–25×15cm (6–10×6in); neat & bushy, for edging, containers, etc; v aromatic finely cut fern-like lvs; profuse yellow to orange starry fls, to 2.5cm (1in) across, early summer to frosts. Vars: 'Golden Gem'; 'Lemon Gem'; 'Lulu' (lemon-yellow); 'Paprika' **3** (gold & mahogany-red bicolour); 'Tangerine Gem'.

T. triploid hybrids (Afro-French marigolds, mule marigolds): F1 hybrids of *T. erecta* & *T. patula* vars; do not set own seed; mainly to 25–40×30cm (10–16×12in), with *T. patula* habit but fls large & mainly double like *T. erecta*. Vars 'Legal Gold'; 'Nell Gwyn' (6cm [2½in] single yellow & red fls, early); 'Nugget' series; 'Red & Gold Hybrids' (to 60cm [2ft]; mixed); 'Seven Star Red' **4** (mahogany-red tinged gold); 'Showboat' (bright yellow).

Mexican sunflower (*Tithonia rotundifolia, T. speciosa*; Helianthus tribe): tall heat-resistant HHA for background planting in full sun; to 1–1.2×0.6–1m (3–4×2–3ft); rather coarse habit; lvs to 30cm (1ft) long; 8–10cm (3–4in) orange-red daisy fls, mid summer to frosts; good for cutting if stems seared. Best var is 'Torch' **5**.

Ursinias (*Ursinia* spp; Anthemis tribe; formerly classed in Arctotis tribe): showy S African HHAs or tender perennials treated thus, for bedding, mixed borders, pots, etc, in sun. Lvs divided, fern-like; 5cm (2in) daisy fls, mainly orange, all summer; cuttable but close at night.

U. (*Sphenogyne*) *anethoides*: best-known sp; to 45×30cm (1½×1ft); fls orange-yellow, purple zone & disc. Var 'Sunstar' has vivid fls with claret-red zone.

U. anthemoides: to 30×20cm (12×10in); purple reverse to petals. Var 'Golden Bedder' has orange disc.

U. cakilifolia: to 30×15cm (12×6in); similar to *U. anethoides*, but hardier & lvs fleshier.

Namaqualand daisies (*Venidium* spp; Arctotis tribe): colourful S African HHAs or tender perennials grown as HHAs; showy, with large daisy fls, early summer to frosts; good for cutting

but close at night; lvs grey-green or silvery, deeply lobed. For full sun.

V. decurrens (*V. calendulaceum*): to 30×30cm (1×1ft); spreading; lvs form rosette; 6cm (2½in) golden-yellow fls with pale zoning & brown disc.

V. fastuosum **6** (Cape daisy, monarch of the veldt): can be treated as HA in mild areas; to 60×30cm (2×1ft); 10cm (4in) glistening orange fls with purplish zone & black disc.

Zinnias (*Zinnia* spp; Helianthus tribe): distinctive & popular summer bedding & border plants from Mexico, also good for containers & cutting; fls single, semi-double & fully double, in wide colour range, all summer to frosts. For well-drained but moist fertile soil in full sun; HHA, but resent root disturbance, so best treated as HA, sowing after frosts; or prick out seedlings into pots under glass & plant our v carefully. Prone to virus & fungal diseases.

Z. angustifolia (*Z. linearis*): to 40×20cm (16×8in); neat narrow lvs; profuse 4cm (1½in) single golden-orange fls. 'Classic' is good var.

Z. elegans (common zinnia): most vars to 60–90×30–45cm (2–3×1–1½ft), but dwarfs to 15–40×20–25cm (6–16×8–10in); fls 4–18cm (1½–7in) across. V numerous vars in several groups, including following (unless stated, double, mixed colours; vars marked † are F1 hybrids):
Giant cactus-fld types (to 60–75cm [2–2½ft]; fls to 18cm [7in] across, petals quilled): 'Big Snowman' (white); 'Big Top' series† (various colours); 'Fruit Bowl'† **7**; 'Zenith' series† (various & mixed colours).
Dahlia-fld types (to 50–75cm [20–30in]; fls to 10cm [4in] across): 'Envy' (chartreuse-green); 'Gold Sun'†; 'Pacific Yellow'†; 'Red Sun'† **8**; 'State Fair' (tetraploid).
Dwarf vars (to 40cm [16in]; fls generally to 4cm [1½in] across): 'Buttons' series, including 'Button Box'; 'Classic' (single, golden-orange); 'Peter Pan'† **9** (various & mixed; 8cm [3in] fls); 'Pulcino'; 'Thumbelina' (to 15cm [6in]).
Other vars: 'Bouquet Hybrids'† (to 60cm [2ft]; semi-ruffled 9cm [3½in] fls; various & mixed); 'Candy Cane' (to 45cm [1½ft]; striped bicolour 9cm [3½in] fls); 'Chippendale Daisy' (dwarf; bicoloured mahogany & yellow 5cm [2in] single fls); 'Early Wonder' (to 45cm [1½ft]; 8cm [3in] double fls, v early); 'Lilliput' ('Pompon'; to 60cm [2ft]; 5cm [2in] pompon fls); 'Ruffles' series† (to 75cm [2½ft]; 8cm [3in] ruffled fls; various & mixed); 'Sombrero' (dwarf; bicoloured red & gold 6cm [2½in] single fls).

Z. haageana (*Z. mexicana*, Mexican zinnia; incorrectly, *Z. angustifolia*): to 40×30cm (16×12in); vars have double & semi-double bicoloured fls with contrasting petal edges & tips. Vars: 'Old Mexico' (tetraploid; 5cm [2½in] mahogany & gold fls); 'Persian Carpet' **10** (4cm [1½in] fls; mixed).

Moonflowers and morning glories

Cultivated relatives of bindweeds; showy annuals or tender perennials mostly grown as half-hardy annuals. Mainly twining climbers with trumpet-shaped, profuse but often transient flowers from mid summer. Leaves usually heart-shaped. Excellent for temporary screening, shade (on pergola) or ground cover. **Cultivation**: For rich, light soil in full sun; provide support. Chip seed to aid germination. Dead-head.

Dwarf morning glory (*Convolvulus tricolor, C. minor*): bushy, to 20–30×30–40cm (8–12×12–16in); dark green lvs; fls to 4cm (1½in) wide, shades of blue or red. Excellent for tubs, window boxes. Can be treated as HA. Vars: 'Blue Flash' (dwarf; blue centred yellow & white); 'Cambridge Blue' (pale blue); 'Crimson Monarch' (cherry-red); 'Minibar Rose' **1** (white-variegated lvs; rose fls edged & centred white); 'Royal Ensign' **2** (royal-blue centred gold & white).

Ipomoeas (true morning glories & relatives, *Ipomoea* spp): nomenclature confused; various spp sometimes listed under *Calonyction, Convolvulus, Mina, Pharbitis, Quamoclit.* Climbers spreading to 1-2m (3–7ft).

I. alba** (*Calonyction aculeatum, I. bona-nox, I. noctiflora, I. roxburghii,* moonflower, moonvine): tender (minimum night temperature 10°C [50°F]); to 3m (10ft); lvs to 20cm (8in) long; fls pure white, to 15cm (6in) across, open at night. Good in tub.

I. (*Q.*) *coccinea* **3** (*M. sanguinea*, red morning glory, star ipomoea): to 1.5–2.5m (5–8ft); lvs to 15cm (6in) long; scarlet starry fls, yellow throat, to 4cm (1½in) long. Var *hederifolia* (correctly, *I. hederifolia*) has lobed lvs.

I.×multifida (*I. cardinalis, Q.×sloteri,* cardinal climber): hybrid of I. coccinea & *I. quamoclit*; to 2.5m (8ft); deeply divided lvs to 11cm (4½in) across; white-centred crimson fls to 5cm (2in) long.

I. hederacea: to 3m (10ft); lvs generally 3-lobed, to 9cm (3½in) long; fls blue or pale purple, to 5cm (2in) long, narrow sepals. May become weedy.

I. (*Convolvulus, P.*) *nil* (Japanese morning glory): to 3m (10ft); shallowly lobed lvs to 15cm (6in) across; fls showy, violet, rose or blue, sometimes fluted & fringed, to 5cm (2in) across. Vars: 'Limbata' (violet-purple edged white); 'Scarlett O'Hara' (large scarlet fls).

I. (*P.*) *purpurea* **4** (*Convolvulus major*, common morning glory): vigorous, to 3m (10ft) or more; lvs to 12cm (5in) long; white, red or purple fls to 8cm (3in) across. Can be weedy.

I. quamoclit (*Q. pennata*, cypress vine; incorrectly, cardinal climber): to 6m (20ft); finely divided lvs; racemes of red & yellow fls to 4cm (1½in) long.

I. tricolor (*I.* [*P.*] *rubro-coerulea, I. violacea*): to 2.5m (8ft); lvs to 25cm (10in) wide; fls to 10cm (4in) long, reddish-purple to blue, yellow throat. Vars: 'Early Call' (rosy-pink, white throat; v early); 'Flying Saucers' **5** (flattened fls, striped blue & white); 'Heavenly Blue' (sky-blue, white throat; early); 'Pearly Gates' (pure white centred cream & gold); 'Wedding Bells (rosy-lavender).

Crimson star glory (*Mina* [*Ipomoea, Quamoclit*] *lobata*): vigorous climber, to 3×1m (10×3ft) or more; lvs heart-shaped to 3-lobed, to 8cm (3in) across; racemes of small crimson fls fading orange & yellow (cuttable).

Wallflowers, stocks and their relatives

Mostly free-flowering annuals & biennials with showy cross-shaped flowers, some very fragrant, good for bedding & often cutting. Best where summers cool. **Cultivation**: Unless stated, for neutral or alkaline, rich soil in full sun. Prone to cabbage root fly, flea beetle, club root.

Sweet alyssum (*Alyssum maritimum***; correctly, *I obularia maritima*): dwarf perennial grown as HA or HHA; excellent for edging. Bushy & spreading, to 8–15×20–30cm (3–6×8–12in); narrow lvs; profuse tiny white, lilac or purple fls in dense racemes, all summer. Vars: 'Lilac Queen'* (pale lilac); 'Little Dorrit'** ('Little Gem'; dwarf; white); 'Minimum'* **6** ('Snow Carpet'; v dwarf; white); 'Oriental Night'* (brilliant purple/violet); 'Pink Heather'* (lavender-pink); 'Rosie O'Day'* **7** (rose); 'Royal Carpet'* (v dwarf; deep purple); 'Tiny Tim'* (v early; white); 'Violet Queen'* **8** (violet-purple); 'Wonderland'* (rose-carmine).

Ornamental kale & cabbage (*Brassica oleracea* vars): colourful forms of common vegetables grown for decorative leaves (good in arrangements); edible. Generally sold as mixtures.

B. o. acephala vars **9** (ornamental or "flowering" kale): biennial grown as HA or HHA; to 30×30cm (1×1ft); rosettes of frilled lvs, white, pink or purple (darker if frosted). Good for winter bedding (moderately to v hardy) or pots.

B. o. capitata vars **10** (ornamental or "flowering" cabbage): biennial grown as HHA for summer & autumn bedding; to 30×30–45cm (1×1–1½ft);

crinkled lvs variegated white, pink/purple in centre, or suffused red.

Wallflowers (*Cheiranthus* spp): short-lived perennials generally grown as HBs for spring/ early summer bedding; propagate good forms by cuttings.

C. (*Erysimum*)×*allionii** (Siberian wallflower; may be listed as *E. asperum*; probably correctly derived from *E. hieraciifolium*): ultra-hardy; to 40×30cm (16×12in); lvs lance-shaped; spikes of yellow to orange fls 1cm (½in) across, late spring to mid summer. Vars: 'Apricot Delight' (apricot-pink); 'Golden Bedder' **1** ('Golden Queen'); 'Orange Queen'.

C. cheiri* (common or English wallflower): v hardy; bushy, to 20–60×25–40cm (8–24×10– 16in); lance-shaped lvs to 8cm (3in) long; dense spikes of yellow to deep crimson fls to 2.5cm (1in) across, mid spring to early summer. Vars (dwarfs marked †): 'Blood Red'; 'Carmine King'; 'Cloth of Gold' (golden-yellow); 'Eastern Queen' **2** (beige flushed pink); 'Fire King' (brilliant scarlet); 'Golden Bedder'†; 'Harpur Crewe'† (double yellow; sterile; raise from cuttings); 'Ivory White'; 'Orange Bedder'†; 'Persian Carpet' (pastel shades); 'Primrose Bedder'† (yellow); 'Ruby Gem' (deep red); 'Scarlet Bedder'†; 'Scarlet Emperor'; 'Tom Thumb Mixed'†; 'Vulcan' **3** (crimson).

Alpine wallflowers (*Erysimum* spp; often listed under *Cheiranthus* spp): short-lived perennials usually grown as HBs; like small wallflowers, with dense heads of 4-petalled fls, spring to summer.

E. asperum (*E. arkansanum*, prairie rocket): ultra-hardy; to 90×60cm (3×2ft); lance-shaped lvs to 10cm (4in) long; fls yellow to orange. Var 'Golden Gem' is dwarf, to 20×15cm (8×6in).

E. (C.) linifolium **4**: moderately hardy; to 45×30cm (1½×1ft); lilac-mauve to violet fls.

Cape stock (*Heliophila longifolia* **5**): HHA for massed planting; to 45×30cm (1½×1ft); narrow lvs 5–25cm (2–10in) long; racemes of fls to 1cm (½in) wide, blue centred white or yellow, mid to late summer.

Candytuft (*Iberis* spp): popular summer-flg spring/autumn-sown HAs or HHAs good for sunny borders on poor soils; tolerate air pollution. Lance-shaped lvs; fl profusely if dead-headed.

I. amara* (*I. coronaria*, rocket candytuft): to 40×15cm (16×6in); white fls in 5–8cm (2–3in) racemes, v good for cutting. Vars: 'Giant Hyacinth-Flowered White'; 'Improved White Spiral' (to 30cm [1ft]).

I. umbellata (common or globe candytuft): to 15–40×25cm (6–16×10in); fls white or pink/ purple shades in flattish umbels; good for edging or rock garden. Vars: 'Albida' (pure white); 'Lilacina' (soft lavender-blue); 'Pink Queen' **6** (pale pink to rose); 'Red Flash' (vivid carmine).

Violet cress (diamond flower, *Ionopsidium*

acaule): HA good for rock gardens, gaps in paving, etc. Creeping, to 8×15cm (3×6in); small, long-stalked lvs; profuse small mauve or white solitary fls all summer. Best in moist soil in part-shade; self-seeds.

Dyer's woad (*Isatis tinctoria* **7**): short-lived perennial grown as HB; erect branching, to 1×0.45m (3×1½ft); oblong lvs to 10cm (4in) long (source of blue dye); erect racemes of small bright yellow fls, early summer. For any soil.

Honesty (money plant, moonwort, satin flower, *Lunaria annua, L. biennis*): HB (sometimes HA) grown for its purple or whitish late spring fls and papery silver disc-shaped frs. To 75×30cm (2½×1ft); lvs coarsely toothed; fls 1cm (½in) across, in loose racemes; frs 2.5cm (1in) across. Best in semi-shade; self-seeds. Vars: 'Munstead Purple Giant'; 'Variegata' **8** (variegated lvs).

Virginia stock (*Malcolmia maritima** **9**): quick HA; to 15–30×10–15cm (6–12×4–6in); grey-green lvs; 1cm (½in) fls, red, lilac, rose or white, from spring (sow in succession). Self-seeds.

Stocks (*Matthiola* spp): popular fragrant annuals & biennials for beds, borders, containers, cutting.

M. bicornis** (night-scented or evening stock; correctly, *M. longipetala bicornis*): HA; rather straggly, to 30–40×20cm (12–16×8in); greyish lvs; fls lilac, open in evenings, summer. Best interplanted with, eg, Virginia stock.

M. incana** (stock, gillyflower): moderately hardy biennial or short-lived perennial, Vars variable, to 30–75×30cm (1–2½×1ft); upright or bushy; downy grey-green narrow lvs; dense erect racemes of 2.5cm (1in) fls, most colours except true blue & orange (sold as separate colours & mixtures), good for cutting. All vars are mixed single & double (latter best for display & cutting), but selectable strains of most types available (generally, pale green seedlings are double, dark green single so long as grown below 10°C [50°F]; in Trysomic strains, sturdier seedlings are double). Vars: 3 main categories. Brompton vars are true biennials (overwintered under glass in cold areas) for spring flg; to 45–60cm (1½–2ft). Intermediate (East Lothian) vars can be treated like Bromptons for spring display outdoors or as winter pot-plants indoors, or as HHAs (winter-sown) to fl outdoors mid–late summer (after true annual vars); to 40–45cm (16–18in); v good for cutting. Annual vars (treated as HHAs or HAs for summer bedding) comprise 3 main sub-groups. Trysomic (Seven-Week) vars **10** are bushy & sturdy, to 30–45cm (1–1½ft) fl 7–8 weeks from sowing; high proportion of doubles. Ten-Week vars fl 10–12 weeks from sowing; varied size & habit, most bushy but 'Excelsior' **11** ('Column') strain are tall, with solitary dense infls, best for cutting. 'Beauty' ('Beauty of Nice') vars are bushy, to 45cm (1½ft), fl 14–16 weeks from sowing.

Ornamental gourds

Half-hardy annual tendrilled climbers related to cucumber & pumpkin, grown for their curiously shaped, often warty fruits, good when dried for arrangements. Leaves generally lobed. Flowers white or yellow, sexes separate (hand-pollinate to ensure fruiting; females have bulbous base). **Cultivation**: For moist fertile soil in full sun. Provide support; pinch out growing tip when tall enough. Pick fruits when fully ripe.

Small gourds (yellow-flowered gourds, *Cucurbita pepo ovifera* vars **1**): to 3–6m (10–20ft); lvs to 10–15cm (4–6in) across; large yellow fls; frs generally 5–25cm (2–10in) across, mainly green, yellow &/or orange. Sold in mixtures and various shapes: 'Apple-Shaped'; 'Miniature Bottle'; 'Orange'; 'Pear-Shaped'; 'Petit Turban Aladdin'; 'Small Warted'; 'Spoon' (ball-shaped, long neck).

Wild or mock cucumber (*Echinocystis lobata* **2**): vigorous, to 6m (20ft); lvs to 12cm (5in) wide; small greenish-white fls; frs spiny, to 5cm (2in) long. Good for hiding ugly objects.

Large or calabash gourds (white-flowered gourds, *Lagenaria siceraria** [*L. vulgaris, L. leucantha*] vars): to 3–9m (10–30ft); lvs not lobed; large white fls; frs to 1m (3ft) long, generally bottle/club-shaped; best in long warm summers. Vars: 'Calabash' ('Bottle'; white); 'Caveman's Club' (knobbly); 'Dipper' ('Siphon'; long-necked, pale green); 'Hercules Club' (*L. longissima*; v long); 'Powder Horn' ('Penguin'; curved neck); 'Turk's Turban' **3**.

Loofah (dishcloth or sponge gourd, *Luffa aegyptiaca, L. cylindrica*): to 3m (10ft); large yellow or whitish fls; frs narrow, to 60cm (2ft) long, pale green, (sponge-like loofah is dried fibrous interior). Needs long hot summer.

Annual grasses

Ornamental spp & vars of annual wild grasses grown for both their foliage & their feathery flower- & seed-heads (from mid summer). Useful for breaking up colour masses & for vertical accent in borders, & for cutting for dried arrangements (cut before fully mature; dry in dark; dye if desired). Tufted. Leaves generally narrow. **Cultivation**: Generally for any well-drained soil in full sun. Treat as hardy annuals unless stated.

Cloud grass (cloud bent, *Agrostis nebulosa*; sometimes incorrectly listed as *A. capillaris*): to 30–45×15cm (12–18×6in); slender, branching; lvs scant; graceful open panicles of v small white fls, giving dainty & haze-like effect.

Animated oat (*Avena sterilis*): to 60–90×30cm (2–3×1ft); spikelets & seed-heads in open 30cm (1ft) panicles, awns to 6cm (2½in) long (twist & flex with changes of moisture in air).

Quaking grass (*Briza* spp): spikelets oval to heart-shaped, drooping & trembling on thin stalks.
B. maxima **4** (greater quaking grass, pearl grass): to 40–60×30cm (16–24×12in); bright green lvs; spikelets 1.5–2.5cm (½–1in) long, silvery, brown & purple.
B. minor (*B. gracilis, B. minima,* lesser quaking grass): to 30×20cm (12×8in); spikelets to 3mm (⅛in) long.

Job's tears (*Coix lacryma-jobi* **5**): HHA; to 60–90×30cm (2–3×1ft) or taller; lvs to 4cm (1½in) wide; drooping clusters of hard-shelled white, grey, brown or black seeds to 1cm (⅜in) long, summer. Soak seeds before sowing.

Love grasses (*Eragrostis* spp): to 60–90×30cm (2–3×1ft).
E. amabilis (feather or Japanese love grass): lvs short; slender panicles to 45cm (1½ft) long; spikelets v small.

E. tef (*E. abyssinica*, teff): lvs long, narrow; loose, open panicles to 30cm (1ft) long; seeds edible.
Squirrel-tail grass (*Hordeum jubatum* **6**): perennial grown as HA; to 75×30cm (2½×1ft); lvs rough & sharp-pointed; drooping 10cm (4in) seed-heads with slender awns to 8cm (3in) long.
Hare's-tail grass (rabbit's-tail grass, *Lagurus ovatus* **7**): to 30–60×15cm (12–24×6in); lvs narrow, soft, hairy; dense woolly white seed heads to 5cm (2in) long. Best in warm areas.
Natal grass (ruby grass, wine grass, *Tricholaena rosea*; correctly *Rhynchelytrum repens*): short-lived perennial grown as HA; clump-forming, to 1–1.2×0.45m (3–4×1½ft); silky infls to 25cm (10in) long, purplish-red fading to pink & silver.
Ornamental corn or maize (*Zea mays* vars): ornamental vars of sweet corn (corn-on-the-cob) grown for coloured lvs or frs (cobs). HHA or HA; to 1–1.5×0.3m (3–5×1ft); broad strap-shaped lvs on stout stems; male fls (tassels) at top, female in lf axils (best hand-pollinated to ensure cobs); seeds not usually edible. Vars: 'Gracillima Variegata' (dwarf; lvs narrow, striped white); *japonica* **8** ('Japonica Variegata', 'Quadricolor'; v tall; lvs variegated yellow, white & often pink); 'Rainbow' **9** ('Calico'; lvs green; seeds yellow, red, orange & purplish; cobs good dried for arrangements); 'Strawberry Popcorn' **10** (dwarf; rounded red cobs to 4cm [1½in] long.

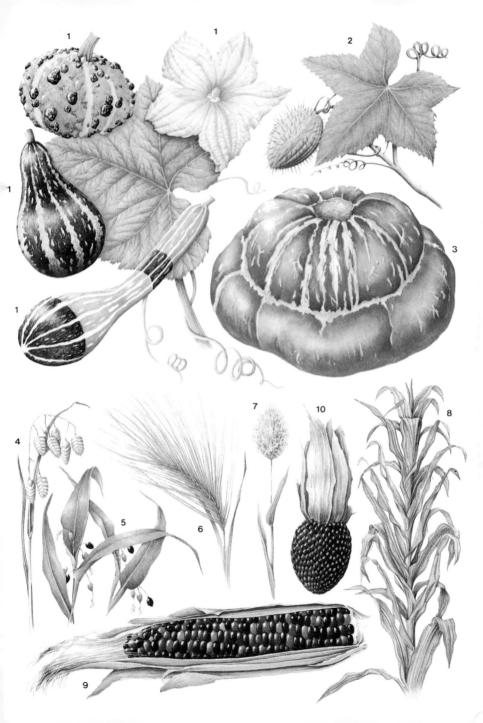

Nemophila and phacelia

Easy hardy annuals of Californian origin with striking flowers, usually vivid blue. **Cultivation**: Best in full sun. Sow spring, or autumn in warm climates for spring display.

Nemophila (*Nemophila* spp): to 20×15cm (8×6in); profuse saucer-shaped 2.5–4cm (1–1½in) fls, early–mid summer. For rock gardens, edging.
N. maculata (five-spot nemophila): fls white, veined & blotched purple. Prefers moist soil.
N. menziesii **1** (*N. insignis*, baby blue-eyes): feathery lvs; sky-blue white-centred fls (all-white in var 'Alba').
Phacelia (*Phacelia* spp): lvs rather fleshy; fls bell-shaped, to 2–2.5cm (¾–1in) wide, showiest when massed in borders; fl all summer where suited, but only for short spring season where summers v hot; attract bees.
P. campanularia **2** (California bluebell): to 25×15cm (10×6in); red-edged oval toothed lvs*, fls gentian-blue. For dry, poor soil. 'Blue Bonnet' is good var.
P. tanacetifolia (tansy phacelia; in US, wild heliotrope): to 60×30cm (2×1ft) or more; hairy; finely divided dark green lvs; lavender-blue fls.
P. (*Eutoca*) *viscida* (sticky phacelia): to 60×30cm (2×1ft) or more; sticky-hairy; roundish toothed lvs; deep blue fls, blue-speckled white throat.

Coleus, salvias and their relatives

Sun-lovers with erect flower heads & generally nettle-like leaves, often superbly coloured or felted & main decorative feature, some pungently fragrant. Useful for bedding or for gaps in borders. **Cultivation**: For most soils in full sun.

Coleus (flame nettle, painted nettle, *Coleus× hybridus* vars **3**; usually listed as *C. blumei*, but in fact hybrids derived from several spp): tender sub-shrubby perennials usually grown as HHAs (sow early) for summer bedding & containers (also pots under glass). To 20–60×20–60cm (8–24×8–24in); grown for nettle-like lvs, 4–15cm (1½–6in) long, brilliantly coloured/variegated in shades of green, yellow, bronze, red, pink, white & purple, deepest in full sun; blue & white fls, rather insignificant & best removed. Pinch back seedlings to induce bushy habit; best colour forms can be propagated by cuttings. Sold as mixtures and colour series: 'Carefree' series (dwarf; scalloped oak-like lvs); 'Dragon' series (medium; large serrated lvs); 'Fashion Parade' (mixed colours & shapes); 'Fiji' (medium-tall; bright colours, fringed); 'Old Lace' series (tall; lvs deeply cut & ruffled); 'Rainbow' series (tall; wide colour range); 'Saber' series (dwarf; base-branching; narrow pointed lvs); 'Seven Dwarfs' (dwarf 'Rainbow' type); 'Wizard' series (like 'Seven Dwarfs' but lvs larger).
Bells of Ireland (shell flower, *Molucella laevis**
4): HHA; to 60×25cm (24×10in); spikes of small white fls with apple-green shell-like calyces; good for cutting/drying.
Basil (sweet basil, *Ocimum basilicum*): HHA culinary herb; to 60×30cm (2×1ft); neat & bushy, with oval glossy lvs*, insignificant white or purplish fls (best removed). Best ornamental var is 'Dark Opal' (dark metallic-purple; goes well with silver-lvd plants, white fls).
Perilla (*Perilla frutescens, P. ocimoides*): HHA grown for foliage; to 60×30cm (2×1ft); toothed oval lvs* 8–15cm (3–6in) long, green or (usually) purplish (associate well with silver foliage). Vars: 'Atropurpurea Laciniata' (bronze-purple deeply cut lvs); 'Crispa' ('Nankinensis'; bronze or purple lvs, wrinkled edges).
Ornamental sages (*Salvia* spp): variable group grown for decorative lvs, bracts or showy fls.
S. argentea (silver sage): moderately hardy perennial usually grown as HB; to 60×60cm (2×2ft); clump of toothed, densely silver-haired lvs; branching stems with pink-tinged white fls, whitish calyces, summer.
S. farinacea (mealy-cup sage): semi-hardy perennial usually grown as HHA; to 60–90×45cm (2–3×1½ft); narrowish lvs; graceful spikes of generally blue fls, powdered calyces, summer to autumn. Vars: 'Blue Bedder'; 'Blue Spike'; 'Catima' (v dark blue); 'Victoria' **5** (to 45cm [1½ft]; violet-blue); 'White Bedder'.
S. horminum (commonly but incorrectly, clary; correctly, *S. viridis*): true H/HHA; to 45×20cm (18×8in); infls of pinkish fls, large colourful bracts, all summer (can be dried). Sold as various red-, pink-, white- & blue-bracted vars & mixtures, including 'Bouquet Mixed' **6**.
S. patens **7** (gentian sage): semi-hardy perennial often grown as HHA; to 60–75×30cm (2–2½×1ft) spikes of dark/gentian-blue fls, from mid summer (paler in var 'Cambridge Blue').
S. sclarea (true clary): HB culinary herb often grown as HA; to 75–90×30cm (2½–3×1ft); hairy lvs* to 20cm (8in) long; branching infls of bluish fls; blue, purple, pink or white bracts, mid summer.
S. splendens **8** (scarlet sage): best-known sp;

semi-hardy sub-shrubby perennial usually grown as HHA for bedding; to 25–60×20–40cm (10–24×8–14in), more as perennial; toothed dark green lvs; erect racemes of usually bright red fls & bracts, early/mid summer to frosts. Numerous dwarf (20–25cm [8–10in]), medium-sized (30–40cm [12–16in]) & tall (45cm [1½ft] or more)

vars with scarlet to red fls, also purple. Other vars: 'Dress Parade' (medium; mixed colours including pastels); 'Panorama' ('Sight Delight'; medium; mixed colours including pastels); 'Rose Flame' (tall; coral-rose); 'Royal Purple' (medium; deep purple); 'White Fire' (medium; creamy-white).

The pea family

Sun-lovers with typical pea flowers & compound leaves with 2–7 leaflets. Several are tendrilled or twining climbers giving quick colourful screen &/or excellent cut flowers. Some have decorative or edible pod fruits. Bacteria in root nodules enrich soil with nitrogen. **Cultivation**: For well-drained soil in full sun; sow spring after chipping &/or soaking seeds in water. Provide support (eg, twiggy sticks, strings, netting) for climbers. For *Pueraria lobata* (perennial often grown as HHA), see p232.

Rattle-box (golden sweet pea, *Crotalaria retusa* **1**): HHA for areas with long hot summers; to 90×30cm (3×1ft); tall racemes of showy golden-yellow fls, 2.5cm (1in) across, streaked red, mid summer (good for cutting); pods contain loose seeds. Needs rich soil, long growing season.

Hyacinth bean (Indian bean, lablab bean, *Dolichos lablab*): semi-hardy sub-shrubby perennial climber usually grown as HA (sown after last frost) or HHA (sown in peat pots; resents root disturbance). Vigorous tendrilled climber, to 3–9m (10–30ft); decorative triangular lfts to 15×15cm (6×6in), sometimes used in salads; tall racemes of purple or white fls, mid summer; 6cm (2½in) pods containing black or white bean-like seeds (edible when cooked).

Sweet pea (*Lathyrus odoratus***): long-favoured H/HHA tendrilled climber (some vars non-climbing) flg all summer (if dead-headed) where night temperatures usually drop below 20°C (68°F). Paired oval lfts; infls of up to 7 delicate-looking 2.5–5cm (1–2in) fls, petals often wavy, in most colours except true yellow & orange. Most vars superb for cutting; also good for screening, etc; dwarf types for beds & borders, flg hedge. Best in deep, rich, neutral or alkaline soil; sow early autumn where winters warm, otherwise autumn or spring; pinch out seedlings to induce branching; mulch, water & feed; dead-head. Numerous vars, generally sold as mixtures in various types/groups, some as colour series &/or individual named vars (selection listed). TALL-GROWING TYPES (to 1.8–3m [6–10ft]): Cuthbertson Floribunda type (v early; medium-sized fls; heat-resistant & best in warm climates or under glass); Galaxy type (vigorous, with infls of 5–7 fls, long season; heat resistant; vars include: 'Amigo' [salmon to coral-pink]; 'Angel Face' [cream edged rose]; 'Blue Argo'* **2**; Cream Whiz'; 'Fancy Free' [cream flushed shell-pink]; 'Great Britain'* **3** [cream flushed rose-pink]; 'Lavender Delight'; 'Scarlet Whiz' [bright scarlet]; also mixtures); Grandiflora** type **4**

(often sold as 'Old Fashioned', etc; rather small fls but strongest scent); Multiflora Gigantea type (vigorous & early, with large infls of 5–6 or more large fls); Royal type ('Royal Family'; similar to Cutherbertson Floribunda but fls larger; early; heat-resistant); Spencer type (v large fls, 4–5 per stem, in wide colour range; v good for cutting, exhibition; vars include: 'Air Warden'* **5** [cerise-scarlet]; 'Beaujolais' **6** [maroon]; 'Carlotta'* [carmine]; 'Elizabeth Taylor'* [mauve]; 'Festival'* [cream-pink]; 'Geranium Pink' [rose suffused salmon]; 'Hunter's Moon'** **7** [deep cream]; 'Leamington'** **8** [deep lilac]; 'Mrs C. Kay' [lavender]; 'Noel Sutton'* [blue]; 'Old Times'** [cream flushed blue]; 'Red Ensign' [bright scarlet]; 'Rosy Frills'** [white edged rose]; 'Southbourne'* [clear pink, white base]; 'Swan Lake' [white]; 'White Ensign'*; 'Winston Churchill' [crimson]).

DWARF & SEMI-DWARF TYPES (support rarely needed; sold as mixtures): 'Bijou' **9** (to 45cm [1½ft]; early; heat-resistant); 'Jet Set' (to 90cm [3ft]); 'Knee-Hi' (to 60–75cm [2–2½ft]); 'Little Elfin' ('Zvolanek'; to 75cm [2½ft]; heat-resistant); 'Little Sweetheart' (to 30cm [1ft]; good for containers); 'Patio' (to 40cm [16in]); 'Snoopea' (to 60cm [2ft]; sprawling, with no tendrils).

Annual lupins (*Lupinus* spp): HAs; generally to 90×30cm (3×1ft); spikes of summer fls. Easy. *L. hartwegii*: white, rose or blue fls, repeat if cut down after 1st flg. Var 'Pixie' **10** is dwarf, to 30–45cm (1–1½ft).

L. pubescens: downy; fls violet-blue & white. *L. texensis* **11** (Texas blue-bonnet): hairy; blue fls marked white or yellow. *L. subcarnosus* is similar.

Scarlet runner (runner bean, *Phaseolus coccineus, P. multiflorus*): tender perennial treated as H/HHA; grown as ornamental in hot-summer areas. Climber, to 1.8–4.5m (6–15ft); deep green lvs; clusters of brilliant scarlet fls, mid–late summer. Best on rich, moist soil; prone to aphids. Var *albus* has white fls.

Hollyhocks and mallows

Sun-loving, free-flowering plants with showy funnel-shaped flowers, single or double, some enormous (though transient), often with prominent stamens. **Cultivation**: Generally for light soil.

Hollyhocks (*Althaea* spp; correctly, *Alcea* spp): ultra-hardy biennials or perennials best grown as HBs or HHAs. Tall, for vertical effect towards rear of borders. Best in rich, heavy, moist soil sheltered by wall, etc; stake tall/exposed plants. Prone to rust, especially if grown as perennials.
A. ficifolia (fig-leaf or Antwerp hollyhock): to 1.8×0.6m (6×2ft); lvs deeply lobed; spikes of single or double yellow fls 8–10cm (3–4in) wide, early summer. Treat as HB; partly rust-resistant.
A. rosea (*A. chinensis*, garden hollyhock): to 1.5–2.75×0.6m (5–9×2ft) as biennial/perennial, shorter as annual; rough hairy lvs, shallowly lobed; spikes of single or double fls to 10cm (4in) or more across, summer, in shades of red, pink, purple, yellow, cream & white. Semi/double vars (mixtures &/or separate colours; v early [HHA] vars marked †): 'Chater's Double' (paeony-fld); 'Majorette'† **1** (to 75cm [2½ft]; fringed fls); 'Powderpuff'; 'Silver Puffs'† (to 75cm [2½ft]; silvery-pink); 'Summer Carnival'† **2**.
Annual hibiscus (rose mallows, *Hibiscus* spp): tender to moderately hardy perennials generally grown as HHAs. Showy plants with v large though transient fls, mid–late summer. May self-seed.
H. (correctly, *Abelmoschus*) *manihot* (sunset hibiscus): to 1.8×0.6m (6×2ft); large deeply lobed lvs to 45cm (1½ft) long; creamy-yellow fls to 20cm (8in) across, maroon centre. Good for screening.

H. moscheutos hybrids (may be listed incorrectly as *H. grandiflorus*): moderately hardy perennial F1 hybrids with various *H.* spp used mainly for bedding or pots; fls 20–25cm (8–10in) across, red, rose, pink or white, some with red eye. Vars (to 60–75×60cm [2–2½×2ft] unless stated): 'Dixie Belle'; 'Frisbee'; 'Rio Carnival'; 'Southern Belle' **3** (to 1.5×1.5m [5×5ft]).
H. trionum **4** (*H. africanus*, flower-of-an-hour): to 75×30cm (2½×1ft); dark green lvs; profuse maroon-eyed creamy-yellow fls 8cm (3in) across, v short-lived. Can be treated as HA.
Lavateras (mallows, *Lavatera* spp): bushy, with maple-like lvs & single hollyhock-like fls.
L. arborea **5** (tree mallow): moderately hardy biennial treated as HB (with winter protection if necessary) or HHA; to 1.8×0.45m (6×1½ft); pale purple 5cm (2in) fls, dark veins, mid summer. Good for wild & coastal gardens; self-seeds.
L. trimestris (*L. rosea*, annual mallow): HA (spring/autumn-sown) or HHA; to 1.2×0.45m (4×1½ft); profuse rose-pink 10cm (4in) fls, mid–late summer. Vars: 'Loveliness' (deep rose); 'Mont Blanc' **6** (white); 'Silver Cup' **7** (silvery-pink, scarlet veins); 'Tanagra' (cerise).
Malope (mallow-wort, *Malope trifida* 'Grandiflora' **8**): HA; to 1×0.3m (3×1ft); mid green lvs; trumpet-shaped fls 5–8cm (2–3in) wide, deep purple-rose with dark veins, all summer (good for cutting). Vars 'Alba' (white); 'Rosea' (rose-red).

Clarkias, godetias and evening primroses

Showy hardy border annuals & biennials with cup/funnel-shaped flowers (some double; most good for cutting). **Cultivation**: For light soil in sun; *Clarkia* & *Godetia* spp best where summers cool. Sow annuals spring or (for earlier flowers) autumn, protecting over winter with cloches where cold.

Clarkias (*Clarkia* spp): slender-stemmed HAs with leafy spikes of semi-double fls, mainly white, pink, red or lavender, mid–late summer.
C. (*Eucharidium*) *concinna* (red ribbons): to 40×20cm (16×8in); bright pink 2.5cm (1in) fls (deep rose-pink in var 'Pink Ribbons').
C. elegans **9** (correctly, *C. unguiculata*); to 60×30cm (2×1ft); fls of vars generally double, to 5cm (2in) across, in wide colour range.
C. pulchella: to 30–45×30cm (1–1½×1ft); white, mauve to carmine frilled fls. 'Filigree' is good var.
Godetias (satin flowers, *Godetia* spp; correctly, *Clarkia* spp): v showy HAs with bright fls, glossy petals, early–mid summer. Like moist soil.
G. (*C.*) *amoena* (farewell-to-spring): to 60×30cm (2×1ft); fls lilac to pink, darker centre.

G. grandiflora (*G. whitneyi*; correctly, *C. amoena whitneyi*): best-known sp; to 25–60×20cm (10–24×8in); fls to 5–10cm (2–4in) across in shades of rose-purple, lavender, pink, salmon, red & white. Sold in mixed & separate colours in tall (60cm [2ft]), semi-dwarf (40cm [16in]) & dwarf (25cm [10in]) vars **10**, single & double, including 'Azalea-Flowered' **11** (frilled petals).
Evening primrose (*Oenothera biennis** **12**): HB; to 1.2×0.3m (4×1ft); lance-shaped lvs to 15cm (6in) long; spikes or panicles of short-lived pale yellow fls to 5cm (2in) across, opening evening, all summer. *O. hookeri* & *O. lamarckiana* (correctly, *O. erythrosepala*) are similar but infls unbranched, & fls fade reddish.

The poppy family

Showy sun-lovers generally with glaucous, finely divided foliage. Large cup-shaped single or double flowers (often crinkled, with satiny texture), generally solitary & long-stalked, mostly short-lived & not for cutting unless noted. Large seed capsules, often attractive & dryable. For beds, borders; smaller types for rock gardens. Good near coast; some naturalize even in salt spray. **Cultivation**: Easy in light, sandy, dryish soil in full sun. Unless stated, sow spring (biennials early summer) in situ; most do not transplant well. For Himalayan blue poppies (*Meconopsis* spp). often grown as biennials, see p312.

Argemones (prickly poppies, *Argemone* spp): HAs with thistle-like spiny lvs containing bright yellow sap; showy fls; prickly seed capsules. Strong-growing, border plants. Self-seed.
A. grandiflora **1**: to 90×30cm (3×1ft); white-veined lvs; glistening white 10cm (4in) fls in clusters, early summer. Var 'Lutea' is yellow.
A. mexicana* **2** (Mexican poppy, devil's fig): to 60×30cm (2×1ft); lvs marked silvery-white; orange or yellow fls to 6cm (2½in) wide, summer.
A. platyceras (crested poppy): to 0.75–1.2×0.4m (2½–4ft×16in); sturdy; lvs bluish; white fls to 10cm (4in) across, late summer, lavender or purplish in var *rosea* (correctly, *A. sanguinea*).
California poppies (*Eschscholzia* spp): HAs with thread-like filigree glaucous lvs & profuse fls all summer if sown in succession. Self-seed.
E. caespitosa (*E. tenuifolia*): to 15×15cm (6×6in); yellow fls 2.5cm (1in) across, close in dull weather. Vars: 'Miniature Primrose', 'Sundew' (both lemon-yellow).
E. californica (common California poppy): to 30–40×15cm (12–16×6in); profuse satiny fls 5–8cm (2–3in) wide, orange or yellow in sp but vars include white, yellow, bronze, orange, pink & red shades, some semi-double; bonnet-like sepals; seed pods 8–10cm (3–4in) long. Vars (mixtures unless stated): 'Alba' (creamy); 'Ballerina' **3** (semi-double; fluted petals); 'Carmine King'; 'Cherry Ripe' (cerise); 'Harlequin Hybrids' (semi-double); 'Mikado' (mahogany-red); 'Mission Bells' (semi-double); 'Monarch Art Shades' (semi-double); 'Orange King'. Often perennial where warm.
Horned poppies (*Glaucium* spp): HAs, or can be treated as HBs where winters moderate; for mixed borders or wild gardens.
G. corniculatum **4** (sea poppy, red horned poppy; may be correctly *G. grandiflorum*): to 25×25cm (10×10in); mid green downy lvs; 5cm (2in) crimson (sometimes orange) fls, black spots, early–mid summer.
G. flavum (*G. luteum*, yellow horned poppy): to 60×45cm (2×1½ft); fleshy lvs; profuse 5–8cm (2–3in) yellow/orange fls all summer.
Mexican tulip poppy (golden cup, *Hunnemannia fumariifolia* **5**): tender perennial treated as HA or HHA; to 60–90×25cm (2–3ft×10in); blue-green lvs; brilliant yellow 6–8cm (2½–3in) satiny fls, all summer (cuttable; sear stem bases in flame). Var 'Sunlight' ('Sunlite') is

semi-double.
True poppies (*Papaver* spp): HAs unless stated; can be autumn-sown.
P. alpinum* (alpine poppy; may be correctly *P. burseri*): short-lived v hardy perennial for rock gardens best treated as HA; to 15–25×20cm (6–10×8in); grey-green lvs; white, yellow, pink apricot or red fls 2.5–5cm (1–2in) across, all summer. Var *rhaeticum* (*P. rhaeticum*) is v dwarf, with yellow or orange fls. Self-seed.
P. commutatum (*P. rhoeas commutatum*): to 50×45cm (20×18in); fls crimson, black blotch, summer. 'Lady Bird' is good var.
P. glaucum (tulip poppy): to 45–50×30cm (18–20×12in); grey-green lvs; profuse tulip-like crimson-scarlet fls to 10cm (4in) wide, black blotch, early summer.
P. nudicaule* (Iceland or arctic poppy): ultra-hardy short-lived perennial best treated as HB; can be treated as HHA. Clump-forming, to 75×45cm (2½×1½ft); soft green lvs in rosettes; 5–10cm (2–4in) often crinkled fls, tissue-paper texture, on slender stems in shades of white, yellow, pink & red, including pastels, all summer (spring in hot climates); good for cutting if stalks seared in flame. Self-seeds. Vars: 'Champagne Bubbles' **6** (F1 hybrid; crimped petals); 'Garden Gnome' (dwarf); 'Kelmscott Strain'.
P. rhoeas (corn, field or Flanders poppy; vars include Shirley poppies): to 60×30cm (2×1ft); hairy; pale green lobed lvs; crinkled 5–8cm (2–3in) fls, early–mid summer, orange-red with black blotch in sp & vars 'American Legion', 'Dwarf Flanders Field' (45cm [1½ft]) & 'Flanders Field'. Shirley vars ('Shirley Double Mixed' **7** & 'Shirley Single Mixed') are shades of white, pink, orange & red, white centre, no blotch.
P. somniferum (opium poppy): to 60–75×30cm (2–2½×1ft); smooth glaucous lvs; fringed fls to 10cm (4in) across, early–mid summer, white, pink, red or purple, often with black blotch; v large seed capsules. Cultivation illegal in many hot areas. Vars: 'Carnation-Flowered' (v fringed double fls; mixed); 'Paeony-Flowered' (double fls; mixed); 'Pink Beauty' (paeony-fld; salmon-pink); 'Pink Chiffon' **8** (paeony-fld; bright pink).
Cream cups (*Platystemon californicus* **9**): compact HA good for edging; to 30×10cm (12×4in); hairy; v narrow grey-green lvs; profuse pale creamy-yellow fls 2.5cm (1in) wide, early summer, pink/green-tipped in var *citrinus*.

Annual phlox and its relatives

Hardy or half-hardy annuals, their flowers often rounded, with a marked central eye. For bedding, the one climbing sp for screening. **Cultivation**: For well-drained soil in sun.

Cathedral bells (cup-&-saucer vine, Mexican ivy, monastery bells, *Cobaea scandens* **1**): semi-hardy tendrilled climber grown outdoors as HHA; to 3–6m (10–20ft); pinnate lvs; bell-like purple fls to 8cm (3in) long, saucer-like green calyx, all summer. Var 'Alba' is greenish-white.

Gilias (*Gilia* spp): HAs unless stated, all with finely divided lvs & profuse fls, mid summer.

G. achilleifolia: bushy, to 60×25cm (24×10in); hairy lvs; clustered blue fls 2.5cm (1in) across.

G. capitata (blue thimble flower): to 45–60×25cm (18–24×10in); globular 2.5cm (1in) heads of tiny lavender fls (good for cutting).

G. lutea hybrids (*G. hybrida*, stardust; often sold as *Leptosiphon hybridus*; correctly, hybrids of *Linanthus androsaceus luteus*): to 10–15×10cm (4–6×4in); pink, yellow or cream 1cm (½in) fls. Good for edging, paving, rock gardens.

G. rubra **2** (*G. coronopifolia*, standing cypress,

skyrocket; correctly, *Ipomopsis rubra*): HHB; to 1–1.8×0.45m (3–6×1½ft); tall spikes of trumpet-shaped scarlet fls 2.5cm (1in) long, yellow with red spots inside. Needs support.

G. tricolor **3** (bird's eyes): bushy, to 60×25cm (24×10in); 2cm (¾in) lilac or violet fls, purple-spotted yellow throat.

Annual phlox (*Phlox drummondii*): popular HHA; to 15–40×15–25cm (6–16×6–10in); lance-shaped lvs to 8cm (3in) long; dense 8cm (3in) heads of 2.5cm (1in) fls in shades of white, pink, purple, red & salmon, all summer if dead-headed (cuttable). Sold as mixtures & separate colours in 3 main groups: Stellaris (*P. cuspidata*, star phlox) vars (to 15–20cm [6–8in]; starry fls; include 'Twinkle'); Nana Compacta vars (to 20cm [8in]; bushy; include 'Beauty' series **4** & 'Cecily'); Grandiflora vars (to 30–40cm [12–16in]; large fls).

Larkspurs and their relatives

Summer-flowering hardy annuals with finely divided foliage. **Cultivation**: For any good soil in sun or partial shade. Sow autumn or early spring (v early for *Delphinium* spp).

Adonis (pheasant's eyes, *Adonis* spp): to 40×30cm (16×12in); cupped fls. Like cool nights.

A. aestivalis (summer adonis): 4cm (1½in) crimson fls. Var *citrina* (*A. citrina*) is pale yellow.

A. autumnalis **5** (autumn adonis [though summer-flg]; correctly, *A. annua*): 2.5cm (1in) scarlet fls, dark eye.

Larkspurs (annual delphiniums, *Delphinium* spp; correctly, *Consolida* spp): generally tall; with erect spikes of 2.5cm (1in) blue, purple, pink or white fls (good for cutting), early–mid summer. Prone to slugs, snails. For perennials that can be treated as HHAs, see p326.

D. ajacis (*C. ambigua*, rocket larkspur; probably correctly, *C. orientalis*): sp rarely grown but probably parent of 'Hyacinth-Flowered' hybrids:

tall form to 60×30cm (2×1ft), dwarf to 30×20cm (12×8in); spikes of double fls, wide colour range.

D. consolida (*C. regalis*, larkspur) vars: to 1.2×0.3m (4×1ft); branch from base. Vars: 'Giant Imperial' strain **6** (to 1.2m [4ft]; single fls in separate colours & mixtures); 'Stock-Flowered' group (to 90cm [3ft]; double fls).

Love-in-a-mist (*Nigella damascena*): bushy, to 40–60×20cm (16–24×8in); saucer-shaped fls to 4cm (1½in) across, thread-like bracts, white to pale blue in sp (good for cutting); striking brown-marked green seed pods (good for drying). Vars (generally semi-double): 'Miss Jekyll' (sky-blue); 'Oxford Blue' (dark blue); 'Persian Jewels' **7** (mixture of white, pink, rose-red, purple, mauve & blue shades). *N. hispanica* **8** is similar but has larger, deep blue fls.

Snapdragons & their relatives

Showy plants for bedding or containers, often perennial in favourable conditions. Tall spp for accent, wild gardens, cutting; climbers for temporary quick cover. Flowers often lipped or pouched. **Cultivation**: Many dislike hot summers, but unless stated for moist but well-drained soil in sun.

Mask flower (*Alonsoa warscewiczii* **9**, *A. grandiflora*): semi-hardy shrubby perennial treated as HHA; bushy, to 45–60×40cm (18–24×16in), dwarf form to 25×20cm (10×8in);

dark green lvs; profuse red to orange fls to 2.5cm (1in) across, all summer to autumn. *A. acutifolia* (*A. myrtifolia*) is similar, with narrower mid green lvs & deep red fls. Both dislike extreme heat.

Snapdragons (*Antirrhinum majus* vars): short-lived moderately to v hardy sub-shrubby perennials best grown as HHAs; bushy if young plants stopped; lance-shaped lvs; fls in spikes (taller vars good for cutting), most colours except blue, mid summer to frosts if dead-headed; fls generally typical "dragon's-mouth" shape but open trumpet-shaped in penstemon-fld vars. Like rich soil; prone to rust in some areas (choose rust-resistant vars marked †). Vars classified in 3 main groups by height (sold as mixtures or colour series unless stated; F1 hybrid vars marked ‡): *A. m. maximum* vars (to 0.75–1.2×0.45m [2½–4×1½ft]): 'Bright Butterflies'‡ (penstemon-fld); 'Madame Butterfly'‡ **1** (double azalea-like fls); 'Rocket'‡ series; 'Wedding Bells'†‡. Tetraploid vars (tetra snaps) have v large ruffled fls. *A. m. nanum* vars (to 30–60×25cm [12–24×10in]): 'Black Prince' (bronze lvs; crimson fls); 'Coronette'‡ series (ring of infls around central spike); 'Dazzler' (scarlet); 'Glamour Parade' (pastel shades); 'Kim'‡ (free-flg); 'Little Darling'‡ (penstemon-fld); 'Malmaison' (silvery-pink); 'Monarch'† series; 'Regal'†‡ series; 'Rembrandt' **2** (orange-scarlet & gold bicolour); 'Sweetheart'‡ (double azalea-like fls). *A. m. pumilum* (*A. m. nanum compactum*) vars (to 25×20cm [10×8in]): 'Floral Carpet'‡; 'Kolibri'‡ (early); 'Magic Carpet'; 'Pixie'‡ series (penstemon-fld); 'Tom Thumb'.

Calceolarias (slipper/pouch flowers, *Calceolaria* spp): tender or semi-hardy perennials grown as HHAs or HHBs, mainly in pots under glass but also for summer bedding or tubs. Lvs usually soft & hairy; showy pouched fls, summer. For light, fairly rich soil; prone to aphids, whitefly.
C.×herbeohybrida vars **3** (florists' calceolarias): hybrids derived mainly from *C. crenatiflora*; to 20–45×20–25cm (8–18×8–10in); fls 4–6cm (1½–2½in) long, yellow, orange or red with heavy spotting. Generally best under glass.
C. integrifolia (bush calceolaria); See p342.
C. mexicana: true HHA; to 45×20cm (18×8in); clusters of pale yellow fls to 1cm (½in) long.

Celsia (*Celsia arcturus*): semi-hardy biennial or perennial treated as HHB; to 45×20cm (18×8in); lower lvs lobed; long spikes of yellow fls, purple anthers, summer. Needs sun & shelter.

Collinsia (Chinese houses, *Collinsia heterophylla* **4**, *C. bicolor*): slender HA, to 60×15cm (24×6in); lance-shaped lvs; whorls of fls 2.5cm (1in) long, upper lip white, lower lilac, all summer. Best in partial shade & cool nights.

Twinspur (*Diascia barberae* **5**): HHA; erect, to 30×15cm (12×6in); dark green glossy lvs; 15cm (6in) racemes of rosy-pink two-spurred fls 2cm (¾in) across, early summer. Dead-head.

Foxgloves (*Digitalis* spp): v hardy biennials or perennials best treated as HBs; tall & stately, with one-sided spikes of drooping tubular fls, early

summer (good for cutting); lvs mainly basal. For rich soil; best in partial shade. Self-seed.
D. ferruginea (rusty foxglove): to 1.5×0.45m (5×1½ft); 60cm (2ft) spikes of golden & reddish-brown hairy fls to 5cm (2in) long.
D. purpurea (common foxglove of Europe): to 1–1.5×0.45–0.6m (3–5×1½–2ft); lvs rough, v poisonous; spikes to 90cm (3ft) long of purplish, red, pink, or white fls, spotted lip. Vars (generally mixtures): 'Alba' (white); 'Excelsior' **6** (to 1.2–1.5m [4–5ft]; fls held horizontally all around stems); 'Foxy' (to 90cm [3ft]; early, can be treated as HHA); 'Shirley' (to 1.5–2m [5–7ft]).

Toadflax (bunny rabbits, *Linaria maroccana*): dainty & colourful HA; to 20–30×15cm (8–12×6in); v narrow lvs; small snapdragon-like spurred fls, lip blotched yellow/white, all summer (good for cutting). Dislikes heat. Vars (mixed violet, blue, red, pink & yellow shades): 'Excelsior'; 'Fairy Bouquet' **7** (dwarf). *L. reticulata* 'Aureo-purpurea' ('Crimson & Gold') is similar but taller, to 1.2m (4ft); deep red fls splashed gold & net-veined.

Maurandias (*Maurandia* [correctly, *Asarina*] spp): tender or semi-hardy climbing perennials sometimes grown outdoors as HHAs; to 1.5–2×1m (5–7×3ft); twining petioles; triangular lvs; showy trumpet-shaped fls, mid–late summer. For rich soil; grow on trellis or in baskets. Can be propagated by cuttings under glass.
M. (A.) barclaiana **8**: fls rose-pink to purple, to 3cm (1¼in) long (deep purple to white in vars).
M. (A.) erubescens (creeping gloxinia; 8cm (3in) fls, pink & white spotted rose-pink.

Nemesia (*Nemesia strumosa*): colourful dwarf HHA for areas where summer nights are cool; to 20–30×15cm (8–12×6in); narrow toothed lvs; profuse funnel-shaped fls to 2.5cm (1in) across in bright & pastel shades of white, yellow, orange, red, purple & blue, often with contrasting eye, early–mid summer, repeating if sheared. Vars: 'Blue Gem' **9** (lavender-blue); 'Carnival' (mixture); 'Fire King' (crimson-scarlet); 'Funfair' (mixture); 'Triumph' (mixture).

Wishbone flower (bluewings, *Torenia fournieri* **10**): HHA for bedding in partial shade & for containers; to 30×20cm (12×8in); narrow toothed lvs; profuse violet, blue & purple trumpet-shaped fls 2.5cm (1in) wide, yellow throat, from mid summer.

Mulleins (*Verbascum* spp): tall grey-green HBs (or short-lived ultra-hardy perennials treated thus) with spikes of 4–5cm (1½–2in) yellow fls, early–mid summer. Unless stated, to 1.5–1.8×0.45m (5–6×1½ft). See also p344.
V. bombyciferum (v hairy; fls pale yellow. Vars: 'Arctic Summer'; 'Silver Lining'.
V. phlomoides **11**: grey & woolly; for wild garden.
V. thapsus (common or flannel mullein): to 1.8m (6ft); v woolly; best in wild garden.

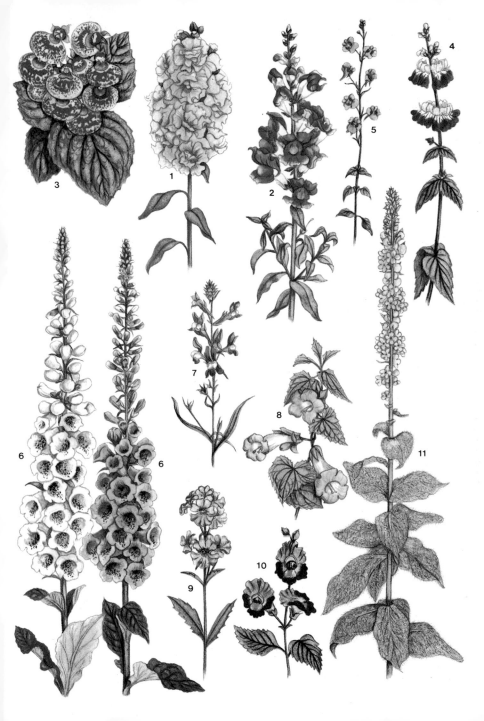

Petunias and their relatives

Sun-lovers, mostly tender perennials treated as annuals, with funnel-shaped flowers, often brightly veined. Some have attractive fruits. Popular subjects for bedding or pots (in open or under glass); some good for cutting. **Cultivation**: Unless stated, treat as HHAs & plant in rich soil in full sun. For *Physalis alkekengi* (Chinese lantern, a perennial often treated as HHA), see p360.

Browallias (*Browallia* spp): bright green pointed lvs; starry cuttable blue or white fls all summer.
B. speciosa: sp to 1.2×0.3m (4×1ft) unstopped for cutting; most vars (& sp if pinched back) to 30–50×25cm (12–20×10in); fls to 5cm (2in) across. Vars: 'Blue Bells Improved'; 'Blue Troll' **1** (to 25cm [10in]); 'Jingle Bells' (mixed); 'Major' (large bright blue fls); 'Marine Bells' (dark blue); 'White Troll' (to 25cm [10in]).
B. viscosa: to 30×15cm (12×6in); sticky. Var 'Sapphire' is dark blue, white eye. *B. americana* (*B. elata*) is similar.
Ornamental peppers (*Capsicum annuum* vars **2**, some possibly hybrids with *C. frutescens*): generally to 20–30×25cm (8–12×10in); pointed lvs, variegated in some vars; fls insignificant; grown for colourful glossy frs, generally cream maturing red, edible but hot-tasting, mid summer onwards if sown in succession. Sold as named vars & mixtures with round frs to 2.5cm (1in) across and conical frs to 5cm (2in) long.
Trumpet flowers (angel's trumpet, *Datura* spp): vigorous & bushy, with v showy trumpet-shaped lily-like fls to 20cm (8in) long, early–mid summer.
D. metel* **3** (*D. chlorantha*, *D. fastuosa*): to 1–1.5×0.45m (3–5×1½ft); lvs to 20cm (8in) long; erect white to creamy fls, double &/or pink to purple in some vars. Poisonous.
D. meteloides* (correctly, *D. inoxia*): to 1×0.6m (3×2ft); grey hairy lvs to 25cm (10in) long; fls white, lilac blush. Poisonous.
Apple of Peru (shoo-fly, *Nicandra physalodes* **4**): HA or HHA; vigorous, to 1×0.6m (3×2ft); wavy-edged lvs to 25cm (10in) long; pale blue bell-shaped fls mid–late summer; small apple-shaped inedible frs within lantern-like green calyx (frtg branches dryable). Said to repel flies.
Flowering tobacco (*Nicotiana* spp): erect, generally sticky-hairy border plants with mid-green lvs to 25cm (10in) long; long-tubed starry fls 2.5–5cm (1–2in) across, all summer, most spp opening (& most fragrant) in evening but garden vars earlier; cuttable. Tolerate shade.
N. alata** (*N. affinis*): to 90×30cm (3×1ft); fls pure white, nocturnal. Tall vars (to 75–90cm [2½–3ft]): 'Lime Green'* ('Lime Sherbet'; good for arrangements); 'Sensation Mixed'* (white, cream, pink, red & purple shades; open in day). Dwarf vars & hybrids (correctly, *N.×sanderae* vars; to 30–60cm [1–2ft]; fls open in day): 'Crimson Rock' **5** (F1 hybrid); '(Dwarf) Crimson Bedder'; '(Dwarf) White Bedder'*; 'Nicki'* series (F1 hybrids); 'Tinkerbell Mixed'*; 'Top

Arts Mixed'*.
N. suaveolens**: to 60×30cm (2×1ft); spikes of white nocturnal fls, purplish veins.
Nierembergias (cup flowers, *Nierembergia* spp): moderately hardy perennials (can be propagated by division, cuttings) grown as HHAs in cool climates. Dainty & branching, with v narrow lvs & 2.5cm (1in) fls, all summer. For sheltered spot.
N. caerulea (correctly, *N. hippomanica*): to 20×20cm (8×8in); fls lavender, yellow throat, but violet-purple in vars 'Purple Robe' **6** & 'Regal Robe' (darkest). For edging.
N. frutescens (correctly, *N. scoparia*): to 45–60×30cm (1½–2×1ft); blue or white fls.
Petunias (*Petunia* hybrids of complex parentage, classified as *P.×hybrida*): to 20–40×25cm (8–16×10in); sticky; pale green lvs; showy single & double fls in all shades of red, purple, blue, pink, salmon, yellow & white, including bicolours, all summer if dead-headed. Best in light soil in some shelter; prone to aphids, virus diseases. Numerous named vars grouped mainly by fl size & type; F1 hybrid vars sturdier, larger-fld & more uniform in habit & colour. Multiflora vars have profuse medium-sized, fls: single F1 vars **7** 5–8cm (2–3in) wide, double F1 vars **8** about 5cm (2in) wide. Grandiflora vars have fewer large fls, less weather-resistant; single F1 vars **9** to 10–12cm (4–5in) wide, double F1 vars **10** to 8–10cm (3–4in) wide & often v frilled. Pendula vars (non-F1) trail, to 15×90cm (6×36in); for ground cover, window boxes, hanging baskets. Nana Compacta vars (non-F1) are dwarf, to 15×20cm (6×8in).
Salpiglossis (painted tongue, velvet flower, *Salpiglossis sinuata*): slender, to 75×30cm (2½×1ft); narrow lvs; 5cm (2in) velvety fls all summer in shades of blue, purple, red, pink & yellow, often splashed gold & dark-veined; cuttable. Showy in sheltered border; give twiggy support. Vars (mixed): 'Bolero'; 'Splash' **11** (F1 hybrid).
Butterfly flower (poor man's orchid, *Schizanthus pinnatus*): to 30–90×30cm (1–3×1ft); sticky; deeply divided lvs; profuse orchid-like fls 4cm (1½in) across, pink, purple, red &/or white, all blotched gold, cuttable. Long season but best in moderate climates (sow autumn for spring display where summers v hot); tall vars generally best under glass. Dwarf vars: 'Dwarf Bouquet'; 'Hit Parade' **12**; 'Star Parade'.

Verbenas

Vervains, *Verbena* spp. Showy, colourful sun-loving perennials, drought-resistant but often rather short-lived, usually best grown as annuals. Toothed leaves; profuse dense heads of small, white rose-pink or purple flowers, summer & autumn. Low-growing spp good for front of borders & ground cover; larger spp for mixed borders. **Cultivation**: For any well-drained soil in full sun; dead-head. Treat as HHAs, or can be propagated by cuttings. Generally moderately hardy as perennials.

V. bonariensis*: to 1.2–1.5×0.6m (4–5×2ft); branching hairy stems; rough dark green lvs to 10cm (4in) long; lilac fls in tufts. Moderately to v hardy but lives only 2–3yrs.

V. canadensis (*V. aubletia*, rose verbena, creeping vervain): semi-prostrate, to 20×40cm (8×16in); white, rose-pink, magenta or violet fls.

V. corymbosa: spreading & self-rooting, to 45×90cm (1½×3ft); coarsely toothed lvs; reddish-purple or lavender fls. Likes moisture.

V.×hybrida (*V.×hortensis*) vars (garden verbenas): hybrids derived from *V. peruviana* & other spp; to 15–45×30cm (6–18×12in); bushy or semi-prostrate; 8cm (3in) heads of bright red-purple, lilac, blue, red, pink or white fls, early summer to frosts. Sold as mixtures & named vars (generally to 25–30cm [10–12in]): 'Amethyst' **1** (violet-blue, white eye); 'Blaze' (bright scarlet,

white eye); 'Delight' (coral-pink); 'Derby' **2** (scarlet, white eye); 'Madame du Barry' **3** (carmine-crimson); 'Sangria' (wine-red, white eye); 'Sissinghurst' **4** (rose-pink); 'Sparkle' (scarlet, white eye; also name of mixture); 'Tropic' (cherry-red).

V. peruviana (*V. chamaedryfolia*): prostrate & mat-forming, to 10×30–60cm (4×12–24in); starry scarlet to crimson fls. Hybrids: see above.

V. rigida (*V. venosa*): upright but creeping, to 30–60×30cm (1–2×1ft), with tuberous root; dark green stiff lvs to 8cm (3in) long; violet-purple fls (white in var 'Alba'); can be propagated by division.

V. tenera maonettii **5**: semi-prostrate & creeping, to 15×30cm (6×12in); deeply lobed hairy lvs; white-edged rosy-lilac fls.

Miscellaneous annuals and biennials

Listed alphabetically by family name; includes short-lived or tender perennials usually treated as annuals. **Cultivation**: Unless stated, for any well-drained soil in sun; sow spring (biennials, early summer). Perennials can be propagated by cuttings & overwintered under glass.

Clock vines (*Thunbergia* spp; Acanthaceae): tender perennial twining climbers treated outdoors (where summers warm) as HHAs; to 3m (10ft); triangular 8cm (3in) lvs; 4–5cm (1½–2in) fls all summer. Useful for trellis & baskets.

T. alata **6** (black-eyed Susan): fls generally orange, centred dark brown. Vars: 'Julietta' (large deep orange fls); 'Susie' series (orange, yellow or white, clear or dark-eyed); 'White Wings' (white, centred cherry-red).

T. gregorii **7** (*T. gibsonii*): pure orange fls.

Mesembryanthemums (*Mesembryanthemum* spp, some often listed as *Dorotheanthus* spp but now correctly *Cleretum* spp; Aizoaceae): low, spreading H/HHAs, to 15×30cm (6×12in); succulent lvs, crystalline secretions; bright daisy-like fls all summer (open only in sun). Need sandy, well-drained soil; for banks, rockeries.

M. criniflorum **8** (*D. bellidiformis*, Livingstone daisy; correctly, *Cleretum bellidiforme*): dark-eyed crimson, pink, orange, buff or yellow fls, often zoned. Sold mainly as mixtures. Vars 'Lunette' **9** & 'Yellow Ice' are yellow.

M. (*Cryophytum*) *crystallinum* (ice plant, sea fig): may spread to 1m (3ft); fls white or rose. For ground cover, sand stabilization. Self-seeds.

M. (*D.*) *tricolor* (correctly, *Cleretum tricolor*): dark-centred white, rose or dark purple fls.

Southern star (*Oxypetalum* [*Tweedia*] *caeruleum**; Asclepiadaceae): tender perennial grown as HHA where summers warm; weakly twining, to 45–90cm (1½–3ft); hairy; silvery-blue star-like fls, darkening, all summer. Likes rich soil; often grown under glass.

Balsams & impatiens (*Impatiens* spp; Balsaminaceae): succulent-stemmed, with spurred fls; include some of best bedding plants for shady gardens (also sun). Like moist fertile soil.

I. balsamina ([rose] balsam, touch-me-not): bushy HHA; sp to 75×45cm (2½×1½ft); single or double cup-shaped fls to 4cm (1½in) wide in white, pink & mauve shades, all summer. For bedding. Double vars (mixed): 'Bush-Flowered' (to 30–40cm [12–14in]); 'Camellia-Flowered' **10** (to 45cm [1½ft]); 'Tom Thumb' (to 25cm [10in]).

I. capensis (*I. biflora*, jewel weed, spotted touch-me-not): erect HA, to 90×60cm (3×2ft); pendent 2.5cm (1in) orange-yellow fls, spotted brown, from mid summer. For mixed borders & wild garden. Self-seeds.

I. glandulifera (*I. roylei*, Himalayan touch-me-

not): erect HA, to 1.5×0.6m (5×2ft); fls deep purple to white, mid–late summer. For mixed borders, wild garden & by water. Self-seeds.
I. wallerana (*I. holstii*, busy Lizzie, patient Lucy, patience; now includes *I. sultanii* [once separate sp]): tender perennial (often grown indoors) excellent as summer bedding HHA for semi-/shade (or full sun where summers not too hot); to 15–60×25–45cm (6–24×10–18in); bright green or bronzed lvs; profuse 2.5–5cm (1–2in) fls in shades of white, pink, scarlet, crimson, orange or maroon, striped white in some vars, v long season. Vars (mixed or colour series & to 20–25cm [8–10in] unless stated; F1 hybrids marked †): 'Baby' (to 15cm [6in]); 'Blitz'† (orange-scarlet); 'Double Up' (to 30cm [1ft]; double; good in hanging baskets); '(Super) Elfin'†; 'Futura'† (good in hanging baskets); 'Gem'†; 'Grand Prix'† (to 30cm [1ft]; v large fls); 'Harlequin'† (to 15–20cm [6–8in]; bicoloured); 'Imp'† (to 25–45cm [10–18in]); 'Minette'† (includes bicolours); 'Novette'† **1** (to 10–15cm [4–6in]); 'Rosette'† (semi-/double); 'Shady Lady'† (to 30–40cm [12–16in]; includes pastel shades); 'Sweet Sue' (6cm [2½in] flame-orange fls); 'Tangeglow' (to 45cm [1½ft]; bright orange); 'Twinkles'† **2** (bicoloured); 'Zig-Zag' (to 15–20cm [6–8in]; bicoloured).
Wax begonias (*Begonia* × *semperflorens-cultorum* vars **3**; Begoniaceae): hybrids derived from *B. cucullata hookeri* (*B. semperflorens*) & other spp; tender dwarf perennials, to 15–30×25cm (6–12×10in), grown as HHAs for summer bedding or pots (also under glass). Glossy oval lvs, green or bronze; profuse fls to 2.5cm (1in) across, red, pink or white, long season. For moist, light soil in sun or partial shade. Sold as mixtures, colour series & individual named vars (including many F1 hybrids) in dwarf (to 15cm [6in]) & tall (to 30cm [1ft]) green- & bronze-lvd forms.
The bellflower family (*Campanula* & *Specularia* spp; Campanulaceae): erect bushy plants with bell-like fls.
Campanula medium **4** (*C. grandiflora*, Canterbury bell): sturdy HB, to 90×30cm (3×1ft); basal rosette of hairy lvs; erect racemes of 2.5–5cm (1–2in) fls in white, pink or blue shades, early summer. For borders in rich, well-drained soil; protect over winter where v cold, or treat early strains as HHAs, sowing early. Vars: 'Bells of Ireland' ('Musical Bells'; to 45cm [1½ft]; single); 'Calycanthema' **5** ("cup & saucer" var; hose-in-hose fls [with deep calyx] to 8cm [3in] long; can be treated as HHA).
C. pyramidalis (chimney bellflower): short-lived v hardy perennial best grown as HB; to 1.2×0.45m (4×1½ft); heart-shaped lvs; blue or white starry fls, mid–late summer.
Specularia (correctly, *Legousia*) *speculum-*

veneris **6**, Venus's looking-glass): HA; to 30×10cm (12×4in); profuse 2cm (¾in) fls, violet-blue centred white, all summer. May self-seed & can be weedy; for mixed borders & wild gardens.
Japanese hop (*Humulus japonicus,*
H. scandens; Cannabaceae): HA twining vine, fast-growing to 6m (20ft) or more; deeply lobed 20cm (8in) lvs; insignificant fls with papery bracts. Useful as summer screen but self-seeds & may become weed. Var 'Variegatus' has lvs splashed white.
Spider flower (*Cleome hasslerana***; generally listed incorrectly as *C. spinosa*; Capparaceae): erect H/HHA, to 1.2×0.45m (4×1½ft); spiny stems; palmate lvs; 15–20cm (6–8in) heads of white, pink or purple fls (rather pungent), long stamens, mid summer to frosts; narrow 5cm (2in) seed pods. For fertile soil. Good as pot plants or in pots. Vars: 'Colour Fountain' (mixed); 'Helen Campbell' (white); 'Pink Queen' (pale pink); 'Purple Queen' (lilac-purple); 'Rose Queen' **7**.
Soapworts (*Saponaria* spp; Caryophyllaceae): HAs (spring/autumn-sown) for bedding, etc, in poor soil; fl early summer.
S. calabrica: compact, to 15×15cm (6×6in); light green sticky lvs; profuse rose-pink fls.
S. vaccaria (cow herb, dairy pink; correctly, *Vaccaria pyramidata*): erect, to 60×25cm (24×10in); pink to purplish fls. Can be weedy.
The beet family (*Atriplex, Beta* & *Kochia* spp; Chenopodiaceae): erect plants grown for colourful foliage; includes 2 decorative vars of vegetables.
Atriplex hortensis 'Rubra' ('Atrosanguinea'; red mountain spinach, red orach): fast-growing HA, to 1.2×0.3m (4×1ft); blood-red triangular lvs to 15cm (6in) long (cuttable; edible). Useful for saline soils, as screen/contrast. Self-seeds.
Beta vulgaris 'Ruby Chard' **8** ('Rhubarb Beet', a leaf-beet var): biennial treated as HA; to 30×30cm (1×1ft); large, puckered dark purplish lvs, red/purple stems (both edible).
Kochia scoparia trichophylla (burning bush, summer cypress): H/HHA; fast-growing neat globular to oval bush, to 90×60cm (3×2ft); grown for profuse pale green narrow lvs **9**, deep red or purple in autumn **10**; fls insignificant. Useful for temporary hedging, as specimen, or as dot plant in bedding schemes. Tolerates heat & wind; self-seeds (weedy in warm climates). Var 'Childsii' is compact, to 75cm (2½ft).
Sweet scabious (pincushion flower, *Scabiosa atropurpurea*** **11**; Dipsacaceae): H/HHA; to 90×30cm (3×1ft); lobed lvs in basal rosettes; stem lvs finely divided; rounded fl heads 5cm (2in) wide, prominent stamens ("pins"), in shades of blue, purple, red, pink & white, all summer if dead-headed (long stems); good for cutting). Give twiggy support. Sold mainly as tall

(90cm [3ft]) & dwarf (45cm [1½ft]) mixtures.

The Spurge family (*Euphorbia* & *Ricinus* spp; Euphorbiaceae): grown mainly for foliage &/or showy bracts or seed-heads (fls insignificant). Sap of *Euphorbia* spp irritating & toxic; all parts (especially seeds) of *Ricinus* sp poisonous & irritating. May become weedy.

Euphorbia heterophylla (annual poinsettia, fire on the mountain, Mexican fire plant, painted spurge; probably correctly *E. cyathophora*): HHA; to 60×30cm (2×1ft); variable dark green lvs; 10cm (4in) whorls of scarlet bracts around small red-orange fls, mid–late summer.

E. lathyris (caper spurge, mole plant): HHA or HB; to 90×45cm (3×1½ft); narrow lvs to 15cm (6in) long in 4s along stems; small yellow fls, early summer. Good in wild garden; said to deter moles. garden; said to deter moles.

E. marginata **1** (*E. variegata*, snow-on-the-mountain): HA; to 60×30cm (2×1ft); oval lvs to 8cm (3in) long; upper lvs & bracts white-edged (can be cut for arrangements if cut stems scalded). Invasive.

Ricinus communis (castor bean, castor-oil plant): tender tree grown as H/HHA; bushy, to 1.5×1m (5×3ft), or to 3–4.5m (10–15ft) with ample heat & moisture; long stalked palmately lobed lvs to 30–90cm (1–3ft) across; insignificant green fls, summer, followed by bristly seed-heads. Used for bold foliage effects, screens, backgrounds, etc. Vars include: 'Cambogensis' (stems purple-black; lvs purple, large); 'Gibsonii' (compact; lvs dark metallic-red); 'Sanguineus' **2** (stems & lvs red); 'Zanzibarensis' (lvs green veined white).

Meadow foam (poached-egg flower, *Limnanthes douglasii** **3**; Limnanthaceae): HA (spring/autumn-sown); to 15×10cm (6×4in); finely divided yellow-green lvs; profuse 2.5cm (1in) fls, white with yellow centre, late spring to mid summer. For moist soil. Self-seeds.

Annual flax (*Linum* spp; Linaceae): erect HAs (spring/autumn-sown); slender stems; narrow lvs; saucer-shaped fls, early–mid summer.

L. grandiflorum: to 45×15cm (18×6in); pink or red 4cm (1½in) fls. Var 'Rubrum' **4** (scarlet flax) is bright red & dwarf (to 30cm [1ft]).

L. usitatissimum (common or annual blue flax): to 60–90×15cm (24–36×6in); blue 1cm (½in) fls.

Blazing star (*Mentzelia lindleyi** **5**, *Bartonia aurea*; Loasaceae): bushy HA, to 45×25cm (18×10in); fleshy stems & lvs; glossy golden 6cm (2½in) fls, pointed petals, early–mid summer. Tolerates wind, heat, sandy soil.

Lobelia (*Lobelia* spp; Lobeliaceae; sometimes classed in Campanulaceae): tender or semi-hardy perennials grown as HHAs; compact plants popular for edging, rock gardens; trailing vars for containers. Profuse blue, carmine, pink or white fls, often white-eyed, all summer.

L. erinus (edging lobelia): 1.2cm (½in) fls.

Compacta vars (bushy, to 10–20×10cm [4–8×4in]): 'Blue Stone' (mid blue); 'Cambridge Blue' **6** (pale blue); 'Crystal Palace' (dark blue); 'Mrs Clibran' **7** ('Bright Eyes'; intense blue, white eye); 'Rosamond' **8** (carmine, white eye); 'Snowball' (white); 'String of Pearls' (mixed); 'White Lady'. Pendula vars (trailing to 60cm [2ft]): 'Blue Cascade' (pale blue); 'Red Cascade' (purple-red, white eye); 'Sapphire' **9** (deep blue, white eye).

L. tenuior: to 30×15cm (12×6in); 2cm (¾in) gentian-blue fls. Good in pots.

Chilean bellflower (*Nolana acuminata*; Nolanaceae): tender perennial grown as HHA; semi-prostrate, to 15×30cm (6×12in); hairy fleshy lvs; trumpet-shaped blue fls 4cm (1½in) wide, white or yellow throat, summer. For hanging baskets, rockeries; likes sandy soil. Var 'Lavender Gown' **10** is lavender-mauve.

N. paradoxa is similar; fls darker blue.

Sand verbena & four-o'clock plants (*Abronia* & *Mirabilis* spp; Nyctaginaceae): semi-hardy or tender perennials generally treated as HHAs (or HAs where summers long).

Abronia umbellata* (pink sand verbena): prostrate, to 15×45cm (6×18in); fleshy lvs; dense 5cm (2in) heads of small rosy-lavender fls, mid–late summer (cuttable). Good near coast; likes sandy soil.

Mirabilis jalapa* **11** (four-o'clock plant, marvel of Peru): to 60–90×30cm (2–3×1ft); heart-shaped lvs; profuse trumpet-shaped fls to 5cm (2in) across (open late afternoon, fade next day) all summer, in shades of white, pink, red & yellow. Sold as mixtures, including bicolours & tricolours in 'Jingles' strain. 'Pygmaea' ('Pygmy') is dwarf, to 50cm (20in). Tuberous; can be lifted like dahlias, or left outdoors in warm climates.

M. longiflora** (sweet four-o'clock): to 90×30cm (3×1ft); grey-green lance-shaped lvs; white, pink or purple fls to 10–15cm (4–6in) long.

Statice (sea lavender, *Limonium* [*Statice*] spp; Plumbaginaceae): annuals, biennials or short-lived perennials all best treated as HHAs; to 45×30cm (1½×1ft); generally lobed lvs in basal rosettes; 8–10cm (3–4in) infls of small funnel-shaped fls from mid summer, good for cutting & drying. Good in coastal gardens.

L. (*S.*) *bonduellii* (Algerian statice): yellow fls.

L. (*S.*) *sinuatum* **12** (notch-leaf or winged statice): hairy; winged stems; fls white, yellow, blue, purple or red, including pastels. Sold in mixtures & separate colours.

L. (*S.*; correctly, *Psylliostachys*) *suworowii* (Russian or rat's-tail statice): rose-pink fls in narrow wavy spikes.

Pink-head knotweed (*Polygonum capitatum*; Polygonaceae): moderately hardy perennial often grown as H/HHA; trailing, to 8×30cm (3×12in); green lvs marbled bronze; dense, soft heads of

pink fls, early–mid summer. Useful for ground cover, hanging baskets, etc. 'Magic Carpet' is good var.

The purslane family (*Calandrinia* & *Portulaca* spp; Portulacaceae): HHAs & tender perennials treated thus, for borders & rock gardens in hot, dry spots; narrow lvs; profuse 2–2.5cm (¾–1in) cup/saucer-shaped fls, all summer.

Calandrinia umbellata (rock purslane): semi-prostrate, to 15×30cm (6×12in); greyish hairy lvs; vivid crimson-magenta fls. Var 'Amaranth' is brilliant crimson.

Portulaca grandiflora **1** (sun plant, rose moss): semi-prostrate, to 20×15cm (8×6in); succulent red stems & bright green lvs; brilliant red, purple, yellow or white fls, boss of yellow stamens (close at night). Sold mainly as mixtures with single or double fls, boldest in F1 hybrid double vars (eg, 'Sunkiss'; 'Sunglo'). 'Tuffet' is a dwarf var, to 10cm (4in). 'Afternoon Delight' fls open all day.

Pimpernels (*Anagallis* spp; Primulaceae): *A. arvensis* (scarlet pimpernel, poor man's weather-glass): HA weed sometimes cultivated, especially in blue-fld var *caerulea* **2**; prostrate, to 5×15cm (2×6in); 10mm (⅜in) fls all summer (close in dull weather). For edging, etc.

A. linifolia (correctly, *A. monelli linifolia*): moderately hardy perennial treated as HHA; to 30×40cm (12×16in); narrow dark green lvs; gentian-blue 2.5cm (1in) fls, red-purple reverse, all summer (best in var 'Phillipsii'). Other colours sometimes available.

Mignonette (*Reseda odorata***; Resedaceae): HA with rather insignificant fls grown for perfume; to 45×25cm (18×10in); erect racemes of yellowish fls, all summer if sown in succession (attract bees). Best in rich alkaline soil; good in pots. Vars 'Crimson Fragrance'**, 'Machet Rubin'** **3** & 'Red Monarch'** have reddish fls.

Annual woodruff (*Asperula orientalis**, *A. azurea*; Rubiaceae): HA for borders & pots; to 30×15cm (12×6in); whorled lvs; clusters of small pale blue fls, mid summer (cuttable). Best in moist semi-shade. May self-seed.

Balloon vine (love-in-a-puff, *Cardiospermum halicacabum*; Sapindaceae): semi-hardy sub-shrubby tendrilled climber usually grown as HA; to 3m (10ft); rather inconspicuous white fls; inflated 2.5cm (1in) frs. Makes fast screen.

Nasturtiums & relatives (*Tropaeolum* spp; Tropaeolaceae): annuals and semi-hardy short-lived perennials all treated as HAs; spp climbing/scrambling by twining petioles; smooth, long-stalked lvs, usually rounded, edible in salads; funnel-shaped spurred fls all summer. Easy on poor, dry soil in sun; prone to black aphids, viruses.

T. majus (garden nasturtium, Indian cress): yellow, orange or red fls to 6cm (2½in) across. Sp and tall garden vars climb to 1.8–2.5m (6–8ft)

or trail. Dwarf & semi-dwarf vars grow to 20–45×15–25cm (8–18×6–10in); fls single or semi-double, in mixtures, colour series & vars: 'Alaska' **4** (lvs marbled green & white; fls single); 'Cherry Rose' (cerise); 'Empress of India' (v dwarf; crimson; single); 'Gleam' series (semi-trailing; good for baskets); 'Jewel' **5**; 'Red Roulette' (orange-scarlet); 'Tom Thumb' (v dwarf; single); 'Whirlybird' (spurless upward-facing single fls).

T. peltophorum (*T. lobbianum*, shield nasturtium): to 1.8m (6ft); tops & undersides of lvs hairy; orange-scarlet 2.5cm (1in) fls.

T. peregrinum **6** (*T. canariense*, canary creeper): to 3.5m (12ft); blue-green 5-lobed lvs, bright yellow fringed 2.5cm (1in) fls, green spurs.

Blue lace flower (*Didiscus* [correctly, *Trachymene*] *caerulea* **7**; Umbelliferae): H/HHA; to 45×30cm (1½×1ft); sticky; finely divided lvs; scabious-like lavender-blue fls in flattish umbels to 5cm (2in) across, long-stemmed & good for cutting. Give twiggy support. Grown in pots under glass.

Pansies (*Viola* spp; Violaceae): short-lived dwarf perennials best treated as H/HHBs, HHAs or HAs; long-stalked rounded & blunt-toothed lvs; 5-petalled asymmetrical rounded fls, wide colour range, often blotched or bicoloured. Excellent for bedding, edging, containers. Best in moist, fertile soil in sun or semi-shade; dead-head. For true perennial spp, see p348.

V. tricolor **8** (heartsease, wild pansy; in US, Johnny-jump-up): treat as HB or H/HHA; to 8–15×15–30cm (3–6×6–12in); 2.5cm (1in) fls, cream, yellow, purple-red or blue, mid summer.

V. × *wittrockiana* (*V. tricolor hortensis*) vars (garden pansies): hybrids of *V. tricolor* & other spp, generally treated as H/HHBs or HHAs; similar to above but sturdier, to 15–25×20–30cm (6–10×8–12in); fls 5–10cm (2–4in) across, mainly late spring to early autumn (good for cutting). Sold as mixtures, colour series & numerous named vars (selection listed). F1 hybrid vars (vigorous; large fls) include: 'Azure Blue' **9**; 'Imperial Light Blue' (light blue, dark eye); 'Imperial Orange' (deep apricot); 'Orange Prince' **10** (apricot-orange, black blotch); 'Sunny Boy' **11** (yellow, dark blotch). Swiss Giant vars (v large velvety fls, late) include: 'Alpenglow' (mahogany-red, dark blotch); 'Berna' (dark blue); 'Coronation Gold'; 'Lake Thun' (mid blue, dark blotch); 'Rheingold' (golden-yellow, dark blotch); 'Ullswater' (rich blue, dark blotch); 'White Lady' (creamy-white). Other named vars include: 'Arkwright Ruby'* **12** (brown-red); 'Bowles' Black' (almost black); 'Chantreyland' (apricot). Winter-flg (Hiemalis) vars fl late autumn to spring in mild, sheltered sites or under glass if sown early summer; sold mainly as mixtures.

Water lilies

Nymphaea spp & vars. Showy, long-lived herbaceous aquatics, rhizomatous unless noted, with floating rounded to heart-shaped leaves & solitary many-petalled waxy flowers (cup-shaped & often starry, usually semi-/double, with golden stamens) at or just above water surface, all summer. Generally classed here as very vigorous (water depth 75–90cm [2½–3ft] × surface spread 1–1.5m [3–5ft]), vigorous (45–60×75–90cm [1½–2×2½–3ft]), moderately vigorous (30–45×30–75cm [1–1½×1–2½ft]) & dwarf (15–30×30–45cm [6–12×12–18in]). Leaves glossy & leathery, often purplish beneath; provide shade for fish. Night-flowering spp & vars marked †. **Cultivation**: Plant rhizomes horizontally, tubers vertically, 10–25cm (4–10in) deep (most vigorous types deepest) direct in mud at bottom of pool or in perforated plastic containers of stiff loam; top with gravel. For full sun. Prone to aphids. **Propagation**: Division; seed.

Hardy species: can generally overwinter in pool. *N. alba* (European white water lily): moderately to v hardy; v vigorous; 30cm (1ft) lvs, reddish when young; white 10–12cm (4–5in) fls. *N. candida* is similar; moderately vigorous; smaller fls. *N. odorata** (fragrant water lily): ultra-hardy; vigorous; 10–25cm (4–10in) dull green lvs; 5–12cm (3–5in) white fls, open mornings. Vars & hybrids: *minor** (moderately vigorous; small white fls); *rosea** (Cape Cod pink water lily; purplish lvs; deep pink fls); 'Sulphurea' (moderately hardy hybrid with *N. mexicana*; lvs mottled red-brown; deep sulphur-yellow 8cm [3in] fls above water; 'Sulphurea Grandiflora' is similar, with larger fls); 'Turicensis'* (moderately vigorous; soft pink fls); 'W. B. Shaw'* **1** (moderately vigorous; pink fls, darker centre). *N. tuberosa* (magnolia water lily): ultra-hardy; v vigorous; tuberous; bold deep green 40cm (16in) lvs; 10–20cm (4–8in) white fls, open mornings. Vars: 'Richardsonii' **2** (larger rounded fls, prominent sepals); 'Rosea'* (apple-green lvs; smaller soft pink fls).

Hardy hybrids: generally v hardy. V VIGOROUS VARS (fls to 20–25cm [8–10in] across): 'Attraction' **3** (garnet-red tipped pink, darkening); 'Charles de Meurville' (wine-red); 'Gladstoniana' (white); 'Picciola' (moderately hardy; crimson). VIGOROUS VARS (fls to 15–20cm [6–8in] across): 'Conqueror' (moderately hardy; deep red, dark centre, whitish sepals; free-flg); 'Escarboucle' **4** (deep crimson; v free-flg); 'James Brydon' (moderately to v hardy; young lvs purplish; fls carmine-red); 'Marliacea Albida'* (moderately to v hardy; white; free-flg); 'Marliacea Carnea' (moderately to v hardy; white tinged pink); 'Marliacea Rosea'* (moderately to v hardy; rose-pink, deeper centre); 'Masaniello'* (moderately to v hardy; deep rose, white sepals; v free-flg); 'Moorei' (moderately hardy; lvs spotted brown; fls canary-yellow); 'Pink Sensation'* (rich silvery-pink; v free-flg); 'René Gerard' (rich rose-pink marked salmon; v free-flg); 'Sioux' (moderately hardy; lvs mottled brownish; fls rich yellow, coppery centre, ageing red-copper); 'Sunrise'* (moderately hardy; lvs flecked brown; fls golden-yellow); 'Virginalis' (pure white; v free-flg);

'William Falconer' (moderately to v hardy; young lvs reddish, red-veined later; fls dark ruby-red). MODERATELY VIGOROUS VARS (fls to 10–15cm [4–6in] across): 'Albatross' (young lvs purplish; fls white); 'Aurora' (lvs mottled; fls yellow, ageing buff-orange to red); 'Firecrest'* **5** (bright pink, orange-red stamens); 'Froebelii' (blood-red; v free-flg); 'Graziella' (lvs variegated purple; fls red-orange fading yellowish); 'Laydekeri Fulgens' (crimson-magenta, red stamens); 'Laydekeri Lilacea'* (rose-lilac, darkening); 'Laydekeri Purpurata' (rose-crimson, orange-red stamens); 'Marliacea Chromatella' **6** ('Golden Cup'; lvs mottled bronze; fls primrose-yellow); 'Rose Arey'* (rose-pink; v free-flg). DWARF VARS (fls to 5–10cm [2–4in] across): 'Paul Hariot' **7** (lvs spotted maroon; fls apricot, fading orange-pink to coppery-red; v free-flg); 'Pygmaea Alba' (semi-hardy; white); 'Pygmaea Helvola' (semi-hardy; lvs mottled maroon; fls sulphur-yellow).

Tropical species: moderately vigorous. Tender; overwinter in moist soil at 13°C (55°F). *N. capensis** (Cape blue water lily): 15–20cm (6–8in) purple-blotched lvs, scalloped edges; sky-blue 10–15cm (4–6in) fls, above water. Var *zanzibariensis** has larger deep blue fls. *N. lotus**† (Egyptian lotus): tuberous root; large deep green lvs; white 15–25cm (6–10in) fls, pinkish inner petals, open into morning. *N. stellata** (blue lotus): tuberous; scalloped lvs; light blue 10–15cm (4–5in) fls.

Tropical hybrids: fls generally 15–20cm (6–8in) across, stand erect above water (good for cutting). Treat as for tropical spp. Vars: 'Afterglow'* **8** (deep pinkish-orange, yellowish centre); 'Baghdad'* (blue); 'Director George T. Moore'* (deep blue); 'Evelyn Randig'* **9** (lvs mottled purple; fls magenta-rose); 'H. C. Haarstick'*† (bronze-red lvs; rose-pink fls shading red); 'King of the Blues'* **10** (deep velvety-blue); 'Missouri'* (fluted lvs; large white fls); 'Mrs Edward Whitaker'* (light blue); 'Mrs George C. Hitchcock'* (v large deep pink fls); 'Mrs G. H. Pring'* (v large creamy fls); 'Panama Pacific'* (violet, lilac-purple sepals); 'Red Flare'*† (bronze-green lvs; dark red fls); 'St Louis'* (pale yellow); 'Trailblazer'* (yellow).

Other deep-water and floating aquatics

Listed alphabetically by family name. Unless noted, deep-water plants treated like water lilies (p528); generally summer-flowering. Floating plants simply dispersed on water surface. Where tender, overwinter as for tropical water lilies. **Propagation**: Division; seed.

Water hawthorn (*Aponogeton distachyus** 1*; Aponogetonaceae): semi-hardy; water depth 10–60cm (4–24in); spread 45cm (1½ft); light green strap-shaped floating lvs; forked spikes of waxy white 10cm (4in) fls with black stamens, spring to autumn.

Water fringe (*Nymphoides peltata 2*, *Limnanthemum nymphoides*; Gentianaceae; correctly 'Menyanthaceae): v hardy; water depth 10–45cm (4–18in); vigorous & spreading by runners, to 1.8m (6ft); resembles water lily, with floating crinkly-edged round lvs to 5cm (2in) across & fringed golden-yellow fls 2.5cm (1in) wide.

The frogbit family (*Hydrocharis* & *Stratiotes* spp; Hydrocharitaceae): v hardy floating plants; overwinter as submerged dormant buds. *Hydrocharis morsus-ranae 3* (frogbit): like v small floating water lily, with rounded fleshy lvs to 5cm

(12in) across in rosettes & small white 3-petalled 2cm (¾in) fls.
Stratiotes aloides 4 (water soldier): 10–20cm (4–8in) rosettes of spiky, spiny-edged pineapple-like lvs; curious 5cm (2in) white fls (dioecious).

Water hyacinth (*Eichhornia crassipes 5*; Pontederiaceae): tender floating plant (invasive weed in warm climates); buoyant inflated stalks & long black trailing roots; rosettes of small heart-shaped lvs; showy 8–15cm (3–6in) hyacinth-like spikes of 10–30 lavender-blue fls, gold & blue eye.

Fairy moss (*Azolla caroliniana*; Salviniaceae, now correctly Azolliaceae): v hardy tiny floating plant forming colonies & overwintering submerged; trailing roots; minute lacy fern-like fronds of bright green lvs turning pink, then red, then brown from late summer. *A. filiculoides* is similar but less hardy.

Marginal aquatics

Listed alphabetically by family name. Shallow-water perennials (herbaceous unless noted) with foliage &/or flowers above surface, good for planting at edge of pond or (if potted) standing on pool shelf. Many spp rhizomatous & may be invasive (depends on whether roots confined, hence spreads not given). Generally summer-flowering. **Cultivation**: Unless stated, very hardy & for water depth over crown 5–10cm (2–4in); best planted in containers of stiff loam. Best in sun. Spp marked † also suitable for damp soil, bog garden, etc. **Propagation**: Division; seed. See also Perennials section (pp525–361) for some border plants that can grow in water.

The water plantain family (*Alisma, Echinodorus* & *Sagittaria* spp; Alismataceae): tuberous; for water to 15cm (6in) deep.
Alisma plantago-aquatica 6 (*A. plantago*, water plantain, mad-dog weed): to 45–60cm (1½–2ft); plantain-like lance-shaped to oval lvs to 15cm (6in) long, long stalks; panicles of small pale rose-pink to creamy-white fls, opening afternoons. Weedy if not dead-headed.
Echinodorus (*Alisma*, correctly *Baldellia*) *ranunculoides*: to 30cm (1ft); rosettes of dark narrowish lvs to 10cm (4in) long; clusters of small rosy-white fls.
Sagittaria sagittifolia 7 (*S. natans*, arrowhead): to 60cm (2ft); pale green arrow-shaped lvs to 30cm (1ft) long; whorled 30–45cm (1–1½ft) spikes of white fls, brown stamens. Tubers edible. Invasive. *S. japonica 8* (Japanese arrowhead; correctly a var of *S. sagittifolia*) is similar but more vigorous, to 75–90cm (2½–3ft); fls larger, white with yellow stamens (double in var 'Flore Pleno' [plena]).
The arum family (*Acorus, Calla* & *Orontium* spp;

Araceae): rhizomatous, with typical arum fls (see p376, where see also *Lysichiton* & *Zantedeschia* spp, also suitable for shallow water).
Acorus calamus 9 (sweet flag): ultra-hardy; to 60–90cm (2–3ft); iris-like strap-shaped lvs*, striped yellowish in var 'Variegatus' 10; stout brownish spadices to 10cm (4in) long. Root edible (dried & candied).
A. gramineus† (Japanese sweet flag): to 30cm (1ft); v narrow, grassy evergreen lvs, striped white in var 'Variegatus'; rarely flowers. Sometimes grown indoors but v hardy.
Calla palustris† 11 (bog or water arum): ultra-hardy; to 30cm (1ft); glossy heart-shaped lvs to 15cm (6in) long on fleshy stalks; white spathes, yellow spadix; red frs in clusters.
Orontium aquaticum† 12 (golden club): to 45cm (1½ft); metallic blue-green lvs to 30×10cm (12×4in), floating if water deep; 10cm (4in) poker-like spadices on long white stalks, from late spring. For water 8–30cm (3–12in) deep or more.
Water forget-me-not (*Myosotis palustris†*;

correctly, *M. scorpioides*; Boraginaceae); ultra-hardy; to 20cm (8in); v similar to common biennial forget-me-not (p486) but fls deeper blue; evergreen.

Flowering rush (*Butomus umbellatus* **1**; Butomaceae): to 0.6–1.2m (2–4ft); rhizomatous; rush-like narrow lvs, bronze-purple when young; 8–10cm (3–4in) umbels of rose-pink fls 2.5cm (1in) wide on tall stems. Water depth to 15cm (6in).

Brass buttons (*Cotula coronopifolia*†; Compositae): semi-hardy; semi-prostrate, to 15–30cm (6–12in); fleshy lance-shaped lvs* to 8cm (3in) long; profuse golden-yellow button-like fl heads, long season. Short-lived but self-seeds.

The sedge family (*Cyperus, Eriophorum* & *Scirpus* spp): generally rhizomatous, with v narrow, rush-like erect foliage. Spp listed v hardy, but tender *Cyperus alternifolius*† (umbrella plant) & *C. papyrus*† (papyrus), often grown indoors, can spend summer in garden pool.

Cyperus longus **2** (sweet galingale): to 90–120cm (3–4ft); invasive; dark green ribbed stems; red-brown plumes of tiny fls, glossy green pendulous bracts.

Eriophorum angustifolium† (cotton grass): to 45cm (1½ft); dense tufts of lvs; silky white tassel-like infls on slender stems. *E. latifolium* (broad cotton grass) is similar but lvs broader.

Scirpus tabernaemontani 'Zebrinus'† **3**: moderately to v hardy; to 1m (3ft); foliage banded green & white; fls insignificant. Water depth to 15cm (6in); divide regularly. Var 'Albescens' (*S. albescens*) is similar but taller; foliage creamy-white, longitudinally striped green.

Bog bean (buck bean, marsh trefoil, *Menyanthes trifoliata* **4**; Gentianaceae; correctly Menyanthaceae): to 25cm (10in); rhizomatous; trifoliolate bean-like lvs, long stalks; pinkish-white 2.5cm (1in) fringed fls in racemes, spring & early summer. Can be weedy.

Variegated manna-grass (*Glyceria maxima* [*G. aquatica, G. spectabilis*] 'Variegata'†; Gramineae): to 60–90cm (2–3ft); true grass with lvs variegated green, yellow & white, flushed pink spring & autumn. Spreading.

Water irises (*Iris* spp; Iridaceae): aquatic spp of beardless irises (see p386).

I. lacvigata: to 45–75cm (1½–2½ft); pale green grassy lvs; clear deep blue-purple fls 10–15cm (4–6in) wide in 3s. Vars: 'Alba' (white); 'Albopurpurea' (pale blue flecked white); 'Atropurpurea' (violet-purple); 'Colchesteri' (white mottled blue); *elegantissima* **5** (*variegata*; lvs variegated silver; fls pale blue); 'Rose Queen'† (hybrid with *I. kaempferi*; rose-pink); 'Snowdrift' (large white fls, petal bases mottled yellow).

I. pseudacorus† **6** (yellow water iris): vigorous, to 1–1.5m (3–5ft) or more; blue-green lvs; rich

yellow 8cm (3in) fls on branched glossy stems. Vars: 'Golden Queen' (large golden-yellow fls); 'Sulphur Queen' (primrose-yellow); 'Variegata' (young lvs variegated golden).

Corkscrew rush (*Juncus effusus* 'Spiralis'†; Juncaceae): curious ultra-hardy foliage plant, to 45cm (1½ft), with twisted dark green foliage; fls insignificant. *J. e.* 'Vittatus' has straight golden-striped lvs. Good in poor soils.

Water mint (*Mentha aquatica*† **7**; Labiatae): to 30cm (lft); hairy toothed lvs*; spikes of lilac fls in whorls. Can be invasive.

Water canna (*Thalia dealbata*; Marantaceae): moderately hardy; to 1.8m (6ft); canna-like leathery lvs to 50×25cm (20×10in), white-powdered; crowded panicles of small crimson-purple fls on tall stem. Best overwintered under glass unless v mild.

Pickerel weed (*Pontederia cordata* **8**; Pontederiaceae): ultra-hardy; to 60–90cm (2–3ft) or more; rhizomatous; heart-shaped dark glossy green lvs to 25×15cm (10×6in); stout spikes of soft blue fls, yellow eye, late summer. Var *angustifolia* is similar, but lvs lance-shaped.

The buttercup family (*Caltha* & *Ranunculus* spp; Ranunculaceae): ultra-hardy.

Caltha palustris† (marsh marigold, kingcup, water cowslip): to 30–45cm (1–1½ft); clump of heart-shaped 15cm (6in) lvs on fleshy stems; cup-shaped pale to golden-yellow fls 5cm (2in) wide, spring. Vars: 'Alba' (compact; white); 'Plena' **9** ('Monstrosa'; deep yellow double fls).

C. leptosepala is similar but lvs smaller; fls white. *C. polypetala* (giant kingcup) is larger, to 90cm (3ft), with 30cm (1ft) lvs & 8cm (3in) golden-yellow fls; sprawls.

Ranunculus lingua 'Grandiflora'† **10** (great spearwort): to 75cm (2½ft); rhizomatous; dark blue-green erect lvs to 20cm (8in) long; sprays of 5cm (2in) golden-yellow fls, all summer.

Houttuynia (*Houttuynia cordata*†; Saururaceae): to 40cm (16in); rhizomatous & may be invasive; bright red branching stems; metallic bluish-green heart-shaped lvs*; small spikes of white fls, pure white bracts, double in var 'Plena'.

Reedmaces (cat-tails, *Typha* spp; incorrectly, bulrushes; Typhaceae): rhizomatous; long grass-like flat lvs; brown poker-like infls (good for drying). Often v invasive.

T. angustifolia: to 1.8m (6ft); slender, graceful lvs; dark brown infls.

T. minima **11** (dwarf reedmace): to 30–75cm (1–2½ft); light green v narrow lvs; small roundish infls. Not v hardy if rhizome exposed in winter.

Acknowledgments

This book resulted from more than two years of hard work by a large team, and I should like to thank them all for their help – not least the artists who produced the illustrations and the consultants listed who were diligent in correcting both my own and the artists' mistakes. Closer to home, warmest thanks are due to: Sue Minter, who did most of the detailed planning and also (along with Brian Carter) drafted much of the text; Trevor Dolby and, subsequently, Brian Carter, who co-ordinated the work of the artists; Brian again and Jan Roberts for their research work; Maggie Hall and Sue Wright for typing all the words; Mike McGuinness for his guidance on design and artistic problems; Frances Perry for invaluable general advice on matters horticultural; and the many nurserymen in Britain and North America who provided catalogues and information on their plants. — M.W.

Consultants

Trees & shrubs: Roy Lancaster, plus Allen Coombes, Ron Ewart (fuchsias), Michael Gibson (roses), Frank Knight (rhododendrons, camellias & their relatives) & Humphrey Welch (dwarf conifers).
Climbers: Noel J. Prockter & Roy Lancaster, plus Jim Fisk (clematis) & Michael Gibson (roses).
Perennials: Alan Bloom, plus Harold Bagust (pelargoniums), Aidan Brady (grasses), Richard Cawthorne (violets & violas), Reginald Kaye (ferns), David McClintock (bamboos), W. Rickaby (carnations & pinks), Gordon Rowley (cacti & succulents) & James Smith (florists' chrysanthemums).
Bulbs, corms & tubers: Frederick Doerflinger, plus Philip Damp (dahlias) & Ray Jeffs (irises).
Rock plants: Will Ingwersen, plus Frank Knight (heaths, heathers & their relatives).
Annuals & biennials: Arthur Hellyer.
Water plants: Frances Perry.
North American general consultant: John E. Elsley.

Illustration credits

Maps: Eugene Fleury
Colour plates:
Bob Bampton/Garden Studio: 155, 169-71, 175-7, 181-3, 191-9, 203, 215, 219-27
Owain Bell/Garden Studio: 321-5
David Cook: 487-91, 495, 507, 511
Helen Cowcher: 363-79, 385-91, 397-407, 423
Kevin Dean: 205-7
Sarah-Gay Fletcher: 59-61, 121-7, 381-3, 393-5, 409-19
Sarah Fox-Davies: 15-57, 63-5, 83, 107-13, 149, 173, 179
Victoria Goaman: 427-85
Sheila Hadley: 67, 85-99, 133, 151-3, 211
Christine Hart-Davies: 101-5, 141-3, 289, 529-33
Susan Hillier: 253-7, 263, 279-85, 295-7, 493, 497-503, 509, 513-27
Marilyn Leader: 229-39, 247-51, 265-77, 287, 309, 313-9, 327-49, 421
Vanessa Luff: 69, 185-9
Josephine Martin/Garden Studio: 201
Inga Moore: 79-81, 117-19, 129-31, 135-9, 217
Donald Myall: 157-67, 241-5
Sandra Pond: 291-3, 505
Andrew Riley/Garden Studio: 259-61, 299, 311
Nina Roberts: 145-7, 213
David Salariya/Jillian Burgess: 71-7, 209
Sue Wickison: 115, 301-7, 351-61
Catherine Wood: 425

Index

Due to the very large number of species and varieties covered by this book, the index refers to genera and common names only. To find a particular species or one of its varieties, first look up its genus name in the index, then turn to the page number given, where you will find that species listed alphabetically. Where a number of species share a mutual general common name, that name only is listed, e.g. for Turkey oak, English oak, etc, *see* oaks. Where a species bears a misleading common name, or a genus bears a misleading synonymous name, a cross-reference is given to its correct genus name, for example, the entry for lilacs *(Syringa)* has a cross-reference for *Ceanothus,* the Californian lilacs, and the entry for *Aster* has a cross-reference for *Callistephus* (China asters).

Aaron's beard, 108
abele, 194
Abelia, 66
Abeliophyllum, 140
Abelmoschus, 510
Abies, 26, 34
Abronia, 524
absinthe, 270
Abutilon, 132
Acacia, 120, *see also Albizia,* 120, *Robinia,* 126
Acaena, 468
Acantholimon, 456
Acanthopanax, 56
Acanthophyllum, 430
Acanthus, 350
Acer, 46-50
Achillea, 270, 434
Achnatherum, 292
Acidanthera, 392
aconites, 326
Aconitum, 326
Acorus, 530
Acroclinium, 488
Actaea, 328
Actinidia, 248
Adam's needle, 50
adder's-tongues, 396
Adenocarpus, 120
Adenophora, 260
Adiantum, 320
adobe lily, 396
Adonis, 328, 514
Aesculus, 112
Aetheopappus, 278
Aethionema, 440
African blue lilies, 370
African corn lilies, 394
African daisies, 490, 494
African iris, 394
Agapanthus, 370
Agastache, 294
Agathaea, 494
Agathis, 44
Agave, 252
Ageratum, 490
ageratum, hardy, 280
Agrostemma, 488, *see also Lychnis,* 266
Agrostis, 504
Ailanthus, 226
Ajuga, 454
Akebia, 248-50
Albizia, 120
Albizzia, see Albizia, 120
Alcea, 510
Alchemilla, 334
alders, 62, *see also Fothergilla,* 110
Alexandrian laurel, 222
Alisma, 530, *see also Echinodorus,* 530
Alkanets, 256

Allegheny spurge, 64
Allium, 362
almonds, ornamental, 186, 188
Alnus, 62
Alonsoa, 514
Alopecurus, 290
Aloysia, 216
alpenrose, 90
alpine campions, 432
alpine rose, 90
Alstroemeria, 254
Alternanthera, 350
Althaea, 510, see also Hibiscus, 132
Alyssum, 440-2, 500, *see also Ptilotrichum,* 442
Amaracus, 454
Amaranthus, 486
× Amarcrinum, 372
× *Amarygia,* 372
Amaryllis, 368, 372, 374
Amelanchier, 174
American laurels, 102
American pawpaw, 218
Ammobium, 488
Ampelopsis, 246
Amsonia, 350
Amur cork tree, 192-4
Amygdalus, see Prunus, 188
Anacyclus, 434
Anagallis, 526
Anaphalis, 280
Anchusa, 256, 426, 486, *see also Brunnera,* 256
Andromeda, 102-4, 444, 448
Androsace, 464 *see also Douglasia,* 464
Anemone, 328-30, 422, 466
angel's fishing rod, 392
angel's trumpets, 208, 518
angel's wings, 376
Anomatheca, 394
Antennaria, 434
Anthemis, 270, 272, 492
Anthericum, 300, 304
Antholyza, 392
Anthyllis, 120, 124
Antirrhinum, 474, 516
Aphanostephus, 490
Aponogeton, 530
Aporocactus, 260
apple of Peru, 518
apples, ornamental, 180-2
apricots, ornamental, 188
Aquilegia, 330, 466
Arabis, 442

Aralia, 56, *see also Acanthopanax,* 56, *Fatsia,* 56
Araucaria, 44
Araujia, 228
arbor-vitae, 16, 22
Arbutus, 100
Arctostaphylos, 100, 488
Arenaria, 432, *see also Sagina,* 432
Argemone, 512
Argyle apple, 134
Arecastrum, 148
Arisaema, 374-6
Arisarum, 376
Aristolochia, 248
Armeniaca, 188
Armeria, 358, 456
Arnebia, 256
Arnica, 280
aroids, 374-6
Aronia, 174
Arrhenatherum, 290
arrowheads, 530
Artemisia, 78, 270, 434
Arum, 376
arums, 374-6, 530
Aruncus, 336
Arundinaria, 292
Asarina, 474, 516
Asarum, 350
Asclepias, 350-2
ash trees, 142, *see also Sorbus,* 178
Asiatic sweetleaf, 226
Asimina, 218
Asparagus, 250
aspens, 194
Asperula, 360, 484, 526
Asphodeline, 300
asphodels, 300
Asphodelus, 300
Aspidistra, 300
Asplenium, 320
Astelia, 300
Aster, 272-4, 434, 490, *see also Callistephus,* 492, *Felicia,* 494, *Olearia,* 78-80
Asterago, 274
Astilbe, 336-8
Astilboides, 340
Astrantia, 346
Athrotaxis, 42
Athyrium, 320
Atragene, 236
Atriplex, 218, 522
Aubrieta, 442
Aucuba, 80-2
Aunt Eliza, 392
auricula, 460
Aurinia, 442
Australian fuchsias, 192

Australian honeysuckles, 150
autumn amaryllis, 374
autumn crocuses, 418-20
autumn daffodil, 366
avalanche lily, 396
Avena, 290, 504
avens, 334, 468
azaleas, 94-8, deciduous, 94-6, evergreen, 96-8
azaleodendrons, 98
Azara, 108
azarole, 176
Azolla, 530
Aztec lily, 374

Babiana, 392
baboon flower, 392
baby blue-eyes, 506
baby's breath, 266, 488
baby's tears, 360
Baccharis, 78
bald cypresses, 42
Baldellia, 530
balloon flowers, 262, 526
balm of Gilead, 194
balms, 294
balsams, 520
bamboos, 292, *see also Nandina,* 60
Bambusa, 292
bananas, 358
baneberries, 328
Banksia, 150
Baptisia, 298
barberries, 58-60
Barberton daisy, 280
barrenworts, 254
Bartonia, 524
basil, 506
basket flowers, 374, 492
basswood, 214
Bauhinia, 120
bay, 116
bayberries, 222-4
bead tree, 222
beans, 508
bearberry, 448
bear's breeches, 350
beauty-berries, 216
beauty-bush, 66
beavertail grass, 418
bedstraw, 360
beeches, 106
beefsteak plant, 350
Begonia, 424, 522
Belamcanda, 392
Belladonna lily, 372
Bellevalia, 400
bellflowers, 260-2, 426-8, 522, *see also*

Lapageria, 250
Bellis, 490
bells of Ireland, 506
bellwort, 306
Benthamidia, 82
Benzoin, 116
Berberidopsis, 248
Berberis, 58-60, *see also*
 Mahonia, 60
Bergenia, 338
Bessera, 372
Beta, 522
Bethlehem sage, 256
Betonica, 296
betony, 296
Betula, 62
Bignonia, 64, 230
Bilderdykia, 250
bindweeds, 352
birches, 62
bird-of-paradise flower,
 360
bird of paradise shrub,
 120
bird's eyes, 514
bishop's hats, 254
bishop's wort, 296
bistort, 316
bitternut, 112
bitter root, 458
bittersweets, 248
blackberry lily, 392
black-eyed Susans, 496,
 520
black gum, 224
black haw, 72
black snake-root, 328
blackthorn, 188
blackwood, 120
bladder cherry, 360
bladder senna, 122
blanket flowers, 276,
 494
blazing stars, 282, 524
Blechnum, 320
bleeding hearts, 354
Bletilla, 482
blood flower, 372
blood-flower, 352
blood-leaf, 350
blood lilies, 372
bloodroot, 482
bluebeard lilies, 300
bluebeards, 216
bluebells, 256, 398, 428
blueberries, 104, 448
blue-blossom, 154
blue broom, 124
blue buttons, 350
blue cowslip, 256
blue cupidone, 280
blue daisy, 494
blue-dicks, 372
blue dawn flower, 248
blue-eyed grass, 454
blue-eyed Mary, 426
blue grama, 290
blue lace flower, 526
blue thimble flower, 514
bluets, 484
blueweed, 486
bluewings, 516
Bocconia, 312
bog bean, 532
bog myrtle, 222
bog rosemary, 448
Boltonia, 274
bonesets, 256, 280
bonnet bellflowers, 262

Boronia, 190-2
Boston ivy, 248
bottlebrushes, 136-8
Bougainvillea, 234
bouncing Bet, 266
Bouteloua, 290
Bouvardia, 190
bowman's root, 336
box, 64, *see also*
 Pittosporum, 148,
 Sarcococca, 64
box-elder, 48
box-wood, 64
Brachycome, 490
Brachyglottis, 78
Brachysema, 120
Brahea, 148
brambles, 168
brass buttons, 532
Brassica, 500-2
Brazilian coleus, 296
breath of heaven, 192
bridal wreath, 170
briers, 156
Brimeura, 400
Briza, 290, 504
broad-leaved kindling
 bark, 134
broad-leaved Sally, 134
Brodiaea, 366, 372
brooms, 116-8, *see also*
 Erinacea, 124, *Ruscus*,
 222
Broussonetia, 222
Browallia, 518
Bruckenthalia, 444
Brugmansia, 208
Brunfelsia, 208
Brunnera, 256
buck bean, 532
buckeyes, 112
buckthorns, 154, *see*
 also Hippophaë, 84
Buddleia, 128
bugbanes, 328
buffalo berry, 84
bugle lilies, 394
bugles, 454
bugleweeds, 454
bugloss, 256
Bulbocodium, 418
bull bay, 130
bulrushes, 532
bunchberry, 352
bunny ears, 260
bunny rabbits, 516
bunya-bunya, 44
Buphthalmum, 280
Bupleurum, 226, 346
burnets, 336
burning bush, 360,
 522
bush cherry, 186
busy Lizzie, 522
butcher's broom, 222
Butia, 148
Butomus, 532
buttercups, 332, 424,
 466
butterfly bushes, 128
butterfly flower, 518
butterfly irises, 394
butterfly lilies, 360
butterfly tree, 120
butterfly-weed, 352
butternut, 112
buttonwood, 224
butterwort, 480
Buxus, 64

cabbage, ornamental,
 500-2
cabbage tree, 50
Cacalia, 490
cacti, 258-60
Caesalpina, 120
calabash gourds, 504
Caladium, 376
Calamintha, 294
calamints, 294
calamondin, 192
Calandrina, 526
Calceolaria, 342, 474,
 516
Calendula, 490-2
calico bush, 102
California bay, 116
California bluebell, 506
California laurel, 116
Californian fuchsia,
 480-2
Californian lilacs, 154
Californian "tree" poppy,
 314
California poppies, 512
Calla, 530
calla lilies, 376
Calliandra, 120-2
Callicarpa, 216
Calliopsis, 492
Callirhoe, 308
Callisia, 352
Callistemon, 136-8
Callistephus, 492
Calluna, 444
Calocedrus, 16
Calocephalus, 78
Calochortus, 416, 418
Calonyction, 500
Caltha, 532
Calycanthus, 218
camass, 416
Camassia, 416
Camellia, 210
Campanula, 260-2, 426-
 8, 522
campernelle jonquil, 364
camphor tree, 116
campions, 266, 432
Campsis, 230
canary-bird bush, 124
canary clover, 298
canary creeper, 526
candytufts, 442, 502
Canna, 424, *see also*
 Thalia, 532
Canterbury bell, 522
Cantua, 224
Cape daisy, 498
Cape figwort, 344
Cape fuchsia, 344
Cape honeysuckle, 230
Cape jasmine, 190
Cape leadwort, 250
Cape marigolds, 436,
 494
Cape may, 192
Cape plumbago, 250
Cape stock, 502
Capsicum, 518
Caragana, 122
Cardamine, 284
cardinal climber, 500
cardinal flower, 356
Cardiocrinum, 416
Cardiospermum, 526
Carduus, 492
Carex, 354
Carlina, 434

Carmel creeper, 154
Carmichaelia, 122
carnations, 264, 488
carob, 122
Carolina allspice, 218
Carolina jessamine, 250
Carpenteria, 198
Carpinus, 62
Carpobrotus, 252
Carrisa, 218
Carya, 112
Caryopteris, 216
Cassia, 122, 298
Cassiope, 444
Castanea, 106
castor bean, 524
cast-iron plant, 300
caster-oil plant, 524, *see
 also Fatsia*, 56
Catalpa, 64
Catananche, 280
catawbas, 64
catberry, 56
catchflies, 266, 488
Catharanthus, 350
cathedral bells, 514
catmint, 294-6
cat's ear, 418
cat-tails, 532
Caucasian wingnut, 112
Cautleya, 360
Ceanothus, 154
cedars, true, 30, 34, *see
 also Athrotaxis*, 42,
 Chamaecyparis, 14,
 Cryptomeria, 42, 44,
 Cupressus, 16,
 Juniperus, 18, 24,
 Libocedrus, 16, *Thuja*,
 16
Cedrus, 30, 34
celandine, 466
celandine poppy, 314
Celastrus, 248
Celmisia, 274
Celosia, 486
Celsia, 516
Celtis, 214
Cenia, 494
ceniza, 206
Centaurea, 278, 492
Centranthus, 346
century plants, 252
Cephalaria, 354
Cephalocereus, 258
Cephalotaxus, 40
Ceratonia, 122
Ceratostigma, 224, 358
Cercidiphyllum, 62
Cercis, 122
Cereus, 258
Cestrum, 208
Ceterach, 320
Chaenomeles, 180
chalice vines, 246
chalk plant, 266
Chamaecyparis, 14, 20
Chamaedaphne, 100
Chamaemelum, 270
Chamaepericlymenum,
 352-4
Chamaerops, 148, *see
 also Trachycarpus*,
 148
Chamelaucium, 138
chamois cress, 442
chamomile, 270
chaparral broom, 78
chaste tree, 216

checkerberry, 448
Cheiranthus, 442, 502
Chelone, 342
cherries, ornamental,
  184-6
cherry laurels, 184
cherry pie, 486
chestnuts, 106, *see also*
  Aesculus, 112
Chiastophyllum, 440
chicory, 280
Chilean bellflowers, 250,
  524
Chilean fire bush, 150
Chilean glory flower, 230
Chilean guava, 138
Chilean hazel, 150
Chilean jasmine, 228
Chilean nut, 150
Chilean potato tree, 246
Chilean yew, 38
Chimonanthus, 218
China aster, 492
China-berry, 222
chincherinchee, 418
Chinese date, 154
Chinese forget-me-not,
  486
Chinese gooseberry,
  248
Chinese houses, 516
Chinese lantern, 360
Chinese parasol tree,
  226
Chinese sacred bamboo,
  60
Chinese scholar tree,
  126
Chinese swamp cypress,
  42
Chinese tallow tree, 220
Chionanthus, 142
Chionodoxa, 398
chittam wood, 52
chives, ornamental, 362
Chlidanthus, 366
Chlorophytum, 300
Choisya, 192
chokeberries, 174
chollas, 258
Chordospartium, 122
Chorizema, 122
Christmas berry, 174
Christmas rose, 332
Christ's thorn, 154
Chrysanthemum, 268,
  270-2, 434, 492
Chrysogonum, 276
Cichorium, 280
cigar flower, 356
Cimicifuga, 328
Cineraria, 496
Cinnamomum, 116
cinquefoils, 168, 334,
  468
Cirsium, 278
Cissus, 246
Cistus, 76
citrange, 192
× *Citrofortunella*, 192
× *Citroncirus*, 192
Citrus, 192, 194
Cladanthus, 492
Cladrastis, 122
Clarkia, 510, *see also*
  Godetia, 510
clary, 296, 506
Clematis, 236-8, 330
Cleome, 522

Cleretum, 520
Clerodendrum, 216
Clethra, 218-20
Cleyera, 212
Clianthus, 122, 232
climbing bittersweets,
  248
climbing gazanias, 248
Clintonia, 300
Clivia, 372
clock vines, 248, 520
clove pinks, 264
clovers, 298, 480
Cnicus, 278, 492
Cobaea, 514
cobnut, 62
cobra lily, 376
cockscomb, 486
Cocos, 148
Codonopsis, 248, 262
Coix, 504
Colchicum, 418-20
Coleonema, 192
Coleus, 506
Colletia, 154
Collinsia, 516
Colocasia, 376
Colquhounia, 114
columbines, 330, 466
Colutea, 122
comfrey, 256
coneflowers, 276, 496
Confederate jasmine,
  228
Consolida, 514
Convallaria, 300
Convolvulus, 220, 352,
  500
Cooperaria, 366
Coprosma, 190
coralberry, 68
coral drops, 372
coral flower, 348
coral peas, 232
coral plant, 248
coral trees, 124
Cordyline, 50
Coreopsis, 276, 492
corn cockle, 488
Cornelian cherry, 82
cornels, 82, 352-4
cornflower aster, 274
cornflowers, 278, 492
corn lily, 300
corn marigold, 492
corn, ornamental, 504
Cornus, 82, 352-4
Corokia, 82
Coronilla, 122-4
Corsican mint, 454
Cortaderia, 290
Cortusa, 464
Corydalis, 478
Corylopsis, 110
Corylus, 62
Corynabutilon, 132
Coryphantha, 258
cosmea, 494
Cosmos, 494
Cotinus, 52
Cotoneaster, 172
cotton grass, 532
cottonwoods, 194
Cotula, 436, 494, 532
Cotyledon, 440
Coventry bells, 262
cowberry, 448
cow herb, 522
cowslips, 318, 462

coyote bush, 78
crab apples, 180-2
Crambe, 284
cranberry, 448
cranberry bushes, 72
cranesbills, 286, 450-2
crape myrtle, 222
Crassula, 440
× *Crataegomespilus*,
  176
Crataegus, 176
× *Crataemespilus*, 176
cream-bush, 170
cream cups, 512
creeping gloxinia, 516
creeping Jenny, 316
creeping zinnia, 496
Crepis, 436, 494
Cretan dittany, 454
crimson flag, 394
crimson glory vine, 246
crimson star glory, 500
Crinodendron, 200
× *Crinodonna*, 372
Crinum, 372
Crocosmia, 392, *see also*
  Tritonia, 394
Crocus, 380-2
cross vine, 230
Crotalaria, 124, 508
crown imperial fritillary,
  396
cruel plant, 228
Cryophytum, 520
Cryptogramma, 320
Cryptomeria, 42, 44
Cuban lily, 398
cuckoo flower, 284
cucumber tree, 128
Cucurbito, 504
cudweed, 270
Culver's root, 344
Cunninghamia, 42
cup-&-saucer vine,
  514
cup flowers, 518
Cuphea, 356
Cupid's dart, 280
× *Cupressocyparis*,
  14-16
Cupressus, 16, 22
currants, ornamental,
  202-4, *see also*
  Symphoricarpos, 68
curry plant, 282
Curtonus, 392
curuba, 234
cushion bush, 78
cushion pink, 432
Cyananthus, 428
Cycas, 44
Cyclamen, 422
Cydonia, 180, *see also*
  Chaenomeles, 180
cydonia, 180
Cymbalaria, 474
Cynara, 278
Cynoglossum, 256, 486
Cyperus, 532
Cyprepedium, 482
cypresses, true, 16, 22 ,
  see also
  Chamaecyparis, 14,
  20,
  × *Cupressocyparis*,
  14-16, *Glyptostrobus*,
  42, *Taxodium*, 42
cypress vine, 500
Cyprus-turpentine, 52

Cyrilla, 220
Cyrtomium, 320
Cystopteris, 320
Cytisus, 116-8

Daboecia, 444
Dacrydium, 38
Dactylorrhiza, 358
daffodils, 364, 368
Dahlia, 378, 494
dairy pink, 522
daisies, 272, 274, 490
daisy bushes, 78-80
damask violet, 284
dame's rocket, 284
dame's violet, 284
Danaë, 222
Daphne, 212, 484
date palms, 148
Datura, 208, 518
Daubentonia, 126
Davallia, 322
Davidia, 224
daylilies, 302
dead nettles, 294
Decaisnea, 220-2
Decumaria, 244
delicate lily, 366
Delphinium, 326, 514
Dendromecon, 224
Dennstaedtia, 322
Dentaria, 284
deodar, 30
Deschampsia, 290
desert candles, 300
Desfontainea, 128
Desmodium, 298
Deutzia, 198
Devil's club, 56
Devil's fig, 512
diamond flower, 502
Dianthus, 264-6, 430,
  488
Diascia, 516
Dicentra, 354, 480
Dichelostemma, 372
Dicksonia, 322
Dictamnus, 360
Didiscus, 526
Dierama, 392
Diervilla, 66
Dietes, 394
Digitalis, 342, 516
Dimorphotheca, 436,
  494
Dionysia, 464
Diosma, 192
Diospyros, 220
Dipelta, 66
Diplacus, 342
Diplarrhena, 392
Diplazium, 320
Disanthus, 110
Disporum, 300
dittany, 360
Dodecatheon, 464
dog's-tooth violets, 396
dogwoods, 82
Dolichos, 508
Dondia, 484
donkey's tail, 284
Doronicum, 280
Dorotheanthus, 520
Dorycnium, 298
double orange daisy, 274
Douglas fir, 28, 36
Douglasia, 464
dove tree, 224

Doxantha, 230
Draba, 442
dracaenas, 50
Dracocephalum, 296
Dracunculus, 376
dragon plant, 376
Dregea, 228
Drimys, 226
dropwort, 336
Drosanthemum, 252
Dryas, 468
Dryopteris, 322, 324
Duchesnia, 334
Duranta, 216
dusty millers, 270, 278,
    460, 496
Dutchman's pipe, 248
dyer's greenwood, 118
dyer's woad, 502

eastern borage, 256
Eccremocarpus, 230
Echeveria, 284
Echinacea, 276
Echinocactus, 258
Echinocereus, 258
Echinocystis, 504
Echinodorus, 530
Echinops, 278
Echinopsis, 258
Echium, 486
Edgeworthia, 212
edelweiss, 436
Edraianthus, 428
Eichhornia, 530
Elaeagnus, 84
elders, 72
elephant's ear, 376
elms, 214
Elsholtzia, 294
Egyptian taro, 376
Embothrium, 150
Emilia, 490
endive, 280
Enkianthus, 100
Ensete, 358
epaulette tree, 208
epicacti, 260
Epigaea, 448
Epilobium, 308, 480
Epimedium, 254
Epiphyllum, 260
Eragrostis, 504
Eranthis, 422-4
Eremurus, 300
Erica, 100-2, 444-6
Erigeron, 274, 436
Erinacea, 124
Erinus, 474
Eriobotrya, 174
Eriophorum, 358
Erodium, 450-2
Eryngium, 346
Erysimum, 442, 502
Erythea, 148
Erythrina, 124
Erythronium, 396
Escallonia, 202
Eschscholzia, 512
Escobaria, 258
Eucalyptus, 134-6
Eucharidium, 510
Eucomis, 416
Eucryphia, 220
Eugenia, 138
Eulalia, 290
Euodia, 192
Euonymus, 74

Eupatorium, 78, 280
Euphorbia, 286, 524
Euryops, 78
Eutoca, 506
evening primroses, 308,
    480-2, 510
evergreen laburnum, 126
everlasting daisies, 488
everlasting flowers,
    280-2
everlasting peas, 232
Evodia, see Euodia, 192
Exochorda, 170

Fabiana, 208
Fagus, 106
fair maids of February,
    366
fair maids of France, 332,
    472
fair maids of Kent, 332
fairy bells, 300
fairy foxglove, 474
fairy lanterns, 300, 416
fairy moss, 530
fairy's thimble, 426
false acacia, 126
false castor-oil plant, 56
"false" cypresses, 14
false dragonhead, 296
false hellebores, 306
false indigoes, 298
false lupins, 298
false Solomon's seals,
    306
false spikenard, 306
false spiraeas, 170
farewell-to-spring, 510
× Fatshedera, 56
Fatsia, 56
fawn lilies, 396
feathertop, 292
Feijoa, 138
Felicia, 434, 494
fennel, giant ornamental,
    346
fern palm, 44
ferns, 320-4
Ferocactus, 258
Ferula, 346
fescues, 290
Festuca, 290
feverfew, 492
Ficus, 222
fig, 222
filberts, 62
Filipendula, 336
firecracker flower, 372
firecracker plant, 356
fire on the mountain, 524
firethorns, 174
firewheel, 150
firewheel tree, 152
Firmiana, 226
firs, true/silver, 26, 34,
    see also Cunninghamia,
    42, Pseudotsuga, 28,
    36
flags, 530
flame bush, 122
flame creeper, 250
flame nettle, 506
flame pea, 122
flannel bush, 218
flax, 356, 480, 524
fleabanes, 274, 436
fleece flowers, 250, 316
fleur-de-lys, 384

floss flowers, 490
flower-of-an-hour, 510
flower of Jove, 266
flowers of the west wind,
    366
foam flowers, 340
foam of May, 170
forget-me-nots, 256,
    426, 486, 530-2
Forsythia, 140
Fortunella, 192
Fothergilla, 110
four-o'clock plant, 524
foxgloves, 342, 516
foxglove trees, 64
foxtail lilies, 300
Fragaria, 334
Franklinia, 212
Fraxinus, 142
Freesia, 392-4
Fremontia, 218
Fremontodendron, 218
French mulberry, 216
fringe bell, 478
fringecup, 340
fringe trees, 142
Fritillaria, 396
frogbit, 530
Fuchsia, 144-6, 480-2,
    see also Correa, 192

Gaillardia, 276, 494
Galanthus, 366
Galax, 354
Galega, 298
Galeobdolon, 294
Galium, 360
gallberry, 54
Galtonia, 400
gardener's garters, 292
Gardenia, 190
garland flowers, 360, 484
garlic, ornamental, 362,
    see also Tulbaghia,
    374
Garrya, 220
gas plant, 360
× Gaulnettya, 102
Gaultheria, 102, 448
Gaulthettia, 102
Gaura, 308
gayfeathers, 282
Gaylussacia, 102
Gazania, 494, see also
    Mutisia, 248
gean, 184
Gelsemium, 250
Genista, 116-8
Gentiana, 354, 450
Geraldton wax plant, 138
Geranium, 286, 450-2,
    see also Pelargonium,
    288
Gerbera, 280
German catchfly, 266
germanders, 114, 456
Geum, 334, 468
Gevuina, 150
giant club, 258
giant daisy, 272
giant lilies, 416
Gilia, 514
Gillenia, 336
gillyflower, 502
ginger lilies, 360
Ginkgo, 44
gladdon, 388
Gladiolus, 382, see also

Acidanthera, 392
Glaucidium, 330
Glaucium, 512
Glechoma, 296
Gleditsia, 124
globe amaranth, 486
globe artichoke, 278
globe daisies, 480
globeflower, 466
globe flowers, 332
globe thistles, 278
globe tulips, 416
Globularia, 480
Gloriosa, 250
gloriosa daisies, 496
glory lily, 250
glory of the snow, 398
glory pea, 122, 232
Glyceria, 532
Glyptostrobus, 42
goat's beard, 336
goat's rue, 298
Godetia, 510
gold dust, 442
golden chain, 124
golden club, 530
golden cup, 512
golden dewdrop, 216
golden drop, 426
golden-eyed grass,
    454
golden foxtail, 290
golden larch, 30
golden moss, 438
golden rain, 124
golden rain tree, 226
golden rays, 282
golden rods, 274, 436
goldilocks, 272
Gomphrena, 486
Goniolimon, 358
gooseberries,
    ornamental, 202-4,
    see also Actinidia,
    248
Gordonia, 212, see also
    Franklinia, 212
gourds, ornamental, 504
granadillas, 234
granny's bonnet, 330
grape hyacinths, 400
grape ivies, 246
grape vines, 246-8
grasses, ornamental,
    290, 504
grass nut, 372
grass palm, 50
grass-widow, 454
grassy-bells, 428
Greek valerian, 314
green dragon, 374-6
Gregoria, 464
Grevillea, 150-2
Griselinia, 82
ground box, 482
ground ivy, 294-6
guavas, 138
guelder rose, 72
Guernsey lily, 374
Guevina, see Gevuina,
    150
guinea-hen flower, 396
gums, 110, 134-6, see
    also Nyssa, 224
Gunnera, 356
Gymnocarpium, 322
Gymnocladus, 124
Gypsophila, 266, 432,
    488

Haberlea, 452
Habranthus, 366
hackberries, 214
Hacquetia, 484
Haemanthus, 372
Hakea, 152
Halesia, 208
× Halimiocistus, 76
Halimium, 76
Hamamelis, 110
handerkerchief tree, 224
Haplopappus, 436
Hardenbergia, 232
harebell, 428
harebell poppy, 312
hare's ear, 346
harlequin flower, 394
hawkweeds, 282, 436
hawthorns, 176, see also
  Rhaphiolepis, 176
hazels, 62, see also
  Corylopsis, 110,
  Hamamelis, 110
heartsease, 526
heathers, 444-6
heaths, 100-2, 444-6
heavenly bamboo, 60
Hebe, 204-6, 474
Hedera, 56, 228
hedgehog broom, 124
Hedraeanthus, see
  Edraianthus, 428
Hedychium, 360
Hedyotis, 484
Hedysarum, 124
Helenium, 276
Helianthemum, 478
Helianthus, 276, 494-6
Helichrysum, 78, 280-2,
  436, 488
Helictotrichon, 290
Heliophila, 502
Heliopsis, 276
heliotrope, 486
Heliotropium, 486
Helipterum, 488
hellebores, 330-2
helleborines, 306
Helleborus, 330-2
helmet flower, 326
Helonias, 302
Helxine, 360
Hemerocallis, 302
hemlocks, 28-30, 36,
  see also Taxus, 40
hemp agrimony, 280
Hepatica, 466
herb Christopher, 328
herb paris, 306
Hermodactylus, 394
heron's-bills, 452
Hesperis, 284
Heteromeles, 174
Heuchera, 338
× Heucherella, 338
Hiba arbor-vitae, 16
Hibiscus, 132, 308, 510
hickories, 112
Hieracium, 282
Himalayan blue poppies,
  312
Himalayan elecampane,
  282
Himalayan honeysuckle,
  66
Himalayan parsley, 346
Hippophaë, 84
Hoheria, 132
Holcus, 290

hollies, 54-6, see also
  Nemopanthus, 56,
  Olearia, 80
hollyhocks, 510
Holodiscus, 170
honesty, 284, 502
honey flowers, 150, 152,
  358
honey locust, 124
honey myrtles, 138
honeysuckles, 68, 230,
  see also Banksia, 150,
  Tecomaria, 230
Hookera, 372
hop hornbeam, 62
hops, ornamental, 248,
  522
Hordeum, 504
horehound, 294
hornbeams, 62, see also
  Ostrya, 62
horned poppies, 512
horned rampions, 262,
  428
horse chestnuts, 112
horsefly, 298
horsemint, 294
Hosta, 302-4
Hottentot fig, 252
hound's-tongues, 256,
  486
houseleeks, 440
Houstonia, 484
Houttuynia, 532
Hovenia, 154
Hoya, 228
huckleberries, 102
Humulus, 248, 522
Hungarian daisy, 272
Hunnemannia, 512
Hutchinsia, 442
hyacinth bean, 508
Hyacinthella, 400
Hyacinthus, 400, see
  also Galtonia, 400
  Muscari, 400
Hydrangea, 200, 244
Hydrocharis, 530
Hylomecon, 312
Hymenocallis, 372-4
Hypericum, 108, 454
Hypolepis, 322
hyssops, 294
Hyssopus, 294

Iberis, 442, 502
ice plants, 252, 520
Idesia, 108
Ilex, 54-6
immortelle, 488
Impatiens, 520-2
Inca lily, 254
Incarvillea, 352
incense cedars, 16
inch plant, 352
Indian bean, 508
Indian bean trees, 64
Indian chocolate, 334
Indian cress, 526
Indian currant, 68
Indian hawthorn, 176
Indian poke, 306
Indian shot, 524
Indigofera, 124
indigos, 124
inkberry, 54
Inula, 282
Ionopsidium, 502

Ipheion, 366
Ipomoea, 248, 500
Ipomopsis, 514
Iresine, 350
Iris, 384-90,
  bearded 384-6,
  beardless, 386-8,
  bulbous, 390,
  crested, 388-90,
  water, 532,
  see also
  Hermodactylus, 394
ironbarks, 134-6
Isatis, 502
Ismene, 374
Itea, 202
ivies, 56, 228, see also
  Parthenocissus, 246
ivy-leaved toadflax, 474
Ixia, 394

Jack-in-the-pulpit, 376
Jacobaea, 496
Jacobean lily, 374
Jacob's ladders, 314
Jacob's rod, 300
Jankaea, 452
Japanese angelica tree,
  56
Japanese cedars, 42, 44
Japanese hydrangea
  vine, 244
Japanese ivy, 246
Japanese medlar, 174
Japanese pagoda tree,
  126
Japanese raisin tree, 154
japonica, 180
jasmine nightshade, 246
jasmines, 140, 234, 480,
  see also Gardenia,
  190, Mandevilla, 228,
  Trachelospermum,
  228
Jasminum, 140, 234, 480
Jeffersonia, 352
jelly-bean plant, 438
Jerusalem cowslip, 256
Jerusalem cross, 266
Jerusalem sage, 114,
  256
Jerusalem thorn, 126
jessamines, 208, 234,
  250
jetbead, 168
jewel weed, 520
Job's tears, 504
Joe Pye weed, 280
Johnny-jump-up, 526
jonquil, 364, 370
Joseph's coat, 350, 486
Jovibarba, 440
Jubaea, 148
Judas tree, 122
jujube, 154
Juncus, 532
Juneberries, 174
Juniperus, 18, 22-4

Kaffir lilies, 372, 394
kale, ornamental, 500
Kalmia, 102, 448
Kalmiopsis, 448
Kalopanax, 56
kangaroo thorn, 120
kangaroo vine, 246

karo, 148
katsura tree, 218
kaya, 40
kauri, 44
Kenilworth ivies, 474
Kennedia, 232
Kentranthus, 246
Kentucky coffee tree,
  124
kerosene bush, 78
Kerria, 168, see also
  Rhodotypos, 168
kingcup, 532
kingfisher daisy, 494
Kirengeshoma, 338
Kiwi fruit, 248
knapweeds, 278
Knautia, 354
Kniphofia, 304
knotweeds, 316, 524-6
Kochia, 522
Koeleria, 290
Koelreuteria, 224-6
Kolkwitzia, 66
Kolomikta vine, 248
kowhai, 126
kudzu vine, 232
kumquats, 192

lablab bean, 508
Labrador tea, 102
+ Laburnocytisus, 124
Laburnum, 124, see also
  Piptanthus, 126
lacebarks, 132
lad's love, 78
ladybells, 260
lady's mantles, 334
lady's slippers, 482
lady's smock, 284
Lagenaria, 504
Lagerstroemia, 222
Lagurus, 504
lambkill, 102
lamb's ear, 296
lamb's tail, 440
lamb's tongue, 296
Lamiastrum, 294
Lamium, 294
Lampranthus, 252
lancewood, 56
Lantana, 216
lantern tree, 220
Lapageria, 250
Lapeirousia, 394
larches, 30
Lardizabala, 248-50
Larix, 30
larkspurs, 326, 514
Lathyrus, 232, 298,
  508
laurels, 116, see also
  Danaë, 222,
  Daphne, 212, Kalmia,
  102, Prunus, 184
Laurus, 116
laurustinus, 72
Lavandula, 114
Lavatera, 132-4, 510
lavender cotton, 80
lavenders, 114
Layia, 496
lazy daisy, 490
leather-leaf, 100
leatherwood, 220
Ledum, 102
Legousia, 522
Leiophyllum, 488

Lemaireocereus, 260
lemon, 192
lemon verbena, 216
Lenten rose, 332
Lent lily, 364
Leonotis, 114
Leontopodium, 436
Leptospermum, 138
leopard flower, 392
leopard's banes, 280
Leptosiphon, 514
Lespedeza, 298
Leucanthemum, 272, 434
Leucocoryne, 366
Leucodendron, 152
Leucojum, 366
Leucophyllum, 206
Leucospermum, 152
Leucothoë, 102
Lewisia, 458
Leycesteria, 66
Leyland cypresses, 14
Liatris, 282
Libertia, 394
Libocedrus, 16
Ligularia, 282
Ligustrum, 142-4
lilacs, 140-2, see also
  Buddleia, 128,
  Ceanothus, 154,
  Hebe, 206
lilies of the Nile, 370
lilies, true, 408-14
  Lilium, 408-14,
  see also Cardiocrinum,
  416
lily of the field, 366
lily of the valley, 300
lily-of-the-valley tree, 220
lily tree, 130
lily-turfs, 304
limes, 214
Limnanthemum, 530
Limnanthes, 524
Limonium, 358, 524
Linaria, 342, 474, 516
lindens, 214
Lindera, 116
link, 444
Linnaea, 352
Linum, 356, 480, 524
lion's ear, 114
lion's heart, 296
lion's tail, 114
Lippia, 216
Liquidambar, 110
liquorice plant, 282
Liriodendron, 128
Liriope, 304
Lithodora, 426
Lithospermum, 256, 426,
  see also Moltkia, 426
Livingstone daisy, 520
Lobelia, 356, 524
Lobivia, 258
lobster claw, 232
Lobularia, 500
locust bean, 122
locusts, 126, see also
  Gleditsia, 124
Loddon lily, 366
Lomatia, 152
London pride, 340
Lonicera, 68, 230
loofah, 504
loosestrifes, 316, 356
Lophomyrtus, 138

loquat, 174
Loropetalum, 110
Lotus, 298
lotus (water lilies), 528
love-in-a-mist, 514
love-in-a-puff, 526
love-lies-bleeding, 486
Luculia, 190
Luffa, 504
Luma, 138
Lunaria, 284, 502
lungworts, 256
lupins, 126, 298
Lupinus, 126, 298, 508
Lychnis, 266, 432, 488
Lycoris, 374
Lynosyris, 272
Lysichiton, 376
Lysichitum, see
  Lysichiton, 376
Lysimachia, 316

Machaeranthera, 490
Macleaya, 312
mad-dog weed, 530
madrona, 100
magic flower of the Incas, 224
Magnolia, 128-30
magnolia vines, 250
× Mahoberberis, 60
Mahonia, 60
maidenhairs, 320
maidenhair tree, 44
maidenhair vine, 250
maize, ornamental, 504
Malcolmia, 502
mallow-wort, 510
mallows, 132-4, 308, 510
Malope, 510
Maltese cross, 266
Malus, 180-2
Malva, 308
Mammillaria, 258
mandarin, 192
Mandevilla, 228
manna-grass, variegated, 532
manuka, 138
manzanita, 100
maples, 46-50
marguerites, 270, 272, 494
marigolds, 490-2, 496-8, marsh, 532
mariposa lilies, 416
marjoram, 296
marsh trefoil, 532
marvel of Peru, 524
mask flower, 514
masterworts, 344
Matilija poppy, 314
Matricaria, 492
Matteuccia, 322
Matthiola, 502
Maurandia, 516
may, 176
May apple, 352
mayflower, 448
Mazus, 474
meadow cress, 284
meadow foam, 524
meadow rues, 328, 466
meadow saffrons, 418-20
meadowsweets, 336
mealy stringybark, 134
Meconopsis, 312

medlar, 176, see also
  Eriobotrya, 174
medlar-thorn, 176
Megasea, 338
Melaleuca, 138
Melandrium, 266
Melia, 222
Melianthus, 358
Melissa, 294
Melittis, 294
Mentha, 294, 454, 532
menthella, 454
Mentzelia, 524
Menyanthes, 532
Menziesia, 102
merrybells, 306
Mertensia, 256
Mesembryanthemum, 520
Mespilus, 176
mesquite, 126
Metasequoia, 42
Mexican fire plant, 524
Mexican ivy, 514
Mexican orange, 192
Mexican sunflower, 498
Mexican tulip poppy, 512
mezereon, 212
Michaelmas daisies, 272-4
Microcachrys, 38
mignonette, 526
Milium, 290
milkweeds, 350-2
milkworts, 482
milfoil, 270
Milla, 366
mimosa, 120
Mimulus, 342, 474-6
Mina, 500
mind-your-own-business, 360
mint bush, 114
mint shrub, 294
mints, ornamental, 294
Minuartia, 432
Mirabilis, 524
mirror plant, 190
Miscanthus, 290
mistflower, 280
Mitchella, 484
moccasin flower, 482
mock cucumber, 504
mock oranges, 198
mole plant, 524
Molinia, 290
Moltkia, 256, 426
Molucella, 506
monarch of the East, 376
monarch of the veldt, 498
Monarda, 294
monastery bells, 514
mondo grass, 304
money plant, 502
moneywort, 316
Mongolian sweet vetch, 124
monkey flowers, 342, 474
monkey puzzle, 44
monkshoods, 326
Montbretia, 392, see also
  Tritonia, 394
moon daisy, 272
moonflowers, 500
moonvine, 500
moonwort, 502
moosewood, 48
Moraea, 394

Morina, 354
Morisia, 478
morning glories, 220, 248, 500
Morus, 222
moss pink, 458
mother of thousands, 340
mountain ashes, 178
mountain avens, 468
mountain bluet, 278
mountain flax, 252
mountain heaths, 446-8
mountain holly, 56
mountain laurel, 102
mountain pepper tree, 226
mountain silverbell tree, 208
mountain tobacco, 280
Mount Atlas daisy, 434
mourning widow, 286
mouse-ear chickweeds, 432
mouse plant, 376
Muehlenbeckia, 250, 482-4
mugga, 136
mugworts, 270
mulberries, 222, see also
  Callicarpa, 216
mullein pink, 266
mulleins, 344, 476, 516
Musa, 358
musk flower, 476
musk hyacinth, 400
musks, 474
Mutisia, 248
Myosotidium, 256
Myosotis, 426, 486, 530-2
Myrica, 222-4
myrtles, 138, see also
  Lagerstroemia, 222,
  Melaleuca, 138,
  Myrica, 222-4
Myrtus, 138

Namaqualand daisies, 498
Nandina, 60
Narcissus, 364, 368-70
nasturtiums, 250, 526
Natal lilies, 394
Natal plum, 218
navelworts, 426
nectarine, 188
Nectaroscordum, 362
Nemesia, 516
Nemopanthus, 56
Nemophila, 506
Neobesseya, 258
Nepeta, 294-6
Nerine, 374
Nerium, 218
nettle trees, 214
New Zealand burrs, 468
New Zealand flax, 252
New Zealand holly, 80
New Zealand lilac, 206
Nicandra, 518
Nicotiana, 518
Nierembergia, 484, 518
Nigella, 514
ninebark, 170
nodding pincushion, 152

Nomocharis, 418
Nordmannia, 256
Nothofagus, 106
Notholirion, 418
nutgall tree, 52
nutmeg trees, 40
Nymphaea, 528
Nymphoides, 530
Nyssa, 224

oaks, 106
oats, ornamental, 504
obedient plant, 296
ocean spray, 170
Ocimum, 506
Oenothera, 308, 480-2, 510
old man, 78
old man's beard, 142
old woman, 270
Olea, 144
oleander, 218
Olearia, 78-80
oleasters, 84
olive, 144, *see also Elaeagnus*, 84, *Osmanthus*, 144
Omphalodes, 426
onions, ornamental, 362
Onoclea, 322
Ononis, 126, 298
Onopordum, 496
Onosma, 426
Ophiopogon, 304
Oplopanax, 56
Opuntia, 258
orach, 218, 522
orange ball tree, 128
oranges, 192, 194, *see also Maclura*, 222
orchids, 358, 482
orchid trees, 120
Orchis, 358
oregano, 296
Oregon grape, 60
Oreocome, 346
Origanum, 296, 454
Ornithogalum, 418, 420
Orobus, 298
Orontium, 530
orpine, 284, 438
orris, 384
Osage orange, 222
Oscularia, 254
osiers, 196
Osmanthus, 144, *see also* × *Osmarea*, 144, *Phillyrea*, 144
× *Osmarea*, 144
Osmunda, 322
Osteospermum, 436, 494
Ostrya, 82
Oswego tea, 294
Ourisia, 476
Our Lord's candle, 50
Oxalis, 420
ox-eye daisy, 272, 280
Oxycoccus, 448
Oxydendrum, 102-4
Oxypetalum, 520
Ozothamnus, 78

pachistimas, 74
Pachysandra, 64
Pachystegia, 80
Paeonia, 146, 310

paeony, 146, 310
pagoda trees, 126
paint brush, 490
painted daisy, 270-2
painted lady, 306
painted nettle, 506
painted tongue, 518
Paliurus, 154
palmetto, 148
palms, 146-8, *see also Cycas*, 44, *Cordyline*, 50
Palm Springs daisy, 492
Pancratium, 374
Panicum, 290
pansies, 348, 526
Papaver, 512
paperbush, 212
paper mulberry, 222
papyrus, 532
Paradisea, 304
Parahebe, 476
× *Pardancanda*, 392
Pardanthus, 392
Paris, 304-6
Paris daisy, 272
Parrotia, 110, *see also Parrotiopsis*, 110
Parrotiopsis, 110
parrot-leaf, 350
parrot lily, 254
parrot's beak, 298
parrot's bill, 232
Parkinsonia, 126
Parthenocissus, 246
partridge berry, 484
partridge-berry, 448
pasque flower, 466
Passiflora, 234
passionflowers, 234
passionfruits, 234
patience, 522
patient Lucy, 522
Patrinia, 348
Paulownia, 64
Paxistima, 74
peaches, ornamental, 188
peacock iris, 394
peacock orchid, 392
pearl bushes, 170
pearlwort, 432
pears, ornamental, 182
peas, 232, 298, 508
pea shrubs, 122
pea trees, 122
Pelargonium, 288
Peltiphyllum, 338-40
Pennisetum, 290-2
Penstemon, 206, 342, 476
peonies, *see Paeonia*, 310
peppermints, 134
peppers, ornamental, 518
pepper trees, 52
perfumed fairy lily, 366
Perilla, 506
periwinkles, 350
Pernettya, 104
Perovskia, 296
persimmons, 220
Peruvian daffodil, 374
Peruvian lilies, 254
Petrophytum, 468
Petrorhagia, 432
Petunia, 518
Phacelia, 506

Phalaris, 292
Pharbitis, 500
Phaseolus, 508
pheasant's eyes, 514
Phegopteris, 324
Phellodendron, 192-4
Philadelphus, 198
Philesia, 222
Phillyrea, 144
Phlomis, 114, 296
Phlox, 314, 458, 514
Phoenix, 148
Phormium, 252
Photinia, 174, 176
Phygelius, 344
Phyllitis, 320
Phyllodoce, 446-8
Phyllostachys, 292
× *Phyllothamnus*, 448
Physalis, 360
Physocarpus, 170
Physoplexis, 428
Physostegia, 296
Phyteuma, 262, 428
Phytolacca, 358
Picea, 26-8, 34-6
pickerel weed, 532
Pieris, 104
pigeon berry, 216
piggy-back plant, 340
pignut, 112
Pileostegia, 244
pimpernels, 526
pincushion flower, 354
pincushion plant, 494
pincushion trees, 152, 454
pineapple guava, 138
pineapple lilies, 416
Pinellia, 376
pine-mat manzanita, 448
pines, true, 32, 36, *see also Araucaria*, 44, *Athrotaxis*, 42, *Cephalotaxus*, 40, *Dacrydium*, 38, *Phyllocladus*, 38, *Podocarpus*, 38, *Sciadopitys*, 42
Pinguicula, 480
pinks, 264-6, 430, 488
pink siris tree, 120
Pinus, 32, 36
Piptanthus, 126
pistachios, 52
Pistacia, 52
Pittosporum, 148
Plagianthus, 132
planes, 48, 224
plantain lilies, 302
Platanus, 224
Platycladus, 16
Platycodon, 262
Platystemon, 512
pleated leaves, 392
Plectranthus, 296
Pleioblastus, 292
Pleione, 482
Pleistoblastus, 292
pleurisy root, 352
Plumbago, 250, 358
plumbago, 224
plume poppies, 312
plum-fruited yew, 38
plums, ornamental, 188, *see also Carrisa*, 218
plum yews, 40
poached-egg flower, 524
Podalyria, 126
podocarps, 38

Podocarpus, 38
Podophyllum, 352
Poinciana, 120
poinsettia, annual, 524
poison oak, 52
pokeberry, 358
pokeweed, 358
Polemonium, 314
Polianthes, 424
polyanthus, 318
Polygala, 482
Polygonatum, 306
Polygonum, 250, 316, 482-4, 524-6
Polypodium, 324
Polystichum, 320, 324
pomegranate, 224
Poncirus, 194
Pontederia, 532
poor man's orchid, 518
poor man's weather-glass, 526
poplars, 194
poppies, 224, 312, 512
poppy mallows, 308
Populus, 194
Portulaca, 526
potato bush, 208
potato vines, 246
Potentilla, 168, 334, 468
Poterium, 336
pouch flowers, 516
powder-puffs, 120-2
prairie rocket, 502
Pratia, 480
pretty-face, 372
prickly heaths, 456
prickly Moses, 120
prickly pears, 258
prickly thrifts, 456
pride of India, 226
primroses, 318, 460-2
Primula, 318, 460-2
Prince Albert yew, 38
Prince of Wales feathers, 486
princess tree, 64
privets, 142-4
Prophet flower, 256
Prosopis, 126
Prostanthera, 114
Protea, 152
Prunella, 456
Prunus, 184-8
Pseudolarix, 30
Pseudopanax, 56
Pseudotsuga, 28, 36
Pseudowintera, 226
Psoralea, 126
Psylliostachys, 524
Pterocarya, 112
Pterocephalus, 478
Pterostyrax, 208
Ptilotrichum, 442
Pueraria, 232
Pulmonaria, 256
Pulsatilla, 466
Punica, 224
purple coneflower, 276
purslanes, 218, 526
Puschkinia, 398
Puya, 152
Pyracantha, 174
Pyrethrum, 270-2, 534
Pyrola, 358
Pyrus, 182

quamash, 416

Quamoclit, 500
Queen Anne's Irish
  campernelle, 364
queen of the meadow,
  336
queen of the prairie, 336
Quercus, 106
quick, 176
quinces, 180

rain lilies, 366
Ramonda, 452, *see also
  Jankaea*, 452
ramsons, 362
Ranunculus, 332, 424,
  466, 532
Raoulia, 436
*Raphiolepis, see
  Rhaphiolepis*, 174-6
raspberry, flowering, 168
rattlebox, 124, 508
Rebutia, 260
red box, 136
redbuds, 122
red-hot pokers, 304
red ribbons, 510
red valerian, 346
redwoods, 42, 44
reedmaces, 532
Rehderodendron, 208
Reseda, 526
resurrection lily, 374
Retinispora, 14
Rhamnus, 154
Rhaphiolepis, 174-6
Rhapidophyllum, 148
Rhapis, 148
Rhazya, 350
Rheum, 316
Rhipsalidopsis, 260
Rhipsalis, 260
Rhodanthe, 488
Rhodiola, 284
Rhododendron, 84-98,
  species
  rhododendrons, 84-
  90,
  hybrid rhododendrons,
  92-4,
  deciduous azaleas,
  94-6,
  evergreen azaleas, 96-
  8,
  azaleodendrons, 98
Rhodohypoxis, 480
Rhodotypos, 168
rhubarb, ornamental, 316
Rhus, 52, *see also
  Cotinus*, 52
Rhynchelytrum, 504
Rhyncospermum, 228
Ribes, 202-4
rice-paper tree, 56
Richea, 220
Ricinus, 524
rimu, 38
Robinia, 126
rock-cresses, 442
rock jasmines, 464
rock roses, 76, 478
rock spiraea, 468
Rodgersia, 340
Romneya, 314
Romulea, 394
Rondeletia, 190
Rosa, see roses
Roscoea, 360
rose acacia, 126

rose mallee, 136
rose mallows, 308
rosemary, 114, *see also
  Ledum*, 102
rose moss, 526
rose of Sharon, 108, 132
rose-root, 284
roses, 156-66, 240-4,
  albas, 158,
  Bourbons, 158,
  bush, 162, 164 (*see
  also* climbing sports,
  244),
  centifolias, 158,
  China roses, 158,
  climbing, 240, 242,
  cluster-flowering, 164,
  Damasks, 158,
  Floribundas, 164,
  Gallicas, 158,
  Grandifloras, 164,
  hybrid Teas, 162,
  miniatures, 166,
  modern shrub roses,
  160,
  moss roses, 158,
  old garden roses, 158,
  perpetuals, 158,
  Polyanthus, 164,
  Portland roses, 158,
  ramblers, 240,
  rugosas, 160,
  species, 156,
  Tea roses, 158,
  wild, 156
Rosmarinus, 114
rowan, 178
Rubus, 168
Rudbeckia, 276, 496
rue, 360
runner bean, 508
Ruscus, 222
rushes, 532
Russian olive, 84
Russian sage, 296
Russian vine, 250

Sabal, 148
St John's bread, 122
St John's worts, 108,
  454
salal, 102
Salix, 196, 468-70
sallows, 196
sallow thorn, 84
salmonberry, 168
Salpiglossis, 518
Salvia, 114, 296, 506-8
Sambucus, 72
sand cherries, 186
sand flower, 488
sand myrtle, 448
sage brush, 78
sages, ornamental, 114,
  270, 296, 506-8, *see
  also Lantana*, 216
Sagina, 432
Sagittaria, 530
Sago palm, 44
St Bernard's lilies, 300
St Bruno lily, 304
St Dabeoc's heaths, 444
sand verbena, 524
sandworts, 432
Sanguinaria, 482
Sanguisorba, 336
Santolina, 80
Sanvitalia, 496

Sapium, 220
Saponaria, 266, 432,
  488, 522
Sarcococca, 64
Sasa, 292
Sassafras, 116
satin bush, 126
satin flowers, 502, 510
satsuma, 192
Satureja, 294
Sauromatum, 376
savin, 24
Saxegothaea, 38
Saxifraga, 340, 470-2,
  see also Bergenia,
  338, *Peltiphyllum*, 338
Scabiosa, 354, 478,
  522-4
scabious, 354, 522-4
Scarborough lily, 374
scarlet runner, 508
scarlet wisteria tree, 126
Schinus, 52
Schisandra, 250
Schizanthus, 518
Schizocodon, 478
Schizophragma, 244
Schizostylis, 394
Schlumbergera, 260
Sciadopitys, 42
Scilla, 398, *see also
  Hyacinthus*, 400
scimitar shrub, 120
Scirpus, 532
Scolopendrium, 320
Scrophularia, 344
scurfy peas, 126
Scutellaria, 456
sea buckthorn, 84
sea daffodil, 374
sea fig, 520
sea hollies, 346
sea lavenders, 358, 524
sea lilies, 374
sea orach, 218
sea pink, 456
sea-urchin tree, 152
sedges, 354
Sedum, 284, 438
self-heals, 456
Selinum, 346
Semiaquilegia, 466
Sempervivum, 440
Senecio, 80, 282, 496
sennas, 122, *see also
  Colutea*, 122
Sequoia, 42, 44, *see also
  Sequoiadendron*
Sequoiadendron, 42
Serratula, 278
serviceberries, 174
service tree, 178
Sesbania, 126
Setcreasea, 352
shadbushes, 174
Shasta daisy, 272
sheep laurel, 102
shell flowers, 394, 506
Shepherdia, 84
Shibataea, 292
shoo-fly, 518
shooting-stars, 464
Shortia, 478
shrub althaea, 132
Siberian bugloss, 256
Sidalcea, 308
Silene, 432, 488, *see
  also Lychnis*, 266
silk tassel bush, 220

silk tree, 120
silky oak, 150
silver-bells, 208
silverberry, 84
silver lace vine, 250
silver tree, 152
Silybum, 496
Sinarundinaria, 292
Sisyrinchium, 356, 454
Skimmia, 194
skullcaps, 456
skunk cabbage, 376
skyflower, 216
skyrocket, 514
slipper flowers, 516
sloe, 188
Smilacina, 306
smoke bushes, 52
smoke trees, 52
snake's-head iris, 394
snakeweed, 316
snapdragons, 516
sneezeweed, 270, 276
sneezewort, 270
snowballs, 70-2
snowbells, 208, 464
snowberries, 68
snowdrops, 366
snowdrop trees, 208
snowflakes, 366
snow in summer, 78, 432
snow-on-the-mountain,
  524
soapweed, 50
soapworts, 266, 432, 522
Solandra, 246
Solanum, 208, 246
Soldanella, 464
soldiers and sailors, 256
Soleirolia, 360
Solidago, 274, 436
× *Solidaster*, 274
Solomon's seals, 306,
  480
Sophora, 126
Sorbaria, 170
Sorbus, 178
sorrel tree, 102-4
sourwood, 102-4
southern beeches, 106
southern star, 520
southernwood, 78
Spanish bayonet, 50
Spanish broom, 118
Spanish dagger, 50
Spanish gorse, 118
Sparaxis, 394
Spartina, 292
Spartium, 118
spearwort, greater, 532
Specularia, 522
speedwells, 344, 476
Sphenogyne, 498
spice bush, 116
spider flowers, 150-2,
  522
spider lilies, 372-4
spider plants, 300
spiderworts, 352
spike heath, 444
spinach, ornamental, 522
spindle trees, 74
spiny alyssum, 442
Spiraea, 170, *see also
  Filipendula*, 336,
  Holodiscus, 170,
  Petrophytum, 468,
  Sorbaria, 170
spire lily, 400

spleenworts, 320
spotted dog, 256
Sprekelia, 374
spring meadow saffron, 418
spring star-flower, 366
spruces, 26-8, 34-6
spurge laurel, 212
spurges, 286, 524,
see also *Pachysandra*, 64
squills, 398
Stachys, 296
Stachyurus, 226
staff vine, 248
standing cypress, 514
stardust, 514
star-flowered lily of the valley, 306
star jasmines, 228
star of Bethlehem, 262, 418, 420
star tulips, 418
Statice, 358, 524
Stenocarpus, 152
Stenocereus, 260
Stephanandra, 170
Sternbergia, 366
Stewartia, 212
stinking gladwyn, 388
Stipa, 292
stocks, 502
Stokesia, 274
Stokes's aster, 274
stone-cresses, 440
stonecrops, 284, 438
storaxes, 208
storksbills, 450-2
Stranvaesia, 176
× *Stranvinia*, 176
Stratiotes, 530
strawberries, ornamental, 334
strawberry geranium, 340
strawberry trees, 100
strawflowers, 436, 488
Strelitzia, 360
Streptopus, 306
Struthiopteris, 322
Stuartia, 212
Sturt's desert pea, 122
Stylophorum, 314
Styrax, 208
succory, 280
sugarbush, 152
sumachs, 52
sumacs, 52
summer cypress, 522
summer hyacinth, 400
summer lilac, 128
summer-sweets, 218-20
sundrops, 308, 482
sunflowers, 276, 494-6
sun plant, 526
sunrays, 488
sun roses, 76, 478
swamp cypresses, 42,
see also *Glyptostrobus*, 42
swamp pink, 302
Swan River daisy, 490
Swan River pea shrub, 120
Swedish ivy, 296
sweet bays, 116, 130
sweet bergamot, 294
sweet bouvardia, 190

sweet box, 64
sweet flags, 530
sweet gale, 222
sweet galingale, 532
sweet gums, 110
sweet locust, 124
sweet olive, 144
sweet pea bushes, 126
sweet peas, 508
sweet pepper bush, 218
sweet rocket, 284
sweetshrub, 218
sweetspires, 202
sweet sultan, 492
sweet William, 488
Swida, 82
sword lilies, 382
sycamores, 48, 224
Sycopsis, 110
Symphoricarpos, 68
Symphytum, 256
Symplocos, 226
Syringa, 140-2

Tacsonia, 234
Tagetes, 496-8
Tahoka daisy, 490
Taiwania, 42
tamarack, 30
tamarisks, 226
Tamarix, 226
Tanacetum, 272, 434
tangerine, 192
Tasmanian cedars, 42
tassel flowers, 486, 490
tassel hyacinth, 400
Taxodium, 42
Taxus, 40
tea trees, 138
Tecoma, 64
teff, 504
Tellima, 340
Telopea, 152
Tetrapanax, 56
tetra snaps, 516
Teucrium, 114, 456
Texas blue-bonnet, 508
Texas ranger, 206
Thalia, 532
Thalictrum, 228, 466
thorns, 176
Thelypteris, 324
Thermopsis, 298
thistles, 434, 492, 496
thrifts, 358, 456
throatwort, 262
Thunbergia, 248, 520
Thuja, 16, 22, see also *Thujopsis*,
Thujopsis, 16
Thuya, see Thuja, 16, 22
thymes, 456
Thymus, 456
Tiarella, 340
tickseeds, 276, 492
tidy tips, 496
tiger flower, 394
Tigridia, 394
Tilia, 214
Tithonia, 498
toadflax, 342, 474, 516
toad lilies, 306
toadshade, 306
tobacco, flowering, 518
tobira, 148
Tolmeia, 340
toothwort, 284
torch lilies, 304

Torenia, 516
Torreya, 40
totaras, 38
touch-me-nots, 520-2
Townsendia, 436
toyon, 174
Trachelium, 262
Trachelospermum, 228
Trachycarpus, 148
Trachymene, 526
Trachystemon, 256
Tradescantia, 352
trailing arbutus, 448
trailing bellflowers, 428
trailing myrtle, 350
Transvaal daisy, 280
treacle mustards, 442
treasure flowers, 494
tree anemone, 198
tree asters, 78-80
tree daisies, 78-80
tree lupin (lupine), 126
tree mallows, 132-4
tree of heaven, 226
tree paeonies, 146
tree poppy, 224
tree purslane, 218
Tricholaena, 504
Tricuspidaria, 220
Tricyrtis, 306
Trifolium, 480
Trillium, 306
trinity flowers, 352
Triteleia, 366, 372
Tritoma, 304
Tritonia, 394, see also *Crocosmia*, 392
Trollius, 332, 466
Tropaeolum, 250, 484, 526
trout lilies, 396
trumpet creepers, 230
trumpet flowers, 518
trumpet vine, 230
Tsuga, 28-30, 36
tuberose, 424
tufted alkanet, 426
Tulbaghia, 374
Tulipa, 402-6
tulip poplar, 128
tulips, true, 402-6
tulip trees, 128-30
Tunica, 432
tunic flower, 432
tupelo, 224
turtle-heads, 342
Tweedia, 520
twinberry, 68
twinflower, 352
twinleaf, 352
twinspur, 516
twisted-stalks, 306
Typha, 532

Ugni, 138
Ulmus, 214
Umbellularia, 116
umbrella plants, 338-40, 532
Ursinia, 498
Uvularia, 306

Vaccaria, 488, 522
Vaccinium, 104, 448
Valeriana, 348, 484
Vallota, 374
varnish tree, 226

velvet flower, 518
× *Venidio-arctotis*, 282
Venidium, 498
Venus's looking-glass, 522
Veratrum, 306
Verbascum, 344, 476, 516
Verbena, 360, 520, see also *Lippia*, 216
Veronica, 344, 476-8,
see also *Hebe*, 204-6, 474, *Parahebe*, 476
Veronicastrum, 344
vervains, 360, 520
vetchlings, 298
Viburnum, 70-2
Victorian box, 148
Vinca, 350
Viola, 348, 526
violas, 348
violet cress, 502
violets, 348
violettas, 348
viper's bugloss, 486
virgilia, 122
Virginia bluebells, 256
Virginia cowslip, 256
Virginia creepers, 246
Virginia stock, 502
virgin's bower, 236
Viscaria, 432, see also *Lychnis*, 266
Vitadenia, 436
Vitex, 216
Vitis, 246-8, see also *Ampelopsis*, 246
voodoo lily, 376

Wahlenbergia, 428
wake robins, 306
Waldsteinia, 468
wallflowers, 442, 502
wall-pepper, 438
walnuts, 112
wandering Jew, 352
wand flower, 392
waratahs, 152
Washingtonia, 148
water canna, 532
water cowslip, 532
water figwort, 344
water fringe, 530
water hawthorn, 530
water hyacinth, 530
water lilies, 528
water mint, 532
water plantain, 530
water soldier, 530
Watsonia, 394
Wattakaka, 228
wattles, 120
wax myrtles, 222-4
wax plant, 228
wax tree, 52
wayfaring tree, 70
Weigela, 66
wellingtonia, 42
Welsh poppy, 312
whitebeams, 178
white-cup, 484
white kerria, 168
white sanicle, 280
white snakeroot, 280
whitlow grasses, 442
whortleberries, 104
wild cucumber, 504
wild gingers, 350

wild heliotrope, 506
wild hyacinths, 372, 398, 416
wild indigo, 298
wild rosemary, 102
wild senna, 298
willow herb, 480
willows, 196, 468-70
windflowers, 330, 422
wineberry, 168
wine cups, 308
wire-netting bush, 82
winter aconites, 422-4
winterberry, 56
winter daffodil, 366
wintergreens, 358, 448
winter hazels, 110
winter's bark, 226

wintersweets, 218
wire-vine, 250
wishbone flower, 516
Wisteria, 232, see also Sesbania, 126
witch alder, 110
witch hazels, 110
withe-rod, 70
woodbines, 230
wood lilies, 306
wood poppy, 314
woodruffs, 358-60, 526
Woodsia, 324
wood sorrels, 420
Woodwardia, 324
wormwoods, 270, 434
Wulfenia, 478

Xanthoceras, 224-6
Xanthorhiza, 224
Xeranthemum, 488

yarrows, 270, 434
yaupon, 56
yellow archangel, 294
yellow-bells, 64
yellow Chinese poppy, 312
yellowroot, 224
yellow sage, 216
yellowwood, 122
yesterday, today and tomorrow plant, 208
yews, true, 40, see also

Cephalotaxus, 40, Podocarpus, 38, Saxegothaea, 38
Yucca, 50
yulan, 130

Zantedeschia, 376
Zauschneria, 480-2
Zea, 504
Zebrina, 352
Zelkova, 214
Zenobia, 104
Zephyranthes, 366
Zephyr lilies, 366
Zinnia, 498
Ziziphus, 154
Zygocactus, 260